## PORK (180°C, GAS MARK 4)

| CUT AND WEIGHT Start with meat at refrigerator temperature. **Remove roast from oven when it reaches 2-5°C below desired doneness.** | | | MEAT THERMOMETER READING | APPROXIMATE COOKING TIME (per 450 g) |
|---|---|---|---|---|
| Fresh pork | Crown roast | 2.7–3.6 kg | 67°C | 20 mins |
| | Loin roast (with bone) | 1.3–2.2 kg | 67°C | 20 mins |
| | Boneless loin roast | 900 g–1.8 kg | 67°C | 20 mins |
| | Whole leg | 5.4 kg | 67–77°C | 25–30 mins |
| | Leg half, fillet or knuckle end | 1.3–1.8 kg | 67–77°C | 40 mins |
| | Rolled hand | 1.3–2.7 kg | 67–77°C | 45 mins |
| | Tenderloin (roasted at 220–230°C) | 225–750 g | 67°C | 25–35 mins total |
| Smoked, cook before eating | Whole ham | 6.3–7.2 kg | 67°C | 15–18 mins |
| Smoked fully cooked pork (heated at 170°C) | Whole ham | 6.3–7.3 kg | 52–57°C | 1–1¾ hours total |
| | Half ham | 2.7–3.6 kg | 52–57°C | 1 hour total |

## LAMB (160°C, GAS MARK 3)

| CUT AND WEIGHT Start with meat at refrigerator temperature. **Remove roast from oven when it reaches 2-5°C below desired doneness; temperature will rise as roast stands.** | | APPROX. COOKING TIME Medium-rare (67°C) | (MINUTES PER 450 g) Medium (77°C) | Well done |
|---|---|---|---|---|
| Whole leg | 2.2–3.1 kg | 15 mins | 20 mins | 25 mins |
| | 3.1–4.1 kg | 20 mins | 25 mins | 30 mins |
| Leg shank end | 1.3–1.8 kg | 30 mins | 40 mins | 45 mins |
| Leg fillet | 1.3–1.8 kg | 25 mins | 35 mins | 45 mins |
| Leg roast (boneless) | 1.8–3.1 kg | 20 mins | 25 mins | 30 mins |
| Rib roast or rack (cook at 190°C) | 750 g–1.1 kg | 30 mins | 35 mins | 40 mins |
| Crown roast, unstuffed (cook at 190°C) | 900 g–1.3 kg | 25 mins | 30 mins | 35 mins |
| Shoulder roast | 1.8–2.7 kg | 20 mins | 25 mins | 30 mins |
| Shoulder roast (boneless) | 1.5–2.7 kg | 35 mins | 40 mins | 45 mins |

LE CORDON BLEU

# COMPLETE
# COOKING

*Step-by-Step*

LE CORDON BLEU

# COMPLETE
# COOKING

*Step-by-Step*

CASSELL

A CASSELL BOOK
This edition first published in the United Kingdom by
Cassell plc
Wellington House
125 Strand
London WC2R 0BB

First published 1998

Created and produced by
CARROLL AND BROWN LIMITED
20 Lonsdale Road
London NW6 6RD

*Publishing Director* Denis Kennedy
*Art Director* Chrissie Lloyd

*Project Editor* Theresa Reynolds

*Editors* Janet Charatan, Valerie Cipollone, Paula Disbrowe, Kate Fryer,
Joanne Stanford, Madeline Weston

*Cooking Consultants* Beverly LeBlanc, Ilona Robinson

*Senior Art Editor* Sally Powell

*Designers* Paul Stradling, Simon Daley, Hallam Bannister

*Photography* David Murray, Jules Selmes

*Production* Christine Corton, Wendy Rogers, Clair Reynolds

*Nutrition Consultant* Michele C. Fisher, Ph.D., R.D.

*British Library Catalogue-in-Publication Data*
A catalogue record for this book is available from the
British Library

ISBN 0 304 35000 1

Reproduced in Singapore by Colourscan
Printed and bound in Italy by Chromolitho

# FOREWORD

It is with great pleasure that I introduce *Le Cordon Bleu Step-by-Step Cookbook*. Le Cordon Bleu Master Chefs always work with the same publishing team and this book is the latest fruit of those labours. Since the approach of this book is much like that of the teaching methods of our international schools, Le Cordon Bleu is more than delighted to award it the school's seal of approval.

With five schools, in France, Great Britain, Japan, Australia and Northern America, and a student body made up of fifty different nationalities, Le Cordon Bleu is well known and highly regarded around the globe. With its 32 permanent Master Chefs, it has a tradition of excellence in the culinary arts and is committed to furthering the appreciation of fine food and fine living. Already involved in consulting, and the creation and promotion of a variety of culinary products, Le Cordon Bleu defines culinary excellence.

This book provides a fully illustrated step-by-step guide through the preparation of over a thousand finished dishes. Each chapter focuses on a diffcrent food or food category - from Appetisers and Soups to Desserts, Pies and Tarts. Using a typical recipe, the basic method is shown, then alternative recipes follow so you can master the art of cooking many different dishes. Ingredients, basic techniques and equipment are detailed, helping to create a book that removes the mystery of trying something new.

*Le Cordon Bleu Step-by-Step Cookbook* has been created for those who appreciate the value of dining at home. The pleasures of sharing a meal as a family or with friends is a tradition that remains strong in French homes, despite the pressures of the modern world. Recipes range from simple to elaborate, their flavours spanning the globe – working on the premise that a technique once mastered means less time in the kitchen and more time to enjoy the company of family and friends over a delicious meal.

I hope that you will find that this book opens the door to your creativity, when both cooking and entertaining.

Bon Appétit!

André J. Cointreau

# Contents

## POULTRY 131

## MEAT 179

## VEGETABLES 267

## SALADS 313

## PASTA 347

## GRAINS AND PULSES 369

## BREADS AND QUICK CAKES 391

# Equipment KNOW-HOW

There's a piece of equipment available for every cooking method imaginable. No one needs every new gadget on the market, but there are certain items that make kitchen life easier and more enjoyable. Here are all of our favourites, from time-honoured basic cookware to specialized utensils for adventurous home cooks.

## SHOPPING TIPS

Quality cookware can be expensive. But if you get the best, you'll have a lifetime investment that's reliable, durable and a pleasure to use. The first step in judging quality? Check the price: finer metals and manufacturing typically mean you'll pay more. (But not always; cast-iron pans, for instance, are cheap, heavy and durable.) Invest in a few quality pieces, especially knives and sturdy pots and pans. Don't skimp on non-stick pans for low-fat cooking. You can economise on items like pasta pots, which simply boil water. Get extra mileage from your cookware by choosing products that work equally well in the oven and on the stove-top.

## STOVE-TOP STAPLES

Pots and pans come in many materials. Stainless steel is easy to care for but does not conduct heat well, so manufacturers often add an aluminium or copper core to improve its heat-conducting qualities. By contrast, copper is a superb heat conductor and a pleasure to cook in – but it's heavy, expensive and difficult to clean. Aluminium and cast iron are much less costly and easier to care for; both are efficient heat conductors but can react with acidic foods, causing them to taste metallic or discolour.

In general, look for pots and pans with thick bases, which guard against scorching, and ovenproof handles (or ones designed to stay cool). You're better off investing in pieces you know you'll use and avoiding pre-packaged sets, which may contain some pans you won't need. For a well-equipped kitchen, you'll need the following:

**Saucepan** You'll need at least 3 or 4 (ranging from 1-litre to 4-litre), each between 7 and 10cm deep. They should have tight-fitting lids and ovenproof handles.

**Casserole** Great for the stove-top or oven; heavy ones are best, and enamelled pans are pretty enough to serve in. A 5-litre size is the most useful.

**Frying pans** Have at least 3 sizes: small (23cm), medium (26cm) and large (30cm). A good non-stick frying pan is a must if you're trying to cook with less fat.

**Saucepot** This deep, wide, fairly light pot is used for soups, stews and cooking pasta. A 5-litre saucepot with a tight-fitting lid will serve most needs.

**Stockpot** A tall, narrow pot used for cooking soups and stocks as well as bulky foods like corn on the cob and lobster. A 6- or 8-litre stockpot is recommended.

**Double boiler** A set of two saucepans that allows for gentle cooking of foods (in the upper pan) over simmering water (in the lower pan). If you don't own one, it's easy to improvise a double boiler: just nest a metal mixing bowl in a saucepan of simmering water, or stack two saucepans of about the same diameter.

Stockpot

Double boiler

**Stove-top grill pan** This cast-iron pan provides an excellent way to cook foods with little or no fat, giving a similar result to cooking on a barbecue or under a grill. The surface is ridged, allowing fat to drip away from foods and there is a spout to pour off the fat.

### SEASONING A CAST-IRON PAN

Regular (not enamel-coated) cast-iron frying pans require seasoning before the first use to create a non-stick finish. Wash in hot, soapy water; dry. Using a cloth soaked in vegetable oil, rub entire pan – even exterior and lid. Heat upside down in a 180°C (350°F, Gas 4) oven 1 hour. Turn off oven; cool completely in oven.

## FOR THE OVEN

Roasting and baking results depend on how long the food bakes and at how high a temperature, and the dimensions of the vessel. Many materials will do the job: enamelled cast-iron, which is easy to clean and transmits heat well; enamelled steel, which is a reasonably priced, lightweight choice for roasting pans; stainless steel, which is durable and good value; and ovenproof glass and glass-ceramic, which can go directly from the freezer or refrigerator to the oven. Earthenware and stoneware are especially good for long, slow baking. For most cakes, shiny metal tins will yield the most delicate crusts. The following is a review of essentials.

**Baking dish** A large, fairly shallow, open oval or rectangular dish with sides about 5cm high; usually made of glass or ceramic. Choose a variety in different sizes.

**Baking tin** Like a baking dish, but made of metal; the sides of this tin are 4–5cm high. Essential sizes are: a 20cm square; a 22cm square; a rectangular 33 by 20cm tin.

**Casserole** Round, oval, square or rectangular, this dish may be made of glass, ceramic, or enamelled metal, and may have a lid. Have several sizes.

**Roasting tin** A large, deep tin typically made of stainless or enamelled steel or aluminium. A low, open roasting tin with a rack is the most versatile.

**Cake tin** No cook should be without an assortment of round cake tins (20cm and 23cm), plus several square and rectangular baking tins (see page 10). Depending on your baking needs, also consider the following: springform tin (23 by 8cm and 25 by 6cm are useful sizes); angel food cake tin (25cm), bundt or kugelhopf tin (25cm).

**Loaf tin** Vital for quick breads and tea cakes and useful for meat loaves. Standard sizes are 23 by 12cm and 21 by 11cm.

**Pie plate** The standard size is 23cm; deep-dish plates are 24cm. Glass, dark metal or dull metal tins make the best pie crusts – crisp and nicely browned.

**Tart tin** This shallow tin with fluted sides and a removable bottom comes in all shapes and sizes; 28 by 3cm and 23 by 3cm round tins are especially useful. Tartlet tins (7½ to 9½cm) are nice for individual desserts.

**Other baking equipment** The following also come in handy: Swiss roll tin (39 by 27cm, with low rim all around); baking sheets (some with low lip on one or more edges); standard 12 hole muffin tins (each hole 7 by 3cm).

Baking sheet · Roasting tin with rack · Metal baking tin

Casserole · Swiss roll tin · Glass baking dish

## CARE AND CLEANING

**Aluminium** Scrub with a mild abrasive cleanser. If pan has darkened, fill with water and vinegar or lemon juice; boil 15 minutes.

**Cast iron** Wash cast iron briefly so you don't wash away the seasoning (see box, page 10). Clean with boiling water and a paper towel or soft cloth, or use a nylon pad to scrub off food. Dry at once.

**Copper** Wash in hot, soapy water; dry immediately. Copper tarnishes quickly; use a polish to brighten. Most traditional copper tins are lined with tin and will need relining from time to time (reline if you can see copper through the tin).

**Earthenware or stoneware** Cool completely before washing to prevent cracking. Scrub with nylon pad, rinse and air dry. Glazed stoneware is dishwasher-safe.

**Enamelled metals** Soak in hot, soapy water; avoid abrasives.

**Glass, glass-ceramic, porcelain** Soak in hot, soapy water. All are dishwasher-safe.

**Non-stick surfaces** Clean with a sponge and warm, soapy water. Avoid abrasives.

**Stainless steel** Wash in hot, soapy water with a nylon pad. A stainless steel cleaner will help remove stubborn stains.

## MEASURING TINS AND DISHES

To measure the size of a baking dish or tin, measure across the top of the dish from inside edge to inside edge. Measure depth on the inside of the tin as well, from the bottom to the top of the tin.

## TIN SUBSTITUTIONS

Cakes and breads are usually baked in metal baking tins. If necessary, you can substitute a glass or ceramic dish – just reduce the oven temperature by 10°C, since cakes bake faster in these materials than in metal. That way, the outside of the cake won't be over-baked before the centre is cooked.

### TIN VOLUMES

| TIN SIZE | APPROXIMATE VOLUME |
|---|---|
| Each 7 by 3cm muffin tin cup | 90ml |
| 21 by 11 cm loaf tin | 1¼ litres |
| 20cm square baking tin | 1½ litres |
| 22cm square baking tin | 2 litres |
| 23cm pie plate | 1 litre |
| 30 by 18cm baking tin | 1¾ litres |
| 33 by 20cm baking tin | 3 litres |
| 39 by 27cm Swiss roll tin | 1½ litres |

## MICROWAVE TIPS

• Remember that the amount of food affects cooking time. Small or thin pieces cook faster than large or thick ones.
• Avoid microwaving large cuts of meat on the bone. The bones attract microwaves and the meat will cook unevenly.
• Pierce eggs and foods with tight skin (tomatoes, potatoes). If not, they may explode from a build up of steam.
• Use a dish that's large enough for stirring and boiling. Think of how full you'd want a saucepan, not a casserole.
• Don't reheat baked goods in the microwave – they'll be tough. However, you can thaw them in a kitchen towel.
• Use medium power (the microwave will cycle on and off) for delicate tasks such as melting chocolate.
• Clean the oven with soapy water or multi-purpose cleaner.

### MICROWAVE SAFETY

• Use paper products only for cooking less than 10 minutes, or they could ignite. Don't use recycled paper, which can contain metal bits that will spark, or dyed paper products – the dye could leach into food.
• Don't use the twist ties that come with plastic storage bags – the metal could spark and possibly ignite. Also beware of glass or porcelain with a metal trim, or the metal content of some ceramic glazes.
• For safety, use cling film designed for microwave use, and don't let the film touch the food.
• Always remove a tight cover carefully, opening it away from your face – steam can build up under the cover.
• Sugar attracts microwaves, so sweet foods can become extremely hot – be careful when you take a bite.

## UTENSIL ESSENTIALS

**Bristle brushes** Have at least two: one for cleaning pots, and one for scrubbing vegetables. Nylon bristles last the longest.
**Colander** This is indispensable for draining pasta and vegetables. Large colanders are best; look for one with solid feet at the base.
**Cooling racks** Have 2 or 3 if you bake a lot of cakes or biscuits. Avoid racks with large gaps between the wires.
**Chopping boards** To avoid cross-contamination, have one board for raw

Cooling rack

poultry, fish and meat, and another for bread, vegetables and cheese. Scrub with hot soapy water after use, and sterilize weekly in a solution of 1 tablespoon bleach mixed with 4 litres water. Sterilize plastic boards in the dishwasher.

You may want to reserve a board just for fruit, to avoid tragedies like garlic-flavoured apple pie.
**Grater** This flat or box-shaped tool can grate (fine holes), shred (medium holes) or slice (large slots) many foods. Stainless steel won't rust.
**Measuring jugs** These can be glass or plastic; the best ones have metric and imperial markings and American cups.

Chopping boards

**Measuring spoons** Stainless steel are the most durable. For liquids, fill to the rim. For dry ingredients, fill and level off.
**Mixing bowls** A set of these all-purpose bowls is invaluable. Made of glass, stainless steel or plastic, they range from tiny to 8 litres. Avoid beating egg whites in plastic bowls.
**Rolling pins** Heavy rolling pins, hardwood or marble, work best for rolling pastry out smoothly, with less effort. Don't wash wooden rolling pins in the dishwasher.
**Sieve/Strainer** Sifts dry ingredients or strains liquids. Have a few in various sizes and with different gauges of mesh.
**Spatulas** Use wooden or heatproof rubber ones for turning foods during cooking, plastic or rubber for mixing and folding.

Grater    Sieve

**Palette knives** These round-bladed knives are ideal for putting round a tin to loosen a cake and for icing cakes.
**Thermometers** Meat and instant-read thermometers and sugar thermometers measure the temperatures of meats, poultry, liquids, yeast mixtures and sweets, eliminating guesswork when accurate results are important. Test accuracy by immersing in boiling water; thermometer should read 100°C. An oven thermometer indicates if the oven is heating correctly. Store carefully, not loose in a drawer.
**Tongs** Use to pick up foods that are hot, slippery or messy, or turn meats without piercing them.
**Vegetable peeler** Easier than a paring knife for peeling potatoes, apples and other fruit and vegetables. A swivel blade removes less peel than a fixed blade as it conforms to the vegetable's shape. Also great for shaving cheese and making chocolate curls.
**Whisk** A must for mixing smooth sauces, gravies, vinaigrettes and cake mixtures. Have several sizes for different tasks.

Rubber    Palette    Tongs    Whisk
spatula    knife

## ALL THE RIGHT KNIVES

Quality knives are made of high-carbon stainless steel. If the knife has a tang (the narrower metal part at the base of the blade) that goes right through the handle, it's solidly made. A good knife should feel comfortable in your hand. Essential knives include a chef's knife (for chopping, slicing, dicing and mincing; a 15–20cm blade is the most popular), a small paring knife (for fruits and vegetables), and a large serrated knife (for breads, cakes and tomatoes). Useful extras include a carving knife for slicing meats – these often come in a set with a carving fork – and a boning knife. A slicing knife has a scalloped edge and rounded tip, and is good for ham and other cooked meats. Sharp knives are easier to use and safer too because they'll be less likely to slip. Take a cue from chefs, who sharpen their knives every day. For instructions on how to use a sharpening steel, see page 180.

Paring knife   Chef's knife   Serrated knife   Carving fork and knife   Slicing knife

## BLENDING AND MIXING OPTIONS

Blenders and food processors can be used for similar tasks, but they each have their own advantages. The blender makes puréed soups, silky sauces and smooth drinks with ease; its tall, narrow container holds more liquid than a food processor and makes smoother soups. Processor bowls will leak at the base if overloaded. On the other hand, a food processor is better at chopping, shredding and grating; it can also make pastry quickly. If you want a small, portable, hand-held blender choose an immersion blender. This fits right into the cooking pot and, as a benefit, reduces the amount of washing up.

For whipping cream, beating egg whites and mixing cake mixtures, an electric mixer does the job best. A hand-held mixer is convenient because it's light and can be moved around the kitchen. But holding it can be tiring, and it can stall with stiff doughs. A heavy-duty standing mixer easily handles large amounts of thick mixture, cold butter and bread dough, and will free you up to do other things; this type is best for serious bakers. Most standing mixers offer mixing paddles, dough hooks for kneading and balloon whisks for beating eggs and cream. Other accessories range from a food grinder to a sausage stuffer.

## THE LITTLE EXTRAS

**Apple corer** This cylindrical tool neatly cores apples as well as pears. Buy the larger size so you don't miss any core.

**Cocktail sticks** Great for testing cakes and quick breads for doneness. Also handy for serving appetizers and for securing stuffed foods, such as chicken breasts.

**Egg beater** This hand-powered mixer can also be used for whipping cream. Crank gears spin the metal beaters.

**Ice cream maker** They come as manual and electric; used for ice cream, sorbet and frozen yogurt.

**Juicer** A device to extract fruit or vegetable juices – from a simple ridged cone onto which a halved citrus fruit is pressed to elaborate electric models used for carrot juice.

**Kitchen scissors** For cutting kitchen string, snipping fresh herbs and trimming artichoke leaves. Shears, which are larger and spring-loaded, make sectioning poultry simple. Buy sturdy models made of stainless steel.

**Melon baller** Besides scooping perfect globes of melon, this tool cores apples and pears. A large one is most useful.

**Mortar and pestle** For grinding spices, herbs and nuts. You crush with the pestle in a mortar (the bowl).

**Pastry blender** The metal wires on this tool cut the cold fat into flour for pastry without warming it, as your hands would.

**Pastry brush** Used to brush doughs with butter or egg and apply glazes to baked goods; great for dusting off excess flour. Wash immediately after using (especially the base of bristles); dry thoroughly. When buying, look for well-anchored bristles.

**Piping bag** For decorating cakes and pies and forming spritz biscuits and beautifully shaped pastries.

**Potato masher** Perfect for mashing potatoes, other root vegetables and cooked beans into a slightly chunky purée.

**Ruler** Handy for measuring the size of baking tins, and the thickness of meat and fish to gauge cooking times.

**Salad spinner** Uses centrifugal force to dry greens.

**Skewers** A must for making kebabs and trussing turkeys; small, decorative varieties are great for starters.

**Steamer** The collapsible metal style can fit into pots and pans of various sizes. A two-tier steamer pan looks like a double boiler (see page 10) but the top half has a perforated base to allow steam through. Bamboo steamers fit in a wok or over a pot of simmering liquid.

**Zester** Pulled across citrus fruit, it removes only the outer rind, avoiding the bitter pith underneath.

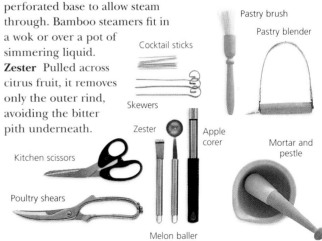

Pastry brush

Pastry blender

Cocktail sticks

Skewers

Zester

Apple corer

Mortar and pestle

Kitchen scissors

Poultry shears

Melon baller

# COOKING BASICS KNOW-HOW

Confidence in the kitchen begins with the basics –
such as mastering the most efficient techniques for
simple procedures like measuring and chopping
ingredients. The following tips and guidelines form
an essential foundation for success and promise to
make any recipe more manageable.

## BEFORE YOU COOK

**Get informed** Read carefully through the recipe before you
start cooking to familiarize yourself with the ingredients
required and the method of working, and to calculate how
much time you are likely to need.

**Shop ahead** Check which of the ingredients listed you have
to hand and make a comprehensive list of all those you
need to buy. Make sure you have the right equipment
before you start. Collect all the ingredients and equipment
together before you begin.

**Preheat** Ovens should be preheated to the specified
temperature at least 15 minutes before you start to cook.
Grills should also be preheated. Grilling always takes place
under a hot grill with the food positioned 5–7.5 cm away
from the source of heat.

**Time it right** Timing is another crucial factor when
cooking. Get into the habit of timing your cooking carefully
(whether on the stove-top or in the oven); using a kitchen
timer is the easiest and most accurate method.

**Oven know-how** Cooking times can vary according to your
oven so it is wise to start checking to see if the dish is ready
towards the end of the cooking time. Whereas conventional
ovens are hotter toward the top, fan-assisted ovens have an
even temperature throughout, so it is unecessary to rotate
baking tins when instructed. As a guide, for fan-assisted
ovens, reduce cooking time by 10 minutes in each hour and
reduce the cooking temperature by about 20°C.

## ALL THE RIGHT MEASURES

The accurate measuring of ingredients is essential for
success, especially when baking.

**Dry ingredients** There are many varieties of scales available
but the most accurate, measuring in increments of 5g, are
the traditional balance scales and the modern digital display
types. Choose a good set with clear numbering and a bowl
that's big enough for measuring larger quantities. Most
electronic scales allow you to reset the reading to zero so
you can weigh each ingredient as you add it to the bowl.

**Liquids** Always measure liquids in a glass or plastic
measuring jug placed on a level surface. Check liquid
measures from eye level as looking down on the measuring
jug will give a distorted view. When measuring syrupy foods

(e.g., molasses, honey, golden syrup), first coat the
measuring spoon or measuring jug with vegetable oil; the
syrup will easily slip out.

**Measuring by spoon** When recipes call for tablespoons or
teaspoon measures of dry or liquid ingredients, measuring
spoon sets are the most accurate. They are available in
metal or plastic sets of 1 tablespoon (15ml), ½ tablespoon
(7.5ml), 1 teaspoon (5ml), ½ teaspoon (2.5ml), ¼ teaspoon
(1.2ml) and, sometimes, ⅛ teaspoon (0.5ml). Hold the
spoon over an empty bowl to catch any excess (do not hold
the spoon over a bowl of ingredients). Always make sure
the spoon measure is full. Level the top by sweeping the
straight edge of a knife blade or a metal spatula across the
spoon from the handle end. Liquids, such as oil, will find
their own level in the measuring spoon

**Measuring the volume of equipment** Some recipes call for
equipment that has a particular volume, such as a 2-litre
soufflé dish. The most accurate way to measure this is to fill
the dish or tin with water from a measuring jug, rather than
the other way round. Using 500ml of cold water at a time,
fill the dish until the water reaches the brim, taking note
each time you fill the jug.

## BOILING AND SIMMERING

Boiling liquid has reached 100°C (212°F) and is ideal for
cooking foods such as vegetables quickly without losing
their nutrients, colour and shape. However, cooking at this
high temperature is not suitable for all foods. Meat, for
example, will become very tough if boiled, while sauces will
evaporate and some may curdle. For this reason, many
recipes instruct to simmer for the remaining cooking time.
Simmering takes place at a slightly lower temperature and is
more gentle than boiling, allowing flavours to mingle and
foods such as meat to tenderize. To tell the difference
between boiling and simmering, look at the surface of the
liquid: when a liquid is boiling, there will be large bubbles
continuously rising and breaking the surface. When a liquid
is simmering, the large bubbles are replaced by a stream of
small bubbles that are just visible on the surface.

## GREASEPROOF OR PARCHMENT?

Greaseproof paper has a waterproof coating which makes it
ideal for wrapping and cooking food in such as fish (see
page 125). It is also used to line cake tins; when lining a tin
with greaseproof paper, you should grease the paper first
with melted butter or margerine, then dust it with plain
flour. If you do a lot of baking, you will probably find it
more convenient to use baking parchment. Because it has
been specially treated with a silicone coating, there is no
need to grease or dust the paper.

## CUT TO SIZE

**Chop** To cut food into small, irregular pieces about the size of peas. Roughly cut up food, then mound pieces in a pile. Hold the handle of a chef's knife with one hand, the tip with the other and chop with a rocking motion.

**Chop finely** To cut food into tiny irregular pieces, less than 3mm. Proceed as for chopping, but cut food smaller.

**Dice** These are small, uniform cubes of about 5mm in size. To dice, first cut food into matchsticks or shreds. Bundle pieces together; slice crosswise into uniform cubes.

**Julienne** These are thin matchsticks about 5cm long. First cut food into slices about 5cm long and 3mm thick. Stack slices; cut lengthwise into 3mm-wide sticks.

## CHOPPING AN ONION

1 Halve onion through the root end; place on chopping board. Make horizontal cuts parallel to board, cutting to, but not through, the root.

2 Make lengthways vertical cuts, almost but not quite through the root.

3 Now cut across the width of the onion to chop into small pieces.

## EMERGENCY SUBSTITUTIONS

**Baking powder** For each 1 teaspoon called for, substitute ¼ teaspoon bicarbonate of soda and ½ teaspoon cream of tartar (make fresh for each use).

**Chives** Substitute spring onions, including the tops.

**Fish sauce (nuoc nam)** For each 1 tablespoon, use 2 teaspoons soy sauce and 1 teaspoon anchovy paste.

**Herbs** For each 1 tablespoon fresh, use 1 tablespoon frozen (use for cooking only, not as a garnish) or ½ teaspoon dried. If you can't find oregano use marjoram, or vice versa.

**Light brown sugar** For each 250g, substitute 250g granulated sugar and 1 tablespoon molasses or treacle; or use dark brown sugar.

**Mustard** For each 1 tablespoon prepared mustard, use 1 teaspoon dry mustard mixed with 2 tablespoons wine vinegar, white wine or water.

**Parma ham** Use ham, preferably Bavarian or country ham.

**Pancetta** Substitute back bacon or ham.

**Pine nuts** Use walnuts or almonds.

**Shallots** Substitute onion.

**Vanilla essence** Use brandy or appropriate flavoured liqueur.

## OVEN TEMPERATURE EQUIVALENTS

| CELSIUS | FARENHEIT | GAS | DESCRIPTION |
| --- | --- | --- | --- |
| 110°C | 225°F | ¼ | Cool |
| 130°C | 250°F | ½ | Cool |
| 140°C | 275°F | 1 | Very low |
| 150°C | 300°F | 2 | Very low |
| 170°C | 325°F | 3 | Low |
| 180°C | 350°F | 4 | Moderate |
| 190°C | 375°F | 5 | Moderately hot |
| 200°C | 400°F | 6 | Hot |
| 220°C | 425°F | 7 | Hot |
| 230°C | 450°F | 8 | Very hot |

## VOLUME EQUIVALENTS

| METRIC | IMPERIAL | METRIC | IMPERIAL |
| --- | --- | --- | --- |
| 25ml | 1 fl oz | 200ml | 7 fl oz (⅓ pint) |
| 50ml | 2 fl oz | 225ml | 8 fl oz |
| 75ml | 2½ fl oz | 250ml | 9 fl oz |
| 100ml | 3½ fl oz | 300ml | 10 fl oz (½ pint) |
| 125ml | 4 fl oz | 350ml | 12 fl oz |
| 150ml | 5 fl oz (¼ pint) | 400ml | 14 fl oz |
| 175ml | 6 fl oz | 500ml | 18 fl oz |

# FOOD SAFETY AND STORAGE KNOW-HOW

The following guidelines are ones that no cook should be without. Keeping food in good condition isn't difficult and shouldn't be daunting. But a safe kitchen does call for a few precautions. Here, we outline safety essentials, including the right way to handle raw meats, and how long you can safely store a range of foods.

## GOLDEN RULES OF FOOD SAFETY

• Keep a clean kitchen. Any area can harbour harmful bacteria, so always wash and dry your hands before handling food. Frequently wash kitchen towels, cloths and sponges. Rinse fresh fruits and vegetables before eating. Wash chopping boards, knives and other utensils with hot soapy water after every use – especially after handling raw meat and poultry. Wash chopping boards occasionally with a solution of 1 tablespoon bleach per 4 litres water to sterilize them.
• Don't put cooked meat (or any ready-to-eat food) on a plate that has come in contact with raw meat, poultry or fish.
• To kill harmful bacteria that may be present in raw eggs, fish, poultry and meat, it's essential to cook these foods thoroughly. A thermometer is the safest method for checking doneness. For a visual check, follow these guidelines: cook red meat at least to medium-rare (pink but not red in centre); pork until juices run clear and meat retains just a trace of pink; poultry until juices run clear; fish just until opaque throughout; and egg yolks and whites until firm and set. Cook minced meat until no pink remains.
• It's unwise to cook foods in stages. Don't start to cook food, stop, and then return to it later. Even when food is stored in the refrigerator between cooking periods, safe temperatures might not be maintained and bacteria may develop.
• Refrigerate leftovers as soon as possible; do not leave at room temperature longer than 2 hours. Divide large amounts among small, shallow containers for quicker cooling.
• In hot weather, don't leave protein foods such as chicken, egg salad, etc., out of the refrigerator for more than 1 hour.

## PACKING A SAFER PICNIC

• Use 2 small coolers rather than one large one – one that will be opened frequently (for fruit and beverages), and one for perishable items like meat, poultry, salads and cheese.
• Chill foods thoroughly before placing them in a cooler (the cooler cannot chill foods that aren't already cold). To preserve the chill, don't open the lid longer than necessary.
• If you're taking raw meat to a barbecue, double-wrap it in sealed plastic bags to prevent juices from tainting other foods.
• Pack perishable items next to ice packs. Keep delicate fruits and lettuce away from ice to prevent freezing.

### WRAP IT UP

**Aluminium foil** This provides optimal protection, moulds easily, and can withstand extreme temperatures. The heavy-duty version is ideal for long-term storage.
**Cling film** The best offer a tight seal and protect food against moisture loss and odour transfer. Thinner wraps often cling better and are ideal for leftovers and brief microwave reheats (but should not be in direct contact with food when microwaved). For freezer storage, choose a heavy plastic wrap intended for that purpose.
**Freezer paper** This old-fashioned favourite protects food from freezer burn and is very easy to label.
**Plastic bags** Food storage bags are intended for room-temperature or refrigerated foods. Freezer bags are the thickest and sturdiest, and can even endure a quick burst in the microwave for defrosting and warming.

## STORE-CUPBOARD STAPLES

Unless otherwise noted, these store-cupboard staples keep best in a cool, dry place. For more information on basic ingredients (e.g., flour, eggs, cheese, pasta and grains), see appropriate Know-How pages.
**Baking powder** Once opened, keep it well sealed and it should be effective for up to 6 months. To test it, add 1 teaspoon to some hot water; it should bubble vigorously.
**Dried breadcrumbs** Store in the cupboard for up to 6 months, or – for better flavour – refrigerate up to 2 years.
**Golden syrup** Once opened, this will keep for 2 years in the cupboard. If it crystallizes, place opened tin or jar in bowl of hot water. Stir syrup until crystals dissolve.
**Honey** It will last indefinitely; if it has crystallized, place opened jar in bowl of hot water. Stir until crystals dissolve.
**Olive oil** Keep in a cool, dark place up to 6 months. Don't buy more than you can use; it may become rancid, especially if stored in a warm place.
**Peanut butter** Unopened, it will last for a year in your cupboard. Refrigerate after opening to avoid rancidity.
**Soy sauce** Unopened, it will keep in the cupboard for a year. Once opened, refrigerate to keep for another year.
**Spices and dried herbs** Keep in lightproof containers in a cool place up to 1 year. Store red spices (paprika, ground red pepper), poppy seeds and sesame seeds in the freezer.
**Tabasco sauce** After opening, store at room temperature up to 3 months or refrigerate for longer storage.
**Vegetable oil** Store in a cool, dark place up to 6 months.
**Vinegar** Unopened, it will keep indefinitely. Sediment that may appear is harmless and can be strained off. Once opened, store in the pantry for 6 months. Vinegar with added flavourings (e.g., fruits, herbs) should be strained into a clean bottle when vinegar level drops below top of ingredients.

## THE RIGHT WAY TO REFRIGERATE

• Make sure your refrigerator temperature remains between 5° and 8°C.
• To prevent spoilage, keep foods on a rotating system. Place new items at the back of the shelves and move older purchases to the front.
• Date all leftovers so you know how long you've had them.
• If you're unsure whether a food is safe to eat, discard it.
• Put packages of fresh meat, poultry and fish on a plate in the refrigerator if you plan to cook them within a day or two; otherwise freeze them immediately.
• Keep eggs in their carton so they don't absorb other food odours. For the same reason, store cheese, cream, milk, yogurt, margarine and butter tightly closed or covered.

## FREEZER FACTS

• Frozen foods retain their colour, texture and nutrients better than foods preserved by other methods.
• Check the temperature of the freezer with a freezer thermometer to be sure that it is at -18°C. (Higher temperatures will draw moisture from the food, resulting in a loss of texture and taste.)
• It's time to defrost whenever there is 1cm of frost on the sides of the freezer. If the frost has not solidified into hard ice, a plastic scraper makes light work of this job.
• Don't overload your freezer or add more than 1kg of food per 8 litres volume of space in a 24-hour period. Either will cause temperature changes that may damage food.
• To avoid ice crystals, colour or texture changes or freezer burn, seal foods in airtight containers, or wrap them tightly in a wrap intended for freezer storage.
• Small 'piece' foods such as individual appetizers (e.g., tartlets, filo triangles), drop biscuits or strawberries keep best when 'tray', or 'dry', frozen. This method freezes foods so they remain separate and you can remove only as many as you need. Simply spread the unwrapped food on a baking sheet; freeze just until firm, then package in sealed plastic bags. Tray freezing is also ideal for firming foods such as cakes and pies so packaging material will not adhere to them.
• Liquid and semi-liquid foods must be stored in leakproof containers; leave space for expansion of liquid during the freezing process (for wide-mouth containers, leave 1cm for 500ml, and 2cm for 1litre cartons; for narrow-mouth containers, leave 2cm for 500ml, and 3cm for litres).
• Don't freeze raw vegetables (they'll lose crispness unless you blanch them first) or fried foods (they'll turn soggy). Also avoid freezing soft cheeses, mayonnaise, soured cream and custard – they'll become watery or may separate.
• Label and date food packets, and note the weight of meats and poultry and number of portions.
• Prepare frozen foods right after thawing; growth of bacteria can occur rapidly in thawed foods left at room temperature (especially casseroles, meat pies and gravy).

## STORING FRESH HERBS

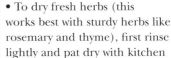

• Most fresh herbs are highly perishable, so buy them in small quantities as needed. To store them for a few days, immerse roots or freshly cut stems in about 5cm of water. Cover the leaves with damp kitchen towels or a plastic bag; refrigerate.
• To dry fresh herbs (this works best with sturdy herbs like rosemary and thyme), first rinse lightly and pat dry with kitchen towels. Hang them upside down by the stems in bunches, in a dry, warm spot out of bright light. When leaves become brittle (typically a few days to a week), pick them off and discard the stems; store dried leaves in tightly covered containers in a cool, dry place.
• To freeze herbs, rinse lightly, pat dry, remove the stems and place in plastic containers or bags. The frozen herbs will darken in colour, but the flavour will be fine. There's no need to thaw frozen herbs; just add them directly to the food you are cooking. Or, place a few herbs (leaves only) in ice cube trays; add just enough water to cover leaves and freeze. Simply add the cube to simmering soups or sauces.

## REFRIGERATOR AND FREEZER STORAGE GUIDE

| FOOD | IN REFRIGERATOR | IN FREEZER |
| --- | --- | --- |
| Raw poultry, fish and meat (small pieces) | 2–3 days | 3–6 months |
| Raw minced meat or poultry | 1–2 days | 3 months |
| Cooked whole roasts or whole poultry | 2–3 days | 9 months |
| Cooked poultry pieces | 1–2 days | 1 month (6 months in stock or gravy) |
| Bread | — | 3 months |
| Ice cream | — | 1–2 months |
| Soups and stews | 2–3 days | 1–3 months |
| Casseroles | 2–3 days | 2–4 weeks |
| Biscuits | — | 6–8 months |

# EATING WELL KNOW-HOW

Establishing good daily eating habits is essential for your health and well-being. Forming poor dietary habits when you're young can lead to health problems later in life. It's essential to go beyond the 'basic four' food groups. The Food Pyramid illustrated below will help you choose what and how much to eat from a variety of food groups to get the nutrients you need without too many calories, or too much fat, saturated fat, cholesterol, sugar or sodium.

## DIETARY GUIDELINES

• Eat a variety of foods to get the calories, protein, vitamins, minerals and fibre needed.
• Balance the food you eat with physical activity to maintain or improve your weight.
• Choose a diet low in fat, saturated fat and cholesterol.
• Choose a diet with plenty of vegetables, fruits and grain products (these fill you up healthfully).
• Use sugar, salt and alcohol only in moderation.
• Eat more fish and white meat and less red meat.

## THE FOOD PYRAMID

The Food Pyramid is an outline of what to eat each day. The research-based plan, originally developed by the United States Department of Agriculture, is meant to serve as a general guide – not a rigid prescription – that encourages you to pick and choose from a vast range of foods to create a healthy diet that's right for you.

• The Pyramid calls for eating a variety of foods to get the nutrients you need along with the right amount of calories to maintain a healthy weight. The Pyramid focuses on controlling fat intake as most American and British diets are too high in fat, especially saturated fat.

• The Pyramid emphasizes foods from five major food groups shown in the three lower sections of the Pyramid. Each group provides some – but not all – of the nutrients you need for a balanced diet. Foods in one category can't replace those in another (and no one group is more important than another); for good health you need them all.

• When planning meals, choose fresh foods whenever possible. Processed foods tend to have fewer nutrients and higher amounts of sugar, fats and sodium than home-prepared ones. When you eat packet foods, check labels to see that the fat content fits your fat allowance (see box, page 19).

**Bread, cereal, rice and pasta** These foods – all from grains – form the base of the Pyramid. You need the most servings (6 to 11) of these foods each day.

**Fruits and vegetables** The next level also comes from plants. Eat fruits (2 to 4 servings daily) and vegetables (3 to 5 servings daily) for vitamins, minerals and fibre.

**Meats and dairy foods** Most of the foods on this level of the Pyramid come from animals. The 'meat' group foods include meat, poultry, fish, dry beans, eggs and nuts. Meats, poultry and fish are rich in protein, B vitamins, iron and zinc. Dry beans, eggs and nuts provide protein along with other vitamins and minerals. Dairy foods – mainly milk, yogurt and cheese – provide protein, bone-building calcium and other nutrients. In general, animal foods are higher in fat than plant foods, but it's not necessary to cut out all meat and dairy products just to keep fat intake low. Low-fat versions of dairy foods and lean, well-trimmed meat and skinless poultry provide the same amounts of vitamins and minerals as their fattier counterparts. Most individuals should aim for 2–3 servings daily from each of these 2 groups. Vegetarians who do not eat animal foods can substitute extra servings of dry beans and nuts for their protein needs but will also need fortified foods, extra servings of other plant foods or supplements to get adequate calcium, iron and vitamin $B_{12}$.

**Fats, oils, and sweets** At the small tip of the Pyramid are foods such as oils, cream, butter, margarine, sugars, soft drinks, sweets and desserts. To maintain a healthy weight, eat them sparingly.

Fats, oils, sweets (use sparingly)

'Meat' group (2–3 servings)    Dairy group (2–3 servings)

Fruit group (2–4 servings)    Vegetable group (3–5 servings)

Bread, cereal, rice and pasta group (6–11 servings)

## WHAT IS A SERVING?

The Pyramid suggests a range of servings for each food group. The number that's right for you depends on your calorie needs, which in turn depends on your age, sex, size and how active you are. What counts as a serving? There's no need to measure everything, but here are some guidelines:
**Bread, cereal, rice, and pasta** 1 slice bread; 30g ready-to-eat cereal; 90g cooked rice, pasta or cereal.
**Vegetables** 50g salad greens; 60g chopped cooked or raw vegetables; 175ml vegetable juice.
**Fruits** 1 medium apple, banana, orange, pear or peach; 125g cooked, canned or frozen fruit; 40g dried fruit; 175ml fruit juice (100 per cent juice).
**Dairy foods** 250ml milk or yogurt; 45g natural cheese; 60g processed cheese.
**Meat group** 60–90g cooked lean boneless meat, fish or poultry (90g is the size of a pack of playing cards). Or, count as 30g of meat any of the following: 90g cooked dry beans; 1 egg; 50g nuts; 2 tablespoons peanut butter.

It's easy to overdo high calorie foods like meat and cheese. Try measuring out the suggested portions at least once; you may be surprised at their size.

## THE RIGHT CARBOHYDRATES

Breads, cereals, grains and pasta provide complex carbohydrates (an important source of energy), vitamins, minerals and fibre. The recommendation of 6–11 servings may seem high, but it adds up more quickly than you'd think: a generous bowl of cereal or pasta could equal 2, 3 or even 4 servings. Starchy foods are often blamed for adding extra pounds, but high-fat toppings (butter on bread, cream sauce on pasta) are the more likely culprits. Avoid foods which may seem high in carbohydrates but are also packed with butter and sugar such as croissants and muesli bars. Wholemeal breads and cereals offer the most fibre.

## FRUITS AND VEGETABLES

Five servings of fruits and vegetables daily (at least) is the rule to remember. Follow these ideas to help get your daily quota:
• For the best range of nutrients – and for delicious variety – don't eat the same fruits and vegetables day after day.
• Include choices high in vitamin C (citrus fruits, kiwifruit, strawberries), and those rich in vitamin A (carrots, winter squash, spinach, kale, cantaloupe).
• Research links cruciferous vegetables such as broccoli, cabbage, cauliflower and Brussels sprouts with reduced risk for certain cancers, so have them several times a week.
• Frozen produce is convenient, and it may be more nutritious than fresh that has been stored or shipped.

## CHOOSING YOUR PROTEINS

**Best choice** Fish and chicken or turkey without skin, dry beans and peas are all high in protein without being too high in fat.
**Leanest red meats** *Beef* topside, top rump, tenderloin, top sirloin, flank steak, minced beef (90–93 per cent); *veal* escalopes (from leg), loin chop; *pork* tenderloin, boneless loin roast, loin chop; *lamb* shank half leg of lamb, loin roast, loin chop, leg and shoulder cubes for kebabs.
**Super seafood** Most fish and seafood is low in fat and rich in helpful Omega-3 oils.
**Go easy on egg yolks** They're high in cholesterol. Many health experts recommend a limit of 4 egg yolks per week.
**Don't go nuts** Nuts and seeds like sesame or sunflower are high in fat; eat in moderation.

## IS THERE A 'GOOD' FAT?

Yes. No healthy diet is without some fat; however, all fats in foods are a mixture of three types of fatty acids: saturated, monounsaturated and polyunsaturated. *Saturated* fat, found in meat and dairy products and coconut, palm, and palm kernel oil, should be limited to 10 per cent of calories (about one third of your total fat intake) or less; too much raises cholesterol and the risk of heart disease. *Monounsaturated* fats (found in olive and peanut oil), and *polyunsaturated* fats (found mainly in vegetable, sunflower, corn, soybean and some fish), are healthier.

### WHAT'S YOUR FAT LIMIT?

Here's an easy way to calculate the maximum amount of fat you should consume each day. For a diet containing 30 per cent fat calories, your ideal body weight in kilograms is roughly equivalent to desirable grams in fat. So if your ideal weight is 60kg, limit your total fat intake to 60g. Fat is an essential nutrient, so don't cut it out completely. Remember that it's your average intake over a period of time – not a single food or meal – that affects your health and weight. Try to avoid eating too many high-fat foods and balance any that you do eat by choosing low-fat foods the next day.

# THE MEDITERRANEAN DIET

For centuries the traditional diet of the sunny countries around the Mediterranean has succeeded in prolonging life and preventing disease. Health experts have taken notice – and suggested that the culinary habits of these countries could help Britons in their quest to cut fat and eat more nutritiously. The result: the 'Mediterranean Pyramid,' a plan not too different from the US-style Pyramid. Both have a foundation of grains, fruits and vegetables. But the Mediterranean model highlights beans and other legumes, limits red meat to a few times per month and promotes the use of olive oil. The model also encourages daily exercise – and even a glass of wine with dinner.

**Go with grains (and pasta!)** Bread, pasta, bulgur and rice are staples on the Mediterranean table. This is a head-start to good health, because grains are naturally high in complex carbohydrates and low in fat. Whole grains boast another healthy bonus – fibre.

**Pack in the produce** The Mediterranean diet abounds in seasonal fresh fruits and vegetables – significantly more than the typical British diet.

**Amazing olive oil** For centuries, people in Mediterranean countries have enjoyed generous amounts of olive oil with no evidence of harm. They cook with it, drizzle it in soup and on salads, and even use it on bread in place of butter. What makes olive oil so good? The main difference between olive oil and other fats is that it's predominantly a heart-healthy monounsaturated fat. When substituted for fats that are more saturated, 'mono' fats tend to lower artery-clogging LDL cholesterol while maintaining levels of the protective HDL cholesterol. But remember, all types of fat are high in calories and excess weight increases the risk of heart disease.

**Focus on fish** Red meat is saved for special occasions (and then usually used in small amounts in grain and vegetable dishes). Fish – low in saturated fat and rich in healthful Omega-3 fatty acids – is eaten several times a week instead.

**Get lean with beans** A key ingredient in Mediterranean salads, soups and stews, these inexpensive foods are low in fat and high in protein, fibre and complex carbohydrates.

**Savour wines** Wine with meals is traditional in Mediterranean cultures, but over-indulgence is rare. Studies have shown that moderate drinking (usually defined as 1 drink per day for women, 2 for men) raises 'good' cholesterol levels and may make blood less likely to form clots in arteries. But moderation is the key – 'one drink' is a 125ml glass of wine, a 175ml serving of beer or a 30ml serving of spirits.

**Finish with fruit** Desserts have a place in the Mediterranean diet, but meals typically end with fresh or dried fruit rather than sugar-laden, high-fat desserts.

**Let yourself relax** Quality of life can't be overlooked as a contributing factor to health and happiness. Meals are savoured slowly with family and friends, and physical activity is a part of daily life.

# LEARNING FROM FOOD LABELS

Food labels can give helpful advice on cooking and serving. However, the most important information that food labels give is the nutritional composition of the food. This helps the consumer make an informed purchase and understand how that particular food fits into their diet.

• Many UK food manufacturers provide NUTRITIONAL INFORMATION showing values for calories, protein, carbohydrate, fat, fibre and sodium contents. This is not yet required by law in Europe, but is mandatory in the US. An example of a typical food label is given below.

• Most packets will supply nutritional information such as calories per 100g and, often, per serving. The vitamin and mineral content may be declared only if 100g or 100ml of the product contains at least 15 per cent of the Recommended Daily Amount (RDA), or if the food is sold in individual portions.

• The large e indicates that when the product was packaged, on average the quantity stated is accurate but the weight of each package may vary slightly.

### Nutritional Information

| Typical values | Per 100g | Per serving (228g) |
|---|---|---|
| Energy | 475kj/115kcal | 1079kj/260kcal |
| Protein | 2.2g | 5g |
| Carbohydrate | 13.6g | 31g |
| of which sugars | 2.2g | 5g |
| Fat | 5.7g | 13g |
| of which saturates | 2.2g | 5g |
| Fibre | 0g | 0g |
| Sodium | .3g | .66g |

Refrigerate after opening. Use within one month
BEST BEFORE DATE ON CAP
456g e

Made in England
Company name
Company address

• Food labels should also carry an ingredient list. Ingredients are listed on food labels in descending order according to their weight. This allows you to, for example, choose muffins with flour, not sugar, at the top of the list.

### USING THE NUTRITIONAL VALUES IN THIS BOOK

With each recipe, you'll find nutritional information that can help you plan a balanced diet. Aim to balance higher-fat recipes with low-fat accompaniments: for example, serve a meat lasagne with a large green salad and a meat curry with a large portion of boiled rice.

• Our nutritional calculations do not include optional ingredients, garnishes or decorations.

• When alternative ingredients are listed (e.g., margarine or butter), our calculations are based on the first one mentioned.

• Unless otherwise noted, whole milk has been used.

## TIPS FOR LOW-FAT COOKING

• Choose lean cuts of meat and trim visible fat before cooking. Remove skin from poultry before or after cooking.
• Grill meats on a rack so the fat can drip away.
• Chill soups and stews overnight so you can easily remove and discard the hardened fat from the top.
• Be skimpy with fat. Use non-stick pans or non-stick cooking spray, or 'sauté' in a small amount of stock or water. Don't pour oil into a frying pan – it's easy to add too much. Measure, or use a pastry brush to coat the pan with a thin layer of oil. When baking, coat tins with a spritz of non-stick cooking spray instead of oils or fats.
• Try semi-skimmed or skimmed milk, low-fat versions of soured cream and cheese and non-fat yogurt; they provide the same calcium and protein as full-fat varieties, with less fat.
• Use fresh herbs and zesty seasonings liberally to replace some of the flavour lost when you cut down on fat.

## SMART SUBSTITUTIONS

• Use low-fat yogurt in dips instead of soured cream.
• Substitute lean ham for streaky bacon and save about 115 calories per 30g.
• Substitute minced chicken or turkey breast for minced beef. (Be sure the package is labelled meat only – if not, it may contain skin and can have as much fat as minced beef.)
• Substitute cooked fibre- and protein-packed dried legumes like beans and lentils for meat in casseroles.
• Replace the cream in cream soups or sauces with evaporated skimmed milk.
• For a leaner hamburger, substitute shredded carrots or cooked rice for a third of the meat.
• Choose angel food cake instead of chocolate cake.
• To reduce fat and cholesterol, use 2 egg whites for 1 whole egg.
• Replace soured cream with buttermilk or yogurt in baking.

## SAMPLE MENUS

The following menus show 3 days of healthy, satisfying meals that meet healthy dietary requirements suggested by most nutritionists: around 2000 calories a day with no more than 30–35 per cent calories from fat. (These values are for a moderately active adult; your calorie requirement may vary from this depending on your metabolism and your level of activity.) The page numbers are listed for the recipes given in this book; all other items are generic. Remember that the key to good health is how you eat over time – not the fat and calorie content of a single meal.

### THREE DAYS OF BALANCED MENUS

| | BREAKFAST | LUNCH | DINNER |
|---|---|---|---|
| Day 1 | 175ml orange juice or orange sections<br>2 slices wholemeal toast spread with<br>    1 tablespoon jam<br>Medium bowl muesli<br>225ml skimmed or semi-skimmed milk<br>Tea, coffee or 125ml fruit juice | Mushroom-Barley Soup (page 61)<br>Crusty bread<br>60g Cheddar cheese<br>1 apple<br>125ml fruit juice or mineral water | Easy Stuffed Sole (page 124)<br>Lime Couscous (page 380)<br>Steamed spinach<br>Peach Sorbet (page 484)<br>Almond-Anise Biscotti (page 518)<br>225ml skimmed or semi-skimmed milk |
| Day 2 | Cantaloupe wedge<br>Boiled egg<br>2 slices wholemeal toast with<br>    polyunsaturated spread<br>225ml skimmed or semi-skimmed milk<br>Tea, coffee or 125ml fruit juice | Turkey sandwich: 60g sliced turkey, 2 slices rye<br>    bread, tomato and onion slices, mustard<br>225ml low-fat yogurt<br>125ml fruit juice or mineral water | Fillets au Poivre (page 199)<br>Steamed new potatoes with dill or parsley<br>Steamed broccoli and carrots<br>Vanilla Chiffon Cake (page 536)<br>Fresh orange segments and strawberries<br>1 glass wine |
| Day 3 | Medium bowl bran-flakes cereal<br>225ml skimmed or semi-skimmed milk<br>225ml low-fat yogurt<br>1 banana<br>Tea, coffee or 125ml fruit juice | Spinach salad: 90g spinach leaves, 1 sliced<br>    hard-boiled egg, 1 grilled and crumbled slice<br>    bacon, 60g crumbled feta cheese, sliced raw<br>    mushrooms, balsamic vinegar<br>Wholemeal roll with polyunsaturated spread<br>80g grapes<br>125ml fruit juice or mineral water | Country French Chicken (page 155)<br>Steamed green beans<br>Lemon-Parsley Rice (page 376)<br>Green salad, with Buttermilk-Chive Dressing<br>    (page 346)<br>Baked Pears with Marsala (page 454)<br>125ml fruit juice or mineral water |

# BARBECUE KNOW-HOW

Back gardens, patios, beaches or a shady spot in a park: no matter where you're planning to hold your barbecue, it is sure to bring together enthusiastic appetites and happy people. Here we explore every detail for delicious results: quick ways to light the coals, the right cooking method for every cut, essential equipment and inspired ways to add flavour.

## GETTING STARTED

Lighting the barbecue becomes easier with practice. To light a standard charcoal barbecue, use a charcoal chimney (a metal cylinder with a rack that stacks briquettes over crumpled newspaper), or an electric starter, which nestles a hot coil among coals. Or, stack coals in a pyramid (for good air circulation) and douse with lighter fluid (instant-lighting charcoal has been pre-treated with lighter fluid). Use enough charcoal to reach 2–3cm beyond the area the food will cover – plus a few more coals if it's cold and windy. The coals will take about 20 minutes to reach the necessary temperature; when they are ready for cooking, they will appear ash grey (during the daytime) or have a slight red glow (at night). Before setting the rack in place, spread the coals in a single layer, or bank them on either side of the barbecue for indirect heat. (Follow the manufacturer's instructions to light gas and electric barbecues.)

## SAFETY TIPS

**Location, location** Place your barbecue on a flat surface so it won't tip over, and away from overhangs, fences and shrubbery that could be ignited by a sudden flare-up.
**Avoid contamination** Use separate dishes for carrying raw and cooked foods. Wash all utensils, containers, chopping boards and work surfaces with hot soapy water after they come into contact with uncooked foods.
**Charcoal smarts** To avoid a build-up of toxic fumes, position the barbecue in a well-ventilated location – and never barbecue indoors. It's dangerous to add lighter fluid to flames or hot coals. Petrol and paraffin are especially dangerous – both can cause an explosion.
**Cut the fat** To avoid grease fires, trim excess fat from meats.
**Stay out of the black** A charred, blackened crust on foods is unhealthy.
**Play it cool** Once you've finished cooking, cover the barbecue, close the vents and allow the coals to burn out completely. Let the ashes cool at least 48 hours and dispose of them in a non-combustible container. If you dispose of coals before they've cooled, remove them with long-handled tongs and bury them in sand or put in a bucket of water.

## THE BEST WAY TO MARINATE

**Nice and easy** Plastic bags provide a great no-fuss method – simply add marinade ingredients and meat, poultry or fish, then seal shut, pressing out excess air and refrigerate. If using a bowl or dish, be sure it's made of a non-reactive material (glass, ceramic, stainless steel) that won't be affected by the acid in the marinade.
**The raw deal** Never let marinades that you've used for raw meat, poultry or fish come into contact with cooked food. Marinate foods (except vegetables) in the refrigerator – never at room temperature, unless marinating time is 30 minutes or less. If using a marinade as a sauce, boil for at least 2 minutes before serving. Discard any unused marinade – do not use again.
**Deepening flavour** Most meat and poultry needs 1 to 3 hours to marinate; seafood, 15 to 30 minutes. But timing also depends on ingredients. The more acid (e.g., lemon juice, vinegar, yogurt) used in your marinade, the less time it will take. Marinating for too long can result in a mushy texture. Marinades penetrate about 1cm deep, so don't expect them to flavour the centre of thick cuts.
**Rub it in!** Seasoning rubs are blends of dried herbs and spices that add flavour (without fat) to grilled meats and other foods. Common ingredients: rosemary, thyme, crushed red pepper, fennel seeds, garlic, dill and cracked peppercorns. Just mix and rub onto meat, pressing it in place, either hours or minutes before barbecuing.

## SKEWER STRATEGIES

• If you favour using metal skewers, you'll have best results with ones that are twisted or square – not round. The reason? Foods tend to twirl on round skewers when you try to turn them, making it difficult to ensure even cooking. (Wooden and skinny bamboo skewers aren't slippery, so their round shape doesn't pose a problem.)
• Be sure to soak wooden or bamboo skewers in water for at least 15 minutes before using, so that they won't burn when exposed to the heat. Then pat them dry.
• To ensure even cooking, don't jam pieces of food up against each other on the skewer – leave a small space between items when you thread them together. Additional safeguards: cut even-sized pieces and combine foods with similar cooking times on the same skewer.

Unwieldy items like large, thick onion slices won't fall apart and slip through the grill rack if you thread them onto 2 parallel skewers.

## DIRECT AND INDIRECT BARBECUING

Different foods require specific heat sources. Follow these guidelines to pick the right method for what you're making. **Direct heat barbecuing** For this method, food is cooked directly over the heat source, and must be turned in order to expose both sides to the fire. Direct barbecuing is best for foods that take less than 30 minutes to cook, such as boneless chicken, steaks, fish fillets, hamburgers and hot dogs. **Indirect heat barbecuing** Similar to oven roasting, this method is for foods that take longer than 30 minutes to cook, including roasts, whole turkeys, bone-in chicken, ribs and briskets; it must be done on a covered barbecue. Bank charcoal on one or both sides of a drip pan on the lower rack. When the coals are ready, place food on the barbecue centred over the pan. For extra moisture, you can add water, stock or fruit juice to the drip pan. Close the lid and keep it closed until the end of cooking time or until you need to add coals (at least an hour); there's no need to turn the food. For a 56cm barbecue, use about 25 briquettes on each side of the drip pan (50 total) for up to an hour of cooking. Add 8 new briquettes to each side for each additional hour of cooking.

## MAKING A FOIL PACKET

Foil packets create a handy pouch for barbecuing small, delicate foods like seafood or vegetables (ideal if you don't own a barbecue tray). You can add flavour with ingredients such as olive oil, citrus zest, Parma ham or fresh herbs. To make a foil packet, centre food on a double thickness of heavy-duty foil. Close packet with a double fold on top and ends (leave space for steam expansion). To avoid punctures, use tongs to turn packets.

## ADDING A DISTINCTIVE FLAVOUR

• Infuse chicken, ham, fish, pork or beef with a hint of citrus by scattering orange, lemon, lime or even grapefruit rind over the coals during the last few minutes of barbecuing time.
• For a smoky flavour, add aromatic wood chips (soak them in water first to bring out their flavour and prolong burning time). Mesquite and hickory are popular choices. More exotic varieties to seek out: alder, fruit-tree woods and grapevines. (Add large chips at the start of grilling, small chips near the end to keep the fire going.)
• Great with barbecued fruits like nectarines, plums, pineapple and peaches: the seductively sweet and smoky flavour of cinnamon sticks, whole cloves, star anise or allspice berries. Simply soak a few in water and add to the coals.
• Enhance the flavour of meats, seafood or vegetables by sprinkling one of the following over coals at the end of cooking time: sturdy herb sprigs (rosemary, thyme); bay leaves; dampened, unpeeled garlic cloves.

## FEEL THE HEAT

• To estimate the temperature of the barbecue, place your hand, palm side down, about 10cm over the heat. Count the seconds ('one thousand one, one thousand two', etc.) until the heat forces you to pull your hand away. If you can keep it in place for 2 seconds, the barbecue is hot (190°C or more); 3 seconds, it's medium-hot (180°–190°C); 4 seconds, it's medium (150°–180°C); 5 seconds, it's low (100°–150°C).
• If the fire is too hot: raise the cooking rack and spread out the charcoal. In a covered cooker, close vents halfway.
• Need more heat? Lower cooking rack; tap ashes from charcoal and push closer together. Add more coals to the edges of hot coals. In covered cooker, open vents fully.

### HELPFUL EQUIPMENT

**Long-handled tongs** Indispensable for turning food and arranging coals. Don't turn meat or poultry with a fork: it can pierce the flesh, releasing juices and flavour.
**Basting brush** For applying sauce or oiling racks.
**Fish slice** Use to support delicate-textured fish (fillets and whole), which otherwise may fall apart as they are being turned. Or use two palette knives together.
**Barbecue brush** Stiff wire bristles make cleaning easy; V–shaped models clean both sides of the grill at once.
**Insulated mitts** Look for mitts that are elbow-length and flameproof.
**Hinged grill basket** A wire basket makes it easy to turn whole fish and other delicate foods.
**Barbecue tray** This small-hole or fine-mesh grid is a must for barbecuing vegetables, seafood and fish fillets.

## CLEANING YOUR BARBECUE

For easiest cleaning, scrub barbecue rack right after using with metal-bristle brush. Let rack cool slightly, then soak it in hot soapy water to loosen grime. If the rack is too large for your sink, let it stand for an hour wrapped in wet kitchen towels; scrub clean. To clean a gas barbecue after use, turn heat to high and let it run for 10–15 minutes with lid closed. Then use a metal-bristle brush to remove any baked-on food. To prevent foods from sticking to racks, rub with vegetable oil or spray with non-stick cooking spray before barbecuing. Do not use spray near hot coals.

Parties are terrific for bringing together favourite foods and friends. What's more, dazzling your guests can take surprisingly little effort. Whether you're an experienced party planner or a beginner, you'll find helpful hints and tips on these pages including ways to get organized, strategies for choosing worry-free menus and how to create the prettiest tables.

## RULES FOR SUCCESS

**Keep it simple**  A few well-planned dishes are more appealing than loads of fussy or rich foods. Remember, the more guests you have, the simpler the food should be.

**Do it ahead**  The more you can do in advance, the more time you'll have to relax and enjoy your guests.

**Be generous**  You're safer having too much food than running out. Don't forget, you can usually freeze the extras.

**Go with the season**  Fruits and vegetables in season are fresher and cost less, so use them as much as possible.

**Make lists**  This is a superb way to get organized. Write a guest list, a menu list and two shopping lists (for nonperishables and perishables). Make a menu preparation timetable that can be checked off as you go.

**Keep a record**  To avoid repeating the same dishes for the same people, write everything down in an entertaining notebook. It's also a useful reminder of which dishes or menus have worked well in the past.

## EASY ENTERTAINING STRATEGIES

• The more dishes you can make ahead, the better. Many soups and stews will actually improve in flavour. it's also a good idea to include some dishes that freeze well, such as Spicy Cheese Sticks (see page 50), cakes or biscuits. For some items, components can be made ahead and stored separately for later assembly.

• Buffets are great for entertaining because once the food is out, all that's needed is to keep the serving bowls and platters full. Don't leave food at room temperature for more than 2 hours (1 hour in hot weather); replenish the table with fresh platters rather than adding more to half-empty ones.

• Create a menu of all room temperature dishes. Try marinated vegetables; savory tarts and quiches; pâtés and terrines; crostini and bruschetta; cold sesame noodles; frittatas; dips and salads; thinly sliced roast beef, turkey or ham; cold poached chicken or fish.

• Feature one centrepiece dish – elegant stuffed roast veal, a hearty lasagne or a big bowl of chilli – and partner with simple side dishes like crisp tossed green salad and crusty bread or rolls.

• Keep prepared foods on hand for easy appetizers. Staples include: caponata; marinated artichokes; tapenade or other spreads; a good pâté; pickled gherkins; jumbo olives; nuts; pitta breads; a selection of biscuits for cheese; etc.

• Plan finishing touches to brighten any menu. A swirl of soured cream on creamy carrot soup; sprigs of fresh herbs on a roast chicken platter; zigzag-cut lemon halves alongside fish; candied violets strewn on a dark chocolate cake – these turn the simple into the sensational.

• Do as much advance preparation as you can to avoid a last-minute panic. Make croûtons and store in an airtight tin at room temperature; rinse, trim and cut vegetables for side dishes and salads (wrap in damp kitchen towels in plastic bags in the refrigerator); prepare salad dressings; and so on.

• Use the food processor and microwave to save time on tasks like shredding cabbage, grating cheese and reheating.

• Avoid labour-intensive tasks. For example, for big parties you may find it easier to buy skinless, boneless chicken breasts than to bone them yourself.

• If it's a big but informal party, ask a few guests to help. For example, delegate barbecue duty for a short while or recruit someone to pass the hors d'oeuvre platter.

## DETAILS, DETAILS

• When inviting your guests, be specific about appropriate dress, the extent of the food and drink, and the expected duration of the party.

• Up to a week ahead, check your supply of chairs, glasses, serving dishes and utensils. Rent, borrow or buy extras if needed. For a large party, you may want to line up help such as waiters or bartenders.

• Check recipes for any special cooking equipment you may need, such as parchment paper.

• Decide on the music in advance. Soft jazz or classical competes less with conversation than other kinds.

• Make sure your bar is stocked; include enough choices (soft drinks, fruit juice, sparkling water, etc.) for non-drinkers. Choose wines to go with dinner.

• Buy enough ice – more than you think you need.

• Make fruited ice cubes to enliven drinks. Freeze tiny strawberries or raspberries in ice cubes. They're lovely in lemon squash, iced tea or a glass of white wine.

• If the refrigerator is full, use a cool box for storing cold drinks, ice and salads.

• Arrange flowers a day ahead so they'll be in full bloom for the day of the party.

• Set the table early in the day or the night before.

• If you're serving messy foods like corn on the cob or spare ribs, have little finger bowls at each place setting – float slices of lemon in warm water in small dishes or ramekins.

• If necessary, put out small bowls for olive stones, cocktail sticks, etc.; put in a stone or stick so people will know.

## STRESS-FREE MENU PLANNING

**Stick with the tried and true**  To minimize potential hitches, serve mostly recipes that you've tried and loved before.
**Consider your guests**  It's important to know of any food restrictions or preferences (e.g., vegetarian, low-cholesterol diet, no fish). Don't forget to ask about food allergies.
**Harmony and order**  The best menus feature foods that complement each other in terms of flavours, colours, textures and richness. Follow a spicy starter with a refreshing salad; a creamy soup with a simple roast instead of a heavily sauced main dish; a light starter salad with a hearty stew. Try to avoid repeating ingredients and flavours. For example, don't have olives in the salad and the stew.
**Think ahead**  Include as many dishes as possible that can be prepared in advance. Soups, stews, casseroles, mousses and sorbets are all good choices. Try not to have more than two dishes that need last-minute attention.
**Room-temperature ready**  It can be tricky to get all the hot foods on the table before something else cools down, so plan at least some dishes to serve at room temperature.
**Bite sized is best**  Foods for hors d'oeuvre should be small enough to be eaten in one bite (or easy to dip).

## SEASONAL ENTERTAINING

Each season brings its own inspiration for party ideas. In spring and summer, think of colourful foods, fresh, light flavours and firing up the barbecue. Winter parties call for richer flavours and heartier foods. Here are some ideas to help you take advantage of seasonal delights.

**Summer/spring sensations**
• Celebrate spring with a buffet of favourites – asparagus spears; grilled salmon; baby vegetables; Strawberry-Rhubarb Pie (see page 490).
• Rub glass rims with lemon wedges and dip in coarse salt (for margaritas or Bloody Marys) or sugar (for Pimms cup).
• Make an outdoor party especially festive by stringing tiny fairy lights around shrubs and small trees.
• Decorate cakes with flowers (see page 316) and chocolate leaves (see page 551).

**Autumn/winter delights**
• Have a halowe'en party with a warming pumpkin soup; use hollowed-out pumpkin as a room decoration.
• Scent the house by simmering cinnamon sticks on the stove.
• Warm up winter with meat-and-potatoes menus: meat loaf with creamy mashed potatoes, or beef tenderloin with roasted potatoes.
• Roast chestnuts (cut the flat side of each first) in a 200°C (400°F, Gas 6) oven for 20 minutes – eat while still hot.
• Bring out hot chocolate with the after-dinner coffee.
• Decorate tables with scented candles and baskets of pine cones and holly.

## ENTERTAINING MENUS

We've created a selection of menus that both you and your guests will love. That's because each is filled with festive and delicious dishes that are simple to make, and many of the recipes can be prepared in advance. Adapt the menu choices as you like to suit individual preferences.

*Healthy Entertaining for 6*
**Marinated Goat's Cheese** (page 41)
**Rolled Silverside with Spring Vegetables** (page 188)
**Crusty bread**
**Apricot Soufflés** (page 461)

•

*Spring Dinner for 8*
**Asparagus with Parmesan Vinaigrette** (page 285)
**Salmon and Vegetables in Parchment** (page 125; double the recipe)
**New potatoes with dill**
**Green salad, with Mustard-Shallot Vinaigrette** (page 345)
**Panna Cotta with Raspberry Sauce** (page 475)

•

*Summer Barbecue for 10 to 12*
**Roasted Aubergine Dip** (page 34), **with pitta wedges**
**Barbecued Pesto Lamb with Tomato-Cucumber Bruschetta** (page 261)
**Barley Salad with Nectarines** (page 331)
**Green Beans with Toasted Sesame Seeds** (page 318)
**Cherry Tomato-Lemon Salad** (page 322)
**Nectarine and Cherry Crisp Oat Cobbler** (page 452), **with vanilla ice cream**

•

*Autumn Dinner for 8*
**Pumpkin and Roasted Garlic Dip** (page 34), **with focaccia strips**
**Roast Duck with Cherry-Port Sauce** (page 141; double the recipe)
**Mashed Root Vegetables** (page 294)
**Green beans**
**Fennel, Pear and Chicory Salad** (page 319)
**Cappuccino Mousse** (page 476)
**Vanilla Wafers** (page 505)

•

*Winter Buffet for 12 to 16*
**Smoked Salmon Terrine** (page 36)
**Apricot-Glazed Smoked Ham** (page 247)
**Vegetables Vinaigrette** (page 276)
**Baked Rigatoni and Peas** (page 364)
**Spinach and Tangerine Salad** (page 319)
**Sweet Potato Scones** (page 402)
**Raspberry-Pear Trifle** (page 473)
**Coconut-Almond Macaroons** (page 508)
**Chocolate and Hazelnut Truffles** (page 524)

## SETTING A PROPER TABLE

A pretty table can set the mood for the meal to follow. Here, a brief guide to setting it.
• Place a dinner plate in the centre of each setting. Add cutlery in the order it will be used, beginning on the outside. (The more formal the setting, the more cutlery there is likely to be, but all settings should follow the order-of-use rule.) Place forks on the left and knives on the right, cutting edge turned in. Place spoons to the right of knives.
• If you have enough pieces, dessert utensils go above the plate (fork next to plate, handle to the left, spoon above fork, handle to the right). If not, clear the table completely and serve dessert cutlery with dessert.
• Set bread plates to the left of the plates, above the forks. Butter knives may be placed on the plates, handle to the right. Place salad plates, if using, to the left of the forks.
• Glasses go on the right, above the knives. Place the water glass closest to the plate, then the white wine glass, and then the red wine glass, if you're serving two wines.
• Place napkins either to the left of the forks, or in the centre of the dinner plate.

## WHICH TABLE COVERING?

**Tablecloths** Measure the table before you buy. For a formal tablecloth, add 40–60cm to both the length and width of the table. For a round table, add 90cm to the diameter. Except for the most formal occasions, choose a tablecloth according to your taste: bright or pastel, textured or patterned. Linen or lace in white and neutrals are most versatile and always look elegant.
**Place mats** These come in all colours, sizes, shapes and materials – from plastic and straw to linen and even metal. The mat should be large enough to hold the entire place setting, but not overlap with the next one.
**Napkins** As with tablecloths, fine cloth napkins in white or neutral colours are the most formal. Otherwise, choose napkins to complement tablecloths or mats.

• Accent each place setting with a miniature bouquet of fresh herbs, tied with a thin ribbon.
• Arrange a few small seashells at each place.
• Seek out one-of-kind linens, glasses, china and napkin rings at car-boot sales and charity shops.
• Illuminate each place setting with a small candle. Chill candles for several hours before lighting for fewer drips.
• For an elegant dinner, write handmade menus for each place setting. Check stationers for small cards.
• Lay a single flower at each place. Small water vials (sold at florists) will keep them fresh for a few hours.

## SUPER CENTREPIECES

Any table looks better with a stylish centrepiece. It's possible to make one from the simplest of raw materials; see the suggestions that follow. Keep the centrepiece low, so guests can see each other across the table. Don't forget to walk around the table so you can check it from all sides.
• Mix flowers, fruits, vegetables and herbs together for a lovely effect. Try shiny plum tomatoes with scarlet poppies; small purple and white aubergines with flowering herbs; pale peaches with lemons and sage leaves.
• Line a basket with an antique cloth; fill with perfect pears.
• Fill a crystal bowl with nuts in their shells.
• Place pots of small flowering plants in a wooden box.
• For a winter party, place chestnuts, pinecones and evergreen boughs in a wide silver bowl.
• Place small gourds and squash in a wicker basket.
• Set orange and red bell peppers in a turquoise bowl.
• Arrange an assembly of cacti in a shallow basket.

## BUFFET BASICS

A buffet is one of the easiest ways to serve a group of eight or more. You can set it up in advance, then mingle with your guests – all you have to do is replenish the food as necessary. If you have room, organize drinks and food in separate places so there's less of a crowd at either place. For a basic buffet, arrange foods in a circle on the table in a logical order: main dish, vegetables, salad, bread. Stack large dinner plates at the start of the buffet and put napkins and cutlery at the end so your guests are freer to fill up their plates. For easy serving, wrap individual place settings (knife and fork) in the napkins.

A two-line buffet is a similar arrangement that's ideal for a bigger crowd. Since you organize the food in two identical lines, one on each side of the table, everyone gets served more quickly. Remember that you'll need double the amount of serving dishes and utensils. For a smaller group, try arranging the buffet on a sideboard or table against the wall.

# WINE KNOW-HOW

Enjoyed the world over, wine can be one of the most pleasurable parts of a meal. Besides being savoured at the table, with dinner or before, wine can also enhance cooking. Here is a guide to serving, storing, and using wine – plus what to expect from some of the more popular varieties.

## SERVING IDEAS

• Stemmed glasses are traditional because the large base allows you to swirl the wine, which helps release its aroma and flavour. Holding the glass by its stem also means you're less apt to warm the wine with the heat of your hand. Fill glasses no more than two-thirds full (for swirling room).
• In general, serve red wines at room temperature. The best red wines need to 'breathe'. If you do wish to aerate wine before serving, decant it or pour it into glasses so that the wine actually comes in contact with air. Some young and fruity reds, such as Beaujolais Nouveau, are best slightly chilled.
• White wines and sparkling wines should be served chilled.
• To quick-chill white wine, submerge the bottle in a bucket or pot filled with half ice and half water for 20 minutes.
• When pairing wine and food, try to match flavour intensities. For example, serve a light wine with a delicate entrée, a spicy, robust wine with a deeply flavoured dish.
• Light wines are best with summer meals, or earlier in the day. Offer heavier wines with winter meals, or late in the day.
• If in doubt, go with the old rule: red wines with meats and cheese, white wines with fish, poultry and vegetable dishes.

## HOW TO STORE

• For long-term storage, keep wine in a cool, humid, dark place (e.g., cupboard, cellar). Store bottles on their side to prevent corks from drying and shrinking, which will let in air.
• It's fine to store leftover wine (without fancy equipment). It may even improve as it has a chance to aerate and release its bouquet. Refrigerate white wine and keep red at room temperature for up to 48 hours, with the original cork.

## COOKING WITH WINE

• Use a decent wine for cooking or marinating – not your absolute best, but something you wouldn't hesitate to drink.
• When adding wine to a sauce or hot dish, let it cook to allow the flavour to mellow and to cook off the alcohol.
• Marinating in wine is a good way to add flavor to meats and poultry. Also, the acid in wine acts as a tenderizer.
• For subtle flavour, use wine in moderation when cooking.
• You can substitute vinegar, stock or juice for wine in recipes.

## KNOW YOUR WINES

### WHITE WINES
**Sauvignon Blanc** This refreshing, clean-flavoured wine has a grassy, herbaceous aroma. Serve with fish and shellfish.
**Chardonnay** One of the most popular white wines, it's produced the world over. Most Chardonnays are fresh, fruity and fairly dry; they are often flavoured by aging in oak. Perfect with light summer foods such as grilled salmon.
**Chenin Blanc** A dry, crisp wine with a spicy, slightly sweet flavour; it complements chicken as well as vegetable dishes.
**Gewürztraminer** A speciality of Alsace, France, though it's produced in other countries as well. A spicy, crisp wine, it can be dry or semi-sweet. Try dry versions with fish, poultry and spicy foods, sweeter ones with desserts.
**Riesling** This favourite has a fruity, slightly sweet taste and a floral fragrance that's faintly like honey. It pairs nicely with veal and shellfish as well as most Oriental foods.
**Sauternes** A rich, sweet wine made primarily from Semillon grapes. The grapes develop a beneficial mould that shrivels them and concentrates their sweetness. Serve as a dessert wine or with rich foods like pâté or Roquefort cheese.

### RED WINES
**Bordeaux** This classic from western France can be light and fruity or rich and fragrant. Roast lamb is the ideal partner.
**Cabernet Sauvignon** Produced in many countries, this well-known wine is full-bodied, fruity and complex. It complements hearty meats, chicken and pasta.
**Chianti** The famous Italian red wine. Sturdy and dry, it goes nicely with pasta, steak, burgers and barbecued foods.
**Côtes du Rhône** A speciality of the Rhone valley, France, ranging from refreshing young reds to more substantial vintages. These wines partner well with game, steak, stews and casseroles.
**Gamay (Beaujolais)** Pleasantly light, this dry, fruity red wine is excellent with meats as well as poultry and pasta.
**Merlot** Rich, fragrant, and smooth-bodied. Serve with robust foods like lamb, sausages and game.
**Pinot Noir** This spicy, intensely flavoured wine can be light and fresh or rich and smooth. It goes with almost any food, but is especially good with salmon, ham and cheeses.

### OTHER WINES
**Fortified** Madeira, sherry and port are all wines that are fortified with a spirit (usually brandy) to increase their alcohol content. They make a fine aperitif or dessert wine.
**Rosé** These wines get their pale pink colour and light-bodied character from a very brief contact with grape skins. Serve rosés well chilled, before dinner or with light foods.
**Sparkling** These bubbly, mild-flavoured wines range from slightly sweet to dry. Champagne is the most famous. Sparkling wines go nicely with many foods, from oysters and smoked salmon to desserts.

# GLOSSARY

**Al dente** Italian for 'to the tooth', describes perfectly cooked pasta and vegetables. If pasta is al dente, it is just tender but offers a slight resistance when it is bitten.

**Baste** To spoon or brush a liquid over food – typically roasted or barbecued meats and poultry – during cooking to keep it moist. The liquid can be a sauce or glaze, stock, melted butter or pan juices.

**Beat** To whip briskly or stir a mixture with a spoon, whisk or electric mixer until it is smooth and light.

**Blanch** To cook foods briefly in boiling water. Blanching locks in textures for tender-crisp vegetables, loosens tomato and peach skins for peeling, and mellows salty foods. Begin timing as soon as the food hits the water – the water needn't return to a boil – then cool in cold water to stop the cooking.

**Blend** To combine two or more ingredients until smooth or uniformly mixed. Blending can be done with a spoon, or an appliance such as an electric mixer or a blender.

**Blind bake** To bake a pie crust before it's filled to create a crisper crust. To prevent the pastry from puffing and slipping during baking, it should be lined with foil and filled with pie weights, dried beans or uncooked rice; these are removed shortly before the end of baking time to allow the pastry to brown.

**Boil** To heat a liquid until bubbles break vigorously on the surface. You can boil vegetables, cook pasta in boiling water or reduce sauces by boiling them. Never boil meats (they'll be tough) or custard sauces (they'll curdle).

**Braise** To cook food in a small amount of liquid in a tightly covered pan, either in the oven or on the stove-top. Braising is an ideal way to prepare less-tender cuts of meat, firm-fleshed fish and vegetables.

**Brown** To cook food quickly on the stove-top (in fat), under a grill or in the oven to develop a richly browned, flavoured surface and help seal in natural juices.

**Butterfly** To split a food, such as shrimp or a boneless lamb leg or pork chop, horizontally in half, cutting almost but not all the way through, then opening (like a book) to form a butterfly shape. Butterflying exposes more surface area so the food cooks evenly and more quickly.

**Caramelize** To heat sugar in a skillet until it becomes syrupy and deep amber brown. Sugary toppings on desserts like crème brûlée can also be caramelized (by heating under the grill until melted), as can onions (by sautéing slowly until deep golden and very tender).

**Chop** To cut food roughly into small, irregular pieces about the size of peas.

**Core** To remove the core or centre of various fruits and vegetables. Coring eliminates small seeds or tough and woody centres (as in pineapple).

**Cream** To beat a fat, such as butter or margarine, alone or with sugar, until it's fluffy and light in colour. This technique whips air into the fat, creating light-textured cakes. An electric mixer makes short work of creaming.

**Crimp** To pinch or press dough edges – especially pie crust edges – to create a decorative finish and/or to seal two layers of dough so the filling doesn't seep out during baking. The edges of a parchment or foil packet may also be crimped to seal in food and its juices during cooking.

**Curdle** To coagulate, or separate, into solids and liquids. Egg- and milk-based mixtures are susceptible to curdling if they're heated too quickly or combined with an acidic ingredient, such as lemon juice or tomatoes.

**Cut in** To work a solid fat, such as vegetable fat, butter or margarine, into dry ingredients by using a pastry blender or two knives used scissor-fashion. The fat and flour should form pea-size nuggets or coarse crumbs for flaky pastry.

**Deglaze** To add a liquid (e.g., water, wine, stock) to a frying pan or roasting tin in which meat or poultry has been cooked to release the caramelized meat juices. After removing the meat and any excess fat, add the liquid to the pan and scrape up the tasty brown bits from the bottom of the pan, to make a quick sauce.

**De-vein** To remove the dark intestinal vein of a prawn. Use the tip of a sharp knife, then rinse the prawn with cold water.

**Dice** To cut food into small cubes of about 5mm.

**Dot** To scatter bits of butter or margarine over a pie, casserole or other dish before baking. This adds extra richness and flavour and helps promote browning.

**Dredge** To coat food lightly with a dry ingredient, typically flour or breadcrumbs. Meats and fish are dredged to create a deliciously crisp, browned exterior. Be sure to shake off excess coating before browning.

**Drizzle** To pour a liquid, such as melted butter or a glaze, in a fine stream, slowly back and forth, over food.

**Dust** To sprinkle very lightly with a powdery ingredient, such as icing sugar (on cakes and pastries) or flour (in a greased cake tin).

**Eau-de-vie** French for 'water of life', describes a colourless brandy distilled from fermented fruit juice. Kirsch (cherry) and framboise (raspberry) are two popular varieties.

**Emulsify** To bind liquids that usually can't blend smoothly, such as oil and water. The trick is to add one liquid, usually the oil, to the other in a slow stream while mixing vigorously. You can also use natural emulsifiers – egg yolks or mustard – to bind mixtures like vinaigrettes and sauces.

**Ferment** To bring about a chemical change in foods and beverages; the change is caused by enzymes produced from bacteria or yeasts. Beer, wine, yogurt, buttermilk, vinegar, cheese and yeast breads all get their distinctive flavours from fermentation.

**Fold** To incorporate a light, airy mixture (such as beaten egg whites) into a heavier mixture (a cake mixture). To fold, use a rubber spatula to cut through the centre of the mixture. Scrape across the bottom of the bowl and up the nearest side. Give the bowl a quarter turn, and repeat just until blended.

**Fork-tender** A degree of doneness for cooked vegetables and meats. You should feel just a slight resistance when the food is pierced with a fork.

**Grill** To cook food with intense, direct dry heat under a grill. For grilled meats, use a rack so the fat drips away. Always preheat the grill, but don't preheat the pan and rack, or the food could stick.

**Julienne** To cut food, especially vegetables, into thin, uniform matchsticks about 5cm long.

**Knead** To work dough until it's smooth, either by pressing and folding with the heel of the hand or in a food processor or an electric mixer with a dough hook. Kneading develops the gluten in the flour, an elastic protein that gives yeast breads their structure.

**Knock back** To deflate yeast dough after it has risen, which distributes the bubbles of carbon dioxide more evenly in the bread dough. Punch your fist into the centre of dough, then pull the edges toward the centre.

**Leavening** Any agent that causes a dough or batter to rise. Common leaveners include baking powder, bicarbonate of soda and yeast. Natural leaveners are air (when beaten into eggs) and steam (in choux pastry and Yorkshire pudding).

**Liqueur** A sweet, high-alcohol beverage made from fruits, nuts, seeds, spices or herbs infused with a spirit, such as brandy or rum. Traditionally served after dinner as a mild digestive, liqueurs can also be used in cooking.

**Marinate** To flavour and/or tenderize a food by letting it soak in a liquid that may contain an acid ingredient (e.g., lemon juice, wine or vinegar), oil, herbs and spices.

**Mince** To chop or cut food into tiny, irregular pieces.

**Pan-fry** To cook food in a small amount of hot fat in a frying pan until browned and cooked through.

**Parboil** To cook a food partially in boiling water. Slow-cooking foods, such as carrots, are often parboiled before they're added to a mixture made of quicker-cooking foods.

**Pare** To cut away the skin or rind of a fruit or vegetable. You can use a vegetable peeler or a paring knife – a small knife with a 7–9cm blade.

**Pasteurize** To sterilize milk by heating, then rapidly cooling it. Most milk sold in the U.K. is pasteurized, which both destroys bacteria that can cause disease and improves shelf life. Ultra-pasteurized (UHT) milk is subjected to very high temperatures – about 150°C – and vacuum-packed for extended storage. It will keep without refrigeration for up to 6 months, but must be refrigerated once it's opened. Ultra-pasteurized cream, however, is not vacuum-packed and should be refrigerated even when unopened.

**Pinch** The amount of a powdery ingredient you can hold between your thumb and forefinger.

**Pipe** To force a food (typically icing or whipped cream) through the nozzle of a piping bag to use as a decoration or garnish, or to shape dough, such as that for éclairs. You can also use a plastic bag with a corner snipped off.

**Poach** To cook food in gently simmering liquid; the surface should barely shimmer. If you plan to use the cooking liquid for a stock or sauce afterward, poach in a pan just

large enough to hold the food. That way, you need less liquid and avoid diluting flavours.

**Pound** To flatten meats and poultry to a uniform thickness using a meat mallet or rolling pin. This ensures even cooking and also tenderizes tough meats by breaking up hard-to-chew connective tissue. Veal and chicken escalopes are often pounded.

**Prick** To pierce a food in many or a few places. You can prick a food to prevent buckling – an empty pie crust before it's baked, for example – or bursting – a potato before baking, or sausages before cooking.

**Proof** To test yeast for potency: if you're not sure yeast is fresh and active, dissolve it in warm water (30°C) with a pinch of sugar. If the mixture foams after 5 to 10 minutes, the yeast is fine to use. Proofing also refers to the rising stage for yeast doughs.

**Purée** To form a smooth mixture by whirling food, usually a fruit or vegetable, in a food processor or blender, working through a food mill, or forcing through a sieve with the back of a wooden spoon.

**Reduce** To boil a liquid rapidly, especially a sauce, so a portion cooks off by evaporation. This creates a thicker sauce with a deeper, more concentrated flavour. If you use a wide pan, the liquid will evaporate faster.

**Render** To melt animal fat slowly (e.g., duck and chicken skin, pork rinds) until it separates from its connective tissue. The clear fat is strained before being used in cooking.

**Roast** To cook food in the oven, in an uncovered tin, by the free circulation of dry heat, usually until the exterior is well browned. Tender cuts of meat as well as poultry and fish are suitable for roasting; so are many vegetables, such as potatoes, parsnips, peppers and tomatoes.

**Sauté** To cook or brown food quickly in a small amount of hot fat in a frying pan; the term derives from the French *sauter* (to jump), and refers to the practice of shaking food in the pan so it browns evenly.

**Scald** To heat milk until tiny bubbles just begin to appear around the edge of the pan – it should not boil. Before milk was pasteurized, scalding was a safeguard used to destroy bacteria and prolong freshness. Today's recipes use scalding for reasons such as dissolving sugar or melting fats.

**Score** To make shallow cuts (usually parallel or crisscross) in the surface of foods before cooking. This is done mainly to aid flavour absorption, as for marinated meats, chicken, and fish, but sometimes also for decorative purposes, as for hams and breads.

**Seal** To brown the surface of meat quickly using very hot heat, either in fat on the stove-top, under the grill or in the oven. The object is to seal in the meat's juices and add flavour by caramelization.

**Shred** To cut, tear or grate food into narrow strips. For some recipes, cooked meat is shredded by pulling it apart with 2 forks.

**Shave** To cut wide, paper-thin slices of food, especially Parmesan cheese, vegetables or chocolate. Shave off slices with a vegetable peeler and use as a garnish.

**Shuck** To remove the shells of oysters, mussels or clams, or the pods of peas.

**Sift** To pass ingredients such as flour or icing sugar through a fine-mesh sifter or sieve. This incorporates air, removes lumps and helps the flour or sugar to mix more readily with liquids.

**Simmer** To cook liquid gently, alone or with other ingredients, over low heat so it's just below the boiling point. A few small bubbles should be visible on the surface.

**Skim** To remove fat or froth from the surface of a liquid, such as boiling stock. A skimmer, with a flat mesh or perforated bowl at the end of a long handle, is the ideal tool for the job.

**Steam** To cook food, covered, in the vapour given off by boiling water. The food is set on a rack or in a basket so it's over, not in, boiling water – since it's not immersed, it retains more nutrients, colour and flavour.

**Stir-fry** To cook small pieces of food quickly in a small amount of oil over high heat, stirring and tossing almost constantly. Vegetables cooked in this way retain their nutrients because of the short cooking time. Stir-frying is much used in Oriental cooking; a wok is the traditional pan, though a frying pan or casserole will do just as well.

**Stock** A thin, clear liquid produced by cooking poultry, meat, fish or vegetables in water, and used as a base for soups, stews, sauces and many other dishes. Stock cubes and granules are convenient as a substitute for home-made.

**Temper** To heat food gently before adding it to a hot mixture so it doesn't separate or curdle. Often eggs are tempered by mixing with a little hot liquid to raise their temperature before they're stirred into a hot sauce or soup.

**Tender-crisp** The ideal degree of doneness for many vegetables, especially green vegetables. Cook them until they're just tender but still retain some texture.

**Toss** To lift and drop pieces of food quickly and gently with two utensils, usually to coat them with a sauce (as for pasta) or dressing (as for salad).

**Whip** To beat an ingredient (especially cream) or mixture rapidly, adding air and increasing volume. Whip with a whisk, egg beater or electric mixer.

**Whisk** To beat ingredients (e.g., cream, eggs, salad dressings, sauces) with a fork or the looped wire utensil called a whisk so as to mix or blend, or incorporate air.

**Zest** To remove the rind of a citrus fruit. Graters, zesters and vegetable peelers remove the rind leaving the bitter white pith underneath. Rind is often referred to as zest.

# MAIL ORDER SOURCES

Carluccio
28a Neal Street
London
WC2H 9PS
0171 240 1487

*Specialists in Italian foods and funghi*

Made in America Ltd
Unit 5b
Hathaway Retail Park
Chippenham
Wiltshire
SN15 1JG
01249 447558

*Large range of imported American foods
and cookware*

Fox's Spices Ltd
Masons Road
Stratford-upon-Avon
Warwickshire
CV37 9NF
01789 266420

*Dried herbs, spices and Oriental seasonings*

Lakeland Limited
Alexandra Buildings
Windermere
Cumbria
LA23 1BQ
015394 88100 (customer services)

*Large selection of food storage containers, labour saving
devices and kitchen tools, utensils and cookware*

Divertimenti (mail order) Ltd
P.O. Box 6611
London SW6 6XU
0171 386 9911

*Cookware and bakeware, books and ingredients*

Andrew Nisbets
1110 Aztec West
Bristol
BS12 4HR
01454 855525

*Speciality cookware and bakeware suppliers to the professional
and domestic markets*

# 1

# STARTERS & FINGER FOODS

Whether you're planning an elaborate drinks party or inviting a few friends for dinner, starters and hors d'oeuvre should appeal to the eye and palate. The flavours, textures and colours of the foods should complement each other as well as the courses that might follow. There should always be a light option, such as fresh salsa or raw vegetables. For inspiration, see what's in season and plentiful at the supermarket.

## PLANNING FOR A PARTY

• To create a festive feel, serve a variety of colourful hors d'oeuvre in assorted shapes.
• Prepare as much as possible in advance. When appropriate, make separate components ahead of time, such as a stuffed vegetable filling, and then refrigerate for later assembly.
• Make only 1 or 2 hot hors d'oeuvre which require last minute preparation, and serve some that require no cooking at all, like cheese, nuts, grapes or assorted salamis.
• If you're passing around an hors d'oeuvre platter, fill it with bite-sized morsels that can be easily eaten.
• Arrange back-up platters; cover with cling film and refrigerate to replenish your table as supplies dwindle.
• Allow 10 to 12 small hors d'oeuvre per guest if no meal follows. Otherwise, allow about 4 to 5 per guest.
• For maximum flavour, remove cold hors d'oeuvre from the refrigerator about 30 minutes before serving.

## STOCKING UP

• Prepare vegetables for crudités up to 1 day ahead. Blanch any vegetables that need to be lightly cooked and rinse with cold running water. Cut up raw vegetables. Wrap both in damp kitchen towels, seal in plastic bags and refrigerate.
• Most pâtés and terrines are best made 1 or 2 days ahead; wrap tightly in cling film or foil and refrigerate.
• Freeze pastry hors d'oeuvre (such as the filo wrapped Mini Spring Rolls and Greek Cheese Bundles on pages 47 and 48, or the Olive Sticks and the pastry cases for the Crab meat Morsels, on pages 49 and 50), raw or baked, up to 1 month ahead. Bake uncooked frozen pastries as the recipe instructs; warm cooked ones in a 180°C (350°F, Gas 4) oven for about 10 minutes.

## SERVING WITH STYLE

Choose interesting serving dishes and garnishes that complement the food. Here are a few attractive ideas:
• Serve crudités on a tray or in a large basket lined with cling film and a bed of rocket, red cabbage, purple kale, spinach or other salad greens.
• Serve cheese on a platter decorated with bunches of fresh herbs, such as thyme or rosemary.
• Serve an assortment of biscuits and breads in wicker baskets lined with colourful napkins.
• Use non-toxic flowers and leaves (see pages 316 and 551) as a lovely garnish. Packed edible flowers are available at some supermarkets or you could pick your own; don't use flowers from a florist as they may have been sprayed.
• For party food that will be served on a buffet, use broad, flat dishes to create the most dramatic presentation.

## QUICK AND EASY HORS D'OEUVRE

The following recipes can be made almost instantly – particularly useful if you are entertaining at short notice:
**White bean and tuna dip** Process a can of drained tuna with a can of drained and rinsed cannellini, a little olive oil, and some coarsely chopped flat-leaf parsley and garlic in a blender or food processor until smooth.
**Devils on horseback** Stuff prunes with chicken liver pâté, then wrap them with strips of streaky bacon. Secure with a cocktail stick and grill 5–8 minutes, turning once until bacon is cooked and crisp, but not dry.
**Stuffed quail's eggs** Hard-boil 6 quail's eggs; cool and peel off the shells. Cut each egg in half and scoop out yolk. Mix yolk with anchovy fillets, mayonnaise and freshly ground black pepper. Pipe filling carefully into egg halves and garnish with snipped chives.
**Quick quesadillas** Sandwich grated cheese and chopped spring onions or salsa between flour tortillas. Heat in a frying pan, turning once, until just beginning to brown on both sides. To serve, cut into wedges.
**Super salsa** Liven up bottled salsa with chopped fresh coriander, or swirl in some soured cream.
**Quick dips** Process mayonnaise and soured cream with bottled pesto, drained bottled roasted red peppers, or drained sun-dried tomatoes in a blender until smooth.
**Mediterranean mezze platter** Assemble bowls of prepared houmous, aubergine dip, and olives; serve with wedges of pitta bread, cucumber and carrot sticks.
**Pizza pronto** Top a large prepared pizza base or focaccia with one of the following: olive oil and crushed dried rosemary; chopped oil-packed sun-dried tomatoes and mozzarella or goat's cheese; crumbled crispy bacon and Cheddar cheese. Bake at 230°C (450°F, Gas 8) for 10 minutes, and cut into small squares.

# CRUDITÉS AND DIPS

Crudités – bite-size whole or cut-up vegetables, raw or lightly cooked – are usually served with a dip or sauce. For the most attractive presentation, choose a colourful variety of vegetable. Ideal for parties or buffets, most crudités can be prepared up to one day in advance. To store, wrap vegetables separately in damp kitchen towels, place in plastic bags and refrigerate.

## CRUDITÉS BASKET

◆◆◆◆◆◆◆◆◆◆◆◆◆

*Prep: 45 minutes*
*Cook: 8–10 minutes*
*Makes 12 first course servings*

**Moroccan Spice Bean Dip (shown above top right) and Parmesan Dip (shown above far right), or other dips of your choice (see page 34)**
450g broccoli
225g mange-tout or sugar snap peas
900g asparagus
3 bunches baby carrots with tops
1 bunch small radishes with tops
2 large red peppers
2 large yellow peppers
2 heads chicory
1 large head radicchio
2 large heads Cos lettuce

1 Prepare dips: cover and refrigerate until ready to use. Cut tough stalks from broccoli. Cut broccoli into 5 by 3cm pieces. Remove tip and strings along both edges of each pea pod. Bend base of asparagus stalks; ends will break off where stalks are tough. Discard ends; trim scales if stalks are gritty.

◆◆◆◆◆◆◆◆◆◆◆◆

### USING BROCCOLI STALKS

Use broccoli stalks as well as florets for crudités. Peel any stalks that seem tough with a vegetable peeler; cut into sticks.

◆◆◆◆◆◆◆◆◆◆◆◆

2 Peel carrots and trim. Trim radishes. Cut peppers into 1cm strips. Separate leaves of chicory, radicchio and lettuce.

3 Blanch broccoli in 4-litre saucepan, in *3cm boiling water*, for 1–2 minutes. Using slotted spoon, place broccoli in colander. Drain, rinse with cold water and drain again. Repeat with asparagus and mange-tout.

4 Line a large shallow basket with cling film or foil. Arrange radicchio and lettuce leaves in basket. Arrange prepared vegetables on top; serve with dips of your choice.

EACH SERVING WITHOUT DIP: ABOUT 75 CALORIES, 4g PROTEIN, 16g CARBOHYDRATE, 1g TOTAL FAT (0g SATURATED), 0mg CHOLESTEROL, 45mg SODIUM

## MOROCCAN SPICE BEAN DIP

*Prep: 10 minutes    Makes about 300g*

1 tsp paprika
¼ tsp fennel seeds, crushed
¼ tsp ground ginger
¼ tsp ground cumin
⅛ tsp ground red pepper
Pinch ground cinnamon
400g canned chick-peas, rinsed and drained
2 tbsp olive oil
1 tbsp fresh lemon juice
½ tsp salt
¼ tsp ground black pepper

◆ Heat first 6 ingredients in 1-litre saucepan over medium-low heat 1–2 minutes, stirring until very fragrant. Remove from heat.

◆ Combine chick-peas, olive oil, lemon juice, salt, black pepper, toasted spices and *4 tablespoons water* in food processor with knife blade attached. Blend until smooth. Transfer to small serving bowl.

**Each 100g: About 225 calories, 7g protein, 25g carbohydrate, 12g total fat (2g saturated), 0mg cholesterol, 920mg sodium**

## PARMESAN DIP

*Prep: 10 minutes, plus chilling
Makes about 300g*

150ml soured cream
75g mayonnaise
40g Parmesan cheese, freshly grated
1 tbsp fresh lemon juice
3 anchovy fillets in oil, drained and mashed
½ tsp coarsely ground black pepper

Using fork or wire whisk, combine all ingredients in small bowl. Cover and refrigerate 2 hours so flavours blend.

**Each 100g: About 335 calories, 7g protein, 4g carbohydrate, 33g total fat (11g saturated), 47mg cholesterol, 470mg sodium**

## GUACAMOLE

*Prep: 15 minutes    Makes about 250g*

2 ripe avocados
2 tbsp finely chopped onion
2 tbsp chopped fresh coriander
1 tbsp fresh lime juice
2 bottled jalapeño chillies, seeded and very finely chopped
½ tsp salt
¼ tsp ground black pepper
1 plum tomato, finely chopped

◆ Cut each avocado in half; remove stone. Using spoon, scoop flesh from peel into medium bowl.

◆ Add next 6 ingredients and coarsely mash avocados with potato masher. Stir in tomato. Transfer to small serving bowl.

**Each 100g: About 265 calories, 4g protein, 5g carbohydrate, 24g total fat (4g saturated), 0mg cholesterol, 450mg sodium**

## PUMPKIN AND ROASTED GARLIC DIP

*Prep: 10 minutes, plus cooling
Bake: 45 minutes    Makes about 450g*

1 whole head garlic
425g canned solid-pack pumpkin
2 tbsp olive oil
1½ tsp salt
1 tbsp chopped fresh parsley

◆ Preheat oven to 230°C (450°F, Gas 8). Discard papery outer layer from garlic; do not separate cloves. Wrap in foil. Roast garlic 45 minutes, or until tender. Remove from oven and allow to cool.

◆ When cool, squeeze garlic from skin. Purée garlic, pumpkin, oil and salt in food processor with knife blade attached. Stir in parsley. Transfer to small serving bowl.

**Each 100g: About 100 calories, 2g protein, 12g carbohydrate, 6g total fat (1g saturated), 0mg cholesterol, 720mg sodium**

## ROASTED AUBERGINE DIP

*Prep: 15 minutes, plus draining    Roast: 1 hour
Makes about 400g*

2 small aubergines (450g each)
2 garlic cloves, cut into thin slivers
2 tbsp olive oil
4 tsp fresh lemon juice
1 tsp salt
¼ tsp ground black pepper
2 tbsp chopped fresh parsley
2 tbsp chopped fresh mint

◆ Preheat oven to 200°C (400°F, Gas 6). Cut slits all over aubergines; insert garlic slivers. Place aubergines on Swiss roll tin and roast 1 hour, or until collapsed. Remove aubergines from oven; cool.

◆ When cool, cut each aubergine in half. Using spoon, scoop flesh from skin into colander set over bowl; discard skin. Let drain 10 minutes.

◆ Transfer aubergine flesh to food processor with knife blade attached. Add oil, lemon juice, salt and pepper. Blend, pulsing processor on and off, until coarsely chopped. Add herbs and pulse to combine. Transfer to small serving bowl.

**Each 100g: About 125 calories, 3g protein, 15g carbohydrate, 7g total fat (1g saturated), 0mg cholesterol, 540mg sodium**

## HONEY-MUSTARD DIP

*Prep: 10 minutes    Makes about 150g*

60g Dijon mustard
80g honey
1 tbsp soy sauce
1 tbsp very finely chopped spring onion
2 tsp very finely chopped peeled fresh ginger

Using fork or wire whisk, mix all ingredients together in small bowl.

**Each 100g: About 235 calories, 3g protein, 50g carbohydrate, 3g total fat, 0mg cholesterol, 1740mg sodium**

# PÂTÉS, TERRINES AND SPREADS

Ideal for light lunches, picnics and cold buffets, pâtés, terrines and spreads can be smooth and satiny or chunky and coarse. A blender or food processor can ensure a smoothly blended, spreadable mixture or, if you prefer, use a wooden spoon or potato masher for a coarser texture. Smoked fish and sautéed chicken livers are classic ingredients for pâtés, while cream cheese is a natural base for quick-to-make spreads – try the Smoked Trout Pâté on this page, or the Tabasco-lime Spread on page 36, flavoured with fresh lime zest.

1 Place smoked trout on chopping board; cut head and tail from each smoked trout. Carefully remove all skin from each trout and discard.

## SMOKED TROUT PÂTÉ

◆◆◆◆◆◆◆◆◆◆◆◆◆◆◆◆◆◆◆◆◆◆◆◆◆◆◆◆

*Prep: 30 minutes*    *Makes* about 800g

3 whole smoked trout (about 550g)
225g cream cheese, softened
75g reduced-fat mayonnaise
3 tbsp fresh lemon juice
⅛ tsp ground black pepper

1 tbsp very finely chopped fresh chives or spring onion
Chives for garnish
Melba Triangles (see page 36) or biscuits for serving
Cucumber slices (optional)

2 Using tweezers, remove all bones from trout. Place trout, cream cheese, mayonnaise, lemon juice and black pepper in blender or food processor with knife blade attached and blend until mixture is smooth.

3 Spoon trout mixture into medium serving bowl and stir in chopped chives until well combined. Smooth top, cover and refrigerate up to 1 day if not serving right away.

4 If pâté has been refrigerated, allow it to stand at room temperature 15 minutes to soften slightly before serving. Garnish with chives. Serve spread on Melba Triangles with cucumber slices, if you like.

### SMOKED FISH PÂTÉS AND SPREADS

Smoked fish makes wonderfully flavourful pâtés and spreads. Those high in natural oils and fat, such as salmon, mackerel and trout, are the ones to look for. Or, if you live near a good deli, seek out a smoked whitefish, such as haddock. As well as being delicious, they're all tender enough to be worked to a smooth consistency. Saltiness and smokiness vary; taste, then adjust the seasoning accordingly. Smoked fish is also good in salads and soufflés. The pâté can be frozen for up to 2 months, provided it is made with fresh fish.

EACH 100g PÂTÉ: ABOUT 205 CALORIES, 20g PROTEIN, 3g CARBOHYDRATE, 13g TOTAL FAT (6g SATURATED), 85mg CHOLESTEROL, 685mg SODIUM

## CHICKEN LIVER PÂTÉ

*Prep:* 15 minutes, plus chilling    *Cook:* 6 minutes
*Makes* about 600g

450g chicken livers, trimmed
  (see page 134)
125g butter
50g very finely chopped
  shallots
½ tsp salt

¼ tsp dried thyme
⅛ tsp ground nutmeg
⅛ tsp ground black pepper
4 tbsp sweet vermouth
Toasts, crackers or thin apple
  slices for serving

◆ Pat chicken livers dry with kitchen towels. Melt 15g butter in 26cm frying pan over medium heat. Add shallots and cook, stirring frequently, 1 minute. Increase heat to high; stir in livers, salt, thyme, nutmeg and pepper. Cook, stirring often, 4 minutes, or until livers are slightly pink in centre. Stir in vermouth and cook 30 seconds.

◆ Transfer mixture to food processor with knife blade attached and blend until smooth. With motor running, add remaining butter through feed tube, a little at a time, until blended. Spoon into serving bowl and refrigerate 6 hours, or until chilled and set. Serve pâté with toasts, crackers or thin apple slices.

**Each 100g pâté: About 275 calories, 19g protein, 3g carbohydrate, 19g total fat (11g saturated), 518mg cholesterol, 375mg sodium**

### TOASTS FOR PÂTÉS, TERRINES AND SPREADS

For the best presentation, serve spreads and pâtés with one of the speciality toasts suggested below. All should be toasted at 190°C (375°F, Gas 5).

**Melba triangles**  Named in honour of the turn-of-the-century Australian opera singer Nellie Melba. Serve with delicate pâtés and spreads. Remove crusts from very thin slices of white bread, then cut each slice diagonally in half. Bake in oven 15 minutes, or until crisp and edges curl slightly, turning once.

**Garlic toast**  Delicious with robust pâtés and spreads. Cut French bread into thin slices and bake in oven 10 minutes, or until lightly toasted, turning once. Peel and halve a garlic clove and immediately rub one side of each slice of warm toast with cut side of garlic.

**Pitta toast**  Serve with Middle Eastern spreads, such as taramasalata (cod roe spread), tzatziki (cucumber yogurt dip) or our Moroccan Spice Bean Dip (see page 34). Cut pitta bread into wedges and bake in oven 15 minutes, or until golden, turning once.

**Italian toast**  Ideal with tomato or olive spreads. Slice ciabatta or focaccia (Italian flat breads) into strips. Bake in oven 15 minutes, or until golden, turning once.

## SMOKED SALMON TERRINE

*Prep:* 40 minutes, plus chilling
*Makes* 32 first course servings

2 tbsp drained capers,
  chopped
1 tbsp chopped fresh dill or
  ¾ tsp dried
½ tsp coarsely ground black
  pepper
900g cream cheese, softened
4 tbsp milk

2 tbsp fresh lemon juice
350g sliced smoked salmon,
  finely chopped
Lemon slices and parsley or
  dill sprigs for garnish
Pumpernickel bread cut into
  small triangles and assorted
  crackers for serving

◆ Using wooden spoon, blend capers, dill, pepper, half of cream cheese, half of milk and half of lemon juice together in medium bowl until smooth.

◆ Using wooden spoon, blend smoked salmon, remaining cream cheese, remaining milk and remaining lemon juice in another medium bowl until smooth.

◆ Line 21 by 11cm loaf tin with cling film; smooth out as many wrinkles as possible. Using spatula, evenly spread half of caper mixture into base of tin. Evenly spread half of smoked-salmon mixture on top. Repeat layering with remaining mixtures. Cover terrine with cling film and refrigerate at least 4 hours, or overnight, until firm.

◆ To serve, invert tin onto platter, remove tin and cling film. Smooth sides of terrine with spatula if necessary. Allow terrine to stand at room temperature 30 minutes to soften slightly. Garnish with lemon slices and parsley sprigs and serve with bread and crackers.

**Each first course serving: About 115 calories, 4g protein, 1g carbohydrate, 11g total fat (6g saturated), 34mg cholesterol, 190mg sodium**

## TABASCO-LIME SPREAD

*Prep:* 10 minutes    *Makes* about 225g

1 lime
225g cream cheese, softened
1 tbsp chopped fresh parsley

1 tsp Tabasco sauce
Crackers or cucumber slices
  for serving

Grate rind and squeeze 2 teaspoons juice from lime. Blend cream cheese, lime rind and juice, parsley and Tabasco sauce in food processor with knife blade attached until smooth. Serve with crackers or cucumber slices.

**Each 100g: About 265 calories, 22g protein, 11g carbohydrate, 111g total fat (67g saturated), 355mg cholesterol, 980mg sodium**

# STUFFED VEGETABLES

Bite-sized vegetables, such as cherry tomatoes, mushrooms or even tiny potato halves, make delicious, fresh vehicles for a variety of delicious fillings. If you're planning a party, most vegetable stuffings can be prepared up to a day in advance, covered tightly with cling film and refrigerated until required. You can stuff vegetables a few hours before serving.

## AUBERGINE-STUFFED CHERRY TOMATOES

Prep: *45 minutes, plus cooling*
Cook: *20 minutes*
Makes 48

½ **small aubergine (about 225g)**
**4cm piece fresh ginger**
**2 tbsp vegetable oil**
**2 tbsp soy sauce**
**2 tsp sugar**
**1 tsp sesame oil**
**24 cherry tomatoes**

### OTHER FILLINGS

• Chopped Kalamata olives and feta cheese

• Guacamole (see page 34)

• Chopped basil, pine nuts, Parmesan and toasted breadcrumbs

**1** Using a large chef's knife, dice aubergine. Peel and very finely chop ginger (you should have about 1 tablespoon).

**2** Heat vegetable oil in 2-litre saucepan over medium heat. Add aubergine and ginger; stir to coat. Add soy sauce, sugar and *4 tablespoons water*. Bring to the boil over high heat. Reduce heat to medium-low.

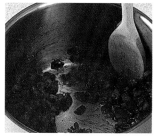

**3** Cover; cook 15 minutes, stirring occasionally and mashing with back of spoon, until aubergine is very tender. Stir in sesame oil. Cool to room temperature. Cover and refrigerate if not using right away.

**4** Meanwhile, cut each tomato in half. Scoop out and discard the seeds, leaving a tomato 'shell'.

**5** Drain tomato halves, cut side down, on kitchen towels. Using small spoon, fill tomato halves with aubergine mixture.

EACH PIECE: ABOUT 10 CALORIES, 0g PROTEIN, 1g CARBOHYDRATE, 1g TOTAL FAT (0g SATURATED), 0mg CHOLESTEROL, 45mg SODIUM

## SMOKED SALMON BOATS

*Prep: 30 minutes    Makes about 36*

225g cream cheese,
    softened
125g sliced smoked salmon,
    chopped
1 tbsp chopped fresh dill or
    1 tsp dried

4 heads chicory
75g red lumpfish caviar
Small dill sprigs, lamb's
    lettuce and zig-zag
    lemon (see page 130)
    for garnish

◆ Blend cream cheese, smoked salmon and dill in food processor with knife blade attached. Separate chicory leaves. Select about 36 large leaves; reserve small leaves for another use. Rinse leaves with cold water and gently pat dry with kitchen towels.

◆ Spoon salmon mixture into piping bag with medium star nozzle (or use a plastic bag and snip one corner for hole). Pipe onto wide end of each leaf. Cover and refrigerate if not serving right away. Just before serving, top with caviar and garnish.

**Each piece: About 30 calories, 2g protein, 1g carbohydrate, 3g total fat (1g saturated), 17mg cholesterol, 50mg sodium**

### PARMA HAM AND CHEESE BOATS

Press 100g ricotta cheese through fine sieve into small bowl; stir in 50g freshly grated Parmesan cheese and 2 tablespoons milk. Cut 175g sliced Parma ham crossways into thin strips. Place a few strips on wide end of each of 36 chicory leaves. Top each with a teaspoon of cheese mixture and sprinkle with ground nutmeg.

Each piece: About 20 calories, 2g protein, 1g carbohydrate, 1g total fat (0g saturated), 5mg cholesterol, 80mg sodium

## CAPONATA-STUFFED MUSHROOMS

*Prep: 50 minutes    Bake: 10 minutes*
*Makes about 48*

48 medium flat or open
    mushrooms
About 4 tbsp olive oil
½ small aubergine (225g),
    coarsely chopped
1 small onion, coarsely
    chopped
1 small celery stalk, coarsely
    chopped

125ml bottled chilli sauce
1 tbsp canned or bottled
    drained capers
¼ tsp dried basil
1 tbsp chopped fresh
    parsley
Salt
2 tbsp toasted flaked
    almonds, finely chopped

◆ Prepare caponata: coarsely chop mushroom stalks; set aside caps. Heat 3 tablespoons olive oil in 26cm frying pan over medium-high heat. Add mushroom stalks, aubergine, onion and celery and cook, stirring frequently, 15 minutes, or until tender and browned. Stir in chilli sauce, capers and basil. Reduce heat to low, cover and simmer 10 minutes. Remove from heat; stir in parsley.

◆ Preheat the oven to 180°C (350°F, Gas 4). Brush mushroom caps lightly with olive oil and sprinkle with salt. Spoon 1 heaped teaspoon filling into each mushroom cap (use any leftover filling to serve on toast another day). Place in Swiss roll tin and bake 10 minutes or until the mushrooms are tender and hot. Sprinkle with almonds.

**Each piece: About 20 calories, 1g protein, 2g carbohydrate, 1g total fat (0g saturated), 0mg cholesterol, 40mg sodium**

## POTATO TOP HATS

*Prep: 30 minutes    Cook: 20 minutes*
*Makes 36*

125ml whipping cream
125g cream cheese, softened
1 tbsp horseradish sauce
1 tbsp chopped fresh chives
18 small new potatoes, boiled
    and chilled

50g bottled salmon caviar or
    orange lumpfish roe
Chopped chives for garnish

Using mixer on medium speed, beat cream in small bowl until stiff peaks form. Using mixer on low speed, beat cream cheese, horseradish and chopped chives in another small bowl until blended. Using rubber spatula, fold whipped cream into cream cheese mixture. Cut each potato in half. Using melon baller, scoop out cavity in each half. Spoon in cream-cheese mixture. Cover loosely and refrigerate if not serving right away. Just before serving, top each potato half with some caviar and garnish with chives.

**Each piece: About 35 calories, 1g protein, 4g carbohydrate, 2g total fat (1g saturated), 7mg cholesterol, 15mg sodium**

# PRAWN STARTERS AND FINGER FOODS

Quick to prepare, prawns have long been a favourite ingredient for starters. Choose from the wide variety of prawns available at fish mongers and supermarket fish counters. Prawns are incredibly versatile because their mild, sweet taste is complemented by a myriad of other flavours. Our Mexican-style Prawn Skewers, for instance, has a tart, zippy dressing of lime juice, coriander and mild green chillies. Cocktail Prawns and Olives has a decidedly Mediterranean spirit, while Potted Shrimp, enhanced with sherry, is an old favourite that's delicious served with crackers or toast.

**1** Bring *2 litres water* to the boil in 4-litre saucepan over high heat. Add prawns and return to the boil. Cook 1–2 minutes, until prawns turn opaque throughout. Drain.

**2** Chop chillies, reserving liquid. Mix chillies with their liquid, lime juice, coriander, oil, salt, sugar and black pepper together in large bowl. Stir in prawns to coat thoroughly with dressing. If not serving kebabs right away, refrigerate prawn mixture. Just before serving, cut each avocado lengthways in half and remove the stone (see below). Peel and cut avocados into 3cm chunks.

**3** Gently stir avocado chunks into prawn mixture to coat thoroughly with chilli dressing, being careful not to bruise avocados.

## MEXICAN-STYLE PRAWN SKEWERS

◆◆◆◆◆◆◆◆◆◆◆◆◆◆◆◆◆◆◆◆◆◆◆◆◆◆◆◆◆◆◆

*Prep: 45 minutes    Cook: 1–2 minutes*
*Makes 20*

40 raw large prawns, peeled and de-veined (see page 90)
125g undrained canned or bottled mild green chillies
2 tbsp fresh lime juice
1 tbsp chopped fresh coriander or 1 tsp dried
1 tbsp olive or vegetable oil

¾ tsp salt
½ tsp sugar
½ tsp ground black pepper
2 medium avocados
20 (30cm) bamboo skewers
Lime and lemon wedges for garnish

**4** Thread 2 prawns and 2 chunks of avocado on each bamboo skewer. Arrange skewers on large platter. Serve immediately, garnished with lime and lemon wedges.

◆◆◆◆◆◆◆◆◆◆◆◆◆◆◆◆◆◆◆◆◆◆◆◆◆◆◆◆◆◆◆

### STONING AVOCADOS

**1** Stoning an avocado doesn't need to be a slippery business. For neat results, using sharp knife, cut avocado lengthways round the stone. Twist gently to separate halves.

**2** Strike the stone with the blade of a chef's knife, so the blade lodges in stone. Twist gently and lift out the stone.

◆◆◆◆◆◆◆◆◆◆◆◆◆◆◆◆◆◆◆◆◆◆◆◆◆◆◆◆◆◆◆

EACH SKEWER: ABOUT 70 CALORIES, 7g PROTEIN, 2g CARBOHYDRATE, 4g TOTAL FAT (1g SATURATED), 61mg CHOLESTEROL, 170mg SODIUM

## COCKTAIL PRAWNS AND OLIVES

*Prep: 20 minutes, plus chilling    Cook: 3 minutes*
*Makes about 12 hors d'oeuvre servings*

750g raw medium or large
prawns, peeled and de-
veined, leaving tail part of
shell on, if you like (see
page 90)
275g large stoned green or
black olives, drained if
canned
2 tbsp olive or vegetable oil
1½ tsp curry powder

½ tsp ground ginger
½ tsp salt
¼ tsp coarsely ground black
pepper
2 tbsp fresh lemon juice
1 tbsp finely chopped fresh
parsley
Lemon slices and celery leaf
for garnish

◆ Bring *2 litres water* to the boil in 4-litre saucepan over
high heat. Add prawns, return to the boil and cook 1–2
minutes, or until they turn opaque throughout. Drain well.
Place prawns and olives in 33 by 20cm ovenproof dish.

◆ Heat oil in large saucepan over medium heat. Add curry
powder, ginger, salt and pepper and cook, stirring
constantly, 1 minute.

◆ Remove pan from heat and stir in lemon juice and
parsley. Pour warm marinade over prawns and olives in
ovenproof dish.

◆ Cover and refrigerate at least 2 hours, tossing
occasionally, until well chilled. Place prawns and olives on
platter and garnish with lemon slices and celery leaf. Serve
with cocktail sticks.

**Each serving: About 90 calories, 10g protein, 1g carbohydrate,
6g total fat (1g saturated), 87mg cholesterol, 725mg sodium**

## PRAWNS WITH TARRAGON DIPPING SAUCE

*Prep: 20 minutes    Cook: 3 minutes*
*Makes about 8 first course servings*

450g raw medium prawns,
peeled and de-veined (see
page 90)
125ml soured cream
60g mayonnaise

15g fresh parsley leaves
1 tbsp chopped fresh
tarragon
1 tsp anchovy paste
¼ tsp ground black pepper

◆ Bring *1½ litres water* to the boil in 3-litre saucepan
over high heat. Add prawns, return to the boil and cook
1–2 minutes, or until they turn opaque throughout. Drain.

◆ Prepare tarragon dipping sauce. Combine soured cream,
mayonnaise, parsley, tarragon, anchovy paste and pepper in
blender and blend until smooth. Transfer dipping sauce to
small serving bowl. Cover sauce and prawns separately and
refrigerate if not serving right away. To serve, arrange
prawns with dipping sauce on platter.

**Each serving: About 125 calories, 10g protein, 1g carbohydrate,
9g total fat (3g saturated), 98mg cholesterol, 155mg sodium**

## POTTED SHRIMP

*Prep: 15 minutes, plus chilling    Cook: 3 minutes*
*Makes about 550g*

125g unsalted butter, softened
450g raw medium prawns,
peeled and de-veined (see
page 90)
¾ tsp salt

¼ tsp ground red pepper
2 tbsp dry sherry
Crackers or toast (see
page 36) for serving

◆ Melt 15g of butter in 26cm frying pan over medium-high
heat. Add prawns, salt and ground red pepper and cook,
stirring often, 2 minutes, or until prawns turn opaque
throughout. Add sherry and boil 30 seconds.

◆ Transfer the mixture to a food processor and blend,
pulsing the processor on and off, until the prawns are finely
chopped. Cut up the remaining butter, then add to
processor and blend until combined.

◆ Transfer mixture to small bowl. Cover and refrigerate up
to 24 hours if not serving right away. If chilled, let potted
shrimp stand at room temperature about 1 hour before
serving. Serve with crackers or toast.

**Each 100g: About 220 calories, 14g protein, 1g carbohydrate,
17g total fat (10g saturated), 172mg cholesterol, 440mg sodium**

# CHEESE STARTERS AND FINGER FOODS

Just a little imagination turns cheese into party fare. For a sit-down starter, marinate creamy goat's cheese with herbs and contrast with delicate greens; for a Tex-Mex taste, use a tortilla chip to scoop up our spicy melted-cheese mixture.

## MARINATED GOAT'S CHEESE

❖❖❖❖❖❖❖❖❖❖❖❖❖

*Prep:* 20 minutes, plus marinating
*Makes* 12 first course servings

**100g goat's cheese**
**60g oil-packed sun-dried tomatoes, drained**
**2 tsp fresh thyme leaves**
**2 tsp fresh rosemary leaves**
**¼ tsp cracked black pepper**
**About 225ml extra virgin olive oil**
**24 Home-made Croûtes (see below)**
**350g mixed salad leaves**

**1** Hold knife under hot water then wipe dry. Use it to cut each cheese log into 8 rounds. Cut sun-dried tomatoes into thin strips.

**2** Layer one quarter of each of the following: goat's cheese rounds, sun-dried tomato strips, thyme leaves, rosemary leaves and black pepper into 500ml jar with tight-fitting lid (a short, wide-mouth jar is best). Repeat layering in same order 3 more times.

❖❖❖❖❖❖❖❖❖❖❖❖❖❖❖❖❖❖❖❖❖❖❖❖❖❖❖❖❖❖❖

### HOME-MADE CROÛTES

Croûtes are the ideal base for creamy cheeses. Use a 6cm biscuit cutter to cut shapes or rounds from slices of bread. Place on a baking sheet. Bake at 190°C (395°F, Gas 6), turning once, for 10–15 minutes until golden. For added flavour, rub the toasted croûtes with a cut clove of garlic, or top with a drizzle of olive oil and chopped fresh rosemary before baking. Croûtes can also be served with soups, stews and pâtés.

**3** Pour olive oil over all. Cover and refrigerate overnight or up to 1 week, turning jar over occasionally for even marinating. Open jar and allow cheese to come to room temperature 30 minutes. Prepare croûtes.

**4** Remove cheese from marinade. Toss salad leaves with some oil from jar; divide among plates. For each serving, place 2 croûtes on top of greens and top each with a slice of marinated goat's cheese.

❖❖❖❖❖❖❖❖❖❖❖❖❖❖❖❖❖❖❖❖❖❖❖❖❖❖❖❖❖

EACH SERVING: ABOUT 310 CALORIES, 9g PROTEIN, 19g CARBOHYDRATE, 23g TOTAL FAT (7g SATURATED), 19mg CHOLESTEROL, 335mg SODIUM

## FIESTA CHILLIES CON QUESO

*Prep: 15 minutes  Bake: 20 minutes*
*Makes 24 hors d'oeuvre servings*

1 tbsp vegetable oil
1 large garlic clove, very
  finely chopped
1 tsp ground cumin
400g canned pinto beans,
  rinsed and drained
125g canned or bottled mild
  green chillies, drained,
  seeded and chopped

350g Cheddar cheese, grated
1 cooked chorizo sausage
  (75g), finely chopped, or
  75g finely chopped
  peperoni
Tortilla chips for serving

◆ Preheat oven to 150°C (300°F, Gas 2). Heat oil in 26cm frying pan over medium heat. Stir in garlic and cumin and cook 30 seconds. Add pinto beans and *4 tablespoons water*; cook, mashing beans with back of spoon, 2–3 minutes longer, until thick. Remove from heat.

◆ Combine next 3 ingredients in large bowl and press half of mixture evenly into 23cm pie plate. Spoon bean mixture evenly on top. Top with remaining cheese mixture. Bake 20 minutes, or until cheese melts. Serve with tortilla chips.

**Each serving without chips: About 75 calories, 5g protein, 3g carbohydrate, 6g total fat (3g saturated), 13mg cholesterol, 165mg sodium**

## ROASTED PEPPER AND MOZZARELLA SANDWICHES WITH BASIL PURÉE

*Prep: 30 minutes  Cook: 20 minutes*
*Makes 16 hors d'oeuvre servings*

3 medium red peppers,
  roasted and peeled (see
  page 310)
5 tbsp olive oil
125g fresh basil or
  watercress leaves

½ tsp salt
1 French stick (about 350g)
450g fresh mozzarella
  cheese, cut into 5mm
  slices

◆ Cut each roasted pepper half lengthways into thirds; set aside. Place oil, basil and salt in blender or food processor with knife blade attached and blend until almost smooth.

◆ Cut French stick horizontally in half. Remove and discard some soft bread from each half. Evenly spread basil mixture on cut side of both halves.

◆ Arrange mozzarella cheese slices on bottom half of French stick then top with roasted peppers. Replace top half of French stick and cut into thin slices.

**Each serving: About 185 calories, 8g protein, 13g carbohydrate, 11g total fat (4g saturated), 22mg cholesterol, 300mg sodium**

## FAST CHEESE BITES

**SMOKY MOZZARELLA SKEWERS** Cut smoked mozzarella (mozzarella affumicata) into 2–3cm cubes. Alternately thread oil-packed sun-dried tomatoes, squares of yellow pepper, fresh basil leaves and mozzarella onto short bamboo skewers. Brush cheese with some oil from sun-dried tomatoes.

**GORGONZOLA-STUFFED DATES** Mix together equal amounts of gorgonzola and softened cream cheese. Split one side of Medjool or other large dates lengthways in half and remove stone. Spread a small amount of cheese mixture into each date with small knife (or use a piping bag to pipe the cheese); top cheese with a walnut half.

**HERB-AND-SPICE COATED GOAT'S CHEESE** Roll logs of goat's cheese in chopped fresh herbs, such as parsley, rosemary, thyme or dill and/or cracked black pepper. Spread desired coatings on greaseproof paper, then roll well-chilled cheese logs over until completely covered. Lift up corners of paper to press in coating gently, if necessary. Wrap logs in cling film until ready to serve.

**PARMA HAM AND GOAT'S CHEESE ROLL-UPS** Mix together 250g softened mild goat's cheese, 2 tablespoons finely chopped spring onions and 1 finely chopped garlic clove. Cut 12 thin slices Parma ham crossways in half. Spoon 2 tablespoons cheese mixture onto base of each strip; top with basil leaf. Roll Parma ham around cheese. Sprinkle with lemon juice, olive oil and ground black pepper.

Smoky mozzarella
skewers

Gorgonzola-stuffed
dates

Herb-and-spice coated
goat's cheese

Parma ham and goat's
cheese roll-ups

# SAVOURY TOASTS

Firm-textured country or French bread slices toast beautifully, and make crisp bases for tasty toppings. Ordinary white bread also lends itself to making delicious toasted miniature sandwiches. Sprouting broccoli is available from large supermarkets in the spring. If you can't find it, spring greens make a good alternative.

## BROCCOLI BRUSCHETTA

❖❖❖❖❖❖❖❖❖❖❖❖❖❖

*Prep: 20 minutes*
*Cook: 6 minutes*
*Makes 8*

1 round crusty loaf
50g Parmesan cheese, freshly grated
900g sprouting broccoli or spring greens, tough stalks trimmed
4 tbsp olive oil
3 garlic cloves, each cut in half
¾ tsp salt
¼ tsp crushed red pepper

**1** Bring *4 litres water* to the boil in 5-litre flameproof casserole over high heat. Meanwhile, preheat the grill. Cut four 2cm thick slices from centre portion of bread, then cut each slice crossways in half. Place the bread slices on rack in large grill pan. Place the pan under the grill at the closest position to the heat. Toast bread 1–2 minutes.

**2** Turn bread and sprinkle with 40g Parmesan. Grill 1–2 minutes longer until cheese melts and edges of bread are lightly toasted. Set aside. Add broccoli to boiling water; cook 2 minutes. Drain; coarsely chop. Wipe casserole dry.

**3** Heat oil in same pan over medium heat. Add garlic and cook until lightly browned. Add sprouting broccoli, salt and red pepper and continue cooking over medium-high heat, stirring, about 5 minutes until tender.

**4** Discard garlic cloves, if you like. Spoon broccoli mixture on top of toasted bread slices. Sprinkle each bruschetta with remaining Parmesan. Serve bruschetta warm or at room temperature.

❖❖❖❖❖❖❖❖❖❖❖❖❖❖❖❖❖❖❖❖❖❖❖❖❖❖❖

### CROSTINI AND BRUSCHETTA

Crostini are thin slices of toasted bread topped with a savoury mixture. Bruschetta (*bru-sket-ta*) are thicker slices of grilled or toasted country bread. Either can be rubbed with a cut clove of garlic (see right) and drizzled with fruity olive oil.

❖❖❖❖❖❖❖❖❖❖❖❖❖❖❖❖❖❖❖❖

EACH PIECE: ABOUT 230 CALORIES, 8g PROTEIN, 29g CARBOHYDRATE, 10g TOTAL FAT (2g SATURATED), 4mg CHOLESTEROL, 585mg SODIUM

## CHICKEN LIVER AND SAGE CROSTINI

*Prep: 15 minutes    Cook: 15 minutes*

*Makes 30*

1 French stick (225g) cut into
  30 thin diagonal slices
2 tbsp olive oil
1 medium onion, finely
  chopped
1 garlic clove, very finely
  chopped
40g plain flour

450g chicken livers, trimmed
  (see page 134) and each cut
  in half
½ tsp dried sage
½ tsp salt
¼ tsp ground black pepper
1 tbsp red wine vinegar
2 tbsp chopped fresh parsley

◆ Preheat oven to 200°C (400°F, Gas 4). Place bread slices on baking sheet and toast in oven 5 minutes, or until lightly toasted. Meanwhile, heat olive oil in 26cm frying pan over medium heat. Add onion; cook 5 minutes, or until tender. Stir in garlic.

◆ Place flour in plastic bag. Add chicken livers and toss to coat; shake off excess. Add chicken livers to pan with sage, salt and pepper. Cook, stirring frequently, 4 minutes, or until livers are browned but still slightly pink in centre. Stir in vinegar; remove from heat. Stir in parsley; mash livers coarsely with back of spoon. Spread 1 tablespoon chicken-liver mixture on each toast slice.

**Each piece: About 60 calories, 5g protein, 5g carbohydrate, 2g total fat (0g saturated), 95mg cholesterol, 90mg sodium**

## RICOTTA BRUSCHETTA

*Prep: 20 minutes    Makes 8*

8 slices (1cm thick) crusty
  country bread, toasted
1 garlic clove, cut in half
450g ripe plum tomatoes,
  seeded and diced
125g ricotta or feta cheese,
  cut into 1cm cubes
2 tbsp extra virgin olive oil

1 tbsp finely chopped red
  onion
1 tbsp chopped fresh basil
2 tsp balsamic vinegar
¼ tsp salt
¼ tsp coarsely ground black
  pepper

◆ Lightly rub one side of each warm toast slice with cut sides of garlic.

◆ Combine tomatoes with remaining ingredients in medium bowl and toss to blend. Spoon tomato and cheese mixture over garlic-rubbed sides of toast slices.

**Each piece: About 130 calories, 4g protein, 15g carbohydrate, 6g total fat (2g saturated), 8mg cholesterol, 215mg sodium**

## BLUE-CHEESE TOASTS

*Prep: 25 minutes    Bake: 12 minutes*

*Makes 64*

16 slices firm white bread,
  crusts removed
125g blue cheese, softened
  and rind removed, if any

25g margarine or butter
2 tbsp finely chopped fresh
  basil

◆ Preheat oven to 200°C (400°F, Gas 6). Grease large baking sheet. Using rolling pin, roll each bread slice paper-thin. Spread about 2 teaspoons softened blue cheese over 1 paper-thin slice of bread; top with second slice, pressing gently to make a sandwich. Repeat with remaining bread and softened cheese.

◆ Melt margarine in small pan over low heat. Remove pan from heat; stir in basil. Brush some basil mixture over top of each sandwich. Cut each sandwich diagonally into quarters; cut each quarter in half. Arrange triangles on baking sheet. Bake 12 minutes, or until golden. Serve hot.

**Each piece: About 25 calories, 1g protein, 3g carbohydrate, 1g total fat (0g saturated), 1mg cholesterol, 65mg sodium**

## MEDITERRANEAN CHEESE TOASTS

*Prep: 25 minutes    Grill: 2 minutes*

*Makes 60*

65g black Mediterranean
  olives, stoned and finely
  chopped
2 tsp canned or bottled
  drained and finely chopped
  capers

4 anchovy fillets, drained and
  finely chopped
1 tbsp Dijon mustard
1 French stick (450g)
275g mozzarella cheese, cut
  into very thin slices

Preheat grill. Combine first 4 ingredients in small bowl. Using serrated knife, cut bread into 60 very thin slices. Place half of bread slices in Swiss roll tin; grill 1 minute or just until golden. Transfer to wire rack. Repeat with remaining bread slices. Place 2 slices cheese on toasted side of each bread slice; top with about ¼ teaspoon olive mixture.

**Each piece: About 35 calories, 2g protein, 4g carbohydrate, 1g total fat (1g saturated), 4mg cholesterol, 85mg sodium**

# TORTILLAS

Tortillas make the perfect base for easy starters. Soft, chewy flour tortillas can be rolled round savoury fillings and sliced to create pinwheels, or filled or sandwiched with enticing ingredients, then grilled or fried to make quesadillas. Use large corn tortilla chips to make individual nachos or dip into our Garden Salsa.

## CORN AND PEPPER QUESADILLAS

✦✦✦✦✦✦✦✦✦✦✦✦✦✦

*Prep: 25 minutes, plus standing*
*Cook: 20–25 minutes*
*Makes 32*

**2 small green peppers**
**2 medium corn on the cob, husks and silk removed**
**2 tsp vegetable oil**
**4 spring onions, sliced**
**1 tsp Tabasco sauce**
**¼ tsp ground cumin**
**¼ tsp salt**
**¼ tsp ground black pepper**
**2 tbsp chopped fresh coriander**
**8 flour tortillas (15–18cm)**
**125g Cheddar cheese, grated**
**Flat-leaf parsley and lime wedges for garnish**
**Mixed pickled chillies (optional)**

1 Preheat grill. Place peppers on rack in grill pan. Place grill pan as close as possible to heat. Grill peppers, turning occasionally, 10–15 minutes, until charred.

2 Transfer peppers to plastic bag, seal and let stand 15 minutes. When peppers are cool enough to handle, remove and discard skin and seeds. Chop peppers. Cut corn kernels from cobs.

3 Heat oil in 26cm frying pan over medium heat. Add corn, spring onions, Tabasco sauce, cumin, salt and pepper and cook, stirring, for 4–5 minutes until corn is tender-crisp. Remove from heat; stir in coriander and chopped peppers. Place 4 tortillas on work surface. Spread corn mixture evenly on top, sprinkle with cheese, then top with remaining tortillas.

### GARDEN SALSA

From 1 lime, grate ½ teaspoon rind and squeeze 1 tablespoon juice. Mix together the grated lime rind, lime juice, diced tomatoes, diced small red onion, 1 seeded and finely diced small jalapeño chilli, 2 tablespoons chopped fresh coriander, ¾ teaspoon salt and ¼ teaspoon coarsely ground black pepper. Serve with tortilla chips. Makes about 750g.

Each 100g: About 25 calories, 1g protein, 5g carbohydrate, 0g total fat, 0mg cholesterol, 275mg sodium

4 Heat 26cm frying pan over medium-high heat. Add 1 quesadilla and cook, turning once, 3–4 minutes, until tortilla is lightly brown and cheese melts. Transfer quesadilla to chopping board. Repeat with remaining quesadillas. Cut each into 8 wedges. Arrange on platter, garnish and serve warm, with pickled chillies, if you like.

EACH PIECE: ABOUT 50 CALORIES, 2g PROTEIN, 6g CARBOHYDRATE, 2g TOTAL FAT (1g SATURATED), 3mg CHOLESTEROL, 80mg SODIUM

## NACHOS

*Prep: 20 minutes    Bake: 5 minutes for each batch*
*Makes 36*

36 large tortilla corn chips
3 large plum tomatoes, finely chopped
40g fresh coriander, finely chopped
¼ tsp salt
1 tbsp vegetable oil
1 medium onion, finely chopped
1 garlic clove, very finely chopped

½ tsp ground cumin
75g cooked chorizo sausage, finely chopped, or 75g peperoni, finely chopped
400g canned black beans, rinsed and drained
125g grated Cheddar cheese
2 pickled jalapeño chillies, very thinly sliced

◆ Preheat oven to 200°C (400°F, Gas 6). Arrange tortilla chips in single layer on 2 or 3 large baking sheets. Combine tomatoes, coriander and salt in small bowl; set aside. Heat oil in 26cm frying pan over medium heat. Add onion, garlic, cumin and chorizo; cook, stirring, 5 minutes, or until onion is tender. Stir in black beans and heat through.

◆ Place 1 tablespoon black-bean mixture on each tortilla chip. Sprinkle cheese over beans and top each nacho with 1 slice jalapeño chilli. Bake 5 minutes, or until cheese begins to melt. Spoon about 1 teaspoon tomato mixture onto each nacho. Transfer nachos to platter and serve warm.

**Each piece: 45 calories, 3g protein, 5g carbohydrate, 3g total fat (1g saturated), 3mg cholesterol, 55mg sodium**

## TOMATO AND GOAT'S CHEESE QUESADILLAS

*Prep: 5 minutes    Cook: 12–16 minutes*
*Makes 32*

8 flour tortillas (15–18cm)
75g goat's cheese, crumbled
1 medium tomato, finely chopped

½ tsp cracked black pepper

◆ Place 4 tortillas on work surface. Sprinkle with crumbled goat's cheese, then chopped tomato and cracked black pepper. Top with remaining tortillas.

◆ Heat heavy 26cm frying pan over medium-high heat. Add 1 quesadilla and cook, turning once, 3–4 minutes until it is lightly browned and cheese just begins to melt. Transfer to chopping board and cut into 8 wedges. Repeat with remaining quesadillas. Serve warm.

**Each piece: 40 calories, 1g protein, 5g carbohydrate, 1g total fat (1g saturated), 2mg cholesterol, 55mg sodium**

## TORTILLA PINWHEELS

*Prep: 15 minutes, plus chilling*
*Makes about 54*

8 flour tortillas (15–18cm)
175g cream cheese, softened
4 spring onions, finely chopped

225g very thinly sliced cooked ham
60g hot pepper relish

◆ Place tortillas on work surface. Mix cream cheese with spring onions in small bowl; spread evenly on tortillas. Arrange layer of ham on top of each, then spread hot pepper relish over ham.

◆ Roll each tortilla up tightly, like a Swiss roll. Wrap each in cling film; refrigerate at least 4 hours, or overnight.

◆ Just before serving, unwrap tortillas and trim ends neatly. Cut each tortilla roll crossways into 1cm slices. To serve, arrange slices on platter.

**Each piece: 30 calories, 1g protein, 2g carbohydrate, 2g total fat (1g saturated), 5mg cholesterol, 75mg sodium**

### CORN VERSUS FLOUR TORTILLAS

Corn and flour tortillas vary in size, taste and texture. Corn tortillas are made from finely ground, soaked and treated corn (called masa harina) and water. They're about 12cm in diameter and the traditional choice for tacos, enchiladas (rolled-up tortillas filled with meat or cheese and baked) and tostadas (salad-topped fried tortillas). Flour tortillas are made from wheat flour and water, and enriched with lard or vegetable shortening. They range from 15–25cm in diameter and have a soft, chewy texture – making them ideal 'wrappers' for burritos (folded tortilla 'sandwiches') and chimichangas (deep-fried burritos).

# FILO PARCELS

Filo pastry can be layered and wrapped around fillings of all sorts. You'll need large sheets for these recipes – look for long (at least 30cm), thin packs. These filo starters can be frozen, unbaked, for up to a month. Bake from frozen, allowing a little longer baking time.

## MINI SPRING ROLLS

◆◆◆◆◆◆◆◆◆◆◆◆◆◆

*Prep: 40 minutes*
*Bake: 15 minutes*
*Makes 36*

**Prawn and Vegetable Filling**
**(see right)**
**12 sheets fresh or frozen**
**(thawed) filo pastry, each**
**about 40 by 30cm (about**
**225g)**
**60g butter, melted**
**Soy sauce for serving**

1 Grease 2 Swiss roll tins. Prepare filling; set aside. Arrange filo sheets in a stack and cut crossways into 3 strips. Place strips on parchment paper; cover with cling film.

3 Roll strip with filling one-third of the way up, then fold the left and right sides in and continue rolling to end.

2 Place 1 strip filo on work surface. Brush top lightly with some melted butter. Drain any liquid from filling. Place 1 scant tablespoon filling in centre at end of strip.

4 Place roll, seam-side down, in Swiss roll tin; brush lightly with melted butter. Repeat with remaining filo strips, filling and melted butter, placing rolls 2–3cm apart. If not serving right away, cover with foil and refrigerate. Preheat oven to 190°C (375°F, Gas 5). Bake egg rolls 15 minutes, or until golden. Serve hot with soy sauce.

## PRAWN AND VEGETABLE FILLING

◆◆◆◆◆◆◆◆◆

**1 tbsp cornflour**
**1 tbsp dry sherry**
**1 tbsp soy sauce**
**¼ tsp sugar**
**4 tbsp vegetable oil**
**225g Chinese cabbage, finely sliced**
**25g spring onions, finely chopped**
**50g mushrooms, chopped**
**225g raw medium prawns, peeled and de-veined (see page 90), chopped**
**½ tsp grated peeled fresh ginger**
**50g bean sprouts, chopped**
**50g canned bamboo shoots, drained and chopped**
**125g cooked ham, chopped**

1 Mix first 4 ingredients in cup; set aside. Heat 2 tablespoons oil in 4-litre saucepan over high heat. Add Chinese cabbage, spring onions and mushrooms and cook, stirring frequently, about 1 minute, just until tender-crisp. Transfer to large bowl with slotted spoon.

2 Heat 2 more tablespoons oil in same pan over high heat. Add prawns and ginger; cook, stirring constantly, 30 seconds, or until prawns turn opaque throughout. Pour in cornflour mixture and stir until thickened. Add prawn mixture to bowl with vegetables. Pat bean sprouts and bamboo shoots dry with kitchen towels. Stir into vegetables and ham.

**EACH PIECE: ABOUT 55 CALORIES, 2g PROTEIN, 4g CARBOHYDRATE, 3g TOTAL FAT (1g SATURATED), 15mg CHOLESTEROL, 120mg SODIUM**

## GREEK CHEESE BUNDLES

*Prep: 40 minutes    Bake: 15–20 minutes*

*Makes 50*

| | |
|---|---|
| 125g feta cheese, crumbled | 1 medium egg |
| 125g ricotta cheese | 8 sheets fresh or frozen |
| 2 tbsp chopped fresh parsley | (thawed) filo pastry, each |
| ¼ tsp coarsely ground black | 40 by 30cm (about 150g) |
| pepper | 50g butter, melted |

◆ Grease two Swiss roll tins. Using fork, combine first 5 ingredients in medium bowl.

◆ Arrange filo sheets in one stack. Cut lengthways into 5 strips; cut each strip crossways into 5 rectangles. Place cut filo on parchment paper and cover with cling film to prevent filo from drying out.

◆ Place 2 rectangles of filo on top of each other on work surface and brush top lightly with melted butter. Place 2 more rectangles crossways on top of first 2 rectangles; brush lightly with more margarine. Place 1 rounded teaspoon filling in centre; crimp filo round filling to form a bundle. Repeat with remaining filo, butter and filling.

◆ Place bundles, crimped-side up, in tins. Brush with melted butter. If not serving right away, cover and refrigerate. Preheat oven to 200°C (400°F, Gas 6). Bake cheese bundles 15–20 minutes until golden. Serve hot.

**Each piece: About 35 calories,
1g protein, 2g carbohydrate,
2g total fat (1g saturated),
11mg cholesterol,
65mg sodium**

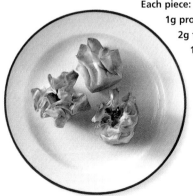

## MUSHROOM TRIANGLES

*Prep: 45 minutes    Bake: 10–12 minutes*

*Makes 35*

| | |
|---|---|
| 2 tbsp vegetable oil | 2 tbsp freshly grated |
| 900g mushrooms, very finely | Parmesan cheese |
| chopped | 7 sheets fresh or frozen |
| 1 large onion, very finely | (thawed) filo pastry, each |
| chopped | 40 by 30cm (about 150g) |
| 1 tsp salt | 45g butter, melted |
| ¼ tsp dried thyme | |

◆ Heat oil in 30cm non-stick frying pan over medium-high heat. Add mushrooms, onion and salt and cook about 15 minutes until mushrooms and onion are golden and all the liquid has evaporated. Remove pan from heat and stir in thyme and Parmesan cheese.

◆ Arrange filo sheets in one stack. Cut stack lengthways into 5 strips. Place cut filo on parchment paper and cover with cling film to prevent filo from drying out.

◆ Place 1 filo strip on work surface; brush top lightly with melted butter. Place about 2 teaspoons mushroom mixture at end of strip. Fold one corner of strip diagonally over filling so that short edge meets long edge of strip, forming a right angle. Continue folding over at right angles to form a triangular-shaped package.

◆ Repeat with remaining filo strips and mushroom filling, brushing each strip with some melted butter. Place triangles, seam-side down, in ungreased Swiss roll tin; brush with remaining butter. If not serving right away, cover and refrigerate. Preheat oven to 220°C (425°F, Gas 7). Bake triangles 10–12 minutes, until golden. Serve hot.

**Each piece: About 35 calories, 1g protein, 4g carbohydrate,
2g total fat (0g saturated), 3mg cholesterol, 100mg sodium**

### DECORATIVE TOUCHES WITH FILO

If you like, for the Mushroom Triangles above, when you reach the last fold at the end of the filo strip, place a tiny sprig of fresh thyme, flat-leaf parsley or other herb on the filo and then fold the filo over to complete the triangular-shaped package. The herb will lend a pleasantly subtle fragrance and flavour.

# PUFF PASTRY BITES

Puff pastry is made of hundreds of layers of pastry, which puff up during baking. It can be twisted and baked to make savoury, flaky sticks, formed into layers or rounds, or baked until golden brown then sandwiched with a flavourful filling.

## OLIVE STICKS

◆◆◆◆◆◆◆◆◆◆◆◆◆◆

*Prep: 30 minutes*
*Bake: 12–15 minutes per batch*
*Makes about 44*

**225g feta cheese, well drained and crumbled**
**2 tbsp finely chopped fresh parsley**
**2 tbsp olive paste or 65g Kalamata olives, stoned and puréed with 1 tbsp olive oil**
**2 medium egg whites**
**500g fresh or frozen (thawed) puff pastry**

**OLIVE PASTE**

This pungent purée is known as *tapenade* in the South of France and *olivada* in Italy; it is traditionally made from black or green olives, garlic, capers, anchovies, herbs and olive oil. Olive paste is delicious spread on toasted bread, added to sandwiches of grilled vegetables or creamy cheeses, or stirred into mayonnaise to make a dip for crudités.

**1** Preheat the oven to 200°C (400°F, Gas 6). Using fork, mix feta cheese, parsley, olive paste and egg whites in small bowl until thoroughly blended. Place half of pastry on lightly floured work surface (keep remainder refrigerated). Roll out pastry with lightly floured rolling pin into 35cm square.

**2** Cut pastry square in half. Spread half of olive paste mixture evenly over one half then top with remaining pastry half.

**3** Gently roll rolling pin over both layers of pastry to seal them together.

**4** Grease large baking sheet. Using large chef's knife, cut pastry rectangle crossways into 1.5cm wide strips, taking care not to tear pastry.

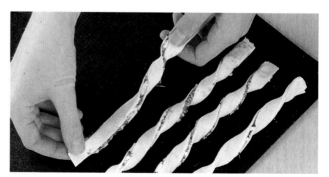

**5** Place pastry strips, 2–3cm apart, on large baking sheet, twisting each strip 3 or 4 times. Bake strips 12–15 minutes until pastry is puffed and lightly browned. Using spatula or wide palette knife, transfer the sticks to wire rack to cool. Repeat with remaining pastry sheet and olive mixture. Serve at room temperature. Store any remaining sticks in an air-tight container.

EACH PIECE: ABOUT 70 CALORIES, 1g PROTEIN, 6g CARBOHYDRATE, 4g TOTAL FAT (1g SATURATED), 5mg CHOLESTEROL, 100mg SODIUM

## SPICY CHEESE STICKS

*Prep: 30 minutes    Bake: 15–20 minutes per batch*
*Makes about 36*

500g fresh or frozen (thawed)
  puff pastry
225g mature Cheddar
  cheese, grated

1 tsp hot chilli powder
1 tsp salt
1 large egg, beaten

◆ Preheat oven to 190°C (375°F, Gas 5). Grease large baking sheet. Place half of pastry on lightly floured work surface (keep remainder refrigerated). Roll out pastry into 36cm square; cut in half. Sprinkle half of grated cheese onto half of pastry; top with remaining pastry half. Roll out pastry into 36 by 25cm rectangle.

◆ Sprinkle rectangle with half of chilli powder and half of salt; press in gently with rolling pin. Turn rectangle over and brush with some beaten egg. Cut rectangle crossways into eighteen 25 by 2cm strips.

◆ Place pastry strips, 1cm apart, on baking sheet, twisting each strip 3 or 4 times. Bake 15–20 minutes until sticks are crisp and lightly browned. Transfer to wire rack to cool.

◆ Repeat with remaining pastry, cheese, chilli powder, salt and egg. Serve warm or at room temperature. Store in an air-tight container.

**Each piece: About 95 calories, 2g protein, 8g carbohydrate, 5g total fat (2g saturated), 12mg cholesterol, 150mg sodium**

## CRAB MEAT MORSELS

*Prep: 20 minutes    Bake: 15 minutes*
*Makes 42*

250g fresh or frozen (thawed)
  puff pastry
225g canned white crab meat,
  flaked and picked over
50g mayonnaise

1 tbsp fresh lemon juice
2 tsp chopped fresh
  tarragon
¼ tsp ground black pepper

◆ Preheat oven to 200°C (400°F, Gas 6). Place pastry on lightly floured work surface; roll out into 25 by 30cm rectangle. Using 4cm fluted biscuit cutter, cut out 42 rounds. Place on ungreased large baking sheet. Bake 15 minutes, or until golden. Transfer to wire rack to cool.

◆ Mix the crab meat, mayonnaise, lemon juice, tarragon and pepper in bowl. Cut each pastry puff horizontally in half; remove top halves. Place 1 level teaspoon crab meat mixture on each bottom half and replace tops.

**Each piece: About 45 calories, 1g protein, 3g carbohydrate, 3g total fat (1g saturated), 4mg cholesterol, 45mg sodium**

## STILTON AND APPLE MILLEFEUILLES

*Prep: 30 minutes    Bake: 17–20 minutes*
*Makes about 32*

250g frozen or frozen
  (thawed) puff pastry
45g unsalted butter, softened
2 large Golden Delicious
  apples, peeled, cored and
  chopped

65g Stilton cheese, softened
50g walnuts, toasted
  and finely chopped
1 tbsp chopped fresh parsley
Thin apple slices, walnuts and
  parsley sprigs for garnish

◆ Preheat oven to 200°C (400°F, Gas 6). Place pastry on lightly floured surface; roll out pastry into 38 by 24cm rectangle. Transfer to ungreased large baking sheet. Using ruler as guide, cut pastry lengthways into 38 by 4cm strips; place second baking sheet on top of pastry to keep it flat. Bake 15–20 minutes until pastry is golden. Transfer pastry to wire rack to cool.

◆ Melt 15g butter in 26cm frying pan over medium heat. Stir in apples, cover and cook 10–15 minutes until tender and beginning to brown. Remove from heat and mash with back of wooden spoon.

◆ Combine cheese with remaining 30g butter in small bowl until well blended. Stir in chopped walnuts and parsley.

◆ Spread cheese mixture evenly over 2 pastry strips. Spread apple mixture evenly over another 2 pastry strips. Stack apple layers on cheese layers; top with remaining pastry strips. Using serrated knife, trim ends and cut each stack crossways into 2cm slices. Garnish with apple, walnuts and parsley; serve at room temperature.

**Each piece: About 60 calories, 1g protein, 6g carbohydrate, 4g total fat (1g saturated), 4mg cholesterol, 55mg sodium**

# FLAKY TURNOVERS

Our easy-to-make basic recipe for turnover pastry can be used to enfold a tempting assortment of delicious fillings, from a fragrant Mexican meat mixture to an Indian-spiced vegetable blend. Perfect for entertaining, these inviting little hors d'oeuvre can all be prepared ahead, and frozen for up to 1 month. Reheat them, from frozen, at 220°C (425°F, Gas 7) for about 10 minutes.

## MEXICAN-STYLE EMPANADITAS

❖❖❖❖❖❖❖❖❖❖❖❖❖❖❖❖❖❖❖❖❖❖❖❖❖❖❖❖

*Prep: 1¼ hours    Bake: 12 minutes per batch*

*Makes about 60*

| | |
|---|---|
| 2 tsp vegetable oil | 3 tbsp chopped sultanas |
| 1 small onion, finely chopped | 3 tbsp chopped pimiento-stuffed olives |
| 1 large garlic clove, very finely chopped | 225g canned tomatoes with their juice |
| ¼ tsp ground cinnamon | Flaky Turnover Pastry (see page 52) |
| ¼ tsp ground red pepper | |
| 125g minced beef | 1 medium egg |
| ¼ tsp salt | |

**1** Prepare filling: heat oil in 30cm frying pan over medium heat. Add onion and cook, stirring often, 5 minutes, or until tender. Stir in garlic, cinnamon and ground red pepper and cook for a further 30 seconds. Add minced beef and salt and cook, stirring often, 5 minutes, or until beef begins to brown.

**2** Stir in sultanas, olives and tomatoes and break up tomatoes with back of spoon. Increase heat to high and cook 10 minutes, or until almost all liquid evaporates. Remove from heat. Preheat oven to 220°C (425°F, Gas 7).

**3** Divide pastry into quarters. Roll out one quarter of pastry less than 2mm thick on lightly floured work surface with floured rolling pin (keep remainder of pastry covered with cling film).

**4** Using 7–8cm round plain cutter, cut out as many pastry rounds as possible, reserving any trimmings to re-roll.

**5** Using spatula, carefully transfer pastry rounds to ungreased large baking sheet. Place 1 level teaspoon filling in centre of each round; fold rounds in half to enclose filling. Crimp edges together with your fingers or fork to seal.

**6** Beat egg with *2 tablespoons water* in cup to make glaze. Brush egg glaze lightly over turnovers and bake 12 minutes, or until golden. Transfer to wire rack. Repeat with remaining pastry and filling. Serve warm.

EACH EMPANADITA: ABOUT 80 CALORIES, 1g PROTEIN, 7g CARBOHYDRATE, 5g TOTAL FAT (1g SATURATED), 5mg CHOLESTEROL, 105mg SODIUM

## MUSHROOM TURNOVERS

*Prep: 1¼ hours   Bake: 12 minutes per batch*
*Makes about 60*

| | |
|---|---|
| 1 tbsp olive oil | ⅛ tsp dried thyme |
| 1 medium onion, finely chopped | 1 garlic clove, very finely chopped |
| 225g white mushrooms, thinly sliced | 125ml whipping cream |
| 125g shiitake mushrooms, stalks discarded, thinly sliced | 2 tbsp chopped fresh parsley |
| | Flaky Turnover Pastry (see below) |
| ¾ tsp salt | 1 medium egg, beaten with 2 tbsp water, for glaze |
| ¼ tsp ground black pepper | |

◆ Prepare mushroom filling: heat olive oil in 30cm frying pan over medium-high heat. Add onion and cook, stirring often, 3 minutes, or until tender. Stir in white and shiitake mushrooms, salt, pepper and thyme and cook, stirring often, 10 minutes, or until liquid evaporates.

◆ Stir in garlic and cook 30 seconds. Stir in cream and boil 5 minutes, or until mixture is reduced and thickened. Remove from heat and stir in parsley.

◆ Prepare pastry. Cut out, fill and bake as directed in Steps 3 to 6 of Mexican-style Empanaditas (see page 51).

**Each turnover: About 90 calories, 1g protein, 8g carbohydrate, 6g total fat (2g saturated), 6mg cholesterol, 100mg sodium**

## SPICY POTATO CRESCENTS

*Prep: 1¼ hours   Bake: 12 minutes per batch*
*Makes about 60*

| | |
|---|---|
| 1 tbsp vegetable oil | ½ tsp ground cumin |
| 1 medium onion, finely chopped | ¼ tsp ground red pepper |
| 2 medium potatoes, peeled and diced | 1 tsp salt |
| | 75g frozen petit pois |
| 1 tbsp very finely chopped, peeled fresh ginger | 15g fresh coriander, finely chopped |
| 1 large garlic clove, very finely chopped | Flaky Turnover Pastry (see below) |
| 1 tsp curry powder | 1 medium egg, beaten with 2 tbsp water, for glaze |

◆ Prepare spicy potato filling: heat oil in 26cm frying pan over medium heat. Add onion and cook 5 minutes, or until tender. Add potatoes and cook, stirring often, 10 minutes, or until beginning to brown. Stir in ginger and next 4 ingredients; cook 30 seconds. Add salt and *225ml water* and bring to the boil. Reduce heat to medium-low, cover and simmer 10–15 minutes until potatoes are tender. Stir in peas; cook, uncovered, until liquid evaporates. Remove from heat; stir in chopped coriander, mashing potatoes roughly with back of spoon.

◆ Prepare pastry. Cut out, fill and bake as directed in Steps 3 to 6 of Mexican-style Empanaditas (see page 51).

**Each crescent: About 80 calories, 1g protein, 7g carbohydrate, 5g total fat (1g saturated), 4mg cholesterol, 110mg sodium**

## FLAKY TURNOVER PASTRY

◆◆◆◆◆◆◆◆◆◆◆◆◆

This pastry is extra light and flaky, thanks to the baking powder. To make in a food processor with the knife blade attached, blend dry ingredients in bowl then add white vegetable fat and blend until the mixture resembles coarse crumbs. Add *7 tablespoons iced water* all at once and pulse just until pastry forms a ball.

**600g plain flour, sifted**
**2 tsp baking powder**
**2 tsp salt**
**300g white vegetable fat**

1 Combine dry ingredients in large bowl. Using pastry blender or two knifes used scissor fashion, cut in fat until the mixture resembles coarse crumbs.

2 Add about *8 table-spoons iced water*, 1 tablespoon at a time, tossing with fork until pastry begins to hold together. Transfer to lightly floured work surface and knead lightly to form ball.

### WHAT'S IN A NAME?

◆◆◆◆◆◆◆◆◆◆

In Spain and Mexico, the *empanada* (Spanish for 'baked in pastry') or *empanadita*, a smaller version, is a flaky pastry turnover stuffed with either sweet or savoury fillings. The classic empanada comes from Galicia and is made with chicken, onions and peppers. Other typical fillings include seafood or minced meats mixed with vegetables, herbs and spices. Shapes can vary from turnovers (with scalloped edges in Chile and Argentina) to small individual pies.

# PARTY SKEWERS

Tender morsels of chicken, meat or seafood, imaginatively seasoned and threaded on bamboo skewers, make ideal party or buffet fare. Satay is the Indonesian version – ours (see page 54) highlights marinated pork with a peanut dipping sauce.

## SESAME CHICKEN

❖❖❖❖❖❖❖❖❖❖❖❖❖

*Prep: 30 minutes, plus marinating*
*Grill: 7 minutes*
*Makes 24*

**5cm piece fresh ginger**
**1 spring onion**
**1 tbsp chopped fresh coriander**
**3 tbsp soy sauce**
**1 tbsp dry sherry**
**1 tbsp vegetable oil**
**4 boneless chicken breasts (about 750g), skinned**
**Coriander Sauce (see below)**
**24 (15cm) bamboo skewers**
**4 tsp sesame seeds**
**Coriander sprigs for garnish**

1 Peel and very finely chop ginger (you should have about 4 teaspoons). Very finely chop spring onion. Mix ginger, spring onion and coriander in large bowl. Add soy sauce, sherry and oil and stir until well combined.

2 Using chef's knife, cut each chicken breast lengthways into six equal strips on chopping board.

3 Add chicken to mixture in bowl and stir to coat. Cover and refrigerate for at least 2 hours, or up to 6.

### CORIANDER SAUCE

Combine 4 tablespoons water, 50g fresh coriander sprigs, 1 chopped spring onion, 1 jalapeño chilli, seeded if desired and chopped, 1 teaspoon fresh lemon juice, ½ teaspoon sugar, ½ teaspoon very finely chopped peeled fresh ginger, and ¼ teaspoon salt. Blend until smooth. Transfer to small bowl and refrigerate until serving time. Makes about 125ml.

4 Prepare Coriander Sauce. Soak skewers (see page 54). Cook sesame seeds in non-stick frying pan over medium heat, shaking pan and stirring often, until golden. Remove from heat. Preheat grill.

5 Thread 1 chicken strip on each skewer. Arrange skewers on rack in grill pan; sprinkle with half of toasted sesame seeds. Place pan at closest position to heat and grill 4 minutes.

6 Turn skewers over and sprinkle with remaining sesame seeds. Grill 3 minutes, or until juices run clear. Arrange chicken skewers on serving platter and garnish with coriander sprigs. Serve hot with Coriander Sauce.

EACH SKEWER: 45 CALORIES, 7g PROTEIN, 1g CARBOHYDRATE, 2g TOTAL FAT (0g SATURATED), 17mg CHOLESTEROL, 170mg SODIUM

Add minced beef and next 5 ingredients to bowl with breadcrumbs; stir until well combined. Shape mixture into forty-eight 4cm balls. On each skewer, thread 2 meatballs alternately with spring-onion pieces. Grill at closest position to heat, turning once, 8–10 minutes, just until cooked through. Serve hot.

**Each skewer:** About 115 calories, 7g protein, 1g carbohydrate, 8g total fat (3g saturated), 46mg cholesterol, 220mg sodium

## SCALLOPS WITH SAGE AND BACON

*Prep: 15 minutes, plus marinating   Barbecue/grill: 5 minutes*
*Makes 20*

| | |
|---|---|
| 2 tbsp olive oil | 5 rashers bacon, rind |
| 1 tsp grated lemon rind | removed if necessary |
| ½ tsp coarsely ground | 20 (15cm) bamboo skewers, |
| black pepper | soaked (see below) |
| 40 shucked medium scallops, | 1 bunch fresh sage |
| about 625g | Salt |

◆ Mix oil, lemon rind and pepper together in a large bowl. Pull tough crescent-shaped muscle from side of each scallop. Add scallops to bowl and stir gently to coat. Cover and refrigerate at least 30 minutes or up to 6 hours.

◆ Prepare barbecue or preheat grill. Fry bacon over medium heat 5 minutes, or just until beginning to brown. Transfer to kitchen towels to drain. Cut each slice bacon crossways into 4 pieces. On each skewer, thread 1 scallop, 1 small sage leaf (or ½ large leaf), 1 piece of bacon and another scallop. Sprinkle with salt.

◆ Grill at closest position to heat, turning once, 5 minutes, or just until scallops turn opaque throughout. Serve hot.

**Each skewer:** About 50 calories, 5g protein, 1g carbohydrate, 2g total fat (0g saturated), 11mg cholesterol, 70mg sodium

## HERBED MEATBALLS

*Prep: 20 minutes   Barbecue/grill: 8–10 minutes*
*Makes 24*

| | |
|---|---|
| 2 slices firm white bread, torn | 1 tsp dried mint |
| 2 bunches spring onions | 2 tsp salt |
| 900g minced beef | ¾ tsp ground black pepper |
| 2 medium eggs | 24 (15cm) bamboo skewers, |
| 2 tbsp chopped fresh parsley | soaked (see right) |

◆ Prepare barbecue or preheat grill. Place bread in blender or food processor with knife blade attached and blend until fine crumbs form. Transfer to large bowl. Chop 125g of spring onions and add them to bowl; cut remainder into 2–3cm lengths.

## PORK SATAY

*Prep: 25 minutes, plus marinating   Barbecue/grill: 3–4 minutes per batch*
*Makes 24*

| | |
|---|---|
| 225g lean boneless pork | 2 tsp vegetable oil |
| tenderloin | 1 small onion, finely chopped |
| 3 tbsp soy sauce | ½ tsp crushed red pepper |
| 1 tbsp fresh lime juice | 60g peanut butter |
| 1 tsp grated peeled fresh | 1 tbsp light molasses or |
| ginger | golden syrup |
| 1 tsp sugar | 24 (15cm) bamboo skewers, |
| 1 garlic clove, very finely | soaked (see below) |
| chopped | |

◆ Slice pork 5mm thick, then cut each slice lengthways in half to make strips. Mix 2 tablespoons soy sauce with lime juice, ginger, sugar and garlic in small bowl. Add pork, stirring to coat. Cover and refrigerate 1–4 hours.

◆ Prepare dipping sauce: heat oil in 1-litre saucepan over medium heat. Add onion and cook, stirring frequently, 5 minutes, or until tender. Stir in crushed red pepper and cook 30 seconds. Transfer to blender, add peanut butter, light molasses, remaining 1 tablespoon soy sauce and *4 tablespoons water* and blend until smooth. Set aside until ready to serve.

◆ Prepare barbecue or preheat grill. Thread pork strips loosely on skewers. Grill pork strips at closest position to heat, turning once, 3–4 minutes, just until pork is cooked through. Serve hot with dipping sauce.

**Each skewer:** About 40 calories, 3g protein, 2g carbohydrate, 2g total fat (1g saturated), 6mg cholesterol, 150mg sodium

### SOAKING BAMBOO SKEWERS

Delicate bamboo skewers are ideal for individual first course servings. Before using for cooking, however, soak bamboo skewers in water to prevent them burning on the barbecue or under the grill. Fill a shallow bowl with water. Add skewers and allow to soak at least 15 minutes, then remove and pat dry.

# Soups

2

Few foods are more inviting than a steaming bowl of home-made soup. Comforting to eat and easy to prepare, most require little more than some initial chopping. Depending on its richness, soup can play various roles in your weekly menus. A simple broth or purée makes an elegant first course; a hearty bean soup creates a meal on its own when served with crusty bread and a crisp salad. Garnishes are great – they add extra fragrance and colour, making any soup more appetizing. Add fresh herbs just before serving.

## KNOW YOUR SOUPS

**Bisque** A rich, creamy soup with a velvety texture, usually made with shellfish.
**Broth** A tasty liquid made by simmering meat, fish, poultry and/or vegetables. Broth makes a light soup on its own and an excellent base for most other soups.
**Chowder** A hearty soup containing chunks of fish, shellfish and/or vegetables of which clam chowder is the most well known.
**Consommé** A clear soup, made by reducing stock and then filtering it meticulously. Good consommé has a heady aroma and strong flavour.
**Gumbo** A traditional Cajun dish from New Orleans, gumbo is a thick soup served over rice. It may contain a variety of vegetables, seafood and meats, and may be thickened with okra. The name gumbo comes from an African word for okra.
**Stock** A clear rich liquid made by simmering poultry, meat, or fish bones in water with vegetables. The strained mixture is used as a base for soups, stews and sauces.

## FINISHING TOUCHES

• Stir chopped fresh parsley, dill, basil or mint into soured cream or yogurt and spoon onto a creamed soup.
• Toasted nuts or crumbled crispy bacon are delicious sprinkled over Broccoli Soup (see page 60), or Split Pea Soup with Smoked Ham (see page 66).
• Garlic-flavoured home-made crôutons, grated Parmesan or Gruyère, pesto and slices of fresh lemon or lime are other tasty options.
• As a pretty garnish for chilled soups, freeze ice cubes with tiny sprigs of fresh herbs or berries. Add just before serving.

## STORING

• Cool leftover soup; refrigerate in a sealed container up to 3 days. Chilling can thicken soup, so add extra stock, water, cream or milk when reheating.
• Most soups freeze well in airtight containers for up to 3 months. Place in a large, shallow container for quicker freezing; leave a little air space to allow for expansion.
• Don't add cream, yogurt or eggs to soup bases before freezing; they will curdle when the soup is reheated.
• It's best to thaw frozen soup in the refrigerator before reheating. Since freezing may diminish some flavours, be sure to taste before serving and adjust seasonings if needed.

## QUICK HOME-MADE SOUPS

Making soup can be simple. Select your favourite from the chart, then just follow the steps below.

1 Heat 1 tablespoon vegetable oil, margarine or butter in 3-litre saucepan over medium heat. Add 1 medium onion, finely chopped; cook 5 minutes, or until tender.

2 Add Flavouring (below) for chosen soup; cook 30 seconds. Add 225ml chicken or vegetable stock, 225ml water and ¼ teaspoon salt; heat to boiling over high heat.

3 Stir in Vegetables and return the mixture to boiling. Reduce heat to medium and cook 10 to 20 minutes, until vegetables are very tender. Liquidize soup in blender in small batches until smooth. Season to taste. Makes 4 servings.

### SOUP SELECTION

| SOUP | FLAVOURING | VEGETABLES |
|------|-----------|-----------|
| Spinach | 1 garlic clove, finely chopped | 300g frozen spinach |
| Pea | 1 garlic clove, finely chopped and pinch dried mint or sprig of fresh mint, chopped | 300g frozen peas |
| Carrot | ⅛ tsp ground nutmeg | 450g chopped carrots |
| Potato | ⅛ tsp ground nutmeg and ¼ tsp dried thyme | 450g chopped potatoes |
| Courgette | 1 tsp curry powder | 450g chopped courgettes |

# CLEAR SOUPS

Clear soups may be light – or they can be hearty main dishes loaded with tender meat and chunky vegetables. Our Latin Chicken Soup creates its own aromatic broth as chicken and vegetables gently simmer; fresh lime juice, coriander and crisp tortilla chips lend additional flavour. Where the recipe calls for stock, you can save time by using stock cubes or the cartons of ready-made stock that you'll find in the chilled cabinets of your supermarket, but home-made stock will always give the best result.

**1** Combine chicken, next 6 ingredients, 450g whole potatoes and *2½ litres water* in 8-litre flameproof casserole and bring to the boil over high heat.

**2** Reduce heat to low, cover and simmer 35–45 minutes until chicken is cooked through and potatoes are fork-tender. Using slotted spoon, transfer chicken and potatoes to separate bowls. Pour cooking liquid through strainer into large bowl; skim and discard fat. Return all but 225ml cooking liquid to casserole and discard vegetables.

## LATIN CHICKEN SOUP

◆◆◆◆◆◆◆◆◆◆◆◆◆◆◆◆◆◆◆◆◆◆◆◆◆◆◆◆

*Prep: 25 minutes    Cook: 1¼ hours*
*Makes 8 main dish servings*

1.5kg chicken, cut into
  8 pieces (see page 134)
3 large celery stalks, each cut
  into thirds
3 medium carrots, each cut
  into thirds
2 medium onions, unpeeled
  and each cut into quarters
10 fresh coriander sprigs
2 bay leaves
1 tsp whole black
  peppercorns

1kg potatoes, peeled
400g canned sweetcorn,
  drained
2 tsp salt
60ml fresh lime juice
2 tbsp chopped fresh
  coriander
Tortilla chips and lime wedges
  (optional)

**3** Add reserved liquid to potatoes in bowl and mash. Add to casserole and stir well. Dice remaining potatoes. Add to casserole and bring to the boil.

**4** Reduce heat to low, cover and simmer 10 minutes, or until potatoes are tender. Meanwhile, discard skin and bones from chicken and cut it into bite-sized pieces.

**5** Stir chicken pieces, corn and salt into soup and heat through. Just before serving, add lime juice and chopped coriander. Serve with tortilla chips and lime wedges, if you like.

EACH SERVING: ABOUT 380 CALORIES, 33g PROTEIN, 39g CARBOHYDRATE, 10g TOTAL FAT (3g SATURATED), 82mg CHOLESTEROL, 835mg SODIUM

## RAVIOLI IN BROTH WITH VEGETABLES

*Prep:* 10 minutes   *Cook:* 20 minutes
*Makes* 3 main dish servings

350g fresh cheese ravioli
400ml chicken or beef stock
1 medium carrot, cut into
   matchstick-thin strips
1 small courgette (175g), diced
2 tsp grated peeled fresh ginger
¼ bunch watercress, tough stalks
   removed

◈ Cook ravioli as packet instructs.
Drain and cover to keep warm.

◈ Meanwhile, bring stock and carrot
strips to the boil in 3-litre saucepan
over high heat. Reduce heat to low,
cover and simmer 5 minutes.

◈ Add diced courgette and grated
ginger to pan. Stir to combine and
return to the boil.

◈ Reduce heat to low; cover and
simmer 5 minutes, or just until
vegetables are tender.

◈ To serve, divide watercress sprigs
and cheese ravioli between 3 shallow
serving bowls. Spoon broth with
vegetables over ravioli.

**Each serving: About 405 calories,
20g protein, 46g carbohydrate, 16g total
fat (8g saturated), 103mg cholesterol,
545mg sodium**

## MUSHROOM AND WILD RICE SOUP

*Prep:* 45 minutes   *Cook:* 1 hour
*Makes* 8 first course servings

100g wild rice
15g dried mushrooms
2 tbsp olive oil
2 medium celery stalks, finely chopped
1 large onion, finely chopped
300g white mushrooms, thinly sliced
900ml chicken stock
1 tbsp soy sauce
½ tsp dried thyme
¼ tsp coarsely ground black pepper
60ml cream sherry

◈ Bring wild rice and *600ml water* to
the boil in 3-litre saucepan over high
heat. Reduce heat to low, cover and
simmer 45 minutes, or until rice is
tender and most of water is absorbed.
Meanwhile, combine dried mushrooms
and *450ml boiling water* in medium
bowl, then set aside.

◈ Heat 1 tablespoon oil in 30cm non-
stick frying pan over medium heat.
Add celery, onion and *2 tablespoons
water* and cook about 10 minutes until
vegetables are tender and lightly
browned. Transfer to 4-litre saucepan.
In same frying pan, heat remaining
1 tablespoon olive oil over medium-
high heat. Add sliced fresh mushrooms
and cook about 10 minutes, until
tender and lightly browned. Transfer
to saucepan with celery mixture.

◈ Using slotted spoon, remove dried
mushrooms from liquid and coarsely
chop, then strain liquid. Add
mushrooms and liquid to celery
mixture. Stir in stock, soy sauce,
thyme, pepper and wild rice with any
cooking liquid and bring to the boil.
Reduce heat to low; cover and simmer
5 minutes. Stir in sherry.

**Each serving: About 120 calories,
4g protein, 15g carbohydrate, 5g total
fat (1g saturated), 8mg cholesterol,
575mg sodium**

## MISO SOUP

*Prep:* 20 minutes   *Cook:* 35 minutes
*Makes* 5 main dish servings

1 tbsp vegetable oil
2 large carrots, thinly sliced
1 small onion, diced
2 garlic cloves, very finely chopped
1 tbsp grated peeled fresh ginger
1 small head Chinese cabbage (450g),
   cut crossways into 1cm thick slices
1 tbsp rice vinegar
¼ tsp coarsely ground black pepper
60g red miso
450g firm tofu, drained and cut into
   1cm cubes
2 spring onions, thinly sliced

◈ Heat oil in 5-litre flameproof
casserole over medium heat. Add
carrots, onion, garlic and grated
ginger and cook, stirring occasionally,
about 10 minutes, or until onion is
lightly browned.

◈ Add cabbage, vinegar, pepper and
*1½ litres water* and bring to the boil
over high heat. Reduce heat to low,
cover and simmer 20 minutes, or until
vegetables are tender. In cup, mix miso
and *60ml hot water*; add to soup. Stir in
tofu and heat through, about
5 minutes. Sprinkle with spring onions.

**Each serving: About 225 calories,
18g protein, 16g carbohydrate, 12g total
fat (2g saturated), 0mg cholesterol,
545mg sodium**

---

### MISO

A highly concentrated fermented soya
bean paste, made from a combination of
soya beans and grains such as rice or
barley, miso is widely used in Japanese
cooking – from sauces and soups to main
dishes – and is made in different
strengths, varying by colour. Red miso
(far right) has the strongest flavour,
golden (right) is fairly mild, and
white is mellow and slightly
sweet. Look for miso in
health food shops and
Oriental supermarkets.

# PURÉED SOUPS

Perfectly smooth, silky textured soups make an elegant starter to almost any meal. Blenders produce the smoothest soups; remove the centre part of the blender lid to prevent overflow and splatter. Hand-held immersion blenders work well, but it is necessary to cool the soup slightly before using one. For the smoothest texture, use a wooden spoon to push the pureé through a fine-mesh sieve.

## WINTER SQUASH AND APPLE SOUP

◆◆◆◆◆◆◆◆◆◆◆◆◆◆◆◆

*Prep: 35 minutes*
*Cook: 40 minutes*
*Makes 8 first course servings*

**2 medium Golden Delicious apples (about 350g)**
**2 medium butternut squash (about 800g each)**
**2 tbsp vegetable oil**
**1 small onion, chopped**
**400ml vegetable stock**
**1 tbsp chopped fresh thyme, or ¼ tsp dried**
**1 tsp salt**
**⅛ tsp coarsely ground black pepper**
**225ml single cream**
**Chopped fresh thyme or parsley for garnish**

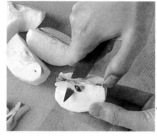

**1** Peel, quarter and core each apple. Cut each into 2cm chunks.

**2** Using large chef's knife, cut each squash into 2 pieces and slice off peel. Remove and discard seeds.

**3** Cut squash into 2cm chunks. Heat oil in 4-litre saucepan over medium heat. Add onion and cook until tender.

**4** Stir in apples, squash, stock, 1 tablespoon thyme, salt, pepper and *350ml water*. Bring to the boil over high heat. Reduce heat to low, cover and simmer, stirring frequently, 20–25 minutes, until squash is tender.

**5** Spoon one-third of mixture into blender. Cover (with centre part of blender lid removed) and blend on low speed until very smooth. Pour mixture into bowl. Repeat with remaining mixture.

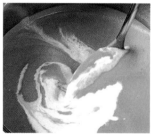

**6** Return puréed soup to rinsed-out pan. Stir in cream and heat through over medium heat, stirring occasionally. Do not boil. Serve garnished with chopped fresh thyme.

EACH SERVING: ABOUT 175 CALORIES, 3g PROTEIN, 29g CARBOHYDRATE, 7g TOTAL FAT (3g SATURATED), 11mg CHOLESTEROL, 305mg SODIUM

# BROCCOLI SOUP

*Prep: 10 minutes    Cook: 30 minutes*
*Makes 8 first course servings*

1 large bunch broccoli (750g)
1 tbsp margarine or butter
1 medium onion, finely chopped
900ml chicken stock
½ tsp salt
¼ tsp ground black pepper
¼ tsp dried thyme
Pinch grated nutmeg
125ml single cream

◆ Cut stalks from broccoli; peel stalks and thinly slice. Cut tops into florets. Melt margarine in 3-litre saucepan over medium heat. Add onion and cook, stirring often, 5 minutes, or until tender. Add broccoli stalks and florets, stock, next 4 ingredients and *450ml water*. Bring to the boil over high heat and boil 15 minutes, or until broccoli stalks are tender.

◆ Spoon small amount of broccoli mixture into blender. Cover (with centre part of blender removed) and blend on low speed until smooth.

◆ Pour mixture into bowl. Repeat with remaining broccoli mixture. Return mixture to rinsed-out pan. Stir in cream and heat through over medium heat; do not boil.

**Each serving: About 80 calories, 4g protein, 8g carbohydrate, 4g total fat (2g saturated), 13mg cholesterol, 615mg sodium**

◆◆◆◆◆◆◆◆◆◆◆◆◆◆◆◆◆◆◆

### CREAM GARNISH

Drizzle 1 tablespoon crème fraîche or soured cream in ring onto soup. Draw tip of knife through ring at intervals, alternately moving towards the centre, then towards the outside, until it forms a flower shape.

◆◆◆◆◆◆◆◆◆◆◆◆◆◆

# FRESH TOMATO AND BASIL SOUP

*Prep: 15 minutes    Cook: 25 minutes*
*Makes 4 first course servings*

4 large ripe tomatoes (900g)
1 medium bunch basil
2 tbsp vegetable oil
1 large onion, chopped
1 small carrot, grated
½ tsp sugar
900ml chicken stock
½ tsp salt
Soured cream (optional)

◆ Cut each tomato horizontally in half; squeeze out and discard seeds. Chop tomatoes. Reserve 4 small basil sprigs; chop 50g of remaining basil.

◆ Heat oil in 3-litre saucepan over medium heat. Add onion and carrot and cook, stirring occasionally, until just tender.

◆ Add chopped tomatoes and sugar; bring to the boil over high heat. Reduce heat to low, cover and simmer, stirring occasionally, 15 minutes, or until tomatoes are very soft.

◆ Spoon half of tomato mixture into blender. Cover (with centre part of blender lid removed) and blend on low speed until smooth. Pour mixture into bowl. Repeat with remaining tomato mixture. Return mixture to rinsed-out pan. Stir in chopped basil, stock and salt and heat through over medium heat.

◆ Serve soup hot or allow to cool, cover and refrigerate to serve chilled later. To serve, spoon soup into 4 soup bowls. Top each serving with a spoonful of soured cream, if you like. Garnish with basil sprigs.

**Each serving: About 155 calories, 4g protein, 19g carbohydrate, 9g total fat (2g saturated), 8mg cholesterol, 725mg sodium**

# ROASTED GARLIC AND POTATO SOUP

*Prep: 1 hour 5 minutes, plus cooling*
*Cook: 30 minutes    Makes 6 first course servings*

1 whole head garlic
3 tbsp olive or vegetable oil
2 medium onions, diced
600g potatoes, peeled and diced
900ml chicken stock
225ml single cream
1¼ tsp salt

◆ Preheat oven to 180°C (350°F, Gas 4). Remove any loose papery skin from garlic, leaving head intact. Place garlic in small ovenproof dish; pour oil over. Cover with foil and bake 1 hour, or until soft. Cool garlic until easy to handle. Separate head into cloves and press soft, cooked garlic from each clove into small bowl; discard skin. Reserve 1 tablespoon oil from dish.

◆ Heat reserved oil in 4-litre saucepan over medium-high heat. Add onions and cook, stirring often, 10 minutes, or until golden brown and tender.

◆ Add potatoes to the pan with garlic, stock and *750ml water*. Bring to the boil over high heat. Reduce heat to low, cover and simmer, stirring occasionally, about 10 minutes, until potatoes are tender.

◆ Spoon half of potato mixture into blender. Cover (with centre part of blender lid removed) and blend on low speed until smooth. Pour mixture into bowl. Repeat with remaining potato mixture. Return soup to rinsed-out pan. Stir in cream and salt. Heat through over medium-high heat, stirring constantly; do not boil. Serve hot or allow to cool, cover and refrigerate to serve chilled later.

**Each serving: About 235 calories, 5g protein, 28g carbohydrate, 12g total fat (4g saturated), 20mg cholesterol, 755mg sodium**

# HEARTY VEGETABLE SOUPS

Packed with chunky vegetables and greens, these long-simmered soups extract the maximum flavour from a few simple ingredients. The addition of grains, pulses or beans makes a humble vegetable soup substantial enough for supper – so hearty, in fact, that you'll never miss the meat.

## MUSHROOM-BARLEY SOUP

❖❖❖❖❖❖❖❖❖❖❖

*Prep: 20 minutes*
*Cook: 1¼ hours*
*Makes 6 main dish servings*

**125g pearl barley**
**750g mushrooms**
**5 medium carrots**
**2 tbsp olive oil**
**3 medium celery stalks, sliced**
**1 large onion, coarsely chopped**
**2 tbsp tomato purée**
**900ml beef stock**
**60ml dry sherry**
**Fresh oregano leaves for garnish**
**Crusty bread (optional)**

**1** Bring barley and *1 litre water* to the boil in 3-litre saucepan over high heat. Reduce heat to low. Cover; simmer 30 minutes. Drain.

**2** Meanwhile, cut mushrooms into thick slices. Cut carrots lengthways in half, then crossways into 5mm slices.

**3** Heat olive oil in 5-litre flameproof casserole over medium-high heat. Add celery and onion and cook, stirring occasionally, 8–10 minutes until golden brown. Increase heat to high; add mushrooms and cook, stirring occasionally, 10–12 minutes until liquid evaporates and mushrooms are lightly browned.

❖❖❖❖❖❖❖❖❖❖❖❖❖❖❖❖❖❖❖❖❖❖❖❖❖

### GARNISHING HEARTY SOUPS

Top steaming soup with one of the following for extra colour, texture or flavour: soured cream or yogurt; fresh herbs; crumbled bacon; thin strips of ham; chopped hard-boiled egg; shredded Gruyère; grated Parmesan; pesto tossed with chopped tomato; crumbled tortilla chips.

For crumbled bacon, cook bacon until crisp. Break into tiny pieces to use as garnish.

**4** Reduce heat to medium-high, stir in tomato purée and cook, stirring, 2 minutes. Add beef stock, carrots, sherry, barley and *900ml water*. Bring to the boil over high heat. Reduce heat to low, cover and simmer 20–25 minutes, until carrots and barley are tender. Garnish and serve hot, with crusty bread, if you like.

Pesto tossed with chopped tomato

Chopped hard-boiled egg

Chopped fresh parsley

❖❖❖❖❖❖❖❖❖❖❖❖❖❖❖❖❖❖❖❖❖❖❖❖❖❖❖❖❖

EACH SERVING: ABOUT 220 CALORIES, 8g PROTEIN, 34g CARBOHYDRATE, 6g TOTAL FAT (1g SATURATED), 0mg CHOLESTEROL, 575mg SODIUM

## LENTIL-VEGETABLE SOUP

*Prep: 20 minutes    Cook: 40 minutes*
*Makes 4 main dish servings*

| | |
|---|---|
| 900ml chicken or vegetable stock | 1 medium yellow courgette or acorn squash, cut into 1cm pieces |
| 75g lentils | |
| 2 tbsp vegetable oil | 1 garlic clove, very finely chopped |
| 2 medium carrots, cut into 1cm thick slices | ½ medium head batavia (curly lettuce), coarsely chopped |
| 1 medium onion, coarsely chopped | |
| 1 medium courgette, cut into 1cm pieces | 900g canned tomatoes |
| | 25g plain dried breadcrumbs |

◆ Bring stock and lentils to the boil in 4-litre saucepan over high heat. Reduce heat to low, cover and simmer 20 minutes, or until lentils are almost tender.

◆ Meanwhile, heat oil in 30cm frying pan over medium-high heat. Add carrots and onion and cook about 5 minutes until lightly browned. Add green and yellow courgettes and garlic; cook about 5 minutes until lightly browned. Stir in batavia and cook about 2 minutes until tender.

◆ Add tomatoes with their juice, breadcrumbs, vegetables in frying pan and *225ml water* to lentil mixture. Bring to the boil over high heat, breaking up tomatoes with back of spoon. Reduce heat to low, cover and simmer 5 minutes.

**Each serving: About 300 calories, 13g protein, 43g carbohydrate, 9g total fat (1g saturated), 0mg cholesterol, 675mg sodium**

## MINESTRONE WITH PESTO

*Prep: 30 minutes, plus soaking and cooking beans    Cook: 1 hour*
*Makes 6 main dish servings*

| | |
|---|---|
| 2 tbsp olive oil | 1 large garlic clove, very finely chopped |
| 3 medium carrots, sliced | |
| 2 medium celery stalks, thinly sliced | 900ml chicken stock |
| 1 large onion, diced | 400g canned chopped tomatoes |
| 60g pancetta, sliced, or bacon, diced | 175g dried cannellini beans, soaked (see page 370) and cooked |
| 3 potatoes (450g), peeled and cut into 1cm cubes | |
| 2 medium courgettes, diced | ½ tsp salt |
| 450g Savoy cabbage, thinly sliced (about ½ head) | 75g Pesto (see page 354) |

◆ Heat oil in 5-litre flameproof casserole over medium-high heat. Add carrots, celery, onion and pancetta; cook, stirring occasionally, 10 minutes, or until onion begins to brown. Add potatoes, courgettes, cabbage and garlic; cook, stirring, until cabbage wilts. Add stock, tomatoes with their juice and *225ml water*. Bring to the boil over high heat. Reduce heat to low, cover and simmer 30 minutes, or until vegetables are tender.

◆ Purée 50g cooked beans with 225ml soup in blender or food processor with knife-blade attached. Stir salt, bean purée and remaining cooked beans into soup, and bring to the boil over high heat. Reduce heat to low, cover and simmer 10 minutes. Serve hot with Pesto.

**Each serving: About 450 calories, 19g protein, 54g carbohydrate, 19g total fat (4g saturated), 10mg cholesterol, 510mg sodium**

## BORSCHT

*Prep: 25 minutes    Cook: 1½ hours*
*Makes 4 main dish servings*

| | |
|---|---|
| 2 tbsp margarine or butter | 1 tbsp tomato purée |
| 225g green cabbage, sliced | 900ml beef stock |
| 2 medium carrots, sliced | 1 tbsp sugar |
| 2 medium celery stalks, sliced | ¼ tsp salt |
| 1 medium onion, diced | ⅛ tsp ground black pepper |
| 450g beetroot, peeled and cut into matchstick-thin sticks | Celery leaves for garnish |
| | Pumpernickel bread (optional) |
| 400g canned chopped tomatoes | |

◆ Melt margarine in 5-litre flameproof casserole over medium heat. Add cabbage, carrots, celery and onion, cover and cook, stirring frequently, until tender and browned. Add beetroot, tomatoes with their juice, tomato purée, stock, sugar, salt, pepper and *350ml water*. Bring to the boil over high heat. Reduce heat to low; cover and simmer, stirring, 45 minutes, or until vegetables are tender.

◆ Spoon 450ml soup into blender. Cover (with centre part of lid removed) and purée on low speed until smooth. Return soup to rinsed-out casserole and heat through. Garnish and serve hot with pumpernickel bread, if you like. Or, cool, cover and refrigerate to serve chilled later.

**Each serving: About 220 calories, 7g protein, 37g carbohydrate, 7g total fat (1g saturated), 0mg cholesterol, 1465mg sodium**

# HEARTY SEAFOOD SOUPS

Cook shellfish or tasty chunks of fish in a spicy, flavourful stock to produce sensational soups – from Mediterranean Fish Soup, based on the Provençal classic bouillabaisse that varies with the day's catch, to a traditional Louisiana gumbo based on a dark *roux* of flour and oil thickened with okra. Just add crusty bread and a fresh green salad to make a memorable meal.

## MEDITERRANEAN FISH SOUP

❖❖❖❖❖❖❖❖❖❖❖❖❖

*Prep:* 35 minutes
*Cook:* 30 minutes
*Makes* 12 main dish servings

**Rouille (see page 64)**
**450g scallops**
**12 medium or 24 small hard-shell clams**
**12 medium mussels**
**450g tiger prawns**
**2 tbsp olive oil**
**3 medium leeks (450g), cut into 2cm pieces**
**1 garlic clove, very finely chopped**
**1 tsp salt**
**¾ tsp dried thyme**
**½ tsp saffron threads**
**800g canned tomatoes**
**900g cod fillets, cut into 4cm chunks**
**2 tbsp chopped fresh parsley**

**1** Prepare Rouille. Rinse scallops under cold running water, then pull tough crescent-shaped muscle from side of each scallop. Slice each scallop horizontally in half. Using stiff brush, scrub clams and mussels under cold running water to remove any sand. Remove beards from mussels (see page 88). Peel and de-vein prawns (see page 90) and rinse well.

**2** Bring *225ml water* to the boil in 8-litre flameproof casserole over high heat. Add clams and mussels; return to the boil. Reduce heat to medium; cover and cook, stirring occasionally, about 5 minutes, just until shells open. Discard any clams or mussels that do not open.

**3** Using slotted spoon, transfer cooked shellfish to bowl; set aside.

**4** Allow cooking liquid to stand until sand settles to bottom of casserole. Ladle as much clear liquid as possible through strainer into measuring jug or bowl; discard remaining gritty liquid from casserole. Rinse and dry casserole.

**5** Heat oil in casserole over medium heat. Add leeks and garlic; cook until tender. Stir in salt, thyme, saffron, tomatoes with their juice, clam cooking liquid and *450ml water*. Bring to the boil over high heat, breaking up tomatoes with back of spoon.

**6** Add cod, prawns and scallops and return to the boil. Reduce heat to medium-low, cook, uncovered, 5–8 minutes, until seafood is opaque throughout. Add clams and mussels and heat through. Sprinkle with parsley and top with a dollop of Rouille.

EACH SERVING: ABOUT 230 CALORIES, 30g PROTEIN, 12g CARBOHYDRATE, 6G TOTAL FAT (1g SATURATED), 110mg CHOLESTEROL, 565mg SODIUM

## PERUVIAN SEAFOOD SOUP

*Prep: 30 minutes   Cook: 25 minutes*
*Makes 6 main dish servings*

1 tbsp vegetable oil
1 medium onion, chopped
2 garlic cloves, very finely chopped
2 serrano chillies, seeded and very finely chopped
450g red potatoes, cut into 2cm chunks
750ml fish stock
¾ tsp salt
⅛ tsp dried thyme
½ medium lime
450g monkfish, dark membrane removed and cut into 2–3cm pieces
450g medium prawns, peeled and de-veined (see page 90)
25g fresh coriander, chopped
Lime wedges for serving

◆ Heat oil in 4-litre saucepan over medium heat. Add onion and cook 5 minutes, or until tender. Add garlic and chillies and cook 30 seconds. Add potatoes, next 3 ingredients and *450ml water* and bring to the boil over high heat. Boil 10 minutes.

◆ Add lime half and monkfish; cover and cook 5 minutes. Stir in prawns, cover and cook for 3–5 minutes, just until prawns are opaque throughout. Remove lime half, pressing to squeeze juice into soup. Sprinkle soup with coriander and serve with lime wedges.

**Each serving: About 225 calories, 26g protein, 20g carbohydrate, 4g total fat (1g saturated), 135mg cholesterol, 665mg sodium**

## MUSSEL SOUP

*Prep: 15 minutes   Cook: 20 minutes*
*Makes 4 main dish servings*

1 tbsp olive oil
1 large onion, sliced
2 garlic cloves, very finely chopped
800g canned tomatoes in juice
1 tbsp tomato purée
225ml fish stock
60ml dry white wine
⅛ tsp crushed red pepper
900g small mussels, scrubbed and beards removed (see page 88)
2 tbsp chopped fresh parsley

◆ Heat oil in 5-litre flameproof casserole over medium heat. Add onion and cook about 10 minutes, until golden. Add garlic and cook for 2 minutes longer. Stir in tomatoes with their juice, tomato purée, the next 3 ingredients and *450ml water*. Bring to the boil over high heat, breaking up tomatoes with back of spoon. Boil 3 minutes.

◆ Add mussels and return to the boil. Reduce heat to low; cover and simmer about 4 minutes, until mussels open. Discard any mussels that do not open. Stir in parsley.

**Each serving: About 185 calories, 12g protein, 18g carbohydrate, 6g total fat (1g saturated), 21mg cholesterol, 1000mg sodium**

## RED-SNAPPER GUMBO

*Prep: 20 minutes   Cook: 40 minutes*
*Makes 6 main dish servings*

200g long-grain rice
3 tbsp vegetable oil
3 tbsp plain flour
1 medium green pepper, seeded, cored and chopped
1 medium celery stalk, chopped
1 medium onion, chopped
400g canned tomatoes
400ml chicken stock
300g okra, sliced
300g frozen sweetcorn
1 tbsp Worcestershire sauce
½ tsp salt
¼ tsp ground red pepper
⅛ tsp dried thyme
1 bay leaf
300g red snapper fillet, cut into bite-sized chunks

◆ Prepare rice as packet instructs. Drain well and keep warm. Meanwhile, heat oil in 5-litre flameproof casserole over medium heat. Stir in flour and cook, stirring constantly, about 10 minutes, until flour is dark brown but not burned (mixture will be thick).

◆ Add green pepper, celery and onion to flour mixture and cook, stirring occasionally, 8–10 minutes, until vegetables are tender.

◆ Gradually stir in tomatoes and chicken stock, breaking up tomatoes with back of spoon. Stir in okra, next 6 ingredients and *225ml water*. Bring to the boil over high heat. Reduce heat to low, cover and simmer 10 minutes.

◆ Stir in red snapper and simmer until opaque throughout. To serve, discard bay leaf. Ladle soup into 6 soup bowls and top each with a scoop of rice.

**Each serving: About 330 calories, 16g protein, 49g carbohydrate, 9g total fat (2g saturated), 22mg cholesterol, 705mg sodium**

### ROUILLE

Soak 1 slice firm white bread, crusts removed, in water to cover 5 minutes; squeeze out water. Purée bread, 1 red pepper, roasted and peeled (see page 310) 2 tablespoons extra virgin olive oil and ⅛ teaspoon ground red pepper in blender or food processor with knife blade attached.

Finely chop 1 garlic clove and mash to a paste with ¼ teaspoon salt; stir into bread mixture. Makes 125ml.

**Each 100ml: About 265 calories, 2g protein, 14g carbohydrate, 22g total fat (3g saturated), 0mg cholesterol, 535mg sodium**

# HEARTY MEAT AND POULTRY SOUPS

A bowl of thick, steaming soup, loaded with vegetables, beans or pasta, can be a wonderfully welcome and satisfying meal in itself. Alternatively, a mugful can be served with a sandwich or salad as a light lunch. Sweet sausage, smoked ham and tasty meatballs are so full of flavour that a small amount goes a long way in these chunky soups. Each of these specialities takes very little effort to prepare – just remember to allow plenty of simmering time so that the individual flavours can mingle. If preparing these soups in advance, add any leafy vegetables, such as spinach, just before serving.

1 Heat 5-litre flameproof casserole over medium-high heat. Add sausage and cook, stirring frequently and breaking up with spoon, until browned. Using slotted spoon, transfer sausage to bowl.

2 Reduce heat to medium. Add oil to drippings in casserole. Add onions and cook until golden. Add garlic and cook 1 minute. Stir in tomatoes with their juice, breaking up tomatoes with back of spoon.

3 Add chicken stock and *450ml water*. Bring mixture to the boil over high heat. Reduce heat to low, cover and simmer 20–25 minutes.

4 Meanwhile, cook ditalini or tubetti in 3-litre saucepan as packet instructs but do not add salt to water. Drain pasta thoroughly.

5 Add cooked sausage and cannellini to soup. Stir well to mix; heat through. Add cooked pasta and spinach to soup. Stir well to mix; heat through. Serve soup hot with crusty bread and Parmesan cheese shavings, if you like.

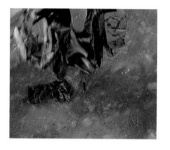

## ITALIAN SAUSAGE AND CANNELLINI SOUP

*Prep: 15 minutes*    *Cook: 50–55 minutes*
*Makes 8 main dish servings*

450g mild Italian sausages, casings removed

1 tbsp olive oil

2 medium onions, chopped

2 garlic cloves, very finely chopped

800g canned tomatoes

900ml chicken stock

175g ditalini or tubetti pasta

225g canned cannellini beans, rinsed and drained

150g spinach, tough stalks removed and leaves cut into 3cm strips

Crusty bread and Parmesan cheese shavings (optional)

### ITALIAN SAUSAGE

Made from coarsely ground pork and often redolent of fennel seeds, Italian sausage packs plenty of flavour. The hot version is spiced up with ground red pepper. In their casings, Italian sausages can be fried, grilled, or braised (be sure to cook fully). Or, remove the casings to crumble and sauté the meat as in our hearty Italian Sausage and Cannellini Soup.

EACH SERVING: ABOUT 435 CALORIES, 24g PROTEIN, 45g CARBOHYDRATE, 18g TOTAL FAT (6g SATURATED), 44mg CHOLESTEROL, 900mg SODIUM

## MEATBALL AND BATAVIA SOUP

*Prep:* 20 minutes    *Cook:* 35 minutes
*Makes* 6 main dish servings

| | |
|---|---|
| 450g lean minced beef | 2 spring onions, thinly sliced |
| 50g plain dried breadcrumbs | 750ml beef stock |
| 25g Parmesan cheese, freshly grated | ½ tsp dried marjoram |
| ¼ tsp salt | 1 small head batavia (curly lettuce), about 225g, cut into bite-sized pieces |
| ¼ tsp ground black pepper | |
| 1 medium egg | 1 large tomato, cut into 1cm pieces |
| 1 tbsp olive or vegetable oil | |

◆ Mix minced beef, breadcrumbs, Parmesan cheese, salt, pepper, egg and *60ml water* in large bowl. Shape into 30 meatballs.

◆ Heat oil in 5-litre flameproof casserole over medium-high heat. Add meatballs, half at a time, and cook until browned, transferring them to clean bowl as they brown.

◆ Cook spring onions 1 minute in drippings remaining in casserole. Add stock, marjoram, meatballs and *750ml water* and bring to the boil over high heat.

◆ Reduce heat to low, cover and simmer 5 minutes. Stir in batavia and tomato and cook just until batavia is wilted.

**Each serving: About 315 calories, 20g protein, 10g carbohydrate, 21g total fat (8g saturated), 95mg cholesterol, 820mg sodium**

## SPLIT-PEA SOUP WITH SMOKED HAM

*Prep:* 10 minutes    *Cook:* 1¼ hours
*Makes* 6 main dish servings

| | |
|---|---|
| 450g dried split peas | 2 smoked ham hocks |
| 2 tbsp vegetable oil | ¼ tsp ground allspice |
| 350g turnips, peeled and cut into 1cm cubes | 1 bay leaf |
| | 1 tsp salt |
| 2 medium carrots, diced | Chopped fresh parsley for garnish |
| 2 medium celery stalks, diced | |
| 1 medium onion, finely chopped | |

◆ Rinse split peas with cold running water and discard any stones or shrivelled peas.

◆ Heat oil in 5-litre flameproof casserole over medium-high heat. Add next 4 ingredients and cook, stirring frequently, 10 minutes, or until vegetables are tender-crisp.

◆ Add split peas, ham hocks, allspice, bay leaf, salt and *4 litres water*. Bring to the boil over high heat. Reduce heat to low, cover and simmer 45 minutes.

◆ Discard bay leaf. Remove ham hocks; discard skin and bones and finely chop meat. Return meat to casserole. Heat through; garnish with parsley.

**Each serving: About 415 calories, 30g protein, 54g carbohydrate, 10g total fat (2g saturated), 28mg cholesterol, 1115mg sodium**

## CHICKEN MINESTRONE

*Prep:* 15 minutes    *Cook:* 35 minutes
*Makes* 6 main dish servings

| | |
|---|---|
| 375g boneless chicken breast | 225g yellow courgettes or acorn squash, cut into 1cm slices |
| 75g tubetti or ditalini pasta | |
| 1 tbsp vegetable oil | |
| 1 medium onion, chopped | 400g canned cannellini beans, rinsed and drained |
| 1 medium carrot, chopped | |
| 2 large tomatoes, chopped | 300g frozen chopped spinach, thawed |
| 225g green beans, trimmed and each cut in half | |
| | Freshly grated Parmesan cheese (optional) |
| 750ml chicken stock | |

◆ Cut each chicken breast in half lengthways, then crossways into 5mm strips. Prepare tubetti as packet instructs; drain well. Meanwhile, heat oil in 5-litre flameproof casserole over medium-high heat. Add chicken and cook, stirring frequently, just until it loses its pink colour throughout. Transfer to bowl.

◆ In drippings in casserole, cook onion and carrot over medium heat until tender but not browned. Add tomatoes, green beans, stock and *450ml water*. Bring to the boil over high heat. Reduce heat to low; cover and simmer 5 minutes.

◆ Add squash and simmer 5 minutes, or until vegetables are tender. Stir in chicken, tubetti, cannellini and spinach; heat through over medium-high heat. Serve with grated Parmesan, if you like.

**Each serving: About 260 calories, 22g protein, 32g carbohydrate, 6g total fat (1g saturated), 45mg cholesterol, 920mg sodium**

◆◆◆◆◆◆◆◆◆◆◆◆◆◆◆◆◆◆◆◆◆◆◆◆

### COOKING WITH HAM HOCKS

Smoked ham hocks impart a depth of flavour to long-simmering soups and stews. After cooking, remove hocks from soup and cut through the skin. Peel away the skin and cut round bone to release meat. Chop the ham and return it to the soup.

◆◆◆◆◆◆◆◆◆◆◆◆◆◆◆◆◆◆◆◆◆◆◆◆

# CHOWDERS

Named after the French *chaudière*, a cauldron used to cook the catch of the day, chowder is a thick, creamy soup traditionally made with fish. Corn and other vegetables also feature in contemporary versions. Versatile and warming, chowders can be served as the main dish or in mugs as a substantial first course.

## OYSTER-CORN CHOWDER

◆◆◆◆◆◆◆◆◆◆◆◆◆

*Prep:* 20 minutes
*Cook:* 10 minutes
*Makes* 8 first course servings

3 medium corn on the cob,
   husks and silk removed or
   400g canned sweetcorn
450g shucked oysters
   (about 24), with their juices
600g potatoes, peeled
   and diced
450ml fish stock
225ml single cream
450ml milk
1 tsp salt
¼ tsp coarsely ground black
   pepper
Chopped chives or parsley
   for garnish

1 If using fresh corn, hold each cob firmly on chopping board and cut kernels away from cobs with sharp knife. Scrape the cobs with back of knife to release milk.

2 Drain oysters (reserve 150ml juices). Bring potatoes, stock and reserved oyster juices to the boil in 4-litre flameproof casserole over high heat. Reduce heat to low, cover and simmer about 10 minutes until potatoes are fork-tender.

3 Remove casserole from heat. Using slotted spoon, transfer 350g potatoes to blender. Cover (with centre part of blender lid removed) and blend with cream on low speed until smooth. Pour potato mixture back into casserole. Stir in milk, corn kernels with their milk, salt and pepper; heat just to boiling over medium-high heat.

4 Add oysters and cook, stirring often, 5 minutes, or until edges ruffle and centres are firm. Garnish; serve immediately.

EACH SERVING: ABOUT 200 CALORIES, 8g PROTEIN, 29g CARBOHYDRATE, 7g TOTAL FAT (4g SATURATED), 36mg CHOLESTEROL, 500mg SODIUM

## CORN CHOWDER

*Prep:* 20 minutes
*Cook:* 25 minutes
*Makes* 4 main dish servings

1 tbsp margarine or butter
1 medium onion, finely chopped
1 red pepper, cored, seeded and finely
    chopped
450g potatoes, peeled and cut into
    1cm chunks
400ml chicken stock
⅛ tsp dried thyme
¾ tsp salt
Ground black pepper
4 medium corn on the cob, husks and
    silk removed
225ml single cream
3 rashers bacon, cooked and crumbled

◆ Melt margarine in 4-litre saucepan
over medium heat. Add chopped
onion and red pepper and cook,
stirring often, 5 minutes, or until
vegetables are tender.

◆ Add potatoes, stock, thyme, salt,
⅛ teaspoon pepper and *225ml water.*
Bring to the boil and boil 10 minutes,
or until potatoes are fork-tender.

◆ Meanwhile, cut kernels from corn
cobs (you should have about 300g).
With back of knife, scrape cobs to
release milk. Add kernels and their
milk to pan and cook 5 minutes.

◆ Stir in cream and heat through (do
not boil). Spoon soup into bowls;
sprinkle with crumbled bacon and a
little black pepper.

**Each serving: About 380 calories,
11g protein, 59g carbohydrate, 14g total
fat (6g saturated), 34mg cholesterol,
975mg sodium**

## GARDEN VEGETABLE CHOWDER

*Prep:* 20 minutes
*Cook:* 30 minutes
*Makes* 4 main dish servings

1 tbsp margarine or butter
350g leeks, white and light green parts,
    each cut lengthways in half and sliced
    5mm thick
2 medium carrots, sliced 5mm thick
1 medium celery stalk, sliced 5mm thick
450g potatoes, cut into 1cm chunks
400ml chicken or vegetable stock
⅛ tsp dried thyme
¾ tsp salt
⅛ tsp ground black pepper
60g French beans, cut into 1cm pieces
1 medium courgette (300g) cut into
    1cm chunks
225ml single cream
1 tbsp chopped fresh dill

◆ Melt margarine in 3-litre saucepan
over medium heat. Stir in leeks,
carrots and celery. Cover and cook,
stirring occasionally, 10 minutes, or
until vegetables are tender.

◆ Stir in potatoes, chicken stock,
thyme, salt, pepper and *225ml water.*
Bring to the boil over high heat and
boil, uncovered, 5 minutes.

◆ Stir in French beans and cook
5 minutes. Stir in courgette and cook
5 minutes longer. Stir in cream and
heat through (do not boil). Remove
from heat and stir in dill.

**Each serving: About 285 calories,
7g protein, 42g carbohydrate, 11g total fat
(5g saturated), 30mg cholesterol,
925mg sodium**

## NEW ENGLAND-STYLE COD CHOWDER

*Prep:* 20 minutes
*Cook:* 30 minutes
*Makes* 5 main dish servings

4 rashers bacon
3 medium carrots, each cut lengthways
    in half, then sliced
450g fennel, diced, or 3 medium celery
    stalks, diced
1 medium onion, diced
450g potatoes, peeled and cut into
    1cm chunks
750ml fish stock
400ml chicken stock
1 bay leaf
450g cod fillet, cut into 4cm pieces
225ml single cream
Chopped fresh parsley for garnish

◆ Cook bacon in 5-litre flameproof
casserole over medium heat until
browned. Transfer to kitchen towels to
drain, then crumble.

◆ Discard all but 2 tablespoons
bacon drippings from casserole. Add
chopped carrots, diced fennel and
onion and cook, stirring occasionally,
6–8 minutes, until lightly browned.
Add potatoes, fish stock, chicken stock
and bay leaf and bring to the boil over
high heat. Reduce heat to low, cover
and simmer 10–15 minutes, until
vegetables are tender.

◆ Add cod, cover and cook
3–5 minutes, until fish is opaque
throughout. Stir in cream and heat
through (do not boil). Discard bay
leaf. Serve soup hot, topped with
crumbled bacon and chopped parsley.

**Each serving: About 320 calories,
24g protein, 35g carbohydrate, 10g total
fat (5g saturated), 68mg cholesterol,
850mg sodium**

# CHILLED SOUPS

Chilled soups of all kinds make refreshing first courses or main dishes in the summer; cold fruit soups make unusual desserts any time of year. Because they must be made in advance, they're ideal for easy entertaining. Chilling diminishes flavour, so always taste the soup before serving and add extra seasoning if it seems bland.

## SPICY CURRIED CARROT SOUP

◆◆◆◆◆◆◆◆◆◆◆◆◆◆

*Prep:* 30 minutes, plus chilling
*Cook:* 1 hour
*Makes* 12 first course servings

**1.5kg carrots**
**450g onions**
**4cm piece fresh ginger**
**2 tbsp olive oil**
**4 tsp curry powder**
**800ml chicken stock**
**1½ tsp salt**
**225ml single cream**
**Fresh coriander for garnish**

1 Peel carrots and cut into 2cm slices. Coarsely chop onion. Peel ginger (see below) and grate 1 tablespoon ginger.

◆◆◆◆◆◆◆◆◆◆◆◆◆

**PEELING GINGER**

Using small knife, peel away the rough outer skin that covers the aromatic flesh. To prevent drying, peel only the amount to be grated.

◆◆◆◆◆◆◆◆◆◆◆◆◆

2 Heat oil in 5-litre flameproof casserole over medium heat. Add onion and cook, stirring frequently, 15–20 minutes until tender and golden.

4 Using hand-held immersion blender, blend soup until puréed. (Or, in a blender on low speed, with centre part of blender lid removed, purée in batches until smooth.) Return to casserole.

3 Add curry powder and grated ginger to casserole and cook, stirring constantly, 1 minute. Add carrots, stock, salt and *450ml water* and bring to the boil. Reduce heat to low, cover and simmer 30–40 minutes until carrots are very tender. Remove casserole from heat and allow soup to cool slightly.

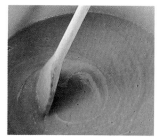

5 Stir in cream and *1 litre water.* Cool, cover and refrigerate at least 4 hours, or until very cold. Garnish with coriander. (This is also good served hot. After adding cream and water, heat through over medium heat; do not boil.)

EACH SERVING: ABOUT 120 CALORIES, 3g PROTEIN, 16g CARBOHYDRATE, 6g TOTAL FAT (2g SATURATED), 13mg CHOLESTEROL, 605mg SODIUM

## CALIFORNIAN SPICY AVOCADO AND VEGETABLE SOUP

*Prep: 20 minutes, plus chilling*
*Makes 5 main dish servings*

| | |
|---|---|
| 2 large tomatoes | 60ml red wine vinegar |
| 1 medium yellow pepper | ¼ tsp salt |
| 1 medium cucumber | 1½ tsp chopped |
| 1 large celery stalk | fresh coriander or parsley |
| ½ bunch radishes | ½ tsp chilli powder |
| 2 medium avocados | |
| 900ml spicy cocktail vegetable juice, chilled | |

◆ Seed and coarsely chop tomatoes. Cut yellow pepper into 1cm pieces. Cut cucumber lengthways in half, scoop out seeds and cut into 1cm pieces.

◆ Thinly slice celery. Finely chop radishes. Halve, seed and peel avocados and cut into 2cm pieces.

◆ Transfer vegetables to large bowl. Add spicy cocktail vegetable juice, red wine vinegar, salt, coriander and chilli powder and stir well to combine.

◆ Allow to cool, then cover and refrigerate soup at least 30 minutes, or until very cold.

**Each serving: About 195 calories, 4g protein, 22g carbohydrate, 12g total fat (2g saturated), 0mg cholesterol, 825mg sodium**

## PEACHY MELON SOUP

*Prep: 15 minutes*
*Makes 5 first course or dessert servings*

| | |
|---|---|
| 1 small cantaloupe (1kg), chilled | 2 tbsp fresh lime juice |
| 225ml peach nectar or apricot nectar, chilled | Lime slices for garnish |

◆ Cut cantaloupe in half. Using spoon, scoop out and discard seeds. Cut rind away from cantaloupe and discard. Cut cantaloupe into bite-sized chunks.

◆ Blend cantaloupe, peach nectar and lime juice in blender on medium speed (with centre part of blender lid removed) until smooth. Increase speed to high and blend 1 minute longer.

◆ If not serving right away, pour into large bowl, cool, cover and refrigerate up to 6 hours. Garnish with lime slices.

**Each serving: About 100 calories, 2g protein, 25g carbohydrate, 0g total fat, 0mg cholesterol, 50mg sodium**

## PEAR AND RED WINE SOUP

*Prep: 10 minutes, plus chilling    Cook: 15–20 minutes*
*Makes 5 first course or dessert servings*

| | |
|---|---|
| 225ml red wine | 4 fully ripe pears (750g), |
| 100g sugar | peeled, cored and each cut |
| 1 lemon | into quarters |

◆ Heat red wine, sugar and *225ml water* in 2-litre saucepan over high heat, stirring to dissolve sugar. Bring to the boil.

◆ Meanwhile, using vegetable peeler or small sharp knife, remove two 8cm strips rind from lemon and squeeze 1 tablespoon juice.

◆ Add pears and lemon rind to pan and return to the boil. Reduce heat to low and simmer 10–15 minutes, until pears are very tender. Remove and discard rind.

◆ Blend pear mixture, in batches, in blender (with centre part of lid removed), until smooth. Transfer to bowl and stir in lemon juice. Cool, then cover and refrigerate soup at least 4 hours, or until very cold.

**Each serving: About 195 calories, 1g protein, 44g carbohydrate, 1g total fat (0g saturated), 0mg cholesterol, 30mg sodium**

◆◆◆◆◆◆◆◆◆◆◆◆◆◆◆◆◆◆◆◆◆◆◆◆◆◆◆

### USING LEMON RIND

The outer, yellow part of a lemon contains a fragrant oil that imparts a zesty flavour to all kinds of savoury and sweet dishes. Remove the rind with a vegetable peeler or small sharp knife, taking care to leave behind the white pith, which is unpleasantly bitter. (The same holds true for lime and orange rinds.)

◆◆◆◆◆◆◆◆◆◆◆◆◆◆◆◆◆◆◆◆◆◆◆◆◆◆◆

# 3

# EGGS & CHEESE

Boiled, fried, poached, baked, scrambled or whipped into a frothing meringue, eggs are one of our most versatile foods. The yolks can be used to thicken and enrich custards and the whites to aerate cakes and soufflés. Nutritionally speaking, eggs are a good and inexpensive source of protein, riboflavin, vitamins A and D, choline and phosphorus. While the yolks are relatively high in fat and cholesterol, egg whites are completely fat- and cholesterol-free.

Treat eggs with care – their delicate structure is sensitive to handling and heat. To ensure that your egg dishes have a fluffy, light texture, use low to medium heat and do not overcook, or the yolks may toughen and the whites become rubbery.

## BUYING, STORING AND USING

• When buying eggs, reject any that are dirty, cracked or leaking. Move each egg in the carton to make sure it isn't stuck to the bottom.
• The colour of an egg – white or brown – is determined by the breed and diet of the hen and has no bearing on taste, nutritional value or cooking performance.
• The 'use-by' date printed on the egg carton is an excellent way to determine the freshness of the eggs. In some cases, the 'use-by' date is also printed on the egg itself. This is helpful if newly purchased eggs are stored with older ones.
• A blood spot does not signal a fertilized or bad egg. It can, in fact, be an indication of freshness. It means that while the egg was forming, a blood vessel ruptured on the egg's surface. The spot can be removed with the tip of a knife.
• Store eggs in the coldest part of the refrigerator – not in the refrigerator door. Keep them in their carton to prevent the porous shells from absorbing other odours and place the carton away from strong smelling foods such as onions.
• Store eggs pointed end down to keep the yolk centred.
• For baked goods, bring eggs out of the refrigerator about 30 minutes before you are going to use them, or place them in a bowl of warm (not hot) water for 5 minutes. Room-temperature eggs will beat to a greater volume, yielding lighter cakes and soufflés. However, cold eggs are easier to separate; so do this as soon as you take them out of the refrigerator. For all other recipes, you can use eggs straight from the refrigerator.
• Cover unused, unbroken egg yolks with cold water and refrigerate. Use within 2 days and drain before using.

• Refrigerate leftover egg whites in a tightly covered container; use within 4 days.
• You can safely refrigerate hard-boiled eggs in their shells for up to 7 days (mark to identify them as cooked).
• All recipes in this book use medium eggs.
  1 medium egg white = about 2 tablespoons
  1 medium egg yolk = about 1 tablespoon
  5 medium eggs = about 225ml
  8 medium egg whites = about 225ml

## FREEZING FACTS

To freeze leftover raw eggs, beat to blend the whites and yolks, transfer to a freezer container, and seal. Egg whites can be frozen on their own. Egg yolks, however, must have salt or sugar added, depending on whether they will be used in a sweet or savoury dish, to prevent the yolks from thickening. For every 4 yolks, stir in ⅛ teaspoon salt or 1½ teaspoons sugar then freeze as usual. Thaw frozen eggs in the refrigerator.

## TESTING FOR FRESHNESS

Crack the egg onto a saucer. A fresh egg has a round yolk and a thick, translucent white. An older egg's yolk is flat, the white thin and runny. For poaching or frying, use a fresh egg so it holds its shape. Use older eggs for scrambling or baking.

To test without breaking the egg, place in a glass of cold water: if fresh, it will stay on the bottom or stand upright if less fresh. If older, it will float. For hard-boiling, a less fresh egg is easier to peel.

## EGGS TO ORDER

**Scrambled** For each serving, beat together 2 eggs, 2 tablespoons milk, and salt and pepper to taste until blended. Heat 2 teaspoons butter or margarine in frying pan over medium heat until hot. Add eggs and, as they begin to set, draw an inverted spatula across the bottom of the pan, forming large soft curds; stir occasionally. Continue cooking until eggs are thickened and set.

**Poached** Bring 7–8cm of water in frying pan to the boil. Reduce heat so water gently simmers. Break cold eggs, 1 at at time, into a cup; holding cup close to water, slip in egg. Cook 3 to 5 minutes, until whites are set and yolks begin to thicken. Lift out each egg using a slotted spoon. Drain the egg in the spoon over kitchen towels before using.

**Fried** Heat 1 tablespoon butter or margarine in 20cm frying pan over medium-high heat. Break 2 eggs into pan; reduce heat to low. For 'sunny-side up', cover and cook slowly until whites are set and yolks have thickened. For 'sunny-side down', carefully turn eggs to cook second side.
**Boiled** Place eggs in saucepan of gently bubbling water; add a pinch of salt. Start timing from the moment the water returns to the boil. Reduce the heat and simmer gently, 3–4 minutes for soft boiled or 6–10 minutes for hard boiled. To prevent hard boiled eggs from greying around the yolks, immediately plunge them into cold water after cooking.

## SMART SEPARATING

Many recipes call for separated eggs. An egg separator is handy, but the half-shell method (below) works just as well.
• It is easiest to separate refrigerated eggs.
• Remove any trace of egg yolk in the whites using a half-shell as a scoop.
• When separating several eggs, transfer the whites to a different bowl as you go in case a yolk breaks.

Tap the egg sharply on the side of the bowl to crack the shell. With your thumbs, carefully pull shell open along the crack, letting some of the white run into the bowl. Transfer the yolk back and forth from one half-shell to the other until all the white has emptied into the bowl.

## EGG WHITE MAGIC

• For maximum volume, use room-temperature whites.
• Fat inhibits whites from foaming. Avoid all traces of yolk. Don't use plastic bowls; they absorb fat.
• If whites are under-whisked, the result will not be as light. Over-whisked whites won't blend well with other ingredients.
• Soft peaks: When whisk is lifted, peaks form and curl over slightly.
• Stiff peaks: Whites do not slip when bowl is tilted.
• To salvage over-whisked whites, stir an additional unbeaten white in a small bowl, add some of over-whisked whites. Add mixture to over-whisked whites; whisk 30 seconds.
• When folding whisked whites into another mixture, first fold a small amount of whites into the heavier mixture to lighten it. To fold, use a rubber spatula, and cut through centre of mixture to bottom of bowl, then lift it up side of bowl. Repeat, giving bowl a quarter-turn after each stroke.
• Cream of tartar helps stabilize whisked egg whites.
• Meringue powder and powdered egg whites have been pasteurized and are a safe substitute for raw eggs in recipes calling for uncooked whites.

### EGGS AND SALMONELLA

The risk of salmonella, a bacterium that can cause food poisoning, is relatively low and can be avoided by thorough cooking. Most cases come from eating under-cooked eggs or foods containing raw eggs. People most at risk are the elderly, pregnant women, infants and anyone who is ill or whose immune system is compromised. To ensure safety, cook eggs to 60°C and keep at that temperature for 3½ minutes, or cook to 70°C.

# CHEESE KNOW-HOW

## KNOW YOUR CHEESES

To make cheese, milk is usually combined with a starter such as rennet, so that it separates into curds (solids) and whey (liquid). The whey is drained off; the curds are used as fresh cheese or cured by pressing, cooking or adding bacterial cultures. Most cheese falls into the following categories:
• Hard, such as Parmesan and Pecorino Romano.
• Semi-hard, such as Cheddar, Gruyère and Emmenthal.
• Semi-soft, such as Gouda and Edam.
• Soft, such as Brie and Camembert; this category includes 'washed' rind cheeses such as Pont l'Evêque and Livarot.
• Fresh, including such perishable mild-tasting cheeses as ricotta, cottage cheese, mascarpone and cream cheese.
• Goat's and sheep's milk cheeses, which may be fresh and mild, or aged and sharp.

The wide range in the taste and texture of individual cheeses is the result of the type of milk used, the manufacturing process and the length of aging. In general, the longer cheese has been aged, the stronger the flavour, the harder the cheese, and the longer it will keep. Ideal with bread and wine, cheese also has many culinary uses: it can be spread, piped, sliced, grated, melted and mixed into batters and doughs. Cheese can also be used as a central ingredient in soups, tarts and casseroles – and many other dishes.

• Blue cheeses, such as Stilton and Roquefort, and injected or sprayed with *penicillium* moulds.
• Processed cheese, made by combining one or more cheeses with an emulsifier and pasteurizing the mixture; processed cheese spreads have ingredients added to make them soft, moist and spreadable.

## BUYING

• When choosing hard or semi-hard cheeses, avoid those with small beads of moisture on the surface or dry, cracked rinds.
• Reject any cheese that smells of ammonia. Be sure wrapped cheeses are not wet or sticky.
• If possible, sample first.
• Semi-soft or soft cheeses should be slightly springy to the touch and soft in the middle (or very soft for immediate use). Any 'bloomy' (white and powdery) rind should be even in colour and slightly moist.

## SERVING AND STORING

Before serving most cheeses, let stand at room temperature about 1 hour to bring out flavour and texture. Fresh cheeses, such as cottage and ricotta, should be eaten chilled.
• As a rule of thumb, the harder the cheese, the longer it will keep. Fresh soft cheeses, particularly goat's cheese, should be eaten as soon as possible. Firmer, drier cheeses, such as Cheddar, will keep for a month or longer if well wrapped. Hard cheeses will last several months.
• Store all cheese in the refrigerator, tightly wrapped to prevent drying. Leave the original wrapping intact, or re-wrap in greaseproof paper or foil and cling film. Cheese will last longer if the wrapping is changed every few days.
• Strong-smelling cheeses, such as Gorgonzola, should be wrapped and placed in an airtight container.
• Even when stored correctly, the surface of hard cheese may turn mouldy; simply cut off the mouldy part or scrape the surface clean. The cheese will be fine to eat. However, soft cheeses with mould should be discarded, as the mould may have permeated the cheese.
• If cheese has dried out in the refrigerator, grate it and use it for cooking purposes.
• Hard or semi-hard cheeses can be frozen up to 3 months if wrapped tightly in moisture-proof wrapping. Cheeses that are frozen may lose moisture and become crumbly – use them for cooking rather than eating.

## TO GRATE OR NOT TO GRATE

How you prepare cheese – by grating, or shaving – affects the qualities it lends to a dish.
**Finely grated** Classic for pasta. Hard-grating cheeses such as Parmesan or Pecorino Romano work best to coat pasta evenly.

**Coarsely grated** Cheeses prepared this way hold their own in salads and add noticeable texture to pasta dishes. Coarse shreds melt evenly to create smooth sauces or toppings.
**Cheese shavings** Thick, sturdy curls of hard cheese such as Parmesan add strong, individual bites of flavour that create an interesting element in many salads and pasta dishes.

Cheese shavings are simple to make. Use a vegetable peeler to pare off pieces from a block of hard cheese such as Parmesan.

## COOKING SUCCESS

• Cheese reacts quickly when heated. Cook briefly over low heat for best results; high heat or long cooking can make cheese tough and leathery. Processed cheese melts smoothly without becoming grainy or stringy.
• Grate or slice cheese for quick, even melting. For easier grating, use cold cheese; if grating a soft cheese such as mozzarella, put it in the freezer for about 30 minutes.
• Stir cheese into sauces at the end of cooking and heat just until cheese melts and blends in. Don't overheat, or sauce may become stringy. If re-heating, use a double boiler.
• Sprinkle cheese toppings over stove-top dishes when they are fully cooked. Remove the pan from the heat and cover; the heat from the food will melt the cheese.
• Grill cheese toppings 8–10cm from the heat, until melted.
• To blend cream cheese with other ingredients, let it stand, wrapped, at room temperature to soften. Alternatively, unwrap the cheese and microwave for 15–20 seconds.
• If you need to substitute one cheese for another in a recipe, use one with a similar fat and moisture content. For example, replace a full-fat Cheddar with Gruyère or Fontina, not a low-fat goat's cheese.
• Reduced-fat cheeses need extra care while cooking to prevent them from turning rubbery.

## ASSEMBLING A CHEESE BOARD

A cheese board works nicely as a light meal or alternative to dessert. To create a nice variety, choose at least three different types of cheese. Make sure they vary in flavour from mild to sharp, and in texture from soft or creamy to firm. Include wedges of blue cheese, soft cheese, hard or semi-hard cheese and perhaps some goat's cheese.

Avoid crowding the board, and accompany with crackers, toast or thinly sliced French or Italian bread. Add fresh fruit, if desired, such as seedless grapes or apple or pear wedges.

# BAKED EGGS

Perfect for brunch or supper, baked egg dishes lend themselves equally well to sweet and savoury flavours. For true convenience, the egg bake below can be assembled the night before and baked in the morning. *Chiles rellenos*, or stuffed chillies, are a favourite Mexican snack – here we've baked them in an egg mixture to make a tasty and substantial main dish.

## BRUNCH BRIOCHE AND EGG BAKE

❖❖❖❖❖❖❖❖❖❖❖❖❖

*Prep:* 20 minutes, plus chilling
*Bake:* 45 minutes
*Makes* 8 main dish servings

**1 loaf unsliced rich egg bread, such as Brioche or challah, about 450g, cut into 2–3cm thick slices**
**750ml milk**
**½ tsp salt**
**10 medium eggs**
**50g plus 1 tbsp sugar**
**1 tsp ground cinnamon**
**2 tbsp margarine or butter**
**Maple-Banana Sauce (see below right)**
**Cooked bacon (optional)**

**1** Grease shallow 3½–4-litre ovenproof dish. Arrange bread slices, overlapping slightly, in dish. Whisk milk, salt, eggs and 50g sugar together in medium bowl until well mixed. Slowly pour over bread.

**2** Prick bread with fork so it absorbs egg mixture. Spoon any unabsorbed egg mixture over bread. Mix cinnamon with remaining 1 tablespoon sugar, in cup, then sprinkle over bread and dot with margarine. Cover and refrigerate at least 30 minutes, or overnight.

**MAPLE-BANANA SAUCE**

Melt 2 tablespoons butter or margarine in 30cm non-stick frying pan over medium-high heat. Add 6 thinly sliced medium bananas and cook about 3 minutes until lightly browned. Add 225ml maple syrup; boil 2–3 minutes until slightly thickened. Serve warm. Makes about 750ml.

**3** Preheat oven to 170°C (325°F, Gas 3). Remove Brioche bake from refrigerator; uncover. Bake 45 minutes, or until knife inserted in centre comes out clean. Meanwhile, prepare Maple-Banana Sauce. Serve egg bake warm with sauce and bacon, if you like.

EACH SERVING: ABOUT 570 CALORIES, 17g PROTEIN, 85g CARBOHYDRATE, 19g TOTAL FAT (6g SATURATED), 307mg CHOLESTEROL, 605mg SODIUM

## PUFFY APPLE PANCAKE

*Prep:* 25 minutes    *Bake:* 15 minutes
*Makes* 6 main dish servings

| | |
|---|---|
| 6 medium Granny Smith's apples (900g) | 3 medium eggs |
| | 175ml milk |
| 2 tbsp margarine or butter | 90g plain flour |
| 100g plus 2 tbsp sugar | ¼ tsp salt |

◆ Peel and core apples; cut each into 8 wedges. Preheat oven to 220°C (425°F, Gas 7). Melt margarine with 100g sugar and *60ml water* in 30cm frying pan with ovenproof handle. Bring to the boil over medium-high heat.

◆ Add apple wedges to mixture in pan and cook, stirring occasionally, about 15 minutes until apples are golden and sugar mixture begins to caramelize.

◆ Meanwhile, blend eggs, milk, flour, salt and remaining 2 tablespoons sugar together in blender or food processor with knife blade attached until smooth. When apples are golden and lightly caramelized, pour egg mixture over.

◆ Place pan in oven and bake 15 minutes, or until puffed and golden. Serve immediately.

**Each serving: About 310 calories, 6g protein, 57g carbohydrate, 8g total fat (2g saturated), 111mg cholesterol, 180mg sodium**

### PUFFY PEAR PANCAKE

Prepare Puffy Apple Pancake as above, but substitute 6 ripe Bosc pears (about 900g) for the apples, and add 1 tablespoon pear-flavoured liqueur and a generous pinch of ground nutmeg to the egg mixture when blending.

Each serving: About 355 calories, 6g protein, 66g carbohydrate, 8g total fat (2g saturated), 111mg cholesterol, 180mg sodium

## SAVOURY CHEESE BAKE

*Prep:* 20 minutes    *Bake:* 50–60 minutes
*Makes* 6 main dish servings

| | |
|---|---|
| 30g margarine or butter | 225g Cheddar cheese, grated |
| 1 tsp salt | 1 tsp Tabasco sauce |
| 800ml milk | ¼ tsp ground black pepper |
| 200g coarse white or yellow cornmeal | 5 medium eggs |

◆ Preheat oven to 170°C (325°F, Gas 3). Grease shallow 2½-litre ovenproof dish.

◆ Melt margarine with salt, 350ml milk and *450ml water* in 3-litre saucepan. Bring to the boil over medium-high heat.

◆ Gradually stir in cornmeal, whisking constantly to prevent lumping. Reduce heat to low and cook, stirring occasionally, until mixture is very stiff. Remove pan from heat and stir in cheese until blended.

◆ Whisk Tabasco sauce, black pepper, eggs and remaining 450ml milk together until blended. Using wire whisk or fork, gradually whisk egg mixture into cheese mixture; pour into prepared dish.

◆ Bake 50–60 minutes, or until knife inserted in centre comes out clean. Serve immediately.

**Each serving: About 445 calories, 22g protein, 30g carbohydrate, 26g total fat (13g saturated), 236mg cholesterol, 760mg sodium**

## CHILES RELLENOS

*Prep:* 20 minutes    *Bake:* 35 minutes
*Makes* 4 main dish servings

| | |
|---|---|
| 350g canned mild whole green chillies, drained | 5 medium eggs |
| | 60g plain flour |
| 225g Cheddar cheese | 125ml milk |

◆ Preheat oven to 180°C (350°F, Gas 4). Grease shallow 2-litre ovenproof serving dish. Carefully slit each chilli down one side and remove seeds (do not cut chillies in half); pat chillies dry with kitchen towels. Slice cheese into same number of pieces as there are chillies. Insert 1 slice cheese in each chilli. Arrange stuffed chillies in prepared dish.

◆ Beat eggs, flour and milk together in medium bowl until blended. Pour egg mixture over chillies.

◆ Bake 35 minutes, or until top is golden brown and knife inserted in centre comes out clean. Serve immediately.

**Each serving: About 405 calories, 24g protein, 19g carbohydrate, 25g total fat (13g saturated), 321mg cholesterol, 1050mg sodium**

# OMELETTES

A perfectly plump, golden omelette is one of the most enticing dishes, and one of the fastest to prepare. For a light, fluffy texture, cook the eggs quickly and keep the mixture moving freely in the frying pan. This is easiest to accomplish in a non-stick pan.

## BIG WESTERN OMELETTE

❖❖❖❖❖❖❖❖❖❖❖❖❖

*Prep:* 15 minutes
*Cook:* 15 minutes
*Makes* 3 main dish servings

**6 medium eggs**
**¼ tsp ground black pepper**
**Salt**
**3 tbsp vegetable oil**
**1 small onion, diced**
**1 medium green pepper, cored, seeded and diced**
**225g sliced cooked ham, diced**
**225g mushrooms, each cut in half**
**Tomato wedges, shredded fresh basil and flat-leaf parsley sprigs for garnish**

**1** Using wire whisk or fork, beat eggs, pepper, ½ teaspoon salt and *75ml water* in medium bowl until blended. Heat 1 tablespoon oil in heavy based 30cm non-stick frying pan over medium-high heat. Add onion, green pepper and ¼ teaspoon salt and cook until vegetables are tender. Add ham and heat through. Transfer mixture to bowl; keep warm.

**2** In same pan, heat 1 tablespoon oil. Add mushrooms and cook until tender. Transfer to another bowl and keep warm.

**3** In same pan, heat remaining 1 tablespoon oil over medium heat. Add eggs; cook until edge sets. Gently lift edge as it sets, tilting pan so uncooked egg runs underneath.

### NON-STICK PANS

The specially formulated surface on non-stick frying pans or saucepans requires a bit of respect. For best results, use wooden, plastic, or other non-metal utensils to prevent scratching. Do not use over extremely high heat, and never plunge the hot pan into cold water.

**4** Shake pan occasionally to keep omelette moving freely in pan. When it is set but still moist, spoon ham and vegetable mixture over half of omelette.

**5** Tilt pan and, using spatula, fold omelette in half. To serve, cut omelette into 3 pieces; top with mushrooms. Garnish with tomato wedges, basil and parsley sprigs.

EACH SERVING: ABOUT 365 CALORIES, 23g PROTEIN, 10g CARBOHYDRATE, 26g TOTAL FAT (6g SATURATED), 437mg CHOLESTEROL, 1095mg SODIUM

# BASIC OMELETTE

◆ ◆ ◆ ◆ ◆ ◆ ◆ ◆ ◆ ◆ ◆ ◆ ◆ ◆

*Prep: 2 minutes    Cook: 2–3 minutes*
*Makes 1 serving*

2 medium eggs                  2 tsp margarine or butter
Pinch each salt and ground
    black pepper

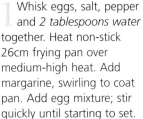

1 Whisk eggs, salt, pepper and *2 tablespoons water* together. Heat non-stick 26cm frying pan over medium-high heat. Add margarine, swirling to coat pan. Add egg mixture; stir quickly until starting to set.

2 With handle of pan towards you, place filling on half of eggs and cook 30 seconds, or until almost set. Using heatproof rubber spatula, loosen omelette and roll, starting from unfilled side, onto a warm plate.

**Each serving: About 220 calories, 13g protein, 1g carbohydrate, 18g total fat (5g saturated), 426mg cholesterol, 320mg sodium**

## RATATOUILLE OMELETTE

*Prep: 15 minutes    Cook: 40 minutes*
*Makes 4 main dish servings*

1 olive oil                              1 large garlic clove, very finely
1 small onion, finely chopped                chopped
450g aubergine (about             225g canned tomatoes with
    ½ large), cut into 1cm pieces        juice
½ tsp salt                            Pinch dried thyme
⅛ tsp ground black pepper      2 tbsp chopped fresh basil or
½ yellow or red pepper,              parsley
    cored, seeded and diced      4 Basic Omelettes (see above)
1 small courgette (125g),         60g Parmesan cheese, freshly
    diced                                    grated (optional)

◆ Heat oil in non-stick 30cm frying pan over medium heat. Add onion; cook until tender. Add aubergine, salt and black pepper. Cook, stirring often, 10 minutes, or until aubergine begins to brown. Stir in diced pepper, courgette and garlic; cook 1 minute. Stir in tomatoes with their juice and thyme, breaking up tomatoes with back of spoon. Bring to the boil. Reduce heat to low; cover and simmer 15 minutes, or until aubergine is tender. Remove from heat; stir in basil.

◆ Prepare Basic Omelettes. Fill each omelette with quarter of ratatouille mixture, and 1 tablespoon grated Parmesan cheese, if you like.

**Each serving: About 240 calories, 11g protein, 12g carbohydrate, 17g total fat (4g saturated), 320mg cholesterol, 895mg sodium**

## SPINACH, CHEDDAR AND BACON OMELETTE

*Prep: 5 minutes    Cook: 5 minutes*
*Makes 4 main dish servings*

1 medium bunch spinach          4 rashers streaky bacon,
    (300–350g)                            cooked crisp and crumbled
125g Cheddar cheese, grated   4 Basic Omelettes (see left)

Wash spinach. Cook spinach in 2-litre saucepan with water clinging to its leaves over high heat, stirring frequently, until just wilted. Drain in colander, pressing out excess liquid, then coarsely chop; set aside. Prepare Basic Omelettes. Fill each omelette with a quarter of spinach, cheese and bacon.

**Each serving: About 335 calories, 21g protein, 5g carbohydrate, 26g total fat (11g saturated), 355mg cholesterol, 765mg sodium**

## LIGHT TOMATO OMELETTE

*Prep: 5 minutes    Cook: 5 minutes*
*Makes 4 main dish servings*

1 tsp olive oil                         ⅛ tsp ground black pepper
1 garlic clove, very finely          2 tbsp chopped fresh parsley
    chopped                              4 Basic Omelettes (see above
4 large plum tomatoes, diced        left)
¼ tsp salt                            Tossed salad (optional)

Heat oil in non-stick 26cm frying pan over medium-high heat. Add garlic and next 3 ingredients; cook, stirring often, 5 minutes, or until almost dry. Remove from heat; stir in parsley. Prepare Basic Omelettes, but, for each one, use 1 medium egg and 1 medium egg white instead of 2 medium eggs and 1 teaspoon olive oil instead of margarine. Fill each with quarter of tomato mixture. Serve with salad, if you like.

**Each serving: About 165 calories, 11g protein, 9g carbohydrate, 10g total fat (2g saturated), 213mg cholesterol, 530mg sodium**

# FRITTATAS AND TORTILLAS

A frittata is a flat Italian omelette; a tortilla is a flat Spanish omelette. They differ from French omelettes in that the filling ingredients are set in the eggs as they cook, not rolled up in the omelette at the end. Frittatas and tortillas cook slowly, either on the hob or in the oven. You can brown the top of the frittata under the grill before serving; be sure the frying pan and its handle are heatproof. (Or wrap a plastic handle in heavy-duty foil.)

## ASPARAGUS, TOMATO AND CHEESE FRITTATA

❖ ❖ ❖ ❖ ❖ ❖ ❖ ❖ ❖ ❖ ❖

*Prep:* 30 minutes
*Cook:* 20 minutes
*Makes* 4 main dish servings

350g asparagus
1 medium onion
1 medium tomato
125g Jarlsberg or
    Emmental cheese
20g margarine or butter
8 medium eggs
½ tsp dried marjoram
¼ tsp salt

**1** Bend base of asparagus stalks; ends will break off where stalks are tough. Discard ends; trim if gritty. Cut stalks diagonally into 5cm pieces.

**2** Thinly slice onion. Cut tomato into 8 wedges and remove seeds. Finely grate cheese.

**3** Melt margarine in 26cm non-stick frying pan with ovenproof handle over medium heat. Add asparagus and onion; cook 10 minutes.

**4** Preheat grill. Using fork, beat eggs, marjoram, salt, half grated cheese and *60ml water* in medium bowl until blended.

**5** Pour egg mixture over vegetables in pan and arrange tomato wedges on top. Cover and cook over medium heat 10 minutes, or until set. Sprinkle with remaining cheese.

**6** Grill frittata at closest position to heat 1 minute, or until cheese is bubbly. Loosen frittata and slide onto platter; cut into wedges. Serve hot or at room temperature.

EACH SERVING: ABOUT 340 CALORIES, 23g PROTEIN, 9g CARBOHYDRATE, 23g TOTAL FAT (4g SATURATED), 442mg CHOLESTEROL, 470mg SODIUM

## POTATO AND HAM FRITTATA

*Prep: 10 minutes    Cook: 50–55 minutes*
*Makes 6 main dish servings*

| | |
|---|---|
| 4 tbsp vegetable oil | Salt |
| 225g cooked ham in one piece, diced | 8 medium eggs |
| 1 medium onion, cut into 5mm thick slices | 1 tsp dried thyme |
| 450g potatoes, peeled and cut into 5mm slices | ¼ tsp coarsely ground black pepper |

❖ Heat 2 tablespoons oil in 26cm non-stick frying pan over medium-high heat. Add ham; cook until browned. Transfer to plate. Add onion to pan; cook over medium heat until golden. Transfer to another plate. Heat remaining 2 tablespoons oil in same pan. Add potatoes and ½ teaspoon salt; cook 15 minutes, or until golden. Remove from heat. Spoon off excess oil. Stir ham into potatoes; sprinkle with onion.

❖ Beat eggs, thyme, black pepper, ¼ teaspoon salt and *60ml water* together in medium bowl. Pour into pan and cook, covered, over low heat 25–30 minutes until set. Serve hot or at room temperature.

**Each serving: About 315 calories, 19g protein, 18g carbohydrate, 18g total fat (4g saturated), 305mg cholesterol, 855mg sodium**

## LOW-FAT VEGETABLE FRITTATA

*Prep: 30 minutes    Bake: 10 minutes*
*Makes 4 main dish servings*

| | |
|---|---|
| Non-stick cooking spray | ¾ tsp salt |
| 1 medium onion, diced | ¼ tsp coarsely crushed black pepper |
| 1 medium red pepper, cored, seeded and diced | 4 tbsp finely chopped fresh basil |
| 1 medium green pepper, cored, seeded and diced | 6 medium egg whites |
| 1 medium courgette (225g), diced | 2 medium eggs |
| 1 tsp sugar | 50g feta cheese, crumbled |

❖ Preheat oven to 190°C (375°F, Gas 5). Spray 30cm non-stick frying pan with cooking spray. Add onion and cook over medium-high heat until golden. Add peppers and next 4 ingredients; cook, stirring frequently, until tender-crisp. Stir in *60ml water*, bring to the boil. Reduce heat to low, cover and simmer 10 minutes, or until tender. Remove from heat; stir in 3 tablespoons basil.

❖ Using wire whisk or fork, beat egg whites, eggs, 30g feta and remaining basil in medium bowl. Spray 26cm frying pan (with ovenproof handle) with cooking spray. Add egg mixture and cook over medium-high heat 1–2 minutes until it begins to set. Remove from heat. Using slotted spoon,

spoon vegetable mixture over egg mixture; sprinkle with remaining 20g feta. Bake 10 minutes, or until set. If desired, grill 1–2 minutes to brown top of frittata. Serve hot or at room temperature.

**Each serving: About 140 calories, 12g protein, 10g carbohydrate, 6g total fat (3g saturated), 119mg cholesterol, 675mg sodium**

## SPANISH POTATO TORTILLA

*Prep: 20 minutes    Cook: 40 minutes*
*Makes 4 main dish servings*

| | |
|---|---|
| 4 tbsp olive or vegetable oil | Salt |
| 600g potatoes, peeled and thinly sliced | 5 medium eggs |
| 1 medium red pepper, cored, seeded and diced | 25g Parmesan cheese, freshly grated |
| 1 medium green pepper, cored, seeded and diced | 2 tbsp chopped fresh parsley |
| 1 onion, thinly sliced | ½ tsp coarsely ground black pepper |

❖ Heat 2 tablespoons oil in 26cm non-stick frying pan over medium heat. Add potatoes, peppers, onion and ½ teaspoon salt; cook until vegetables are slightly browned. Reduce heat to low, cover and cook, stirring occasionally, about 15 minutes, until vegetables are fork-tender. Transfer to bowl to cool. Wipe pan clean. Using wire whisk or fork, beat eggs, Parmesan, parsley, pepper and ½ teaspoon salt together in large bowl. Stir in vegetables.

❖ Heat 1 tablespoon of oil in clean pan over medium-low heat. Add egg mixture; cook until set around edge. Using spatula, lift edge as it sets, tilting pan to allow uncooked portion to run under; shake pan occasionally. When set but still moist on top, increase heat slightly to brown base.

❖ Loosen tortilla from pan. Invert plate over pan and flip tortilla onto plate. Wipe pan clean. Add remaining 1 tablespoon oil to pan and heat over medium heat. Slide tortilla into pan, browned-side up. Cook about 5 minutes until base is golden then invert tortilla onto warm platter. Cut into wedges. Serve hot or at room temperature.

**Each serving: About 345 calories, 12g protein, 35g carbohydrate, 18g total fat (4g saturated), 269mg cholesterol, 680mg sodium**

# CRÊPES

Our Basic Crêpes (see page 82) can be stuffed with a variety of fillings. Here they're rolled into cylinders round a traditional rustic French mixture of sautéed peppers called *pipérade*, but they can also be folded over a hearty chicken and vegetable filling or an apple and Gruyère cheese combination. You can prepare the crêpes ahead and refrigerate them overnight, or freeze them for up to one month.

## CRÊPES WITH PIPÉRADE FILLING

❖❖❖❖❖❖❖❖❖❖❖❖❖

*Prep: 40 minutes, plus making crêpes*
*Bake: 15 minutes*
*Makes 4 main dish servings*

**8 Basic Crêpes (see page 82)**
**1 tbsp olive oil**
**1 medium onion, thinly sliced**
**1 medium red pepper, cored, seeded and thinly sliced**
**1 medium yellow or green pepper, cored, seeded and thinly sliced**
**¾ tsp salt**
**1 garlic clove, very finely chopped**
**⅛ tsp ground red pepper**
**450g canned tomatoes**
**75g Gruyère cheese, grated**
**Diced red and yellow pepper and chopped fresh parsley for garnish**

**1** Prepare Basic Crêpes (see page 82). Prepare *pipérade* filling: heat olive oil in 26cm frying pan over medium heat. Add onion, sliced red and yellow peppers and salt; cover and cook 15 minutes, or until vegetables are tender. Stir in garlic and ground red pepper and cook, uncovered, 30 seconds.

### QUICK CRÊPE FILLINGS

Filling a crêpe can be as easy as assembling your favourite sandwich. Any combination of the following makes a tasty treat: thinly sliced ham, smoked chicken or turkey; diced tomatoes; chopped rochet, crumbled feta or goat cheese; chopped fresh herbs; sautéed sliced mushrooms; cottage cheese; or smoked fish.

**2** Stir in tomatoes with their juice, breaking them up with back of spoon. Cook, uncovered, 15 minutes, or until thick.

**4** Place generous 2 table-spoons pipérade filling in centre of each crêpe.

**3** Preheat oven to 200°C (400°F, Gas 6). Place crêpes on work surface; sprinkle evenly with cheese, leaving 2cm border.

**5** Roll up crêpes and place, seam-side down, in 33 by 20cm ovenproof dish. Bake 15 minutes, or until crêpes are heated through. To serve, sprinkle with diced pepper and chopped parsley.

EACH SERVING: ABOUT 345 CALORIES, 15g PROTEIN, 25g CARBOHYDRATE, 21g TOTAL FAT (10g SATURATED), 153mg CHOLESTEROL, 940mg SODIUM

## CHICKEN AND VEGETABLE CRÊPES

*Prep: 40 minutes, plus making crêpes   Bake: 15–20 minutes*
*Makes 4 main dish servings*

8 Basic Crêpes (see right)
45g margarine or butter
1 medium onion, very finely chopped
4 large skinless, boneless chicken breasts, cut into bite-sized pieces
1 medium courgette (about 300g), cut into 1cm pieces

1 medium yellow courgette (300g), cut into 1cm pieces
½ tsp salt
¼ tsp coarsely ground black pepper
125ml milk
30g plain flour
125g Jarlsberg or Emmental cheese, grated

◆ Prepare Basic Crêpes. Preheat oven to 200°C (400°F, Gas 6). Melt margarine in 3-litre saucepan over medium-high heat. Add onion and cook until tender. Add chicken and cook, stirring frequently, about 3 minutes until it loses its pink colour. Stir in green and yellow courgettes, salt and pepper.

◆ Whisk milk with flour in small bowl; stir into chicken mixture. Cook, stirring, until liquid thickens and boils. Stir in half of cheese.

◆ Place crêpes on work surface. Spoon 3–4 tablespoons of chicken mixture over each crêpe; fold 2 sides over, slightly over-lapping. Place filled crêpes, seam-side up, in 33 by 20cm ovenproof baking dish. Spoon any remaining mixture around crêpes and sprinkle with remaining cheese. Bake 15–20 minutes, until chicken mixture is bubbly.

Each serving: About 600 calories, 49g protein, 30g carbohydrate, 31g total fat (9g saturated), 236mg cholesterol, 885mg sodium

## APPLE AND GRUYÈRE CRÊPES

*Prep: 15 minutes, plus making crêpes   Bake: 5 minutes*
*Makes 4 dessert servings*

8 Basic Crêpes (see right)
2 Golden Delicious apples (about 450g)

15g margarine or butter
125g Gruyère cheese, grated

◆ Prepare Basic Crêpes. Preheat oven to 200°C (400°F, Gas 6). Grease large baking sheet. Peel and core each apple; cut into thin slices. Melt margarine in 26cm non-stick frying pan over medium-high heat. Add apples and cook, stirring often, 5 minutes, or until tender and beginning to brown.

◆ Place crêpes on work surface and sprinkle cheese over half of each one. Arrange apple slices over cheese. Fold crêpes in half to enclose filling, then place on baking sheet. Bake 5 minutes, or until hot.

Each serving: About 380 calories, 15g protein, 30g carbohydrate, 23g total fat (12g saturated), 161mg cholesterol, 425mg sodium

## BASIC CRÊPES

◆ ◆ ◆ ◆ ◆ ◆ ◆ ◆ ◆ ◆ ◆ ◆ ◆ ◆

Crêpes, made from a smooth egg batter, are used in both sweet and savoury dishes. It's important to let the batter rest before cooking; the resting process relaxes the gluten in the flour for tender crêpes. This recipe makes about 12 crêpes; the leftovers can be frozen for later use or rolled up with jam and eaten as a quick snack.

*Prep: 5 minutes, plus chilling   Cook: 20 minutes*

3 medium eggs
350ml milk
80g plain flour

½ tsp salt
About 60g butter, melted

1 Mix eggs, milk, flour, salt and 30g melted butter in blender on medium speed until smooth and free from lumps.

2 Transfer batter to medium bowl and refrigerate for at least 1 hour, or overnight. Whisk batter thoroughly just before you want to use it.

3 Heat 26cm non-stick frying pan over medium-high heat; brush lightly with melted butter. Pour 60ml batter into pan and tip to coat base. Cook 1½ minutes, or until top is set and underside is lightly browned.

4 Using plastic spatula, loosen crêpe, then turn it over and cook other side 30 seconds. Slip onto parchment paper. Repeat with remaining batter, brushing pan lightly with butter before cooking each crêpe. Stack cooked crêpes.

Each crêpe: About 80 calories, 3g protein, 6g carbohydrate, 4g total fat (2g saturated), 62mg cholesterol, 140mg sodium

# SOUFFLÉS

Few dishes impress like a golden, high-rising soufflé. Eggs provide a rich flavour – and dramatic results. To begin, a cooked base of flour, butter and milk is enriched with egg yolks, cheese and other flavourings. Egg whites are beaten to stiff peaks and folded into the mixture to create a light, airy texture.

## CRAB SOUFFLÉ

❖❖❖❖❖❖❖❖❖❖❖❖❖❖❖❖❖❖❖❖❖❖❖❖

*Prep: 20 minutes    Bake: 40–45 minutes*
*Makes 4 main dish servings*

225g canned white crab meat
60g butter
40g plain flour
½ tsp dry mustard
225ml milk
1 tbsp dry sherry
50g Emmental or Gruyère
  cheese, grated

2 tbsp coarsely chopped fresh
  parsley
1 tbsp dried breadcrumbs
4 medium eggs, separated
1 medium egg white
  (optional)
½ tsp cream of tartar

1 Preheat oven to 180°C (350°F, Gas 4). Pick over crab meat to remove any pieces of shell or cartilage. Flake crab meat; set aside.

2 Melt butter in 3-litre saucepan over medium heat. Stir in flour and mustard. Cook, stirring, 1 minute. Gradually whisk in milk and sherry; cook, whisking constantly, until mixture thickens and boils. Remove from heat.

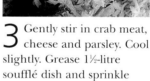

3 Gently stir in crab meat, cheese and parsley. Cool slightly. Grease 1½-litre soufflé dish and sprinkle with breadcrumbs.

4 Beat egg whites with cream of tartar in medium bowl with electric mixer on high speed, until stiff peaks form.

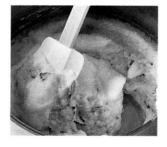

5 Stir egg yolks into cheese mixture, then, using rubber spatula, fold in egg whites, one-third at a time, until just blended. Pour into soufflé dish. Bake 40–45 minutes, until puffy and golden. Serve immediately.

❖❖❖❖❖❖❖❖❖❖❖❖❖❖❖❖❖❖❖❖❖❖

### MAKING A 'TOP-HAT' SOUFFLÉ

If you want the centre of your cooked soufflé to puff up dramatically, make a 3cm deep indentation all the way round the top of the uncooked soufflé mixture with the back of a metal spoon, 3cm in from the edge of the dish.

❖❖❖❖❖❖❖❖❖❖❖❖❖❖❖❖❖❖❖❖❖❖❖❖

EACH SERVING: ABOUT 315 CALORIES, 22g PROTEIN, 9g CARBOHYDRATE, 21g TOTAL FAT (9g SATURATED), 314mg CHOLESTEROL, 720mg SODIUM

## CORN-CHEESE SOUFFLÉ

*Prep: 15 minutes   Bake: 40–45 minutes*
*Makes 4 main dish servings*

60g butter
1 spring onion, chopped
30g plain flour
½ tsp dry mustard
½ tsp salt
175ml milk
50g Cheddar or other cheese with
   jalapeño chillies, grated
225g canned creamed sweetcorn
4 medium eggs, separated
1 medium egg white (optional),
   see below
½ tsp cream of tartar

◆ Melt butter in 3-litre saucepan over medium heat. Add spring onion and cook until tender. Stir in flour, mustard and salt; cook, stirring, 1 minute. Gradually whisk in milk and cook, whisking constantly, until mixture thickens and boils. Stir in cheese and sweetcorn until cheese melts. Remove from heat.

◆ Preheat oven to 180°C (350°F, Gas 4). Grease 1½-litre soufflé dish. Follow instructions in Steps 4 and 5 of Crab Soufflé (see page 83).

**Each serving: About 330 calories, 13g protein, 20g carbohydrate, 22g total fat (10g saturated), 264mg cholesterol, 730mg sodium**

## HAM AND SPINACH SOUFFLÉ

*Prep: 15 minutes   Bake: 35–40 minutes*
*Makes 4 main dish servings*

60g butter
30g plain flour
½ tsp dry mustard
225ml milk
300g frozen chopped spinach, thawed
   and squeezed dry
125g Cheddar cheese, grated
50g cooked ham, chopped
1 tbsp plain breadcrumbs
4 medium eggs, separated
1 medium egg white (optional),
   see below
½ tsp cream of tartar

◆ Melt butter in 3-litre saucepan over medium heat. Stir in flour and mustard; cook, stirring, 1 minute. Gradually whisk in milk; cook, whisking constantly, until mixture thickens and boils. Stir in spinach, cheese and ham until cheese melts. Remove from heat.

◆ Preheat oven to 180°C (350°F, Gas 4). Grease 1½-litre soufflé dish; sprinkle with breadcrumbs. Follow instructions in Steps 4 and 5 of Crab Soufflé (see page 83), but bake only 35–40 minutes until puffy and golden.

**Each serving: About 405 calories, 22g protein, 15g carbohydrate, 29g total fat (14g saturated), 281mg cholesterol, 665mg sodium**

## TOMATO SOUFFLÉ

*Prep: 45 minutes   Bake: 45 minutes*
*Makes 8 accompaniment servings*

1 tbsp vegetable oil
1 medium onion, chopped
900g tomatoes, peeled and diced with
   juices reserved
½ tsp sugar
Salt
¼ tsp ground black pepper
60g butter
30g plain flour
300ml milk
1 tbsp dried breadcrumbs
6 medium eggs, separated
2 tbsp freshly grated Parmesan cheese

◆ Heat oil in 30cm frying pan over medium heat. Add onion and cook 10 minutes, until tender. Add tomatoes with their juice, sugar, ½ teaspoon salt and pepper. Increase heat to high and cook, stirring often, 15 minutes, or until juices evaporate. Meanwhile, melt butter in 2-litre saucepan over medium heat. Stir in flour and ¾ teaspoon salt; cook, stirring, 1 minute. Gradually whisk in milk and cook, whisking constantly, until mixture thickens and boils. Remove from heat and stir in tomato mixture.

◆ Preheat oven to 170°C (325°F, Gas 3). Grease 2-litre soufflé dish and sprinkle with breadcrumbs. Beat egg yolks slightly in large bowl, then beat in small amount of tomato mixture. Gradually stir yolk mixture into tomato mixture, stirring rapidly to prevent lumping. Pour mixture back into bowl.

◆ Beat egg whites in medium bowl with electric mixer on high speed until stiff peaks form. Using rubber spatula, gently fold beaten egg whites, one-third at a time, into tomato mixture just until blended, then pour into soufflé dish. Sprinkle with Parmesan. Bake 45 minutes, or until puffy and golden. Serve immediately.

**Each serving: About 200 calories, 8g protein, 13g carbohydrate, 13g total fat (5g saturated), 182mg cholesterol, 510mg sodium**

### SOUFFLÉ TIPS

**Extra volume**  Adding an extra egg white gives the soufflé extra lightness and also lends volume to the finished dish.

**The right dish**  For a tall and impressive-looking soufflé, use a straight-sided soufflé dish or casserole of medium depth. Fill the dish three-quarters full to ensure the soufflé puffs up well above the rim during baking.

**Make it ahead**  Prepare the soufflé and let it stand in its dish at room temperature for up to 30 minutes before baking.

**Keep it puffy**  During baking, avoid opening the oven door to check the soufflé or the cold draught could cause the delicate mixture to collapse. Always serve a soufflé as soon as it has finished baking, before it deflates.

# QUICHES

A savoury egg custard, often with cheese added, is baked together with other ingredients in a flaky pastry case to make a traditional quiche. Our variations on the filling include a selection of exotic mushrooms, tender cabbage spiked with mustard, and plum tomatoes roasted for sweetness and depth of flavour. Each quiche may be served hot or at room temperature.

## MUSHROOM AND CHEESE QUICHE

◆ ◆ ◆ ◆ ◆ ◆ ◆ ◆ ◆ ◆ ◆ ◆

*Prep: 45 minutes, plus chilling*
*Bake: 50–55 minutes*
*Makes 6 main dish servings*

**Pastry for 28cm tart (see page 487)**
**5 medium eggs**
**450ml milk**
**1 tbsp chopped fresh parsley**
**¾ tsp salt**
**¼ tsp coarsely ground black pepper**
**125g Gruyère or Emmenthal cheese, grated**
**1 tbsp olive or vegetable oil**
**350g shiitake mushrooms, stalks removed and caps thinly sliced**
**125g chestnut or button mushrooms, thinly sliced**
**125g oyster mushrooms, thinly sliced**

1 Prepare pastry and chill. Preheat oven to 200°C (400°F, Gas 6). Roll out pastry into 33cm round on lightly floured surface with floured rolling pin. Ease into 28 by 3cm round tart tin with removable base.

2 Trim pastry, leaving 1cm overhang. Fold overhang in and press against side of tart tin to form rim 3mm above edge of tin.

3 Line pastry case with foil and fill with dried beans, pie weights or uncooked rice. Bake 15 minutes; remove foil and beans. Return pastry case to oven and bake 10 minutes longer or until golden.

4 Meanwhile, using fork, beat eggs, milk, parsley, salt and pepper in medium bowl until blended. Stir in half of cheese.

5 Heat oil in 30cm non-stick frying pan over medium-high heat. Add all mushrooms and cook, stirring frequently, 15 minutes, or until tender and liquid evaporates.

6 Spoon mushrooms into pastry case; top with remaining cheese, then egg mixture. Bake quiche 25–30 minutes until custard is set and top is browned.

EACH SERVING: ABOUT 530 CALORIES, 18g PROTEIN, 36g CARBOHYDRATE, 35g TOTAL FAT (11g SATURATED), 209mg CHOLESTEROL, 690mg SODIUM

## DIJON CABBAGE QUICHE

*Prep: 55 minutes, plus chilling    Bake: 55–60 minutes*

*Makes 8 main dish servings or 16 first course servings*

Pastry for 28cm Tart (see
   page 487), made with single
   cream instead of water
900g green cabbage
2 tbsp vegetable oil
1 large onion, thinly sliced
3 medium eggs
1 tbsp chopped fresh parsley
3 tbsp Dijon mustard

¾ tsp salt
¾ tsp coarsely ground black
   pepper
225ml single cream
175g Gruyère cheese,
   grated
Flat-leaf parsley and sliced
   tomatoes for garnish

◆ Prepare pastry and chill. Thinly slice cabbage, discarding tough ribs. Heat oil in 30cm non-stick frying pan over high heat. Stir in cabbage and onion until coated. Reduce heat to low, cover and cook, stirring occasionally, 30 minutes, or until cabbage is very tender.

◆ Preheat oven to 200°C (400°F, Gas 6). Follow instructions in Steps 1 to 3 of Mushroom and Cheese Quiche (see page 85). Using fork, whisk eggs with next 5 ingredients in medium bowl. Stir in 125g of Gruyère cheese.

---

### MUSTARD

When ground mustard seeds are combined with liquid, enzymes react to form fiery mustard oil. Prepared mustard varies in pungency, flavour and colour, depending on the type of mustard seeds and additional ingredients used.
Varieties include grainy (made with both ground and partly crushed seeds), Dijon (made with wine or sour grape juice) and hot English (made with flour and turmeric). Refrigerate prepared mustard after opening.

Dijon

Grainy

English

---

◆ Sprinkle remaining 50g cheese over base of baked pastry case. Spoon cabbage mixture over cheese, then top with egg mixture. Arrange a few parsley leaves on top of quiche.

◆ Bake quiche 25–30 minutes until custard is set and top is browned. Garnish and serve hot. Or, cool completely on wire rack and re-heat to serve later.

**Each main dish serving: About 445 calories, 14g protein, 27g carbohydrate, 32g total fat (11g saturated), 116mg cholesterol, 680mg sodium**

## ROASTED TOMATO AND CHEESE QUICHE

*Prep: 35 minutes, plus chilling    Bake: 1¼ hours*

*Makes 9 main dish servings*

Pastry for 28cm Tart (see
   page 487)
350g plum tomatoes
½ tsp coarsely ground black
   pepper
Salt

8 large eggs
750ml milk
125–150g full-fat soft cheese
   with garlic and herbs,
   softened
25g fresh basil, chopped

◆ Prepare pastry and chill. Meanwhile, preheat oven to 230°C (450°F, Gas 8). Grease 1 or 2 Swiss roll tins; cut each plum tomato crossways into 1cm thick slices.

◆ Arrange slices in single layer in Swiss roll tins; sprinkle with pepper and ½ teaspoon salt. Bake 30 minutes, or until tomatoes are lightly browned. Remove from oven and lower temperature to 190°C (375°F, Gas 5).

◆ Roll out pastry on lightly floured surface with floured rolling pin into square 2cm larger all round than an inverted 20 by 20cm ovenproof dish.

◆ Gently ease pastry into dish, allowing it to hang over edges. Fold overhang under to form stand-up edge; make fluted edge (see page 488). Refrigerate pastry while preparing filling.

◆ Whisk eggs, milk, cheese and ¼ teaspoon salt together in large bowl until blended. Reserve 1 tablespoon chopped basil for topping; stir remaining basil into egg mixture. Pour egg mixture into pastry case.

◆ Carefully remove tomatoes from tin and arrange tomatoes over egg mixture. Sprinkle quiche with reserved basil. Bake 40–45 minutes until knife inserted in centre comes out clean. Serve hot, or cool completely on wire rack and re-heat to serve later.

**Each serving: About 365 calories, 12g protein, 24g carbohydrate, 25g total fat (8g saturated), 212mg cholesterol, 530mg sodium**

# SHELLFISH

# SHELLFISH KNOW-HOW

Prawns, lobster, oysters and scallops are succulent fruits of the sea that add a tasty diversity to any diet. There are two main categories: molluscs (clams, mussels, oysters, scallops and squid), which have soft bodies and hard, rigid shells, and crustaceans (prawns, crab and lobster), with long bodies and jointed shells. Like fish, shellfish is high in Omega-3 fatty acids, which can help lower cholesterol levels. Never overcook delicate shellfish, or its tender flesh will turn tough.

## BUYING AND STORING

Freshness is paramount, since shellfish is highly perishable. Buy only fresh shellfish from a reliable source. Shellfish should be undamaged and, like fish, should have a fresh, clean odour. When buying frozen shellfish, look for firm, thoroughly frozen, undamaged packages. To thaw, place the shellfish in its wrapping on a plate to catch drips, and thaw overnight in the refrigerator. Once thawed, cook quickly and do not refreeze.

## CLAMS AND COCKLES

• When buying clams and cockles, be sure the shells are tightly closed and not broken. If slightly apart, they should snap shut when tapped; discard any that stay open.
• Refrigerate live clams and cockles, covered with a damp tea towel, for up to 3 days, and shucked, with their liquid, for up to 1 day. Dead clams and cockles should be discarded before cooking.
• Clean most clams by scrubbing with a stiff brush under cold running water to remove any sand. Cockles may require only rinsing.
• Clams and cockles are shucked in the same way as oysters (see page 89).
• When cooking in the shell, discard any that do not open.
• When serving clams, allow about 400g clams or cockles per main dish serving.

## MUSSELS

• The blue mussel is the type most commonly sold in the U.K.; it has a bluish-black shell. You may also come across New Zealand green mussels, which are larger with a bright green shell. They have a similar flavour to blue mussels.

• Mussels are at their best in the cold winter months, although imported and farmed varieties are available throughout the year.
• Buy mussels with undamaged, tightly closed shells or with shells that snap shut when tapped. Any that remain open should be discarded. Avoid those that feel heavy (they may be full of sand) and any that feel light and are loose when shaken (the mussel may be dead).
• Store live mussels, covered with a damp tea towel, in a single layer in the refrigerator. Use within 2 days. Discard any dead mussels before cooking.
• Always de-beard just before you're ready to cook; once de-bearded, mussels soon die and spoil.
• After you've cooked the mussels, check that all shells have opened and discard any that have not.
• Plan on about 1½ dozen mussels per main dish serving.

1  Scrub mussels with a stiff brush under cold running water to remove any sand. Scrape any barnacles off with a knife.

2  To de-beard, grasp the hair-like beard with your thumb and forefinger and pull it away, or scrape it off with a knife.

## OYSTERS

• Fresh oysters can be bought year-round but are considered at their best during autumn and winter.
• Buy oysters with undamaged, tightly closed shells.
• Fresh shucked oysters are also available. They should be plump and uniform in size, smell fresh, and be packed in clear, not cloudy, liquid.
• Cover live oysters with a damp tea towel and store flat, preferably on ice, in the refrigerator for up to 5 days. Refrigerate shucked oysters in a container with their liquid for up to 1 day. The liquid should cover the oysters. If it doesn't, top it with a mixture made by dissolving ½ teaspoon salt in 1 cup water.
• Clean oysters by scrubbing with a stiff brush under cold running water to remove any sand.
• Shuck oysters just before serving or cooking; discard open or damaged oysters.
• For serving raw on the half-shell, allow 6 oysters per diner.

## SHUCKING OYSTERS AND CLAMS

Oysters and clams are shucked using the same technique. An oyster knife (see page 96), which can be used for both, is shown here. You can also open clams (but not oysters) with a clam knife, which has a long blade and a rounded tip designed to accommodate the shape of the clam shell. To protect your hands, hold the oyster or clam in a heavy cloth or oven mitt. This will also make the shell easier to grip.

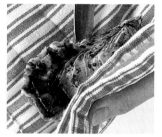 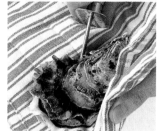

Hold oyster in oven mitt, flat side up. Insert point of oyster knife between top and bottom shells next to the hinge.

Push knife blade further into the shell and then twist the knife to prise top and bottom shells apart.

Carefully loosen flesh from top shell, taking care not to spill any liquid. Discard top shell.

Run knife blade under the oyster to loosen flesh from bottom shell. Remove any broken shell.

## SCALLOPS

• Some scallops are shucked at sea but they are also available on the half shell. The part we eat is actually the adductor muscle and the crescent-shaped coral, or roe.

To prepare scallops, first remove the tough little side muscle using your fingers. Rinse under cold running water to remove any sand from crevices, then pat dry with kitchen towels.

• Queen scallops are smaller than sea scallops and are usually sold frozen. Calico scallops are even smaller, but because they are shucked by commercial steaming, they are less tender and sweet.
• Choose sweet-smelling scallops that are almost 'dry'. Avoid those that have been soaked in phosphates (to plump and preserve them); these are bright white, wet, and shiny.
• Scallops shrink and toughen if over-cooked. For best results, cook only until just opaque throughout.
• Allow about 125g shucked scallops per person.

## SQUID

• Buy whole squid that are small with bright white flesh, clear eyes and a mild ocean smell. Check that the skin and tentacles are intact.
• Fresh squid should be refrigerated in a tightly sealed container for no more than a day or two. Rinse thoroughly before and after cleaning.
• As a guide when estimating how much squid to buy, 750g whole squid should yield about 450g cleaned meat. Allow 125g meat per serving.
• Although cleaned squid is quite widely available at fishmongers and some supermarkets, it's easy to clean your own – follow the simple steps below.

 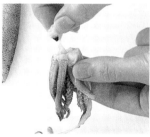

Hold squid body firmly in one hand, and grip head and tentacles with the other. Pull gently to remove the body contents.

Cut off tentacles in front of eyes. Remove and discard beak from centre of tentacles. Discard head and ink sac.

Pull out the clear plastic-like quill from body pocket and discard.

Rub off thin dark outer skin from body; discard skin. Rinse body well inside and out under cold running water; rinse tentacles.

## PRAWNS

- Most of the prawns sold in the U.K. have been previously frozen, so you can buy prawns all year round.
- Depending on variety, prawn shells can be light grey, brownish pink or red, but when cooked all will turn reddish.
- Select raw prawns with firm-looking meat and shiny shells that feel full. Avoid black spots, which are a sign of aging. Prawns are usually sold without the heads; if not, gently pull the head away from the body before shelling. Cooked, shelled prawns should be plump with white flesh and a mild odor.
- When buying prawns in their shells, always buy more than you need to account for the shelled weight. For example, 600g prawns yields 450g shelled and de-veined.
- Prawns can be shelled before or after cooking. While unpeeled can be more flavourful, it's often more convenient to shell before cooking.
- De-veining small and medium prawns is optional, but do remove the vein of large prawns, which can contain grit.
- Although small prawns are cheaper, they are harder to peel and may not be as good value.
- Cook raw prawns briefly, just until opaque throughout; heat cooked prawns just until warmed through.
- Allow about 125g shelled prawns per serving.

The recipes in this book call for prawns by size as well as by weight. To give you an idea of what is meant by 'small', 'medium', and so on, the chart at right tells you the number of prawns you should get per 500g for different sizes.

### PRAWN SIZES

| SIZE | PRAWNS PER 500g |
| --- | --- |
| Small | 36–45 |
| Medium | 25–40 |
| Large | 21–30 |
| Extra large | 16–20 |
| Jumbo | 10 |

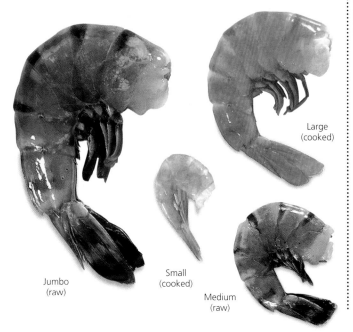

Jumbo (raw)

Small (cooked)

Medium (raw)

Large (cooked)

## PEELING AND DE-VEINING

1 Using kitchen scissors or small knife, cut prawn shell along outer curve, just deep enough into flesh to expose the dark vein.

2 Peel back shell from the cut and gently separate shell from prawn. Discard shell or use to make stock.

3 Holding prawn under cold running water, remove vein with tip of a knife.

## BUTTERFLYING

1 Shell prawn as above, leaving tail segment intact. Using kitchen scissors or knife, cut prawn along centre back, about three-quarters of the way into the flesh.

2 Spread the flesh open, and remove the dark vein with tip of a knife. Rinse the butterflied shrimp under cold running water.

### WHAT'S IN A NAME?

Large Dublin Bay prawns (30 or fewer per 500g) are sometimes sold as 'prawns'. They are a separate species, however, and are part of the lobster family. Resembling miniature lobsters, Dublin Bay prawns are also called saltwater crayfish or langoustines; their tails are used to make scampi. There is a freshwater version, crayfish, which look like a cross between shrimp and lobster.

# CRABS

• Crabs are popular for their tasty succulent meat and are readily available all year round.

• Crabs are sold whole, cooked or live, as frozen cooked legs or claws, or flaked meat (light and dark meat from the body and claws).

• When buying whole crabs, choose cooked ones with bright red shells or live crabs that are active. Cooked crabmeat should be white tinged with pink, and sweet-smelling; when preparing it, check for any small pieces of shell and cartilage. Frozen crabmeat is a convenient alternative to fresh.

• Hard-shell varieties of crab should be cooked before you remove the meat. Soft-shell crabs, which are available fresh from specialist suppliers only from late spring until early autumn, are eaten shell and all, and must be cleaned thoroughly (see below right) before cooking.

To remove meat from a cooked hard-shell crab, first twist off legs and claws close to the body. Break each claw and leg with a nutcracker; remove meat using a lobster pick or skewer.

Using your fingers, pull off the 'apron' from underside of crab and discard it.

Holding crab in both hands, insert your thumb under shell by apron hinge. Pull body away from shell.

Using a spoon, remove meat and roe from shell. Discard stomach sac located between eyes. Discard shell or scrub to use as serving container.

Pull away the inedible feathery gills, or 'dead man's fingers', from the body and discard.

Using kitchen scissors, cut body down centre; trim any jagged edges of shell.

Using fingers or lobster pick, remove meat from each body section.

## CLEANING SOFT-SHELL CRABS

Soft-shell crabs are blue crabs or green shore crabs that have shed their shells and are growing new ones. To clean, using kitchen scissors, cut across each crab 5mm behind eyes; discard front portion. Cut off flat, pointed apron on underside. Bend back top shell on each side and pull off spongy gills. Rinse with cold running water; pat dry with kitchen towels.

# LOBSTER

• There are two types of lobster: the larger, meatier, clawed lobster, found in the North Atlantic and Mediterranean, and the rock or spiny lobster. The rock lobster, commercially harvested off Florida, southern California, Australia, New Zealand and South America, has no claws. It is often sold frozen as lobster tail.

• When buying a live lobster, pick it up near its head – the tail should curl under and it should feel heavy for its size; if too light it is not fresh and the meat has had time to dry out. Check that both claws are intact.

• Purchase frozen lobster tails in untorn packets with no evidence of frost; the lobster meat should have no dry areas.

• Live lobsters must be purchased the day they will be cooked because they can't be stored for very long. Store for no more than a few hours, wrapped in a wet cloth or wet newspaper, on a bed of ice in the refrigerator.

• When buying whole lobsters, allow a 600–750g lobster for each serving. If you are buying tails only, allow one 175–225g tail or 2–3 smaller ones per serving.

## BOILING LOBSTERS

To boil live lobsters, bring enough water to cover the lobsters to the boil in a 12-litre stockpot over high heat. Add lobsters, head first. Return water to the boil, then reduce heat to medium; cover and simmer for about 10 minutes per 450g lobster. When cooked, the lobster shells will turn red. Using tongs, transfer lobsters to a colander to drain.

1 To remove meat from a cooked lobster, break off claws and legs. Using nutcracker or lobster cracker, crack large claws and remove meat.

2 Twist off head from tail. Using kitchen scissors, cut down centre of thin shell on underside of tail to expose meat. Gently pull meat from shell in one piece.

3 Cut along outer curve of tail meat, about 5mm deep, to expose dark vein. Remove vein and discard.

4 Spoon any green tomalley (liver) or coral roe (found only in females) into a bowl. Serve with the lobster meat, if desired.

5 Lift out rigid portion from head shell, then spoon out any additional tomalley or roe and add to bowl. Remove and discard sac and spongy gills from head.

6 Break rigid portion into several pieces. Pick out meat with lobster pick or fork.

# CLAMS AND MUSSELS

Cleaning mussels and clams is very simple and straightforward; once prepared, they take only minutes to cook. Hard-shell clams come in various sizes; medium and smaller clams are more tender than the larger ones used to make chowder or for stuffing and grilling. Clams can be eaten raw or used in a variety of cooked dishes from stuffed clams to richly flavoured pasta sauces. The briny liquid they release adds wonderful flavour to dishes but varies in saltiness – taste after cooking and season accordingly.

1 Using stiff brush, scrub clams under cold water. Shuck them and release meat from bottom shells (see page 89).

2 Preheat oven to 200°C (400°F, Gas 6). Place clams in bottom shells in small ovenproof dish. Place in refrigerator.

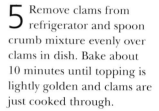

3 Process bread into fine crumbs in food processor with knife blade attached. Spread crumbs on baking sheet and bake 5 minutes, or until golden. Cook bacon in 26cm non-stick frying pan over medium-low heat until browned. Using slotted spoon, transfer bacon to kitchen towels to drain. Discard drippings from pan.

4 Add oil to skillet; add onion and cook, stirring occasionally, 3 minutes, or until tender. Add garlic and pepper; cook 30 seconds. Remove from heat; stir in parsley, crumbs and bacon.

5 Remove clams from refrigerator and spoon crumb mixture evenly over clams in dish. Bake about 10 minutes until topping is lightly golden and clams are just cooked through.

## STUFFED CLAMS

❖❖❖❖❖❖❖❖❖❖❖❖

*Prep: 20 minutes*
*Bake: 15 minutes*
*Makes 4 first course servings*

**12 medium hard-shell clams**
**2 slices white bread, torn**
**2 rashers bacon, trimmed if**
  **necessary and finely**
  **chopped**
**1 tbsp olive oil**
**1 small onion, finely chopped**
**1 small garlic clove, very**
  **finely chopped**
**¼ tsp ground black pepper**
**2 tbsp chopped fresh parsley**

### WHAT'S IN A NAME?

**Large hard-shell** Suitable for chowder, these clams are gathered from British shores and can be as much as 9cm long.
**Surf** These smaller, Scottish hard-shell clams are similar to Venus clams (below) but can be sandy; clean thoroughly.
**Mediterranean** These are smaller than British clams. The most expensive are Palourdes, which are very popular in France. Venus clams are less costly and have more fragile shells.

EACH SERVING: ABOUT 115 CALORIES, 6g PROTEIN, 10g CARBOHYDRATE, 6g TOTAL FAT (1g SATURATED), 12mg CHOLESTEROL, 135mg SODIUM

## CLAMS AND MUSSELS IN BROTH

*Prep: 25 minutes    Cook: 20 minutes*
*Makes 4 main dish servings*

| | |
|---|---|
| 24 medium or small hard-shell clams | 1 small onion, diced |
| 24 large mussels | 1 bay leaf |
| 25g margarine or butter | 225ml dry vermouth |
| 3 medium celery stalks, diced | Coarsely chopped celery leaves for garnish |
| 3 medium carrots, diced | |

◆ Using stiff brush, scrub clams and mussels under cold water to remove any sand. Remove beards from mussels (see page 88).

Melt margarine in 8-litre flameproof casserole over medium heat. Add celery, carrots, onion and bay leaf and cook, stirring occasionally, 8–10 minutes until vegetables are tender. Stir in vermouth, clams and mussels and bring to the boil over high heat.

◆ Reduce heat to medium-low; cover and cook, stirring occasionally, about 10 minutes until mussels and clams open. Discard any that do not open. Remove and discard bay leaf. Serve clams and mussels in bowls with liquid and vegetables, garnished with chopped celery leaves.

**Each serving: About 245 calories, 16g protein, 14g carbohydrate, 8g total fat (4g saturated), 65mg cholesterol, 300mg sodium**

## LINGUINE WITH CLAMS AND MUSSELS

*Prep: 20 minutes    Cook: 20 minutes*
*Makes 6 main dish servings*

| | |
|---|---|
| 24 medium or small hard-shell clams | 4 tbsp chopped fresh parsley |
| 12 mussels | 800g canned chopped tomatoes |
| 450g dried linguine | 175g tomato purée |
| 1 tsp salt | 125ml chicken stock |
| 60ml dry white wine | 1 tbsp sugar |
| 2 tbsp olive or vegetable oil | |
| 1 garlic clove, very finely chopped | |

◆ Using stiff brush, scrub clams and mussels under cold water. Remove beards from mussels (see page 88). Prepare linguine as packet instructs, using 1 teaspoon of salt in water, drain. Return linguine to pan and keep warm.

◆ Meanwhile, toss clams with wine, oil, garlic and 2 tablespoons parsley in 30cm frying pan. Cover pan; cook over medium-high heat, stirring occasionally, 8–10 minutes, until clams open. Using slotted spoon, transfer clams to bowl as they open; discard any clams that do not open.

◆ Add mussels to liquid remaining in pan and bring to the boil over high heat. Reduce heat to medium, cover and cook, stirring occasionally, 3–5 minutes until shells open.

◆ Using slotted spoon, transfer mussels to bowl with clams as they open. Discard any mussels that do not open.

◆ Heat remaining ingredients and remaining 2 tablespoons parsley in same pan over medium-high heat until boiling. Stir in shellfish; heat through. Spoon sauce and shellfish over linguine and serve.

**Each serving: About 445 calories, 17g protein, 73g carbohydrate, 9g total fat (1g saturated), 18mg cholesterol, 885mg sodium**

## ASIAN-STYLE ANGEL HAIR PASTA WITH CLAMS

*Prep: 20 minutes    Cook: 25 minutes*
*Makes 4 main dish servings*

| | |
|---|---|
| 1 tbsp olive oil | 24 hard-shell clams, scrubbed |
| 3 garlic cloves, cut in half | 225g dried angel hair pasta |
| 1½ tsp grated peeled fresh ginger | Salt |
| ¼ tsp crushed red pepper | 1¼ tsp cornflour |
| 225ml chicken stock | 2 tbsp chopped fresh coriander |
| 75ml dry white wine | |
| 3 strips lemon rind, each 7 by 3cm, finely sliced lengthways | |

◆ Heat oil in 30cm frying pan over medium heat. Add garlic, ginger and crushed red pepper; cook, stirring, 3 minutes. Stir in chicken stock, wine and lemon rind; bring to the boil over high heat.

◆ Add clams and return to the boil. Reduce heat to medium-low; cover and cook 10–15 minutes until clams open. Using slotted spoon, transfer clams to bowl as they open. Discard any that do not open.

◆ After clams have cooked about 5 minutes, cook pasta as packet instructs, using 1 teaspoon salt in water. Drain pasta and divide between 4 large soup bowls.

◆ Meanwhile, mix cornflour with *1 tablespoon water* in small bowl until smooth. Whisk mixture into stock mixture remaining in pan; cook over medium heat until mixture boils. Boil, stirring, 1 minute. Discard garlic.

◆ Return clams to pan; heat through. To serve, spoon clam sauce over pasta in bowls. Sprinkle with coriander.

**Each serving: About 310 calories, 15g protein, 47g carbohydrate, 5g total fat (1g saturated), 23mg cholesterol, 340mg sodium**

# OYSTERS

Shuck oysters just before using; be sure to save their savoury juices if making a sauce. The most popular way of eating oysters is raw on the half shell, but for a special occasion, try them warm topped with spicy spinach and breadcrumbs, or baked in a creamy sauce. If you're not using the shells, you can ask your fishmonger to shuck the oysters for you. Keep shucked oysters refrigerated for no longer than 24 hours.

## OYSTERS ROCKEFELLER

❖❖❖❖❖❖❖❖❖❖❖❖❖

*Prep: 30 minutes*
*Bake: 10 minutes*
*Makes 4 first course servings*

**12 oysters, scrubbed**
**Rock or coarse sea salt**
**(optional)**
**300–350g spinach**
**15g plus 2 tsp butter**
**25g onion, very finely**
**chopped**
**Pinch ground nutmeg**
**Pinch ground red pepper**
**Pinch salt**
**1 tbsp Pernod or other anise-**
**flavoured apéritif**
**60ml whipping cream**
**2 tbsp dried breadcrumbs**
**Lemon wedges and dill sprigs**
**for garnish**

**1** Preheat oven to 220°C (425°F, Gas 7). Shuck oysters and release meat from bottom shells (see page 89). Remove any pieces of broken shell.

### ROCK SALT

Rock salt can be a greyish colour because it retains more minerals than other salts. This is the salt that is refined to make fine cooking salt, or the coarser crystals of salt that are freshly ground before use. In this recipe, a bed of coarse salt crystals is used to hold the oyster shells flat while they bake.

**2** Place oysters in bottom shells in shallow baking tray on 1cm layer of rock salt, if desired; this will keep the oysters flat. Refrigerate until ready to bake.

**4** In same pan, melt 15g butter over medium heat. Add onion and cook 3 minutes until tender. Stir in spinach, nutmeg, red pepper, salt, Pernod and cream. Cook over high heat, stirring, until reduced and thick. Remove from heat. Melt remaining 2 teaspoons butter in small saucepan and stir in breadcrumbs.

**3** Wash spinach. Cook it with water clinging to its leaves in 2-litre saucepan over high heat, stirring, until wilted. Drain well and chop very fine.

**5** Spoon spinach mixture evenly on top of oysters. Sprinkle with breadcrumbs. Bake 10 minutes. Serve garnished with lemon wedges and dill sprigs.

EACH SERVING: ABOUT 170 CALORIES, 6g PROTEIN, 9g CARBOHYDRATE, 12g TOTAL FAT (7g SATURATED), 51mg CHOLESTEROL, 270mg SODIUM

## GLAZED OYSTERS WITH LEEK AND CARROT

*Prep: 15 minutes   Grill 2–3 minutes*
*Makes 4 first course servings*

12 oysters, scrubbed
Rock or coarse sea salt
  (optional)
Salt
1 medium leek, cut into
  matchstick-thin strips
1 medium carrot, cut into
  matchstick-thin strips

2 tbsp very finely chopped
  shallots
2 tbsp dry white wine
60ml whipping cream
Chopped fresh tarragon for
  garnish

◆ Preheat grill. Shuck oysters and release meat from bottom shells (see page 89); save as much oyster liquor as possible. Arrange bottom shells in shallow baking tray on 1cm layer of rock salt, if desired, to keep them flat. Refrigerate the oysters, reserving their liquor.

◆ Bring *1½ litres water* and 1 teaspoon salt to the boil in 2-litre saucepan over high heat. Add leek and carrot and cook 2–3 minutes until tender. Drain.

◆ Boil shallots, wine and reserved oyster liquor in 1-litre saucepan over high heat until liquid is reduced to about 1 tablespoon. Add cream; boil until mixture is reduced to 60ml. Remove from heat.

◆ Arrange leek and carrot strips evenly in shells and place oysters on top. Spoon sauce on top. Place pan under grill at closest position to heat; grill 2 minutes. Garnish and serve.

**Each serving: About 115 calories, 4g protein, 9g carbohydrate, 7g total fat (4g saturated), 43mg cholesterol, 120mg sodium**

---

### OYSTER KNIFE

This knife is indispensable when it comes to opening oysters. It has a short blade and pointed end to pry the shells apart. Choose a knife with a guard that protects your fingers from the sharp edges of the shell. The short, stubby handle enables you to keep a firm grip, which is important when it comes to this difficult culinary task. It does become easier with practice. The knife can also be used for opening clams. Buy the sturdiest knife available; a flimsy one may break off in your hand.

---

## OYSTERS WITH GINGER MIGNONETTE

*Prep: 15 minutes   Makes 2 first course servings*

12 oysters, scrubbed
60ml rice vinegar
2 spring onions, finely
  chopped

½ tsp grated peeled fresh
  ginger
½ tsp coarsely ground black
  pepper

◆ Shuck oysters and release meat from bottom shells (see page 89). Arrange in bottom shells on platter.

◆ Combine rice vinegar, spring onions, ginger and pepper in small bowl, stirring until well combined. To serve, spoon mignonette sauce onto oysters.

**Each serving: About 60 calories, 6g protein, 4g carbohydrate, 2g total fat (0g saturated), 46mg cholesterol, 95mg sodium**

---

## SCALLOPED OYSTERS

*Prep: 15 minutes   Bake: 35 minutes*
*Makes 6 first course servings*

225g unsliced white bread
60g butter or margarine,
  melted
18 shucked oysters (about
  600g)

125ml whipping cream
¼ tsp salt
⅛ tsp ground black pepper
2 tbsp chopped fresh parsley

◆ Preheat oven to 200°C (400°F, Gas 6). Tear bread into 2cm pieces and place in shallow baking tray. Drizzle with butter and toss to coat. Bake 25 minutes, or until bread is golden and crisp. Set toasted bread aside.

◆ Drain oysters, reserving oyster liquor.

◆ Boil reserved oyster liquor in 1-litre saucepan over high heat until reduced to about 2 tablespoons. Add cream, salt and pepper and return to the boil; remove from heat.

◆ Combine toasted bread, oysters and 1 tablespoon parsley in 23 by 23cm ovenproof dish. Pour cream mixture on top and toss to coat.

◆ Bake 10 minutes. Sprinkle with remaining 1 tablespoon chopped parsley and serve.

**Each serving: About 285 calories, 8g protein, 24g carbohydrate, 18g total fat (9g saturated), 70mg cholesterol, 535mg sodium**

# SCALLOPS

Scallops can be bought on the shell or ready cleaned and shucked and are the easiest shellfish to prepare. Before using, remove and discard the hard muscle found on the side – the creamy white meat can then be lightly sautéed or quickly grilled. Accent the delicate flavour of scallops with a tangy vinaigrette or sauce, or complement their soft texture with a breadcrumb topping. Scallops become tough if over-cooked, so cook just until they turn opaque.

## SCALLOPS AND PRAWN VINAIGRETTE

◆◆◆◆◆◆◆◆◆◆◆◆◆◆◆◆◆◆◆◆◆◆◆◆◆◆◆◆◆◆◆◆◆◆

*Prep: 25 minutes, plus chilling    Cook: 5 minutes*
*Makes 6 main dish servings*

60ml plus 3 tbsp olive or
  vegetable oil
60ml white wine vinegar
1½ tsp salt
1 tsp dried tarragon
1 tsp sugar
½ tsp Tabasco sauce
⅛ tsp ground black pepper
450g raw unpeeled large
  prawns

450g shucked large scallops
3 medium heads chicory,
  sliced crossways
25g fresh parsley, finely
  chopped
Rocket and sliced red onion
  (optional)

**1** Prepare vinaigrette: whisk together 60ml oil with white wine vinegar, salt, tarragon, sugar, Tabasco sauce and black pepper until blended. Set aside.

**2** Peel and de-vein prawns (see page 90); rinse under cold running water. Rinse scallops to remove any sand. Pull tough crescent-shaped muscle from side of each scallop. Pat prawns and scallops dry with kitchen towels. Cut each scallop horizontally in half.

**3** Heat remaining 3 tablespoons oil in 30cm frying pan over medium-high heat. Add prawns and scallops; cook, stirring, 5 minutes, or until opaque throughout. Add shellfish to vinaigrette in bowl; toss to coat. Cover and refrigerate at least 2 hours.

**4** Just before serving, add chicory and parsley to seafood mixture; toss well to combine. Serve with arugula and sliced red onion, if you like.

### SCALLOPS

There are many species of scallops, with those on sale in the U.K. coming from Atlantic and Mediterranean waters, and increasingly shipped frozen from the Pacific. King scallops, about 4cm across, are the most commonly available. Bay scallops from the States, are about 1cm in diameter with a sweet flavour and most delicate texture. They are occasionally sold in the U.K. Calico scallops, from the Gulf of Mexico, have speckled shells; similar to bay scallops in size, they're tougher, with a coarser taste.

EACH SERVING: ABOUT 280 CALORIES, 26g PROTEIN, 5g CARBOHYDRATE, 17g TOTAL FAT (2g SATURATED), 142mg CHOLESTEROL, 800mg SODIUM

## SCALLOPS WITH WATERCRESS AND LEMON-CAPER SAUCE

*Prep: 10 minutes   Cook: 8–10 minutes*
*Makes 4 main dish servings*

| | |
|---|---|
| 600g shucked large scallops | 2 bunches watercress |
| 75g butter | 1 tbsp fresh lemon juice |
| ⅛ tsp ground black pepper | 1 tbsp canned or bottled |
| Salt | drained and chopped |
| 1 tbsp vegetable oil | capers |

◈ Rinse scallops with cold water to remove sand from crevices. Pull tough crescent-shaped muscle from side of each scallop. Pat dry with kitchen towels. Heat 30g butter in 26cm frying pan over medium-high heat. Add scallops, black pepper and ½ teaspoon salt and cook about 5 minutes, or until scallops are just browned on both sides and opaque throughout.

◈ Meanwhile, heat oil in large flameproof casserole or 5-litre saucepan over high heat. Add watercress and ¼ teaspoon salt and cook, stirring, about 2 minutes until watercress just wilts.

◈ Transfer scallops to 4 warm plates and keep warm. Bring lemon juice, capers and *2 tablespoons water* to the boil in same frying pan over medium-high heat.

◈ Reduce heat to medium and add remaining 45g butter, a quarter at at a time, beating with a wire whisk until butter just melts and mixture thickens. (Do not use margarine; the sauce will not be thick.) Pour sauce over scallops and arrange watercress on plates.

**Each serving: About 310 calories, 25g protein, 4g carbohydrate, 22g total fat (11g saturated), 93mg cholesterol, 895mg sodium**

## PEPPERY SCALLOPS

*Prep: 10 minutes   Grill: 5 minutes*
*Makes 4 main dish servings*

| | |
|---|---|
| 600g shucked large scallops | 1 tbsp chopped fresh basil |
| 25g margarine or butter, melted | ½ tsp ground black pepper |
| | ¼ tsp salt |
| 2 tbsp dried breadcrumbs | Lemon slices or wedges |

◈ Preheat grill. Rinse scallops under cold water to remove sand from crevices. Pull tough crescent-shaped muscle from side of each scallop. Pat dry with kitchen towels. Toss scallops in bowl with melted margarine to coat. Mix breadcrumbs, basil, pepper and salt on sheet of greaseproof paper. Dip top of each scallop into breadcrumb mixture.

◈ Place scallops, breaded-side up, on rack in grill pan. Grill scallops close to heat, without turning, 5 minutes, or until topping is golden and scallops are opaque throughout. Serve with lemon slices.

**Each serving: About 190 calories, 24g protein, 6g carbohydrate, 7g total fat (1g saturated), 47mg cholesterol, 455mg sodium**

## SAUTÉED SCALLOPS AND VEGETABLES

*Prep: 25 minutes   Cook: 20 minutes*
*Makes 4 main dish servings*

| | |
|---|---|
| 2 bunches rocket | 350g medium mushrooms, quartered |
| 450g shucked large scallops | |
| 4 tsp olive or vegetable oil | 225g sugar snap peas, strings removed |
| 1 large red pepper, cored, seeded, and thinly sliced | |
| | 2 tbsp soy sauce |
| 1 medium onion, thinly sliced | |

◈ Arrange rocket on platter; set aside. Rinse scallops under cold water to remove sand from crevices. Pull tough crescent-shaped muscle from side of each scallop. Pat dry with kitchen towels. Heat 2 teaspoons oil in 30cm non-stick frying pan over medium-high heat. Add red pepper and onion; cook until onion is golden. Transfer mixture to plate. Heat 1 teaspoon oil in same pan. Add mushrooms and cook until golden brown. Add sugar snap peas and cook, stirring, 2 minutes longer, or until tender-crisp. Transfer to same plate.

◈ Heat remaining 1 teaspoon oil in same pan over medium-high heat. Add scallops and cook, stirring occasionally, 3–4 minutes until scallops are opaque throughout. Return vegetable mixture to pan with scallops; stir in soy sauce. Heat through over medium-high heat. Spoon scallop mixture over rocket on platter.

**Each serving: About 215 calories, 24g protein, 19g carbohydrate, 6g total fat (1g saturated), 37mg cholesterol, 780mg sodium**

# SQUID

Squid, also known by its Italian name, *calamari*, makes a special treat whether it is coated and pan fried for crunch, simmered in a sauce, or quickly grilled. For speediest preparation, buy cleaned squid; if you clean it yourself (see page 89), allow 750g whole squid to yield 450g, cleaned. Cook squid either very briefly – less than a minute – or for more than 30 minutes to prevent it from turning rubbery.

## CALAMARI WITH SPICY TOMATO SAUCE

❖❖❖❖❖❖❖❖❖❖❖❖❖

*Prep:* 30 minutes
*Cook:* 10 minutes
*Makes* 4 first course servings

**1 tbsp vegetable oil, plus additional for frying**
**1 small onion, finely chopped**
**225ml tomato passata**
**3 tbsp red wine vinegar**
**1½ tsp sugar**
**½ tsp salt**
**¼ tsp dried chilli flakes**
**¼ tsp dried oregano**
**450g cleaned squid**
**1 medium egg, lightly beaten**
**150g plain flour**
**Lemon wedges and parsley sprigs for garnish**

**1** Prepare spicy tomato sauce: heat 1 tablespoon oil in 1-litre saucepan over medium heat. Add chopped onion and cook until tender. Add tomato passata and next 5 ingredients and bring to the boil.

**2** Reduce heat to low; cover and simmer 5 minutes. Keep sauce warm. Slice squid bodies crossways into 2cm rings. Cut tentacles into several pieces if they are large.

**3** Toss squid pieces with egg to coat. Place flour on greaseproof paper. Heat 1cm oil in 26cm frying pan over medium heat. Dip squid in flour; add to frying pan and cook in small batches until golden.

### SQUID INK

If you clean and prepare squid yourself, you will see the ink sac; this contains a brownish-black liquid and is usually discarded. Squid and cuttlefish both have this sac; they squirt ink as a defence mechanism to cloud the water round them.

In Italy, where squid is much more commonly eaten than in the U.K., cooks add squid or cuttlefish ink to pasta dough and risotto to give a deep black colour and deep-sea flavour. If you live near a good Italian market, you may be able to find squid-ink pasta. For a dramatic presentation, try squid-ink pasta instead of linguine in our Linguine with Squid Sauce (see page 100).

**4** Using slotted spoon, transfer squid to kitchen towels to drain. Serve with warm tomato sauce, garnished with lemon wedges and parsley sprigs.

EACH SERVING: ABOUT 300 CALORIES, 22g PROTEIN, 24g CARBOHYDRATE, 13g TOTAL FAT (3g SATURATED), 317mg CHOLESTEROL, 680mg SODIUM

## LINGUINE WITH SQUID SAUCE

*Prep: 40 minutes   Cook: 1¼ hours*
*Makes 6 main dish servings*

900g cleaned squid
1 tbsp olive oil
1 medium onion, chopped
2 large garlic cloves, very
    finely chopped
1 tsp fennel seeds

¼ tsp crushed red pepper
800g canned tomatoes
Salt
450g dried linguine
25g fresh flat-leaf parsley,
    finely chopped

◆ Slice squid bodies into 1cm rings. Cut tentacles into several pieces if they are large.

◆ Heat oil in 4-litre saucepan over medium heat. Add onion and cook, stirring often, 5–8 minutes until tender.

◆ Stir in garlic, fennel seeds and crushed red pepper, and cook 30 seconds. Stir in tomatoes with their juice and 1¼ teaspoons salt, breaking up tomatoes with back of spoon. Bring to the boil.

◆ Stir in squid pieces and return to the boil. Reduce heat to low, cover and simmer 30 minutes. Uncover and simmer 30 minutes longer. Meanwhile, prepare linguine as packet instructs, using 2 teaspoons salt in water; drain. Toss linguine with squid sauce and parsley in large bowl.

**Each serving: About 480 calories, 35g protein, 70g carbohydrate, 6g total fat (1g saturated), 352mg cholesterol, 735mg sodium**

## THAI SQUID SALAD

*Prep: 30 minutes   Cook: 30 seconds*
*Makes 4 first course servings*

Salt
3 tbsp fish sauce (*nuoc nam*,
    see page 30)
3 tbsp fresh lime juice
1 tbsp caster sugar
¼ tsp dried chilli flakes
½ small onion, very thinly
    sliced

1 medium carrot, grated
450g cleaned squid
1 large loose-leaf lettuce, torn
    into bite-sized pieces
25g fresh mint leaves
25g fresh coriander leaves

◆ Bring *3 litres water* with 2 teaspoons salt to the boil in 4-litre saucepan over high heat.

◆ Meanwhile, prepare dressing: stir together fish sauce, lime juice, caster sugar, dried chilli flakes and ¼ teaspoon salt in large bowl until sugar dissolves. Stir in sliced onion and grated carrot.

◆ Slice squid bodies into very thin rings. Cut tentacles into several pieces if they are large.

◆ Add squid pieces to boiling water and cook 30 seconds. Drain. Add to dressing in bowl. Add lettuce, mint and coriander and toss to coat.

**Each serving: About 150 calories, 19g protein, 13g carbohydrate, 2g total fat (0g saturated), 264mg cholesterol, 565mg sodium**

## GRILLED SQUID

*Prep: 15 minutes   Barbecue/grill: 1–2 minutes*
*Makes 4 first course servings*

450g cleaned squid
1 tbsp extra virgin olive oil
1 tbsp fresh lemon juice
¼ tsp salt

⅛ tsp ground black pepper
1 tbsp chopped flat-leaf
    parsley
Lemon wedges for garnish

◆ Prepare barbecue or preheat grill. Slice squid bodies down one side to open flat. Toss bodies and tentacles with olive oil, lemon juice, salt and pepper in medium bowl.

◆ Thread squid bodies onto metal skewers so they lie flat; thread tentacles onto separate skewers. Place on barbecue over high heat or under grill and cook 1–2 minutes, turning once, just until opaque throughout.

◆ Remove squid pieces from skewers and transfer to serving platter; sprinkle with parsley. Serve garnished with lemon wedges.

**Each serving: About 135 calories, 18g protein, 4g carbohydrate, 5g total fat (1g saturated), 264mg cholesterol, 185mg sodium**

# Prawns

Sweet-tasting prawns are the most popular of all shellfish. They can be cooked in or out of their shells, but are most often peeled and de-veined before serving. Whether they are simply sautéed, lightly marinated and grilled, or simmered in a tangy tomato sauce, prawns take only minutes to cook; as soon as they turn opaque throughout, they're done. Don't overcook prawns or they will be tough.

## GARLIC PRAWNS AND BEANS

❖❖❖❖❖❖❖❖❖❖❖❖❖❖❖❖❖❖❖❖❖❖❖❖❖❖

*Prep:* 20 minutes  *Cook:* 20 minutes
*Makes* 4 main-dish servings

600g raw unpeeled large prawns

2 tbsp olive oil

1 small aubergine (350g), cut into 5mm slices

2 garlic cloves, crushed with side of knife

½ tsp salt

1 tbsp plain flour

¼ tsp dried chilli flakes (optional)

225ml chicken stock

1 tbsp fresh lemon juice

450g canned cannellini beans, rinsed and drained

Capers, lemon wedges and flat-leaf parsley sprigs for garnish

**1** Peel and de-vein prawns (see page 90); rinse under cold water. Preheat grill and lightly oil grill rack. Brush aubergine with 1 tablespoon oil and place on rack.

**2** Grill at closest position to heat, turning once, 8–10 minutes, until tender. Transfer aubergine to plate and keep warm.

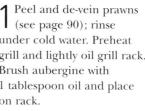

**3** Heat remaining 1 tablespoon oil in 30cm non-stick frying pan over medium-high heat. Add garlic, prawns and salt; cook until prawns begin to turn opaque.

**4** Meanwhile, mix flour, dried chilli flakes (if using), chicken stock and lemon juice together in small bowl until smooth. Add flour mixture to prawns in frying pan.

**5** Discard garlic from prawn mixture; stir in beans. Bring to the boil over high heat, stirring. Boil, stirring, 1 minute, or until thickened. Serve prawn mixture with aubergine and garnish with capers, lemon wedges and parsley.

### CRUSHING GARLIC

Garlic is crushed to make it easier to peel, and to release the cloves' aromatic oils. The crushed cloves can easily be removed from a finished dish. To crush, press clove with flat side of knife until skin breaks.

EACH SERVING: ABOUT 335 CALORIES, 32g PROTEIN, 30g CARBOHYDRATE, 10g TOTAL FAT (2g SATURATED), 218mg CHOLESTEROL, 690mg SODIUM

## PRAWN CURRY

*Prep: 20 minutes   Cook: 8–10 minutes*
*Makes 4 main dish servings*

| | |
|---|---|
| 2 tbsp margarine or butter | Salt |
| 2 garlic cloves, very finely chopped | 1 medium courgette (225g) |
| 2 tsp very finely chopped, peeled fresh ginger | 450g raw medium prawns, peeled and de-veined (see page 90) |
| 2 tsp curry powder | ½ tsp ground black pepper |
| ½ tsp ground coriander | 2 tbsp chopped fresh coriander |
| ½ tsp ground cumin | Hot cooked rice (optional) |
| 175ml whipping cream | |

◆ Melt 1 tablespoon margarine in 2-litre saucepan over medium heat. Stir in garlic and next 4 ingredients; cook, stirring, 1 minute. Stir in cream and ½ teaspoon salt; increase heat to high and boil 5 minutes, or until thickened. Meanwhile cut courgette lengthways in half; thinly slice.

◆ Melt remaining 1 tablespoon margarine in 26cm frying pan over medium-high heat. Add courgette; cook, stirring, 3 minutes until beginning to brown. Stir in prawns, ½ teaspoon salt and pepper; cook, stirring, 2 minutes, or until prawns are opaque throughout. Stir prawn mixture into cream sauce in saucepan; sprinkle with coriander. Serve over rice, if you like.

**Each serving: About 310 calories, 21g protein, 5g carbohydrate, 23g total fat (12g saturated), 236mg cholesterol, 815mg sodium**

## BARBECUED PRAWN TOSTADAS

*Prep: 30 minutes   Barbecue/grill: 2–3 minutes*
*Makes 6 main dish servings*

| | |
|---|---|
| 1 large lime | Salt |
| 3–4 avocados (900g total) | Coarsely ground black pepper |
| 2 small tomatoes, seeded and cut into 1cm chunks | 750g raw unpeeled large prawns |
| 1 tbsp canned drained and chopped pickled jalapeño-chilli slices | 1 tbsp olive oil |
| | 6 corn tortillas (15cm) |

◆ Prepare barbecue or preheat grill. Grate 1 teaspoon rind and squeeze 2 tablespoons juice from lime. Peel and cube avocados; mash in bowl. Stir in tomato chunks, 1 tablespoon lime juice, jalapeño chilli slices, ½ teaspoon salt and ¼ teaspoon pepper. Press cling film directly onto surface of mixture to prevent discolouration until ready to use.

◆ Peel and de-vein prawns, leaving tail part on, if you like (see page 90). Combine prawns, oil, ¾ teaspoon salt, ½ teaspoon pepper, lime rind and remaining lime juice in medium bowl; toss to coat.

◆ Thread prawns onto metal skewers and barbecue over medium heat or grill, turning occasionally, 2–3 minutes until prawns are opaque throughout. Place tortillas directly on barbecue or under grill and cook 1–2 minutes per side until lightly browned.

◆ To serve, arrange tortillas on 6 dinner plates. Divide avocado mixture and prawns between tortillas. Garnish with diced tomato and lime wedges.

**Each serving: About 420 calories, 23g protein, 26g carbohydrate, 27g total fat (4g saturated), 175mg cholesterol, 720mg sodium**

## PRAWNS IN FETA-TOMATO SAUCE

*Prep: 20 minutes   Cook: 50 minutes*
*Makes 4 main dish servings*

| | |
|---|---|
| 1 tbsp olive oil | ½ tsp salt |
| 2 medium onions, chopped | 400g canned tomatoes |
| 750g potatoes, peeled and cut into 3cm pieces | 450g raw medium prawns, peeled and de-veined (see page 90) |
| 1 large garlic clove, very finely chopped | 450g feta cheese, diced |
| Pinch ground red pepper | 15g fresh dill, chopped |

◆ Heat oil in 26cm frying pan over medium heat. Add onions and cook, stirring often, 10 minutes, or until tender. Add potatoes and cook, stirring occasionally, 10 minutes, or until beginning to brown. Stir in garlic and ground red pepper and cook 30 seconds.

◆ Stir in *175ml water* and salt; cover and simmer over low heat 10 minutes, or until potatoes are almost tender.

◆ Add tomatoes with their juice, breaking up tomatoes with back of spoon. Cook, uncovered, over medium heat 10 minutes, or until juices are slightly thickened.

◆ Stir in prawns and feta. Cover and cook 3–5 minutes until prawns are opaque throughout. Remove from heat and stir in chopped dill.

**Each serving: About 390 calories, 28g protein, 47g carbohydrate, 11g total fat (5g saturated), 200mg cholesterol, 955mg sodium**

## SPICY STIR-FRIED PRAWNS

*Prep: 15 minutes    Cook: 8 minutes*
*Makes 4 main dish servings*

60ml bottled chilli sauce
2 tbsp soy sauce
2 tbsp dry sherry
4 spring onions
2 tbsp vegetable oil

800g raw large prawns, peeled and de-veined (see page 90)
¼ tsp dried chilli flakes
1 tbsp chopped fresh parsley

❖ Mix chilli sauce, soy sauce and sherry in small bowl until well combined. Cut spring onions into 8cm pieces.

❖ Heat oil in 4-litre saucepan over high heat. Add spring onions and cook, stirring frequently, about 3 minutes until lightly browned.

❖ Stir in prawns and dried chilli flakes and cook, stirring constantly, 2 minutes. Stir in chilli sauce mixture and cook 2 minutes longer, or until prawns turn opaque throughout. Remove from heat and stir in parsley.

**Each serving: About 205 calories, 24g protein, 5g carbohydrate, 8g total fat (2g saturated), 219mg cholesterol, 965mg sodium**

## PRAWNS WITH BLACK-BEAN SAUCE

*Prep: 25 minutes plus soaking    Cook: 25 minutes*
*Makes 6 main dish servings*

300g dried black beans
4 tbsp vegetable oil
1 large onion, chopped
1 large celery stalk, diced
2 tbsp chilli powder
800g canned tomatoes
Salt

1¼ tsp dried oregano
¼ tsp dried chilli flakes
15g fresh parsley, chopped
2 tbsp red wine vinegar
600g raw large prawns, peeled and de-veined (see page 90)

❖ Rinse black beans; discard stones or shrivelled beans. Soak black beans in *water* to cover by 5cm in large bowl overnight. Drain. Place beans and *1.3 litres water* in 5-litre flameproof casserole and bring to the boil over high heat. Reduce heat to low. Cover and simmer 40 minutes, or until beans are tender. Drain.

❖ Heat 2 tablespoons oil in 30cm frying pan over high heat. Add onion and celery and cook, stirring frequently, about 5 minutes until tender and lightly browned. Add chilli powder; cook 1 minute.

❖ Add tomatoes with their juice, 1 teaspoon salt, 1 teaspoon oregano and ⅛ teaspoon dried chilli flakes. Return to the boil, breaking up tomatoes with spoon. Reduce heat to low; simmer, stirring occasionally, 10 minutes. Stir in black beans, parsley and vinegar and heat through.

❖ Meanwhile, heat remaining 2 tablespoons oil in 26cm frying pan over high heat. Add prawns, ½ teaspoon salt, remaining ¼ teaspoon oregano and remaining ⅛ teaspoon chilli flakes; cook, stirring constantly, just until prawns are opaque throughout. To serve, spoon bean mixture onto 6 warm plates and top with prawn mixture.

**Each serving: About 285 calories, 26g protein, 41g carbohydrate, 11g total fat (2g saturated), 117mg cholesterol, 945mg sodium**

## GINGERED PRAWNS AND ASPARAGUS

*Prep: 20 minutes    Cook: 10 minutes*
*Makes 4 main dish servings*

750g asparagus, tough ends removed
450g raw unpeeled large prawns
1 tbsp balsamic vinegar
1 tbsp soy sauce

2 tbsp olive or vegetable oil
1 tbsp very finely chopped, peeled fresh ginger
¼ tsp dried chilli flakes
1 bunch rocket or watercress

❖ Cut asparagus into bite-sized pieces. Peel and de-vein prawns, leaving tail part on, if you like (see page 90).

❖ Mix balsamic vinegar, soy sauce and *1 tablespoon water* together in medium bowl; add prawns to mixture in bowl. Cover with cling film and refrigerate 30 minutes.

❖ Heat oil in 30cm non-stick frying pan over medium-high heat. Add asparagus and cook, stirring frequently, about 5 minutes, until just tender-crisp.

❖ Stir in prawn mixture, chopped ginger and dried chilli flakes and cook, stirring constantly, about 4 minutes until prawns are opaque throughout and asparagus is tender.

❖ To serve, arrange rocket on 4 warm plates and top with prawn mixture.

**Each serving: About 195 calories, 23g protein, 5g carbohydrate, 9g total fat (1g saturated), 175mg cholesterol, 480mg sodium**

## BAKED LEMON-GARLIC PRAWNS

*Prep: 25 minutes    Bake: 12–15 minutes*
*Makes 4 main dish servings*

600g raw unpeeled large prawns
300–350g spinach, chopped
2 medium tomatoes, halved, seeded and
    cut into 1cm chunks
2 tbsp olive or vegetable oil
Salt
1 garlic clove, very finely chopped
1 tbsp chopped fresh parsley
1 tbsp fresh lemon juice
¼ tsp grated lemon rind mixed with
    ¼ tsp ground black pepper
Parsley sprigs for garnish

◆ Preheat oven to 220°C (450°F, Gas 8). Peel and de-vein prawns (see page 90).

◆ Combine spinach, tomatoes, 1 tablespoon oil and ½ teaspoon salt in bowl. Place spinach mixture in four 15cm round gratin dishes.

◆ Stir together prawns, garlic, next 3 ingredients, remaining 1 tablespoon oil and ½ teaspoon salt in same bowl. Arrange prawn mixture over spinach mixture. Bake 12–15 minutes until prawns are opaque throughout. Place each dish on plate; garnish with parsley sprigs.

**Each serving: About 205 calories, 26g protein, 6g carbohydrate, 8g total fat (1g saturated), 219mg cholesterol, 865mg sodium**

### PRAWN SHELLS FOR FISH STOCK

Instead of discarding prawn shells, use them to make stock. Place the shells in a pan with water to cover. Bring to the boil over high heat, then reduce the heat to low and simmer 30 minutes. Leave the shells in the liquid to cool, then strain the liquid into a bowl. Store up to 1 week in an air tight container in the fridge, or up to 3 months in the freezer.

## CREOLE PRAWNS AND PEPPERS

*Prep: 35 minutes    Bake: 20 minutes*
*Makes 6 main dish servings*

750g raw unpeeled large prawns
1 large lemon
60g margarine or butter
1 medium onion, chopped
2 medium celery stalks, thinly sliced
1 large red pepper, cored, seeded and
    cut into 2–3cm pieces
1 large green pepper, cored, seeded and
    cut into 2–3cm pieces
450g canned chopped tomatoes
1 tsp salt
1 tsp sugar
1 tsp dried basil
½ tsp Tabasco sauce
1 bay leaf
2 tbsp chopped fresh parsley
Hot cooked rice (optional)

◆ Peel and de-vein prawns (see page 90). Grate 1 teaspoon rind and squeeze 2 teaspoons juice from lemon.

◆ Preheat oven to 190°C (375°F, Gas 5). Melt margarine in 30cm frying pan over medium-high heat. Add onion and celery and cook, stirring frequently, 5 minutes, or until tender. Add peppers and cook, stirring frequently, 10 minutes longer, or until peppers are tender.

◆ Stir in lemon rind, lemon juice, tomatoes, salt, sugar, basil, Tabasco sauce and bay leaf and cook for 1 minute. Stir in prawns.

◆ Spoon prawn mixture into shallow 2-litre ovenproof dish. Bake 20 minutes, or until prawns are opaque throughout. Remove dish from oven and discard bay leaf. Stir in parsley. Serve with rice, if you like.

**Each serving: About 210 calories, 21g protein, 13g carbohydrate, 9g total fat (2g saturated), 175mg cholesterol, 845mg sodium**

## SEAFOOD AND SAFFRON-RICE CASSEROLE

*Prep: 35 minutes    Bake: 40 minutes*
*Makes 6 main dish servings*

450g raw unpeeled large prawns
350g shucked large scallops
2 tsp very finely chopped, peeled
    fresh ginger
¼ tsp dried chilli flakes
3 tbsp coarsely chopped fresh parsley
Salt
2 tbsp vegetable oil
1 medium onion, diced
1 medium red pepper, cored, seeded
    and diced
300g long-grain rice
400ml chicken stock
¼ tsp crushed saffron threads

◆ Peel and de-vein prawns (see page 90). Rinse scallops with cold water to remove sand from crevices. Pull tough muscle from side of each scallop.

◆ Toss prawns and scallops with ginger, dried chilli flakes, 2 tablespoons of parsley and ½ teaspoon salt in bowl. Cover and refrigerate.

◆ Preheat oven to 190°C (375°F, Gas 5). Heat oil in flameproof casserole over medium-high heat. Add onion and red pepper and cook until tender-crisp. Stir in rice, stock, saffron, ½ teaspoon salt and *300ml water*. Bring to the boil over high heat. Cover and bake in oven 20 minutes.

◆ Remove casserole from oven. Reserve 6 prawns and 6 scallops; stir remaining seafood into rice mixture. Tuck reserved prawns and scallops into top. Bake, uncovered, for 20 minutes longer, or until all the liquid is absorbed and seafood is opaque throughout. To serve, sprinkle with remaining 1 tablespoon parsley.

**Each serving: About 345 calories, 26g protein, 42g carbohydrate, 7g total fat (1g saturated), 141mg cholesterol, 870mg sodium**

# CRAB

When serving whole crab, provide nutcrackers, extra bowls for the shells and plenty of napkins, and don't stand on ceremony. Live blue crabs are traditionally used for the time-honoured American crab boil, but you can substitute frozen blue crab or blue coral crabs, available from specialist suppliers. Soft-shell crabs are a speciality of the East Coast of the U.S.; they are in season in the summer months and may be available, frozen, from specialist suppliers or Chinese supermarkets. Canned white crab meat, which provides the taste of real crab without the trouble of picking meat out of the shell, is the ideal choice for crab cakes.

**1** Coarsely chop onions, carrot and celery. Cut lemon into thin slices. Transfer onions, carrot, celery and lemon to 12-litre stockpot.

**2** Add seasoning, dried chilli flakes, lager, salt and *4 litres water*. Bring to the boil over high heat and boil 15 minutes. Pour into large colander and rinse crabs with cold water.

## CRAB BOIL

◆◆◆◆◆◆◆◆◆◆◆◆◆◆◆◆◆◆◆◆◆◆◆◆◆◆◆◆◆◆

*Prep:* 5 minutes    *Cook:* 20 minutes
*Makes* 4 main dish servings

2 medium onions
1 medium carrot
1 medium celery stalk
1 lemon
100g Old Bay seasoning
  (available from speciality
  shops, see below)

1 tbsp dried chilli flakes
350ml lager
1 tbsp salt
24 live hard-shell blue crabs
Corn on the cob (optional)

**3** Add crabs to stockpot holding from behind with tongs. Cover stockpot tightly and bring to the boil over high heat.

**4** Boil 5 minutes, or until crabs turn red. Transfer crabs to colander to drain. Serve crabs with corn on the cob, if you like.

### OLD BAY SEASONING

The water for a crab boil is traditionally highly seasoned with Old Bay seasoning, a mixture that may contain anything from hot chillies, fresh ginger and bay leaves to whole allspice and peppercorns. The blend of herbs and spices can vary, and ready-prepared blends are available from speciality food shops that stock American ingredients. If you can't find any, make your own blend; try a mixture of celery salt, ground red pepper and dry mustard, combined with a few of your favourite herbs and spices.

EACH SERVING:  ABOUT 115 CALORIES, 23g PROTEIN, 2g CARBOHYDRATE, 1g TOTAL FAT (0g SATURATED), 96mg CHOLESTEROL, 395mg SODIUM

## THIN PASTA WITH CRAB MEAT SAUCE

*Prep:* 15 minutes  *Cook:* 30 minutes
*Makes* 6 main dish servings

| | |
|---|---|
| 1 tbsp olive or vegetable oil | ¼ tsp white pepper |
| 1 garlic clove, cut in half | Salt |
| 1 small onion, diced | 450g canned white crab meat, |
| 2 medium plum tomatoes, | picked over |
| seeded and diced | 350g dried angel hair pasta or |
| 450ml fish stock | thin spaghetti |
| 2 tbsp dry sherry | 1 tbsp chopped fresh parsley |

◆ Heat oil in 3-litre saucepan over medium heat. Add garlic and cook, stirring, until golden. Using slotted spoon, remove and discard garlic. Add onion to oil; cook about 5 minutes until tender and golden. Stir in tomatoes, stock, sherry, pepper and ¾ teaspoon salt. Bring to the boil over high heat. Reduce heat to low; cover and simmer 10 minutes. Stir in crab meat; heat through, stirring occasionally, 1–2 minutes.

◆ Meanwhile, prepare pasta as packet instructs, using 2 teaspoons salt in water. Drain and serve pasta in 6 bowls, topped with crab mixture and sprinkled with parsley.

Each serving: About 320 calories, 21g protein, 47g carbohydrate, 4g total fat (1g saturated), 45mg cholesterol, 695mg sodium

## SOFT-SHELL CRABS WITH LEMON-CAPER SAUCE

*Prep:* 15 minutes  *Cook:* 10 minutes
*Makes* 4 first course or 2 main dish servings

| | |
|---|---|
| 1 small lemon | 40g butter |
| 2 tbsp chopped fresh parsley | 4 tbsp plain flour |
| 2 tbsp canned or bottled | ¼ tsp ground black pepper |
| drained capers | 40g shallots, very finely |
| 4 live large soft-shell crabs, | chopped |
| about 175g each | |

◆ Cut both ends from lemon. Place upright on chopping board; cut off rind and white pith. Slice lemon 5mm thick, discarding seeds, then finely chop. Stir lemon, parsley and capers together, set aside.

◆ To clean crabs, cut across each crab 5mm just behind eyes with kitchen shears; discard front portion. Cut off flat, pointed apron on underside. Bend back top shell on each side and pull off spongy gills. Rinse crabs with cold water; pat dry with kitchen towels.

◆ Melt 30g butter in 26cm non-stick frying pan over medium heat. Meanwhile, spread flour on greaseproof paper; coat crabs evenly with flour. Add crabs to pan, sprinkle with pepper, and cook, turning once, 8 minutes, or until crabs are golden and cooked through. Transfer to serving platter and keep warm.

◆ Add remaining 10g butter and shallots to pan and cook 1 minute. Stir in lemon mixture and heat through; spoon mixture over crabs.

Each first course serving: About 250 calories, 32g protein, 9g carbohydrate, 10g total fat (5g saturated), 151mg cholesterol, 750mg sodium

## CRAB CAKES RÉMOULADE

*Prep:* 35 minutes  *Cook:* 10 minutes
*Makes* 4 main dish servings

| | |
|---|---|
| Rémoulade Sauce (see below) | 1 tbsp plain flour |
| 45g margarine or butter | 1 tsp dry mustard |
| ½ small onion, grated | 125ml milk |
| 1 large celery stalk, very finely | 450g canned white crab meat, |
| chopped | picked over |
| ½ small red pepper, cored, | 25g dried breadcrumbs |
| seeded and very finely | 1 tbsp fresh lemon juice |
| chopped | |

◆ Prepare Rémoulade Sauce; cover and refrigerate. Melt 15g margarine in 3-litre saucepan over medium heat.

◆ Add onion, celery and red pepper and cook, stirring occasionally, until tender. Stir in flour and mustard; cook, stirring, 1 minute. Gradually stir in milk; cook, stirring, until mixture thickens. Remove pan from heat; stir in crab meat, breadcrumbs and lemon juice.

◆ Melt remaining 30g margarine in 30cm non-stick frying pan over medium heat. Spoon 8 mounds of crab mixture into pan and press into cakes. Cook 10 minutes, or until browned on both sides. Serve with Rémoulade Sauce.

Each serving: About 680 calories, 24g protein, 23g carbohydrate, 55g total fat (9g saturated), 103mg cholesterol, 1115mg sodium

### RÉMOULADE SAUCE

Mix 225g mayonnaise, 60g tomato ketchup, 15g very finely chopped fresh parsley, 1 tablespoon horseradish sauce, 2 teaspoons distilled white vinegar, 1 teaspoon grated lemon rind and 1 teaspoon Tabasco sauce in bowl. Makes about 375g.

# LOBSTER

Buy lobsters the day you plan to serve them and to cook them live (see page 92). Enjoy lobster meat straight from the shell accompanied by a simple stuffing or mix it with an exotic curry sauce for a light meal. Use the shells to add flavour to savoury fish soups.

**1** Preheat oven to 230°C (450°F, Gas 8). Bring *5cm water* to the boil over high heat. Add lobsters, head down. Cover and return to the boil over high heat; boil 2 minutes.

**2** Using tongs, transfer lobsters to colander to drain; allow to cool slightly. Using large chef's knife or kitchen shears, cut each lobster in half lengthways, cutting through shell as cleanly as possible.

## STUFFED LOBSTER

◆◆◆◆◆◆◆◆◆◆◆◆◆◆

*Prep: 20 minutes*
*Bake: 12–15 minutes*
*Makes 2 main dish servings*

**2 live lobsters (600g each)**
**4 slices firm white bread, torn**
**45g margarine or butter**
**40g shallots, very finely chopped**
**15g fresh basil, chopped**
**⅛ tsp salt**
**⅛ tsp ground black pepper**
**Lemon wedges**

**3** Using tip of sharp knife, remove and discard head sac and intestinal vein. Using spoon, remove green tomalley (see below). Place lobster halves, cut-side up, in shallow baking tray.

**4** Process bread to fine crumbs in blender or food processor with knife blade attached. Melt margarine in 26cm frying pan over medium heat. Add shallots and cook 2 minutes, or until tender. Remove pan from heat and stir in breadcrumbs, basil, salt and pepper. Spoon stuffing onto body cavities and tails of lobsters. Bake lobsters 12–15 minutes until tail meat is opaque throughout. Serve with lemon wedges.

### TOMALLEY AND CORAL

Tomalley is the green-coloured liver of the lobster and is considered a great delicacy. The female lobster is prized for its roe, or eggs, otherwise known as coral. When raw, the coral is black, but when cooked, it turns bright red. The tomalley and roe can be eaten alone, used in a sauce or made into a flavoured butter to spread on the lobster before grilling it.

EACH SERVING: ABOUT 560 CALORIES, 58g PROTEIN, 30g CARBOHYDRATE, 22g TOTAL FAT (4g SATURATED), 270mg CHOLESTEROL, 605mg SODIUM

# LOBSTER IN COCONUT MILK CURRY

*Prep: 20 minutes    Cook: 20 minutes*
*Makes 4 main dish servings*

2 live lobsters
  (600–750g each)
2 limes
15g margarine or butter
1 small onion, finely chopped
2 tsp very finely chopped,
  peeled fresh ginger
⅛–¼ tsp ground red pepper
400ml canned coconut milk

1 medium carrot, grated
½ tsp salt
60g mange-tout, cut into
  matchstick-thin strips
15g fresh basil, chopped
Hot cooked jasmine or
  regular long-grain rice
  (optional)

◆ Cook lobsters and remove meat (see page 92), then coarsely chop meat.

◆ Using vegetable peeler, remove two 8cm long strips of rind from limes; set aside. Squeeze 2 tablespoons lime juice into small bowl.

◆ Melt margarine in 3-litre saucepan over medium heat. Add chopped onion and cook, stirring frequently, 5 minutes, or until tender. Stir in ginger and ground red pepper; cook 30 seconds.

◆ Stir in coconut milk, grated carrot, salt and lime rind; bring to the boil. Stir in lobster, lime juice and mange-tout; heat through. Remove from heat; stir in chopped basil. Serve lobster over rice, if you like.

**Each serving: About 420 calories, 30g protein, 16g carbohydrate, 28g total fat (22g saturated), 135mg cholesterol, 325mg sodium**

# THE ULTIMATE LOBSTER CLUB SANDWICH

*Prep: 15 minutes    Cook: 12 minutes*
*Makes 2 main dish servings*

1 live lobster (600–750g)
60g mayonnaise
2 tsp chopped fresh tarragon
1 tsp fresh lemon juice
⅛ tsp ground black pepper
6 thin slices brioche or
  challah bread, toasted

½ avocado, thinly sliced
4 rashers bacon, cooked until
  crisp and drained
4 slices tomato
2 lettuce leaves

◆ Cook lobsters and remove meat (see page 92), then chop the meat and place in small bowl.

◆ Combine mayonnaise, chopped tarragon, lemon juice and black pepper in another small bowl; stir 1 tablespoon of mayonnaise mixture into chopped lobster meat. Spread remaining mayonnaise mixture on one side of each toasted brioche slice.

◆ Arrange avocado on 2 toast slices; top with bacon, then tomato. Place lettuce on another 2 brioche slices and top with lobster mixture. Stack on top of avocado layer. Top with remaining brioche slices.

**Each serving: About 710 calories, 40g protein, 47g carbohydrate, 41g total fat (8g saturated), 196mg cholesterol, 765mg sodium**

# LOBSTER BISQUE

*Prep: 15 minutes    Cook: 1¼ hours*
*Makes about 1.2 litres or 4 first course servings*

30g margarine or butter
1 medium onion, chopped
1 medium carrot, chopped
1 medium celery stalk,
  chopped
1 garlic clove, very finely
  chopped
3 tablespoons tomato purée
Leftover shells and heads
  from 4 steamed lobsters

2 tbsp brandy
450ml fish stock, or leftover
  water from steaming lobsters
3 parsley sprigs
⅛ tsp dried thyme
Pinch nutmeg
Pinch ground red pepper
175ml whipping cream
3 tbsp plain flour
French bread slices (optional)

◆ Melt margarine in 12-litre stockpot over medium heat. Add onion, carrot, celery and garlic and cook 5 minutes, or until tender. Stir in tomato purée.

◆ Increase heat to high, add lobster shells and cook, stirring occasionally, 5 minutes. Stir in brandy and cook until it has evaporated. Add fish stock, parsley, thyme, nutmeg, ground red pepper and *1½ litres water*. Bring to the boil; reduce heat to low, cover and simmer 30 minutes.

◆ Strain soup, discarding lobster shells and vegetables. Transfer soup to saucepan and boil over high heat 10–15 minutes until reduced to about 1.2 litres. Place cream in small bowl; whisk in flour until smooth. Whisk cream mixture into soup; return to the boil, whisking constantly. Reduce heat and simmer 2 minutes. Serve bisque with French bread slices, if you like.

**Each serving: About 280 calories, 3g protein, 14g carbohydrate, 22g total fat (11g saturated), 61mg cholesterol, 440g sodium**

# F5ISH

Fish is becoming more and more popular. This is particularly noticeable with the increased variety of fish now available in fishmongers and supermarkets. The recognition of its nutritional value continues to grow; fish is a rich source of protein, vitamins and minerals, and is also relatively low in fat and calories. Even fatty fish, such as tuna and salmon, contain only about 15 per cent fat, far less than most meats, while white fish such as cod or haddock contain less than 2 per cent. Fish is a delicate food to handle and its freshness is very important. Just remember the golden rule – don't overcook it.

## KNOW YOUR FISH

Fish are usually divided into two categories, 'round' and 'flat'. They have very different bone structures and consequently are prepared and cut differently.

**Round fish** These have a plump, rounded body, and eyes that lie on either side of the head. The backbone runs along the centre of the fish, separating the two thick fillets on either side. Round fish are generally filleted or cut into steaks.

Red snapper fillet

Red snapper

**Flat fish** Almost two-dimensional, flat fish have both eyes on the same side of the head. The backbone runs through the centre of the fish, with two lines of bones fanning out on either side, separating the top and bottom fillets. Flat fish are usually filleted but, if very large like halibut, can be cut into steaks.

Lemon sole

Lemon sole fillet

## FISH SENSE

| HOW FISH IS SOLD | HOW MUCH TO BUY |
|---|---|
| **WHOLE** Fish that has not been prepared in any way, sold fully intact with the head, scales, fins and guts. | 450g per serving |
| **CLEANED AND SCALED** A whole fish that has been gutted and scaled, with the gills removed. | 450g per serving |
| **CLEANED, SCALED AND HEAD REMOVED** A whole fish, gutted and scaled, with the gills, fins, head and tail removed. (Smaller fish prepared this way may have the tail left on.) | 225–450g per serving |
| **STEAKS** Cross-section cuts from large fish, 2–4.5cm thick, usually containing a section of backbone and skin. If cut from very large fish, such as swordfish or tuna, the steaks are usually boneless and may be skinless as well. | 125–225g per serving |
| **FILLETS** The meaty sides of fish that are cut off the backbone. Fillets are boneless and may or may not be skinned. Although usually sold in single pieces, butterfly fillets (both sides of the fish taken off the bone held together by the skin) are also available. | 125–225g per serving |

## BUYING FRESH FISH

• Buy fresh fish from a reliable source, either an independent fishmonger, or from the fish counter in a local supermarket that has a quick turnover. The fish should be displayed on ice in a refrigerated case. Packaged fish should have no visible liquid inside.
• Fresh fish should smell fresh and clean; avoid any with a strong or 'fishy' odour.
• For whole fish, look for bright, clear, full eyes (if the eyes are cloudy or sunken, the fish is old) and shiny, brightly coloured skin with scales tightly in place. The flesh should feel firm and spring back when pressed with a finger. Gills should be bright pink or red, not dull or brown, and should not show any white slime. The tail should not be curled up or look dried out.
• Fish fillets and steaks should be neatly cut with no torn edges. Check the flesh is moist but not wet, with no signs of dryness or discoloration. The flesh should be dense rather

than flaky with no visible gaps. Fillets should look freshly cut with an almost translucent appearance rather than opaque. Any visible bones should be firmly embedded in the flesh.

• When choosing smoked fish, the smoky smell should be mild and not pungent, and the flesh plump, pale in colour and fresh looking with a good sheen.

## STORING FRESH FISH

• Once you've chosen your fish, it is important to get it home in good condition. If you're travelling any distance, or if the weather is extremely hot, have it packed in ice, or use a cool box or bag.

• To store fresh fish, rinse and dry, then place it in a dish, covered, in the coldest part of the refrigerator, 1–5°C. Fresh fish is best used within 1 day.

• Always keep fish cold until you're ready to cook it – bacteria can multiply at room temperature. Don't leave it out while you're preparing the other ingredients.

• Do not store ungutted fish; bacteria in the guts will multiply and can cause the fish to spoil very quickly.

• You may be tempted to freeze a surplus of fresh fish, but home freezers are never as cold as commercial ones, and can spoil the flavour and texture of fish. This is due to the slow formation of ice crystals during the freezing process.

• If you must freeze fish, be sure it's extremely fresh and of high quality. Rinse and dry, then carefully wrap it in freezer bags or freezer food wrap and freeze for up to 3 months.

• Fish with the skin left on, whether whole (gutted) or steaks or fillets, freezes best because the skin helps protect the flesh from the drying effects of the freezer. (To thaw or cook frozen fish, see below.)

## BUYING, USING AND STORING FROZEN FISH

• Packaged frozen raw fish should be tightly wrapped in sealed, undamaged packaging; the flesh should be frozen solid with no visible ice crystals. Avoid fish with white or discoloured portions, which may indicate freezer burn or deterioration. There should be no detectable odour.

• Keep frozen fish for no more than 3 months.

• In many cases, frozen fish can be cooked from frozen, but remember to add a few more minutes to the cooking time.

• The best way to thaw frozen fish is overnight in the refrigerator. Put the fish, in its original wrapping, on a plate to catch the drips. Once thawed, open the packaging, drain well and pat dry with kitchen towels before cooking. Don't defrost fish in water as valuable nutrients will be lost and the texture and flavour of the fish will be affected.

• Don't thaw fish at room temperature unless you are using it as soon as it has defrosted. Being left in warm conditions can cause any naturally occurring bacteria to multiply.

• Never refreeze frozen fish unless it is cooked first.

## SCALING A WHOLE FISH

Fresh whole fish are usually sold cleaned and scaled, but some may need additional scaling. Scaling can be messy, so it's best to work on newspapers in or near the sink. Rinse the fish frequently under cold running water to make scaling easier. Use the back of a knife or a fish scaler, a small tool with rows of rounded 'teeth' that scrape the fish's skin.

Hold the fish firmly by the tail (dip your fingers in coarse salt or use kitchen towels to help grip more easily) and, holding the back edge of a knife at a right angle to the body, scrape towards the head to remove the scales. Turn the fish over and repeat on the other side.

## SKINNING A FISH FILLET

Round and flat fish fillets are skinned the same way; the procedure is not difficult to master. Use a knife with a long blade; a sharp blade is essential. Before you begin, dip your fingers in coarse salt for a better grip, or hold the tail end with kitchen towels.

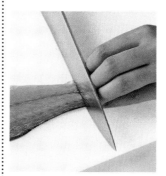

1 Place the fillet skin-side down on a chopping board. Make a small cut through to the skin at the base of the tail, then loosen the flesh from the skin just a little with the knife.

2 Pull the skin taut at the tail end. Hold the knife at 45° to the skin and, with a gentle sawing action, work the knife between the skin and flesh. Using tweezers, remove any pin bones.

## COOKING SUCCESS

• Fish is best cooked briefly. Overcooking can toughen the flesh or cause it to fall apart; it can also ruin the flavour.
• Fish is done as soon as the flesh is no longer translucent and turns opaque all the way through. Remember that fish continues to cook after it has been removed from the heat.
• For steaks and fillets, test they are cooked by inserting the point of a knife deep into the thickest part and gently parting the flesh, which should be just opaque throughout.
• For a whole fish, insert the point of a small knife into the backbone to see if the flesh is opaque.
• To ensure that fish fillets cook evenly, tuck the thin end underneath if necessary to create a more uniform thickness.
• To estimate cooking time for whole, stuffed or rolled fish, as well as steaks and fillets, use the '10 minute rule'. Allow 10 minutes of cooking time for every 2.5cm of thickness. Fish with a sauce or frozen fish require more time; see the chart below. (Do not use this rule for microwave or deep-frying, as these cooking methods are much quicker.) Use the rule only as a guideline, checking the fish is cooked just before the cooking time indicated.

### COOKING TIMES

| | |
|---|---|
| Fresh fish | 10 minutes per 2.5cm |
| Fresh fish in sauce | 15 minutes per 2.5cm |
| Frozen fish | 20 minutes per 2.5cm |

To determine the cooking time, measure the fish at the thickest part. Then time as directed in the chart.

## FANTASTIC (NO-FUSS) FLAVOURINGS

You don't have to coat fish in a rich, fancy sauce to give it flavour – here are some easy ways to add an exciting taste:
**Add a little lemon** Or any citrus fruit for that matter. Cover fish fillets with paper-thin lemon slices before baking; add citrus wedges to poaching liquid; or, simply serve cooked fish with a drizzle of juice for a fresh flavour.
**For a Mexican taste** Add some diced avocado and chopped fresh coriander to ready-made salsa. Serve with grilled fish.
**Low-fat alternative** For a 'creamy' sauce, swirl whole-grain mustard, a handful of capers and a little chopped spring onion into plain low-fat yogurt or reduced-fat mayonnaise.
**Oriental style** Marinate fish steaks in a little oil, vinegar, soy sauce, sherry and grated fresh ginger before cooking.
**Indian flavour** Prepare a dry blend of your favourite Indian spices to rub over the skin of whole fish. Drizzle with a little oil before baking or grilling.

## SUBSTITUTING FISH

When you want to try a recipe but the tuna or salmon it calls for isn't available, don't worry. Substituting one fish for another is nearly always an option, and doing so will add more variety to your recipes.

Fish, a naturally low-fat food, is generally categorized by its fat content, ranging from white fish with very low amounts of fat to oily fish. As a rule, the oilier the fish, the darker and richer the flesh. When choosing a substitute, go for a fish that is in the same fat category as the one used in the recipe (see chart below). Before you make a decision, also consider the flavour and texture of the fish. Most thin, white-fleshed fish fillets, for example, are mild tasting and flaky. And, of course, if the recipe calls for fish steaks, it's best to stick with steaks although if necessary you could use firm fillets.

**White fish** The majority of readily available fish fall in this group. Fish with the lowest fat content, or white fish, have the most delicate texture and mildest flavour. Their fat content may be as little as 2.5 per cent, as the oil is concentrated in the liver (which is generally not eaten).

**Moderately oily fish** This category contains fish with a slightly higher fat content, about 6 per cent. They have a moderately firm texture and fairly neutral flavour.

**Oily fish** The average fat content of oily fish is 12 per cent but this can vary with the season and can be as high as 20 per cent. The fat is distributed throughout the flesh, which has a strong flavour and meaty texture. Oily fish are rich in Omega-3 fatty acids. Unlike the saturated fats found in meat, Omega-3 fatty acids are a type of polyunsaturated fat which is believed to help reduce the risk of heart disease.

### THE FISH EXCHANGE

| LEAN | MODERATE | OILY |
|---|---|---|
| Bream | Bass | Eel |
| Brill | Catfish | Herring |
| Cod | Mullet | Mackerel |
| Coley | Swordfish | Salmon |
| Dab | | Sardine |
| Haddock | | Smelt |
| Hake | | Sprat |
| Halibut | | Trout |
| Hoki | | Whitebait |
| Huss (dogfish) | | Yellowfin tuna |
| Monkfish | | |
| Pollack | | |
| Red snapper | | |
| Skate | | |
| Sole | | |
| Turbot | | |
| Whiting | | |

# GRILLED FISH

Salmon, tuna and swordfish are all high in natural oils, which means they will remain moist and tender when they are quickly cooked under a grill. Brushing the fish with a sauce before grilling will also add flavour. The skin can be left on for easier handling; trim it off with a paring knife before serving, if you like.

## SALMON WITH DILL AND CAPER SAUCE

❖❖❖❖❖❖❖❖❖❖❖❖❖

*Prep:* 10 minutes
*Grill:* 10 minutes
*Makes* 6 main dish servings

**Vegetable oil**
**1 small bunch fresh dill**
**2 tbsp fresh lemon juice**
**45g canned or bottled drained and chopped capers**
**2 tsp sugar**
**2 tsp anchovy paste**
**1 salmon fillet (about 900g), with skin**
**¼ tsp salt**
**Lemon slices for garnish**
**Sautéed potatoes (optional)**

**1** Preheat grill. Grease grill rack. Prepare sauce: chop 2 tablespoons dill. Mix dill, lemon juice and next 3 ingredients together in small bowl.

**2** Place salmon fillet on work surface, skin-side down. Using tweezers, remove any small bones. Sprinkle salmon fillet with salt on flesh side only.

### ANCHOVY PASTE

Available in tubes, anchovy paste has a slightly more delicate flavour than whole anchovy fillets. Made from pounded salt-cured anchovies mixed with vinegar and spices, it has many uses as a piquant seasoning. Use it to enhance the dill and caper sauce on this page; mix it with butter or margarine to top grilled fish steaks; stir a little into dips and salad dressings; or add to fresh tomato pasta sauces. As a guide: ½ teaspoon paste is equivalent to 1 anchovy fillet.

**3** Place salmon on rack in grill pan and brush sauce on flesh side only. Place pan 10–15cm from heat. Grill 10 minutes, without turning, or until salmon is opaque throughout. Cut into 6 pieces. Garnish with dill sprigs and lemon slices, and serve with sautéed potatoes, if you like.

EACH SERVING: ABOUT 195 CALORIES, 31g PROTEIN, 3g CARBOHYDRATE, 6g TOTAL FAT (1g SATURATED), 80mg CHOLESTEROL, 680mg SODIUM

## SALMON WITH CORN-TOMATO SALSA

*Prep: 10 minutes    Grill: 6–7 minutes*
*Makes 4 main dish servings*

2 corn on the cob, husks and
   silk removed
1 tbsp olive oil
1 small red onion, chopped
¼ tsp salt
1 medium tomato, diced
125g canned or bottled mild
   green chillies, drained and
   chopped

2 tbsp chopped fresh parsley
2 tbsp fresh lemon juice
1 tsp sugar
4 salmon fillets (about
   175g each), with skin
1 tbsp bottled teriyaki sauce
½ tsp coarsely ground black
   pepper

◆ Preheat grill. Grease grill rack. Prepare corn-tomato salsa: cut corn kernels from cobs.

◆ Heat oil in 1-litre saucepan over medium heat. Add onion, corn and salt and cook until onion is tender.

◆ Stir in tomato, chillies, parsley, lemon juice and sugar and heat through. Keep warm.

◆ Place salmon fillets, skin-side down, on grill rack in grill pan. Brush tops of fillets with teriyaki sauce; sprinkle with black pepper. Place pan in grill; grill at closest position to heat 6–7 minutes, without turning, until golden brown and opaque throughout. Serve with corn-tomato salsa.

**Each serving:** About 295 calories, 36g protein, 16g carbohydrate, 9g total fat (1g saturated), 88mg cholesterol, 530mg sodium

## HALIBUT WITH PARMESAN TOMATOES

*Prep: 10 minutes    Grill: 14 minutes*
*Makes 4 main dish servings*

2  medium tomatoes
2 tbsp dried breadcrumbs
15g Parmesan cheese, freshly
   grated
1 tbsp chopped fresh parsley
1 halibut steak, 4cm thick
   (600g), skinned

60g mayonnaise
1 tbsp chopped oil-packed
   sun-dried tomato
Parsley sprigs and lemon
   wedges for garnish

◆ Preheat grill. Cut each tomato in half. Place tomato halves, cut-side up, on rack in grill pan.

◆ Mix breadcrumbs, Parmesan cheese and parsley together in small bowl; sprinkle on top of tomatoes.

◆ Place halibut steak on rack with tomatoes. Place pan in grill about 15cm from heat and grill 6 minutes. Meanwhile, mix mayonnaise with sun-dried tomato in small bowl.

◆ Turn halibut over and cover tomatoes loosely with foil to prevent them over-browning. Grill 6 minutes longer, or just until fish is opaque throughout.

◆ Remove pan from grill and spread mayonnaise mixture over halibut. Continue grilling until topping is browned.

◆ To serve, arrange halibut and tomatoes on platter. Serve garnished with parsley and lemon wedges.

**Each serving:** About 290 calories, 31g protein, 6g carbohydrate, 15g total fat (2g saturated), 54mg cholesterol, 235mg sodium

## FIVE-SPICE SALMON

*Prep: 5 minutes    Grill: 6–7 minutes*
*Makes 4 main dish servings*

2 tsp Chinese five-spice
   powder
1 tsp plain flour
½ tsp salt

¼ tsp cracked black pepper
4 pieces salmon fillet (about
   125g each), with skin

◆ Preheat grill. Grease grill rack. Mix Chinese five-spice powder, flour, salt and black pepper together in small bowl. Use to coat flesh side of salmon fillets.

◆ Place salmon fillets, skin-side down, on grill rack in grill pan. Place pan in grill and grill at closest position to heat 6–7 minutes, without turning, until salmon is opaque throughout.

**Each serving:** About 155 calories, 23g protein, 1g carbohydrate, 6g total fat (1g saturated), 59mg cholesterol, 370mg sodium

---

### CHINESE FIVE-SPICE POWDER

Used widely in Chinese cooking, five-spice powder may include cinnamon, cloves, fennel seeds, star anise and Sichuan peppercorns, ground to a fine powder. It is available ready-made from Oriental specialists and many supermarkets. Every blend is different, and may not contain exactly five spices.

The blend lends pungency to Chinese red-cooked meats and poultry (pork, beef, chicken or duck simmered in soy sauce with ginger), and is also used in marinades and dipping sauces. Sometimes the whole spices are tied like a bouquet garni in a muslin bag and added to simmered dishes to impart flavour; the bag is discarded from the finished dish before serving.

## GREEK-STYLE SWORDFISH

*Prep: 10 minutes   Grill: 8 minutes*
*Makes 4 main dish servings*

4 swordfish steaks, each 2cm
  thick (about 175g each),
  skinned
1 tbsp olive oil
400g canned tomatoes with
  herbs

1 medium tomato, chopped
25g feta cheese, crumbled
40g stoned black olives, sliced

◆ Preheat grill. Grease grill rack. Brush both sides of swordfish steaks with olive oil; place swordfish steaks on grill rack in grill pan.

◆ Place pan in grill at closest position to heat and grill swordfish steaks 8 minutes, turning once, or until fish is opaque throughout.

◆ Meanwhile, bring tomatoes with herbs to the boil in 2-litre saucepan over medium-high heat; boil about 5 minutes until mixture is slightly thickened.

◆ Spoon tomatoes with herbs onto 4 warm dinner plates. Arrange swordfish on top of tomatoes; sprinkle with chopped tomato, feta cheese and sliced olives.

**Each serving: About 295 calories, 36g protein, 6g carbohydrate, 13g total fat (3g saturated), 72mg cholesterol, 480mg sodium**

## THYME-GRILLED SWORDFISH STEAKS

*Prep: 5 minutes   Grill: 8 minutes*
*Makes 4 main dish servings*

4 swordfish steaks, each 2cm
  thick (about 175g each),
  skinned
1 tsp fresh thyme
¾ tsp salt

½ tsp coarsely ground black
  pepper
2 tsp olive oil
Thyme or parsley sprigs for
  garnish

◆ Preheat grill. Place swordfish steaks on parchment paper and sprinkle both sides with thyme, salt and black pepper.

◆ Place swordfish on rack in grill pan. Drizzle each steak with ½ teaspoon olive oil.

◆ Place pan in grill at closest position to heat; grill 8 minutes, without turning, or until fish is opaque throughout. Serve garnished with thyme sprigs.

**Each serving: About 225 calories, 34g protein, 0g carbohydrate, 9g total fat (2g saturated), 66mg cholesterol, 550mg sodium**

## SWORDFISH STEAKS STUFFED WITH SUN-DRIED TOMATOES

*Prep: 15 minutes   Grill: 11–13 minutes*
*Makes 4 main dish servings*

2 tbsp finely chopped drained
  oil-packed sun-dried
  tomatoes
1 tsp grated lemon rind
4 swordfish steaks, each
  2–3cm thick (about 175g
  each), skinned

30g butter or margarine,
  softened
2 tbsp chopped fresh parsley
¼ tsp salt
Lemon slices for garnish
Cooked pasta (optional)

◆ Preheat grill. Reserve 2 teaspoons of chopped sun-dried tomatoes and ½ teaspoon of grated lemon rind for topping. Stir together remaining sun-dried tomatoes and lemon rind in small bowl.

◆ Cut each swordfish steak horizontally through centre along a long edge, almost but not all the way through, to form pocket. Spread some sun-dried tomato mixture in each pocket.

◆ Place swordfish steaks on rack in grill pan. Place pan in grill at closest position to heat; grill swordfish steaks 5 minutes. Turn swordfish over; grill 5–7 minutes longer until fish is opaque throughout.

◆ Meanwhile, mix butter, parsley, salt, reserved sun-dried tomatoes and lemon rind together in small bowl. Spread parsley mixture over tops of grilled swordfish steaks; grill for 1 minute longer. Garnish with lemon slices and serve with pasta, if you like.

**Each serving: About 265 calories, 34g protein, 1g carbohydrate, 13g total fat (4g saturated), 82mg cholesterol, 360mg sodium**

## FRESH TUNA AND VEGETABLE SALAD

*Prep:* 35 minutes    *Grill:* 8 minutes

*Makes* 4 main dish servings

8 tbsp vegetable oil

750g potatoes, peeled and cut into 4cm chunks

1 medium onion, chopped

Salt and ground black pepper

2 medium courgettes, cut into 4cm chunks

1½ tsp fresh rosemary or ½ tsp dried, crushed

2 tuna steaks, each 2cm thick (about 225g each), skinned

2 tbsp chopped oil-packed sun-dried tomatoes, 2 tbsp of the oil reserved

3 tbsp white wine vinegar

1½ tsp sugar

Lettuce leaves

2 medium tomatoes, cut into bite-sized chunks

◆ Heat 3 tablespoons oil in 30cm frying pan over medium heat. Add potatoes, onion, ½ teaspoon salt and ¼ teaspoon pepper; cover and cook about 20 minutes, turning potatoes occasionally, until potatoes are golden and tender. Transfer potato mixture to bowl.

◆ In same pan, heat 1 tablespoon oil over medium-high heat. Add courgettes, rosemary and ¼ teaspoon salt and cook, stirring frequently, until courgettes are lightly browned and tender-crisp. Transfer to another bowl.

◆ Preheat grill. Place tuna on grill rack in grill pan. Spoon reserved oil from sun-dried tomatoes into cup; brush tops of tuna steaks with some tomato oil. Sprinkle lightly with salt and pepper.

◆ Place pan in grill at closest position to heat; grill tuna 4 minutes. Turn tuna steaks; brush with remaining tomato oil. Sprinkle with salt and pepper and grill 4 minutes longer, or until pale pink in centre when cut with knife for medium, or until desired doneness.

◆ Meanwhile, prepare vinaigrette: whisk white wine vinegar, sugar, remaining 4 tablepoons vegetable oil, ¾ teaspoon salt and ¼ teaspoon pepper together in small bowl until well combined.

◆ To assemble salad: using fork, break tuna steaks into large chunks. Arrange lettuce leaves on large platter; arrange tuna, tomato chunks, potato mixture and courgettes on top. Sprinkle sun-dried tomatoes over tuna. Drizzle vinaigrette over tuna and vegetables. Serve tuna salad at room temperature.

**Each serving: About 795 calories, 32g protein, 48g carbohydrate, 54g total fat (10g saturated), 43mg cholesterol, 875mg sodium**

## SICILIAN TUNA

*Prep:* 30 minutes, plus chilling    *Grill:* 8 minutes

*Makes* 8 main dish servings

4 anchovy fillets, chopped

1 garlic clove, very finely chopped

¼ tsp dried thyme

⅛ tsp ground black pepper

6 tbsp olive oil

5 tbsp fresh lemon juice

8 tuna steaks, each 2cm thick (about 125g each), skinned

1 large celery stalk, sliced

3 medium plum tomatoes, diced

2 spring onions, sliced

45g stoned black olives, thinly sliced

2 tbsp canned or bottled drained and chopped capers

15g fresh basil, chopped

Mix anchovies, garlic, thyme, pepper, 3 tablespoons oil and 3 tablespoons lemon juice together in non-metallic dish. Add tuna, turning to coat. Refrigerate, turning once, at least 45 minutes. Preheat grill. Heat remaining 3 tablespoons oil in 2-litre saucepan over medium heat. Add celery and cook 5 minutes. Add plum tomatoes, spring onions, olives and capers and cook 5 minutes. Stir in basil and remaining 2 tablespoons lemon juice; keep warm. Meanwhile, place tuna on grill rack in grill pan. Grill at closest position to heat about 8 minutes, turning once, until pale pink in centre when cut with knife for medium, or until desired doneness. Serve with sauce.

**Each serving: About 275 calories, 28g protein, 3g carbohydrate, 17g total fat (3g saturated), 44mg cholesterol, 220mg sodium**

## COD WITH TOMATO RELISH

*Prep:* 10 minutes    *Grill:* 6–8 minutes

*Makes* 4 main dish servings

3 tsp vegetable oil

1 small onion, diced

800g canned tomatoes, drained and cut into quarters

60ml red wine vinegar

2 tbsp brown sugar

Salt

4 pieces cod fillet (about 175g each), skinned

¼ tsp coarsely ground black pepper

Prepare tomato relish: heat 2 teaspoons oil in 2-litre saucepan over medium heat. Add onion and *2 tablespoons water* and cook for 10 minutes until onion is tender and golden. Stir in tomatoes, vinegar, brown sugar and ¼ teaspoon salt; bring to the boil over high heat. Continue cooking, stirring frequently, 10–15 minutes until relish thickens. Meanwhile, preheat grill. Place cod on grill rack in grill pan. Sprinkle with pepper, ¼ teaspoon salt and remaining 1 teaspoon oil. Grill at closest position to heat 6–8 minutes, without turning, until opaque throughout. To serve, spoon tomato relish over cod.

**Each serving: About 245 calories, 32g protein, 19g carbohydrate, 5g total fat (1g saturated), 73mg cholesterol, 685mg sodium**

# PAN-FRIED FISH

Dip fish in seasoned flour, cornmeal or grated potatoes, then pan-fry to create a golden-crisp crust. These pieces of fish become fragile when cooked, so turn them carefully only once.

## COD WITH CRISPY POTATO CRUST

❖❖❖❖❖❖❖❖❖❖❖❖

*Prep: 20 minutes*
*Cook: 20–30 minutes*
*Makes 4 main dish servings*

4 tbsp olive or vegetable oil
1 medium onion, very finely chopped
2 medium egg whites
⅛ tsp ground white pepper
3 tbsp cornflour
450g baking potatoes
4 pieces cod fillet, each 2–3cm thick (about 175g each), skinned
1 tsp salt
Balsamic Sauce (see below)
Green beans and drained and chopped oil-packed sun-dried tomatoes (optional)

### BALSAMIC SAUCE

Combine 1 tablespoon sugar, 2 tablespoons balsamic vinegar, 1 crumbled vegetable stock cube, 1 teaspoon cornflour and 175ml water in 1-litre saucepan. Bring to the boil, stirring constantly. Reduce heat and simmer 1 minute, stirring, or until sauce thickens slightly. Keep warm. Makes about 175ml.

**1** Heat 1 tablespoon oil in small saucepan over medium-high heat. Add onion and cook until lightly browned. Transfer to bowl and cool slightly. Stir in egg whites, pepper and 1 tablespoon cornflour.

**2** Peel potatoes and grate onto tea towel. Wrap potatoes in tea towel and squeeze out as much liquid as possible. Stir potatoes into egg-white mixture in bowl.

**3** Sprinkle cod fillets with salt. Place remaining 2 tablespoons cornflour on sheet of greaseproof paper. Carefully dip cod into cornflour, turning to coat both sides.

**4** Spread about 4 tablespoons potato mixture on top of each cod fillet, pressing firmly. Turn fillets over and spread each with another 4 tablespoons potato mixture.

**5** Heat 2 tablespoons oil in 30cm non-stick frying pan over medium heat. Add 2 cod fillets; cook 10–15 minutes, turning once, until opaque throughout. Transfer to plate; keep warm. Heat remaining oil; repeat with remaining cod. Meanwhile, prepare sauce. Serve cod with sauce, and beans and sun-dried tomatoes, if you like.

EACH SERVING: ABOUT 395 CALORIES, 34g PROTEIN, 38g CARBOHYDRATE, 11g TOTAL FAT (2g SATURATED), 74mg CHOLESTEROL, 830mg SODIUM

## TROUT WITH A CORNMEAL CRUST

*Prep:* 25 minutes    *Cook:* 6 minutes
*Makes* 4 main dish servings

Spicy Corn Relish (see below)
4 rainbow trout fillets (about 125g each),
    skinned
¾ tsp salt
½ tsp ground black pepper
3 tbsp yellow cornmeal
1 tbsp plain flour
1 tsp paprika
2 tbsp vegetable oil

◆ Prepare Spicy Corn Relish; set aside. Sprinkle fillets with salt and pepper. Mix cornmeal, flour and paprika on greaseproof paper. Dip fillets into cornmeal mixture, turning to coat.

◆ Heat oil in 30cm frying pan over medium-high heat. Add fish fillets and cook, carefully turning fillets once, 6 minutes until golden brown and opaque throughout. Serve with Spicy Corn Relish.

**Each serving: About 325 calories, 27g protein, 24g carbohydrate, 14g total fat (2g saturated), 65mg cholesterol, 600mg sodium**

### SPICY CORN RELISH

Cook 4 corn on the cob; cut kernels from cobs. Mix corn, 1 diced large red pepper, 2 very finely chopped jalapeño chillies, 2 tablespoons cider vinegar, 1 tablespoon olive oil, 1 tablespoon chopped fresh coriander, ½ teaspoon sugar and ¼ teaspoon salt. Makes about 450g.

## HADDOCK WITH CHICORY-ORANGE SALAD

*Prep:* 20 minutes    *Cook:* 5 minutes
*Makes* 2 main dish servings

2 tsp red wine vinegar
2 tbsp olive or vegetable oil
¼ tsp sugar
Salt
125g chicory leaves
1 medium cucumber, seeded and cut into
    1cm chunks
1 navel orange, peeled and sliced
1 small red pepper, cored, seeded and
    diced
1 small red onion, thinly sliced
2 tsp plain flour
⅛ tsp ground black pepper
2 pieces of haddock fillet (175g each),
    skinned
2 tbsp pesto

◆ Prepare chicory-orange salad: mix red wine vinegar, 1 tablespoon oil, sugar and ¼ teaspoon salt in large bowl until blended. Add chicory leaves, cucumber, orange, red pepper and onion; toss to coat. Set aside.

◆ Mix flour, black pepper and ¼ teaspoon salt on greaseproof paper. Dip fish fillets into flour mixture, turning to coat.

◆ Heat remaining 1 tablespoon oil in 26cm non-stick frying pan over medium-high heat. Add fish fillets and cook about 5 minutes, carefully turning them once, until they are golden brown and opaque throughout. Spread top of fillets with pesto.

◆ To serve, arrange haddock fillets and chicory-orange salad on 2 plates.

**Each serving: About 420 calories, 30g protein, 26g carbohydrate, 23g total fat (3g saturated), 36mg cholesterol, 800mg sodium**

## RED SNAPPER WITH SPRING GREENS

*Prep:* 15 minutes    *Cook:* 20 minutes
*Makes* 4 main dish servings

2 tbsp vegetable oil
1 medium onion, coarsely chopped
600g spring greens, coarsely chopped
Salt
400g canned black-eyed beans, rinsed
    and drained
1 tbsp plain flour
1 tsp paprika
½ tsp dried thyme
⅛ tsp ground red pepper
4 red snapper fillets (125g each),
    with skin
1 tbsp fresh lemon juice
Lemon slices and parsley sprigs for
    garnish

◆ Heat 1 tablespoon oil in 3-litre saucepan over medium-high heat. Add onion and cook, stirring frequently, until tender. Add spring greens and ½ teaspoon salt and cook until vegetables begin to brown. Add *60ml water*. Reduce heat to low; cover and simmer, stirring occasionally, 5 minutes, or until greens are tender. Stir in black-eyed beans; heat through. Keep warm over low heat.

◆ Combine flour, paprika, thyme, red pepper and ¾ teaspoon salt on sheet of greaseproof paper. Press flesh side of fillets into flour mixture to coat.

◆ Heat remaining 1 tablespoon oil in 30cm non-stick frying pan over medium-high heat. Add fillets and cook 5–7 minutes, turning once, until fish is golden brown and opaque throughout. Transfer to warm platter.

◆ Add lemon juice and *1 tablespoon water* to pan. Bring to the boil, then pour over snapper fillets. To serve, arrange greens on platter with snapper fillets. Garnish with lemon slices and parsley sprigs.

**Each serving: About 375 calories, 35g protein, 39g carbohydrate, 9g total fat (2g saturated), 41mg cholesterol, 770mg sodium**

# FISH CAKES

Delicate-flavoured cod fillets make excellent fish-cakes, though other fish, such as fresh or even canned salmon, also give delicious results. For light cakes, chop fish finely by hand – minced fish tends to become compact when the other ingredients are mixed in with it, resulting in dense and heavy cakes.

## CODFISH CAKES

❖❖❖❖❖❖❖❖❖❖❖❖❖❖❖

*Prep: 20 minutes, plus chilling*
*Cook: 10–12 minutes*
*Makes 4 main dish servings*

**Tartar Sauce (optional, see below)**
**3 tbsp vegetable oil**
**2 large celery stalks, chopped**
**1 small onion, chopped**
**3 slices firm white bread**
**450g cod fillet, skinned**
**1 medium egg**
**2 tbsp reduced-fat mayonnaise**
**1 tbsp chopped fresh parsley**
**1 tsp Tabasco sauce**
**1 tsp fresh lemon juice**
**½ tsp salt**
**Rocket for garnish**
**Lemon wedges (optional)**

### TARTAR SAUCE

Combine 100g reduced-fat mayonnaise, 2 tablespoons chopped fresh parsley, 2 teaspoons Dijon mustard, 2 teaspoons sweet pickle relish and 2 teaspoons fresh lemon juice in small bowl until blended. Cover with cling film and refrigerate. Makes about 75g.

**1** Prepare Tartar Sauce, if you like; set aside. Heat 1 tablespoon oil in 30cm frying pan over medium heat. Add celery and onion; cover and cook until tender and lightly browned, stirring occasionally. Remove from heat; set aside. Process bread to fine crumbs in blender or food processor with knife blade attached. Place two-thirds of breadcrumbs on sheet of greaseproof paper. Place remaining crumbs in bowl.

**2** Using tweezers, pull out any bones from cod. Finely chop fish; add to bowl with breadcrumbs. Mix in celery and onion mixture, egg, mayonnaise, parsley, Tabasco sauce, lemon juice and salt until well combined.

**3** Shape fish mixture into four 8cm round patties (mixture will be very soft and moist). Refrigerate until firm (at least 30 minutes) for easier handling. Wipe pan clean.

**4** Carefully dip patties, one at a time, into crumbs on greaseproof paper, turning to coat. In same frying pan, heat remaining 2 tablespoons oil over medium-low heat.

**5** Add patties to frying pan and fry 10–12 minutes, turning once, until cooked through. Garnish, and serve with lemon and Tartar Sauce, if you like.

EACH SERVING: ABOUT 285 CALORIES, 24g PROTEIN, 16g CARBOHYDRATE, 14g TOTAL FAT (2g SATURATED), 110mg CHOLESTEROL, 600mg SODIUM

## MEXICAN FISH CAKES

*Prep: 25 minutes    Cook: 12–15 minutes*
*Makes 4 main dish servings*

2 tbsp vegetable oil
1 medium onion, finely chopped
1 large garlic clove, very finely chopped
¼ tsp ground cinnamon
¼ tsp ground cumin
Pinch ground cloves
3 slices firm white bread
450g cod fillet, skinned
1 medium egg
1 tbsp fresh lime juice
1 jalapeño chilli, seeded and very
    finely chopped
½ tsp salt
3 tbsp chopped fresh coriander
15g margarine or butter
Lime wedges for serving

◆ Heat 1 tablespoon oil in 30cm
frying pan over medium heat. Add
chopped onion and cook 5 minutes,
or until tender. Stir in garlic, cinnamon,
cumin and cloves; cook 30 seconds.
Transfer onion mixture to medium
bowl. Wipe pan clean.

◆ Process 1 slice of bread to fine
crumbs in blender or food processor
with knife blade attached. Add to
onion mixture. Process remaining
2 slices bread to fine crumbs and place
on greaseproof paper.

◆ Using tweezers, pull out bones from
fish. Finely chop fish; add to bowl with
crumbs. Stir in egg, next 3 ingredients
and 2 tablespoons coriander. Shape
fish mixture into four 8cm round
patties. Toss remaining coriander with
crumbs; carefully dip patties, one at a
time, into mixture, turning to coat.

◆ In same pan, melt margarine with
remaining 1 tablespoon oil over
medium-low heat. Add patties and fry
12–15 minutes, turning once, until
browned and cooked through. Serve
with lime wedges.

**Each serving: About 270 calories,
24g protein, 14g carbohydrate, 12g total
fat (2g saturated), 103mg cholesterol,
500mg sodium**

## SALMON BURGERS

*Prep: 15 minutes    Cook: 10 minutes*
*Makes 4 main dish servings*

Pickled Ginger (optional, see below)
450g salmon fillet, skinned
2 spring onions, thinly sliced
2 tbsp soy sauce
1 tsp grated peeled fresh ginger
¼ tsp ground black pepper
15g dried breadcrumbs
2 tbsp sesame seeds
1 tbsp vegetable oil

◆ Prepare Pickled Ginger, if you like;
set aside. Using tweezers, pull out any
bones from salmon fillet. Finely chop
salmon fillet. Place in bowl and stir in
spring onions, soy sauce, fresh ginger
and black pepper. Shape into four
8cm round patties.

◆ Combine breadcrumbs and sesame
seeds on greaseproof paper. Carefully
dip patties, one at a time, into mixture,
turning to coat.

◆ Heat oil in 26cm non-stick frying
pan over medium heat. Add patties
and fry 10 minutes, turning once, until
browned and cooked through. Serve
with Pickled Ginger, if you like.

**Each serving: About 220 calories,
25g protein, 6g carbohydrate, 10g total fat
(2g saturated), 59mg cholesterol,
650mg sodium**

### PICKLED GINGER

Combine 125ml white vinegar, 60g sugar
and 225ml water in 1-litre pan over high
heat. Bring to the boil, then add 60g
peeled, thinly sliced fresh ginger. Reduce
heat to low and simmer 30 minutes, or
until tender. Drain well.

## SALMON PATTIES WITH CAPER SAUCE

*Prep: 15 minutes    Cook: 5–10 minutes*
*Makes 6 main dish servings*

125g mayonnaise
1 tbsp fresh lemon juice
1 tbsp very finely chopped fresh parsley
1 tbsp canned or bottled drained and
    very finely chopped capers
2 slices firm white bread
600g canned salmon, drained, skinned
    and boned
1 medium egg
3 spring onions, chopped
60ml milk
2 tbsp Dijon mustard
2 tsp Worcestershire sauce
¼ tsp Tabasco sauce
25g dried breadcrumbs
2 tbsp vegetable oil
30g margarine or butter

◆ Prepare caper sauce: stir
mayonnaise, lemon juice, parsley and
capers together in small bowl; cover
and refrigerate.

◆ Process bread to fine crumbs in
blender or food processor with knife
blade attached; place in large bowl.
Add salmon, egg, spring onions, milk,
mustard, Worcestershire and Tabasco
sauce. Mix lightly until blended,
leaving salmon in large chunks. Shape
salmon mixture into six 1cm thick
round patties.

◆ Place dried breadcrumbs on
greaseproof paper. Carefully dip
patties, one at a time, into crumbs,
turning to coat.

◆ Heat oil with margarine in 30cm
frying pan over medium heat. Add
salmon patties and cook 5–10 minutes,
turning once, until browned and
heated through. Serve patties with
caper sauce.

**Each serving: About 440 calories,
25g protein, 13g carbohydrate, 32g total
fat (6g saturated), 106mg cholesterol,
1075mg sodium**

# POACHED AND STEAMED FISH

Delicate foods such as fish are often poached – cooked in gently simmering liquid. Poached fish can be served hot or cold. Steamed fish does not come in contact with the liquid but is cooked by a surrounding vapour bath. Both poached and steamed fish tend to be pale in colour, so they are especially good paired with colourful sauces.

## COLD POACHED SALMON WITH SAUTÉED CUCUMBERS

◆◆◆◆◆◆◆◆◆◆◆◆◆◆

*Prep:* 10 minutes, plus chilling
*Cook:* 12–15 minutes
*Makes* 4 main dish servings

1 medium lemon
1 bunch watercress
125ml soured cream
2 tsp chopped fresh tarragon
 or ¼ tsp dried
1½ tsp sugar
Salt
4 salmon steaks (about 175g
 each), skinned
½ tsp coarsely ground black
 pepper
1 medium onion, sliced
1 tbsp vegetable oil
3 medium cucumbers (about
 800g), seeded and cut into
 4cm chunks
1 tbsp soy sauce
¼ tsp crushed red pepper
Radishes and watercress
 sprigs for garnish

**1** Squeeze 1 tablespoon juice from lemon; set juice and lemon shell aside. Prepare watercress sauce: remove tough stalks from watercress. Blend watercress, soured cream, tarragon, 1 teaspoon sugar, 1 teaspoon salt and reserved lemon juice together in blender or food processor with knife blade attached, until smooth. Cover and refrigerate. Rub salmon steaks with black pepper and ¾ teaspoon salt.

**SEEDING CUCUMBERS**

To sauté cucumbers, you'll need to remove the seeds first, or they will stew and become mushy. (Large cucumbers in particular have very watery centres.) Trim ends from cucumbers, then halve each lengthways. Using a small spoon, scoop out the seeds and discard.

**2** Bring *1–2cm water* to the boil in 30cm frying pan over high heat. Add lemon shell, onion and salmon; return to the boil. Reduce heat, cover and simmer for 5–8 minutes until fish is opaque throughout.

**3** Carefully transfer salmon to platter; cool slightly and refrigerate until cold. Meanwhile, heat oil in washed pan over medium-high heat. Add cucumbers, soy sauce, red pepper and remaining ½ teaspoon sugar; cook, stirring constantly, until cucumbers are coated.

**4** Reduce heat to medium; cook, stirring frequently, 5 minutes longer, or until cucumbers are just tender-crisp. To serve, divide cucumbers and salmon steaks between 4 dinner plates. Spoon watercress sauce over salmon steaks and serve garnished with radishes and watercress sprigs.

EACH SERVING: ABOUT 460 CALORIES, 36g PROTEIN, 11g CARBOHYDRATE, 31g TOTAL FAT (10g SATURATED), 106mg CHOLESTEROL, 520mg SODIUM

## MONKFISH ESCABÈCHE

*Prep: 20 minutes, plus chilling    Cook: 30 minutes*
*Makes 4 main dish servings*

750g monkfish or cod fillets,
  skinned
2 tbsp fresh lemon juice
Salt
3 tbsp olive or vegetable oil
1 small onion, finely chopped
1 medium red pepper, cored,
  seeded and finely chopped
1 medium green pepper,
  cored, seeded and finely
  chopped

1 small tomato, peeled and
  finely chopped
125ml dry white wine
2 tbsp red wine vinegar
1 tsp dried oregano
¼ tsp coarsely ground black
  pepper

◆ Pull tough, greyish membrane from monkfish fillets. Slice fillets crossways into 2cm thick pieces. Bring monkfish, lemon juice, ½ teaspoon salt and *350ml water* to the boil in large frying pan over high heat. Reduce heat to low; cover and simmer about 8 minutes, or until fish is pierced easily with knife. Transfer monkfish to plate lined with kitchen paper to drain. Discard poaching liquid. Wipe pan dry.

◆ Heat oil in same pan over medium-high heat. Add onion and red and green peppers and cook 10 minutes, or until tender. Add tomato, white wine, vinegar, oregano, pepper and 1¼ teaspoons salt; bring to the boil. Cook, stirring frequently, about 5 minutes, or until liquid is reduced by half. Spoon half of sauce onto platter; arrange monkfish pieces on top. Spoon remaining sauce over monkfish. Cover and refrigerate until monkfish is well chilled.

**Each serving: About 265 calories, 26g protein, 8g carbohydrate, 13g total fat (1g saturated), 42mg cholesterol, 730mg sodium**

## MEDITERRANEAN SWORDFISH

*Prep: 15 minutes    Cook: 30 minutes*
*Makes 4 main dish servings*

1 swordfish steak, about 4cm
  thick (800g), skinned
2 tbsp olive or vegetable oil
450g small red or white
  potatoes, quartered
Salt
2 medium courgettes (about
  450g), thickly sliced
1 bunch radishes, each cut in
  half

1 tbsp fresh lemon juice
1 tbsp canned or bottled
  drained and chopped capers
½ chicken stock cube,
  crumbled
½ tsp dried rosemary
¼ tsp ground black pepper
1 tbsp very finely chopped
  fresh parsley
1 tbsp grated lemon rind

◆ Remove any skin and bone from swordfish; cut fish into 4cm chunks. Heat oil in 26cm frying pan over medium-high heat. Add potatoes and cook about 10 minutes until browned. Using slotted spoon, transfer to bowl. Cook swordfish with ¼ teaspoon salt in oil remaining in pan about 1 minute, stirring, just until fish is lightly browned. Transfer fish to bowl with potatoes. Cook courgettes and radishes with ¼ teaspoon salt in same pan, stirring, until tender-crisp. Transfer to another bowl.

◆ Add lemon juice, next 4 ingredients and *60ml water* to pan. Return potatoes and swordfish to pan and bring to the boil over high heat. Reduce heat to low, cover and simmer 10–12 minutes until potatoes are tender and swordfish is opaque throughout. Stir in parsley and courgette mixture and heat through. Sprinkle with lemon rind.

**Each serving: About 420 calories, 43g protein, 27g carbohydrate, 15g total fat (3g saturated), 77mg cholesterol, 760mg sodium**

## STEAMED PLAICE

*Prep: 15 minutes    Cook: 10–15 minutes*
*Makes 6 main dish servings*

2 large spring onions
1 piece fresh ginger, about
  5cm long, peeled
2 tbsp dry sherry
2 tsp soy sauce
½ chicken stock cube,
  crumbled

6 plaice fillets (about 750g),
  skinned
1 tbsp very finely chopped
  cooked ham

◆ Slice spring onions and ginger into 5cm long matchstick-thin strips. Mix sherry, soy sauce and stock cube together in large bowl. Add fish fillets, turning to coat; fold each fillet in half and arrange, slightly overlapping, in shallow casserole that will fit in large wok or roasting tin. Sprinkle spring onions, ginger and any remaining sherry mixture over fish.

◆ Pour *3–5cm water* into wok. Place steamer or rack in wok. Set platter with fish on steamer. Bring water to the boil over high heat. Reduce heat to medium. Cover and steam fish 10–15 minutes until opaque throughout. Sprinkle with ham.

**Each serving: About 115 calories, 22g protein, 1g carbohydrate, 1g total fat (0g saturated), 56mg cholesterol, 300mg sodium**

---

### BAMBOO STEAMER

Instead of using a platter on a rack, use a traditional bamboo steamer. Line steamer with lettuce or cabbage leaves and arrange the fish on top. Set steamer in a wok over boiling water, cover and steam as instructed.

# BAKED FISH

Baking is one of the easiest ways to cook fish. Mild fish, such as cod, haddock and red snapper, gain added moisture and flavour when they are baked with vegetables. As is true for all fish recipes, the most important rule for baking is not to over-cook the fish.

**1** Preheat oven to 220°C (425°F, Gas 7). Using chef's knife cut each potato crossways into thin slices.

**2** Trim root end and stalk from fennel bulb, and cut bulb crossways into thin slices. Toss potatoes, fennel, garlic, olive oil, ¾ teaspoon salt and ¼ teaspoon pepper together in 2½-litre ovenproof dish.

## BAKED COD WITH FENNEL AND POTATOES

◆◆◆◆◆◆◆◆◆◆◆◆◆

*Prep: 15 minutes*
*Bake: 55–60 minutes*
*Makes 4 main dish servings*

**750g red or white potatoes**
**1 medium fennel bulb**
**1 garlic clove, very finely chopped**
**2 tbsp olive oil**
**Salt and coarsely ground black pepper**
**1 piece cod fillet (600g), cut into 4 pieces, skinned**
**1 medium tomato, seeded and diced**
**Feathery fennel tops for garnish**

### RING THE CHANGES

Cod is ideal for this dish because of its thick, meaty flesh that stays moist during baking. Other fresh fish, however, are also suitable, producing succulent results. Try this recipe with haddock fillet or monkfish tail to replace the cod fillet.

**3** Bake 45 minutes, stirring once, or until vegetables are fork-tender and lightly browned. Sprinkle fish with ¼ teaspoon pepper and ⅛ teaspoon salt. Arrange in single layer on top of potato mixture.

**4** Bake 10–15 minutes longer until fish is opaque throughout when tested with a fork. Sprinkle with diced tomato and serve garnished with fennel tops.

EACH SERVING: ABOUT 365 CALORIES, 29g PROTEIN, 37g CARBOHYDRATE, 8g TOTAL FAT (1g SATURATED), 61mg CHOLESTEROL, 565mg SODIUM

## HADDOCK WITH LEMON-GARLIC BREADCRUMBS

*Prep:* 10 minutes  *Bake:* 10–15 minutes
*Makes* 4 main dish servings

2 slices firm white bread
30g margarine or butter
1 garlic clove, very finely
  chopped
4 pieces haddock or cod fillet
  (about 175g each), skinned

2 tbsp fresh lemon juice
¾ tsp salt
Lemon wedges (optional)
Parsley sprigs for garnish

◆ Preheat oven to 230°C (450°F, Gas 8). Process bread in food processor with knife blade attached or in blender until fine crumbs form. Melt margarine in 26cm frying pan over medium heat; add garlic and cook until golden. Add breadcrumbs and cook, stirring often, until lightly toasted. Remove pan from heat.

◆ Arrange haddock fillets in 33 by 20cm ovenproof dish. Sprinkle fillets with lemon juice and salt. Press breadcrumb mixture onto tops of fillets. Bake 10–15 minutes until fish is opaque throughout. To serve, arrange haddock fillets on platter; serve with lemon wedges, if you like, and garnish with parsley sprigs.

**Each serving: About 225 calories, 31g protein, 7g carbohydrate, 7g total fat (1g saturated), 73mg cholesterol, 625mg sodium**

## RED SNAPPER WITH OLIVES

*Prep:* 20 minutes  *Bake:* 30 minutes
*Makes* 4 main dish servings

1 medium lemon
1 small red pepper
60g Niçoise olives, stoned, or
  60g stoned black olives,
  sliced
2 medium shallots or 1 small
  onion, thinly sliced and
  separated into rings
2 tbsp canned or bottled
  drained and chopped
  capers

2 tbsp olive or vegetable oil
½ tsp salt
½ tsp ground black pepper
2 whole red snapper (about
  800g each), gutted and
  scaled, with head and tail
  left on
225ml chicken stock
1 large tomato, peeled,
  seeded and diced
2 tbsp chopped fresh parsley

◆ Preheat oven to 180°C (350°F, Gas 4). Grate rind and squeeze 2 tablespoons juice from lemon. Core and seed red pepper, then cut into matchstick-thin 3cm long strips. Mix lemon rind, red-pepper strips, olives, shallots, capers and 1 tablespoon oil together in small bowl. Mix salt, black pepper and remaining 1 tablespoon oil together in cup.

◆ Rinse fish with cold water and pat dry with kitchen towels. Place fish in large roasting tin; brush with olive oil mixture, then sprinkle with olive mixture. Pour stock and reserved lemon juice round fish; sprinkle diced tomato round fish. Bake 30 minutes, or until fish is opaque throughout.

◆ Using spatula, carefully transfer fish to warm platter. Stir 1 tablespoon parsley into sauce in tin, then spoon sauce round fish. Sprinkle with remaining parsley.

**Each serving: About 400 calories, 60g protein, 10g carbohydrate, 13g total fat (2g saturated), 103mg cholesterol, 680mg sodium**

## EASY STUFFED SOLE

*Prep:* 20 minutes  *Bake:* 20 minutes
*Makes* 6 main dish servings

225g large scallops
1 bunch watercress, stalks
  removed and leaves
  chopped
40g butter or margarine
1 medium carrot, coarsely
  grated
1 spring onion, very finely
  chopped

1 medium egg white
¼ tsp ground black pepper
1 tbsp plus 125ml dry white
  wine
Salt
4 sole fillets (about 225g
  each), skinned
1 slice white bread, torn into
  tiny pieces

◆ Preheat oven to 180°C (350°F, Gas 4). Rinse scallops with cold water to remove any sand and pull tough crescent-shaped muscle from side of each scallop; pat dry. Reserve 1 tablespoon watercress. Melt 15g butter in 26cm frying pan over medium heat. Add carrot, spring onion and remaining watercress and cook until tender. Remove pan from heat.

◆ Blend scallops to paste in food processor with knife blade attached. Blend in egg white, pepper, 1 tablespoon wine and ½ teaspoon salt; slowly pour in *60ml water* and blend just until mixed. Stir in cooled vegetable mixture.

◆ Grease 33 by 20cm ovenproof dish. Arrange 2 fillets in dish. Sprinkle with ⅛ teaspoon salt; spread evenly with scallop mixture. Top with remaining fillets and sprinkle with ⅛ teaspoon salt. Pour remaining wine over; dot with 15g butter. Bake 15 minutes, basting occasionally.

◆ Meanwhile, melt remaining 10g butter over medium heat. Add bread pieces and cook until golden. Remove from heat; stir in reserved watercress. Sprinkle bread mixture over fillets; bake 5 minutes longer, or until fish is opaque throughout. Serve with pan juices.

**Each serving: About 255 calories, 36g protein, 5g carbohydrate, 7g total fat (2g saturated), 99mg cholesterol, 510mg sodium**

# Wrapped Baked Fish

Baking fish wrapped in paper – *en papillote* – allows it to steam in its own juices, locking in moistness and flavour. For even cooking, choose fillets of equal thickness.

## SALMON AND VEGETABLES IN PARCHMENT

❖❖❖❖❖❖❖❖❖❖❖❖❖

*Prep: 15 minutes*
*Bake: 15 minutes*
*Makes 4 main dish servings*

2 medium carrots
½ bunch watercress
125g mushrooms, sliced
¾ tsp lemon and dill
   seasoning
1 piece salmon fillet (600g),
   skinned
4 heart-shaped pieces or
   squares (30cm) baking
   parchment paper or foil
   (see below)
30g butter or margarine,
   cut up

### PAPER PACKETS

To make a heart, fold a 30cm sheet of baking parchment paper or foil in half, and draw half a heart shape with the centre on the fold. Cut just inside the line; the open heart should be 8cm larger than the fillet. Or, simply use a 30cm square of parchment paper or foil. Parchment paper makes the best presentation as it puffs nicely when baked.

1 Preheat oven to 200°C (400°F, Gas 6). Using vegetable peeler, shave each carrot lengthways into strips.

2 Remove tough stalks from watercress. Toss watercress, carrots, mushrooms and lemon and dill seasoning together in bowl. Remove salmon skin, if any; cut salmon into 4 equal pieces.

3 Reserve one quarter of watercress mixture. Arrange remaining watercress on half of each piece of parchment paper. Top with salmon, then reserved watercress mixture. Dot with butter; fold other half of parchment paper over ingredients.

4 To seal packets, begin at one corner and fold edges of paper over about 1cm all round, overlapping folds. Place packets on shallow baking tray. Bake 15 minutes. Cut packets open to serve.

EACH SERVING: ABOUT 240 CALORIES, 30g PROTEIN, 5g CARBOHYDRATE, 11g TOTAL FAT (3g SATURATED), 89mg CHOLESTEROL, 200mg SODIUM

## RED SNAPPER IN PARCHMENT

*Prep: 15 minutes   Bake: 15 minutes*
*Makes 4 main dish servings*

1 tbsp olive oil
1 large garlic clove, very finely chopped
450g plum tomatoes, peeled, seeded and
   finely chopped
Salt and ground black pepper
65g fresh basil, chopped
4 red snapper fillets (175g each), skinned
4 squares (30cm) baking parchment
   paper or foil

◆ Preheat oven to 200°C (400°F, Gas 6). Heat oil in 30cm frying pan over medium-high heat. Add garlic; cook, stirring, 30 seconds. Add tomatoes, ¼ teaspoon salt and ⅛ teaspoon pepper. Cook, stirring continuously, 5 minutes, or until pan is almost dry. Remove from heat; stir in chopped basil.

◆ Using tweezers, remove any bones from fish. Place one fillet on half of each parchment paper square; sprinkle with salt and pepper. Top with tomato mixture. Fold other half of paper over ingredients. To seal packets, begin at one corner and fold edges of paper over 1cm all round, overlapping the folds. Place packets on shallow baking tray. Bake 15 minutes. Cut packets open to serve.

**Each serving: About 230 calories,
36g protein, 6g carbohydrate, 6g total fat
(1g saturated), 62mg cholesterol,
320mg sodium**

### 'EN PAPILLOTE' TIPS

• Cut any firm vegetables (carrots and peppers) into thin or small pieces for even cooking. Precook slow-cooking vegetables (potatoes and cabbage) and allow to cool.

• Fold the edges of the packet tightly so no steam can escape.

• Take care when opening the packets to avoid escaping steam.

## COD WITH SAVOY CABBAGE IN PARCHMENT

*Prep: 20 minutes   Bake: 20 minutes*
*Makes 4 main dish servings*

2 rashers bacon, rinded, if necessary, and
   chopped
2 tsp vegetable oil
½ head Savoy cabbage, thinly sliced
Pinch dried thyme
Salt and ground black pepper
4 squares (30cm) baking parchment
   paper or foil
4 pieces thick cod fillet (175g each),
   skinned
15g butter or margarine, cut up

◆ Preheat oven to 200°C (400°F, Gas 6). Cook bacon in 30cm frying pan over medium-low heat until browned. Using slotted spoon, transfer bacon to kitchen towels to drain. Discard drippings from pan.

◆ In same pan, heat oil over high heat. Add cabbage, thyme, ½ teaspoon salt and ¼ teaspoon pepper and cook, stirring often, until cabbage is tender. Stir in cooked bacon and allow to cool.

◆ Arrange cabbage mixture on half of each parchment paper square. Remove any bones from cod; place fish on top of cabbage. Sprinkle lightly with salt and pepper and dot with butter. Fold other half of paper over ingredients.

◆ To seal packets, begin at one corner and fold edges of paper over 1cm all round, overlapping the folds. Place packets on shallow baking tray. Bake 20 minutes. Cut packets open to serve.

**Each serving: About 230 calories,
33g protein, 6g carbohydrate, 8g total fat
(3g saturated), 85mg cholesterol,
565mg sodium**

## SEAFOOD IN PARCHMENT PACKETS

*Prep: 20 minutes   Bake: 12 minutes*
*Makes 4 main dish servings*

12 small prawns (about 175g)
1 tbsp vegetable oil
1 medium onion, chopped
450g mushrooms, sliced
Salt
2 tbsp dry white wine
2 bunches rocket
4 squares (30cm) baking parchment
   paper or foil
4 small sole or plaice fillets (about
   125g each), skinned
1 tbsp canned or bottled drained capers
1 tbsp chopped fresh parsley

◆ Preheat oven to 230°C (450°F, Gas 8). Peel and de-vein prawns (see page 90). Heat oil in 30cm frying pan over medium-high heat. Add onion and cook until lightly browned. Add mushrooms and ½ teaspoon salt; cook, stirring, about 10 minutes, or until mushrooms are browned and liquid evaporates. Add wine; cook 1 minute longer. Transfer mushroom mixture to bowl using slotted spoon.

◆ Add rocket and ¼ teaspoon salt to pan, cover and cook 1 minute, or until rocket wilts. Remove from heat and allow to cool.

◆ Place rocket on half of each parchment paper square. Top with fish and mushroom mixture. Place 3 prawns on top of each. Sprinkle with capers. Fold other half of paper over ingredients.

◆ To seal packets, begin at one corner and fold edges of paper over 1cm all round, overlapping the folds. Place packets on shallow baking tray. Bake 12 minutes. Cut packets open to serve; sprinkle seafood with chopped parsley.

**Each serving: About 230 calories,
33g protein, 10g carbohydrate, 6g total fat
(1g saturated), 119mg cholesterol,
645mg sodium**

# FISH CASSEROLES AND STEWS

When selecting fish for casseroles and stews, choose firm-textured fish that retains its shape during cooking – cod, haddock and monkfish are ideal, or use a variety, for contrasting tastes and textures. Accompany with some good crusty bread for mopping up all the delicious sauce.

## SEAFOOD STEW

❖❖❖❖❖❖❖❖❖❖❖❖❖

*Prep:* 25 minutes
*Cook:* 45–55 minutes
*Makes* 10 main dish servings

600g raw large prawns
750g red snapper or cod
  fillets, skinned
450g large scallops
1 medium lime, halved
1 tsp ground coriander
3 tbsp olive or vegetable oil
2 large onions, diced
2 large celery stalks, diced
2 medium carrots, diced
1 medium red pepper, cored,
  seeded and diced
1kg canned tomatoes
1 vegetable or chicken stock
  cube
125ml dry white wine
1 tsp sugar
1 tsp salt
¼ tsp dried chilli flakes
2 tbsp chopped fresh parsley

**1** Hold each prawn curved-side up; insert tip of kitchen scissors under shell. Cut about 5mm deep along back through to tail to expose vein. De-vein and rinse; do not remove shells.

**2** Cut red snapper into 8 by 5cm pieces. Rinse scallops to remove any sand from crevices. Pull tough muscle from side of each scallop. Squeeze juice from lime into large bowl; stir in coriander. Add prawns, red snapper and scallops; toss to coat. Set aside.

**3** Heat oil in 8-litre flameproof casserole over medium heat. Add sliced vegetables and cook, stirring occasionally, about 25 minutes until tender and browned.

**4** Stir in tomatoes with their juice, next 5 ingredients and *175ml water*, breaking up tomatoes with back of spoon. Bring to the boil over high heat.

**5** Reduce heat to medium-low; cook 5 minutes to blend flavours. Stir seafood mixture into tomato mixture and return to the boil over high heat. Reduce heat to medium-low; cook, stirring occasionally, 5–10 minutes until seafood is opaque throughout. Stir in parsley.

EACH SERVING: ABOUT 250 CALORIES, 33g PROTEIN, 12g CARBOHYDRATE, 6g TOTAL FAT (1g SATURATED), 127mg CHOLESTEROL, 790mg SODIUM

## EASY COD STEW

*Prep: 15 minutes    Cook: 25 minutes*
*Makes 4 main dish servings*

1 tbsp olive or vegetable oil
1 large onion, halved and
    thinly sliced
¾ tsp salt
350g red or white potatoes,
    cut into 2cm chunks

400ml chicken stock
400g canned tomatoes
600g cod fillet, skinned and
    cut into 4cm chunks
300–350g fresh spinach,
    coarsely sliced

◆ Heat oil in 4-litre saucepan over medium heat.
Add onion and salt and cook, stirring, until onion is tender
but not browned.

◆ Add potatoes, stock, tomatoes and *225ml water*; bring to
the boil over high heat. Reduce heat to low, cover and
simmer 10 minutes, or until potatoes are almost tender.

◆ Stir in cod and spinach; cook 5 minutes longer, or until
cod is opaque throughout and potatoes are fork-tender.

**Each serving: About 290 calories, 31g protein, 31g carbohydrate,
5g total fat (1g saturated), 62mg cholesterol, 815mg sodium**

## LETTUCE-WRAPPED SEAFOOD

*Prep: 25 minutes    Bake: 30–35 minutes*
*Makes 6 main dish servings*

225g large scallops
225g raw large prawns
40g plain flour
½ tsp salt
900g cod fillets, cut into
    6 pieces, skinned

3 tbsp vegetable oil
800ml chicken stock
12 large Cos lettuce leaves
3 spring onions, sliced

◆ Preheat oven to 220°C (425°F, Gas 7). Rinse scallops with
cold water to remove any sand from crevices. Pull tough
muscle from side of each scallop, then cut each horizontally
in half. Peel and de-vein prawns (see page 90).

◆ Mix flour and salt together on greaseproof paper. Dip
cod fillets into flour mixture, turning to coat.

◆ Heat oil in 26cm frying pan over medium-high heat. Add
cod fillets, 3 pieces at a time, and cook, turning once, until
golden brown. Transfer cod fillets to plate.

◆ Discard any oil remaining in frying pan. Pour chicken
stock into pan; bring to the boil over high heat. Remove
pan from heat.

◆ Line shallow 2½-litre casserole with 8 lettuce leaves,
allowing them to overhang side slightly. Arrange cod,
scallops, prawns and spring onions on top.

◆ Pour stock over seafood; fold lettuce over top. Arrange
remaining lettuce leaves on top. Cover; bake 30–35 minutes
until seafood is opaque throughout. To serve, fold back
lettuce; spoon seafood and lettuce into bowls.

**Each serving: About 295 calories, 42g protein, 8g carbohydrate,
9g total fat (2g saturated), 137mg cholesterol, 430mg sodium**

## LOUISIANA SEAFOOD CASSEROLE

*Prep: 30 minutes    Bake: 45–50 minutes*
*Makes 8 main dish servings*

350g hot Italian sausages
2 medium celery stalks, cut
    into 1cm pieces
1 large red pepper, cored,
    seeded and cut into 1cm
    pieces
1 large green pepper, cored,
    seeded and cut into 1cm
    pieces
1 medium onion, diced
450g easy-cook rice

400g canned tomatoes
800ml chicken stock
1 bay leaf
½ tsp Tabasco sauce
¼ tsp dried thyme
450g monkfish, cod or
    haddock fillets, skinned
350g raw large prawns
350g large scallops
2 tbsp chopped fresh parsley

◆ Preheat oven to 180°C (350°F, Gas 4). Cook sausages in
8-litre flameproof casserole over medium-high heat until
browned. Using slotted spoon, transfer sausages to kitchen
towels to drain.

◆ Cook celery, red and green peppers and onion in
drippings in casserole, stirring occasionally, until tender.
Meanwhile, cut sausages into 1cm thick diagonal slices.

◆ Add rice to vegetables in casserole; cook, stirring, until
rice is opaque. Stir in tomatoes, next 4 ingredients and
sausages; bring to the boil. Bake, covered, 25 minutes.

◆ Meanwhile, pull tough, greyish membrane from
monkfish fillets; cut monkfish into 4cm pieces. Peel and
de-vein prawns (see page 90). Pull tough muscle from side
of each scallop. Rinse shellfish with cold running water.

◆ Stir monkfish, prawns and scallops into rice mixture.
Cover and bake, stirring occasionally, 20–25 minutes longer
until rice is tender and seafood is opaque throughout.
Discard bay leaf. Stir in parsley and serve.

**Each serving: About 500 calories, 37g protein, 56g carbohydrate,
13mg total fat (4g saturated), 127mg cholesterol, 720mg sodium**

# BARBECUED FISH

The 'meaty' flavour and firm texture of fish such as tuna, salmon, halibut and red snapper make them well suited to barbecuing. Because fish contains little fat, it can dry out quickly over fierce heat. For best results, it should either be marinated or brushed with olive oil before cooking to keep it moist. As a further safeguard, lightly grease the grill rack to prevent the fish sticking. As with all fish, freshness – and a brief cooking time – is paramount. While an outdoor barbecue is best for an authentic char-grilled taste, you can also cook fish for a similar result on the hob in a ridged cast-iron grill pan or under the grill.

**1** Prepare barbecue. Rinse scallops with cold water to remove sand from crevices. Pull tough crescent-shaped muscle from side of each scallop.

**2** Blend chutney, lemon juice and salt together in food processor with knife blade attached until smooth. Reserve 3 tablespoons mixture for dressing salad. Pour remaining mixture into large bowl; stir in curry powder until blended. Toss scallops, salmon and red peppers with chutney mixture in bowl.

## CURRIED SEAFOOD KEBABS

❖❖❖❖❖❖❖❖❖❖❖❖❖❖❖❖❖❖❖❖❖❖❖❖❖❖❖❖

*Prep: 20 minutes    Barbecue: 7–8 minutes*
*Makes 6 main dish servings*

450g large scallops
125g mango chutney
60ml fresh lemon juice
1¼ tsp salt
1 tsp curry powder
450g salmon fillet, skinned and cut into 12 chunks

2 large red peppers, each cored, seeded and cut into 9 pieces
6 (23cm) bamboo skewers
Summer Salad with Chutney Dressing (see below right)
Lime wedges and cooked parslied rice (optional)

**3** Alternately thread red peppers, salmon and scallops on skewers. Place kebabs on barbecue over high heat. Cook, turning occasionally, 7–8 minutes, until seafood is opaque throughout. Meanwhile, prepare salad. Pour pan juices over salad. Serve kebabs with salad, lime wedges and rice, if you like.

### CURRY POWDER

A mixed blend of up to 20 pulverized spices, herbs and seeds, curry powder can vary widely in content. Dried red chillies give heat, and turmeric gives the characteristic rich yellow colour; ginger, cumin, black pepper and coriander seeds are also often included. Curry powder is rarely used in India, where spices are freshly ground every day. It should be stored in an air-tight container in the refrigerator for up to 6 months.

### SUMMER SALAD WITH CHUTNEY DRESSING

Place reserved chutney mixture in large bowl. Slowly beat in 2 tablespoons olive or vegetable oil until slightly thickened. Add 1 head red leaf lettuce, torn into bite-sized pieces, 1 bunch watercress, stalks removed, and 225g seedless green grapes. Toss well to coat.

EACH SERVING: ABOUT 275 CALORIES, 29g PROTEIN, 22g CARBOHYDRATE, 8g TOTAL FAT (1g SATURATED), 64mg CHOLESTEROL, 635mg SODIUM

## SALMON TERIYAKI WITH SQUASH

*Prep: 15 minutes   Barbecue: 18–20 minutes*
*Makes 4 main dish servings*

60ml bottled teriyaki sauce
125g peeled and grated fresh
  horseradish root
2 tbsp olive or vegetable oil
2 medium courgettes (about
  600g)
2 medium yellow courgettes
  (about 600g)

¼ tsp lemon-pepper seasoning
  or ⅛ tsp grated lemon rind
  mixed with ⅛ tsp ground
  black pepper
4 salmon steaks, each 2cm
  thick (about 175g each),
  skinned

◆ Mix teriyaki sauce, 60g grated horseradish root and
1 tablespoon olive oil together in small bowl; set aside.
Prepare barbecue.

◆ Cut all courgettes lengthways in half. Brush halves with
remaining 1 tablespoon oil; sprinkle with lemon-pepper
seasoning. Place courgettes on barbecue over medium
heat. Barbecue 12–15 minutes, or until tender, turning
courgettes occasionally.

◆ Meanwhile, arrange salmon steaks on barbecue over
medium heat. Barbecue 8–10 minutes, brushing
occasionally with teriyaki sauce and turning once, until
salmon is opaque throughout. Transfer salmon and squash
to platter. Serve with remaining grated horseradish.

**Each serving: About 325 calories, 38g protein, 14g carbohydrate,
13g total fat (2g saturated), 88mg cholesterol, 815mg sodium**

◆◆◆◆◆◆◆◆◆◆◆◆◆◆◆◆◆◆◆◆◆◆◆◆◆◆

### LEMON GARNISHES

**Knots**  Score rind of lemon to divide it into
quarters; remove rind. Using tip of spoon,
scrape away most of white pith. Stack
pieces; cut into long, thin strips, then
tie into knots.

**Scalloped slices**  Use a zester to cut
lengthways strips of rind from lemon
to give striped effect. Cut lemon
crossways into thin slices.

**Twists**  Cut lemon into thin slices;
make cut from edge to centre of each
slice. Twist into a curl.

**Zig-zags**  Draw zig-zag pattern round
centre of lemon. Using sharp knife,
cut through pattern to halve lemon.

◆◆◆◆◆◆◆◆◆◆◆◆◆◆◆◆◆◆◆◆◆◆◆◆◆◆

*Prep: 5 minutes, plus marinating   Barbecue: 10 minutes*
*Makes 4 main dish servings*

60ml white wine
1 tsp Worcestershire sauce
2 tbsp fresh lemon juice
1 tbsp very finely chopped
  fresh dill or ¾ tsp dried

1 tbsp olive or vegetable oil
¼ tsp ground black pepper
2 halibut steaks, each 2–3cm
  thick (about 350g), skinned

◆ Mix first 6 ingredients together in 33 by 20cm non-
metallic dish. Add halibut, turning to coat. Cover and
refrigerate at least 2 hours, turning once. Meanwhile,
prepare barbecue.

◆ Place halibut on barbecue over low heat, reserving
marinade. Barbecue 10 minutes, turning occasionally and
basting frequently, or until opaque throughout.

**Each serving: About 220 calories, 35g protein, 4g carbohydrate,
7g total fat (1g saturated), 54mg cholesterol, 240mg sodium**

## STUFFED RED SNAPPER

*Prep: 20 minutes   Barbecue: 15–20 minutes*
*Makes 6 main dish servings*

1 large lemon
4 tbsp olive or vegetable oil
2 medium carrots, grated
1 medium onion, very finely
  chopped
⅛ tsp ground black pepper

Salt
15g fresh parsley, finely
  chopped
3 whole red snapper (750g
  each), filleted
Lemon wedges for garnish

◆ Prepare barbecue. Grate rind and squeeze juice from
lemon. Heat 2 tablespoons oil in 26cm frying pan over
medium-high heat. Add carrots, onion, pepper and
½ teaspoon salt; cook until vegetables are tender and
golden. Stir in parsley and lemon rind; remove from heat.
Arrange 3 fillets, skin-side down, on work surface; sprinkle
with ½ teaspoon salt. Spread vegetable mixture over fillets;
top with remaining fillets, skin-side up. Tie each snapper
securely with string at about 5cm intervals.

◆ Mix lemon juice and remaining 2 tablespoons oil
together in small bowl. Brush fish with some lemon juice
mixture. Place red snapper on greased grill topper or
greased grill rack. Barbecue snapper over medium heat,
15–20 minutes, carefully turning fish once and brushing
frequently with remaining lemon juice mixture, until fish is
opaque throughout. Remove string from fish and garnish
with lemon wedges.

**Each serving: About 410 calories, 63g protein, 7g carbohydrate,
13g total fat (2g saturated), 110mg cholesterol, 560mg sodium**

# 6

# POULTRY

# Poultry KNOW-HOW

Chickens, ducks, geese, turkeys and poussins, farmed or free-range, are appreciated worldwide for their versatility. Most poultry recipes are simple to prepare and offer a wide array of delicious flavour options. Lower in fat and, weight for weight, generally less expensive than red meat, chicken and turkey are an ideal choice for those watching their waistline. White meat has less fat and fewer calories than dark meat, and skinless breast meat is the leanest of all. For maximum flavour and moistness, cook poultry with the skin on. Remove it before eating, if you like, and you will slash the fat content by about half.

## BUYING

• Choose fresh whole birds that seem plump, with meaty breasts. Meatier birds are a better buy because you're paying for less bone per kilo. Chicken parts should also look plump.
• Poultry skin should be smooth, moist and free of bruises. Bone ends should be pinkish-white. The colour of the skin can range from creamy white to yellow; it depends on the bird's feed and breed and has no effect on taste.
• Avoid packets that are broken or leaking.
• Most poultry is sold oven-ready, which means it has been plucked and cleaned, ready to cook. In traditional butchers and poulterers poultry, which has been hung with the guts still inside to develop its flavour, is weighed after plucking but before cleaning and with the head and feet still attached. An oven-ready bird will be about one-third lighter.
• To check freshness of packed poultry, note the 'sell-by' date on the packet. You can safely buy poultry through that date, and then refrigerate it for up to 2 days afterwards.
• Most free-range chickens are those fed on at least 70 per cent cereal diet and allowed continuous access to open-air runs. As a result, they develop more muscle, which creates fuller-flavoured meat. Free-range chickens are usually more expensive than confined chickens. Corn-fed chickens are now readily available and are easily identified by their yellow tinged flesh.
• When buying frozen poultry, be sure the meat is rock-hard and without signs of freezer burn. The quick commercial freezing process should guarantee that poultry has not absorbed excess water. Check by making sure there are no ice crystals. The packaging should be tightly sealed and intact; frozen liquid in the bottom can mean the bird was thawed and refrozen.

## POULTRY SENSE

| POULTRY/READY-TO-COOK WEIGHT | | SERVINGS | STUFFING |
|---|---|---|---|
| Small to medium | 1.1–1.5kg | 2–4 | 350–500g |
| Roasting chicken | 2.2–3.1kg | 6–7 | 800g–1kg |
| Capon | 2.7–3.6kg | 6–8 | 800g–1kg |
| Poussin | 500g | 1 | 175g |
| Turkey | 3.6–5.4kg | 6–8 | 1–1.8kg |
| | 5.4–7.3kg | 12–16 | 1.8–2.5kg |
| | 7.3–9.1kg | 16–20 | 2.5–3kg |
| | 9.1–10.8kg | 20–24 | 3–3.8kg |
| Turkey breast | 1.8–2.7kg | 5–8 | — |
| Turkey breast (boneless) | 1.1–1.3kg | 6–9 | — |
| Duckling | 1.8–2.2kg | 4 | 500–700g |
| Goose | 4.5–5.4kg | 6–8 | 1–1.8kg |

## HANDLING AND STORING

• Raw poultry can harbour salmonella, a prime source of food poisoning. Always wash your hands, chopping board and all utensils in hot, soapy water after handling it; do not deal with other foods until you have done this. Chopping boards should be occasionally bleached with a solution of 1 tablespoon bleach to 4 litres water.
• Store raw poultry in its original wrapping in the coldest part of the refrigerator for up to 2 days for small birds and up to 4 days for goose and turkey; keep it separate from cooked and ready-to-eat foods.
• If poultry is wrapped in butcher's paper, or if the wrapping is leaking, unwrap it, place in a dish, and cover loosely with foil or greaseproof paper before refrigerating.
• Some wrappings can transfer their odour to poultry. After unwrapping, check that any smell disappears quickly. Do not use if any 'off' odours linger.
• Rinse poultry inside and out with cold running water and pat dry with kitchen towels before using.
• Store any giblets separately in the refrigerator and use within a day. They are an excellent addition to gravy.
• Freeze whole uncooked poultry up to 6 months and pieces 3–6 months. Minced poultry will keep in the refrigerator 1 day, or in the freezer up to 3 months.

• Carve leftover meat from a cooked, cooled bird, cover in foil and refrigerate for use within 2–3 days or freeze up to 3 months. The carcass can be used to make stock which can then be covered and frozen for use within 3 months. Wrap leftover stuffing separately from meat and refrigerate to use within 3 days or freeze for up to 1 month.

## THAWING

For safety, it's important to thaw poultry in one of two ways: either in the refrigerator or by immersing it in cold water (see below). Never thaw poultry on the kitchen worktop, because bacteria can multiply rapidly at room temperature. Follow the label instructions for frozen poultry and keep these important guidelines in mind:
• Frozen poultry should be thawed completely before cooking, so allow sufficient time, especially for large birds.
• Remove giblets as soon as possible during thawing, then wrap and refrigerate and use for stock or gravy, if desired.
• If all ice crystals have disappeared from the body cavity and the legs are soft and flexible, then the bird has thawed.
• Once thawed, cook the bird within 12 hours. Wipe out the body and neck cavities with kitchen towels; pat the skin dry.
• For reasons of texture, not safety, do not refreeze poultry once it has been thawed.

**Thawing in the refrigerator** Leave the bird in its original wrapper and place it on a tray to catch drips. Thawing time will depend both on the size of the bird and the temperature of the refrigerator (ideally 1.6° to 4°C). As a general rule, allow about 12 hours per kilo.

**Thawing in cold water** If there's no time to thaw the bird in the refrigerator, try the cold-water method, which takes less time but requires more attention. Place the bird, in its original wrapper or a watertight plastic bag, in a large pan or in the sink with cold water to cover. Warm water thaws poultry too quickly and can cause bacteria to grow. Change the water regularly – every 30 minutes – to maintain the temperature. Allow about 1 hour of thawing time per kilo, then add 1 hour to that total.

| REFRIGERATOR | | COLD WATER | |
| --- | --- | --- | --- |
| WEIGHT (g/kg) | APPROXIMATE THAWING TIME | WEIGHT (g/kg) | APPROXIMATE THAWING TIME |
| 450g–1kg | 12 hours | 450g–1kg | 1½–2 hours |
| 900g–1.8kg | 12–24 hours | 900g–2.7kg | 2–4 hours |
| 1.8–2.7kg | 24–36 hours | 3.1–5.4kg | 4½–7 hours |
| 2.7–5.4kg | 1½–2 days | 5.4–9.1kg | 7–11 hours |
| 5.4–9.1kg | 2–3 days | 9.1–10.8kg | 11–13 hours |
| 9.1–10.8kg | 3–3½ days | Parts | 2–4 hours |

## STUFFING

Whole birds don't have to be stuffed. You can place a quartered onion or lemon inside the cavity or spread fragrant herbs or spices under the skin. However, a traditional stuffing, deliciously flavoured with sautéed vegetables, sausage or other savory ingredients, will accent the flavour of the meat. Follow the rules below:
• Before stuffing, rinse the bird inside and out and pat dry.
• Cool any cooked stuffing before filling the bird, unless roasting immediately .
• Stuff the bird just before roasting, never in advance. It's fine to prepare a stuffing recipe ahead, but remember to refrigerate it separately and then add it before roasting.
• Lightly stuff the body and neck cavities; do not pack. Stuffing needs room because it expands during cooking.
• Stuffing temperature in body cavity should reach 74°C.
• Bake extra stuffing in a separate covered casserole for the last 30 minutes of roasting. Since this stuffing is not as moist, you may want to drizzle the top with some stock or melted butter or margarine before cooking.

Stand the bird, neck-end up, in a bowl just big enough to hold it upright. Lightly spoon stuffing into neck cavity. Secure neck flap over opening with skewers. Tuck wing tips under back of bird. Loosely stuff body cavity (left); fold skin over opening. Using string, tie legs and tail-flap together to hold stuffing.

### WHITE VERSUS DARK MEAT

The white breast meat is the most tender part of the bird – and the leanest. A 100g portion of breast meat without skin has about 4 grams of fat. The same amount of skinless dark meat has about 10 grams of fat. Remember that by removing the skin, before or after cooking, fat content is trimmed by about 50 per cent.

White meat is ideal for quick stir-frying and pan-frying or moist cooking methods such as poaching. It also takes well to dry-heat methods like grilling, but take care not to overcook, because white meat can dry out quickly. The more richly flavoured and moister dark meat remains succulent in casseroles and stews. Or, coat thighs and drumsticks with crumbs and bake or sauté. Dark meat pieces also cook well on the barbecue.

Boneless thighs and breasts cook more quickly and are often more convenient. However, poultry cooked on the bone has the best flavour and tends to be juicier; the bones also help the bird or bird part hold its shape.

# CUTTING UP A CHICKEN

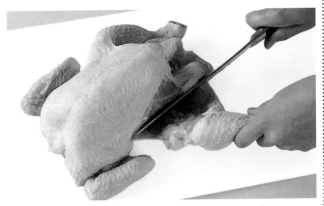

1 Place chicken breast-side up on chopping board. To remove leg and thigh portion, cut down between thigh and body. Bend leg portion back; twist to break hip joint. Cut through joint. Repeat for other leg.

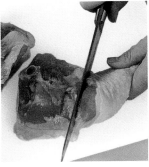

2 To separate drumstick from thigh, place leg portion skin-side down and cut through joint. Repeat for other leg.

3 To remove wing, pull away from body, then cut between joint and breast. Repeat for other wing. Remove wing tips, if desired; freeze to use in stock.

4 Using poultry shears or kitchen scissors, cut through rib cage along one side of backbone from tail end to neck. Repeat on other side to remove backbone in one piece.

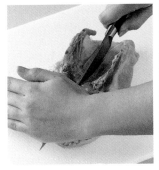

5 With skin-side down, cut breast in half by placing knife along one side of breastbone. Press knife down to cut through bone and meat. Cut each breast half crosswise, if you like.

# SKINNING AND BONING A CHICKEN BREAST

1 To remove skin from chicken, grasp skin at thickest end of breast and pull it away. If you like, use a kitchen towel or dip your fingers in a little coarse salt for a better grip.

2 To bone a chicken breast, holding knife as close as possible to bone, work blade over rib bones, gently pulling meat away with the other hand.

3 The white tendon found on the underside of the breast is tough and should be removed. Holding end of tendon, scrape from meat with knife as you pull the tendon away.

# TRIMMING CHICKEN LIVERS

Before cooking chicken livers, trim any fat and membranes with a small sharp knife. Any green-tinged portions should also be cut away.

## QUARTERING A DUCKLING

1 Using poultry shears or kitchen scissors, cut away neck flap of duckling skin. Pull off any large pieces of fat. Use fat to roast potatoes, if you like.

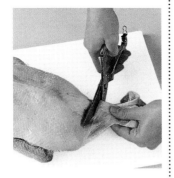

2 Keeping duckling breast-side up, and working from body cavity to neck, cut duckling along one side of breastbone.

3 Open duckling to expose rib cage and backbone. Cut along one side of backbone to split duckling into two halves.

4 Place duckling halves skin-side up. To divide into quarters, cut each half diagonally midway between wing and leg.

## ROASTING AND CARVING POULTRY

Use the chart at right to estimate roasting times for different weights of poultry. To be sure a whole bird is fully cooked, always use a meat thermometer. Before cooking, insert the meat thermometer into thickest part of inner thigh, but not touching the bone, and pointing toward the body. When it reads 80–83°C, the bird is done. The temperature will continue to rise as you let the bird stand, so the final temperature will be 2–5°C higher than this. As a second test for doneness, insert a small knife into the thickest part of the thigh; the juices should run clear.

Also check that the leg moves easily. Once cooked, bones darken in colour, though the bones of very young chicken may remain pink even if thoroughly cooked.

Letting the bird rest after roasting results in firmer, juicier meat that is easier to carve. Poultry should stand at least 10 minutes before serving. To carve, select a knife with a slender blade long enough to slice off the breast of large birds like turkey or long-bodied birds such as duck and goose. The blade should extend about 5cm beyond the meat on both sides to accommodate the sawing action of carving. For the most tender slices, carve across the grain rather than parallel to the fibres of the meat.

| ROASTING TIMES AT 180°C (350°F, GAS 4) | | | |
|---|---|---|---|
| POULTRY TYPE AND WEIGHT | | COOKING TIME (UNSTUFFED) | COOKING TIME (STUFFED) |
| Chicken | 1.1–1.3kg | 1¼–1½ hrs | 1¼–1½ hrs |
| | 1.3–1.8kg | 1½–1¾ hrs | 1½–1¾ hrs |
| | 1.8–2.7kg | 1¾–2 hrs | 1¾–2 hrs |
| Capon roasted at 160°C (325°F, Gas 3) | 2.2–2.7kg | 2–2½ hrs | 2½–3 hrs |
| | 2.7–3.6kg | 2½–3½ hrs | 3–4 hrs |
| Poussin | 450g | 1–1¼ hrs | 1–1¼ hrs |
| Turkey roasted at 160°C (325°F, Gas 3) | 3.6–5.4kg | 2¾–3 hrs | 3–3½ hrs |
| | 5.4–6.3kg | 3–3¾ hrs | 3½–4 hrs |
| | 6.3–8.2kg | 3¾–4¼ hrs | 4–4¼ hrs |
| | 8.2–9.1kg | 4¼–4½ hrs | 4¼–4¾ hrs |
| | 9.1–10.8kg | 4½–5 hrs | 4¾–5½ hrs |
| Duckling | 1.8–2.2kg | 2½–2¾ hrs | 2½–2¾ hrs |
| Goose | 4.5–5.4kg | 2¾–3¼ hrs | 3–3½ hrs |

## ROASTING IT RIGHT

• Roast poultry on a rack in the roasting tin to allow heat to circulate freely under the bird.

• When roasting fattier birds such as duck or goose, prick the skin all over with a 2-tine fork so the fat can drain away. Spoon off the fat from the tin occasionally.

• For moist meat and crisp skin, baste occasionally during cooking.

• If the skin is becoming too brown, cover the bird with a loose tent of foil.

• After roasting, transfer the bird to a warm platter and let the pan juices stand for a minute. Then spoon off most or all of the fat from the top. The juices remaining in the pan can be used to make a gravy or sauce.

## CARVING A ROAST TURKEY (TRADITIONAL METHOD)

1 To remove turkey leg, force it outward with a carving fork, then cut between thigh and body and through joint. If you like, cut drumstick from thigh through centre joint.

2 To carve leg, holding it steady with carving fork, slice thigh meat parallel to the bone. Slice drumstick meat parallel to bone. Repeat with second thigh and drumstick.

3 To carve breast, make a horizontal cut above wing joint along the length of the bird, making sure it goes right to the bone.

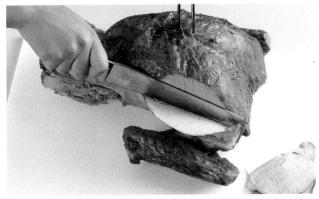

4 With knife blade parallel to rib cage, beginning halfway up breast, cut thin slices. Continue slicing, starting a little higher each time. Cut off wing. Repeat on other side.

## CARVING A ROAST TURKEY BREAST (KITCHEN METHOD)

After removing turkey leg (see left), remove turkey breast in one piece; transfer to chopping board. Hold meat still with carving fork; beginning at tip of breast, carve thin slices.

## CARVING A ROAST DUCK

1 To remove wing, cut through joint between wing and body. To remove leg, cut through skin around leg, then cut down between thigh and body to reveal joint; cut through joint to separate. Cut drumstick from thigh through centre joint. Repeat with second wing and leg.

2 Holding knife blade at a 45° angle to meat, cut long, thin slices from one side of breast. Repeat on other side.

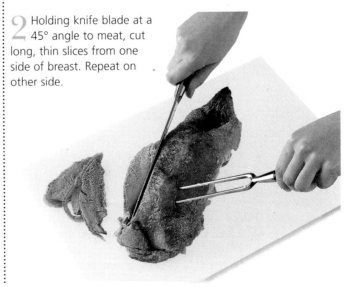

# ROAST TURKEY AND GOOSE

A perfectly roasted bird has a rich, golden skin and tender, succulent meat. To avoid bacterial growth, don't stuff birds until just before cooking; and don't pack stuffing tightly or it may not cook through. Using a meat thermometer ensures your bird is fully cooked.

## GOLDEN ROAST TURKEY WITH GIBLET GRAVY

◆◆◆◆◆◆◆◆◆◆◆◆◆◆

*Prep: 15 minutes, plus standing and making the stuffing and gravy*
*Roast: About 3¾ hours*
*Makes 14 main dish servings*

**Cranberry Pear Relish (optional, see page 138)**
**Country Sausage and Nut Stuffing (see page 138)**
**1 oven-ready turkey, (6.3kg), giblets and neck reserved for gravy**
**1½ tsp salt**
**½ tsp ground black pepper**
**Giblet Gravy (see page 138)**
**Roasted potato wedges and sugar snap peas (optional)**

### CHECKING TURKEY FOR DONENESS
◆◆◆◆◆◆◆◆◆◆◆◆

Turkey is done when the thigh temperature reaches 77–79.5°C and the leg moves up and down easily. Breast temperature should be 72–74.5°C; stuffing temperature should be 74°C.

**1** Prepare Cranberry Pear Relish, if you like, and stuffing. Preheat oven to 170°C (325°F, Gas 3). Rinse turkey; drain well. Spoon some stuffing lightly into neck cavity.

**2** Fold neck skin over stuffing. Fasten neck skin to back with 1 or 2 skewers. Spoon remaining stuffing lightly into body cavity. Fold skin over opening; skewer closed.

**3** Using string, tie legs and tail together. Place turkey, breast-side up, on rack in large roasting tin. Rub turkey all over with salt and black pepper.

**4** Insert meat thermometer into thickest part of thigh next to body, being careful that pointed end of thermometer does not touch bone. Cover turkey with loose foil.

**5** Roast turkey about 3¾ hours. Start checking for doneness during last hour of roasting (see left). To brown, remove foil during last hour of roasting and baste with roasting juices occasionally.

**6** Meanwhile, prepare stock for Giblet Gravy, steps 1 and 2. Place turkey on warm large platter. Allow to stand 15 minutes for easier carving; keep warm. Reserve roasting juices. Prepare Giblet Gravy. Serve turkey with stuffing, gravy, relish, potato wedges and sugar snap peas, if you like.

EACH SERVING WITHOUT GRAVY: ABOUT 390 CALORIES, 53g PROTEIN, 0g CARBOHYDRATE, 18g TOTAL FAT (5g SATURATED), 181mg CHOLESTEROL, 365mg SODIUM

## COUNTRY SAUSAGE AND NUT STUFFING

*Prep: 45 minutes    Bake: 45 minutes*
*Makes enough to stuff a 5.4–7.3kg bird*

450g pork sausage meat
60g margarine or butter
3 medium celery stalks, diced
1 large onion, diced
1 medium red pepper, cored, seeded and diced
½ tsp coarsely ground black pepper

300ml chicken stock
400–450g breadcrumbs made from day-old bread
75g pecans, toasted and coarsely chopped
15g chopped fresh parsley

◆ Heat 30cm frying pan over medium-high heat. Add sausage meat and cook, stirring frequently to break up, about 10 minutes until browned. Using slotted spoon, transfer sausage to large bowl.

◆ Discard all but 2 tablespoons drippings from pan. Add margarine, celery, onion and red pepper; cook, stirring occasionally, until vegetables are browned.

◆ Stir in black pepper and stock. Bring to the boil, stirring to loosen brown bits from base of pan.

◆ Add vegetable mixture, breadcrumbs, pecans and parsley to sausage meat, then mix well. Use to stuff a 5.4–7.3kg turkey. (Place any leftover stuffing in greased, covered ovenproof dish and add to oven 30 minutes before end of roasting time.)

**Each 100g: About 265 calories, 8g protein, 21g carbohydrate, 17g total fat (4g saturated), 17mg cholesterol, 600mg sodium**

### CRANBERRY PEAR RELISH

Bring 350g cranberries, 250g brown sugar, 50ml balsamic vinegar and 125ml water to the boil over high heat, stirring. Reduce heat to low; simmer, uncovered, 8 minutes, or until most of cranberries pop. Add 1 peeled, cored and diced pear to pan; cover and cook 2–3 minutes. Transfer to bowl, cover and refrigerate relish about 4 hours until chilled. If you like, transfer relish to air-tight container and refrigerate up to 2 days. Makes about 500g.

**Each 100g: About 290 calories, 0g protein, 67g carbohydrate, 0g total fat, 0mg cholesterol, 50mg sodium**

## GIBLET GRAVY

◆◆◆◆◆◆◆◆◆◆◆◆◆

Turkey giblets and neck
Roast turkey pan drippings
½ tsp salt

2 tbsp plain flour

1 Bring turkey gizzard, heart, neck and *water* to cover to the boil in 3-litre saucepan over high heat. Reduce heat to low, cover and simmer 45 minutes. Add liver and cook 15 minutes.

2 Strain stock into large bowl. Pull meat from neck; discard bones. Coarsely chop neck meat and giblets. Cover and refrigerate meat and stock separately.

3 Remove rack from roasting tin. Pour roasting juices through sieve into 1-litre glass measuring jug. Add 225ml stock to roasting tin. Stir until brown bits are loosened; pour into juices in jug. Let stand until fat separates.

4 Spoon 2 tablespoons fat from roasting juices in jug into 2-litre saucepan. Skim and discard remaining fat. Stir salt and flour into pan. Cook over medium heat, stirring constantly, until golden.

5 Add remaining stock and enough *water* to roasting juices in jug to make 750ml. Gradually stir into pan; cook, stirring, until gravy thickens and boils. Stir in reserved meat and heat through. Makes about 800ml.

**Each ¼ cup: About 50 calories, 4g protein, 1g carbohydrate, 3g total fat (1g saturated), 34mg cholesterol, 85mg sodium**

## TURKEY WITH PORT SAUCE AND RICE STUFFING

*Prep: 35 minutes, plus standing    Roast: About 3 hours*
*Makes 6 main dish servings*

300g aromatic rice (such as jasmine) or regular long-grain rice
Salt
3 medium celery stalks
1 medium onion
2 tbsp vegetable oil
50g currants
1 oven-ready turkey (about 3.6kg), giblets and neck reserved for another use
½ tsp dried thyme
450ml cranberry-raspberry juice
2 tbsp brown sugar
40g cranberries, chopped
2 tbsp port
2 tsp cornflour
½ chicken stock cube

◆ Prepare stuffing: cook rice as packet instructs in large saucepan using ¾ teaspoon salt. Meanwhile, thinly slice celery and finely chop onion. Heat oil in 26cm frying pan over medium heat. Add celery and onion and cook until vegetables lightly browned. Stir in *125ml water*; bring to the boil over high heat. Reduce heat to low; simmer, uncovered, until water evaporates and vegetables are tender. Stir vegetable mixture into rice with currants. Set stuffing aside.

◆ Preheat oven to 180°C (350°F, Gas 4). Prepare turkey for roasting and stuff as in Steps 1 to 5 of Golden Roast Turkey with Giblet Gravy (see page 137), but rub turkey all over with dried thyme and 1 teaspoon salt and roast 3 hours, or until meat thermometer inserted in thickest part of thigh registers 77–79.5°C. (Place any leftover stuffing in greased, covered ovenproof dish and add to oven 30 minutes before end of roasting time.)

◆ Prepare glaze: bring cranberry-raspberry juice and brown sugar to the boil in 3-litre saucepan over high heat. Cook, uncovered, 15 minutes, or until mixture has reduced to 75ml. Cover and set aside.

◆ Place turkey on warm platter. Let stand 15 minutes for easier carving; keep warm. Reserve roasting juices.

◆ Prepare port sauce: remove rack from roasting tin; skim and discard fat from juices. Add *125ml water* to juices; stir until brown bits are loosened. Strain into 1-litre saucepan. Add cranberries and 60ml glaze. Bring to the boil over high heat and boil 1 minute, or until thickened.

◆ Mix port, cornflour, stock cube and *175ml water* together in small bowl. Stir into sauce; bring to the boil and boil 1 minute. Pour into gravy boat. Brush turkey with remaining glaze. Serve with sauce and stuffing.

**Each serving: About 825 calories, 72g protein, 65g carbohydrate 28g total fat (8g saturated), 233mg cholesterol, 895mg sodium**

## APPLE-GLAZED TURKEY WITH MULTI-GRAIN BREAD STUFFING

*Prep: 30 minutes, plus standing and making gravy*
*Roast: About 3¾ hours*
*Makes 14 main dish servings*

45g margarine or butter
7 medium celery stalks, chopped
3 medium onions, chopped
¾ tsp dried oregano
750g multi-grain bread, cut into 1cm cubes
400ml chicken stock
Coarsely ground black pepper
1 oven-ready turkey (about 6.3kg), giblets and neck reserved for Giblet Gravy (see page 138)
1½ tsp salt
Apple Glaze (see below)

◆ Prepare stuffing: melt margarine in 30cm frying pan over medium heat. Add celery and onions and cook, stirring frequently, until golden. Stir in *125ml water*; reduce heat to low, cover and cook until vegetables are tender. Toss vegetables with oregano, bread, stock, ¾ teaspoon pepper and *350ml water* in very large bowl; set aside.

◆ Preheat oven to 170°C (325°F, Gas 3). Prepare turkey for roasting and stuff as in Steps 1 to 5 of Golden Roast Turkey with Giblet Gravy (see page 137), but rub turkey all over with salt and ½ teaspoon pepper.

◆ Roast 3¾ hours, or until meat thermometer inserted in thickest part of thigh registers 77–79.5°C. (Place any leftover stuffing in greased, covered ovenproof dish and add to oven 30 minutes before end of roasting time.)

◆ Meanwhile, prepare stock for Giblet Gravy steps 1 and 2. Prepare Apple Glaze. About 10 minutes before end of roasting time, brush turkey with glaze. Place turkey on warm platter. Let stand 15 minutes for easier carving; keep warm. Reserve juices in roasting tin.

◆ Prepare Giblet Gravy. Serve turkey with stuffing and gravy.

**Each serving: About 630 calories, 61g protein, 36g carbohydrate, 25g total fat (7g saturated), 215mg cholesterol, 855mg sodium**

---

### APPLE GLAZE

Bring 150g apple jelly, 3 tablespoons balsamic vinegar, ½ teaspoon ground cinnamon and ¼ teaspoon ground cloves to the boil in 1-litre saucepan over a medium-high heat. Boil about 2 minutes, stirring constantly, until mixture thickens slightly.

## ROAST GOOSE WITH WILD RICE AND CHESTNUT STUFFING

*Prep: 2 hours    Roast: 3 hours*
*Makes 8 main dish servings*

| | |
|---|---|
| 25g margarine or butter | ¼ tsp dried thyme |
| 1 large Granny Smith's apple, peeled, cored and chopped | 500ml chicken stock |
| | 150g wild rice, rinsed |
| 1 large celery stalk, diced | 200g easy-cook white rice |
| 1 medium carrot, diced | 450g fresh chestnuts |
| 1 small onion, diced | 1 goose (about 5.4kg) |
| Salt and ground black pepper | |

◆ Prepare stuffing: melt 15g margarine in 3-litre saucepan over medium heat. Add apple and cook until softened. Transfer to bowl. In same pan, melt 10g remaining margarine. Add celery, carrot, onion, ¼ teaspoon each salt and pepper and thyme and cook, stirring frequently, until vegetables are golden.

◆ Stir in stock and wild rice; bring to the boil over high heat. Reduce heat to low; cover and simmer 35 minutes. Stir in easy-cook rice and bring to the boil over high heat. Reduce heat to low; cover and simmer 25 minutes longer, or until liquid is absorbed and rice is tender.

◆ Meanwhile, prepare chestnuts: bring chestnuts and *water* to cover to the boil in 4-litre saucepan over high heat. Reduce heat to medium; cook 10 minutes. Remove from heat. Transfer chestnuts, 3 or 4 at a time, to chopping board and cut each in half. Scrape out chestnut from shell (the skin will stay in shell), then chop any large pieces. When rice is done, stir in chestnuts and apple. Set stuffing aside.

◆ Preheat oven to 180°C (350°F, Gas 4). Remove giblets and neck from goose and discard fat from body cavity. Rinse goose with cold water; drain well. Fasten neck skin to back with 1 or 2 skewers. Place breast-side up and lift wings towards neck, then fold them under back of goose so they stay in place. Spoon stuffing lightly into body cavity. Tie legs and tail together with kitchen string.

◆ Place goose, breast-side up, on rack in large roasting tin. Prick skin in several places to drain fat during roasting. Rub goose with 1 teaspoon salt and ¼ teaspoon pepper. Insert meat thermometer into thickest part of thigh next to body, being careful that pointed end does not touch bone.

◆ Roast goose for 3 hours, spooning off fat from pan occasionally, or until thermometer reaches 77–79.5°C. During last hour of roasting, if necessary, cover goose with foil to prevent over-browning. Place goose on warm large platter; let stand 15 minutes for easier carving.

**Each serving: About 1180 calories, 83g protein, 47g carbohydrate, 71g total fat (22g saturated), 280mg cholesterol, 765mg sodium**

## GLAZED GOOSE

*Prep: 20 minutes    Roast: 3–3½ hours*
*Makes 10 main dish servings*

| | |
|---|---|
| 1 goose (about 6.3kg) | 3 tbsp red wine vinegar |
| 1 tsp salt | 1 tbsp finely chopped peeled fresh ginger |
| ½ tsp ground black pepper | |
| ½ tsp ground sage | 3 tbsp plain flour |
| 3 tbsp caster sugar | ½ beef stock cube |
| 3 tbsp soy sauce | Fresh sage leaves for garnish |

◆ Preheat oven to 180°C (350°F, Gas 4). Remove giblets and neck from goose; discard fat from body cavity. Rinse the goose with cold water; drain well. Place breast-side up and lift wings towards neck, then fold them under back of goose so they stay in place. Tie legs and tail together with string.

◆ Place goose, breast-side up, on rack in large roasting tin. Prick skin in several places to drain fat during roasting. Rub goose with salt, pepper and ground sage. Insert meat thermometer into thickest part of thigh next to body, being careful that pointed end of thermometer does not touch bone. Roast goose 3–3½ hours, spooning off fat occasionally, or until thermometer reaches 77–79.5°C. During last hour of roasting, if necessary, cover goose with foil to prevent over-browning.

◆ Meanwhile, prepare glaze: stir sugar, soy sauce, vinegar and ginger together in small bowl. After goose has roasted 2½ hours, use pastry brush to brush occasionally with glaze.

◆ Place goose on warm large platter and let stand 15 minutes for easier carving; keep warm. Reserve roasting juices in tin.

◆ Prepare gravy: remove rack from roasting tin. Pour roasting juices through sieve into large measuring jug or bowl. Set roasting tin aside. Let juices stand a few seconds until fat separates. Spoon 2 tablespoons fat from juices into 2-litre saucepan; skim and discard remaining fat. Add *125ml water* to roasting tin; stir until brown bits are loosened. Add to meat juice in measuring jug with enough additional *water* to make 450ml.

◆ Stir flour into fat in saucepan over medium heat. Gradually stir in meat-juice mixture and stock cube; cook, stirring constantly, until mixture thickens slightly and boils. Pour gravy into gravy boat. To serve, garnish platter with sage leaves. Serve with gravy.

**Each serving: About 905 calories, 73g protein, 6g carbohydrate, 63g total fat (20g saturated), 263mg cholesterol, 810mg sodium**

# ROAST DUCK

The trick to producing crispy duck is to pierce the skin and roast the duck on a rack, allowing the fat to drain. Serve as a festive meal or for a treat on a winter evening.

## ROAST DUCK WITH CHERRY-PORT SAUCE

❖❖❖❖❖❖❖❖❖❖❖❖

*Prep: 10 minutes, plus preparing stock*
*Roast: 2½ hours*
*Makes 4 main dish servings*

**1 duckling (about 2kg), giblets and neck reserved for Giblet Stock (see below)**
**½ tsp dried thyme**
**¼ tsp salt**
**¼ tsp ground black pepper**
**2 Conference pears, each cut into quarters and cored**
**2 tsp sugar**
**60g shallots, finely chopped**
**75ml port**
**60g dried sour cherries**
**Roasted potatoes, Brussels sprouts and carrots (optional)**

### GIBLET STOCK

Discard liver from duckling giblets. Bring remaining giblets and neck, 400ml chicken stock and 450ml water to the boil in 2-litre saucepan over high heat. Reduce heat to low and simmer, uncovered, for 1½ hours (if liquid evaporates too quickly, add 125ml more water). Strain, discarding the giblets. Makes 125–175ml.

**1** Preheat oven to 180°C (350°F, Gas 4). Discard fat from body cavity of duckling. Rinse and drain well. Lift wings towards neck and fold under back so they stay in place. Prick skin in several places to drain fat during roasting. Sprinkle ¼ teaspoon thyme inside body cavity.

**2** Tie legs and tail together with kitchen string. Place duckling, breast-side up, on rack in medium roasting tin. Sprinkle with salt, pepper and remaining thyme.

**3** Insert meat thermometer into thickest part of thigh next to body (pointed end should not touch bone). Roast 2½ hours, spooning off fat occasionally, or until thermometer reaches 77–79.5°C. Meanwhile, prepare Giblet Stock. After duckling has roasted 2 hours, place pears in small ovenproof dish. Sprinkle with sugar and bake 30 minutes, or until pears are tender. Transfer duckling and pears to platter. Let stand 15 minutes; keep warm.

**4** Prepare Cherry-Port Sauce: discard fat from roasting tin. Add shallots; cook over medium-high heat, stirring, 2 minutes. Stir in port, dried cherries and Giblet Stock. Bring to the boil, stirring until brown bits are loosened; simmer 5 minutes. Pour into small bowl. Serve duckling with Cherry-Port Sauce and vegetables, if you like.

EACH SERVING: ABOUT 790 CALORIES, 39g PROTEIN, 25g CARBOHYDRATE, 57g TOTAL FAT (19g SATURATED), 171mg CHOLESTEROL, 685mg SODIUM

# ROASTED DUCK WITH CRANBERRY-DATE COMPÔTE

*Prep:* 10 minutes   *Roast:* 2½ hours
*Makes* 4 main dish servings

1 duckling (about 2kg), giblets
  and neck reserved for Giblet
  Stock (see page 141)
1 orange, cut into quarters
¼ tsp salt
¼ tsp ground black pepper
100g sugar

300g cranberries
125ml dry red wine
75g stoned dates, chopped
Flat-leaf parsley and orange
  slices for garnish
Roasted potatoes (optional)

◆ Preheat oven to 180°C (350°F, Gas 4). Discard fat from body cavity of duckling. Rinse; drain well. Lift wings towards neck, then fold them under back so they stay in place. Prick skin of duckling in several places to drain fat during roasting. Place orange quarters in cavity. Tie legs and tail together with string.

◆ Place duckling, breast-side up, on rack in medium roasting tin. Sprinkle with salt and pepper. Insert meat thermometer into thickest part of thigh next to body, being careful that pointed end does not touch bone. Roast for 2½ hours, spooning fat from pan occasionally, or until meat thermometer reaches 77–79.5°C. Transfer to platter and let stand 15 minutes for easier carving; keep warm.

◆ Meanwhile, prepare Giblet Stock. Prepare compôte: cook sugar in 26cm frying pan over medium-high heat, stirring, until melted and amber in colour. Remove from heat; stir in cranberries, wine, dates and Giblet Stock (the mixture will bubble). Cook over medium-low heat, stirring, until cranberries pop. Spoon into bowl. To serve, carve duckling (see page 136); garnish with parsley and orange slices and serve with compôte, and potatoes, if you like.

**Each serving: About 890 calories, 39g protein,
54g carbohydrate, 57g total fat (19g saturated),
171mg cholesterol, 705mg sodium**

# CHILLI-GLAZED DUCK

*Prep:* 10 minutes   *Roast:* 2 hours 10 minutes
*Makes* 4 main dish servings

1 duckling (about 2 kg), cut
  into quarters (see page 135)
1 tbsp chilli sauce

2 tbsp light molasses or
  golden syrup

◆ Preheat oven to 180°C (350°F, Gas 4). Discard fat from duckling quarters. Rinse and drain well. Prick skin in several places to drain fat during roasting.

◆ Place duckling quarters, skin-side up, on rack in large foil-lined roasting tin. Roast 2 hours, spooning off fat from tin occasionally.

◆ Meanwhile, prepare glaze: combine chilli sauce and light molasses in small bowl.

◆ Increase temperature to 230°C (450°F, Gas 8). Remove duckling from oven and brush on both sides with chilli glaze. Return to oven and roast 10 minutes longer.

**Each serving: About 685 calories, 37g protein, 7g carbohydrate,
55g total fat (19g saturated), 163mg cholesterol, 170mg sodium**

# GINGER-GLAZED DUCK

*Prep:* 10 minutes   *Roast:* 2 hours 10 minutes
*Makes* 4 main dish servings

1 duckling (about 2kg), cut
  into quarters (see page 135)
½ tsp salt
¼ tsp ground black pepper

3 tsp grated peeled fresh
  ginger
2 tbsp honey
1 tbsp soy sauce

◆ Preheat oven to 180°C (350°F, Gas 4). Discard fat from duckling quarters. Rinse and drain well. Prick skin in several places to drain fat during roasting.

◆ Combine salt, pepper and 1 teaspoon ginger, then rub on inner side of duckling quarters. Place duckling quarters, skin-side up, on rack in large foil-lined roasting tin. Roast 2 hours, spooning off fat from tin occasionally.

◆ Meanwhile, combine remaining 2 teaspoons ginger with honey and soy sauce. Increase oven temperature to 230°C (450°F, Gas 8). Remove duckling from oven and brush on both sides with ginger glaze. Return duckling to oven and roast 10 minutes longer.

**Each serving: About 695 calories, 37g protein, 9g carbohydrate,
55g total fat (19g saturated), 163mg cholesterol, 640mg sodium**

# ROAST CHICKEN

A crisp, golden roasted chicken is a timeless favourite: homely and succulently satisfying. Dress up the flavour with a simple stuffing or rich glaze, or by placing aromatic ingredients such as fresh herbs or thin slices of lemon under the skin. To keep the bird moist and juicy, baste it occasionally during roasting.

## ROAST CHICKEN WITH LEMON AND HERBS

❖❖❖❖❖❖❖❖❖❖❖❖❖❖❖❖❖❖❖❖❖❖❖❖❖❖❖❖❖❖

*Prep: 15 minutes, plus standing and making gravy   Roast: About 2 hours*
*Makes 8 main dish servings*

| | |
|---|---|
| 1 roasting chicken (about 3.1kg), giblets and neck reserved for another use | A few thyme and sage sprigs |
| | 1 tbsp chopped fresh thyme |
| | ½ tsp paprika |
| 4 thin slices lemon | Pan Gravy (see page 144) |
| 4 large fresh sage leaves | Fresh sage leaves for garnish |
| 2 garlic cloves | Roasted potatoes and broccoli |
| 1 lemon, cut in half | (optional) |

### CHECKING CHICKEN FOR DONENESS

You can check chicken for doneness by inserting a knife into thickest part of thigh: the juices should run clear. For complete accuracy, use a meat thermometer; the chicken is done when the reading reaches 74.5–77°C.

1 Preheat oven to 190°C (375°F, Gas 5). Carefully push your fingers between skin and chicken breast to loosen skin. Place lemon slices and large sage leaves under skin.

2 Place garlic cloves, lemon halves and sprigs of thyme and sage inside cavity of chicken.

3 Sprinkle chicken with chopped thyme and paprika. Place chicken breast-side up, lift wings up towards neck and fold them under back so they stay in place. Tie legs together with kitchen string.

4 Place chicken, breast-side up, on rack in medium roasting tin. Insert meat thermometer into thickest part of thigh, next to body, being careful that pointed end of thermometer does not touch bone.

5 Roast, basting occasionally with roasting juices, about 2 hours. When chicken turns golden, cover loosely with tent of foil. Start checking for doneness during last 30 minutes of roasting (see above left).

6 When chicken is cooked through, place on large warm platter and let stand 15 minutes for easier carving; keep warm. Reserve juices and prepare Pan Gravy. To serve, garnish platter with fresh sage leaves. Serve chicken with Pan Gravy, and roasted potatoes and broccoli, if you like.

EACH SERVING: ABOUT 505 CALORIES, 53g PROTEIN, 5g CARBOHYDRATE, 29g TOTAL FAT (8g SATURATED), 211mg CHOLESTEROL, 375mg SODIUM

## Granny's Roast Chicken with Rice and Spinach Stuffing

*Prep: 35 minutes, plus standing    Roast: 2½ hours*
*Makes 8 main dish servings*

2 tbsp vegetable oil
1 onion, diced
200g easy-cook rice
300g frozen chopped spinach, thawed and squeezed dry
2 tbsp fresh lemon juice
1 roasting chicken (about 3.1kg), giblets and neck reserved for another use

1 tsp grated lemon rind
1 tsp dried rosemary, crushed
1 tsp salt
½ tsp ground black pepper
Pan Gravy (see below)

◆ Prepare stuffing: heat 1 tablespoon oil in 3-litre saucepan over medium heat. Add onion and cook until golden. Prepare rice as packet instructs, in pan with onion, but do not use butter. Stir spinach and lemon juice into cooked rice.

◆ Preheat oven to 180°C (350°F, Gas 4). Spoon some stuffing lightly into neck cavity of chicken. Fold neck skin over stuffing; fasten to back with 1 or 2 skewers. Place chicken breast-side up and lift wings up towards neck, then fold them under back of chicken so they stay in place.

◆ Spoon more stuffing lightly into body cavity. Close by folding skin lightly over opening, using skewer if necessary. Tie legs and tail together with string. (Bake any leftover stuffing in small covered ovenproof dish during last 30 minutes of roasting time.)

◆ Place chicken, breast-side up, on rack in medium roasting tin. Mix lemon rind, rosemary, salt, pepper and remaining 1 tablespoon oil together. Rub chicken all over with herb mixture. Insert meat thermometer into thickest part of thigh, next to body, being careful that pointed end of thermometer does not touch bone.

### PAN GRAVY

Remove rack from roasting tin. Add 60ml dry vermouth to juices in tin. Bring to the boil over high heat, stirring to loosen brown bits. Add 300ml chicken stock and boil 3 minutes. Pour stock mixture into measuring jug or gravy separator; let stand a few seconds until fat separates from liquid. Return 2 tablespoons fat to roasting tin; skim and discard remaining fat. Add 2 tablespoons plain flour to roasting tin and cook over low heat, stirring, 1 minute. Gradually stir in stock mixture, and ¼ teaspoon each salt and ground black pepper. Return to the boil, stirring; boil 1 minute. Makes about 300ml.

Each 100ml: About 135 calories, 0g protein, 7g carbohydrate, 7g total fat (0g saturated), 13mg cholesterol, 600mg sodium

◆ Roast, basting occasionally with roasting juices, about 2½ hours. When chicken turns golden, cover loosely with foil. Start checking for doneness during last 30 minutes of roasting. Chicken is done when temperature reaches 74.5–77°C and juices run clear when thickest part of thigh is pierced with tip of knife. Place chicken on warm platter; let stand 15 minutes, keep warm. Reserve roasting juices. Prepare Pan Gravy. Serve chicken with stuffing and gravy.

Each serving: About 645 calories, 56g protein, 27g carbohydrate, 34g total fat (9g saturated), 215mg cholesterol, 925mg sodium

## Mahogany Roast Chicken

*Prep: 10 minutes, plus standing    Roast: 1¼ hours*
*Makes 4 main dish servings*

1 chicken (about 1.5kg), giblets and neck reserved for another use
¾ tsp salt
½ tsp coarsely ground black pepper

2 tbsp dry vermouth
2 tbsp dark brown sugar
2 tbsp balsamic vinegar

◆ Preheat oven to 190°C (375°F, Gas 5). Prepare chicken for roasting as in Steps 3 and 4 of Roast Chicken with Lemon and Herbs (see page 143), but sprinkle chicken with salt and pepper.

◆ Roast chicken 45 minutes. Meanwhile, prepare glaze: stir vermouth, brown sugar and vinegar together in small bowl until sugar dissolves. After 45 minutes, brush chicken with some glaze. Increase temperature to 200°C (400°F, Gas 6); roast 30 minutes longer, brushing with glaze twice more, or until thermometer reaches 74.5–77°C and juices run clear when thickest part of thigh is pierced with tip of knife.

◆ Place chicken on warm platter and let stand 15 minutes; keep warm. Meanwhile, add *60ml water* to juices in roasting tin and bring to the boil over medium heat, stirring until brown bits are loosened. Remove from heat, skim and discard fat. Serve chicken with pan juices.

Each serving: About 450 calories, 47g protein, 9g carbohydrate, 23g total fat (6g saturated), 186mg cholesterol, 540mg sodium

### GRAVY SEPARATOR

This handy tool makes it easy to skim fat. Simply fill the jug with stock or roasting juices and let it stand for a moment. The fat will rise to the top, so the fat-free liquid can be poured out of the spout from the bottom.

# ROAST POUSSINS

Poussins are small chickens, less than six weeks old. Weighing slightly less than half a kilogram, each poussin will feed one to two people. A favourite for entertaining, poussins are easy to prepare and make an elegant entrée served alongside an innovative pilaf or colourful vegetables. Roasting offers the best results: crisp, golden skin and moist, tender meat.

## POUSSINS WITH WILD-RICE PILAFF

❖❖❖❖❖❖❖❖❖❖❖❖❖❖❖❖❖❖❖❖❖❖

*Prep: 60–65 minutes*    *Roast: 35 minutes*
*Makes 2 main dish servings*

1 tbsp olive oil
1 large carrot, diced
1 medium yellow pepper, diced
1 medium onion, diced
75g wild rice, rinsed
Salt
1 garlic clove, very finely chopped

1 tsp chopped fresh oregano or ¼ tsp dried
¼ tsp ground black pepper
1 poussin (450g), cut lengthways in half (see page 146)

**1** Prepare pilaf: heat oil over medium-high heat in 2-litre saucepan. Add carrot, yellow pepper, and onion and cook, stirring frequently, until tender and lightly browned.

**2** Stir in wild rice, ¼ teaspoon salt, and *60ml water*. Heat to boiling over high heat. Reduce heat to low; cover and simmer 45–50 minutes, until wild rice is tender and liquid is absorbed. Keep warm.

**3** Meanwhile, preheat oven to 220°C (425°F, Gas 7). Mix garlic, oregano, ¼ teaspoon salt and black pepper together in small bowl; rub over poussin halves. Place halves, skin-side up, in small roasting tin.

**4** Roast, brushing occasionally with roasting juices, about 35 minutes, until browned and juices run clear when poussin is pierced with tip of knife. Transfer poussin halves to 2 warm plates; keep warm.

**5** Using large spoon, skim fat from roasting juices in tin; discard fat. Stir *3 tablespoons hot water* into juices in tin. Stir until brown bits are loosened. Spoon juices over poussin halves; serve with wild-rice pilaf.

---

### WILD RICE

Prized for its nutty flavour and chewy texture, wild rice isn't really a rice at all. It's actually a marsh grass native to the northern part of the U.S., around the Great Lakes. Because it requires special harvesting methods, wild rice is expensive. You can make it go further, however, by combining it with other grains. Wild rice should always be rinsed before using. Depending on the variety of the rice used, it can take up to an hour to cook.

EACH SERVING: ABOUT 510 CALORIES, 40g PROTEIN, 45g CARBOHYDRATE, 19g TOTAL FAT (4g SATURATED), 90mg CHOLESTEROL, 640mg SODIUM

## POUSSINS PROVENÇALE

*Prep: 15 minutes    Roast: 35 minutes*
*Makes 6 main dish servings*

1 tbsp olive or vegetable oil
1 small garlic clove, very
  finely chopped
½ tsp dried thyme
½ tsp salt
¼ tsp ground black pepper
3 poussins (450g each), each
  cut lengthways in half (see
  below)

2 large onions, each cut into
  quarters
10 medium stoned ripe olives,
  coarsely chopped
3 large tomatoes, each cut
  into quarters

◆ Preheat oven to 220°C (425°F, Gas 7). Mix oil, garlic, thyme, salt and pepper in small bowl. Rub poussin halves with oil mixture; place skin-side up in large roasting tin.

◆ Arrange onion quarters and chopped olives around poussins and roast 25 minutes, brushing poussins occasionally with roasting juices. Add tomatoes and cook about 10 minutes longer, or until juices run clear when poussins are pierced with tip of knife. Transfer poussins with olives and vegetables to platter. Skim and discard fat from juices; serve poussins with juices.

**Each serving: About 310 calories, 33g protein, 10g carbohydrate, 15g total fat (4g saturated), 90mg cholesterol, 320mg sodium**

## CITRUS-GLAZED POUSSINS

*Prep: 10 minutes    Roast: 35 minutes*
*Makes 4 main dish servings*

2 poussins (450g each), each
  cut lengthways in half (see
  below)

1 small lemon
4 tbsp orange marmalade
2 tsp soy sauce

◆ Preheat oven to 220°C (425°F, Gas 7). Place poussins, skin-side up, in large roasting tin. Roast poussins, brushing occasionally with roasting juices, about 35 mintues, until juices run clear when poussins are pierced with tip of knife. Meanwhile, grate 1 teaspoon peel and squeeze 1 tablespoon juice from lemon into 1-litre saucepan. Add marmalade and soy sauce; heat over low heat until marmalade melts.

### HALVING SMALL BIRDS

Small poultry can be cut in half before or after cooking. Poultry shears are easiest but a large knife will also work well. Place bird on a chopping board, back down. Slit closely along breastbone with a knife to loosen the meat. Cut along one side of the breastbone with shears. Turn bird over; cut along each side of backbone and discard it.

◆ Brush poussin halves with marmalade mixture frequently during last 10 minutes of roasting time. Skim and discard fat from roasting juices; serve poussins with roasting juices.

**Each serving: About 300 calories, 32g protein, 15g carbohydrate, 12g total fat (3g saturated), 92mg cholesterol, 260mg sodium**

## POUSSINS WITH ACORN SQUASH

*Prep: 20 minutes    Roast: 1¼ hours*
*Makes 6 main dish servings*

2 medium acorn squash
  (about 600g each)
3 poussins (450g each)
¾ tsp salt
½ tsp coarsely ground black
  pepper

225ml cider or apple juice
90g pitted prunes
2 cinnamon sticks
  (7–8cm each)

◆ Preheat oven to 190°C (375°F, Gas 5). Cut each acorn squash lengthways in half; remove and discard seeds. Cut each squash half lengthwise into 3 wedges; remove peel from wedges. Cut each wedge diagonally in half.

◆ Lift wings of poussins toward neck, then fold them under back of poussins so they stay in place. With string, tie legs of each poussin together.

◆ Place poussins, breast-side up, in large roasting tin; rub with salt and pepper. Arrange squash in roasting tin around poussins.

◆ Roast poussins and squash 30 minutes. Add cider, prunes, and cinnamon sticks to tin. Roast, basting poussins occasionally with roasting juices, 45 minutes longer, or until squash is tender and juices run clear when poussins are pierced with tip of knife.

◆ Cut each poussin lengthways in half (see below left). To serve, arrange poussins, squash, prunes and cinnamon sticks on large platter. Skim and discard fat from roasting juices; serve poussins with juices.

**Each serving: About 380 calories, 34g protein, 36g carbohydrate, 12g total fat (3g saturated), 92mg cholesterol, 360mg sodium**

### POULTRY SHEARS

These curved shears are used to split both large and small birds. The serrated blades are spring-loaded, which forces them apart. After using, wash in hot, soapy water to avoid the risk of salmonella.

# ROAST TURKEY BREAST

Ideal for white-meat-only fans, a turkey breast is deliciously versatile. Pound it flat and roll round a tasty filling, then slice and serve hot or cold for an easy but impressive main dish. Or, alternatively, simply roast it whole and serve with all the traditional accompaniments.

## STUFFED TURKEY BREAST WITH BASIL SAUCE

◆ ◆ ◆ ◆ ◆ ◆ ◆ ◆ ◆ ◆ ◆ ◆

*Prep: 25 minutes, plus standing*
*Roast: 1¼–1½ hours*
*Makes 8 main dish servings*

1 skinless, boneless turkey-
    breast (about 900g)
75g fresh basil leaves
125g cooked ham, thinly
    sliced
125g Jarlsberg cheese, thinly
    sliced
1 tbsp olive oil
½ tsp dried basil
½ tsp coarsely ground black
    pepper
¼ tsp salt
Basil Sauce (see right)
Basil sprigs and cherry
    tomatoes for garnish

**1** Preheat oven to 170°C (325°F, Gas 3). Holding knife parallel to work surface, cut turkey breast horizontally almost but not all the way through.

**2** Open out turkey breast. Using rolling pin, pound breast between 2 sheets of cling film into 30 by 25cm rectangle.

**3** Cover turkey breast with basil leaves; top with ham and then cheese. Starting from a long side, roll up Swiss roll style to enclose stuffing completely.

### BASIL SAUCE

Mix 225g mayonnaise, 2 teaspoons white wine vinegar, ½ teaspoon sugar, 15g chopped fresh basil and ½ teaspoon salt together in medium bowl. Chill until ready to serve. Makes 8 servings.

**4** Tie roll securely with string at 4cm intervals. Place on rack in small roasting tin. Mix olive oil, dried basil, black pepper and salt together in small bowl; brush over turkey-breast roll.

**5** Insert meat thermometer into centre of roll. Roast 1¼–1½ hours, brushing occasionally with roasting juices, until thermometer reaches 72°C. Meanwhile, prepare Basil Sauce. Transfer turkey to chopping board; discard string. Let stand 15 minutes for easier slicing. Cut crossways into 1cm thick slices and arrange on warm large platter. Garnish with basil sprigs and cherry tomatoes. Serve turkey with Basil Sauce.

EACH SERVING: ABOUT 415 CALORIES, 35g PROTEIN, 2g CARBOHYDRATE, 28g TOTAL FAT (4g SATURATED), 99mg CHOLESTEROL, 640mg SODIUM

# TURKEY PINWHEELS

*Prep: 45 minutes, plus standing   Roast: 1¼–1½ hours*
*Makes 12 main dish servings*

2 tbsp plus 2 tsp vegetable oil
450g carrots, diced
2 medium onions, diced
1 large red pepper, cored,
    seeded and diced
1 medium celery stalk, diced
Salt
2 tbsp dried breadcrumbs

25g Parmesan cheese, freshly
    grated
15g fresh parsley, chopped
1 skinless, boneless turkey-
    breast (1.1kg)
1 tsp coarsely ground black
    pepper

◆ Heat 2 tablespoons oil in 30cm frying pan over medium-high heat. Add carrots, onions, red pepper, celery and 1 teaspoon salt and cook, stirring frequently, about 15 minutes until vegetables are well browned.

◆ Add *125ml water* and bring to the boil over high heat. Reduce heat to low; cover and simmer 5 minutes, or until vegetables are tender. Uncover and continue cooking until any liquid in pan evaporates.

◆ Remove pan from heat. Stir in breadcrumbs, Parmesan cheese and half of chopped parsley.

◆ Preheat oven to 170°C (325°F, Gas 3). Holding knife parallel to work surface, and starting from long side of turkey breast, cut horizontally almost, but not all the way, through. Open out turkey breast to make a butterflied breast. Using rolling pin, pound butterflied breast between 2 sheets of cling film into 35 by 30cm rectangle.

◆ Spread vegetable mixture evenly over entire turkey breast. Starting from long side, roll up turkey, Swiss-roll style, to enclose stuffing completely. Tie roll securely with string at 4cm intervals. Place on rack in small roasting tin.

◆ Mix black pepper, ¾ teaspoon salt and remaining 2 teaspoons oil and chopped parsley together in small bowl; pat over roll. Insert meat thermometer into centre of roll. Roast 1¼–1½ hours, brushing occasionally with roasting juices, until thermometer reaches 72°C.

◆ Transfer turkey to chopping board and discard string. Let roll stand 15 minutes for easier slicing. To serve, cut roll crossways into 1cm thick slices. Arrange turkey slices on warm large platter.

**Each serving: About 175 calories, 25g protein, 8g carbohydrate, 4g total fat (1g saturated), 60mg cholesterol, 405mg sodium**

# HERB-ROASTED TURKEY BREAST

*Prep: 10 minutes plus, refrigerating and standing*
*Roast: 2–2¼ hours*
*Makes 8 main dish servings*

15g fresh basil, chopped
1 tbsp salt
1 tsp fennel seeds, crushed
¼ tsp coarsely ground black
    pepper

1 whole turkey breast,
    including both breast fillets
    (about 2.2kg)
Vegetable oil

◆ Mix basil, salt, fennel seeds and pepper together in small bowl and rub mixture all over turkey. Place turkey breast in large bowl, cover with cling film and refrigerate overnight.

◆ Preheat oven to 170°C (325°F, Gas 3). Place turkey breast, skin-side up, on rack in medium roasting tin and rub skin with oil.

◆ Insert meat thermometer into thickest part of meat, being careful that pointed end of thermometer does not touch bone. Cover with loose tent of foil.

◆ Roast 2–2¼ hours. Start checking for doneness during last 30 minutes. To brown turkey breast, remove foil during last 20–30 minutes of roasting, and brush generously with roasting juices for an attractive sheen. The turkey breast is done when thermometer reaches 72°C.

◆ When turkey breast is cooked through, place it on warm large platter and let stand 15 minutes for easier slicing. Or, to serve cold, allow to cool completely then cover and refrigerate at least 3 hours. Cut into thin slices.

**Each serving: About 345 calories, 58g protein, 0g carbohydrate, 11g total fat (3g saturated), 108mg cholesterol, 870mg sodium**

◆◆◆◆◆◆◆◆◆◆◆◆◆◆◆◆◆◆◆◆◆◆◆◆◆

## BONING A TURKEY BREAST

1 Hold sharp knife almost flat against the bone and rib-cage, then gently cut and scrape meat away, pulling it off in one piece as you cut.

2 Discard the bones. Remove skin, then use knife to gently cut away the white tendon.

◆◆◆◆◆◆◆◆◆◆◆◆◆◆◆◆◆◆◆◆◆◆◆◆◆

# ROASTED OR BAKED CHICKEN PIECES

Roasting is a terrific way to cook chicken pieces coated with aromatic seasonings, such as thyme, rosemary and paprika, or enhanced with spicy marinades like the Indian-style yogurt mixture used in our Tandoori-style Chicken. Vegetables roasted in the roasting tin along with the chicken and basted with the roasting juices add flavour to the dish and keep preparation simple. Make sure your roasting tin is large enough so that the chicken pieces roast evenly, and remove quicker-cooking breast pieces first. To keep cooked chicken warm, just cover the pieces loosely with a sheet of foil.

**1** Preheat oven to 230°C (450°F, Gas 8). Cut potatoes into 5cm chunks. Trim fennel bulb, reserving some feathery tops for garnish; cut bulb into 8 wedges. Cut red onion into 8 wedges.

**2** Toss chicken and vegetables with olive oil in large roasting tin. Sprinkle with chopped thyme, salt and pepper.

## THYME-ROASTED CHICKEN AND VEGETABLES

◆◆◆◆◆◆◆◆◆◆◆◆◆◆◆◆◆◆◆◆◆◆◆◆◆

*Prep:* 20 minutes   *Roast:* 50 minutes
*Makes* 4 main dish servings

450g potatoes, unpeeled
1 large fennel bulb (about 750g)
1 large red onion
1 chicken (about 1.3kg), cut into 8 pieces (see page 134) and skin removed

2 tbsp olive oil
1 tbsp chopped fresh thyme or 1 tsp dried
1¼ tsp salt
¼ tsp ground black pepper
Thyme sprigs for garnish

**3** Roast chicken and vegetables 20 minutes, basting with roasting juices. Roast chicken 20 minutes longer, basting once, until juices run clear when chicken breasts are pierced with tip of knife. Transfer chicken breasts to large serving bowl and keep warm.

**4** Roast remaining chicken pieces and vegetables 10 minutes longer, or until the juices run clear when chicken pieces are pierced with tip of knife and vegetables are tender. Transfer to serving bowl with chicken breasts.

**5** Add *75ml hot water* to juices in pan, stirring until brown bits are loosened. Spoon juices over chicken and vegetables. Garnish with thyme sprigs and reserved fennel tops.

EACH SERVING: ABOUT 430 CALORIES, 38g PROTEIN, 36g CARBOHYDRATE, 16g TOTAL FAT (3g SATURATED), 101mg CHOLESTEROL, 860mg SODIUM

# BAKED LIME CHICKEN

*Prep: 15 minutes   Bake: 50 minutes*
*Makes 4 main dish servings*

2 small limes
1 chicken (about 1.5kg), cut
   into 8 pieces (see page 134)
45g margarine or butter
40g plain flour
¾ tsp salt
½ tsp ground black pepper

2 tbsp light brown sugar
400ml chicken stock
Lime rind strips and lime
   wedges for garnish
Carrots and mashed potatoes
   (optional)

◆ Preheat oven to 200°C (400°F, Gas 6). Grate all rind and squeeze 2 tablespoons juice from limes. Toss chicken with lime juice in large bowl. Melt margarine in large roasting tin in oven. Remove tin from oven.

◆ Mix flour, salt and pepper together on sheet of greaseproof paper and use to coat chicken pieces. Dip chicken pieces, one at a time, into melted margarine in roasting tin, turning to coat. Arrange chicken, skin-side up, in tin. (Do not use smaller tin and crowd chicken pieces; they won't brown.)

◆ Mix grated lime rind and brown sugar together in small bowl; sprinkle over chicken pieces. Pour stock into tin. Bake 50 minutes, basting chicken with pan juices occasionally, or until chicken is tender and juices run clear when pierced with tip of knife.

◆ To serve, transfer chicken to 4 plates. Skim fat from roasting juices. Spoon juices over chicken. Garnish with lime rind strips and lime wedges. Serve with carrots and mashed potatoes, if you like.

**Each serving: About 505 calories, 43g protein, 14g carbohydrate, 29g total fat (7g saturated), 166mg cholesterol, 650mg sodium**

# HERB CHICKEN

*Prep: 10 minutes   Roast: 40 minutes*
*Makes 8 main dish servings*

2 tbsp chopped fresh thyme
   or 2 tsp dried
2 tbsp chopped fresh
   rosemary or 2 tsp dried,
   crushed
1 tbsp olive oil
2 tsp paprika

1½ tsp salt
1 tsp coarsely ground black
   pepper
2 chickens (1.5kg each), each
   cut into quarters
Fresh thyme and rosemary
   sprigs for garnish

◆ Preheat oven to 200°C (425°F, Gas 6). Mix thyme and rosemary, olive oil, paprika, salt and pepper together in small bowl; rub over chicken quarters. Place chicken, skin-side up, on rack in large roasting tin. Roast chicken (do not turn) 40 minutes, or until golden and juices run clear when pierced with tip of knife.

◆ Serve hot, or allow to cool and refrigerate to serve cold later. To serve, arrange chicken on platter. Tuck thyme and rosemary sprigs among chicken quarters.

**Each serving: About 380 calories, 42g protein, 1g carbohydrate, 22g total fat (6g saturated), 166mg cholesterol, 520mg sodium**

# TANDOORI-STYLE CHICKEN

*Prep: 10 minutes, plus marinating   Roast: 30 minutes*
*Makes 6 main dish servings*

225g plain low-fat yogurt
½ small onion, chopped
2 tbsp fresh lime juice
1 tbsp finely chopped peeled
   fresh ginger
1 tbsp paprika
1 tsp ground cumin
1 tsp ground coriander

¾ tsp salt
¼ tsp ground red pepper
Pinch ground cloves
6 chicken breasts (about
   1.3kg), skin removed
Lime wedges for garnish
Cooked basmati rice
   (optional)

◆ Blend all ingredients, except chicken, lime wedges and rice, in blender on high speed or food processor with knife blade attached until smooth. Place chicken in bowl with yogurt marinade, turning to coat. Marinate in refrigerator at least 30 minutes.

◆ Preheat oven to 230°C (450°F, Gas 8). Place chicken on rack in medium roasting tin. Spoon half of marinade over chicken (discard remaining marinade). Roast 30 minutes, or until juices run clear when pierced with tip of knife. Garnish with lime. Serve with basmati rice, if you like.

**Each serving: About 210 calories, 36g protein, 5g carbohydrate, 5g total fat (1g saturated), 94mg cholesterol, 375mg sodium**

# OVEN-FRIED CHICKEN

You get all the crispness of fried chicken – without the extra fat and fuss of deep-frying – in the oven. Remove the skin before coating to cut the fat further. Use herbs, spices and other flavourings to add variety to the crust – or use a little cornmeal for some crunch.

## CHICKEN MEXICANA

❖❖❖❖❖❖❖❖❖❖❖❖❖

*Prep:* 15 minutes
*Bake:* 40–45 minutes
*Makes* 8 main dish servings

125g canned or bottled mild green chillies, drained and chopped
8 tbsp Dijon mustard
1 tbsp fresh lime juice
½ tsp ground black pepper
35g dried breadcrumbs
35g yellow cornmeal
1 tbsp paprika
2 tbsp coarsely chopped fresh coriander or parsley
½ tsp salt
1 tsp dried oregano
2 chickens (1.3kg each), each cut into 8 pieces (see page 134) and skin removed
2 tbsp olive or vegetable oil
Tomato-Cucumber Salsa (optional, see right)
Lime slices, coriander and sliced pickled jalapeño chillies for garnish
Warm flour tortillas (optional)

**1** Mix chillies, mustard, lime juice and pepper together in bowl. Mix breadcrumbs and next 5 ingredients together on sheet of greaseproof paper.

**2** Preheat oven to 220°C (425°F, Gas 7). Brush mustard mixture evenly onto chicken. Coat with breadcrumb mixture, firmly pressing onto chicken.

**3** Grease large roasting tin. Place chicken pieces in roasting tin in single layer. Using pastry brush, lightly dab oil onto chicken.

---

### TOMATO-CUCUMBER SALSA

Cut 2 medium cucumbers, unpeeled, lengthways in half, then remove seeds and dice. Whisk 3 tablespoons olive or vegetable oil, 3 tablespoons red wine vinegar, ¾ teaspoon sugar, ¾ teaspoon salt and ½ teaspoon coarsely ground black pepper together in large bowl until blended. Stir in diced cucumbers, 4 seeded and diced medium tomatoes and 2 diced medium green peppers until well combined. Refrigerate until ready to serve. Makes 8 servings.

Each serving: About 75 calories, 1g protein, 7g carbohydrate, 5g total fat (1g saturated), 0mg cholesterol, 205mg sodium

**4** Bake chicken (do not turn) 40–45 minutes, until crisp and juices run clear when pierced with tip of knife. Meanwhile, prepare Tomato-Cucumber Salsa, if desired. Garnish and serve with salsa and tortillas, if you like.

---

EACH SERVING: ABOUT 365 CALORIES, 38g PROTEIN, 18g CARBOHYDRATE, 14g TOTAL FAT (3g SATURATED), 109mg CHOLESTEROL, 760mg SODIUM

# 'FRIED' CHICKEN

*Prep: 25 minutes   Bake: 40 minutes*
*Makes 8 main dish servings*

4 chicken breasts (about 1kg)
4 large chicken legs
  (about 1kg)
225g plain very low-fat yogurt
1¼ tsp salt
100g dried breadcrumbs
2 tbsp chopped fresh
  coriander or parsley
¾ tsp coarsely ground black
  pepper
Coriander or parsley sprigs
  for garnish

◆ Preheat oven to 220°C (425°F, Gas 7). Remove skin and fat from chicken. Cut each leg at joint, separating drumstick from thigh.

◆ Mix yogurt and salt together in shallow dish. Mix breadcrumbs, chopped coriander and black pepper together on sheet of greaseproof paper. Coat each piece of chicken lightly with yogurt mixture, then coat with breadcrumb mixture.

◆ Arrange chicken pieces in single layer in large roasting tin. Bake chicken (do not turn) 40 minutes, or until juices run clear when pierced with tip of knife.

◆ When chicken is cooked through, if you like, turn on grill. Grill chicken in tin 4–5 minutes until coating is golden brown. To serve, arrange chicken on warm large platter. Garnish with coriander sprigs.

Each serving: About 365 calories, 43g protein, 12g carbohydrate, 15g total fat (4g saturated), 124mg cholesterol, 580mg sodium

# 'FRIED' CHICKEN WITH CORNMEAL CRUST

*Prep: 15 minutes   Bake: 35 minutes*
*Makes 4 main dish servings*

Olive-oil non-stick cooking
  spray
50g dried breadcrumbs
25g Parmesan cheese, freshly
  grated
2 tbsp yellow cornmeal
½ tsp ground red pepper
1 medium egg white
½ tsp salt
1 chicken, 1.5kg, cut into
  8 pieces (see page 134)
  and skin removed

◆ Preheat oven to 220°C (425°F, Gas 7). Spray shallow baking tray with olive-oil non-stick cooking spray.

◆ Mix breadcrumbs, Parmesan, cornmeal and ground red pepper together on sheet of greaseproof paper.

◆ Beat egg white and salt together in shallow dish. Coat each piece of chicken with egg-white mixture, then coat with breadcrumb mixture. Place chicken on baking tray and spray lightly with cooking spray.

◆ Bake chicken (do not turn the pieces) 35 minutes, or until coating is crisp and golden and juices run clear when chicken is pierced with tip of knife.

Each serving: About 370 calories, 47g protein, 14g carbohydrate, 13g total fat (4g saturated), 132mg cholesterol, 635mg sodium

# CRISPY CHICKEN WITH PARMESAN TOMATOES

*Prep: 15 minutes   Bake: 35–40 minutes*
*Makes 2 main dish servings*

25g dried breadcrumbs
1 tbsp chopped fresh parsley
1 small garlic clove, very
  finely chopped
2 tsp olive or vegetable oil
Coarsely ground black pepper
2 tbsp Dijon mustard
2 chicken breasts (about
  750g)
350g plum tomatoes
25g Parmesan cheese, freshly
  grated
1 tsp dried oregano

◆ Preheat oven to 200°C (400°F, Gas 6).

◆ Mix breadcrumbs, parsley, garlic, olive oil and ¼ teaspoon pepper together in small bowl until blended. Brush mustard onto skin side of each chicken breast, then coat with crumb mixture, firmly pressing crumb mixture onto chicken.

◆ Grease an ovenproof dish. Place chicken, skin-side up, in dish and bake (do not turn) 20 minutes.

◆ Meanwhile, cut each tomato lengthways in half. Mix Parmesan cheese, oregano and ¼ teaspoon pepper together on sheet of greaseproof paper. Sprinkle mixture evenly over tomato halves.

◆ Add tomatoes to dish and bake 15–20 minutes longer, until coating is crisp and browned and juices run clear when chicken is pierced with tip of knife.

Each serving: About 550 calories, 62g protein, 21g carbohydrate, 23g total fat (6g saturated), 161mg cholesterol, 1055mg sodium

## COOKING SPRAYS

Cooking sprays provide a quick, easy way to grease frying pans, baking tins and ovenproof dishes and are especially helpful for ornate, fluted tube tins or barbecue grill racks (make sure to spray unheated rack). Although they add very little taste, olive-oil- or butter-flavoured varieties are available. For an instant snack, lightly spray triangles of pitta bread, top with crumbled oregano and bake until golden.

# STUFFED CHICKEN PIECES

Imaginative stuffings can dress up chicken pieces as well as whole birds. One technique is to form a 'pocket' by separating the skin from the meat and then tucking the stuffing into the space formed. The skin will keep the filling next to the meat, infusing it with flavour. Alternatively, a flattened boneless chicken breast can be rolled around a filling and then secured with cocktail sticks. Aromatic basil and dried tomatoes, summer-ripe courgettes, and tangy feta cheese all feature in the stuffings given here.

## CHICKEN BREASTS STUFFED WITH SUN-DRIED TOMATOES AND BASIL

*Prep:* 20 minutes   *Bake:* 35–40 minutes
*Makes* 4 main dish servings

1 bunch basil
60g oil-packed sun-dried
   tomatoes, drained
Coarsely ground black pepper
25g Parmesan cheese, freshly
   grated
4 chicken breasts (about
   1.1kg)

1 tbsp oil from sun-dried
   tomatoes
½ tsp salt
Courgette Ribbons with Mint
   (optional, see page 304)

1 Preheat oven to 220°C (425°F, Gas 7). Chop 15g basil; reserve remaining sprigs for garnish. Coarsely chop sun-dried tomatoes.

2 Mix basil, tomatoes, ½ teaspoon pepper and Parmesan together in bowl. Push fingers between skin and meat of each chicken breast to form pocket.

3 Place some basil mixture in each pocket. Place chicken breasts, skin-side up, in 33 by 20cm ovenproof dish.

4 Brush chicken with oil from sun-dried tomatoes; sprinkle with salt and ½ teaspoon pepper. Bake, basting occasionally with juices, 35–40 minutes until browned and juices run clear when chicken is pierced with tip of knife. Serve chicken garnished with remaining basil sprigs and Courgette Ribbons with Mint, if you like.

### FRESH BASIL

Fresh basil has a warm, sweet aroma quite unlike the dried herb (which has a more grassy, minty flavour). Purple opal basil is a pretty variety that has a spicier taste. To store, place basil in a jar, with stems in 5cm water, then cover with a plastic bag and secure with a rubber band.

**EACH SERVING: ABOUT 365 CALORIES, 48g PROTEIN, 2g CARBOHYDRATE, 17g TOTAL FAT (5g SATURATED), 133mg CHOLESTEROL, 450mg SODIUM**

## CHEESE-STUFFED CHICKEN

*Prep:* 30 minutes   *Bake:* 45 minutes

*Makes* 6 main dish servings

1 tbsp olive oil

1 medium onion, very finely chopped

1 small carrot, grated

1 bunch watercress, tough stalks trimmed, chopped

225g ricotta cheese

25g Parmesan cheese, freshly grated

60g Emmental cheese, grated

⅛ tsp coarsely ground black pepper

3 chicken breasts (about 800g)

3 chicken-leg quarters (about 750g)

½ tsp salt

◆ Heat oil in 26cm frying pan over medium heat. Add onion and carrot. Cover and cook 5 minutes, stirring occasionally. Add watercress and cook, uncovered, until just wilted, stirring. Remove from heat and cool slightly. Preheat oven to 200°C (400°F, Gas 6).

◆ Add cheeses and pepper to vegetable mixture in pan; stir to combine. Push fingers between chicken skin and meat to form pocket; fill with stuffing. Place chicken, stuffing-side up, in large roasting tin; sprinkle with salt.

◆ Bake 45 minutes, basting frequently, or until juices run clear when chicken is pierced with tip of knife. Serve chicken with roasting juices.

**Each serving: About 425 calories, 45g protein, 5g carbohydrate, 24g total fat (10g saturated), 143mg cholesterol, 420mg sodium**

## COURGETTE-STUFFED CHICKEN

*Prep:* 20 minutes   *Bake:* 50 minutes

*Makes* 4 main dish servings

2 tbsp olive oil

2 medium courgettes (450g), grated

3 slices white bread, torn into fine crumbs

60g Emmental cheese, grated

1 medium egg

½ tsp salt

⅛ tsp ground black pepper

1 chicken (about 1.3 kg), cut into quarters

2 tbsp honey

◆ Preheat oven to 200°C (400°F, Gas 6). Heat olive oil in 2-litre saucepan over medium heat. Add courgettes and cook, stirring, about 2 minutes. Remove from heat. Stir in bread and cheese, then egg, salt and pepper.

◆ Carefully push fingers between chicken skin and meat to form pocket; fill with stuffing. Place chicken, skin-side up, in roasting tin. Bake 50 minutes, or until juices run clear when chicken is pierced with tip of knife. Brush with honey.

**Each serving: About 540 calories, 44g protein, 22g carbohydrate, 30g total fat (9g saturated), 208g cholesterol, 530g sodium**

## GREEK-STYLE CHICKEN

*Prep:* 25 minutes   *Cook:* 25 minutes

*Makes* 6 main dish servings

125g feta cheese, crumbled

1 tbsp fresh lemon juice

1 tsp dried oregano

6 skinless, boneless chicken breasts (about 900g)

¾ tsp salt

¼ tsp ground black pepper

2 tbsp plain flour

2 tbsp olive oil

¼ chicken stock cube, crumbled

1 tomato, peeled and diced

300–350g spinach, coarsely sliced

Toasted pitta wedges (optional)

◆ Using fork, mix feta cheese, lemon juice and oregano in small bowl until smooth. Using rolling pin or meat mallet, pound each chicken breast between 2 sheets cling film to 1cm thickness.

◆ Spread cheese mixture over each breast to within 1cm of edge. Fold each chicken breast crossways in half to enclose filling; secure with wooden cocktail stick. Mix salt, pepper and 1 tablespoon flour on sheet greaseproof paper; coat chicken with flour mixture.

◆ Heat oil in 30cm frying pan over medium-high heat. Add chicken and cook until golden brown on both sides, turning once. Meanwhile, mix stock cube, remaining 1 tablespoon flour and *225ml water* together in small bowl until smooth. Add to pan with tomato and spinach; bring to the boil over high heat. Reduce heat to low; cover and simmer 8–10 minutes, until juices run clear when chicken is pierced with tip of knife. To serve, remove and discard cocktail sticks. Serve chicken with pitta wedges, if you like.

**Each serving: About 285 calories, 37g protein, 5g carbohydrate, 12g total fat (5g saturated), 125mg cholesterol, 690mg sodium**

# PAN-FRIED POULTRY

Lean, quick-cooking cuts of poultry benefit from pan-frying. Sealing keeps in the juices; a light coating of flour gives a golden crust. Use the pan drippings in a sauce, with a medley of mushrooms, or just a dash of wine and some stock.

## FRENCH COUNTRY CHICKEN

◆◆◆◆◆◆◆◆◆◆◆◆◆◆

*Prep:* 20 minutes
*Cook:* 30 minutes
*Makes* 6 main dish servings

**750g skinless, boneless chicken breasts**
**3 tbsp plain flour**
**½ tsp salt**
**¼ tsp ground black pepper**
**2 tbsp chopped fresh tarragon, or 1 tsp dried**
**2 tbsp olive oil**
**450g assorted mushrooms, such as button, brown and shiitake, sliced**
**1 large shallot, finely chopped**
**225ml chicken stock**
**60ml dry white wine**
**Chopped fresh tarragon or parsley for garnish**

### FRYING PANS

A good frying pan has a thick base so heat spreads evenly, low sides so steam can escape and a heat-proof handle. Stainless steel with a copper core, anodized aluminium and heavier cast iron are all excellent heat conductors.

**1** Cut each chicken breast into 3–4 pieces. If pieces are not evenly thin, pound to 3mm thickness (see page 156). Mix flour, salt, pepper and 1 tablespoon chopped tarragon on greaseproof paper; use to coat chicken.

**2** Heat 1 tablespoon oil in 30cm frying pan over medium-high heat. Add mushrooms and shallot and cook, stirring, 12–15 minutes, until any liquid evaporates. Transfer mixture to bowl.

**3** Heat remaining 1 tablespoon oil in same pan. Add half of chicken breasts; cook about 4 minutes per side, until golden. Transfer to platter; keep warm. Repeat with remaining chicken.

**4** Add chicken stock, white wine, mushroom mixture and remaining 1 tablespoon chopped tarragon to drippings in pan. Bring to the boil and boil 1 minute. Pour mushroom sauce over chicken; garnish with chopped tarragon.

EACH SERVING: ABOUT 230 CALORIES, 28g PROTEIN, 10g CARBOHYDRATE, 8g TOTAL FAT (2g SATURATED), 84mg CHOLESTEROL, 395mg SODIUM

## CHICKEN WITH PRAWNS AND CAPERS

*Prep: 25 minutes    Cook: 25 minutes*
*Makes 6 main dish servings*

| | |
|---|---|
| 450g raw large prawns | 300g large mushrooms, sliced |
| 450g skinless, boneless chicken breasts | 1 shallot or small onion, very finely chopped |
| 3 tbsp plain flour | 60ml dry white wine |
| Salt | 2 tbsp canned or bottled drained capers |
| 3 tbsp olive or vegetable oil | |

✦ Peel and de-vein prawns, leaving tail part of shell on, if you like (see page 90). If chicken breasts are not evenly thin, pound to 2mm thickness (see below). Cut chicken into 8 by 5cm pieces. Combine 2 tablespoons flour and ¾ teaspoon salt on greaseproof paper; use to coat chicken.

✦ Heat 1 tablespoon oil in 30cm frying pan over medium-high heat. Add mushrooms and cook, stirring often, 10 minutes, or until golden. Using slotted spoon, transfer mushrooms to large bowl.

✦ Heat 2 teaspoons oil in same pan over medium-high heat. Add prawns and shallot and cook, stirring often, until prawns are opaque throughout. Transfer to bowl with mushrooms. Heat 1 tablespoon oil in same pan over medium-high heat. Add chicken, half at a time, and cook 2–3 minutes, until chicken loses its pink colour throughout. Transfer to same bowl.

✦ Heat remaining oil with drippings in pan over medium-high heat. Stir in remaining 1 tablespoon flour; cook, stirring constantly, about 30 seconds until flour begins to brown slightly. Gradually stir in wine, ½ teaspoon salt and *300ml water*. Cook over high heat until sauce thickens slightly and boils; boil 1 minute. Return chicken mixture to pan, stir in capers and heat through.

**Each serving: About 270 calories, 34g protein, 8g carbohydrate, 10g total fat (2g saturated), 171mg cholesterol, 690mg sodium**

✦✦✦✦✦✦✦✦✦✦✦✦✦✦✦✦✦✦✦✦✦✦✦✦✦✦

### POUNDING POULTRY PIECES

Pounding boneless pieces to a uniform thickness ensures even cooking and helps to tenderize the meat. Place each piece between 2 sheets of parchment paper or cling film and pound with a rolling pin or meat mallet.

✦✦✦✦✦✦✦✦✦✦✦✦✦✦✦✦✦✦✦✦✦✦✦✦✦✦

## SPRING TURKEY AND VEGETABLE PICCATA

*Prep: 25 minutes    Cook: 20 minutes*
*Makes 6 main dish servings*

| | |
|---|---|
| 3 tbsp olive or vegetable oil | 2 medium courgettes (450g), cut into 8cm matchsticks |
| 1 large fennel bulb (about 600g), trimmed and cut into 5mm thick slices | 600g turkey escalopes |
| 3 large carrots, cut into 8cm matchsticks | ½ tsp coarsely ground black pepper |
| 1 medium onion, diced | ¼ tsp dried thyme |
| Salt | 1 large lemon |

✦ Heat 2 tablespoons oil in 30cm non-stick frying pan over medium-high heat. Add fennel, carrots, onion and ½ teaspoon salt and cook, stirring occasionally, until vegetables are lightly browned. Stir in courgettes and cook until vegetables are tender. Transfer vegetable mixture to large bowl.

✦ If turkey escalopes are thick, pound to 2mm thickness (see below left). Cut into 8 by 5cm pieces. Sprinkle with pepper, thyme and ½ teaspoon salt.

✦ Heat remaining 1 tablespoon oil in same pan over medium-high heat. Add turkey, a few pieces at a time, and cook 2–3 minutes until turkey just loses its pink colour throughout. Transfer to bowl with vegetables.

✦ Squeeze juice from half lemon and slice remaining half for garnish. Pour lemon juice and *75ml water* into juices in pan, stirring until brown bits are loosened. Return turkey and vegetables to pan; heat through. Serve garnished with lemon slices.

**Each serving: About 245 calories, 27g protein, 18g carbohydrate, 8g total fat (1g saturated), 59mg cholesterol, 470mg sodium**

### COOKING WITH WINE

◆◆◆◆◆◆◆◆◆◆◆◆◆◆◆◆◆◆◆◆◆◆◆◆◆◆◆◆◆◆

Wine gives sauces, stews and braised dishes an acid balance and a delicious depth of flavour. To avoid a sharp, raw taste, boil the wine to reduce it by at least half. This evaporates the alcohol and concentrates the wine, creating a mellow flavour. Wine can also be used to deglaze pan juices, or as a poaching liquid for fruit. It's essential to use a good-tasting wine, as the flavour in the bottle will be passed on to the final dish. White wines blend with delicate poultry and fish; red wines create a deeper flavour and go well with red meats and game. Salty, smoked or acidic foods can make wine taste flat. Avoid cooking wine in an aluminium pan, or the finished dish may have a metallic taste.

## CHICKEN WITH LEMON-CAPER SAUCE

*Prep:* 15 minutes
*Cook:* 10 minutes
*Makes* 4 main dish servings

2 tbsp plus 1½ tsp plain flour
½ tsp salt
1 medium egg
4 skinless, boneless chicken breasts
　　(about 600g)
2 tsp olive or vegetable oil
30g margarine or butter
125ml chicken stock
60ml dry white wine
2 tbsp fresh lemon juice
3 garlic cloves, cut in half
2 tbsp canned or bottled drained and
　　chopped capers
Chopped fresh parsley for garnish

＊ Mix 2 tablespoons flour with salt on greaseproof paper. Beat egg in shallow dish. Coat chicken with flour mixture, then dip in egg.

＊ Heat oil and 1 tablespoon margarine in 30cm non-stick frying pan over medium-high heat. Add chicken; cook 3 minutes. Reduce heat to medium; turn chicken and cook about 5 minutes longer until juices run clear when chicken is pierced with tip of knife. Transfer to warm platter.

＊ Mix chicken stock, wine, lemon juice and remaining 1½ teaspoons flour in small bowl until smooth. Add garlic to juices in pan and cook until golden. Stir in stock mixture and bring to the boil over high heat. Boil 1 minute. Stir in capers and remaining 1 tablespoon margarine until melted. Discard garlic. Pour sauce over chicken. Garnish with parsley.

**Each serving: About 290 calories, 34g protein, 5g carbohydrate, 13g total fat (3g saturated), 157mg cholesterol, 675mg sodium**

## CHICKEN BREASTS WITH TARRAGON SAUCE

*Prep:* 15 minutes
*Cook:* 25 minutes
*Makes* 4 main dish servings

2 tsp plus 1 tbsp olive or vegetable oil
2 large shallots, thinly sliced
1 tsp salt
1 tbsp chopped fresh tarragon or
　　½ tsp dried
5 tbsp plain flour
4 chicken breasts (about 1.1kg), skin
　　removed
½ chicken stock cube

＊ Heat 2 teaspoons oil in 30cm non-stick frying pan over medium heat. Add shallots and cook until tender and lightly browned. Using slotted spoon, transfer shallots to small bowl.

＊ Mix salt, tarragon and 3 tablespoons flour together on greaseproof paper; use to coat chicken breasts. Heat remaining 1 tablespoon oil in same pan over medium-high heat. Add chicken and cook, turning once, until golden brown. Reduce heat to medium-low, cover and cook about 10 minutes longer, until juices run clear when chicken is pierced with the tip of knife. Place chicken breasts on 4 plates. Keep warm.

＊ Mix remaining 2 tablespoons flour with *350ml water* in small bowl until smooth. Add flour mixture, stock cube and sautéed shallots to juices in pan and bring to the boil over high heat, stirring until brown bits are loosened. Boil 1 minute. To serve, pour sauce over chicken.

**Each serving: About 335 calories, 44g protein, 14g carbohydrate, 11g total fat (2g saturated), 114mg cholesterol, 860mg sodium**

## CHICKEN BREASTS WITH TOMATO-OLIVE SAUCE

*Prep:* 15 minutes
*Cook:* 20 minutes
*Makes* 4 main dish servings

1 tbsp olive or vegetable oil
4 skinless, boneless chicken breasts
　　(about 600g)
1 medium onion, finely chopped
1 tbsp red wine vinegar
750g plum tomatoes, peeled, seeded and
　　chopped
½ cup Kalamata olives, stoned
Cooked pasta (optional)
Flat-leaf parsley sprigs for garnish

＊ Heat oil in 30cm frying pan over medium-high heat. Add chicken breasts and cook about 8 minutes until golden and juices run clear when chicken is pierced with tip of knife. Transfer chicken to plate.

＊ Add onion to drippings in pan and cook over medium heat until tender-crisp. Add vinegar and cook until onion is very tender. Stir in chopped tomatoes and olives and bring to the boil over high heat.

＊ Return chicken to pan and heat through. Serve with pasta, if you like; garnish with parsley.

**Each serving: About 300 calories, 34g protein, 13g carbohydrate, 13g total fat (2g saturated), 101mg cholesterol, 615mg sodium**

## SMOTHERED CHICKEN AND PEPPERS

*Prep: 15 minutes    Cook: 30 minutes*
*Makes 4 main dish servings*

3 tbsp plain flour
Salt and ground black pepper
6 skinless, boneless chicken
   thighs, each cut in half
   (about 600g)
2 tbsp olive oil
450g medium red potatoes,
   each cut in half

1 medium red pepper, cored,
   seeded and diced
1 medium yellow pepper,
   cored, seeded and diced
2 tbsp brown sugar
2 tbsp cider vinegar

◆ Mix flour, 1 teaspoon salt and ¼ teaspoon black pepper together; use to coat chicken.

◆ Heat oil in 30cm non-stick frying pan over medium-high heat. Add chicken thighs and cook until golden brown; transfer to bowl.

◆ Add potatoes, peppers, ½ teaspoon salt and ¼ teaspoon black pepper to pan; cook until vegetables are golden.

◆ Return chicken to frying pan. Reduce heat to medium; cover and cook, stirring often, 10–15 minutes, or until juices run clear when chicken is pierced with tip of knife and potatoes are fork-tender. Stir in brown sugar and cider vinegar; heat through.

**Each serving: About 430 calories, 31g protein, 39g carbohydrate, 17g total fat (4g saturated), 132mg cholesterol, 930mg sodium**

## TURKEY ESCALOPES WITH CHOPPED SALAD

*Prep: 20 minutes    Cook: 8–10 minutes*
*Makes 4 main dish servings*

1 spring onion, thinly sliced
2 tbsp freshly grated
   Parmesan cheese
1 tbsp red wine vinegar
½ tsp Dijon mustard
¼ tsp salt
¼ tsp coarsely ground black
   pepper

3–4 tbsp olive or vegetable oil
450g plum tomatoes, cut into
   2cm pieces
2 bunches rocket, coarsely
   chopped
4 large turkey escalopes
   (about 450g)
35g dried breadcrumbs

◆ Using wire whisk or fork, mix spring onion with next 5 ingredients and 2 tablespoons oil in medium bowl. Add tomatoes and rocket and toss to mix well.

◆ Pound turkey pieces to 5mm thickness (see page 156). Place breadcrumbs on greaseproof paper; use to coat turkey. Heat 1 tablespoon oil in 30cm non-stick frying pan over medium-high heat.

◆ Add turkey to pan, 2 pieces at a time and cook 2–3 minutes per side, until golden and they lose their pink colour throughout, adding remaining 1 tablespoon oil if necessary. To serve, place turkey escalopes on 4 plates and pile chopped salad on top.

**Each serving: About 300 calories, 32g protein, 13g carbohydrate, 13g total fat (2g saturated), 73mg cholesterol, 345mg sodium**

## POTATO-CRISP CHICKEN

*Prep: 20 minutes    Cook: 15 minutes*
*Makes 2 main dish servings*

2 skinless, boneless chicken
   breasts (about 350g)
1 large baking potato, peeled
Salt

¼ tsp coarsely ground black
   pepper
2 tbsp vegetable oil
Parsley sprigs for garnish

◆ Pound chicken breasts to 5mm thickness (see page 156).

◆ Using sharp knife, cut wide portion of potato crossways into 24 paper-thin slices, immediately placing cut potato slices into bowl of cold water to prevent discoloration. Drain; pat dry with kitchen towels.

◆ Arrange 6 potato slices into an oval same size as a chicken breast on work surface, overlapping slices to fit. Place chicken breast on top of potato slices; sprinkle with ⅛ teaspoon salt. Top chicken with another 6 potato slices. Repeat with remaining potato slices and chicken.

◆ Heat oil in 30cm frying pan over medium-high heat. Add chicken and cook until potatoes are golden on bottom. Reduce heat to medium and cook 2–3 minutes longer until potatoes are browned.

◆ Using spatula, carefully turn over chicken; sprinkle with pepper and ¼ teaspoon salt. Cook over medium-high heat until potatoes are golden on second side. Reduce heat to medium and cook 2–3 minutes longer until potatoes are browned and fork-tender and juices run clear when chicken is pierced with tip of knife. To serve, arrange chicken breasts on 2 serving plates and garnish with parsley sprigs.

**Each serving: About 430 calories, 41g protein, 26g carbohydrate, 18g total fat (4g saturated), 122mg cholesterol, 460mg sodium**

# PAN-BRAISED CHICKEN

These full-bodied dishes extract maximum flavour from the chicken by cooking it in two steps. First it's sealed in hot oil to lock in the juices and create a rich, browned flavour. Next, it's simmered in liquid until tender and cooked through. Serve these dishes with vegetable purées, polenta or crusty bread, to soak up all the delicious juices.

## CHICKEN OSSO-BUCO STYLE

❖❖❖❖❖❖❖❖❖❖❖❖

*Prep:* 20 minutes
*Cook:* 45 minutes
*Makes* 4 main dish servings

2 tbsp vegetable oil
8 chicken thighs (about 1.1kg), skin and fat removed
1 tsp salt
1 large onion
4 medium carrots
1 large celery stalk
400g canned tomatoes with herbs
Chopped fresh parsley and grated lemon rind for garnish

**1** Heat oil in 30cm frying pan over medium-high heat. Add chicken thighs and sprinkle with salt. Cook until golden on all sides. Transfer to bowl.

**2** Meanwhile, coarsely chop onion on chopping board. Dice carrots and celery. Add onion, carrots and celery to juices in pan and cook, stirring frequently, 10 minutes, or until vegetables are lightly browned.

### WHAT'S IN A NAME?

*Osso buco* is the Italian name both for veal shanks and the classic Milanese method of cooking them: they are first braised with aromatic vegetables and tomatoes, then enlivened with a last-minute sprinkling of lemon rind, parsley and garlic. The same delicious flavour – in much less time – can be achieved with chicken.

**3** Return chicken thighs to pan. Stir in stewed tomatoes and bring to the boil over high heat.

**4** Reduce heat to low. Cover and simmer 25 minutes, or until juices run clear when chicken is pierced with tip of knife. Serve chicken sprinkled with chopped parsley and lemon rind.

EACH SERVING: ABOUT 440 CALORIES, 42g PROTEIN, 18g CARBOHYDRATE, 21g TOTAL FAT (5g SATURATED), 190mg CHOLESTEROL, 935mg SODIUM

## CHICKEN WITH OLIVES AND THYME

*Prep: 15 minutes    Cook: 45 minutes*
*Makes 4 main dish servings*

| | |
|---|---|
| 1 tbsp olive oil | 175ml chicken stock |
| 8 skinless chicken thighs (about 1kg) | 75g Kalamata olives, stoned |
| | 1 tsp chopped fresh thyme or ¼ tsp dried |
| Salt | |
| 2 small onions, each cut into 6 wedges | 2 tsp plain flour |

◆ Heat oil in 30cm non-stick frying pan over medium-high heat. Add chicken, sprinkle with ¼ teaspoon salt and cook until lightly browned on all sides. Transfer to plate.

◆ Add onions to juices in pan and cook, shaking pan occasionally, until golden. Stir in chicken stock, olives and thyme; return chicken to pan.

◆ Reduce heat to low; cover and simmer 20–25 minutes until juices run clear when chicken is pierced with tip of knife. Transfer chicken to warm platter.

◆ Mix flour, ¼ teaspoon salt and *1 tablespoon water* together in small bowl until smooth. Stir flour mixture into pan and bring to the boil over high heat, stirring. Boil about 1 minute until sauce thickens slightly. Pour sauce over chicken and serve.

**Each serving: About 420 calories, 42g protein, 8g carbohydrate, 24g total fat (5g saturated), 190mg cholesterol, 1005mg sodium**

## ORANGE-ROSEMARY CHICKEN

*Prep: 15 minutes    Cook: 30 minutes*
*Makes 4 main dish servings*

| | |
|---|---|
| 2 tbsp olive or vegetable oil | 4 medium red potatoes (about 350g) |
| 6 skinless, boneless chicken thighs (about 600g), each cut in half | 1 medium orange |
| | 60ml chicken stock |
| | 1 tbsp plain flour |
| 1 large onion (225g), thinly sliced | 1 tsp chopped fresh rosemary or ¼ tsp dried |
| Salt | |

◆ Heat oil in 30cm frying pan over medium-high heat. Add chicken, onion and 1 teaspoon salt and cook about 15 minutes until onion is tender and chicken thighs are browned on all sides and lose their pink colour throughout. Transfer chicken to bowl, leaving onions in pan.

◆ Meanwhile, cut potatoes into 3cm chunks. Using vegetable peeler, cut two 6 by 2cm strips of rind from orange; reserve. Squeeze 60ml juice from orange, then stir in stock, flour and *175ml water* until smooth.

◆ Add potatoes, orange juice mixture and ¼ teaspoon salt to onions and bring to the boil over high heat, stirring. Reduce heat to low, cover and simmer 10 minutes, or until potatoes are almost tender.

◆ Return chicken thighs to pan; stir in rosemary. Cook until potatoes are tender and chicken is heated through. Meanwhile, cut reserved orange rind into thin strips. Serve garnished with orange rind.

**Each serving: About 395 calories, 33g protein, 25g carbohydrate, 18g total fat (4g saturated), 144mg cholesterol, 865mg sodium**

## HARVEST DINNER

*Prep: 25 minutes    Cook: 40 minutes*
*Makes 6 main dish servings*

| | |
|---|---|
| 1 medium butternut squash (900g) | ¾ tsp salt |
| | 400ml chicken stock |
| 450g onions | 1 tbsp plain flour |
| 450g fresh kale | 45g dried cranberries or raisins |
| 1 tsp vegetable oil | |
| 6 chicken thighs (about 1.1kg), skin and fat removed | Crusty bread (optional) |

◆ Cut squash lengthways in half and remove seeds; cut each half crossways into 2–3cm thick slices. Cut skin from slices; cut into bite-sized chunks. Cut onions into thick slices. Remove tough stalks from kale leaves; tear leaves into bite-sized pieces.

◆ Heat oil in deep 30cm non-stick frying pan over medium-high heat. Add chicken and cook until browned on all sides; transfer to plate.

◆ Add squash, onions, salt and *2 tablespoons water* to juices in pan; cook until vegetables are browned. Stir together stock and flour in small bowl, then add to pan along with kale and cranberries. Return chicken to pan; bring to the boil over high heat. Reduce heat to low, cover and simmer 20 minutes, or until vegetables are tender and juices run clear when chicken is pierced with tip of knife. Serve with bread, if you like.

**Each serving: About 290 calories, 25g protein, 31g carbohydrate, 9g total fat (2g saturated), 100mg cholesterol, 655mg sodium**

## SWEET-AND-SPICY CHICKEN

*Prep:* 10 minutes
*Cook:* 40 minutes
*Makes* 6 main dish servings

1 tbsp vegetable oil
1 chicken (about 1.3kg), cut into 8 pieces (see page 134)
1 medium onion, diced
1 medium green pepper, cored, seeded and diced
75g blanched whole almonds
2 tsp chilli powder
225g canned tomatoes
1 tsp salt
¼ tsp ground cinnamon
900g sweet potatoes, peeled and cut into 1cm slices
1 large cooking apple, cut into wedges
Coriander sprigs for garnish

◆ Heat oil in 30cm frying pan over medium-high heat. Add chicken and cook about 10 minutes, until browned on all sides; transfer to plate.

◆ Discard all but 2 tablespoons juices from pan. Add onion, pepper and almonds; cook over medium heat about 10 minutes until vegetables are tender and almonds are lightly browned.

◆ Stir in chilli powder; cook, stirring constantly, 1 minute. Remove pan from heat; stir in tomatoes with their juice, salt, cinnamon and *300ml water*, stirring until brown bits are loosened.

◆ Blend tomato mixture in blender on low speed until smooth. Return tomato mixture and chicken to pan; add sweet potatoes. Bring to the boil over high heat.

◆ Reduce heat to low, cover and simmer, stirring occasionally, 20 minutes, or until juices run clear when chicken is pierced with tip of knife. Add apple wedges to pan; heat through. Garnish and serve.

**Each serving: About 520 calories, 34g protein, 49g carbohydrate, 22g total fat (5g saturated), 111mg cholesterol, 525mg sodium**

## CHICKEN AND MUSHROOMS

*Prep:* 5 minutes
*Cook:* 1 hour
*Makes* 4 main dish servings

1 tbsp vegetable oil
1 chicken (about 1.5kg), cut into quarters
1 small onion, very finely chopped
1¼ tsp salt
¼ tsp dried thyme
450g small mushrooms
30g plain flour
60ml single cream
1 small bunch dill
Hot cooked rice (optional)

◆ Heat oil in 30cm frying pan over medium heat. Add chicken and cook until lightly browned on all sides; transfer to plate. Add chopped onion to juices in pan; cook until onion is tender but not browned.

◆ Return chicken to pan. Add salt, thyme and *450ml water*; bring to the boil over high heat. Reduce heat to low, cover and simmer for 30 minutes.

◆ Add mushrooms to pan; cover and simmer 15 minutes longer, or until chicken is tender.

◆ Using slotted spoon, transfer chicken and mushrooms to warm large platter. Skim fat from liquid in pan.

◆ Stir flour and *75ml water* until blended in small bowl; slowly add to pan and cook, stirring constantly, until sauce thickens slightly and boils. Stir in cream and heat through.

◆ To serve, pour some sauce over chicken; pour remainder into sauce-boat. Chop 1 tablespoon dill and sprinkle over chicken and mushrooms. Garnish with remaining dill. Serve with sauce, and rice, if you like.

**Each serving: About 630 calories, 61g protein, 15g carbohydrate, 35g total fat (11g saturated), 237mg cholesterol, 850mg sodium**

## CHICKEN MOLE

*Prep:* 10 minutes
*Cook:* 45 minutes
*Makes* 6 main dish servings

400g canned chopped tomatoes
125g canned or bottled mild green chillies, drained and chopped
75g blanched whole almonds
½ small onion, cut into chunks
1 small garlic clove
1 tbsp chilli powder
1 tsp ground cumin
1 tsp ground coriander
1 tsp salt
¾ tsp ground cinnamon
½ tsp sugar
1 tbsp olive oil
1.3kg bone-in chicken parts, skin removed
15g plain chocolate, chopped
Chopped fresh coriander for garnish
Sautéed peppers and onions (optional)

◆ Prepare mole sauce: combine first 11 ingredients in blender and blend on high speed until smooth.

◆ Heat oil in 30cm non-stick frying pan over medium-high heat. Add chicken in batches and cook until golden; transfer to plate. Add sauce, chocolate and *60ml water* to pan; cook, stirring, until chocolate melts. Add chicken and bring to the boil over high heat. Reduce heat to low; cover and simmer 30–35 minutes until juices run clear when chicken is pierced with tip of knife. Garnish; serve with peppers and onions, if you like.

**Each serving: About 305 calories, 38g protein, 10g carbohydrate, 13g total fat (2g saturated), 91mg cholesterol, 745mg sodium**

## CHICKEN WITH MUSSELS AND CLAMS

*Prep: 10 minutes    Cook: 55 minutes*
*Makes 6 main dish servings*

1 chicken (about 1.5kg), cut into 8 pieces (see page 134)
½ tsp ground black pepper
Salt
2 tbsp vegetable oil
400g canned tomatoes
125g canned or bottled mild green chillies, drained and chopped
1 tbsp chilli powder
1 tsp sugar
12 small clams
12 small mussels
1 tbsp chopped fresh parsley
15g margarine or butter
¼ tsp ground turmeric (optional)
150g couscous
Parsley sprigs for garnish

◆ Remove skin from all chicken pieces except wings. Sprinkle chicken with pepper and ½ teaspoon salt. Heat oil in 30cm frying pan over medium-high heat.

◆ Add chicken to pan and cook until browned on all sides; pour off fat from pan. Stir in tomatoes, green chillies, chilli powder, sugar and *225ml water*; bring to the boil over high heat. Reduce heat to low; cover and simmer 30 minutes.

◆ Meanwhile, using stiff brush, scrub clams and mussels with cold water to remove any sand; remove beards from mussels (see page 88). Add clams and mussels to pan; cover and cook 8–10 minutes until shells open. Discard any that do not open. Sprinkle shellfish and chicken with parsley.

◆ While shellfish is cooking, prepare couscous: melt margarine with turmeric, ½ teaspoon salt and *350ml water* in 2-litre saucepan. Bring to the boil over high heat. Stir in couscous. Cover pan and remove from heat; let stand 5 minutes. Fluff couscous with fork. Serve chicken with couscous. Garnish with parsley.

**Each serving: About 490 calories, 40g protein, 32g carbohydrate, 22g total fat (5g saturated), 136mg cholesterol, 815mg sodium**

## SPICY PEANUT CHICKEN

*Prep: 15 minutes    Cook: 1 hour*
*Makes 4 main dish servings*

1 tsp ground cumin
¼ tsp ground cinnamon
4 chicken quarters (about 1kg), skin removed
1 tbsp vegetable oil
1 medium onion, sliced
800g canned tomatoes, drained and chopped with juice reserved
65g smooth peanut butter
15g fresh coriander leaves
2 garlic cloves
½ tsp salt
¼ tsp crushed red pepper

Mix cumin and cinnamon together in small bowl; rub over chicken. Heat oil in 30cm frying pan over medium-high heat. Add chicken and cook until browned. Add onion and cook 5 minutes. Purée reserved tomato juice and remaining ingredients in blender on high speed; pour over chicken. Stir in tomatoes and bring to the boil over high heat. Reduce heat to low; cover and simmer 40 minutes, or until juices run clear when chicken is pierced with tip of knife.

**Each serving: About 385 calories, 35g protein, 16g carbohydrate, 21g total fat (5g saturated), 98mg cholesterol, 765mg sodium**

## CHICKEN RAGOÛT

*Prep: 15 minutes    Cook: 55 minutes*
*Makes 4 main dish servings*

3 tbsp vegetable oil
1 chicken (about 1.1kg), cut into quarters and skin removed
1 tsp salt
¼ tsp coarsely ground black pepper
½ tsp dried thyme
2 courgettes, cut into chunks
3 medium carrots, chopped
1 large onion, chopped
2 tsp plain flour
800g canned tomatoes

◆ Heat 1 tablespoon oil in 30cm non-stick frying pan over medium-high heat. Add chicken and sprinkle with salt, pepper and thyme and cook until browned. Transfer to plate. Add courgettes to juices in pan. Cook until tender; transfer to bowl. Heat remaining 2 tablespoons oil in same pan. Add carrots and onion and cook until browned.

◆ Mix flour and *2 tablespoons water* in small bowl until smooth; add to pan. Add tomatoes with their juice, breaking up tomatoes with back of spoon. Return chicken to pan; bring to the boil over high heat. Reduce heat to low; cover and simmer 25 minutes, or until juices run clear when chicken is pierced with tip of knife. Stir in courgettes, heat through and serve.

**Each serving: About 390 calories, 34g protein, 24g carbohydrate, 19g total fat (4g saturated), 90mg cholesterol, 965mg sodium**

# POULTRY CASSEROLES AND STEWS

Casseroles and stews provide hearty and delicious meals that are easily prepared. After browning chicken or duck – which seals in the juices and adds a slightly caramelized flavour – cover the casserole and leave the meat to simmer with a variety of vegetables in an aromatic broth on the stove-top or in the oven. Fluffy rosemary dumplings absorb the stock in the recipe below, while our delicate anise-perfumed Chicken Bouillabaisse simply calls out for crusty French bread.

## CHICKEN AND VEGETABLES WITH ROSEMARY DUMPLINGS

*Prep:* 20 minutes    *Cook:* 1 hour
*Makes* 6 main dish servings

2 tbsp vegetable oil
6 chicken breasts (about 1.4kg), skin removed
½ tsp salt
4 large carrots, cut into 5mm thick slices
2 large celery stalks, cut into 5mm thick slices
1 medium onion, diced

Rosemary Dumplings (see below right)
400ml chicken stock
¼ tsp ground black pepper
2 tbsp plain flour
225ml milk
300g frozen peas, thawed
Rosemary sprigs and chopped fresh chives for garnish

**1** Heat 1 tablespoon oil in 8-litre flameproof casserole over medium-high heat. Add chicken, half at a time, sprinkling each batch with ¼ teaspoon salt; cook 8–10 minutes, until lightly browned. Transfer to bowl.

**2** Heat remaining 1 tablespoon oil in juices in casserole. Add carrots, celery and onion and cook, stirring frequently, about 10 minutes, until browned and tender.

**3** Meanwhile, prepare dumplings. Return chicken to pan. Add stock, black pepper and *450ml water*. Bring to the boil over high heat.

**4** Drop dumpling mixture by rounded tablespoons into casserole to make 12 dumplings. Cover, reduce the heat to low and simmer 15 minutes.

**5** Using slotted spoon, transfer dumplings, chicken and vegetables to large shallow bowl; reserve stock in casserole. Beat flour with milk in small bowl; whisk into stock.

**6** Bring to the boil over high heat; boil, stirring, 3 minutes, or until sauce thickens slightly. Add peas; heat through. Pour sauce over chicken and vegetables; garnish and serve.

### ROSEMARY DUMPLINGS

Mix 2 teaspoons baking powder, 1½ teaspoons chopped fresh rosemary or ½ teaspoon crushed dried rosemary, 125g plain flour and ½ teaspoon salt together in small bowl. Beat 125ml milk with 1 large egg. Stir milk mixture into flour mixture just until blended. Shape and cook dumplings as directed in Step 4, above. Makes 12 dumplings.

EACH SERVING: ABOUT 460 CALORIES, 46g PROTEIN, 37g CARBOHYDRATE, 13g TOTAL FAT (4g SATURATED), 143mg CHOLESTEROL, 585mg SODIUM

# COUNTRY CASSEROLE

*Prep: 1 hour    Bake: 1 hour*
*Makes 8 main dish servings*

2 tbsp plus 1 tsp vegetable oil
2 chickens (about 1.3kg), each
    cut into 8 pieces (see page
    134) and skin removed
2 medium onions, chopped
1 large Granny Smith's apple,
    peeled, cored and diced
1 large green pepper, cored,
    seeded and diced
3 large garlic cloves, very
    finely chopped

1 tbsp grated peeled fresh
    ginger
3 tbsp curry powder
¼ tsp ground cumin
1 tsp salt
½ tsp coarsely ground black
    pepper
800g canned tomatoes
1 tbsp tomato purée
400ml chicken stock
75g seedless raisins

◆ Preheat oven to 180°C (350°F, Gas 4). Heat 2 tablespoons oil in 8-litre flameproof casserole over medium-high heat. Add chicken in batches and cook until browned; transfer to bowl. Add remaining 1 teaspoon oil to casserole. Add onions and next 4 ingredients and cook, stirring frequently, 2 minutes. Reduce heat to low; cover and cook 5 minutes.

◆ Stir in curry powder and cumin; cook 1 minute. Stir in remaining ingredients. Return chicken to pan and bring to the boil over high heat. Boil 1 minute. Cover and bake 1 hour, or until juices run clear when chicken is pierced with tip of knife.

**Each serving: About 400 calories, 44g protein, 22g carbohydrate, 16g total fat (4g saturated), 131mg cholesterol, 935mg sodium**

# CHINESE-SPICED DUCK CASSEROLE

*Prep: 30 minutes    Bake: 2 hours*
*Makes 4 main dish servings*

1 duckling (about 2kg), cut
    into quarters (see page 135)
4 medium red onions, halved
60ml soy sauce
2 tbsp dry sherry
1 tbsp grated peeled fresh
    ginger

1 tsp sugar
2 star anise or ¼ tsp anise
    seeds
600g Brussels sprouts,
    trimmed, each cut in half
    if large

◆ Place duckling in 5-litre flameproof casserole and cook over high heat until browned; transfer to large bowl. Discard all but 1 tablespoon of juices from casserole. To juices in casserole, add onions and cook 10 minutes, or until golden. Transfer to bowl with duckling.

◆ Preheat oven to 180°C (350°F, Gas 4). Stir soy sauce, sherry, ginger, sugar, star anise and *60ml water* into casserole. Bring to the boil over high heat, stirring until brown bits are loosened. Return duckling and onions to casserole. Cover and bake, basting occasionally with cooking

liquid, 1¼ hours. Stir in Brussels sprouts. Cover and bake 45 minutes longer, or until duckling is tender. Skim fat from liquid in casserole before serving.

**Each serving: About 740 calories, 57g protein, 30g carbohydrate, 43g total fat (13g saturated), 178mg cholesterol, 1205mg sodium**

# CHICKEN BOUILLABAISSE

*Prep: 30 minutes    Bake: 1 hour*
*Makes 4 main dish servings*

1 tbsp olive oil
8 chicken thighs (about
    1.1kg), skin removed
2 large carrots, diced
1 medium onion, diced
1 medium fennel bulb,
    trimmed and sliced
3 garlic cloves, very finely
    chopped
900g canned chopped
    tomatoes

125ml dry white wine
400ml chicken stock
2 tbsp Pernod or other anise-
    flavour apéritif (optional)
¼ tsp dried thyme
⅛ tsp ground red pepper
1 bay leaf
Pinch saffron threads

◆ Heat oil in 5-litre flameproof casserole over medium-high heat. Add chicken thighs, half at a time and cook about 12 minutes, until browned. Transfer to bowl. Add carrots and onion to juices in casserole; cook, stirring occasionally, about 10 minutes until tender and golden. Transfer to same bowl.

◆ Preheat oven to 180°C (350°F, Gas 4). Add fennel and *125ml water* to pan, stirring until all brown bits are loosened. Cook, stirring occasionally, about 7 minutes until fennel is tender and browned. Add garlic and cook 3 minutes longer.

◆ Return chicken and carrot mixture to casserole. Add tomatoes with their juice and remaining ingredients. Bring to the boil over high heat. Cover and bake 30 minutes, or until juices run clear when chicken is pierced with tip of knife. Remove bay leaf before serving.

**Each serving: About 415 calories, 36g protein, 23g carbohydrate, 18g total fat (4g saturated), 116mg cholesterol, 555mg sodium**

---

### BAY LEAVES

Available fresh or dried, aromatic bay leaves, also called sweet bay or laurel, impart a deep, heady flavour to long-simmered dishes. Fresh leaves are vibrant green and deliver a sharp, pungent flavour. Turkish bay leaves offer a sweet, subtle taste. To avoid any danger of swallowing, always discard the bay leaves before serving the food.

---

# POACHED POULTRY

Poaching is the perfect low-fat cooking method, resulting in tender, succulent meat. Aromatic vegetables, herbs and spices may be simmered with the poultry to infuse both the meat and the stock with flavour. Reserve the stock to create a sauce for the dish, or refrigerate it to use as a base for soups, sauces, pilafs or risottos.

## TURKEY AND PRAWN BLANQUETTE

*Prep: 40 minutes, plus cooling    Cook: 1½ hours*
*Makes 10 main dish servings*

| | |
|---|---|
| 3 medium onions | Salt |
| 450g carrots | 40g plain flour |
| 1 large celery stalk, thickly sliced | 450ml milk |
| 1 turkey breast (about 1.1kg), skin removed | 375g raw large prawns, peeled and de-veined (see page 90) |
| 125ml dry white wine | 300g frozen peas |
| 10 black peppercorns | 2 tbsp chopped fresh dill |
| 1 whole clove | Dill sprigs for garnish |
| 4 tbsp olive oil | Mashed potatoes and French bread (optional) |
| 350g mushrooms, sliced | |

**1** Thickly slice 1 onion and 1 carrot; place in 5-litre flameproof casserole with turkey, wine, peppercorns, clove and *900ml water*, and bring to the boil over high heat. Reduce heat to low, cover and simmer, turning turkey occasionally, 30 minutes, or until it loses its pink colour throughout.

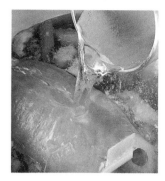

**2** Meanwhile, dice remaining onions. Cut remaining carrots diagonally into thin slices. Transfer turkey breast to bowl and set aside. Strain turkey stock through sieve into 4-litre saucepan; discard cooked vegetable mixture.

**3** Bring stock to the boil over high heat. Reduce heat to medium and cook 30 minutes until reduced to 450ml.

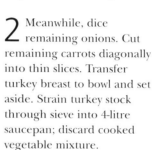

**4** When cool enough to handle, discard bones from turkey. Cut meat into bite-sized chunks; return to bowl. Heat 2 tablespoons olive oil in same casserole over high heat.

**5** Add sliced carrots, mushrooms and ½ teaspoon salt; cook until carrots are tender. Transfer to bowl with turkey.

**6** Heat remaining 2 tablespoons oil in same casserole over medium heat. Add diced onions and 1 teaspoon salt; cook until onions are tender but not browned. Stir in flour; cook, stirring constantly, 1 minute. Gradually stir in milk and turkey stock; bring to the boil, stirring.

**7** Reduce heat to low; simmer, stirring constantly, about 1 minute until sauce thickens slightly. Stir in prawns, turkey, carrots, mushrooms and peas. Simmer just until prawns are opaque throughout and blanquette is heated through. Stir in chopped dill. Garnish with dill sprigs and serve with mashed potatoes and French bread, if you like.

EACH SERVING: ABOUT 290 CALORIES, 31g PROTEIN, 20g CARBOHYDRATE, 8g TOTAL FAT (2g SATURATED), 152mg CHOLESTEROL, 535mg SODIUM

## POULE AU POT WITH TARRAGON

*Prep: 15 minutes    Cook: 1 hour*
*Makes 4 main dish servings*

1 chicken (about 1.5kg),
  cut into 8 pieces (see
  page 134)
450g small red potatoes
450g carrots, each quartered
  lengthways and cut into
  8cm pieces
3 medium leeks, cleaned and
  cut into 8cm pieces
400ml chicken stock
½ tsp salt
¼ tsp ground black pepper
¼ tsp dried thyme
1 small bunch tarragon

◆ Combine chicken, potatoes, carrots, leeks, chicken stock, salt, black pepper, thyme, 1 large sprig tarragon and *900ml water* in 6- to 8-litre flameproof casserole. Bring to the boil over high heat. Reduce heat to low; cover and simmer 45 minutes, or until chicken loses its pink colour throughout.

◆ Using slotted spoon, transfer chicken to plate; remove and discard skin. Using slotted spoon, transfer vegetables to serving bowl; add chicken and 225ml stock from casserole (reserve remaining stock for another use). Chop 1 tablespoon tarragon and sprinkle on top.

Each serving: About 570 calories, 48g protein, 45g carbohydrate, 22g total fat (6g saturated), 166mg cholesterol, 485mg sodium

## TURKISH CHICKEN IN WALNUT SAUCE

*Prep: 20 minutes, plus cooling    Cook: 30–35 minutes*
*Makes 4 main dish servings*

4 chicken breasts (about
  1.1kg)
400ml chicken stock
1 small bunch parsley
200g walnuts, toasted
3 slices firm white bread, torn

1 small garlic clove, very
  finely chopped
¾ tsp salt
½ tsp paprika
⅛ tsp ground red pepper

◆ Place chicken breasts, chicken stock, 3 parsley sprigs and *225ml water* in a 4-litre flameproof casserole. Bring to the boil over high heat. Reduce heat to low; cover and simmer 20–25 minutes, until chicken loses its pink colour throughout. Remove from heat and allow chicken to cool in liquid 30 minutes. Drain chicken, reserving stock. Remove and discard skin and bones. Cut chicken meat into 1cm strips; transfer to bowl.

◆ Prepare walnut sauce: blend walnuts and bread, in food processor with knife blade attached, until walnuts are finely ground and mixture is smooth. Add 225ml stock from pan (reserve remaining stock for another use), garlic, salt, paprika and ground red pepper; blend until well combined.

◆ Add half of walnut sauce to chicken in bowl and stir to combine. Spoon onto platter. Pour remaining walnut sauce on top. Garnish with parsley.

Each serving: About 575 calories, 51g protein, 19g carbohydrate, 34g total fat (4g saturated), 119mg cholesterol, 855mg sodium

## CHICKEN BREASTS WITH TUNA SAUCE

*Prep: 15 minutes, plus chilling    Cook: 15–20 minutes*
*Makes 6 main dish servings*

6 skinless, boneless chicken
  breasts (about 800g)
1 medium onion, thinly sliced
175g white tuna in oil
75ml olive oil
3 tbsp milk
2 tbsp fresh lemon juice

2 tbsp canned or bottled
  drained capers
¼ tsp salt
1 bunch rocket or watercress
Lemon slices and capers
  for garnish

◆ Place chicken breasts, onion and *450ml water* in 26cm frying pan and bring to the boil.

◆ Reduce heat to low, cover and simmer 5–10 minutes, turning chicken once, until it loses its pink colour throughout.

◆ Transfer chicken breasts to plate; cover and refrigerate until well chilled.

◆ Meanwhile, prepare tuna sauce: blend tuna with its oil, olive oil, milk, lemon juice, 2 tablespoons capers and salt in food processor with knife blade attached or in blender on high speed, until smooth.

◆ To serve, line platter with rocket. Dip each piece of cold chicken into tuna sauce to coat and arrange over rocket. Pour any remaining sauce over chicken breasts. Garnish with lemon slices and capers.

Each serving: About 330 calories, 38g protein, 3g carbohydrate, 17g total fat (3g saturated), 104mg cholesterol, 355mg sodium

# MINCED POULTRY

Minced poultry is as versatile as minced beef, with much less fat – but be sure to read the label. Cheaper products may contain a high proportion of dark meat or even skin, increasing the fat content to rival that of red meat. Like any minced meat, minced poultry should always be thoroughly cooked.

**1** Finely chop bread. Grate 1 tablespoon onion and set aside; chop remainder. Cut aubergine and courgettes into 3cm chunks.

**2** Combine bread, grated onion, turkey, Parmesan cheese, basil, egg and salt in medium bowl. Using wet hands, shape mixture into 25 meatballs.

**3** Heat 2 tablespoons oil in 30cm frying pan over medium heat. Add meatballs, half at a time, and cook until browned. Transfer meatballs to plate as they brown.

## TURKEY MEATBALLS

❖❖❖❖❖❖❖❖❖❖❖❖

*Prep: 30 minutes*
*Cook: 50 minutes*
*Makes 5 main dish servings*

2 slices firm white bread
1 medium onion
1 small aubergine (about 450g)
2 small courgettes (about 350g)
600g minced turkey
30g Parmesan cheese, freshly grated
2 tbsp chopped fresh basil or ¾ tsp dried
1 medium egg
½ tsp salt
4 tbsp olive or vegetable oil
800g canned tomatoes
½ tsp sugar
Olives and chopped flat-leaf parsley for garnish
Crusty bread (optional)

**4** Add remaining 2 tablespoons olive oil to juices in same pan and heat over medium-high heat. Add aubergine, courgettes and chopped onion and cook, stirring frequently, 5 minutes, or until onion is golden. Stir in *60ml water*. Reduce heat to low; cover and simmer, stirring occasionally, 10 minutes.

**5** Add tomatoes with their juice and sugar, breaking up tomatoes with back of spoon. Return meatballs to pan, and bring to the boil over high heat. Reduce heat to low; simmer, uncovered, 15 minutes, or until cooked through. Garnish and serve with crusty bread, if you like.

EACH SERVING: ABOUT 400 CALORIES, 27g PROTEIN, 23g CARBOHYDRATE, 23g TOTAL FAT (5g SATURATED), 134mg CHOLESTEROL, 695mg SODIUM

## TURKEY MEATBALL PITTAS

*Prep: 15 minutes    Bake: 12–15 minutes*
*Makes 5 main dish servings*

450g minced turkey
2 slices firm white bread,
   finely chopped
2 tbsp grated onion
1 medium egg white
1½ tsp ground cumin
Salt
5 wholewheat pittas
   (15cm each)

½ large cucumber, peeled and
   cut into 2cm pieces
225g very low-fat plain yogurt
2 tbsp chopped fresh
   coriander
225g Cos lettuce, thinly sliced

◆ Preheat oven to 220°C (425°F, Gas 7). Grease baking tray. Mix minced turkey, bread, onion, egg white, cumin, ¼ teaspoon salt and *3 tablespoons water* together in medium bowl. Using wet hands, shape mixture into 25 meatballs. Place on baking tray and bake 12–15 minutes until cooked through (meatballs will not brown).

◆ Meanwhile, cut off 2cm across top of each pitta. Wrap pittas in foil. After meatballs have baked 5 minutes, place pittas in oven to warm. Combine cucumber, yogurt, coriander and ¼ teaspoon salt in small bowl. Fill pittas with lettuce and meatballs; top with cucumber mixture.

**Each serving: About 375 calories, 27g protein, 46g carbohydrate, 10g total fat (2g saturated), 73mg cholesterol, 745mg sodium**

## TEXAS CHICKEN BURGERS

*Prep: 15 minutes    Cook: 12–15 minutes*
*Makes 4 main dish servings*

450g minced chicken
2 spring onions, chopped
1 small courgette (about
   150g), grated
1 medium carrot, grated
1 tbsp chilli powder
¼ tsp ground cumin
⅛ tsp ground red pepper

450g baked beans
1 tbsp prepared mustard
1 tbsp light molasses or
   golden syrup
Non-stick cooking spray
4 whole-grain sandwich rolls,
   split
Lettuce leaves

◆ Mix minced chicken, spring onions, courgette, carrot, chilli powder, cumin and ground red pepper in medium bowl until well mixed. Using wet hands, shape mixture into four 9cm round patties; set aside.

◆ Bring baked beans, mustard and molasses to the boil in medium saucepan over medium heat, stirring occasionally.

◆ Meanwhile, spray heavy 30cm frying pan with non-stick cooking spray. Heat pan over medium-high heat until very hot. Using spatula, transfer chicken patties to hot pan. Cook 5 minutes, then turn patties and cook 5 minutes longer, or

until they lose their pink colour throughout. Arrange patties on sandwich rolls with lettuce leaves. Serve with baked beans.

**Each serving: About 410 calories, 28g protein, 48g carbohydrate, 16g total fat (4g saturated), 154mg cholesterol, 745mg sodium**

## CHICKEN MEATBALL CHILLI

*Prep: 30 minutes    Cook: 45 minutes*
*Makes 10 main dish servings*

3 tbsp vegetable oil
2 medium celery stalks, finely
   chopped
1 medium onion, finely
   chopped
3 slices firm white bread,
   finely chopped
900g minced chicken
1 medium egg

Salt
3 large carrots, thinly sliced
2 tbsp chilli powder
800g canned tomatoes
1.2kg canned cannellini
   beans, rinsed and drained
Chopped fresh coriander for
   garnish
Corn bread (optional)

◆ Heat 1 tablespoon oil in 5-litre flameproof casserole over medium heat. Add celery and onion; cook, stirring occasionally, until tender. Combine celery mixture with bread in large bowl. Mix in minced chicken, egg, ½ teaspoon salt and *60ml water*. Using wet hands, shape into 4cm meatballs.

◆ Heat remaining oil in same casserole over medium heat. Add meatballs, half at a time, and cook until browned, transferring meatballs to bowl as they brown. Add carrots to juices in casserole and cook over medium-high heat 5 minutes, or until tender-crisp. Stir in chilli powder, tomatoes with their juice, ¼ teaspoon salt and *450ml water*; bring to the boil over high heat.

◆ Return meatballs to casserole. Reduce heat to low; cover and simmer 10 minutes. Stir in beans and heat through over medium heat. Garnish with coriander and serve with corn bread, if you like.

**Each serving: About 345 calories, 23g protein, 31g carbohydrate, 15g total fat (4g saturated), 139mg cholesterol, 910mg sodium**

# STIR-FRIED POULTRY

Stir-frying is the world's fastest cooking technique. You don't need a wok; a large frying pan works just as well. For a successful result, follow these simple rules: cut the ingredients into small, even pieces for quick, uniform cooking; stir constantly; and don't be afraid of high heat. Since the cooking is so quick, have all ingredients and utensils at hand before you begin.

## INDONESIAN CHICKEN

*Prep: 25 minutes, plus marinating    Cook: 10 minutes*
*Makes 4 main dish servings*

| | |
|---|---|
| 1 tsp plus 1 tbsp vegetable oil | ½ tsp dried chilli flakes |
| 1 spring onion, thinly sliced | ½ tsp ground cumin |
| 1 garlic clove, very finely chopped | ½ tsp ground coriander |
| 1 medium lime | 4 skinless, boneless chicken breasts (about 950g) |
| 1 medium orange | 1 tsp cornflour |
| 2 tbsp soy sauce | Fresh coriander leaves for garnish |
| 1 tbsp honey | |

**1** Heat 1 teaspoon oil in non-stick wok or 30cm frying pan over medium heat. Add spring onion and garlic; cook 2–3 minutes until beginning to brown. Transfer to bowl.

**2** Grate rind and squeeze juice from lime and orange; set aside orange juice. Add all rind and lime juice to bowl with spring onion, soy sauce, honey, dried chilli flakes, cumin and coriander.

**3** Cut chicken breasts lengthways into 1cm wide strips, then add to soy sauce mixture and stir to coat. Cover and marinate 15 minutes. Using slotted spoon, remove chicken from marinade; reserve marinade.

**4** Heat remaining 1 tablespoon oil in same wok over medium-high heat. Add chicken strips and cook, stirring constantly, 5 minutes, or until chicken just loses its pink colour throughout. Transfer to clean bowl.

### JUICING CITRUS FRUITS

For best yield, use room-temperature fruit. Before juicing, roll the fruit under the palm of your hand, which loosens inner membranes, helping to release as much juice from the fruit as possible.

**5** Using fork, mix cornflour with orange juice in small bowl. Add to wok with reserved chicken marinade. Cook over medium heat, stirring constantly, until mixture boils and thickens slightly; boil 1 minute. Return chicken to wok; heat through. Serve garnished with coriander.

**EACH SERVING: ABOUT 220 CALORIES, 26g PROTEIN, 12g CARBOHYDRATE, 7g TOTAL FAT (2g SATURATED), 81mg CHOLESTEROL, 555 mg SODIUM**

## CHICKEN AND AUBERGINE

*Prep:* 20 minutes  *Cook:* 30 minutes
*Makes* 6 main dish servings

2 tbsp vegetable oil
6 skinless, boneless chicken breasts
  (about 800g), cut lengthways into 1cm
  wide strips
6 small aubergines (about 900g), each cut
  lengthways in half
1 tbsp grated peeled fresh ginger
1 garlic clove, very finely chopped
60ml soy sauce
60ml red wine vinegar
3 tbsp sugar
2 tbsp sesame oil
2 tsp cornflour
¼ tsp dried chilli flakes
Hot cooked rice (optional)

◆ Heat oil in 30cm frying pan or wok over high heat. Add chicken and cook, stirring constantly, until it loses its pink colour throughout. Transfer to bowl. Add aubergines, ginger, garlic and *60ml water* to juices in pan and bring to the boil. Reduce heat to medium-low; cover and stir-fry about 20 minutes, until liquid evaporates. Mix soy sauce with next 5 ingredients in small bowl.

◆ Return chicken to pan. Add soy sauce mixture and bring to the boil over high heat. Reduce heat to medium; cook, stirring, until sauce thickens slightly and boils. Serve with rice, if you like.

**Each serving: About 310 calories, 32g protein, 18g carbohydrate, 12g total fat (3g saturated), 95mg cholesterol, 730mg sodium**

## EASY CHINESE CHICKEN AND VEGETABLES

*Prep:* 25 minutes  *Cook:* 12 minutes
*Makes* 4 main dish servings

4 skinless, boneless chicken breasts
  (about 600g)
60ml soy sauce
2 tbsp balsamic vinegar
2 tsp brown sugar
2 tbsp vegetable oil, plus more if needed
5 medium carrots, thinly sliced
  diagonally
2 large red peppers, cored, seeded and
  cut into 4cm pieces
1 bunch spring onions, cut into 3cm
  pieces
Lettuce leaves (optional)
60g cashew nuts

◆ Using knife held in slanting position, almost parallel to chopping board, slice each chicken breast into 2mm thin slices. Mix soy sauce with vinegar and brown sugar.

◆ Heat 1 tablespoon oil in 30cm frying pan or wok over high heat. Add chicken and cook, stirring constantly, just until chicken loses its pink colour throughout. Transfer to bowl.

◆ Heat remaining 1 tablespoon oil in same pan over medium-high heat. Add carrots and red peppers and stir-fry 4 minutes. Add spring onions and stir-fry until vegetables are tender-crisp, adding additional oil if necessary.

◆ Return chicken to pan. Stir in soy sauce mixture; cook 1 minute, or until chicken is heated through. To serve, arrange lettuce leaves on platter, if you like; spoon chicken mixture over. Sprinkle with cashew nuts.

**Each serving: About 370 calories, 36g protein, 22g carbohydrate, 16g total fat (4g saturated), 101mg cholesterol, 1110mg sodium**

## CHICKEN WITH SESAME NOODLES

*Prep:* 20 minutes  *Cook:* 10 minutes
*Makes* 4 main dish servings

225g dried linguine
1 medium red pepper
1 medium cucumber
2 tbsp cornflour
¼ tsp salt
4 skinless, boneless chicken breasts
  (about 450g), cut crossways into
  2.5cm thick strips
2 tbsp vegetable oil
65g smooth peanut butter
3 tbsp soy sauce
1 tbsp sesame oil
1 tbsp distilled white vinegar
2 tsp sugar
1 spring onion, thinly sliced
¼ tsp dried chilli flakes (optional)

◆ Prepare linguine as packet instructs; drain. Meanwhile, cut red pepper and cucumber into matchstick strips.

◆ Combine cornflour and salt in medium bowl. Add chicken strips and toss to coat. Heat oil in 30cm frying pan or wok over high heat. Add chicken and stir-fry until it loses its pink colour throughout. Transfer to plate; keep warm.

◆ Add peanut butter, soy sauce, sesame oil, vinegar, sugar and *175ml water* to pan; cook over medium heat, stirring constantly, until smooth. Stir in linguine and heat through. Spoon linguine mixture onto warm platter. Top with red pepper and cucumber strips, chicken strips and spring onion. Sprinkle with dried chilli flakes, if you like. Toss to serve.

**Each serving: About 570 calories, 38g protein, 56g carbohydrate, 22g total fat (4g saturated), 81mg cholesterol, 1025mg sodium**

# POULTRY PIES

Tender chunks of chicken or turkey with vegetables in a creamy sauce, topped with crisp golden pastry, make poultry pies a favourite winter dish. For simplicity, use leftover cooked poultry or buy some ready-cooked.

## CHICKEN PIE WITH CORNMEAL CRUST

◆ ◆ ◆ ◆ ◆ ◆ ◆ ◆ ◆ ◆ ◆ ◆

*Prep:* 1 hour
*Bake:* 35–40 minutes
*Makes* 10 main dish servings

**800g potatoes**

**600g swedes**

**3 medium carrots**

**1 large onion**

**2 large celery stalks**

**1 tbsp olive or vegetable oil**

**½ tsp salt**

**300g frozen peas**

**450g cooked chicken, cut into bite-sized pieces**

**225ml milk**

**30g plain flour**

**750ml chicken stock**

**¼ tsp ground black pepper**

**Cornmeal Pastry (see page 172)**

**25g celery leaves, very finely chopped**

**1 medium egg white, lightly beaten**

**Celery leaves for garnish**

**1** Peel and dice potatoes and swedes; dice carrots, onion and celery. Heat oil in 30cm non-stick frying pan over medium-high heat. Add swedes, carrots and onion and cook for 10 minutes. Stir in potatoes, celery and salt and cook, stirring often, 10 minutes longer or until vegetables are tender. Stir in peas and chicken; spoon mixture into 33 by 20cm ovenproof dish. Beat milk and flour together in small bowl.

**2** Bring chicken stock to the boil in 3-litre saucepan; stir in milk mixture and pepper. Cook, stirring, until sauce boils. Stir into chicken mixture. Preheat oven to 220°C (425°F, Gas 7).

**3** Prepare Cornmeal Pastry. Roll out pastry on lightly floured surface, using floured rolling pin into rectangle 5cm larger all around than top of dish; sprinkle with chopped celery leaves. Using rolling pin, press leaves into pastry.

**4** Place topping over filling and trim, leaving 2cm overhang; reserve trimmings. Fold overhang under and crimp edge. Brush with some egg white. Re-roll trimmings and cut into leaves to decorate edge of pie. Brush pastry leaves with egg white.

**5** Cut several slits in crust to allow steam to escape during baking. Crimp 45cm piece of foil. Place foil on oven rack directly below pie to catch any drips while baking. Bake 35–40 minutes, until crust is golden brown and filling is hot and bubbling. Towards end of baking time, cover edge of crust with foil to prevent over-browning. Garnish with celery leaves.

EACH SERVING: ABOUT 455 CALORIES, 23g PROTEIN, 49g CARBOHYDRATE, 19g TOTAL FAT (6g SATURATED), 47mg CHOLESTEROL, 755mg SODIUM

## Fiesta turkey pie

*Prep: 55 minutes    Bake: 40–45 minutes*
*Makes 8 main dish servings*

300g plain flour
225g mature Cheddar cheese, finely grated
150g white vegetable fat
225g potatoes, peeled and cut into 1cm pieces
1 tbsp vegetable oil
1 medium onion, diced

450g cooked turkey, cut into bite-sized pieces
400g canned cannellini, rinsed and drained
400g canned tomatoes
325g canned sweetcorn, drained
1 tsp chilli powder

◆ Mix flour and 60g cheese in large bowl. With pastry blender or two knives used scissor-fashion, cut in vegetable fat until mixture resembles coarse crumbs. Add *5–6 tablespoons cold water*, 1 tablespoon at a time, mixing with a fork after each addition, until pastry is just moist enough to hold together. Shape into a ball. Cover pastry ball with cling film.

◆ Bring potatoes and enough *water* to cover to the boil in 2-litre saucepan over high heat. Reduce heat to low; cover and simmer 5 minutes, or until potatoes are tender. Drain.

◆ Heat oil in 30cm frying pan over medium-high heat. Add onion and cook, stirring occasionally, until tender. Stir in turkey, cannellini, tomatoes, sweetcorn, chilli powder and potatoes and bring to the boil. Remove from heat and stir in remaining cheese.

## CORNMEAL PASTRY

◆◆◆◆◆◆◆◆◆◆◆◆◆◆

30g coarse yellow cornmeal
225g plain flour

1 tsp salt
150g white vegetable fat

1 Mix cornmeal, flour and salt together in large bowl. With pastry blender or two knives used scissor-fashion, cut in white vegetable fat until mixture resembles coarse crumbs.

2 Sprinkle *6–7 tablespoons cold water*, 1 tablespoon at a time, into the flour mixture, mixing with a fork after each addition until the pastry is just moist enough to hold together.

◆ Preheat oven to 200°C (400°F, Gas 6). Roll out two-thirds of pastry on lightly floured surface, using floured rolling pin, into round 6cm larger all round than inverted 23cm deep-dish pie dish. Gently ease pastry into pie dish; trim edge, leaving 2–3cm overhang. Spoon filling into pie dish.

◆ Roll remaining pastry into 28cm round; lift onto pie. Trim edge, leaving 2–3cm overhang. Fold overhang under and make fluted edge (see page 488). Cut several slits in crust to allow steam to escape during baking. Bake pie 40–45 minutes, until crust is golden and filling is bubbling.

**Each serving:** About 570 calories, 32g protein, 47g carbrohydrate, 29g total fat (11g saturated), 77mg cholesterol, 600mg sodium

## FILO-CRUST CHICKEN PIES

*Prep: 55 minutes    Bake: 20–25 minutes*
*Makes 4 main dish servings*

1 tbsp vegetable oil
1 medium onion, diced
225g potatoes, peeled and cut into 1cm pieces
2 medium carrots, sliced
1 tsp salt
½ tsp ground black pepper
¼ tsp dried tarragon
150g frozen peas

300ml milk
2 tbsp plain flour
450g cooked chicken, cut into bite-sized pieces
3 sheets fresh or frozen (thawed) filo pastry, about 40 by 30cm each (about 60g)
15g butter, melted

◆ Heat oil in 26cm frying pan over medium-high heat. Add onion and cook until tender. Add potatoes, carrots, salt, pepper, tarragon and *225ml water*; bring to the boil. Reduce heat to low; cover and simmer 20 minutes, or until vegetables are tender. Stir in frozen peas.

◆ Mix milk and flour together in small bowl until smooth; stir into liquid in pan. Cook over medium heat, stirring constantly, until mixture boils and thickens. Stir in chicken; spoon chicken mixture into four 300ml ramekins or small ovenproof dishes.

◆ Preheat oven to 220°C (425°F, Gas 7). Place 1 sheet of filo pastry on work surface; lightly brush with some melted butter. Top with second sheet of filo, lightly brushing with more butter. Top with remaining sheet, brushing with remaining butter. Cut stack in half crossways, then lengthways to make 4 stacks.

◆ Gently arrange 1 stack on top of each ramekin, scrunching centre so edge is within rim. Place ramekins in shallow baking tray. Bake 20–25 minutes until crust is golden and filling is hot.

**Each serving:** About 455 calories, 43g protein, 35g carbohydrate, 15g total fat (5g saturated), 114mg cholesterol, 800mg sodium

# USING COOKED POULTRY

Use cooked poultry to create satisfying meals with an international flair in no time. We've paired chicken and turkey with bold flavours to create a spicy Thai stir-fry, a Mexican-inspired tortilla dish with creamy avocado and melted cheese, zesty burritos and even a quick French-style cassoulet. Always keep cooked poultry refrigerated until you are ready to use it.

1 Prepare rice: Bring *450ml water* to the boil in 2-litre saucepan. Add rice, salt and black pepper and return to the boil. Reduce heat to low; cover and simmer 20 minutes, or until rice is tender and liquid absorbed. Stir in parsley. Set aside and keep warm.

## THAI TURKEY

◆◆◆◆◆◆◆◆◆◆◆◆◆◆◆◆◆◆◆◆◆◆◆◆◆◆◆◆◆◆◆◆

*Prep:* 20 minutes    *Cook:* 25 minutes
*Makes* 4 main dish servings

| | |
|---|---|
| **200g long-grain rice** | **1 tbsp chopped fresh coriander** |
| **¾ tsp salt** | **1 tbsp honey** |
| **¼ tsp coarsely ground black pepper** | **1½ tsp curry powder** |
| **2 tsp chopped fresh parsley** | **1 tsp sesame oil** |
| **350g cooked turkey breast meat** | **½ tsp cornflour** |
| **3 spring onions** | **¼ tsp dried chilli flakes** |
| **1 medium red pepper** | **1 tbsp vegetable oil** |
| **1 garlic clove, finely chopped** | **Chopped fresh coriander and sliced spring onions for garnish** |
| **2 tbsp soy sauce** | |

2 Meanwhile, coarsely shred turkey meat. Thinly slice spring onions and cut red pepper into 5cm long matchstick strips.

3 Mix garlic, soy sauce, 1 tablespoon chopped coriander, honey, curry powder, sesame oil, cornflour, dried chilli flakes and *75ml water* together in small bowl.

4 Heat vegetable oil in wok or 30cm frying pan over high heat. Add spring onions and red pepper and cook, stirring frequently, until tender and golden. Stir in soy sauce mixture and turkey; cook, stirring to coat turkey well, until heated through. Serve over rice, garnished with coriander and spring onions.

### SOME LIKE IT HOT

Dried chillies are prized round the globe for their flavour – and fire. Ground red pepper blends easily with other ingredients; a pinch will heat up an entire dish. Dried chilli flakes can be sautéed or used as a condiment. Whole dried chillies are best suited to simmered dishes.

**EACH SERVING: ABOUT 355 CALORIES, 30g PROTEIN, 45g CARBOHYDRATE, 6g TOTAL FAT (1g SATURATED), 71mg CHOLESTEROL, 965mg SODIUM**

# TRIPLE-DECKER TORTILLA MELT

*Prep: 25 minutes    Bake: 12–15 minutes*
*Makes 4 main dish servings*

1 medium avocado
3 tbsp mayonnaise
1 tbsp milk
2 tsp fresh lemon juice
¼ tsp salt
⅛ tsp ground black pepper
450g cooked chicken breast
   meat

3 flour tortillas (about 20cm
   each)
125g canned or bottled mild
   green chillies, drained and
   chopped
125g Cheddar cheese, grated
3 medium plum tomatoes,
   thinly sliced

◆ Cut avocado lengthways in half; remove stone and peel. Mash avocado with next 5 ingredients in small bowl. Discard skin and bones from chicken; cut into bite-sized pieces.

◆ Preheat oven to 190°C (375°F, Gas 5). Heat 1 tortilla in 26cm frying pan over high heat, turning once, 40 seconds, or until slightly crisp. Repeat with remaining 2 tortillas.

◆ Place 1 tortilla on ungreased baking sheet; top with half of chicken. Spread half of avocado mixture over chicken; sprinkle with half of chillies and one-third of cheese. Arrange one-third of tomato slices over cheese.

◆ Top with second tortilla; top with remaining chicken, avocado mixture and chillies, then half of remaining cheese and half of remaining tomato slices. Top with third tortilla; arrange remaining tomato on top. Sprinkle with remaining cheese. Bake 12–15 minutes until heated through and cheese on top is browned. To serve, cut into 4 wedges.

**Each serving: About 505 calories, 37g protein, 24g carbohydrate, 30g total fat (9g saturated), 101mg cholesterol, 650mg sodium**

# CHICKEN BURRITOS

*Prep: 25 minutes    Bake: 35 minutes*
*Makes 4 main dish servings*

1.3kg roasted chicken
200g canned tomatoes
1 jalapeño chilli, diced
60ml soured cream
1 tbsp chilli powder
450g canned refried beans

8 flour tortillas (about 20cm
   each)
175g Cheddar cheese, grated
60g iceberg lettuce, sliced
Avocado and lime slices for
   garnish

◆ Discard skin and bones from chicken and pull meat into thin shreds. Mix shredded chicken, tomatoes with their liquid, jalepeño chilli, soured cream and chilli powder together in large bowl.

◆ Preheat oven to 220°C (425°F, Gas 7). Spread one-eighth of beans over each tortilla. Spoon one-eighth of chicken mixture across centre of each bean-topped tortilla. Sprinkle half of cheese evenly over chicken; roll up tortillas and place, seam-side down, in ovenproof dish.

◆ Cover with foil and bake 30 minutes, or until heated through. Remove foil; sprinkle burritos with remaining cheese. Bake 5 minutes longer, or until cheese melts. Serve with lettuce; garnish with avocado and lime slices.

**Each serving: About 825 calories, 63g protein, 65g carbohydrate, 34g total fat (15g saturated), 170mg cholesterol, 1345mg sodium**

# QUICK TURKEY CASSOULET

*Prep: 25 minutes    Cook: 40 minutes*
*Makes 8 main dish servings*

450g smoked Polish sausage,
   cut into 1cm slices
2 tbsp vegetable oil
450g carrots, cut into 2.5cm
   pieces
2 large onions, sliced
2 medium celery stalks, sliced
1.2kg canned cannellini
   beans, rinsed and drained

300g cooked turkey, cut into
   bite-sized pieces
400g canned tomatoes
½ beef stock cube, crumbled
1 bay leaf
60g fresh breadcrumbs
1 tbsp plus 15g chopped fresh
   parsley

◆ Cook sausage in 5-litre flameproof casserole over medium heat until browned. Transfer to plate. Heat 1 tablespoon oil in juices in casserole. Add carrots, onions and celery and cook 10 minutes, or until tender.

◆ Return sausage to casserole; add cannellini, turkey, tomatoes with their juice, stock cube, bay leaf and *350ml water*. Bring to the boil over high heat; reduce heat to low; simmer 15 minutes.

◆ Meanwhile, heat remaining 1 tablespoon oil in 1-litre saucepan over medium-high heat. Add breadcrumbs and 1 tablespoon parsley; cook until crumbs are golden.

◆ To serve, discard bay leaf. Stir remaining 15g parsley into cassoulet; sprinkle with toasted breadcrumbs.

**Each serving: About 445 calories, 29g protein, 38g carbohydrate, 20g total fat (6g saturated), 67mg cholesterol, 1480mg sodium**

# GRILLED POULTRY

Grilling is an ideal cooking method – simple, fast and requiring a minimum of fat – and it's suitable for all kinds of poultry cuts. Our recipes range from tender nuggets of boneless chicken breast in a spicy marinade to poussin halves with a simple herb and lemon seasoning. Make sure to preheat the grill for 10 minutes before using. Grills vary in the degree of heat they generate, so check the food carefully for doneness. To avoid flare-ups when grilling, never line the rack of the grill pan with foil – the fat should be allowed to drip through into the pan below (if you like, for easy cleaning, line the grill pan only).

**1** Mix first 9 ingredients together in 30 by 18cm ovenproof dish. Add chicken and turn to coat. Cover with cling film and refrigerate 3 hours.

**2** Preheat grill. Lightly grease rack in grill. Arrange chicken on rack. Spread any mixture left in dish over chicken.

## ISLAND CHICKEN WITH FRUIT

❖❖❖❖❖❖❖❖❖❖❖❖❖❖❖❖❖❖❖❖❖❖❖❖❖❖❖

*Prep: 25 minutes, plus marinating    Grill: 12–15 minutes*
*Makes 4 main dish servings*

1 small onion, grated
225g plain low-fat yogurt
1 tbsp vegetable oil
2 tsp grated peeled fresh
   ginger
1 tsp salt
½ tsp ground cumin
¼ tsp chilli powder
¼ tsp ground turmeric
¼ tsp ground cinnamon

4 skinless, boneless chicken
   breasts (about 750g)
½ small honeydew melon
2 large mangoes
2 tbsp peach jam
1 tbsp fresh lime juice
¼ tsp coarsely ground black
   pepper
Lime rind slivers for garnish
Couscous (optional)

**3** Grill chicken about 12cm from heat, without turning, 12–15 minutes, until chicken loses its pink colour throughout.

**4** Meanwhile, remove peel from melon and mangoes. Cut both into 4cm chunks. Gently toss fruit with peach jam, lime juice and pepper together in large bowl.

**5** Slice each chicken breast on slight diagonal into 6 pieces. Arrange on 4 plates, keeping original shape intact. Spoon fruit mixture on the side and garnish with lime rind slivers. Serve with couscous, if you like.

EACH SERVING: ABOUT 420 CALORIES, 42g PROTEIN, 44g CARBOHYDRATE, 9g TOTAL FAT (3g SATURATED), 125mg CHOLESTEROL, 640mg SODIUM

## JAMAICAN JERK CHICKEN KEBABS

*Prep: 20 minutes, plus marinating*    *Grill: 10 minutes*
*Makes 4 main dish servings*

| | |
|---|---|
| 2 spring onions, chopped | 3 tsp vegetable oil |
| 1 jalapeño chilli, seeded and chopped | Salt |
| 1 tbsp chopped peeled fresh ginger | 4 skinless, boneless chicken breasts (about 450g), cut into 12 pieces |
| 2 tbsp white wine vinegar | 2 medium red peppers, cored, seeded and cut into 2.5cm pieces |
| 2 tbsp Worcestershire sauce | |
| 1 tsp ground allspice | |
| 1 tsp dried thyme | 4 long all-metal skewers |

◆ Blend spring onions, jalapeño chilli, ginger, white wine vinegar, Worcestershire sauce, allspice, thyme, 2 teaspoons oil and ½ teaspoon salt together in blender on high speed until combined.

◆ Place chicken pieces in medium bowl. Add spring onion mixture, stirring to coat. Cover with cling film and refrigerate 30 minutes.

◆ Preheat grill. Meanwhile, toss pepper pieces with remaining 1 teaspoon oil and ⅛ teaspoon salt in small bowl.

◆ Alternately thread chicken and pepper pieces on 4 long metal skewers. Place on rack in grill and brush with any remaining marinade. Grill at closest position to heat, turning once, 10 minutes, or until chicken just loses its pink colour throughout.

**Each serving: About 185 calories, 26g protein, 5g carbohydrate, 6g total fat (2g saturated), 81mg cholesterol, 485mg sodium**

## GRILLED POUSSINS WITH LEMON

*Prep: 5 minutes*    *Grill: 30 minutes*
*Makes 4 main dish servings*

| | |
|---|---|
| 2 poussins, about 500g each, each cut lengthways in half (see page 146) | ¼ tsp dried rosemary, crushed |
| | ½ tsp dried thyme |
| | ¼ tsp ground black pepper |
| Salt | 2 tbsp fresh lemon juice |

◆ Preheat grill. Arrange poussin halves in small roasting tin, skin-side down, and sprinkle with ¼ teaspoon salt. Grill about 15cm from heat 15 minutes.

◆ Mix rosemary, thyme, black pepper and ½ teaspoon salt together in small bowl. Turn poussins over; sprinkle with herb mixture.

◆ Grill, basting once or twice with juices from roasting tin, 15 minutes longer, or until golden and juices run clear when thickest part of poussin is pierced with tip of knife.

◆ Transfer to warm platter; skim fat from juices in roasting tin. Add lemon juice to roasting tin, stirring until brown bits are loosened. Spoon juices over poussins.

**Each serving: About 245 calories, 32g protein, 1g carbohydrate 12g total fat (3g saturated), 92mg cholesterol, 480mg sodium**

## CHILLI-SPICED CHICKEN LEGS

*Prep: 15 minutes*    *Broil: 45–50 minutes*
*Makes 8 main dish servings*

| | |
|---|---|
| 350ml bottled chilli sauce | 1 tbsp olive oil |
| 1 small onion, grated | 2 tsp chilli powder |
| 1 garlic clove, very finely chopped | 1 tsp salt |
| | ½ tsp Tabasco sauce |
| 3 tbsp brown sugar | 3 tbsp chopped fresh parsley |
| 1 tbsp white wine vinegar | 8 chicken leg quarters |

◆ Preheat grill. Mix first 9 ingredients together with 2 tablespoons chopped parsley and *1 tablespoon water* in medium bowl until blended.

◆ Arrange chicken quarters, skin-side down, on rack in grill pan and brush chicken with some chilli mixture. Grill about 15cm from heat 25 minutes.

◆ Turn chicken over and grill 20–25 minutes longer, brushing occasionally with chilli mixture, until juices run clear when chicken is pierced with tip of knife. To serve, sprinkle with remaining 1 tablespoon chopped parsley.

**Each serving: About 380 calories, 34g protein, 18g carbohydrate, 19g total fat (5g saturated), 116mg cholesterol, 955mg sodium**

# BARBECUED POULTRY

Except for quick-cooking escalopes and boneless breasts, poultry should be barbecued over medium-hot coals, so that it cooks through without charring or drying out. For safety, use long-handled tongs and basting brushes designed for barbecuing.

## POUSSINS WITH FRUIT SALSA

◆◆◆◆◆◆◆◆◆◆◆◆◆

*Prep: 30 minutes*
*Barbecue: 30 minutes*
*Makes 4 main dish servings*

**1 large red or green jalapeño chilli**
**2 medium peaches**
**2 medium kiwifruit**
**225g canned crushed pineapple in its own juice, drained**
**1 tbsp very finely chopped fresh coriander**
**½ tsp sugar**
**Salt**
**Grated rind of 1 medium lime**
**3 tbsp fresh lime juice**
**2 garlic cloves, very finely chopped**
**4 tsp chilli powder**
**1 tbsp olive oil**
**2 poussins (450g each), each cut lengthways in half (see page 146)**

**1** Prepare barbecue. Prepare fruit salsa: cut jalapeño chilli lengthways in half; discard seeds and very finely chop chilli.

**2** Peel, halve, and stone peaches; peel kiwifruit. Dice peaches and 1 kiwifruit. Slice remaining kiwifruit and place in medium bowl; using fork, coarsely crush.

**3** Stir in diced peaches and kiwifruit, jalapeño chilli, pineapple, chopped coriander, sugar, ½ teaspoon salt, lime rind and 2 tablespoons lime juice. Cover and refrigerate.

### JALAPEÑO CHILLIES

....................

Jalapeño chillies spice up countless dishes from salsas to bean or grain salads and dips. Most of the heat lies in the ribs and seeds; for extra kick, leave them in. Green jalapeños have a green-pepper flavour. Red jalapeños are the ripe form of the green; they offer a sweeter flavour.

**4** Mix garlic, chilli powder and oil with remaining lime juice and 1 teaspoon salt in bowl; rub over poussins. Put poussins on side of barbecue (not over hottest point) over medium heat. Barbecue, turning often, 30 minutes, or until juices run clear when pierced with knife. Serve with salsa.

EACH SERVING: ABOUT 370 CALORIES, 33g PROTEIN, 23g CARBOHYDRATE, 16g TOTAL FAT (4g SATURATED), 92mg CHOLESTEROL, 930mg SODIUM

## HERBED TURKEY ESCALOPES

*Prep: 10 minutes    Barbecue: 5–7 minutes*
*Makes 4 main dish servings*

2 medium lemons
1 tbsp chopped fresh sage or
   ¾ tsp dried
1 tbsp vegetable oil
½ tsp salt
¼ tsp coarsely ground black
   pepper

1 garlic clove, crushed
4 turkey escalopes
   (about 450g)
Sage leaves and barbecued
   lemon slices for garnish
Sautéed peppers and lamb's
   lettuce (optional)

◆ Prepare barbecue. Grate 2 teaspoons rind from lemons. Cut each lemon in half and squeeze juice from 3 halves into small bowl. Stir lemon rind, chopped sage, vegetable oil, salt, black pepper and crushed garlic into lemon juice in bowl until combined. Place turkey escalopes on barbecue over high heat. Barbecue, brushing with lemon mixture often and turning once, 5–7 minutes until turkey just loses its pink colour throughout.

◆ Place turkey escalopes on 4 plates. Squeeze juice from remaining lemon half over them. Garnish with sage leaves and barbecued lemon slices, and serve with sautéed peppers and lamb's lettuce, if you like.

**Each serving: About 175 calories, 29g protein; 3g carbohydrate, 4g total fat (1g saturated), 71mg cholesterol, 325mg sodium**

◆◆◆◆◆◆◆◆◆◆◆◆◆◆◆◆◆◆◆◆◆◆◆◆◆◆

### BARBECUED CITRUS GARNISHES

Barbecued slices of oranges, lemons or limes make attractive and flavourful garnishes for barbecued foods. Slice thinly; carefully remove seeds. Barbecue slices 2–5 minutes on each side, until grill marks appear.

◆◆◆◆◆◆◆◆◆◆◆◆◆◆◆◆◆◆◆◆◆◆◆◆◆◆

## APRICOT-GINGER CHICKEN LEGS

*Prep: 10 minutes    Barbecue: 35 minutes*
*Makes 6 main dish servings*

2 spring onions, chopped
175g apricot jam
90g tomato ketchup
2 tbsp cider vinegar
1 tbsp plus 1 tsp grated
   peeled fresh ginger

1 tbsp plus 1 tsp soy sauce
6 chicken leg quarters
   (about 1.6kg)

◆ Prepare barbecue. Mix spring onions, apricot jam, tomato ketchup, cider vinegar, grated ginger and soy sauce together in small bowl.

◆ Place chicken quarters on barbecue over medium heat. Barbecue about 10 minutes until golden on both sides. Then, to avoid charring, stand chicken quarters upright, leaning one against the other. Barbecue about 25 minutes longer, rearranging pieces from time to time, until juices run clear when chicken is pierced with tip of knife.

◆ During last 10 minutes of cooking, brush chicken quarters frequently with apricot mixture.

**Each serving: About 425 calories, 37g protein. 26g carbohydrate, 19g total fat (5g saturated), 129mg cholesterol, 625mg sodium**

## SWEET-AND-SOUR CHICKEN WINGS

*Prep: 5 minutes    Barbecue: 25–30 minutes*
*Makes 4 main dish servings*

60ml red wine vinegar
60ml soy sauce
50g sugar
1 tbsp cornflour
2 tbsp sesame oil

12 chicken wings (about 900g)
¼ tsp ground black pepper
Chopped spring onion for
   garnish

◆ Prepare barbecue. Prepare sweet-and-sour sauce: combine vinegar, soy sauce, sugar, cornflour, sesame oil and *60ml water* in 1-litre saucepan. Cook over medium-high heat, stirring, until sauce boils and thickens; boil 1 minute. Remove pan from heat.

◆ Sprinkle chicken wings with pepper and place on barbecue over medium heat. Barbecue 25–30 minutes until tender and golden and juices run clear when chicken is pierced with tip of knife, turning chicken wings frequently and brushing with sweet-and-sour sauce during last 10 minutes of cooking. To serve, sprinkle chicken wings with chopped spring onion.

**Each serving: About 440 calories, 31g protein, 17g carbohydrate, 29g total fat (8g saturated), 188mg cholesterol, 1140mg sodium**

# M7EAT

Whether preparing beef, pork, lamb or veal, the same basic cooking techniques apply. The method you choose depends largely on the cut. Here is the essential guide for making the best decisions on choosing, cooking and carving a joint of meat.

## BUYING AND STORING

• The U.K. has stringent hygiene standards. 'Quality' rating standards are voluntary. The current system, devised by the wholesaler to enable the retailer to estimate the yield of the carcass, only indicates the age and size of the carcass.
• Select joints with a good colour and even marbling; any fat should be creamy white. Check that bones are cut cleanly, with no obvious splintering. Be sure to note the sell-by date on the label; cuts in vacuum packaging have a longer shelf life.
• For boneless cuts and minced meat, allow about 125–150g per serving. For cuts with some bone, such as chops, allow 150–225g; for bony cuts, such as ribs, 350–450g.
• Store raw meat in the coldest part of the refrigerator, away from cooked and ready-to-eat foods. Refrigerate uncooked meats 2 to 3 days or freeze up to 6 months. Refrigerate minced meat only 1 to 2 days or freeze up to 3 months.
• For short-term storage, up to 2 days in the refrigerator or 2 weeks in the freezer, leave the meat in its original wrapping if intact. For longer freezing, or if wrapping is torn, carefully re-wrap meat in freezer wrap, heavy-duty plastic wrap or foil, pressing out air. Layer steaks, chops and patties with freezer bags before wrapping. Label packets with the name of the cut, the number of servings and the date.
• Thaw frozen meat on a plate to catch drips overnight in the refrigerator – never on the worktop. Use thawed meat as soon as possible; never re-freeze, or the texture of the meat will suffer.

## COOKING SUCCESS

### Roasting
• When roasting boneless joints, place the meat on a rack in the roasting tin. That way, the heat can circulate under the meat and prevent it from steaming in its juices. For some joints, such as rib roasts, the bones act as a built-in rack.
• Use a meat thermometer to determine doneness. Insert it into the thickest part of the meat without touching bone.
• Remove the roast from the oven when it reaches 2–5°C less than the desired temperature; the temperature will continue to rise as the meat stands.

### Pan-frying and sautéing
• Pat meat dry with kitchen towels; it will brown more easily.
• Use a heavy-bottomed pan, which will conduct heat evenly.
• Use just enough oil to prevent meat from sticking and make sure the pan is hot before adding the meat.
• Avoid crowding the pan, or meat will steam, not brown.
• After cooking meat, pour off any fat and then de-glaze the pan by adding a little liquid to release the caramelized meat juices and create a quick sauce.

### Braising and stewing
• Cut meat into cubes of about the same size for uniform cooking, then pat dry with kitchen towels before browning.
• Simmer over low heat; do not boil or meat will toughen.
• Use a pan with a tight-fitting lid to keep in steam.
• To test braised or simmered meat for doneness, pierce with a fork; the fork should slip in easily.
• Many stews taste even better if cooked a day ahead, then chilled overnight to allow flavors to build and mellow. Remove any solidified surface fat before reheating.

### Grilling and barbecuing
• Grill or barbeque thinner cuts close to the heat. Thicker cuts need more distance so the inside has time to cook through before the outside burns.
• To prevent flare-ups when grilling, do not line the rack with foil; the fat must be able to drip through. If you like, for easy cleaning, line the pan below the rack with foil.
• To avoid piercing meat and releasing its juices, use tongs rather than a fork to turn it over.

## CARVING IT RIGHT

• Let steaks and roasts stand, covered in foil, for 10–15 minutes before slicing. The juices settle, enriching the flavour and firming the meat so it's easier to carve.
• Place a cloth under the chopping board to prevent slipping and always use a sharp knife.
• Carve across the grain, not parallel to the fibres of the meat – this produces shorter fibres for more tender meat.

## SHARPENING A CARVING KNIFE

Rest one end of sharpening steel on work surface. Position the widest part of blade at a 20° angle on the underside of the steel near finger guard. Draw knife downward, pulling the handle toward you gradually, until you have sharpened the full length of the blade; repeat on other side of knife. Continue, alternating strokes, until sharp.

# BEEF KNOW-HOW

Virtually any cut of beef can be a delicious meal if it's cooked correctly. What determines the best method is the quality of the cut; the part of the animal from which the cut comes; and the animal's age (older meat will be tougher). Read on for helpful hints and tips to ensure you get juicy, tender results from every cut you cook.

## THE 'LEAN' STORY

Thanks to improved raising methods, trim butchering and consumer demand for healthier foods, beef is leaner than in the past.

• Although there are strict rules throughout the U.K. governing hygiene standards, this is not true regarding grading the quality of the meat. Any voluntary grading is meant to communicate carcass age and yield between the wholesaler and retailer. Moreover, cutting methods may vary from region to region, but the names assigned to carcass parts are generally consistent.

• Cuts of beef labelled 'rump' or 'topside' are lean.

• Lighter, pinker minced beef has a higher percentage of fat, around 25 per cent. Leaner options are available up to 10 per cent. Check with your butcher or check most packets of lean mince for the percentage of lean meat.

• To eliminate the danger of E. coli and other bacteria, minced beef, lean or otherwise, should always be cooked to medium doneness – until barely pink in the centre.

• To be tender, lean cuts should either be pan-fried or roasted briefly, just until medium-rare so they do not dry out, or else braised for a long time.

## BUYING BEEF

• For all beef, colour is a good indicator of quality. Beef should be bright to deep red. Any fat should be dry and creamy white. Cut edges should look freshly cut and moist, but never wet.

• Minced beef should look bright and cherry red. Don't worry if the centre of the packet looks darker than the exterior. The darker colour comes from a lack of oxygen; when exposed to air, the dark meat should return to red. Vacuum-packed beef is darker and more purple in colour.

• All beef is aged to improve its texture and flavour; for supermarket beef the process is quite short. Traditional aging can take up to six weeks; such cuts are more expensive and are generally found only at family butchers and restaurants.

## CHOOSING THE RIGHT CUT

With appropriate cooking methods, any cut of beef can be tender. Cook lean cuts by dry-heat methods (roasting, grilling, barbecuing, pan-frying); for less-tender cuts use a moist-heat method (stewing, braising) until meat fibres are fork-tender.

**For grilling or pan-frying** Lean, tender cuts work best for these quick methods. When grilling steaks 2–3cm thick or more, position them further from the heat so the outside isn't charred before the inside is done.

**Suitable cuts** Porterhouse steak, T-bone steak (below), rump, forerib, rib-eye, sirloin steaks, fillet, flank (or goose) steak, minced beef.

Trim away excess fat before cooking

Look for lightly marbled meat with fat in broken lines

Steaks for grilling should be at least 2cm thick

**For braising or stewing** Less tender cuts of beef become deliciously tender when simmered in a well-flavoured liquid for a long time. Such cuts are often less expensive too.

**Suitable cuts** Chuck steak, blade, silverside (below, unrolled), brisket, short ribs, shin, blade steak, oxtails. Cubes for stew are usually cut from boneless beef round or chuck. Bones add flavour and body to stews.

Trim away excess fat before cooking in liquid

Whole cuts keep their shape during long, slow cooking

Coarse grained, less tender cuts require moist-heat cooking

**For roasting** Large, tender cuts with some internal fat will give best results. Roast boneless cuts on a rack in a shallow roasting pan so the meat doesn't stew in its juices; bone-in roasts don't need a rack.

**Suitable cuts** Standing rib roast (below), sirloin, fillet and whole rib-eye.

A thin covering of fat ensures meat stays moist during cooking

Bones should be cleanly cut

Meat should have some marbling for tenderness

# ROASTING BEEF

To roast to perfection, use a meat thermometer to judge accurately when the meat is 'done' – 59.5°C for medium-rare and 67°C for medium. The roasting chart on the right gives guidelines for cooking a variety of joints. Start with the meat at refrigerator temperature, and **remove the roast from the oven when it reaches 2–5°C below the desired doneness; the temperature will rise as the roast stands**. For juiciest meat, allow the roast to stand for 15 minutes before carving.

## ROASTING TIMES

| CUT | OVEN TEMPERATURE | WEIGHT | APPROXIMATE COOKING TIME Medium-rare (59.9°C) | Medium (67°C) |
|---|---|---|---|---|
| Rib roast (chine bone removed) | 180°C (350°F, Gas 4) | 1.8–2.7kg<br>2.7–3.6kg | 1¾–2¼ hrs<br>2¼–2½ hrs | 2¼–2¾ hrs<br>2¾–3 hrs |
| Rib eye roast | 180°C (350°F, Gas 4) | 1.8–2.7kg | 1¾–2 hrs | 2–2½ hrs |
| Whole fillet | 220°C (425°F, Gas 7) | 1.8–2.2kg | 50–60 mins | 60–70 mins |
| Half fillet | 220°C (425°F, Gas 7) | 900g–1.3kg | 35–40 mins | 45–50 mins |
| Silverside | 160°C (325°F, Gas 3) | 1.3–1.8kg<br>2.7–3.6kg | 1¾–2 hrs<br>2½–3 hrs | 2¼–2½ hrs<br>3–3½ hrs |
| Topside | 160°C (325°F, Gas 3) | 900g–1.3kg | 1½–1¾ hrs | — |

## SLICING A RUMP STEAK

Use a 2-pronged carving fork to steady the meat. Cut steak across the grain for tender slices.

Starting at thin end of steak, position carving knife at a 45° angle to meat, with blade facing away from you. Use a sawing motion to cut slices along length of steak.

## CARVING A RIB ROAST

The chine bone should be removed by your butcher so that you can carve the roast between the rib bones. Carving will be easier, and the meat will be juicier, if you allow the roast to stand for at least 15 minutes after you have removed it from the oven.

1 Place roast, rib-side down, on cutting board. With a carving knife, cut down toward ribs to make a slice about 5mm thick.

2 Release the meat slice by cutting along edge of rib bone. Transfer slice to warm platter.

3 Repeat to cut more slices. As each rib bone is exposed, cut it away from roast and add to platter. This will make it easier to carve the rest of the roast.

## STEAK SUCCESS

Cut into steaks to check for doneness, following our visual guide at right. Always use a meat thermometer to check roasts.

Rare steak

Medium-rare steak

Well-done steak

# ROAST BEEF

Roast beef is superb when rubbed with a herb coating, which flavours the meat and the roasting juices. The roasting tin should be kept uncovered; placing the meat fat-side up keeps it moist. Since no two cuts of meat are exactly alike, a meat thermometer is the best guide to when the roast is cooked to perfection.

## BEEF RIB ROAST WITH MADEIRA GRAVY

*Prep: 15 minutes, plus standing and making Yorkshire Pudding*
*Roast: 2 hours 20 minutes*
*Makes 12 main dish servings*

| | |
|---|---|
| 1 tbsp fennel seeds | Yorkshire Pudding (optional, see page 184) |
| 1 tsp coarsely ground black pepper | 60ml Madeira or dry sherry |
| 1 tsp salt | 2 tbsp plain flour |
| 2 tbsp chopped fresh parsley | 1 stock cube, crumbled |
| 1 (3-rib) beef rib roast, (about 3.1kg), chine bone removed | Chopped fresh parsley for garnish |
| | Courgettes and carrots (optional) |

1 Preheat oven to 170°C (325°F, Gas 3). Using a pestle and mortar, crush fennel seeds. Stir in pepper, salt and parsley. Pat roast dry with kitchen towels. Rub fennel mixture over roast. Place roast, fat-side up, on rack in large roasting tin.

2 Insert meat thermometer into centre of roast. Roast 2 hours 20 minutes (20 minutes per 450g), or until thermometer reaches 57°C. Internal temperature of meat will rise to 59.5°C (medium-rare) upon standing. Or, roast until desired doneness.

3 Transfer beef to warm large platter; let stand 15 minutes for easier carving. Keep warm. Remove rack from roasting tin. Pour pan drippings into 1-litre measuring jug; let stand a few seconds until fat separates from meat juice. Skim 2 tablespoons fat from juices into 2-litre saucepan. Skim remaining fat; discard or reserve for Yorkshire Pudding. Prepare Yorkshire Pudding, if you like.

4 Prepare gravy: add Madeira and *125ml water* to roasting tin; stir over medium heat until brown bits are loosened. Add Madeira mixture to meat juice in measuring jug with enough *water* to make 900ml; set aside. Stir flour into fat in saucepan until blended. Cook over medium heat, stirring constantly, until flour turns golden.

5 Gradually stir in meat-juice mixture and stock cube; cook, stirring, until gravy boils and thickens slightly. To serve, slice beef. Arrange slices on 12 plates; sprinkle with chopped parsley. Serve with gravy, and Yorkshire Pudding, courgettes, and carrots, if you like.

EACH SERVING: ABOUT 530 CALORIES, 70g PROTEIN, 1g CARBOHYDRATE, 24g TOTAL FAT (9g SATURATED), 167mg CHOLESTEROL, 320mg SODIUM

## MUSTARD-CRUSTED RIB-EYE ROAST

*Prep: 25 minutes, plus standing    Roast: 80 minutes*
*Makes 12 main dish servings*

1 boned and rolled beef
  rib-eye roast (about 1.8kg)
½ tsp dried thyme
Salt and ground black pepper
6 medium red onions, each
  cut lengthways in half
1 tbsp horseradish sauce

90g course-grained Dijon
  mustard
750g green beans, ends
  trimmed
2 tbsp olive or vegetable oil
450g mange-tout or sugar
  snap peas, strings removed

◆ Preheat oven to 180°C (350°F, Gas 4). Pat roast dry with kitchen towels. Mix thyme, 1 teaspoon salt and ½ teaspoon pepper together in small bowl; use to rub over roast. Place roast, fat-side up, in large roasting tin with onions. Insert meat thermometer into centre of roast; roast 1 hour, turning onions occasionally.

◆ In small bowl, mix horseradish and mustard. After meat has roasted 1 hour, spread top with mustard mixture. Roast 20 minutes longer, or until thermometer reaches 57°C. Internal temperature of meat will rise to 59.5°C (medium-rare) upon standing. Or, roast until desired doneness. Transfer roast to warm large platter; let stand 15 minutes.

◆ Meanwhile, bring *2–3cm water* to the boil in 30cm frying pan over high heat. Add green beans; return to the boil. Reduce heat to low; cover and simmer 8–10 minutes, until tender-crisp. Drain. Wipe pan dry. In same pan, heat oil over high heat; add green beans and mange-tout and cook, stirring constantly, until coated. Sprinkle with 1 teaspoon salt and ¼ teaspoon pepper; cook, stirring, 5 minutes longer, or until mange-tout are tender-crisp. Slice roast; arrange vegetable mixture on platter with roast.

**Each serving: About 505 calories, 30g protein, 14g carbohydrate, 36g total fat (14g saturated), 103mg cholesterol, 545mg sodium**

## ROAST BEEF WITH TWO SAUCES

*Prep: 25 minutes, plus standing    Roast: 1½ hours*
*Makes 8 main dish servings*

1 topside roast (about 1.7kg)
2 tsp dried thyme
1 tsp dried sage
4 garlic cloves, very finely
  chopped
¼ tsp salt
Coarsely ground black pepper
175ml olive or vegetable oil

75g canned or bottled drained
  and chopped capers
90g Dijon mustard
1 tbsp chopped chives
175g horseradish sauce
110g mayonnaise
1 tsp sugar
125g whipping cream

◆ Preheat oven to 170°C (325°F, Gas 3). Trim any fat from roast; pat dry with kitchen towels. In cup, mix thyme, sage, garlic, salt and 1¼ teaspoons pepper. Use to rub over roast. Place roast on rack in small roasting tin. Insert meat thermometer into centre of roast.

◆ Roast beef 1½ hours, or until thermometer reaches 57°C. Internal temperature of meat will rise to 59.5°C (medium-rare) upon standing. Or, roast until desired doneness. Transfer roast to warm large platter; let stand 15 minutes.

◆ Meanwhile, prepare sauces. For caper sauce: mix oil, capers, Dijon mustard, chives, ¾ teaspoon pepper and *60 ml water* in small bowl until blended.

◆ For horseradish sauce: mix horseradish, mayonnaise and sugar in small bowl until blended. Using an electric mixer at medium speed, whip cream to stiff peaks; fold into horseradish mixture.

◆ Slice roast; serve with caper sauce and horseradish sauce.

**Each serving: About 730 calories, 44g protein, 5g carbohydrate, 59g total fat (16g saturated), 153mg cholesterol, 1055mg sodium**

## YORKSHIRE PUDDING

◆ ◆ ◆ ◆ ◆ ◆ ◆ ◆ ◆ ◆ ◆ ◆ ◆

For individual puddings, use eighteen 6 by 4 cm muffin-tin cups; bake puddings only 12–15 minutes.

3 medium eggs
350ml milk
225g plain flour
¾ tsp salt
3 tbsp roast-beef pan juices

1 Preheat oven to 230°C (450°F, Gas 8). Whisk eggs, milk, flour and salt in medium bowl until smooth. Place drippings in 33 x 20cm metal baking tin; place in oven for 2 minutes. Remove tin from oven.

2 Pour milk mixture over hot drippings. Bake 25 minutes, or until puffed and lightly browned. Cut into squares; serve hot. Makes 12 accompaniment servings.

**Each serving: About 105 calories, 4g protein, 13g carbohydrate, 4g total fat (2g saturated), 59mg cholesterol, 165mg sodium**

# ROAST BEEF FILLETS

This premium cut of beef, a boneless strip from the loin, is the most tender and makes a wonderful roast. Unlike larger cuts of beef, the fillet roasts quickly at a high temperature. If cooking a whole, unstuffed fillet, tuck the thin end under so the roast is an even thickness.

## STUFFED BEEF FILLET

◆ ◆ ◆ ◆ ◆ ◆ ◆ ◆ ◆ ◆ ◆ ◆ ◆

*Prep:* 30 minutes, plus standing
*Roast:* 45–50 minutes
*Makes* 10 main dish servings

2 tbsp vegetable oil
1 medium onion, very finely
  chopped
300–350g spinach, chopped
½ tsp salt
¼ tsp ground black pepper
30g Parmesan cheese, freshly
  grated
30g sun-dried oil-packed
  tomatoes, drained and
  finely chopped
1 centre-cut beef fillet
  (about 1.3 kg)
1 beef stock cube, crumbled
60ml dry sherry
Chopped sun-dried oil-packed
  tomatoes for garnish
Assorted sautéed vegetables
  (optional)

**1** Preheat oven to 220°C (425°F, Gas 7). Heat oil in frying pan over medium heat. Add onion; cook until tender. Add spinach, salt and pepper; cook, stirring until spinach just wilts.

**2** Remove mixture from heat; stir in Parmesan cheese and 30g sun-dried tomatoes. Set aside. Make a lengthways cut along centre of fillet, cutting almost but not all the way through.

**3** Ease fillet open. Spoon spinach-cheese mixture evenly into cut in fillet, pressing firmly. Close fillet, packing mixture into cut.

**4** Using kitchen string, tie fillet securely in several places to hold cut edges of meat together. Place fillet, cut-side up, on rack in small roasting tin.

**5** Roast beef fillet 45–50 minutes for medium-rare, or until desired doneness. After meat has roasted 30 minutes, if necessary, cover stuffing with foil to prevent it from drying out.

**6** Transfer meat to chopping board. Let stand 10 minutes; keep warm. Meanwhile, remove rack from roasting tin. Skim and discard fat from juices; add stock cube, sherry, and *350ml water* to roasting tin. Bring to the boil over medium-high heat; stir until brown bits are loosened. To serve, remove strings from beef; slice beef. Arrange slices on 10 plates; garnish with sun-dried tomatoes and serve with gravy, and sautéed vegetables, if you like.

EACH SERVING: ABOUT 270 CALORIES 31g PROTEIN, 4g CARBOHYDRATE, 13g TOTAL FAT (4g SATURATED), 73mg CHOLESTEROL, 335mg SODIUM

## BEEF FILLET WITH WILD MUSHROOMS

*Prep: 25 minutes, plus standing   Roast: 45–55 minutes*
*Makes 8 main dish servings*

1 centre-cut beef fillet (about 1.1kg), tied
2 tsp vegetable oil
Salt and ground black pepper
Dried thyme
30g margarine or butter
50g very finely chopped shallots
350g white mushrooms, sliced

125g shiitake mushrooms, stems discarded, sliced
125g oyster mushrooms, each cut in half if large
75ml Madeira
75ml whipping cream
1tbsp chopped fresh parsley
Steamed mange-tout and tomatoes (optional)

◆ Preheat oven to 220°C (425°F, Gas 7). Pat beef fillet dry with kitchen towels. Combine oil, 1 teaspoon salt, ¼ teaspoon pepper and ¼ teaspoon thyme in small bowl; use to rub over fillet.

◆ Place beef on rack in small roasting tin. Insert meat thermometer into centre of thickest part of meat. Roast 45–55 minutes, until meat thermometer reaches 57°C. Internal temperature of meat will rise to 59.5°C (medium-rare) upon standing. Or, roast until desired doneness.

◆ Meanwhile, in 30cm frying pan, melt margarine over medium-high heat. Add shallots and cook, stirring often, 1 minute. Stir in all mushrooms, ¾ teaspoon salt, ⅛ teaspoon pepper, and ⅛ teaspoon thyme. Cook, stirring often, 10 minutes, or until mushrooms are lightly browned and liquid evaporates. Stir in Madeira and cook until pan is almost dry. Stir in cream; boil 1 minute. Remove from heat.

◆ Transfer fillet to warm large platter. Let stand 10 minutes; keep warm. Remove rack from roasting tin. Add *60ml water* to tin and bring to the boil over medium-high heat. Stir until brown bits are loosened; stir into mushroom mixture with parsley.

◆ Thinly slice fillet; serve with mushrooms, and mange-tout and tomatoes, if you like.

**Each serving: About 360 calories, 34g protein, 15g carbohydrate, 17g total fat (7g saturated), 87mg cholesterol, 375mg sodium**

## ORIENTAL BEEF FILLET

*Prep: 10 minutes, plus marinating and standing   Roast: 50–60 minutes*
*Makes 16 main dish servings*

125ml soy sauce
3 tbsp grated, peeled fresh ginger
1½ tsp fennel seeds, crushed
½ tsp dried chilli flakes

½ tsp cracked black pepper
¼ tsp ground cloves
1 beef fillet (about 2.2kg), tied
1 tbsp vegetable oil
Parsley sprigs for garnish

◆ Mix soy sauce, ginger, fennel seeds, dried chilli flakes, black pepper and cloves in large bowl. Add fillet, turning to coat with marinade.

◆ Cover bowl securely with cling film and refrigerate 6 hours, or overnight, turning fillet occasionally to coat.

◆ Preheat oven to 220°C (425°F, Gas 7). Place fillet on rack in large roasting tin; discard marinade. Brush fillet with oil. Insert meat thermometer into centre of thickest part of meat.

◆ Roast fillet 50–60 minutes until meat thermometer reaches 57°C. Internal temperature of meat will rise to 59.5°C (medium-rare) upon standing. Or, roast until desired doneness.

◆ Transfer fillet to chopping board. Let stand 10 minutes; keep warm. Thinly slice fillet; arrange on warm large platter. Garnish with parsley sprigs.

**Each serving: About 225 calories, 31g protein, 0g carbohydrate, 10g total fat (4g saturated), 74mg cholesterol, 195mg sodium**

---

### FENNEL SEEDS

Native to the Mediterranean, fennel has been prized for its delicate, liquorice-like flavour for thousands of years. The bulb, feathery leaves, stalks, flowers and seeds were popular with the Romans and ancient Greeks, as well as in the cuisines of ancient China, India and Egypt. Fennel seeds are small, greenish-brown ovals that are available whole and ground. They enhance sweet and savoury dishes such as fish soups, breads, sausages, roasted meats, curries, cabbage and even apple pie. To release the flavour fully , lightly crush the seeds in a mortar with a pestle before adding them to a dish. Indian restaurants often serve plain or sugar-coated fennel seeds after dinner as a digestive and breath freshener.

# BRAISED BEEF

Braising, or pot roasting, makes tougher cuts of meat tender. The meat is first browned to seal in flavour, then gently simmered with vegetables and herbs in liquid. Serve the vegetables whole with the meat, or purée them to make a delicious savoury sauce.

**1** Mix first 6 ingredients in small bowl. Pat roast dry with kitchen towels. Rub 2½ teaspoons spice mix over roast; reserve remaining mix.

**2** Heat oil in 5-litre flame-proof casserole over medium-high heat. Add roast; brown well on all sides; transfer to plate.

**3** Add onions, celery and green pepper to juices in casserole. Cover and cook, stirring often, over medium heat until tender.

## CAJUN-STYLE POT ROAST

◆◆◆◆◆◆◆◆◆◆◆◆◆◆

*Prep: 15 minutes*
*Cook: 2½–3 hours*
*Makes 12 main dish servings*

1½ tsp salt
1 tsp paprika
1 tsp dry mustard
½ tsp dried thyme
½ tsp ground red pepper
½ tsp ground black pepper
1 beef silverside or topside roast (about 1.3kg)
1 tbsp vegetable oil
2 medium onions, each cut into wedges
2 large celery stalks, sliced diagonally into 4cm pieces
1 medium green pepper, cut into 4cm pieces
400g canned tomatoes
1 bay leaf
1 garlic clove, very finely chopped
600g frozen whole baby okra
Celery leaves for garnish

**4** Stir in tomatoes with their juice, bay leaf, garlic and remaining spice mix. Return roast to casserole; bring mixture to the boil over high heat. Reduce heat to low. Cover and simmer 2–2½ hours until roast is fork-tender, turning it occasionally. About 10 minutes before roast is done, add frozen okra to casserole; heat through.

**5** To serve, transfer roast and vegetables to warm deep platter. Discard bay leaf. Skim and discard fat from stock in casserole. Slice roast; garnish and serve with stock and vegetables.

EACH SERVING: ABOUT 195 CALORIES, 23g PROTEIN, 8g CARBOHYDRATE, 7g TOTAL FAT (2g SATURATED), 66mg CHOLESTEROL, 190mg SODIUM

## COUNTRY POT ROAST

*Prep: 15 minutes    Cook: 3–3½ hours*
*Makes 12 main dish servings*

| | |
|---|---|
| 1 boneless chuck-eye roast or brisket (about 1.8kg) | 2 large celery stalks, sliced |
| 30g plain flour | 2 garlic cloves, crushed |
| 2 tbsp vegetable oil | 1 tsp dried oregano |
| 350ml tomato juice | ½ tsp salt |
| 2 medium onions, chopped | ¼ tsp ground black pepper |
| 2 medium carrots, sliced | Mashed potatoes (optional) |
| | Flat-leaf parsley for garnish |

◆ Pat roast dry with kitchen towels. Spread flour on greaseproof paper; coat roast with flour.

◆ Heat oil over medium-high heat in 5-litre flameproof casserole. Add roast and brown on all sides; discard fat in casserole.

◆ Add tomato juice, onions, carrots, celery, garlic, oregano, salt and pepper to roast in casserole, stirring to combine. Bring to the boil over high heat.

◆ Reduce heat to low; cover and simmer 2½–3 hours, until roast is fork-tender, turning roast occasionally.

◆ Transfer roast to warm large platter; keep warm. Skim and discard fat from stock in casserole. Fill blender about half-full with stock and vegetables from casserole. Cover (with centre part of blender lid removed) and blend on low speed until mixture is smooth; pour into large bowl. Repeat until all of mixture is blended.

◆ Return gravy mixture to casserole and bring to the boil over high heat. Thinly slice roast; serve with gravy, and mashed potatoes, if you like. Garnish with parsley.

Each serving: About 420 calories, 31g protein, 7g carbohydrate, 29g total fat (11g saturated), 117mg cholesterol, 285mg sodium

## ROLLED SILVERSIDE WITH SPRING VEGETABLES

*Prep: 25 minutes    Cook: 70 minutes*
*Makes 8 main dish servings*

| | |
|---|---|
| 1 rolled silverside or topside (about 900g), tied | 1 bay leaf |
| ½ tsp coarsely ground black pepper | ½ tsp dried tarragon |
| | 750g baby carrots, trimmed |
| 2 tsp vegetable oil | 800g small white and/or red potatoes |
| 1 beef stock cube (5g), crumbled | 750g thin asparagus, tough ends removed |
| 1 garlic clove, cut in half | |

◆ Pat beef dry with kitchen towels; rub with pepper. Heat oil over medium-high heat in 5-litre flameproof casserole; add meat and brown on all sides.

◆ Add stock cube, garlic, bay leaf, tarragon and *600ml water*; bring to the boil. Reduce heat to low; cover and simmer 20 minutes. Add carrots and potatoes; return to the boil over high heat.

◆ Reduce heat to low; cover and simmer 30 minutes longer, or until vegetables are tender and temperature of meat reaches 57°C on instant-read meat thermometer inserted in thickest part of meat. The internal temperature of meat will rise to 59.5°C (medium-rare) upon standing. Transfer meat to warm large platter; keep warm.

◆ Meanwhile, bring *1cm water* to the boil in 30cm frying pan over high heat; add asparagus and cook 3–5 minutes until tender-crisp; drain.

◆ Transfer carrots and potatoes to platter with meat, reserving stock in casserole. Discard garlic and bay leaf. Skim and discard fat from stock. Thinly slice meat; serve with stock, carrots, potatoes and asparagus.

Each serving: About 285 calories, 26g protein, 28g carbohydrate, 6g total fat (2g saturated), 55mg cholesterol, 310mg sodium

# BEEF PIES

These savoury meat pies make a perfect meal anytime of the year but are particularly warming in winter. Crusts, flecked with herbs, enriched with cheese, or made with puff pastry provide perfect toppings to enrich the hearty fillings.

## BEEF CURRY PIE

❖❖❖❖❖❖❖❖❖❖❖❖❖❖

*Prep: 1¼ hours*
*Bake: 35 minutes*
*Makes 6 main dish servings*

**Parsley Crust (see below)**
**450g lean boneless beef chuck, cut into 1cm cubes**
**3 tsp olive or vegetable oil**
**1 garlic clove, very finely chopped**
**2 tbsp curry powder**
**2 medium carrots, sliced**
**1 medium onion, diced**
**1 beef stock cube, crumbled**
**½ tsp salt**
**1 tbsp cornflour**
**300g frozen peas**

### PARSLEY PASTRY

Mix 300g plain flour, 30g chopped fresh parsley and 1 teaspoon salt in large bowl. Using a pastry blender or two knives used scissor-fashion, cut in 175g white vegetable fat until mixture resembles coarse crumbs. Stir in 5–6 tablespoons cold water, 1 tablespoon at a time, mixing lightly with fork after each addition until pastry just holds together. Divide pastry in half; shape each into a ball.

1 Prepare Parsley Pastry; wrap and refrigerate. Pat beef dry with kitchen towels. Heat 2 teaspoons oil in 26cm non-stick frying pan over medium-high heat. Add beef and brown on all sides. Stir in garlic and curry powder; cook 1 minute longer. Using slotted spoon, transfer beef mixture to bowl. Heat remaining 1 teaspoon oil in same frying pan; add carrots and onion and cook 10 minutes, or until browned.

2 Add beef, stock cube, salt and *300ml water*. Bring to the boil over high heat. Reduce heat to low; cover and simmer 30 minutes. Mix cornflour and *60ml water*; gradually add to pan. Cook over high heat, stirring, until mixture thickens; boil 1 minute. Stir in peas; remove from heat.

3 Preheat oven to 220°C (425°F, Gas 7). Using floured rolling pin, roll out half of pastry on lightly floured surface into round 3cm larger than inverted 23cm pie plate. Ease pastry into pie plate. Spoon in filling; trim pastry edge leaving 2cm overhang.

4 Roll remaining pastry into 25cm round. Cut into 1½cm strips. Place half of strips about 2cm apart across pie; do not seal ends. Fold every other strip back halfway from centre.

5 Place centre cross strip on pie; replace folded part of strips. Fold back alternate strips; add second cross strip. Repeat to weave strips into lattice. Seal ends. Fold over-hang under; make fluted edge (see page 488). Bake on baking sheet 35 minutes until pastry is golden and filling is bubbly.

EACH SERVING: ABOUT 645 CALORIES, 23g PROTEIN, 44g CARBOHYDRATE, 42g TOTAL FAT (13g SATURATED), 56mg CHOLESTEROL, 855mg SODIUM

# DEEP-DISH BEEF PIE

*Prep: 2 hours   Bake: 25–30 minutes*
*Makes 8 main dish servings*

2 tablespoons vegetable oil
450g pearl onions, peeled
900g beef for stew, cut into
 5cm chunks
400ml beef stock
300ml ginger beer
1½ tsp salt
¼ tsp coarsely ground black
 pepper
450g small white or red
 potatoes, each cut into
 quarters

450g carrots, cut into 5cm
 pieces
3 medium parsnips (about
 225g), cut into bite-sized
 chunks
225g French beans, trimmed,
 each cut in half
250g fresh or frozen (thawed)
 puff pastry
1 medium egg, lightly beaten
50g plain flour

◈ Heat oil in a 8-litre flameproof casserole over medium-high heat. Add onions; cook until browned. Using slotted spoon, transfer to plate. Pat beef dry with kitchen towels. Heat oil remaining in casserole over medium-high heat. Add beef, one-third at a time; cook until well browned; transfer to plate.

◈ Return all beef to casserole; stir in stock, ginger beer, salt and pepper. Bring to the boil over high heat. Reduce heat to low; cover and simmer 30 minutes. Add onions; return to the boil. Cover and simmer 30 minutes. Add potatoes, carrots, parsnips and green beans; return to the boil. Cover and simmer, stirring occasionally, 30 minutes longer, or until meat and vegetables are tender.

◈ Meanwhile, using floured rolling pin, roll out pastry on lightly floured surface into 33cm square. Trim pastry into round 1cm larger all round than 3-litre casserole. Brush pastry round with beaten egg. Keep pastry cold.

◈ Preheat oven to 180°C (375°F, Gas 5). Mix flour and *225ml water* together in small bowl; stir into stew. Cook over medium-high heat, stirring gently, until mixture thickens and boils. Spoon stew into casserole. Place pastry round on casserole, leaving over-hang; pinch edge to seal. Bake 25–30 minutes until pastry is golden.

Each serving:
About 525 calories,
32g protein,
53g carbohydrate,
21g total fat
(6g saturated),
82mg cholesterol,
790mg sodium

# CHEDDAR-CRUST CHILLI CASSEROLE

*Prep: 35 minutes   Bake: 40–45 minutes*
*Makes 8 main dish servings*

1 tbsp vegetable oil
750g lean minced beef
1 medium onion, coarsely
 chopped
2 tbsp chilli powder
400g canned kidney beans,
 rinsed and drained
400g canned cannellini beans,
 rinsed and drained
300g frozen cut green beans
400g canned chopped
 tomatoes

300g frozen sweetcorn
1 tbsp chopped fresh
 coriander or parsley
415g plain flour
60g Cheddar cheese, grated
½ tsp salt
225g white vegetable fat
1 medium egg, lightly beaten

◈ Heat oil in a 30cm frying pan over medium-high heat; add beef and onion and cook, stirring frequently, until pan juices evaporate and beef is well browned.

◈ Stir in chilli powder; cook, stirring constantly, 1 minute. Stir in kidney beans, cannellini beans, green beans, tomatoes, corn and coriander.

◈ Mix 40g flour with *300ml water* together in small bowl; stir into minced-beef mixture and bring to the boil over high heat. Spoon mixture into 33 by 20cm glass or ceramic baking dish. Cool slightly. Preheat oven to 190°C (375°F, Gas 5).

◈ Meanwhile, prepare pastry: with fork, mix cheese, salt, and remaining 375g flour in large bowl. Using pastry blender or two knives used scissor-fashion, cut in vegetable fat until mixture resembles coarse crumbs.

◈ Sprinkle *6–7 tablespoons cold water*, 1 tablespoon at a time, into flour mixture, mixing lightly with fork after each addition, until pastry is just moist enough to hold together.

◈ Using floured rolling pin, roll out pastry on lightly floured surface into a rectangle about 5cm larger all round than top of ovenproof dish.

◈ Place pastry over filling. Trim edge, leaving 2–3cm overhang. Fold over-hang under; make fluted edge (see page 488). Make several cuts in top to allow steam to escape during baking. Brush pastry with beaten egg. Bake on baking sheet 40–45 minutes until pastry is golden.

Each serving: About 825 calories, 31g protein, 66g carbohydrate, 49g total fat (17g saturated), 97mg cholesterol, 585mg sodium

# BEEF CASSEROLES AND STEWS

A rich beef stew makes a traditional meal in many countries. It's easy to make in advance, as flavours improve the next day, and it's easier to skim off fat if the stew is refrigerated overnight. To avoid scorching, add a little water when reheating.

## BEEF AND MIXED MUSHROOM STEW

*Prep:* 30 minutes   *Bake:* 1½ hours
*Makes* 6 main dish servings

15g dried mushrooms
900g beef for stew, cut into
  4cm chunks
2 tbsp vegetable oil
450g mushrooms, each cut
  in half
1 large onion, diced
2 garlic cloves, very finely
  chopped
2 tbsp tomato purée
225ml beef stock

175ml dry red wine
2 medium carrots, each cut
  lengthways in half, then
  crossways into thirds
¾ tsp salt
¼ tsp dried thyme
1 bay leaf
Chopped fresh parsley for
  garnish
Wide egg noodles (optional)

1 Place dried mushrooms in small bowl; add *225ml boiling water*. Set mixture aside for about 30 minutes so mushrooms can soften. Meanwhile, pat beef dry with kitchen towels.

2 Heat 1 tablespoon oil in 5-litre flameproof casserole over medium-high heat. Add fresh mushrooms and cook about 10 minutes, or until lightly browned and most of liquid evaporates. Transfer to small bowl.

3 Heat remaining 1 tablespoon oil in same casserole over medium-high heat. Add beef chunks, half at a time, and brown well; transfer beef to plate as it browns.

4 Using slotted spoon, remove dried mushrooms from soaking liquid and coarsely chop; strain liquid through sieve lined with muslin or kitchen towels. Preheat oven to 180°C (350°F, Gas 4).

5 Add onion and *2 tablespoons water* to juices in casserole; cook over medium heat about 10 minutes, until onion is lightly browned. Add garlic and cook 30 seconds longer. Stir in tomato purée; cook, stirring, 1 minute.

6 Return browned beef to casserole; add dried mushrooms with their liquid, beef stock, wine, carrots, salt, thyme and bay leaf. Bring to the boil over high heat. Cover and bake 1¼ hours. Add sautéed mushrooms; bake 15 minutes longer, or until beef is tender. Skim and discard fat; discard bay leaf. Sprinkle with chopped parsley. Serve stew with egg noodles, if you like.

EACH SERVING: ABOUT 360 CALORIES, 37g PROTEIN, 13g CARBOHYDRATE, 16g TOTAL FAT (5g SATURATED), 77mg CHOLESTEROL, 610mg SODIUM

## SAUERBRATEN STEW

*Prep: 45 minutes    Bake: 1¼ hours*
*Makes 8 main dish servings*

900g beef for stew, cut into
   4cm chunks
2 tbsp vegetable oil
1 large onion, sliced
750g butternut squash,
   peeled, seeded, and cut into
   4cm chunks
750g small red potatoes, cut
   into quarters

225ml cider vinegar
70g light brown sugar
2 tsp salt
1 bay leaf
8 gingernut biscuits, finely
   crumbled
75g dark seedless raisins
450g green beans, trimmed

◆ Preheat oven to 180°C (350°F, Gas 4). Pat beef dry with kitchen towels. Heat oil in 5-litre flameproof casserole over medium-high heat. Add beef, one-third at a time, and brown on all sides Using slotted spoon, transfer meat to plate as it browns. Cook onion in drippings in casserole about 5 minutes until tender. Stir in squash, potatoes, vinegar, brown sugar, salt, bay leaf and *675ml water*. Return meat to casserole; bring to·the boil over high heat. Cover and bake 1¼ hours, or until meat is tender.

◆ Stir in gingernut biscuit crumbs and raisins until well blended; stir in green beans. Cover and bake 30 minutes longer, or until meat and vegetables are tender. Skim and discard fat; discard bay leaf before serving.

**Each serving: About 420 calories, 29g protein, 52g carbohydrate, 12g total fat (4g saturated), 55mg cholesterol, 665mg sodium**

## BRAISED RIB CASSEROLE

*Prep: 30 minutes    Bake: 2½ hours*
*Makes 6 main dish servings*

1.8kg beef short back ribs
1 tbsp vegetable oil
450g carrots, cut into 3cm
   pieces
2 large onions, sliced
2 tbsp plain flour
400g canned chopped
   tomatoes

1½ tsp salt
800g canned cannellini or
   other small white beans,
   rinsed and drained
Chopped fresh parsley and
   grated lemon rind for
   garnish
Hot cooked rice (optional)

◆ Preheat oven to 180°C (350°F, Gas 4). Pat ribs dry with kitchen towels. Heat oil in 5-litre flameproof casserole over medium-high heat. Add ribs, half at a time, and brown on all sides; transfer ribs to bowl as they brown. Cook carrots and onions in drippings in casserole, stirring occasionally, until lightly browned.

◆ Mix flour and *225ml water* together in small bowl. Return ribs to casserole; stir in flour mixture, tomatoes and salt. Bring to the boil over high heat.

◆ Cover casserole and bake 2 hours, stirring occasionally. Stir in beans; bake 30 minutes longer, or until ribs are tender.

◆ Skim and discard all fat. Sprinkle with chopped parsley and grated lemon rind and serve with rice, if you like.

**Each serving: About 895 calories, 82g protein, 49g carbohydrate, 40g total fat (16g saturated), 174mg cholesterol, 875mg sodium**

## PAPRIKASH CASSEROLE

*Prep: 30 minutes    Bake: 1¼ hours*
*Makes 6 main dish servings*

750g beef for stew, cut into
   3cm chunks
2 tbsp vegetable oil
2 large onions, thinly sliced
350g mushrooms
2 tbsp paprika

1 tbsp plain flour
1¼ tsp salt
125ml soured cream
2 tbsp chopped fresh parsley
Cooked wide egg noodles
   (optional)

◆ Preheat oven to 180°C (350°F, Gas 4). Pat beef dry with kitchen towels. Heat 1 tablespoon oil in 5-litre flameproof casserole over medium-high heat. Add beef, half at a time, and brown on all sides; transfer meat to bowl as it browns.

◆ Add remaining 1 tablespoon oil to drippings in casserole; cook onions and mushrooms until lightly browned. Stir in paprika; cook 1 minute, stirring.

◆ Mix flour and *350ml water* together in small bowl; stir into onion mixture with salt. Return meat to casserole; bring to the boil over high heat. Cover casserole and bake 1¼ hours, or until meat is tender, stirring once halfway through cooking time.

◆ Skim and discard all fat. Stir in soured cream. Sprinkle with parsley and serve with egg noodles, if you like.

**Each serving: About 405 calories, 31g protein, 36g carbohydrate, 15g total fat (4g saturated), 61mg cholesterol, 555mg sodium**

## ORANGE BEEF AND BARLEY STEW

*Prep:* 35 minutes  *Bake:* 1½–1¾ hours
*Makes* 6 main dish servings

| | |
|---|---|
| 750g beef for stew, cut into 4cm chunks | 800g canned plum tomatoes |
| 2 tbsp vegetable oil | 400ml beef stock |
| 4 carrots, cut into 5cm pieces | 225ml dry red wine |
| 2 medium onions, each cut into 6 wedges | 3 strips orange rind (7 by 3cm each) |
| 2 garlic cloves, very finely chopped | 1 bay leaf |
| | ½ tsp salt |
| | 150g pearl barley |

◈ Preheat oven to 180°C (350°F, Gas 4). Pat beef dry with kichen towels. Heat 1 tablespoon oil in 5-litre flameproof casserole over medium-high heat; add beef in batches and brown on all sides; transfer to bowl. Add remaining 1 tablespoon oil to drippings in casserole; cook carrots and onions until browned. Add garlic; cook 1 minute, stirring. Return beef to casserole; add tomatoes with their liquid, stock, wine, orange rind, bay leaf and salt. Bring to the boil over high heat, breaking up tomatoes with back of spoon.

◈ Cover casserole and bake 45 minutes. Stir in barley; cover and bake 45–60 minutes longer, until beef and barley are tender. Skim and discard fat; discard bay leaf.

**Each serving:** About 410 calories, 31g protein, 36g carbohydrate, 14g total fat (4g saturated), 55mg cholesterol, 750mg sodium

## OXTAIL STEW

*Prep:* 15 minutes  *Cook:* 3½ hours
*Makes* 6 main dish servings

| | |
|---|---|
| 450g carrots | 225ml dry red wine |
| 6 medium celery stalks | 2 tbsp tomato purée |
| 1.8kg oxtails | 800g canned tomatoes |
| 1 tsp vegetable oil | 1 tsp salt |
| 1 large onion, finely chopped | ¼ tsp ground black pepper |
| 2 garlic cloves, very finely chopped | ¼ tsp dried thyme |
| | ¼ tsp dried rosemary, crushed |
| 2 tbsp plain flour | |

◈ Finely chop 1 carrot and 1 celery stalk. Cut remaining carrots and celery lengthways in half, then crosswise into 8cm pieces; set aside.

◈ Pat oxtails dry with kitchen towels. Heat 1 teaspoon oil in 5-litre flameproof casserole over medium-high heat. Add half of oxtails and brown on all sides; transfer to bowl. Repeat with 1 teaspoon oil and remaining oxtails. Heat remaining 1 teaspoon oil in drippings in casserole; add finely chopped carrot, celery and onion and cook 5 minutes, or until tender. Stir in garlic; cook 30 seconds. Add flour and cook, stirring, 1 minute. Stir in wine; bring to the boil,

stirring, over high heat. Add tomato purée and tomatoes, breaking them up with back of spoon. Return oxtails to casserole. Add salt, pepper, thyme and rosemary; bring to the boil over high heat.

◈ Reduce heat to low; cover and simmer 2½ hours, or until meat is very tender. Stir in reserved carrot and celery pieces; bring to the boil over high heat. Reduce heat to low; cover and simmer 30 minutes longer, or until vegetables are tender. Skim and discard fat before serving.

**Each serving:** About 535 calories, 61g protein, 22g carbohydrate, 19g total fat (6g saturated), 177mg cholesterol, 975mg sodium.

## ROPA VIEJA

*Prep:* 30 minutes, plus standing  *Cook:* 3–3½ hours
*Makes* 6 main dish servings

| | |
|---|---|
| 800g beef flank steak | 1 green pepper, cored, seeded and cut into strips |
| 1 medium onion, chopped | 3 garlic cloves, very finely chopped |
| 1 medium carrot, chopped | 3 serrano or jalapeño chillies, seeded and very finely chopped |
| ½ bay leaf | |
| Salt | |
| 4 tsp olive oil | ¼ tsp ground cinnamon |
| 1 large onion, sliced | 400g canned tomatoes |
| 1 red pepper, cored, seeded and cut into strips | Canned or bottled drained capers for garnish |
| 1 yellow pepper, cored, seeded and cut into strips | |

◈ Cut steak crossways in half. Bring steak, chopped onion, carrot, bay leaf, ½ teaspoon salt and *1 litre water* to the boil in 5-litre flameproof casserole over high heat. Reduce heat to low; cover and simmer 2½–3 hours until meat is very tender. Remove from heat; let stand, uncovered, 30 minutes. Transfer beef to chopping board. Strain stock and reserve. Using fork or fingers, shred beef into fine strips.

◈ Heat oil in 30cm frying pan over medium-high heat. Add sliced onion, peppers and ½ teaspoon salt. Cook, stirring, frequently, 10 minutes or until vegetables are tender. Stir in garlic, serranos and cinnamon; cook 30 seconds. Stir in tomatoes with their liquid, breaking up tomatoes with back of spoon; cook 5 minutes.
Stir in 450ml stock (reserve remaining stock for use another day) and beef; simmer, stirring occasionally, 10 minutes. To serve, sprinkle with capers.

**Each serving:** About 305 calories, 28g protein, 13g carbohydrate, 16g total fat (6g saturated), 67mg cholesterol, 760mg sodium

## HEARTY BEEF STEW

*Prep:* 30 minutes   *Cook:* 2¼–2¾ hours

*Makes* 6 main dish servings

2 rashers bacon, trimmed if
   necessary and chopped
900g boneless beef chuck, cut
   into 4cm pieces
1–2 tsp vegetable oil
1 large onion, finely chopped
2 medium carrots, finely
   chopped
2 garlic cloves, very finely
   chopped
2 tbsp plain flour
2 tsp tomato purée

450ml dry red wine
½ bay leaf
¼ tsp dried thyme
Salt and ground black pepper
450g small white onions,
   peeled
1 tsp sugar
30g margarine or butter
450g mushrooms, each cut
   into quarters if large
Chopped fresh parsley for
   garnish

◆ Cook bacon in 5-litre flameproof casserole over medium heat until beginning to brown; transfer to bowl. Pat beef dry with kitchen towels. Add 1 teaspoon oil to drippings in casserole; increase heat to medium-high. Add beef in batches and brown on all sides, adding 1 teaspoon more oil if necessary; transfer to bowl with bacon.

◆ Reduce heat to medium. Add chopped onion, carrots and garlic and cook, stirring, until tender. Stir in flour and cook 1 minute. Stir in tomato purée and cook 1 minute. Add wine, bay leaf, thyme, 1 teaspoon salt, and ¼ teaspoon pepper; stir until brown bits are loosened.

◆ Return browned beef and bacon to casserole and bring to the boil over high heat. Reduce heat to low; cover and simmer 1½–2 hours, until beef is very tender. Skim fat; discard bay leaf.

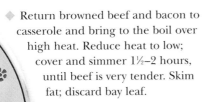

◆ Meanwhile, bring small white onions, sugar, 1 tablespoon margarine and *1 cup water* to the boil in 26cm frying pan over high heat. Reduce heat to low; cover and simmer 10 minutes, or until onions are tender. Uncover; cook over medium-high heat, shaking pan occasionally, until water evaporates and onions are golden.

◆ Melt remaining 1 tablespoon margarine in 30cm frying pan over medium-high heat. Add mushrooms and a pinch each salt and pepper; cook, stirring often, until mushrooms are tender and liquid evaporates. Stir onions and mushrooms into stew. Garnish and serve.

**Each serving: About 560 calories, 35g protein, 20g carbohydrate, 32g total fat (12g saturated), 119mg cholesterol, 620mg sodium**

## SCANDINAVIAN BEEF STEW

*Prep:* 25 minutes   *Cook:* 2½–3 hours

*Makes* 8 main dish servings

900g boneless beef chuck, cut
   into 5cm pieces
2 tsp vegetable oil
1 large onion, finely chopped
1 tbsp ground coriander
2 tsp ground ginger
¼ tsp ground nutmeg

1 tsp salt
¼ tsp dried thyme
¼ tsp ground black pepper
450g carrots
2 large parsnips (about 225g)
½ small swede
450g small red potatoes

Pat beef dry. Heat 1 teaspoon oil in 5-litre flameproof casserole over medium-high heat. Add half beef; brown on all sides. Transfer to plate. Repeat with remaining oil and beef. Reduce heat to medium. Add onion to drippings in casserole; cook until tender. Stir in coriander, ginger and nutmeg; cook 30 seconds. Add beef, salt, thyme, pepper and *750ml water*; bring to the boil over high heat. Reduce heat to low; simmer, covered, 1½–2 hours, until beef is tender. Meanwhile, cut vegetables into 4cm pieces. Add vegetables to casserole and return to the boil. Reduce heat to low; cover and simmer 30–40 minutes longer, until tender. Skim fat.

**Each serving: About 400 calories, 26g protein, 26g carbohydrate, 21g total fat (8g saturated), 88mg cholesterol, 355mg sodium**

## CHINESE-SPICED BEEF STEW

*Prep:* 15 minutes   *Cook:* 2–2½ hours

*Makes* 8 main dish servings

900g boneless beef chuck, cut
   into 5cm pieces
2 tsp vegetable oil
75ml dry sherry
3 tbsp soy sauce
2 tbsp sugar
60g fresh ginger, peeled
   and sliced
2 garlic cloves, peeled

2 star anise
4 strips orange rind,
   7 by 3cm each
1 bunch broccoli (about
   750g), cut into spears
125g mange-tout, trimmed
1 bunch spring onions, each
   cut into 5cm pieces

Pat beef dry. Heat 1 teaspoon oil in 5-litre flameproof casserole over medium-high heat. Add half of beef; cook until browned. Transfer to plate. Repeat with remaining 1 teaspoon oil and remaining beef. Return beef to casserole. Add sherry, next 6 ingredients and *675ml water*; bring to the boil over high heat. Reduce heat to low; cover and simmer 1½–2 hours, until beef is very tender. Transfer beef to bowl; keep warm. Boil liquid in casserole 10 minutes. Meanwhile, bring *2–3cm water* to the boil in saucepan. Add broccoli. Cover; cook 5 minutes. Add mange-tout and spring onions; cook, covered, 1 minute longer. Drain; stir into casserole. Spoon over beef.

**Each serving: About 355 calories, 27g protein, 11g carbohydrate, 22g total fat (8g saturated), 88mg cholesterol, 465mg sodium**

# CHILLI

This American south-western speciality, originating in Texas, has become an English favourite. It is excellent whether made with cubes of beef or with minced meat; some chillies include beans and vegetables as well. Use leftover chilli spooned over a jacket potato or fluffy white rice.

## TEXAS-STYLE CHILLI

❖ ❖ ❖ ❖ ❖ ❖ ❖ ❖ ❖ ❖ ❖

*Prep:* 25 minutes
*Cook:* 2 hours 20 minutes
*Makes* 12 main dish servings

**1.5kg beef for stew, cut into 1cm cubes**
**60ml vegetable oil**
**3 medium green peppers, cored, seeded and diced**
**2 medium onions, chopped**
**4 garlic cloves, very finely chopped**
**1.6kg canned tomatoes**
**350g tomato purée**
**40g chilli powder**
**50g sugar**
**2 tsp salt**
**2 tsp dried oregano**
**¾ tsp cracked black pepper**
**Grated Cheddar cheese and sliced spring onions for garnish**
**Tortilla chips (optional)**

**1** Pat beef dry with kitchen towels. Heat oil in 8-litre flameproof casserole over medium-high heat. Add beef, one-third at a time; brown on all sides. Transfer beef to bowl as it browns.

**2** Add green peppers, onions and garlic to drippings in casserole; cook over medium-high heat, stirring occasionally, 10 minutes.

**3** Return beef to casserole; stir in tomatoes with their juice, tomato purée, chilli powder, sugar, salt, oregano and black pepper, breaking up tomatoes with back of spoon.

---

### TOUCH OF SPICE

Deep red in colour, with a hot and spicy flavour, chilli powder may be purely one variety of chilli, dried and ground, or more often, a seasoning blend of ground dried chillies, oregano, cumin, garlic and salt. Depending on the brand, the flavour can range from mild to fiery hot, and the saltiness varies, too. The best chilli powders contain only pure ground chillies, and are deep red in colour, rather than brown. There are hundreds of different chillies, with different flavours and heat levels. Mexican and American south-western cooks prefer to grind their own chillies. For freshness, store chilli powder in the freezer.

**4** Stir in *450ml water*. Bring to the boil over high heat. Reduce heat to low; cover and simmer, stirring occasionally, 1½ hours, or until beef is tender. To serve, spoon into bowls and garnish; serve with tortilla chips, if you like.

---

EACH SERVING: ABOUT 345 CALORIES, 33g PROTEIN, 21g CARBOHYDRATE, 15g TOTAL FAT (4g SATURATED), 64mg CHOLESTEROL, 910mg SODIUM

## CHILLI-BEEF CASSEROLE

*Prep:* 40 minutes    *Bake:* 1 hour
*Makes* 8 main dish servings

| | |
|---|---|
| 3 tbsp olive or vegetable oil | 2 tbsp chilli powder |
| 1 large onion, chopped | 1 tsp salt |
| 1 small red pepper, cored, seeded and diced | 450g canned tomatoes |
| | 2 tbsp tomato purée |
| 1 small green pepper, cored, seeded and diced | 1 medium tomato, diced |
| | 90g small pimiento-stuffed olives |
| 900g beef for stew, cut into 1cm pieces | 75g raisins |
| 2 tbsp plain flour | 30g flaked almonds, toasted |

◆ Heat 1 tablespoon oil in 5-litre flameproof casserole over medium-high heat. Add diced onion and peppers and cook until tender and golden. Using slotted spoon, transfer vegetables to bowl.

◆ Preheat oven to 200°C (400°F, Gas 6). Pat beef dry with kitchen towels. Toss beef with flour, chilli powder and salt in a large bowl.

◆ Heat 1 more tablespoon oil in same casserole over medium-high heat. Add half of beef and cook until browned; using slotted spoon, transfer to bowl with vegetables. Repeat with remaining beef and remaining 1 tablespoon oil.

◆ Return beef and vegetables to casserole. Add tomatoes, tomato purée and *175ml water*; stir until brown bits are loosened. Bring to the boil over high heat. Cover casserole; bake 45 minutes, or until beef is almost tender.

◆ Stir in tomato, olives and raisins. Cover and bake 15 minutes longer, or until beef is tender. To serve, skim and discard fat and sprinkle with toasted almonds.

**Each serving:** About 415 calories, 26g protein, 17g carbohydrate, 28g total fat (9g saturated), 88mg cholesterol, 745mg sodium

## CHILLI CON CARNE

*Prep:* 10 minutes    *Cook:* 55 minutes
*Makes* 8 main dish servings

| | |
|---|---|
| 900g minced beef | ½ tsp ground black pepper |
| 1 large onion, diced | 800g canned tomatoes |
| 1 garlic clove, very finely chopped | 900g canned red kidney beans, rinsed and drained |
| 30g chilli powder | 425ml tomato passata |

◆ Cook minced beef, onion and garlic, stirring often, in 5-litre flameproof casserole over high heat until all pan juices evaporate and beef is well browned. Stir in chilli powder and pepper; cook 1 minute.

◆ Stir in tomatoes with their liquid and next 2 ingredients. Bring to the boil over high heat. Reduce heat to low, cover. Simmer, stirring often, 30 minutes. Skim fat before serving.

**Each serving:** About 455 calories, 29g protein, 30g carbohydrate, 25g total fat (10g saturated), 84mg cholesterol, 955mg sodium

## GREEN CHILLI AND TOMATILLO STEW

*Prep:* 30 minutes, plus standing    *Bake:* 2½–3 hours
*Makes* 8 main dish servings

| | |
|---|---|
| 4 poblano chillies or 2 green peppers | 2 medium onions, finely chopped |
| 1 bunch coriander | 1 tsp ground cumin |
| 3 garlic cloves, very finely chopped | ¼ tsp ground red pepper |
| 1½ tsp salt | 900g tomatillos, husked, rinsed and each cut into quarters |
| 900g boneless beef chuck, cut into 2cm pieces | 400g canned sweetcorn, drained |
| 3 serrano or jalapeño chillies, seeded and very finely chopped | Soured cream (optional) |

◆ Preheat grill. Line grill pan with foil. Place poblanos in pan without rack. Place pan in grill; grill at closest position to heat, turning occasionally, about 15 minutes until charred all over. Wrap foil round poblanos; let stand until cool enough to handle. Remove and discard skin and seeds; cut poblanos into 2cm pieces.

◆ Preheat oven to 175°C (325°F, Gas 3). Chop 15g coriander leaves and stalks; chop and reserve another 15g leaves for garnish. Mash garlic to paste with salt; add to 5-litre flame-proof casserole. Add chopped coriander leaves and stalks, beef and next 4 ingredients; mix well. Cover and bake 1 hour. Stir in poblanos and tomatillos. Cover; bake 1½–2 hours longer, until beef is very tender. Stir in corn; cover and bake 5 minutes. Skim and discard fat. Garnish and serve with soured cream, if you like.

**Each serving:** About 385 calories, 26g protein, 23g carbohydrate, 22g total fat (8g saturated), 88mg cholesterol, 790mg sodium

---

### TOMATILLOS

These small, pale green, tart-tasting fruits are encased in a slightly sticky papery husk, which is removed before cooking. In Mexican recipes they are simmered, dry roasted or puréed for sauces. Canned varieties are available but fresh tomatillos yield the best flavour. Look for them in specialist greengrocers.

# PAN-FRIED BEEF

Pan-frying is suited to tender fillets and sirloins, but it also works well for less-tender cuts – just take care not to overcook them, and slice the cooked meat thinly across the grain. The pan drippings can be used to create a quick sauce. Stir in a little liquid such as wine or stock, then boil until the sauce is reduced and the flavours are concentrated.

## FILET MIGNON IN SHERRY SAUCE

*Prep: 10 minutes    Cook: 15 minutes*
*Makes 4 main dish servings*

3 oil-packed sun-dried
  tomatoes
1 bunch rocket
1 small head loose-leaf lettuce
60g margarine or butter
2 shallots, very finely
  choppped

½ tsp salt
¼ tsp coarsely ground black
  pepper
4 beef fillet steaks, each 3cm
  thick (about 125g each)
60ml dry sherry
Sourdough bread (optional)

**1** Cut sun-dried tomatoes into thin slices; set aside. Arrange rocket and lettuce on 4 plates; set aside.

**2** Melt margarine in 30cm frying pan over medium-high heat. Add shallots, salt and pepper; cook, stirring, until lightly browned.

**3** Pat steaks dry with kitchen towels. Add steaks to pan; cook about 5 minutes, until underside of meat is browned. Turn and cook about 5 minutes longer for medium-rare, or until desired doneness.

**4** Place steaks on salad greens on plates. Sprinkle with sun-dried tomatoes; keep warm. Add sherry to pan; bring to the boil over high heat. Boil 1 minute; pour sherry over steaks and salad. Serve with sourdough bread, if you like.

### SUN-DRIED TOMATOES

These tomatoes, available packed in oil or dried, have an intense tomato flavour and pleasantly chewy texture. Those in oil can be used straight from the jar, while the dried must be re-hydrated: soak them in boiling water to cover about 5 minutes; drain. You can rehydrate a batch of dried tomatoes and store them in oil for future use: squeeze out any excess water, pack the tomatoes loosely in a jar, cover with olive oil and add dried herbs, if you like. Store your 'oil-packed' tomatoes in the refrigerator for up to 2 weeks.

Dried

Oil packed

PER SERVING: ABOUT 435 CALORIES, 21g PROTEIN, 6g CARBOHYDRATE, 34g TOTAL FAT (11g SATURATED), 73mg CHOLESTEROL, 475mg SODIUM

## FILLETS WITH TOMATOES AND ROQUEFORT

*Prep:* 10 minutes    *Cook:* 30 minutes
*Makes* 4 main dish servings

350g French beans or other
   green beans, trimmed
3 tsp margarine or butter
125g oyster mushrooms or
   white mushrooms, sliced
2 tsp soy sauce
¾ tsp cornflour
¼ beef stock cube, crumbled
4 beef fillet steaks, each
   2–3cm thick (about
   125g each)

½ tsp salt
4 thick tomato slices
2 tbsp dry white wine
   (optional)
30g Roquefort or other blue
   cheese, crumbled
French bread (optional)

◆ Add green beans to *2–3cm boiling water* in 4-litre saucepan. Return to the boil over high heat. Reduce heat to low; cover and simmer 5–8 minutes until tender-crisp. Drain; place in bowl. Wipe saucepan dry. Melt 2 teaspoons margarine in same pan over medium-high heat; add mushrooms and cook, stirring frequently, until golden. Stir in green beans and soy sauce; keep warm. Mix cornflour, stock cube and *125ml water* together in small bowl until blended. Set aside.

◆ Pat steaks dry. Melt remaining 1 teaspoon margarine in 26cm non-stick frying pan over medium-high heat; add steaks with salt and cook 10 minutes, turning once, for medium-rare, or until desired doneness. Transfer to plate; keep warm. Cook tomato in drippings in pan, turning once, just until hot. Transfer to 4 warm plates; keep warm.

◆ If using wine, add to pan; cook 30 seconds, stirring. Stir in cornflour mixture; boil 1 minute, stirring constantly, until sauce thickens slightly. Top each tomato slice with a steak. Spoon sauce over steaks; sprinkle with cheese. Serve with bean mixture, and bread, if you like.

**Each serving: About 380 calories, 24g protein, 10g carbohydrate, 27g total fat (11g saturated), 78mg cholesterol, 700mg sodium**

## FILLETS WITH SHIITAKE CREAM SAUCE

*Prep:* 10 minutes    *Cook:* 30 minutes
*Makes* 2 main dish servings

2 beef fillet steaks, each
   2–3cm thick (about
   125g each)
1 tbsp olive oil
125g mange-tout, strings
   removed
90g radishes, each cut in half
   if large

Salt
4 tsp margarine or butter
1 small onion, diced
½ tsp chopped fresh thyme
125g shiitake mushrooms,
   stalks discarded
75ml single cream

◆ Pat steaks dry. Heat oil in 3-litre saucepan over high heat. Add mange-tout, radishes and ¼ teaspoon salt; cook, stirring often, until radishes are lightly browned and mange-tout are tender-crisp. Keep warm.

◆ Melt 2 teaspoons margarine in 26cm non-stick frying pan over medium heat. Add onion and cook until tender. Transfer to plate. Add steaks to pan with thyme and ¼ teaspoon salt. Cook steaks over medium-high heat 10 minutes, turning once, for medium-rare. Transfer to 2 warm plates; keep warm.

◆ Melt remaining 2 teaspoons margarine in same pan. Stir in shiitake mushrooms; cook until lightly browned. Stir in cream and cooked onion; bring to the boil over high heat. Spoon mushroom sauce over steaks; serve with vegetable mixture.

**Each serving: About 685 calories, 29g protein, 56g carbohydrate, 42g total fat (14g saturated), 87mg cholesterol, 700mg sodium**

## TUSCAN-STYLE STEAK

*Prep:* 5 minutes, plus standing    *Cook:* 20 minutes
*Makes* 4 main dish servings

1 beef rump steak,
   3–4cm thick (about 800g)
2 tsp olive oil
½ tsp dried rosemary
¼ tsp dried thyme

¼ tsp coarsely ground black
   pepper
Salt
1 lemon, cut into wedges

Pat steak dry. Mix oil, rosemary, thyme and pepper together in small bowl. Use to rub over steak. Heat 26cm frying pan over medium-high heat until hot. Add steak; reduce heat to medium and cook 20 minutes, turning once, for medium-rare, or until desired doneness. Sprinkle steak generously with salt; transfer to warm large platter. Let stand 10 minutes; keep warm. Cut steak into thin slices and serve with lemon wedges.

**Each serving: About 340 calories, 44g protein, 3g carbohydrate, 16g total fat (6g saturated), 93mg cholesterol, 220mg sodium**

## BLACK PEPPER STEAK

*Prep: 10 minutes    Cook: 12 minutes*
*Makes 8 main dish servings*

| | |
|---|---|
| 1 beef rump steak, 3–4cm thick (about 1.1 kg) | 60ml whipping cream |
| 1 tbsp cracked black pepper | 1 tbsp plain flour |
| 1 tsp salt | 1 beef stock cube, crumbled |
| 2 tbsp olive oil | 60ml brandy |

❖ Cut steak crossways into 4 pieces; then cut each piece horizontally in half to make 8 steaks. Pat steaks dry with kitchen towels. Sprinkle steaks on both sides with cracked black pepper and salt.

❖ Heat oil in 30cm frying pan over high heat. Add steaks to pan and cook 8–10 minutes, turning once, for medium-rare, or until desired doneness. Transfer steaks to platter and keep warm.

❖ Prepare sauce: whisk cream, flour, stock cube and *175ml water* together in small bowl. Pour off fat from pan. Add brandy to pan; cook 2 minutes, stirring until brown bits are loosened from bottom of pan.

❖ Add cream mixture to pan; bring to the boil over high heat. Reduce heat to medium and cook, stirring constantly, until sauce thickens slightly and boils. Pour sauce over steaks.

**Each serving: About 315 calories, 27g protein, 2g carbohydrate, 20g total fat (7g saturated), 88mg cholesterol, 440mg sodium**

## FILLETS AU POIVRE

*Prep: 10 minutes    Cook: 10 minutes*
*Makes 4 main dish servings*

| | |
|---|---|
| 4 beef fillet steaks, each 2–3cm thick (about 125g each) | ½ tsp salt |
| | 75ml brandy |
| 2 tsp cracked black pepper | 1 tbsp coarse-grained French mustard |

❖ Pat steaks dry with kitchen towels. Mix pepper and salt together on greaseproof paper; use to coat steaks. Heat 30cm non-stick frying pan over medium-high heat until hot. Add steaks and cook 8–10 minutes, turning once, for medium-rare, or until desired doneness.

❖ Transfer steaks to plate; keep warm. Add brandy and mustard to pan and heat to boiling, stirring frequently; boil 30 seconds. Pour sauce onto 4 plates; place steaks on top.

**Each serving: About 335 calories, 20g protein, 1g carbohydrate, 22g total fat (9g saturated), 73mg cholesterol, 415mg sodium**

### CRACKING PEPPERCORNS

Cracked peppercorns give steak a crunchy, piquant crust. Seal a handful of black peppercorns in a heavy-weight plastic bag. Using rolling pin, tap the peppercorns until they crack open but are not crushed.

## FLANK STEAK WITH RED-ONION MARMALADE

*Prep: 10 minutes, plus standing    Cook: 35 minutes*
*Makes 6 main dish servings*

| | |
|---|---|
| 45g margarine or butter | 1 beef flank steak (about 800g) |
| 2 medium red onions (about 450g), thinly sliced | ¼ tsp coarsely ground black pepper |
| 3 tbsp sugar | Boiled parslied potatoes (optional) |
| 3 tbsp distilled white vinegar | |
| Salt | |

❖ Prepare onion marmalade: melt 2 tablespoons margarine in 30cm non-stick frying pan over medium heat. Add onions; cook, stirring occasionally, 15 minutes, or until tender. Stir in sugar, vinegar and ½ teaspoon salt. Reduce heat to low; simmer 5 minutes. Spoon into small bowl; keep warm.

❖ Wash pan and wipe dry. Pat steak dry with kitchen towels; sprinkle with black pepper and ½ teaspoon salt. Melt remaining 1 tablespoon margarine in same pan over medium-high heat. Add steak and cook 12–15 minutes, turning once, for medium-rare, or until desired doneness. Transfer steak to chopping board. Let stand 10 minutes; keep warm. Return onion marmalade to pan; heat through. Using knife almost parallel to cutting surface, thinly slice steak crossways against the grain. Serve with marmalade, and boiled potatoes, if you like.

**Each serving: About 325 calories, 27g protein, 13g carbohydrate, 18g total fat (6g saturated), 67mg cholesterol, 505mg sodium**

## STEAK WITH RED WINE SAUCE

*Prep:* 5 minutes
*Cook:* 15 minutes
*Makes* 4 main dish servings

2 tsp vegetable oil
2 sirloin steaks, each 2–3cm thick (about 300g each)
Salt and ground black pepper
40g shallots, very finely chopped
225ml dry red wine

Pinch dried thyme
20g butter, cut up
2 tsp chopped fresh tarragon or parsley
Sautéed julienned vegetables (optional)

◆ Heat oil in 26cm frying pan over medium-high heat until very hot. Pat steaks dry with kitchen towels. Sprinkle steaks with salt and pepper. Add to pan, and cook 7–8 minutes, turning once, for medium-rare, or until desired doneness. Transfer steaks to warm platter; keep warm.

◆ Pour off drippings from pan. Add shallots to pan; cook 1 minute, or until tender. Stir in red wine and thyme; boil over high heat about 5 minutes until reduced to 75ml. Remove from heat; stir in butter until incorporated.

◆ Cut steaks into thin slices and pour sauce on top. Sprinkle with tarragon. Serve with sautéed vegetables, if you like.

**Each serving: About 345 calories, 32g protein, 3g carbohydrate, 18g total fat (8g saturated), 82mg cholesterol, 295mg sodium**

◆◆◆◆◆◆◆◆◆◆◆◆◆◆◆◆◆◆◆◆◆◆◆◆◆◆◆◆◆◆◆◆

### CHOPPING SHALLOTS

To very finely chop a shallot, separate and peel the individual sections. Place each section, flat-side down, on the chopping board. Slice parallel to cutting board, keeping root end intact. Then slice shallot lengthways, still keeping root end intact. Slice across the shallot at right angles to the previous cut, making a fine dice. Discard the root end. Chop onions the same way.

◆◆◆◆◆◆◆◆◆◆◆◆◆◆◆◆◆◆◆◆◆◆◆◆◆◆◆◆◆◆◆◆

## RIB-EYE STEAKS WITH MADEIRA

*Prep:* 5 minutes   *Cook:* 15 minutes
*Makes* 4 main dish servings

1 tbsp olive or vegetable oil
1 small onion, chopped
2 beef rib-eye steaks, each 1cm thick (about 225g each)
¼ tsp salt
⅛ tsp cracked black pepper
2 tbsp Madeira or beef stock

◆ Heat oil in 26cm frying pan over medium-high heat; add onion and cook, stirring often, until tender. Transfer to small bowl. Pat steaks dry with kitchen towels. In oil remaining in pan, cook steaks, turning once, 6–8 minutes for medium-rare, or until desired doneness. Sprinkle steaks with salt and cracked black pepper. Transfer steaks to warm platter; keep warm.

◆ Pour off pan drippings. Add Madeira, onion and *2 tablespoons water* to pan; stir over medium heat until brown bits are loosened. Cut steaks into thin slices; pour Madeira sauce on top.

**Each serving: About 250 calories, 25g protein, 3g carbohydrate, 14g total fat (5g saturated), 58mg cholesterol, 185mg sodium**

## BEEF FILLETS WITH GRILLED-TOMATO SAUCE

*Prep:* 30 minutes, plus cooling   *Cook:* 15 minutes
*Makes* 4 main dish servings

1.1kg plum tomatoes, each cut lengthways in half
1 medium onion, coarsely chopped
4 beef fillet steaks, each 4cm thick (about 150g each)
1 tsp coarsely ground black pepper
Salt
1 tbsp vegetable oil
½ tsp sugar
½ tsp dried basil

◆ Preheat grill. Place tomatoes, cut-side up, and onion in grill pan. Grill at closest position to heat 15–20 minutes, or until tomatoes and onion are lightly charred. Remove pan from oven; set aside to cool. When tomatoes are cool enough to handle, peel and coarsely chop.

◆ Pat steaks dry with kitchen towels; sprinkle with pepper and 1 teaspoon salt. Heat oil in 30cm frying pan over medium-high heat. Add steaks and cook 10–12 minutes, turning once, for medium-rare, or until desired doneness.

◆ Transfer steaks to warm platter; keep warm. To drippings in pan, add tomatoes, onion, sugar, basil and ½ teaspoon salt; bring to the boil over high heat, stirring frequently. Spoon sauce onto warm platter; arrange steaks on sauce.

**Each serving: About 460 calories, 28g protein, 18g carbohydrate, 32g total fat (11g saturated), 91mg cholesterol, 885mg sodium**

# STIR-FRIED BEEF

For speed and ease of preparation, nothing is better than a stir-fry. Cut the meat and vegetables into uniform pieces to ensure even cooking. A wok is made for the job, but a large frying pan with high sides or a flameproof casserole will work just as well but may take slightly longer to heat.

## ORANGE BEEF AND PEPPERS

*Prep: 25 minutes    Cook: 15 minutes*
*Makes 4 main dish servings*

| | |
|---|---|
| 1 beef rump steak, 2cm thick (about 450g) | 1 tsp grated orange rind |
| 2 tbsp soy sauce | 125ml fresh orange juice |
| 2 tbsp vegetable oil | 1½ tsp grated, peeled fresh ginger |
| 1 large red pepper, cut into 5mm slices | ¾ tsp cornflour |
| 1 large yellow pepper, cut into 5mm slices | 2 large oranges, peeled and white pith removed, cut lengthways in half, and thinly sliced |
| 1 bunch spring onions, cut into 5cm pieces | 2 bunches rocket |

**1** Cut steak lengthways in half. Using knife held in slanting position, almost parallel to cutting surface, slice each half of steak crossways into 3mm thick slices. In medium bowl, toss steak with soy sauce.

**2** Heat 2 teaspoons oil in 30cm non-stick frying pan or wok over medium-high heat. Add red and yellow peppers; cook, stirring frequently, until tender-crisp. Transfer peppers to bowl.

**3** Heat 1 teaspoon oil in same pan over medium-high heat. Add spring onions; cook, stirring often, until tender-crisp. Transfer to bowl with peppers. Mix orange rind and next 3 ingredients together in small bowl until smooth.

**4** Heat remaining 1 tablespoon oil in same pan over medium-high heat. Add half of beef mixture and cook, stirring, just until beef loses its pink colour; transfer to bowl with vegetables.

**5** Repeat with remaining beef mixture. Return vegetables and all beef to pan. Stir in orange-juice mixture and oranges; cook, stirring constantly, until liquid thickens and boils. Serve over rocket.

---

### SOY SAUCE

The unique flavour of this ancient seasoning comes from fermented soya beans that are mixed with roasted wheat and aged up to two years. Dark soy sauce traditionally flavours and darkens hearty meat dishes; light-coloured soy sauce is saltier with a less pungent flavour, and is best with seafood, vegetables and soups.

---

**EACH SERVING: ABOUT 330 CALORIES, 25g PROTEIN, 19g CARBOHYDRATE, 18g TOTAL FAT (5g SATURATED), 62mg CHOLESTEROL, 575mg SODIUM**

## GINGER BEEF

*Prep: 25 minutes    Cook: 20 minutes*
*Makes 4 main dish servings*

1 beef flank steak (about 450g)
2 tbsp soy sauce
2 tbsp dry sherry
2 tsp grated, peeled fresh ginger
1 garlic clove, very finely chopped
3 tbsp vegetable oil
225g mushrooms, sliced

1 large red pepper, cored, seeded and thinly sliced
225g sugar snap peas or mange-tout, strings removed
2 large celery stalks, cut into 2–3cm pieces
1 medium onion, thinly sliced
225g fresh bean sprouts
2 tsp cornflour

◆ Cut steak lengthways in half. Using knife held in slanting position, almost parallel to cutting surface, slice steak crossways into 3mm thick slices. Mix steak, soy sauce, sherry, ginger and garlic in bowl; set aside. Heat 1 tablespoon oil in 30cm non-stick frying pan or wok over medium-high heat. Add mushrooms and red pepper; cook, stirring, until liquid evaporates. Transfer to large bowl.

◆ Heat 1 tablespoon oil in same pan over medium-high heat; add sugar snap peas, celery and onion and cook, stirring, until tender-crisp. Stir in bean sprouts; cook 2 minutes, stirring. Spoon vegetables into bowl with mushroom mixture. Mix cornflour and *125ml water* together in small bowl until smooth.

◆ Heat remaining 1 tablespoon oil in same pan over medium-high heat until very hot. Add half of steak mixture and cook, stirring constantly, until beef loses its pink colour. Transfer to bowl with mushrooms. Repeat with remaining steak mixture. Return vegetables and all beef to pan. Stir in cornflour mixture and cook, stirring constantly, until liquid thickens slightly and boils.

**Each serving: About 380 calories, 28g protein, 18g carbohydrate, 21g total fat (6g saturated), 58mg cholesterol, 620mg sodium**

### GRATING FRESH GINGER

Fresh ginger has a pungent, sweet-hot flavour. When buying, look for firm, heavy knobs. Grating is easy, as the fibres remain in the grater. Simply rub the peeled ginger across a fine grating surface or a ginger grater (available from Oriental supermarkets).

## THAI BEEF WITH BASIL

*Prep: 15 minutes, plus standing    Cook: 6 minutes*
*Makes 4 main dish servings*

3 tbsp fish sauce (nuoc nam)
1 tbsp soy sauce
1 tbsp brown sugar
1 beef rump steak (about 450g)
450g sweet onions
1 tbsp plus 1 tsp vegetable oil

3 long red or serrano chillies, seeded and cut into slivers
3 garlic cloves, very finely chopped
2 tsp peeled fresh ginger, very finely chopped
60g fresh basil leaves

Mix first 3 ingredients together in large bowl. Cut steak lengthways in half, then slice across grain into 3mm thick slices; stir into sauce mixture. Let stand 30 minutes. Thinly slice onion. Heat 1 tablespoon oil in 30cm frying pan or wok over high heat until very hot. Add beef mixture and cook, stirring constantly, 1 minute, or just until beef loses its pink colour; transfer to plate. Add remaining 1 teaspoon oil to pan; add onion and cook, stirring, 3 minutes. Add chillies, garlic and ginger; cook 30 seconds. Return beef to pan with basil; heat through.

**Each serving: About 280 calories, 29g protein, 20g carbohydrate, 10g total fat (3g saturated), 56mg cholesterol, 755mg sodium**

## SPICY BEEF BUNDLES

*Prep: 15 minutes    Cook: 20 minutes*
*Makes 6 main dish servings*

3 tbsp vegetable oil
225g mushrooms, very finely chopped
4 spring onions, very finely chopped
225g canned bamboo shoots, drained and very finely chopped
1 tbsp fresh ginger, peeled and very finely chopped

750g minced beef
60ml dry sherry
2 tbsp cornflour
3 tbsp soy sauce
1 tsp sugar
½ tsp Tabasco sauce
Iceberg lettuce leaves
2 tbsp pine nuts, toasted

Heat 1 tablespoon oil in 30cm frying pan or wok over medium-high heat. Add mushrooms, spring onions, and bamboo shoots; cook, stirring often, 10 minutes. Transfer to bowl. Heat remaining 2 tablespoons oil in same pan over high heat. Add ginger and beef; cook until liquid evaporates and beef is browned. Return mushroom mixture to pan. Mix sherry and next 4 ingredients together in small bowl; stir into pan. Cook over medium heat, stirring constantly, until thickened. Let each person spoon some beef mixture and pine nuts onto a lettuce leaf, fold over and eat out of hand.

**Each serving: About 435 calories, 23g protein, 9g carbohydrate, 33g total fat (11g saturated), 84mg cholesterol, 605mg sodium**

# MEAT LOAF

An easy-to-prepare family favourite, meat loaf lends itself to a range of simple variations. Try our meat loaf with a savoury spinach-mushroom filling, or a version with the robust flavours found in a bowl of chilli. To avoid a heavy, tough-textured loaf, don't over-blend the meat mixture.

## MUSHROOM-AND-SPINACH-STUFFED MEAT LOAF

❖❖❖❖❖❖❖❖❖❖❖❖

*Prep:* 30 minutes
*Bake:* 1 hour
*Makes* 8 main dish servings

2 tbsp vegetable oil
2 medium celery stalks, chopped
1 medium onion, chopped
225g mushrooms, sliced
300g frozen chopped spinach, thawed
125g pimiento-stuffed olives, chopped
750g minced beef
60g rolled oats
1 tbsp Worcestershire sauce
1½ tsp salt
1 medium egg
175g bottled chilli sauce
Mashed potatoes and steamed sliced carrots (optional)

1 Preheat oven to 190°C (375°F, Gas 5). Heat 1 tablespoon oil in 26cm frying pan over medium heat; add celery and onion and cook, stirring occasionally, until very tender. Transfer to bowl.

2 Heat remaining 1 tablespoon oil in same pan over medium-high heat; add mushrooms and cook, stirring occasionally, until golden brown. Remove mushrooms from heat. Squeeze spinach dry.

3 Stir spinach and chopped olives into mushrooms; set aside. Mix minced beef, oats, Worcestershire, salt, egg, celery mixture, 50g chilli sauce and *60ml water* together in large bowl.

4 Fill and shape meat mixture into a roll: on sheet of greaseproof paper, pat meat mixture into 30 by 25cm rectangle. Spread spinach mixture on meat rectangle.

5 From a long side, carefully roll meat mixture, Swiss-roll fashion, lifting paper and using long spatula to loosen meat from paper.

6 Place loaf, seam-side down, in 35 by 24cm roasting tin. Bake 50 minutes. Spread remaining 125g chilli sauce over loaf; bake 10 minutes longer. Serve with mashed potatoes and carrots, if you like.

EACH SERVING: ABOUT 350 CALORIES, 20g PROTEIN, 16g CARBOHYDRATE, 23g TOTAL FAT (8g SATURATED), 90mg CHOLESTEROL, 910mg SODIUM

## CHILLI MEAT LOAF

*Prep: 20 minutes    Bake: 1¼ hours*
*Makes 8 main dish servings*

| | |
|---|---|
| 1 tbsp vegetable oil | 1 medium egg |
| 1 large celery stalk with leaves, chopped | 125g canned or bottled mild green chillies, drained (liquid reserved) and chopped |
| 1 medium onion, chopped | |
| 2 tsp chilli powder | |
| 2 slices firm white bread | 1½ tsp salt |
| 750g minced beef | ¼ tsp ground black pepper |
| 450g canned red kidney beans, rinsed and drained | 175g mild chunky salsa |
| | 225g soured cream |

◆ Preheat oven to 180°C (350°F, Gas 4). Heat oil in large frying pan over medium heat; add celery with leaves and onion and cook, stirring, until tender.

◆ Stir in chilli powder; cook, stirring, 1 minute. Remove pan from heat.

◆ Tear bread into crumbs and put in large bowl; add cooked celery mixture, minced meat, kidney beans, egg, green chillies with their liquid, salt and black pepper; mix well to combine.

◆ Shape meat mixture into 25 by 10cm loaf in a 33 by 20cm roasting tin, pressing mixture firmly together. Spread 50g salsa over loaf. Bake 1¼ hours.

◆ Using 2 spatulas, carefully place meat loaf on platter. Serve meat loaf warm or cover and refrigerate at least 3 hours to serve chilled.

◆ To serve, gently stir together soured cream and remaining 125g salsa in small bowl until blended; serve soured-cream salsa with meat loaf.

**Each serving: About 330 calories, 21g protein, 17g carbohydrate, 20g total fat (9g saturated), 92mg cholesterol, 955mg sodium**

### THE DEEP FREEZE

Meat loaf freezes beautifully, so consider doubling the recipe and making an extra loaf for storing in the freezer. Cool completely, wrap tightly in plastic, then over-wrap in heavy-duty foil or freezer paper, label and date. Plan to use within 1 month. Thaw in the refrigerator or microwave oven before re-heating. Or, serve at room temperature. For almost-instant sandwiches, freeze meat-loaf slices individually in heavy-duty foil or freezer paper. Make up the sandwiches in the morning with the still-frozen slices. By noon, the sandwiches will be thawed and ready to eat.

## CONFETTI MEAT LOAF

*Prep: 25 minutes    Bake: 1¼ hours*
*Makes 8 main dish servings*

| | |
|---|---|
| 2 tbsp vegetable oil | 1 medium egg |
| 2 large carrots, diced | 750g minced beef |
| 1 large onion, diced | 225g canned sweetcorn |
| 1¼ tsp salt | 150g frozen peas, thawed |
| 1 tsp fennel seeds | 90g dried breadcrumbs |
| ½ tsp coarsely ground black pepper | |

◆ Preheat oven to 180°C (350°F, Gas 4). Heat oil in 26cm frying pan over medium-high heat. Add carrots, onion, salt, fennel seeds and pepper; cook, stirring often, about 15 minutes until tender.

◆ Transfer to large bowl. Add remaining ingredients and *125ml water*; mix well. Shape meat mixture into 22 by 15cm loaf in 33 by 20cm roasting tin, pressing firmly. Bake 1¼ hours. To serve, using 2 spatulas, place meat loaf on warm platter.

**Each serving: About 300 calories, 19g protein, 20g carbohydrate, 16g total fat (5g saturated), 79mg cholesterol, 715mg sodium**

## MEAT LOAF WITH SUN-DRIED TOMATOES

*Prep: 25 minutes    Bake: 1¼ hours*
*Makes 8 main dish servings*

| | |
|---|---|
| 1 tbsp olive oil | 750g minced beef |
| 2 medium carrots, grated | 75g oil-packed sun-dried tomatoes, drained and chopped |
| 1 medium celery stalk, chopped | |
| 1 medium onion, chopped | 3 slices firm white bread, torn into small crumbs |
| 1 tsp salt | |
| ¼ tsp ground black pepper | 2 tbsp freshly grated Parmesan cheese |
| 300–350g spinach, coarsely chopped | 2 medium egg whites |

◆ Preheat oven to 180°C (350°F, Gas 4). Heat oil in 30cm non-stick frying pan over medium-high heat; add carrots, celery, onion, salt and pepper and cook, stirring occasionally, until tender. Stir in spinach and cook, stirring constantly, until spinach wilts.

◆ Transfer vegetable mixture to large bowl. Add remaining ingredients; mix well. Shape meat mixture into 20 by 12cm loaf in 33 by 20cm roasting tin, pressing firmly. Bake 1¼ hours. To serve, using 2 spatulas, place meat loaf on warm platter.

**Each serving: About 250 calories, 19g protein, 11g carbohydrate, 15g total fat (5g saturated), 54mg cholesterol, 460mg sodium**

# BURGERS

Whether barbecued or pan-fried, beef burgers should be handled as little as possible during their preparation, and cooked to medium – with just a trace of pink in the centre.

## TEX-MEX STUFFED BURGERS

◆◆◆◆◆◆◆◆◆◆◆◆◆

*Prep: 20 minutes*
*Barbecue: 10 minutes*
*Makes 4 main dish servings*

**450g minced beef**
**16 water biscuits, crushed**
**1 small green pepper, very finely chopped**
**1 small red pepper, very finely chopped**
**1 tsp grated onion**
**¾ tsp salt**
**¼ tsp coarsely ground black pepper**
**125g Cheddar cheese, grated**
**4 hamburger buns with sesame seeds, split**
**4 lettuce leaves**
**1 small tomato, diced**
**Potato crisps, pickles and tomato wedges (optional)**
**Flat-leaf parsley for garnish**

### TO GRILL

Preheat grill and place burgers on rack in grill pan. Place pan in grill at closest position to heat and grill, turning once, about 10 minutes for medium, or until desired doneness; top with cheese as instructed.

1 Prepare barbecue. Mix first 7 ingredients in medium bowl.

2 Shape mixture into 4 balls, handling as little as possible. Make indentation in centre of each ball; place 1 heaped tablespoon grated cheese in each indentation. Shape ball round cheese to enclose completely; flatten each ball into a 2cm thick round patty. Place burgers on barbecue over medium heat.

3 Cook burgers, turning once, 10 minutes for medium, or until desired doneness. During last few minutes of cooking, top burgers with remaining grated cheese and place hamburger buns, cut-side down, on barbecue; cook until cheese melts and buns are lightly toasted.

### ROQUEFORT BURGERS

Mix 450g minced beef, 1 tablespoon Worcestershire sauce and ½ teaspoon coarsely ground black pepper. Shape burgers as above; stuff with 60g crumbled Roquefort or other blue cheese. Barbecue; top with thinly sliced red onion, if you like. Makes 4 main dish servings.

Each serving: About 475 calories, 28g protein, 22g carbohydrate, 30g total fat (13g saturated), 97mg cholesterol, 575mg sodium

4 To serve, arrange lettuce leaves on bottom halves of toasted buns; top with burgers. Spoon diced tomato on top. Replace tops of buns. Serve with potato crisps, pickles, and tomato wedges, if you like. Garnish with parsley.

EACH SERVING: ABOUT 590 CALORIES, 33g PROTEIN, 32g CARBOHYDRATE, 37g TOTAL FAT (15g SATURATED), 114mg CHOLESTEROL, 950mg SODIUM

## CAJUN BURGERS WITH RÉMOULADE SAUCE

*Prep:* 20 minutes    *Cook:* 8 minutes

*Makes* 4 main dish servings

| | |
|---|---|
| 1 tbsp vegetable oil | Tabasco sauce |
| 1 small red pepper, cored, seeded and very finely chopped | 450g minced beef |
| | 125g mayonnaise |
| 1 small onion, very finely chopped | 1 tbsp fresh lemon juice |
| | 1 tbsp ketchup |
| 2 garlic cloves, very finely chopped | 2 tsp horseradish sauce |
| | 4 muffins, split and lightly toasted |
| ¼ tsp dried thyme | 4 lettuce leaves |
| Salt | 4 tomato slices |

◆ Heat oil in 26cm frying pan over medium heat. Add red pepper, onion, garlic, thyme, ½ teaspoon salt and ¼ teaspoon Tabasco sauce; cook, stirring occasionally, until vegetables are tender. Transfer to medium bowl. Add minced beef and mix just until blended. Shape beef mixture into four 2cm thick round patties, handling meat as little as possible. Cook patties in same pan over high heat, shaking pan occasionally and turning patties once, 8 minutes for medium, or until desired doneness.

◆ Meanwhile, prepare rémoulade sauce: combine next 4 ingredients, ¼ teaspoon salt, and ¼ teaspoon Tabasco sauce in bowl until blended. To serve, spread sauce on toasted muffins; sandwich with lettuce, burgers and tomato.

**Each serving: About 690 calories, 26g protein, 34g carbohydrate, 50g total fat (13g saturated), 100mg cholesterol, 980mg sodium**

### SWEET-AND-TANGY ONIONS

Peel 6 medium red onions (about 750g); cut each into 8 wedges, leaving a little of the root end to help hold shape during cooking. Bring onions, 125ml water, 125ml distilled white vinegar, 100g sugar and 1 teaspoon salt to the boil in 26cm frying pan over high heat. Reduce heat to low; cover and simmer 3–5 minutes, until onions are tender-crisp. Transfer to bowl; cover and refrigerate until well chilled. Drain to serve with your favourite burgers. Makes about 750g.

Each 100g: About 85 calories, 1g protein, 22g carbohydrate, 0g total fat, 0mg cholesterol, 290mg sodium

## STEAKHOUSE BURGERS WITH HORSERADISH SOURED CREAM

*Prep:* 10 minutes    *Cook:* 6 minutes

*Makes* 4 main dish servings

| | |
|---|---|
| 600g minced beef | 75ml soured cream |
| Salt and coarsely ground black pepper | 4 muffins, split and lightly toasted |
| 2½ tsp horseradish sauce | 4 lettuce leaves |

◆ Shape minced beef into four 1cm thick round patties, handling meat as little as possible. Sprinkle patties with ½ teaspoon salt, then with 1 teaspoon pepper, pressing pepper lightly into patties. Heat 30cm non-stick frying pan over medium-high heat until hot. Add patties and cook, shaking pan occasionally and turning patties once, about 6 minutes for medium, or until desired doneness.

◆ Meanwhile, stir horseradish sauce, ⅛ teaspoon salt, and ⅛ teaspoon black pepper into soured cream in small bowl. Serve patties on toasted muffins with lettuce leaves and horseradish sauce.

**Each serving: About 555 calories, 30g protein, 28g carbohydrate, 34g total fat (14g saturated), 113mg cholesterol, 745mg sodium**

## HAMBURGERS WITH MUSHROOM AND ONION TOPPING

*Prep:* 15 minutes    *Cook:* 20 minutes

*Makes* 4 main dish servings

| | |
|---|---|
| 450g minced beef | 225g mushrooms, sliced |
| Salt and coarsely ground black pepper | 15g fresh parsley, chopped |
| | 8 slices Italian bread, each 5mm thick, toasted |
| 2 tbsp olive oil | 1 tomato, sliced |
| 1 large onion, sliced | |

◆ Shape minced beef into 2cm thick round patties, handling meat as little as possible. Cook patties in 26cm frying pan over high heat, turning patties once and sprinkling with ¼ teaspoon each salt and pepper, 8 minutes for medium, or until desired doneness.

◆ Meanwhile, heat oil in another 26cm frying pan over medium-high heat; add onion and cook until tender-crisp and golden. Stir in mushrooms, ½ teaspoon salt and ¼ teaspoon pepper; cook over high heat, stirring often, until mushrooms are golden and tender. Stir in parsley.

◆ To serve, arrange 2 toasted bread slices on each plate; top with 1 or 2 slices tomato, 1 hamburger and some mushroom mixture to make open-faced sandwich.

**Each serving: About 565 calories, 27g protein, 39g carbohydrate, 33g total fat (11g saturated), 84mg cholesterol, 840mg sodium**

# MEATBALLS

Pan-fried meatballs make an easy main dish. For best results, blend the meat mixture until the ingredients are just evenly combined – over-mixing creates tough meatballs. Form the meat into uniform balls, and avoid crowding the pan when cooking, or the meatballs will stew instead of fry. Mashed potatoes, rice or pasta are ideal side dishes for meatballs.

## MEATBALLS IN LIGHT TOMATO SAUCE

✦✦✦✦✦✦✦✦✦✦✦✦✦✦✦✦✦✦✦✦✦✦✦✦✦✦✦

*Prep: 25 minutes    Cook: 45 minutes*
*Makes 6 main dish servings*

| | |
|---|---|
| 750g minced beef | 1 medium carrot, sliced |
| 90g fresh breadcrumbs (about 3 slices white bread) | 1 medium celery stalk, sliced |
| | 400g canned tomatoes |
| 1 medium egg | 60ml dry white wine or |
| ¼ tsp ground black pepper | chicken stock |
| Salt | ½ tsp dried basil |
| 2 tbsp vegetable oil | 1 tbsp chopped fresh parsley |
| 1 medium onion, cut into thin wedges | 2 tsp grated lemon rind |
| | Cooked pasta (optional) |

**1** Mix minced beef, breadcrumbs, egg, pepper, 1 teaspoon salt and *60ml water* together in large bowl. Shape meat mixture into 18 meatballs.

**2** Heat oil in 30cm frying pan over medium-high heat; add meatballs, half at a time, and cook until browned on all sides. Transfer to plate.

**3** Add onion, carrot and celery to drippings in pan and cook, stirring often, 10 minutes, or until vegetables are tender and lightly browned.

**4** Add tomatoes with their juice, wine, basil and ½ teaspoon salt, breaking up tomatoes with spoon. Return meatballs to pan; bring to the boil over high heat.

### FRESH TOMATO SAUCE

This recipe uses canned tomatoes, which are already peeled. However, peeled fresh tomatoes can easily be substituted, especially in summer when they are at their ripest and tastiest. Peel 450g tomatoes (see page 314), then proceed as instructed in Steps 4 and 5 of the recipe. If the tomato sauce seems too thick at the end of simmering, stir in a little chicken stock or water to thin.

**5** Reduce heat to low; cover and simmer, turning meatballs occasionally, 20 minutes, or until they are cooked through. To serve, sprinkle meatballs with parsley and lemon rind. Serve with pasta, if you like.

EACH SERVING: ABOUT 425 CALORIES, 23g PROTEIN, 13g CARBOHYDRATE, 29g TOTAL FAT (11g SATURATED), 119mg CHOLESTEROL, 815mg SODIUM

## SWEDISH MEATBALLS

*Prep: 20 minutes    Cook: 20 minutes*
*Makes 6 main dish servings*

25g margarine or butter
1 medium onion, finely chopped
2 slices firm white bread, torn
750g minced beef
1 medium egg
1 tsp salt
¼ tsp ground black pepper
¼ tsp ground nutmeg
Pinch ground allspice
2 tsp vegetable oil
2 tbsp plain flour
400ml chicken stock
60ml whipping cream
15g fresh dill, chopped

◆ Melt 15g margarine in 26cm frying pan over medium heat. Add onion and cook, stirring often, 8 minutes, or until tender. Transfer to large bowl and wipe pan clean.

◆ Meanwhile, process bread to fine crumbs in blender or food processor with knife blade attached. Add breadcrumbs, minced beef, egg, salt, black pepper, ground nutmeg and allspice to onion and mix until blended. Shape into 4cm meatballs.

◆ Melt 5g margarine with 1 teaspoon oil in same pan over medium heat. Add half of meatballs and cook, turning occasionally, 10 minutes, or until browned on all sides and just cooked through; transfer to plate and keep warm. Repeat with remaining 5g margarine and 1 teaspoon oil and remaining meatballs; transfer to plate.

◆ Add flour to drippings in pan and cook, stirring constantly, 1 minute. Gradually whisk in chicken stock and whipping cream; bring to the boil, stirring, over high heat. Reduce heat to low and simmer 5 minutes. Return meatballs to pan, stirring gently to coat with sauce. Sprinkle with chopped dill and serve.

**Each serving: About 440 calories, 23g protein, 9g carbohydrate, 34g total fat (13g saturated), 138mg cholesterol, 820mg sodium**

### SHAPING MEATBALLS

To make uniform meatballs, try this: for 3cm meatballs, pat the meat mixture out on greaseproof paper into a 3cm thick square. Cut the square into 3cm cubes and, with wet hands, roll each cube into a ball. For 5cm meatballs, cut a 5cm thick square into 5cm cubes.

## MEXICAN MEATBALLS

*Prep: 20 minutes    Cook: 45 minutes*
*Makes 6 main dish servings*

750g minced beef
1 medium egg
90g dried breadcrumbs
1 tsp salt
½ tsp ground black pepper
3 garlic cloves, very finely chopped
2 tsp vegetable oil
1 small onion, very finely chopped
1 tsp ground cumin
800g canned tomatoes
225ml chicken stock
1 tbsp chilli sauce
15g fresh coriander, chopped

◆ Mix minced beef, egg, breadcrumbs, salt, pepper, *60ml water* and one-third of garlic in large bowl until blended. Shape into 3cm meatballs.

◆ Heat oil in 5-litre flameproof casserole over medium heat. Add onion and cook, stirring often, 5 minutes, or until tender. Stir in cumin and remaining garlic; cook 30 seconds. Stir in tomatoes, chicken stock and chilli sauce; bring mixture to the boil over high heat.

◆ Add meatballs; return to the boil. Reduce heat to low and simmer, uncovered, 30 minutes, or until meatballs are cooked through. Sprinkle with coriander.

**Each serving: About 425 calories, 25g protein, 19g carbohydrate, 27g total fat (10g saturated), 123mg cholesterol, 990mg sodium**

## CLASSIC ITALIAN MEATBALLS

*Prep: 15 minutes    Cook: 15 minutes*
*Makes 6 main dish servings*

2 slices firm white bread, torn
750g minced beef
1 medium egg
15g fresh flat-leaf parsley, chopped
45g Pecorino Romano or Parmesan cheese, freshly grated
1 garlic clove, very finely chopped
1 tsp salt
¼ tsp ground black pepper
2 tsp olive oil

◆ Process bread to fine crumbs in blender or food processor with knife blade attached. Transfer to large bowl. Add minced beef, egg, chopped parsley, grated cheese, garlic, salt and black pepper. Mix until combined. Shape into twelve 5cm meatballs.

◆ Heat oil in 26cm frying pan over medium heat. Add meatballs and cook, gently turning occasionally, 15 minutes, or until browned all over and just cooked through.

**Each serving: About 370 calories, 24g protein, 5g carbohydrate, 27g total fat (11g saturated), 123mg cholesterol, 570mg sodium**

# GRILLED BEEF

A prime cut of beef, grilled to tender, juicy perfection, is a treat that's easy to prepare. The method is simple: season the meat or spread it with a herb butter and grill it, close to the heat (but don't over-cook), turning the meat only once during cooking.

## LEMON-PEPPER STEAK

❖❖❖❖❖❖❖❖❖❖❖❖

*Prep: 10 minutes, plus standing*
*Grill: 16 minutes*
*Makes 8 main dish servings*

30g butter, softened
2 tbsp grated lemon rind
2 tsp cracked black pepper
1½ tsp salt
1 garlic clove, very finely chopped
1 beef rump steak, 3cm thick (about 900g)
Steamed broccoli and sautéed mushrooms (optional)

**1** Preheat grill. Prepare lemon butter: mix butter, grated lemon peel, pepper, salt and garlic together in small bowl until mixture is smooth and well blended.

**2** Place steak on grill rack; spread with half of lemon butter. Place under grill at closest position to heat; grill 8 minutes.

**3** Using tongs, turn steak over; spread with remaining lemon butter. Grill about 8 minutes longer for medium-rare, or until desired doneness.

## A SAMPLER OF SAVOURY BUTTERS

### Parsley-caper butter
Mix 30g softened butter, 2 tablespoons chopped fresh parsley, 2 tablespoons chopped capers, 1 tablespoon very finely chopped shallot, ½ teaspoon salt and ¼ teaspoon ground black pepper in small bowl.

### Chilli-lime butter
Mix 30g softened butter with 1 tablespoon grated lime rind, 2 teaspoons chilli powder, ¾ teaspoon salt and ⅛ teaspoon ground red pepper in small bowl.

### Ginger-tarragon butter
Mix 30g softened butter with 2 teaspoons grated, peeled fresh ginger, 2 teaspoons chopped fresh tarragon, ¾ teaspoon salt and ¼ teaspoon ground black pepper in small bowl.

**4** To serve, transfer steak to chopping board. Let stand 10 minutes; keep warm. Cut steak across the grain into thin slices. Serve with broccoli and mushrooms, if you like.

EACH SERVING: ABOUT 180 CALORIES, 26g PROTEIN, 1g CARBOHYDRATE, 8g TOTAL FAT (4g SATURATED), 64mg CHOLESTEROL, 470mg SODIUM

## STEAK WITH YELLOW-PEPPER CHUTNEY

*Prep: 25 minutes, plus standing    Grill: 13–15 minutes*

*Makes 6 main dish servings*

1 beef flank steak (750g)
Salt and coarsely ground
   black pepper
1 tbsp vegetable oil
4 large yellow peppers, cored,
   seeded and cut into
   1cm thick slices
1 large onion, thinly sliced
225g cherry tomatoes, each
   cut in half

225g mango chutney
2 tbsp chopped fresh parsley
2 pitta breads (each 15cm)
10g butter or margarine,
   softened
1 tbsp freshly grated
   Parmesan cheese

◈ Preheat grill. Place steak on rack in grill pan; sprinkle with ¾ teaspoon salt and ½ teaspoon black pepper. Place under grill at closest position to heat; grill steak 5 minutes. Turn steak over; sprinkle with ½ teaspoon salt and ¼ teaspoon black pepper and grill 8–10 minutes longer for medium-rare, or until desired doneness. Transfer to chopping board. Let steak stand 10 minutes; keep warm. Keep grill on.

◈ Meanwhile, prepare yellow-pepper chutney: heat oil in 30cm non-stick frying pan over medium-high heat; add peppers and onion and cook until tender-crisp. Stir in tomatoes, chutney and *125ml water*; heat through. Remove from heat. Stir in parsley.

◈ Split each pitta horizontally in half. Spread butter over pitta halves; sprinkle with cheese. Cut each half into 6 pieces. Place on baking sheet. Place baking sheet under grill at closest position to heat; grill until pitta pieces are lightly toasted. To serve, thinly slice flank steak across the grain. Serve with chutney and pitta slices.

**Each serving: About 425 calories, 27g protein, 51g carbohydrate, 13g total fat (5g saturated), 62mg cholesterol, 670mg sodium**

## FILLETS ON A BED OF GREENS

*Prep: 20 minutes    Grill: 14–15 minutes*

*Makes 4 main dish servings*

1 medium head radicchio,
   coarsely chopped
1 large head chicory, coarsely
   chopped
1 bunch watercress, coarsely
   chopped
2 tbsp plain dried
   breadcrumbs
15g margarine or butter,
   softened
1 tbsp grated lemon rind

1 tbsp very finely chopped
   fresh parsley
¼ tsp coarsely ground black
   pepper
Salt
4 beef fillet steaks, each
   4cm thick (about 125g each)
75ml olive or vegetable oil
2 tbsp fresh lemon juice
1 tbsp white wine vinegar
1½ tsp sugar

◈ Preheat grill. Mix radicchio, chicory and watercress in large bowl; refrigerate. Prepare breadcrumb topping: mix breadcrumbs, margarine, lemon rind, parsley, pepper and ½ teaspoon salt in small bowl.

◈ Place steaks on rack in grill pan; place pan in grill at closest position to heat. Grill steaks 8 minutes. Turn steaks over; grill 3–4 minutes longer for medium-rare, or until desired doneness.

◈ Remove pan from grill ; spread tops of steaks with breadcrumb topping. Grill steaks 3 minutes longer, or until topping is golden.

◈ Meanwhile, bring oil, lemon juice, vinegar, sugar and ½ teaspoon salt to the boil over medium heat. Pour over chopped salad; toss to mix well. Arrange salad on platter. To serve, arrange steaks on salad.

**Each serving: About 505 calories, 22g protein, 9g carbohydrate, 43g total fat (12g saturated), 73mg cholesterol, 670mg sodium**

◆◆◆◆◆◆◆◆◆◆◆◆◆◆◆◆◆◆◆◆◆◆◆◆◆◆◆

### COATING STEAKS WITH CRUMBS

For a tasty and crunchy finishing touch, top grilled steaks with a savoury breadcrumb mixture. Grill the steaks as instructed above, turning once. A few minutes before they're done, use a heatproof rubber spatula to spread the tops of the steaks with the breadcrumb mixture. Grill just until topping is golden.

◆◆◆◆◆◆◆◆◆◆◆◆◆◆◆◆◆◆◆◆◆◆◆◆◆◆◆

## RUMP STEAK OREGANATO

*Prep: 10 minutes, plus standing     Grill: 12–15 minutes*
*Makes 6 main dish servings*

| | |
|---|---|
| 1 medium lemon | 1 tsp dried oregano |
| 2 garlic cloves, very finely chopped | ¾ tsp coarsely ground black pepper |
| 1 tbsp olive oil | 1 rump steak, 3cm thick (about 750g) |
| 1 tsp salt | |

♦ Preheat grill. Grate rind and squeeze juice from lemon. Mix lemon rind, lemon juice, garlic, oil, salt, oregano and pepper in 30 by 21cm ovenproof dish. Add steak, turning to coat both sides.

♦ Place steak on rack in grill pan. Place in grill at closest position to heat. Grill steak, turning once and brushing with any remaining marinade after turning, 12–15 minutes for medium-rare, or until desired doneness.

♦ Transfer to platter. Let stand 10 minutes; keep warm. To serve, thinly slice steak. Spoon any juices from grill pan over steak slices.

Each serving: About 190 calories, 23g protein, 3g carbohydrate, 10g total fat (3g saturated), 68mg cholesterol, 405mg sodium

## BARBECUE-STYLE STEAK AND ONION RINGS

*Prep: 25 minutes, plus marinating and standing     Grill: 16–20 minutes*
*Makes 6 main dish servings*

| | |
|---|---|
| 60ml bottled barbecue sauce | 2 large onions (about 750g), cut crossways into 2cm thick slices |
| 2 tbsp tomato ketchup | |
| 1 garlic clove, very finely chopped | 125ml milk |
| 1 beef rump steak, 4cm thick (about 1.1kg) | 225g plain flour |
| | 1 tsp salt |
| Vegetable oil for deep-frying | |

♦ Mix barbecue sauce, ketchup and chopped garlic in 30 by 21cm ovenproof dish. Add steak, turning to coat. Cover and refrigerate at least 1 hour.

♦ Heat 5cm oil in 3–4-litre saucepan over medium heat to 190°C (375°F) on deep-fat thermometer or heat oil in deep-fat fryer set at 190°C (375°F). Meanwhile, separate onion slices into rings. Place milk in small bowl. Mix flour and salt in another bowl.

♦ Dip onion rings into milk, then into flour mixture. Repeat to coat twice. Add onion rings to hot oil in batches and fry, turning once, 3–5 minutes, until golden brown. Transfer onion rings as they brown to kitchen towels to drain thoroughly. Keep warm.

♦ Meanwhile, preheat grill. Place steak on rack in grill pan; grill about 12cm from heat, brushing once with marinade, 10 minutes. Turn steak; grill, brushing with marinade, 6–10 minutes longer for medium-rare or until desired doneness. Transfer to chopping board. Let stand 10 minutes; keep warm. Thinly slice; serve with onion rings.

Each serving: About 530 calories, 47g protein, 31g carbohydrate, 23g total fat (6g saturated), 96mg cholesterol, 645mg sodium

## FILLETS WITH BALSAMIC-FRUIT SAUCE

*Prep: 20 minutes     Grill: 14–15 minutes*
*Makes 4 main dish servings*

| | |
|---|---|
| ½ beef stock cube, crumbled | ¼ tsp cracked black pepper |
| 1 tsp vegetable oil | 1 tbsp balsamic vinegar |
| 2 medium shallots, very finely chopped | 1 tsp grated lemon rind |
| | ½ tsp sugar |
| 8 stoned prunes, coarsely chopped | 4 small fillet steaks, each 2cm thick (about 90g each) |

♦ Preheat grill. Meanwhile, make balsamic-fruit sauce: dissolve stock cube in *125ml very hot water* in small bowl. Heat oil in saucepan over medium heat. Add shallots; cook until softened, adding stock cube mixture as needed to prevent shallots sticking. Stir in prunes, pepper and any remaining stock cube mixture; reduce heat to low and simmer 5 minutes. Stir in balsamic vinegar, lemon rind and sugar; keep warm.

♦ Place steaks on rack in grill pan; place pan in grill at closest position to heat. Grill steaks 4 minutes.

♦ Turn steaks and grill 4–6 minutes longer for medium-rare, or until desired doneness. To serve, arrange steaks on 4 warm plates; spoon balsamic-fruit sauce over.

Each serving: About 295 calories, 16g protein, 18g carbohydrate, 18g total fat (7g saturated), 55mg cholesterol, 255mg sodium

### LOW-FAT 'SAUTÉING'

When sautéing shallots or onions, prevent them sticking by adding enough liquid just to cover the base of the pan to a minimal amount of oil or butter – you'll save fat and calories. Here, we've used a small amount of beef stock.

## BEEF FILLETS WITH ONION AND RED-PEPPER CONFIT

*Prep:* 30 minutes  *Grill:* 12 minutes

*Makes* 4 main dish servings

1 tbsp olive or vegetable oil
2 medium onions, diced
1 large red pepper, cored, seeded and diced
1 tsp sugar
½ tsp dried basil
Salt and coarsely ground black pepper

1 tbsp red wine vinegar
1 tbsp chopped fresh parsley
4 beef fillet steaks, each 3.5cm thick (about 125g each)
Sautéed spinach (optional)

◆ Prepare red-pepper confit: heat oil in saucepan over medium heat; add onions and cook, stirring occasionally, until tender and golden.

◆ Stir in red pepper, sugar, basil, ¾ teaspoon salt and ¼ teaspoon black pepper; cook, stirring frequently, until red pepper is tender-crisp. Stir in vinegar and *2 tablespoons water*; bring to the boil over high heat. Reduce heat to low; cover and simmer 5 minutes, or until red pepper is tender. Stir in parsley; keep warm.

◆ Preheat grill. Place steaks on rack in grill pan; place pan in grill at closest position to heat. Grill steaks 6 minutes. Turn steaks and sprinkle with ¾ teaspoon black pepper and ¼ teaspoon salt. Grill 6 minutes longer for medium-rare, or until desired doneness.

◆ Transfer steaks to chopping board; slice each steak horizontally in half. Spoon red-pepper confit onto 4 plates, reserving about 4 tablespoons. Arrange steaks over confit, slightly overlapping top and bottom halves; spoon reserved confit over steaks. Serve with sautéed spinach, if you like.

Each serving: About 355 calories, 21g protein, 10g carbohydrate, 25g total fat (9g saturated), 73mg cholesterol, 585mg sodium

## STEAK AND PEPPER FAJITAS

*Prep:* 25 minutes, plus standing  *Grill:* 12–14 minutes

*Makes* 4 main dish servings

1 beef rump steak, 2.5cm thick (about 350g)
225g bottled medium-hot salsa
1 tbsp vegetable oil
1 medium red onion, sliced
1 each medium green and red pepper, cored, seeded and sliced

2 tbsp chopped fresh coriander
8 flour tortillas (15–18cm), warmed according to packet instructions
225ml soured cream
125g mature Cheddar cheese, grated

◆ Preheat grill. Place steak on rack in grill pan; spread steak with 4 tablespoons salsa. Place pan under grill at closest position to heat; grill steak 6 minutes. Turn steak and spread with 4 tablespoons salsa; grill 6–8 minutes longer for medium-rare, or until desired doneness. Transfer steak to chopping board. Let stand 10 minutes; keep warm.

◆ Meanwhile, heat oil in 30cm non-stick frying pan over medium-high heat. Add red onion and both sliced peppers; cook, stirring often, until tender-crisp. Stir in coriander. Spoon into serving bowl. To serve, using knife held almost parallel to cutting surface, thinly slice steak across the grain. Serve steak with pepper mixture, flour tortillas, soured cream, grated cheese and remaining salsa.

Each serving: About 640 calories, 35g protein, 50g carbohydrate, 33g total fat (16g saturated), 96mg cholesterol, 840mg sodium

## HERBED SIRLOIN STEAK

*Prep:* 10 minutes, plus standing  *Grill:* 13–17 minutes

*Makes* 6 main dish servings

20g fresh parsley, coarsely chopped
1 tbsp chopped fresh thyme or ½ tsp dried
2 tbsp dried breadcrumbs
1 tbsp reduced-fat mayonnaise

½ tsp coarsely ground black pepper
1 sirloin steak, 3cm thick (about 750g)
½ teaspoon salt

Preheat grill. Mix first 5 ingredients in small bowl; set aside. Sprinkle steak with salt. Place steak on rack in grill pan; place under grill at closest position to heat. Grill steak, turning once, 12–15 minutes for medium-rare, or until desired doneness. Remove pan from grill; spread herb mixture on top of steak. Grill 1–2 minutes longer, until topping is golden. Transfer steak to chopping board. Let stand 10 minutes; keep warm. Thinly slice steak.

Each serving: About 180 calories, 23g protein, 2g carbohydrate, 8g total fat (3g saturated), 69mg cholesterol, 250mg sodium

# BARBECUED BEEF

Steaks, ribs and kebabs all lend themselves to barbecuing, and they are even better when enhanced with a marinade, spice rub or tangy sauce. The marinade serves the dual purpose of adding flavour and making the meat more tender. If you're using a charcoal barbecue, prepare the fire 20–30 minutes before cooking to be sure the coals are hot. They are ready when a light-grey ash covers the coals (in daylight) or they glow red (at night).

## T-BONE STEAK WITH CHAR-GRILLED SALAD

❖❖❖❖❖❖❖❖❖❖❖❖

*Prep: 10 minutes, plus standing*
*Barbecue: 25–40 minutes*
*Makes 6 main dish servings*

**1 large head radicchio**
**3 medium heads chicory**
**3 tbsp olive oil**
**1 tbsp chopped fresh
  rosemary or 1 tsp dried,
  crushed**
**Salt**
**60g bottled chilli sauce**
**60ml balsamic vinegar**
**1 garlic clove, crushed with
  side of knife**
**1 beef T-bone steak,
  5cm thick (about 1kg)**

**1** Prepare barbecue. Prepare char-grilled salad: cut radicchio into 6 wedges. Cut each head of chicory lengthwise in half. Mix oil, chopped rosemary and ½ teaspoon salt in cup. Set aside. Prepare chilli mixture: mix chilli sauce, vinegar, ¾ teaspoon salt and garlic in shallow dish until well combined.

**2** Add steak to chilli mixture; turn to coat. Place steak on barbecue over medium heat; brush with half of chilli mixture.

**3** Cook steak, turning occasionally, 20–30 minutes for medium-rare, or until desired doneness; brush with remaining chilli mixture halfway through cooking time. Transfer to chopping board. Let stand 10 minutes; keep warm.

**4** Meanwhile, place vegetables on barbecue; brush with oil mixture. Cook, turning occasionally, 5–10 minutes, until tender-crisp. Thinly slice steak; arrange on serving platter with char-grilled salad.

---

### BARBECUE EQUIPMENT

The long handles on these tools make it easier – and safer – to manoeuvre foods over hot fires. Shown here (left to right): a brush for basting; a fork for moving vegetables and meat (don't pierce meat, or you will lose juices); and tongs for turning and picking up. A spatula is indispensable for burgers. Another useful tool is a grill topper. This flat, perforated grate fits over a grilling rack and is ideal for unskewered small foods such as scallops, prawns and vegetables, which can fall through the rack.

---

EACH SERVING: ABOUT 490 CALORIES, 33g PROTEIN, 9g CARBOHYDRATE, 35g TOTAL FAT (12g SATURATED), 104mg CHOLESTEROL, 675mg SODIUM

## LIME BEEF WITH TORTILLAS

*Prep:* 25 minutes, plus marinating and standing
*Barbecue:* 10–12 minutes
*Makes* 6 main dish servings

4 medium limes
1 small onion, chopped
1 tsp chilli powder
½ tsp salt
¼ tsp dried chilli flakes
1 beef skirt steak or flank
   steak (about 750g)
60ml olive or vegetable oil

2 medium avocados, peeled,
   stoned, and cut into thin
   wedges
4 small tomatoes, cut into thin
   wedges
12 flour tortillas (15–18cm),
   warmed according to packet
   instructions

◆ Grate rind and squeeze juice from limes. Mix grated lime rind and juice, onion, chilli powder, salt and dried chilli flakes in an ovenproof dish. Add steak to marinade and turn to coat. Cover and refrigerate steak at least 4 hours, turning occasionally.

◆ Prepare barbecue. Prepare lime dressing: remove meat from marinade; pour marinade into saucepan. Bring to the boil over high heat; boil 5 minutes. Pour marinade into small bowl. Gradually whisk oil into marinade in a thin stream; set dressing aside.

◆ Place steak on barbecue over medium-high heat; cook steak, turning once, 6–8 minutes for skirt steak, 10–12 minutes for flank steak, for medium-rare, or until desired doneness. Place steak on large chopping board. Let stand 10 minutes; keep warm.

◆ To serve, using knife held almost parallel to cutting surface, thinly slice steak across the grain. Arrange avocado and tomato wedges on chopping board. Place lime dressing and warm tortillas next to steak. Let each person arrange some sliced meat, avocado and tomato on a tortilla, then spoon on some dressing, roll up tortilla and eat out of hand.

**Each serving: About 640 calories, 31g protein, 53g carbohydrate, 35g total fat (8g saturated), 58mg cholesterol, 600mg sodium**

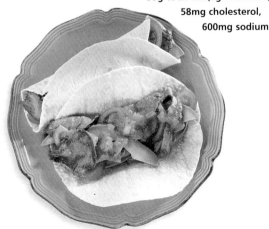

## SPICE-RUBBED BEEF FILLET

*Prep:* 5 minutes   *Barbecue:* 30–40 minutes
*Makes* 10 main dish servings

1 tbsp fennel seeds, crushed
2 tsp salt
½ tsp ground ginger

½ tsp dried chilli flakes
1 beef fillet roast
   (about 1.1kg)

◆ Mix first 4 ingredients on greaseproof paper. Use mixture to rub on beef. If you like, cover and refrigerate spice-rubbed beef overnight before barbecuing.

◆ Prepare barbecue. Cook beef, covered, over medium heat, turning occasionally, 30–40 minutes for medium-rare, or until desired doneness. Temperature on instant-read thermometer should reach 57°C (internal temperature of meat will rise to 59.5°C upon standing). Transfer beef to chopping board. Let stand 10 minutes; keep warm. Thinly slice.

**Each serving: About 175 calories, 24g protein, 0g carbohydrate, 8g total fat (3g saturated), 59mg cholesterol, 480mg sodium**

## FILLETS WITH RED-PEPPER AND ONION STUFFING

*Prep:* 35 minutes   *Barbecue:* 10–15 minutes
*Makes* 4 main dish servings

1 tbsp plus 2 tsp olive or
   vegetable oil
1 large onion, chopped
1 tbsp red wine vinegar
1 tsp sugar
¾ tsp dried basil
Salt

100g bottled roasted red
   peppers, drained and
   chopped
4 beef fillet steaks, each
   4cm thick (125g each)
½ tsp coarsely ground black
   pepper

◆ Heat 1 tablespoon oil in 2-litre saucepan over medium-high heat; add onion and cook, stirring frequently, until golden. Stir in vinegar, sugar, basil, ¼ teaspoon salt and *1 tablespoon water*; bring to the boil over high heat. Reduce heat to low; cover and simmer 15 minutes. Uncover; stir in roasted peppers and cook, stirring, until liquid evaporates. Remove from heat; cool to room temperature.

◆ Prepare barbecue. Using sharp knife, cut a horizontal slit in each steak, almost but not all the way through, to form a deep pocket. Spoon onion mixture into pockets. Brush steaks with remaining 2 teaspoons oil; sprinkle with black pepper and ½ teaspoon salt.

◆ Place steaks on barbecue over medium heat; cook, turning once, 10–15 minutes for medium-rare, or until desired doneness.

**Each serving: About 360 calories, 21g protein, 7g carbohydrate, 28g total fat (9g saturated), 73mg cholesterol, 455mg sodium**

## Beef satay with Peanut sauce

*Prep: 20 minutes*
*Barbecue: 3–4 minutes*
*Makes 6 main dish servings*

30 (25–30cm) bamboo skewers
1 medium lemon
1 small garlic clove, very finely chopped
1 tbsp Dijon mustard
¼ tsp dried chilli flakes
60ml plus 2 tbsp soy sauce
1 tbsp plus 1 tsp sugar
1 beef flank steak (about 750g)
65g smooth peanut butter
1 tbsp white wine vinegar

◈ Prepare barbecue. Soak bamboo skewers in *water* to cover for 15 minutes; drain and pat dry. Meanwhile, grate rind and squeeze 1 tablespoon juice from lemon.

◈ Mix lemon rind, lemon juice, garlic, mustard, dried chilli flakes, 60ml soy sauce and 1 tablespoon sugar in large ovenproof dish. Holding knife almost parallel to work surface, cut flank steak crossways into 30 slices, each about 5mm thick. Add steak to soy sauce mixture in baking dish; toss to coat. Set aside.

◈ Prepare peanut sauce: bring peanut butter, vinegar, *¼ cup water*, remaining 2 tablespoons soy sauce and remaining 1 teaspoon sugar to the boil in small saucepan, stirring constantly, over medium-high heat. Reduce heat to low; simmer, stirring, until mixture is smooth. Remove pan from heat. Keep warm.

◈ Loosely thread 1 slice steak, accordion style onto each skewer. Place skewers on barbecue over medium heat. Cook, turning once, 3–4 minutes for medium-rare, or until desired doneness. Arrange skewers on warm large platter. Serve with warm peanut sauce.

**Each serving: About 280 calories, 26g protein, 9g carbohydrate, 16g total fat (6g saturated), 58mg cholesterol, 1215mg sodium**

## Sirloin steak kebabs with Caesar salad

*Prep: 25 minutes*
*Barbecue: 10–12 minutes*
*Makes 6 main dish servings*

Caesar Salad (see below)
70g tomato ketchup
3 tbsp light molasses or golden syrup
2 tbsp Worcestershire sauce
1 tbsp German mustard
1 tbsp grated onion
½ tsp salt
1 sirloin or rump steak, 3cm thick (about 900g), cut into 5cm chunks
6 (35cm) all-metal skewers

◈ Prepare barbecue. Prepare Caesar Salad but do not toss with dressing; refrigerate. Mix tomato ketchup and next 5 ingredients in large bowl; add steak and toss to coat.

◈ Thread steak chunks onto skewers. Place skewers on barbecue over medium heat. Cook, turning occasionally and brushing with remaining ketchup mixture, 10–12 minutes for medium-rare, or until desired doneness. Toss salad with dressing; serve with kebabs.

**Each serving: About 230 calories, 30g protein, 10g carbohydrate, 10g total fat (4g saturated), 91mg cholesterol, 445mg sodium**

### CAESAR SALAD

Tear or cut 2 heads Cos lettuce into bite-sized pieces; place in bowl with 90g plain croûtons. Blend 40g freshly grated Parmesan cheese, 60ml olive oil, 2 tablespoons fresh lemon juice, 2 teaspoons Dijon mustard, ½ teaspoon each salt and coarsely ground black pepper, 4 anchovy fillets and 1 garlic clove in a blender until smooth. Add to salad; toss. Makes 6 accompaniment servings.

## Spicy beef kebabs

*Prep: 15 minutes*
*Barbecue: 10–12 minutes*
*Makes 4 main dish servings*

1 tbsp chilli powder
1 tbsp soy sauce
1 tsp jalapeño chilli sauce
2 tbsp vegetable oil
1 beef sirloin steak, 3cm thick (about 750g), cut into 12 chunks
½ tsp salt
3 spring onions, cut into 8cm long pieces
8 large mushrooms
1 medium courgette (about 350g), cut into bite-sized chunks
4 (35cm) all-metal skewers
8 cherry tomatoes
Couscous (optional)

◈ Prepare barbecue. Mix chilli powder, soy sauce, jalapeño chilli sauce and 1 tablespoon oil in medium bowl. Add beef to chilli mixture; stir to coat.

◈ Mix salt and remaining 1 tablespoon oil in large bowl. Add spring onions, mushrooms and courgette; toss to coat.

◈ Alternately thread beef, spring onion pieces, mushrooms, courgette and tomatoes on to skewers. Place skewers on barbecue over medium heat. Cook, turning once, 10–12 minutes, until beef is medium-rare and vegetables are tender. Serve kebabs with couscous, if you like.

**Each serving: About 450 calories, 37g protein, 24g carbohydrate, 22g total fat (7g saturated), 98mg cholesterol, 980mg sodium**

## SPICY BEEF RIBS WITH CHAR-GRILLED PINEAPPLE

*Prep: 20 minutes*
*Barbecue: 25–30 minutes*
*Makes 4 main dish servings*

1 garlic clove, very finely
  chopped
1 tbsp olive or vegetable oil
1½ tsp coarsely ground black
  pepper
1½ tsp dry mustard
1½ tsp fennel seeds, crushed
1 tsp salt

½ tsp ground cloves
1.8kg beef thin ribs, cut into
  1-rib portions
1 medium pineapple
2 tbsp brown sugar
Flat-leaf parsley sprigs for
  garnish

◆ Prepare barbecue. Mix garlic, oil, pepper, dry mustard, fennel seeds, salt and ground cloves in small bowl. Use to rub over ribs.

◆ Cut off rind from pineapple. Slice pineapple lengthways in half, then cut each half crossways into 2cm thick slices; remove centre core from each slice.

◆ Place ribs on barbecue over medium heat; cook, turning frequently, 15–20 minutes for medium-rare, or until desired doneness. Transfer ribs to board or large platter.

◆ Toss pineapple slices with brown sugar in large bowl. Place pineapple slices on barbecue; cook, turning frequently, 10 minutes, or until browned on both sides. Serve ribs with pineapple slices. Garnish with parsley sprigs.

Each serving: About 1070 calories, 105g protein, 25g carbohydrate, 59g total fat (24g saturated), 261mg cholesterol, 735mg sodium

### BARBECUED FRUIT

Barbecued fruit makes a striking garnish or delicious dessert. Use firm-textured fruits that aren't overly ripe, such as nectarines, peaches, plums or pineapple. Halve fruit or cut into fairly thick slices or wedges so it won't slip through the grill.

## DOUBLE CHILLI BEEF KEBABS

*Prep: 15 minutes   Barbecue: 9–11 minutes*
*Makes 4 main dish servings*

1 tbsp vegetable oil
1 tbsp chilli powder
125ml bottled chilli sauce
1 tbsp honey
½ tsp salt

4 (25cm) all-metal skewers
600g beef rump steak or
  sirloin, cut into 2–3cm cubes
2 bunches spring onions, cut
  into 5cm pieces

◆ Prepare barbecue. Prepare double-chilli sauce: heat oil over medium heat in saucepan. Add chilli powder; cook, stirring constantly, 1 minute. Stir in chilli sauce, honey and salt; cook 1 minute longer. Remove from heat.

◆ Alternately thread beef cubes and spring-onion pieces onto skewers.

◆ Place skewers on barbecue over medium heat; cook, turning once, 5 minutes. Brush with double-chilli sauce; turn and cook, turning occasionally and brushing with remaining sauce, 4–6 minutes longer, until beef is medium-rare, or until desired doneness. To serve, transfer kebabs to large platter.

Each serving: About 325 calories, 29g protein, 14g carbohydrate, 17g total fat (6g saturated), 72mg cholesterol, 775mg sodium

## KOREAN-STYLE SESAME-GINGER SHORT RIBS

*Prep: 15 minutes, plus marinating   Grill: 20–25 minutes*
*Makes 5 main dish servings*

1.8kg beef thin ribs, cut into
  5cm pieces (ask your
  butcher to cut up the ribs)
3 large garlic cloves, very
  finely chopped

125ml soy sauce
4 tsp very finely chopped,
  peeled fresh ginger
2 tsp sesame oil

◆ Using sharp knife, slash meaty side of ribs at 1cm intervals, 5mm deep.

◆ Mix garlic, soy sauce, ginger and sesame oil in large bowl. Add ribs, turning to coat well with mixture.

◆ Cover bowl securely with cling film and refrigerate overnight, turning ribs once to coat.

◆ Prepare barbecue. Place ribs on barbecue over medium heat; brush with remaining marinade. Cook, turning occasionally, 20–25 minutes for medium, or until desired doneness. To serve, transfer ribs to large platter.

Each serving: About 785 calories, 85g protein, 3g carbohydrate, 46g total fat (19g saturated), 209mg cholesterol, 1805mg sodium

No matter how you cook veal, do it with care. Lean and delicate, veal should actually be cooked more like poultry than beef. As with other meats, the proper cooking method depends on the cut. Whether you grill a thick, juicy chop or create an aromatic stew, do not overcook veal, or you will toughen its delicate texture.

## KNOW YOUR VEAL

Veal calves are raised to an age of 4–5 months. The finest and most expensive of all veal is milk fed. It comes from animals that are fed on their mothers' milk or a special milk formula. The meat is light pink – almost white – and mildly flavoured, with a firm but velvety texture.

Grain-fed veal comes from calves that are reared to a similar age but fed a diet of grain or grass. It has a rosier colour and a slightly stronger flavour than milk-fed veal.

## BUYING AND STORING

• Look for fine-textured pale to creamy pink veal with little marbling. Any fat should be firm and very white. The bones of milk-fed veal will have reddish marrow.
• The high costs of farming quality milk-fed veal in the dairy herds of the U.K. and France are reflected in the price. Veal from grain-fed calves, where available will cost less.
• Because veal is a moist meat, it is fairly perishable. It will last, tightly wrapped, for only two days in the refrigerator.

## STUFFING A VEAL BREAST

1 Make stuffing; cool. To make a pocket, work boning or paring knife between the two main layers of muscle. Extend the space until pocket is deep and wide.

2 Spoon stuffing into pocket (fill loosely because stuffing will expand during cooking). Thread a metal skewer through meat at pocket opening to secure.

## CHOOSING THE RIGHT CUT

Veal is especially good cooked by moist-heat methods such as braising so the meat stays juicy and full of flavour. Roasting at moderate temperatures also works well, and pan-frying (in butter or oil) is ideal for thin cutlets.

**For grilling, barbecuing or pan-frying** These dry-heat methods are suitable for a variety of thin cuts. For grilling and barbecuing, choose fairly thick chops and steaks; cuts that are too thin will dry out. Use veal escalopes for pan-frying only. Since they will cook quickly, keep a close watch.
**Suitable cuts** Best end of neck, cutlets (below right), loin chops, minced veal and escalopes (below left).

Escalopes of even thickness cook uniformly – pound lightly if necessary

Trim fat to 5mm before cooking

Cutlets for grilling should be at least 2cm thick

**For braising or stewing** Bone-in pieces are especially suited to long cooking, as they yield the best flavour. Veal shanks have meaty-tasting marrow in the centre, which helps enrich stews. When done, braised or stewed veal should be fork-tender.
**Suitable cuts** Shank and shin crosscuts (below right), neck or middle neck, breast, shoulder. Veal cubes for stew (below left) are cut from the neck or shoulder.

Chunky veal cubes stand up to long, slow cooking

Marrow in veal shanks adds richness to stews

Pieces should have a good proportion of meat to bone

Connective tissue around muscles helps meat hold its shape during long cooking

**For roasting** Many large cuts of veal will roast nicely. Since veal roasts are generally very lean, ensure juicy results by cooking only to medium doneness 67°C, basting occasionally with the pan juices.
**Suitable cuts** Shoulder (below), middle or best end of neck, loin roast, rump and breast.

Veal has little internal fat, so should be basted during roasting

A well-trimmed roast should be free of cartilage, sinews and membranes

Boneless roasts will keep their shape and cook evenly if they're tied or netted

## ROASTING TIMES AT 170°C (325°F, GAS 3)

| CUT AND WEIGHT<br>Start with meat at refrigerator temperature. **Remove roast from oven when it reaches 2–5°C below desired doneness; temperature will rise as it stands.** | | MEAT THERMOMETER READING | APPROXIMATE COOKING TIME (MINUTES PER 450g) |
| --- | --- | --- | --- |
| Boneless shoulder roast | 1.3–2.2kg | 67°C | 35–40 mins |
| Leg rump roast (boneless) | 1.3–2.2kg | 67°C | 35–40 mins |
| Boneless loin roast | 1.3–2.2kg | 67°C | 25–30 mins |
| Middle or best end of neck | 1.3–2.2kg | 67°C | 30–35 mins |

## FLAVOURS FOR VEAL

Many flavours marry well with delicate, elegant veal. Fresh herbs – tarragon, sage, or rosemary – are lovely. For zesty flavour, try lemon and capers (a must for veal piccata), vinegars, tomatoes, olives, orange and fortified wines such as Madeira or Marsala.

## CARVING A VEAL BREAST ROAST

A veal breast is very easy to carve if the rib bones have been cracked by the butcher before cooking, but even if ribs are not cracked, the breast should still be easy to carve after its long cooking. Place roast on a chopping board, cover with loose tent of foil and let stand 15 minutes. Remove the metal skewer.

1 Steady veal roast with a 2-pronged carving fork. Carve slices from veal breast by cutting down through meat following the line of the rib bone.

2 Cut away exposed rib and continue carving even slices of meat, working along breast. Transfer slices to warm platter.

## MAKING VEAL STOCK

Veal bones produce a rich and full-bodied stock that makes a wonderful substitute for stock cubes in soups, stews and sauces. It becomes thick when reduced and has a depth of flavour that is superior to stock cubes. Ask your butcher for veal bones cut into 5–8cm pieces, or buy knuckle, shin or neck pieces and use the bones for stock and the meat for stew. This recipe makes about 2½ litres.

**1.8kg veal knuckle bones or other veal bones**
**4 carrots**
**2 celery stalks**
**2 onions, each cut in half**
**1 bay leaf**
**8 whole black peppercorns**
**¼ tsp dried thyme**

1 Rinse veal bones; place in 6-litre stockpot with 4 litres cold water. Bring mixture to the boil over high heat. Reduce heat to low; skim and discard froth from top of liquid.

2 Add remaining ingredients; simmer 4–6 hours. Do not boil vigorously, and do not stir, or stock will not be clear. Continue to skim any froth that rises to top. Strain stock through colander; discard veal bones and vegetables. Strain stock through fine sieve. Transfer to small containers and refrigerate to use within 4 days, or freeze up to 4 months. Before using, skim and discard any surface fat.

# Roast veal

A naturally tender meat with a delicate flavour, veal is best roasted at a moderate temperature. Be sure to baste it from time to time while cooking – the result will be a most delicious roast. If you add potatoes or other vegetables to the roasting tin, they will also be flavoured with the roasting juices.

**1** Heat 2 tablespoons oil in 30cm frying pan over medium-high heat. Add mushrooms, onion, ½ teaspoon salt and ¼ teaspoon pepper and cook, stirring often, until liquid evaporates.

**2** Reduce heat to medium; cook until vegetables are golden. Set aside. Untie veal roast. To make veal evenly thick, pound it, fat-side down, between 2 sheets cling film into 30 by 25cm rectangle.

**3** Preheat oven to 170°C (325°F, Gas 3). Arrange spinach over veal; top with mushroom mixture. Starting from a narrow end, roll veal, Swiss-roll fashion. Tie roast with string at 5cm intervals.

## STUFFED VEAL WITH ROASTED POTATOES

❖ ❖ ❖ ❖ ❖ ❖ ❖ ❖ ❖ ❖ ❖

*Prep: 50 minutes, plus standing*
*Roast: 2¼ hours*
*Makes 8 main dish servings*

**3 tbsp olive or vegetable oil**
**350g mushrooms, finely chopped**
**1 medium onion, finely chopped**
**Salt and coarsely ground black pepper**
**1 rolled boneless veal shoulder roast (about 1.3kg)**
**1 bunch spinach (300–350g), stalks removed, rinsed and dried**
**½ tsp dried thyme**
**1.5kg potatoes, peeled and cut into 5cm chunks**
**Thyme sprigs for garnish**

**4** Mix dried thyme, ¾ teaspoon salt and ½ teaspoon pepper in small bowl. Use to rub over veal; place roast on small rack in large roasting tin. Insert meat thermometer into centre of roast.

**5** Roast veal 1¼ hours, brushing occasionally with pan drippings. Toss potatoes with remaining 1 tablespoon oil, ½ teaspoon salt and ¼ teaspoon pepper in large bowl.

**6** Add potatoes to roasting tin, turning to coat with drippings. Roast veal and potatoes 1 hour longer, turning potatoes occasionally, or until potatoes are fork-tender and temperature on meat thermometer reaches 67°C for medium. Transfer veal with potatoes to warm large platter; let stand 10 minutes for easier carving. Keep warm. To serve, slice veal roast. Arrange veal and potatoes on 8 plates and garnish with thyme sprigs.

EACH SERVING: ABOUT 395 CALORIES, 33g PROTEIN, 41g CARBOHYDRATE, 12g TOTAL FAT (3g SATURATED), 112mg CHOLESTEROL, 600mg SODIUM

## VEAL ROAST WITH ROSEMARY AND GARLIC

*Prep: 20 minutes, plus standing    Roast: 2 hours*
*Makes 8 main dish servings*

3 garlic cloves, very finely chopped
½ tsp dried rosemary
¼ tsp dried thyme
1 tsp salt
½ tsp ground black pepper
1 rolled boneless veal shoulder roast (about 1.3kg)

1 tbsp olive oil
1 small onion, finely chopped
1 medium carrot, finely chopped
125ml dry white wine

◆ Preheat oven to 180°C (350°F, Gas 4). Mash garlic, rosemary, thyme, salt and pepper to a paste on chopping board. Pat veal dry with kitchen towels. Rub paste all over veal and in crevices.

◆ Heat oil in 26cm ovenproof frying pan over medium-high heat. Add veal and brown all over, 10 minutes. Add chopped onion and carrot and place veal on top. Pour in wine. Insert meat thermometer into centre of roast.

◆ Transfer pan to oven and roast veal 2 hours, basting with pan juices every 30 minutes and adding *125ml water* if pan is dry, or until meat thermometer reaches 67°C for medium.

◆ Transfer veal to warm large platter; let stand 10 minutes for easier carving. Keep warm. Meanwhile, add *175ml water* to same pan and bring to the boil; stir until brown bits are loosened. Simmer 2 minutes. Skim and discard fat from pan juices. Strain pan juices and vegetables through coarse sieve, pressing hard on vegetables. Discard chopped vegetables. Slice veal thin and serve with pan juices.

**Each serving: About 205 calories, 27g protein, 3g carbohydrate, 8g total fat (3g saturated), 112mg cholesterol, 365mg sodium**

## STUFFED BREAST OF VEAL

*Prep: 30 minutes, plus cooling    Roast: 2 hours*
*Makes 6 main dish servings*

800ml chicken stock
100g easy-cook rice
2 tbsp olive oil
1 medium onion, diced
1 large celery stalk, diced
1 small head batavia (curly lettuce), about 350g, chopped
45g raisins, chopped

1¼ tsp dried sage
Salt and ground black pepper
1 veal breast (about 2.7kg) with pocket (see page 217) for stuffing (ask your butcher to crack bones for easier carving)
Warm Plum Tomato Salad (optional, below left)

◆ Prepare stuffing: bring 300ml stock to the boil in saucepan over high heat; stir in rice. Reduce heat to low. Cover; simmer 20 minutes, or until rice is tender and all liquid is absorbed.

◆ Meanwhile, heat 1 tablespoon oil in 30cm frying pan over medium-high heat. Add onion and celery; cook, stirring occasionally, until lightly browned. Add batavia; cook, stirring, until it just wilts. Remove from heat; stir in rice, raisins and ¼ teaspoon each sage, salt and pepper. Cool to room temperature.

◆ Preheat oven to 180°C (350°F, Gas 4). Spoon stuffing into pocket of veal; skewer closed if necessary (see page 217). Place veal, meat-side up, in roasting tin. Mix remaining 1 tablespoon oil with remaining 1 teaspoon sage, ¼ teaspoon salt and ¼ teaspoon pepper in small bowl. Use to rub over veal. Roast veal 1 hour. Pour remaining 500ml stock into roasting tin. Roast 1 hour longer, basting often, until tender when pierced with tip of knife.

◆ Just before veal is done, prepare Warm Plum Tomato Salad, if you like; keep warm. Place veal on warm large platter. Let stand 15 minutes for easier carving; keep warm.

◆ Pour stock in roasting tin into 2-litre saucepan; let stand a few seconds, until fat separates from stock. Skim and discard fat. Add *350ml water* to roasting tin; stir until brown bits are loosened; stir into stock in pan and heat through. Serve veal with sauce, and tomato salad, if you like.

**Each serving: About 455 calories, 48g protein, 23g carbohydrate, 18g total fat (4g saturated), 193mg cholesterol, 435mg sodium**

---

### WARM PLUM TOMATO SALAD

Heat 3 tablespoons olive oil in 30cm frying pan over medium heat. Add 1 very finely chopped small onion; cook until tender. Add 12 halved small plum tomatoes, ½ teaspoon salt and ¼ teaspoon cracked black pepper. Cook, stirring occasionally, until heated through. Just before serving, sprinkle with 2 tablespoons freshly grated Parmesan cheese and 1 tablespoon fresh lemon juice. Makes 6 accompaniment servings.

Each serving: About 105 calories, 2g protein, 8g carbohydrate, 8g total fat (1g saturated), 2mg cholesterol, 230mg sodium

# PAN-FRIED VEAL

Delicate veal stays tender when it's pan-fried very quickly over fairly high heat. For moist and tender results, do not cook the meat beyond medium. The mild flavour of veal is enhanced by fresh, lively flavours, such as the rocket and tomato salad accompanying it here.

## VEAL WITH TOMATO AND ROCKET SALAD

❖❖❖❖❖❖❖❖❖❖❖

*Prep: 20 minutes*
*Cook: 5 minutes*
*Makes 4 main dish servings*

**2 tsp fresh lemon juice**
**6 tbsp olive oil**
**Salt and ground black pepper**
**1 large tomato, coarsely chopped**
**15g fresh basil leaves**
**45g red onion, coarsely chopped**
**450g veal escalopes**
**2 medium eggs**
**75g plain flour**
**125g dried breadcrumbs**
**1 bunch rocket**
**Toasted Italian bread (optional)**

**1** Prepare salad: mix lemon juice, 2 tablespoons oil, ½ teaspoon salt and ¼ teaspoon pepper in medium bowl. Stir in tomato, basil and red onion until combined; set aside.

**2** Using rolling pin, pound veal between 2 sheets of parchment paper or cling film to 3mm thickness. Pat veal dry. Whisk eggs with ½ teaspoon each salt and pepper in shallow dish.

**3** Spread flour on sheet of greaseproof paper; spread breadcrumbs on another sheet of paper. Dip veal, one piece at a time, first in flour, turning to coat and shaking off excess, then in egg, then in bread-crumbs, shaking off excess.

**4** Heat 2 tablespoons oil in 30cm non-stick frying pan over medium-high heat until very hot. Add half of veal; cook 1 minute per side, or until browned. Transfer to platter in single layer. Keep warm.

**5** Repeat with remaining 2 tablespoons oil and remaining veal escalopes. Add rocket to tomato mixture in bowl; toss well to combine. To serve, spoon tomato and rocket salad on top of hot veal escalopes. Serve with toasted Italian bread, if you like.

EACH SERVING: ABOUT 565 CALORIES, 40g PROTEIN, 35g CARBOHYDRATE, 29g TOTAL FAT (5g SATURATED), 221mg CHOLESTEROL, 865mg SODIUM

# VEAL CUTLETS AU POIVRE WITH POTATO-CARROT FRITTERS

*Prep: 20 minutes    Cook: 20 minutes*

*Makes 2 main dish servings*

| | |
|---|---|
| 1 large baking potato (about 350g) | Salt |
| 1 medium egg | 3 tbsp olive or vegetable oil |
| 1 large carrot, grated | 2 veal cutlets, each 3cm thick (about 350g each) |
| 3 tbsp plain flour | 2 tsp cracked black pepper |
| 1 tbsp chopped fresh parsley | 3 tbsp dry white wine |

◆ Peel potato. Coarsely grate potato into medium bowl half-filled with cold *water*. Drain potato, discarding water. Wrap potato in clean tea towel; squeeze to remove as much water as possible. Beat egg in same bowl. Stir in potato, carrot, flour, parsley and ½ teaspoon salt until well mixed.

◆ Heat 2 tablespoons oil in 30cm frying pan over medium heat. Drop potato mixture into pan to make 6 mounds, each about 4 tablespoons. Using spatula, flatten each to make 10cm fritters.

◆ Cook fritters about 4 minutes or until golden brown on bottom; turn over and brown other side. Transfer to baking sheet lined with kitchen towels to drain; keep warm.

◆ Pat veal cutlets dry with kitchen towels. Press cracked pepper and ¼ teaspoon salt into meat. Heat remaining 1 tablespoon oil over medium-high heat; add veal cutlets and cook, turning once, until browned.

◆ Reduce heat to medium; cook 6 minutes longer for medium-rare, or until desired doneness.

◆ Place veal cutlets on 2 warm plates; keep warm. Skim and discard fat from drippings in pan; stir in wine and simmer 1 minute. Spoon sauce over veal; serve with potato fritters.

**Each serving: About 725 calories, 53g protein, 45g carbohydrate, 35g total fat (8g saturated), 286mg cholesterol, 1025mg sodium**

# STUFFED VEAL ESCALOPES

*Prep: 25 minutes    Cook: 7 minutes*

*Makes 4 main dish servings*

| | |
|---|---|
| 3 tbsp olive or vegetable oil | 4 large veal escalopes, each 5mm thick (about 125g each) |
| 1 medium onion, thinly sliced | 2 tbsp plus ½ tsp plain flour |
| 60ml oil-packed sun-dried tomatoes, drained and thinly sliced | ½ tsp salt |
| 1 tbsp red wine vinegar | ¼ chicken stock cube, crumbled |
| Ground black pepper | ¼ tsp dried basil |
| 20g fresh basil leaves, thinly sliced, or 1 teaspoon dried | |

◆ Heat 1 tablespoon oil in 2-litre saucepan over medium heat; add onion and cook, stirring occasionally, until very tender. Stir in sun-dried tomatoes, vinegar and ¼ teaspoon pepper. Cook, stirring, until vinegar evaporates; remove from heat. Stir in fresh basil.

◆ If veal escalopes are thick, using rolling pin or meat mallet, pound between 2 sheets of parchment paper or cling film to 5mm thickness. Pat dry with kitchen towels. Combine 2 tablespoons flour, salt and ¼ teaspoon pepper on sheet of greaseproof paper.

◆ Spoon one quarter of onion mixture on to half of each escalope; fold other half over filling. Carefully dip veal into flour mixture, turning to coat; shake off excess.

◆ Heat remaining 2 tablespoons oil in 30cm frying pan over medium-high heat; add veal and cook 5 minutes, or until browned all over. Transfer veal to warm platter.

◆ Stir stock cube and dried basil into drippings in pan. Mix remaining ½ teaspoon flour and *125ml water* in small bowl until blended; stir into pan. Bring to the boil; boil 30 seconds, or until thickens slightly. Pour juices over veal.

**Each serving: About 305 calories, 32g protein, 9g carbohydrate, 16g total fat (3g saturated), 114mg cholesterol, 455mg sodium**

### VEAL ESCALOPE SUBSTITUTE

Thin, tender veal escalopes are ideal for special occasions or everyday meals. But if they're not available in the supermarket, or if you're watching your budget, try a favourite veal escalope recipe using chicken or turkey escalopes. Cooking time for poultry will be a minute or two longer; while it's fine to serve veal on the medium side of doneness, poultry should always be fully cooked. For best results, buy chicken or turkey escalopes about 5mm thick. If they are thicker, simply pound them to a uniform thickness.

# VEAL CASSEROLES AND STEWS

To transform veal into a sumptuous casserole or stew, the pieces are first browned in hot oil for best flavour and colour, and then slowly simmered until very tender. The bone-in veal shin slices make an especially delicious, full-bodied stew.

## VEAL AND SPAETZLE CASSEROLE

❖❖❖❖❖❖❖❖❖❖❖❖❖❖❖❖❖❖❖❖❖❖❖

*Prep:* 45 minutes    *Bake:* 1¾–2 hours
*Makes* 4 main dish servings

3 tbsp olive or vegetable oil
2 large celery stalks, cut into
   1cm thick slices
2 medium carrots, cut into
   1cm thick slices
1 large onion, cut into
   1cm pieces
4 veal shin slices with bone,
   each 5cm thick
   (about 450g each)

400g canned tomatoes
125ml dry white wine
¼ tsp ground black pepper
¼ tsp dried oregano
225g plain flour
30g fresh basil, finely
   chopped
2 medium eggs
½ tsp salt

**1** Heat oil in 8-litre flameproof casserole over medium-high heat. Add celery, carrots and onion and cook, stirring occasionally, until golden and tender-crisp; transfer to bowl using slotted spoon.

**2** Preheat oven to 190°C (375°F, Gas 5). Pat veal dry with kitchen towels. Brown veal in drippings in casserole over high heat on all sides. Return sautéed vegetables to casserole.

**3** Add tomatoes with their juice, white wine, pepper and oregano, breaking up tomatoes with back of spoon; bring to the boil. Cover and bake 1¾–2 hours, or until veal is very tender.

**4** When veal is almost done, prepare basil spaetzle: bring *3½ litres water* to the boil in 4-litre saucepan over high heat. Using wooden spoon, beat flour, basil, eggs, salt and *⅓ cup water* in medium bowl until smooth.

**5** Reduce heat under pan to medium. Drop dough by measuring teaspoons into simmering water, stirring water gently so spaetzle pieces do not stick together.

**6** Cook spaetzle 2–3 minutes, until tender but firm; drain well. To serve, skim and discard any fat from liquid in casserole. Gently stir in spaetzle and transfer casserole to large serving dish.

EACH SERVING: ABOUT 620 CALORIES, 56g PROTEIN, 47g CARBOHYDRATE, 20g TOTAL FAT (5g SATURATED), 278mg CHOLESTEROL, 590mg SODIUM

## VEAL STEW WITH ORANGE GREMOLATA

*Prep: 30 minutes    Bake: 1¼ hours*
*Makes 6 main dish servings*

900g veal for stew, cut into 3–4cm chunks
2 tbsp vegetable oil
4 medium carrots, cut into 5cm pieces
1 medium onion, chopped
225ml chicken stock
400g canned tomatoes
1 tbsp tomato purée
¾ tsp salt
¼ tsp coarsely ground black pepper
¼ tsp dried thyme
2 garlic cloves, very finely chopped
2 tbsp chopped fresh parsley
1 tbsp grated orange rind

◆ Pat veal dry. Heat 1 tablespoon oil in 5-litre flameproof casserole over medium-high heat. Add veal, half at a time; brown on all sides. Transfer veal to bowl as it browns.

◆ Preheat oven to 180°C (350°F, Gas 4). Heat remaining 1 tablespoon oil in same casserole over medium heat. Add carrots and onion; cook 10 minutes, or until browned. Add stock, stirring until brown bits are loosened. Return veal to casserole. Stir in tomatoes and next 4 ingredients; bring to the boil over high heat. Cover; bake 1¼ hours, or until veal and vegetables are tender. Mix next 3 ingredients in bowl; stir into stew.

**Each serving: About 320 calories, 38g protein, 12g carbohydrate, 13g total fat (3g saturated), 136mg cholesterol, 815mg sodium**

## VEAL AND MUSHROOM STEW

*Prep: 30 minutes*
*Bake: 1–1¼ hours*
*Makes 6 main dish servings*

750g veal for stew, cut into 3–4cm chunks
¾ tsp salt
¼ tsp ground black pepper
3 tbsp vegetable oil
450g medium mushrooms, each cut in half
125g shiitake mushrooms, stalks removed
75ml Marsala
300g frozen peas

◆ Pat veal dry with kitchen towels; sprinkle with salt and pepper. Heat 2 tablespoons oil in 5-litre flameproof casserole over medium-high heat. Add veal chunks, half at a time, and brown on all sides. Transfer veal to bowl as it browns.

◆ Preheat oven to 180°C (350°F, Gas 4). Heat remaining 1 tablespoon oil in same casserole over medium-high heat; cook all mushrooms, stirring occasionally, until mushrooms are lightly browned.

◆ Return veal to casserole; stir in Marsala and *125ml water*, stirring until brown bits are loosened. Bring to the boil over high heat. Cover and bake 1–1¼ hours, stirring occasionally, until veal is tender. Stir in peas; heat through.

**Each serving: About 310 calories, 31g protein, 15g carbohydrate, 13g total fat (3g saturated), 99mg cholesterol, 390mg sodium**

## VEAL AND VEGETABLE RAGOÛT

*Prep: 25 minutes    Cook: 2 hours*
*Makes 10 main dish servings*

3 tbsp olive oil
1 large onion, very finely chopped
1.3kg veal for stew, cut into 5cm chunks
1 tsp salt
¼ tsp ground black pepper
5 tbsp plain flour
60ml dry red wine
1 beef stock cube, crumbled
750g turnips, peeled and cut into 3–4cm wedges
450g carrots, cut lengthways in half, then crossways into 5cm pieces
6 medium celery stalks, cut into 5cm pieces
450g medium mushrooms

◆ Heat oil in 8-litre flameproof casserole over medium-high heat. Add onion and cook 10 minutes, or until tender; transfer to bowl.

◆ Pat veal dry with kitchen towels. Mix salt, pepper and 3 tablespoons flour together in large bowl; add veal and toss to coat.

◆ Heat oil remaining in casserole over medium-high heat. Add veal, half at a time, and brown well on all sides, adding more oil if necessary; transfer veal to bowl with cooked onion as it browns.

◆ Return onion and veal to casserole. Mix red wine, stock cube and 2 tablespoons flour in small bowl until smooth; add to casserole with *450ml water*; bring to the boil, stirring. Reduce heat to low; cover and simmer 45 minutes.

◆ Add turnips, carrots, celery, and mushrooms to casserole; bring to the boil over high heat. Reduce heat to low; cover and simmer 40 minutes, or until veal and vegetables are tender.

**Each serving: About 305 calories, 35g protein, 15g carbohydrate, 11g total fat (2g saturated), 119mg cholesterol, 465mg sodium**

◆◆◆◆◆◆◆◆◆◆◆◆◆◆◆◆◆◆◆◆◆◆◆◆◆◆◆◆◆◆◆◆◆◆◆◆◆◆◆◆

### PATTING MEAT DRY

When sealing meat, for the best 'browned' flavour and colour, it must be as dry as possible. This is easily done by patting raw meat with kitchen towels. This helps meat absorb seasonings, and prevents any excess moisture creating steam, which inhibits the browning process.

◆◆◆◆◆◆◆◆◆◆◆◆◆◆◆◆◆◆◆◆◆◆◆◆◆◆◆◆◆◆◆◆◆◆◆◆◆◆◆◆

# GRILLED VEAL

When a premium cut of veal is grilled, it requires very few embellishments to enhance its flavour. Our selection uses a simple Fontina cheese and Parma ham stuffing, a caper and Dijon mustard topping, a quick sherry marinade with yellow peppers, and, easiest of all, a rub made of fresh sage and olive oil. Serve with lightly cooked vegetables or a green salad for an easy, elegant meal.

## VEAL STUFFED WITH FONTINA, PARMA HAM AND BASIL

◆◆◆◆◆◆◆◆◆◆◆◆◆◆◆◆◆◆◆◆◆◆◆◆◆◆◆◆◆◆◆◆◆◆

*Prep:* 15 minutes    *Grill:* 10–12 minutes
*Makes* 4 main dish servings

60g Fontina cheese, grated
30g Parma ham, chopped
15g fresh basil, chopped
Ground black pepper
4 veal cutlets or loin chops,
  each 2–3cm thick
  (about 225g each)

1 tsp olive oil
¼ tsp salt
Sautéed peppers and grilled
  tomatoes (optional)

**1** Preheat grill. Mix Fontina, Parma ham, basil and ⅛ teaspoon black pepper together in small bowl until evenly combined.

**2** Pat veal chops dry with kitchen towels. Holding knife parallel to work surface, cut a horizontal pocket in each cutlet.

### PARMA HAM

Lending flavour to the veal in this classic dish, Parma ham, from Parma in northern Italy, is the best known proscuitto. These hams have been cured, aged for up to 14 months and air dried. Parma ham is considered by many to be the finest, although some prefer the saltier cure from San Daniele, near Venice.

Parma ham is available in Italian food shops or in supermarkets, pre-packaged or freshly cut at the deli counter. It makes an ideal partner for chicken as well as veal and can also be used in stuffings for pasta, or as a first course, served in paper-thin slices accompanied with fresh melon or figs.

**3** Stuff one-quarter of cheese mixture into pocket in each cutlet. Rub cutlet with oil; sprinkle with salt and ¼ teaspoon black pepper. Place cutlet on rack in grill pan.

**4** Place pan under grill at closest position to heat. Grill, turning once, 10–12 minutes for medium-rare. Serve with sautéed peppers and grilled tomatoes, if you like.

EACH SERVING: ABOUT 355 CALORIES, 37g PROTEIN, 1g CARBOHYDRATE, 22g TOTAL FAT (10g SATURATED), 151mg CHOLESTEROL, 470mg SODIUM

## ZESTY VEAL CHOPS

*Prep: 5 minutes    Grill: 10–13 minutes*
*Makes 4 main dish servings*

2 tbsp canned or bottled
  drained and chopped
  capers
1 tbsp chopped fresh parsley
1 tbsp Dijon mustard

1 tbsp olive oil
4 veal loin chops or cutlets,
  each 2cm thick (about 225g
  each)
Parsley sprigs for garnish

◈ Preheat grill. Mix capers, chopped parsley, mustard and oil together in small bowl.

◈ Place veal chops on rack in grill pan. Place pan in grill at closest position to heat; grill veal chops 5 minutes.

◈ Turn veal chops; spoon caper mixture evenly over chops. Grill 5–8 minutes longer for medium, or until desired doneness. Place veal chops on 4 plates. Garnish and serve with salad greens, if you like.

**Each serving: About 310 calories, 32g protein, 0g carbohydrate, 19g total fat (7g saturated), 130mg cholesterol, 375mg sodium**

### CAPERS

The flower buds of a shrub native to eastern Asia, capers are used only in their preserved form. Their firm texture and pungent taste make them ideal partners for smooth-textured or delicately flavoured foods, such as veal. They are usually sold pickled in vinegar, but can also be found layered in salt in Italian shops. In either case, you can rinse capers before using to remove excess salt. Capers keep well for months and are good in pasta sauces and pizza toppings, or with sautéed fish, lamb, beef and poultry; they are also a classic ingredient in salad Niçoise and black butter sauce.

## GINGERED VEAL CUTLETS WITH SAUTÉED PEPPERS

*Prep: 25 minutes    Grill: 10–12 minutes*
*Makes 4 main dish servings*

75ml dry sherry
3 tbsp soy sauce
2 tbsp grated, peeled fresh
  ginger
4 veal cutlets, each
  2cm thick (about 225g each)

1 tbsp olive oil
4 medium yellow peppers,
  cored, seeded and cut into
  2–3cm strips
½ tsp sugar
1 bunch rocket

◈ Preheat grill. Mix sherry, soy sauce and ginger together in a baking tin large enough to take the cutlets in a single layer. Add veal cutlets, turning to coat thoroughly with mixture.

◈ Heat oil in 30cm frying pan over high heat; add peppers and sugar and cook, stirring occasionally, 10 minutes, or until peppers are tender and lightly browned.

◈ Meanwhile, place baking tin with veal cutlets and sherry mixture in grill at closest position to heat; grill cutlets, turning once, 10–12 minutes for medium, or until desired doneness.

◈ To serve, line large platter with rocket leaves; spoon peppers evenly on top. Tuck veal cutlets into peppers; pour pan juices over cutlets and serve.

**Each serving: About 345 calories, 36g protein, 16g carbohydrate, 13g total fat (3g saturated), 145mg cholesterol, 905mg sodium**

## GRILLED CUTLETS WITH SAGE

*Prep: 5 minutes    Grill: 8 minutes*
*Makes 2 main dish servings*

2 veal cutlets, each 1cm thick
  (350–400g each)
1 tbsp chopped fresh sage
2 tsp olive oil

½ tsp salt
¼ tsp ground black pepper
Lemon wedges (optional)

◈ Preheat grill. Pat veal cutlets dry with kitchen towels. Mix chopped fresh sage, olive oil, salt and pepper together in small bowl. Use to rub over cutlets.

◈ Place cutlets on rack in grill pan. Place pan under grill at closest position to heat. Grill veal cutlets, turning once, 8 minutes for medium, or until desired doneness. Serve with lemon wedges, if you like.

**Each serving: About 295 calories, 40g protein, 0g carbohydrate, 13g total fat (4g saturated), 168mg cholesterol, 675mg sodium**

# PORK KNOW-HOW

Today's pork is bred leaner than it used to be and benefits from a vast range of seasonings and cooking methods. To guarantee tenderness, cook it only to 67°C. It will have just a hint of pink in the centre with a deeper pink colour near the bone, but the juices will be clear.

## BUYING PORK

• Look for fresh pork that is pinkish-white to greyish-pink. Leg and shoulder joints tend to be darker than loin cuts. The flesh should be firm to the touch and moist but not wet. Fat marbling should be minimal; any fat should be white, firm and well trimmed.
• Cured and smoked pork products are darker in colour due to the curing process. They should be rosy pink.
• The quality of pork is consistent but there may be slight regional differences in how the joints are cut. Simply check the label for the cut you need, remembering that meat from the loin, especially the fillet, or leg is the leanest.

## KNOW YOUR PORK PRODUCTS

**Fresh**  Fresh pork has not been salted, brined, smoked or cured in any way.
**Cured**  Pork is cured by salting with a dry rub or brine; once cured, it can be smoked for added flavour. Curing and smoking were originally methods of preserving pork, enabling it to be stored at room temperature. Today they're mainly intended for flavour.
**Smoked**  Smoking takes place after curing and is generally done as a separate process to impart flavour to the pork. Wrap and seal smoked products before storing.
**Ham**  Cut from the hind leg of pork, ham is usually cured and may then be smoked. Some hams are aged several months for even more flavour. Some hams are heavily salted and require soaking before they are cooked. Italian Parma ham is cured, dried ham that is not smoked.
**Bacon**  Pork belly is used to make streaky bacon, which is cured and sometimes smoked. Smoked bacon has deeper pink meat and yellower fat than unsmoked bacon. Italian pancetta is a type of unsmoked bacon that is often sold rolled in a Swiss roll shape, then sliced.
**Back bacon**  Closer in flavour and texture to ham than to bacon, back bacon is cut from the loin rather than the belly, and is therefore much leaner than streaky bacon.
**Salt pork or Petit Salé**  Salt pork is cut from pork belly. It is salt-cured but not smoked, and is fattier than back bacon.

## CHOOSING THE RIGHT CUT

Pork does not vary as much in tenderness as beef, so many joints are equally suitable for dry-heat and moist-heat cooking methods. If grilling, barbecuing or roasting pork, do not overcook it or it will become tough and dry.

**For grilling, barbecuing or pan-frying**  A wide range of lean pork cuts lend themselves to these quick cooking methods. **Suitable cuts**  Tenderloin (below left), fore or middle loin chops (below right), chump or blade chops are ideal. Spare and back ribs are good for grilling and barbecuing after pre-cooking.

Lean cuts like tenderloin are best for quick cooking methods

For grilling or barbecuing, chops should be at least 1cm thick

**For braising or stewing**  Many cuts of pork stand up well to long, slow cooking in liquid. Well-marbled cuts are especially succulent when braised or stewed. Avoid using very lean cuts, such as tenderloin, which toughen from long cooking. **Suitable cuts**  Blade or shoulder, whole or chops (below right), leg chops, whole hand and hock, neck end and belly spare ribs. Pork cubes for stew (below left) are cut from the shoulder or leg.

Moist-heat cooking makes less-lean cuts especially tender

Trim excess fat before cooking

**For roasting**  Use tender cuts for roasting. Cuts from the loin (the back of the pig from shoulder to hip) are especially suitable. Good cuts also come from the leg and shoulder.
**Suitable cuts**  Rib crown roast, rolled hand roast, leg (bone-in or boneless), whole tenderloin, bone-in loin (below), boneless loin, neck end and belly spare ribs.

A covering of fat keeps meat from drying out but should be no more than 5mm thick

Any fat should be firm and white

# TESTING PORK FOR DONENESS

**What's the minimum cooking temperature?** The rule used to be to cook pork until it was well done – and often overdone – to eliminate the risk of trichinosis, a disease caused by parasitic worms that are killed at 59°C. But modern production methods have virtually eradicated trichinosis. Today's fresh pork can be juicy and succulent – and perfectly safe to eat – if is cooked to an internal temperature of 67°C, 77°C for very large joints, such as leg of pork.

**Medium or well done?** Pork cooked to medium (67°C) has a pink-tinged centre and is slightly deeper pink near any bone. Well-done pork is less pink. Avoid cooking pork to a higher internal temperature, or the meat will become dry and tough. Minced pork should be cooked until no pink remains.

**The right test** To check pork chops and other small cuts for doneness, make a tiny slit near the centre with a sharp knife. The meat is done if the juices run clear. To test roasts, use a meat thermometer inserted in the thickest part but without touching any bone which would throw off the reading. Remove roast from the oven when the temperature reaches 2°C below the desired doneness, then let it stand 10 to 15 minutes. The meat will continue to cook as it stands.

## ROASTING TIMES AT 180°C (350°F, GAS 4)

| CUT AND WEIGHT<br>Start with meat at refrigerator temperature. **Remove roast from oven when it reaches 2–5°C below desired doneness.** | | | MEAT THERMOMETER READING | APPROXIMATE COOKING TIME (PER 450g) |
|---|---|---|---|---|
| Fresh pork | Crown roast | 2.7–3.6kg | 67°C | 20 mins |
| | Loin roast (with bone) | 1.3–2.2kg | 67°C | 20 mins |
| | Boneless loin roast | 900g–1.8kg | 67°C | 20 mins |
| | Whole leg | 5.4kg | 67–77°C | 25–30 mins |
| | Leg half, fillet or knuckle end | 1.3–1.8kg | 67–77°C | 40 mins |
| | Rolled hand | 1.3–2.7kg | 67–77°C | 45 mins |
| | Tenderloin roasted at 220–230°C (425–450°F, Gas 7–8) | 225–750g | 67°C | 25–35 mins total |
| Smoked, cook before eating | Whole ham | 6.3–7.3kg | 67°C | 15–18 mins |
| Smoked fully cooked ham heated at 170°C (325°F, Gas 3) | Whole ham | 6.3–7.3kg | 52–57°C | 1–1¾ hours total |
| | Half ham | 2.7–3.6kg | 52–57°C | 1 hour total |

### RE-HEATING HAMS

Whole smoked hams labelled 'fully cooked' can be purchased at most delicatessens and butchers. This type of ham could be a welcome addition to a buffet table. While such hams can be eaten as is, additional heating will improve their flavour and texture. Bake ham until thermometer inserted in the centre registers 52–57°C. Smoked hams that are not marked 'fully cooked' must be cooked to an internal temperature of 67°C.

## CARVING A WHOLE HAM

1 Place ham on cutting board. Using a carving fork to steady ham, cut a few slices from thin side of ham. Turn ham over onto cut surface; this will form a level base, making carving easier.

2 Cut out a small wedge of meat at shank end. Cut even slices along ham right to bone.

3 Use a sawing action to work blade under slices to release them from bone. Transfer to warm platter.

# ROAST PORK

The wide range of cuts available mean that a pork roast is ideal for any occasion. Try an imposing crown roast for a dinner party; a whole leg of pork served with a choice of sauces as the centrepiece for a buffet; or, for a smaller gathering, a succulent tenderloin seasoned with Caribbean-style spices that takes just half an hour to cook.

## GOLDEN CROWN ROAST OF PORK

◆ ◆ ◆ ◆ ◆ ◆ ◆ ◆ ◆ ◆ ◆ ◆ ◆ ◆ ◆ ◆ ◆ ◆ ◆ ◆ ◆ ◆ ◆ ◆ ◆

*Prep:* 25 minutes, plus standing   *Roast:* 3 hours
*Makes* 14 main dish servings

| | |
|---|---|
| **1 crown roast of pork (about 2kg), about 16 ribs** | **3 tbsp plain flour** |
| **1 tsp dried thyme** | **Sautéed cherry tomatoes and courgettes (optional)** |
| **½ tsp ground black pepper** | **Thyme sprigs and cranberries for garnish** |
| **Salt** | |
| **Cranberry and Hazelnut Stuffing (see page 230)** | |

**1** Preheat oven to 170°C (325°F, Gas 3). Pat roast dry with kitchen towels. Mix dried thyme, pepper and 1 teaspoon salt in bowl. Use to rub inside and outside of roast. Place roast, rib-ends down, in large roasting tin. Roast 2 hours.

**2** Meanwhile, prepare Cranberry and Hazelnut Stuffing. After pork has roasted 2 hours, remove from oven and turn rib-ends up. Using large spoon, fill cavity of pork roast with stuffing.

**3** Insert meat thermometer into thickest part of meat, being careful that pointed end does not touch bone. Roast 1 hour longer, or until thermometer reaches 64.5°C (internal temperature of meat will rise to 67°C upon standing). If stuffing browns too quickly, cover with foil.

**4** Transfer roast to warm large platter. Let stand 15 minutes; keep warm. Meanwhile, prepare gravy: pour pan drippings into 500ml measuring jug; let stand a few seconds, until fat separates from meat juices.

**5** Spoon 3 tablespoons fat from drippings into 2-litre saucepan; skim and discard remaining fat. Add *225ml water* to roasting tin; stir over medium heat until brown bits are loosened.

**6** Add liquid in roasting tin to meat juices in jug with enough *water* to equal 450ml. Stir flour and ½ teaspoon salt into fat in saucepan over medium heat; cook 1 minute. Gradually stir in meat-juice mixture and cook, stirring constantly, until gravy boils and thickens. Pour into sauce boat. Garnish roast; serve with stuffing and gravy, and cherry tomatoes and courgettes, if you like.

EACH SERVING: ABOUT 635 CALORIES, 39g PROTEIN, 38g CARBOHYDRATE, 36g TOTAL FAT (11g SATURATED), 84mg CHOLESTEROL, 470mg SODIUM

## PORK ROAST WITH CARAWAY SEEDS

*Prep: 15 minutes, plus standing   Roast: 2½ hours*
*Makes 10 main dish servings*

| | |
|---|---|
| 1 pork loin roast (about 2.7kg) | 1 tsp dry mustard |
| 2 tbsp caraway seeds, crushed | ½ tsp dried thyme |
| 1 tbsp vegetable oil | ½ tsp dried oregano |
| 1 tsp salt | 3 tbsp plain flour |
| | 1 beef stock cube, crumbled |

◆ Preheat oven to 170°C (325°F, Gas 3). Pat pork dry with kitchen towels. Mix caraway seeds with next 5 ingredients in small bowl; use to rub over fat side of pork.

◆ Place roast, fat-side up, in 38 by 28cm roasting tin. Insert meat thermometer into centre of roast, being careful that pointed end does not touch bone. Roast pork about 2½ hours, or until thermometer reaches 64.5°C (internal temperature of meat will rise to 67°C upon standing).

◆ Transfer roast to warm large platter. Let stand 15 minutes for easier carving; keep warm.

◆ Meanwhile, prepare gravy: pour drippings from roasting tin through sieve into 2-litre measuring jug; let stand a few seconds, until fat separates from meat juices. Spoon 2 tablespoons fat from drippings into roasting tin; skim and discard any remaining fat. Add *water* to meat juices in jug to equal 600ml.

◆ Stir flour into fat in tin over low heat until blended. Gradually stir in meat juice mixture and stock cube; stir until brown bits are loosened. Cook, stirring constantly, until gravy thickens and boils. Serve roast with gravy.

**Each serving: About 375 calories, 45g protein, 2g carbohydrate, 20g total fat (6g saturated), 96mg cholesterol, 405mg sodium**

### CRANBERRY AND HAZELNUT STUFFING

Chop 2 large celery stalks and 1 large onion. Melt 25g margarine or butter in 30cm frying pan over medium heat; add celery and onion and 1 tablespoon dried sage; cook until tender and transfer to large bowl. Coarsely chop 350g cranberries with 100g sugar in food processor with knife blade attached; add to celery mixture in bowl. Stir in 450g breadcrumbs made from day-old bread, 100g chopped, roasted hazelnuts and about 100ml water; mix well. Use to stuff Golden Crown Roast of Pork (see page 229); bake any leftover stuffing in small covered casserole with pork during last 40 minutes of roasting. Makes 1.1kg.

**Each 100g: About 240 calories, 5g protein, 37g carbohydrate, 9g total fat (1g saturated), 0mg cholesterol, 240mg sodium**

## CABBAGE-WRAPPED PORK ROAST

*Prep: 30 minutes, plus standing   Roast: 1 hour*
*Makes 10 main dish servings*

| | |
|---|---|
| 6 large outer leaves green cabbage | 1 tsp salt |
| | ½ tsp ground black pepper |
| 1 bunch spring onions | ½ chicken stock cube |
| 1 boneless pork loin roast (about 1.3kg) | 2 tsp cornflour |
| 1 tbsp very finely chopped fresh thyme or ½ tsp dried | |

◆ Bring *3 litres water* to the boil in 5-litre flameproof casserole over high heat. Meanwhile, trim tough ribs from cabbage leaves. Cut off root ends of spring onions; separate into leaves. Add cabbage to boiling water and cook 3–5 minutes until wilted. Using slotted spoon, transfer to colander to drain. Add spring onions to boiling water; blanch 10 seconds, or until wilted. Drain spring onions; pat dry with kitchen towels.

◆ Preheat oven to 180°C (350°F, Gas 4). Pat pork dry with kitchen towels. Mix thyme, salt and pepper in cup. Use to rub over pork.

◆ Lay cabbage leaves flat, overlapping them. Place seasoned pork roast on cabbage; be sure leaves extend beyond roast on both ends. Lift leaves up over roast to enclose meat completely.

◆ To secure cabbage leaves, tie 2 blanched spring onions together (they should be long enough to wrap around width of roast); slip onions underneath wrapped roast, pull ends up, and tie in a knot. Repeat with remaining onions, tying at 2–3cm intervals.

◆ Place pork roast in 35 by 24cm roasting tin. Insert meat thermometer into centre of roast. Dissolve stock cube in *450ml hot water* in 500ml measuring jug; pour into roasting pan. Roast 1 hour, or until meat thermometer reaches 64.5°C, basting occasionally with pan juices (internal temperature will rise to 67°C upon standing).

◆ Transfer pork to warm large platter. Let stand 15 minutes; keep warm. Mix cornflour with *2 tablespoons water* in small bowl. Stir into drippings in roasting tin and bring to the boil over high heat; boil, stirring constantly, 1 minute. Spoon over pork.

**Each serving: About 215 calories, 22g protein, 3g carbohydrate, 12g total fat (4g saturated), 66mg cholesterol, 355mg sodium**

## PORK ROAST WITH FRESH SAGE

*Prep: 15 minutes, plus standing    Roast: 2–2¼ hours*

*Makes 8 main dish servings*

| | |
|---|---|
| 2 garlic cloves, very finely chopped | 1 tsp salt |
| 15g fresh parsley, very finely chopped | ½ tsp ground black pepper |
| 2 tbsp chopped fresh sage | 1 pork loin roast (about 1.8kg) |
| ½ tsp dried thyme | 75ml dry white wine |
| | 150ml chicken stock |

◆ Preheat oven to 180°C (350°F, Gas 4). Using flat side of chef's knife, on chopping board, mash garlic with parsley, sage, thyme, salt and pepper to make a thick paste.

◆ Pat pork dry with kitchen towels. Place pork in roasting tin; rub herb paste over pork. Insert meat thermometer into thickest part of roast, being careful that pointed end does not touch bone. Roast 2–2¼ hours until thermometer reaches 64.5°C (internal temperature of meat will rise to 67°C upon standing).

◆ Transfer roast to warm large platter. Let stand 15 minutes for easier carving; keep warm. Add wine to roasting tin and bring to the boil over high heat; stir until brown bits are loosened. Add stock and return to the boil. Skim and discard fat from pan juices. Serve roast with pan juices.

**Each serving: About 305 calories, 37g protein, 1g carbohydrate, 15g total fat (5g saturated), 81mg cholesterol, 445mg sodium**

## LEG OF PORK WITH TWO SAUCES

*Prep: 30 minutes, plus standing    Roast: 5½ hours*

*Makes 30 main dish servings*

| | |
|---|---|
| 1 whole pork leg (about 6.7kg) | 125ml soured cream |
| 2 tsp dried sage | 85g coarse-grained French mustard |
| 2 tsp salt | 75ml milk |
| 1 tsp ground black pepper | Mushroom Pan Gravy (see right) |
| 1 tbsp vegetable oil | |
| 3 spring onions, thinly sliced | |

◆ Preheat oven to 170°C (325°F, Gas 3). Remove skin and trim excess fat from pork leg, leaving thin covering of fat. Place pork, fat-side up, on rack in large roasting tin. Score fat on top of pork leg in shallow parallel lines. Mix sage, salt and pepper in small bowl; use to rub over pork.

◆ Insert meat thermometer into centre of thickest part of pork, being careful that pointed end does not touch bone.

◆ Roast pork about 5½ hours, or until meat thermometer reaches 67°C. If pork begins to brown too quickly, cover loosely with tent of foil. Pork near bone will be slightly pink.

◆ Meanwhile, prepare mustard sauce: heat oil in 2-litre saucepan over medium-high heat; add spring onions and cook 5 minutes, or until tender and lightly browned. Remove from heat. Stir in soured cream, mustard and milk until blended. Refrigerate until ready to serve.

◆ When pork is done, transfer to warm large platter. Let stand 30 minutes; keep warm. Prepare Mushroom Pan Gravy. Thinly slice pork; serve with gravy and mustard sauce.

**Each serving: About 385 calories, 55g protein, 1g carbohydrate, 16g total fat (6g saturated), 131mg cholesterol, 360mg sodium**

## MUSHROOM PAN GRAVY

| | |
|---|---|
| Pan drippings from Leg of Pork with Two Sauces (see left) | 3 tbsp plain flour |
| | Chicken stock (optional) |
| 450g mushrooms, sliced | |

1 Remove rack from pork roasting tin; pour drippings into 2-litre measuring jug (set roasting tin aside). Let drippings stand a few seconds until fat separates from meat juices; spoon 2 tablespoons fat into 30cm frying pan. Skim and discard remaining fat.

2 Cook mushrooms in fat in frying pan over high heat until browned. Reduce heat to medium. Stir in flour; cook until lightly browned. Add *water* or chicken stock to juices in jug to make 400ml. Add about 125ml juice mixture to roasting tin; stir over high heat until brown bits are loosened.

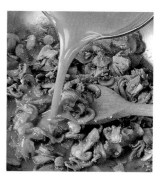

3 Stir liquid from roasting tin and remaining meat-juice mixture into mushrooms. Cook, stirring, over high heat until gravy boils and thickens. Makes about 675ml.

**Each 100ml: About 70 calories, 3g protein, 7g carbohydrate, 3g total fat (1g saturated), 7mg cholesterol, 285mg sodium**

## SPICE-ROASTED PORK

*Prep: 10 minutes, plus standing*
*Roast: 1–1¼ hours*
*Makes 6 main dish servings*

1 boneless pork loin roast (about 900g)
1 tsp salt
¾ tsp dried thyme
½ tsp ground cinnamon
½ tsp ground black pepper
Pinch ground nutmeg
Pinch ground cloves
175ml dry white wine
150ml chicken stock
Thyme sprigs for garnish
Peas and apple sauce (optional)

◆ Preheat oven to 180°C (350°F, Gas 4). Pat pork dry with kitchen towels. Mix salt and next 5 ingredients in small bowl; use to rub over pork. Place pork in small roasting tin; insert meat thermometer into thickest part of pork. Roast 1–1¼ hours, or until thermometer reaches 64.5°C (internal temperature will rise to 67°C upon standing).

◆ Transfer pork to platter. Let stand 10 minutes; keep warm. Meanwhile, add wine to roasting tin. Bring to the boil over high heat; stir until brown bits are loosened. Add stock; return to the boil. Boil 2 minutes. Skim fat from pan juices. Slice pork thin; garnish and serve with peas and apple sauce, if you like, and pan juices.

**Each serving:** About 235 calories, 24g protein, 1g carbohydrate, 13g total fat (5g saturated) 75mg cholesterol, 525mg sodium

## JAMAICAN ROAST PORK TENDERLOINS

*Prep: 10 minutes, plus standing*
*Roast: 30–35 minutes*
*Makes 6 main dish servings*

2 pork tenderloins (350g each)
1 garlic clove, very finely chopped
1 tbsp brown sugar
1 tsp grated lime rind
½ tsp ground ginger
½ tsp salt
¼ tsp ground black pepper
Pinch ground nutmeg
Pinch ground allspice
Pinch ground red pepper
2 tsp plus 2 tbsp dark rum
300ml chicken stock

◆ Preheat oven to 230°C (450°F, Gas 8). Pat pork dry with kitchen towels. Place pork in small roasting tin, tucking thin ends under for even thickness.

◆ Mix garlic, brown sugar, lime rind, ginger, salt, black pepper, nutmeg, allspice, ground red pepper and 2 teaspoons rum together in small bowl. Use mixture to rub over pork. Insert meat thermometer into thickest part of pork. Pour 60ml chicken stock in pan around pork.

◆ Roast pork 30–35 minutes, or until thermometer reaches 64.5°C (internal temperature of meat will rise to 67°C upon standing), adding 60ml more stock to roasting tin after 10 and then after 20 minutes to prevent juices in tin from burning.

◆ Transfer pork to platter. Let stand 10 minutes; keep warm. Add remaining 2 tablespoons rum to roasting tin and bring to the boil over high heat; stir until brown bits are loosened. Boil 1 minute. Add remaining 120ml stock to tin; heat to boiling. Slice pork thin and serve with pan juices.

**Each serving:** About 170 calories, 24g protein, 3g carbohydrate, 5g total fat (2g saturated), 70mg cholesterol, 445mg sodium

## ORANGE ROAST PORK WITH CUMIN

*Prep: 15 minutes, plus standing*
*Roast: 1–1¼ hours*
*Makes 6 main dish servings*

1 boneless pork loin roast (about 900g)
1 garlic clove, very finely chopped
2 tsp grated orange rind
1 tsp salt
¾ tsp ground cumin
½ tsp dried oregano
½ tsp dried thyme
¼ tsp ground red pepper
1 medium onion, finely chopped
2 tbsp cider vinegar
175ml chicken stock

◆ Preheat oven to 180°C (350°F, Gas 4). Pat pork dry with kitchen towels. Using small knife, cut several 1cm deep cuts in pork.

◆ Mix garlic, orange rind, salt, cumin, oregano, thyme and ground red pepper in small bowl. Use to rub over pork, pressing into crevices and cuts.

◆ Spread chopped onion in 28 by 19cm roasting tin; place pork roast on top. Insert meat thermometer into thickest part of pork.

◆ Roast pork 1–1¼ hours, or until thermometer reaches 64.5°C (internal temperature of meat will rise to 67°C upon standing).

◆ Transfer pork to platter. Let stand 10 minutes; keep warm. Skim and discard fat from roasting tin. Add vinegar to roasting tin and bring to the boil over high heat; stir until brown bits are loosened. Boil 1 minute.

◆ Add chicken stock to juices in tin and bring to the boil over high heat; boil 3 minutes. Slice pork thin and serve with pan juices.

**Each serving:** About 240 calories, 25mg protein, 4g carbohydrate, 13g total fat (5g saturated), 76mg cholesterol, 535mg sodium

# PORK CASSEROLES AND STEWS

Laden with fragrant spices such as chilli powder, cumin, paprika and allspice, pork makes an especially tender, succulent casserole. These hearty dishes have bold, assertive flavours that capture the tastes of the American southwest, Caribbean or Eastern Europe. For best results, cut the pork into equal-sized cubes for even cooking, then brown them in batches to seal in the juices before finishing them in the oven or on the hob. The chilli versions are even better the next day. Warm corn bread, noodles or rice all make great accompaniments to soak up the delicious liquid.

## PORK AND BLACK BEAN CHILLI

❖❖❖❖❖❖❖❖❖❖❖❖❖❖❖❖❖❖❖❖❖❖❖❖❖

*Prep:* 50 minutes, plus standing    *Cook:* 1¾ hours
*Makes* 10 main dish servings

| | |
|---|---|
| **450g dried black beans** | **1 medium onion, diced** |
| **750g boneless shoulder of pork** | **40g chilli powder** |
| | **800g canned tomatoes** |
| **3 tbsp vegetable oil** | **2 tbsp tomato purée** |
| **1 large red pepper, cored, seeded and cut into 1cm pieces** | **1¾ tsp salt** |
| | **Tabasco sauce** |
| **1 large green pepper, cored, seeded and cut into 1cm pieces** | **Corn bread (optional)** |

**1** Rinse beans with cold water; discard any shrivelled beans. Bring beans and *1½ litres water* to the boil in 4-litre saucepan over high heat; boil 3 minutes. Remove saucepan from heat; cover and let stand 1 hour. Drain and rinse beans. Cut pork into 1cm cubes. Pat dry with kitchen towels. Preheat oven to 190°C (375°F, Gas 5).

**2** Heat oil in 5-litre flameproof casserole over medium heat; add pork, half at a time, and cook, stirring, until browned. Transfer to bowl.

**3** Add peppers and onion to drippings in casserole; cook, stirring occasionally, until tender-crisp. Stir in chilli powder; cook, stirring, 2 minutes.

**4** Add tomatoes and tomato purée, stirring and breaking up tomatoes with back of spoon. Stir in salt, black beans, browned pork and *1 litre water*. Bring to the boil over high heat. Cover and bake, stirring occasionally, about 1¾ hours until pork is cooked through and beans are tender. Stir in Tabasaco sauce to taste. Serve chilli in bowls, with corn bread, if you like.

## TABASCO SAUCE

Made by steeping chillies in vinegar, this fiery condiment adds a kick to our Pork and Black Bean Chilli, and can be added to all kinds of soups, stews, sauces, omelettes and marinades. The sauce is surprisingly strong, so add only a few drops and taste the dish to check the degree of heat. Refrigerate after opening.

EACH SERVING: ABOUT 315 CALORIES, 26g PROTEIN, 36g CARBOHYDRATE, 16g TOTAL FAT (5g SATURATED), 38mg CHOLESTEROL, 735mg SODIUM

## ADOBO-STYLE CHILLI

*Prep: 15 minutes    Cook: 2½ hours*
*Makes 6 main dish servings*

900g boneless shoulder of
   pork, cut into 5cm chunks
2 tsp vegetable oil
2 medium onions, finely
   chopped
4 garlic cloves, very finely
   chopped
3 tbsp chilli powder
1 tbsp ground cumin

¼ tsp ground cinnamon
¼ tsp ground red pepper
Pinch ground cloves
800g canned tomatoes
60ml cider vinegar
¾ tsp salt
½ tsp dried oregano
1 bay leaf

◆ Pat pork dry with kitchen towels. Heat 1 teaspoon oil in
5-litre flameproof casserole over medium-high heat. Add
half of pork and brown all over. Transfer to plate; repeat
with remaining 1 teaspoon oil and remaining pork.

◆ Add onions to drippings in casserole; cook 5 minutes
over medium heat. Stir in garlic and next 5 ingredients;
cook 1 minute. Add tomatoes with their juice, breaking up
with spoon, vinegar, salt, oregano, bay leaf and pork. Bring
to the boil over high heat. Reduce heat to low; cover and
simmer 2 hours. Discard bay leaf. Skim fat before serving.

**Each serving: About 445 calories, 40g protein, 14g carbohydrate,
26g total fat (9g saturated), 96mg cholesterol, 630mg sodium**

## HUNGARIAN PORK GOULASH

*Prep: 20 minutes    Bake: 1½ hours*
*Makes 6 main dish servings*

2 tbsp vegetable oil
2 large onions, chopped
1 garlic clove, very finely
   chopped
30g paprika
900g boneless pork shoulder
   blade roast, cut into
   4cm chunks

450g bottled sauerkraut,
   drained and rinsed
450g canned chopped
   tomatoes
400ml beef stock
¼ tsp ground black pepper
225ml soured cream

◆ Preheat oven to 170°C (325°F, Gas 3). Heat oil in 5-litre
flameproof casserole over medium heat. Add onions; cook
10 minutes, or until tender. Add garlic; cook, stirring,
1 minute. Add paprika; cook 1 minute. Add pork,
sauerkraut, tomatoes with their juice, stock and pepper;
bring to the boil over high heat.

◆ Cover and bake 1½ hours, or until pork is tender.
Remove from oven; stir in soured cream. Heat through over
medium heat (do not boil).

**Each serving: About 520 calories, 42g protein, 17g carbohydrate,
31g total fat (9g saturated), 109mg cholesterol, 960mg sodium**

## CARIBBEAN PORK CASSEROLE

*Prep: 40 minutes, plus marinating    Bake: 45 minutes*
*Makes 6 main dish servings*

4 spring onions
2 pork tenderloins (about
   350g each), cut into
   2–3cm thick slices
2 tbsp very finely chopped,
   peeled fresh ginger
2 tbsp soy sauce
2 tbsp Worcestershire sauce
1 tbsp chopped fresh thyme
   or ½ tsp dried

½ tsp ground allspice
½ tsp ground red pepper
750g sweet potatoes, peeled
   and cut into 1cm thick slices
1 large red pepper, cored,
   seeded and cut into
   bite-sized pieces
2 tbsp vegetable oil
400g canned pineapple
   chunks in their own juice

◆ Preheat oven to 220°C (425°F, Gas 7). Very finely chop
2 spring onions. Cut remaining green onions into 5cm
pieces. Toss spring onions with pork, ginger, soy sauce,
Worcestershire, thyme, allspice and red pepper together
in large bowl. Cover pork and marinate 30 minutes.

◆ Toss sweet potatoes, red pepper and spring onion pieces
and 1 tablespoon oil together in 26 by 40cm ovenproof
baking dish. Bake, uncovered, 15 minutes.

◆ While vegetables are baking, heat remaining 1 tablespoon
oil in 26cm frying pan over medium-high heat; add half of
pork, reserving any marinade, and brown all over. Transfer
pork to bowl; repeat with remaining pork.

◆ Pour pineapple chunks with their juice into drippings in
pan; stir until brown bits are loosened. Add pineapple
mixture, pork and reserved marinade to vegetables in
baking dish. Bake, uncovered, stirring occasionally,
30 minutes longer, or until pork and vegetables are tender.

**Each serving: About 330 calories, 26g protein, 36g carbohydrate,
9g total fat (2g saturated), 65mg cholesterol, 450mg sodium**

# PAN-BRAISED PORK

Pork chops stay moist and juicy when browned in oil then braised in liquid in a tightly covered pan; the resulting juices form the basis for a quick and delicious sauce. Maintain a gentle simmer for tender chops.

## SICILIAN STUFFED PORK CHOPS

❖ ❖ ❖ ❖ ❖ ❖ ❖ ❖ ❖ ❖ ❖ ❖ ❖ ❖

*Prep:* 30 minutes
*Cook:* 70 minutes
*Makes* 4 main dish servings

**350g Swiss chard**
**1 tsp plus 1 tbsp olive oil**
**1 garlic clove, very finely**
**    chopped**
**40g sultanas**
**2 tbsp pine nuts, toasted and**
**    chopped**
**Salt**
**4 pork loin chops, each**
**    3–4cm thick (300g each)**
**¼ tsp ground black pepper**
**225ml chicken stock**
**75ml dry white wine**
**Confetti Pasta (see below)**

### CONFETTI PASTA

Cook 175g orzo (rice-shaped pasta) as label instructs; drain. Heat 2 teaspoons olive oil in 26cm non-stick frying pan over medium heat. Add 2 grated medium carrots, 1 grated courgette (225g), 1 very finely chopped garlic clove, ¾ teaspoon salt and ¼ teaspoon ground black pepper. Cook 5 minutes. Stir in orzo; heat through. Makes 4 accompaniment servings.

**1** Finely slice Swiss chard; bring to the boil with *2–3cm water* in 2-litre saucepan over high heat. Cover and cook 5 minutes. Drain, pressing hard to squeeze out excess liquid.

**2** Heat 1 teaspoon oil in same pan over medium heat. Add garlic and cook 30 seconds. Remove from heat; stir in Swiss chard, raisins, pine nuts and ¼ teaspoon salt.

**3** Cut a pocket from rib side of each chop, inserting knife near bone. Slice parallel to surface, widening pocket as you go. Do not cut through to edge.

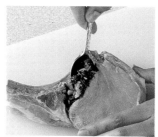

**4** Fill pockets with Swiss chard stuffing; gently press closed. Pat chops dry. Sprinkle with pepper and ¼ teaspoon salt. Heat remaining 1 tablespoon oil in 30cm frying pan over medium-high heat.

**5** Add chops to pan and brown on both sides. Add stock and wine; bring to the boil. Reduce heat to low; cover and simmer 1 hour, or until chops are tender. Prepare Confetti Pasta; keep warm.

**6** Transfer chops to platter; keep warm. Increase heat to high; boil pan juices until reduced to 175ml. Skim fat from juices. Serve chops with juices poured over, accompanied by Confetti Pasta.

EACH SERVING: ABOUT 725 CALORIES, 60g PROTEIN, 47g CARBOHYDRATE, 31g TOTAL FAT (9g SATURATED), 113mg CHOLESTEROL, 955mg SODIUM

## ORANGE PORK CHOPS

*Prep:* 5 minutes
*Cook:* 50–65 minutes
*Makes* 4 main dish servings

4 pork loin chops, each 2cm thick
   (about 175g each)
1 tbsp vegetable oil
2 large onions, cut into 5mm thick slices
60ml dry sherry
60ml soy sauce
60g orange marmalade
Orange slices for garnish
Steamed French beans (optional)

◆ Pat pork chops dry with kitchen
towels. Heat oil in 30cm frying pan
over medium-high heat. Add pork
chops and cook until lightly browned
on both sides; transfer chops to plate
as they brown.

◆ Add onions to drippings in pan;
cook, stirring frequently, until lightly
browned. Return chops to pan. Stir in
sherry, soy sauce and marmalade;
bring to the boil over high heat.

◆ Reduce heat to low; cover pan and
simmer 30–45 minutes, or until chops
are tender. Remove cover; increase
heat to medium-high and cook
3 minutes longer, or until liquid in
pan is almost evaporated.

◆ To serve, place chops on 4 plates.
Garnish with orange slices. Serve with
French beans, if you like.

**Each serving: About 390 calories,
31g protein, 25g carbohydrate, 16g total
fat (5g saturated), 64mg cholesterol,
1100mg sodium**

## PORK CHOPS WITH APPLES AND CREAM

*Prep:* 10 minutes
*Cook:* 1–1¼ hours
*Makes* 4 main dish servings

4 pork loin chops, each 2cm thick
   (about 175g each)
½ tsp salt
¼ tsp ground black pepper
2 tsps vegetable oil
1 small onion, finely chopped
60ml Calvados or brandy
225ml chicken stock
Pinch dried thyme
3 medium Golden Delicious apples,
   peeled, cored and each cut into
   quarters
125ml whipping cream
Chopped fresh parsley for garnish

◆ Pat pork chops dry with kitchen
towels. Sprinkle with salt and pepper.
Heat oil in 30cm frying pan over
medium-high heat. Add pork chops
and lightly brown on both sides.
Transfer chops to plate as they brown.

◆ Add onion to drippings in pan and
cook over medium heat 3 minutes, or
until tender. Add Calvados and cook
until liquid is almost evaporated.

◆ Return chops to pan. Add stock,
thyme and apples; bring to the boil
over high heat. Reduce heat to low;
cover pan and simmer 30–45 minutes,
until chops are tender.

◆ Transfer chops and apples to warm
platter; keep warm. Increase heat
under pan to high; boil, uncovered,
5 minutes, or until liquid is reduced to
125ml. Add cream and return to the
boil. Boil 3 minutes. To serve, spoon
cream sauce over pork chops. Sprinkle
with parsley.

**Each serving: About 485 calories,
31g protein, 23g carbohydrate, 27g total
fat (12g saturated), 110mg cholesterol,
610mg sodium**

## PORK CHOPS WITH SPROUTING BROCCOLI

*Prep:* 5 minutes
*Cook:* 30 minutes
*Makes* 4 main dish servings

2 tbsp olive oil
1 garlic clove, cut in half
4 pork loin foreloin, middle loin or
   chump end chops, each 1cm thick
   (about 150g each)
75ml dry vermouth or chicken stock
1 tsp sugar
¼ tsp ground black pepper
Salt
900g sprouting broccoli or spring greens,
   tough stalks removed

◆ Bring *6 litres water* to the boil in
8-litre saucepan over high heat.
Meanwhile, heat 1 tablespoon oil in
30cm frying pan over medium heat;
add garlic and cook until lightly
browned. Using slotted spoon, remove
garlic from pan and discard.

◆ Pat pork chops dry with kitchen
towels. Add pork chops to oil in frying
pan and cook over medium-high heat
until well browned on both sides.

◆ Add vermouth, sugar, pepper and
½ teaspoon salt to chops in frying pan.
Reduce heat to low; cover and simmer
20 minutes, or until pork chops are
tender, turning chops once.

◆ Meanwhile, add sprouting broccoli
and 1 tablespoon salt to boiling water
in saucepan. Return to the boil; boil
2 minutes. Drain thoroughly.

◆ Heat remaining 1 tablespoon oil in
same saucepan over high heat. Add
sprouting broccoli and ¼ teaspoon salt
and cook, stirring, until well coated.
Set aside.

◆ When pork chops are done, add
sprouting broccoli to frying pan; cover
and cook until heated through.

**Each serving: About 335 calories,
31g protein, 10g carbohydrate, 18g total
fat (5g saturated), 54mg cholesterol,
765mg sodium**

# PAN-FRIED PORK

Juicy and succulent, pan-fried pork chops offer the best flavour when simply prepared with herbs, spices or a crispy coating. The following recipes range from an Italian-style dish with ham and melted cheese to a spicy Tex-Mex variation using black-eyed beans and tomatoes, and served with a refreshing corn salad. To avoid tough meat, it's essential not to overcook the chops. To test for doneness without using a meat thermometer, make a small cut in the thickest part of the meat or near the bone: the inside should have just lost its pink colour.

**1** Heat 2 teaspoons oil in 30cm non-stick frying pan over medium heat. Add onion; cook until tender. Transfer to small bowl.

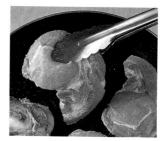

**2** Pat chops dry with kitchen towels. Cook chops in same pan 5 minutes over medium-high heat, or until underside is browned.

## BONELESS PORK CHOPS WITH SAUTÉED APPLES

*Prep:* 10 minutes   *Cook:* 25 minutes
*Makes* 4 main dish servings

4 tsp vegetable oil
1 medium red onion, thinly sliced
4 boneless pork loin chops, each 3cm thick (225g each)
Salt
½ tsp dried thyme
¼ tsp coarsely ground black pepper

2 medium Golden Delicious apples, unpeeled, cored and cut into 5mm thick wedges
1 tbsp sugar
125ml apple juice or cider
1 tsp cornflour
Cooked pasta or mashed potatoes (optional)

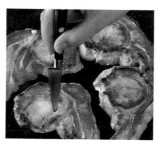

**3** Sprinkle chops with ½ teaspoon salt. Turn chops; sprinkle with thyme, pepper and ½ teaspoon salt. Cook 3–5 minutes longer, until pork just loses its pink colour throughout.

**4** Transfer chops to 4 warm plates; keep warm. Heat remaining 2 teaspoons oil in same pan. Add apples. Sprinkle with sugar; cook until browned. Transfer to plates with chops.

**5** Mix apple juice and cornflour in small bowl. Stir apple juice mixture and onion into pan; bring to the boil over high heat, stirring. Boil 1 minute. Pour apple juice mixture over pork chops and apple wedges. Serve with pasta or mashed potatoes, if you like.

EACH SERVING: ABOUT 510 CALORIES, 49g PROTEIN, 21g CARBOHYDRATE, 25g TOTAL FAT (8g SATURATED), 106mg CHOLESTEROL, 650mg SODIUM

## PORK CHOPS ROMANO

*Prep: 5 minutes    Cook: 15 minutes*
*Makes 6 main dish servings*

1 tbsp plain flour
1 tbsp balsamic vinegar
6 boneless pork loin chops,
    each 2cm thick
    (about 125g each)
2 tbsp vegetable oil

6 thin slices cooked ham,
    about 125g
6 thin slices Emmenthal
    cheese, about 125g
Steamed broccoli (optional)

◆ Using fork, mix flour, vinegar and *175ml water* in measuring jug until smooth; set aside.

◆ Place pork chops between 2 sheets of cling film. Using rolling pin or meat mallet, pound each chop into 5mm thick; pat dry with kitchen towels.

◆ Heat 1 tablespoon oil in 30cm frying pan over medium-high heat; add half of pork and cook about 4 minutes, turning once, until browned on both sides and pork just loses its pink colour throughout. Transfer pork to plate. Repeat with remaining 1 tablespoon oil and pork.

◆ Stir vinegar mixture into drippings in pan; cook over medium heat, stirring constantly, until sauce thickens slightly and boils.

◆ Top each piece of pork with a slice of ham and cheese. Return pork to pan; cover and simmer until cheese just melts. Serve with broccoli, if you like.

**Each serving: About 395 calories, 32g protein, 2g carbohydrate, 28g total fat (11g saturated), 77mg cholesterol, 320mg sodium**

## BREADED PORK CHOPS

*Prep: 10 minutes    Cook: 16–20 minutes*
*Makes 6 main dish servings*

60g plain dried breadcrumbs
1 tsp salt
¼ tsp ground black pepper
2 tbsp milk
1 medium egg

6 pork foreloin, middle loin
    or chump end chops, each
    2cm thick
    (about 175g each)
2 tbsp vegetable oil

◆ Mix breadcrumbs, salt and pepper on a piece of greaseproof paper. Using fork, beat milk and egg together in a shallow dish. Dip pork chops in milk mixture, then in breadcrumb mixture to coat.

◆ Heat 1 tablespoon oil in 26cm frying pan over medium-high heat. Add half of chops; cook 8–10 minutes, turning once, until golden brown on both sides and pork just loses its pink colour throughout.

◆ Transfer chops to platter; keep warm. Repeat with remaining chops, adding remaining 1 tablespoon oil to pan.

**Each serving: About 325 calories, 31g protein, 7g carbohydrate, 19g total fat (6g saturated), 99mg cholesterol, 510mg sodium**

## CHILLI PORK CHOPS WITH
## CORN SALAD

*Prep: 15 minutes    Cook: 8 minutes*
*Makes 4 main dish servings*

1 medium tomato, seeded
    and cut into 2–3cm chunks
400g canned sweetcorn,
    drained
400g canned black-eyed
    beans, rinsed and drained
1 tbsp chopped fresh
    coriander or parsley
1 tbsp fresh lime juice

½ tsp sugar
1 tbsp plain flour
1 tbsp chilli powder
¼ tsp salt
4 small pork loin chops,
    each 1cm thick
    (about 150g each)
1 tbsp vegetable oil

◆ Prepare corn salad: mix first 6 ingredients in medium bowl; set aside.

◆ Mix flour, chili powder and salt together on greaseproof paper. Pat pork chops dry with kitchen towels. Coat chops with chilli powder mixture.

◆ Heat oil in 30cm non-stick frying pan over medium-high heat; add pork chops and cook about 8 minutes, until golden brown on both sides and pork just loses its pink colour throughout. Serve pork with corn salad.

**Each serving: About 420 calories, 33g protein, 38g carbohydrate, 16g total fat (5g saturated), 54mg cholesterol, 860mg sodium**

# MINCED PORK

Deliciously imbued with herbs and spices from fresh ginger to delicate dill, minced pork is juicy and full of flavour. It is the basis for favourites from around the world, such as stuffed cabbage, Chinese dumplings or classic French pâté.

## CHINESE DUMPLINGS

❖❖❖❖❖❖❖❖❖❖❖❖

*Prep:* 45 minutes
*Cook:* 5 minutes
*Makes* 4 main dish servings

180g Chinese cabbage, sliced
225g minced pork
2 tbsp soy sauce
1 tbsp dry sherry
2 tsp cornflour
1½ tsp very finely chopped, peeled fresh ginger
1 spring onion, very finely chopped
36 fresh or frozen (thawed) wonton wrappers, each about 9 by 9cm (available from Chinese supermarkets)
1 medium egg white, beaten
Soy Dipping Sauce (below)
Sautéed asparagus and sesame seeds (optional)
Spring onions for garnish

### SOY DIPPING SAUCE

Mix 60ml soy sauce, 60ml rice vinegar or white wine vinegar and 2 tablespoons very fine strips peeled fresh ginger in small bowl. Makes about 125ml.

**1** Prepare filling: bring cabbage and *2–3cm boiling water* to the boil in 2-litre saucepan over high heat. Cook 1 minute; drain. Immediately rinse with cold water until cool.

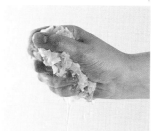

**2** Squeeze as much water out of cabbage as possible. Finely chop cabbage. Squeeze any liquid from chopped cabbage; place it in bowl. Stir in pork and next 5 ingredients.

**3** Arrange half of wonton wrappers on sheet of parchment paper. Using pastry brush, brush each wrapper lightly with egg white. Spoon 1 rounded teaspoon filling onto centre of each wrapper.

**4** Bring opposite corners of wrapper up over filling; pinch and pleat edges together to seal. Repeat with remaining wrappers, egg white and filling.

**5** Heat *1cm water* to the boil in deep 30cm frying pan over high heat. Place all dumplings, pleated edges up, in one layer in pan. Stir gently to prevent sticking.

**6** Bring dumplings to the boil over high heat. Reduce heat to low, cover pan, and simmer 5 minutes, or until dumplings are cooked through. Meanwhile, prepare Soy Dipping Sauce. Using slotted spoon, transfer dumplings to 4 plates; serve with asparagus and sesame seeds, if you like. Garnish, and pass dipping sauce separately.

EACH SERVING: ABOUT 320 CALORIES, 22g PROTEIN, 46g CARBOHYDRATE, 4g TOTAL FAT (1g SATURATED), 42mg CHOLESTEROL, 2020mg SODIUM

## STUFFED CABBAGE WITH DILL

*Prep: 40 minutes   Bake: 1 hour*
*Makes 4 main dish servings*

1 medium head green
  cabbage (about 1.3kg)
100g long-grain rice
30g margarine or butter
2 medium onions, finely
  chopped
450g minced pork

15g fresh dill, chopped
¼ tsp ground nutmeg
¼ tsp salt
Ground black pepper
800g canned tomatoes
1 tsp sugar

◆ Bring *6 litres water* to the boil in an 8-litre saucepan. Cut and discard core from cabbage. Add cabbage to boiling water, cut-side up. Using 2 large spoons, gently separate outer leaves as they soften slightly; remove 12 large leaves and drain on kitchen towels. (Drain and reserve remaining cabbage for another day.) Spread cabbage leaves on work surface; trim thick ribs almost to thinness of leaves, for easy rolling.

◆ Meanwhile, prepare rice as packet instructs. Melt 15g margarine in 26cm frying pan over medium heat. Add half of onions and cook, stirring often, 5 minutes, or until tender. Transfer to medium bowl with rice, pork, dill, nutmeg, salt and ¼ teaspoon pepper. Mix well. Preheat oven to 190°C (375°F, Gas 5). Place about 4 tablespoons filling in centre of each cabbage leaf. Fold 2 sides of cabbage leaf over filling, overlapping edges, then roll up Swiss-roll style. Arrange cabbage rolls in 2-litre shallow casserole.

◆ Melt remaining 15g margarine in same frying pan over medium heat. Add remaining onions and cook, stirring often, 5 minutes, or until tender. Add tomatoes with their juice, sugar and ⅛ teaspoon pepper and bring to the boil, breaking up tomatoes with back of spoon. Pour evenly over cabbage rolls. Cover with foil and bake 1 hour.

**Each serving: About 445 calories, 32g protein, 54g carbohydrate, 13g total fat (3g saturated), 65mg cholesterol, 675mg sodium**

◆◆◆◆◆◆◆◆◆◆◆◆◆◆◆◆◆◆◆◆◆◆◆◆◆◆◆◆◆◆

### PREPARING CABBAGE ROLLS

Place blanched cabbage leaves, rib-side up, on work surface. Holding knife almost parallel to surface, trim thick rib so leaves lie almost flat. Place about 4 tablespoons filling in centre of each leaf. Fold sides over filling, over-lapping edges, then roll leaf up to form a neat package.

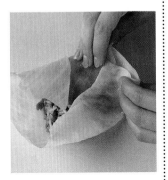

◆◆◆◆◆◆◆◆◆◆◆◆◆◆◆◆◆◆◆◆◆◆◆◆◆◆◆◆◆◆

## PORCUPINE MEATBALLS

*Prep: 20 minutes   Cook: 45 minutes*
*Makes 4 main dish servings*

400ml chicken stock
1 tbsp dry sherry
¼ tsp sesame oil
100g long-grain rice
4 spring onions, chopped
450g minced pork

1 medium egg
2 tbsp soy sauce
2 tsp grated, peeled fresh
  ginger
¼ tsp ground black pepper

◆ Bring the stock, sherry, sesame oil and *350ml water* to the boil in 26cm frying pan over high heat. Meanwhile, combine uncooked rice with remaining ingredients in large bowl; mix well. On greaseproof paper, form mixture into 1½-inch meatballs (mixture will be soft).

◆ Carefully place meatballs in stock mixture; return to the boil. Reduce heat to low; cover and simmer 45 minutes. Serve meatballs with stock.

**Each serving: About 285 calories, 28g protein, 21g carbohydrate, 9g total fat (3g saturated), 127mg cholesterol, 650mg sodium**

## COUNTRY PÂTÉ

*Prep: 20 minutes plus chilling   Bake: 1¾ hours*
*Makes 30 first course servings*

15g butter
1 medium onion, finely
  chopped
450g chicken livers, trimmed
  (see page 134)
1.1kg minced pork
2 medium eggs

75ml brandy
½ tsp dried thyme
¼ tsp ground nutmeg
Pinch ground cloves
2½ tsp salt
½ tsp ground black pepper
2 bay leaves

◆ Preheat oven to 180°C (350°F, Gas 4). Melt butter in 2-litre saucepan over medium heat. Add onion and cook, stirring, 4 minutes, or until tender. Transfer to electric blender. Add livers and blend until smooth.

◆ Combine pork, eggs, brandy, thyme, nutmeg, cloves, salt and pepper in large bowl until evenly blended. Stir in liver mixture until smooth. Spoon into 23 by 12cm loaf tin. Smooth top. Place bay leaves down centre.

◆ Cover tin tightly with foil. Bake pâté on baking tray 1¾ hours, or until instant-read thermometer inserted in centre reaches 67°C. Place on wire rack. Place a second loaf tin on top of pâté; weight down with heavy cans. Cool to room temperature. Refrigerate pâté, with weights, overnight. Unmould pâté, discarding bay leaves. Slice thin.

**Each serving: About 85 calories, 11g protein, 1g carbohydrate, 3g total fat (1g saturated), 97mg cholesterol, 220mg sodium**

# STIR-FRIED PORK

Coming from the Orient, this method of cooking strips of meat and assorted vegetables in a tasty sauce is a quick route to a delicious meal.

## SESAME PORK STIR-FRY

❖❖❖❖❖❖❖❖❖❖

*Prep: 20 minutes*
*Cook: 20 minutes*
*Makes 4 main dish servings*

Watercress Rice (optional, see below)
1 pork tenderloin (about 350g), cut into 1cm by 5mm strips
2 tbsp soy sauce
1 tbsp very finely chopped, peeled fresh ginger
1 tsp sesame oil
1 garlic clove, very finely chopped
175ml chicken stock
1¼ tsp cornflour
2 tsp olive oil
3 medium carrots, cut into 5cm by 5mm sticks
1 medium red pepper, cored, seeded and cut into 5mm wide strips
1 small courgette (225g), cut into 5cm by 5mm sticks

1 Prepare Watercress Rice, if you like; keep warm. Meanwhile, toss pork and next 4 ingredients together in medium bowl. Mix chicken stock and cornflour in small bowl; set aside.

2 Heat 1 teaspoon olive oil in 30cm non-stick frying pan or wok over medium-high heat. Add carrots and red pepper; cook, stirring, 5 minutes, or until lightly browned.

3 Add *1 tablespoon water;* cook 3–5 minutes longer, until tender-crisp. Transfer to bowl. Heat remaining 1 teaspoon oil in same pan. Add courgette; cook, stirring, 3 minutes.

### WATERCRESS RICE

Bring 350ml water and 150g long-grain rice to the boil in 1-litre saucepan over high heat. Reduce heat to low; cover and simmer 15–20 minutes, until rice is tender and water is absorbed. Stir in 60g coarsely chopped watercress leaves (about ½ bunch). Makes 4 accompaniment servings.

Each serving: About 130 calories, 3g protein, 28g carbohydrate, 0g total fat, 0mg cholesterol, 10mg sodium

4 Transfer courgette to bowl with carrot and red pepper mixture. Cook pork mixture, stirring constantly, in same pan until pork just loses its pink colour. Stir stock mixture; add to pork. Stir in vegetables; bring to the boil. Boil 1 minute, stirring, or until mixture thickens. Serve with Watercress Rice, if you like.

EACH SERVING: ABOUT 185 CALORIES, 20g PROTEIN, 11g CARBOHYDRATE, 7g TOTAL FAT (2g SATURATED), 53mg CHOLESTEROL, 770mg SODIUM

# PORK LO MEIN

*Prep:* 30 minutes    *Cook:* 15 minutes
*Makes* 4 main dish servings

| | |
|---|---|
| **1 pork tenderloin (about 350g) cut into very thin slices** | **1 head bok choy (about 750g), sliced crossways into 2–3cm wide strips** |
| **2 tbsp oyster sauce** | **175g radishes, each cut in half if large** |
| **2 tbsp dry sherry** | **1 bunch spring onions, cut into 5cm pieces** |
| **2 tbsp soy sauce** | **400g canned Chinese straw mushrooms, or 2 jars (200g each) whole mushrooms, drained** |
| **1 tsp grated, peeled fresh ginger** | |
| **225g linguine** | |
| **4 tbsp vegetable oil** | |
| **½ tsp salt** | |

◆ Mix pork, oyster sauce, sherry, soy sauce and ginger together in medium bowl; set aside. Cook linguine in large saucepan as packet instructs.

◆ Meanwhile, heat 2 tablespoons oil in 30cm frying pan or wok over high heat. Add salt and bok choy and cook, stirring, until bok choy is tender-crisp; transfer to bowl. Add 1 tablespoon oil to oil remaining in pan; add radishes and cook, stirring frequently, until tender-crisp. Transfer to bowl with bok choy.

◆ Add remaining 1 tablespoon oil to oil remaining in pan; heat over high heat. Add spring onions and cook, stirring frequently, until tender-crisp. Add pork mixture; cook, stirring constantly, about 3 minutes, until pork just loses its pink colour throughout. Return bok choy and radishes to pan. Add mushrooms and heat through.

◆ Drain linguine. Return linguine to saucepan and add pork mixture; toss to mix well.

**Each serving: About 500 calories, 31g protein, 52g carbohydrate, 20g total fat (4g saturated), 115mg cholesterol, 1330mg sodium**

# STIR-FRIED PORK WITH ASPARAGUS AND SHIITAKE MUSHROOMS

*Prep:* 25 minutes    *Cook:* 15 minutes
*Makes* 4 main dish servings

| | |
|---|---|
| **1 pork tenderloin (about 350g), cut into very thin slices** | **900g asparagus, trimmed and cut diagonally into 2–3cm pieces** |
| **2 tbsp soy sauce** | **4 tsp very finely chopped, peeled fresh ginger** |
| **1 tbsp plus 2 tsp vegetable oil** | **1 garlic clove, very finely chopped** |
| **225g shiitake mushrooms, stalks discarded and cut into wedges** | **225ml chicken stock** |
| **225g white mushrooms, each cut into quarters** | **1 tbsp hoisin sauce** |

◆ Toss pork with soy sauce in medium bowl. Heat 1 tablespoon oil in 26cm frying pan or wok over high heat. Add pork mixture and cook, stirring, 2 minutes, until pork just loses its pink colour throughout. Transfer to plate.

◆ Add 1 more teaspoon oil to oil in pan; heat over high heat. Add mushrooms and cook, stirring frequently, 5 minutes, or until mushrooms are browned and liquid has evaporated. Transfer to plate with pork.

◆ Add remaining 1 teaspoon oil to oil in pan; heat over high heat. Add asparagus, ginger and garlic; cook, stirring frequently, 2 minutes. Stir in stock and hoisin sauce; bring to the boil. Boil 2–4 minutes, until asparagus is tender-crisp. Return pork and mushrooms to pan; heat through.

**Each serving: About 270 calories, 26g protein, 24g carbohydrate, 10g total fat (2g saturated), 54mg cholesterol, 980mg sodium**

## STIR-FRYING HINTS

• Have all ingredients cut and measured, and sauces or thickening agents mixed, before you start cooking.

• Foods that are at room temperature will cook more evenly than those that are cold. About 30 minutes before cooking, bring out any refrigerated items.

• Cut ingredients into pieces of roughly the same size to ensure even cooking.

• The oil should be very hot. To test, add a piece of vegetable to the oil; if it sizzles, the oil is hot enough.

• Don't crowd the pan; the food will stew rather than fry.

• Stir the food almost continuously in the pan so everything cooks evenly.

# GRILLED PORK

The tenderloin is both the leanest and most tender cut of pork, and its long, narrow shape means it cooks quickly and evenly. For a fast and low-fat meal, grill it with an Oriental-style marinade, a fragrant spice rub or skewer cubes of pork with sweet red plums then baste with redcurrant jelly. Whatever your choice, in about fifteen minutes you'll have a sizzling meal.

## MARINATED PORK FILLET

*Prep: 20 minutes, plus marinating and standing    Grill: 15–20 minutes*
*Makes 4 main dish servings*

- 2 tbsp soy sauce
- 2 tbsp dry sherry
- 2 tsp grated, peeled fresh ginger
- 2 garlic cloves, very finely chopped
- 1 pork tenderloin (450g)
- 1 tbsp vegetable oil
- 2 medium spring onions, each cut lengthways in half, then cut into 5cm pieces
- 3 small courgettes (225g each), each quartered lengthways, then cut in 5cm pieces
- 1 large red pepper, cored, seeded and cut into thin 5cm strips
- ½ tsp salt
- 1¾ tsp sugar
- ½ tsp cornflour

1 Put soy sauce, sherry, ginger and garlic in glass dish large enough to take pork tenderloin; mix until well combined. Add pork tenderloin, turning to coat. Cover and refrigerate, turning tenderloin occasionally, 40 minutes. About 20 minutes before serving, preheat grill. Place tenderloin on rack in grill pan; reserve marinade in dish. Place pan in grill about 15cm from heat.

2 Grill 15–20 minutes, turning pork once, until browned and internal temperature of meat reaches 64.5°C on instant-read thermometer (it will rise to 67°C upon standing). Transfer to chopping board; let stand 10 minutes.

3 Meanwhile, heat oil in 26cm non-stick frying pan over medium-high heat. Add spring onions, courgettes, red pepper and salt; cook, stirring often, until golden and tender-crisp.

4 Bring reserved marinade and sugar to the boil in small saucepan over medium heat. Mix cornflour and *125ml cold water* in small bowl; stir into saucepan. Return to the boil; boil, stirring, 1 minute.

5 Cut pork tenderloin on slight diagonal into 1cm thick slices. To serve, arrange vegetable mixture and pork on warm large platter; spoon sauce evenly over pork.

EACH SERVING: ABOUT 225 CALORIES, 26g PROTEIN, 11g CARBOHYDRATE, 8g TOTAL FAT (2g SATURATED), 65mg CHOLESTEROL, 835mg SODIUM

## CHILLI KEBABS WITH PLUMS

*Prep: 15 minutes   Grill: 8 minutes*
*Makes 4 main dish servings*

2 tsps chilli powder
1 tsp ground cumin
1 tsp brown sugar
⅛ tsp ground red pepper
½ tsp salt
1 pork tenderloin, (about
   350g), cut into 4cm cubes

4 plums, each stoned and cut
   into quarters
4 (25cm) all-metal skewers
3 tbsp redcurrant jelly, melted

◈ Preheat broiler. Mix first 5 ingredients together in medium bowl. Pat pork dry with kitchen towels; add to spice mixture and toss to coat evenly.

◈ Thread pork alternately with plum quarters on skewers. Place skewers on rack in grill pan.

◈ Place pan in grill at closest position to heat. Grill 7 minutes, turning once. Brush kebabs with half of redcurrant jelly; grill 20 seconds.

◈ Turn kebabs and brush with remaining redcurrant jelly. Grill kebabs 20 seconds longer, or until pork is browned and just cooked through.

**Each serving: About 185 calories, 18g protein, 20g carbohydrate, 4g total fat (1g saturated), 49mg cholesterol, 320mg sodium**

## CURRIED PORK TENDERLOIN

*Prep: 5 minutes, plus standing   Grill: 15–20 minutes*
*Makes 4 main dish servings*

1 pork tenderloin (450g)
1 tbsp curry powder
1 tsp ground cumin

¾ tsp salt
¼ tsp ground cinnamon
2 tsp vegetable oil

◈ Preheat grill. Pat pork dry with kitchen towels. Mix next 5 ingredients together in small bowl; use to rub over pork. Place pork on rack in grill pan. Place pan in grill about 15cm from heat; grill 15–20 minutes, turning once, until pork is browned and internal temperature reaches 64.5°C on instant-read thermometer (temperature will rise to 67°C upon standing).  Transfer pork to platter. Let stand 10 minutes; keep warm. To serve, thinly slice pork.

**Each serving: About 165 calories, 24g protein, 1g carbohydrate, 7g total fat (2g saturated), 65mg cholesterol, 450mg sodium**

## PORK WITH SAUTÉED VEGETABLES

*Prep: 40 minutes, plus standing   Grill: 15–20 minutes*
*Makes 6 main dish servings*

2 tbsp brown sugar
1 tbsp dry mustard
2 tbsp balsamic vinegar
2 tbsp soy sauce
2 pork tenderloins (350g each)
3 tsp vegetable oil
5 large carrots, thinly sliced
1 medium onion, thinly sliced
4 large celery stalks, thinly
   sliced

2–3cm piece fresh ginger,
   peeled and thinly sliced
Salt
2 large red peppers, cored,
   seeded and cut into 5mm
   wide strips
1 large green pepper, cored,
   seeded and cut into
   5mm wide strips

◈ Mix first 4 ingredients together in non-metallic dish large enough to take pork tenderloins. Add pork, turning to coat; set aside while cooking vegetables.

◈ Heat 2 teaspoons oil in 30cm non-stick frying pan over medium-high heat. Add carrots, onion, celery, ginger and ½ teaspoon salt and cook 10–12 minutes, until vegetables are browned; transfer to bowl.

◈ Preheat grill. Heat remaining 1 teaspoon oil in same frying pan. Add peppers and ½ teaspoon salt; cook until browned. Return carrot mixture to pan; keep warm.

◈ Brush rack in grill pan with oil. Place pork on rack; reserve marinade. Place pan under grill about 15cm from heat; grill 15–20 minutes, turning once, until pork is browned and internal temperature reaches 64.5°C on instant-read thermometer (temperature will rise to 67°C upon standing).

◈ Transfer pork to platter. Let stand 10 minutes; keep warm.

◈ Place marinade in 1-litre saucepan with *125ml water*; bring to the boil over high heat. Reduce heat to medium-low; boil sauce 3 minutes.

◈ Thinly slice pork; serve with vegetables and sauce.

**Each serving: About 250 calories, 26g protein, 21g carbohydrate, 7g total fat (2g saturated), 65mg cholesterol, 805mg sodium**

# PORK RIBS

Rubbed with spices or brushed with a sweet or tangy glaze, barbecued ribs are one of the joys of summer. Simmering the ribs before cooking guarantees tenderness and removes excess fat. Turn ribs often during cooking to avoid burning, especially when they are coated with a sweet barbecue sauce or glaze. If the weather doesn't permit cooking on the barbecue, these recipes will be just as fast under the grill.

## TERIYAKI-GLAZED RIBS

*Prep: 1½ hours*   *Barbecue: 15 minutes*
*Makes 5 main dish servings*

4 racks pork baby back ribs
  (450g each)
1 tbsp olive or vegetable oil
4 spring onions, thinly sliced
75ml teriyaki sauce
2 tbsp cornflour
3 tbsp finely chopped, peeled
  fresh ginger

350g apricot or peach jam
5 medium nectarines, each
  cut in half and stoned
2 tbsp sugar
Grilled French bread
  (optional)

**1** Put ribs in 8-litre saucepan or casserole. Add enough *water* to cover and bring to the boil over high heat. Reduce heat to low; cover and simmer 45–60 minutes, until tender. Transfer to platter. If not serving right away, cover and refrigerate. Prepare barbecue.

**2** Prepare glaze: heat oil in 1-litre saucepan over medium heat. Add spring onions and cook, stirring frequently, until golden. Stir in teriyaki sauce, next 3 ingredients and *60ml water*; cook, stirring, until mixture thickens and boils. Boil 1 minute. Sprinkle nectarines with sugar.

**3** Place ribs on barbecue over medium heat. Barbecue 15 minutes, turning frequently, and brushing with glaze during last 5 minutes of cooking, until heated through.

### TERIYAKI SAUCE

A blend of Japanese wines, soy sauce and sugar, this salty-sweet condiment gives a glossy sheen to barbecued or grilled fish, chicken and meats – baste near the end of cooking to avoid burning. Or, use as a marinade to give meat a delicious flavour and tenderize it, too.

**4** After ribs have been on barbecue 5 minutes, add nectarines. Cook 10 minutes, turning often, or until browned. Serve ribs and nectarines with French bread, if you like.

EACH SERVING: ABOUT 890 CALORIES, 47g PROTEIN, 77g CARBOHYDRATE, 44g TOTAL FAT (15g SATURATED), 164mg CHOLESTEROL, 850mg SODIUM

## RIBS WITH CHILLI-HERB COATING

*Prep:* 1½ minutes
*Barbecue:* 15–20 minutes
*Makes* 4 main dish servings

1.8kg pork spareribs, cut into
  2-rib portions
3 tbsp chilli powder
2 tsp dried oregano
1 tsp dry mustard
1 tsp salt
Chopped fresh parsley for garnish
Potato salad (optional)

◆ Put ribs in 8-litre saucepan or casserole. Add enough *water* to cover and bring to the boil over high heat. Reduce heat to low; cover and simmer 45–60 minutes, or until ribs are tender. Transfer to platter. If not serving right away, cover and refrigerate. Prepare barbecue.

◆ Pat ribs dry with kitchen towels. Mix chilli powder, oregano, mustard and salt together in small bowl. Use to rub over ribs.

◆ Place ribs on barbecue over medium heat; barbecue 15–20 minutes, turning ribs often, until heated through. Garnish, and serve with potato salad, if you like.

Each serving: About 720 calories,
57g protein, 4g carbohydrate, 52g total
fat (19g saturated), 205mg cholesterol,
730mg sodium

## SWEET-AND-SPICY RIBS

*Prep:* 1½ hours
*Barbecue:* 15–20 minutes
*Makes* 4 main dish servings

1.8kg pork spareribs, cut into
  2-rib portions
125ml bottled chilli sauce
125ml hoisin sauce
60g brown sugar
¾ tsp ground allspice
½ tsp Tabasco sauce
4 medium-sized ripe peaches, each cut in
  half and stoned
2 tbsp peach jam

◆ Put ribs in 8-litre saucepan or casserole. Add enough *water* to cover and bring to the boil over high heat. Reduce heat to low; cover and simmer 45–60 minutes, or until tender. Transfer to platter. If not serving right away, cover and refrigerate. Prepare barbecue.

◆ Mix chilli sauce and next 4 ingredients together in small bowl. Place spareribs on barbecue over medium heat. Barbecue 15–20 minutes, turning ribs often and brushing with sauce frequently during last 10 minutes, until heated through.

◆ After ribs have cooked 10 minutes, add peaches to barbecue. Cook about 5 minutes, turning once and brushing once with jam. Serve ribs with peaches.

Each serving: About 905 calories,
57g protein, 56g carbohydrate, 51g total
fat (19g saturated), 205mg cholesterol,
1630mg sodium

### ORANGE-ROSEMARY GLAZE

If you're having a big barbecue, you may want to make a variety of glazes. This recipe makes enough for 1.8kg of spareribs. Mix 225g orange marmalade, 60ml fresh lemon juice, 2 tablespoons chopped fresh rosemary or 2 teaspoons dried rosemary, crushed, and 1½ teaspoons salt together in small bowl until combined. Makes about 300ml.

## COUNTRY-STYLE RIBS WITH JALAPEÑO BARBECUE SAUCE

*Prep:* 1½ hours
*Barbecue:* 15–20 minutes
*Makes* 6 main dish servings

1.8kg pork back ribs
125ml cider vinegar
60ml chilli sauce
2 tbsp brown sugar
2 tbsp drained, chopped canned mild
  green chillies
1 tbsp drained, chopped pickled jalapeño
  chillies, stems and seeds removed
1 tbsp vegetable oil
1 tsp salt
⅛ tsp dried oregano

◆ Put ribs in 8-litre saucepan or casserole. Add enough *water* to cover and bring to the boil over high heat. Reduce heat to low; cover and simmer 45–60 minutes, or until ribs are tender. Transfer to platter. If not serving right away, cover and refrigerate. Prepare barbecue.

◆ Prepare barbecue sauce: blend remaining ingredients in blender on medium speed or in food processor with knife blade attached, until smooth. Place ribs on grid over medium heat. Cook, turning often and brushing with sauce during last 10 minutes, 15–20 minutes, until heated through.

Each serving: About 610 calories,
65g protein, 9g carbohydrate, 34g total fat
(11g saturated), 134mg cholesterol,
645mg sodium

### THE INDOOR ALTERNATIVE

To grill, rather than barbecue, ribs, first simmer as directed in recipes. Arrange ribs meat-side down on grill rack in grill pan. Place pan in grill about 20cm from heat; cook ribs, turning and brushing with glaze or sauce as instructed in recipe, 20 minutes, or until they are heated through.

# SMOKED PORK

Smoked pork is usually brine-cured, then flavoured with hardwood smoke, such as apple or occasionally mesquite; it is usually but not always fully cooked. Its robust flavour goes well with the sweet-sour combinations of preserves and mustard, apple juice and vinegar, or brown sugar and sauerkraut. Half and fully cooked smoked ham is becoming increasingly available in butchers and supermarkets. A good butcher, however, will smoke any cut of pork for you if you give him a few day's notice.

## APRICOT-GLAZED SMOKED HAM

*Prep:* 10 minutes, plus standing    *Bake:* 2 hours
*Makes* 12 main dish servings

| | |
|---|---|
| Half fully-cooked bone-in ham (3.1kg) | 3 tbsp plain flour |
| | 400ml chicken stock |
| 175g apricot jam | Rosemary sprigs for garnish |
| 3 tbsps Dijon mustard | Brussels sprouts and sweet |
| ½ tsp ground ginger | potato wedges (optional) |

**1** Preheat oven to 170°C (325°F, Gas 3). Remove skin and trim all but 5mm fat from ham. Score fat, just through to the meat, into 2cm diamonds. Place ham on rack in medium roasting tin.

**2** Insert meat thermometer into centre of ham, being careful that pointed end does not touch bone. Bake 1½ hours. Meanwhile, prepare glaze: mix jam, mustard and ginger together in small bowl until blended. Brush glaze over ham. Bake ham 30 minutes longer, or until thermometer reaches 57°C. Place on warm large platter. Let stand 15 minutes; keep warm.

**3** Prepare gravy: remove rack from roasting tin. Pour drippings through sieve into 2-litre measuring jug; let stand a few seconds, until fat separates from meat juice. Spoon 3 tablespoons fat from drippings into 2-litre saucepan; skim and discard remaining fat.

**4** Add *225ml water* to roasting tin; stir until brown bits are loosened. Pour through sieve into meat juice in measuring jug. Stir flour into fat in saucepan over medium heat; cook 1 minute. Gradually stir in meat juice mixture and stock; cook, stirring, until gravy thickens. Thinly slice ham; garnish and serve with gravy, and sprouts and sweet potatoes, if you like.

EACH SERVING: ABOUT 260 CALORIES, 34g PROTEIN, 12g CARBOHYDRATE, 8g TOTAL FAT (2g SATURATED), 76mg CHOLESTEROL, 1845mg SODIUM

## SMOKED PORK CHOP CASSEROLE

*Prep: 30 minutes    Bake: 1–1¼ hours*
*Makes 6 main dish servings*

1 small head green cabbage
  (about 750g)
450g small red potatoes
2 tbsp vegetable oil
3 large onions, each cut into
  quarters
6 smoked pork loin chops,
  each 1cm thick (about
  150g each)

125ml apple juice
60ml cider vinegar
½ tsp coarsely ground black
  pepper
325g dried fruit salad

◈ Preheat oven to 190°C (375°F, Gas 5). Cut cabbage into 6 wedges; remove core. Arrange cabbage and potatoes in shallow 5-litre casserole or roasting tin.

◈ Heat oil in 30cm frying pan over medium-high heat; add onions and cook, stirring often, until golden brown. Transfer onions to casserole with cabbage and potatoes.

◈ Pat pork chops dry with kitchen towels. Cook chops, half at a time, in oil remaining in pan until lightly browned on both sides. Tuck chops into vegetables in casserole.

◈ Add remaining ingredients to drippings remaining in pan; bring to the boil over high heat; stir until brown bits are loosened.

◈ Pour apple juice mixture over pork chops and vegetables. Cover and bake 1–1¼ hours, basting meat and vegetables with liquid in casserole several times, until tender.

Each serving: About 515 calories, 30g protein, 68g carbohydrate, 16g total fat (5g saturated), 54mg cholesterol, 790mg sodium

## FRUITED SMOKED PORK WITH CABBAGE

*Prep: 40 minutes    Bake: 45–60 minutes*
*Makes 6 main dish servings*

1 medium head green
  cabbage (about 1.3kg)
3 tbsp vegetable oil
2 large onions, each cut into
  8 wedges
1 smoked pork shoulder roll
  (900g)
750g canned pear halves in
  syrup

500g canned apricots in syrup
2 tbsp brown sugar
3 tbsp white wine vinegar
3 tbsp German mustard
½ tsp ground allspice

◈ Preheat oven to 170°C (325°F, Gas 3). Cut cabbage into quarters; remove core. Cut cabbage crossways into 2–3cm wide slices; discard tough ribs.

◈ Heat oil in 8-litre flameproof casserole over medium heat. Add onions; cook until tender. Stir in cabbage; cover and cook, stirring occasionally, 20 minutes, or until cabbage is tender. Meanwhile, remove string casing (if any) from pork; cut pork into 5mm thick slices. Drain canned fruit. Stir brown sugar, vinegar, mustard, and allspice into cabbage. Spoon cabbage mixture into 33 by 20cm ovenproof dish. Tuck pork and fruit into cabbage. Cover with foil; bake 45–60 minutes, until pork is tender.

Each serving: About 625 calories, 34g protein, 55g carbohydrate, 32g total fat (10g saturated), 84mg cholesterol, 1145mg sodium

## SMOKED PORK CHOP DINNER

*Prep: 10 minutes    Cook: 50 minutes*
*Makes 4 main dish servings*

4 smoked pork loin or rib
  chops, each 2cm thick
  (about 175g each)
1 tbsp vegetable oil
1 Granny Smith's apple,
  unpeeled
450g carrots, cut into
  2–3cm pieces

750g sauerkraut, drained
  and rinsed
350ml lager or non-alcoholic
  lager
60g brown sugar
2 tsp caraway or fennel seeds,
  crushed

◈ Pat chops dry with kitchen towels. Heat oil in 30cm frying pan over high heat; add chops and cook until browned on both sides. Meanwhile, grate half of apple; reserve the rest.

◈ Add carrots, grated apple, sauerkraut, beer, brown sugar, caraway seeds and *120ml water* to pan. Bring to the boil. Reduce heat to low; cover and simmer 35 minutes.

◈ Cut remaining apple into wedges; add to pan. Cover and cook 10 minutes longer, occasionally spooning liquid over chops, or until carrots and pork are tender.

Each serving: About 500 calories, 37g protein, 41g carbohydrate, 19g total fat (6g saturated), 74mg cholesterol, 2195mg sodium

◆◆◆◆◆◆◆◆◆◆◆◆◆◆◆◆◆◆◆◆◆◆◆◆◆◆◆

### SAUERKRAUT SECRET

Sauerkraut is shredded cabbage that has been pickled for several weeks in cabbage juice and salt, which gives it a unique sour taste. To mellow the pungent salty flavour, rinse sauerkraut with cold running water, then drain it well before using.

◆◆◆◆◆◆◆◆◆◆◆◆◆◆◆◆◆◆◆◆◆◆◆◆◆◆◆

# PORK SAUSAGES

Pork sausages are found in many cuisines, and the variety is huge: the recipes here feature Italian sausage, smoked Polish kielbasa and coriander-flavoured bratwurst. As with all pork, fresh sausages must be cooked thoroughly.

## TORTA RUSTICA

❖❖❖❖❖❖❖❖❖❖❖❖❖❖❖❖❖

*Prep: 40 minutes, plus preparing pizza dough and cooling*
*Bake: 25 minutes*
*Makes 6 main dish servings*

**Double quantity Basic Pizza Dough (see page 418)**
**450g mild Italian sausages, casings removed**
**1 medium egg**
**225g ricotta cheese**
**225g mozzarella cheese, grated**
**200g bottled roasted red peppers, drained, cut into 1cm wide slices, and patted dry with kitchen towels**
**30g fresh basil leaves**

**1** Prepare Basic Pizza Dough as instructed in steps 1 and 2. Cook sausage in frying pan over medium heat, stirring to break up meat, about 20 minutes. Drain on kitchen towels.

**2** Separate egg, placing white in cup. Reserve egg white in refrigerator, covered. Using fork, stir ricotta cheese into egg yolk until smooth and blended. Prehcat oven to 220°C (425°F, Gas 7).

**3** Using floured rolling pin, roll out half pizza dough on lightly floured surface to 33cm square. Use to line 24cm deep-dish pie plate. Trim edge, leaving 2–3cm over-hang; reserve trimmings. Sprinkle half of mozzarella over crust; top with half of sausage. Add all of roasted red peppers, ricotta mixture and basil.

**4** Top layers with remaining sausage, spreading evenly, then remaining mozzarella.

**5** Roll out second half of pizza dough on lightly floured surface. Using tip of knife, make small cuts in dough. Place over filling; fold over-hang over top crust; pinch edges to seal.

**6** Cut several leaves from reserved trimmings to decorate torta. Beat reserved egg white lightly with fork; brush top of torta with some egg white. Arrange leaves on top; brush with more egg white. Bake torta 15 minutes. Cover loosely with foil; bake 10 minutes longer. Transfer to wire rack to cool slightly. Serve warm or at room temperature. Or, cover and refrigerate torta to serve later.

EACH SERVING: ABOUT 610 CALORIES, 28g PROTEIN, 53g CARBOHYDRATE, 29g TOTAL FAT (13g SATURATED), 114mg CHOLESTEROL, 1350mg SODIUM

## POLENTA AND SAUSAGE CASSEROLE

*Prep: 70 minutes    Bake: 35 minutes*

*Makes 8 main dish servings*

225g mild Italian sausages, casings removed
225g hot Italian sausages, casings removed
1 tbsp olive oil
1 large onion, chopped
1 large celery stalk, chopped
1 medium carrot, chopped
800g canned tomatoes

2 tbsp tomato purée
240g coarse yellow cornmeal
400ml chicken stock
¼ tsp salt
60g Parmesan cheese, grated
225g Fontina or mozzarella cheese, grated
Celery leaves for garnish

◆ Prepare tomato-sausage sauce: cook all sausages in 5-litre flameproof casserole over medium-high heat until browned, stirring to break up. Transfer to bowl. Heat oil in drippings in casserole over medium-high heat; add onion, celery and carrot and cook, stirring often, until browned. Stir in sausage meat, tomatoes and tomato purée; bring to the boil over high heat. Reduce heat to low; cover and simmer 10 minutes. Remove cover and simmer 10 minutes longer, breaking up tomatoes with back of spoon.

◆ Preheat oven to 180°C (350°F, Gas 4). Prepare polenta: using wire whisk, mix cornmeal, chicken stock and salt in 4-litre saucepan. Over medium-high heat, gradually add *1 litre boiling water*, whisking constantly, about 5 minutes, or until mixture thickens. Whisk in Parmesan cheese. Remove from heat.

◆ Grease 33 by 20cm ovenproof dish. Spread half of polenta in dish; top with half of tomato-sausage sauce, then half of Fontina cheese. Repeat with remaining polenta and sauce. Bake casserole, uncovered, 15 minutes. Sprinkle with remaining Fontina; bake 20 minutes longer, or until casserole is hot and bubbling. Let stand 15 minutes for easier serving. Garnish with celery leaves.

**Each serving: About 420 calories, 20g protein, 36g carbohydrate, 22g total fat (10g saturated), 64mg cholesterol, 1100mg sodium**

## KIELBASA WITH CABBAGE AND FRUIT

*Prep: 10 minutes    Cook: 25 minutes*

*Makes 6 main dish servings*

1 small head Savoy or green cabbage (900g)
15g margarine or butter
1 medium onion, finely chopped
125ml dry white wine
225g mixed dried fruit

125ml chicken stock
¼ tsp dried thyme
¼ tsp salt
¼ tsp ground black pepper
450g fully cooked kielbasa (Polish sausage), cut into 2–3cm pieces

Cut cabbage into quarters; remove core. Thinly slice cabbage, discarding any tough ribs. Melt margarine in 8-litre flameproof casserole over medium heat. Add onion and cook 5 minutes, or until tender. Add wine and dried fruit and bring to the boil over high heat. Stir in stock, thyme, salt, pepper and cabbage. Cover and cook over high heat 5 minutes. Stir in kielbasa and cook 15 minutes longer, or until cabbage is tender and kielbasa is heated through.

**Each serving: About 440 calories, 14mg protein, 40g carbohydrate, 25g total fat (10g saturated), 47mg cholesterol, 905mg sodium**

## BEER-BRAISED BRATWURST DINNER

*Prep: 30 minutes    Bake: 1½ hours*

*Makes 6 main dish servings*

750g bratwurst
1 small head green cabbage (about 900g), cut into 6 wedges with core removed
1 tbsp vegetable oil
450g red potatoes, cut into 4cm chunks

2 medium onions, sliced
325–350ml lager or non-alcoholic lager
1 tbsp caraway seeds
½ chicken stock cube, crumbled
¼ tsp ground black pepper

◆ Cook sausages in 30cm frying pan over medium-high heat, turning frequently, until browned; drain on kitchen towels. Place sausages and cabbage in shallow 3½-litre casserole.

◆ Preheat oven to 190°C (375°F, Gas 5). Heat oil in drippings in pan over medium-high heat. Add potatoes and onions; cook until lightly browned, stirring often; add to casserole.

◆ Add remaining ingredients to the pan. Bring to the boil over high heat; stir until brown bits are loosened. Pour over mixture in casserole. Cover and bake 1½ hours, or until vegetables are tender.

**Each serving: About 385 calories, 13g protein, 30g carbohydrate, 24g total fat (9g saturated), 45mg cholesterol, 680mg sodium**

Sweet, succulent lamb is both elegant and earthy. Once a symbol of spring, lamb is now bred so it can be enjoyed all year round. Roasted whole leg of lamb makes for an impressive centrepiece while diced lamb can be made into a comforting stew.

## KNOW YOUR LAMB

Most lamb sold today is marketed as spring lamb – usually 3–9 months old. Baby lamb, or milk-fed lamb, has an even milder flavour and paler colour; it comes from sheep under 3 months of age. Meat from sheep butchered between 12 and 24 months is sold as yearling lamb, and sheep over 2 years as mutton. These meats have a more gamey flavour than younger lambs, and are seldom sold in the usual retail outlets. Most imported lamb comes from New Zealand, and the cuts are slightly smaller since they come from a smaller – though not younger – animal.

## BUYING AND SERVING

• Select lamb that is light red. Darker meat is from an older animal and will have a stronger flavour. Any fat should be white, firm and waxy. Bones should be porous and unsplintered, with a reddish tinge at the cut end.
• A leg of lamb may be covered with 'fell', a moist, pliable paper-thin membrane that surrounds the fat and may be strongly flavoured. You can trim it off or not, as you prefer.
• Each 450g of raw lamb serves the following: boneless roasts, 3–4 servings; bone-in roasts and chops, 2–3 servings; bony cuts like neck chops and shanks, 1–2 servings.

### MARINADES FOR LAMB

• Olive oil, red wine, thyme and Dijon mustard
• Yogurt, garlic, cumin and crushed cardamom seeds
• Balsamic vinegar, olive oil, garlic, fresh mint leaves and rosemary
• Lemon juice, lemon peel, olive oil, fresh mint leaves and oregano
• Paste of crushed fennel seeds, cumin seeds, coriander seeds, garlic and olive oil
• Dry rub of chilli powder, ground cumin and thyme
• Soy sauce, garlic and Chinese five-spice powder

## CHOOSING THE RIGHT CUT

When preparing any cut of lamb, remember that it can dry out quickly if overcooked. So unless you prefer well-done meat, cook lamb just to medium-rare for the best results.

**For grilling, barbecuing or pan-frying** Tender cuts work best; avoid overcooking.
**Suitable cuts** Rib and neck chops, loin chops (below right), chump chops (below left), leg steaks, butterflied leg.

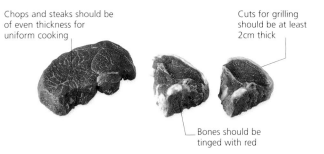

Chops and steaks should be of even thickness for uniform cooking

Cuts for grilling should be at least 2cm thick

Bones should be tinged with red

**For braising or stewing** These moist-heat cooking methods are best reserved for slightly less tender and more economical cuts. Remember to cook at a gentle simmer.
**Suitable cuts** Blade chops, scrag end of neck (below left), shanks (below right), breast. Lamb cubes for stew are cut from the shoulder.

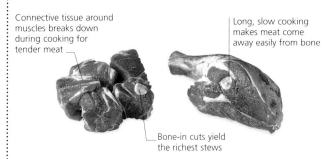

Connective tissue around muscles breaks down during cooking for tender meat

Long, slow cooking makes meat come away easily from bone

Bone-in cuts yield the richest stews

**For roasting** Many cuts of lamb are good for roasting, but the leg, shoulder and rib sections are the most popular. Place lamb roasts fat-side up on a rack in a roasting pan, which will help keep the meat moist.
**Suitable cuts** Whole leg of lamb, leg shank end, shoulder, rack (rib roast).

Layer of fell surrounding fat may be removed, if you like

Any bones should be cleanly cut, not splintered

Thin covering of fat keeps juices in

# BONING AND BUTTERFLYING A LEG

1 Place lamb, fat-side down, on cutting board. Using sharp boning or paring knife, cut through meat to expose main leg bone.

2 Keeping knife blade against bone, scrape all meat around bone until you reach the knee joint.

3 Turn leg slightly and cut around knee joint. Continue to cut meat from knee down to second leg bone. Remove leg bone.

1 So leg can lie flat for easier carving, cut a slice from thin side of leg; turn leg cut-side down. Holding meat steady with a carving fork, make a vertical cut to bone about 2–3cm from shank. From shank end, make a horizontal cut parallel to bone to release the wedge of meat.

4 Since the boned leg of lamb is uneven in thickness, cut the thicker muscles horizontally almost in half, then open like a book to make meat flatter and a more even thickness. Trim excess fat from meat.

2 Cut even slices of meat, slicing perpendicular to bone and working along leg away from the shank.

## ROASTING TIMES AT 170°C (325°F, GAS 3)

| CUT AND WEIGHT<br>Start with meat at refrigerator temperature. **Remove roast from oven when it reaches 2–5°C below desired doneness; temperature will rise as it stands** | | APPROXIMATE COOKING TIME (MINUTES PER 450g) | | |
| --- | --- | --- | --- | --- |
| | | Medium-rare (67°C) | Medium (77°C) | Well done |
| Whole leg | 2.2–3.1kg | 15 mins | 20 mins | 25 mins |
| | 3.1–4.1kg | 20 mins | 25 mins | 30 mins |
| Leg shank end | 1.3–1.8kg | 30 mins | 40 mins | 45 mins |
| Leg fillet | 1.3–1.8kg | 25 mins | 35 mins | 45 mins |
| Leg roast (boneless) | 1.8–3.1kg | 20 mins | 25 mins | 30 mins |
| Rib roast or rack at 190°C (375°F, Gas 5) | 750g–1.1kg | 30 mins | 35 mins | 40 mins |
| Crown roast, unstuffed at 190°C (375°F, Gas 5) | 900g–1.3kg | 25 mins | 30 mins | 35 mins |
| Shoulder roast | 1.8–2.7kg | 20 mins | 25 mins | 30 mins |
| Shoulder roast (boneless) | 1.5–2.7kg | 35 mins | 40 mins | 45 mins |

3 Turn leg over. With knife blade almost flat and working away from you, cut long slices following line of the bone.

# ROAST LAMB

Crowned with a crust of buttery crumbs, rolled round a fragrant onion-and-herb stuffing, or served bistro-style on a bed of potatoes, lamb roasts beautifully. Rosemary, thyme, mint and garlic are classic complements to its distinctive flavour. Whatever cut you choose, for the juiciest, tastiest lamb, roast just until the interior is still slightly pink.

## ROASTED LEG OF LAMB WITH PISTACHIO-MINT CRUST

*Prep: 30 minutes, plus standing*  *Roast: 2¼–2½ hours*
*Makes 14 main dish servings*

1 whole leg of lamb (3.1kg)
2 large garlic cloves, sliced
Salt
30g margarine or butter
1 small onion, chopped
1½ slices firm white bread, torn into 5mm crumbs
60g shelled pistachios, finely chopped

2 tbsp coarsely chopped fresh mint
¼ tsp coarsely ground black pepper
125ml port
3 tbsp plain flour
400ml chicken stock
Asparagus and boiled potatoes (optional)

**1** Preheat oven to 170°C (325°F, Gas 3). Trim fat from lamb. Make about a dozen 1cm wide cuts all over lamb; place a slice of garlic in each cut. Rub lamb with 1 teaspoon salt.

**2** Place lamb, fat-side up, on rack in large roasting tin. Insert meat thermometer into thickest part of lamb, being careful that pointed end does not touch bone. Roast 1 hour.

**3** Meanwhile, melt margarine in small saucepan over medium heat. Add onion; cook about 10 minutes, until lightly browned and tender; remove from heat. Stir in bread crumbs, pistachios, mint, pepper and ½ teaspoon salt.

**4** After lamb has cooked 1 hour, carefully pat bread mixture on top. Roast 1¼–1½ hours longer, until thermometer reaches 57°C for medium-rare (internal temperature of meat will rise to 59.5°C upon standing).

**5** Transfer to warm platter; let stand 15 minutes. Prepare gravy: remove rack from roasting tin; pour pan drippings into 1-litre measuring jug. Add port to roasting tin. Bring to the boil over high heat; stir until brown bits are loosened.

**6** Add port mixture to meat juice in jug; let stand a few seconds, until fat separates from meat juice. Skim 2 tablespoons fat into roasting tin; discard any remaining fat. Stir flour into fat in roasting tin and cook over medium-high heat until blended. Gradually whisk in meat juice mixture and stock and cook, stirring, until gravy boils and thickens slightly; boil 1 minute. Thinly slice lamb; serve with gravy, and asparagus and potatoes, if you like.

EACH SERVING: ABOUT 285 CALORIES, 33g PROTEIN, 6g CARBOHYDRATE, 13g TOTAL FAT (4g SATURATED), 99mg CHOLESTEROL, 460mg SODIUM

## LAMB ROASTED OVER POTATOES

*Prep: 15 minutes, plus standing    Roast: 1½–1¾ hours*
*Makes 8 main dish servings*

15g margarine or butter
2 medium onions, sliced
350ml chicken stock
750g potatoes, peeled
   and thinly sliced
Salt
Ground black pepper

1 tsp olive oil
1 garlic clove, very finely
   chopped
½ tsp dried thyme
1 shank half of leg of lamb,
   about 1.5kg

◆ Preheat oven to 220°C (425°F, Gas 7). Melt margarine in 26cm frying pan over medium heat. Add onions; cook, stirring often, until tender. Stir in stock; bring to the boil over high heat. Remove from heat. Toss potatoes with onion mixture, ½ teaspoon salt and ¼ teaspoon pepper in roasting tin; spread evenly in tin. Roast 15 minutes.

◆ Meanwhile, mix olive oil, garlic, thyme, ½ teaspoon salt, and ¼ teaspoon black pepper in small bowl; rub over lamb. Insert meat thermometer in thickest part of lamb, being careful that pointed end does not touch bone. Stir potatoes; place lamb on top. Roast 1¼ hours longer, stirring potatoes every 20 minutes, or until thermometer reaches 57°C for medium-rare (internal temperature of meat will rise to 59.5°C upon standing). Transfer lamb to warm large platter. Let stand 15 minutes; keep warm. (If potatoes are not yet tender, roast 15 minutes longer.) Thinly slice lamb; serve with potatoes.

Each serving: About 435 calories, 46g protein, 35g carbohydrate, 12g total fat (4g saturated), 133mg cholesterol, 590mg sodium

## HERB-CRUSTED RACKS OF LAMB

*Prep: 15 minutes, plus standing    Roast: 65–70 minutes*
*Makes 8 main dish servings*

2 racks of lamb, 8 ribs each
   (1.1kg each); ask butcher to
   loosen backbone from ribs
½ tsp salt
4 slices firm white bread, torn
60g margarine or butter

2 tsp dried rosemary, crushed
¼ tsp ground black pepper
2 tbsp very finely chopped
   fresh parsley
2 tbsp Dijon mustard

◆ Preheat oven to 190°C (375°F, Gas 5). Place lamb in large roasting tin, meat-side up. Sprinkle with salt. Insert meat thermometer into centre of 1 roast, being careful that pointed end does not touch bone. Roast lamb 50 minutes.

◆ Meanwhile, process bread in food processor with knife blade attached or in blender (in batches) on medium speed until fine crumbs form. Melt margarine in 26cm frying pan over medium heat. Add breadcrumbs, rosemary and pepper; cook until crumbs are golden brown. Stir in parsley.

◆ Remove roasting tin from oven. Spread top of each rack of lamb with mustard. Carefully pat crumb mixture on top. Roast lamb 15–20 minutes longer, until thermometer reaches 57°C for medium-rare (internal temperature of meat will rise to 59.5°C upon standing).

◆ Transfer roasts to chopping board. Let stand 15 minutes; keep warm. Cut backbone from each lamb rack; place on warm large platter. To serve, carve between ribs.

Each serving: About 485 calories, 46g protein, 7g carbohydrate, 29g total fat (9g saturated), 147mg cholesterol, 505mg sodium

## ONION-STUFFED BUTTERFLIED LEG OF LAMB

*Prep: 20 minutes, plus standing    Roast: 1¼ hours*
*Makes 10 main dish servings*

60g margarine or butter
1 large onion, very finely
   chopped
1 garlic clove, very finely
   chopped
Salt
1½ tsp dried rosemary,
   crushed

1½ tsp dried thyme
Ground black pepper
1.3kg boneless butterflied leg
   of lamb (ask your butcher
   to do this)
1 tbsp olive or vegetable oil
125ml dry white wine

◆ Preheat oven to 170°C (325°F, Gas 3). Melt margarine in 26cm frying pan over medium heat; add onion, garlic, 1 teaspoon salt, ¾ teaspoon rosemary, ¾ teaspoon thyme and ¼ teaspoon pepper and cook until onion is tender. Remove from heat.

◆ Place lamb flat on work surface, cut-side up; spread onion mixture evenly over lamb. Cut three 60cm lengths and one 85cm length of string. Place long string horizontally on work surface, and short strings vertically across it. Roll lamb tightly. Set lamb, seam-side up, lengthways along long string. Tie strings securely round meat.

◆ Place lamb on rack in large roasting tin. Rub with oil and remaining ¾ teaspoon each rosemary and thyme; sprinkle with salt and pepper. Insert meat thermometer into centre of lamb. Roast 1¼ hours, or until thermometer reaches 57°C for medium-rare (internal temperature of meat will rise to 59.5°C upon standing).

◆ Transfer lamb to warm large platter. Let stand 15 minutes; keep warm. Add wine and *125ml water* to roasting tin. Bring to the boil over high heat; stir until brown bits are loosened. Skim and discard fat. Remove string from lamb; thinly slice and serve with gravy.

Each serving: About 250 calories, 29g protein, 2g carbohydrate, 13g total fat (3g saturated), 88mg cholesterol, 360mg sodium

# LAMB SHANKS

Lamb shanks have excellent flavour but are not as tender as other cuts. The solution is to cook them by moist-heat methods such as braising, resulting in deliciously tender meat in a rich sauce. Lemon, tomatoes and dried fruit are some of the piquant ingredients that enhance the robust taste of the meat. Each shank yields enough meat for one serving.

## BRAISED LAMB SHANKS WITH COUSCOUS

❖❖❖❖❖❖❖❖❖❖❖❖

*Prep:* 15 minutes
*Cook:* 2½ hours
*Makes* 4 main dish servings

2 tsp vegetable oil
4 small lamb shanks (about 450g each), patted dry with kitchen towels
2 medium carrots, cut into 5mm thick slices
1 large celery stalk, cut into 5mm slices
1 medium onion, coarsely chopped
800g canned tomatoes
2 tbsp tomato purée
2 tbsp chopped fresh rosemary or 2 tsp dried, crushed
2 tsp sugar
½ beef stock cube, crumbled
1 bay leaf
1 cinnamon stick (7–8cm)
225g canned chick-peas, rinsed and drained
125g couscous

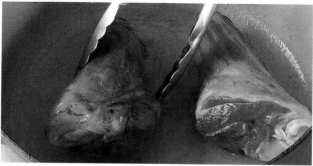

**1** Heat oil in 8-litre flameproof casserole over medium-high heat. Add lamb shanks, 2 at a time; brown on all sides. Transfer to bowl as they brown.

**2** Reduce heat to medium. Add carrots, celery, and onion to drippings in casserole; cook, stirring occasionally, until golden brown on all sides.

**3** Add tomatoes and next 6 ingredients, and *225ml water*; bring to the boil over high heat, breaking up tomatoes with back of spoon.

**4** Return shanks to casserole. Bring to the boil; reduce heat to low. Cover; simmer 2 hours, or until tender, turning meat once. Discard bay leaf and cinnamon stick; skim and discard fat. Add chick-peas to casserole; heat through over high heat. Meanwhile, prepare couscous as label instructs, but do not add margarine or butter. Serve lamb shanks and sauce with couscous.

EACH SERVING: ABOUT 490 CALORIES, 32g PROTEIN, 56g CARBOHYDRATE, 15g TOTAL FAT (5g SATURATED), 77mg CHOLESTEROL, 1180mg SODIUM

## MOROCCAN LAMB SHANKS

*Prep: 30 minutes    Bake: 2 hours*
*Makes 4 main dish servings*

4 small lamb shanks (about 450g each)
1 tbsp plus 1 tsp vegetable oil
2 medium onions, finely chopped
3 garlic cloves, very finely chopped
1 tsp ground ginger
¼ tsp ground cinnamon
¼ tsp ground red pepper
400ml chicken stock
75g stoned prunes
40g dried ready-to-eat apricots
1 tsp salt
¼ tsp ground black pepper
15g fresh coriander, chopped

◆ Preheat oven to 180°C (350°F, Gas 4). Pat lamb shanks dry with kitchen towels. Heat 1 tablespoon oil in 8-litre flameproof casserole over medium-high heat. Add shanks, 2 at a time; brown on all sides. Transfer shanks to bowl as they brown.

◆ Reduce heat to medium. Add remaining 1 teaspoon oil and onions to casserole; cook 5 minutes, or until onion is tender. Stir in garlic and next 3 ingredients; cook 30 seconds.

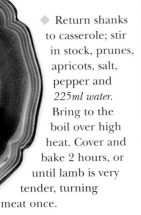

◆ Return shanks to casserole; stir in stock, prunes, apricots, salt, pepper and *225ml water*. Bring to the boil over high heat. Cover and bake 2 hours, or until lamb is very tender, turning meat once.

◆ Skim and discard fat from sauce in casserole. To serve, sprinkle with chopped coriander.

**Each serving: About 355 calories, 26g protein, 29g carbohydrate, 16g total fat (5g saturated), 85mg cholesterol, 1025mg sodium**

## LAMB AND BEAN CASSEROLE

*Prep: 30 minutes*
*Bake: 2 hours*
*Makes 4 main dish servings*

4 small lamb shanks (about 450g each)
2 tbsp plain flour
2 tbsp vegetable oil
1 large celery stalk, diced
1 medium onion, diced
400g canned tomatoes
400ml beef stock
1 garlic clove, very finely chopped
1 bay leaf
½ tsp dried thyme
½ tsp salt
¼ tsp coarsely ground black pepper
400g canned cannellini beans, rinsed and drained
1 tsp chopped fresh parsley
1 tsp grated lemon rind

◆ Preheat oven to 180°C (350°F, Gas 4). Pat lamb shanks dry with kitchen towels. Coat shanks with flour. Heat oil in 8-litre flameproof casserole over medium-high heat; add lamb shanks, 2 at a time; brown on all sides. Transfer shanks to bowl as they brown.

◆ Reduce heat to medium. Add celery and onion to casserole; cook until well browned. Return shanks to casserole; stir in tomatoes, stock, garlic, bay leaf, thyme, salt and pepper; bring to the boil over high heat.

◆ Cover casserole and bake 2 hours, or until lamb shanks are tender, turning meat once.

◆ Skim and discard fat from sauce in casserole. Stir in cannellini beans; heat through on top of hob over medium heat. Discard bay leaf. To serve, sprinkle with parsley and lemon rind.

**Each serving: About 395 calories, 30g protein, 29g carbohydrate, 18g total fat (6g saturated), 77mg cholesterol, 1000mg sodium**

## GREEK-STYLE LAMB SHANKS

*Prep: 30 minutes*
*Bake: 2½ hours*
*Makes 4 main dish servings*

4 small lamb shanks (about 450g each)
1 tbsp vegetable oil
2 medium onions, diced
1 large carrot, diced
2 garlic cloves, very finely chopped
400g canned chopped tomatoes
225ml chicken stock
¾ tsp salt
750g medium potatoes, unpeeled and each cut into quarters
350g French beans, ends trimmed and cut into 5cm pieces
2 medium lemons
2 tbsp chopped fresh dill
2 tbsp chopped fresh parsley

◆ Preheat oven to 180°C (350°F, Gas 4). Pat lamb shanks dry with kitchen towels. Heat oil in 8-litre flameproof casserole over medium-high heat. Add shanks, 2 at a time; brown on all sides. Transfer shanks to bowl as they brown.

◆ Add diced onions and carrot to drippings in casserole; cook over medium heat 12 minutes, or until tender and lightly browned. Add garlic; cook 1 minute longer.

◆ Return shanks to casserole. Stir in tomatoes with their juice, stock and salt; bring to the boil over high heat.

◆ Cover casserole and bake 1¼ hours. Turn shanks over; add potatoes and French beans. Cover and bake 1¼ hours longer, or until lamb and potatoes are tender.

◆ Skim and discard fat from sauce in casserole. Grate 1 tablespoon rind and squeeze 2 tablespoons juice from lemons. Stir lemon rind and juice, dill and parsley into sauce.

**Each serving: About 490 calories, 32g protein, 63g carbohydrate, 16g total fat (5g saturated), 81mg cholesterol, 1090mg sodium**

# LAMB CASSEROLES AND STEWS

The distinctive flavour of lamb holds its own in stews packed with chunky vegetables and flavoured with pungent herbs and spices. The long, slow cooking time both tenderizes the meat and allows the seasonings to permeate the lamb and vegetables for a warming, substantial meal.

## LAMB CURRY

❖ ❖ ❖ ❖ ❖ ❖ ❖ ❖ ❖ ❖ ❖ ❖ ❖ ❖ ❖ ❖ ❖ ❖ ❖ ❖ ❖ ❖ ❖

*Prep:* 25 minutes   *Cook:* 2¼–2½ hours
*Makes* 6 main dish servings

2 tbsp vegetable oil
1.8kg bone-in lamb shoulder, cut up for stew, patted dry with kitchen towels
6 medium onions, finely chopped
2 tbsp very finely chopped, peeled fresh ginger
4 garlic cloves, very finely chopped
12 cardamom pods
1 cinnamon stick (8cm)

2 tsp ground cumin
¼ tsp ground red pepper
2 tbsp tomato purée
1½ tsp salt
900g baking potatoes, peeled and cut into 4cm pieces
15g fresh coriander, chopped
Naan bread and steamed spinach (optional)

**1** Heat 1 teaspoon oil in 5-litre flameproof casserole over medium-high heat. Add one-third of lamb and brown all over; transfer to bowl. Repeat in 2 more batches with 2 teaspoons oil and remaining lamb.

**2** Add remaining 1 tablespoon oil to drippings in casserole; heat until hot. Stir in onions; cook, stirring, 15 minutes, or until tender. Stir in ginger and next 5 ingredients; cook, stirring, 1 minute.

### CARDAMOM

A member of the ginger family, cardamom is a spice prized for its aromatic seeds and is commonly used in Indian and Scandinavian cooking. Each whole pod, which may be pale green or bleached white, holds a cluster of tiny, hard black seeds, which have a flowery, lemony taste. Cardamom is sold in the pod or as ground seeds. The pods retain more fragrance than the ground version, which loses flavour quickly. Try adding whole pods, slightly crushed to release the fragrant oils, to a stew, curry or rice. Ground cardamom added to freshly ground coffee beans imparts a Middle Eastern flavour.

**3** Add tomato purée and cook, stirring, 1 minute. Return lamb to casserole; stir in salt and *450ml water*; bring to the boil over high heat. Reduce heat to low; cover and simmer 1½ hours.

**4** Stir in potatoes; return to the boil. Reduce heat to low, cover and simmer 30–45 minutes, until potatoes are tender. Skim and discard fat. Sprinkle with coriander. Serve with spinach and naan bread, if you like.

EACH SERVING: ABOUT 610 CALORIES, 62g PROTEIN, 43g CARBOHYDRATE, 20g TOTAL FAT (6g SATURATED), 183mg CHOLESTEROL, 710mg SODIUM

## LAMB STEW PROVENÇAL

*Prep: 45 minutes    Bake: 1¼–1½ hours*
*Makes 6 main dish servings*

900g boneless lamb, cut into
   4cm pieces
2 tsp plus 1 tbsp vegetable oil
4 medium onions, thinly sliced
2 red peppers, cored, seeded
   and thinly sliced
1 tsp salt
3 garlic cloves, finely chopped

400g canned tomatoes
¼ tsp dried thyme
¼ tsp fennel seeds
¼ tsp ground black pepper
3 strips (8 by 1cm) orange
   rind
15g fresh basil, chopped

Preheat oven to 180°C (350°F, Gas 4). Pat lamb dry with kitchen towels. Heat 1 teaspoon oil in 5-litre flameproof casserole over medium-high heat. Add half of lamb; brown all over. Using slotted spoon, transfer to plate. Repeat with 1 teaspoon oil and remaining lamb. Add 1 tablespoon oil and next 3 ingredients to drippings in casserole. Cook, stirring often, 25 minutes, or until very tender. Add garlic; cook 1 minute. Add tomatoes with their juice, stirring to break them up, next 4 ingredients and lamb. Bring to the boil. Cover; bake 1¼–1½ hours, until lamb is tender. Skim and discard fat. To serve, sprinkle with basil.

**Each serving:** About 325 calories, 40g protein, 15g carbohydrate, 14g total fat (4g saturated), 122mg cholesterol, 550mg sodium

## ROMAN LAMB STEW WITH MARSALA

*Prep: 15 minutes    Cook: 2 hours*
*Makes 6 main dish servings*

900g boneless lamb, cut into
   4cm pieces
3 tsp vegetable oil
450g carrots
1 medium onion, finely
   chopped
1 celery stalk, finely chopped
1 garlic clove, finely chopped

225ml Marsala
400g canned tomatoes
1¼ tsp salt
¼ tsp ground black pepper
¼ tsp dried rosemary
¼ tsp dried thyme
300g frozen peas

◆ Pat lamb dry with kitchen towels. Heat 1 teaspoon oil in 5-litre flameproof casserole over medium-high heat. Add half of lamb and brown all over; using slotted spoon,

transfer to plate. Repeat with 1 more teaspoon oil and remaining lamb. Meanwhile, finely chop 1 carrot. Cut remaining carrots lengthways in half, then crosswise into 7–8cm lengths.

◆ Reduce heat to medium. Add remaining 1 teaspoon oil, carrot, onion and celery to drippings in casserole; cook 5 minutes, or until tender. Stir in garlic and cook 30 seconds. Add Marsala and bring to the boil over high heat. Stir in tomatoes with their juice, salt, pepper, rosemary, thyme and lamb. Bring to the boil, breaking up tomatoes with back of spoon. Reduce heat to low; cover and simmer 1 hour. Stir in remaining carrots; cover and cook 30–45 minutes longer, until lamb and carrots are tender. Skim and discard fat. Stir in peas; cover and cook 5 minutes longer.

**Each serving:** About 405 calories, 42g protein, 21g carbohydrate, 13g total fat (4g saturated), 122mg cholesterol, 710mg sodium

## LAMB AND VEGETABLE RAGOÛT

*Prep: 25 minutes    Cook: 80 minutes*
*Makes 4 main dish servings*

450g boneless lamb, cut into
   2–3cm pieces
1 tbsp vegetable oil
½ tsp salt
2 large celery stalks, chopped
1 large onion, chopped
400g canned tomatoes
400ml beef stock
750g potatoes

3 medium turnips (350g)
3 medium carrots, cut into
   2cm chunks
1 tbsp soy sauce
1 tsp sugar
2 tbsp plain flour
300g frozen peas
2 tbsp grated lemon rind

◆ Pat lamb dry with kitchen towels. Heat oil in 5-litre flameproof casserole over medium-high heat. Add lamb and salt; brown lamb all over. Using slotted spoon, transfer lamb to bowl. Add celery and onion to drippings in casserole; cook until lightly browned. Stir in lamb, tomatoes, beef stock and *225ml water*. Bring to the boil over high heat. Reduce heat to low; cover and simmer 25 minutes.

◆ Peel potatoes and turnips; cut into 4cm chunks. Stir into casserole with next 3 ingredients. Return to the boil over high heat. Reduce heat to low; cover and simmer 20 minutes longer, or until lamb and vegetables are tender.

◆ Mix flour and *2 tablespoons water* in small bowl; stir into ragoût. Cook, stirring, over medium-high heat until mixture thickens and boils. Skim and discard fat. Stir in peas; cook 5 minutes longer. To serve, sprinkle with lemon rind.

**Each serving:** About 525 calories, 40g protein, 67g carbohydrate, 12g total fat (4g saturated), 92mg cholesterol, 1360mg sodium

# LAMB CHOPS

Delicate rib chops and larger loin chops are luxury cuts, immensely satisfying to eat and easy to cook. Grilled with a fragrant rosemary and apple-jelly glaze or coated in a fiery mustard crust, pan-fried and served with a sweet walnut-fig sauce or a piquant pepper relish, they're a treat in any guise. More economical meaty shoulder chops offer plenty of flavour but, as they're less tender, they're more suitable for braising. Lamb freezes well, making it available all year round, so don't hesitate to choose frozen lamb if the cut you want is not available fresh.

1 Preheat grill. Rub both sides of each lamb chop with cut sides of garlic; discard garlic. Sprinkle lamb chops with rosemary, salt and black pepper. Mix redcurrant jelly and balsamic vinegar in small bowl until well combined.

## GLAZED ROSEMARY LAMB CHOPS

*Prep:* 10 minutes   *Grill:* 10 minutes
*Makes* 4 main dish servings

8 lamb loin chops, each 2–3cm thick (125g each)
1 large garlic clove, cut in half
2 tsp chopped fresh rosemary or ½ tsp dried, crushed
¼ tsp salt

¼ tsp coarsely ground black pepper
60g redcurrant jelly
1 tbsp balsamic vinegar
Rosemary sprigs for garnish
Italian green beans (optional)

2 Place chops on rack in grill pan. Place in grill at closest position to heat; grill chops 4 minutes. Brush chops with half of jelly mixture and grill 1 minute. Turn chops and grill 4 minutes longer.

3 Brush on remaining jelly mixture and grill 1 minute longer for medium-rare. Transfer to 4 plates; skim fat from drippings in pan. Garnish and serve with pan juices, and green beans, if you like.

### BALSAMIC VINEGAR

This distinctive vinegar, from the area around Modena, Italy, is made from white Trebbiano grape juice. Aged in wooden barrels for at least 10 years, balsamic vinegar has an intense, tangy-sweet flavour that is especially good in marinades and salad dressings. Strawberries, peaches and other fruits are also enhanced by a splash of balsamic vinegar.

EACH SERVING: ABOUT 350 CALORIES, 39g PROTEIN, 14g CARBOHYDRATE, 14g TOTAL FAT (5g SATURATED), 127mg CHOLESTEROL, 235mg SODIUM

## LAMB CHOPS WITH WALNUT-FIG SAUCE

*Prep:* 5 minutes    *Cook:* 25 minutes
*Makes* 4 main dish servings

4 lamb loin chops, each
   4cm thick (225g each)
1 tbsp vegetable oil
Salt

30g coarsely chopped walnuts
175ml apple juice
8 dried figs, each cut in half

◆ Pat lamb chops dry with kitchen towels. Heat oil in 26cm frying pan over medium-high heat; add lamb chops and cook about 5 minutes, until browned on both sides. Reduce heat to low; cover and cook 12–15 minutes longer for medium-rare, or until desired doneness, turning chops occasionally.

◆ Transfer lamb chops to warm platter. Sprinkle with ¼ teaspoon salt; keep warm. Pour off all drippings in pan. Add walnuts to pan and cook over low heat, stirring frequently, until lightly toasted.

◆ Add apple juice, figs and ¼ teaspoon salt to walnuts in pan. Bring to the boil over high heat. Cook 2–3 minutes, until liquid is slightly thickened. Pour walnut-fig sauce over lamb chops.

**Each serving: About 500 calories, 41g protein, 39g carbohydrate, 21g total fat (6g saturated), 127mg cholesterol, 370mg sodium**

### MINT JELLY

The fresh taste of mint makes it a perfect partner for lamb. Although mint sauce or mint jelly is traditionally served with roast leg of lamb, it works just as well with smaller cuts.

Mix 1 tablespoon cider vinegar and 1 teaspoon dried mint in small bowl; let stand 5 minutes. Meanwhile, melt 125g apple jelly in 1-litre saucepan over medium heat. Stir in mint mixture and bring to the boil. Strain mixture through sieve. Makes 125g.

Each tablespoon: About 50 calories, 0g protein, 13g carbohydrate, 0g total fat, 0mg cholesterol, 5mg sodium

## LAMB CHOPS WITH RED PEPPER RELISH

*Prep:* 30 minutes    *Grill:* 10 minutes
*Makes* 4 main dish servings

75ml cider vinegar
50g sugar
Pinch dried thyme
Pinch fennel seeds, crushed
Salt
1 medium Golden Delicious
   apple, peeled, cored and
   diced

2 small red peppers, cored,
   seeded and diced
2 jalapeño chillies, seeded
   and finely chopped
8 lamb loin chops, each
   2–3cm thick (125g each)

◆ Combine vinegar, sugar, thyme, fennel and 1 teaspoon salt in 2-litre saucepan; bring to the boil over high heat. Add apple, peppers and jalapeño chillies; bring to the boil.

◆ Reduce heat to medium-low; simmer, stirring occasionally, 15–20 minutes, until mixture is thickened and most of liquid has evaporated.

◆ Meanwhile, preheat grill. Sprinkle lamb chops with ¼ teaspoon salt. Place chops on rack in grill pan. Place pan in grill at closest position to heat; grill chops 5 minutes.

◆ Turn chops; grill 5 minutes longer for medium-rare, or until desired doneness. Serve with warm red pepper relish.

**Each serving: About 370 calories, 39g protein, 21g carbohydrate, 14g total fat (5g saturated), 127mg cholesterol, 970mg sodium**

## GRILLED LAMB CHOPS WITH MUSTARD-PARSLEY CRUST

*Prep:* 10 minutes    *Grill:* 8–9 minutes
*Makes* 4 main dish servings

8 lamb loin chops, each
   2–3cm thick (90g each)
2 tbsp dried breadcrumbs
2 tbsp Dijon mustard

2 tbsp chopped fresh parsley
2 tsp olive or vegetable oil
½ tsp salt

◆ Preheat grill. Place chops on rack in grill pan. Place pan in grill 10–12cm from heat; grill chops 5 minutes.

◆ Meanwhile, mix breadcrumbs, mustard, parsley, oil and salt in small bowl. Turn chops; spread breadcrumb mixture over meaty portion. Grill chops 3–4 minutes longer for medium-rare, or until desired doneness.

**Each serving: About 265 calories, 30g protein, 3g carbohydrate, 14g total fat (4g saturated), 97mg cholesterol, 570mg sodium**

# BARBECUED BUTTERFLIED LAMB

If you're having a special occasion barbecue, butterflied leg of lamb makes a spectacular meal that is easy to prepare. Ask the butcher to butterfly and bone a 1.8–2.2kg half-leg, to yield 1.3–1.5kg meat. The thickness of the piece will vary in places; slice off the thinner pieces as soon as they are done.

## BARBECUED PESTO LAMB

✦✦✦✦✦✦✦✦✦✦✦✦✦

*Prep:* 25 minutes
*Barbecue:* 15–25 minutes
*Makes* 10 main dish servings

**180g basil leaves**
**60g pine nuts**
**80g Parmesan cheese, freshly grated**
**3 tbsp olive oil**
**2 tbsp fresh lemon juice**
**¾ tsp salt**
**2 garlic cloves**
**1.3kg boneless butterflied leg of lamb (ask your butcher to do this)**
**Tomato-Cucumber Bruschetta (optional, see below)**
**Basil sprigs for garnish**

**1** Prepare barbecue. Prepare pesto: blend basil leaves and next 6 ingredients in food processor with knife blade attached or in blender. Place lamb in 33 by 20cm non-metallic dish; spread pesto on both sides of lamb.

**2** Place lamb on barbecue over medium heat; reserve any pesto. Cook, brushing with reserved pesto several times and turning occasionally, 15–25 minutes for medium-rare, or until desired doneness. Cut off sections as they are done.

**3** Transfer lamb to chopping board; let stand 10 minutes for easier carving. Meanwhile, prepare Tomato-Cucumber Bruschetta, if desired. Cut lamb into thin slices. Garnish and serve with bruschetta, if you like.

### TOMATO-CUCUMBER BRUSCHETTA

Mix 1 seeded and chopped medium tomato, 1 peeled and chopped medium cucumber, 1 tablespoon olive oil, 2 teaspoons fresh lemon juice and ¼ teaspoon ground black pepper in medium bowl. Cut one 225g loaf Italian bread diagonally into 1cm thick slices (reserve ends for another use). Toast slices on barbecue over medium heat, turning once. Spread slices with 4 tablespoons bottled tapenade; top with tomato mixture. Makes 10 servings.

Each serving: About 100 calories, 2g protein, 13g carbohydrate, 4g total fat (1g saturated), 0mg cholesterol, 180mg sodium

### PINE NUTS

The seed of a stone pine, pine nuts ('pignoli' in Italian) are a much-loved Mediterranean ingredient, used in stuffings for meat and vine leaves, pesto, vegetable sautés, and cakes and biscuits. Because pine nuts are high in fat, they turn rancid quickly. To prolong flavour, buy the freshest nuts and store them in the freezer.

EACH SERVING: ABOUT 255 CALORIES, 31g PROTEIN, 2g CARBOHYDRATE, 14g TOTAL FAT (4g SATURATED), 91mg CHOLESTEROL, 290mg SODIUM

## YOGURT-MARINATED BUTTERFLIED LEG OF LAMB

*Prep: 10 minutes, plus marinating*
*Barbecue: 15–25 minutes*
*Makes 10 main dish servings*

225g low-fat yogurt
15g fresh parsley, chopped
60ml fresh lemon juice
2½ tsp salt
2 tsp coarsely ground black pepper
2 garlic cloves, very finely chopped
1.3kg butterflied boneless leg of lamb
  (ask your butcher to do this)
Grilled peppers (optional)

◆ Mix first 6 ingredients in 33 by 20cm non-metallic dish. Add lamb, turning to coat with marinade. Cover dish with cling film and refrigerate, turning lamb occasionally, at least 3 hours.

◆ Prepare barbecue. Place lamb on grid over medium heat, reserving marinade in dish. Cook, brushing with reserved marinade and turning occasionally, 15–25 minutes for medium-rare, or until desired doneness.

◆ Transfer lamb to chopping board; let stand 10 minutes for easier carving. Cut into bite-sized chunks, and serve with grilled peppers, if you like.

**Each serving: About 200 calories, 30g protein, 3g carbohydrate, 7g total fat (3g saturated), 90mg cholesterol, 615mg sodium**

## BARBECUED LAMB WITH MINT AND OREGANO

*Prep: 25 minutes, plus marinating*
*Barbecue: 15–25 minutes*
*Makes 10 main dish servings*

1 large bunch fresh mint
1 large bunch fresh oregano
3 tbsp plus 60ml olive oil
3 tbsp plus 60ml fresh lemon juice
1 garlic clove, very finely chopped
Salt and ground black pepper
1.3kg butterflied boneless leg of lamb
  (ask your butcher to do this)

◆ Chop 15g mint and 15g oregano into 33 by 20cm non-metallic dish. Add 3 tablespoons each olive oil and lemon juice, garlic, 1 teaspoon salt and ½ teaspoon pepper in; stir until well blended.

◆ Add lamb to dish, turning to coat with marinade and spooning marinade over. Cover dish with cling film and refrigerate, turning lamb occasionally, at least 8 hours, or overnight.

◆ Prepare barbecue. Prepare sauce: chop remaining mint and oregano (about 2 tablespoons of each); stir into small bowl with remaining ¼ cup each olive oil and lemon juice, ½ teaspoon salt and ¼ teaspoon pepper.

◆ Place lamb on barbecue over medium heat, discarding marinade in dish. Cook, turning lamb occasionally, 15–25 minutes for medium-rare, or until desired doneness.

◆ Transfer lamb to chopping board; let stand 10 minutes for easier carving. Cut lamb into thin slices and arrange on large platter. Spoon herb sauce on top of lamb; garnish with any remaining herbs.

**Each serving: About 275 calories, 29g protein, 2g carbohydrate, 16g total fat (4g saturated), 88mg cholesterol, 390mg sodium**

## LEG OF LAMB WITH COCONUT COUSCOUS

*Prep: 10 minutes    Barbecue: 15–25 minutes*
*Makes 10 main dish servings*

240g couscous
150g currants or raisins
50g desiccated coconut, toasted
1 tbsp dried rosemary, crushed
1 tbsp olive or vegetable oil
2 tsp salt
1 tsp coarsely ground black pepper
1 garlic clove, very finely chopped
1.3kg butterflied boneless leg of lamb
  (ask your butcher to do this)
Parsley sprigs for garnish
75g Kalamata olives, stoned, or other
  stoned black olives

◆ Prepare barbecue. Prepare couscous as label instructs; stir in currants and toasted coconut. Keep warm.

◆ Mix rosemary, oil, salt, pepper and garlic in small bowl; rub over lamb. Place lamb on barbecue over medium heat. Cook turning lamb occasionally, 15–25 minutes for medium-rare, or until desired doneness.

◆ Transfer lamb to chopping board; let stand 10 minutes for easier carving. Cut lamb into thin slices; arrange on large platter with couscous. Tuck parsley sprigs in between lamb slices. Scatter olives over top.

**Each serving: About 420 calories, 34g protein, 43g carbohydrate, 12g total fat (4g saturated), 88mg cholesterol, 630mg sodium**

### TOASTING COCONUT

Toasted coconut has a sweet, nutty taste and an appealing crunchy texture. To toast coconut, preheat the oven to 180°C (350°F, Gas 4). Spread coconut in a single layer in a shallow pan. Bake for about 10 minutes or until coconut is lightly toasted, stirring occasionally so it browns evenly. Cool slightly before using.

# Barbecued Lamb Cuts

Small cuts of lamb such as chops and steaks or cubes threaded on skewers cook beautifully on the barbecue. The meat can be marinated to absorb the flavours of herbs and spices, then cooked alongside colourful vegetables such as courgettes, tomatoes and onions. A simple salad makes the perfect accompaniment.

1 Bring shallots with *water* to cover to the boil in 3-litre saucepan over high heat. Reduce heat to low; cover and simmer 5 minutes. Drain shallots and peel.

2 Mix lemon juice, rosemary, oil, salt and pepper together in medium non-metallic bowl. Add lamb, courgettes, and shallots; toss to coat. Cover; refrigerate, tossing occasionally, 2 hours.

3 Prepare barbecue. Prepare Greek salad, but do not toss with dressing. Thread lamb, courgettes and shallots. Cook kebabs over medium heat, turning occasionally, 8–10 minutes for medium-rare.

## LAMB KEBABS WITH GREEK SALAD

❖❖❖❖❖❖❖❖❖❖❖❖

*Prep:* 30 minutes, plus marinating
*Barbecue:* 8–10 minutes
*Makes* 4 main dish servings

12–16 large unpeeled shallots
3 tbsp fresh lemon juice
1 tbsp chopped fresh rosemary or 1 tsp dried, crushed
2 tbsp olive oil
1 tsp salt
1 tsp coarsely ground black pepper
750g lamb cubes for kebabs, about 4cm each
2 small courgettes (350g), cut into 2–3cm thick slices
Greek Salad (see above right)
4 (25cm) metal skewers
Rosemary sprigs for garnish

### GREEK SALAD

Toss 1 small head Cos lettuce, cut into 5cm pieces, 2 small tomatoes cut into 2–3cm chunks, 1 small cucumber, cut into 5mm thick slices, 75g stoned Kalamata olives, and ½ diced small red onion in a bowl. Prepare dressing: mix 2 tablespoons red wine vinegar, 1 tablespoon olive oil, ½ teaspoon dried oregano and ½ teaspoon each salt and ground black pepper in small bowl. Chill salad and dressing separately. Just before serving, toss salad with dressing. Makes 4 servings.

Each serving: About 110 calories, 2g protein, 9g carbohydrate, 8g total fat (1g saturated), 0mg cholesterol, 580mg sodium

4 Arrange lamb kebabs on large platter. Garnish with rosemary sprigs. Toss Greek salad gently with dressing and serve with kebabs.

EACH SERVING (KEBABS ONLY): ABOUT 390 CALORIES, 45g PROTEIN, 11g CARBOHYDRATE, 18g TOTAL FAT (5g SATURATED), 137mg CHOLESTEROL, 630mg SODIUM

## MARINATED LAMB CHOPS WITH CHAR-GRILLED TOMATOES

*Prep: 15 minutes, plus marinating   Barbecue: 8–10 minutes*
*Makes 4 main dish servings*

2 garlic cloves, very finely chopped
60ml red wine vinegar
2 tsp dried rosemary, crushed
1¼ tsp salt
Coarsely ground black pepper
8 lamb loin chops, each 2–3cm thick (90g each)

2 large tomatoes, each cut horizontally in half
1 tbsp olive or vegetable oil
30g Parmesan cheese, freshly grated
1 tbsp chopped fresh parsley

◆ Prepare barbecue. Mix first 4 ingredients and ½ teaspoon pepper in 33 by 20cm non-metallic dish. Arrange lamb chops in single layer in dish, turning to coat with marinade. Let lamb chops stand, turning occasionally, 15 minutes.

◆ Place lamb chops on barbecue over medium heat, reserving marinade in dish. Brush tomatoes with oil; place tomatoes, cut-side down, on barbeque with chops. Cook 8–10 minutes for medium-rare, or until desired doneness, turning chops and tomatoes once, and brushing chops with reserved marinade halfway through cooking time. To serve, sprinkle tomato halves with Parmesan cheese, chopped parsley, and ¼ teaspoon pepper. Serve with chops.

**Each serving: About 300 calories, 29g protein, 6g carbohydrate, 18g total fat (6g saturated), 91mg cholesterol, 815mg sodium**

## OREGANO LAMB STEAK

*Prep: 15 minutes, plus marinating and standing   Barbecue: 8–10 minutes*
*Makes 4 main dish servings*

2 tbsp chopped fresh oregano or 1 tsp dried
1 tbsp red wine vinegar
1 garlic clove, very finely chopped
1 tsp grated orange rind
¼ tsp ground black pepper
1 tbsp plus 1 tsp olive oil
Salt

1 lamb steak, 2–3cm thick (450g)
2 small red onions, cut crossways into 1cm thick slices
4 plum tomatoes, each cut lengthways in half
4 pitta breads (15cm)

◆ Combine oregano, vinegar, garlic, orange rind, pepper, 1 tablespoon olive oil and ½ teaspoon salt in shallow non-metallic dish. Add lamb, turning to coat with marinade. Cover and refrigerate at least 4 hours, or overnight.

◆ Prepare barbecue. Secure red onion slices with cocktail sticks to hold rings in place. Drizzle onions with remaining 1 teaspoon olive oil in medium bowl and toss gently to coat. Place lamb and onions on barbecue over medium heat. Cook 10–12 minutes for medium, or until desired doneness,

turning lamb and onions once. Meanwhile, sprinkle tomatoes lightly with salt, place cut-side down on barbeque, and cook, turning once, 5 minutes. Grill pitta breads 30–60 seconds on each side, until lightly toasted. Transfer lamb, vegetables and pitta breads to platter. Let lamb stand 10 minutes; keep warm. To serve, thinly slice lamb; cut each pitta crosswise in half.

**Each serving: About 505 calories, 26g protein, 42g carbohydrate 26g total fat (9g saturated), 80mg cholesterol, 985mg sodium**

## BARBECUED LAMB STEAK WITH SPICE CRUST

*Prep: 5 minutes, plus standing   Barbecue: 8–10 minutes*
*Makes 4 main dish servings*

1 tsp coriander seeds
1 tsp cumin seeds
1 tsp fennel seeds
½ tsp salt

½ tsp black peppercorns
1 lamb steak, 2–3cm thick (450g)

◆ Prepare barbecue. Heat coriander, cumin and fennel seeds in 1-litre saucepan over medium-low heat, shaking pan occasionally, 1–2 minutes, until very fragrant. Transfer to mortar with salt and peppercorns; coarsely crush spices. Or, place in heavy-duty plastic bag; crush with rolling pin.

◆ Pat lamb dry with kitchen towels. Press crushed spice mixture all over lamb. Place lamb on barbecue over medium heat. Cook 8–10 minutes, turning once, for medium, or until desired doneness. Transfer lamb to platter. Let stand 10 minutes; keep warm. To serve, thinly slice lamb.

**Each serving: About 265 calories, 19g protein, 1g carbohydrate, 20g total fat (9g saturated), 80mg cholesterol, 320mg sodium**

❖❖❖❖❖❖❖❖❖❖❖❖❖❖❖❖❖❖❖❖❖❖❖

### MARINATING HINTS

When marinades contain acidic ingredients, such as vinegar, wine or citrus juice, marinate food in non-metallic containers such as glass and ceramic (stainless steel is also suitable as it is a non-reactive metal). Heavy-duty plastic bags also work well. Aluminium can react with the acid and create an  unpleasant metallic taste. Foods can be marinated up to 30 minutes at room temperature. If longer marinating is called for, keep the food refrigerated.

❖❖❖❖❖❖❖❖❖❖❖❖❖❖❖❖❖❖❖❖❖❖❖

# MINCED LAMB

Minced lamb is great for classic dishes, from spicy Middle-Eastern style meatballs and a delectable casserole with aubergine, to shepherd's pie.

## AUBERGINE AND LAMB CASSEROLE

❖❖❖❖❖❖❖❖❖❖❖

*Prep:* 55 minutes
*Bake:* 35–40 minutes
*Makes* 10 main dish servings

2 small aubergines (600g each), cut lengthways into 1cm thick slices
5 tbsp olive oil
900g ground lamb
1 large onion, chopped
2 garlic cloves, very finely chopped
1 tsp ground cumin
½ tsp ground cinnamon
Salt and coarsely ground black pepper
800g canned tomatoes
2 tbsp tomato purée
50g plain flour
675ml milk
4 medium eggs, lightly beaten
¼ tsp ground nutmeg
Crusty bread (optional)

1 Preheat oven to 230°C (450°F, Gas 8). Place aubergine on 2 greased baking sheets. Use 3 tablespoons oil to brush both sides. Bake 20 minutes, or until soft, switching position of sheets between racks after 10 minutes. Remove from oven; turn oven control to 190°C (375°F, Gas 5).

2 Heat 1 tablespoon oil in deep 30cm frying pan over medium-high heat; add lamb, onion and garlic and cook 15 minutes, or until all are browned.

3 Stir in cumin, cinnamon, 1 teaspoon salt, and ¼ teaspoon pepper; cook 1 minute. Remove pan from heat; add tomatoes and tomato purée, breaking up tomatoes with back of spoon.

4 Heat 1 tablespoon oil in 3-litre saucepan over medium heat; add flour and cook 1 minute. Gradually whisk in milk; cook about 15 minutes until thick. Remove from heat.

5 Gradually whisk small amount of hot milk mixture into eggs. Return egg mixture to pan, whisking. Whisk in nutmeg, ½ teaspoon salt and ¼ teaspoon pepper.

6 Arrange half of aubergine slices, overlapping slices to fit if necessary in shallow 3½–4-litre ovenproof casserole or baking dish; top with half of lamb mixture. Repeat with remaining aubergine slices and lamb mixture; pour milk mixture evenly over top. Bake 35–40 minutes, until top is puffed and golden and casserole is heated through. Serve with crusty bread, if you like.

EACH SERVING: ABOUT 400 CALORIES, 24g PROTEIN, 20g CARBOHYDRATE, 25g TOTAL FAT (9g SATURATED), 160mg CHOLESTEROL, 700mg SODIUM

## SHEPHERD'S PIE

*Prep: 40 minutes    Bake: 20 minutes*
*Makes 4 main dish servings*

900g potatoes, peeled and cut
   into 4cm chunks
Salt
125ml milk
45g butter or margarine
5 tbsp freshly grated
   Parmesan cheese
Ground black pepper
1 medium onion, chopped

2 carrots, finely chopped
450g minced lamb
2 tbsp tomato purée
2 tbsp plain flour
60ml dry red wine
225ml chicken stock
¼ tsp dried thyme
150g frozen peas

◆ Preheat oven to 220°C (425°F, Gas 7). Bring potatoes with ¼ teaspoon salt and *water* to cover to the boil in 4-litre saucepan over high heat. Reduce heat to low; cover and simmer 20 minutes, or until potatoes are tender. Drain and return to pan. Using potato masher, mash potatoes with milk and 30g butter. Stir in 30g Parmesan cheese and ¼ teaspoon pepper.

◆ Meanwhile, melt remaining 1 tablespoon butter in 26cm frying pan over medium heat. Add onion and carrots; cook until tender. Add lamb and cook over medium-high heat, breaking it up with spoon, until no longer pink.

◆ Add tomato purée; cook, stirring, 1 minute. Add flour and cook, stirring, 1 minute. Stir in wine; cook until evaporated. Add stock, thyme, ¼ teaspoon salt and ⅛ teaspoon black pepper; stir until brown bits are loosened. Bring to the boil. Stir in peas.

◆ Spoon lamb mixture into 24cm deep-dish pie plate; spoon potatoes evenly on top. Sprinkle with remaining 1 tablespoon Parmesan. Bake on baking sheet 20 minutes, or until browned.

**Each serving: About 650 calories, 34g protein, 61g carbohydrate, 30g total fat (13g saturated), 121mg cholesterol, 745mg sodium**

## TURKISH MEATBALLS

*Prep: 15 minutes    Cook: 8–10 minutes*
*Makes 4 main dish servings*

1 slice firm white bread
450g minced lamb
1 medium egg
15g fresh parsley, chopped
1 small garlic clove, very
   finely chopped

Pinch ground red pepper
½ tsp ground cumin
½ tsp salt
2 tbsp plain flour
1 tbsp vegetable oil

◆ In blender or food processor with knife blade attached, process bread to fine crumbs. Mix breadcrumbs with lamb and next 6 ingredients in large bowl until combined. Shape mixture into 4cm meatballs.

◆ Roll meatballs in flour on greaseproof paper to coat evenly. Heat oil in 30cm frying pan over medium-high heat. Add meatballs and cook, turning occasionally, 8–10 minutes, until just cooked through. Transfer to paper towels to drain.

**Each serving: About 320 calories, 24g protein, 7g carbohydrate, 22g total fat (8g saturated), 135mg cholesterol, 390mg sodium**

## LAMB IN PITTAS WITH YOGURT SAUCE

*Prep: 20 minutes    Cook: 30 minutes*
*Makes 6 main dish servings*

2 tbsp vegetable oil
2 medium onions, chopped
750g minced lamb
1 medium aubergine (600g),
   diced
350ml tomato juice
½ tsp coarsely ground black
   pepper
Salt

1 small cucumber, seeded and
   diced
225g low-fat yogurt
1 tbsp chopped fresh dill or
   ¼ tsp dried
1 bunch watercress
3 wholemeal pittas (15cm),
   each cut in half

◆ Heat 1 tablespoon oil in 30cm frying pan over medium-high heat. Add onions; cook 5 minutes. Add minced lamb, breaking it up with spoon; cook until browned and juices have evaporated.

◆ Add aubergine and remaining 1 tablespoon oil; cook until aubergine is tender. Stir in tomato juice, pepper and 1 teaspoon salt; heat through. Meanwhile, prepare yogurt sauce: mix cucumber, yogurt, dill, and ¼ teaspoon salt together in small bowl.

◆ Divide half of watercress among 6 plates. Tuck remaining watercress into pitta halves. Spoon lamb mixture into pittas. Arrange filled pittas on plates with watercress. To serve, spoon yogurt sauce over filling in pittas.

**Each serving: About 410 calories, 25g protein, 34g carbohydrate, 20g total fat (7g saturated), 70mg cholesterol, 930mg sodium**

# Vegetables

8

# VEGETABLES KNOW-HOW

Packed with fibre, vitamins and minerals, vegetables are vital for a balanced diet. With hundreds of varieties to choose from, and many ways to prepare them, there is a vegetable suited to everyone's taste. Supermarkets offer a large range and are introducing us to new and exotic vegetables all the time, while farm shops offer local produce, picked at it's peak. Their tomatoes, potatoes and beans are generally more full of flavour than the mass-produced equivalent. If you have a garden, grow your own for the ultimate in freshness.

## BUYING AND STORING

As a rule, buy vegetables in season and you will get them at their peak of flavour and freshness and prices will be lower, too. In general, choose firm, brightly coloured vegetables without blemishes or wilted leaves. Smaller vegetables tend to be sweeter and more tender. Avoid buying vegetables in packets if you can, because the quality is harder to check.

Most vegetables stay freshest if they are stored in the coldest part of the refrigerator – usually the bottom shelf or the salad drawer – in loosely sealed paper or plastic bags. Don't make the wrapping airtight, because condensation can form on the surface and speed deterioration. Store potatoes, onions, garlic and winter squash in a cool, dark, well-ventilated place. For most vegetables, the sooner you use them, the more flavourful and nutritious they will be.

## PREPARATION

• Shake or brush off loose dirt before washing, then use a soft vegetable brush for scrubbing. Rinse in lukewarm water to remove sand and grit from leafy vegetables and courgettes.
• Wash vegetables just before you use them.
• Peel off only a thin layer of skin, or don't peel at all, to cut the loss of vitamins, minerals and fibre.
• Vegetables such as artichokes and celeriac discolour quickly when cut. To reduce discoloration, use a stainless steel knife and rub the cut portions with a lemon half. Or, immediately place prepared vegetables in a bowl of acidulated water (combine 1 litre water with 3 tablespoons lemon juice).
• To revive limp cut vegetables or slightly wilted greens, soak them in iced water for about 15 minutes. Avoid soaking vegetables in water for longer than necessary, as it leaches out nutrients and creates waterlogged vegetables.

## COOKING SUCCESS

• Most vegetables should be cooked as briefly as possible to retain the best colour, texture and flavour. Unless the recipe directs otherwise, cook in the minimum amount of lightly salted water so you don't drain away nutrients.
• Most vegetables can be cooked in the microwave. The short cooking time means that they retain their colour and texture, as well as more of their nutrients.
• If you are cooking vegetables to serve cold or re-heat later, after steaming or boiling, drain and then immediately rinse under cold running water to halt the cooking.
• Don't discard vegetable cooking water; it's full of nutrients. Save to use in sauces, soups, stocks and gravies.

## THE RIGHT CUT

A sharp knife is essential for cutting vegetables. For speedy slicing, you can use an adjustable-blade slicer (see page 297) or a food processor.

Cut vegetables into same-sized pieces for even cooking and a more attractive finished dish.

Dice – small, even cubes

Julienne – fine strips the size of a matchstick

Chop – small, irregular-shaped pieces

### ORGANIC VEGETABLES

Concern about chemicals in food has led to the wider availability of organic produce. Produced without the use of chemical fertilizers and pesticides, these vegetables are not only healthier, but can have more flavour as well. Since production is labour-intensive and yields relatively low, organic vegetables are more expensive than their supermarket counterparts. At present there are no consistent government regulations guiding the standards of growers. If in doubt, ask what voluntary standards are being met – a reputable supplier will be happy to answer your questions.

# CABBAGE FAMILY

**Broccoli and sprouting broccoli** Choose broccoli with firm, tightly closed buds (either dark green or purplish green) and no sign of yellowing or flowering. The stems should be firm; if they seem tough, peel away the outer layer with a vegetable peeler. Sprouting broccoli has leafy stalks with clusters of tiny broccoli-like buds; the flavour is pleasantly bitter. Look for sturdy stalks and fresh, dark-green leaves.

**Brussels sprouts** Buy bright green, firm, tight heads. Small are best; large sprouts can be bitter. If boiling or steaming, cut an X in the base of each sprout first for even cooking.

**Cauliflower** When buying cauliflower, choose firm heads that feel heavy for their size. Check that florets are tightly packed and unblemished; leaves should look fresh and green. The size of the head has no bearing on quality.

**Chinese cabbage** Resembling lettuce more than cabbage, Chinese cabbage has an elongated shape and pale green leaves that curl at the tips – look for crisp, firm leaves and a freshly cut stalk end. Bok choy has wide white or pale green stalks gathered in a loose head flowing to large green leaves. Choose bok choy with crisp, firm, stalks and moist, deep green leaves.

**Head cabbage (green, red, Savoy)** Of these cabbages, Savoy has the most mellow flavour. Buy heads that feel heavy for their size with fresh, unwilted leaves free of browning. Although you will probably discard the outer leaves, they protect the centre, so choose heads with some still attached.

Baby bok choy

Kohlrabi

Cauliflower

Red cabbage

Chinese cabbage

Savoy cabbage

Green cabbage

**Kohlrabi** This pale green or purple bulb has leafy shoots at the top; the bulb tastes like turnip, while the leaves have a spinach flavour. Choose small, heavy bulbs with dark green leaves; larger bulbs can be woody. Always peel before using.

# LEAFY GREENS

Vitamin-rich leafy greens can be young and tender and eaten raw, or mature and strong flavoured and better cooked. Greens cook down a lot; 450g yields only 125g cooked. Look for crisp, unblemished, brightly coloured greens; small leaves with thin stems are the most tender. To store, wash greens in several changes of water and pat dry with kitchen towels. Line a plastic bag with a damp kitchen towel, loosely fill with greens and use within 3 days.
• Mild-flavoured greens include spinach, lettuce and Swiss chard, with stalks that taste like celery and leaves that taste like spinach. Spinach is great in salads; chard is best cooked.
• For a moderately strong flavour, choose spring greens, chicory and batavia (curly lettuce).
• Pungent greens include curly endive, kale, dandelion greens, mustard greens and turnip greens. Except when very young and tender, these greens are bitter raw, but are delicious sautéed with garlic and olive oil, or added (at the end of cooking time) to soups and stews.

# ARTICHOKES, ASPARAGUS, CELERY AND FENNEL

**Artichokes** Choose globe artichokes that feel heavy for their size, with compact heads and tightly closed green leaves. Heavily browned artichokes are old, but a little brown at the ends of the leaves is fine. For baby artichokes, look for compact heads with soft leaves and soft stalks.

**Asparagus** Look for brightly coloured, firm spears with tight buds; choose even-sized spears for uniform cooking. White asparagus is more expensive. Peeling is optional; if you do peel, remove only the tough peel at the stem end. You can also remove the scales with a small knife, if you prefer. To store, trim ends and stand spears upright, loosely covered, in a tall glass with 2–3cm of water in the bottom.

**Celery** A head of celery should look moist and crisp. Look for tight, compact heads with unblemished stalks and fresh leaves. In general, a darker colour indicates a stronger taste. If you like, use a vegetable peeler to remove the outer strings.

**Fennel** All parts of fennel are edible, from the bulb to the celery-like stalks and feathery leaves (add to salads or use as a garnish). Fennel can be eaten raw (slice it thin and add to salads or crudités platters) or cooked. Slow-cooking fennel by roasting or braising brings out its sweetness and tames the liquorice flavour. Look for compact, uncracked, whitish-green bulbs free of discoloration; the leaves should look fresh and green. Bulbs that are spreading at the top indicate an older, tougher vegetable.

| Carrots | Swede | Celeriac |

## BEANS, CORN, OKRA AND PEAS

**Beans** The beans with edible pods include green beans, yellow wax beans, runner beans and haricots verts, a slender French variety (see page 292). Beans should have a good colour and firm, unblemished pods that snap crisply when bent (though haricots verts tend to be less crisp).

**Corn on the cob** Always cook corn soon after purchase, before the natural sugars turn to starch and reduce sweetness. Look for green, healthy husks that fit the cob tightly. The silk should be moist and fresh-looking – dry silk indicates old corn. Kernels should be plump and milky and grow in tight rows right to the tip. Avoid corn that's sold husked as it deteriorates faster – shuck just before cooking.

**Okra** Buy small, bright green pods that are firm, not limp. Avoid large pods, which can be fibrous or tough. Okra becomes slippery when cooked and acts as a thickener for sauced dishes. Don't cook okra in a cast-iron or aluminum pot – these metals can cause okra to discolour.

**Edible-pod peas** These crisp treats are eaten pod and all. Mange-tout have flat, almost translucent pods, while sugar snap peas have plumper, rounder pods. For either variety, look for firm, crisp pods with a good green colour. Sugar snaps should be plump but not bursting at the seam.

**Peas** Choose fresh peas with plump, firm, bright green pods. The sugars in peas turn to starch soon after picking, so buy and cook as fresh as possible. Shell just before using. 450g of peas in the pod yields about 2 servings shelled peas.

## ROOT VEGETABLES

**Beetroot** Loved for its sweetness, beetroot has the highest sugar content of any vegetable and is very low in calories. Choose firm, unblemished, small to medium-sized beetroots. If possible, buy bunches with the green tops on, which can be cooked like spinach. The leaves should look fresh and healthy.

**Carrots and parsnips** Buy firm, smooth, slender roots without cracks or blemishes. Small parsnips have the sweetest flavour; large parsnips may have a woody centre. Baby carrots look great on a plate, but mature, dark orange carrots actually have the sweetest taste and most vitamins.

**Celeriac** This aromatic knobbly root tastes like a cross between celery and parsley. Small, firm roots have the best texture; for easy peeling, look for a minimum

Turnips

Beetroot

Parsnips

of rootlets and knobs. Celeriac can be grated and dressed for salad; it's also delicious cooked in soups or purées.

**Radish** Look for smooth radishes that feel firm, not spongy. They vary in colour (from white through red and purple to black), shape (round, oval, elongated), and flavour (from hot to mild).

**Swede** Choose firm, heavy swedes with smooth skin. When cooked, their yellow flesh takes on a creamy texture.

**Jerusalem artichokes** Look for small, firm roots free of soft or green-tinged spots (see page 296).

**Turnips** Buy small turnips that feel heavy for their size, with smooth, unbruised skins. Large turnips can be woody.

## POTATOES

Potatoes vary in their starch content, which affects the texture of the finished dish. Baking potatoes have a fluffy, mealy texture that makes them good for frying and baking but means that they may fall apart a little when boiled. Waxy potatoes such as Desirée, King Edward and Maris Piper have less starch and hold their shape when cooked, whatever the method. They are ideal for boiling and salads. Tiny new potatoes are perfect steamed whole, while yellow-fleshed potatoes have a creamy texture ideal for making mashed potatoes.

Sweet potatoes can be yellow or orange. The yellow-fleshed variety is drier and less sweet than the orange-fleshed sweet potato.

Whatever the variety, choose dry, smooth potatoes without sprouts. Reject potatoes with a greenish cast, the result of prolonged exposure to light, because they'll taste bitter. Store potatoes in a cool, dark, well-ventilated place – not the refrigerator. Older potatoes will keep for about 2 weeks; new and sweet potatoes will keep for about a week.

Peeling or not is a matter of choice, but do cut off any green areas or sprouts.

Sweet potato

Desirée

Baking potato

Maris Piper

# ONION FAMILY

These vegetables range from 'dry' ones with papery outer skins, such as onions and garlic, to 'green' varieties that have a bulb at one end, such as spring onions. Dry onions are categorized either as storage onions, which are firm, compact, available year-round, and strongly flavoured (freeze for 20 minutes before chopping for fewer tears), or sweet onions, like Spanish and large mild types. Sweet onions, ripe in spring and summer, have a higher water and sugar content and are more fragile. Of all the onion family, leeks alone need thorough cleaning: slit lengthwise from top to bottom and rinse well, fanning the leaves to remove all grit.

Choose dry onions that feel heavy for their size with dry, papery skins. Avoid any with sprouts or soft spots. Spring onions should have clean white bulbs and fresh-looking tops. Store dry onions, preferably in a single layer, in a cool, dry, dark, airy place. Refrigerate spring onions up to 2 weeks. (For more information on garlic, see page 351.)

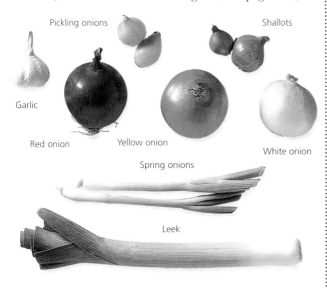

Pickling onions

Shallots

Garlic

Red onion

Yellow onion

White onion

Spring onions

Leek

# SQUASH

Squash are divided into two groups, summer and winter, but most are available year-round. Summer squash have tender flesh and seeds and soft edible skins. Winter squash have hard, thick skins and seeds and firm flesh. When buying summer squash, choose ones that feel firm. Winter squash should have hard, blemish-free skin. For both types, look for dry, well-shaped squash with good colour; a squash should feel heavy for its size. Store summer squash in the refrigerator and winter squash in a cool, dry place.

## SUMMER SQUASH

**Pattypan** This small, bowl-shaped squash has a scalloped edge; it can be white, yellow or pale green. The sculptural shape of this quick-cooking squash makes it perfect for grilling or, if large, for stuffing.

**Courgettes** In addition to the regular green courgettes, there are yellow and grey ones – all can be eaten raw or cooked. Younger varieties tend to have the sweetest flavour.
**Marrow** These are courgettes which have been left on the vine to grow large. They should be firm, heavy and longer than 30cm. This versatile vegetable can be steamed, boiled, stuffed or baked au gratin.

## WINTER SQUASH
**Acorn** This round, deeply ridged squash has a dark green skin, sometimes with an orange blotch, and a sweet orange flesh. There is also an orange-skinned variety. It is often stuffed with savoury fillings or simply sliced and baked.
**Butternut** With one end shaped like a bulb, this large tan squash has deep orange flesh that is moist and sweet. It is used in soups and pies as well as served on its own – peel off the skin before cooking.
**Chayote** Also called christophine, this pear-shaped, pale green squash has a large centre seed and a slight apple taste. Although it is a winter squash, prepare it as you would courgettes. Look for small, firm chayotes.
**Pumpkin** Large, round pumpkins have stringy flesh, which should be strained after cooking; smaller pumpkins, with more flesh and fewer fibres, make better eating. Cut in half or into wedges, remove the seeds, and bake as you would other squash. Buy blemish-free, heavy pumpkins.
**Spaghetti** This watermelon-shaped squash has yellow-gold flesh that separates into spaghetti-like strands when cooked. Look for pale yellow skin; greenish skin indicates that the squash is under-ripe.

Yellow courgettes

Acorn squash

Pattypan squash

Baby pumpkin

Spaghetti squash

## MUSHROOMS

Fresh or dried, mushrooms come in great variety (see page 305). Buy plump, firm, unblemished fresh mushrooms with an even colour. To store, refrigerate mushrooms in a loosely closed paper bag (so they can breathe), loosely covered with a damp kitchen towel. Avoid storing in plastic bags – they'll become too moist, acquire a slimy texture, and deteriorate faster. Clean mushrooms just before using with a soft brush or wipe of a damp cloth. Never subject mushrooms to a long rinsing or soak them in water – they will absorb water and become soggy. Don't peel mushrooms; much of their flavour is concentrated in the skin so you'll peel away their flavour. Mix and match any of the following varieties of mushrooms for a dish with a rich depth of taste.

**White (button)** This common cultivated mushroom can also be cream or brown-coloured. White mushrooms have a mild flavour, with caps that range in diameter from 5mm to 7cm.

**Flat** A dark brown mushroom measuring as much as 15cm in diameter. They have open caps with exposed gills and are prized for their rich flavour and meaty texture. The woody stalks can be used in stocks.

**Chestnut** A brown, full-flavoured variety of the white (button) mushroom.

**Shiitake** A brown Oriental mushroom with a flat cap and a rich, meaty flavour. The stalks are usually too tough to eat.

**Oyster** A delicate-tasting Oriental variety with a soft cream or grey colour, large, ruffled cap and a short, fat stalk.

**Morel** A golden-brown mushroom with a honeycombed, elongated cap and unusual spongy texture. Morels are available in speciality food stores; they have a hearty, woody flavour and tender texture when cooked.

**Porcini** Also called cèpes, these delicious mushrooms are pale brown and range in weight from 30–450g. They have a meaty texture and strong, earthy flavour. Choose porcini with firm, large caps and pale undersides.

**Chanterelle** A trumpet-shaped mushroom that ranges in colour from bright yellow to orange. Chanterelles have a delicate, nutty flavour and chewy texture. When buying, avoid any with broken or shrivelled caps. They should be cooked gently and briefly.

## AUBERGINE

This vegetable comes in many guises – including the coomon pear-shaped Western aubergine; small baby (Italian) or long, slender Japanese aubergine; and elegant creamy-white varieties (see page 308). Choose aubergines that feel heavy for their size with smooth, glossy, taut skins free of soft or brown spots. Avoid hard aubergines, which are under-ripe. Unlike many vegetables, aubergine will not suffer if it's overcooked – it will simply have a softer texture. Peeling is optional; the skin is edible and adds a beautiful colour to dishes.

## PEPPERS AND CHILLIES

Although peppers are classed as fruits, sweet peppers are used as a vegetable, while chillies, the hot variety of peppers, are used as a seasoning. As sweet peppers ripen they become even sweeter. Red peppers are simply green peppers that have been left on the vine to ripen. The sweetest pepper is the pimiento, which is sold tinned or bottled.

Chillies vary widely in flavour, from mild to burning. As a broad rule, the smaller the chilli, the hotter it is. Tiny Thai chillies, habaneros and Scotch bonnets are searingly hot; jalapeños and serranos are a bit less so. Capsaicin is the compound that gives chillies their heat, and most of the capsaicin is in the seeds and veins. To tame the fire, remove the seeds and veins, but take care – the oils released can irritate the skin. If you have sensitive skin, wear rubber gloves when preparing chillies, and wash your hands well when you have finished.

Choose sweet peppers and chillies with a good bright colour for their variety and firm, smooth skins. Reject shrivelled, blemished, or bruised peppers. Chillies are also sold dried; soak them in hot water for about 30 minutes before using.

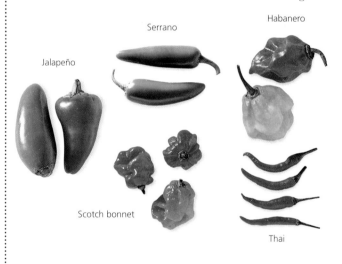

Jalapeño

Serrano

Habanero

Scotch bonnet

Thai

## TOMATOES

Tomatoes, in their many forms (see page 312), vary in sweetness and acidity. Cherry tomatoes, red or yellow, are reliably sweet all year round. Yellow tomatoes are lower in acid than red varieties. Plum tomatoes have thick, meaty walls and are ideal for cooked sauces.

Select firm (but not hard), heavy tomatoes with deeply coloured, unblemished skins. Don't store tomatoes in the refrigerator because cold kills their flavour; the only time to refrigerate a tomato is when it's over-ripe. Otherwise, store them at room temperature out of direct sunlight where they can turn soft. Unripe tomatoes can be placed in a paper bag with an apple to speed ripening.

Canned tomatoes are preferable to fresh in cooking when good quality fresh tomatoes are unavailable.

# CABBAGE FAMILY

The cabbage family includes green, red, Savoy and Chinese varieties, plus broccoli, Brussels sprouts, and cauliflower. A lesser-known member is kohlrabi, which resembles a knobby pale green beetroot and is a cross between cabbage and turnip. Best known for being nutritious and economical, these underrated vegetables are tasty both raw in salads or cooked. The freshest vegetables have the mildest, most delicate flavour. Red cabbage is sweeter than green, ideal for pickling or sautéing with apples or sultanas. Its sturdy structure demands a slightly longer cooking time than for green.

## VEGETARIAN STUFFED CABBAGE

*Prep: 50 minutes    Cook: 1 hour*
*Makes 4 main dish servings*

| | |
|---|---|
| 1 large head Savoy cabbage (750–850g), tough outer leaves discarded | 1 garlic clove, very finely chopped |
| 2 tbsp vegetable oil | 1 tbsp very finely chopped peeled fresh ginger |
| 1 red pepper, cored, seeded and finely chopped | 50g long-grain rice, cooked as packet instructs |
| 1 yellow pepper, cored, seeded and finely chopped | 200g canned cannellini beans, rinsed and drained |
| 1 medium onion, finely chopped | 100g canned water chestnuts, drained and finely chopped |
| 1 tbsp rice vinegar | 400g canned tomatoes |
| 1 tbsp soy sauce | French bread (optional) |

1. Remove 2 large cabbage leaves; set aside. Cut out core and centre of cabbage, leaving a 2–3cm shell. Dice 100g of cabbage leaves removed from centre.

2. Heat 1 tablespoon oil in 30cm non-stick frying pan over medium-high heat. Add peppers and half of onion; cook, stirring often, 8–10 minutes until tender.

3. Add diced cabbage, rice vinegar, ½ tablespoon soy sauce, garlic and ½ tablespoon ginger; cook 5 minutes. Remove from heat; stir in rice, beans and water chestnuts.

4. Stuff cabbage shell with vegetable mixture firmly but gently. Cover opening with reserved leaves, overlapping slightly, then tie with string. Heat remaining 1 tablespoon oil in 8-litre flameproof casserole over medium heat. Add remaining onions and cook 5 minutes, or until tender. Add remaining ½ tablespoon ginger; cook 30 seconds.

5. Add tomatoes with their juice, remaining ½ tablespoon soy sauce and *225ml water*, breaking up tomatoes with back of spoon. Place stuffed cabbage, core-end down, in tomato sauce and bring to the boil over high heat. Reduce heat to low; cover and simmer 30–40 minutes, basting cabbage occasionally. To serve, place cabbage in deep platter and discard string. Spoon sauce round cabbage. Cut into wedges. Serve with French bread, if you like.

EACH SERVING: ABOUT 275 CALORIES, 9g PROTEIN, 43g CARBOHYDRATE, 8g TOTAL FAT (1g SATURATED), 0mg CHOLESTEROL, 605mg SODIUM

## KOHLRABI AND CARROTS WITH DILL

*Prep: 25 minutes    Cook: 25 minutes*
*Makes 6 accompaniment servings*

6 medium kohlrabi (about 900g), peeled
450g carrots
2 tbsp vegetable oil
60g butter or margarine
2 tsp plain flour
1 chicken stock cube, crumbled
1 tbsp chopped fresh dill or ½ tsp dried

◆ Cut each kohlrabi into 1cm thick slices, then cut each slice into 1cm wide sticks. Cut each carrot crossways into 3 pieces, then cut each piece lengthways into quarters. Heat oil in 30cm frying pan over medium-high heat. Add vegetables and cook, stirring often, about 15 minutes until browned. Add *75ml water* and reduce heat to low. Cover and cook 10 minutes, or until vegetables are tender-crisp and liquid evaporates.

◆ Meanwhile, melt butter in 1-litre saucepan over low heat. Stir in flour and cook 1 minute. Add stock cube; gradually stir in *125ml water*. Cook, stirring constantly, until mixture thickens slightly and boils. Pour sauce over vegetables and sprinkle with dill. Gently toss to coat well.

**Each serving: About 185 calories, 4g protein, 18g carbohydrate, 12g total fat (4g saturated), 21mg cholesterol, 295mg sodium**

## RED CABBAGE WITH APPLES

*Prep: 15 minutes    Cook: 25 minutes*
*Makes 8 accompaniment servings*

2 tbsp olive oil
About 1kg red cabbage, quartered, cored and coarsely sliced
2 Golden Delicious apples, peeled, cored and chopped
1 tbsp sugar
2 tbsp red wine vinegar
2 tsp salt
Chopped fresh parsley for garnish

◆ Heat olive oil in 30cm frying pan over high heat. Add cabbage and apples; toss to coat. Stir in sugar, vinegar and salt.

◆ Reduce heat to medium; cook, stirring occasionally, about 20 minutes until cabbage is tender. To serve, sprinkle with parsley.

**Each serving: About 90 calories, 2g protein, 15g carbohydrate, 4g total fat (1g saturated), 0mg cholesterol, 550mg sodium**

## SAUTÉED CABBAGE AND FRESH PEAS

*Prep: 25 minutes    Cook: 15–20 minutes*
*Makes 6 accompaniment servings*

3 tbsp vegetable oil
1 medium onion, chopped
About 1kg green cabbage, quartered, cored and cut into 2cm slices
900g fresh peas, shelled, or 300g frozen peas
1¼ tsp salt
¼ tsp dried chilli flakes
1 tbsp chopped fresh thyme or parsley

◆ Heat oil in 5-litre flameproof casserole over medium heat. Add onion and cook, stirring occasionally, 5 minutes, or until tender and golden.

◆ Stir in cabbage, peas, salt, dried chilli flakes and *2 tablespoons water*. Increase heat to high and cook, stirring frequently, 10–12 minutes until cabbage is tender-crisp. To serve, sprinkle with thyme.

**Each serving: About 135 calories, 4g protein, 16g carbohydrate, 7g total fat (1g saturated), 0mg cholesterol, 480mg sodium**

## CABBAGE AND ONION WITH CARAWAY

*Prep: 10 minutes    Cook: 15 to 20 minutes*
*Makes 6 accompaniment servings*

About 1kg green cabbage
2 tbsp vegetable oil
1 large onion, diced
1 tsp salt
¾ tsp caraway seeds, crushed
¼ tsp ground black pepper

◆ Carefully remove several large cabbage leaves and use to line serving platter, if you like. Set platter aside.

◆ Cut cabbage into quarters; cut out core. Coarsely slice cabbage and discard tough ribs.

◆ Heat 2 tablespoons oil in 5-litre flameproof casserole over medium heat. Add onion and cook, stirring occasionally, 5 minutes, or until tender and golden.

◆ Stir in cabbage, salt, caraway seeds and pepper. Increase heat to high and cook, stirring frequently, for 10–12 minutes until cabbage is tender-crisp. To serve, spoon cabbage mixture onto platter lined with cabbage leaves.

**Each serving: About 100 calories, 3g protein, 13g carbohydrate, 5g total fat (1g saturated), 0mg cholesterol, 390mg sodium**

## SAUTÉED BRUSSELS SPROUTS

*Prep:* 15 minutes   *Cook:* 5 minutes
*Makes* 6 accompaniment servings

600g Brussels sprouts,      45g butter
   trimmed                  ½ tsp salt

Thinly slice Brussels sprouts. Melt butter in 30cm frying pan over high heat. Add Brussels sprouts; sprinkle with salt and cook, stirring, 5 minutes, or until sprouts are tender-crisp and beginning to brown.

Each serving: About 90 calories, 3g protein, 9g carbohydrate, 6g total fat (2g saturated), 16mg cholesterol, 265mg sodium

## CURRIED CAULIFLOWER WITH POTATOES AND PEAS

*Prep:* 15 minutes   *Cook:* 30 minutes
*Makes* 8 accompaniment servings

1 tbsp vegetable oil          1 tsp curry powder
1 large onion, finely chopped ¼ tsp ground cumin
2 potatoes, peeled and cut    1 tsp salt
   into 1cm pieces            1 small head cauliflower
1 tbsp very finely chopped       (900g), cut into small florets
   peeled fresh ginger        150g frozen peas
2 garlic cloves, very finely  15g fresh coriander, chopped
   chopped

Heat oil in 26cm frying pan over medium heat. Add onion and cook 5 minutes, or until tender. Add potatoes and next 4 ingredients; cook, stirring, 2 minutes. Stir in salt and *350ml water*; bring to the boil over high heat.

Reduce heat to medium; cover and cook 10 minutes. Stir in cauliflower; cover and cook 10 minutes longer, or until tender. Stir in peas and cook, uncovered, until most of liquid evaporates. To serve, stir in coriander.

Each serving: About 120 calories, 5g protein, 21g carbohydrate, 2g total fat (0g saturated), 0mg cholesterol, 295mg sodium

## BRUSSELS SPROUTS WITH BACON

*Prep:* 15 minutes   *Cook:* 15 minutes
*Makes* 10 accompaniment servings

850g Brussels sprouts,        ½ tsp salt
   trimmed                    ¼ tsp coarsely ground black
6 rashers bacon, trimmed if      pepper
   necessary                  45g pine nuts, toasted
1 tbsp olive oil
2 garlic cloves, very finely
   chopped

Bring *10–12cm water* to the boil in 4-litre saucepan over high heat. Add Brussels sprouts and return to the boil. Reduce heat to low; cover and simmer 5 minutes, or until sprouts are tender-crisp. Drain.

Fry bacon in 30cm non-stick frying pan over medium-low heat until browned. Transfer bacon to kitchen paper to drain, then crumble. Spoon off all but 1 tablespoon bacon fat from pan. Heat fat and olive oil over medium-high heat. Add Brussels sprouts, garlic, salt and pepper. Cook, stirring frequently, 5 minutes or until sprouts are browned. To serve, sprinkle with pine nuts and crumbled bacon.

Each serving: About 85 calories, 4g protein, 9g carbohydrate, 5g total fat (1g saturated), 3mg cholesterol, 185mg sodium

### PREPARING BRUSSELS SPROUTS

First, remove any yellow or wilted leaves, then trim the stalk. If boiling the sprouts, use a small knife to make an X-shaped cut in the stalk end for faster and more uniform cooking.

## VEGETABLES VINAIGRETTE

*Prep:* 20 minutes    *Cook:* 25–30 minutes

*Makes* 8 accompaniment servings

75ml olive or vegetable oil
60g coarse-grained Dijon
    mustard
60ml white wine vinegar
¾ tsp salt
1 large head cauliflower
    (1.3kg), cut into 6 by 2cm
    pieces

1 large bunch broccoli, cut
    into 6 by 2cm pieces
450g carrots, cut into 5mm
    thick diagonal slices

◆ Whisk oil, mustard, vinegar and salt together in large bowl until blended; set aside.

◆ Bring *10–12cm water* to the boil in 8-litre saucepan over high heat. Add cauliflower and return to the boil. Reduce heat to low; cover and simmer 5–7 minutes until tender-crisp. Using slotted spoon, transfer cauliflower to colander; rinse with cold water.

◆ Bring water remaining in pan to the boil; add broccoli. Reduce heat to low; cover and simmer 5–7 minutes, until tender-crisp. Using slotted spoon, transfer to colander with cauliflower; rinse with cold water.

◆ In water remaining in pan (adding more *water* if necessary to equal 2–3cm), bring carrots to the boil over high heat. Reduce heat to low; cover and simmer 5 minutes, or until tender-crisp. Transfer to colander with cauliflower and broccoli; rinse with cold water.

◆ Add drained vegetables to bowl with vinaigrette; toss until coated. Serve vegetables warm; or, cover and refrigerate to serve cold later.

**Each serving: About 180 calories, 7g protein, 19g carbohydrate, 10g total fat (1g saturated), 0mg cholesterol, 455mg sodium**

## WARM BROCCOLI AND POTATO SALAD

*Prep:* 15 minutes    *Cook:* 25 minutes

*Makes* 8 accompaniment servings

6 rashers bacon, trimmed and
    cut into 1cm pieces
3 medium red potatoes, cut
    into 5mm thick slices
1 medium onion, chopped
3 tbsp red wine vinegar

2 tsp sugar
1½ tsp salt
¼ tsp dried chilli flakes
1 large bunch broccoli, cut
    into 7 by 3cm pieces

◆ Cook bacon in 30cm frying pan over medium-low heat until browned; drain on kitchen paper. Spoon off all but 3 tablespoons fat from pan. Increase heat to medium. Add potatoes and onion; cook, turning potatoes occasionally, about 10 minutes until browned. Add *125ml water*; reduce heat to medium-low. Cover and cook 5 minutes longer until potatoes are tender. Stir in vinegar and next 3 ingredients; cook, stirring, until liquid boils and thickens slightly.

◆ Meanwhile, place broccoli in *10–12cm boiling water* in saucepan over high heat. Reduce heat to low; cover and simmer, stirring occasionally, 8–10 minutes until tender-crisp. Drain broccoli. Stir broccoli and bacon into potato mixture until broccoli is coated with dressing.

**Each serving: About 110 calories, 5g protein, 18g carbohydrate, 3g total fat (1g saturated), 4mg cholesterol, 505mg sodium**

## BROCCOLI AND RED-PEPPER AMANDINE

*Prep:* 10 minutes    *Cook:* 15 minutes

*Makes* 5 accompaniment servings

2 tbsp olive or vegetable oil
1 red pepper, cored, seeded
    and cut into 1cm wide strips
1 large bunch broccoli, cut
    into florets

½ tsp salt
1 tbsp fresh lemon juice
2 tbsp sliced almonds, toasted

◆ Heat 1 tablespoon oil in 30cm frying pan over medium-high heat. Add red pepper and cook until tender-crisp and browned. Using slotted spoon, transfer to plate.

◆ Heat remaining 1 tablespoon oil in same pan. Add broccoli and cook, stirring constantly, until coated with oil. Add salt and *3 tablespoons water*. Reduce heat to medium; cover and cook 2 minutes. Uncover; stir-fry 5 minutes longer, or until broccoli is tender-crisp. Stir in red pepper and mix thoroughly. Spoon mixture onto platter. Sprinkle with lemon juice and almonds.

**Each serving: About 110 calories, 5g protein, 9g carbohydrate, 7g total fat (1g saturated), 0mg cholesterol, 250mg sodium**

# LEAFY GREENS

Packed with flavour and nutrients, leafy greens range in texture and taste from tender and mild to resilient and slightly peppery or bitter – depending on type, age and growing conditions. In general, the darker the greens, the more vitamins and minerals they contain. Spinach is especially delicate and versatile, but you can mix and match most greens for variety (tougher or stronger-flavoured greens will need longer cooking). Squeeze excess moisture from cooked or thawed spinach to avoid a watery end result.

## SPINACH AND RICOTTA DUMPLINGS

*Prep: 50 minutes*
*Bake: 15–20 minutes*
*Makes 4 main dish servings*

700g fresh spinach or 600g frozen chopped spinach, thawed and squeezed dry
225g ricotta cheese
2 medium eggs
¼ tsp ground black pepper
125g Parmesan cheese, freshly grated
75g plus 2 tbsp plain flour
30g butter or margarine
450ml milk

**1** If using fresh spinach, remove tough stalks; wash well. Cook spinach with water clinging to its leaves in 5-litre flameproof casserole over high heat, stirring, until wilted. Drain. Squeeze dry; coarsely chop. Prepare dumplings: mix spinach, ricotta, eggs, pepper, 60g Parmesan and 75g flour. Using floured hands, shape spinach mixture into 5 by 3cm ovals.

**2** Meanwhile, half fill 5-litre saucepan with *water*. Bring to the boil over high heat. Reduce heat to medium. Add dumplings, half at a time.

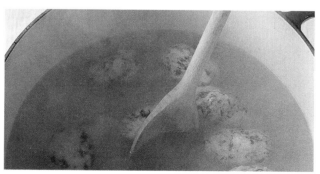

**3** Cook the dumplings in simmering water, gently stirring occasionally, 3–5 minutes until they float to the top. Using a slotted spoon, transfer them to kitchen paper to drain. Preheat oven to 180°C (350°F, Gas 4).

**4** Melt butter in 2-litre saucepan over medium heat. Stir in remaining 2 tablespoons flour; cook 1 minute. Gradually whisk in milk and cook, whisking constantly, until sauce thickens slightly and boils. Remove pan from heat; stir in 30g grated Parmesan. Place dumplings in single layer in shallow 2-litre casserole; spoon sauce over. Sprinkle remaining 35g grated Parmesan over top. Bake dumplings 15–20 minutes until sauce is hot and bubbly.

EACH SERVING: ABOUT 475 CALORIES, 30g PROTEIN, 27g CARBOHYDRATE, 28g TOTAL FAT (15g SATURATED), 187mg CHOLESTEROL, 785mg SODIUM

## ITALIAN SPINACH WITH CHICK-PEAS AND RAISINS

*Prep: 15 minutes    Cook: 6 minutes*

*Makes 4 accompaniment servings*

1 tbsp olive oil

1 garlic clove, crushed with side of knife

¼ tsp dried chilli flakes

400g canned chick-peas, rinsed and drained

700g spinach, washed and dried very well

40g sultanas

½ tsp salt

◆ Heat oil with garlic in 5-litre flameproof casserole over medium heat until golden; discard garlic. Add dried chilli flakes to oil remaining in pan and cook 15 seconds.

◆ Stir in chick-peas and cook, stirring, 2 minutes, or until hot. Increase heat to high. Add spinach, sultanas and salt. Cook, stirring, 2–3 minutes, just until spinach wilts.

**Each serving: About 200 calories, 9g protein, 31g carbohydrate, 6g total fat (1g saturated), 0mg cholesterol, 805mg sodium**

## SPICY INDIAN CREAMED SPINACH

*Prep: 20 minutes    Cook: 12 minutes*

*Makes 4 accompaniment servings*

15g butter or margarine

1 medium onion, finely chopped

2 tsp finely chopped peeled fresh ginger

2 garlic cloves, very finely chopped

½ tsp ground coriander

½ tsp ground cumin

⅛ tsp ground red pepper

700g spinach, washed and dried very well

½ tsp salt

60ml whipping cream

◆ Melt butter in 5-litre flameproof casserole over medium heat. Add chopped onion and cook, stirring often, 5 minutes, or until tender. Add chopped ginger, garlic, ground coriander, ground cumin and ground red pepper and cook, stirring, 1 minute longer.

◆ Increase heat to high. Add spinach and salt; cook, stirring, 2–3 minutes, just until spinach wilts. Stir in cream and boil 2 minutes until thickened.

**Each serving: About 130 calories, 5g protein, 10g carbohydrate, 9g total fat (5g saturated), 28mg cholesterol, 420mg sodium**

## BAKED SPINACH AND RICE BALLS

*Prep: 45 minutes    Bake: 25–30 minutes*

*Makes 4 main dish servings*

100g long-grain rice

700g spinach or 600g frozen chopped spinach, thawed and squeezed dry

3 tbsp olive or vegetable oil

2 large onions, diced

¼ tsp salt

Ground black pepper

60g Parmesan cheese, freshly grated

30g dried breadcrumbs

1 medium egg

1 large carrot, diced

½ tsp dried basil

400g canned tomatoes

400ml vegetable or beef stock

2 tsp sugar

◆ Prepare rice in 1-litre saucepan as packet instructs. Meanwhile, if using fresh spinach, remove tough stalks; wash spinach. Dry well and chop.

◆ Heat 2 tablespoons oil in 30cm frying pan over medium-high heat. Add half of onions with salt and ½ teaspoon pepper and cook, stirring often, until tender and golden.

◆ Stir in spinach and cook, stirring, just until spinach wilts; remove pan from heat. Stir in Parmesan cheese, breadcrumbs, egg and cooked rice until well blended. When cool enough to handle, shape mixture into 12 balls; set aside.

◆ Preheat oven to 190°C (375°F, Gas 5). Heat remaining 1 tablespoon oil over medium-high heat. Add carrot, basil, ¼ teaspoon pepper and remaining onion and cook, stirring often, until onion and carrot are tender.

◆ Add tomatoes with their juice, stock and sugar, breaking up tomatoes with back of spoon. Bring mixture to boil over high heat; pour into shallow 2-litre ovenproof serving dish.

◆ Arrange spinach balls in sauce in dish. Bake for 25–30 minutes until sauce is hot and bubbly and spinach balls are heated through.

**Each serving: About 400 calories, 16g protein, 50g carbohydrate, 17g total fat (4g saturated), 63mg cholesterol, 765mg sodium**

## SPINACH WITH MUSHROOMS AND BACON

*Prep: 20 minutes    Cook: 15 minutes*
*Makes 4 accompaniment servings*

3 rashers bacon, trimmed if
  necessary
1 tbsp olive oil
2 garlic cloves, crushed with
  side of knife
225g mushrooms, cut into
  5mm thick slices

⅛ tsp ground black pepper
Salt
700g spinach, washed and
  dried very well
1 tbsp red wine vinegar
  (optional)

◈ Cook bacon in 5-litre flameproof casserole over medium-low heat until browned; transfer to kitchen paper to drain. Discard drippings from casserole

◈ Heat oil with garlic in same casserole over medium heat until garlic is golden; discard garlic. Add mushrooms, pepper and ¼ teaspoon salt to oil; cook about 5 minutes until mushrooms are tender and liquid has evaporated.

◈ Increase heat to high. Add spinach to casserole, sprinkle with ¼ teaspoon salt and cook, stirring, 2–3 minutes, just until spinach wilts. Stir in vinegar, if using. To serve, crumble bacon on top.

**Each serving: About 105 calories, 7g protein, 8g carbohydrate, 6g total fat (1g saturated), 4mg cholesterol, 455mg sodium**

## BATAVIA PIE

*Prep: 50 minutes, plus chilling and standing    Bake: 40–45 minutes*
*Makes 6 main dish servings*

Pastry for a 2-Crust Pie (see
  page 487) or 300g ready-
  made shortcrust pastry
3 tbsp olive oil
1 large onion, finely chopped
2 garlic cloves, very finely
  chopped
2 large heads batavia (curly
  lettuce), about 1kg, cut into
  bite-sized pieces

60g plus 2 tbsp freshly grated
  Parmesan cheese
½ tsp dried chilli flakes
½ tsp salt
2 tbsp dried breadcrumbs

◈ Prepare Pastry for 2-Crust Pie. Shape pastry into 2 balls, one slightly larger. Wrap and chill 30 minutes, or overnight.

◈ Meanwhile, heat 2 tablespoons oil in 8-litre flameproof casserole over medium heat. Add onion and garlic; cook 10–15 minutes until onion is very tender.

◈ Increase heat to high. Stir in batavia; cook about 10 minutes, stirring often, just until tender. Drain well, pressing out excess liquid.

◈ Return batavia to casserole; stir in 60g Parmesan, dried chilli flakes, salt and remaining 1 tablespoon oil, set aside. Preheat oven to 190°C (375°F, Gas 5).

◈ Roll out larger ball of pastry on lightly floured surface 4cm larger all round than inverted 23cm pie plate; use to line pie plate. Sprinkle crumbs over pastry; top with batavia filling.

Roll smaller ball of pastry into 25cm round. Make several cuts in pastry and place over filling. Trim edge, leaving 1cm overhang; fold overhang under and press gently all round rim to make stand-up edge. Sprinkle pastry with remaining 2 tablespoons Parmesan. Bake 40–45 minutes until crust is golden. Let pie stand 10 minutes; cut into wedges.

**Each serving: About 540 calories, 15g protein, 45g carbohydrate, 35g total fat (8g saturated), 8mg cholesterol, 945mg sodium**

## BRAISED CHICORY

*Prep: 5 minutes    Cook: 15–25 minutes*
*Makes 6 accompaniment servings*

6 large heads chicory
2 tbsp vegetable oil
30g butter or margarine
1 tsp sugar

½ tsp salt
Fresh basil or parsley leaves
  for garnish

◈ Cut each chicory lengthways in half. Heat oil and butter in 30cm frying pan over medium-high heat. Arrange chicory cut-side down, in 1 layer in pan. Cook, uncovered 5–10 minutes until cut sides are lightly browned.

◈ Turn chicory cut-side up. Reduce heat to low; add *125ml water*. Sprinkle chicory with sugar and salt; cover and cook 10–15 minutes until tender. Transfer to warm large platter; garnish with basil.

**Each serving: About 85 calories, 1g protein, 3g carbohydrate, 8g total fat (1g saturated), 11mg cholesterol, 235mg sodium**

# STIR-FRYING GREENS

One of the best ways to prepare leafy green vegetables is to stir-fry them – just enough to wilt them while retaining their bright colour. Some of the tougher or more bitter greens, such as spring and mustard greens, should be blanched (cooked briefly in boiling water first) to mellow and tenderize them. See below for instructions on how to prepare, blanch and stir-fry some of the most common varieties of greens. If you like, use a combination. The cooking times are short; be sure to keep an eye on the greens so they don't overcook.

## EXTRAS FOR STIR-FRIES

Enhance the flavour and texture of stir-fried greens with any of the following easy additions:

**Flavour with oil**  Drizzle cooked greens with extra virgin olive oil, walnut oil, or a few drops of sesame oil.

**Extra dimension**  Stir in a little soy sauce, lemon juice, vinegar or oyster sauce at the end of cooking.

**Extra spice**  Add grated fresh ginger, mustard seeds or cumin seeds with the dried chilli flakes.

**Crunchy toppings**  Sprinkle cooked greens with toasted sesame seeds, almonds, walnuts or pine nuts.

**Preparation and blanching**
Prepare 450g greens (see chart, right) and discard any discoloured leaves. To blanch, if recommended, add greens to 5–6 litres boiling water and cook as directed and drain.

**Stir-frying**
Heat 1 tablespoon olive oil in a large frying pan or wok over a high heat. Add 2 garlic cloves, crushed with side of knife and cook, stirring frequently, until golden. Add ⅛ teaspoon dried chilli flakes and cook for 30 seconds. Add the prepared greens and sprinkle with ¼ teaspoon salt and cook, stirring. Discard the garlic, if desired.

## PREPARING AND STIR-FRYING GREENS

| TYPE OF GREENS | PREPARE | BLANCH | STIR-FRY |
|---|---|---|---|
| Beetroot greens | Wash; chop stalks | No | 5 minutes |
| Bok choy (pak choi; pak choy; Chinese mustard cabbage) | Wash; thinly slice stalks; cut leaves into 2–3cm slices | No | 5 minutes |
| Sprouting broccoli (rape; rapini) | Wash; trim thick stalks | Yes, 5 minutes | 5 minutes |
| Chicory (curly endive) | Wash; tear leaves | No | 5 minutes |
| Spring greens | Wash; discard stalks; cut leaves into 2–3cm slices | Yes, 3 minutes | 5 minutes |
| Dandelion greens | Wash | Yes, 3 minutes | 5 minutes |
| Batavia (curly lettuce) | Wash; tear leaves | No | 5 minutes |
| Kale | Wash; discard stalks; tear leaves | Yes, 5 minutes | 5 minutes |
| Mustard greens | Wash | Yes, 5 minutes | 5 minutes |
| Chinese cabbage (celery cabbage) | Wash; thinly slice | No | 3 minutes |
| Spinach | Wash very well | No | 3 minutes |
| Swiss chard (chard) | Wash; thinly slice stalks; cut leaves into 2–3cm slices | No | 3 minutes |
| Watercress | Wash | No | 3 minutes |

# ARTICHOKES

With just a little more work than is required for most vegetables, fresh artichokes offer high rewards both in great taste and presentation.

## STUFFED ARTICHOKES, CAESAR-STYLE

❖❖❖❖❖❖❖❖❖❖❖❖

*Prep:* 1 hour
*Bake:* 15–20 minutes
*Makes* 4 main dish servings

4 large artichokes
4 slices firm white bread, torn
  into 5mm crumbs
2 tbsp olive oil
1 large garlic clove, very finely
  chopped
4 anchovy fillets, chopped
75g pine nuts, lightly toasted,
  or walnuts, toasted and
  chopped
40g Parmesan cheese, freshly
  grated
2 tbsp chopped fresh parsley
1 tbsp fresh lemon juice
¼ tsp salt
175ml chicken stock
Flat-leaf parsley for garnish

1 Prepare and cook artichokes (see below). Preheat oven to 200°C (400°F, Gas 6). Bake breadcrumbs in baking tray 5 minutes, or until golden. Heat oil over medium heat in 1-litre saucepan. Add garlic and anchovies; cook until almost dissolved and garlic is golden. Dice artichoke stalks. Mix stalks, crumbs, garlic mixture, pine nuts, Parmesan, parsley, lemon juice, salt and 60ml stock in bowl.

2 Pour remaining 115ml chicken stock into shallow ovenproof dish large enough to hold cooked artichokes (about 33 by 20cm). Add artichokes.

3 Spoon crumb mixture between artichoke leaves and into centre cavities. Bake 15–20 minutes until artichokes are hot. Serve garnished with parsley.

---

### PREPARING AND COOKING ARTICHOKES

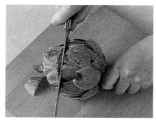

1 Using sharp knife, cut 2–3cm straight across top of each artichoke. Cut off stalk; peel stalk with vegetable peeler; reserve.

2 Pull loose dark green outer leaves from artichoke base. Using kitchen scissors, trim thorny tips of the leaves.

3 Spread artichoke open and carefully cut round choke with small knife. Scrape out fuzzy centre portion with spoon; discard.

4 Rinse artichoke well. Bring 1 tablespoon fresh lemon juice and 2–3cm water to the boil in 5-litre saucepan over a high heat. Add artichoke, stalk-end down, with stalk; return to the boil. Reduce heat to low; cover and simmer for 30–40 minutes until knife inserted in centre goes through base easily. Drain.

---

EACH SERVING: ABOUT 335 CALORIES, 16g PROTEIN, 33g CARBOHYDRATE, 19g TOTAL FAT (4g SATURATED), 14mg CHOLESTEROL, 915mg SODIUM

## BRAISED BABY ARTICHOKES WITH OLIVES

*Prep: 20 minutes    Cook: 15 minutes*
*Makes 8 first-course servings*

16 baby artichokes (about
  900g)
60ml olive oil
3 medium garlic cloves, sliced
½ tsp coarsely ground black
  pepper

½ tsp salt
50g oil-cured or Kalamata
  olives, stoned and coarsely
  chopped
Lemon wedges for garnish

◆ Trim baby artichokes: bend back outer green leaves and snap off at base until leaves are half-green (at top) and half-yellow (at bottom). Cut off stalk and across top of each artichoke at point where yellow meets green. Cut each artichoke lengthways in half.

◆ Bring *2–3cm water* to the boil in 30cm frying pan over high heat. Add artichokes and cook 5 minutes; drain.

◆ Dry pan. Heat olive oil in same pan over medium-high heat. Add garlic and cook, stirring, until lightly browned. Add artichokes; cook 2 minutes, or until lightly browned.

◆ Stir in pepper, salt and *225ml water*; cover and cook 5 minutes longer, or until knife inserted in base of artichoke goes through easily. Stir in olives; heat through. Spoon into bowl; garnish with lemon wedges.

**Each serving: About 100 calories, 2g protein, 6g carbohydrate, 8g total fat (1g saturated), 0mg cholesterol, 280mg sodium**

## ARTICHOKES WITH ROASTED RED PEPPER AND BASIL SAUCE

*Prep: 25 minutes    Cook: 35–45 minutes*
*Makes 8 first course or accompaniment servings*

4 medium artichokes
175g reduced-fat mayonnaise
200g bottled roasted red
  peppers, drained
1 tsp sugar
¾ tsp salt

½ tsp Tabasco sauce
1 tbsp fresh lemon juice
30g fresh basil or parsley,
  chopped
Shredded fresh basil for
  garnish

◆ Prepare and cook artichokes (see page 281), but omit Step 3. Meanwhile, blend mayonnaise, roasted red peppers, sugar, salt, Tabasco sauce and lemon juice in food processor with knife blade attached or in blender on medium speed until smooth. Spoon red-pepper sauce into bowl; stir in basil. Cover and refrigerate.

◆ Cut each artichoke into 4 wedges. Cut out and discard fuzzy centres. Serve artichokes warm or cover and refrigerate to serve cold later. To serve, arrange artichoke

wedges round bowl of red-pepper sauce on platter; garnish sauce with shredded basil. Let each person dip artichoke leaves and hearts in sauce.

**Each serving: About 110 calories, 2g protein, 10g carbohydrate, 6g total fat (1g saturated), 8mg cholesterol, 300mg sodium**

## COUSCOUS-STUFFED ARTICHOKES

*Prep: 1 hour    Bake: 15–20 minutes*
*Makes 4 main dish servings*

4 large artichokes
3 tbsp olive oil
2 medium carrots, diced
2 garlic cloves, very finely
  chopped
15g fresh mint, chopped
3 tbsp chopped fresh parsley

175g couscous
350ml chicken stock
½ tsp salt
¼ tsp coarsely ground black
  pepper
1 lemon, cut into wedges

◆ Prepare and cook artichokes (see page 281). Meanwhile, preheat oven to 200°C (400°F, Gas 6). Heat 1 tablespoon olive oil in 26cm non-stick frying pan over medium heat. Add carrots and cook about 10 minutes until tender. Stir in garlic; cook 1 minute longer. Transfer carrots and garlic to medium bowl. Dice artichoke stalks; add to carrot mixture with mint and parsley.

◆ Prepare couscous as packet instructs, but use 225ml chicken stock in place of water. When couscous is done, stir in salt, pepper, carrot mixture and remaining oil.

◆ Pour remaining 125ml chicken stock into shallow ovenproof dish large enough to hold all artichokes (about 33 by 20cm); place artichokes in dish. Spoon couscous mixture between leaves and into centre cavities. Bake 15–20 minutes until artichokes are heated through. Serve with lemon wedges.

**Each serving: About 375 calories, 13g protein, 61g carbohydrate, 12g total fat (2g saturated), 7mg cholesterol, 830mg sodium**

# FENNEL AND CELERY

Cool, crunchy raw celery is a popular staple on crudité platters, but many people are not aware that cooking transforms it into an appealing side dish. Paired with parsnips, toasted walnuts and a hint of brown butter, for example, it makes a delicate winter sauté. A relative of celery, fennel shares its crisp texture but offers a distinctive, sweet anise flavour. While fennel is delicious raw, simply sliced thin and drizzled with vinaigrette, cooked fennel has a more subtle flavour and melting texture. Roast it in olive oil to accompany roasted chicken or fish, or slice and layer it in a cheese-rich gratin. When purchasing either vegetable, choose firm, crisp specimens with fresh-looking leaves.

## BRAISED FENNEL WITH TWO CHEESES

❖❖❖❖❖❖❖❖❖❖❖❖❖❖❖❖❖❖❖❖❖❖❖

*Prep: 15 minutes    Cook: 45 minutes, plus grilling*
*Makes 6 accompaniment servings*

**3 small fennel bulbs (225g each)**
**400ml chicken stock**
**175g mozzarella cheese, grated**

**30g Parmesan cheese, freshly grated**
**1 tbsp chopped fresh parsley**

1 Rinse fennel bulbs with cold water; cut off root ends and stalks. Slice each bulb lengthways in half. Bring chicken stock and *350ml water* to the boil in deep 30cm frying pan over high heat. Add fennel; return to the boil.

2 Reduce heat to low; cover and simmer 35 minutes, turning bulbs once, or until fennel is fork-tender; drain. Preheat grill. Place fennel, cut-side up, in a shallow 1½-litre flameproof casserole. Mix mozzarella and Parmesan cheeses and parsley in small bowl.

3 Sprinkle cheese mixture over fennel. Place casserole in grill at closest position to heat. Grill 1–2 minutes until cheese topping is golden and bubbly and fennel is heated through.

**BRAISED CELERY WITH GRUYÈRE**

Substitute 2 bunches celery for fennel; trim stalks from bases. Cut each stalk in half to give 5–6cm lengths. Proceed as above but simmer only 20 minutes in Step 2 and use 125g Gruyère or Emmental cheese, grated, instead of mozzarella.

Each serving: About 125 calories, 8g protein, 7g carbohydrate, 8g total fat (4g saturated), 28mg cholesterol, 530mg sodium

EACH SERVING: ABOUT 135 CALORIES, 8g PROTEIN, 10g CARBOHYDRATE, 8g TOTAL FAT (4g SATURATED), 29mg CHOLESTEROL, 490mg SODIUM

## ROASTED FENNEL

*Prep: 5 minutes    Roast: 1 hour*
*Makes 6 accompaniment servings*

3 large fennel bulbs (about           ½ tsp salt
  600g each)                          ¼ tsp ground black pepper
1 tbsp olive oil

◆ Preheat oven to 220°C (425°F, Gas 7). Trim fennel bulbs
and cut each into 6 wedges. Place fennel in baking tray and
toss with olive oil, salt and pepper to coat evenly.

◆ Roast fennel about 1 hour, or until browned at the edges
and tender when pierced with tip of knife.

**Each serving: About 110 calories, 4g protein, 21g carbohydrate,
3g total fat (0g saturated), 0mg cholesterol, 325mg sodium**

## CELERY AND PARSNIPS IN BROWN BUTTER

*Prep: 20 minutes    Cook: 25–30 minutes*
*Makes 5 accompaniment servings*

2 tbsp coarsely chopped              6 stalks celery, cut into
  walnuts                                7–8cm long matchstick-thin
1 tbsp vegetable oil                   strips
225g parsnips, peeled                ¼ tsp salt
  and cut into 7–8cm long              2 tbsp butter
  matchstick-thin strips

◆ Toast walnuts in 26cm frying pan over medium heat until
lightly browned; transfer to small bowl. Wipe pan clean with
kitchen towels.

◆ Heat oil in same pan over medium heat. Add parsnips,
celery and salt and cook about 20 minutes, stirring
frequently, until vegetables are tender.

◆ Transfer vegetables to warm platter; keep warm. Melt
butter in same pan; cook until it turns golden, stirring (if
butter gets dark, it will be bitter). Add walnuts and toss to
coat. Spoon mixture over vegetables.

**Each serving: About 120 calories, 2g protein, 11g carbohydrate,
9g total fat (3g saturated), 12mg cholesterol, 200mg sodium**

## FENNEL AND POTATO GRATIN

*Prep: 20 minutes    Bake: About 1 hour 20 minutes*
*Makes 8 accompaniment servings*

1 large fennel bulb (600g),           225ml whipping cream
  trimmed, cored and very             1 garlic clove, crushed with
  thinly sliced                          side of knife
750g potatoes, peeled and             Pinch ground nutmeg
  very thinly sliced                   30g Parmesan cheese, freshly
1 tsp salt                              grated
¼ tsp ground black pepper

◆ Preheat oven to 200°C (400°F, Gas 6). Toss fennel with
potatoes, salt and pepper in large bowl. Spread evenly in
shallow ovenproof 2-litre serving dish. Cover tightly with foil
and bake 1 hour.

◆ Combine cream, garlic and nutmeg in 1-litre saucepan;
bring to the boil over high heat. Discard garlic. Pour cream
mixture over fennel mixture. Sprinkle with Parmesan. Bake,
uncovered, 20 minutes longer, or until golden.

**Each serving: About 215 calories, 4g protein, 23g carbohydrate,
12g total fat (7g saturated), 43mg cholesterol, 375mg sodium**

### PREPARING FENNEL

Also known as anise, sweet
anise and finocchio, fennel
is a vegetable valued for all
its parts: bulb, leaves, stalks
and seeds. The bulb is the
part most often eaten, but
young fennel stalks can be
served as crudités. The
feathery leaves can be added
to salads or used as a
stuffing for fish; they also
make an attractive garnish.

1 To prepare fennel, rinse
the bulb in cold water.
Trim root end with a large
chef's knife.

2 Cut off stalks and
feathery leaves, reserving
them for other uses, if you
like. Remove any bruised or
discoloured outer stalks;
halve or quarter, cut out
core, if you like, and slice the
bulb as recipe instructs.

# ASPARAGUS

Asparagus is at its best cooked simply and briefly, just until the spears are slightly limp. When buying, look for stalks with tips that are dry, tight and purplish in colour. The thickness of the spear makes no difference in the taste, but do select spears of uniform size so they cook evenly.

## ASPARAGUS WITH PARMESAN VINAIGRETTE

❖❖❖❖❖❖❖❖❖❖❖❖❖

*Prep:* 20 minutes
*Cook:* 10–15 minutes
*Makes* 8 accompaniment servings

1.3kg asparagus
125ml olive or vegetable oil
60ml red wine vinegar
1 tbsp Dijon mustard
1 tsp salt
45g Parmesan cheese, freshly grated
60g Parma ham or cooked ham, chopped

**1** Hold base of each asparagus stalk firmly and bend; end will break off at spot where it becomes too tough to eat. Discard ends; trim scales if stalks are gritty.

**2** In *2–3cm boiling water* bring asparagus to the boil in deep 30cm frying pan. Reduce heat to medium-low; simmer 5–10 minutes, just until tender. Drain well.

**3** Prepare vinaigrette in 33 by 20cm baking dish. Whisk oil, vinegar, mustard, salt and 30g Parmesan cheese together.

### PREPARING ASPARAGUS

Asparagus may need only minimal trimming, but if the end of the stalk looks tough and woody, simply bend the stalk to snap the end off. Rinse the asparagus thoroughly under cold running water. You can trim the scales with a paring knife or vegetable peeler, if you like, though this is not really necessary – do so only if the stalks seem gritty.

Asparagus may be peeled for an elegant presentation or if the skin is thick and tough, but we prefer to leave them unpeeled; the outside of the stalk is rich in vitamin C, folic acid and thiamine, which are lost in peeling. Store asparagus upright in 2–3cm water, loosely covered, in the refrigerator.

**4** Add hot asparagus to vinaigrette; turn to coat. Serve at room temperature or cover and refrigerate, turning occasionally, 2 hours. To serve, spoon asparagus and vinaigrette onto serving platter. Sprinkle with Parma ham and remaining 15g Parmesan cheese.

EACH SERVING: ABOUT 180 CALORIES, 7g PROTEIN, 7g CARBOHYDRATE, 15g TOTAL FAT (2g SATURATED), 4mg CHOLESTEROL, 460mg SODIUM

## ASPARAGUS GRATIN

*Prep: 25 minutes    Cook: 10–15 minutes, plus grilling*

*Makes 6 accompaniment servings*

2 tbsp plus 2 tsp olive oil
1 large shallot, finely chopped
2 slices firm white bread
900g asparagus, tough ends removed

Salt
30g Parmesan cheese, freshly grated
1 tbsp chopped fresh parsley
1 tbsp fresh lemon juice

◆ Preheat oven to 200°C (400°F, Gas 6). Heat 2 tablespoons olive oil in 1-litre saucepan over medium-low heat. Add shallot; cook about 6 minutes until golden. Remove from heat.

◆ Process bread to fine crumbs in blender or tear bread into small crumbs. Spread crumbs in baking tray and bake for 3–6 minutes until golden; set aside.

◆ Bring asparagus and ½ teaspoon salt to the boil in *2–3cm boiling water* in 30cm frying pan over high heat. Reduce heat to medium-low and simmer, uncovered, 5–10 minutes until just tender; drain. Place asparagus in shallow, flameproof dish; drizzle with remaining 2 teaspoons oil. Preheat grill.

### GRATIN DISHES

Designed for grilling or baking at high temperatures, a gratin dish is shallow so that food heats through quickly and achieves the maximum browned top.

◆ Toss breadcrumbs with Parmesan cheese, parsley, lemon juice, shallot and ¼ teaspoon salt in medium bowl. Sprinkle breadcrumb mixture over asparagus. Grill about 12cm from heat for 3 minutes, or until crumbs are lightly browned.

Each serving: About 130 calories, 6g protein, 11g carbohydrate, 8g total fat (2g saturated), 3mg cholesterol, 265mg sodium

## CHILLED ASPARAGUS WITH WATERCRESS MAYONNAISE

*Prep: 20 minutes, plus chilling    Cook: 10–15 minutes*

*Makes 6 accompaniment servings*

900g asparagus, tough ends removed
1 bunch watercress
125g mayonnaise
2 tbsp milk

2 tbsp canned or bottled drained and very finely chopped capers
1 tbsp fresh lemon juice
Lemon slices for garnish

◆ Bring asparagus to the boil in *2–3cm boiling water* in 30cm frying pan over high heat. Reduce heat to medium-low and simmer, uncovered, 5–10 minutes until asparagus is just tender; drain. Place on serving platter; cover and refrigerate 2 hours, or until chilled.

◆ Prepare watercress mayonnaise: chop three-quarters of watercress; reserve remaining watercress for garnish. Combine chopped watercress, mayonnaise, milk, capers and lemon juice in medium bowl; spoon over chilled asparagus. Garnish with lemon slices and reserved watercress.

Each serving: About 170 calories, 4g protein, 7g carbohydrate, 15g total fat (2g saturated), 11mg cholesterol, 235mg sodium

## SESAME STIR-FRIED ASPARAGUS

*Prep: 5 minutes    Cook: 10 minutes*

*Makes 4 accompaniment servings*

450g thin asparagus, tough ends removed
1 tbsp sesame seeds

1 tbsp vegetable oil
½ tsp sesame oil
¼ tsp salt

◆ Cut asparagus diagonally into 2–3cm pieces. Toast sesame seeds in 26cm frying pan over medium heat, shaking pan frequently, 5 minutes, or until fragrant and pale golden. Remove from pan. Heat vegetable oil and sesame oil in same pan over high heat until very hot.

◆ Add asparagus; sprinkle with salt and cook, stirring constantly, 5 minutes, or until tender-crisp. To serve, sprinkle with sesame seeds.

Each serving: About 70 calories, 3g protein, 5g carbohydrate, 5g total fat (1g saturated) 0mg cholesterol, 145mg sodium

# SWEETCORN

At its peak between May and September, corn on the cob is a perennial summer delight. For added flavour, tuck a sprig of rosemary or some sage leaves right into the husk and barbecue the cob for a sweet, roasted flavour. Cut from the cob, the fresh kernels can be transformed into a quick sauté with chives, a savoury corn pudding with a comforting texture, or combined with broad beans to make succotash, a favourite from the American south. Once sweetcorn is picked, its sugar content begins to turn to starch, so for maximum sweetness cook it as soon as possible after buying. (New hybrids retain their sugars longer and can be stored for several days in the refrigerator.)

## ROASTED SUCCOTASH IN CORN HUSKS

*Prep: 30 minutes   Roast: 35 minutes*

*Makes 6 accompaniment servings*

| | |
|---|---|
| 6 large corn on the cob with husks | 45g butter or margarine, melted |
| 300g frozen broad beans, thawed | 1 tsp sugar |
| 1 large tomato, diced | ¼ tsp grated lemon rind |
| 125g smoked Cheddar cheese, grated | ¼ tsp ground black pepper |
| | ½ tsp salt |

**1** Peel husks back from each cob; cut cob at its base to remove husk intact. Remove silk from husks and soak with string in *water* to cover in bowl 20 minutes.

**2** Meanwhile, cut 450g corn kernels from cobs; place in another bowl (reserve remaining corn for another day). Stir in remaining ingredients.

**3** Preheat oven to 220°C (425°F, Gas 7). Drain husks and string. Shake off excess water. Carefully place about 150g corn mixture in each husk.

**4** Bring husks together, enclosing filling completely. Tie open end of each husk tightly with string; cut off loose ends of string.

**5** Place filled corn husks in baking tray; roast 35 minutes, or until corn is tender and filling is heated through. To serve, place filled corn husks on platter and remove string.

EACH SERVING: ABOUT 340 CALORIES, 14g PROTEIN, 47g CARBOHYDRATE, 14g TOTAL FAT (8g SATURATED), 37mg CHOLESTEROL, 500mg SODIUM

## CREAMY SWEETCORN BAKE

*Prep: 30 minutes   Bake: 1¼ hours*
*Makes 8 accompaniment servings*

2 medium corn on the cob,
  husks and silk removed, or
  300g frozen sweetcorn,
  thawed
30g margarine or butter
1 small onion, very finely
  chopped

30g plain flour
1 tsp salt
¼ tsp coarsely ground black
  pepper
450ml single cream
225ml milk
4 medium eggs

◆ Preheat oven to 170°C (325°F, Gas 3). Cut corn kernels from cobs. Melt margarine in 2-litre saucepan over medium heat. Add onion and cook, stirring occasionally, about 10 minutes until tender and golden brown.

◆ Stir in flour, salt and pepper until blended. Gradually stir in cream and milk and cook, stirring constantly, until mixture thickens slightly and boils. Remove pan from heat; stir in corn.

◆ Using wire whisk or fork, beat eggs slightly in deep 2-litre casserole or soufflé dish. Gradually beat in corn mixture. Set casserole in larger roasting tin; place tin on oven rack. Pour *boiling water* into tin to come halfway up side of casserole.

◆ Bake 1¼ hours or until knife inserted in centre of bake comes out clean.

**Each serving: About 210 calories, 8g protein, 16g carbohydrate, 13g total fat (6g saturated), 133mg cholesterol, 375mg sodium**

## BARBECUED HERBED SWEETCORN

*Prep: 25 minutes, plus soaking   Barbecue: 30–40 minutes*
*Makes 8 accompaniment servings*

8 medium corn on
  the cob with
  husks

8 tsp olive oil
Several sprigs each basil,
  rosemary and sage or thyme

◆ Prepare barbecue. Soak cobs with husks in *cold water* to cover for 15 minutes. (Soaking keeps the husks from burning on barbecue.)

◆ Drain corn well. Gently pull back husks to about three-quarters of way down; remove the silk.

◆ Using pastry brush, brush each cob with 1 teaspoon olive oil. Tuck several sprigs of herbs into each cob.

◆ Re-wrap cobs with husks, removing 1 strip of husk from each cob and tying tops of husks together with the removed strip of husk.

◆ Place cobs on barbecue over medium heat and cook, turning occasionally, 30–40 minutes until tender when pierced with tip of sharp knife.

**Each serving: About 155 calories, 4g protein, 28g carbohydrate, 5g total fat (1g saturated), 0mg cholesterol, 5mg sodium**

## SAUTÉED FRESH SWEETCORN

*Prep: 10 minutes   Cook: 5 minutes*
*Makes 4 accompaniment servings*

6 medium corn on the cob,
  husks and silk removed
30g butter or margarine
½ tsp salt

¼ tsp coarsely ground black
  pepper
15g fresh chives, chopped, or
  spring onions, thinly sliced

Cut sweetcorn kernels from cobs. Melt butter in 26cm frying pan over medium-high heat. Add sweetcorn kernels, salt and black pepper and cook, stirring frequently, 4 minutes, or until sweetcorn is tender. Remove from heat; stir in chopped chives.

**Each serving: About 225 calories, 6g protein, 42g carbohydrate, 7g total fat (2g saturated) 16mg cholesterol, 340mg sodium**

**MAKE YOUR OWN HERB BRUSH**

If you have an abundance of garden herbs, try making a fragrant herb brush, which can be used for brushing oil or melted butter or margarine over grilled or barbecued fish, meat or poultry, garlic bread, or focaccia, as well as corn on the cob. Or, use it to dab vinaigrette over salads and steamed vegetables. Choose herbs such as rosemary, sage and thyme for your herb brush.

1 Tie a small bouquet of herb sprigs together at the stalk end with a piece of string or another sprig.

2 Dip in olive oil or melted butter or margarine and brush over grilled corn on the cob or other food.

# PEAS, SUGAR SNAPS AND MANGE-TOUT

Tender peas and mange-tout are very easy to overcook while it's almost impossible to under-cook them. Fresh green peas from a garden or the supermarket are a spring and summer treat that is well worth the extra time and effort of shelling; eat them as soon as possible after picking or buying, because, like sweetcorn, their sugars quickly convert to starch. Frozen peas are often sweeter than 'fresh' peas that have been off the vine for some time. Both flat mange-tout and plump sugar snap peas are meant to be eaten whole, pod and all – simply pull off the tough string first.

**1** If using fresh peas, shell them. Bring *175ml water* to the boil in 3-litre saucepan over high heat. Add fresh or frozen peas and return to the boil.

**2** Reduce heat to low, cover pan and simmer 3–5 minutes until peas are just tender. Drain in colander and rinse peas with cold water until they are cool; set aside.

## SWEET SUMMER PEAS

*Prep: 25 minutes    Cook: 8–10 minutes*
*Makes 6 accompaniment servings*

| | |
|---|---|
| 1.1kg fresh peas or 600g frozen peas, thawed | ¾ tsp salt |
| 60g mayonnaise | ⅛ tsp ground black pepper |
| 1 tbsp chopped fresh parsley | 175g radishes, finely chopped |
| 1 tbsp tarragon vinegar | Lettuce leaves |

**3** Prepare dressing: whisk mayonnaise, parsley, tarragon vinegar, salt and pepper together in a large bowl until smooth and well combined.

**4** Add cooked peas and chopped radishes to dressing; toss to coat. Cover and refrigerate if not serving right away. To serve, line bowl with lettuce; spoon salad over lettuce.

### HOME-MADE TARRAGON VINEGAR

Wash 900ml bottle with cork in hot soapy water. Boil the bottle in a large pan, and the cork in a small pan, for 5 minutes, then drain. Place 3 or 4 sprigs tarragon in the bottle, pushing in with a skewer if necessary. Bring 900ml white wine vinegar to the boil over a high heat in non-reactive saucepan (stainless steel or enamel). Pour through a funnel into the bottle. Cork and let stand in cool, dark place for 2 weeks.

Strain through a fine sieve into a glass measuring jug. Discard the tarragon sprigs. Return the vinegar to bottle and add fresh tarragon. This can be stored up to 3 months at cool room temperature; if stored in a warm place, it may ferment and develop an off flavour. If the cork pops, discard the vinegar.

EACH SERVING: ABOUT 110 CALORIES, 3g PROTEIN, 9g CARBOHYDRATE, 8g TOTAL FAT (1g SATURATED), 5mg CHOLESTEROL, 370mg SODIUM

## SUGAR SNAPS AND YELLOW PEPPERS

*Prep:* 20 minutes    *Cook:* 15 minutes

*Makes* 6 accompaniment servings

1 tbsp plus 2 tsp olive or vegetable oil

1 large yellow pepper, cored, seeded and cut into 5 by 2cm pieces

2 large celery stalks, cut diagonally into 5mm thick slices

Salt

Coarsely ground black pepper

450g sugar snap peas or mange-tout, strings removed

◆ Heat 1 tablespoon oil in 30cm non-stick frying pan over medium-high heat. Add yellow pepper, celery, ¾ teaspoon salt and ¼ teaspoon black pepper and cook, stirring frequently, about 10 minutes until vegetables are tender and lightly browned. Transfer to bowl.

◆ Heat remaining 2 teaspoons oil in same pan. Add sugar snap peas, ½ teaspoon salt and ¼ teaspoon black pepper and cook, stirring frequently, about 4 minutes until peas are tender-crisp. Stir in pepper mixture until well combined.

◆ Spoon vegetable mixture onto platter. If not serving right away, cover and refrigerate to serve cold later.

Each serving: About 75 calories, 3g protein, 8g carbohydrate, 4g total fat (1g saturated), 0mg cholesterol, 460mg sodium

**PREPARING MANGE-TOUT AND SNAP PEAS**

Rinse mange-tout well. To remove the string, pull off the tip of the pod, keeping the string intact. Pull the string down along the length of the pod. With sugar snap peas, the string runs along both sides of the pod.

## MIXED PEA POD STIR-FRY

*Prep:* 15 minutes    *Cook:* 8 minutes

*Makes* 4 accompaniment servings

225g green beans, ends trimmed

1 tsp salt

2 tsp vegetable oil

125g mange-tout, strings removed

125g sugar snap peas, strings removed

1 garlic clove, very finely chopped

1 tbsp soy sauce

◆ Bring *2–3cm water* to the boil in 30cm frying pan. Add green beans and salt and return to the boil. Reduce heat to low and simmer, uncovered, 3 minutes; drain in colander. Wipe pan dry.

◆ Heat oil in same pan over high heat until hot. Add green beans and cook, stirring often, 1 minute, or until beginning to brown.

◆ Add mange-tout, sugar snap peas and garlic; cook, stirring, 2–3 minutes until peas are tender-crisp. Remove from heat and stir in soy sauce.

Each serving: About 60 calories, 3g protein, 8g carbohydrate, 2g total fat (0g saturated), 0mg cholesterol, 295mg sodium

## SAUTÉED PEAS WITH SPRING ONIONS

*Prep:* 30 minutes    *Cook:* 15 minutes

*Makes* 6 accompaniment servings

1.8kg fresh peas, shelled, or 600g frozen peas, (thawed)

30g butter or margarine

1 bunch spring onions, cut into 5mm pieces

½ tsp salt

¼ tsp ground black pepper

15g fresh mint, chopped

◆ If using fresh peas, bring *225ml water* to the boil in saucepan over high heat. Add peas and return to the boil. Reduce heat to low; cover and simmer 3 minutes, or until just tender. Drain; set aside.

◆ Melt butter in 26cm frying pan over medium heat. Add spring onions and cook 2 minutes, or until tender. Add fresh or frozen thawed peas, salt and pepper and cook, stirring often, for 3–5 minutes longer, or until peas are hot. Remove from heat and stir in chopped mint. Spoon into warm serving bowl.

Each serving: About 110 calories, 5g protein, 14g carbohydrate, 4g total fat (2g saturated), 11mg cholesterol, 305mg sodium

# GREEN BEANS

Green beans of all kinds take well to simple preparations – roasted in a very hot oven, blanched and then stir-fried with Oriental seasonings, or sautéed in a little olive oil. Whatever variety you choose, buy firm, straight, slender beans without blemishes. To test for freshness, try breaking one in half: if it bends, the bean is past its prime; if it snaps easily, the bean should be tender and sweet.

## ROASTED GREEN BEANS WITH DILL VINAIGRETTE

❖❖❖❖❖❖❖❖❖❖❖

*Prep: 20 minutes*
*Roast: 20–30 minutes*
*Makes 8 accompaniment servings*

**900g green beans, trimmed**
**3 tbsp olive oil**
**Salt**
**2 tbsp white wine vinegar**
**1½ tsp Dijon mustard**
**½ tsp sugar**
**½ tsp coarsely ground black pepper**
**2 tbsp chopped fresh dill**

**1** Preheat oven to 230°C (450°F, Gas 8). Combine green beans, 1 tablespoon olive oil and ½ teaspoon salt in large roasting tin and toss to coat.

**2** Roast beans, uncovered, for 20–30 minutes, until tender and slightly browned, stirring twice during roasting for even cooking. Meanwhile, prepare the vinaigrette: whisk vinegar, mustard, sugar, pepper and ¼ teaspoon salt together in a small bowl.

### DILL

A member of the parsley family, dill is both a herb and a spice. Fresh dill has feathery green leaves and a slightly lemony anise flavour. It's a favourite for yogurt-based dips, cream sauces, soups and salads, especially fish and cucumber salads. It loses its flavour quickly on heating, so when used in hot dishes it should be added towards the end of cooking. (Dried dill, or dillweed, does not have quite the same flavour.) Dill seeds are more pungent and are good in pickles, breads and vegetable dishes.

**3** Slowly whisk in remaining 2 tablespoons olive oil; whisk in dill. When beans are done, add them to bowl and toss with vinaigrette. Serve warm or at room temperature.

EACH SERVING: ABOUT 75 CALORIES, 1g PROTEIN, 7g CARBOHYDRATE, 5g TOTAL FAT (1g SATURATED), 0mg CHOLESTEROL, 240mg SODIUM

## ROMAN-STYLE GREEN BEANS

*Prep:* 15 minutes  *Cook:* 20–25 minutes
*Makes* 8 accompaniment servings

**900g green beans, ends trimmed**
**125g sliced pancetta or sliced bacon,**
  **cut into 1cm strips**
**1 tbsp olive oil**
**½ tsp salt**
**40g pine nuts, toasted**

◆ Bring *2–3cm water* to the boil in 5-litre saucepan over high heat. Add beans and return to the boil. Reduce heat to low and simmer, uncovered, 5–10 minutes until beans are tender-crisp; drain.  Wipe pan dry.

◆ Cook pancetta, stirring frequently, in same pan over medium heat until golden. Using slotted spoon, transfer pancetta to kitchen paper to drain; set aside.

◆ Add olive oil to drippings in pan and heat over medium-high heat until hot. Add green beans with salt and cook, stirring frequently, until beans are lightly browned and tender.

◆ Spoon green beans onto warm large platter; sprinkle with pancetta and toasted pine nuts.

**Each serving: About 90 calories, 6g protein, 7g carbohydrate, 5g total fat (1g saturated), 8mg cholesterol, 365mg sodium**

## GREEN BEANS WITH HAZELNUTS

*Prep:* 20 minutes  *Cook:* 10–15 minutes
*Makes* 6 accompaniment servings

**750g green beans, ends trimmed**
**Salt**
**30g butter or margarine**
**75g hazelnuts, toasted and skinned (see**
  **page 522)**
**1 tsp grated lemon rind**
**¼ tsp ground black pepper**

◆ Bring *2–3cm water* to the boil in 5-litre saucepan over high heat. Add beans and 2 teaspoons salt and return to the boil.

◆ Reduce heat to low and simmer, uncovered, for 5–10 minutes, or until tender-crisp; drain. Wipe pan dry.

◆ Melt butter in same pan over medium heat. Add hazelnuts and cook, stirring, 3 minutes, or until butter just begins to brown.

◆ Stir in lemon rind, pepper, beans and ¼ teaspoon salt and cook, stirring, 5 minutes.

**Each serving: About 120 calories, 3g protein, 8g carbohydrate, 10g total fat (1g saturated), 0mg cholesterol, 140mg sodium**

## SESAME GREEN BEANS

*Prep:* 15 minutes  *Cook:* 10–15 minutes
*Makes* 8 accompaniment servings

**900g green beans, ends trimmed**
**1 tbsp sesame seeds**
**2 tbsp soy sauce**
**2 tsp sesame oil**
**1 tbsp very finely chopped, peeled fresh**
  **ginger or ¾ tsp ground ginger**

◆ Bring *2–3cm water* to the boil in 5-litre saucepan over high heat. Add beans and return to the boil. Reduce heat to low and simmer, uncovered, 5–10 minutes until beans are tender-crisp.

◆ Meanwhile, toast sesame seeds in small saucepan over medium heat, stirring and shaking pan frequently, until golden brown.

◆ Drain beans. Wipe pan dry. Return beans to pan. Stir in soy sauce, sesame oil and ginger; heat through.

◆ Sprinkle beans with toasted sesame seeds. Serve beans warm or cover and refrigerate to serve cold later.

**Each serving: About 45 calories, 2g protein, 7g carbohydrate, 2g total fat (0g saturated), 0mg cholesterol, 270mg sodium**

---

### GREEN BEANS

Regular green beans are widely available; Italian green beans may be easier to come by at specialist shops. Haricots verts, a slender, tender but expensive French bean, are increasingly available at supermarkets. Feel free to substitute a different bean in a favourite recipe. Before using, remove ends of beans (top and tail) and for runner beans remove the long fibrous strings.

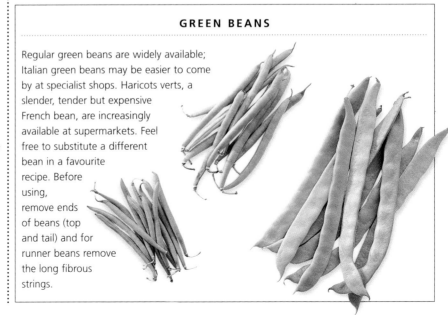

# ROOT VEGETABLES

Many of nature's edible gifts come from beneath the ground. Besides potatoes, which fall into their own category, carrots are perhaps the favourite root. But beetroots, turnips, parsnips, celeriac, swedes and Jerusalem artichokes are equally delicious – sweet and earthy – whether mashed, baked, roasted or glazed.

## HARVEST BAKE

◆◆◆◆◆◆◆◆◆◆◆◆

*Prep: 40 minutes*
*Bake: 1 hour*
*Makes 8 accompaniment servings*

**75g margarine or butter**
**450g onions, cut into 5mm thick slices**
**2 garlic cloves, very finely chopped**
**6 medium carrots (about 450g), peeled and thinly sliced**
**6 medium parsnips (about 450g), peeled, cored and thinly sliced**
**1 small swede (about 450g), peeled, cut into quarters and thinly sliced**
**3 tbsp plain flour**
**1½ tsp salt**
**¼ tsp coarsely ground black pepper**
**¼ tsp ground nutmeg**
**600ml milk**
**30g Parmesan cheese, freshly grated**
**Chopped fresh parsley for garnish**

**1** Preheat oven to 170°C (375°F, Gas 5). Melt 45g margarine in non-stick frying pan over medium heat. Add onion and garlic; cook 15–20 minutes, stirring often, until golden.

### SWEDE

A cross between a cabbage and a turnip, swedes have yellow-orange flesh and a thick skin, which is often waxed to prevent drying out. They will keep for up to 2 weeks in the refrigerator, and can be prepared as for turnips.

**2** Toss carrots, parsnips, swede and onion mixture together in shallow 2½-litre baking dish until well combined. Cover and bake 45 minutes, or until vegetables are fork-tender.

**3** Meanwhile, melt remaining 30g margarine in 2-litre saucepan over medium heat. Stir in flour and next 3 ingredients and cook, stirring, 1 minute.

**4** Gradually stir milk into flour mixture in saucepan; cook, stirring constantly, until sauce thickens slightly and boils.

**5** Stir sauce into vegetables. Sprinkle grated Parmesan cheese evenly on top. Bake, uncovered, 15 minutes longer, or until sauce is bubbly and top is golden brown. To serve, sprinkle with parsley.

EACH SERVING: ABOUT 245 CALORIES, 7g PROTEIN, 32g CARBOHYDRATE, 11g TOTAL FAT (4g SATURATED), 13mg CHOLESTEROL, 615mg SODIUM

Also known as celery root, celeriac is a special variety of celery grown for its knobby, round root rather than its stalks. At its peak in the winter months, it has a pronounced celery flavour and a firm, dense texture similar to that of turnips. The flesh of the larger roots, however, can be woody and tough. Celeriac can discolour when cut; sprinkling it with lemon juice will prevent this. Try it boiled or braised, or shredded raw for a salad.

## CELERIAC RÉMOULADE

*Prep: 20 minutes, plus chilling*
*Makes 6 accompaniment servings*

| | |
|---|---|
| 2 tbsp fresh lemon juice | 1 tbsp finely chopped fresh |
| 750g celeriac | parsley |
| 60g mayonnaise | ¼ tsp ground black pepper |
| 2 tbsp Dijon mustard | |

◆ Place lemon juice in large bowl. Peel celeriac. Using adjustable-blade slicer, or mandoline, or very sharp knife, cut celeriac into 3mm thick matchstick strips. As you cut it, add celeriac to lemon juice and toss to prevent discoloration.

◆ Mix mayonnaise, mustard, parsley and pepper together in small bowl until well combined. Add to celeriac in large bowl and toss to combine well. Cover and refrigerate for at least 1 hour, or overnight.

**Each serving: About 160 calories, 2g protein, 6g carbohydrate, 15g total fat (2g saturated), 11mg cholesterol, 340mg sodium**

## MASHED ROOT VEGETABLES

*Prep: 15 minutes    Cook: 25 minutes*
*Makes 8 accompaniment servings*

| | |
|---|---|
| 900g carrots, celeriac, | Salt |
| parsnips, white turnips | 45g butter or margarine |
| and/or swede | Pinch ground nutmeg |
| 450g potatoes | ¼ tsp ground black pepper |

◆ Peel vegetables and potatoes and cut into 2–3cm pieces. Bring root vegetables, potatoes, 2 teaspoons salt and *water* to cover to the boil in 4-litre saucepan over high heat. Reduce heat to low, cover and simmer 15 minutes, or until vegetables are tender. Drain and return to pan.

◆ Add butter, ground nutmeg, black pepper and ½ teaspoon salt and mash with potato masher until potatoes are smooth and creamy.

**Each serving: About 135 calories, 2g protein, 23g carbohydrate, 5g total fat (2g saturated), 13mg cholesterol, 250mg sodium**

## VEGETABLE COBBLER

*Prep: 30 minutes    Bake: 1¼ hours*
*Makes 6 main dish servings*

| | |
|---|---|
| 1 medium butternut squash (about 900g), peeled, seeded and cut into 4cm chunks | 400ml vegetable stock |
| | ½ tsp grated lemon rind |
| | 1 small bunch broccoli (about 175g), cut into 5 by 2–3cm pieces |
| 450g red potatoes, cut into 4cm chunks | |
| | 275ml milk |
| 3 medium parsnips (about 225g), peeled and cut into 2–3cm pieces | 1 tbsp cornflour |
| | 240g plain flour |
| | 1½ tsp baking powder |
| 1 medium red onion, cut into 6 wedges | ½ tsp bicarbonate of soda |
| | ½ tsp salt |
| 2 tbsp olive oil | 60g white vegetable fat |
| ¼ tsp salt | 175ml buttermilk or soured milk (see page 392) |
| ½ tsp dried tarragon | |

◆ Preheat oven to 230°C (450°F, Gas 8). Toss first 7 ingredients together in 33 by 20cm ovenproof dish until vegetables are well coated with oil. Bake, uncovered, 1 hour, or until vegetables are fork-tender and lightly browned, stirring once.

◆ Meanwhile, after vegetables have cooked about 45 minutes, bring stock and lemon rind to the boil in 3-litre saucepan over high heat. Add broccoli and return to the boil. Reduce heat to low; cover and simmer 1 minute.

◆ Mix 125ml milk with cornflour and stir into broccoli mixture. Cook, stirring constantly, until mixture thickens slightly and boils; boil 1 minute. Pour broccoli mixture over vegetables and stir until brown bits are loosened from base of ovenproof dish. Remove from heat.

◆ Make scone topping: mix flour and next 3 ingredients in large bowl. Using pastry blender or two knives used scissor fashion, cut in vegetable fat until mixture resembles coarse crumbs. Add buttermilk and stir just until moistened. Turn out dough onto lightly floured surface; knead 6–8 times, just until smooth. Roll out to 1cm thick and cut out 12 rounds using 6cm biscuit cutter. Place rounds of dough on top of vegetable mixture. Bake cobbler, uncovered, for a further 15 minutes, or until scone topping is browned.

**Each serving: About 505 calories, 13g protein, 78g carbohydrate, 18g total fat (5g saturated), 8mg cholesterol, 790mg sodium**

## CARROTS AND PARSNIPS AU GRATIN

*Prep: 45 minutes   Bake: 20 minutes*
*Makes 8 accompaniment servings*

450g carrots, peeled and cut
   diagonally into 5mm thick
   slices
450g parsnips, peeled and cut
   diagonally into 5mm thick
   slices
30g margarine or butter

1 small onion, finely chopped
125g mayonnaise
2 tbsp horseradish sauce
¼ tsp salt
⅛ tsp ground black pepper
1 slice firm white bread, torn
   into 5mm crumbs

❖ Bring *4cm water* to the boil in 30cm frying pan over high heat. Add carrots and parsnips and return to the boil. Reduce heat to low; cover and simmer 20 minutes, or until vegetables are tender. Drain, reserving 60ml cooking liquid Transfer vegetables to 1½-litre ovenproof dish.

❖ Preheat oven to 180°C (350°F, Gas 4). Melt 15g margarine in 1-litre saucepan over medium heat. Add onion and cook, stirring occasionally, until tender. Remove from heat.

❖ Stir in mayonnaise, horseradish, salt, pepper and reserved cooking liquid. Gently fold sauce into vegetables.

❖ Melt remaining 15g margarine in small frying pan over low heat. Stir in breadcrumbs; mix until coated with margarine. Scatter over vegetables in dish. Bake 20 minutes, or until crumbs are browned and vegetables are hot.

**Each serving: About 210 calories, 2g protein, 21g carbohydrate, 14g total fat (2g saturated), 8mg cholesterol, 260mg sodium**

## ROASTED CARROTS AND PARSNIPS

*Prep: 15 minutes   Roast: 1 hour*
*Makes 8 accompaniment servings*

450g carrots, peeled and cut
   into 5cm pieces
450g parsnips, peeled and cut
   into 5cm pieces
225g large shallots, peeled

1 tbsp olive oil
⅛ tsp dried thyme
½ tsp salt
¼ tsp ground black pepper

Preheat oven to 220°C (425°F, Gas 7). Toss carrots, parsnips and shallots with olive oil, thyme, salt and pepper until evenly coated in large roasting tin. Roast 1 hour, or until vegetables are tender when pierced with knife.

**Each serving: About 105 calories, 2g protein, 22g carbohydrate, 2g total fat (0g saturated), 0mg cholesterol, 160mg sodium**

## MAPLE-GLAZED CARROTS WITH PISTACHIOS

*Prep: 30 minutes   Cook: 30–40 minutes*
*Makes 10 accompaniment servings*

1.3kg carrots, peeled and cut
   into 8 by 1cm sticks
60g butter or margarine,
   cut up
1 tsp salt

175ml maple syrup
60g pistachios, chopped and
   toasted

❖ Bring *2–3cm water* to the boil in 30cm frying pan over high heat. Add carrots and return to the boil. Reduce heat to low; cover and simmer 8–10 minutes, until carrots are tender-crisp. Drain.

❖ Wipe pan dry. Return carrots to pan. Add butter and salt and cook, uncovered, over medium-high heat, gently stirring occasionally, 10–15 minutes, until carrots are glazed and golden.

❖ Add maple syrup and bring to the boil. Boil 2 minutes, stirring frequently, until carrots are lightly coated with glaze. Transfer to bowl; sprinkle with pistachios.

**Each serving: About 175 calories, 3g protein, 25g carbohydrate, 8g total fat (3g saturated), 13mg cholesterol, 315mg sodium**

### PARSNIPS

Available all year round, parsnips are at their peak in winter. Their creamy texture lends itself to cold-weather favourites such as smooth mashes, purées and soups, while their sweet nutty flavour makes them excellent in stews or roasted as an accompaniment. When buying, look for firm, smooth, medium-sized parsnips without cracks. Large, older parsnips have a stronger flavour than younger ones; they may also have a woody core, which should be removed before cooking.

## BEETROOTS WITH BASIL VINAIGRETTE

*Prep: 30 minutes, plus cooling    Cook: 45 minutes*
*Makes 8 accompaniment servings*

2.7kg beetroots with tops
  (about 12 medium)
3 tbsp cider vinegar
2 tbsp olive or vegetable oil
2 tsp sugar
1 tsp salt
15g fresh basil, chopped
½ small onion, cut into paper-
  thin slices

❖ Trim stalks and leaves from beetroots, reserving several leaves for garnish. Scrub beetroots. Bring beetroots with *water* to cover to the boil in 5-litre saucepan over a high heat. Reduce heat to low; cover and simmer 30 minutes, or until beetroots are tender when pierced with knife.

❖ Drain and leave until cool enough to handle. Peel beetroots and cut into bite-sized chunks.

❖ Whisk vinegar, oil, sugar and salt together in large bowl. Add basil, onion and beetroots; toss to combine. Serve at room temperature or cover and refrigerate to serve cold later. To serve, line platter with reserved beetroot leaves and spoon beetroots on top.

**Each serving: About 125 calories, 3g protein, 21g carbohydrate, 4g total fat (0g saturated), 0mg cholesterol, 410mg sodium**

## ROASTED BEETROOTS WITH CARDAMOM-SPICE BUTTER

*Prep: 20 minutes, plus cooling    Roast: 1–1½ hours*
*Makes 4 accompaniment servings*

1.2kg beetroots with tops
  (about 6 medium)
½ tsp ground cardamom
¼ tsp ground cumin
Pinch ground cloves
15g butter or margarine
¼ tsp salt

❖ Preheat oven to 220°C (425°F, Gas 7). Trim stalks and leaves from beetroots. Scrub beetroots.

❖ Place beetroots in large roasting tin; cover tightly with foil. Roast for 1–1½ hours until tender when pierced with knife. Set aside until cool enough to handle. Peel beetroots and cut into wedges.

❖ Heat cardamom, cumin and cloves in 3-litre saucepan over low heat, shaking pan occasionally, 2 minutes, or until very fragrant. Add butter and heat until bubbling. Add beetroots and salt; increase heat to medium and cook, stirring often, 5 minutes, or until hot.

**Each serving: About 115 calories, 3g protein, 20g carbohydrate, 3g total fat (1g saturated), 8mg cholesterol, 310mg sodium.**

## GLAZED TURNIPS

*Prep: 10 minutes    Cook: 20 minutes*
*Makes 6 accompaniment servings*

750g turnips, peeled and cut
  into 2–3cm wedges
1 tsp salt
30g butter or margarine
70g sugar

❖ Combine turnips with salt and *water* to cover and bring to the boil in 30cm frying pan over high heat.

❖ Reduce heat to low; cover and simmer 7–10 minutes, just until turnips are tender when pierced with knife. Drain.

❖ Wipe pan dry. Melt butter in same pan over high heat. Add sugar and cook, stirring occasionally, about 2 minutes until amber in colour. Add turnips and cook, stirring often, 5 minutes, or until well coated.

**Each serving: About 95 calories, 1g protein, 16g carbohydrate, 4g total fat (2g saturated), 11mg cholesterol, 455mg sodium**

## ROASTED JERUSALEM ARTICHOKES

*Prep: 15 minutes    Roast: 1 hour*
*Makes 8 accompaniment servings*

900g Jerusalem artichokes
1 tbsp olive oil
1 tsp salt
¼ tsp ground black pepper
Chopped fresh parsley for
  garnish

❖ Preheat oven to 220°C (425°F, Gas 7). Using a vegetable brush, scrub Jerusalem artichokes. Toss with oil, salt and pepper in large roasting tin.

❖ Roast 1 hour, until Jerusalem artichokes are tender when pierced with tip of knife. Garnish with chopped parsley and serve.

**Each serving: About 100 calories, 2g protein, 20g carbohydrate, 2g total fat (0g saturated), 0mg cholesterol, 270mg sodium**

---

### JERUSALEM ARTICHOKES

Neither an artichoke nor from Jerusalem, this brown-skinned tuber is a member of the sunflower family. Crisp, nutty and slightly sweet in taste, Jerusalem artichokes are equally good served raw in a salad or cooked. Peel them or simply scrub the skin well before using. When shopping, choose firm, unblemished tubers free of soft spots and green-tinged portions.

# POTATOES

Potatoes are supremely satisfying in any guise. Here, our side dishes include potatoes baked in layers, mashed to a creamy pulp or roasted with garlic and herbs. For a main dish, try our rich potato and artichoke pancake or a baked jacket potato brimming with a hearty filling.

## TWO-POTATOES ANNA

◆◆◆◆◆◆◆◆◆◆◆◆◆

*Prep: 45 minutes*
*Bake: 25 minutes*
*Makes 10 accompaniment servings*

**900g white potatoes**
**900g orange-fleshed sweet potatoes**
**60ml vegetable oil**
**1 large onion, chopped**
**60g butter or margarine**
**Salt**
**Ground black pepper**
**Parsley sprigs for garnish**

### ADJUSTABLE-BLADE SLICER

To slice, julienne and waffle-cut vegetables easily, use an adjustable-blade slicer. These range from the classic all-metal mandoline to lightweight plastic models. Some have a selection of blades for different functions; the best are adjustable to paper-thinness. To protect your fingers, a safety shield holds the food in place as you slide it over the blade.

**1** Peel potatoes. Using an adjustable-blade slicer or sharp knife, thinly slice potatoes, keeping white and sweet potatoes separate.

**2** Heat oil in 26cm cast-iron frying pan with an ovenproof handle (or wrap handle with double thickness of foil) over medium heat. Add onion and cook until tender. Transfer to bowl.

**3** Arrange white potatoes, overlapping slightly, in same pan. Sprinkle with onion and dot with 30g butter. Sprinkle with ¾ teaspoon salt and ¼ teaspoon pepper.

**4** Arrange sweet potato slices over white potatoes. Dot with remaining 30g margarine; sprinkle with ¾ teaspoon salt and ¼ teaspoon pepper.

**5** Cook layered potatoes over medium heat 15 minutes, or until bottom layer of potatoes is lightly browned. Preheat oven to 230°C (450°F, Gas 8).

**6** Place pan on bottom rack in oven and bake 25 minutes or until potatoes are tender when pierced with knife, pressing them down with spatula occasionally. To serve, loosen edge of potatoes with spatula; carefully invert onto warm platter. Garnish with parsley sprigs; cut into wedges.

EACH SERVING: ABOUT 250 CALORIES, 3g PROTEIN, 37g CARBOHYDRATE, 10g TOTAL FAT (4g SATURATED), 15mg CHOLESTEROL, 385mg SODIUM

## ROASTED POTATOES WITH GARLIC

*Prep:* 20 minutes    *Roast:* 1 hour
*Makes* 10 accompaniment servings

| | |
|---|---|
| 2kg medium red and/or white potatoes, unpeeled and each cut into quarters | 60ml olive oil |
| | 1¼ tsp salt |
| | ½ tsp coarsely ground black pepper |
| 2 medium red onions, each cut into 6 wedges | |
| 1 tbsp chopped fresh thyme or 1 tsp dried | 2 garlic cloves, very finely chopped |

Preheat oven to 220°C (425°F, Gas 7). Toss potatoes with remaining ingredients in roasting tin. Roast, turning occasionally with metal spatula, for 1 hour, or until golden and fork-tender. Serve warm or at room temperature.

Each serving: About 240 calories, 4g protein, 44g carbohydrate, 6g total fat (1g saturated), 0mg cholesterol, 275mg sodium

## POTATO AND ARTICHOKE RÖSTI

*Prep:* 35 minutes    *Bake:* 20–25 minutes
*Makes* 4 main dish servings

| | |
|---|---|
| 4 large baking potatoes (about 1.1kg) | 125g Fontina or mozzarella cheese, grated |
| ¾ tsp salt | 225g bottled marinated artichoke hearts, rinsed, well drained and sliced |
| ¼ tsp coarsely ground black pepper | |
| 2 tbsp olive oil | |

◆ Preheat oven to 200°C (400°F, Gas 6). Peel and coarsely grate potatoes; pat dry. Toss potatoes with salt and pepper.

◆ Heat 1 tablespoon oil in 26cm frying pan with an ovenproof handle (or wrap handle with double thickness of foil) over medium heat. Working quickly, add half potatoes, patting with wooden spoon to cover pan. Leaving 1cm border, top potatoes with half cheese, all the artichokes,

then remaining cheese. Cover with remaining potatoes, patting to edge of pan. Cook 10 minutes, or until base is brown, shaking pan occasionally to keep rösti moving freely. Carefully invert onto large plate. Add remaining 1 tablespoon oil to pan; slide rösti back into pan. Cook 10 minutes longer, gently shaking pan. Place in oven and bake 20–25 minutes until potatoes are tender.

Each serving: About 475 calories, 15g protein, 71g carbohydrate, 16g total fat (6g saturated), 33mg cholesterol, 700mg sodium

## CLASSIC MASHED POTATOES

*Prep:* 20 minutes    *Cook:* 30 minutes
*Makes* 8 accompaniment servings

| | |
|---|---|
| 1.3kg potatoes | 1½ tsp salt |
| 60g butter or margarine | 225ml hot milk |

◆ Peel potatoes and cut into 2–3cm chunks. Bring potatoes and enough *water* to cover to the boil in 3-litre saucepan over high heat. Reduce heat to low, cover and simmer 15 minutes, or until fork-tender. Drain.

◆ Return potatoes to pan. Mash potatoes with butter and salt. Gradually add milk; mash until smooth.

Each serving: About 215 calories, 4g protein, 36g carbohydrate, 7g total fat (3g saturated), 20mg cholesterol, 490mg sodium

### MASHED POTATOES PLUS

**Garlic and lemon** Prepare Classic Mashed Potatoes as above as far as draining potatoes. Meanwhile, heat the butter and salt called for in recipe with 2 finely chopped garlic cloves in 1-litre saucepan over a low heat for 3 minutes. Add to potatoes and mash. Add the milk as instructed, then stir in 2 tablespoons finely chopped fresh parsley and 1 teaspoon grated lemon rind.

Each serving: About 215 calories, 4g protein, 36g carbohydrate, 7g total fat (3g saturated), 20mg cholesterol, 490mg sodium

**Horseradish** Prepare Classic Mashed Potatoes as above, but add 2 tablespoons undrained horseradish sauce with the milk.

Each serving: About 215 calories, 4g protein, 36g carbohydrate, 7g total fat (3g saturated), 20mg cholesterol, 530mg sodium

**Parsnip** Prepare Classic Mashed Potatoes as above, but substitute 450g parsnips, peeled and cut into 2–3cm pieces, for 450g potatoes and use only 175ml milk.

Each serving: About 210 calories, 4g protein, 35g carbohydrate, 7g total fat (3g saturated), 19mg cholesterol, 490mg sodium

## JACKET POTATOES

*Prep: 15–25 minutes    Bake: 45 minutes*
*Makes 4 main dish servings*

**4 large baking potatoes,**    **Choice of Jacket Potato**
**(350g each)**    **Topping (see below)**

Preheat oven to 230°C (450°F, Gas 8). Pierce potatoes with a fork. Bake directly on oven rack for 45 minutes, or until fork-tender. Meanwhile, prepare Jacket Potato Topping. When potatoes are done, slash tops; press to open slightly, then spoon topping on top.

**For nutritional values, see below.**

## CHUNKY HOME-FRIED POTATOES

*Prep: 5 minutes    Cook: 25 minutes*
*Makes 4 accompaniment servings*

**750g medium red potatoes**    **½ tsp salt**
**2 tbsp olive oil**

✦ Cut potatoes into 4cm chunks. Heat oil in 30cm frying pan over medium-high heat. Add potatoes and salt and cook, turning occasionally, until golden brown.

✦ Reduce heat to medium; cover pan and continue cooking potato chunks, turning once or twice, until potatoes are fork-tender.

**Each serving: About 205 calories, 3g protein, 34g carbohydrate, 7g total fat (1g saturated), 0mg cholesterol, 275mg sodium**

## BAKED POTATO WEDGES

*Prep: 10 minutes    Bake: 45 minutes*
*Makes 4 accompaniment servings*

**3 medium baking potatoes or**    **1 tbsp vegetable oil**
**orange-fleshed sweet**    **½ tsp salt**
**potatoes**    **⅛ tsp ground black pepper**

✦ Preheat oven to 220°C (425°F, Gas 7). Cut each potato lengthways into quarters, then cut each quarter lengthways into 3 wedges.

✦ Toss potato wedges with oil, salt and black pepper until evenly coated on baking tray. Bake 45 minutes, or until potatoes are golden.

**Each serving: About 195 calories, 3g protein, 38g carbohydrate, 4g total fat (1g saturated), 0mg cholesterol, 280mg sodium**

## JACKET POTATO TOPPINGS (EACH TOPS 4 POTATOES)

**CHILLI** Heat 30cm non-stick frying pan over medium-high heat. Add 175g minced beef and 1 chopped small onion; cook, stirring, until meat is browned and onion is tender. Stir in 3 tablespoons chilli powder; cook 1 minute. Add 400g canned chopped tomatoes with chilli, 175ml water and 1 teaspoon sugar; cook 1 minute longer.

Each serving: About 435 calories, 11g protein, 96g carbohydrate, 3g total fat (1g saturated), 4mg cholesterol, 500mg sodium

**HAM AND EGG** Melt 30g butter or margarine in 30cm non-stick frying pan over medium heat. Add 1 diced medium green pepper and 1 diced medium onion; cook until tender and browned. Stir in 125g diced cooked ham and 6 medium eggs, beaten with 60ml water and ¼ teaspoon each salt and coarsely ground black pepper. Stir until eggs are cooked.

Each serving: About 595 calories, 24g protein, 92g carbohydrate, 15g total fat (5g saturated), 344mg cholesterol, 645mg sodium

**CHUNKY VEGETABLE** Cut 1 small aubergine, 1 medium courgette and 1 large red pepper into 1cm pieces. Heat 2 tablespoons olive oil in 30cm non-stick frying pan over medium-high heat. Add vegetables; cook 15 minutes. Stir in 400g canned tomatoes with herbs, 60ml water, 1 tablespoon balsamic vinegar and 1 teaspoon salt. Heat through.

Each serving: About 490 calories, 10g protein, 99g carbohydrate, 7g total fat (1g saturated), 0mg cholesterol, 760mg sodium

**SPINACH AND FETA** Melt 30g butter or margarine in 2-litre saucepan over medium heat. Stir in 2 tablespoons plain flour. Add 375ml milk and bring to the boil, stirring. Stir in 1300g thawed frozen chopped spinach, ¼ teaspoon each dried dill and ground black pepper, and 60g crumbled feta; heat through. Top with 60g feta.

Each serving: About 590 calories, 18g protein, 99g carbohydrate, 16g total fat (9g saturated), 55mg cholesterol, 520mg sodium

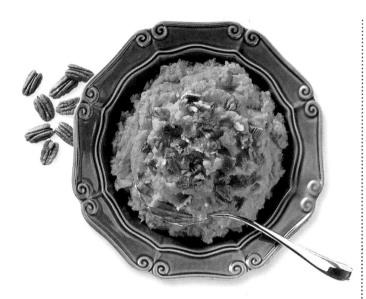

## PRALINE SWEET POTATOES

*Prep: 15 minutes, plus cooling    Cook: 35–40 minutes*
*Makes 10 accompaniment servings*

2.2kg orange-fleshed sweet
  potatoes, peeled and each
  cut crossways into thirds
50g sugar

125g pecans
75g butter or margarine
125ml milk
1¼ tsp salt

◆ Bring sweet potatoes and enough *water* to cover to the boil in 8-litre saucepan over high heat. Reduce heat to low; cover and simmer for 20–25 minutes, until potatoes are fork-tender. Drain and return to pan.

◆ Meanwhile, grease baking sheet. Heat sugar and *60ml water*, stirring gently, in 1-litre saucepan over low heat until sugar dissolves. Increase heat to medium and boil rapidly, without stirring, about 7 minutes until syrup turns a light golden brown.

◆ Working quickly, stir in pecans and 30g butter until combined. Spread pecan mixture in a thin layer on baking sheet; set aside to cool.

◆ Add milk, salt and remaining 45g butter to potatoes. Mash them until almost smooth. Heat mixture through over low heat.

◆ To serve, spoon mashed sweet potatoes into large bowl. Break pecan mixture into small pieces; sprinkle on top of sweet potatoes.

**Each serving: About 335 calories, 4g protein, 51g carbohydrate, 14g total fat (3g saturated), 18mg cholesterol, 360mg sodium**

## SWEET POTATO CASSEROLE

*Prep: 20 minutes    Bake: 60–70 minutes*
*Makes 8 accompaniment servings*

1.8kg orange-fleshed sweet
  potatoes, peeled and cut
  into 2cm thick slices
75g dark brown sugar
Salt

¼ tsp coarsely ground black
  pepper
60g butter or margarine, cut
  into small pieces
60g walnuts, coarsely chopped

◆ Preheat oven to 200°C (400°F, Gas 6). Arrange half the potato slices in a 33 by 20cm ovenproof serving dish. Sprinkle with half of sugar, ¼ teaspoon salt and all the pepper. Dot with 30g butter. Top with remaining potatoes. Sprinkle with remaining sugar and ¼ teaspoon salt; dot with remaining 30g butter.

◆ Cover with foil and bake 30 minutes. Uncover; sprinkle with walnuts and bake 30–40 minutes longer, until potatoes are tender, basting with syrup in dish 3 times during baking.

**Each serving: About 300 calories, 4g protein, 52g carbohydrate, 9g total fat (2g saturated), 16mg cholesterol, 225mg sodium**

## TWO-POTATO CASSEROLE

*Prep: 1 hour, plus cooling    Bake: 45 minutes*
*Makes 8 accompaniment servings*

900g baking potatoes,
  unpeeled
900g orange-fleshed sweet
  potatoes, unpeeled
45g butter or margarine
1 small onion, finely chopped
3 tbsp plain flour

2 tsp salt
¼ tsp coarsely ground black
  pepper
600ml milk
600g frozen chopped spinach,
  thawed and squeezed dry

◆ Bring baking and sweet potatoes and enough *water* to cover to the boil in 8-litre saucepan over high heat. Reduce heat to low; cover and simmer 20–30 minutes until potatoes are just fork-tender but not soft. Drain and cool.

◆ Preheat oven to 190°C (375°F, Gas 5). Melt butter in 2-litre saucepan over medium heat. Add onion and cook until tender. Stir in flour, salt and ground black pepper. Gradually whisk in milk and cook, whisking, until sauce boils; set aside.

◆ Peel all potatoes; cut into 5mm thick slices. Arrange half potato slices in greased deep 2-litre casserole. Top with all spinach; pour half of sauce on top. Repeat with remaining potatoes and sauce. Cover and bake 30 minutes. Uncover; bake 15 minutes longer, or until top is browned.

**Each serving: About 335 calories, 9g protein, 61g carbohydrate, 7g total fat (3g saturated), 10mg cholesterol, 700mg sodium**

# ONION FAMILY

Leeks, garlic and onions are the foundation of some fragrant and appetizing side dishes. Leeks can be marinated in oil and herbs and then grilled to bring out their fresh, delicate flavour. Onions and garlic become sweet, succulent and considerably milder in flavour when roasted or cooked with a small amount of preserves or sugar in a frying pan until glazed. Try any of these recipes with roasted meats or poultry.

## GRILLED LEEKS

*Prep: 25 minutes, plus marinating*  *Grill: 10 minutes*
*Makes 6 accompaniment servings*

6 large leeks
Salt
60ml olive or vegetable oil
2 tbsp tarragon vinegar
1½ tsp finely chopped fresh
   oregano

½ tsp sugar
½ tsp coarsely ground black
   pepper
Oregano or parsley sprigs for
   garnish

**1** Cut off roots from base of leeks and trim tops. Cut each lengthways in half to within 5cm of root ends.

**2** Separate leaves of each leek slightly and rinse thoroughly with cold water. (Sand and grit often lodges between the leaves.)

**3** Bring *5cm water* to the boil in 8-litre saucepan over high heat. Add leeks and 2 teaspoons salt and return to the boil. Reduce heat to low; cover and simmer 5–10 minutes until leeks are just tender. Drain well, shaking to remove excess water.

**4** Prepare marinade: whisk oil, tarragon vinegar, oregano, sugar, black pepper and ½ teaspoon salt together in shallow non-metallic dish. Add leeks to marinade and turn to coat. Cover dish with cling film and refrigerate at least 2 hours, turning leeks occasionally.

**5** Preheat grill. Place leeks on grill rack, reserving marinade. Grill about 15cm from heat, 10 minutes, or until leeks are hot and lightly browned, turning once and brushing with reserved marinade.

**6** Transfer leeks to large serving platter. Pour juices in grill pan over leeks. Serve warm or cover with cling film and refrigerate to serve cold later. Garnish with oregano sprigs.

EACH SERVING: ABOUT 130 CALORIES, 1g PROTEIN, 13g CARBOHYDRATE, 9g TOTAL FAT (1g SATURATED), 0mg CHOLESTEROL, 230mg SODIUM

## CARAMELIZED ONIONS

*Prep: 45 minutes, plus cooling*
*Cook: 30 minutes*
*Makes 4 accompaniment*
*servings*

**750g pearl onions**
**75g sultanas**
**2 tbsp sugar**
**2 tbsp vegetable oil**
**½ tsp salt**

◆ Bring onions and *2–3cm water* to the boil in deep 30cm frying pan over high heat. Reduce heat to low; cover and simmer 15 minutes, or until onions are tender. Drain. Cool onions under cold water; drain again.

◆ Peel onions, leaving a little of root end on to help hold shape while cooking.

◆ Wipe frying pan dry. Cook onions, sultanas, sugar, oil and salt in same pan over medium-high heat, stirring and shaking pan often, about 5 minutes until onions are glazed and browned.

**Each serving: About 210 calories, 3g protein, 37g carbohydrate, 7g total fat (1g saturated), 0mg cholesterol, 275mg sodium**

## GLAZED PEARL ONIONS

*Prep: 45 minutes, plus cooling*    *Cook: 25 minutes*
*Makes 6 accompaniment servings*

**900g pearl onions**
**45g butter or margarine**
**2 tbsp redcurrant jelly**

**2 tsp sugar**
**¼ tsp salt**

◆ Bring onions and *2–3cm water* to the boil in deep 30cm frying pan over high heat. Reduce heat to low; cover and simmer 5–10 minutes until onions are tender. Drain. Cool onions under cold water; drain again.

◆ Peel onions, leaving a little of root end of each to help hold shape while cooking. Wipe frying pan dry.

◆ Cook onions and remaining ingredients in same pan over medium-high heat, stirring and shaking pan often, about 5 minutes until onions are glazed and browned.

**Each serving: About 130 calories, 2g protein, 19g carbohydrate, 6g total fat (1g saturated), 0mg cholesterol, 160mg sodium**

## OVEN-ROASTED ONIONS

*Prep: 10 minutes    Roast: About 1¼ hours*
*Makes 12 accompaniment servings*

**4 tbsp olive or vegetable oil**
**2kg large red or white onions, cut crossways into 2cm thick slices**

**Salt**
**2 tbsp brown sugar**
**1 tbsp cider vinegar**

◆ Preheat oven to 200°C (400°F, Gas 6). Grease each of 2 baking sheets with 1 tablespoon oil. Place onion slices in single layer in each.

◆ Mix remaining 2 tablespoons oil with 1 teaspoon salt. Brush onion slices with half of oil mixture. Place baking sheets on 2 oven racks and roast onions 45 minutes.

◆ Using spatula, turn onion slices over; brush with remaining oil mixture. Rotate baking sheets between upper and lower racks and roast onions 30 minutes longer.

◆ Mix brown sugar, cider vinegar and ½ teaspoon salt together in small bowl. Brush onion slices with brown sugar mixture and roast 5 minutes longer, or until onions are tender and golden.

**Each serving: About 110 calories, 2g protein, 19g carbohydrate, 4g total fat (1g saturated), 0mg cholesterol, 275mg sodium**

## PAN-ROASTED GARLIC

*Prep: 15 minutes, plus cooling    Cook: 30 minutes*
*Makes about 225g*

**4 heads garlic (about 350g), separated into cloves, unpeeled**

**1 tbsp sugar**
**1 tbsp vegetable oil**
**½ tsp salt**

◆ Bring garlic cloves and *1.3 litres water* to the boil in 3-litre saucepan over high heat.

◆ Reduce heat to low, cover and simmer 15 minutes, or until garlic cloves are fork-tender. Drain. Cool garlic under cold water; drain again.

◆ Peel garlic cloves. Cook garlic, sugar, oil and salt in 26cm frying pan over medium-high heat, stirring and shaking pan often, about 5 minutes until garlic cloves are caramallized and browned.

◆ Use pan-roasted garlic as a condiment to sprinkle over salads or cooked vegetables, serve alongside roasted meats and poultry or spread like butter on bread.

**Each 100g: About 300 calories, 10g protein, 56g carbohydrate, 7g total fat (1g saturated), 0mg cholesterol, 500mg sodium**

# Squash

Squash are grouped into summer and winter varieties, although most are available all year round. Winter varieties (including butternut, acorn and spaghetti squash) have hard skin and seeds, and typically contain a firm, orange-coloured flesh; they are equally good large or small. By contrast, soft-skinned summer squash, such as green and yellow courgettes, have a creamy-white flesh and are most tender and flavourful when small. Cooking options for both are plentiful; squash can be sliced and sautéed in garlic-flavoured oil, grated and fried for crisp, golden fritters, halved and baked with a buttery pecan topping or roasted with fragrant herbs.

**1** Using a coarse grater, grate carrot and courgettes. Pat vegetables very dry with kitchen towels.

**2** Mix grated vegetables with flour, Parmesan, salt, pepper and egg in medium bowl.

## Vegetable fritters

*Prep:* 20 minutes  *Cook:* 5 minutes per batch
*Makes* 4 accompaniment servings

1 large carrot
1 medium courgette (300g)
1 medium yellow courgette (300g)
40g plain flour
40g Parmesan cheese, freshly grated

½ tsp salt
⅛ tsp ground black pepper
1 medium egg
125ml vegetable oil

**3** Heat oil in 26cm frying pan over medium heat. Gently drop one-eighth of vegetable mixture at a time into oil in pan, flattening slightly to about 8cm round.

**4** Cook 3 fritters at a time, turning once, 5 minutes until golden brown. Using spatula, transfer to kitchen towels to drain. Keep warm in low oven while cooking remainder.

### MINI FRITTERS

Try tiny fritters with a basil dipping sauce. For sauce, in blender blend 150ml soured cream, 40g fresh basil, 1 teaspoon fresh lemon juice and ¼ teaspoon each salt and black pepper until smooth. In Step 3, drop mixture into pan 1 tablespoon at a time. Cook until golden, turning once. Makes about 32 mini fritters.

Each fritter with 1 teaspoon sauce: About 40 calories, 1g protein, 2g carbohydrate, 3g total fat (2g saturated), 9mg cholesterol, 75mg sodium

EACH SERVING: ABOUT 245 CALORIES, 8g PROTEIN, 15g CARBOHYDRATE, 18g TOTAL FAT (4g SATURATED), 60mg CHOLESTEROL, 450mg SODIUM

## ACORN SQUASH WITH BROWN SUGAR-PECAN TOPPING

*Prep: 15 minutes     Bake: 45 minutes*
*Makes 4 accompaniment servings*

2 small acorn squash (450g each)
½ tsp salt
60g pecans or walnuts, chopped

50g light brown sugar
30g margarine or butter, melted

◆ Preheat oven to 190°C (375°F, Gas 5). Cut each acorn squash lengthways in half; discard seeds. Cut squash crossways into 2–3cm slices. Place slices, in a single layer, in baking sheet and sprinkle with salt. Drizzle *2 tablespoons water* round squash. Cover sheet tightly with foil. Bake 30 minutes.

◆ Meanwhile, stir nuts with brown sugar and margarine in small bowl until combined. Spoon evenly over squash. Bake, uncovered, 15 minutes longer.

**Each serving:** About 320 calories, 4g protein, 49g carbohydrate, 15g total fat (2g saturated), 0mg cholesterol, 350mg sodium

## COURGETTE RIBBONS WITH MINT

*Prep: 10 minutes     Cook: 3 minutes*
*Makes 4 accompaniment servings*

2 medium courgettes (225g each)
1 tbsp olive oil
2 garlic cloves, each cut in half

½ tsp salt
2 tbsp chopped fresh mint
Mint sprig for garnish

◆ Trim ends from courgettes. Using vegetable peeler or adjustable-blade slicer, shave courgettes lengthways into long strips (if courgettes are wider than peeler, first cut each lengthways in half). Heat olive oil with garlic in 30cm frying pan over medium heat until garlic is golden; discard garlic.

◆ Increase heat to high. Add courgettes and salt and cook, stirring, 2 minutes, or just until courgette wilts. Remove from heat; stir in chopped mint. To serve, garnish with mint sprig.

**Each serving:** About 50 calories, 1g protein, 4g carbohydrate, 4g total fat (0g saturated), 0mg cholesterol, 270mg sodium

## ROSEMARY-ROASTED BUTTERNUT SQUASH

*Prep: 20 minutes     Roast: 35 minutes*
*Makes 10 accompaniment servings*

60g margarine or butter
3 medium butternut squash (about 800g each)
1 medium onion, diced
1¾ tsp salt

1¼ tsp dried rosemary, crushed
½ tsp coarsely ground black pepper

◆ Preheat oven to 200°C (400°F, Gas 6). Place margarine in roasting tin and place in oven until margarine melts. Meanwhile, cut each squash lengthways in half; discard seeds. Cut squash into 5cm chunks. Cut peel from chunks.

◆ Remove roasting tin from oven. Add squash, onion, salt, rosemary and pepper; toss to coat with margarine. Arrange squash in single layer; roast 35 minutes, or until tender.

**Each serving:** About 145 calories, 2g protein, 27g carbohydrate, 5g total fat (1g saturated), 0mg cholesterol, 435mg sodium

## THREE-SQUASH SAUTÉ

*Prep: 20 minutes     Cook: 45 minutes*
*Makes 6 accompaniment servings*

1 medium spaghetti squash
3 tbsp olive oil
1 garlic clove, crushed with side of knife
1 small courgette (175g), cut into 1cm pieces
1 small yellow courgette (175g), cut into 1cm pieces

225g cherry tomatoes, each cut in half
2 tbsp finely chopped fresh basil
¾ tsp salt
¼ tsp ground black pepper
2 tbsp pine nuts, toasted

◆ Cut spaghetti squash lengthways in half; discard seeds. Bring *2–3cm water* to the boil in 8-litre flameproof casserole. Add spaghetti squash, cut side up and return to the boil. Reduce heat to low; cover and simmer 30 minutes, or until tender.

◆ Remove spaghetti squash from casserole; drain. Using 2 forks, gently scrape squash lengthways, lifting out pulp as it becomes free. Drain pulp thoroughly on kitchen towels. Discard squash skin.

◆ Wipe casserole dry. Heat oil in same casserole over medium-high heat. Add garlic and cook until lightly browned; discard garlic. Stir in courgettes; cook until tender. Add spaghetti squash, cherry tomatoes, basil, salt and pepper; heat through. Sprinkle with pine nuts.

**Each serving:** About 110 calories, 2g protein, 9g carbohydrate, 9g total fat (1g saturated), 0mg cholesterol, 275mg sodium

# Mushrooms

There's a world of mushrooms beyond the common cultivated white variety. Exotics, such as shiitake and porcini with their big, meaty flavour and the contrastingly delicate oyster mushroom, are increasingly available.

## Warm Mushroom Salad

❖❖❖❖❖❖❖❖❖❖❖❖❖

*Prep: 20 minutes*
*Cook: 35 minutes*
*Makes 6 appetizer or accompaniment servings*

1 bunch rocket
225g shiitake mushrooms
3 tbsp vegetable oil
1 large red onion, cut into 1cm wedges
1.1kg chestnut and/or white button mushrooms, each cut in half if large
2 tbsp soy sauce
2 tbsp red wine vinegar
30g pine nuts, toasted (optional)
Parsley sprigs for garnish

1 Arrange rocket on platter; set aside. Cut and discard stalks from shiitake mushrooms, then cut mushroom caps into 1cm wide strips.

2 Heat 1 tablespoon oil in 30cm frying pan over medium heat. Add onion and cook just until tender. Using slotted spoon, transfer to medium bowl.

3 Heat 1 tablespoon oil in same pan over medium-high heat. Add half of all mushrooms; cook until liquid evaporates. Stir in 1 tablespoon soy sauce.

4 Transfer mushrooms to bowl with onion. Repeat with remaining 1 tablespoon oil, remaining mushrooms and remaining 1 tablespoon soy sauce. Add vinegar to mushroom mixture in bowl; toss to coat. Spoon mushroom mixture on top of rocket on platter. Sprinkle with pine nuts, if using; garnish with parsley.

---

### MUSHROOMS

These mushrooms generally have a more intense flavour than white button; use a selection to add interest to almost any mushroom recipe. Morels, porcini (*cèpe* in French) and shiitake are available fresh or dried. Don't throw away the soaking water from dried mushrooms – it is full of flavour and can be used in stocks, soups and sauces.

Dried porcini (cèpe)

Chestnut

Fresh shiitake

Dried morel

Chanterelle

Flat

Dried shiitake

Oyster

---

**EACH SERVING: ABOUT 150 CALORIES, 6g PROTEIN, 19g CARBOHYDRATE, 8g TOTAL FAT (1g SATURATED), 0mg CHOLESTEROL, 360mg SODIUM**

## MUSHROOM, ASPARAGUS AND GRUYÈRE STRUDEL

*Prep: 40 minutes, plus cooling    Bake: 25 minutes*
*Makes 6 main dish servings*

350g asparagus
Salt
105g margarine or butter
450g mushrooms, thinly sliced
2 tsp fresh lemon juice
40g walnuts, toasted and
  finely chopped

2 tbsp dried breadcrumbs
12 sheets fresh or frozen
  (thawed) filo pastry, each
  about 40 by 30cm
  (about 225g)
125g Gruyère cheese, grated

◆ Cut asparagus into 15cm long spears. Bring *1cm water* to the boil in 30cm frying pan over medium-high heat. Add asparagus and ½ teaspoon salt; return to the boil. Reduce heat to medium-low; cook for 4–8 minutes, until tender. Drain. Wipe pan dry.

◆ Melt 15g margarine in same pan over medium-high heat. Add mushrooms and ½ teaspoon salt; cook until mushrooms are browned and liquid evaporates. Add lemon juice; cook 30 seconds. Transfer to plate; cool.

◆ Preheat oven to 190°C (375°F, Gas 5). Lightly grease baking sheet. Melt remaining 90g margarine. Mix walnuts and breadcrumbs together in small bowl.

◆ Place 1 filo sheet on work surface with short side facing you; brush lightly with some melted margarine. Sprinkle all over with one-sixth of walnut-breadcrumb mixture. Top with another filo sheet; brush with some margarine, being careful not to tear pastry.

◆ Spoon one-sixth of cheese in a strip on filo 5cm from edge facing you and leaving 4cm border on both sides. Arrange one-sixth of asparagus on cheese; top with one-sixth of mushrooms. Fold bottom of filo over to enclose filling, then fold left and right sides in towards centre. Roll up pastry, Swiss-roll fashion, forming a packet.

◆ Place packet, seam-side down, on baking sheet. Brush lightly with some margarine. Repeat to make 5 more packets. Bake 25 minutes, or until slightly puffed and golden brown.

**Each serving: About 375 calories, 13g protein, 28g carbohydrate, 25g total fat (7g saturated), 21mg cholesterol, 645mg sodium**

## CHAR-GRILLED MUSHROOM SALAD

*Prep: 15 minutes    Barbecue/grill: 8–9 minutes*
*Makes 4 first course servings*

1 wedge Parmesan cheese
2 bunches rocket
2 tbsp balsamic vinegar
2 tbsp olive oil
2 tbsp finely chopped shallots

2 tbsp chopped fresh parsley
¼ tsp salt
⅛ tsp ground black pepper
450g flat mushrooms, stalks
  discarded

◆ Prepare barbecue or preheat grill. Using vegetable peeler, shave 30g curls from Parmesan cheese; set aside. Reserve remaining Parmesan for use another day. Arrange rocket on platter.

◆ Prepare dressing: whisk vinegar, oil, shallots, parsley, salt and pepper together in small bowl. Place mushrooms, top-side up, on barbecue rack or on grill rack in pan at position closest to heat. Brush mushroom tops with 1 tablespoon dressing. Barbecue or grill 4 minutes. Turn mushrooms over; brush with 1 more tablespoon dressing. Cook 4–5 minutes longer, or until tender.

◆ Slice mushrooms and arrange on arugula. Spoon remaining dressing over salad. Top with Parmesan curls.

**Each serving: About 150 calories, 6g protein, 14g carbohydrate, 10g total fat (2g saturated), 6mg cholesterol, 280mg sodium**

## SAUTÉED MIXED MUSHROOMS

*Prep: 15 minutes    Cook: 10 minutes*
*Makes 4 accompaniment servings*

30g butter or margarine
40g shallots, finely chopped
225g button mushrooms, each
  cut into quarters
125g shiitake mushrooms,
  stalks discarded, cut into
  2–3cm wedges
125g oyster mushrooms, each
  cut in half if large

⅛ tsp dried thyme
¼ tsp salt
⅛ tsp ground black pepper
1 small garlic clove, finely
  chopped
1 tbsp chopped fresh parsley

Melt butter in 30cm frying pan over medium-high heat. Add shallots and cook, stirring, 1 minute. Stir in all mushrooms. Sprinkle with thyme, salt and pepper and cook, stirring often, until mushrooms are tender and liquid evaporates. Stir in garlic and parsley; cook 1 minute longer.

**Each serving: About 100 calories, 3g protein, 10g carbohydrate, 6g total fat (2g saturated), 16mg cholesterol, 205mg sodium**

# AUBERGINE

Deep purple or creamy white, aubergine has a hearty, meaty texture and a neutral taste that readily absorbs the flavours of whatever ingredients are cooking with it. Aubergine marries particularly well with strong flavours, such as garlic, olive oil and balsamic vinegar. Purchase plump, shiny, unblemished aubergines that feel heavy for their size; light ones may be spongy.

## ITALIAN AUBERGINE WITH GARLIC

*Prep: 25 minutes     Grill: 40 minutes*
*Makes 10 accompaniment servings*

| | |
|---|---|
| 60ml olive oil | ½ tsp cracked black pepper |
| 3 garlic cloves, sliced | 4 aubergines (350g each) |
| 15g fresh basil, finely | or 10 small aubergines |
| chopped | (90g each) |
| 1½ tsp salt | 1 tbsp grated lemon peel |

1 Heat olive oil in 1-litre saucepan over medium heat. Add garlic slices and cook, stirring occasionally, until lightly browned. Remove pan from heat; stir in basil, salt and pepper.

2 Preheat grill. Cut each aubergine lengthways into 2cm thick slices. Lightly score both sides of each slice in criss-cross pattern. (If using small aubergines cut each lengthways in half. Score cut sides only.)

3 Place half aubergine slices in single layer on rack in grill pan. Brush lightly with some olive oil mixture from pan. Grill about 20cm from heat for 10 minutes. Turn slices and lightly brush with some remaining olive oil mixture, gently pressing garlic slices and basil into the cuts in aubergine.

4 Grill aubergine 10 minutes longer, or until fork-tender; transfer to platter. Repeat with remaining aubergine slices and olive oil mixture. Sprinkle aubergine with lemon rind. Serve at room temperature or cover with cling film and refrigerate to serve later.

EACH SERVING: ABOUT 135 CALORIES, 1g PROTEIN, 9g CARBOHYDRATE, 11g TOTAL FAT (1g SATURATED), 0mg CHOLESTEROL, 325mg SODIUM

# AUBERGINE LASAGNE

*Prep: 50 minutes plus standing    Bake: 40 minutes*

*Makes 10 main dish servings*

2 medium aubergines (about 750g each), cut into 5mm thick slices
5 tbsp olive or vegetable oil
1 small onion, chopped
2 tsp sugar
1½ tsp salt
1 tsp dried basil
400g canned tomatoes
12 lasagne sheets
30g Parmesan cheese, freshly grated
225g mozzarella cheese, grated

◆ Preheat grill. Place half of aubergine slices on rack in grill pan; brush on both sides with 2 tablespoons oil. Grill 10 minutes at closest position to heat, or until browned, turning once halfway through cooking. Transfer to plate. Repeat with remaining aubergine and 2 more tablespoons oil. Preheat oven to 190°C (375°F, Gas 5).

◆ Meanwhile, prepare tomato sauce: heat remaining 1 tablespoon oil in 4-litre saucepan over medium heat. Add onion and cook until tender. Stir in sugar, salt, basil and tomatoes with their juice; bring to the boil over high heat, breaking up tomatoes with back of spoon. Reduce heat to low and simmer, uncovered, 15 minutes, stirring occasionally.

◆ Meanwhile, prepare lasagne sheets as packet instructs; drain. Spread 225ml tomato sauce in base of 33 by 20cm ovenproof serving dish. Arrange half of lasagne sheets over sauce, overlapping to fit. Arrange half of aubergine slices over lasagne and top with half remaining sauce, then half Parmesan and half mozzarella. Repeat with remaining lasagne sheets, aubergine, tomato sauce, Parmesan cheese and mozzarella.

◆ Bake 40 minutes, or until heated through. Remove from oven; let stand 10 minutes for easier serving.

Each serving: About 325 calories, 12g protein, 41g carbohydrate, 14g total fat (5g saturated), 20mg cholesterol, 715mg sodium

# AUBERGINE STEW

*Prep: 25 minutes    Cook: 30–35 minutes*

*Makes 8 accompaniment servings*

3 tbsp olive oil
1 large onion, cut into 2cm pieces
2 medium aubergines (about 750g each), cut into 5cm pieces
75g pimiento-stuffed olives
2 tbsp dark brown sugar
1 tbsp balsamic vinegar
¾ tsp salt
250g fresh mozzarella cheese balls (bocconcini), drained and each cut in half (optional)
225g tomatoes, peeled and cut into 2cm pieces
15g basil leaves, coarsely chopped

◆ Heat 1 tablespoon oil in 30cm non-stick frying pan, 5cm deep, over medium heat. Add onion and cook, stirring often, 10 minutes, or until golden.

◆ Increase heat to medium-high. Add remaining 2 tablespoons oil and aubergine; cook, stirring often, about 10 minutes, or until aubergines are browned. Stir in olives, next 3 ingredients and *125ml water;* bring to the boil over high heat. Reduce heat to low; cover and simmer 10–15 minutes longer, until aubergine is tender. Remove from heat; stir in mozzarella cheese balls, if using, tomatoes and chopped basil.

Each serving: About 125 calories, 2g protein, 18g carbohydrate, 6g total fat (1g saturated), 0mg cholesterol, 290mg sodium

## AUBERGINES

Aubergines come in different shapes, sizes and colours, ranging from tiny green Thai pea aubergines and baby white to the large, purple Western variety, which can be oval or egg-shaped.

Aubergines can be peeled or not, depending on the type of dish you are preparing and whether the skin is tough or tender. For example, dips are best made with peeled aubergine. Always cook aubergines until completely tender and creamy.

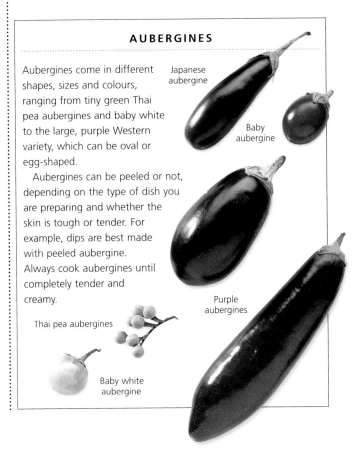

Japanese aubergine

Baby aubergine

Purple aubergines

Thai pea aubergines

Baby white aubergine

# PEPPERS

Sweet peppers can be green, red, yellow, orange or even purple. Unlike hot peppers, or chillies, sweet peppers lack a fiery bite since they contain no capsaicin, the chemical substance responsible for the heat. Roasting and grilling intensifies the subtle sweetness of peppers and makes them easy to peel. Sweet peppers are also natural candidates for stuffing and baking whole.

## PEPPER AND AUBERGINE SALAD

❖❖❖❖❖❖❖❖❖❖❖❖❖

*Prep: 30 minutes*
*Grill: 35 minutes*
*Makes 8 accompaniment servings*

**1 medium aubergine (about 750g)**
**1 medium onion**
**Salt**
**2 medium yellow peppers**
**2 medium red peppers**
**60g basil leaves, cut into thin strips**
**2 tbsp olive or vegetable oil**
**1 tbsp fresh lemon juice**
**1 tsp sugar**
**½ tsp coarsely ground black pepper**
**Basil sprigs for garnish**

1 Preheat grill. Cut aubergine crossways into 1cm thick slices, then cut into 1cm wide strips. Cut onion in half through root end; cut each half into thin wedges, discarding tough root end.

2 Toss aubergine and onion with ½ teaspoon salt in large bowl. Spread on grill rack. Grill at closest position to heat, turning strips occasionally, 20 minutes, or until aubergine is browned on all sides.

3 Meanwhile, cut yellow and red peppers into 1cm wide strips. Toss pepper strips with ½ teaspoon salt in medium bowl. When aubergine mixture is done, return it to large bowl.

4 Spoon pepper strips onto grill rack. Grill at closest position to heat, turning strips occasionally, 15 minutes, or until browned on all sides. Add to aubergine.

5 Add basil strips, next 4 ingredients, and *1 tablespoon water* to aubergine mixture, then toss to mix. Spoon onto platter. Serve warm or cover and refrigerate to serve cold later. Garnish with basil.

EACH SERVING: ABOUT 80 CALORIES, 2g PROTEIN, 12g CARBOHYDRATE, 4g TOTAL FAT (0g SATURATED), 0mg CHOLESTEROL, 270mg SODIUM

## BARLEY-STUFFED PEPPERS

*Prep: 1¼ hours*   *Bake: 1 hour*
*Makes 6 main dish servings*

175g pearl barley
625ml vegetable or chicken
  stock
2 tbsp olive or vegetable oil
1 large onion, chopped
3 medium carrots, grated
½ tsp salt
150g frozen peas

2 tbsp chopped fresh parsley
175g mature Cheddar cheese,
  grated
800g canned Italian-style
  tomatoes
2 medium red peppers
2 medium green peppers
2 medium yellow peppers

◈ Bring barley and stock to the boil in 3-litre saucepan over high heat. Reduce heat to low; cover and simmer 1 hour, or until barley is tender and liquid is absorbed.

◈ Meanwhile, heat oil in 26cm frying pan over medium-high heat. Add onion and cook, stirring often, until almost tender. Stir in carrots and salt; cook 5 minutes, or until vegetables are tender and lightly browned.

◈ When barley is tender, stir in carrot mixture, peas, parsley and 125g of cheese. Blend tomatoes in food processor with knife blade attached or in blender on medium speed until almost smooth; pour into shallow 2½-litre casserole.

◈ Preheat oven to 180°C (350°F, Gas 4). Cut off top from each pepper and reserve for garnish. Remove seeds. Cut thin slice from base of each pepper, if necessary, so they will stand level. Fill peppers with barley mixture. Stand peppers in tomato sauce and sprinkle with remaining 50g cheese.

◈ Bake for 1 hour, or until tender when pierced with a knife. Loosely cover peppers with foil during last 30 minutes of baking to prevent over-browning. To serve, arrange reserved pepper tops on stuffed peppers.

**Each serving: About 405 calories, 15g protein, 55g carbohydrate, 15g total fat (7g saturated), 30mg cholesterol, 695mg sodium**

## RED AND YELLOW PEPPER SAUTÉ

*Prep: 15 minutes*   *Cook: 15 minutes*
*Makes 6 accompaniment servings*

2 tbsp olive or vegetable oil
2 large red peppers, cored,
  seeded and cut into 2–3cm
  wide slices
2 large yellow peppers, cored,
  seeded and cut into 2–3cm
  wide slices

½ tsp dried oregano
¼ tsp salt

Heat oil in 30cm frying pan over medium-high heat. Add pepper slices, oregano and salt, and cook, stirring frequently, until peppers are golden and tender-crisp.

**Each serving: About 70 calories, 1g protein, 7g carbohydrate, 5g total fat (1g saturated), 0mg cholesterol, 90mg sodium**

## ROASTED PEPPER AND WALNUT DIP

*Prep: 20 minutes, plus standing*   *Grill: 10 minutes*
*Makes 400ml*

60g walnuts
½ tsp ground cumin
4 medium red peppers,
  roasted and peeled (see
  below)

2 slices firm white bread, torn
1 tbsp olive oil
2 tbsp raspberry vinegar
⅛ tsp ground red pepper
½ tsp salt

Preheat oven to 180°C (350°F, Gas 4). Spread walnuts in pie plate; bake 8–10 minutes until toasted. Toast cumin in 1-litre saucepan over low heat 1–2 minutes until very fragrant. Blend walnuts until ground, in food processor with knife blade attached. Add cumin and remaining ingredients; blend until smooth. Transfer to bowl. Cover and refrigerate if not serving right away (remove 1 hour before serving).

**Each 100ml: About 180 calories, 4g protein, 14g carbohydrate, 13g total fat (1g saturated), 0mg cholesterol, 330mg sodium**

### ROASTING PEPPERS

Preheat grill and line grill pan with foil. Cut peppers lengthways in half; discard stalks and seeds. Place peppers, skin-side up, in pan. Grill at closest position to heat 10 minutes, or until charred. Wrap in foil; let stand 15 minutes. Remove foil and peel off skin.

# TOMATOES

It's worth waiting all year for garden-ripe juicy tomatoes. Here we celebrate them in a tomato and goat cheese tart and grilled tomatoes topped with Parmesan. For gardeners who are left with an under-ripe crop at the end of the summer, we even turn green tomatoes into a tempting treat, fried for a BLT. For maximum flavour, store tomatoes at room temperature rather than in the refrigerator, unless they are over-ripe.

## SAVOURY TOMATO TART

❖❖❖❖❖❖❖❖❖❖❖❖❖

*Prep:* 30 minutes
*Cook:* 35 minutes
*Makes* 6 main dish servings

**Pastry for 28cm Tart (see page 487)**

**1 tbsp olive or vegetable oil**

**3 medium onions (about 450g), thinly sliced**

**Salt**

**85g goat's cheese, crumbled**

**3 large tomatoes (about 750g), cut into 5mm thick slices**

**½ tsp coarsely ground black pepper**

**40g Kalamata olives, stoned and chopped**

**Sliced fresh basil leaves for garnish**

**1** Prepare pastry and use to line tart tin as instructed. Preheat oven to 220°C (425°F, Gas 7). Line tart case with foil; fill with pie weights, dry beans or uncooked rice. Bake 20 minutes; remove foil and weights. Bake pastry case 10 minutes longer, or until golden. (If crust puffs up during baking, gently press it down with back of spoon.)

**3** Preheat grill. Spoon onions in an even layer over the base of the pastry case. Sprinkle with half of goat's cheese.

**2** Meanwhile, heat oil over medium heat in 30cm non-stick frying pan. Add onions and ¼ teaspoon salt and cook, stirring frequently, about 15 minutes until onions are tender and browned.

**4** Arrange tomato slices in concentric circles over onion layer. Sprinkle black pepper and ¼ teaspoon salt over tomatoes. Sprinkle remaining goat's cheese over top. Place pan in grill about 15cm from heat. Grill tomatoes about 5 minutes until cheese just melts. Sprinkle with olives and sliced basil leaves. To serve, cut tart into wedges.

EACH SERVING: ABOUT 415 CALORIES, 8g PROTEIN, 33g CARBOHYDRATE, 28g TOTAL FAT (7g SATURATED), 15mg CHOLESTEROL, 650mg SODIUM

## CHERRY TOMATO GRATIN

*Prep: 10 minutes*
*Bake: 20 minutes*
*Makes: 6 accompaniment servings*

30g dried breadcrumbs
30g Parmesan cheese, freshly
  grated
1 garlic clove, finely chopped
¼ tsp coarsely ground black
  pepper
1 tbsp olive oil
900g cherry tomatoes
2 tbsp chopped fresh parsley

◆ Preheat oven to 220°C (425°F, Gas 7). Combine breadcrumbs, Parmesan cheese, garlic, pepper and olive oil in small bowl.

◆ Place cherry tomatoes in deep 23cm ovenproof serving dish. Sprinkle breadcrumb mixture on top of tomatoes. Sprinkle with parsley. Bake 20 minutes, or until breadcrumb topping is golden.

**Each serving: About 85 calories, 3g protein, 9g carbohydrate, 4g total fat (1g saturated), 3mg cholesterol, 130mg sodium**

## GRILLED PARMESAN TOMATOES

*Prep: 10 minutes   Grill: 3–4 minutes*
*Makes: 4 accompaniment servings*

15g butter or margarine
1 small garlic clove, very
  finely chopped
30g Parmesan cheese, freshly
  grated
350g plum tomatoes, each cut
  lengthways in half

◆ Preheat grill. Melt butter in 1-litre saucepan over low heat. Add garlic and cook just until golden; remove pan from heat.

◆ Spread Parmesan cheese on greaseproof paper. Dip cut side of each tomato half in butter, then in Parmesan. Place on grill rack. Spoon any remaining cheese on top of tomatoes and drizzle with any remaining butter.

◆ Grill at position closest to heat 3–4 minutes until cheese is golden brown.

**Each serving: About 70 calories, 3g protein, 4g carbohydrate, 5g total fat (3g saturated), 13mg cholesterol, 155mg sodium**

## FRIED GREEN TOMATO SANDWICHES

*Prep: 10 minutes   Cook: 20 minutes*
*Makes: 4 sandwiches*

1 medium egg white
¼ tsp salt
60g coarse yellow cornmeal
Coarsely ground black pepper
3 medium green tomatoes,
  cut into 1cm thick slices
225g bacon rashers
60g reduced-fat mayonnaise
60g low-fat plain yogurt
2 tbsp chopped fresh chives
8 slices white bread, toasted
4 lettuce leaves

◆ Beat egg white and salt together in shallow dish. Combine cornmeal with ¼ teaspoon pepper on greaseproof paper. Dip tomato slices in egg mixture to coat both sides, then dip into cornmeal mixture to coat both sides thoroughly. Place coated slices on greaseproof paper.

◆ Fry bacon in 30cm frying pan over medium-low heat until browned. Transfer to kitchen towels to drain.

◆ Increase heat to medium-high. Cook tomato slices, a few at a time, in drippings in frying pan until golden brown on both sides. Drain on kitchen towels.

◆ Combine mayonnaise, yogurt, chives and ¼ teaspoon pepper in small bowl. Spread mayonnaise mixture on toast. Arrange lettuce, tomato slices, then bacon on 4 pieces of toast. Top with remaining toast to make 4 sandwiches.

**Each sandwich: About 350 calories, 12g protein, 45g carbohydrate, 13g total fat (3g saturated), 17mg cholesterol, 645mg sodium**

### TOMATOES

Tomatoes come in many shapes and sizes, especially at good supermarkets. Large red beefsteak tomatoes are juiciest, while cherry tomatoes are sweet all year round. Yellow tomatoes are less acidic than red ones, and can be mixed with the red for a pretty effect. For sauces, nothing can beat plum tomatoes, which have the meatiest flesh.

Yellow pear

Cherry

Vine-ripened

Beefsteak

Plum

# SALADS
# 9

# $S$ALADS <u>KNOW-HOW</u>

Gone are the days when a salad meant skimpy diet fare. Today's creations are inspired mixtures of bold flavours, colours and varied textures. Crisp green salads are the classic starter, while mixed greens combined with vegetables, fruits, cheese and meat can make substantial meals.

## PREPARING SALAD INGREDIENTS

The most basic steps of salad preparation, such as washing and storing lettuce, are crucial. Since fresh, uncooked ingredients hide few flaws, nothing spoils a salad faster than biting down on a bit of grit. Tear lettuce into smaller pieces by hand; a knife will bruise the leaves. Most vegetables can be sliced a day in advance; sturdy ones (e.g., cabbage, carrots or cooked beetroot) will keep longer. To retain moisture, store prepared vegetables wrapped in damp kitchen towels in food-storage bags in the salad drawer in the refrigerator. Don't chop fresh herbs in advance – they will blacken.

## PEELING TOMATOES

1 Cut a shallow X in the bottom end of each tomato; drop into pan of boiling water for 10 seconds.

2 Using slotted spoon, transfer tomatoes to bowl of ice water. Use a knife to peel off the skin.

## STORING AND PREPARING LETTUCE

Wash and dry lettuce leaves carefully. Remove and discard any wilted outer leaves along with any that are bruised, or spotted leaves which will deteriorate rapidly. A salad spinner makes short work of drying lettuce; the kind with a pull cord is especially good. Be careful not to overload the spinner, or the lettuce will become bruised. To keep lettuce crisp, place clean, dry leaves in a food storage bag, along with a few damp kitchen towels and seal. Most varieties, including the popular Butterhead and Cos will only keep

for 2 to 3 days; Iceberg, Little Gem and other more sturdy heads will keep up to a week. Fresh herbs such as parsley, basil, chervil or dill make delightful additions to salads, but don't chop the leaves in advance, or they will blacken.

To avoid a soggy salad or diluted dressing, dry rinsed lettuce well before using. Place leaves on a clean tea towel; pat dry with another towel. (Or, simply pat leaves dry with kitchen towels or spin dry in a salad spinner.)

## CORING FIRM-HEAD LETTUCE

Using small knife, cut all the way around core in a cone shape. Holding lettuce head firmly with one hand, twist out the loosened core.

## PREPARING LOOSE-LEAF LETTUCE

1 Gently break off leaves at stem end. Discard any bruised or wilted leaves.

2 Swish leaves briefly in cold water. Gently remove and grit will sink to bottom.

### CHOOSING THE RIGHT LETTUCE

Lettuces fall into four basic types: crisphead varieties such as Iceberg are crisp but bland; loose-leaf lettuces like Butterhead are soft and delicate or tender and sweet. Long-leaf lettuces such as Cos or Little Gem have a crisp, mild flavour. For variety, choose two types of lettuce or buy a ready-to-eat mixed leaf pack.

## ASSEMBLING SALADS

Whether tossing leafy greens or making a main dish salad, aim for a balance of texture, colour and flavour. Cut or tear ingredients into manageable pieces, but don't make them too small. It is also important to pick the right serving dish. A jumble of curly leaves is most manageable in a bowl, while neatly arranged sliced ingredients look best on a plate. Chilled plates help keep ingredients cool. To avoid a watered-down dressing, vegetables must be thoroughly dried. When making a salad of rice, beans or potatoes, toss the cooked ingredients with the dressing while still warm so they will soak it up.

### SALAD STATISTICS

| LETTUCE | APPROXIMATE YIELD* |
| --- | --- |
| 1 medium crisphead lettuce | 550g prepared leaves |
| 1 medium Butterhead lettuce | 250g prepared leaves |
| 1 medium Cos lettuce | 450g prepared leaves |

* Allow about 100g prepared leaves per serving

## SALAD LEAVES

**Rocket** An Italian favourite, this highly perishable green has a hot peppery taste that is stronger in older leaves. The leaves tend to be gritty and need thorough rinsing.
**Spinach** Sweet and earthy-tasting, spinach is delicious raw or cooked. Whether flat or crinkly, leaves should be crisp and dark with a fresh smell; spinach harbours grit, so rinse well.
**Iceberg** Juicy but bland-tasting leaves give this crisphead more crunch than flavour; good with creamy dressings.
**Butterhead** One of the most inexpensive and easily-available lettuces, Butterhead has a mild flavour. It can be crisp at its heart and its outer leaves have a slight bite.
**Cos (Romaine)** Long-leaf lettuce with thick, firm leaves with stout central ribs.
**Red chicory** A variety of chicory with crimson-tipped leaves and a slightly bitter taste.
**Mâche** Also called lamb's lettuce or corn salad, this tender green has a nutty taste.
**Chicory** The shoots of a curly endive root, with tightly packed leaves and a strong, slightly bitter taste.

**Watercress** This lively green has a peppery bite and can stand on its own or pair with other lettuces; also delicious used in sandwiches, soups and omelettes.
**Radicchio** Burgundy-coloured leaves and a slightly bitter flavour of this Italian lettuce gives a welcome contrast to the salad bowl. In the Italian tradition, pair it with rocket and chicory for a colourful and flavourful mix.
**Frisée** A member of the endive family, frisée has slender, curly leaves that range in colour from yellow-white to pale green; it has a delicately bitter flavour.
**Red oak leaf** This variety of loose-leaf lettuce has crisp, ruffled leaves with a fuller flavor than other loose-leaf varieties.

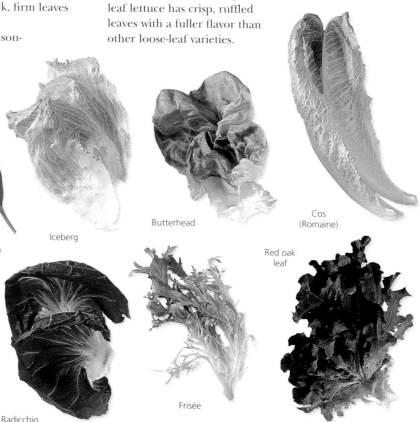

Rocket

Spinach

Iceberg

Butterhead

Cos (Romaine)

Red chicory

Mâche

Red oak leaf

Chicory

Watercress

Radicchio

Frisée

## THE BEST-DRESSED SALAD

Dressings should enhance but not overpower the taste and texture of salad greens. Sturdy lettuces such as Cos and Iceberg stand up to thick creamy dressings such as Caesar or Thousand Island. By contrast, delicate greens, such as loose-leaf varieties, pair best with simple vinaigrettes. For the crispest results, toss salads just before serving. To create a new taste, you can vary the oils and vinegars used in dressings. Extra virgin olive oil is classic, or substitute walnut or hazelnut oil for half the olive oil, or add just a drop of sesame oil. Vinegars range from dark, mellow balsamic to the more subtle varieties made from wine, champagne, cider or sherry. Other delicious options include vinegars infused with fruit (e.g. raspberry, blueberry) or a fresh herb like tarragon.

The best way to emulsify a vinaigrette dressing is first to whisk together the mustard, vinegar or lemon juice, and seasonings. Than add the oil, in a slow, steady stream, while whisking constantly .

## QUICK SALAD FIXINGS

Choose a basic ingredient, then enhance the flavour with store-cupboard staples or easy additions:

**Tossed greens**  Enliven with herb leaves or sprigs, warm garlic croûtons and Parmesan shavings; add substance with grilled meat or chicken strips or cubes of smoked ham.

**Steamed new potatoes**  Dress with vinaigrette and add gutsy flavour with bacon bits, anchovies, capers, olives or crumbled tangy cheese such as feta, blue or goat's cheese.

**Rice or couscous**  Add interest with grapes, sliced apple or pear, orange chunks, or dried apricots or raisins. Toasted nuts, pine kernels or sunflower seeds give crunch.

### SLIM SALADS

You can make low-fat salad dressings by substituting buttermilk or plain yogurt for mayonnaise or soured cream. Zesty salsa, or an Oriental-style vinaigrette of seasoned rice vinegar, soy sauce and fruit juice are two ways to boost flavour without any fat at all. For toppings, use crunchy vegetables but avoid fat boosters like avocados, nuts, bacon and cheese. For a main dish salad, use skinless chicken, tuna in brine, prawns or beans.

## GLORIOUS GARNISHES

Edible flowers lend a unique flavour and dazzling colour to salads. The fragile blossoms are typically left whole (tiny herb flowers should be plucked from the stem) and sprinkled on before serving so they are not discoloured by the dressing. Always use the flowers sparingly, as some have a strong flavour. Small herb flowers, such as mint, thyme, oregano or lavender blossoms can be particularly pungent, so check before using. You will need flowers that have not been treated with pesticides or other chemical sprays; flowers from the florist have usually been sprayed. Some supermarkets carry edible flowers, or check your own garden for unsprayed blossoms. However, not all flowers are edible, and some can be downright dangerous to eat. Non-toxic flowers include carnations, pansies, borage, geraniums, nasturtiums, roses, sweet peas, marigolds, cornflowers, gypsophila. Most herb flowers can also be used, including chive, marjoram, mint, oregano and thyme. Salad bowls are not the only thing that benefit from these colourful blooms. Add them to iced punch, herbal teas, desserts, or use to garnish soup, roasted fish or meats. Flowers such as roses, pansies or violets are often crystallized and used to decorate cakes.

Oregano flowers

Nasturtiums

Chive flowers

Pinks

Marjoram flowers

Mint flowers

Thyme flowers

# VEGETABLE SALADS

Whether your supply of fresh produce is reaped from your own garden, a farm shop, market or the local supermarket, a warm or cold salad of tasty, vibrantly coloured vegetables is sure to make an irresistible side dish. For the best texture, cook the vegetables just until they are tender.

## SUMMER BEETROOT AND ASIAN PEAR SALAD

◆◆◆◆◆◆◆◆◆◆◆◆◆◆◆◆◆◆◆◆◆◆◆◆◆◆◆◆◆

*Prep: 20 minutes    Cook: 40 minutes*
*Makes 6 accompaniment servings*

8 medium beetroots (about 1.8kg), with tops
1 tbsp light brown sugar
1 tbsp red wine vinegar
1 tbsp olive or vegetable oil
2 tsp Dijon mustard
½ tsp salt

1 large Asian pear or Red Delicious apple, peeled, cored and cut into thin wedges
1 tbsp chopped fresh parsley
Lettuce leaves

**1** Trim any stalks from beetroots; scrub them. Bring beetroots and enough *water* to cover to the boil in 4-litre saucepan over high heat. Reduce heat to low; cover and simmer 30 minutes, or just until beetroots are tender.

**2** Drain cooked beetroots and cool thoroughly with cold water. When they are cool enough to handle, use paring knife to peel. Cut each in half or into quarters, if large.

**3** Prepare vinaigrette: whisk brown sugar, red wine vinegar, oil, Dijon mustard and salt together in large bowl. Add beetroots, Asian pear and chopped parsley to vinaigrette.

**4** Toss beetroot mixture to coat with vinaigrette. Serve at room temperature or cover and refrigerate to serve cold later. To serve, line serving platter with lettuce leaves and spoon salad on top.

### ASIAN PEAR

Also called 'Chinese Pear' or 'Apple Pear', this delicious fruit is available in supermarkets during their season – our winter. They can be smooth skinned or speckled with a matte russeting. Unlike regular pears, they are low in acid and aroma, and quite hard even when ripe. This firm texture means that thin slices will hold up to tossing – making them perfect in salads. Asian pears can be stored in the refrigerator for at least 2 weeks. Crunchy and juicy at the same time, delicate in flavour, they make a light, refreshing dessert and remain crisp even when cooked.

EACH SERVING: ABOUT 130 CALORIES, 3g PROTEIN, 24g CARBOHYDRATE, 3g TOTAL FAT (0g SATURATED), 0mg CHOLESTEROL, 350mg SODIUM

## CHUNKY VEGETABLE SALAD

*Prep: 20 minutes*   **Makes** *4 accompaniment servings*

2 tbsp olive or vegetable oil
2 tbsp red wine vinegar
¾ tsp salt
½ tsp sugar
¼ tsp coarsely ground black
  pepper
2 large tomatoes, cut into thin
  wedges
1 large yellow pepper, cored,
  seeded and cut into bite-
  sized chunks

1 medium cucumber,
  unpeeled, cut into bite-sized
  chunks
½ small red onion, finely
  chopped
1 tbsp chopped fresh chervil,
  coriander or parsley

◆ Prepare dressing: whisk olive oil, red wine vinegar, salt, sugar and pepper until blended in medium bowl.

◆ Add vegetables and chopped herbs to dressing in bowl; toss well to coat. Transfer to serving platter.

**Each serving: About 110 calories, 2g protein, 12g carbohydrate, 7g total fat (1g saturated), 0mg cholesterol, 410mg sodium**

## WARM PEAS AND CARROTS SALAD

*Prep: 15 minutes*   *Cook: 10 minutes*
**Makes** *4 accompaniment servings*

150g frozen peas
1 tbsp vegetable oil
3 medium carrots, thinly
  sliced
1 small onion, thinly sliced

Salt
1 tbsp fresh lemon juice
1 small head Cos lettuce,
  washed and well dried

◆ Bring small saucepan of salted *water* to the boil over high heat. Add peas; return to the boil and cook 5 minutes. Drain; set aside.

◆ Meanwhile, heat oil in 26cm non-stick frying pan over medium-high heat. Add carrots, onion and ½ teaspoon salt. Cook, stirring often, until vegetables are tender and lightly browned. Stir peas into carrot-onion mixture in pan. Stir in lemon juice; remove pan from heat.

◆ Tear or cut lettuce leaves crossways into 5mm wide strips. Toss lettuce and vegetable mixture together to mix well.

**Each serving: About 115 calories, 5g protein, 17g carbohydrate, 4g total fat (1g saturated), 0mg cholesterol, 330mg sodium**

## GREEN BEANS WITH TOASTED SESAME SEEDS

*Prep: 25 minutes*   *Cook: 20 minutes*
**Makes** *8 accompaniment servings*

3 tbsp olive oil
2 tbsp fresh lemon juice
2 tsp Dijon mustard
½ tsp salt

900g green beans, ends
  trimmed
1 tbsp sesame seeds, toasted

◆ Prepare dressing: whisk olive oil, lemon juice, mustard and salt until blended together in large bowl; set aside.

◆ Bring *2–3cm water* to the boil in 8-litre flameproof casserole over high heat. Add beans and return to the boil.

◆ Reduce heat to low and simmer, uncovered, 5–10 minutes until beans are tender. Transfer to colander to drain well.

◆ Add warm beans to dressing in bowl and toss to mix well. Cover and refrigerate if not serving right away. Just before serving, toss beans with sesame seeds.

**Each serving: About 80 calories, 2g protein, 7g carbohydrate, 6g total fat (1g saturated), 0mg cholesterol, 180mg sodium**

❖❖❖❖❖❖❖❖❖❖❖❖❖❖❖❖❖❖❖❖❖❖

**TOASTING SESAME SEEDS**

Sesame seeds are the tiny, oval seeds of a tropical herb. They have a mild, nutty flavour that is best brought out by toasting: toast sesame seeds in small frying pan over a medium-low heat 1–2 minutes, stirring and shaking the pan often to prevent burning, until the seeds are lightly browned.

❖❖❖❖❖❖❖❖❖❖❖❖❖❖❖❖❖❖❖❖❖

# WATERCRESS, ORANGE AND BEETROOT SALAD

*Prep: 45 minutes   Cook: 40 minutes*
*Makes 10 accompaniment servings*

10 medium beetroots (about 2kg), trimmed
4 large navel oranges
60ml olive oil
60ml red wine vinegar
1 tbsp Dijon mustard
1 tsp sugar
¾ tsp salt
¼ tsp coarsely ground black pepper
350g watercress, tough stalks removed
1 medium red onion, thinly sliced

◆ Bring beetroots and enough *water* to cover to the boil in 4-litre saucepan over high heat. Reduce heat to low; cover and simmer 30 minutes, or until beetroots are tender.

◆ Meanwhile, grate 1 teaspoon rind from 1 orange; set aside. Cut rind and white pith from all oranges and discard. Holding oranges over large bowl to catch juice, cut out sections between membranes. Place orange sections on plate; reserve juice.

◆ Prepare dressing: whisk olive oil, red wine vinegar, Dijon mustard, sugar, salt, black pepper and grated orange into orange juice in bowl.

◆ Drain beetroots and cool with cold water. Peel and cut each beetroot lengthways in half, then cut each half crossways into 5mm thick slices.

◆ Add beetroots, orange sections, watercress and red-onion slices to dressing in bowl. Toss beetroot mixture to coat with dressing.

Each serving: About 150 calories, 4g protein, 23g carbohydrate, 6g total fat (1g saturated), 0mg cholesterol, 310mg sodium

# FENNEL, PEAR AND CHICORY SALAD

*Prep: 35 minutes*
*Makes 8 accompaniment servings*

60ml extra virgin olive oil
60ml tarragon vinegar
1 tbsp Dijon mustard
¾ tsp salt
¼ tsp coarsely ground black pepper
5 medium Bartlett or Red Williams pears (about 900g), unpeeled, each cored and sliced into 12 wedges
3 fennel bulbs (about 300g each)
4 medium heads chicory (2 red, if available)
75g walnuts, toasted and coarsely chopped

◆ Prepare dressing: whisk olive oil, tarragon vinegar, Dijon mustard, salt and pepper together in small bowl until blended; set aside.

◆ Place pear wedges into large bowl. Trim top and bottom from each fennel bulb; slice each lengthways in half and remove and discard core. Slice fennel halves crossways into paper-thin slices. Place in bowl with pear wedges.

◆ Cut 2 heads chicory (1 yellow and 1 red, if using both colours) crossways into 2–3mm thick slices; toss with fennel mixture. Separate leaves from remaining chicory.

◆ Add dressing to fennel mixture; toss well to coat with dressing.

◆ Arrange chicory leaves around edge of large shallow bowl or platter. Top with fennel salad and sprinkle with toasted walnuts.

Each serving: About 245 calories, 4g protein, 30g carbohydrate, 15g total fat (2g saturated), 0mg cholesterol, 320mg sodium

# SPINACH AND TANGERINE SALAD

*Prep: 30 minutes*
*Makes 8 accompaniment servings*

4 medium tangerines or navel oranges
350g spinach trimmed, washed and well dried
2 small heads loose-leaf lettuce, (about 225g)
3 tbsp extra virgin olive oil
3 tbsp cider vinegar
1 tsp sugar
1 tsp Dijon mustard
⅛ tsp salt
⅛ tsp coarsely ground black pepper

◆ Coarsely grate rind from 1 tangerine; set aside. Cut remaining rind and white pith from all tangerines; discard. Cut each tangerine in half (from top to bottom), then cut each half cross-ways into 5mm thick slices. Tear spinach and lettuce into bite-sized pieces.

◆ Prepare vinaigrette: whisk olive oil, cider vinegar, sugar, Dijon mustard, salt, black pepper and tangerine rind together in large bowl.

◆ Add spinach, lettuce and tangerine slices to vinaigrette and toss well.

Each serving: About 75 calories, 2g protein, 8g carbohydrate, 5g total fat (1g saturated), 0mg cholesterol, 80mg sodium

## BABY GREENS SALAD WITH GRAPEFRUIT VINAIGRETTE

*Prep: 25 minutes    Makes 8 accompaniment servings*

| | |
|---|---|
| 2 medium grapefruits | ½ tsp sugar |
| 2 medium heads chicory | ½ tsp salt |
| 1 tbsp balsamic vinegar | 60ml olive or vegetable oil |
| 1 tbsp Dijon mustard | 450g mixed baby salad greens |
| 2 tsp canned or bottled | or mixed salad greens |
| drained capers | |

◆ Using small paring knife, cut slice of rind from both ends of one grapefruit on chopping board. Stand grapefruit upright and cut away rind and white pith, following contours of fruit. Repeat with remaining grapefruit; discard rind and white pith.

◆ Holding grapefruits over small bowl to catch juice, cut out sections between membranes. Place grapefruit sections on plate; reserve juice in bowl. Cut each chicory lengthways into matchstick-thin strips.

◆ Prepare vinaigrette: combine balsamic vinegar, mustard, capers, sugar, salt and 2 tablespoons grapefruit juice (reserve remaining juice for another use) in large bowl. Slowly whisk in oil. Add greens, grapefruit sections and chicory to vinaigrette in bowl; toss to coat.

**Each serving: About 105 calories, 2g protein, 10g carbohydrate, 7g total fat (1g saturated), 0mg cholesterol, 230mg sodium**

## CHAR-GRILLED VEGETABLES VINAIGRETTE

*Prep: 15 minutes    Barbecue: 15–20 minutes*
*Makes 4 accompaniment servings*

| | |
|---|---|
| 6 tbsp olive or vegetable oil | 1 medium yellow pepper, |
| 6 tbsp white wine vinegar | cored, seeded and |
| 2 tbsp chopped fresh tarragon | quartered |
| 1 tsp salt | 2 small courgettes |
| 1 tsp coarsely ground black | (175g each), halved |
| pepper | lengthways |
| 1 tsp sugar | 2 baby aubergines |
| 4 large flat mushrooms | (125g each), halved |
| (125g), stalks trimmed | lengthways |
| 1 medium red pepper, cored, | Tarragon sprigs for garnish |
| seeded and quartered | |

◆ Prepare barbecue. Prepare vinaigrette: whisk olive oil, white wine vinegar, chopped tarragon, salt, black pepper and sugar together in large bowl.

◆ Wipe mushrooms clean with damp kitchen towels. Add mushrooms, both peppers, courgettes and aubergines to vinaigrette in bowl; toss to coat.

◆ Place vegetables on barbecue over medium heat. Barbecue, turning occasionally and brushing with some of vinaigrette remaining in bowl, until vegetables are browned and tender when pierced with a fork.

◆ Remove vegetables from barbecue, slice mushrooms and toss all vegetables in remaining vinaigrette. Garnish with tarragon sprigs.

**Each serving: About 235 calories, 3g protein, 14g carbohydrate, 21g total fat (3g saturated), 0mg cholesterol, 540mg sodium**

## BABY GREENS WITH RASPBERRY VINAIGRETTE

*Prep: 20 minutes    Makes 4 accompaniment servings*

| | |
|---|---|
| 1 tbsp sugar | 125g feta cheese, crumbled |
| 3 tbsp white wine vinegar | 8 quail's eggs or 4 small eggs, |
| 1 tbsp Dijon mustard | hard-boiled and each cut |
| 175g raspberries | lengthways in half |
| 60ml extra virgin olive oil | |
| 225g mixed baby salad greens | |
| or mixed salad greens | |

◆ Prepare vinaigrette: mix sugar, white wine vinegar and mustard together in large bowl. Add 85g raspberries to vinaigrette and crush berries slightly with fork. Slowly pour in olive oil, mixing gently.

◆ Add salad greens to vinaigrette in bowl and toss to coat well. To serve, place dressed salad greens on 4 side plates. Sprinkle with feta cheese and remaining 90g raspberries; tuck eggs into greens.

**Each serving: About 295 calories, 10g protein, 12g carbohydrate, 24g total fat (7g saturated), 185mg cholesterol, 470mg sodium**

# TOMATO SALADS

No flavour captures the essence of summer as well as vine-ripened tomatoes. Simply drizzle with vinaigrette or team with goat's cheese and salad leaves for a colourful side dish. Alternatively, add cubes of toasted bread and pancetta to create a main dish salad. We've also included an easy method for making home-dried tomatoes which can be used to enrich dishes all year round. Once cut, fresh tomatoes release juices that dilute dressings, so serve immediately.

## DRIED TOMATO, GOAT'S CHEESE AND ROCKET

◆◆◆◆◆◆◆◆◆◆◆◆◆◆

*Prep: 15 minutes, plus preparing Home-dried Tomatoes (optional)*
*Makes 6 accompaniment servings*

**Home-dried Tomatoes (see right) or 24 oil-packed sun-dried tomatoes, drained well**
**Coarsely ground black pepper**
**3 logs goat's cheese, about 90g each**
**2 tbsp red wine vinegar**
**1 tbsp extra virgin olive oil**
**½ tsp dried basil**
**¼ tsp sugar**
**2 bunches rocket or watercress**

**1** Prepare Home-Dried Tomatoes a day ahead, if using. Sprinkle 2 tablespoons black pepper on greaseproof paper. Roll cheese logs in pepper; slice each into 6 pieces.

**2** Prepare vinaigrette: whisk vinegar, olive oil, basil, sugar and ¼ teaspoon coarsely ground black pepper together in small bowl until well combined.

**3** Arrange rocket on 6 plates with goat's cheese pieces. Arrange tomatoes over rocket and cheese; drizzle salad with vinaigrette and serve.

## HOME-DRIED TOMATOES

◆◆◆◆◆◆◆◆◆◆◆◆◆◆

Store in a sealed plastic bag in the refrigerator for up to 2 months or in the freezer up to 6 months. Makes 24.

**12 plum tomatoes (about 1.3kg)**
**2 tbsp extra virgin olive oil**
**½ tsp dried basil**
**½ tsp dried thyme**
**½ tsp salt**
**¼ tsp coarsely ground black pepper**

**1** Preheat oven to 130°C (250°F, Gas 2). Peel tomatoes (see page 314). Halve each lengthways and remove seeds. Toss tomatoes with remaining ingredients.

**2** Arrange tomatoes, cut side down, on wire rack on baking sheet. Bake 5½ hours, or until tomatoes are shrivelled and partially dried. Cool completely.

EACH SERVING: ABOUT 220 CALORIES, 8g PROTEIN, 14g CARBOHYDRATE, 16g TOTAL FAT (1g SATURATED), 44mg CHOLESTEROL, 365mg SODIUM

## PANZANELLA SALAD WITH TOMATO VINAIGRETTE

*Prep: 30 minutes    Cook: 15 minutes*
*Makes 6 main dish servings*

225g pancetta or bacon, cut
   into 5mm pieces
3 tbsp olive oil
175g sourdough bread, cut
   into 1cm cubes
2 tbsp freshly grated
   Parmesan cheese
Ground black pepper
175g tomatoes, peeled (see
   page 314) and coarsely
   chopped
1 small shallot, chopped
1 tbsp red wine vinegar

1 tbsp balsamic vinegar
1 tsp sugar
1 tsp chopped fresh oregano
2 tsp coarse-grained French
   mustard
¼ tsp salt
450g rocket
450g red cherry and/or
   yellow pear-shaped
   tomatoes, each cut in half,
   or 450g tomatoes, cut into
   1cm chunks

◆ Cook pancetta in 30cm non-stick frying pan over medium heat until lightly browned. Using slotted spoon, transfer pancetta to large bowl.

◆ Pour off all but 2 tablespoons drippings from pan and add 1 tablespoon olive oil. Add bread cubes and cook, stirring frequently, about 10 minutes until lightly browned on all sides. Add toasted bread cubes to bowl with pancetta; add Parmesan cheese and ¼ teaspoon pepper; toss to combine and set aside.

◆ Prepare tomato vinaigrette: blend peeled tomatoes, shallot, red wine vinegar, balsamic vinegar, sugar, oregano, mustard, salt, ¼ teaspoon pepper and remaining 2 tablespoons olive oil in blender on medium speed until blended and smooth.

◆ Toss pancetta mixture with tomato vinaigrette, rocket and cherry tomatoes.

**Each serving: About 225 calories, 10g protein, 25g carbohydrate, 11g total fat (2g saturated), 11mg cholesterol, 615mg sodium**

## TWO-TOMATO SALAD

*Prep: 30 minutes    Cook: 10 seconds*
*Makes 8 accompaniment servings*

15g fresh basil, chopped
2 tbsp olive or vegetable oil
2 tbsp white wine vinegar
1 tsp Dijon mustard
¾ tsp salt

½ tsp sugar
900g cherry tomatoes
2 medium tomatoes, sliced
Basil sprigs for garnish

◆ Prepare vinaigrette: whisk basil, oil, vinegar, Dijon mustard, salt and sugar together in large bowl until blended, set aside.

◆ Bring *3 litres water* to the boil in 5-litre saucepan over high heat. Fill large bowl with *ice water*. Meanwhile, cut small X in the stalk end of each cherry tomato.

◆ Add half cherry tomatoes to boiling water; blanch 5 seconds. Using slotted spoon, transfer tomatoes to ice water to cool. Repeat with remaining cherry tomatoes, returning water in pan to the boil before adding.

◆ Drain cherry tomatoes. Using fingers, slip tomatoes from their skins, one at a time, and add to vinaigrette; toss to coat.

◆ To serve, arrange tomato slices on serving platter. Spoon cherry tomatoes and vinaigrette over tomato slices; garnish with basil sprigs.

**Each serving: About 55 calories, 1g protein, 6g carbohydrate, 4g total fat (1g saturated), 0mg cholesterol, 225mg sodium**

## CHERRY TOMATO-LEMON SALAD

*Prep: 20 minutes    Makes 8 accompaniment servings*

2 medium lemons
900g red cherry tomatoes,
   each cut in half
450g yellow cherry tomatoes,
   each cut in half
1 tbsp sugar

2 tbsp chopped fresh chives
2 tbsp extra virgin olive oil
¾ tsp salt
½ tsp coarsely ground black
   pepper

◆ Cut rind and white pith from lemons; discard. Cut each lemon crossways into slightly less than 5mm thick slices.

◆ Toss lemon slices, tomatoes and remaining ingredients together in medium bowl.

**Each serving: About 65 calories, 1g protein, 9g carbohydrate, 4g total fat (1g saturated), 0mg cholesterol, 210mg sodium**

# Potato salads

These lively potato salads are ideal to serve at a picnic or barbecue, or as part of a buffet of cold meats and salads. Toss potato chunks with roasted green beans and blue cheese; with fresh herbs and cool, crunchy celery; or with ripe olives, balsamic vinegar and feta cheese. You don't need to peel the potatoes and red potatoes, unpeeled, add colour. For the best results, add the potatoes to the dressing while they are still warm and prepare them several hours in advance: these steps allow the potatoes to absorb the dressing for a fuller flavour. Serve the salads warm or refrigerate until 30 minutes before serving.

**1** Preheat the oven to 220°C (425°F, Gas 7). If using onions, peel and cut each lengthways in half. Cut potatoes into 4cm chunks.

**2** Combine shallots, potatoes, salt and 1 tablespoon oil in large roasting tin. Roast 30 minutes.

## ROASTED POTATO SALAD WITH GREEN BEANS AND BLUE CHEESE

*Prep: 25 minutes    Roast: 45 minutes*
*Makes 6 accompaniment servings*

16 shallots, peeled, or 8 small
   white onions
900g red potatoes, unpeeled
1 tsp salt
3 tbsp olive or vegetable oil
225g French green beans or
   green beans, ends trimmed

1 tbsp fresh lemon juice
1 tsp Dijon mustard
30g Danish blue or dolcelatte
   cheese, crumbled

**3** After vegetables have roasted 30 minutes, stir in green beans and 1 more tablespoon oil. Roast 15 minutes longer, or until vegetables are tender.

**4** Meanwhile, prepare vinaigrette: whisk lemon juice, Dijon mustard and remaining oil together in large bowl. Add roasted vegetables to bowl, tossing to coat with vinaigrette. Serve salad warm or cover and refrigerate to serve later. To serve, place potato salad in serving dish or on platter; sprinkle with crumbled Danish blue.

### GREEK ROASTED POTATO SALAD

Prepare salad as instructed but add 75g stoned Kalamata olives when tossing vegetables with vinaigrette, and 2–4 tablespoons chopped fresh oregano, mint or parsley, if desired. Omit Danish blue cheese. Instead sprinkle with 60g crumbled feta cheese.

Each serving: About 280 calories, 5g protein, 39g carbohydrate, 12g total fat (3g saturated), 8mg cholesterol, 700mg sodium

EACH SERVING: ABOUT 235 CALORIES, 5g PROTEIN, 37g CARBOHYDRATE, 8g TOTAL FAT (2g SATURATED), 3mg CHOLESTEROL, 455mg SODIUM

## CLASSIC POTATO SALAD

*Prep:* 25 minutes, plus cooling
*Cook:* 45–50 minutes
*Makes* 8 accompaniment servings

1.3kg potatoes, peeled and cut
   in half if large
Salt
2 large celery stalks, thinly sliced
225g mayonnaise
125ml milk
2 tbsp white wine vinegar
1 tbsp grated onion
1 tsp sugar
¼ tsp coarsely ground black
   pepper

◆ Bring potatoes, 1 teaspoon salt, and enough *water* to cover to the boil in 4-litre saucepan over high heat. Reduce heat to low, cover and simmer for 25–30 minutes until potatoes are fork-tender. Drain and allow to cool slightly. Cut potatoes into 2cm cubes.

◆ Mix celery, mayonnaise, milk, white wine vinegar, onion, sugar, black pepper and 2 teaspoons salt together in large bowl. Add potatoes and gently toss to coat. If not serving right away, cover and refrigerate.

**Each serving: About 360 calories,
4g protein, 37g carbohydrate, 23g total fat
(4g saturated), 18mg cholesterol,
740mg sodium**

## MEDITERRANEAN POTATO SALAD

*Prep:* 15 minutes, plus cooling
*Cook:* 40–45 minutes
*Makes* 6 accompaniment servings

900g red potatoes, unpeeled and cut
   in half if large
Salt
6 oil-packed sun-dried tomatoes, drained
125g feta cheese, crumbled
1 tbsp fresh shredded basil
75g stoned black olives, finely chopped
3 tbsp olive oil
2 tbsp balsamic vinegar
Basil sprigs for garnish

◆ Bring potatoes, 1 teaspoon salt and enough *water* to cover to the boil in 4-litre saucepan over high heat. Reduce heat to low, cover and simmer 20–25 minutes until potatoes are fork-tender. Drain and allow to cool slightly. Cut potatoes into 1cm pieces.

◆ Cut sun-dried tomatoes into thick slices. Mix tomatoes, feta cheese, basil, olives, olive oil, balsamic vinegar and ½ teaspoon salt together in large bowl. Add potatoes and gently toss to coat. If not serving right away, cover and refrigerate. Garnish before serving.

**Each serving: About 285 calories,
6g protein, 35g carbohydrate, 14g total fat
(4g saturated), 18mg cholesterol,
575mg sodium**

## LEMON-CHIVE POTATO SALAD

*Prep:* 25 minutes, plus cooling
*Cook:* 30 - 35 minutes
*Makes* 12 accompaniment servings

2.2kg small new potatoes
Salt
2 lemons
3 tbsp olive oil
1 tsp sugar
175ml mayonnaise
125ml milk
75ml soured cream
5 large celery stalks, thinly sliced
30g fresh chives or spring onion tops,
   chopped

◆ Bring potatoes, 2 teaspoons salt and enough *water* to cover to the boil in 8-litre saucepan. Reduce heat to low, cover and simmer 12–15 minutes, until potatoes are fork-tender.

◆ Meanwhile, prepare lemon dressing: grate 1½ teaspoons rind and squeeze 60ml juice from lemons. Whisk lemon rind and juice, oil, sugar and 1½ teaspoons salt in large bowl until blended.

◆ Drain potatoes. Add hot potatoes to dressing. Using wooden spoon, stir gently to coat thoroughly with dressing. Allow potatoes to cool at room temperature 30 minutes, stirring occasionally.

◆ Meanwhile stir mayonnaise, milk, soured cream and ½ teaspoon salt together in bowl until mixture is smooth. Add mayonnaise mixture, celery and chives to cooled potatoes; stir gently to coat well. If not serving right away, cover and refrigerate.

**Each serving: About 320 calories,
5g protein, 41g carbohydrate, 16g total fat
(3g saturated), 12mg cholesterol,
505mg sodium**

### PERFECT POTATO SALADS

• Waxy new and red potatoes are ideal for salads because they retain their firm texture when cut. Avoid using baking potatoes, which can fall apart in salads.

• Choose potatoes of about the same size so they cook evenly.

• It's important that potatoes are neither under- nor over-cooked. They are ready if just tender when tested with the tip of a knife. If over-cooked, they will absorb too much dressing and fall apart.

• When adding the dressing, don't overdo it. Potatoes taste best when they are lightly coated rather than swimming in dressing.

• Always make potato salad with warm, freshly cooked potatoes. Cold leftover potatoes will not absorb the dressing as well.

• If your finished potato salad still needs a flavour boost, try adding some chopped cooked bacon, capers, anchovy fillets or drained sun-dried tomatoes.

# VEGETABLE COLESLAWS

As good as basic coleslaw can be, coleslaw-style salads are not limited to cabbage and mayonnaise alone. Celeriac and broccoli add their crunch and flavour, while coriander and sesame oil lend Oriental nuances to special coleslaws. There's even a coleslaw without cabbage: a crunchy carrot, apple and date blend that's especially good with grilled meats.

## CELERIAC COLESLAW

◆ ◆ ◆ ◆ ◆ ◆ ◆ ◆ ◆ ◆ ◆ ◆

*Prep: 1 hour, plus chilling*
*Makes 10 accompaniment servings*

125g reduced-fat mayonnaise
60g coarse-grained French mustard
60ml fresh lemon juice
1 tbsp sugar
1 tbsp rice vinegar
¼ tsp salt
¼ tsp coarsely ground black pepper
450g celeriac (if you can't find celeriac, use another 3 medium carrots and ¼ teaspoon celery seeds)
3 medium carrots
1 small head green cabbage (about 500g), quartered and cored

1 Prepare dressing: whisk mayonnaise, mustard, lemon juice, sugar, vinegar, salt and pepper together in small bowl.

2 Peel and finely grate celeriac and carrots. Thinly slice cabbage; discard tough ribs. Cut cabbage into quarters using chef's knife. Cut out core.

3 Place vegetables in large bowl. Add dressing and toss to coat well. Cover and refrigerate at least 1½ hours to allow flavours to blend.

◆ ◆ ◆ ◆ ◆ ◆ ◆ ◆ ◆ ◆ ◆ ◆ ◆ ◆ ◆ ◆ ◆ ◆ ◆ ◆ ◆ ◆ ◆ ◆

### GOOD GRATING

• Use a stainless steel knife for slicing cabbage; carbon steel may react with the juices in the cabbage, causing the cut edges to discolour (this will turn green cabbage black, and red cabbage blue).

• Slicing or grating vegetables in advance causes a loss of vitamin C. If you must do this, seal the grated vegetables tightly in a plastic bag and refrigerate.

• For grating, use the coarse side of a grater, the shredding disk in a food processor or an adjustable-blade slicer (right), which makes short work of grating and gives attractive long, fine, uniform shreds.

◆ ◆ ◆ ◆ ◆ ◆ ◆ ◆ ◆ ◆ ◆ ◆ ◆ ◆ ◆ ◆ ◆ ◆ ◆ ◆ ◆ ◆ ◆ ◆ ◆ ◆ ◆ ◆ ◆ ◆

EACH SERVING: ABOUT 80 CALORIES, 2g PROTEIN, 10g CARBOHYDRATE, 4g TOTAL FAT (0g SATURATED), 4mg CHOLESTEROL, 250mg SODIUM

## ASIAN COLESLAW

*Prep: 40 minutes*  *Makes 12 accompaniment servings*

75ml rice vinegar
2 tbsp vegetable oil
2 tsp sesame oil
¾ tsp salt
450g carrots, grated

1 large head Savoy cabbage
  (about 1.1kg), thinly sliced
  and tough ribs removed
4 spring onions, thinly sliced
30g fresh coriander, chopped

◆ Prepare vinaigrette: whisk rice vinegar, vegetable oil, sesame oil and salt together in large bowl until blended.

◆ Add carrots, cabbage, spring onions and coriander to vinaigrette and toss to mix well.

Each serving: About 80 calories, 2g protein, 12g carbohydrate, 3g total fat (1g saturated), 0mg cholesterol, 280mg sodium

## CABBAGE AND SPINACH COLESLAW

*Prep: 35 minutes, plus chilling*  *Makes 12 accompaniment servings*

1 medium head green
  cabbage (900g)
1 medium head red cabbage
  (900g)
1 medium red onion
175g mayonnaise
60ml cider vinegar

2 tbsp sugar
2 tbsp Dijon mustard
1 tsp salt
½ tsp coarsely ground black
  pepper
150g spinach leaves

◆ Quarter, core and thinly slice both cabbages, and discard tough ribs. Place cabbage in large bowl. Cut red onion lengthways in half, then cut each half crossways into paper-thin slices. Add onion to cabbage.

◆ Prepare dressing: whisk mayonnaise, cider vinegar, sugar, Dijon mustard, salt and coarsely ground black pepper together in small bowl. Add dressing to cabbage mixture and toss to coat well. Cover bowl with cling film and refrigerate for at least 3 hours before serving to allow the flavours to blend.

◆ Meanwhile, rinse spinach with cold water and pat dry with kitchen towels; tear into strips then wrap with cling film and refrigerate until ready to serve slaw.

◆ To serve, add julienned spinach to cabbage mixture and toss to mix well.

Each serving: About 160 calories, 3g protein, 14g carbohydrate, 12g total fat (2g saturated), 8mg cholesterol, 400mg sodium

## CARROT AND APPLE COLESLAW WITH DATES

*Prep: 20 minutes*  *Makes 6 accompaniment servings*

1 tbsp fresh lemon juice
1 tsp honey
¼ tsp dried mint
¼ tsp salt
450g carrots, grated

2 Granny Smith's apples,
  peeled, cored and grated
35g stoned dates, chopped
2 tbsp chopped fresh parsley

◆ Prepare dressing: whisk lemon juice, honey, mint and salt together in large bowl until combined.

◆ Add carrots, apples, dates and parsley to dressing in bowl; toss to mix well.

Each serving: About 90 calories, 1g protein, 23g carbohydrate, 0g total fat, 0mg cholesterol, 25mg sodium

## SWEET BROCCOLI AND WATERCRESS COLESLAW

*Prep: 10 minutes*  *Makes 4 accompaniment servings*

450g broccoli
75g mayonnaise
60ml cider vinegar
4 tsp sugar

2 tsp celery seeds
75g watercress, tough stalks
  removed

◆ Trim tough stalks and any leaves from broccoli. Using coarse side of grater, grate broccoli. Prepare dressing: whisk mayonnaise, cider vinegar, sugar and celery seeds together in large bowl.

◆ Remove tough stalks from watercress. Add watercress and broccoli to dressing in bowl; toss to mix well.

Each serving: About 185 calories, 2g protein, 14g carbohydrate, 15g total fat (2g saturated), 11mg cholesterol, 140mg sodium

### MORE VARIATIONS

Every cook will have their favoured versions of coleslaw, the possibilities are endless. Try adding some of the following to a basic mix of grated cabbage and carrot tossed in a mayonnaise dressing:

• Meats such as pancetta or bacon, diced or cut into thin strips and cooked until crispy.

• Dried fruit such as apricots, sultanas or raisins.

• Nuts such as pine nuts, chopped walnuts, unsalted peanuts or chopped pecans.

• Fresh fruits such as apple or pineapple.

# PASTA SALADS

Pasta salads are served at room temperature: they pack well for a picnic, and are the ideal addition to any barbecue. Eat pasta salads the same day they're made because pasta continues to absorb dressing as it stands. After cooking, rinse the hot pasta under cold running water – this stops the cooking and ensures a firm texture.

## SZECHUAN PEANUT-NOODLE SALAD

❖❖❖❖❖❖❖❖❖❖❖

*Prep:* 25 minutes
*Cook:* 12 minutes
*Makes* 5 main dish or
8 accompaniment servings

**450g linguine or spaghetti**
**125g mange-tout, strings removed**
**80g smooth peanut butter**
**3 tbsp soy sauce**
**2 tbsp vegetable oil**
**1 tbsp sesame oil**
**1 tbsp cider vinegar**
**2 tsp grated peeled fresh ginger**
**1 medium red pepper, cored, seeded and thinly sliced**
**Dry-roasted peanuts and chopped spring onion (optional)**

### SESAME OIL

Pressed from sesame seeds, sesame oil has a rich, light brown colour with a distinctive smell and strong, nutty flavour. An important ingredient in Japanese and Chinese cooking, toasted sesame oil is even stronger with a deep golden colour. Both are easily available.

**1** Prepare linguine as packet instructs. Drain, reserving 225ml pasta cooking water. Rinse linguine with cold water; drain well.

**2** Bring *2–3cm water* to the boil in 3-litre saucepan. Add mange-tout and return to the boil. Reduce heat to low; simmer 1 minute, or until tender-crisp.

**3** Rinse mange-tout with cold water to stop cooking; drain and cut into matchstick-thin strips.

**4** Prepare peanut-butter dressing: whisk peanut butter, soy sauce, vegetable oil, sesame oil, cider vinegar, ginger and reserved pasta cooking water together in large bowl until mixture is thoroughly blended and smooth.

**5** Add linguine, mange-tout strips and sliced red pepper to peanut-butter dressing; toss to coat well. Sprinkle with dry-roasted peanuts and chopped spring onion, if you like. Serve noodle salad immediately or cover and refrigerate to serve later. If noodles become too sticky upon standing, toss with a little hot water until dressing is of desired consistency.

EACH MAIN DISH SERVING: ABOUT 595 CALORIES, 21g PROTEIN, 62g CARBOHYDRATE, 32g TOTAL FAT (6g SATURATED), 101mg CHOLESTEROL, 835mg SODIUM

## ORZO SALAD WITH FETA CHEESE

*Prep:* 20 minutes   *Cook:* 10 minutes

*Makes* 6 accompaniment servings

| | |
|---|---|
| 175g orzo (rice-shaped pasta) | 40g stoned Kalamata olives, chopped |
| 2 tbsp fresh lemon juice | |
| 2 tbsp olive oil | 15g fresh parsley, chopped |
| ¾ tsp salt | 1 large ripe tomato, diced |
| ½ tsp ground black pepper | 75g feta cheese, crumbled |

◆ Cook orzo as packet instructs. Drain and rinse with cold water; drain again.

◆ Prepare vinaigrette: whisk lemon juice, olive oil, salt and pepper together in large bowl.

◆ Add orzo to vinaigrette in bowl and toss to coat. Stir in olives and parsley. Add tomato and feta cheese and toss gently, just until combined.

**Each serving: About 260 calories, 9g protein, 33g carbohydrate, 10g total fat (3g saturated), 12mg cholesterol, 530mg sodium**

## MACARONI SALAD

*Prep:* 15 minutes   *Cook:* 20 minutes

*Makes* 6 accompaniment servings

| | |
|---|---|
| 175g dried tubetti or ditalini pasta | 1 tbsp fresh lemon juice |
| | ½ tsp salt |
| 3 medium carrots, diced | ½ tsp ground black pepper |
| 75g mayonnaise | 3 medium celery stalks, diced |
| 15g fresh dill, chopped | 150g frozen peas, thawed |

◆ Prepare tubetti as packet instructs in 5-litre flameproof casserole, but cook for only 8 minutes.

◆ Add carrots to tubetti and cook 3 minutes longer. Drain and rinse with cold water; drain again.

◆ Prepare dressing: stir mayonnaise, dill, lemon juice, salt and pepper together in large bowl until blended.

◆ Add tubetti and carrots to dressing; toss to coat. Add celery and peas and toss again to combine.

**Each serving: About 225 calories, 5g protein, 28g carbohydrate, 10g total fat (2g saturated), 7mg cholesterol, 300mg sodium**

## TORTELLINI SALAD WITH ARTICHOKES AND PEPPERS

*Prep:* 25 minutes   *Cook:* 10–15 minutes

*Makes* 6 main dish servings

| | |
|---|---|
| 500g fresh cheese tortellini | 1 medium yellow pepper, cored, seeded and cut into thin strips |
| 60ml white wine vinegar | |
| 3 tbsp extra virgin olive oil | |
| 1 tsp sugar | 1 medium tomato, seeded and diced |
| ½ tsp salt | |
| ¼ tsp coarsely ground black pepper | 175g bottled marinated artichoke hearts, drained and each cut in half |
| 1 medium red pepper, cored, seeded and cut into thin strips | 225g rocket or watercress |

◆ Prepare tortellini as packet instructs. Drain and rinse with cold water; drain again.

◆ Prepare dressing: whisk white wine vinegar, oil, sugar, salt and black pepper together in large bowl.

◆ Add red and yellow peppers, tomato, artichokes and tortellini to dressing in bowl; toss to coat. Cover and refrigerate if not serving right away.

◆ To serve, set aside a few whole rocket leaves for garnish. Tear remaining rocket leaves into bite-sized pieces; toss with tortellini mixture. Garnish with rocket leaves.

**Each serving: About 350 calories, 14g protein, 46g carbohydrate, 13g total fat (3g saturated), 40mg cholesterol, 540mg sodium**

# RICE SALADS

If you're celebrating summer with a picnic or throwing a holiday buffet party, a rice salad is a side dish to consider. Vegetables or chunks of fresh or dried fruit make welcome additions. Tossing the hot rice with the dressing allows it to absorb maximum flavour as it cools. Rice salads are best eaten within two hours of preparation as rice hardens when it's refrigerated.

## MINTED RICE SALAD WITH CORN

❖❖❖❖❖❖❖❖❖❖❖❖❖❖❖

*Prep:* 20 minutes, plus cooling
*Cook:* 20 minutes
*Makes* 8 accompaniment servings

**200g long-grain rice**
**Salt**
**2 tbsp fresh lemon juice**
**2 tbsp olive oil**
**¼ tsp ground black pepper**
**3 medium corn on the cob,**
**  husks and silk removed**
**120g radishes, finely diced**
**120g frozen peas, thawed**
**15g fresh mint, chopped**

**1** Prepare rice as packet instructs, using ½ teaspoon salt. Meanwhile, prepare vinaigrette: whisk lemon juice, oil, pepper and ¾ teaspoon salt together in large bowl.

**2** Add drained rice to vinaigrette and toss gently but thoroughly to coat. Allow to cool 30 minutes, tossing mixture occasionally with fork.

**3** Meanwhile, bring *3 litres water* to the boil in 5-litre flameproof casserole. Add corn and cook 5 minutes. Drain and cool.

### ALMOST-INSTANT RICE SALADS

Make a rice salad with any vinaigrette plus a few choice leftover meats or vegetables, or try the following:

• Canned tuna, diced tomatoes, capers, chopped flat-leaf parsley and a lemon juice and olive oil vinaigrette.

• Diced cooked chicken, celery, apple, chopped walnuts and a mayonnaise and lemon juice dressing.

• Rinsed and drained canned black beans, crumbled feta cheese, some diced avocado and a dressing of fresh lime juice, olive oil, garlic and ground cumin.

**4** Cut kernels from cobs and add to rice with diced radishes, peas and chopped fresh mint. Toss to combine.

EACH SERVING: ABOUT 160 CALORIES, 3g PROTEIN, 28g CARBOHYDRATE, 4g TOTAL FAT (1g SATURATED), 0mg CHOLESTEROL, 325mg SODIUM

## WHITE AND WILD RICE SALAD WITH DRIED CRANBERRIES AND GRAPES

*Prep:* 20 minutes, plus cooling    *Cook:* 50–60 minutes
*Makes* 8 accompaniment servings

100g wild rice
Salt
150g long-grain rice
60g dried cranberries or
  currants
2 tbsp red wine vinegar
2 tbsp olive oil
½ tsp grated orange rind
¼ tsp ground black pepper

300g seedless red grapes,
  each cut in half
2 medium celery stalks, thinly
  sliced
2 tbsp chopped fresh parsley
Lettuce leaves (optional)
60g pecans, toasted and
  coarsely chopped

◆ Cook wild rice as packet instructs, using ½ teaspoon salt. Meanwhile, cook long-grain rice as packet instructs, using ¼ teaspoon salt.

◆ Drain and rinse white and wild rice with *boiling water*. Drain again; transfer to bowl and set aside.

◆ Combine dried cranberries with enough *boiling water* just to cover in a small bowl; let stand for 5 minutes. Drain.

◆ Prepare dressing: mix vinegar, olive oil, orange rind, pepper and ¾ teaspoon salt together in large bowl.

◆ Add wild rice, long-grain rice and cranberries to dressing in bowl; toss to coat. Allow to cool 30 minutes, tossing occasionally with fork.

◆ Add grapes, celery and chopped parsley to rice salad; toss until evenly combined.

◆ To serve, line salad bowl or platter with lettuce leaves, if you like. Spoon rice salad over lettuce and sprinkle with chopped pecans.

**Each serving: About 205 calories, 4g protein, 32g carbohydrate, 8g total fat (1g saturated), 0mg cholesterol, 410mg sodium**

## JAPANESE RICE SALAD

*Prep:* 20 minutes, plus cooling    *Cook:* 20 minutes
*Makes* 8 accompaniment servings

300g long-grain rice
Salt
3 tbsp rice vinegar
2 tbsp vegetable oil
1 tsp grated, peeled fresh
  ginger
¼ tsp ground black pepper

125g green beans, ends
  trimmed and cut into
  5mm pieces
2 medium carrots, grated
3 spring onions, thinly sliced
Watercress (optional)

◆ Prepare rice as packet instructs, using ½ teaspoon salt. Drain and rinse with *boiling water*. Drain again; transfer to bowl and set aside.

◆ Prepare dressing: whisk seasoned rice vinegar, oil, ginger, pepper and ½ teaspoon salt together in large bowl.

◆ Add rice and toss to coat. Allow to cool for 30 minutes, tossing occasionally with a fork.

◆ Meanwhile, bring *450ml water* and 1 teaspoon salt to the boil in 2-litre saucepan. Add green beans and cook for 5 minutes. Drain and rinse with cold water.

◆ Add green beans to rice with carrots and spring onions; toss to combine. To serve, arrange watercress, if using, round edge of platter; spoon rice salad into centre.

**Each serving: About 175 calories, 3g protein, 32g carbohydrate, 4g total fat (1g saturated), 0mg cholesterol, 395mg sodium**

## BROWN RICE AND MANGO SALAD

*Prep:* 25 minutes    *Cook:* 1 hour
*Makes* 8 accompaniment servings

200g long-grain brown rice
Salt
1 large lime
2 tbsp olive oil
¼ tsp ground black pepper

1 ripe mango, peeled and cut
  into 1cm cubes
15g fresh coriander, chopped
2 spring onions, thinly sliced

◆ Prepare brown rice as packet instructs, using ½ teaspoon salt. Rinse rice with cold water and drain well; tranfer to bowl and set aside. Meanwhile, grate ½ teaspoon rind and squeeze 2 tablespoons juice from lime.

◆ Prepare dressing: whisk lime rind, lime juice, olive oil, pepper and ½ teaspoon salt together in large bowl. Add rice and toss to coat. Add mango, coriander and spring onions; toss until evenly combined.

**Each serving: About 135 calories, 2g protein, 24g carbohydrate, 4g total fat (1g saturated), 0mg cholesterol, 205mg sodium**

# GRAIN SALADS

Barley and wheat, both whole (wheat grains) and cracked (bulgar), contribute to some wonderfully satisfying salads. Cooked (or soaked, for bulgar) until just tender but still slightly firm, they lend excellent texture and a delicately nutty flavour to these nutritious and unusual salads. If the grains in these recipes aren't available at the supermarket, look for them in health food shops.

## BARLEY SALAD WITH NECTARINES

❖❖❖❖❖❖❖❖❖❖❖❖❖❖❖❖❖❖❖❖❖❖❖❖❖❖❖❖

*Prep:* 30 minutes    *Cook:* 40–50 minutes
*Makes* 12 accompaniment servings

450g pearl barley
Salt
3 or 4 medium limes
75ml olive oil
1 tbsp sugar
¾ tsp coarsely ground black pepper

750g nectarines (about 4), stoned and cut into 1cm pieces
450g tomatoes, seeded and cut into 1cm pieces
4 spring onions, thinly sliced
30g fresh mint, chopped

1 Bring *1½ litres water* to the boil in 4-litre saucepan. Add barley and 1½ teaspoons salt; return to the boil. Reduce heat to low; cover and simmer 35–45 minutes until barley is tender and most of liquid has been absorbed. Drain and rinse barley with cold water. Drain well.

2 Meanwhile, prepare lime dressing: grate 1 tablespoon rind and squeeze 125ml juice from limes. Place rind and lime juice in large bowl. Add olive oil, sugar, pepper and 1¼ teaspoons salt; whisk together until blended.

3 Add barley, nectarines, tomatoes, spring onions and mint to dressing; stir gently to coat. If not serving right away, cover and refrigerate.

### BARLEY

This hearty, ancient grain is often identified with beer, breads, cereals and soups, but it also makes delicious, healthy salads. When cooked until tender, the whole grain has a nutty taste and chewy texture, making it the perfect partner for piquant vinaigrettes, herbs, crunchy vegetables and even fruit. Instead of rice, try barley as an easy side dish. Pearl barley is scoured six times to remove the bran and husk for quicker cooking.

EACH SERVING: ABOUT 230 CALORIES, 5g PROTEIN, 40g CARBOHYDRATE, 7g TOTAL FAT (1g SATURATED), 0mg CHOLESTEROL, 405mg SODIUM

## WHEAT-GRAIN SALAD WITH SPINACH

*Prep: 15 minutes, plus soaking    Cook: 1½ hours*
*Makes 4 main dish servings*

250g wheat grains
350g spinach, tough stalks
    removed
1 medium tomato
10 sun-dried tomatoes
    (about 30g)
3 tbsp olive oil

2 tbsp red wine vinegar
1 tsp salt
½ tsp sugar
½ tsp Dijon mustard
¼ tsp coarsely ground black
    pepper
150g sultanas

◆ Soak wheat grains in *water* to cover by 5cm in large bowl
overnight.

◆ Drain wheat grains. Bring *1½ litres water* to the boil in
4-litre saucepan. Add wheat grains and return to the boil.
Reduce heat to low; cover and simmer 1 hour, or until
wheat grains are tender. Drain.

◆ Meanwhile, coarsely chop spinach. Dice tomato. Place
sun-dried tomatoes in small bowl; pour *225ml boiling water*
over them. Let stand 5 minutes to soften; drain well.
Coarsely chop sun-dried tomatoes.

◆ Prepare dressing: whisk oil, red wine vinegar, salt, sugar,
mustard and black pepper together in medium bowl. Add
sultanas, diced tomato, chopped sun-dried tomatoes,
spinach and wheat grains; toss until blended.

Each serving: About 455 calories, 12g protein, 82g carbohydrate,
12g total fat (1g saturated), 0mg cholesterol, 625mg sodium

## BARLEY, CORN AND BEAN SALAD

*Prep: 15 minutes, plus cooling    Cook: 40–50 minutes*
*Makes 6 accompaniment servings*

135g pearl barley
Salt
150g frozen baby broad beans
3 corn on the cob, husks and
    silk removed

2 tbsp cider vinegar
1 tbsp olive oil
¼ tsp ground black pepper
15g fresh parsley, chopped

◆ Bring *600ml water* to the boil in 2-litre saucepan over
high heat. Add barley and ½ teaspoon salt; return to the
boil. Reduce heat to low; cover and simmer 35–45 minutes
until tender. Drain and rinse with cold water. Drain again.

◆ Meanwhile, cook broad beans as packet instructs. Drain
and rinse with cold water; drain again.

◆ Bring *4 litres water* to the boil in 5-litre flameproof
casserole. Add corn on the cob; cook 5 minutes. Drain and
allow to cool. Cut kernels from cobs.

◆ Prepare dressing: whisk cider vinegar, olive oil, black
pepper and ¾ teaspoon salt together in large bowl. Add
barley, broad beans, corn kernels and chopped parsley;
toss until blended.

Each serving: About 180 calories, 6g protein, 35g carbohydrate,
3g total fat (0g saturated), 0mg cholesterol, 320mg sodium

## TOMATO AND MINT TABBOULEH

*Prep: 20 minutes, plus standing and chilling*
*Makes 8 accompaniment servings*

250g bulgar (cracked wheat)
60ml fresh lemon juice
450g medium-size ripe
    tomatoes, cut into 1cm
    pieces
1 medium cucumber (about
    225g), peeled and cut into
    1cm pieces
3 spring onions, chopped

45g fresh parsley, chopped
30g fresh mint leaves,
    chopped
1 tbsp olive oil
¾ tsp salt
¼ tsp coarsely ground black
    pepper

◆ Combine bulgar, lemon juice and *350ml boiling water* in
large heatproof bowl, stirring to mix. Allow to stand about
30 minutes until liquid is absorbed.

◆ When mixture is cool, stir in tomatoes, cucumber pieces,
chopped spring onions and remaining ingredients. Cover
and refrigerate bulgar mixture at least 1 hour to allow
flavours to blend.

Each serving: About 125 calories, 4g protein, 24g carbohydrate,
2g total fat (0g saturated), 0mg cholesterol, 215mg sodium

# BEAN SALADS

With their soft texture and mild taste, beans absorb the flavours of any dressing and make a wonderful foundation for a salad. If you cannot find one variety, simply substitute another. For the freshest taste and consistency – and to reduce some of the sodium – always rinse canned beans before using. Keep your store cupboard stocked with a good assortment of canned beans and you'll always be able to prepare delicious salads at a moment's notice. Dried beans take a little longer to prepare but are equally suited to salads once they have been re-hydrated and cooked.

1 Cook black beans as black-eyed beans in Step 1 of Texas Caviar, page 386. Cut green beans into 4cm pieces. Bring green beans and *2.5cm water* to the boil in 3-litre saucepan. Reduce heat to low; cover and simmer 5–10 minutes until tender-crisp. Drain. Meanwhile, chop onion.

## FIESTA BEAN SALAD

❖◆❖◆❖◆❖◆❖◆❖◆❖◆❖◆❖◆❖◆❖◆❖◆❖◆❖◆❖

*Prep:* 20 minutes, plus soaking and chilling    *Cook:* 20 minutes
*Makes* 12 accompaniment servings

**200g dried black beans,**
    **soaked using 1-hour method**
    **on page 385 and drained**
**450g green beans**
**1 small onion**
**60ml olive or vegetable oil**
**1 tbsp chilli powder**
**75ml distilled white vinegar**
**1½ tsp sugar**
**1½ tsp salt**

**400g canned red kidney**
    **beans, rinsed and drained**
**400g canned cannellini beans,**
    **rinsed and drained**
**400g canned sweetcorn,**
    **drained**
**15g fresh coriander or**
    **parsley, chopped**
**400g canned flageolet beans,**
    **rinsed and drained**

2 Heat oil over medium-high heat in 2-litre saucepan. Add onion and cook, stirring, 10 minutes, or until tender.

3 Stir chilli powder into onions and cook, stirring 1 minute. Remove from heat; stir in vinegar, sugar and salt.

4 Place red kidney beans, cannellini beans and black beans in large bowl. Add corn, coriander, green beans, flageolet beans and onion mixture; toss to coat. Cover with cling film and refrigerate at least 1 hour to blend flavours.

❖◆❖◆❖◆❖◆❖◆❖◆❖◆❖◆❖◆❖

### LEFTOVER CORIANDER

Left with half a bunch? Add coriander to omelettes, tuna salads or mixed greens, or use it instead of basil in your favourite pesto recipe. To avoid discoloration, don't chop coriander in advance.

❖◆❖◆❖◆❖◆❖◆❖◆❖◆❖

EACH SERVING: ABOUT 190 CALORIES, 9g PROTEIN, 32g CARBOHYDRATE, 5g TOTAL FAT (1g SATURATED), 0mg CHOLESTEROL, 790mg SODIUM

## AVOCADO AND BLACK BEAN SALAD

*Prep: 20 minutes, plus soaking*
*Makes 4 accompaniment servings*

2 small avocados
2 medium plum tomatoes
2 medium navel oranges
200g dried black beans

1 tbsp chopped fresh
    coriander or parsley
1 tsp salt

◆ Soak beans in *water* to cover by 5cm in large bowl overnight. Cut each avocado in half; discard stones. Peel avocados. Cut avocados and tomatoes into bite-sized chunks.

◆ Cut rind and white pith from oranges and discard. Cut each orange crossways into 5mm thick slices. Using wooden spoon, toss avocados, tomatoes, orange slices and remaining ingredients together in large bowl to mix well.

**Each serving: About 335 calories, 15g protein, 49g carbohydrate, 20g total fat (3g saturated), 0mg cholesterol, 580mg sodium**

## CHICK-PEA SALAD

*Prep: 20 minutes*
*Makes 4 accompaniment servings*

2 tbsp red wine vinegar
2 tbsp olive oil
1 tsp Dijon mustard
¼ tsp salt
350g small tomatoes, each cut
    into 8 wedges
75g Kalamata olives, stoned
    and coarsely chopped

1 spring onion, thinly sliced
400g canned chick-peas,
    rinsed and drained
2 tbsp chopped fresh
    oregano, basil or parsley

Prepare vinaigrette: whisk red wine vinegar, olive oil, mustard and salt together in large bowl. Add tomato wedges, olives, spring onion, chick-peas and oregano and toss to mix well.

**Each serving: About 235 calories, 6g protein, 24g carbohydrate, 14g total fat (2g saturated), 0mg cholesterol, 900mg sodium**

## BLACK-EYED BEAN SALAD

*Prep: 10 minutes, plus chilling   Cook: 20 minutes*
*Makes 8 accompaniment servings*

600g canned black-eyed
    beans, rinsed and drained
1 large red pepper, cored,
    seeded and diced
75g red onion, chopped
300g frozen peas, thawed
3 tbsp cider vinegar
2 tbsp olive oil

1 tsp sugar
1 tsp chopped fresh thyme or
    ¼ tsp dried
¾ tsp salt
¼ tsp coarsely ground black
    pepper
1 large tomato

◆ Toss black-eyed beans with remaining ingredients, except tomato. Cover and refrigerate at least 3 hours to blend the flavours.

◆ To serve, cut the tomato into 5mm thick slices. Arrange the tomato slices and black-eyed pea salad on a large platter.

**Each serving: About 165 calories, 8g protein, 25g carbohydrate, 4g total fat (1g saturated), 0mg cholesterol, 235mg sodium**

## TWO-BEAN AND TOMATO SALAD

*Prep: 20 minutes   Cook: 10 minutes*
*Makes 6 accompaniment servings*

350g French green beans or
    green beans, ends trimmed
2 tbsp extra virgin olive oil
1 tbsp fresh lemon juice
½ large shallot, finely chopped
½ tsp Dijon mustard
¼ tsp salt

¼ tsp coarsely ground black
    pepper
2 medium tomatoes, each cut
    into 12 wedges
400g canned cannellini beans,
    rinsed and drained

◆ Bring *2cm water* to the boil in 26cm frying pan over high heat. Add beans and return to the boil. Reduce heat to medium and cook, uncovered, for 3–5 minutes until beans are tender-crisp. Drain. Rinse beans with cold water, then drain again and pat dry with kitchen towels.

◆ Prepare dressing: whisk olive oil, lemon juice, chopped shallot, mustard, salt and pepper together in large bowl until blended.

◆ Add green beans, tomato wedges and cannellini beans; gently toss to mix well.

**Each serving: About 145 calories, 6g protein, 21g carbohydrate, 5g total fat (1g saturated), 0mg cholesterol, 115mg sodium**

# MOULDED SALADS

A colourful, shimmering gelatine salad, studded with fruit, makes an eye-catching addition to a cold buffet. Infused with spices or flecked with herbs, these salads are cool and refreshing (in summer, try the simple tomato aspic). Always make sure the gelatine is completely dissolved: all granules must disappear.

## SPICED WINE AND FRUIT MOULD

❖❖❖❖❖❖❖❖❖❖❖❖❖

*Prep: 40 minutes, plus standing and chilling*
*Cook: 30 minutes*
*Makes 16 accompaniment servings*

250g sugar
3 cinnamon sticks, 7–8cm each
2 tsp whole allspice
½ tsp salt
5 sachets (11g each) powdered gelatine
1 bottle (750 ml) sweet white wine
2 tbsp grenadine syrup
2 tbsp fresh lemon juice
6 bottled maraschino cherries
475g canned whole figs in syrup, drained
900g canned pear halves in syrup, drained
100g green candied cherries, each cut in half, for garnish
Flat-leaf parsley sprigs for garnish

**1** Bring first 4 ingredients and *225ml water* to the boil in 2-litre saucepan over high heat. Reduce heat to low; simmer 15 minutes. Discard spices. Sprinkle gelatine over *350ml cold water* in measuring jug; let stand for 2 minutes to soften gelatine. Stir into syrup; cook over medium heat, stirring, until the gelatine completely dissolves (do not boil). Remove from heat.

**2** Combine sweet white wine, grenadine, lemon juice and *350ml water* in large bowl. Stir in gelatine mixture. Arrange maraschino cherries and half of figs in attractive design in base of 2½-litre fluted mould.

**3** Carefully pour 1cm gelatine mixture over fruit; place mould in large bowl of *ice water* until gelatine is set but not firm (it should be sticky to the touch). Add enough gelatine mixture to cover fruit by 1cm.

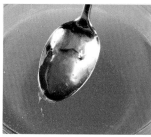

**4** Let mould stand in ice-water bath until next layer is set but not firm. Meanwhile, place bowl of gelatine mixture in another large bowl of *ice water* just until it mounds slightly when dropped from spoon, stirring often. Reserve enough pears to fit round edge of mould.

**5** Dice remaining pears and figs; gently fold into gelatine mixture in bowl. Ladle fruit mixture into mould; edge should immediately gel (remove mould from ice-water bath if mixture sets too quickly).

**6** Working quickly, arrange reserved pear halves round edge of mould, rounded-side out and pointed-end down. Refrigerate at least 6 hours, or until set. To serve, unmould salad onto chilled platter and garnish.

EACH SERVING: ABOUT 175 CALORIES, 2g PROTEIN, 35g CARBOHYDRATE, 0g TOTAL FAT, 0mg CHOLESTEROL, 75mg SODIUM

## ROYAL CRANBERRY MOULD

*Prep: 30 minutes, plus standing and chilling*
*Makes 16 accompaniment servings*

3 sachets (11g each) powdered gelatine
350g fresh cranberries, coarsely chopped
300g sugar
800g canned sliced peaches, drained and diced
2 medium navel oranges, rind and white pith removed, coarsely chopped

◆ Evenly sprinkle gelatine over *675ml cold water* in 2-litre saucepan; let stand for 2 minutes to soften slightly. Cook over medium heat, stirring frequently, until gelatine completely dissolves (do not boil). Remove from heat.

◆ Pour gelatine mixture into large bowl; stir in *900ml cold water*. Refrigerate about 2 hours just until it mounds slightly when dropped from spoon.

◆ Meanwhile, place cranberries in large bowl and stir in sugar until it completely dissolves, then stir in peaches and oranges. When gelatine mixture is ready, fold fruit into thickened gelatine.

◆ Pour gelatine-fruit mixture into 25cm Bundt or Kugelhopf tin or 2½-litre mould. Cover and refrigerate at least 6 hours, until set.

◆ To serve, unmould salad onto a chilled platter.

Each serving: About 170 calories, 2g protein, 43g carbohydrate, 0g total fat, 0mg cholesterol, 35mg sodium

## RED WINE AND BEETROOT MOULD

*Prep: 20 minutes, plus standing and chilling*
*Makes 16 accompaniment servings*

450g bottled sliced beetroots
4 sachets (11g each) powdered gelatine
125ml cider vinegar
1 bottle (750ml) red wine
¼ tsp salt
1 medium carrot
3 tbsp chopped fresh dill or 2 tsp dried

◆ Drain liquid from beetroots into 2-litre saucepan. Add *500ml cold water,* then evenly sprinkle gelatine over liquid and let stand 2 minutes.

◆ Cook beetroot mixture over medium heat, stirring frequently, until gelatine completely dissolves (do not boil). Remove from heat.

◆ Pour beetroot mixture into large bowl; stir in cider vinegar, salt and red wine. Refrigerate about 2 hours; mixture is ready when it mounds slightly when dropped from spoon.

◆ Meanwhile coarsely chop beetroots and grate carrot. When gelatine mixture is ready, fold in beetroots, carrot and dill. Pour into 2½-litre mould. Cover and refrigerate mixture at least 6 hours until set. To serve, unmould salad onto chilled platter.

Each serving: About 85 calories, 2g protein, 13g carbohydrate, 0g total fat, 0mg cholesterol, 170mg sodium

## TOMATO ASPIC

*Prep: 10 minutes, plus standing and chilling    Cook: 20 minutes*
*Makes 8 accompaniment servings*

900ml tomato juice
15g celery leaves
6 whole allspice
2 whole cloves
2 sachets (11g each) powdered gelatine
2 tbsp fresh lemon juice
1 tbsp sugar
½ tsp Tabasco sauce
225ml soured cream
2 tbsp mayonnaise
2 tbsp chopped fresh dill

◆ Pour 125ml tomato juice into large bowl; set aside. Bring remaining tomato juice with celery leaves, allspice and cloves to the boil in 3-litre saucepan over high heat. Reduce heat to low; simmer for 15 minutes. Sprinkle gelatine over juice in bowl; let stand for 2 minutes to soften gelatine slightly.

◆ Strain hot juice mixture over softened gelatine; stir until it dissolves. Stir in lemon juice, sugar and Tabasco sauce. Pour into a 21 by 11cm loaf tin or 1.2-litre mould.

◆ Cover and refrigerate at least 6 hours until set. To serve, unmould aspic onto chilled platter. Stir soured cream, mayonnaise and dill together; serve with aspic.

Each serving: About 120 calories, 3g protein, 8g carbohydrate, 9g total fat (4g saturated), 15mg cholesterol, 480mg sodium

### EASY UNMOULDING

To unmould a gelatine salad, dip the base of the mould or tin into a large bowl of warm water for 10 seconds – no longer, or the gelatine will begin to melt. Place a chilled serving platter that's been moistened with a little cold water over the mould, invert the two together quickly, and give the mould a firm shake or tap to release the salad. (If the mould comes out off centre, you can easily slide it back over the moistened platter.) If the salad fails to come out, hold the mould on its side until the salad begins to loosen from the top side. Or, turn the mould right-side up and run a round bladed knife between the gelatine mixture and the mould. Then try again.

# MAIN DISH MEAT SALADS

Steak, smoked ham, Parma ham and minced beef team up with crisp greens, crunchy vegetables and spicy dressings to make salads into main dishes. Fresh mint and coriander round out Thai flavours in the most refreshing way, while juicy pears and shaved Parmesan provide the Italian solution to using greens like radicchio, which can be bitter.

## BEEF CAESAR SALAD

❖ ❖ ❖ ❖ ❖ ❖ ❖ ❖ ❖ ❖ ❖ ❖ ❖ ❖ ❖ ❖ ❖ ❖ ❖ ❖ ❖ ❖ ❖ ❖ ❖ ❖

*Prep: 25 minutes, plus standing    Grill: 12–15 minutes*
*Makes 4 main dish servings*

| | |
|---|---|
| 450g beef flank steak | 1 garlic clove, finely chopped |
| ½ tsp salt | 2 tbsp freshly grated |
| ½ tsp coarsely ground black | Parmesan cheese |
| pepper | 1 medium head Cos lettuce |
| 3 tbsp olive oil | 1 medium head red leaf |
| 2 tbsp mayonnaise | lettuce |
| 1 tbsp Dijon mustard | 1 medium cucumber |
| 1 tbsp fresh lemon juice | Parmesan shavings for garnish |
| ½ tsp anchovy paste | Crusty bread (optional) |

**1** Preheat grill. Place steak on grill rack; sprinkle with salt and black pepper. Place under grill at closest position to heat source; grill 12–15 minutes for medium-rare, or until desired doneness, turning steak once. Transfer to chopping board; let stand 10 minutes.

**2** Meanwhile, prepare dressing: using wire whisk or fork, mix olive oil, mayonnaise, Dijon mustard, lemon juice, anchovy paste, chopped garlic and grated Parmesan cheese together in large bowl.

**3** Wash and thoroughly dry lettuces. Tear both lettuces into bite-sized pieces; add to dressing in bowl and toss gently to coat.

**4** Peel several strips of skin from cucumber, leaving some green. Thinly slice and toss with lettuce mixture. Place salad on 4 plates. Slice steak thinly across the grain and arrange on salads. Sprinkle with Parmesan shavings; serve with crusty bread, if you like.

### CAESAR SALAD PLUS

Though originally concocted simply with Cos lettuce (in Tijuana, Mexico, in 1924), Caesar salad can be turned into a main dish by the addition of meat, such as the flank steak here. Other good choices are skinless, boneless chicken breasts, grilled and sliced, or skewered prawns, grilled and piled on top.

EACH SERVING: ABOUT 395 CALORIES, 27g PROTEIN, 8g CARBOHYDRATE, 28g TOTAL FAT (7g SATURATED), 65mg CHOLESTEROL, 655mg SODIUM

## THAI BEEF SALAD

*Prep:* 45 minutes   *Cook:* 10 minutes
*Makes* 4 main dish servings

2 large bunches coriander
2 large bunches fresh mint
60ml rice vinegar
3 tbsp vegetable oil
4 tbsp fish sauce (nuoc nam, see page 30)
4 tsp grated peeled fresh ginger
1 jalapeño chilli, seeded and finely chopped
Salt
1 large carrot, cut into 5cm long matchstick-thin strips
1 medium red pepper, cored, seeded and cut into 5cm long matchstick-thin strips
2 large spring onions, cut into 5cm long matchstick-thin strips
450g minced beef
1 garlic clove, finely chopped
1 head Butterhead lettuce, torn into bite-sized pieces

◈ From coriander, remove 30g leaves; set aside. Chop 15g coriander leaves. Repeat with mint. Prepare dressing: whisk chopped coriander and mint, rice vinegar, next 4 ingredients and ⅛ teaspoon salt together in medium bowl. Spoon half of dressing into large bowl; set aside. Add carrot, red pepper and spring onions to dressing remaining in medium bowl.

◈ Fry minced beef in 26cm frying pan over medium-high heat until browned, breaking it up. Spoon off and discard fat.

◈ Add garlic and ¼ teaspoon salt to beef in frying pan and cook 1 minute, stirring. Add to carrot mixture; toss well. Add lettuce and reserved coriander and mint to dressing in large bowl. Toss. Spoon onto 4 plates and top with beef mixture.

**Each serving: About 380 calories, 20g protein, 12g carbohydrate, 27g total fat (8g saturated), 69mg cholesterol, 840mg sodium**

## QUESADILLA SALAD

*Prep:* 30 minutes   *Cook:* 10 minutes
*Makes* 4 main dish servings

2–3 limes
¾ tsp chilli powder
½ tsp ground coriander
½ tsp sugar
4 tsp olive oil
1 head Cos lettuce, cut crossways into 2cm wide strips
350g cherry tomatoes, each cut in half
1 small avocado, peeled and cut into 1cm wedges
125g sliced smoked ham, cut into 1cm strips
2 spring onions, thinly sliced
8 flour tortillas (about 15cm each)
175g Cheddar cheese, grated
¾ tsp crushed dried chillies

◈ Prepare vinaigrette: grate ¼ teaspoon rind and squeeze 3 tablespoons juice from limes. Whisk lime rind, lime juice, chilli powder, ground coriander and sugar together in large

bowl. Whisk in oil in thin stream until blended. Add lettuce cherry tomatoes, avocado, smoked ham strips and spring onions; toss well. Arrange salads on 4 plates.

◈ Heat 26cm frying pan over medium heat. Place 1 tortilla in pan; sprinkle with one-quarter of cheese; top with second tortilla, pressing lightly. Cook quesadilla, turning once, for about 2 minutes until lightly toasted and cheese melts.

◈ Transfer to chopping board. Cut into 8 wedges; keep warm. Repeat with remaining tortillas and cheese. To serve, tuck quesadillas into salads.

**Each serving: About 610 calories, 27g protein, 54g carbohydrate, 35g total fat (11g saturated), 62mg cholesterol, 950mg sodium**

## PARMA HAM AND PEAR SALAD WITH PARMESAN AND PECANS

*Prep:* 25 minutes   *Makes* 3 main dish servings

1 piece Parmesan cheese
1 tbsp red wine vinegar
1 tsp Dijon mustard
¼ tsp ground black pepper
2 tbsp olive oil
1 small head radicchio (about 125g), torn into pieces
1 head chicory, separated into leaves
1 bunch rocket
2 ripe pears, peeled, cored and each cut into eighths
125g Parma ham, thinly sliced
30g toasted pecans, broken into pieces

◈ Using vegetable peeler, shave 60g curls from Parmesan; set aside. Prepare vinaigrette: whisk vinegar, mustard and pepper together in large bowl; slowly whisk in oil.

◈ Add radicchio, chicory, rocket and pears to vinaigrette; toss well. Arrange salad on 3 plates. Arrange Parma ham on top. Sprinkle with Parmesan curls and pecans.

**Each serving: About 365 calories, 18g protein, 23g carbohydrate, 23g total fat (6g saturated), 26mg cholesterol, 845mg sodium**

# MAIN DISH POULTRY SALADS

Use quick-cooking boneless chicken breasts, or simply purchase a roasted chicken from the supermarket, for these simple salads. We've added exotic ingredients such as lime, mango, fresh ginger and tangy feta cheese to complement the delicate taste of chicken. Each makes a colourful and delicious one-dish meal.

## CURRIED CHICKEN SALAD WITH MANGO

◆ ◆ ◆ ◆ ◆ ◆ ◆ ◆ ◆ ◆ ◆ ◆

*Prep:* 25 minutes, plus cooling
*Cook:* 15 minutes
*Makes* 4 main dish servings

**450g skinless, boneless chicken breasts**
**Salt**
**1 tsp curry powder**
**75g plain low-fat yogurt**
**60g mayonnaise**
**2 tbsp mango chutney**
**2 tbsp fresh lime juice**
**¼ tsp ground black pepper**
**1 large ripe mango, diced (see right)**
**3 celery stalks, thinly sliced**
**15g fresh coriander, chopped**
**Lettuce leaves**
**2 tbsp sliced almonds, toasted (optional)**

**1** Bring chicken, 1 teaspoon salt and *water* to cover by 2–3cm to the boil in 3-litre saucepan over high heat. Reduce heat to low; simmer 10 minutes, or until cooked through. Cool in liquid 30 minutes.

**2** Meanwhile, toast curry powder in 1-litre saucepan over low heat, stirring constantly with wooden spoon to prevent burning, 1 minute, or until very fragrant.

**3** Prepare dressing: whisk curry powder, yogurt, mayonnaise, chutney, lime juice, pepper and ½ teaspoon salt together in large bowl.

◆ ◆ ◆ ◆ ◆ ◆ ◆ ◆ ◆ ◆ ◆ ◆ ◆ ◆ ◆ ◆ ◆ ◆

### PREPARING A MANGO

Slice mango down both sides of long, flat stone. Run small paring knife between skin and flesh of each half, 2–3cm deep, then turn back the 2–3cm border of skin. Cut away rest of peel in a few strokes, then dice or slice as desired.

**4** Drain chicken; cut into bite-sized pieces. Toss chicken, mango, celery and coriander in dressing. Line platter with lettuce; top with salad and almonds, if using.

EACH SERVING: ABOUT 310 CALORIES, 28g PROTEIN, 18g CARBOHYDRATE, 14g TOTAL FAT (3g SATURATED), 90mg CHOLESTEROL, 560mg SODIUM

## WARM CHICKEN, SPINACH AND FETA SALAD

*Prep:* 20 minutes    *Cook:* 20 minutes

*Makes* 4 main dish servings

5 tbsp olive or vegetable oil

1 medium red pepper, cored, seeded and cut into 5mm wide strips

1 medium yellow pepper, cored, seeded and cut into 5mm wide strips

750g skinless, boneless chicken breasts, cut crossways into 2–3cm wide strips

Salt

3 tbsp white wine vinegar

1 tsp sugar

½ tsp coarsely ground black pepper

350g spinach, tough stalks removed

125g feta cheese

◆ Heat 3 tablespoons oil in 30cm large frying pan over medium-high heat. Add pepper strips and cook, stirring frequently, about 10 minutes until tender and lightly browned. Using slotted spoon, transfer pepper strips to large serving bowl.

◆ Add chicken strips and ½ teaspoon salt to oil remaining in pan; cook, stirring frequently, about 10 minutes until chicken is lightly browned and loses its pink colour throughout. Using slotted spoon, transfer chicken strips to bowl with peppers.

◆ Prepare dressing: remove pan from heat. Add vinegar, sugar, remaining oil, black pepper and ¼ teaspoon salt to juices in pan; stir until brown bits are loosened.

◆ Add vinegar mixture and spinach to bowl with chicken; toss gently to mix. Finely crumble feta onto salad.

**Each serving:** About 460 calories, 45g protein, 10g carbohydrate, 27g total fat (8g saturated), 147mg cholesterol, 825mg sodium

## SESAME NOODLE SALAD WITH CHICKEN

*Prep:* 25 minutes    *Cook:* 12 to 15 minutes

*Makes* 4 main dish servings

350g linguine or spaghetti

175g mange-tout, strings removed, each cut crossways into thirds

65g smooth peanut butter

3 tbsp rice vinegar

3 tbsp soy sauce

1 tbsp brown sugar

1 tbsp finely chopped peeled fresh ginger

1 tbsp sesame oil

¼ tsp ground red pepper

1 small garlic clove, crushed

2 medium carrots, grated

½ small head red cabbage (150g), thinly sliced

175g boneless roasted chicken, pulled into thin strips

◆ Prepare linguine as packet instructs. During last minute of cooking, add mange-tout. Drain and rinse with cold water to cool. Drain again; set aside.

◆ Prepare peanut-butter sauce: whisk peanut butter, next 7 ingredients and *175ml very hot tap water* together in a small bowl until blended. Toss linguine, mange-tout, carrots, red cabbage and chicken with peanut-butter sauce in large bowl. If not serving right away, cover and refrigerate. If noodles become too sticky after standing, toss with a little *hot water* until dressing is desired consistency.

**Each serving:** About 615 calories, 34g protein, 86g carbohydrate, 15g total fat (3g saturated), 44mg cholesterol, 1095mg sodium

## SMOKED TURKEY, SPINACH AND CHICK-PEA SALAD

*Prep:* 25 minutes    *Makes* 4 main dish servings

60ml fresh lemon juice

3 tbsp olive oil

½ tsp sugar

½ tsp ground cumin

¼ tsp coarsely ground black pepper

1 small garlic clove, finely chopped

3 medium nectarines, stoned and cut into 5mm wedges

400g canned chick-peas, rinsed and drained

225g sliced smoked turkey, cut into 5 by 1cm strips

350g spinach, tough stalks removed and leaves torn into 5cm pieces

Prepare vinaigrette: whisk lemon juice, olive oil, sugar, cumin, pepper and garlic together in large salad bowl until blended. Add nectarines, chick-peas, turkey and spinach to bowl and toss to mix well.

**Each serving:** About 330 calories, 20g protein, 35g carbohydrate, 14g total fat (2g saturated), 26mg cholesterol, 920mg sodium

# MAIN DISH FISH SALADS

Salmon and tuna make elegant salads, either warm or chilled. Tuna grilled with fragrant thyme is redolent of the Mediterranean, and canned tuna with chunky vegetables comes straight from Tuscany. Salmon with asparagus celebrates spring in a fresh, appealing way.

**1** Prepare lemon-caper dressing: combine first 8 ingredients in small bowl. Slowly whisk in the olive oil until mixture thickens slightly; set aside.

**2** Bring *2–3cm water* to boil in 26cm frying pan. Add salmon and next 2 ingredients; bring to the boil. Reduce heat to low, cover and simmer 8 minutes, or until opaque.

**3** Drain salmon; chill. Meanwhile, bring potatoes and enough *water* to cover to the boil in 3-litre saucepan over high heat. Reduce heat to low; cover and simmer 15–20 minutes until they are fork-tender. Drain potatoes thoroughly; cut each in half, or into quarters if large. While potatoes are still warm, toss with 60ml dressing in medium bowl.

## SALMON AND ASPARAGUS SALAD

❖❖❖❖❖❖❖❖❖❖❖❖❖

*Prep:* 30 minutes
*Cook:* 30 minutes
*Makes* 4 main dish servings

**75ml fresh lemon juice**

**1 tsp grated lemon rind**

**2 tbsp canned or bottled drained and chopped capers**

**2 tbsp coarse-grained Dijon mustard**

**2 tbsp chopped fresh dill**

**1 tsp sugar**

**½ tsp salt**

**¼ tsp coarsely ground black pepper**

**75ml olive oil**

**450g salmon fillet, skin and small bones removed, if any**

**1 large lemon, sliced**

**1 tsp whole black peppercorns**

**450g new potatoes, unpeeled**

**450g asparagus, tough ends removed, cut into 5cm pieces**

**1 medium head lettuce, torn into bite-sized pieces**

**2 medium hard-boiled eggs, each cut into quarters**

**4** Bring asparagus and *2–3cm water* to the boil in 2-litre saucepan over high heat. Reduce heat to low; simmer, uncovered, 5 minutes, or until tender-crisp. Drain and chill briefly.

**5** Using fork, break salmon into 2–3cm chunks. Add asparagus to potatoes in bowl; toss with 60ml dressing. Divide lettuce among 4 plates; arrange potato mixture, eggs and salmon on top. Drizzle with remaining dressing.

EACH SERVING: ABOUT 470 CALORIES, 31g PROTEIN, 32g CARBOHYDRATE, 25g TOTAL FAT (4g SATURATED), 164mg CHOLESTEROL, 750mg SODIUM

**OLIVES**

It only takes a few olives to perk up seafood, meat and green salads, as well as pasta sauces. Imported varieties such as Kalamata offer the deepest flavours. Taste before using; olives vary greatly in flavour and saltiness. Loose olives should be used within 2–3 days, while those packed in brine will keep, unopened, for a year or so.

## FRESH TUNA NIÇOISE

*Prep: 25 minutes    Grill: 8–10 minutes*
*Makes 4 main dish servings*

4 medium plum tomatoes, peeled (see page 314), seeded and diced
6 Kalamata olives, stoned and coarsely chopped
3 anchovy fillets, chopped
2 tbsp canned or bottled drained and chopped capers
2 tbsp chopped fresh parsley
½ tsp coarsely ground black pepper

1 tsp dried thyme
2 tbsp olive oil
4 tuna steaks, 2–3cm thick and about 175g each
2 tbsp cider vinegar
¼ tsp salt
1 small head frisée or 1 head curly endive (inner leaves)
125g watercress

◆ Preheat grill. Mix first 5 ingredients together in medium bowl; set aside. Combine pepper, thyme and 1 tablespoon oil in small bowl; rub over tuna. Grease rack in grill pan; place tuna on rack. Grill at closest position to heat, turning once, 8–10 minutes until pale pink in centre for medium.

◆ Meanwhile, whisk vinegar, remaining 1 tablespoon oil and ¼ teaspoon salt together in large bowl. Add frisée and watercress; toss well. Arrange salad on 4 plates and place tuna on top. Spoon tomato mixture over tuna.

**Each serving: About 400 calories, 45g protein, 16g carbohydrate, 18g total fat (4g saturated), 67mg cholesterol, 700mg sodium**

## WARM SALMON SALAD

*Prep: 30 minutes    Cook: 8 minutes*
*Makes 4 main dish servings*

1 piece salmon fillet (about 450g), skin and small bones removed, if any
1 bunch spring onions (about 125g)
4 large navel oranges
2 tbsp light soy sauce

2 tbsp balsamic vinegar
2 tsp brown sugar
1 tbsp olive oil
2 small heads Butterhead lettuce, torn
2 small plum tomatoes, diced

◆ Using knife held in slanting position, almost parallel to cutting surface, slice salmon crossways into 5mm thick slices. Cut spring onions into 2–3cm pieces.

◆ Cut rind and white pith from 3 oranges; discard. Holding 1 orange at a time over strainer set over measuring jug, cut out sections between membranes; drop sections into strainer and set aside. Squeeze juice from membranes into measuring jug. Squeeze juice from remaining orange to equal 175ml juice in all. Stir in soy sauce, vinegar and sugar.

◆ Heat olive oil in 30cm non-stick frying pan over medium-high heat. Add salmon slices in batches; cook 1–2 minutes until golden, carefully turning once. Transfer to plate.

◆ Cook spring onions in juices in pan, stirring often, until golden; stir in juice mixture. Bring to the boil; boil 1 minute. To serve, arrange lettuce, orange sections, and salmon on 4 plates. Spoon spring onion mixture over salmon; sprinkle with diced tomatoes.

**Each serving: About 275 calories, 25g protein, 28g carbohydrate, 8g total fat (1g saturated), 58mg cholesterol, 395mg sodium**

## TUSCAN TUNA AND BEAN SALAD

*Prep: 25 minutes, plus cooling    Cook: 10 minutes*
*Makes 4 main dish servings*

2 tbsp plus 60ml olive oil
125g Italian bread, cut into 2–3cm cubes
2 large garlic cloves, crushed with side of knife
225g green beans, ends trimmed
60ml red wine vinegar
2 tbsp canned or bottled drained and chopped capers
1 tsp sugar
1 tsp Dijon mustard
¼ tsp coarsely ground black pepper

350g canned white tuna in brine, drained and broken into large pieces
400g canned cannellini beans, rinsed and drained
2 medium tomatoes, each cut into 8 wedges
1 head lettuce, torn
½ small head curly endive, torn
1 small red onion, cut in half and thinly sliced

◆ Prepare croûtons: heat 2 tablespoons olive oil in 30cm non-stick frying pan over medium heat. Add bread cubes and garlic and cook, stirring occasionally, until bread is lightly browned. Remove pan from heat; discard garlic.

◆ Bring *2–3cm water* to the boil in 2-litre saucepan. Add green beans and return to the boil over high heat. Reduce heat to low; simmer, uncovered, 5–10 minutes until beans are tender-crisp. Drain and rinse with cold water to cool slightly. Prepare vinaigrette: whisk vinegar, capers, sugar, mustard, pepper and remaining 60ml olive oil together in large bowl. Add remaining ingredients, green beans and croûtons; toss to serve.

**Each serving: About 525 calories, 34g protein, 45g carbohydrate, 24g total fat (4g saturated), 35mg cholesterol, 1125mg sodium**

# MAIN DISH SEAFOOD SALADS

Salads made from crab, prawns and lobster create elegant meals for entertaining that are quick to prepare and require minimal cooking time. Try substituting other shellfish; for example, you can replace the crab meat with cooked prawns or surimi (imitation crab meat).

## LAYERED CRAB SALAD

◆◆◆◆◆◆◆◆◆◆◆◆◆◆◆◆◆◆◆◆◆◆◆◆◆◆◆◆◆◆◆◆◆◆◆◆

*Prep: 30 minutes    Cook: 5 minutes*
*Makes 4 main dish servings*

225ml chicken stock
100g couscous
1 medium tomato
1 small cucumber
2 tbsp vegetable oil
1 small onion, finely chopped
2 tbsp dry white wine
450g canned white crab meat, picked over
1 tbsp chopped fresh parsley

2 tbsp mayonnaise
⅛ tsp ground black pepper
1 medium avocado, halved lengthways, stoned, peeled and thinly sliced
225g mixed baby salad greens or mixed salad greens
2 tsp white wine vinegar
¼ tsp salt

**1** Bring stock to the boil in 1-litre saucepan over high heat. Stir in couscous; cover and remove from heat. Let stand 5 minutes. Uncover; fluff couscous with fork. Cool slightly.

**2** Remove both ends from an empty food can (about 7–8cm in diameter and 7–8cm tall) to make a hollow cylinder. Wash and dry can thoroughly. Seed and dice tomato and cucumber. Combine couscous, tomato and cucumber; set aside. Heat 1 tablespoon oil in small frying pan over medium-high heat. Add onion and cook, stirring occasionally, until very lightly browned. Stir in wine.

**3** Mix crab meat, onion mixture, parsley, mayonnaise and black pepper together. Place can on a plate; spoon in one-quarter of couscous mixture. Gently press with back of spoon.

**4** Top couscous with one-quarter of avocado slices, then one-quarter of crab mixture, pressing after each layer. While pressing with back of spoon, slowly lift off can. Repeat to make 3 more salads.

### VARIATION: LAYERED CRAB SALAD PLATTER

Prepare Layered Crab Salad as above, but to assemble salad, line a 1½-litre soufflé dish or bowl with cling film. Fill evenly with crab mixture and press down firmly with spoon. Arrange avocado slices on top. Spoon in couscous and spread over avocado layer; press down firmly. Carefully invert salad onto platter. Dress greens as in step 5 and arrange round crab salad.

**5** Toss greens with vinegar, remaining 1 tablespoon oil and salt in bowl. Arrange round crab salads.

EACH SERVING: ABOUT 450 CALORIES, 27g PROTEIN, 36g CARBOHYDRATE, 22g TOTAL FAT (4g SATURATED), 76mg CHOLESTEROL, 545mg SODIUM

## PRAWN AND WATERCRESS SALAD

*Prep:* 45 minutes    *Cook:* 1–2 minutes
*Makes* 4 main dish servings

450g raw large prawns, peeled
  and de-veined (see page 90)
Salt
600g medium jicama or
  mooli, peeled and cut into
  4cm by 5mm sticks
225g watercress (about
  2 bunches), tough stalks
  removed

2 medium navel oranges
1 large lime
15g fresh coriander leaves
60g mayonnaise
1 tsp sugar
¼ tsp ground red pepper
225g plain low-fat yogurt

◆ Cut each prawn horizontally in half; rinse with cold water. Bring *7–8cm water* to the boil in 3-litre saucepan over high heat. Add prawns and 1 teaspoon salt; return to the boil. Cook 1 minute, or until prawns turn opaque throughout. Drain; rinse. Drain again and refrigerate.

◆ Combine jicama and watercress in large salad bowl. Cut rind and white pith from oranges; discard. Cut out sections between membranes and add (without juice) to bowl.

◆ Prepare yogurt dressing: grate 1 teaspoon rind and squeeze 2 tablespoons juice from lime. Process lime rind, lime juice, coriander, mayonnaise, sugar, ground red pepper and ½ teaspoon salt 30 seconds in food processor with knife blade attached or blender on medium speed, until blended. Add yogurt, pulsing just until blended. Just before serving, add prawns to bowl with jicama mixture. Add dressing and toss to combine.

**Each serving:** About 320 calories, 24g protein, 29g carbohydrate, 13g total fat (2g saturated), 185mg cholesterol, 720mg sodium

## ITALIAN SEAFOOD SALAD

*Prep:* 50 minutes, plus chilling    *Cook:* 20 minutes
*Makes* 8 main dish servings

450g sea scallops
900g cleaned squid
900g raw large prawns, peeled
  and de-veined (see page 90)
1 small garlic clove, finely
  chopped
150ml fresh lemon juice
75ml olive oil

2 tbsp Dijon mustard
½ tsp coarsely ground black
  pepper
150g Kalamata olives, stoned
  and coarsely chopped
4 large celery stalks, sliced
15g parsley leaves

◆ Rinse scallops with cold water to remove any sand from crevices. Pull tough crescent-shaped muscle from side of each scallop. Rinse squid; slice bodies crossways into 2cm thick rings. Cut tentacles into several pieces if large. Bring *6cm water* to the boil in 5-litre saucepan over high heat. Add prawns; return to the boil. Reduce heat to medium; cook

1–2 minutes, until prawns turn opaque throughout. Using slotted spoon, transfer prawns to colander to drain; transfer to large bowl.

◆ Add scallops to boiling water in pan; return to the boil. Reduce heat to medium; cook 2–3 minutes until scallops turn opaque throughout. Using slotted spoon, transfer to colander to drain, then add to bowl with prawns. Add squid to boiling water in pan; return to the boil. Squid should be tender and turn opaque throughout when water returns to the boil. If not, cook for 30–60 seconds longer. Drain well in colander; add to prawns and scallops.

◆ Prepare dressing: whisk garlic and next 4 ingredients together in small bowl. Add to bowl with seafood with olives, celery and parsley; toss to combine. Cover and refrigerate at least 3 hours to blend flavours.

**Each serving:** About 390 calories, 47g protein, 10g carbohydrate, 17g total fat (2g saturated), 463mg cholesterol, 795mg sodium

## LOBSTER AND MANGO SALAD

*Prep:* 30 minutes    *Cook:* 12 minutes
*Makes* 4 main dish servings

2 live lobsters, 600–750g each,
  or 225g cooked lobster
  meat
1 medium cucumber, peeled
  and diced
Salt
1 medium navel orange

2 tbsp fresh lemon juice
⅛ tsp ground black pepper
2 tbsp olive oil
1 mango, peeled and diced
  (see page 339)
1 tbsp chopped fresh mint
125g mixed baby salad greens

◆ Cook live lobsters, if using, and remove meat from shells (see page 92). Chop lobster meat coarsely; set aside. Toss cucumber with ¼ teaspoon salt in small bowl. Transfer to sieve and set over bowl to drain.

◆ Prepare dressing: using vegetable peeler, remove several strips of rind from orange, then cut 1 tablespoon very fine strips. Squeeze 2 tablespoons juice. Whisk orange and lemon juice, pepper and ½ teaspoon salt together in small bowl; slowly whisk in olive oil. Stir in rind.

◆ Combine 2 tablespoons dressing with lobster in small bowl. Pat cucumber dry. Combine cucumber with mango, mint and 2 tablespoons dressing in another bowl. Arrange greens on 4 plates; spoon mango mixture in centre. Arrange lobster on top. Drizzle remaining dressing over greens.

**Each serving:** About 185 calories, 13g protein, 18g carbohydrate, 7g total fat (1g saturated), 41mg cholesterol, 620mg sodium

# SALAD DRESSINGS

Fast to prepare, fresh and delicious, these salad dressings provide infinite possible combinations. From a creamy buttermilk and chive dressing to a classic vinaigrette flavoured with Dijon mustard and shallots, there's something here to suit every salad.

Each of these dressings can be prepared a day or two in advance and refrigerated in a jar with a tight-fitting lid. If made ahead, bring the dressing to room temperature for fullest flavour, and shake the jar well before tossing the dressing with salad greens.

## MUSTARD-SHALLOT VINAIGRETTE

*Prep:* 10 minutes    *Makes* about 175ml

| | |
|---|---|
| 6 tbsp olive oil | ½ tsp salt |
| ⅓ cup red wine vinegar | ½ tsp coarsely ground black |
| 4 tsp Dijon mustard | pepper |
| 1 tbsp finely chopped shallot | ½ tsp sugar |

Whisk all ingredients together in small bowl.

Each 100ml: About 430 calories, 1g protein, 6g carbohydrate, 47g total fat (6g saturated), 0mg cholesterol, 840mg sodium

## JAPANESE MISO VINAIGRETTE

*Prep:* 10 minutes    *Makes* about 225ml

| | |
|---|---|
| 2 tbsp miso (fermented soya bean paste, see page 58) | 1 tbsp finely chopped, peeled fresh ginger |
| 125ml rice vinegar | 1 tbsp sugar |
| 60ml olive oil | |

Stir miso into rice vinegar in small bowl until smooth. Process with remaining ingredients in blender until smooth.

Each 100ml: About 265 calories, 2g protein, 10g carbohydrate, 25g total fat (3g saturated), 0mg cholesterol, 550mg sodium

### VINAIGRETTE VARIATIONS

**Blue cheese vinaigrette** Prepare Mustard-Shallot Vinaigrette, adding 60g crumbled blue cheese to ingredients. Makes about 225ml.

Each 100ml: About 420 calories, 6g protein, 5g carbohydrate, 43g total fat (9g saturated), 18mg cholesterol, 995mg sodium

**Balsamic vinaigrette** Prepare Mustard-Shallot Vinaigrette, using balsamic vinegar instead of red wine vinegar. Makes about 175ml.

Each 100ml: About 475 calories, 1g protein, 14g carbohydrate, 47g total fat (6g saturated), 0mg cholesterol, 845mg sodium

### HERB VINEGARS

Wash several 675–900ml capacity bottles with corks (or jars with clamp-top lids) in hot soapy water. To sterilize, put bottles in large pan (and corks in small pan) with water to cover and bring to the boil over high heat. Boil for 15 minutes; drain.

Place 3 or 4 sprigs of desired herbs (washed and dried) and other ingredients (see below) in each bottle; you may need a skewer to push them in. For each bottle, bring 675–900ml vinegar to the boil in non-reactive pan. Pour through funnel into bottle. Cork; let stand in cool, dark place about 2 weeks (it is not necessary to refrigerate). Strain through fine sieve into measuring jug. Discard herbs and fruits; return vinegar to bottle; add sprigs of fresh herbs, if you like. Store at room temperature up to 3 months. If the cork pops, discard the vinegar.

**Chive-garlic** Rice vinegar, 2–3 peeled garlic cloves, chives.

**Dill-peppercorn** Cider vinegar, 1 tablespoon whole black peppercorns, dill sprigs.

**Sage-rosemary** Red wine vinegar, sage and rosemary sprigs.

**Basil-orange** White wine vinegar, strips of rind of 1 orange, basil sprigs.

**Raspberry-mint** (below left) White wine vinegar, 350ml fresh raspberries, mint sprigs.

**Chilli-coriander** (below centre) Distilled white vinegar, 1–4 fresh chillies, coriander sprigs.

**Lemon-thyme** (far right) White wine vinegar, strips of rind of 1 lemon, thyme sprigs.

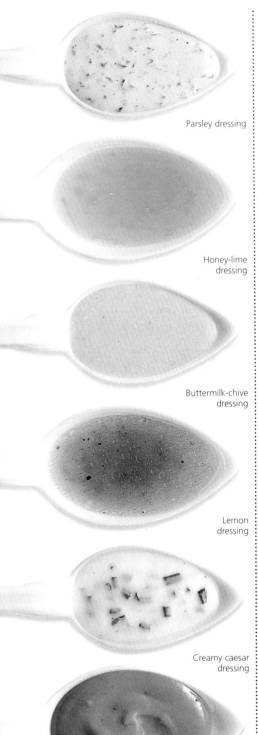

Parsley dressing

Honey-lime dressing

Buttermilk-chive dressing

Lemon dressing

Creamy caesar dressing

Tahini dressing

## PARSLEY DRESSING

*Prep:* 10 minutes    *Makes* about 175ml

125g mayonnaise
30g fresh parsley leaves
60ml soured cream
1 tbsp red wine vinegar
1 tsp anchovy paste
¼ tsp ground black pepper

Process all ingredients in blender until smooth, scraping sides as necessary.

Each 100ml: About 550 calories, 4g protein,
5g carbohydrate, 59g total fat
(12g saturated), 54mg cholesterol,
865mg sodium

## HONEY-LIME DRESSING

*Prep:* 5 minutes    *Makes* about 125ml

75ml fresh lime juice
4 tsp honey
1 tbsp rice vinegar
⅛ tsp salt

Whisk all ingredients together in small bowl until well combined.

Each 100ml: About 85 calories, 0g protein,
24g carbohydrate, 0g total fat,
0mg cholesterol, 215mg sodium

## BUTTERMILK-CHIVE DRESSING

*Prep:* 5 minutes    *Makes* about 175ml

225ml buttermilk
2 tbsp distilled white vinegar
2 tbsp chopped fresh chives
1 tbsp reduced-fat mayonnaise
¼ tsp salt
¼ tsp coarsely ground black pepper

Whisk all ingredients together in small bowl until well combined.

Each 100ml: About 53 calories, 2g protein,
5g carbohydrate, 3g total fat
(1g saturated), 6mg cholesterol,
380mg sodium

## LEMON DRESSING

*Prep:* 5 minutes    *Makes* about 175ml

60ml fresh lemon juice
½ tsp salt
¼ tsp ground black pepper
125ml olive oil

Whisk lemon juice, salt and pepper together in small bowl. Gradually whisk in oil in thin, steady stream.

Each 100ml: About 550 calories, 0g protein,
3g carbohydrate, 62g total fat
(8g saturated), 0mg cholesterol,
610mg sodium

## CREAMY CAESAR DRESSING

*Prep:* 10 minutes    *Makes* about 300ml

75ml olive oil
40g Parmesan cheese, freshly grated
60ml fresh lemon juice
60g mayonnaise
1 tsp anchovy paste
½ tsp coarsely ground pepper
1 small garlic clove, very finely chopped

Whisk all the ingredients together in small bowl until smooth.

Each 100ml: About 285 calories, 5g protein,
3g carbohydrate, 29g total fat
(6g saturated), 11mg cholesterol,
490mg sodium

## TAHINI DRESSING

*Prep:* 10 minutes    *Makes* about 175ml

125g tahini (sesame seed paste)
2 tbsp fresh lemon juice
4 tsp soy sauce
1 tbsp honey (optional)
½ tsp ground black pepper
½ small garlic clove, very finely chopped

Whisk all ingredients together in small bowl until smooth.

Each 100ml: About 265 calories, 8g protein,
13g carbohydrate, 23g total fat
(3g saturated), 0mg cholesterol,
795mg sodium

# PASTA

Delicious, nutritious and easy to prepare, pasta is the perfect 'fast' food for today's busy lifestyle. The variety of shapes, sizes and flavours make pasta an even more attractive mealtime option. Here is a guide to pasta which will help you ensure great results every time.

## BUYING AND STORING

For the best taste and texture, buy dried pasta made from durum wheat or semolina flour (semolina is more coarsely ground durum wheat). Good quality pasta will have a clear yellow colour and feel hard and smooth. Stored in a cool, dry, dark place, dried pasta will keep up to 1 year (wholemeal pasta up to 6 months). Store commercially made fresh pasta in the refrigerator according to package directions – or up to 1 week – or freeze up to 1 month.

## HOME-MADE PASTA

It's easy to make your own fresh pasta. Although the dough can be rolled out with a rolling pin, a pasta machine makes it easy. A machine thins the dough gradually – through a series of thickness settings controlled by a knob – which results in an even, chewy texture. Support longer strips of dough as they come through the machine so that they do not fold and stick together. Cut unwieldy lengths into more manageable pieces. You can refrigerate homemade pasta, tightly covered, up to 3 days, or freeze up to 1 month. Do not thaw before cooking.

1 Using machine on widest setting, pass through portion of dough. Fold dough into thirds and roll again. Repeat folding and rolling 8 to 10 times, until dough is smooth and elastic.

2 Continue rolling unfolded dough, reducing thickness setting by 1 notch each time, until it reaches the desired thickness; pass dough through cutting blades. Cut pasta into lengths.

## THE SECRETS OF PERFECT PASTA

**Start with plenty of water** Use at least 4 litres of water for every 450g of pasta. Add the pasta and salt after the water comes to a rapid boil. (If the water stops boiling when you add the pasta, cover pot until it returns to the boil.)

**Stir frequently** This ensures even cooking and prevents strands from clumping or sticking to the bottom of the pot.

**Check early (and often) for doneness** Cooking times on packets are guides, not rules; begin checking doneness early.

**Test the texture** Perfectly cooked pasta should feel firm to the bite. This texture is described in Italian as *al dente*, or 'to the tooth'. At this stage, the pasta will have no raw flour taste, but will reveal a tiny chalky-white centre. Residual heat will continue to cook pasta as it is drained and tossed, so gauge cooking time accordingly.

**Avoid a soggy sauce** Drain cooked pasta thoroughly by shaking excess moisture through the colander. Unless it's indicated in a recipe, never rinse pasta. (Except for lasagne, pasta is rinsed only when it is to be used in a cold salad.)

**Serve it hot** Pasta will cool down quickly and noodles tend to absorb liquid – creamy sauces can practically disappear. For best results, call everyone to the table while you are tossing, and serve the pasta in pre-warmed bowls.

## TO SALT OR NOT TO SALT

Almost all pasta recipes suggest adding salt to the pasta cooking water. Most purists would not have it any other way. However, some people shy away from this step because they are worried about adding too much sodium to their diet. The amount of salt (we recommend 2 teaspoons per 450g of pasta) added to the water isn't all absorbed by the noodles, it merely seasons them. When you drain the noodles, you are draining much of the sodium away as well (only about 10 per cent is absorbed by the pasta). The sodium analyses for all our pasta recipes are based on pasta cooked in salted water. Most importantly, salting the water results in noodles with a much fuller flavour.

### FRESH VERSUS DRIED

There is no doubt that fresh, tender pasta is a delight to eat, but it is not superior to dried – it is simply different. Fresh noodles, typical of the cooking of northern Italy, are finer-textured and richer because they are made with eggs, and pair best with delicate sauces. By contrast, dried pasta, favoured by southern Italian cooks, is made from flour and water. It is more economical, lower in fat, and the best choice for robust, highly flavoured sauces.

## A MORE NUTRITIOUS PASTA

Storing pasta in a clear glass or plastic container on an open shelf or counter exposes it to light, which destroys riboflavin, a B vitamin which is the key nutrient in pasta. Instead, store pasta in an opaque container or in the cupboard, or buy pasta sold in cardboard cartons, which keep out the light.

## COOKING LONG PASTA

Add pasta all at once to boiling water, pushing ends down as they soften and all strands are immersed. Cover pot until water returns to a boil.

To prevent noodles from sticking to the bottom of the pot, stir often. A spaghetti fork grips and separates strands, allowing for easier draining and neater serving.

## COMMON PASTA DILEMMAS – SOLVED

**How much do I make?** Most packets list a 75g serving size, but a more generous main dish measure is 125g dry pasta, 90g fresh, per person. For rich dishes you are apt to use less. The cooked yield depends on the shape: 100g of dried *penne, ziti, fusilli* create more volume than the same amount of *spaghetti, fettuccine* and *linguine* .

**How should I store leftover pasta?** Toss it with a small amount of oil and store in a sealed plastic bag.

**What's the best way to reheat pasta?** Microwave it in a microwave-safe container or glass bowl for about 2 minutes on high. Alternatively, place pasta in a colander and hold under hot running water until warm; toss with hot sauce.

**What can I do with leftover pasta?** Layer it with sautéed vegetables and tomato sauce in a gratin dish, top with grated Parmesan cheese, and bake; use as an omelette or frittata filling; toss with salad dressing and a variety of crisp, colourful vegetables for a quick lunch.

**How can I keep cooked lasagne sheets from sticking together?** Rinse cooked sheets under cold running water, then return to pan and cover with cold water. Drain on a clean tea towel before using.

## KNOW YOUR PASTA

These days pasta can be purchased in a wide variety of shapes and sizes; each one has a special texture and its own cooking time. Many shapes have amusing Italian names that reflect their shape. For example ditalini means 'thimbles'; penne, 'quills'; orecchiette, 'little ears' and linguine, 'little tongues'. One shape may be referred to by different names in different regions, and one name may refer to several different shapes.

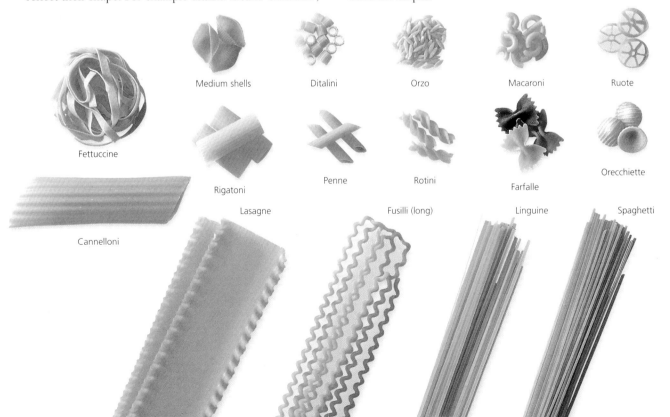

Fettuccine

Medium shells

Ditalini

Orzo

Macaroni

Ruote

Rigatoni

Penne

Rotini

Farfalle

Orecchiette

Cannelloni

Lasagne

Fusilli (long)

Linguine

Spaghetti

# PASTA PARTNERS

**Tiny shapes and skinny strands**  Alphabets, acini di pepe, stars, ditalini, orzo and vermicelli are excellent in soups, particularly home-made broths.

**Long, thin strands**  Spaghetti or linguine go well with smooth tomato or seafood sauces. You should use just enough sauce to keep the strands wet and slippery.

**Stout, hollow, medium-sized shapes**  Rigatoni, ziti and similar shapes are good for baked dishes, since their thick walls will withstand prolonged cooking. Their sturdiness also makes them suitable for robust meat sauces and grilled vegetables.

**Wide, flat pasta**  Pastas such as pappardelle, tagliatelle and fettuccine are best with simple, rich sauces made with cream, butter or a selection of cheeses.

**Ridged, curved shapes**  Penne, farfalle, gemelli, fusilli, orecchiette or conchiglie are designed to catch chunky sauces that contain chopped vegetables, olives or chunks of cheese. These also make terrific pasta salads, because they cradle other ingredients and can stand up to assertive vinaigrettes or creamy dressings.

**Large shapes**  Canneloni and lumache are strictly for stuffing with vegetables, meat and/or cheese mixtures.

# NEARLY-INSTANT PASTA DISHES

- Mix diced ham, frozen peas (add to the pasta cooking water before draining noodles to thaw), some chopped fresh rosemary, Parmesan cheese and olive oil with penne.
- Toss slivered roasted red peppers, quartered oil-packed artichoke hearts, chunks of smoked mozzarella and a generous amount of chopped flat-leaf parsley with rigatoni; thin slightly with chicken stock.
- Sauté shrimp or scallops in hot olive oil with some fresh breadcrumbs and crushed red pepper; toss with spaghetti.
- Mix rotini pasta with chunks of roasted turkey, a handful of toasted pine nuts, sultanas, some crushed red pepper and a little olive oil.
- Toss farfalle with ricotta cheese, chopped toasted walnuts, a spoonful of milk and some grated Parmesan.
- Cook cheese tortellini in chicken stock to cover until almost tender; stir in sliced spinach leaves until wilted. Serve in soup bowls with freshly grated Parmesan cheese.
- Heat canned, drained chickpeas and diced salami in chicken stock; toss with ruote. Stir in olive oil, freshly grated Parmesan cheese and cracked black pepper.

# KNOW YOUR ORIENTAL PASTA

Unlike most Western pastas, which are made from wheat flour, Oriental noodles are made from a variety of flours, including rice, bean or vegetable starches such as yam, soybean or potato. The versatility of these delicious noodles is limited only by your imagination. They can be served alongside meat and fish dishes, as salads with tasty Oriental-style vinaigrettes and other ingredients such as crisp vegetables, fresh herbs or seafood, or added to steaming stock to make a nourishing soup. Thinner noodles can be softened in hot water; others are boiled like spaghetti.

**Soba**  These thin, brownish-grey noodles are made from buckwheat flour; they are served cold with a dipping sauce or in hot soup.

**Flat rice noodles**  Made from rice flour, these noodles are typically boiled or stir-fried for salads or soups.

**Rice stick noodles**  These thread-like sticks can be softened in hot water for soups and salads, or deep-fried, which causes them to puff dramatically into crunchy strands used in salads.

**Cellophane noodles**  When softened these thin, translucent strands, made from mung bean flour, become slippery and transparent.  They are used in stir-fries, soups and salads.

**Chinese-style egg noodles**  Made from wheat flour, these tender strands are similiar in texture and flavour to Western egg noodles. Available fresh or dried in a variety of widths, they are added to soups, topped with meat, stir-fried or eaten cold with sesame dressing.

**Udon noodles**  These long, thick, chewy Japanese noodles made from wheat flour can be flat or round; they are usually eaten in soup.

Soba

Udon noodles

Chinese-style egg noodles

Rice stick noodles

Flat rice noodles

Cellophane noodles

# TOMATO PASTA SAUCES

With a few choice ingredients or a clever cooking technique, a simple tomato sauce can become the base for a sensational meal. We've roasted plum tomatoes and garlic, for example, to create a rich and incredibly sweet sauce. There's also a fresh tomato sauce with chunks of mozzarella; a rich tomato-cream sauce; and a marinara with a host of tasty variations.

## ROASTED TOMATO SAUCE

*Prep:* 20 minutes, plus cooling    *Roast:* 50–60 minutes
*Makes* 4 main dish servings

| | |
|---|---|
| 750g medium-size ripe plum tomatoes | ¼ tsp coarsely ground black pepper |
| 6 medium garlic cloves, unpeeled | 450g penne or corkscrew pasta, cooked |
| 2 tbsp olive oil | Grated Pecorino Romano cheese (optional) |
| ¾ tsp salt | |

**1** Preheat oven to 230°C (450°F, Gas 8). Cut each tomato lengthways in half. Toss tomatoes and garlic cloves with 1 tablespoon olive oil in 37 by 29cm roasting tin. Roast 50–60 minutes until tomatoes are well browned and garlic cloves are soft.

**2** Allow mixture to cool 20 minutes in tin. When tomatoes and garlic are cool, peel tomatoes over bowl to catch all juices. Squeeze garlic from skins into same bowl.

**3** Using spoon, break up tomatoes and garlic. Stir in salt, pepper and remaining 1 tablespoon olive oil until blended. To serve, toss cooked pasta with sauce. Sprinkle with grated Pecorino Romano cheese, if you like.

**GARLIC**

• Choose plump, rock-hard heads of garlic with dry, papery skins. Avoid soft or moist heads, as well as those that are refrigerated at the grocery store.

• Store garlic in an open container in a cool, dry place for up to 2 months. If a clove begins to sprout, cut it in half and cut out the bitter-tasting green core.

• For easy peeling, crush the clove with the flat side of a chef's knife to loosen the skin.

• When sautéing garlic, stir it often to prevent it over-browning and taking on a bitter taste.

• Raw, garlic is pungent (and its flavour in a dish builds if it sits); roasting or blanching sweetens and mellows it.

EACH SERVING: ABOUT 560 CALORIES, 18g PROTEIN, 102g CARBOHYDRATE, 10g TOTAL FAT (1g SATURATED), 0mg CHOLESTEROL, 545mg SODIUM

## SUMMER TOMATO SAUCE WITH MOZZARELLA

*Prep: 15 minutes, plus standing*   *Makes 4 main dish servings*

600g ripe tomatoes, cut into 1cm pieces
225g fresh mozzarella cheese, cut into 1cm pieces
60g fresh basil leaves
1 tbsp olive oil

1 tbsp red wine vinegar
1 tsp salt
¼ tsp coarsely ground black pepper
450g penne or ziti, cooked

Combine tomatoes with their juice and remaining ingredients, except pasta, in medium bowl, stirring gently. Allow sauce to stand 15 minutes to develop flavour. To serve, toss cooked pasta with sauce.

Each serving: 665 calories, 28g protein, 99g carbohydrate, 18g total fat (8g saturated), 44mg cholesterol, 885mg sodium

## MARINARA SAUCE

*Prep: 10 minutes*   *Cook: 35 minutes*
*Makes 4 main dish servings*

2 tbsp olive oil
1 small onion, chopped
1 garlic clove, very finely chopped
800g canned tomatoes

175g tomato purée
2 tbsp chopped fresh basil or parsley (optional)
450g spaghetti or rigatoni, cooked

Heat oil in 3-litre saucepan over medium heat. Add onion and garlic and cook until tender. Stir in tomatoes with their juice, tomato purée and basil, if using. Bring to the boil over high heat, breaking up tomatoes with back of spoon. Reduce heat to low. Partially cover pan; simmer, stirring occasionally, 20 minutes. To serve, toss cooked pasta with sauce, or use in your favourite recipe.

Each serving: About 570 calories, 18g protein, 104g carbohydrate, 9g total fat (1g saturated), 0mg cholesterol, 1130mg sodium

### MARINARA PLUS

Our Marinara Sauce is so versatile, it's worth doubling the recipe – make it in 5-litre flameproof casserole and simmer for 30 instead of 20 minutes – and freezing half to use another day. Try adding any of the following:

• 225g mushrooms, sliced and sautéed

• 225g Italian sausages (casings removed), crumbled and cooked

• 2 green or red peppers, sliced and sautéed

## CREAMY TOMATO SAUCE WITH PEAS

*Prep: 10 minutes*   *Cook: 10 minutes*
*Makes 4 main dish servings*

1 tbsp olive oil
1 medium onion, chopped
800g canned chopped tomatoes
300g frozen peas, thawed
15g fresh basil leaves, chopped

125ml whipping cream
½ tsp salt
¼ tsp dried chilli flakes
450g medium shell or corkscrew pasta, cooked

◈ Heat oil in 30cm non-stick frying pan over medium heat. Add onion and cook until tender.

◈ Add tomatoes with their juice and remaining ingredients, except pasta. Heat through, stirring constantly. To serve, toss cooked pasta with sauce.

Each serving: 665 calories, 21g protein, 108g carbohydrate, 17g total fat (8g saturated), 41mg cholesterol, 790mg sodium

## TOMATO-SAGE SAUCE

*Prep: 15 minutes*   *Cook: 1 hour*
*Makes 6 main dish servings*

2 tbsp olive oil
1 small onion, finely chopped
1.3kg ripe plum tomatoes, peeled (see page 314) and chopped
125ml chicken stock

75ml dry white wine
30g butter
1 tbsp chopped fresh sage
1 tsp salt
750g spaghetti or cavatelli, cooked

◈ Heat olive oil in 26cm frying pan over medium-low heat. Add chopped onion; cook 15–20 minutes until very tender and slightly golden.

◈ Stir in tomatoes with their juice, chicken stock and white wine. Bring to the boil over high heat.

◈ Reduce heat to low; cover and simmer 30 minutes, stirring occasionally and pressing on tomatoes with back of slotted spoon to crush.

◈ Uncover and simmer, stirring occasionally, 25 minutes longer, or until sauce has reduced and thickened slightly. Stir in butter, sage and salt and stir until butter melts. To serve, toss cooked pasta with sauce.

Each serving: 420 calories, 12g protein, 69g carbohydrate, 11g total fat (3g saturated), 12mg cholesterol, 580mg sodium

# OLIVE OIL PASTA SAUCES

A bottle of good olive oil comes in handy for creating a variety of easy pasta sauces. By adding a few tasty ingredients such as sprouting broccoli, anchovies, dried tomatoes or Kalamata olives, you can create a splendid sauce in next to no time. Or, try our classic Italian pesto – packed with fresh basil taste. Because these sauces are simple, it's essential to use good-quality ingredients so that the pure flavours shine through.

## LINGUINE WITH SPROUTING BROCCOLI AND ANCHOVIES

❖❖❖❖❖❖❖❖❖❖❖❖

*Prep:* 5 minutes
*Cook:* 15 minutes
*Makes* 4 main dish servings

**450g linguine or spaghetti**
**900g sprouting broccoli or**
**    spring greens**
**2 tsp salt**
**3 tbsp olive oil**
**3 garlic cloves, crushed with**
**    side of knife**
**60g canned anchovy fillets,**
**    undrained**
**¼ tsp dried chilli flakes**
**75g sultanas**

**1** Prepare pasta as packet instructs. Drain, reserving 60ml pasta cooking water. Return pasta to pan; keep warm. Meanwhile, trim ends of stalks from sprouting broccoli. Bring *4 litres water* to the boil in 5-litre flameproof casserole over high heat. Add sprouting broccoli and salt; return to the boil. Boil 2 minutes; drain. Wipe casserole dry.

**2** Heat oil in same casserole over medium heat. Add garlic; cook until golden. Add anchovies with their oil and dried chilli flakes; cook, stirring, until anchovies begin to dissolve.

**3** Add sprouting broccoli and raisins to mixture in casserole and cook, stirring, until sprouting broccoli is heated through and well coated with oil.

### OLIVE OIL

The fragrant oil pressed from tree-ripened olives is prized round the world for cooking and salads. Olive oil is classified in categories that indicate colour and taste Extra virgin, with a greenish hue, fruity aroma and taste, and the lowest acidity, is the finest. It is cold-pressed, a process that relies only on pressure and yields the most flavour. Virgin olive oil is slightly more acidic, and regular olive oil contains blends of refined and virgin oils. Light olive oil isn't low-fat, but instead has been filtered for a neutral aroma and taste. Stored in a cool, dark place, olive oil will last up to 6 months.

**4** Stir in pasta and reserved pasta cooking water; toss well to combine.

EACH SERVING: ABOUT 660 CALORIES, 27g PROTEIN, 111g CARBOHYDRATE, 14g TOTAL FAT (2g SATURATED), 12mg CHOLESTEROL, 1075mg SODIUM

# PESTO

*Prep:* 10 minutes    *Makes* 4 main dish servings

125g fresh basil leaves

60ml olive oil

60g Parmesan cheese, freshly grated

2 tbsp pine nuts or chopped walnuts

½ tsp salt

450g long fusilli or linguine, cooked

Fresh basil leaves for garnish

Process all ingredients except pasta and basil leaves in a food processor with knife blade attached or in blender on medium speed, adding *60ml water* until smooth. To serve, toss cooked pasta with pesto and garnish.

Each serving: About 590 calories, 18g protein, 86g carbohydrate, 19g total fat (4g saturated), 5mg cholesterol, 500mg sodium

## OIL AND GARLIC SAUCE

*Prep:* 10 minutes    *Cook:* 10 minutes
*Makes* 4 main dish servings

60ml olive oil

1 large garlic clove, very finely chopped

2 tbsp finely chopped fresh parsley

30g Parmesan cheese, freshly grated

¼ tsp salt

¼ tsp ground black pepper

450g spaghetti or linguine, cooked

2 tbsp pine nuts, toasted (optional)

◆ Heat olive oil in 1-litre saucepan over medium heat. Add garlic and cook just until golden. Remove pan from heat; stir in parsley, Parmesan cheese, salt and pepper.

◆ To serve, toss cooked pasta with sauce. Sprinkle pine nuts over pasta, if you like.

Each serving: About 555 calories, 16g protein, 85g carbohydrate, 16g total fat (3g saturated), 2mg cholesterol, 310mg sodium

## SPINACH, CHICK-PEA AND RAISIN SAUCE

*Prep:* 15 minutes    *Cook:* 10 minutes
*Makes* 4 main dish servings

3 tbsp olive oil

4 garlic cloves, very finely chopped

350g spinach, tough stalks removed

400g canned chick-peas, rinsed and drained

75g sultanas

¼ tsp salt

¼ tsp dried chilli flakes

125ml chicken stock

450g penne or corkscrew pasta, cooked

Heat oil in a 30cm non-stick frying pan over medium heat. Add garlic and cook until golden. Increase heat to medium-high. Stir in spinach, chick-peas, raisins, salt and chilli flakes and cook until spinach wilts. Stir in chicken stock and heat through. To serve, toss cooked pasta with sauce.

Each serving: 700 calories, 23g protein, 122g carbohydrate, 14g total fat (2g saturated), 0mg cholesterol, 740mg sodium

## SUN-DRIED TOMATO AND OLIVE SAUCE

*Prep:* 15 minutes    *Cook:* 15 minutes
*Makes* 4 main dish servings

2 tbsp olive oil

3 garlic cloves, very finely chopped

30g sun-dried tomatoes, chopped

400ml chicken stock

75g Kalamata olives, stoned

15g parsley leaves, chopped

450g spaghetti or corkscrew pasta, cooked

60g goat's cheese, crumbled

Heat oil in 30cm non-stick frying pan over medium heat. Add garlic and cook 30 seconds. Add sun-dried tomatoes and chicken stock. Bring to the boil over medium-high heat. Reduce heat to low and simmer 10 minutes. Stir in olives and parsley. To serve, toss cooked pasta with sauce. Sprinkle with goat's cheese.

Each serving: 580 calories, 19g protein, 92g carbohydrate, 15g total fat (4g saturated), 14mg cholesterol, 745mg sodium

# CREAMY PASTA SAUCES

Besides being rich and satisfying, cream-based pasta sauces are generally very quick to prepare: in the time it takes to boil water and cook the pasta, the sauce can be ready. To keep fat and calories within reasonable limits, we've used single cream in all of the recipes here except the Classic Alfredo Sauce which demands a richer cream such as whipping cream for authenticity. Sauces can be enlivened with a range of tastes and textures such as vegetables, strong cheeses and fresh herbs.

## SMOKED SALMON AND CREAM SAUCE

*Prep:* 10 minutes   *Cook:* 10 minutes
*Makes* 4 main dish servings

1 large carrot
225g sliced smoked salmon
75ml dry vermouth or dry
  white wine
225ml single cream
½ tsp salt

¼ tsp ground black pepper
1 tbsp chopped fresh dill
450g bow-tie or medium shell
  pasta, cooked
Dill sprigs for garnish

### SMOKED SALMON

Smoking salmon requires a long, slow process: the fish is first cured, either with a dry rub of salt (and sometimes sugar and spices) for several hours or even days, or in a brine. It is then smoked, at a temperature of 32°C or less. Its flavour and texture vary with the variety of salmon, the cure, the duration and temperature of the smoking process and the wood used for smoking (usually oak in Scotland, juniper in Norway and alder in the American Pacific Northwest).

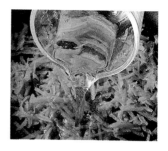

**1** Grate carrot. Bring carrot and *125ml water* to the boil in 26cm non-stick frying pan over medium-high heat. Boil 5 minutes, or until carrot is tender.

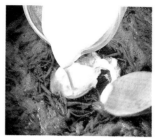

**2** Meanwhile, cut salmon into 5cm pieces. Add vermouth to carrot mixture in frying pan and boil 1 minute. Add cream, salt and pepper; return to the boil, stirring constantly. Simmer 1 minute longer.

**3** Remove pan from heat; stir in salmon and dill. To serve, toss cooked pasta with salmon mixture until pasta is well coated. Garnish with dill sprigs.

EACH SERVING: ABOUT 595 CALORIES, 27g PROTEIN, 90g CARBOHYDRATE, 11g TOTAL FAT (5g SATURATED), 35mg CHOLESTEROL, 860mg SODIUM

## LIGHT ALFREDO SAUCE

*Prep: 15 minutes    Cook: 15 minutes*
*Makes 4 main dish servings*

450g dried fettuccine
1 bunch broccoli, cut into
  small florets (optional)
2 tsp vegetable oil
1 small onion, diced
1 garlic clove, very finely
  chopped
450g skimmed milk

225ml chicken stock
3 tbsp plain flour
½ tsp salt
¼ tsp coarsely ground black
  pepper
125g Parmesan cheese,
  freshly grated

❖ Prepare fettuccine as packet instructs. If using broccoli, when pasta has cooked for 9 minutes, add florets to water; cook for 3 minutes longer. Drain.

❖ Meanwhile, heat oil in 30cm non-stick frying pan over medium heat. Add onion and garlic and cook until golden.

❖ Whisk milk, chicken stock, flour, salt and pepper together until blended. Add milk mixture to onion and garlic in frying pan and cook, stirring occasionally, until mixture thickens and boils. Stir in Parmesan cheese. To serve, toss cooked fettuccine and broccoli with sauce.

Each serving: About 495 calories, 23g protein, 78g carbohydrate, 11g total fat (3g saturated), 17mg cholesterol, 850mg sodium

## CLASSIC ALFREDO SAUCE

*Prep: 5 minutes    Cook: 10 minutes*
*Makes 6 main dish servings*

450ml whipping cream
125g Parmesan cheese,
  freshly grated
30g butter or margarine

½ teaspoon salt
¼ tsp coarsely cracked black
  pepper
450g fettuccine, cooked

❖ Bring cream to the boil in 2-litre saucepan over medium-high heat, stirring frequently. Reduce heat to medium; gradually stir in 60g Parmesan cheese.

❖ Add butter, 15g at a time, stirring. Add salt and pepper. To serve, toss cooked pasta with sauce. Sprinkle with remaining Parmesan cheese.

Each serving: About 605 calories, 17g protein, 45g carbohydrate, 41g total fat (23g saturated), 133mg cholesterol, 650mg sodium

## MUSHROOM SAUCE

*Prep: 10 minutes    Cook: 20 minutes*
*Makes 4 main dish servings*

2 tbsp olive or vegetable oil
750g mushrooms, thinly sliced
225ml single cream

2 tbsp soy sauce
450g linguine or fettuccine,
  cooked

❖ Heat oil in 30cm frying pan over high heat. Add mushrooms and cook, stirring frequently, 15 minutes, or until browned and all liquid has evaporated.

❖ Stir in cream and soy sauce; cook, stirring constantly, about 3 minutes until sauce reduces slightly. To serve, toss cooked pasta with sauce.

Each serving: About 515 calories, 18g protein, 75g carbohydrate, 19g total fat (5g saturated), 22mg cholesterol, 675mg sodium

## BLUE CHEESE AND WALNUT SAUCE

*Prep: 5 minutes    Cook: 10–15 minutes*
*Makes 6 main dish servings*

225ml single cream
175ml chicken stock
125g Gorgonzola or
  blue cheese, crumbled
¼ tsp coarsely ground black
  pepper

450g bow-tie or corkscrew
  pasta, cooked
60g chopped walnuts, toasted

❖ Bring cream and stock to the boil in 2-litre saucepan over medium-high heat. Reduce heat to medium; cook 5 minutes. Add Gorgonzola and pepper and cook, whisking constantly, until melted and smooth.

❖ To serve, toss cooked pasta with sauce. Sprinkle with toasted walnuts.

Each serving: About 470 calories, 17g protein, 61g carbohydrate, 18g total fat (7g saturated), 31mg cholesterol, 505mg sodium

# SEAFOOD PASTA SAUCES

From tender clams to meaty cubes of swordfish, the sweet, delicate flavours of seafood pair beautifully with pasta. These recipes rely on a few choice ingredients (olives, capers, fresh orange rind) that offer bold, exciting tastes. Because, as with all seafood, it's essential not to overcook the fish or shellfish, these sauces are also quick to prepare. In order not to interfere with the flavours of fish, do not serve cheese with seafood pastas.

## WHITE CLAM SAUCE

*Prep:* 15 minutes    *Cook:* 15 minutes
*Makes* 4 main dish servings

24 fresh small clams
125ml dry white wine
60ml olive oil
1 large garlic clove, very finely chopped

¼ tsp dried chilli flakes
15g fresh flat-leaf parsley, chopped
450g linguine or spaghetti, cooked

**1** Using stiff brush, scrub clams thoroughly with cold running water to remove any sand. Discard any clams that do not close tightly when shells are lightly tapped. Combine clams and wine in 5-litre flameproof casserole. Cover and cook over high heat 5 minutes. Using slotted spoon, transfer all opened clams to bowl.

**2** Cover and cook all remaining unopened clams for 3–5 minutes longer, removing clams as they open. Discard any clams that do not open.

**3** Remove clams from shells and chop coarsely; set aside. Strain cooking liquid through strainer lined with kitchen paper into small bowl; set aside.

**4** Wipe casserole clean. Add olive oil, garlic, and chilli flakes and cook over medium heat, stirring occasionally, just until garlic begins to turn golden.

**5** Stir in chopped parsley, reserved clams and reserved clam stock until well combined; heat sauce just to simmering. To serve, toss clam sauce with cooked pasta.

### MUSSEL SAUCE

Substitute 900g fresh mussels for the clams. Scrub and de-beard mussels (see page 88). Prepare as directed for clam sauce, but in Step 3, do not chop mussels; if you like, leave mussels in their shells. For a flavour twist, add one of the following or a combination: the grated rind of 1 lemon or orange; 30g chopped fresh basil leaves; 4 chopped plum tomatoes. Or, sprinkle the finished dish with fresh, coarse breadcrumbs, lightly toasted.

Each serving: About 640 calories, 27g protein, 88g carbohydrate, 17g total fat (2g saturated), 48mg cholesterol, 365mg sodium

EACH SERVING: ABOUT 600 CALORIES, 22g PROTEIN, 87g CARBOHYDRATE, 16g TOTAL FAT (2g SATURATED), 18mg CHOLESTEROL, 150mg SODIUM

## SICILIAN BARBECUED SWORDFISH SAUCE WITH MINT AND ORANGE

*Prep: 15 minutes, plus standing   Barbecue/grill: 8–10 minutes*
*Makes 6 main dish servings*

| | |
|---|---|
| 2 large tomatoes, cut into 1cm cubes | Salt and coarsely ground black pepper |
| 15g fresh mint, chopped | 1 tsp grated orange rind |
| 1 tbsp red wine vinegar | 1 swordfish steak (about 450g), 2.5cm thick |
| 1 small garlic clove, very finely chopped | 450g penne or bow-tie pasta, cooked |
| 3 tbsp olive oil | |

◆ Combine tomatoes with their juice, mint, red wine vinegar, garlic, 2 tablespoons olive oil, ¾ teaspoon salt and ¼ teaspoon pepper. Let stand 30 minutes.

◆ Prepare barbecue or preheat grill. Combine orange rind, remaining 1 tablespoon olive oil, ¼ teaspoon salt and ¼ teaspoon pepper until blended; use to brush over both sides of swordfish steak.

◆ Barbecue swordfish over medium-high heat, or grill on grill rack in grill pan at position closest to heat, turning once, 8–10 minutes, just until opaque throughout.

◆ Transfer swordfish to chopping board; cut into 2cm cubes. Add to tomato mixture in bowl. To serve, toss cooked pasta with sauce.

**Each serving: About 445 calories, 25g protein, 59g carbohydrate, 11g total fat (2g saturated), 29mg cholesterol, 505mg sodium**

## SEAFOOD FRA DIAVOLO

*Prep: 20 minutes   Cook: 1 hour*
*Makes 6 main dish servings*

| | |
|---|---|
| 1 tbsp olive oil | 225g raw medium prawns peeled and de-veined (see page 90), tail left on, if you like |
| 1 large garlic clove, very finely chopped | |
| ¼ tsp dried chilli flakes | |
| 800g canned tomatoes | 15g fresh parsley, chopped |
| ½ tsp salt | 450g linguine or spaghetti, cooked |
| 225g cleaned squid, cut into 5mm thick rings | |
| 12 mussels, scrubbed and de-bearded (see page 88) | |

◆ Heat oil in 4-litre saucepan over medium heat. Add chopped garlic and dried chilli flakes; cook 30 seconds, just until very fragrant. Stir in tomatoes with their juice and salt, breaking up tomatoes with back of spoon. Bring to the boil over high heat. Add squid and return to the boil. Reduce heat to low; cover and simmer 30 minutes. Uncover and simmer 15 minutes longer.

◆ Increase heat to high. Add mussels; cover and cook 3 minutes. Stir in prawns; cover and cook 2 minutes longer, or until mussels open and prawns turn opaque throughout. Discard any mussels that do not open. Stir in parsley. To serve, toss cooked pasta with sauce.

**Each serving: About 420 calories, 27g protein, 65g carbohydrate, 5g total fat (1g saturated), 162mg cholesterol, 635mg sodium**

## TUNA, OLIVE AND CAPER SAUCE

*Prep: 20 minutes   Cook: 10 minutes*
*Makes 6 main dish servings*

| | |
|---|---|
| 2 tbsp olive oil | 60g Kalamata olives, stoned and chopped |
| 1 large garlic clove, very finely chopped | |
| 450g tomatoes, cut into 1cm cubes | 20g fresh flat-leaf parsley, chopped |
| ¼ tsp salt | 2 tbsp canned or bottled drained and chopped capers |
| ¼ tsp ground black pepper | 450g penne or corkscrew pasta, cooked |
| 350g canned tuna in brine, drained | |

Heat oil in 26cm frying pan over medium heat. Add garlic; cook 30 seconds, just until very fragrant. Stir in tomatoes with their juice, salt and pepper. Cook, stirring occasionally, 5 minutes. Stir in tuna, breaking up chunks with spoon, and cook until heated through. Stir in olives, parsley and capers. To serve, toss cooked pasta with sauce.

**Each serving: About 430 calories, 25g protein, 61g carbohydrate, 9g total fat (1g saturated), 23mg cholesterol, 575mg sodium**

# MEAT PASTA SAUCES

The heartiest pastas are the ones tossed with a thick meat sauce. Classic Bolognese, enriched with red wine, cream and tomatoes, is a well known favourite that never palls. For something out of the ordinary, try the Sicilian sauce with pork and raisins. Both these recipes require plenty of simmering time so that they develop their wonderful depth of flavour. Quicker, but just as delicious, is the tasty Sausage and Butternut Squash Sauce and the Amatriciana Sauce, another Italian classic with a garlic and red pepper kick.

## CLASSIC BOLOGNESE SAUCE

*Prep: 10 minutes    Cook: 1½ hours*
*Makes 6 main dish servings, plus extra sauce*

2 tbsp olive oil
1 medium onion, finely
  chopped
1 carrot, finely chopped
1 celery stalk, finely chopped
750g minced beef, or 225g
  each minced beef, veal, and
  pork
60ml dry red wine
800g canned tomatoes,
  chopped, juice reserved

2 tsp salt
¼ tsp ground black pepper
⅛ tsp ground nutmeg
60ml whipping cream
450g spaghetti or fettuccine,
  cooked
Freshly grated Parmesan
  cheese (optional)

**1** Heat olive oil in 5-litre flameproof casserole over medium heat. Add onion, carrot and celery and cook, stirring occasionally, 10 minutes, or until tender.

**2** Add minced meat to vegetables in casserole and cook, stirring frequently to break up meat, until meat is no longer pink.

**3** Stir in red wine and bring to the boil over high heat. Stir in tomatoes with their juice, salt, pepper and nutmeg.

**4** Return mixture to the boil; reduce heat to low and simmer, uncovered, stirring occasionally, 1 hour. Stir in cream and heat through, stirring. To serve, use half of sauce to toss with cooked pasta. (Cool remaining sauce, then freeze for use another day.) Serve with freshly grated Parmesan cheese, if you like.

**BOLOGNESE PLUS**

Known to Italians as *il ragù*, Bolognese sauce is one of the very few recipes in Italy to have an official standard version. All cooks have their own variations, though: try sautéing some chopped Parma ham or chicken livers with the meat. Stir in a little grated lemon rind or earthy dried porcini mushrooms with the tomatoes, or add chopped fresh herbs such as parsley or marjoram at the end of cooking.

EACH SERVING: ABOUT 475 CALORIES, 21g PROTEIN, 62g CARBOHYDRATE, 15g TOTAL FAT (5g SATURATED), 47mg CHOLESTEROL, 585mg SODIUM

## SAUSAGE AND BUTTERNUT SQUASH SAUCE

*Prep: 15 minutes    Cook: 20 minutes*

*Makes 6 main dish servings*

450g dried corkscrew or other short pasta

1 medium butternut squash (about 850g)

350g mild Italian sausages, casings removed

¼ tsp salt

¼ tsp coarsely ground black pepper

20g fresh basil leaves, chopped

30g Parmesan cheese, freshly grated

Basil leaves for garnish

◆ Prepare pasta as packet instructs. Drain, reserving 175ml cooking water. Return pasta to pan; keep warm.

◆ Meanwhile, cut squash into large chunks; cut peel from chunks and cut into 1cm pieces. Set aside.

◆ Cook sausages in 30cm non-stick frying pan over medium-high heat, stirring frequently to break up meat, about 7 minutes, until browned. Using slotted spoon, transfer sausage meat to bowl, discarding all but 2 tablespoons drippings from pan.

◆ Add squash, salt and pepper to drippings in pan. Reduce heat to medium; cover and cook, stirring occasionally, about 10 minutes until squash is tender.

◆ To serve, add chopped basil, Parmesan, sausage meat and reserved pasta cooking water to pan; toss pasta with sauce. Garnish with basil leaves.

**Each serving: About 545 calories, 19g protein, 72g carbohydrate, 19g total fat (6g saturated), 47mg cholesterol, 770mg sodium**

## AMATRICIANA SAUCE

*Prep: 10 minutes    Cook: 45 minutes*

*Makes 4 main dish servings*

1 tbsp olive oil

125g pancetta, chopped

1 small onion, finely chopped

1 garlic clove, very finely chopped

¼ tsp dried chilli flakes

800g canned tomatoes

450g spaghetti or rigatoni, cooked

15g fresh parsley, chopped

◆ Heat oil in 5-litre flameproof casserole over medium heat. Add pancetta and cook, stirring often, 5 minutes, or until lightly browned.

◆ Stir in onion; cook about 3 minutes until tender. Stir in garlic and dried chilli flakes; cook 15 seconds. Add tomatoes with their juice. Bring to the boil over high heat, breaking up tomatoes with back of spoon.

◆ Reduce heat to low and simmer, uncovered, stirring occasionally, 30 minutes. To serve, toss cooked pasta with sauce and parsley.

**Each serving: About 545 calories, 23g protein, 97g carbohydrate, 8g total fat (1g saturated), 14mg cholesterol, 805mg sodium**

## HEARTY SICILIAN MEAT SAUCE

*Prep: 15 minutes    Cook: 1¾ hours*

*Makes 6 main dish servings*

2 tbsp vegetable oil

750g pork shoulder, cut into 4cm cubes

450g onions, cut into 1cm thick slices

4 medium carrots, diced

800g canned tomatoes

1 tbsp sugar

1 tsp salt

40g raisins

2 tbsp chopped fresh parsley

450g rigatoni or ziti, cooked

◆ Heat 1 tablespoon oil in 5-litre flameproof casserole over medium-high heat. Add pork cubes in batches and cook until browned; transfer pork to bowl as it browns.

◆ Add remaining 1 tablespoon oil to drippings in casserole. Add onions and carrots; cook until lightly browned. Return pork to casserole; stir in tomatoes with their juice, sugar and salt. Bring to the boil over high heat, breaking up tomatoes with back of spoon.

◆ Reduce heat to low; cover and simmer 1¼ hours, or until pork is very tender. Using 2 forks, pull pork into shreds. Stir raisins and parsley into pork mixture in casserole. Reduce heat to low; cover and simmer 5 minutes. To serve, toss cooked pasta with sauce.

**Each serving: About 565 calories, 38g protein, 81g carbohydrate, 10g total fat (2g saturated), 57mg cholesterol, 750mg sodium**

# HOME-MADE PASTA

It is not at all difficult to make your own pasta, and the results are delicious as well as impressive. Use a pasta machine if you have one; or, follow our easy instructions for hand-rolling tortelli, pappardelle spiced with lemon and pepper, or pretty herb squares.

## HAM AND CHEESE TORTELLI

*Prep: 1½ hours, plus standing*    *Cook: 15 minutes*
*Makes 6 main dish servings*

Spinach Pasta (see below)
425g ricotta cheese
225g cooked ham, diced
⅛ tsp ground nutmeg
⅛ tsp ground black pepper
2 medium eggs

Plain flour for dusting
1 tsp salt
90g butter or margarine, melted
60g Parmesan cheese, freshly grated

**1** Prepare Spinach Pasta. Prepare filling: mix ricotta cheese, cooked ham, nutmeg, black pepper and 1 egg together in small bowl until blended; cover and refrigerate. When pasta dough has rested 30 minutes, cut dough in half; cover one half with cling film. Roll out remaining dough into 50 by 45cm rectangle on well-floured work surface with floured rolling pin.

**2** Trim edges and cut dough lengthways into six 6cm wide strips. Cut strips crossways into 5 pieces, making thirty 10 by 6cm rectangles. Cover with cling film while you assemble tortelli.

**3** Line 2 large baking sheets with cling film; dust with flour. Place 1 slightly rounded teaspoon ham and cheese filling in 5cm long strip lengthways down centre of each pasta rectangle. Beat remaining egg in small bowl.

**4** Fold 1 long side of pasta rectangle over filling. Lightly brush edge of other long side with egg; fold it over filling. Pinch gently to seal; twist ends to close. Place tortelli in single layer on baking sheet.

### SPINACH PASTA

Boil 125g spinach leaves with any tough stalks removed in 5mm water in 2-litre saucepan. Reduce heat; simmer 1 minute. Drain; rinse with cold running water. Squeeze dry; finely chop. Place spinach in large bowl; stir in 4 medium eggs and 1 teaspoon salt. Gradually stir in 450g plain flour to make stiff dough. Knead about 20 times on well-floured surface, until smooth and not sticky. Cover with cling film. Allow to rest for 30 minutes.

Each serving: About 265 calories, 11g protein, 45g carbohydrate, 4g total fat (1g saturated), 142mg cholesterol, 415mg sodium

**5** Repeat shaping with remaining dough and filling. Cover baking sheets loosely with cling film; let tortelli dry 30 minutes, turning once.

**6** To cook, bring *6 litres water* and salt to the boil in 8-litre saucepan over high heat. Add tortelli, stirring gently to separate; return to the boil. Reduce heat to medium; cook 10 minutes, until *al dente*. Drain. Gently toss with melted butter and half of Parmesan cheese. To serve, sprinkle with remaining Parmesan cheese.

EACH SERVING: ABOUT 605 CALORIES, 32g PROTEIN, 48g CARBOHYDRATE, 30g TOTAL FAT (15g SATURATED), 299mg CHOLESTEROL, 1030mg SODIUM

# BASIC PASTA DOUGH

*Prep: 25 minutes, plus standing*
*Makes about 450g pasta, enough for 8 accompaniment*
*or 4 main dish servings*

Follow the steps, or, blend ingredients in food processor with knife blade attached 10–15 seconds to form smooth ball (do not knead). Cover and let rest 30 minutes.

About 335g plain flour
1 tbsp olive oil

1 tsp salt
2 medium eggs

**1** Stir 335g flour with olive oil, salt, eggs and *60ml water* to make a stiff dough.

**2** Knead dough on well-floured surface about 20 times, or until smooth and not sticky. Cover with cling film; allow to rest 30 minutes for easier rolling.

**Each accompaniment serving: About 150 calories, 5g protein, 25g carbohydrate, 3g total fat (1g saturated), 53mg cholesterol, 335mg sodium**

## HERB SQUARES

*Prep: 30 minutes, plus standing    Cook: 5–8 minutes*
*Makes 8 accompaniment or 4 main dish servings*

◆ Prepare Basic Pasta Dough (see above).

◆ After dough has rested 30 minutes, cut in half. Follow pasta machine instructions; roll to thinnest setting to make 2 equal strips. Alternatively, place half dough on well-floured surface (keep remaining dough in cling film) and roll into 30cm square with floured rolling pin. Cover with cling film. Repeat with other half of dough, but do not cover with cling film.

◆ Cover surface of 1 strip of dough, or uncovered square of dough, with small pieces of herbs, such as parsley, dill, chervil or tarragon, stalks removed. Remove cling film from first piece of dough and carefully place on top of herb-covered dough.

◆ Roll dough strip through pasta machine or roll dough square into 40cm square with floured rolling pin. Cut dough crossways into eight 5cm wide strips, then lengthways into 8 pieces, making sixty-four 5cm squares. Sprinkle pasta squares with flour to prevent sticking.

◆ Line baking sheet with cling film; dust with flour. Place pasta squares on baking sheet, layering with cling film. If not cooking pasta immediately, cover with cling film and refrigerate.

◆ To cook, bring *6 litres water* and 2 teaspoons salt to the boil in 8-litre saucepan over high heat. Add pasta, stirring gently to separate and return to the boil. Reduce heat to medium; cook 3–5 minutes until *al dente*.

◆ Drain pasta well and toss with olive oil or butter. Alternatively, serve floated in chicken broth.

## LEMON-PEPPER PAPARDELLE

*Prep: 25 minutes, plus standing    Cook: 5–8 minutes*
*Makes 8 accompaniment or 4 main dish servings*

◆ Prepare Basic Pasta Dough, but add 1 tablespoon finely grated lemon rind and ½ teaspoon coarsely ground black pepper to dough.

◆ After dough has rested 30 minutes, cut in half. Follow pasta machine instructions; roll to thinnest setting. Or, place half dough on well-floured surface (keep remaining dough in cling film), and roll into 30cm square with floured rolling pin.

◆ Cut dough into twelve 2–3cm wide strips. Sprinkle strips with flour to prevent them from sticking.

◆ Line baking sheet with cling film; dust with flour. Place pasta strips on baking sheet, layering with floured cling film. Repeat with remaining dough. If not cooking pasta immediately, cover with cling film and refrigerate.

◆ To cook, bring *6 litres water* and 2 teaspoons salt to the boil in 8-litre saucepan over high heat. Add pasta, stirring gently to separate and return to the boil. Reduce heat to medium; cook 3–5 minutes until *al dente*.

◆ Drain pasta well and serve with olive oil or butter.

# BAKED AND STUFFED PASTA

Ever popular as a comforting family meal and for fuss-free entertaining, baked pastas are loved by all for their fragrant, zesty sauces and gooey strings of melted cheese. When cooking the pasta for these recipes, it's essential to under-cook it slightly, so it doesn't become soft and mushy during baking.

## COURGETTE AND CHEESE CANNELLONI

*Prep: 40 minutes   Bake: 40 minutes*
*Makes 7 main dish servings*

14 cannelloni shells
2 small courgettes (about 350g)
1 small onion
2 tbsp olive oil
425g ricotta cheese
125g mozzarella cheese, grated
125g Provolone cheese, grated

2 medium eggs
Marinara Sauce (see page 352)
1 tbsp chopped fresh basil or parsley
Basil sprigs for garnish
Italian bread (optional)

**1** Prepare cannelloni tubes as packet instructs but do not add salt to water. Drain. Meanwhile, grate courgettes and very finely chop onion.

**2** Heat oil in 26cm frying pan over high heat. Add courgettes and onion and cook, stirring often, until lightly browned and all liquid evaporates. Remove from heat.

**3** Prepare filling: combine ricotta cheese, mozzarella, Provolone and eggs in large bowl, stirring until well mixed. Stir in courgette mixture. Set aside.

**4** Preheat oven to 190°C (375°F, Gas 5). Measure and reserve 125g marinara sauce. Spoon remaining sauce into base of 33 by 20cm ovenproof serving dish or 3½ to 4-litre shallow casserole; spread in even layer.

**5** Spoon filling into cooked cannelloni tubes. Or, pipe filling into tubes. Arrange tubes in sauce in dish in single layer, making sure they do not touch sides of dish.

**6** Spoon reserved marinara sauce over top of cannelloni tubes. Cover dish with foil and bake 40 minutes, or until pasta is heated through and sauce is bubbly. To serve, sprinkle with chopped basil. Garnish with basil sprigs. Serve cannelloni with Italian bread, if you like.

EACH SERVING: ABOUT 485 CALORIES, 23g PROTEIN, 41g CARBOHYDRATE, 26g TOTAL FAT (12g SATURATED), 115mg CHOLESTEROL, 1010mg SODIUM

## BAKED RIGATONI AND PEAS

*Prep: 35 minutes   Bake: 30–35 minutes*
*Makes 8 main dish servings*

450g dried rigatoni or ziti
Salt
105g margarine or butter
30g plain flour
675ml milk
125g Parmesan cheese,
  freshly grated

300g frozen peas, thawed
400g canned chopped
  tomatoes
30g fresh basil leaves, cut into
  strips
30g dried breadcrumbs

◈ Prepare rigatoni as packet instructs, using 2 teaspoons salt in water; drain. Return rigatoni to pan; keep warm. Preheat oven to 180°C (350°F, Gas 4). Meanwhile, melt 75g of margarine in 2-litre pan over low heat. Stir in flour; cook, stirring 2 minutes. Using wire whisk, gradually blend in milk. Increase heat to medium; cook, stirring frequently, about 15 minutes until mixture thickens slightly and boils. Stir in 1 teaspoon salt and 90g Parmesan.

◈ Pour sauce over rigatoni, stirring to combine. Stir in peas, tomatoes with their juice and basil. Spoon rigatoni mixture into shallow 3½ to 4-litre casserole or 33 by 20cm ovenproof serving dish. Melt remaining margarine in small saucepan over low heat. Remove pan from heat; stir in breadcrumbs and remaining 35g Parmesan. Sprinkle topping over rigatoni. Bake 30–35 minutes until top is golden brown.

**Each serving: About 485 calories, 19g protein, 60g carbohydrate, 19g total fat (7g saturated), 24mg cholesterol, 870mg sodium**

## REDUCED-FAT MACARONI CHEESE

*Prep: 30 minutes   Bake: 20 minutes*
*Makes 6 main dish servings*

350g elbow macaroni twists
450g low-fat cottage cheese
2 tbsp plain flour
450ml skimmed milk
125g mature Cheddar cheese,
  grated

1 tsp salt
¼ tsp ground black pepper
¼ tsp ground nutmeg
30g Parmesan cheese, freshly
  grated

◈ Prepare macaroni as packet instructs but do not add salt to water; drain. Preheat oven to 190°C (375°F, Gas 5). Spray 2½-litre shallow, flameproof casserole with non-stick cooking spray. Blend cottage cheese until smooth in food processor with knife blade attached. (Alternatively, blend cottage cheese with 60ml of the milk called for in recipe in blender on high speed.)

◈ Whisk flour with 60ml milk in 2-litre saucepan until smooth. Gradually stir in remaining milk until blended. Cook over medium heat, stirring frequently, until mixture

thickens slightly and just boils. Remove pan from heat and stir in cottage cheese, mature Cheddar, salt, pepper and ground nutmeg.

◈ Place macaroni in casserole; pour cheese sauce over. Bake, uncovered, 20 minutes. Meanwhile, remove casserole from oven; preheat grill. Sprinkle Parmesan on top. Grill at closest position to heat for 2–3 minutes until top is golden brown and bubbling.

**Each serving: About 400 calories, 26g protein, 51g carbohydrate, 9g total fat (6g saturated), 28mg cholesterol, 900mg sodium**

## TEX-MEX STYLE PASTA

*Prep: 35 minutes   Bake: 15 minutes*
*Makes 4 main dish servings*

225g dried wagon wheel or
  corkscrew pasta
225g fully cooked chorizo
  sausage, thinly sliced
1 large green pepper, cored,
  seeded and diced
1 large onion, diced
800g canned tomatoes
1 small courgette (about
  175g), diced

450g canned sweetcorn,
  drained
125g canned or bottled mild
  green chillies, chopped,
  liquid reserved
60g Cheddar cheese, coarsely
  grated

◈ Prepare pasta as packet instructs but do not add salt to water; drain. Meanwhile, preheat oven to 200°C (400°F, Gas 6). Cook sausage, green pepper and onion in 26cm frying pan over medium-high heat, stirring frequently, until vegetables are tender. Spoon off and discard any fat in pan.

◈ Stir in tomatoes, courgette, sweetcorn and chillies with their liquid; bring to the boil. Reduce heat to low; cook 5 minutes. Stir in pasta. Spoon into shallow 2-litre casserole or 30 by 18cm ovenproof dish. Sprinkle with grated cheese and bake 15 minutes, or until top is golden brown.

**Each serving: About 445 calories, 31g protein, 86g carbohydrate, 29g total fat (11g saturated), 13mg cholesterol, 1305mg sodium**

# LASAGNE

A pan of hot, bubbly lasagne has timeless appeal. Here are lasagne recipes for every taste, from a robust beef and sausage version to tempting cheese-filled lasagne rolls. Because lasagne freezes beautifully, it's a perfect dish to make in advance

1 Prepare lasagne sheets as packet instructs. Drain and rinse with cold water. Return lasagne to pan with *cold water* to cover. Meanwhile, combine tomatoes and tomato passata in 3-litre ovenproof serving dish; break up tomatoes with back of spoon. Prepare filling: mix all cheeses, pepper and 3 tablespoons chopped basil together in large bowl.

2 Preheat oven to 190°C (375°F, Gas 5). Drain lasagne on clean tea towels. Cut in half lengthways. Spread filling on lasagne sheets, dividing it equally between them, and roll up Swiss-roll style. Slice each lasagne roll crossways in half.

## THREE-CHEESE LASAGNE ROLLS

❖❖❖❖❖❖❖❖❖❖❖❖❖

*Prep: 35 minutes*
*Bake: 35–40 minutes*
*Makes 8 main dish servings*

**6 lasagne sheets**
**800g canned tomatoes**
**225ml tomato passata**
**425g ricotta cheese**
**175g half-fat mozzarella**
**cheese, grated**
**45g Parmesan cheese, freshly grated**
**½ tsp coarsely ground black pepper**
**4 tbsp chopped fresh basil**
**2 tsp olive oil**
**1 small onion, chopped**
**1 small courgette (about 125g), diced**
**1 small tomato, diced**
**1 tbsp canned or bottled drained and chopped capers**

3 Arrange lasagne rolls, cut-side down, in sauce in ovenproof dish; cover loosely with foil. Bake 35–40 minutes until hot.

4 Meanwhile, prepare topping: heat oil in 26cm non-stick frying pan over medium heat. Add onion and cook until tender and browned. Stir in courgette; cook until tender.

5 Stir in diced tomato, capers and remaining 1 tablespoon basil; heat through. To serve, place sauce and lasagne rolls on 6 plates; spoon diced vegetable topping over.

EACH SERVING: ABOUT 290 CALORIES, 18g PROTEIN, 32g CARBOHYDRATE, 11g TOTAL FAT (5g SATURATED), 30mg CHOLESTEROL, 680mg SODIUM

## BEEF AND SAUSAGE LASAGNE

*Prep: 1 hour, plus standing*  **Bake:** *45 minutes*
**Makes** *10 main dish servings*

12 dried lasagne sheets

225g hot Italian sausages, casings removed

225g minced beef

1 medium onion, diced

800g canned tomatoes

2 tbsp tomato purée

1 tsp salt

1 tsp sugar

¾ tsp dried mixed herbs

425g ricotta cheese

1 medium egg

15g fresh parsley, chopped

225g half-fat mozzarella cheese, grated

◆ Prepare lasagne sheets as packet instructs but do not add salt to water; drain and rinse with cold water. Return to pan with *cold water* to cover, set aside.

◆ Meanwhile, prepare meat sauce: cook sausages, minced beef and onion in 4-litre saucepan over high heat, stirring often to break up sausages, until meat is browned. Spoon off and discard fat. Add tomatoes with their juice and next 4 ingredients. Bring to the boil, breaking up tomatoes with back of spoon. Reduce heat to low; cover and simmer, stirring occasionally, 30 minutes. Set aside.

◆ Preheat oven to 190°C (375°F, Gas 5). Mix ricotta, egg and parsley together in medium bowl. Drain lasagne sheets on clean kitchen towels.

◆ Arrange half of the lasagne sheets, overlapping slightly, in 33 by 20cm ovenproof serving dish. Top with ricotta mixture. Sprinkle with half of mozzarella; top with half of meat sauce. Layer with remaining lasagne sheets and meat sauce and top with remaining mozzarella. Cover with foil; bake 30 minutes.

◆ Uncover and bake 15 minutes longer or until sauce is bubbly and top is lightly browned. Let stand 15 minutes for easier serving.

**Each serving: About 400 calories, 23g protein, 27g carbohydrate, 22g total fat (10g saturated), 90mg cholesterol, 785mg sodium**

## MUSHROOM LASAGNE

*Prep: 1 hour, plus standing*  **Bake:** *50 minutes*
**Makes** *12 main dish servings*

15g dried porcini mushrooms

16 dried lasagne sheets

1.2 litres milk

75g butter or margarine

40g plain flour

Pinch ground nutmeg

Salt and ground black pepper

75g shallots, finely chopped

750g button mushrooms, sliced

2 tbsp chopped fresh parsley

425g ricotta cheese

300g frozen chopped spinach, thawed and squeezed dry

125g Parmesan cheese, freshly grated

◆ Combine porcini and *175ml hot water* in bowl; let stand 30 minutes. Using slotted spoon, remove porcini; rinse to remove any grit. Chop and set aside. Strain liquid through sieve lined with kitchen towels; set aside. Meanwhile, prepare lasagne sheets as packet instructs, but do not add salt to water; drain and rinse with cold water. Return lasagne sheets to pan with *cold water* to cover. Set aside.

◆ Prepare béchamel sauce: bring milk to the boil in 3-litre saucepan over medium-high heat. Meanwhile, melt 45g butter in 4-litre saucepan over medium heat. Stir in flour; cook, stirring, 1 minute. Gradually whisk in milk, nutmeg, ½ teaspoon salt and ⅛ teaspoon pepper. Return to the boil. Reduce heat to low; simmer 5 minutes, stirring. Remove from heat.

◆ Melt remaining butter in 30cm frying pan over medium-high heat. Add shallots; cook 1 minute. Stir in mushrooms, ½ teaspoon salt and ⅛ teaspoon pepper and cook 10 minutes, or until liquid has evaporated. Stir in porcini and soaking liquid; cook until liquid has evaporated. Remove from heat; stir in parsley.

◆ Preheat oven to 190°C (375°F, Gas 5). Mix ricotta, spinach, 30g Parmesan, ½ teaspoon salt, ¼ teaspoon pepper and 125ml béchamel. Drain lasagne sheets on clean tea towels.

◆ Spread 125ml béchamel sauce in 13 by 20cm ovenproof serving dish. Arrange 4 lasagne sheets over sauce, overlapping slightly. Top with half of mushroom mixture, 225ml béchamel, 30g Parmesan and 4 more lasagne sheets. Add all of ricotta mixture, 4 more lasagne sheets, remaining mushrooms, 225ml béchamel and 30g Parmesan. Top with remaining lasagne sheets, béchamel and Parmesan. Cover with foil; bake 30 minutes.

◆ Uncover and bake 20 minutes longer or until sauce is bubbly and top is lightly browned. Let stand 15 minutes.

**Each serving: About 355 calories, 18g protein, 36g carbohydrate, 16g total fat (9g saturated), 51mg cholesterol, 580mg sodium**

# ORIENTAL NOODLES

With a few speciality ingredients, it's surprisingly easy to create the exotic flavours of your favourite Oriental noodle dishes. Oriental food shops and most supermarkets will carry the products called for in these recipes. But if you can't find rice noodles, you can substitute spaghetti or linguine.

## CANTONESE NOODLE PANCAKE

❖❖❖❖❖❖❖❖❖❖❖❖

*Prep:* 25 minutes
*Cook:* 35–45 minutes
*Makes* 6 main dish servings

450g Chinese-style egg noodles or spaghetti
350g pork tenderloin, thinly sliced
2 tbsp dry sherry
4 tbsp soy sauce
2 tbsp plus 4 tsp vegetable oil
1 large red pepper, cored, seeded and cut into 2–3cm pieces
4 large spring onions, cut into 4cm pieces
350g bok choy, cut crossways into 5cm pieces
125g mange-tout, strings removed
2 tsp cornflour
2 tbsp very finely chopped peeled fresh ginger
425g canned Chinese straw mushrooms, drained

**1** Prepare noodles as packet instructs but do not add salt to water. Drain. Meanwhile, mix pork slices, sherry and 2 tablespoons soy sauce together in 30 by 18cm glass baking dish; set aside. Heat 1 tablespoon oil in 30cm non-stick frying pan over medium heat. Place noodles in pan to form 30cm round pancake. Cook 5–8 minutes until golden on bottom.

### TOFU TOPPING

If you prefer, make a light and easy vegetarian version of this pancake by substituting 450g firm tofu for the pork tenderloin. Cut the tofu into 2–3cm cubes. Proceed as instructed for pork, but cook tofu for about 5 minutes in Step 5.

**2** Carefully invert pancake onto plate. Slide pancake back into pan and cook for 5–8 minutes longer, until golden on other side. Transfer to large warm platter; keep warm.

**4** Transfer onion mixture to bowl with pork slices. Heat 2 teaspoons oil in same casserole. Add bok choy and mange-tout; cook until tender-crisp. Transfer to bowl with onion mixture.

**3** While pancake is cooking, heat 2 teaspoons oil in 5-litre flameproof casserole over medium-high heat. Add red pepper and spring onions; cook until tender-crisp.

**5** Mix cornflour, *225ml water*, and remaining soy sauce in small bowl. Heat remaining 1 tablespoon oil in same casserole. Add pork mixture and ginger; cook until pork loses its pink colour. Return vegetables to casserole; stir in cornflour mixture and mushrooms. Cook over medium-high heat, stirring, until mixture thickens slightly and boils. Spoon pork mixture onto pancake; cut into wedges.

EACH SERVING: ABOUT 465 CALORIES, 25g PROTEIN, 64g CARBOHYDRATE, 11g TOTAL FAT (2g SATURATED), 33mg CHOLESTEROL, 945mg SODIUM

## JAPANESE NOODLE SOUP

*Prep: 25 minutes    Cook: 20 minutes*
*Makes 4 main dish servings*

1 tbsp vegetable oil
175g firm tofu, cut into
   2–3cm pieces
3 spring onions, thinly sliced
   on the diagonal
1 tbsp grated peeled fresh
   ginger
25g instant shiro miso soup
   mix (white soya bean paste
   soup), or 1½ vegetable stock
   cubes
225g dried udon noodles
   (thick rice flour noodles) or
   linguine

1 large carrot, cut crossways
   into thirds, then lengthways
   into matchstick-thin strips
1 medium red pepper, cored,
   seeded and cut into thin
   strips
3 strips (each 7 by 1cm)
   lemon rind
¼ tsp dried chilli flakes
1 small bunch watercress,
   tough stalks removed

◆ Heat vegetable oil in 26cm non-stick frying pan over medium-high heat. Add tofu, spring onions and ginger and cook 5 minutes, or until golden. Set aside.

◆ Bring *2 litres water* to the boil in 4-litre saucepan over high heat. Add soup mix, next 5 ingredients and tofu mixture; return to the boil. Reduce heat to low; simmer 8–10 minutes until noodles are cooked (linguine will take slightly longer). Stir in watercress until it wilts. Serve immediately (udon noodles absorb liquid quickly).

**Each serving: About 355 calories, 17g protein, 54g carbohydrate, 9g total fat (2g saturated), 0mg cholesterol, 540mg sodium**

## THAI CHICKEN AND NOODLES

*Prep: 25 minutes    Cook: 35 minutes*
*Makes 4 main dish servings*

225g flat dried rice noodles or
   linguine
1 stalk fresh lemon grass
4 large spring onions
2 large skinless, boneless
   chicken breasts (about
   450g)
1 tbsp vegetable oil
300g mushrooms, sliced

1 tbsp very finely chopped,
   peeled fresh ginger
2 tsp red curry paste (see
   page 30)
2 tbsp soy sauce
400ml canned coconut milk
1 medium red pepper
2 tbsp chopped fresh
   coriander

◆ Prepare rice noodles or linguine as packet instructs; drain. Return to pan; keep warm. (If packet has no instructions, cook as for regular pasta 5 minutes, or just until tender.) Meanwhile, remove outer layer from lemon grass. Trim and cut 15cm long piece from bulb end; discard top. Cut stalk lengthways in half. Slice 2 spring onions into 2–3cm pieces; reserve remaining 2 for garnish. Cut chicken breasts into 2–3cm wide strips.

◆ Heat oil in 30cm non-stick frying pan over medium-high heat. Add mushrooms and spring onions and cook until golden. Using slotted spoon, transfer to small bowl.

◆ Add ginger and red curry paste to pan; cook, stirring, 1 minute. Add lemon grass, chicken strips, soy sauce, coconut milk and *225ml water* and bring to the boil. Reduce heat to low; cover and simmer 10 minutes, or until chicken just loses its pink colour throughout.

◆ While chicken is cooking, cut red pepper and reserved spring onions into 7–8cm long paper-thin strips. Remove lemon grass from chicken mixture and discard. Stir in mushroom mixture and coriander; heat through. To serve, arrange noodles in large bowl; top with chicken mixture. Garnish with red pepper and spring onion strips.

**Each serving: About 450 calories, 35g protein, 52g carbohydrate, 11g total fat (4g saturated), 81mg cholesterol, 660mg sodium**

## PAD THAI

*Prep: 25 minutes, plus soaking    Cook: 5 minutes*
*Makes 4 main dish servings*

225g rice stick noodles, or
   angel hair pasta
60ml fresh lime juice
60ml fish sauce (nuoc nam,
   see page 30)
2 tbsp sugar
1 tbsp vegetable oil
225g raw medium prawns,
   shelled and de-veined (see
   page 90), each cut
   lengthways in half

2 garlic cloves, very finely
   chopped
¼ tsp dried chilli flakes
3 medium eggs, lightly beaten
175g bean sprouts, rinsed
60g unsalted roasted peanuts,
   coarsely chopped
3 spring onions, thinly sliced
30g fresh coriander leaves
Lime wedges

◆ Soak rice stick noodles if using, in large bowl, in *hot water* to cover for 20 minutes. Drain and cut into 10cm lengths. Or, break angel hair pasta in half, cook as packet instructs; drain and rinse with *cold water*. Mix lime juice, fish sauce and sugar together in small bowl. Assemble remaining ingredients before beginning to cook.

◆ Heat oil in 30cm frying pan over high heat. Add prawns, garlic and dried chilli flakes and cook, stirring, for 1 minute. Add eggs and cook, stirring, 20 seconds, or just until set. Add noodles and cook, stirring, 2 minutes. Add lime juice mixture, half of bean sprouts, half of peanuts, and half of spring onions; cook, stirring, 1 minute. Transfer noodle mixture to platter. Top with remaining bean sprouts, peanuts and spring onions. Sprinkle with coriander; serve with lime wedges.

**Each serving: About 440 calories, 28g protein, 47g carbohydrate, 16g total fat (3g saturated), 297mg cholesterol, 1170mg sodium**

# GRAINS &
PULSES

11

# GRAINS AND PULSES KNOW-HOW

Long a staple and source of protein in the cuisines of cultures around the globe, grains and pulses also take a prominent place on the British table – and it's easy to see why. Grains and pulses are inexpensive, low in fat, rich in nutrients, and, if served together, form a complete protein. When it comes to meal planning, few foods are as versatile, creating satisfying side dishes and salads or hearty entrées in bold, robust flavours.

## BUYING AND STORING

Dried pulses and grains will keep for a year or longer, but they become less flavourful and drier with time. For best results, buy them in small quantities and use within 6 months. Avoid packages with any hint of dust or mould. Store grains and pulses in airtight containers in a cool, dry place. The bran left in brown rice and other whole grains makes them more perishable, so refrigerate or freeze them for longer storage.

Cooked beans can be refrigerated, tightly covered, for 4 or 5 days or frozen for 6 months (thaw them at room temperature for about 1 hour). Cooked grains can be refrigerated for up to 5 days. Since they keep so well, it's a good idea to cook extra beans and grains to use for fast salads, soups, pilafs, and stir-fries. Cooked rice becomes hard if refrigerated, but re-heats beautifully in the microwave.

## SOAKING BEANS

There are two reasons to soak dried beans in water before they're cooked. The first is that this process softens and returns moisture to the beans, which will reduce cooking time. The second is that soaking allows some of the gas-causing oligosaccharides (complex sugars that the human body cannot digest) to dissolve in the water, which makes digestion easier. Always discard the soaking liquid and cook the beans in fresh water.

To soak, combine beans with enough cold water to cover by 5cm. (Remember that beans will rehydrate to triple their dry size, so start with a large enough bowl or pot.) The standard soaking time is overnight, or about 8 hours. It's not true that longer is better, though; if left to soak too long, beans may start to ferment, so follow the recipe or package instructions. When time is of the essence, you can use the quick-soak method instead. To do this, simply boil the water and beans for 3 minutes; remove from heat. Cover and set aside for 1 hour; discard the soaking liquid.

## REASONS TO RINSE

There's no need to rinse most domestic packaged rice before cooking. That's because the rice has already been cleaned during milling – and you'll rinse away the starchy coating on enriched rice that contains nutrients such as thiamin, niacin and iron. You should, however, rinse wild rice and imported varieties such as basmati or jasmine, which may be dirty or dusty.

By contrast, dried beans and lentils should be picked over to remove any shrivelled beans, stones or twigs, then rinsed with cold running water to remove dust before cooking. Canned beans of all kinds should also be rinsed, for the best appearance and texture in the finished dish.

## COOKING SUCCESS

• For the lightest texture, be sure to allow cooked rice a 5-minute 'standing time' before fluffing and serving.
• For enhanced flavour, cook rice in stock.
• Don't lift the lid when cooking rice. This allows steam and heat to escape from the pan and results in a mushy texture.
• Never add anything acidic (e.g., tomatoes, vinegar, wine or citrus juices) or salt to beans at the start of cooking. These can toughen the skins and result in a longer cooking time, so add toward the end of cooking.
• Test rice and beans for doneness by tasting: freshness and variety can influence their cooking times. Rice should be soft and fluffy; beans should be creamy, not mushy, in texture.
• Cool cooked beans in their cooking liquid to prevent them from drying out.

### RICE COOKING METHODS

There are two basic methods of cooking rice, immersion and absorption. For the immersion method, rice is boiled like pasta, in a large amount of salted water until tender, then drained; the disadvantage is that nutrients are poured away with the cooking water. The most popular method of cooking is the absorption method, where rice is cooked in a measured quantity of liquid, all of which is absorbed, thus conserving nutrients. (Rice cookers use the absorption method and have a built-in timer; some also double up as steamers for other foods.) The cooking time and amount of liquid will vary depending on the variety of rice (see chart on page 371). For long-grain white rice, combine 400g rice with 450ml cooking liquid, 1 teaspoon salt (optional), and 1 tablespoon butter or margarine (optional) in a 2–3-litre saucepan. Heat to boiling. Reduce heat; cover and simmer 18–20 minutes. Remove from heat; let stand, covered, 5 minutes.

# KNOW YOUR RICE

**Long-grain** Slender, polished white elongated grains; it cooks into dry grains that separate easily.

**Easy-cook** Rice that has been steamed and pressure-treated; the grains remain firm and separate after cooking.

**Instant** Rice that has been partially or fully cooked, then dehydrated. It cooks in minutes but remains dry and chewy.

**Arborio** The traditional rice for Italian risotto; this fat, almost round grain has a high starch content and yields a moist, creamy texture. Vialone Nano and Carnaroli rice varieties have a similar starch content.

**Brown** The least processed form of rice; it has the outer hull removed but retains the nutritious, high-fibre bran layers that give it its light tan colour, nutty flavour and chewy texture.

**Basmati** A long-grain rice native to India; valued for its fragrant perfume, delicate taste and fluffy texture. When cooked, the slender grains swell only lengthwise, resulting in thin, dry grains perfect for pilafs.

**Wild rice** Not truly a rice but the seed of an aquatic grass. The long, dark-brown grains have a chewy texture and nutty, earthy flavour; rinse well before cooking.

Long-grain · Instant · Arborio

Brown · Basmati · Wild

### WHAT IS STICKY RICE?

Sticky, or glutinous, rice is a short-grain Asian rice with a slightly sweet taste and soft, sticky texture resulting from a high starch content. Typically used in dim sum, sushi and desserts, it can be purchased in Oriental or Caribbean markets.

## RICE SENSE

| RICE VARIETY (200g) | AMOUNT OF LIQUID | COOKING TIME | COOKED YIELD |
| --- | --- | --- | --- |
| Long-grain | 400–450ml | 18–20 mins | 600g |
| Medium- or short-grain | 350–400ml | 18–20 mins | 600g |
| Brown | 450–575ml | 45–50 mins | 600–800g |
| Wild | 450–575ml | 45–60 mins | 450g |

# KNOW YOUR GRAINS

**Couscous** Grains of pre-cooked semolina; in North African cooking, it is steamed and served with spiced meats and vegetables to make a dish of the same name.

**Bulgar** Wheat kernels that have been steamed, dried and crushed. A staple in Middle Eastern cuisine and the grain for tabbouleh, bulgar has a tender, chewy texture.

**Barley** An ancient grain used to make cereal, bread, salads and soups. Pearl barley has been polished to remove the outer hull; quick-cooking pearl barley has been pre-steamed.

**Wheat grains** Unprocessed whole wheat kernels with a chewy texture; used for salads, pilafs, breakfast porridge or baking.

**Quinoa** A staple grain of the ancient Incas, quinoa is rich in protein and vital nutrients. The tiny seeds cook quickly; they have a slightly earthy taste and springy texture.

**Cornmeal** Dried corn kernels (yellow or white) ground to a fine, medium or coarse texture. Much used in baking, it is also cooked to make polenta, a staple dish in Northern Italy. Stone-ground cornmeal still contains the germ of the corn and has the best flavour; store in the freezer or refrigerator.

Couscous · Bulgar · Barley

Wheat grains · Quinoa · Cornmeal

**Buckwheat** A grain with an earthy flavour. The kernels may be cooked like rice. Kasha is roasted buckwheat kernels. Buckwheat flour is used in blinis.

## KNOW YOUR BEANS

**Black beans** Also called turtle beans, these are a staple bean in South and Central America, Mexico and Caribbean countries. With a slightly sweet taste, they're prized as the base for black bean soup, as a partner with rice or as a robust filling for burritos.

**Haricot** A small white bean, also called the pea bean. Widely used for tinned baked beans, they are ideal for slow cooking dishes such as casseroles as they retain their shape well.

**Yellow or green split peas** Dried peas that have been husked and split in half, these have a slightly sweet flavour that pairs well with ham, and can be cooked to a soft purée that makes excellent soup.

**Borlotti** These plump, beautiful beans are cream-coloured with red streaks, but become uniform in colour during cooking. They have a bitter-sweet flavour.

**Pink** A smooth, reddish-brown dry bean popular in the western states of America where it's used to make refried beans and chilli; interchangeable with pinto beans.

**Flageolet** These pale green beans have a delicate flavour. Popular in soup, as a side dish and in salads, they can be substituted for white beans in most recipes.

**Black-eyed beans** An oval, beige-coloured bean with a black circular 'eye'. Used to make soups and salads; they have a mealy texture and earthy taste.

**Chick-peas** Also called garbanzos, they're perhaps best known as the base for hummous, a creamy Middle Eastern dip; they're also a favourite in Italian and Indian cooking. Their cooking time can vary greatly, so always taste for doneness.

**Red kidney** The choice for chilli, this medium-size bean has a firm, burgundy-coloured skin, pale flesh, and a sweet, meaty flavour.

**Cannellini** Also called white kidney beans, they have a creamy texture and milder taste than the red variety. Cannellini are common in Italian cooking, where they're used for soup or pasta dishes, or with tuna to make a salad.

**Pinto** Spanish for 'painted', these pale pink beans are splotched with reddish-brown streaks. Grown in the Southwest and prized in most Spanish-speaking countries, pinto beans are used to make refried beans or used in soup or stew. Pinto beans are interchangeable with pink beans.

**Broad beans (dried)** Also called fava, these flat, light brown beans resemble large butter beans. They have a tough skin that should be removed by blanching before cooking; commonly used to make salads and soups in Mediterranean and Middle Eastern countries.

**Butter beans** Also called giant lima, these large oval, cream-coloured beans hold their shape well when cooked; often served alone as a hot vegetable or in salads.

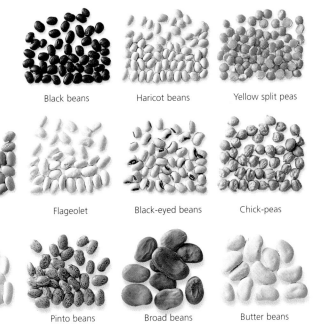

Black beans     Haricot beans     Yellow split peas

Borlotti     Pink beans     Flageolet     Black-eyed beans     Chick-peas

Red kidney     Cannellini     Pinto beans     Broad beans     Butter beans

## KNOW YOUR LENTILS

Protein-packed lentils, one of our oldest cultivated crops, cook into countless savoury, satisfying dishes including Indian dal (a rich, spicy dish made with tomatoes, onions and seasonings) and hearty stews and salads. They don't need to be pre-soaked and cook faster than dried beans.

**Small green French lentils (Puy)** Considered to have the best flavour, these tiny, plump lentils cook quickly, hold their shape and have a nutty taste.

**Red** A smaller, round variety, these lighten to yellow and become very soft when cooked. They are often used in Indian dal.

**Green lentils** Popular in European cooking; they have a firm texture and a nutty, earthy taste.

**Brown lentils** The most common variety; they have a firm texture and a mild nutty flavour.

Puy     Red     Green     Brown

# RICE

Perhaps the world's most versatile staple, rice is the basis of traditional dishes from around the globe. Here, we feature recipes that reflect the cuisines of Spain, Mexico, China, India and the Middle East. Our Flavoured Rice ideas on page 376 illustrate how plain white rice can be transformed with a dash of herbs or spice into a tempting side dish.

1 Preheat oven to 230°C (450°F, Gas 8). Brush aubergine slices on both sides with 2 tablespoons oil. Place on baking sheet; bake for 15 minutes, turning slices once. Set aside. Reduce temperature to 180°C (350°F, Gas 4).

## VEGETABLE PAELLA

**Prep:** *40 minutes plus standing* **Bake:** *50 minutes*

**Makes** *8 main dish servings*

1 small aubergine (about 450g), cut lengthways in half, then crossways into 1cm thick slices

2 tbsp plus 60ml olive or vegetable oil

1 medium onion, diced

225g mushrooms, each cut in half or quarters

2 small courgettes (about 350g), cut into 2–3cm pieces

2 medium tomatoes, cut into 2cm pieces

80ml vegetable stock

450g easy-cook rice

400g canned artichoke hearts, drained

¼ tsp salt

½ tsp crushed saffron threads

¼ tsp ground black pepper

400g canned chick-peas, rinsed and drained

300g frozen peas

40g pimiento-stuffed olives, rinsed and drained

½ tsp chopped fresh thyme

2 Meanwhile, heat remaining 60ml oil in 30cm frying pan over medium-high heat. Add onion and cook, stirring occasionally, until tender.

3 Add mushrooms and cook, stirring occasionally, until tender and brown. Stir in the courgettes; cook 1 minute.

4 Stir in tomatoes, vegetable stock, rice, artichoke hearts, salt, saffron, pepper and aubergine; bring to the boil over high heat. Transfer rice mixture to shallow 4-litre casserole. Bake, uncovered, about 50 minutes, until rice is tender and liquid is absorbed.

5 Remove casserole from oven; stir in chick-peas, peas, olives and thyme. Let paella stand 10 minutes to allow ingredients to heat through.

**SAFFRON**

The most expensive spice you can buy, saffron is the yellow-orange stigmas of the crocus flower, which are hand-picked and dried. Available as threads or powder, saffron should be used sparingly – too much produces a medicinal flavour. Use the threads in preference to powder, which loses its pungency in storage. The golden colour and distinct flavour of saffron are traditional in paella, bouillabaisse and risotto Milanese.

EACH SERVING: ABOUT 475 CALORIES, 12g PROTEIN, 78g CARBOHYDRATE, 13g TOTAL FAT (2g SATURATED), 0mg CHOLESTEROL, 715mg SODIUM

## ARROZ CON POLLO

*Prep: 15 minutes, plus standing    Cook: 40 minutes*
*Makes 4 main dish servings*

1 tbsp vegetable oil
750g chicken thighs, skin removed
1 medium onion, chopped
1 medium red pepper, cored, seeded and cut into 1cm pieces
1 garlic clove, very finely chopped
⅛ tsp ground red pepper

200g long-grain rice
1 strip (7 by 1cm) lemon rind
¼ tsp dried oregano
400ml chicken stock
150g frozen peas
60g pimiento-stuffed olives, chopped
15g fresh coriander, chopped
Lemon wedges for garnish

◆ Heat oil in a 5-litre flameproof casserole over medium-high heat. Add chicken thighs and cook 8–10 minutes, turning once, until well browned. Transfer to bowl. Reduce heat to medium. Add onion and pepper pieces to casserole; cook 5 minutes, or until tender. Stir in garlic and ground red pepper and cook 30 seconds. Add rice and cook, stirring, 1 minute. Stir in lemon rind, oregano and stock plus *50ml water*. Return chicken to casserole and bring to the boil over high heat. Reduce heat to low; cover and simmer 20 minutes, or until juices run clear when chicken is pierced with tip of knife.

◆ Stir in peas; cover and heat through. Remove from heat; let stand 5 minutes. Spoon into serving bowl and sprinkle with olives and coriander. Serve garnished with lemon wedges.

**Each serving: About 440 calories, 27g protein, 52g carbohydrate, 14g total fat (3g saturated), 77mg cholesterol, 450mg sodium**

## CHINESE FRIED RICE

*Prep: 5 minutes    Cook: 30 minutes*
*Makes 4 main dish servings*

200g long-grain rice
6 medium eggs
½ tsp salt
3 tbsp vegetable oil

125g cooked ham, diced
75g frozen peas, thawed
1 tbsp chopped spring onion

◆ Prepare rice as packet instructs. Meanwhile, lightly beat eggs and salt until just blended; set aside.

◆ Heat 2 tablespoons oil in 30cm non-stick frying pan over medium heat, Add rice and stir gently until it is well coated with oil. Push rice to one side of pan.

◆ Add remaining 1 tablespoon oil to pan and heat over medium-high heat until very hot. Pour in eggs and cook, stirring constantly, until egg mixture is the size of peas and leaves side of the pan.

◆ Stir rice into eggs. Stir in ham and peas; heat through. Sprinkle with spring onion.

**Each serving: About 430 calories, 21g protein, 41g carbohydrate, 20g total fat (5g saturated), 335mg cholesterol, 755mg sodium**

## JAMBALAYA

*Prep: 20 minutes    Cook: 45 minutes*
*Makes 6 main dish servings*

225g hot Italian sausages, pricked all over with fork
1 medium onion, finely chopped
1 medium green pepper, cored, seeded and diced
1 medium celery stalk, diced
1 garlic clove, very finely chopped
⅛ tsp ground red pepper
300g long-grain rice

⅛ tsp dried thyme
¼ tsp salt
400ml chicken stock
400g canned tomatoes, drained and chopped
450g raw medium prawns, peeled, and de-veined (see page 90)
2 spring onions, thinly sliced
Tabasco sauce (optional)

◆ Cook sausages in 5-litre flameproof casserole over medium heat about 10 minutes until browned all over. Transfer to kitchen paper to drain; allow to cool. Slice sausages into 1cm pieces.

◆ Add onion, green pepper and celery to casserole and cook 10 minutes, or until tender. Stir in garlic and ground red pepper; cook, stirring, 30 seconds.

◆ Add rice and cook, stirring, 1 minute. Stir in thyme, salt and stock and *350ml water*. Return sausages to casserole and bring to the boil over high heat. Reduce heat to low; cover and simmer 15 minutes.

◆ Stir in tomatoes; cover and cook 5 minutes. Stir in prawns; cover and cook 5 minutes longer, or until prawns turn opaque throughout.

◆ Spoon mixture into serving bowl and sprinkle with spring onions. Serve with Tabasco sauce, if you like.

**Each serving: About 385 calories, 22g protein, 45g carbohydrate, 13g total fat (4g saturated), 152mg cholesterol, 710mg sodium**

## CUMIN RICE WITH BLACK-EYED BEANS

*Prep: 10 minutes, plus standing    Cook: 30 minutes*
*Makes 6 accompaniment servings*

| | |
|---|---|
| 1 tbsp vegetable oil | ¼ tsp salt |
| 1 medium onion, finely chopped | 400g black-eyed beans, rinsed and drained |
| 1 garlic clove, very finely chopped | 2 tbsp chopped fresh coriander |
| 2 tsp cumin seeds | Lime wedges |
| 300g long-grain rice | |
| 400ml chicken or vegetable stock | |

❖ Heat oil in 3-litre saucepan over medium heat. Add onion and cook 5 minutes, or until tender. Stir in garlic and cumin seeds; cook until fragrant. Add rice and cook, stirring, 1 minute.

❖ Stir in chicken stock plus *375ml water* and salt. Bring to the boil over high heat. Reduce heat to low. Cover and simmer 15 minutes.

❖ Stir black-eyed beans into rice. Cover and simmer 5 minutes longer. Remove from heat and let stand 5 minutes. Spoon rice mixture into serving bowl and sprinkle with coriander. Serve with lime wedges.

**Each serving: About 265 calories, 8g protein, 51g carbohydrate, 4g total fat (1g saturated), 5mg cholesterol, 580mg sodium**

## INDIAN-SPICED RICE

*Prep: 2 minutes, plus standing    Cook: 25 minutes*
*Makes 4 accompaniment servings*

| | |
|---|---|
| 1 tbsp vegetable oil | 4 whole cloves |
| 1 cinnamon stick, 7–8cm long | 200g long-grain rice |
| 10 black peppercorns | ½ tsp salt |
| 6 cardamom pods | |

❖ Heat oil in 2-litre saucepan over medium heat. Add cinnamon stick, peppercorns, cardamom and cloves and cook, stirring often, just until spices begin to darken. Add rice and cook, stirring, 1 minute.

❖ Stir in salt and *450ml water*. Bring rice to the boil over high heat. Reduce heat to low; cover and simmer 20 minutes. Remove rice from heat and let stand 5 minutes. Fluff with fork.

**Each serving: About 205 calories, 3g protein, 38g carbohydrate, 4g total fat (1g saturated), 0mg cholesterol, 270mg sodium**

## PERSIAN RICE PILAFF

*Prep: 10 minutes, plus standing    Cook: 30 minutes*
*Makes 4 accompaniment servings*

| | |
|---|---|
| 15g butter or margarine | Pinch ground cinnamon |
| 1 small onion, finely chopped | ⅛ tsp ground black pepper |
| 200g long-grain rice | ½ tsp grated orange rind |
| 400ml chicken or vegetable stock | 60g pine nuts, toasted |
| 40g currants | 15g fresh parsley, chopped |

❖ Melt butter in 2-litre saucepan over medium heat.

❖ Add chopped onion and cook, stirring often, 4 minutes, or until tender. Add rice and cook, stirring, 1 minute.

❖ Stir in chicken stock and *50ml water*, currants, ground cinnamon and ground black pepper. Bring to the boil over high heat. Reduce heat to low; cover and simmer 20 minutes.

❖ Remove rice from heat and allow to stand 5 minutes. Add orange rind; fluff with fork until combined. Gently stir in pine nuts and parsley.

**Each serving: About 285 calories, 7g protein, 49g carbohydrate, 8g total fat (2g saturated), 10mg cholesterol, 475mg sodium**

### WORLD OF RICE

There are more than 40,000 varieties of rice, and more than half the world's people eat rice as their main sustenance. Specialities come from all over the world: in the Near East and India, rice pilaff is prepared by browning rice in hot oil or butter before cooking it in stock, which helps keep the grains separate. Japanese cooks prefer a starchier variety of rice, while in northern Thailand, sticky rice holds together enough to be eaten with the hands. In China, rice is served as a breakfast porridge called *congee*.

*Rijsttafel*, Dutch for 'rice table', is an adaptation of an Indonesian meal that's popular in Holland: a platter of hot spiced rice is accompanied by various small side dishes, including fried seafood and meats, curries and relishes. In Spain and Mexico, *arroz con pollo*, or 'rice with chicken', may get added flavour from tomatoes, pimientos, onions, peppers and peas. Paella is a Spanish rice dish that usually contains a combination of chicken, seafood, sausages, pork and vegetables, with saffron for a bright yellow colour. Jambalaya, the New Orleans version of paella, may include ham and prawns and replaces the saffron with ground red pepper. 'Dirty' rice was also created in New Orleans; it gets its 'dirty' appearance from chicken livers.

# FLAVOURED RICE

**ORANGE-CORIANDER RICE** Bring 200g long-grain rice, 225g chicken or vegetable stock, 175ml water and ¼ teaspoon salt to the boil in 2-litre saucepan over high heat. Reduce heat to low; cover and simmer 18–20 minutes until rice is tender and liquid absorbed. Stir in 2 tablespoons chopped fresh coriander and ½ teaspoon grated orange rind. Makes 4 accompaniment servings.

Each serving: About 180 calories, 4g protein, 38g carbohydrate, 1g total fat (0g saturated), 5mg cholesterol, 400mg sodium

**GREEN RICE** Bring 200g long-grain rice, 225ml chicken or vegetable stock, 175ml water and ¼ teaspoon salt to the boil in 2-litre saucepan over high heat. Reduce heat to low; cover and simmer 15 minutes. Stir in 300g frozen chopped spinach, thawed and squeezed dry; cover and cook 5 minutes. Stir in 60g finely crumbled feta cheese. Makes 4 accompaniment servings.

Each serving: About 235 calories, 8g protein, 42g carbohydrate, 4g total fat (2g saturated), 17mg cholesterol, 620mg sodium

Parsley-walnut rice

Soy-sesame rice

**LEMON-PARSLEY RICE** Bring 200g long-grain rice, 225ml chicken or vegetable stock, 175ml water and ¼ teaspoon salt to the boil in 2-litre saucepan over high heat. Reduce heat to low; cover and simmer 18–20 minutes until rice tender and liquid is absorbed. Stir in 2 tablespoons chopped fresh parsley and 1 teaspoon grated lemon rind until blended. Makes 4 accompaniment servings.

Each serving: About 180 calories, 4g protein, 38g carbohydrate, 1g total fat (0g saturated), 5mg cholesterol, 405mg sodium

**PARSLEY-WALNUT RICE** Bring 200g long-grain rice, 225ml chicken or vegetable stock, 175ml water and ¼ teaspoon salt to the boil in 2-litre saucepan over high heat. Reduce heat to low; cover and simmer 18–20 minutes until rice is tender and liquid is absorbed. Stir in 30g chopped toasted walnuts, 2 tablespoons chopped fresh parsley and 15g butter or margarine until blended. Makes 4 accompaniment servings.

Each serving: About 250 calories, 5g protein, 39g carbohydrate, 8g total fat (1g saturated), 13mg cholesterol, 435mg sodium

**SOY-SESAME RICE** Bring 200g long-grain rice, 225ml chicken or vegetable stock, 175ml water and ¼ teaspoon salt to the boil over high heat. Reduce heat to low; cover and simmer 18–20 minutes until rice is tender and liquid is absorbed. Stir in 2 chopped spring onions, 2 teaspoons soy sauce and ¼ teaspoon sesame oil. Makes 4 accompaniment servings.

Each serving: About 180 calories, 4g protein, 38g carbohydrate, 1g total fat (0g saturated), 13mg cholesterol, 575mg sodium

**CHEDDAR RICE** Bring 200g long-grain rice, 225ml chicken or vegetable stock, 175ml water and ¼ teaspoon salt to the boil in 2-litre saucepan over high heat. Reduce heat to low, cover and simmer 18–20 minutes until rice is tender and liquid is absorbed. Stir in 60g grated Cheddar cheese, 2 teaspoons drained and chopped canned or bottled mild green chilli and 3 thinly sliced spring onions. Makes 4 accompaniment servings.

Each serving: About 240 calories, 8g protein, 38g carbohydrate, 6g total fat (3g saturated), 21mg cholesterol, 505mg sodium

**COCONUT RICE** Bring 200g long-grain rice, 225ml chicken or vegetable stock, 175ml water and ¼ teaspoon salt to the boil in 2-litre saucepan over high heat. Reduce heat to low; cover and simmer 18–20 minutes until rice is tender and liquid is absorbed. Stir in 125ml unsweetened coconut milk, ½ teaspoon grated lime rind and pinch ground red pepper. Makes 4 accompaniment servings.

Each serving: About 245 calories, 5g protein, 39g carbohydrate, 8g total fat (7g saturated), 5mg cholesterol, 405mg sodium

**LEMON-PARMESAN RICE** Bring 200g long-grain rice, 225ml chicken or vegetable stock, 175ml water and ¼ teaspoon salt to the boil in 2-litre saucepan over high heat. Reduce heat to low; cover and simmer 18–20 minutes until rice is tender and liquid is absorbed. Stir in 30g freshly grated Parmesan cheese, 1 teaspoon grated lemon rind and ¼ teaspoon ground black pepper. Makes 4 accompaniment servings.

Each serving: About 205 calories, 7g protein, 38g carbohydrate, 3g total fat (1g saturated), 10mg cholesterol, 520mg sodium

# RISOTTO

Rich, creamy risotto, a speciality from northern Italy, relies on starchy, short-grain Arborio rice – and a little patience. The grains of rice are first sautéed, then hot stock is added gradually as it is absorbed. Almost constant stirring ensures even cooking. Perfect risotto is just tender, yet still slightly *al dente*.

## SPRING RISOTTO

❖❖❖❖❖❖❖❖❖❖❖❖❖

*Prep:* 30 minutes
*Cook:* 55 minutes
*Makes* 4 main dish servings

**400ml vegetable or chicken stock**
**2 tbsp olive oil**
**3 medium carrots, diced**
**350g asparagus, tough ends removed, cut into 5cm pieces**
**175g sugar snap peas, strings removed and each cut crossways in half**
**¼ tsp coarsely ground black pepper**
**Salt**
**1 small onion, chopped**
**400g Arborio rice (Italian short-grain rice)**
**125ml dry white wine**
**60g Parmesan cheese, freshly grated**
**15g fresh basil or parsley, chopped**

**1** Bring stock and *800ml water* to the boil in 2-litre saucepan over high heat. Reduce heat to low to maintain simmer; cover. Heat 1 tablespoon olive oil in 4-litre saucepan over medium heat. Add carrots and cook 10 minutes. Add asparagus, sugar snap peas, pepper and ¼ teaspoon salt; cover and cook about 5 minutes, until tender-crisp. Transfer vegetables to bowl; set aside.

**2** Heat remaining 1 tablespoon oil in same pan over medium heat. Add onion and cook 5 minutes, or until tender. Add rice and ¼ teaspoon salt; cook, stirring, until rice is opaque.

**3** Add white wine; cook, stirring constantly, until wine is absorbed. Add about 125ml simmering stock to rice mixture, stirring until liquid is absorbed.

**4** Continue cooking, adding simmering stock, 125ml at a time, and stirring after each addition, about 25 minutes until all liquid is absorbed and rice is tender but still firm.

**5** When risotto is done (it should have a creamy consistency), stir in vegetables; heat through. Stir in Parmesan and basil. Spoon risotto into 4 shallow bowls and serve hot.

### RISOTTO TIPS

• Serve risotto at once; it continues to absorb liquid as it stands.

• Use a heavy pan with a thick base that heats evenly; maintain the rice at a steady, gentle simmer.

• Keep the stock at a constant simmer, or the risotto will cook too slowly and become gluey.

EACH SERVING: ABOUT 645 CALORIES, 18g PROTEIN, 107g CARBOHYDRATE, 12g TOTAL FAT (4g SATURATED), 18mg CHOLESTEROL, 965mg SODIUM

## PRAWN RISOTTO WITH BABY PEAS

*Prep:* 35 minutes  *Cook:* 35 minutes
*Makes* 4 main dish servings

450g raw medium prawns
400ml chicken or vegetable stock
15g butter or margarine
⅛ tsp ground black pepper
½ tsp salt
1 tbsp olive oil
1 small onion, finely chopped
400g Arborio rice (Italian short-grain rice)
125ml dry white wine
150g frozen baby peas
15g fresh parsley, chopped

◆ Peel and de-vein prawns (see page 90), reserving shells. Bring stock, *900ml water* and reserved shells to the boil in 3-litre saucepan over high heat. Reduce heat to low; simmer 20 minutes. Strain stock through sieve; if necessary, add *water* to equal 1.2 litres. Return stock to clean pan and bring to the boil over high heat. Reduce heat to low to maintain simmer; cover.

◆ Melt butter in 4-litre saucepan over medium-high heat. Add prawns, pepper and salt; cook, stirring, 2 minutes, or just until prawns are opaque. Transfer to bowl.

◆ Heat oil in same pan over medium heat. Add onion; cook 5 minutes, until tender. Add rice and cook, stirring often, until grains are opaque. Add wine; cook until wine is absorbed. Add 125ml simmering stock; stir until stock is absorbed.

◆ Continue cooking, adding stock, 125ml at a time, and stirring after each addition, about 25 minutes until all liquid is absorbed and rice is tender and creamy but still firm. Stir in peas and cooked prawns and heat through. Stir in parsley.

**Each serving: About 645 calories, 30g protein, 100g carbohydrate, 8g total fat (3g saturated), 191mg cholesterol, 565mg sodium**

## MUSHROOM RISOTTO

*Prep:* 20 minutes, plus standing
*Cook:* 50 minutes
*Makes* 4 main dish servings

15g dried porcini mushrooms
400ml chicken or vegetable stock
30g butter or margarine
450g button mushrooms, sliced
¼ tsp ground black pepper
½ tsp salt
Pinch dried thyme
1 tbsp olive oil
1 small onion, finely chopped
400g Arborio rice (Italian short-grain rice)
125ml dry white wine
60g Parmesan cheese, freshly grated
2 tbsp chopped fresh parsley

◆ Combine porcini with *175ml boiling water* in small bowl; let stand 30 minutes. Using slotted spoon, remove porcini; rinse and chop. Strain soaking liquid through sieve lined with kitchen towels. Bring stock, *750ml water* and porcini liquid to the boil in 2-litre saucepan over high heat. Reduce heat to low to maintain simmer; cover.

◆ Melt butter in 4-litre saucepan over medium heat. Add mushrooms, pepper, salt and thyme; cook, stirring occasionally, 10 minutes. Stir in porcini. Using slotted spoon, transfer mushroom mixture to bowl.

◆ Heat oil in same pan over medium heat. Add onion; cook 5 minutes. Add rice and cook, stirring often, until grains are opaque. Add wine; cook until absorbed. Add 125ml simmering stock; stir until absorbed.

◆ Continue cooking, adding stock, 125ml at a time, and stirring after each addition, about 25 minutes until all liquid is absorbed and rice is tender and creamy but still firm. Stir in mushroom mixture and Parmesan; heat through. Stir in parsley.

**Each serving: About 645 calories, 17g protein, 102g carbohydrate, 14g total fat (5g saturated), 34mg cholesterol, 600mg sodium**

## BUTTERNUT SQUASH RISOTTO WITH SAGE

*Prep:* 20 minutes  *Cook:* 50 minutes
*Makes* 4 main dish servings

1 medium butternut squash (900g)
400ml chicken or vegetable stock
30g butter or margarine
¼ tsp ground black pepper
3 tbsp chopped fresh sage
¼ tsp salt
1 tbsp olive oil
1 small onion, finely chopped
400g Arborio rice (Italian short-grain rice)
75ml dry white wine
60g Parmesan cheese, freshly grated

◆ Cut squash into chunks; cut off and discard peel. Cut half squash into 1cm pieces. Grate remaining squash. Bring stock and *800ml water* to the boil in 2-litre saucepan over high heat. Reduce heat to low to maintain simmer; cover.

◆ Melt butter in 4-litre saucepan over medium heat. Add squash pieces, pepper, 2 tablespoons sage and salt. Cook, stirring often, 10 minutes, or until squash is tender (add *2–4 tablespoons water* if squash sticks to pan before it is tender). Transfer to small bowl.

◆ Add oil, onion and grated squash to same pan; cook, stirring frequently, until vegetables are tender. Add rice; cook, stirring often, until grains are opaque. Add wine; cook until absorbed. Add 125ml simmering stock; stir until absorbed.

◆ Continue cooking, adding stock 125ml at a time, and stirring after each addition, about 25 minutes until all liquid is absorbed and rice is tender and creamy but still firm. (Add *125ml water* if necessary.) Stir in squash pieces, Parmesan and remaining sage; heat through.

**Each serving: About 690 calories, 17g protein, 119g carbohydrate, 14g total fat (5g saturated), 34mg cholesterol, 470mg sodium**

# Couscous

The granular semolina called couscous, originally from North Africa, is quickly transformed into a refreshing main-course salad or an exotic side dish for chicken, lamb or beef. The boxed supermarket version is ready in about five minutes – traditional couscous is soaked, steamed and dried several times.

## Nutty couscous salad

*Prep: 20 minutes    Cook: 5 minutes*
*Makes 8 accompaniment servings*

300g couscous
75g stoned dates
1 bunch flat-leaf parsley
1 large orange
2 tbsp olive or vegetable oil
2 tbsp cider vinegar
½ tsp sugar

¼ tsp salt
150g currants or dark seedless raisins
2 tbsp coarsely chopped crystallized ginger
175g salted cashews

**1** Prepare couscous as packet instructs. Cut each date crossways into 3 pieces. Reserve a few sprigs parsley for garnish.

**2** Using large chef's knife, finely chop enough remaining parsley to equal 3 tablespoons. Set aside.

**3** Prepare orange dressing: grate rind and squeeze juice from orange. Whisk orange rind, orange juice, oil, cider vinegar, sugar and salt together in large bowl until blended.

**4** Add couscous, dates, chopped parsley, currants, ginger and cashews to dressing; toss to mix well. Garnish with parsley sprigs. Cover and refrigerate if not serving right away.

---

### DATES

With at least 50 per cent sugar, dates are the sweetest of fruits. They are categorized as soft, semi-soft or dry, according to how soft they are when ripe: the Deglet Noor, the most commonly available, is a medium-size semi-soft date, while the Medjool, a very large premium date, is the best known of the soft dates.

Dates are available both fresh on the stalk and dried; most supermarket dates have been dried and partially rehydrated. When buying, avoid very shrivelled dates (though a wrinkled skin is normal) and any with mould or sugar crystals on the skin. Dates will last up to a year in an air-tight container in the refrigerator and up to five years in the freezer.

Dates are frequently used in baking (you can substitute chopped dates for raisins), and are good in salads, pilaffs, poultry stuffings and lamb stews.

Medjool

Deglet Noor

---

EACH SERVING: ABOUT 410 CALORIES, 9g PROTEIN, 60g CARBOHYDRATE, 17g TOTAL FAT (4g SATURATED), 8mg CHOLESTEROL, 370mg SODIUM

## FLAVOURED COUSCOUS

Couscous easily takes on a variety of flavours enabling you to vary it to your taste – try one of the following:

**Lime couscous** Prepare 175g couscous as packet instructs, but add 1 tablespoon fresh lime juice and ½ teaspoon grated lime rind to water before boiling. Makes 4 accompaniment servings.

Each serving: About 210 calories, 6g protein, 36g carbohydrate, 5g total fat (1g saturated), 0mg cholesterol, 245mg sodium

**Moroccan couscous** Prepare 175g couscous as packet instructs, but add 40g sultanas, ¼ teaspoon ground cinnamon, ¼ teaspoon ground turmeric, and ¼ teaspoon ground cumin to water before boiling. Makes 4 accompaniment servings.

Each serving: About 245 calories, 6g protein, 44g carbohydrate, 5g total fat (1g saturated), 0mg cholesterol, 255mg sodium

**Spring onion and dried tomato couscous** Prepare 175g couscous as packet instructs, but add 1 sliced medium spring onion and 5 chopped oil-packed sun-dried tomatoes to water before boiling. Makes 4 accompaniment servings.

Each serving: About 225 calories, 6g protein, 37g carbohydrate, 6g total fat (1g saturated), 0mg cholesterol, 270mg sodium

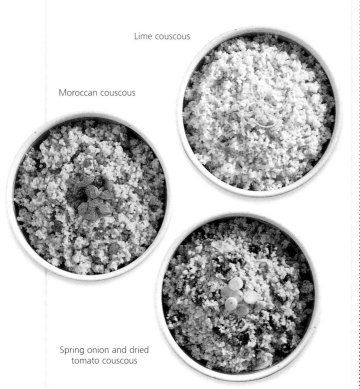

Lime couscous

Moroccan couscous

Spring onion and dried tomato couscous

# FRAGRANT VEGETABLE COUSCOUS

*Prep: 10 minutes, plus standing    Cook: 15 minutes*
*Makes 4 accompaniment servings*

| | |
|---|---|
| 1 tbsp olive or vegetable oil | ⅛ tsp ground cinnamon |
| 3 spring onions, finely chopped | 400ml chicken stock |
| 2 medium carrots, peeled and diced | 175g couscous |
| Salt and freshly ground black pepper | ½ tsp grated orange rind (optional) |

◆ Heat oil in 3-litre saucepan over medium-high heat. Add spring onions, carrots, ¼ teaspoon salt and ¼ teaspoon pepper and cook, stirring occasionally, until carrots are tender-crisp. Stir in cinnamon.

◆ Using wooden spoon, stir chicken stock into vegetable mixture; bring to the boil over high heat. Stir in couscous to combine well. Cover pan; remove from heat and allow to stand 5 minutes.

◆ Fluff couscous mixture with fork. Stir in grated orange rind, if you like.

Each serving: About 235 calories, 7g protein, 40g carbohydrate, 5g total fat (1g saturated), 8mg cholesterol, 585mg sodium

# COUSCOUS SALAD WITH RADISHES

*Prep: 15 minutes    Cook: 5 minutes*
*Makes 8 accompaniment servings*

| | |
|---|---|
| 300g couscous | 150g frozen peas, thawed |
| 400ml vegetable stock | 3 tbsp olive oil |
| 1 bunch radishes, coarsely chopped | 1 tsp grated lemon rind |
| 150g frozen sweetcorn, thawed | ½ tsp salt |

◆ Prepare couscous as packet instructs, but use vegetable stock plus *water* to equal amount of water called for on label, and do not use butter, margarine or salt.

◆ Mix chopped radishes, sweetcorn, peas, olive oil, lemon rind and salt together in large bowl. Stir in couscous until well combined. Cover salad and refrigerate if not serving right away.

Each serving: About 220 calories, 6g protein, 36g carbohydrate, 5g total fat (1g saturated), 0mg cholesterol, 180mg sodium

# CORNMEAL

Cornmeal – ground dried corn kernels – is the key ingredient of polenta, the silky cornmeal mush of northern Italy. It can be served as a side dish, like mashed potatoes; layered with cheese; or cooled and sliced to be grilled or fried. Spoonbread, an American soufflé-like casserole, is the fancy southern version of cornmeal mush. Always add cornmeal gradually to a liquid, and stir well to prevent lumps.

## POLENTA WITH MUSHROOMS

❖❖❖❖❖❖❖❖❖❖❖❖❖❖❖

*Prep:* 15 minutes, plus standing
*Cook:* 35 minutes
*Makes* 3 main dish servings

**15g dried porcini mushrooms**
**225g shiitake mushrooms**
**225g chestnut or button mushrooms**
**2 tbsp olive oil**
**1 medium onion, coarsely chopped**
**30g butter or margarine**
**1 tsp very finely chopped fresh oregano or ¼ tsp dried**
**¼ tsp coarsely ground black pepper**
**½ tsp salt**
**450ml milk**
**125g coarse yellow cornmeal**
**30g Parmesan cheese, freshly grated**
**Oregano sprigs for garnish**

**1** Combine porcini and *225ml boiling water*; let stand 30 minutes. Meanwhile, cut stalks from shiitakes; trim stalk ends from chestnut mushrooms. Rinse and thickly slice shiitake and chestnut mushrooms. Heat 1 tablespoon olive oil in 30cm frying pan over medium heat. Add onion and cook 5 minutes, or until tender; transfer to small bowl. Heat butter and remaining oil in same pan over medium-high heat.

**PERFECT POLENTA**

This is our tried-and-tested method for lump-free polenta: in pan you intend to cook in, place one-third of cold liquid called for in recipe, then gradually whisk in cornmeal. In another pan, heat remaining liquid to boiling. Add hot liquid to cornmeal mixture, whisking constantly.

**2** Add shiitakes and chestnut mushrooms, oregano and pepper; cook, stirring, 10 minutes. Meanwhile, drain porcini in sieve lined with kitchen towels; reserve 175ml liquid. Rinse porcini; chop.

**4** Prepare polenta: place salt and 300ml milk in 3-litre saucepan. Gradually whisk in cornmeal until smooth. Bring remaining 150ml milk and *450ml water* to the boil over high heat; whisk into cornmeal mixture. Return to the boil over medium-high heat, whisking. Reduce heat to low.

**3** Return onion to pan. Stir in porcini and reserved liquid; bring to the boil. Boil 1 minute. Remove from heat; keep warm.

**5** Cook polenta, stirring constantly, 5 minutes, or until thick. Stir in grated Parmesan until well combined. Serve polenta topped with mushroom mixture. Garnish with oregano.

EACH SERVING: ABOUT 545 CALORIES, 16g PROTEIN, 65g CARBOHYDRATE, 26g TOTAL FAT (10g SATURATED), 49mg CHOLESTEROL, 690mg SODIUM

## ROSEMARY POLENTA WEDGES

*Prep: 15 minutes, plus standing*
*Grill: 5–10 minutes*
*Makes 8 accompaniment servings*

1½ tsp salt
187g coarse yellow cornmeal
675ml milk
15g butter or margarine

½ tsp very finely chopped
   fresh rosemary or
¼ tsp dried, crushed
Rosemary sprigs for garnish

◆ Line two 2cm round cake tins with foil; grease foil. Place salt and *300ml water* in 3-litre saucepan; gradually whisk in cornmeal.

◆ Bring milk to the boil in 2-litre saucepan over medium-high heat; whisk into cornmeal mixture. Return to the boil over medium-high heat, whisking. Reduce heat to low and cook, stirring constantly, 3–5 minutes until mixture is thick.

◆ Spoon mixture into prepared tins; allow to stand 10 minutes, or until firm. If not serving right away, cover and refrigerate.

◆ About 20 minutes before serving, preheat grill. Grease rack in grill pan. Remove polenta from tins; discard foil. Cut each polenta round into 8 wedges. Place wedges on grill rack.

◆ Melt butter with rosemary in small saucepan over medium heat. Brush polenta wedges with butter mixture; garnish each with small rosemary sprig. Grill about 15cm from heat for 5–10 minutes until lightly browned and heated through.

**Each serving: About 165 calories, 5g protein, 24g carbohydrate, 5g total fat (2g saturated), 17mg cholesterol, 460mg sodium**

## SPOONBREAD

*Prep: 15 minutes plus standing   Bake: 40 minutes*
*Makes 8 accompaniment servings*

750ml milk
½ tsp salt
¼ tsp ground black pepper
125g coarse yellow cornmeal

60g butter or margarine,
   cut up
3 medium eggs, separated

◆ Preheat oven to 200°C (400°F, Gas 6). Grease 1½-litre shallow ovenproof serving dish. Bring milk, salt and pepper to the boil in 4-litre saucepan over medium-high heat. Remove from heat; gradually whisk in cornmeal. Whisk in butter until melted. Allow to stand 5 minutes.

◆ Whisk in egg yolks, one at a time. Beat egg whites to soft peaks in medium bowl with electric mixer on high speed. Fold half of whites into cornmeal mixture, then fold in remaining whites. Pour into prepared dish. Bake 35–40 minutes, or until set. Serve immediately.

**Each serving: About 200 calories, 7g protein, 18g carbohydrate, 11g total fat (5g saturated), 108mg cholesterol, 270mg sodium**

## THREE-CHEESE POLENTA

*Prep: 45 minutes, plus standing   Bake: 20 minutes*
*Makes 10 main dish servings*

Chunky Tomato Sauce (see
   below)
450ml single cream
1 tsp salt
½ tsp ground black pepper
375g coarse yellow cornmeal

15g butter or margarine
125g mozzarella cheese,
   grated
125g Fontina cheese, grated
125g Parmesan cheese,
   freshly grated

◆ Prepare Chunky Tomato Sauce; keep warm. Meanwhile, place cream, salt, pepper and *225ml water* in 5-litre flameproof casserole. Gradually whisk in cornmeal until smooth. Whisk in *1½ litres boiling water* and bring to the boil over medium-high heat. Reduce heat to low; cook, stirring constantly, about 5 minutes until mixture is very thick. Stir in butter until melted. Remove polenta from heat.

◆ Preheat oven to 220°C (425°F, Gas 7). Grease 33 by 20cm ovenproof serving dish. Mix Mozzarella, Fontina and Parmesan together in medium bowl. Spread one-third of polenta in dish. Reserve 60g cheese mixture for topping; sprinkle polenta with half remaining cheese. Top with one-third of polenta, remaining cheese, then remaining polenta. Sprinkle with reserved 60g cheese.

◆ Bake 20 minutes, or until top is browned. Remove from oven; allow to stand 10 minutes for easier serving.

◆ Cut polenta lengthways into 2 strips. Cut each strip crossways into 5 pieces. Serve with Chunky Tomato Sauce.

**Each serving: About 500 calories, 17g protein, 50g carbohydrate, 26g total fat (11g saturated), 51mg cholesterol, 1355mg sodium**

---

### CHUNKY TOMATO SAUCE

Melt 30g butter or margarine in 4-litre saucepan over medium heat. Stir in 3 large diced celery stalks and 3 large diced carrots, until coated. Cover and cook 20 minutes, stirring occasionally, until vegetables are very tender. Add 1.2 litres bottled tomato pasta sauce and bring to the boil. Reduce heat to low; cover and simmer for 15 minutes.

---

# OTHER GRAINS

There are a variety of grains to discover beyond the ever-popular rice and couscous. For a flavour-packed side dish or a hearty, healthy lunch, choices such as quinoa (see box, below), bulgar wheat, pearl barley and wheat all offer unique textures and tastes. These delicious and wholesome grains are even more appealing when they're enlivened with a variety of tasty ingredients – from nuts and fresh herbs to crunchy vegetables and dried fruits.

## QUINOA WITH SWEETCORN

❖❖❖❖❖❖❖❖❖❖❖❖❖❖❖❖❖❖❖❖❖❖❖❖❖❖❖❖❖❖❖

*Prep:* 10 minutes   *Cook:* 20 minutes
*Makes* 6 accompaniment servings

175g quinoa
Salt
3 medium corn on the cob,
   silk and husks removed

4 spring onions
15g butter or margarine
¼ tsp ground black pepper
½ tsp grated lemon rind

**1** Thoroughly rinse quinoa in fine-mesh sieve with cold water. Place in 2-litre saucepan with ½ teaspoon salt and *400ml water*; bring to the boil over high heat.

**2** Reduce heat to low; cover pan and simmer 15 minutes, or until water is absorbed. Meanwhile, cut corn kernels from cobs. Thinly slice spring onions.

**3** Melt butter in 26cm frying pan over medium-high heat. Add corn, spring onions, pepper and ¼ teaspoon salt. Cook, stirring often, 3 minutes, or until tender-crisp. Add quinoa and lemon rind. Cook, stirring, until combined.

### THE HIGH-PROTEIN GRAIN

Native to the Andes mountains in South America, quinoa was cultivated by the ancient Incas. Unlike any other grain or vegetable quinoa is a complete protein (containing all eight essential amino acids). It is also high in iron.

Available from health food shops, quinoa cooks quickly and has a light, springy texture. It can be cooked by any method that suits rice. Rinse quinoa before using to remove the saponin, a bitter, soapy tasting coating that acts as a natural insecticide.

Try lightly browning quinoa in a dry frying pan for 5 minutes before cooking to give it a delicious toasted flavour. For a salad, toss cooked quinoa with finely chopped raw vegetables and a vinaigrette. Quinoa can also be served with fruit and a little sugar or honey as a breakfast cereal.

EACH SERVING: ABOUT 165 CALORIES, 5g PROTEIN, 29g CARBOHYDRATE, 4g TOTAL FAT (2g SATURATED), 5mg CHOLESTEROL, 300mg SODIUM

## BULGAR PILAFF

*Prep:* 10 minutes, plus standing    *Cook:* 30 minutes
*Makes* 6 accompaniment servings

30g butter or margarine
1 medium onion, finely
   chopped
150g bulgar wheat
400ml chicken or vegetable
   stock
1 cinnamon stick, about
   7–8cm

400g canned chick-peas,
   rinsed and drained
60g dried apricots, diced
¼ tsp salt
⅛ tsp ground black pepper
15g fresh parsley, chopped

◆ Melt butter in 3-litre saucepan over medium heat. Add chopped onion and cook, stirring often, 5 minutes, or until onion is tender. Add bulgar wheat and cook, stirring, for 2 minutes longer.

◆ Stir in stock, cinnamon stick, chick-peas, dried apricots, salt and pepper; bring to the boil over high heat.

◆ Reduce heat to low; cover and simmer 15 minutes. Remove from heat; allow to stand 5 minutes. Stir in parsley; fluff bulgar mixture with fork.

**Each serving: About 220 calories, 7g protein, 37g carbohydrate, 6g total fat (2g saturated), 16mg cholesterol, 350mg sodium**

## WHEAT WITH BROWN BUTTER AND PECANS

*Prep:* 10 minutes, plus soaking    *Cook:* 1¼ hours
*Makes* 6 accompaniment servings

175g wheat grains
30g butter or margarine
1 medium onion, finely
   chopped

Salt and freshly ground black
   pepper
60g pecans, coarsely chopped
2 tbsp chopped fresh parsley

◆ Soak wheat grains overnight in medium bowl in enough *water* to cover by 5cm.

◆ Drain wheat grains. Place in 3-litre saucepan with *675ml water* and bring to the boil over high heat.

◆ Reduce heat to low; cover and simmer 1 hour, or just until tender but still firm. Drain. Wipe pan clean.

◆ Melt butter in same saucepan over medium heat. Add onion and cook, stirring frequently, 5 minutes, or until onion is tender.

◆ Stir in ½ teaspoon salt, ⅛ teaspoon pepper and chopped pecans. Cook, stirring, about 3 minutes until pecans are lightly toasted and butter begins to brown.

◆ Add wheat grains and *1 tablespoon water* to pecan mixture; stir until well combined. Heat through, stirring. Remove from heat; stir in parsley.

**Each serving: About 235 calories, 6g protein, 31g carbohydrate, 11g total fat (2g saturated), 11mg cholesterol, 225mg sodium**

## MUSHROOM-BARLEY PILAFF

*Prep:* 15 minutes    *Cook:* 55 minutes
*Makes* 6 accompaniment servings

200g pearl barley
30g butter or margarine
1 medium onion, finely
   chopped
2 medium celery stalks, cut
   into 5mm thick slices
350g mushrooms, sliced

400ml chicken or vegetable
   stock
½ tsp salt
⅛ tsp ground black pepper
⅛ tsp dried thyme
15g fresh parsley, chopped

◆ Toast barley in 3-litre saucepan over medium heat, shaking pan occasionally, 4 minutes, or until beginning to brown. Transfer to bowl.

◆ Melt butter in same pan over medium heat. Add onion and celery and cook 5 minutes, or until tender. Stir in mushrooms; cook about 10 minutes until tender and liquid has evaporated.

◆ Stir in barley, stock and *200ml water,* salt, pepper and thyme. Bring to the boil over high heat. Reduce heat to low; cover and simmer 30 minutes, or until barley is tender. Remove from heat and stir in parsley.

**Each serving: About 190 calories, 6g protein, 32g carbohydrate, 5g total fat (2g saturated), 16mg cholesterol, 530mg sodium**

# DRIED BEANS

Prized for their value and versatility, dried beans turn up in favourite dishes round the globe. Before cooking, soak dried beans overnight, or follow the quick (1 hour) method used in our Cassoulet. For digestibility, it's best to drain soaked beans, then cook them in fresh water. Cooking time will vary with both age and variety.

## CASSOULET

❖ ❖ ❖ ❖ ❖ ❖ ❖ ❖ ❖ ❖ ❖ ❖ ❖ ❖

*Prep:* 45 minutes, plus standing
*Bake:* 1½ hours
*Makes* 12 main dish servings

**450g dried cannellini beans**
**125g salt pork, diced**
**900g boneless fresh pork shoulder, cut into 4cm chunks**
**450g lamb for stew, cut into 4cm chunks**
**4 parsley sprigs**
**2 bay leaves**
**6 whole cloves**
**450g smoked Polish sausage, cut into 4cm chunks**
**6 large carrots, cut into bite-sized chunks**
**3 large celery stalks, thickly sliced**
**2 medium onions, each cut into quarters**
**175g tomato purée**
**225ml dry white wine or chicken stock**
**1½ tsp salt**
**½ tsp dried thyme**
**Crusty bread (optional)**

1 Rinse beans; discard any stones or shrivelled beans. Soak in *water* to cover by 5cm in large bowl overnight. (Or, to quick-soak: bring beans and *1½ litres water* to the boil in 4-litre saucepan over high heat; cook 3 minutes. Remove from heat. Cover; let stand for 1 hour.) Drain. Bring beans and *1.2 litres water* to the boil in 4-litre saucepan over high heat. Reduce heat to low; cover and simmer 30 minutes.

2 Meanwhile, cook salt pork in 8-litre flameproof casserole over medium heat until fat is rendered. Transfer to bowl. Pour off all but 2 table-spoons fat from casserole.

3 Preheat oven to 180°C (350°F, Gas 4). Cook pork and lamb in fat in casserole, in small batches, over medium-high heat until browned, transferring pieces to bowl with salt pork.

4 Tie parsley, bay leaves and cloves together in piece of muslin. Return meats to casserole; add spice bag, beans with their liquid, sausage and next 7 ingredients.

5 Bring to the boil over high heat, stirring occasionally. Cover and bake, stirring occasionally, for 1½ hours, or until meat and beans are fork-tender. To serve, discard spice bag and skim fat from cassoulet. (Cassoulet will become very thick upon standing. Stir in enough *hot water* to reach desired consistency.) Serve in soup bowls with bread, if you like.

### BOUQUET GARNI

The traditional bouquet garni is made of sprigs of thyme and parsley and 1 or 2 bay leaves, in a muslin bag or tied together with string. The bouquet garni is always discarded at the end of cooking. To make it easy to remove, tie one end of the string to the pan handle.

EACH SERVING: ABOUT 415 CALORIES, 41g PROTEIN, 34g CARBOHYDRATE, 17g TOTAL FAT (6g SATURATED), 95mg CHOLESTEROL, 975mg SODIUM

## TEXAS CAVIAR

*Prep: 20 minutes, plus standing and chilling*
*Cook: 45 minutes    Makes 10 accompaniment servings*

450g dried black-eyed beans
125ml cider vinegar
60ml olive or vegetable oil
1 tbsp salt
2 tsp sugar
¼ tsp ground red pepper
1 small garlic clove, very finely chopped

30g fresh parsley, chopped
3 spring onions, very finely chopped
2 medium celery stalks, thinly sliced
1 hard-boiled medium egg, chopped, for garnish

◆ Rinse black-eyed beans with cold water and discard any stones or shrivelled beans. Soak beans in *water* to cover by 5cm in large bowl overnight. Drain beans and place them and *1.3 litres water* in 5-litre flameproof casserole and bring to the boil over high heat. Reduce heat to low. Cover and simmer 40 minutes, or until beans are tender. Drain.

◆ Prepare dressing: whisk vinegar, oil, salt, sugar, ground red pepper and garlic together in medium bowl. Add black-eyed beans, parsley, spring onions and celery; toss gently to coat. Cover bowl; refrigerate for at least 2 hours to blend flavours, stirring occasionally. Serve garnished with egg.

**Each serving: About 185 calories, 12g protein, 31g carbohydrate, 8g total fat (1g saturated), 21mg cholesterol, 675mg sodium**

## THREE-BEAN CASSEROLE

*Prep: 20 minutes, plus standing    Cook: about 2¾ hours*
*Makes 8 main dish servings*

125g dried cannellini beans
125g dried red kidney beans
125g dried pinto beans
2 tbsp vegetable oil
450g boneless fresh pork shoulder, cut into 2–3cm chunks
135g tomato ketchup

110g dark molasses
50g dark brown sugar
1 tbsp Worcestershire sauce
2 tsp salt
1 tsp mustard seeds
1 medium onion, thinly sliced

◆ Rinse all beans with cold water and discard any stones or shrivelled beans. Soak beans in *water* to cover by 5cm in large bowl overnight. (Or, to quick soak: bring beans and *1.3 litres water* to the boil in 5-litre flameproof casserole over high heat; boil 3 minutes. Remove from heat; cover and allow to stand 1 hour.) Drain and rinse beans.

◆ Preheat oven to 180°C (350°F, Gas 4). Heat oil in 5-litre flameproof casserole over medium-high heat. Add pork and cook until well browned. Add beans and *850ml water* to casserole; bring to the boil over high heat. Cover; bake 1 hour. Stir in tomato ketchup and remaining ingredients; re-cover and bake 1 hour longer, stirring occasionally. Uncover; bake for a further 45–50 minutes, until beans are tender, stirring occasionally.

**Each serving: About 255 calories, 21g protein, 44g carbohydrate, 5g total fat (1g saturated), 28mg cholesterol, 790mg sodium**

## HOPPIN' JOHN

*Prep: 15 minutes    Cook: 1 hour*
*Makes 8 main dish servings*

450g dried black-eyed beans
1 tbsp vegetable oil
2 medium celery stalks, coarsely chopped
1 large onion, coarsely chopped
1 medium red pepper, cored, seeded and coarsely chopped

2 garlic cloves, very finely chopped
350g smoked ham hock
800ml chicken stock
¼ tsp dried chilli flakes
1 bay leaf
Salt
400g long-grain rice
Tabasco sauce (optional)

◆ Rinse black-eyed beans with cold water; discard any stones or shrivelled beans. Soak beans in *water* to cover by 5cm in large bowl overnight. Drain and rinse beans. Heat oil in 4-litre saucepan over medium-high heat. Add next 3 ingredients; cook 10 minutes, or until golden. Add garlic; cook 30 seconds. Stir in black-eyed beans, ham hock, next 3 ingredients, ½ teaspoon salt and *900ml water*. Bring to the boil over high heat. Reduce heat to low; cover and simmer 40 minutes, or until beans are tender.

◆ Meanwhile, prepare rice as packet instructs, but use 1 teaspoon salt and do not add butter or margarine. Discard ham hock and bay leaf from beans. Gently mix mixture and cooked rice together in large bowl. Serve with Tabasco sauce, if you like.

**Each serving: About 355 calories, 20g protein, 77g carbohydrate, 3g total fat (1g saturated), 11mg cholesterol, 525mg sodium**

### WHAT'S IN A NAME?

Hoppin' John is an American dish of black-eyed beans and rice, traditionally eaten on New Year's Day. One story attributes its name to the custom of inviting guests to eat by saying 'Hop in, John.' Another story attributes it to a New Year's Day ritual in which children hopped once round the table before eating.

# CANNED BEANS

Canned beans range in colour and flavour from the nutty white chick-pea to the sweet black bean. Keep a variety in your cupboard as they are the secret to many an easy meal, whether baked in a Greek-style pie or tucked into a hearty vegetarian burrito. To achieve the best texture and appearance in your finished dish, rinse beans before using.

## GREEK GREENS AND SPINACH PIE

*Prep: 40 minutes    Bake: 30 minutes*
*Makes 8 main dish servings*

1.2kg canned cannellini beans
2 tbsp olive or vegetable oil
750g kale, tough stalks trimmed, leaves coarsely chopped
600g batavia, chopped
350g spinach, tough stalks removed, leaves coarsely chopped
½ tsp salt
½ tsp coarsely ground black pepper

2 tbsp finely chopped fresh dill or 1 tsp dried
225g feta cheese, crumbled
5 sheets fresh or frozen (thawed) filo, each about 40 by 30cm
30g butter or margarine, melted
Dill sprigs and chopped fresh dill for garnish

1 Rinse and drain 800g cannellini. Using a potato masher, mash drained beans in medium bowl. Spread evenly in 33 by 20cm ovenproof dish. Rinse and drain remaining 400g cannellini; set aside. Heat oil in 8-litre flameproof casserole over high heat. Add greens, one-third at a time, and cook, stirring, just until wilted. While greens are cooking, stir in salt and pepper. Remove from heat.

2 Add drained cannellini, chopped fresh dill and feta cheese to casserole. Spoon mixture evenly over mashed beans in baking dish. Preheat oven to 190°C (375°F, Gas 5).

3 Place 1 sheet filo on top of greens mixture in baking dish; brush filo lightly with some of melted butter.

4 Continue layering with 3 more sheets of filo, brushing each sheet lightly with some of melted butter. Top with dill sprigs arranged in pretty design. Top with remaining sheet of filo; press down gently so dill sprigs are visible through filo. Brush lightly top sheet of filo lightly with remaining butter.

5 Tuck ends of filo into dish. Bake about 30 minutes until filling is heated through and filo is lightly golden. Garnish with chopped dill; cut into squares.

EACH SERVING: ABOUT 345 CALORIES, 18g PROTEIN, 39g CARBOHYDRATE, 14g TOTAL FAT (6g SATURATED), 33mg CHOLESTEROL, 1035mg SODIUM

## ONE-PAN MIXED BEANS AND RICE MEDLEY

*Prep: 15 minutes    Cook: 30 minutes*
*Makes 5 main dish servings*

150g long-grain rice
1 tbsp vegetable oil
1 medium green pepper,
  cored, seeded and cut into
  1cm pieces
1 medium red pepper, cored,
  seeded and cut into 1cm
  pieces
1 medium onion, chopped
400g canned cannellini beans,
  rinsed and drained

400g canned chick-peas,
  rinsed and drained
400g canned red kidney
  beans, rinsed and drained
400g canned pinto beans,
  rinsed and drained
400g canned tomatoes
125ml bottled barbecue sauce

◆ Prepare rice as packet instructs. Heat oil in 30cm frying pan over medium heat. Add green and red pepper and onion and cook until vegetables are tender.

◆ Add all beans, tomatoes, barbecue sauce and *225ml water* to pepper mixture in pan; stir to combine. Bring mixture to the boil over high heat. Reduce heat to low, cover and simmer for 15 minutes.

◆ When rice is done, add rice into bean mixture; stirring until thoroughly combined.

Each serving: About 460 calories, 20g protein, 85g carbohydrate, 6g total fat (1g saturated), 0mg cholesterol, 1180mg sodium

## CORN, KIDNEY BEAN AND RICE BURRITOS

*Prep: 25 minutes    Bake: 15 minutes*
*Makes 4 main dish servings*

200g long-grain rice
400g canned red kidney beans,
  rinsed and drained
400g canned sweetcorn,
  drained
125g canned or bottled mild
  green chillies, drained and
  chopped

125g Cheddar cheese, grated
15g fresh coriander, chopped
Eight 15–18cm flour tortillas
350g bottled salsa

◆ Preheat oven to 220°C (425°F, Gas 7). Prepare rice as packet instructs.

◆ Meanwhile, combine red kidney beans, sweetcorn, green chillies, grated Cheddar and coriander in large bowl.

When rice is done, stir it into bean mixture until thoroughly combined. Spoon about 4 tablespoons rice mixture across centre of each tortilla.

◆ Spoon about 1 tablespoon salsa on top of rice mixture on each tortilla. Fold sides of tortilla over rice mixture, overlapping slightly.

◆ Grease 33 by 20cm ovenproof dish. Place burritos, seam-side down, in dish. Spoon any remaining rice mixture down centre of burritos; top with remaining salsa. Cover loosely with foil and bake 15 minutes, or until burritos are heated through.

Each serving: About 690 calories, 24g protein, 115g carbohydrate, 15g total fat (6g saturated), 25mg cholesterol, 1360mg sodium

## PINTO BEAN AND VEGETABLE HASH

*Prep: 15 minutes    Cook: 30 minutes*
*Makes 4 main dish servings*

750g potatoes, peeled and cut
  into 1cm cubes
2 tbsp vegetable oil
125g back bacon, cut into
  1cm pieces
1 large red pepper, cored,
  seeded and cut into 1cm
  pieces

400g canned pinto beans,
  rinsed and drained
4 medium eggs
Salt and coarsely ground
  black pepper (optional)

◆ Bring potatoes and enough *water* to cover to the boil in 3-litre saucepan over high heat. Reduce heat to low; cover and simmer 4 minutes, or until potatoes are almost tender. Drain.

◆ Heat oil in 30cm frying pan over medium-high heat. Add bacon, red pepper and potatoes; cook, stirring occasionally, about 15 minutes until vegetables are tender and browned. Stir in pinto beans; heat through.

◆ Meanwhile, bring *4cm water* to the boil in 26cm frying pan over high heat. Reduce heat to medium-low. Break 1 egg into cup, then, holding cup close to water's surface, carefully slip egg into simmering water. Repeat with remaining 3 eggs.

◆ Cook eggs 3–5 minutes until desired doneness. When done, carefully remove eggs, one at a time, from water with slotted spoon. Drain each egg (still held in spoon) on kitchen towels. Serve poached eggs on vegetable hash. Sprinkle eggs with salt and pepper, if you like.

Each serving: About 420 calories, 21g protein, 51g carbohydrate, 15g total fat (4g saturated), 229mg cholesterol, 795mg sodium

# LENTILS

Lentils are small, flat pulses which can be brown, red, green or yellow. They are delicious, economical, packed with nutrients and do not require the lengthy soaking and cooking times of most dried beans. In less than an hour, lentils are ready to serve – as an aromatic Indian side dish, a warm salad, a hearty pasta stew or an elegant French-style accompaniment.

## INDIAN-STYLE LENTILS

❖❖❖❖❖❖❖❖❖❖❖❖❖❖❖❖❖❖❖❖❖❖❖❖❖

*Prep:* 20 minutes    *Cook:* 35 - 45 minutes
*Makes* 6 accompaniment servings

450g sweet potatoes

1 medium onion

1 tbsp vegetable oil

1 tbsp very finely chopped peeled fresh ginger

1 large garlic clove, finely chopped

1½ tsp cumin seeds

⅛ tsp ground red pepper

175g lentils, rinsed and picked through

400ml chicken or vegetable stock

¼ tsp salt

225g plain low-fat yogurt

15g fresh mint or coriander, chopped

Mint or coriander leaves for garnish

**1** Peel sweet potatoes and cut into 2cm pieces; set aside. Finely chop onion.

**2** Heat oil in 3-litre saucepan over medium heat. Add onion and cook, stirring occasionally, 5 minutes, or until tender.

**3** Stir in ginger, garlic, cumin seeds and ground red pepper; cook, stirring, 30 seconds. Stir in sweet potatoes, lentils, stock, salt and *225ml water*. Bring to the boil over high heat.

**4** Reduce heat to low; cover and simmer 20–30 minutes, stirring occasionally, until lentils are just tender. Mix yogurt and chopped mint together in small bowl. Garnish and serve with lentils.

### INDIAN LENTIL SOUP

Follow instructions for Indian-Style Lentils, but cut sweet potatoes into 1cm dice and use 800ml stock. Simmer for 45 minutes, or until lentils are very tender. Partly mash with potato masher, if you like. Or, blend in batches in blender, or food processor with knife blade attached. Re-heat if necessary over low heat. Garnish with lemon slices.

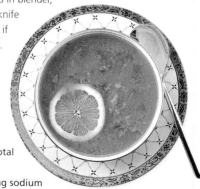

Each serving: About 185 calories, 10g protein, 34g carbohydrate, 5g total fat (1g saturated), 13mg cholesterol, 705mg sodium

**EACH SERVING: ABOUT 175 CALORIES, 9g PROTEIN, 33g CARBOHYDRATE, 4g TOTAL FAT (1g SATURATED), 8mg CHOLESTEROL, 415mg SODIUM**

## WARM LENTIL SALAD

*Prep: 10 minutes    Cook: 30–40 minutes*
*Makes 4 accompaniment servings*

| | |
|---|---|
| 175g lentils | 2 tbsp fresh lemon juice |
| 1 bay leaf | 2 tbsp olive oil |
| 1 small carrot, shredded | ¾ tsp salt |
| 1 tbsp chopped fresh mint or 1 tsp dried | ¼ tsp ground black pepper |

◆ Rinse lentils with cold water and discard any stones or shrivelled lentils.

◆ Bring lentils, bay leaf and enough *water* to cover the lentils by 5cm to the boil in 2-litre saucepan over high heat. Reduce heat to medium-low; cover and simmer 20–30 minutes, until lentils are just tender.

◆ When lentils are done, drain well; discard bay leaf. Mix lentils, carrot, mint, lemon juice, oil, salt and pepper together in medium bowl until blended.

**Each serving: About 140 calories, 8g protein, 21g carbohydrate, 7g total fat (1g saturated), 0mg cholesterol, 410mg sodium**

## LENTILS AND PASTA

*Prep: 15 minutes    Cook: 50 minutes*
*Makes 4 main dish servings*

| | |
|---|---|
| 175g lentils | 1 tbsp olive oil |
| 30g pancetta or cooked ham, chopped | ¾ tsp salt |
| 1 small onion, chopped | ¼ tsp ground black pepper |
| 1 medium carrot, chopped | 150g ditalini or small shell pasta |
| 1 medium celery stalk, chopped | 15g fresh parsley, chopped |
| 1 garlic clove, chopped | Flat-leaf parsley sprig for garnish |

◆ Rinse lentils with cold water and discard any stones or shrivelled lentils. Chop pancetta, onion, carrot, celery and garlic together until very fine.

◆ Heat olive oil in 3-litre saucepan over medium heat. Add pancetta-vegetable mixture and cook, stirring often, 10 minutes, or until tender.

◆ Stir in lentils and *675ml water*; bring to the boil over high heat. Reduce heat to low, cover and simmer 15 minutes. Stir in salt and pepper; re-cover and cook 15 minutes longer, or until lentils are just tender.

◆ Meanwhile, cook ditalini as packet instructs; drain. Stir ditalini and chopped parsley into lentils. Garnish and serve.

**Each serving: About 235 calories, 14g protein, 44g carbohydrate, 5g total fat (1g saturated), 4mg cholesterol, 535mg sodium**

## FRENCH LENTILS WITH SHALLOTS AND BRANDY

*Prep: 10 minutes    Cook: 30–35 minutes*
*Makes 6 accompaniment servings*

| | |
|---|---|
| 175g Puy lentils | 2 tbsp brandy |
| Salt | ¼ tsp ground black pepper |
| 30g butter or margarine | 15g fresh parsley, chopped |
| 50g shallots, finely chopped | |

◆ Rinse lentils with cold water and discard any stones or shrivelled lentils.

◆ Bring lentils and *450ml water* to the boil in 2-litre saucepan over high heat. Reduce heat to low; cover and simmer 20–25 minutes until lentils are just tender, adding ½ teaspoon salt halfway through cooking. Drain. Wipe saucepan clean.

◆ Melt butter in same pan over medium heat. Add chopped shallots ; cook 3 minutes, or until tender. Stir in brandy; cook 1 minute longer until almost evaporated. Stir in cooked lentils, black pepper and ¼ teaspoon salt and heat through. Stir in chopped parsley.

**Each serving: About 100 calories, 6g protein, 14g carbohydrate, 4g total fat (2g saturated), 11mg cholesterol, 315mg sodium**

### LENTILS FOR LUCK

In Italy, lentils are an indispensable part of the festivities for New Year's Eve. Associated with money because they resemble tiny coins, they symbolize prosperity in the coming year. In Tuscany, stewed lentils are served with *cotechino*, a lightly spiced pork sausage that is boiled and served in slices. Further north, in Bologna and Modena, lentils accompany *zampone*, a boned pig's foot stuffed with the same cotechino sausage mixture.

# 12
# BREADS & QUICK CAKES

# QUICK BREADS

Quick breads are wonderfully simple to make. The mixture for muffins and tea loaves, or dough for biscuits and scones, is quick to mix. Best of all, there is no rising time needed since they are leavened with bicarbonate of soda or baking powder instead of yeast.

## WHAT MAKES THEM RISE?

**Bicarbonate of soda** Once combined with an acidic ingredient (e.g., buttermilk or yogurt), it releases carbon dioxide gas that makes a dough or mixture rise. Because it begins working as soon as it is moistened, bake the dough or mixture immediately after mixing. Store bicarbonate of soda in an airtight container in a cool, dry place up to 1 year.
**Baking powder** A mixture of bicarbonate of soda and an acid (usually cream of tartar), baking powder releases some gas when it's moistened and the rest during baking. It should stay potent up to 6 months if stored in a cool, dry place. If you're uncertain if your baking powder is still active, combine ½ teaspoon with 60ml hot water. If the mixture bubbles, the baking powder is fine.

### SOURED MILK

If buttermilk is not to hand, it's easy to make a 'soured' milk that can be substitued for buttermilk in any recipe. Place 1 tablespoon fresh lemon juice or distilled white vinegar in a glass measuring jug, then pour in enough milk to equal 225ml and stir. Let stand about 5 minutes to thicken before using.

## MIXING IT RIGHT

• Be sure the rising agent is fresh (see above).
• Unless cold butter or margarine is used in the cut-in method, always start with room-temperature ingredients.
• When mixing, always combine the wet and dry ingredients just until the flour is moistened. If there are lumps in the mixture, they will smooth out during baking.
• For the cut-in method, blend the solid fat into the dry ingredients until coarse crumbs form. Stir in the liquid only until the dough comes together. Scone dough is sometimes kneaded briefly for a better texture.
• Don't over-mix the mixture or dough, or the result will be a dense, tough bread riddled with tunnels.

## BETTER BAKING

• When making a quick bread, fill the baking tin about two-thirds full. For uniform baking, smooth the top of the mixture with a rubber spatula.
• Fill muffin-tin cups two-thirds to three-quarters full. Fill empty cups half full with water to prevent the tin from warping.
• Always bake quick breads in the centre of the oven. If baking more than two loaves at once, allow some space between the tins so the hot air can circulate.
• The finished loaf often has a cracked centre, which is typical of quick breads and adds to their homely appeal.

## TESTING FOR DONENESS

Insert a cocktail stick into the centre of the loaf – it should come out clean and free of crumbs. If not, bake a few minutes longer, then test again.

## COOLING, STORING AND RE-HEATING

• Cool most quick breads in the tin 10–15 minutes so they can set. Then transfer to a wire rack to cool completely.
• Allow muffins to cool in the tin 5 minutes or they will be difficult to remove intact, then cool on a wire rack.
• The richer the mixture, the longer the bread will stay moist. Rich, dense quick loaves are even better if baked the day before. Flavours develop and they will also be firmer for easier slicing. Most muffins, scones and corn breads are best eaten or frozen the day they are made.
• To store quick breads and muffins, cool completely before wrapping in cling film, over-wrap in foil and keep at room temperature. They should stay fresh up to 3 days.
• Quick breads and muffins freeze well. Wrap tightly, excluding all air. Freeze quick breads up to 3 months, muffins up to 1 month. Thaw, still wrapped, at room temperature.
• Re-heat scones, muffins, loaves and quick cakes, wrapped in foil, at 400°F. Muffins and scones will take about 10 minutes, loaves and quick cakes, 20 minutes.
• Muffins re-heat well in the microwave. Loosely wrap in a kitchen towel and microwave for 20 seconds. Take care – sugary ingredients like jam and chocolate drops get very hot and baked goods can become tough if re-heated too long.
• Day-old muffins, scones and quick breads are good split and toasted under the grill.

# TEA-BREADS

Luscious tea-breads make a cheery breakfast or teatime treat. For a tender texture, mix these breads (leavened with baking powder or bicarbonate of soda, not yeast) just until combined. Let the baked bread rest briefly in the tin to set, then turn it out onto a wire rack to finish cooling. This prevents steam from collecting and making the bread soggy.

## APRICOT-STREUSEL LOAF

◆ ◆ ◆ ◆ ◆ ◆ ◆ ◆ ◆ ◆ ◆

*Prep: 25 minutes, plus cooling*
*Bake: 60–70 minutes*
*Makes 1 loaf, 12 servings*

**175g ready-to-eat dried apricots**
**60g pecans**
**1½ tsp baking powder**
**1 tsp bicarbonate of soda**
**375g plain flour**
**250g caster sugar**
**175g butter or margarine**
**225g soured cream**
**3 medium eggs, beaten**
**2 tsp vanilla essence**

**1** Preheat oven to 180°C (350°F, Gas 4). Grease 23 by 12cm metal loaf tin. Chop apricots and pecans; set aside. Mix baking powder, bicarbonate of soda, 300g flour and 200g sugar in large bowl. Using pastry blender or two knives used scissor-fashion, cut 125g butter into flour mixture until mixture resembles coarse crumbs.

**2** Stir in soured cream, eggs and vanilla just until flour mixture is moistened. Stir in chopped apricots and pecans. Spoon mixture into loaf tin.

**3** Prepare streusel: using your fingertips, mix remaining 75g flour, 50g sugar and 50g butter, softened, until mixture resembles coarse crumbs.

**4** Sprinkle streusel topping over cake. Bake loaf 60–70 minutes until skewer inserted in centre comes out clean. Cool in tin on wire rack 10 minutes; remove from tin. Cool completely on rack.

---

### DRIED APRICOTS

Stoned unpeeled apricots are dried to produce a very sweet, yet tangy fruit that is high in iron and niacin. They are usually treated with sulphur dioxide to preserve their rich orange colour (below, left). Dried apricots from a health food shop may be brown (below, far left) if they have not been treated. Dried apricot halves from California are firmer and more tart than the whole stoned dried apricots from Turkey, which are sweeter, softer and milder in flavour. When chopping dried apricots, dip the blade frequently in hot water to prevent the fruit sticking to it, or snip the fruit with kitchen shears.

---

EACH SERVING: ABOUT 375 CALORIES, 4g PROTEIN, 50g CARBOHYDRATE, 19g TOTAL FAT (8g SATURATED), 39mg CHOLESTEROL, 310mg SODIUM

## BLUEBERRY-LEMON TEA-BREAD

*Prep: 20 minutes, plus cooling    Bake: 65 minutes*
*Makes 1 loaf, 12 servings*

| | |
|---|---|
| 300g plain flour | 265g caster sugar |
| 2 tsp baking powder | 2 medium eggs |
| ½ tsp salt | 125ml milk |
| 125g butter or margarine, softened | 225g blueberries |
| | 60ml fresh lemon juice |

◈ Preheat oven to 180°C (350°F, Gas 4). Grease and flour 23 by 12cm metal loaf tin. Combine flour, baking powder, and salt in medium bowl. Using electric mixer on low speed, beat butter and 200g sugar just until blended in another bowl. Increase mixer speed to medium; beat about 5 minutes until light and creamy.

◈ Reduce mixer speed to low; add eggs, 1 at a time, beating after each addition until well blended, occasionally scraping bowl with rubber spatula. Alternately, beat flour mixture and milk into egg mixture, mixing just until blended. Gently stir in blueberries. Spoon the mixture into loaf tin.

◈ Bake loaf 65 minutes, or until cocktail stick inserted in centre comes out clean. Place sheet of greaseproof paper under wire rack. Cool loaf in tin on wire rack 10 minutes. Remove from tin and place on rack.

◈ Prick top and sides of warm loaf all over with skewer. Prepare lemon glaze: mix lemon juice and remaining 65g sugar together in small bowl. Using a pastry brush, brush top and sides of warm loaf with lemon glaze. Cool loaf completely on rack.

Each serving: About 255 calories, 4g protein, 41g carbohydrate, 9g total fat (4g saturated), 59mg cholesterol, 275mg sodium

◆◆◆◆◆◆◆◆◆◆◆◆◆◆◆◆◆◆◆◆◆◆

### APPLYING A GLAZE

Besides adding flavour to a tea-bread, cake or tart, a glaze gives a smooth, lustrous finish and seal in its moisture. Glazes can be as simple as melted jam, or a mixture of sugar and liquid. Set greaseproof paper under the tea-bread to catch drips. For a flavour that permates, prick the loaf all over, then brush glaze over the top and sides of the warm bread.

◆◆◆◆◆◆◆◆◆◆◆◆◆◆◆◆◆◆◆◆◆◆◆◆◆

## GOLDEN DATE-NUT BREAD

*Prep: 20 minutes, plus cooling    Bake: 1½ hours*
*Makes 1 loaf, 16 servings*

| | |
|---|---|
| 300g plain flour | 175g walnuts, coarsely chopped |
| 150g caster sugar | 225g stoned dates, chopped |
| 1 tsp baking powder | 225ml milk |
| ½ tsp salt | 2 medium eggs, lightly beaten |
| 225g butter or margarine | |

◈ Preheat oven to 190°C (325°F, Gas 5). Grease 23 by 12cm metal loaf tin. Mix flour, sugar, baking powder and salt together in large bowl. Using pastry blender or two knives used scissor-fashion, cut in butter until mixture resembles coarse crumbs. Stir in chopped walnuts, chopped dates, milk and eggs just until flour mixture is moistened. Spoon mixture into loaf tin.

◈ Bake 1½ hours, or until cocktail stick inserted in centre comes out clean. Cool loaf in tin on wire rack 10 minutes; remove from tin and cool completely on rack.

Each serving: About 325 calories, 5g protein, 36g carbohydrate, 20g total fat (6g saturated), 59mg cholesterol, 245mg sodium

## BANANA BREAD

*Prep: 20 minutes, plus cooling    Bake: 50–55 minutes*
*Makes 1 loaf, 12 servings*

| | |
|---|---|
| 300g plain flour | 2 medium eggs |
| ¾ tsp bicarbonate of soda | 2 large ripe bananas (about150g), mashed |
| ½ tsp salt | 60g walnuts, coarsely chopped |
| 150g caster sugar | |
| 90g butter or margarine, softened | |

◈ Preheat oven to 180°C (350°F, Gas 4). Grease and flour 23 by 12cm metal loaf tin. Combine flour, bicarbonate of soda and salt in medium bowl. Using electric mixer on low speed, beat sugar, butter and eggs in large bowl, just until blended. Increase mixer speed to high; beat about 5 minutes, until light and creamy.

◈ Reduce speed to low. Add mashed bananas and *60ml water*; beat until well mixed. Add flour mixture to banana mixture; beat just until blended, occasionally scraping bowl with rubber spatula. Stir in nuts. Spoon mixture into loaf tin.

◈ Bake 50–55 minutes until cocktail stick inserted in centre of loaf comes out clean. Cool in tin on wire rack 10 minutes; remove from tin and cool completely on rack.

Each serving: About 235 calories, 4g protein, 34g carbohydrate, 10g total fat (3g saturated), 52mg cholesterol, 245mg sodium

# QUICK CAKES

These easy-to-make cakes, simply mixed and baked, are just right for mid-morning coffee breaks. As a change from eating them cold, warm through and serve with custard or cream to make a satisfying but not-too-rich dessert. With fillings and toppings to make the most of the season's fruit – and even a choice for chocolate lovers – there's a home-baked treat to tempt everyone.

## APPLE AND WALNUT STREUSEL CAKE

◆◆◆◆◆◆◆◆◆◆◆◆◆◆◆◆◆◆◆◆◆◆◆◆◆

*Prep: 30 minutes, plus cooling    Bake: 45–50 minutes*
*Makes 18 servings*

125g walnuts, chopped
50g brown sugar
1 tsp ground cinnamon
475g plain flour
285g butter or margarine, softened
3 medium Golden Delicious apples

330g caster sugar
450g soured cream
1 tbsp baking powder
2 tsp bicarbonate of soda
2 tsp vanilla essence
4 medium eggs

1 Prepare streusel topping: knead walnuts, brown sugar, cinnamon, 100g flour, and 60g butter together in bowl until mixture forms large pieces.

2 Peel, core and thinly slice apples; toss with 30g caster sugar in medium bowl. Preheat oven to 180°C (350°F, Gas 4). Grease 35 by 24cm roasting tin.

3 Using mixer on medium speed, beat remaining 225g butter and 300g caster sugar together in large bowl until light and fluffy. Add soured cream, baking powder, bicarbonate of soda, vanilla, eggs and remaining 375g flour.

4 Beat mixture on low speed until blended, occasionally scraping bowl. Increase speed to medium; beat 1 minute. Spread mixture in tin to corners. Arrange apple slices on top, to edge of tin.

5 Crumble streusel topping over apple layer. Bake 45–50 minutes until cake pulls away from sides of tin. Cool in tin on wire rack 10 minutes to serve warm. Or, cool to serve later.

### WHAT'S IN A NAME?

The word 'streusel' is German for 'sprinkle' or 'strew'. Similar to a crumble topping, it refers to a sweet topping for breads, pies or cakes. Streusels are made from a mixture of flour, butter or margarine, sugar and, often, nuts and spices such as walnuts and cinnamon.

EACH SERVING: ABOUT 395 CALORIES, 5g PROTEIN, 43g CARBOHYDRATE, 23g TOTAL FAT (9g SATURATED), 93mg CHOLESTEROL, 400mg SODIUM

# RHUBARB CAKE

*Prep: 20 minutes, plus cooling    Bake: 45 minutes*
*Makes 15 servings*

| | |
|---|---|
| 100g light brown sugar | ½ tsp salt |
| 420g plain flour | 2 medium eggs |
| 1 tsp ground cinnamon | 225ml buttermilk or soured |
| 150g butter or margarine | milk (see page 392) |
| 200g caster sugar | 2 tsp vanilla essence |
| 1 tbsp baking powder | 600g rhubarb, cut into 2–3cm |
| 1 tsp bicarbonate of soda | chunks |

◈ Prepare streusel topping: using fingertips, mix brown sugar, 120g flour, cinnamon and 90g butter together in medium bowl until mixture resembles coarse crumbs; set aside. Preheat oven to 190°C (375°F, Gas 5).

◈ Grease and flour 33 by 20cm metal baking tin. Combine remaining 300g flour, caster sugar and next 3 ingredients together in large bowl. Using pastry blender or two knives used scissor-fashion, cut in remaining 60g butter until mixture resembles coarse crumbs.

◈ Using fork or whisk, beat eggs with buttermilk and vanilla in small bowl. Stir into flour mixture just until flour is moistened. Spoon mixture into baking tin.

◈ Place rhubarb chunks evenly over mixture in baking tin. Sprinkle streusel topping over rhubarb. Bake 45 minutes, or until cocktail stick inserted in centre comes out clean.

◈ Cool cake in tin on wire rack 10 minutes to serve warm. Or, cool completely to serve later.

**Each serving: About 250 calories, 4g protein, 40g carbohydrate, 9g total fat (4g saturated), 47mg cholesterol, 370mg sodium**

# GINGER-PEACH CAKE

*Prep: 25 minutes, plus cooling    Bake: 1¼ hours*
*Makes 15 servings*

| | |
|---|---|
| 450g plain flour | 3 medium eggs |
| 1½ tsp bicarbonate of soda | 2 tsp vanilla essence |
| 1½ tsp baking powder | 90g crystallized ginger, finely |
| ½ tsp salt | chopped |
| 300g caster sugar | 4 medium peaches (about |
| 175g butter or margarine, | 750g), peeled, stoned and |
| softened | cut into 1cm wedges |
| 450ml soured cream | |

◈ Preheat oven to 180°C (350°F, Gas 4). Grease and flour 33 by 20cm metal baking tin. Combine flour, bicarbonate of soda, baking powder and salt in medium bowl. Using electric mixer on low speed, beat sugar and butter together in large bowl until blended.

◈ Increase speed to medium; beat 2 minutes, occasionally scraping bowl with rubber spatula. Add soured cream, eggs and vanilla; beat 1 minute, or until blended.

◈ Reduce speed to low. Add flour mixture; beat until well mixed. Increase speed to medium; beat 2 minutes, occasionally scraping bowl. Stir in ginger.

◈ Spread mixture in tin; arrange peach wedges in 3 lengthways rows on top. Bake 1¼ hours, or until cocktail stick inserted in centre of cake comes out clean. Cool in tin on wire rack 10 minutes to serve warm. Or, cool completely to serve later.

**Each serving: About 325 calories, 5g protein, 48g carbohydrate, 12g total fat (4g saturated), 78mg cholesterol, 390mg sodium**

# CHOCOLATE-CHERRY CAKE

*Prep: 30 minutes, plus cooling    Bake: 70 minutes*
*Makes 16 servings*

| | |
|---|---|
| 100g plain chocolate drops | 1½ tsp baking powder |
| 1 tbsp cocoa | 2 tsp vanilla essence |
| 2 tsp ground cinnamon | ½ tsp salt |
| 330g caster sugar | 450ml soured cream |
| 175g butter or margarine, | 3 medium eggs |
| softened | 125g dried cherries |
| 450g plain flour | Icing sugar for decoration |
| 1½ tsp bicarbonate of soda | |

◈ Preheat oven to 170°C (325°F, Gas 3). Grease and flour 25cm Bundt or kugelhopf tin. Combine chocolate drops, cocoa, cinnamon and 65g sugar in small bowl; set aside.

◈ Using electric mixer on low speed, beat butter and remaining 265g sugar in large bowl until blended. Increase speed to medium; beat 2 minutes, or until light and creamy, occasionally scraping bowl with rubber spatula.

◈ Reduce speed to low. Add flour and next 6 ingredients; beat until well mixed. Increase speed to medium; beat 2 minutes, occasionally scraping bowl. Stir in dried cherries.

◈ Spread one-third of cake mixture in Bundt tin; sprinkle with half of chocolate mixture. Top with half of remaining cake mixture; sprinkle with remaining chocolate mixture. Spread remaining cake mixture on top.

◈ Bake 70 minutes, or until cocktail stick inserted in centre comes out clean. Cool cake in tin on wire rack 10 minutes. Invert cake onto rack to cool completely. To serve, sift icing sugar over top of cake.

**Each serving: About 345 calories, 5g protein, 50g carbohydrate, 14g total fat (5g saturated), 72mg cholesterol, 360mg sodium**

# MUFFINS

Warm, fragrant muffins make a delicious snack and can be baked in minutes. A whole host of extras can be added to the basic mixture – juicy berries, moist apples or even chocolate drops. For a tender texture, use a light hand when mixing the wet and dry ingredients (stir the mixture just until the flour is moistened), then gently fold in the added extras, and bake.

## APPLE-BUTTERMILK MUFFINS

❖ ❖ ❖ ❖ ❖ ❖ ❖ ❖ ❖ ❖ ❖

*Prep: 20 minutes*
*Bake: 25 minutes*
*Makes 12*

**2 medium Golden Delicious apples**
**300g plain flour**
**100g light brown sugar**
**2 tsp baking powder**
**1 tsp bicarbonate of soda**
**½ tsp salt**
**225ml buttermilk or soured milk (see page 392)**
**60ml vegetable oil**
**2 tsp vanilla essence**
**1 medium egg**
**60g walnuts, chopped (optional)**
**1 tbsp caster sugar**
**1 tsp ground cinnamon**

**1** Preheat oven to 200°C (400°F, Gas 6). Grease standard 12-hole muffin tin. Peel, core and dice apples. Mix flour, brown sugar, baking powder, bicarbonate of soda and salt in large bowl. Using whisk or fork, mix buttermilk, oil, vanilla essence and egg together in small bowl until blended.

**2** Stir buttermilk mixture into flour mixture just until moistened (mixture will be lumpy). Fold in apples and walnuts, if using. Spoon mixture evenly into muffin tin.

**3** Mix caster sugar and cinnamon together in cup; sprinkle over muffins. Bake 25 minutes, or until cocktail stick inserted in centres comes out clean. Remove muffins from tin and serve warm. Or, cool on wire rack; re-heat if desired.

---

### MUFFIN TINS

A standard muffin tin has 12 holes to the tin, each measuring about 7cm wide by 3cm deep. A mini version is also available, with 12 holes to the tin, each measuring just 4.5cm wide and 2cm deep.

Fill muffin tins two-thirds to three-quarters full with mixture to allow for rising. (If you don't use all the cups, fill the empty ones halfway with water so the tin won't warp while it is in the oven.) Always bake muffins as soon as the mixture is ready, before the leavening loses any of its rising power. Turn muffins out of the tin onto a wire rack as soon as they come out of the oven. If they are left in the tin the bottoms will become soggy from the trapped steam.

---

EACH MUFFIN: ABOUT 210 CALORIES, 4g PROTEIN, 30g CARBOHYDRATE, 8g TOTAL FAT (1g SATURATED), 19mg CHOLESTEROL, 305mg SODIUM

## BASIC MUFFINS

*Prep:* 10 minutes    *Bake:* 20–25 minutes
*Makes 12*

375g plain flour
65g caster sugar
1 tbsp baking powder
½ tsp salt
1 medium egg
225ml milk
75g butter or margarine, melted
1 tsp vanilla essence

◆ Preheat oven to 200°C (400°F, Gas 6). Grease 12-hole standard muffin tin. Mix flour, sugar, baking powder and salt together in large bowl. Using wire whisk or fork, mix egg, milk, melted margarine, and vanilla essence in medium bowl; stir into flour mixture just until moistened (mixture will be lumpy).

◆ Spoon mixture into muffin tin. Bake 20–25 minutes, until cocktail stick inserted in centre of muffins comes out clean. Remove muffins from tin; serve warm. Or, cool on wire rack to serve later; re-heat if desired.

**Each muffin: About 175 calories, 4g protein, 25g carbohydrate, 6g total fat (3g saturated), 34mg cholesterol, 285mg sodium**

### MUFFINS PLUS

Make the Basic Muffins mixture above and then add one of the following:

**Blueberry or raspberry muffins** Fold in 150g blueberries or raspberries.

**Chocolate chip muffins** Fold in 150g plain chocolate drops.

**Walnut or pecan muffins** Fold in 60g chopped toasted walnuts or pecans. Sprinkle with a little sugar before baking.

**Orange muffins** Add 1 teaspoon grated orange rind to dry ingredients. Sprinkle with a little sugar before baking.

## CARROT-BRAN MUFFINS

*Prep:* 15 minutes, plus standing
*Bake:* 30 minutes    *Makes 12*

1 medium egg
225ml milk
60ml vegetable oil
55g all-bran cereal
110g carrots, finely grated
165g plain flour
65g caster sugar
1 tbsp baking powder
½ tsp salt
¼ tsp ground cinnamon
150g raisins

◆ Preheat oven to 200°C (400°F, Gas 6). Grease 12-hole standard muffin tin.

◆ Using wire whisk or fork, combine egg, milk, oil, all-bran cereal and grated carrots in medium bowl until blended; let stand 10 minutes. Mix flour, sugar, baking powder, salt, and cinnamon together in large bowl. Stir bran mixture into flour mixture just until moistened (mixture will be lumpy). Fold in raisins.

◆ Spoon mixture into muffin tin. Bake 30 minutes, or until cocktail stick inserted in centre of muffins comes out clean. Remove muffins from tin; serve warm. Or, cool on wire rack to serve later; re-heat if desired.

**Each muffin: About 190 calories, 4g protein, 34g carbohydrate, 6g total fat (1g saturated), 21mg cholesterol, 350mg sodium**

## BLUEBERRY CORN MUFFINS

*Prep:* 15 minutes    *Bake:* 20–25 minutes
*Makes 12*

150g plain flour
125g coarse yellow cornmeal
100g caster sugar
2 tsp baking powder
1 tsp bicarbonate of soda
½ tsp salt
225ml buttermilk or soured milk (see page 392)
60ml vegetable oil
2 tsp vanilla essence
1 medium egg
225g blueberries or 155g raspberries

◆ Preheat oven to 200°C (400°F, Gas 6). Grease 12-hole standard muffin tin.

◆ Mix first 6 ingredients together in large bowl. Using wire whisk or fork, mix buttermilk, vegetable oil, vanilla essence and egg until blended in small bowl; stir into flour mixture just until moistened (mixture will be lumpy). Fold in berries.

◆ Spoon mixture into muffin tin. Bake 20–25 minutes, until cocktail stick inserted in centre of muffins comes out clean. Remove muffins from tin; serve warm. Or, cool on wire rack to serve later; re-heat if desired.

**Each muffin: About 175 calories, 3g protein, 29g carbohydrate, 5g total fat (1g saturated), 19mg cholesterol, 305mg sodium**

Blueberry corn muffins

Carrot-bran muffins

Chocolate chip muffins

# CORN BREAD

Corn bread is at its best eaten warm and fresh. It's the classic American accompaniment to a bowl of chilli, but it also goes well with lots of other meals. While plain hot corn bread is delicious, flavourings such as cheese, chillies and sweetcorn help make an extra-special bread. For variety, bake a batch of crispy golden corn sticks.

## CHEDDAR AND GREEN CHILLI CORN BREAD

*Prep: 20 minutes    Bake: 25–30 minutes*
*Makes 15 servings*

225g Cheddar cheese
225g plain flour
185g coarse yellow cornmeal
50g caster sugar
1 tbsp baking powder
½ tsp salt
240g canned creamed sweetcorn

125g bottled mild green chillies, drained and chopped
1 small onion, grated
2 medium eggs
175ml milk
60g butter or margarine, melted

**1** Preheat oven to 200°C (400°F, Gas 6). Grease 33 by 20cm metal baking tin. Grate Cheddar cheese. Mix flour and next 4 ingredients together in large bowl.

**2** Beat Cheddar cheese, sweetcorn, chillies, onion, eggs, milk and melted butter in medium bowl until blended; stir into flour mixture just until flour is moistened (mixture will be lumpy).

**3** Spread mixture evenly in tin. Bake 25–30 minutes, until cocktail stick inserted in centre comes out clean. Cut lengthways into 3 strips; cut strips into 5 pieces. Serve warm, or cool in pan on wire rack to serve later.

### THE ALL-AMERICAN BREAD

Corn bread is the classic American bread; native Americans made hundreds of different flat breads using ground sweetcorn, and later colonists developed their own variations. Southerners prefer their corn bread unsweetened and use white rather than yellow cornmeal. For a browned, crisp crust, they bake it in a shallow pan or, better still, in a preheated, greased cast-iron frying pan. In the north, corn bread is on the sweeter, fluffier side, and yellow cornmeal is the rule. Southwestern cooks often use blue cornmeal in the mixture.

A higher proportion of flour makes a lighter corn bread, while more cornmeal makes a denser, drier bread with a more intense flavour. Buttermilk, which frequently appears in recipes of all regions, adds tenderness to the finished bread.

EACH SERVING: ABOUT 225 CALORIES, 8g PROTEIN, 28g CARBOHYDRATE, 9g TOTAL FAT (5g SATURATED), 55mg CHOLESTEROL, 455mg SODIUM

## SWEET-POTATO CORN STICKS

*Prep: 30 to 35 minutes, plus cooling    Bake: 10–15 minutes*
*Makes 15*

250g sweet potatoes, peeled
  and cut into quarters
190g plain flour
125g coarse yellow cornmeal
2½ tsp baking powder

1 tsp salt
60g butter or margarine
280ml milk
165g brown sugar
1 medium egg

◆ Bring sweet potatoes and enough *water* to cover to the boil in 3-litre saucepan over high heat. Reduce heat to low; cover and simmer 15–20 minutes, until sweet potatoes are fork-tender; drain well.

◆ Meanwhile, preheat oven to 200°C (400°F, Gas 6). Generously grease 15 corn-stick moulds (3 pans, 5 moulds each) or 28 by 19cm metal baking tin.

◆ Mix flour and next 3 ingredients together in large bowl. With pastry blender or two knives used scissor-fashion, cut in butter until mixture resembles coarse crumbs.

◆ Using potato masher, mash sweet potatoes with milk and brown sugar in large bowl until smooth; stir in egg. Stir into flour mixture until just blended. Spoon mixture into corn-stick moulds or baking tin.

◆ Bake 10–15 minutes, until cocktail stick inserted in centre of a corn stick comes out clean (if using baking tin, bake 15 minutes).

◆ Cool in moulds on wire rack 5 minutes. Remove corn sticks from moulds (if using baking tin, cut into 14 pieces). Serve warm. Or, cool on wire rack; re-heat just before serving, if desired.

**Each piece: About 160 calories, 3g protein, 26g carbohydrate, 5g total fat (2g saturated), 27mg cholesterol, 295mg sodium**

---

### CORN STICK MOULDS

The secret to making whimsically shaped corn sticks is a special cast-iron mould with depressions shaped like ears of corn. You can find these pans in speciality kitchen shops. Grease the moulds generously to prevent the mixture sticking, and to encourage a crunchy, nicely browned crust. Use a fork to ease the baked corn sticks from the pan.

---

## CORN BREAD IN A PAN

*Prep: 10 minutes    Bake: 25–30 minutes*
*Makes 8 servings*

190g plain flour
155g coarse yellow cornmeal
1 tbsp baking powder
2 tsp caster sugar
1 tsp salt
225ml milk

2 medium eggs
240g canned creamed
  sweetcorn
60g butter or margarine,
  melted

◆ Preheat oven to 220°C (425°F, Gas 7). Generously grease 26cm cast-iron frying pan with ovenproof handle or 20cm square metal baking pan. Mix flour, cornmeal, baking powder, sugar and salt together in large bowl.

◆ Using fork or whisk, mix milk, eggs, corn and melted butter together in medium bowl. Stir milk mixture into flour mixture just until combined; do not overmix.

◆ Pour mixture into frying pan. Bake 25–30 minutes until cocktail stick inserted in centre of bread comes out clean. Serve warm. Or, loosen edge with knife, remove from pan, and cool on wire rack to serve later.

**Each serving: About 260 calories, 7g protein, 39g carbohydrate, 9g total fat (3g saturated), 73mg cholesterol, 635mg sodium**

## SOUTHERN CORN BREAD

*Prep: 10 minutes    Bake: 25 minutes*
*Makes 8 servings*

60g butter or margarine
185g coarse white or yellow
  cornmeal
150g plain flour
2 tsp baking powder

¼ tsp bicarbonate of soda
1 tsp salt
2 medium eggs
400ml buttermilk or soured
  milk (see page 392)

◆ Preheat oven to 230°C (450°F, Gas 8). Place butter in 26cm cast-iron frying pan with ovenproof handle or 22cm square metal baking tin; place in oven 3–5 minutes, just until butter is melted.

◆ Meanwhile, mix cornmeal, flour, baking powder, bicarbonate of soda and salt together in large bowl. Whisk together eggs and buttermilk in medium bowl. Add melted butter to buttermilk mixture; stir into flour mixture just until moistened (mixture will be lumpy; do not overmix).

◆ Pour mixture into frying pan. Bake 25 minutes, or until wooden cocktail stick inserted in centre comes out clean. Serve warm.

**Each serving: 240 calories, 7g protein, 34g carbohydrate, 7g total fat (2g saturated), 71mg cholesterol, 565mg sodium**

# SCONES

Light, fluffy scones, served warm from the oven with golden honey or jam, promise to make any afternoon brighter. Our classic Buttermilk Scones are perfectly simple, but you'll also love our flavoured variations, flecked with fresh herbs, cheese or smoky bacon. Or, try the wholemeal, oatmeal or sweet-potato scones.

## BUTTERMILK SCONES

◆ ◆ ◆ ◆ ◆ ◆ ◆ ◆ ◆ ◆ ◆ ◆

*Prep: 10 minutes*
*Bake: 12 to 14 minutes*
*Makes 13*

**240g unsifted plain flour**
**1½ tsp baking powder**
**½ tsp bicarbonate of soda**
**½ teaspoon salt**
**60g white vegetable fat**
**175ml buttermilk or soured milk (see page 392)**

1 Preheat oven to 230°C (450°F, Gas 8). Mix flour and next 3 ingredients together in large bowl. Using pastry blender, or two knives used scissor-fashion, cut in vegetable fat until mixture resembles coarse crumbs.

2 Add buttermilk and stir just until moistened. Turn dough onto lightly floured surface and knead about 6–8 times, just until smooth. Roll or pat out dough 2cm thick.

3 Cut out scones with 5cm biscuit cutter. Press trimmings together; roll and cut out more scones. Place scones, 2–3cm apart, on ungreased baking sheet. Bake 12–14 minutes, until lightly golden. Serve warm.

### SCONE BASICS

For the lightest scones, handle the dough as little as possible. When cutting them out, 'punch' downward sharply with the cutter and don't twist, or you will seal the edges so the scones will not rise properly.

If you don't have a biscuit cutter, just cut the dough into squares with a sharp knife. Or, even simpler, serve any of these recipes as one giant scone cut into wedges. For a giant scone, follow shaping instructions for Olive-Rosemary Scones, page 404. Place the giant scone on a lightly greased baking sheet, brush the top with milk and score the top to mark out 12 wedges. Bake about 10 minutes longer than for individual scones. Cool slightly on wire rack and serve warm.

### SAVOURY SCONES

**Cheddar scones** Reduce amount of vegetable fat to 30g. Grate 125g Cheddar cheese into flour mixture with vegetable fat.

**Black pepper and bacon scones** Add ½ teaspoon coarsely ground black pepper to flour mixture. After cutting in vegetable fat, stir 3 rashers, cooked and crumbled bacon into flour mixture.

**Parsley-chive scones** After cutting in vegetable fat, stir in 2 tablespoons chopped fresh parsley and 2 tablespoons chopped fresh chives.

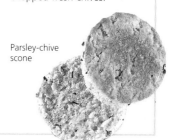

Parsley-chive scone

EACH BISCUIT: ABOUT 100 CALORIES, 2g PROTEIN, 14g CARBOHYDRATE, 4g TOTAL FAT (1g SATURATED), 1mg CHOLESTEROL, 200mg SODIUM

## WHOLEMEAL SESAME SCONES

*Prep:* 15 minutes    *Bake:* 12–15 minutes

*Makes* 12

2 tbsp sesame seeds
150g wholemeal flour
150g plain flour
1 tbsp baking powder
¾ tsp salt
60g butter or margarine
175ml plus 3 tbsp milk

◆ Toast sesame seeds in small frying pan over medium heat, stirring occasionally, about 5 minutes, until lightly browned.

◆ Preheat oven to 220°C (425°F, Gas 7). Reserve 1 teaspoon sesame seeds. Mix wholemeal flour, plain flour, baking powder, salt, and remaining sesame seeds together in large bowl. With pastry blender, or two knives used scissor-fashion, cut in butter until mixture resembles coarse crumbs.

◆ Stir in 175ml plus 2 tablespoons milk just until mixture forms soft dough that leaves side of bowl.

◆ Turn out dough onto lightly floured surface; knead 6–8 times, just until smooth. With floured rolling pin, roll dough 1cm thick.

◆ Using 6cm biscuit cutter, cut out scones. Gently press trimmings together; roll and cut out more scones. Using a metal spatula, place scones 2–3cm apart, on ungreased large baking sheet.

◆ Brush tops of scones with remaining 1 tablespoon milk; sprinkle reserved sesame seeds on top.

◆ Bake scones 12–15 minutes, until golden. Serve scones warm, or cool on wire rack.

**Each scone: About 125 calories, 3g protein, 16g carbohydrate, 5g total fat (2g saturated), 14mg cholesterol, 310mg sodium**

## OATMEAL SCONES

*Prep:* 15 minutes    *Bake:* 12–15 minutes

*Makes* 20

80g rolled oats
525g plain flour
70g light brown sugar
4 tsp baking powder
1½ tsp salt
½ tsp bicarbonate of soda
125g butter or margarine
175g pecans, chopped
½ tsp maple syrup (optional)
350ml plus 2 tbsp buttermilk or soured milk (see page 392)

◆ Preheat oven to 230°C (450°F, Gas 8). Reserve 2 tablespoons oats. Mix flour, next 4 ingredients and remaining oats together in large bowl. Using pastry blender, or two knives used scissor-fashion, cut in butter until mixture resembles coarse crumbs; stir in chopped pecans.

◆ Stir maple syrup, if using, into 350ml buttermilk; stir buttermilk mixture into flour mixture just until soft dough that leaves side of bowl forms.

◆ Turn out dough onto lightly floured surface; knead 6–8 times, just until smooth. Using floured rolling pin, roll dough 1cm thick.

◆ Using 7–8cm biscuit cutter, cut out scones. Gently press trimmings together; roll and cut out more scones. Using a metal spatula, place scones 2–3cm apart, on 2 ungreased large baking sheets.

◆ Brush tops of scones with remaining 2 tablespoons buttermilk; sprinkle reserved oats on top.

◆ Bake scones 12–15 minutes, until golden, rotating baking sheets between upper and lower racks halfway through baking time. Serve scones warm, or cool on wire rack.

**Each scone: About 220 calories, 5g protein, 27g carbohydrate, 11g total fat (3g saturated), 14mg cholesterol, 365mg sodium**

## SWEET POTATO SCONES

*Prep:* 30 minutes, plus cooling

*Bake:* 12–15 minutes    *Makes* 20

450g sweet potatoes, peeled and cut into 5cm chunks
600g plain flour
100g light brown sugar
5 tsp baking powder
1 tsp salt
150g butter or margarine
75ml milk

◆ Bring sweet potatoes and enough *water* to cover to boil in saucepan over high heat. Reduce heat to low; cover and simmer 12–15 minutes, until potatoes are fork-tender. Drain well.

◆ Mash sweet potatoes in medium bowl until smooth using potato masher. Set aside to cool.

◆ Preheat oven to 220°C (425°F, Gas 7). Combine flour, brown sugar, baking powder and salt in large bowl. Using pastry blender, or two knives used scissor-fashion, cut in butter until mixture resembles coarse crumbs.

◆ Stir in milk and cooled mashed sweet potatoes; mix just until combined.

◆ Turn out dough onto lightly floured surface; pat into 20cm square. Cut dough in half. Cut each half into 10 equal pieces. Using metal spatula, place scones 2–3cm apart, on 2 ungreased large baking sheets.

◆ Place baking sheets on 2 oven racks; bake scones 12–15 minutes, until golden, rotating baking sheets between upper and lower racks halfway through baking time. Serve scones warm, or cool on wire rack.

**Each scone: About 175 calories, 3g protein, 28g carbohydrate, 6g total fat (2g saturated), 17mg cholesterol, 300mg sodium**

# SODA BREAD AND MORE SCONES

Although rarely baked today in the traditional cast-iron pot over an open hearth, soda bread is still the staff of life in parts of Ireland. A plain wholemeal version appears at many meals, but the addition of raisins and caraway seeds makes it special. Scones, made from a similar, very lightly kneaded dough, are often richer – especially when served with strawberry jam and clotted cream for a cream tea.

## WHOLE-GRAIN SODA BREAD

❖❖❖❖❖❖❖❖❖❖❖❖❖❖❖❖❖❖❖❖❖❖❖❖❖❖❖❖❖❖❖

*Prep:* 15 minutes, plus cooling   *Bake:* 1 hour
*Makes* 1 loaf, 12 servings

225g plain flour, plus extra
  for sprinkling
225g wholemeal flour
80g rolled oats
50g caster sugar
1 tbsp baking powder
1½ tsp salt

1 tsp bicarbonate of soda
90g butter or margarine
225g sultanas
2 tsp caraway seeds
350ml buttermilk or soured
  milk (see page 392)

**1** Preheat oven to 180°C (350°F, Gas 4). Mix plain flour and next 6 ingredients in large bowl. Using pastry blender or two knives used scissor-fashion, cut in butter until mixture resembles coarse crumbs.

**2** Stir in raisins and caraway seeds. Stir in buttermilk just until flour is moistened (dough will be sticky). Grease baking sheet.

**3** Turn dough onto well-floured surface. Using floured hands, knead 8–10 times to mix thoroughly. (Do not over-mix, or bread will be tough.) Shape into ball; place on baking sheet.

**4** Sprinkle ball lightly with plain flour. Cut 10cm cross in centre, about 5mm deep. Bake 1 hour, or until cocktail stick inserted in centre comes out clean. Remove from baking sheet; cool on wire rack.

### BUTTERMILK

In the past, buttermilk was the liquid left over when cream was churned into butter. Now commercially produced buttermilk is made by adding special bacterial cultures to low-fat milk. These turn the milk's natural sugar to acid, producing a thicker milk with a tangy taste. You can also substitute yogurt, or milk soured with lemon juice or vinegar (see page 392).

Buttermilk is a traditional ingredient in Irish soda bread, and is often used in other tea-breads; its acidity causes the baking powder or bicarbonate of soda to release carbon dioxide gas so the bread can rise. It makes extra-tender pancakes, scones and cakes. Or, add buttermilk to cold soups and salad dressings for a creamy effect with less fat.

EACH SERVING: ABOUT 300 CALORIES, 8g PROTEIN, 54g CARBOHYDRATE, 7g TOTAL FAT (3g SATURATED), 15mg CHOLESTEROL, 595mg SODIUM

# RICH SCONES

*Prep: 15 minutes    Bake: 15–20 minutes*
*Makes 8*

| | |
|---|---|
| 525g plain flour | 90g butter or margarine |
| 2 tbsp baking powder | 2 medium eggs, beaten |
| ½ tsp salt | 225ml plus 1 tbsp single |
| 100g plus 1 tbsp caster sugar | cream |

◆ Preheat oven to 200°C (400°F, Gas 6). Grease large baking sheet.

◆ Mix flour, baking powder, salt and 100g sugar in large bowl. Using pastry blender or two knives used scissor-fashion, cut in butter until mixture resembles coarse crumbs.

◆ Stir eggs and 225ml single cream into mixture in bowl just until ingredients are blended.

◆ Spoon dough onto floured surface (dough will be sticky). Using lightly floured hands, pat dough into 23cm round.

◆ Brush remaining 1 tablespoon cream over dough; sprinkle with remaining 1 tablespoon sugar. Using knife, cut dough into 8 wedges. Using metal spatula, place scones, 7–8cm apart, on baking sheet.

◆ Bake 15–20 minutes until golden. Serve scones warm, or remove from baking sheet and cool on wire rack to re-heat later.

**Each scone: About 365 calories, 8g protein, 54g carbohydrate, 14g total fat (6g saturated), 89mg cholesterol, 630mg sodium**

---

## SCONES PLUS

**Lemon-walnut scones**
Prepare Rich Scones as above, but add 1 teaspoon grated lemon rind with flour mixture; add 125g chopped walnuts with eggs and single cream.

**Currant scones** Prepare Rich Scones as above, but add 90g dried currants with eggs and single cream.

Lemon-walnut scone

Currant scone

---

# OLIVE-ROSEMARY SCONES

*Prep: 15 minutes, plus cooling    Bake: 20–25 minutes*
*Makes 12*

| | |
|---|---|
| 450g plain flour | 1 tsp bicarbonate of soda |
| 60g butter or margarine, cut | ½ tsp salt |
| into 4 pieces | 60ml plus 1 tbsp olive oil |
| 1 tbsp caster sugar | 225ml milk |
| 1 tbsp baking powder | 1 medium egg |
| 2 tsp chopped fresh rosemary | 75g Kalamata olives, stoned |
| or ¼ tsp dried, crushed | and coarsely chopped |

◆ Preheat oven to 220°C (425°F, Gas 7). Lightly grease large baking sheet. Blend flour, butter, caster sugar, baking powder, chopped rosemary, bicarbonate of soda, salt and 60ml olive oil in food processor with knife blade attached, pulsing processor on and off until mixture resembles coarse crumbs.

◆ Mix milk and egg in small bowl; pour mixture through feed tube into flour mixture, pulsing just until blended. Turn dough onto lightly floured surface; using floured hands, press olives into dough. Place dough on baking sheet; pat into 25cm round (dough will be sticky).

◆ Using floured knife, cut round into 12 equal wedges, but do not separate wedges. Brush top with remaining 1 tablespoon olive oil. Bake scones 20–25 minutes, until golden. Remove from baking sheet; cool slightly on wire rack to serve warm.

**Each scone: About 230 calories, 4g protein, 25g carbohydrate, 12g total fat (3g saturated), 32mg cholesterol, 475mg sodium**

---

# BEER BREAD

*Prep: 10 minutes, plus cooling    Bake: 40 minutes*
*Makes 1 loaf, 12 servings*

| | |
|---|---|
| 450g plain flour | 350ml lager |
| 50g light brown sugar | 60g butter or margarine, |
| 1 tbsp baking powder | melted |
| ¾ tsp salt | |

◆ Preheat oven to 190°C (375°F, Gas 5). Grease 23 by 12cm loaf tin. Mix flour, brown sugar, baking powder and salt in large bowl until evenly combined. Stir in beer and melted butter just until moistened (mixture will be lumpy).

◆ Spoon mixture into loaf tin and bake 40 minutes, or until golden and cocktail stick inserted in centre comes out clean. Cool in tin on wire rack 5 minutes; remove from tin and cool completely on rack.

**Each serving: 170 calories, 3g protein, 28g carbohydrate, 4g total fat (2g saturated), 11mg cholesterol, 305mg sodium**

# YEAST BREADS KNOW-HOW

There are dozens of scrumptious breads, rolls, cakes and flat breads that use yeast as a rising agent. While they are not as fast to prepare as quick breads, most yeast breads can be mixed, kneaded and shaped in less than half an hour – the rest is simply unattended rising time. What's more, easy-blend yeast speeds the traditional process considerably.

## TYPES OF YEAST

Yeast is a tiny living organism that causes fermentation. It makes bread rise by converting the natural sugars in flour into bubbles of carbon dioxide gas, which expand during baking and give it a yeasty flavour.

**Dried yeast** Dehydrated granules of baker's yeast; this is the type most commonly used in baking. Easy-blend yeast is a high-activity dry yeast that makes dough rise about 50 per cent faster. It can replace dried yeast in equal amounts; follow the packet instructions carefully. Store either type in a cool, dry place until opened, then refrigerate.

**Fresh yeast** Moist and crumbly, fresh yeast is highly perishable. It is available from some supermarket bakery counters and some delicatessens. Store in the refrigerator up to 2 weeks (or until the expiry date) or freeze up to 3 months. Use any thawed fresh yeast right away.

## DE-MYSTIFYING YEAST

• Yeast should be reliable until the expiry date.
• Since yeast works best in a moderately warm environment, have all ingredients at room temperature before you begin.
• To activate yeast, combine it with warm liquid. Liquid that is too hot kills yeast, while cold liquid slows its growth. To avoid guesswork, use a thermometer to check.
• Yeast doughs require a warm place to rise, ideally 27–29.5°C, so the yeast can grow and the dough expand. Avoid draughty areas, or the dough will rise unevenly. Dough will rise successfully in an unheated oven. Place the dough in a covered bowl on a shelf with a large bowl of hot water underneath it.
• Since sugar speeds yeast growth, it is usually added to the liquid. Fat slows yeast growth, which is why rich doughs are slower to rise. Salt inhibits rising, but a little salt helps control the rate of yeast fermentation.
• Extra yeast is sometimes added to speed up leavening, but produces a more porous loaf with a yeastier flavour. Batter bread recipes often call for more yeast than other types.

## KNOW YOUR FLOURS

A variety of flours can be used for bread-making. Flours vary in their content of gluten, a protein that gives bread its strength and elasticity. Breads typically call for strong plain flour, made entirely from hard wheat. Wholemeal, stoneground and rye flours can also be used, often combined with plain flour for a lighter loaf. Cornmeal, oats and semolina can be added to vary a basic dough.

Store strong plain flour in an airtight container in a cool, dry place for up to 12 months and wholemeal varieties up to 3 months. For longer storage, keep flour in the freezer.

**Strong plain flour** Milled from hard or durum wheat which has a high protein and gluten content, strong plain flour makes an elastic dough and is it the most suitable for bread.
**Rye flour** With a low gluten content, rye flour makes a slightly less elastic dough than flour milled from wheat and for this reason the two are often combined.
**Stoneground flour** Made using the old fashioned method of grinding between two stones rather than the modern milling process, stoneground flour has a better flavour than other flours, but doesn't last well.
**Wholemeal flour** Milled from the whole grain, with nothing added or removed, this is the most nutritious of all flours.

Strong plain    Rye

Stoneground    Wholemeal

## KNEADING

Strong, steady kneading develops the gluten in dough to create an evenly textured loaf that is free of holes or dense spots. Knead for 5 to 10 minutes, working in just as much flour as the dough can absorb. Too much flour makes a dry, heavy loaf. Dough is ready when it is smooth and elastic and tiny blisters appear just below the surface. You can also use a food processor or heavy-duty mixer for kneading, but take care not to overload it or you could damage the motor.

Place dough on lightly floured surface. Using the heel of your hand, push dough down and away with rolling motion. Give it a quarter turn; fold, then push down again. Repeat until dough is smooth and tiny blisters appear.

## RISING AND SHAPING

1 Dough should rise until it doubles in size. To test, press a finger 1cm into centre. If the dent stays, dough has risen sufficiently. If the dent fills in, dough needs more rising time.

2 To knock back dough, push your fist into the centre (this distributes carbon dioxide for a fine-textured result), then work the edges of dough to the centre.

For easier shaping, place risen dough on a lightly floured surface and let rest 15 minutes. For a round loaf, gently pull sides under dough until rounded. Place on a baking sheet and flatten slightly. The shaped dough usually rises a second time, until it is almost doubled in size.

For a rectangular loaf shape, roll dough into rectangle with floured rolling pin. From a narrow end, roll dough tightly, Swiss roll style. Pinch seam and ends to seal; turn ends under. Place, seam-side down, in greased loaf tin.

## WHICH CRUST?

• For a soft, tender crust, brush the unbaked loaf with milk, buttermilk, cream or melted butter or margarine.
• For a crisp, chewy crust, brush or spray loaf with water occasionally during baking.
• For shine and colour, brush loaf with beaten egg mixed with a little water.

## BETTER BAKING

• Some loaves are slashed just before baking. This allows carbon dioxide gas to escape and helps prevent cracks.
• Bake breads in the centre of oven. If baking several tins at once, allow at least 5cm between each tin.
• If top of loaf is over-browning, cover it loosely with foil.
• Bread baked on a baking stone will bake evenly and be extra crisp. Or try unglazed terracotta tiles from tile shops – but make sure they're lead-free.

## TESTING FOR DONENESS

Bread is done when it pulls away from the sides of the tin, is nicely browned and sounds hollow when the bottom is lightly rapped with knuckles. Also check the sides of the loaf – they should feel crisp and firm when pressed.

## COOLING AND STORING

• Cooled bread cuts into neater slices. Most breads should be removed from the tin promptly and cooled right-side up on a wire rack; keep the bread away from draughts, which can cause shrinkage. Cooling can take as long as 3 hours.
• Be sure bread is completely cool before wrapping or freezing. Otherwise, condensation can form on the inside of the wrapper and hasten spoilage.
• Store breads tightly wrapped. Soft breads stay freshest in plastic bags, while crusty breads stay crispest in paper bags.
• Always store breads at room temperature, not in the refrigerator, where they'll turn stale more quickly. Most breads are fine if used within 5 days.
• To freshen a stale loaf, heat in a 180°C (350°F, Gas 4) oven for 5 to 7 minutes. Or, use stale bread to make bread pudding, toast, croûtons or bread crumbs.
• Most breads freeze well for up to 3 months. Cool completely, then place in a freezer bag, pressing out air, or wrap tightly in heavy-duty foil. To thaw, let stand at room temperature for about 1 hour, or wrap frozen bread in foil with an opening at the top so steam can escape and heat in a 150°C (300°F, Gas 2) oven for about 20 minutes.

### TROUBLESHOOTING

**Dough over-rises in bowl** To correct, turn dough onto lightly floured surface and knead 2 to 3 minutes. Cover, let rest 15 minutes and shape as instructed, otherwise loaf could collapse in oven or be heavy-textured.
**Bread is too pale** Place untinned loaf directly on oven rack and bake 5 to 10 minutes longer.
**Bread is dry and crumbly** Dough had too much flour or dough rose too much.
**Bread collapses in oven** The shaped dough over-rose in the tin. Don't let dough rise above the tin's edges.
**Cracks in bread** Dough had too much flour or there was too much dough in the tin.
**Holes in bread** Dough wasn't kneaded enough. It's almost impossible to over-knead by hand. Rising time was too long or in too warm a place.

# BASIC YEAST BREADS

Nothing quite compares to a loaf of home-made bread. There's something satisfying in the mixing and kneading, and especially in the eating. The combination of yeast, liquid and flour is found in all yeast breads; beyond that, the choice of flours and tasty added ingredients makes for marvellous variety.

## BIG ONION BREAD

❖❖❖❖❖❖❖❖❖❖❖❖❖

*Prep: 1 hour, plus rising and cooling*
*Bake: About 1¼ hours*
*Makes 1 loaf, 20 servings*

**175g butter or margarine**
**1.1kg onions, chopped**
**Salt**
**2 sachets (7g each) easy-blend dried yeast**
**About 1.3kg strong plain flour**
**450ml milk**
**80g light molasses or golden syrup**
**4 medium eggs**

**1** Melt 45g butter in large frying pan over medium-high heat. Add onions and 1 teaspoon salt; cook, stirring often, about 30 minutes, until very tender and browned. Remove from heat. Combine yeast, 300g flour and 4 teaspoons salt in large bowl. Heat milk, molasses and remaining 125g butter in saucepan over low heat until very warm (47°–52°C); butter need not melt.

**2** Using electric mixer on low speed, gradually beat liquid into flour mixture just until blended. Increase speed to medium; beat 2 minutes, occasionally scraping bowl with rubber spatula. Beat in 3 eggs and 450g flour to make a thick batter; beat 2 minutes longer, scraping bowl often. Reserve 50g onions. Using wooden spoon, stir in remaining onions then 480g flour to make a soft dough. Turn out onto lightly floured surface.

**3** Knead dough about 10 minutes, until smooth and elastic, working in about 70g flour while kneading. Shape into ball; place in greased large bowl, turning dough to grease top.

**4** Cover dough; let rise in warm place (27°–30°C) about 30 minutes until doubled. To test, press 2 fingers about 1cm into dough then remove. The indentation should remain.

**5** Preheat oven to 180°C (350°F, Gas 4). Grease 25cm tube tin with removable bottom. Knock back the dough by pushing your fist into centre. Turn onto lightly floured surface.

**6** Divide dough in half. Roll each half of dough into a 45cm-long rope. Twist ropes together. Place dough in tin and tuck ends under. Bake 40 minutes.

**7** Lightly beat remaining egg in cup, using fork. When bread has baked 40 minutes, brush top with beaten egg; sprinkle with reserved onions. Bake bread 20–25 minutes longer, until loaf is browned and sounds hollow when lightly tapped with fingers. Cool bread in tin on wire rack 10 minutes; remove side of tube tin. Cool completely on rack.

EACH SERVING: ABOUT 300 CALORIES, 8g PROTEIN, 47g CARBOHYDRATE, 9g TOTAL FAT (4g SATURATED), 65mg CHOLESTEROL, 635mg SODIUM

## WALNUT-OATMEAL BREAD

*Prep: 25 minutes, plus rising and cooling    Bake: 35 to 40 minutes*
*Makes 1 loaf, 12 servings*

| | |
|---|---|
| 1 sachet (7g) easy-blend dried yeast | 1 medium egg |
| 150g light brown sugar | 80g rolled oats |
| 1½ tsp salt | 125g walnuts, coarsely chopped |
| About 675g strong plain flour | 1 tbsp milk |
| 30g butter or margarine | |

◆ Combine yeast, brown sugar, salt and 225g flour in large bowl. Heat butter and *300ml water* in saucepan over low heat until very warm (47–52°C); butter need not melt.

◆ Using electric mixer on low speed, gradually beat liquid into flour mixture just until blended. Increase speed to medium; beat 2 minutes, occasionally scraping bowl with rubber spatula.

◆ Beat in egg and 150g flour to make thick batter; beat 2 minutes longer, scraping bowl often. Reserve 1 tablespoon rolled oats for top of loaf. Using wooden spoon, stir in chopped walnuts, 225g flour and remaining rolled oats to make a soft dough.

◆ Turn out dough onto lightly floured surface; knead about 10 minutes, until smooth and elastic, working in about 75g more flour while kneading. Grease large baking sheet. Shape dough into 12–13cm ball.

◆ Place shaped dough on baking sheet. Cover loosely with cling film; let rise in warm place (27–29.5°C) about 30 minutes, until doubled.

◆ Preheat oven to 180°C (350°F, Gas 4). Using sharp knife or single-edge razor blade, cut 3 slashes across top of loaf. Brush with milk; sprinkle with reserved oats.

### YEAST AND TEMPERATURE

Yeast is the living organism that makes dough rise. Warm liquid activates yeast, allowing it to begin fermentation. Liquid that is too hot will kill the yeast, but if it's not hot enough the yeast will remain dormant. Fresh yeast and active dry yeast are blended with warm liquid, 39.5–44.5°C, and a little sugar, before being mixed with flour and left to become foamy. Easy-blend yeast is added directly to dry ingredients (as in most of these recipes) and dissolved with liquid that is 47–52°C (hot to the touch). For the most accurate results – and the best bread – test the temperature of the liquid with an instant-read thermometer. Always read easy-blend yeast sachets carefully as some breads require 2 risings.

◆ Bake 35–40 minutes, until loaf is golden and bottom sounds hollow when lightly tapped. Remove loaf from baking sheet; cool loaf on wire rack 30 minutes to serve warm. Or, cool completely to serve later.

**Each serving: About 320 calories, 9g protein, 50g carbohydrate, 10g total fat (1g saturated), 23mg cholesterol, 300mg sodium**

## OLIVE AND RED PEPPER BREAD

*Prep: 35 minutes, plus rising and cooling    Bake: 35 minutes*
*Makes 1 loaf, 12 servings*

| | |
|---|---|
| 45g strong plain flour | 150ml milk |
| 1 tsp salt | 75g black olives, chopped |
| 1 sachet (7g) easy-blend yeast | ½ medium red pepper, very finely sliced |
| 1 tsp caster sugar | 1 tsp rock salt |
| 25g butter or margarine | |

◆ Combine flour, salt, yeast and sugar in large bowl. Using fingers, rub in butter.

◆ Heat milk and *175ml water* in small saucepan over low heat until very warm (47–52°C). Make a well in centre of flour mixture and pour in liquid, mixing until blended and soft dough forms.

◆ Turn out dough onto lightly floured surface and knead for about 10 minutes until smooth and elastic, working in olives and red pepper strips while kneading.

◆ Shape dough into ball; place in greased large bowl, turning dough to grease top. Cover dough loosely with cling film; let rise in warm place (27–29.5°C) about 1 hour until doubled and sponge-like in texture.

◆ Knock back dough by pushing your fist into centre. Turn out dough onto lightly floured surface; knead again 3–4 minutes until smooth. Cover loosely with cling film and let rest 15 minutes for easier shaping.

◆ Shape dough into round and place on lightly greased baking sheet. Using sharp knife or single-edge razor blade, slash top of shaped loaf 3 times, cutting about 5mm deep. Cover with oiled cling film and leave in warm place about 1 hour, until doubled. Sprinkle rock salt over loaf.

◆ Preheat oven to 220°C (425°F, Gas 7). Bake 20 minutes. Reduce oven temperature to 180°C (350°F, Gas 4) and bake 15 minutes longer, until bottom of loaf sounds hollow when lightly tapped. Transfer to wire rack to cool.

**Each serving: About 180 calories, 6g protein, 33g carbohydrate, 3g total fat (1g saturated), 2mg cholesterol, 385mg sodium**

## WHOLE-GRAIN BREAD

*Prep: 25 minutes, plus rising and cooling    Bake: 50–60 minutes*
*Makes 1 loaf, 16 servings*

| | |
|---|---|
| 200g rye flour | 1 tbsp salt |
| 60g unprocessed bran | 175ml milk |
| 75g wheatgerm | 125g butter or margarine |
| About 550g strong wholemeal flour | 110g dark molasses or golden syrup |
| 2 sacbets (7g each) easy-blend yeast | 2 medium eggs |
| 3 tbsp caster sugar | 2 tbsp coarse yellow cornmeal |
| | 1 tsp caraway seeds |

◆ Combine rye flour, bran, wheatgerm and 375g wholemeal flour in large bowl. Combine yeast, sugar, salt, and 375g flour mixture in another large bowl. Heat milk, butter, molasses and *225ml water* in 2-litre saucepan over low heat until very warm (47–52°C); butter need not melt.

◆ Gradually beat liquid into yeast mixture, using electric mixer on low speed, just until blended. Increase speed to medium; beat 2 minutes, occasionally scraping bowl with rubber spatula.

◆ Separate 1 egg and reserve white in refrigerator, covered. Beat remaining egg, egg yolk, and 300g flour mixture into yeast mixture; beat 2 minutes longer, scraping bowl often. Using wooden spoon, stir in remaining flour mixture and 112g wholemeal flour to make a soft dough.

◆ Lightly sprinkle work surface with wholemeal flour; turn out dough onto surface and knead about 10 minutes, until smooth and elastic, working in about 60g more wholemeal flour while kneading. Shape dough into ball; place in greased large bowl, turning dough to grease top. Cover loosely with cling film; let rise in warm place (27–29.5°C) about 1 hour until doubled.

◆ Knock back dough; turn onto surface lightly floured with wholemeal flour. Cover loosely with cling film and let rest 15 minutes for easier shaping. Sprinkle baking sheet with cornmeal.

◆ Shape dough into 25 by 12cm oval loaf, tapering ends; place on baking sheet. Cover loosely with cling film; let rise in warm place about 1 hour until doubled.

◆ Preheat oven to 180°C (350°F, Gas 4). Using sharp knife or single-edge razor blade, cut 3 diagonal slashes across top of loaf. Using fork, beat reserved egg white with *1 tablespoon water* in cup; brush over loaf. Sprinkle with caraway seeds. Bake loaf 50–60 minutes, until bottom sounds hollow when lightly tapped. Remove from baking sheet; cool on wire rack.

**Each serving: About 270 calories, 9g protein, 45g carbohydrate, 8g total fat (3g saturated), 45mg cholesterol, 485mg sodium**

## HONEY-WHEAT BREAD

*Prep: 20 minutes, plus rising and cooling    Bake: 30 minutes*
*Makes 1 loaf, 12 servings*

| | |
|---|---|
| 2 sachets (7g each) easy-blend yeast | 170g honey |
| 375g wholemeal flour | 60ml vegetable oil |
| 1½ tsp salt | 1 medium egg |
| | About 600g strong plain flour |

◆ Combine yeast, wholemeal flour and salt in large bowl.

◆ Using electric mixer on low speed, gradually beat *400ml very hot tap water* (47–52°C) into flour mixture just until blended. Increase speed to medium; beat 2 minutes, occasionally scraping bowl with rubber spatula.

◆ Beat in honey, vegetable oil, egg and 150g plain flour to make a thick batter; beat 2 minutes longer, scraping bowl often. Using wooden spoon, stir in 375g plain flour to make a soft dough.

◆ Turn out dough onto floured surface and knead about 10 minutes until smooth and elastic, working in about 75g more plain flour. Cover loosely with cling film and let rest 10 minutes for easier shaping. Shape dough into 25 by 12cm oval loaf and place on large greased baking sheet.

◆ Cover loaf loosely with cling film; let rise in warm place (27–29.5°C) about 30 minutes, until doubled. Using sharp knife or single-edge razor blade, cut three 7–8cm long diagonal slashes across top of loaf.

◆ Preheat oven to 190°C (375°F, Gas 5). Sprinkle loaf lightly with plain flour. Bake 30 minutes, or until bottom of loaf sounds hollow when lightly tapped. Remove loaf from baking sheet; cool on wire rack.

**Each serving: About 335 calories, 9g protein, 63g carbohydrate, 6g total fat (1g saturated), 18mg cholesterol, 275mg sodium**

## BUTTERMILK BREAD

*Prep:* 20 minutes, plus rising and cooling   *Bake:* 25–30 minutes
*Makes* 2 loaves, 12 servings each

1 sachet (7g) easy-blend yeast
2 tsp salt
About 700g strong plain flour
50g caster sugar

400ml buttermilk or soured
  milk (see page 392)
125g butter or margarine

◆ Combine yeast, salt, and 300g flour in large bowl. Heat sugar, buttermilk, and 90g butter in 1-litre saucepan over medium-low heat until very warm (47–52°C); butter need not melt.

◆ Using electric mixer on low speed, gradually beat buttermilk mixture into flour mixture just until blended. Increase speed to medium; beat 2 minutes longer, scraping bowl often with rubber spatula.

◆ Beat in 150g flour to make a thick batter; beat batter 2 minutes longer, scraping bowl often. Using wooden spoon, stir in 220g flour to make a stiff dough.

◆ Turn out dough onto lightly floured surface and knead about 10 minutes, until smooth and elastic, working in about 30g more flour while kneading.

◆ Shape dough into a ball; place in greased large bowl, turning dough to grease top. Cover dough loosely with cling film; let rise in warm place (27–29.5°C) about 1 hour until doubled.

◆ Knock back dough. Turn out dough onto lightly floured surface and cut in half. Cover loosely with cling film and let rest 15 minutes for easier shaping.

◆ Grease two 21 by 11cm loaf tins. Shape each piece of dough into a loaf (see page 406); place, seam-side down, in loaf tins. Cover loosely with cling film; let rise in warm place about 1 hour, until doubled.

◆ Preheat oven to 190°C (375°F, Gas 5). Melt remaining 2 tablespoons butter. Using sharp knife or single-edge razor blade, slash top of each loaf lengthways, cutting about 5mm deep. Brush slashes with melted butter.

◆ Bake 25–30 minutes until loaves are golden and bottoms sound hollow when lightly tapped. Remove loaves from tins; cool on wire racks.

**Each serving: About 135 calories, 3g protein, 20g carbohydrate, 4g total fat (2g saturated), 12mg cholesterol, 240mg sodium**

## 'SOURDOUGH' BREAD

*Prep:* 20 minutes, plus rising and cooling   *Bake:* 25–30 minutes
*Makes* 2 loaves, 16 servings each

2 sachets (7g each) easy-blend
  yeast
2 tbsp caster sugar

2 tsp salt
About 1kg strong plain flour
450g plain low-fat yogurt

◆ Combine yeast, sugar, salt and 900g flour. Heat yogurt and *150ml water* in 2-litre saucepan over medium heat until very warm (47–52°C); stir into flour mixture, mixing until blended and dough forms a ball.

◆ Turn out dough onto lightly floured surface; knead about 10 minutes, until smooth and elastic, working in about 150g flour while kneading. Cut dough in half; cover and let rest 10 minutes for easier shaping. Grease 2 baking sheets.

◆ Shape each piece of dough into 12–13cm round loaf. Place 1 loaf on each baking sheet. Cover loosely with cling film; let rise in warm place (27–29.5°C) about 45 minutes, until doubled. Preheat oven to 200°C (400°F, Gas 6).

◆ Using sharp knife or single-edge razor blade, cut 3 parallel slashes in each loaf; brush loaves with *water*. Bake 25–30 minutes, rotating sheets after 15 minutes, until bottoms of loaves sound hollow when lightly tapped. Remove loaves from baking sheet; cool on wire racks.

**Each serving: About 105 calories, 4g protein, 21g carbohydrate, 1g total fat (0g saturated), 1mg cholesterol, 145mg sodium**

### THE FIRST SOURDOUGH

◆◆◆◆◆◆◆◆◆◆◆◆◆◆◆◆◆◆◆◆◆◆◆◆◆◆◆

Bakers in Europe and the eastern Mediterranean used sourdough starters for thousands of years before commercial yeast became available. Home-made yeast starters – made from flour, water and sometimes sugar – were used to make bread rise. These mixtures would attract wild yeasts naturally present in the air and, after several days, start to ferment. It's this fermentation that gives the bread its characteristic sour taste. Today, sourdough bread is still popular in many countries including France, Germany and the United States. For a loaf reminiscent of the original sourdough taste, but risen with yeast, try our recipe above.

# SAVOURY FILLED BREADS

Our trio of filled breads takes the satisfaction of home-baked bread to new heights. And each recipe is reasonably quick and easy to prepare: mix the dough as usual and roll into a rectangle, then sprinkle it with chopped Kalamata olives, walnuts, sun-dried tomatoes, peperoni or mozzarella cheese. Roll the loaf Swiss-roll fashion and let it rise before baking – the reward will be a truly impressive loaf.

## OLIVE AND WALNUT BREAD

❖❖❖❖❖❖❖❖❖❖❖❖❖❖❖❖❖❖❖❖❖❖❖❖❖❖❖❖❖❖❖❖

*Prep: 30 minutes, plus rising and cooling   Bake: 35–40 minutes*
*Makes 1 loaf, 16 servings*

125g walnuts
1 sachet (7g) easy-blend yeast
1 tsp salt
1 tsp caster sugar
½ tsp coarsely ground black pepper

About 675g strong plain flour plus, additional for dusting
3 tbsp extra virgin olive oil
115g Kalamata olives, stoned and chopped

**1** Coarsely chop walnuts. Toast walnuts in 26cm frying pan over medium heat, stirring occasionally, until toasted. Remove pan from heat. Combine yeast, salt, sugar, pepper and 300g flour in large bowl.

**2** Heat oil and *350ml water* in 1-litre saucepan over low heat until very warm (47–52°C). Using wooden spoon, stir liquid into flour mixture until well blended. Stir in 300g flour to make a soft dough. Turn out dough onto lightly floured surface; knead about 5 minutes, until smooth and elastic, working in about 75g more flour while kneading. Shape into a ball. Cover loosely with cling film and let rest 10 minutes.

**3** Grease large baking sheet. Using floured rolling pin, roll out dough on lightly floured surface to 45 by 30cm rectangle; sprinkle with chopped olives and toasted walnuts. Starting from a short side, tightly roll dough Swiss-roll fashion; pinch seam to seal.

**4** Place loaf, seam-side down, on baking sheet; tuck ends under. Using sharp knife or single-edge razor blade, make parallel 3mm deep slashes on top of loaf. Cover loosely with cling film; let rise in warm place (27–29.5°C) 15 minutes.

**5** Meanwhile, preheat oven to 200°C (400°F, Gas 6). Bake 35–40 minutes, until bottom of bread sounds hollow when lightly tapped. Cool on wire rack slightly to serve warm. Or, cool bread completely to serve later.

EACH SERVING: ABOUT 210 CALORIES, 5g PROTEIN, 27g CARBOHYDRATE, 9g TOTAL FAT (1g SATURATED), 0mg CHOLESTEROL, 250mg SODIUM

## TOMATO AND OLIVE BREAD

*Prep: 35 minutes, plus rising and cooling   Bake: 1 hour*
*Makes 1 loaf, 20 servings*

2 sachets (7g each) easy-blend
  yeast
200g caster sugar
1 tsp salt
About 1.2kg strong plain flour
350ml milk
225g butter or margarine
3 medium eggs

75g Kalamata olives, stoned
  and chopped
240g oil-packed sun-dried
  tomatoes, drained and
  chopped
1 tbsp chopped fresh
  rosemary or 1 tsp dried,
  crushed
Coarse salt (optional)

◆ Combine yeast, sugar, salt and 300g flour in large bowl. Heat milk and butter in 1-litre saucepan over low heat until very warm (47–52°C); butter need not melt.

◆ Using electric mixer on low speed, gradually beat liquid into flour mixture just until blended. Increase mixer speed to medium; beat 2 minutes longer, occasionally scraping bowl with rubber spatula. Separate 1 egg and reserve white in refrigerator, covered. Beat in remaining eggs, egg yolk and 225g flour to make a thick batter; beat 2 minutes longer, scraping bowl often. Stir in 600g flour to make a soft dough.

◆ Turn dough out onto lightly floured surface and knead about 10 minutes, until smooth and elastic, working in about 75g more flour while kneading. Shape dough into ball; cover loosely with cling film and let rest about 10 minutes for easier shaping.

◆ Meanwhile, prepare filling: combine olives, sun-dried tomatoes and rosemary in small bowl.

◆ Grease 25cm tube tin. Using floured rolling pin, roll out dough on lightly floured surface, into 50 by 45cm rectangle. Spread filling evenly over dough, leaving 2–3cm border. Starting from a long side, tightly roll dough Swiss-roll fashion; pinch seam to seal. Place roll, seam-side down, in tube tin; press ends together to seal. Cover loosely with cling film and let rise in warm place (27–29.5°C) about 1 hour, until doubled.

◆ Preheat oven to 180°C (350°F, Gas 5). Using fork, beat reserved egg white with *2 teaspoons water* in cup. Brush loaf with egg white mixture; sprinkle with coarse salt, if using. Bake 1 hour, or until bread sounds hollow when lightly tapped. When bread turns golden (after about 20 minutes), cover loosely with tent of foil to avoid over-browning. Cool bread in tin on wire rack 10 minutes; remove from tin and cool completely on rack.

**Each serving: About 350 calories, 7g protein, 50g carbohydrate, 13g total fat (6g saturated), 58mg cholestrol, 325mg sodium**

## CHEESE AND PEPERONI BREAD

*Prep: 30 minutes, plus rising and cooling   Bake: 45 minutes*
*Makes 1 loaf, 16 servings*

1 sachet (7g) easy-blend yeast
1 tbsp caster sugar
1 tsp salt
About 640g strong plain flour
225ml milk
125g butter or margarine
2 medium eggs

90g peperoni, chopped
225g mozzarella cheese,
  grated
½ tsp dried oregano
½ tsp coarsely ground black
  pepper

◆ Combine yeast, sugar, salt and 150g flour in large bowl. Heat milk and butter in 1-litre saucepan over low heat until very warm (47–52°C); butter need not melt.

◆ Using electric mixer on low speed, gradually beat liquid into flour mixture just until blended. Using fork, beat eggs lightly in cup; reserve 1 tablespoon beaten egg in refrigerator, covered. Beat remaining eggs into mixture. Increase speed to medium; beat 2 minutes, occasionally scraping bowl with rubber spatula. Beat in 150g flour to make a thick batter; beat 2 minutes longer, occasionally scraping bowl. Using wooden spoon, stir in 300g flour to make a soft dough.

◆ Turn dough out onto lightly floured surface and knead about 10 minutes, until smooth and elastic, working in about 30g more flour while kneading. Shape dough into ball; cover loosely with cling film and let rest 10 minutes for easier shaping.

◆ Meanwhile prepare filling: combine peperoni, cheese, and oregano in small bowl.

◆ Grease 23cm round cake tin. Using floured rolling pin, roll out dough on lightly floured surface into 58 by 15cm rectangle. Evenly spoon filling lengthways down centre of dough. Starting from a long side, tightly roll dough Swiss-roll fashion; pinch seam to seal. Place roll, seam-side down, in cake tin to make a ring, overlapping ends slightly; pinch ends together to seal and tuck under. Cover loosely with cling film; let rise in warm place (27–29.5°C) about 30 minutes, until doubled.

◆ Preheat oven to 190°C (375°F, Gas 5). Brush loaf with reserved beaten egg; sprinkle with pepper. Using sharp knife or single-edge razor blade, cut several slashes in top of loaf. Bake 45 minutes, or until bread is golden and bottom sounds hollow when lightly tapped. Remove bread from tin immediately. Let cool on wire rack at least 15 minutes for easier slicing; serve warm. Or, cool completely on rack; refrigerate to re-heat and serve later.

**Each serving: About 260 calories, 9g protein, 26g carbohydrate, 13g total fat (7g saturated), 57mg cholesterol, 410mg sodium**

# ROLLS AND BREADSTICKS

Home-made rolls have an honored place on the dinner table or at a special breakfast or brunch. Making them is fun and easy: just shape the basic yeast dough into small rounds, spirals or knots, or twirl long ropes together to form breadsticks. Brushing with egg before baking will produce an appetizing golden sheen.

## SPIRAL ROLLS

◆◆◆◆◆◆◆◆◆◆◆◆◆

*Prep: 30 minutes, plus*
*rising and cooling*
*Bake: 15–20 minutes*
*Makes 12*

1 sachet (7g) easy-blend yeast
2 tbsp caster sugar
1½ tsp salt
450g plus 2–3 tbsp strong
   plain flour
225ml milk
45g butter or margarine
1 medium egg beaten with
   1 tsp water
Coarse salt

**1** Combine yeast, sugar, salt and 450g flour in large bowl. Heat milk and butter in 1-litre saucepan over low heat until very warm (47–52°C); butter need not melt. Using wooden spoon, gradually stir liquid into flour mixture, adding 2–3 tablespoons more flour if necessary to make a soft dough. Turn out onto lightly floured surface; knead about 5 minutes, until smooth and elastic. Shape into ball.

**2** Place dough in greased bowl, turning to grease top. Cover; let rise in warm place (27–29.5°C) about 30 minutes, until doubled. Preheat oven to 190°C (375°F, Gas 5).

**3** Knock back dough; cut into 12 equal pieces. Roll each piece on lightly floured surface into 30cm rope. Coil each into spiral; tuck end under. Place 5cm apart on greased large baking sheet.

---

### BREAD BASKET BONUSES

Once you've made the basic dough, you can easily create other shapes. Try either of the following variations (pictured above with Spiral Rolls) – or make all three rolls from one batch of dough.

**Knot rolls** Prepare dough as in Steps 1 and 2 above; cut into 12 equal pieces. Roll each

piece of dough into 23cm long rope on lightly floured surface; tie each rope into a knot. Place rolls, 5cm apart, on greased large baking sheet. Dust each roll with flour (omit egg mixture and coarse salt). Bake as instructed.

**Poppy seed rolls** Prepare dough as in Steps 1 and 2 above; cut into 12 equal pieces. Place 3 tablespoons poppy seeds

on plate. Shape each piece of dough into a ball on lightly floured surface; brush top of each with some egg mixture (omit coarse salt). Dip rolls, egg-side down, into poppy seeds. Place rolls, poppy-seed-side up, 5cm apart, on greased large baking sheet. Using kitchen scissors or knife, cut an 'X' in top of each roll. Bake as instructed.

**4** Brush each roll with some egg mixture and sprinkle lightly with coarse salt. Bake 15–20 minutes, until golden. Serve rolls warm. Or, cool completely to serve later.

---

EACH ROLL: ABOUT 165 CALORIES, 5g PROTEIN, 26g CARBOHYDRATE, 4g TOTAL FAT (2g SATURATED), 29mg CHOLESTEROL, 495mg SODIUM

## FENNEL SEED BREADSTICKS

*Prep: 30 minutes, plus rising and cooling*
*Bake: 25 minutes*    *Makes 24*

| | |
|---|---|
| 1 sachet (7g) easy-blend yeast | 300g strong plain flour |
| 1 tsp fennel seeds, crushed | 125g white vegetable fat |
| 1 tsp salt | 1 medium egg |
| 1 tsp cracked black pepper | |

◆ Combine yeast, fennel seeds, salt, pepper and 150g flour in large bowl. Heat vegetable fat and *125ml water* in 1-litre saucepan over low heat until very warm (47°–52°C); vegetable fat need not melt.

◆ Using electric mixer on low speed, gradually beat liquid into flour mixture just until blended. Increase speed to medium; beat 3 minutes, occasionally scraping bowl with rubber spatula. Using wooden spoon, stir in remaining 150g flour to make a soft dough. Knead dough in bowl 2–3 minutes, until smooth and elastic. Cover loosely with cling film; let rise in warm place (27–29.5°C) about 2 hours until doubled.

◆ Preheat oven to 180°C (350°F, Gas 4). Grease 2 baking sheets. Turn out dough onto lightly floured surface. Cut dough into quarters, then cut each quarter into 12 equal pieces. Roll each piece into a 30cm-long rope. Twist 2 ropes of dough loosely together; place on baking sheet. Repeat to make 24 breadsticks in all, placing them 2–3cm apart on baking sheets.

◆ Beat egg in small bowl; brush over breadsticks. Bake breadsticks 25 minutes, or until browned and crisp, rotating baking sheets between upper and lower racks halfway through baking time. Remove from baking sheets; cool on wire racks. Store in tightly covered container.

**Each breadstick: About 75 calories, 1g protein, 8g carbohydrate, 5g total fat (1g saturated), 9mg cholesterol, 90mg sodium**

## POTATO ROLLS

*Prep: 1½ hours, plus rising and chilling*
*Bake: 25–30 minutes*    *Makes 24*

| | |
|---|---|
| 450g potatoes, peeled and cut into 2–3cm chunks | 1 tbsp caster salt |
| 2 sachets (7g each) easy-blend yeast | About 1.4kg strong plain flour |
| | 60g butter or margarine |
| 2 tbsp caster sugar | 2 medium eggs |

◆ Bring potatoes and *900ml water* to the boil in 2-litre saucepan over high heat. Reduce heat to low; cover and simmer 15 minutes, or until potatoes are fork-tender. Drain potatoes, reserving 225ml potato cooking water. Return potatoes to saucepan. Using potato masher, mash potatoes until smooth.

◆ Combine yeast, sugar, salt and 450g flour in large bowl. Heat butter, *225ml water* and reserved potato water in 1-litre saucepan over low heat until very warm (47–52°C); butter need not melt.

◆ Using electric mixer on low speed, gradually beat liquid into flour mixture just until blended. Increase speed to medium; beat 2 minutes, occasionally scraping bowl with rubber spatula. Separate 1 egg and reserve white in refrigerator, covered. Gradually beat remaining egg, egg yolk and 150g flour into flour mixture to make a thick batter; beat 2 minutes longer, scraping bowl often.

◆ Using wooden spoon, stir in mashed potatoes, then 750g flour, 150g at a time, to make a soft dough. (You may want to transfer mixture to a larger bowl for easier mixing.)

◆ Turn out dough onto well-floured surface and knead about 10 minutes, until smooth and elastic, working in about 110g more flour. Cut dough into 24 equal pieces; cover with cling film and let rest 15 minutes for easier shaping. Grease 38 by 28cm roasting tin.

◆ Shape dough into balls and place in roasting tin. Cover tin loosely with cling film and let rise in warm place (27–29.5°C) about 40 minutes, until doubled. (Or, if you like, cover and refrigerate overnight. When ready to bake, let rise in warm place, still covered loosely with cling film, about 30 minutes until doubled).

◆ Preheat oven to 200°C (400°F, Gas 6). Using fork, beat reserved egg white in cup. Brush rolls with egg white. Bake 25–30 minutes, until rolls are golden and sound hollow when lightly tapped. Cool 10 minutes; serve warm. Or, remove from tin and cool on wire rack to serve later; re-heat if desired. To serve, pull rolls apart.

**Each roll: About 215 calories, 6g protein, 41g carbohydrate, 3g total fat (1g saturated), 23mg cholesterol, 295mg sodium**

# FLAT BREADS

Rustic, peasant-style flat breads are enjoyed the world over. Focaccia, a favourite from Italy, is a large, flattened yeast bread that is drizzled with olive oil and sometimes sprinkled with savoury toppings before baking. From the Middle East comes the soft, mild-flavoured pocket bread called pitta. Split for sandwiches, or serve with appetizers, soups or salads.

## GOLDEN ONION FOCACCIA

❖❖❖❖❖❖❖❖❖❖❖❖❖❖❖❖❖❖❖❖❖❖❖❖❖❖❖

*Prep: 30 minutes, plus rising    Bake: 20–25 minutes*
*Makes 8 servings*

1 sachet (7g) easy-
  blend yeast
1 tsp salt
About 300g strong plain flour
4 tbsp olive oil
125g strong wholemeal flour
1 tbsp coarse yellow cornmeal

1 red onion, thinly sliced
2 tbsp freshly grated
  Parmesan cheese
1 tbsp fresh rosemary or
  1 tsp dried, crushed
¼ tsp cracked black pepper
Coarse salt (optional)

**1** Combine yeast, 1 teaspoon salt and 150g plain flour. Heat 2 tablespoons oil and *225ml water* in 1-litre saucepan over medium heat until very warm (47–52°C). Using electric mixer on low speed, gradually beat liquid into flour mixture just until blended. Increase speed to medium; beat 2 minutes. Add 75g plain flour; beat 2 minutes. Using wooden spoon, stir in wholemeal flour to make a soft dough.

**2** Knead dough in bowl 8 minutes, gradually working in about 75g plain flour. Cover loosely with cling film; let rest 15 minutes. Grease 33 by 20cm metal baking tin; sprinkle with cornmeal.

**3** Pat dough into tin, pushing into corners. Cover loosely with cling film; let rise in warm place (27–29.5°C) 30 minutes or until doubled. Heat 1 tablespoon oil in 26cm frying pan over medium heat. Add onion; cook until tender. Preheat oven to 200°C (400°F, Gas 6). Using finger, make deep indentations 2–3cm apart over surface of dough, almost to bottom of tin; drizzle with remaining 1 tablespoon oil.

**4** Spoon onion evenly over dough in tin; sprinkle with remaining ingredients. Bake for 20–25 minutes, until golden. Cool 10 minutes in tin on wire rack. Serve warm. Or, remove from tin and cool completely to serve later.

### OTHER TOPPINGS

**Sweet pepper** Heat 1 tablespoon olive oil in 26cm frying pan over medium heat; add 2 sliced red or yellow peppers and ¼ teaspoon salt; cook, stirring often, 15 minutes, or until peppers are tender.

**Dried tomato and olive** Mix 6 slivered oil-packed sun-dried tomatoes, and 50g chopped, stoned Kalamata olives.

EACH SERVING: ABOUT 235 CALORIES, 6g PROTEIN, 36g CARBOHYDRATE, 8g TOTAL FAT (1g SATURATED), 1mg CHOLESTEROL, 300mg SODIUM

## SEMOLINA FOCACCIA WITH FENNEL AND SULTANAS

*Prep: 20 minutes, plus rising and cooling    Bake: 25 minutes*
*Makes 12 servings*

1 sachet (7g) easy-blend yeast
2 tbsp caster sugar
2 tsp salt
240g plus 2 tbsp semolina flour (see below)
60ml plus 2 tbsp olive oil
115g sultanas
1 tbsp fennel seeds, crushed
About 225g strong plain flour

◆ Combine yeast, sugar, salt and 240g semolina flour in large bowl. Heat 60ml oil and *225ml water* in 1-litre saucepan over low heat until very warm (47–52°C).

◆ Using electric mixer on low speed, gradually beat liquid into flour mixture just until blended, scraping bowl often with rubber spatula. Increase speed to medium; beat 2 minutes, scraping bowl often. Using wooden spoon, stir in sultanas, fennel and 150g plain flour to make a soft dough.

◆ Turn out dough onto lightly floured surface and knead about 8 minutes, until smooth and elastic, working in about 75g more plain flour. Shape dough into a ball; cover with cling film and let rest 15 minutes.

◆ Grease shallow 39 by 27cm Swiss-roll tin. Sprinkle with remaining 2 tablespoons semolina flour. Using floured rolling pin, roll out dough on floured surface into 38 by 25cm rectangle. Place in Swiss-roll tin, pushing dough into corners. Cover loosely with cling film and let rise in warm place (27–29.5°C) about 30 minutes until doubled.

◆ Preheat oven to 200°C (400°F, Gas 6). Using fingers, make indentations 2–3cm apart over surface of dough, almost to base of tin. Drizzle with remaining 2 tablespoons oil. Bake 25 minutes, or until golden. Remove from tin and cool on wire rack.

**Each serving: About 220 calories, 4g protein, 35g carbohydrate, 7g total fat (1g saturated), 0mg cholesterol, 360mg sodium**

---

### SEMOLINA FLOUR

A high-protein, high-gluten flour milled from durum wheat, semolina flour has a nutty flavour and a texture that resembles cornmeal. Commonly used for making commercial dried pastas, it is also good for breads and gnocchi. Also known as 'soft wheat flour (type 00)', semolina flour is available in Italian grocery stores, some supermarkets or by mail-order (see page 30).

---

## WHOLEMEAL PITTAS

*Prep: 1¼ hours, plus cooling, standing, chilling and rising*
*Bake: 5 minutes per batch    Makes 16*

300g potatoes, peeled and cut into 2–3cm chunks
1 sachet (7g) easy-blend yeast
1 tsp salt
80g strong wholemeal flour
About 485g strong plain flour
225g plain low-fat yogurt
1 tbsp honey

◆ Heat potatoes and enough *water* to cover to boil in 2-litre saucepan over high heat. Reduce heat to low; cover and simmer 15 minutes, or until potatoes are fork-tender.

◆ Drain potatoes; return to pan. Using potato masher, mash potatoes until smooth; let cool to room temperature.

◆ Combine yeast, salt, wholemeal flour and 110g plain flour in large bowl. Heat yogurt, honey, and *60ml water* in 1-litre saucepan over medium-low heat until very warm (47–52°C); stir into flour mixture until blended.

◆ Stir in potatoes and 225g plain flour to make a soft dough. Knead dough in bowl to shape into a ball. Cover bowl loosely with cling film and refrigerate overnight.

◆ When ready to bake, turn out dough onto well-floured surface and knead about 10 minutes, until smooth and elastic, working in about 150g plain flour while kneading.

◆ Cut dough into 16 equal pieces; shape each piece into a ball. Cover loosely with cling film and let rise in warm place (27–29.5°C) about 40 minutes until doubled.

◆ Preheat oven to 230°C (450°F, Gas 8). Place oven rack in centre of oven. Using floured rolling pin and working with 4 pieces of dough at a time, roll each piece of dough on lightly floured surface into a 15cm round, being careful to keep thickness of dough even. (If dough is too thick or too thin, pittas will not rise uniformly when baked.) Using pastry brush, brush excess flour from pittas.

◆ Heat large baking sheet in oven 5–7 minutes. Place 4 pitta rounds on preheated baking sheet; bake 5 minutes, or until golden and puffed. Cool on wire rack. Repeat with remaining dough, heating baking sheet for each batch.

**Each pitta: About 135 calories, 4g protein, 28g carbohydrate, 1g total fat (0g saturated), 1mg cholesterol, 145mg sodium**

# HOME-MADE PIZZAS

Pizza is a dish that inspires healthy appetites and plenty of creativity – we've topped ours with ingredients such as marinated artichokes, aubergine and mild goat's cheese. We've even char-grilled pizza for an extra-crisp crust and a slightly smoky flavour. Or, you could try adding flavourings to the crust itself for a simple but delicious variation.

## ARTICHOKE AND CHEESE PIZZA

◆◆◆◆◆◆◆◆◆◆◆◆◆

*Prep: 40 minutes, plus resting*
*Bake: 25–30 minutes*
*Makes 4 main dish servings*

**Basic Pizza Dough (see page 418)**

**Coarse yellow cornmeal, for sprinkling**

**15g fresh basil leaves**

**175g marinated artichoke hearts with marinade**

**1 small aubergine (about 350g), cut lengthways in half, then cut crossways into 5mm thick slices**

**3 small tomatoes, cut into thin wedges**

**175g goat's cheese such as Montrachet, broken into chunks, or mozzarella cheese, thinly sliced**

**1** Prepare Basic Pizza Dough as in Step 1. Sprinkle 2 large baking sheets with cornmeal. Shape pizza dough into 2 balls; place 1 on each baking sheet, about 7–8cm from edges. Cover with cling film and let rest 15 minutes. Meanwhile, preheat grill. Reserve a few basil leaves for garnish; thinly slice remaining basil leaves. Drain artichoke hearts, reserving marinade. Cut each artichoke heart lengthways in half.

**2** Toss aubergine slices with 2 tablespoons reserved artichoke marinade in shallow baking tray, then arrange in a single layer. Grill for 7–10 minutes, turning once, until tender and brown. Remove aubergine slices from grill. Preheat oven to 220°C (425°F, Gas 7). Toss aubergine, artichokes, tomatoes and half sliced basil with remaining artichoke marinade in bowl.

**3** Pat 1 ball dough from centre outward to make 26cm round on baking sheet. (Dough will extend over edge of sheet until you form rim.) If dough shrinks back, let it rest a few minutes.

**4** Arrange half aubergine mixture and half goat's cheese on the patted-out pizza base, leaving 2–3cm border.

**5** Pinch and press edge up to make high rim. Repeat with second pizza. Cover; let rest 15 minutes. Bake 25–30 minutes, rotating sheets halfway through, until crust is browned. Sprinkle on remaining basil and garnish with basil leaves.

### FLAVOURED BASES

◆◆◆◆◆◆◆◆◆◆◆◆◆

To vary the Basic Pizza Dough on page 418, add any of the following:

• 1 teaspoon cracked black pepper or crushed fennel seeds

• 1 tablespoon finely chopped fresh rosemary or 1 teaspoon dried, crushed

• 50g chopped, stoned Kalamata olives

EACH SERVING: ABOUT 435 CALORIES, 18g PROTEIN, 56g CARBOHYDRATE, 16g TOTAL FAT (9g SATURATED), 33mg CHOLESTEROL, 695mg SODIUM

## BASIC PIZZA DOUGH

◆◆◆◆◆◆◆◆◆◆◆◆◆

300g strong plain flour
1 sachet (7g) easy-blend yeast
¾ tsp salt

2 tsp olive oil
Coarse yellow cornmeal

1 Combine flour, yeast and salt in large bowl. Stir in *175ml very hot tap water* (47–52°C) and oil until blended and dough comes away from side of bowl. Turn out onto lightly floured surface; knead 5 minutes.

2 Sprinkle 2 baking sheets with cornmeal. Shape dough into 1, 2 or 4 balls (for 1 large rectangular, two 26cm or four 15cm pizzas). Place on large baking sheet (for 2 or 4 balls, use 2 baking sheets). Cover with cling film; let rest 15 minutes.

3 Shape dough: to make 1 large pizza, roll dough ball into 35 by 24cm rectangle on baking sheet; add topping. Bring edges of dough up; fold to make 2–3cm rim. For two 26cm pizzas, pat and stretch 1 ball into 26cm round. Add topping; make 2–3cm rim. Repeat to make second pizza. For four 15cm pizzas, pat and stretch 1 ball into 15cm round. Add topping; make 1cm rim. Repeat to make 3 more pizzas.

## BISTRO PIZZA

*Prep: 55 minutes, plus resting*  **Bake:** *20–30 minutes*
**Makes** *4 main dish servings*

2 medium red peppers, roasted and peeled (see page 310), or 200g bottled roasted red peppers, drained
Basic Pizza Dough (see above)
450g thin asparagus, trimmed

1 tsp olive oil
¼ tsp salt
175g smoked mozzarella cheese, grated
¼ tsp coarsely ground black pepper

◆ Prepare roasted red peppers; cut into strips. Set aside. Prepare pizza dough as in Steps 1 and 2, making 1, 2 or 4 balls as desired. While dough is resting, cut asparagus into 5cm pieces. Toss asparagus with olive oil and salt in bowl.

◆ Shape dough as in Step 3; top with mozzarella, red-pepper strips and asparagus. Sprinkle with black pepper. Let rest 15 minutes. Meanwhile, preheat oven to 220°C (425°F, Gas 7). Bake in oven 20–30 minutes until base is browned.

**Each serving: About 425 calories, 18g protein, 50g carbohydrate, 14g total fat (6g saturated), 33mg cholesterol, 740mg sodium**

## GARDEN PIZZA

*Prep: 30 minutes, plus resting*  **Bake:** *20–30 minutes*
**Makes** *4 main dish servings*

Basic Pizza Dough (see left)
1 tbsp vegetable oil
1 small courgette (about 175g), diced
1 small yellow courgette (about 175g), diced
300g frozen chopped spinach, thawed and squeezed dry

1 large tomato, seeded and diced
½ tsp dried oregano
¼ tsp ground black pepper
225g half-fat mozzarella cheese, grated

Prepare pizza dough as in Steps 1 and 2, making 1, 2 or 4 balls as desired. While dough is resting, heat oil in large frying pan over medium-high heat; add courgettes; cook until tender. Stir in spinach, tomato, oregano, and pepper; remove pan from heat. Shape dough as in Step 3; top with vegetable mixture and mozzarella. Let rest 15 minutes. Preheat oven to 220°C (425°F, Gas 7). Bake in oven 20–30 minutes, until base is browned.

**Each serving: About 450 calories, 24g protein, 55g carbohydrate, 16g total fat (7g saturated), 32mg cholesterol, 730mg sodium**

## CHAR-GRILLED PIZZA

*Prep: 15 minutes, plus resting*  **Barbecue:** *5–10 minutes*
**Makes** *4 main dish servings*

Basic Pizza Dough (see above left)
2 tbsp olive oil
225g fresh mozzarella cheese, thinly sliced

12 basil leaves
2 small tomatoes, thinly sliced
Salt and ground black pepper

◆ Prepare a barbecue. Prepare pizza dough as in Step 1. Let rest 15 minutes, then shape into two 26cm rounds or four 15cm rounds on work surface as in Steps 2 and 3, but do not add toppings or form rims.

◆ Place pizza bases on barbecue rack; cook over medium heat 2–5 minutes, until underside turns golden and grill marks appear. Using tongs, turn bases over. Brush lightly with some olive oil. Top with mozzarella, then basil and tomato slices. Grill 3–5 minutes longer, until cheese begins to melt. Transfer pizzas to plates. Drizzle with remaining olive oil; sprinkle with salt and pepper.

**Each serving: About 470 calories, 18g protein, 49g carbohydrate, 22g total fat (9g saturated), 44mg cholesterol, 750mg sodium**

# QUICKER HOME-MADE PIZZAS

Here are some quick pizza recipes for when time is of the essence. Try our simple Basil and Feta Pizza enhanced with a refreshing dressed salad topping or to make life even easier, use a ready-to-use pizza base, available at your supermarket. All of your energy can then go towards preparing tempting toppings: sweet caramelized onions with nutty-tasting Gruyère and smoked salmon with cream cheese are just some of the inspired ideas you will find here. Ready-made pizza bases and our alternative instant bases (see box, below) will not be as crisp as a base made with pizza dough – to avoid a soggy base, it's best to serve these pizzas immediately.

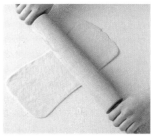

1 Preheat oven to 220°C (425°F, Gas 7). Prepare Basic Pizza Dough. Halve dough; using floured rolling pin, roll each half into a 28 by 15cm rectangle on lightly floured surface.

2 Place rectangles on 2 greased baking sheets. Sprinkle dough with basil and half feta cheese. Bake 12–15 minutes, rotating sheets after 7 minutes, until crust is golden brown.

## BASIL AND FETA PIZZA WITH FRESH SALAD TOPPPING

❖❖❖❖❖❖❖❖❖❖❖❖❖❖❖❖❖❖❖❖❖❖❖❖❖❖❖❖

*Prep: 30 minutes, plus resting*   *Bake: 12–15 minutes*
*Makes 2 main dish servings*

Basic Pizza Dough (see page 418)
30g fresh basil leaves, chopped
30g feta cheese, crumbled
60g reduced-fat mayonnaise
2 tbsp milk

¼ tsp coarsely ground black pepper
1 small head Cos lettuce (about 350g)
1 small red onion
30g Parmesan cheese, freshly grated

3 Meanwhile, prepare dressing: using fork, mix mayonnaise, milk, pepper and remaining feta together in large bowl.

4 Thinly slice lettuce and onion; toss with dressing in bowl. Pile salad on top of hot pizza bases; sprinkle with Parmesan.

### INSTANT PIZZA BASES

You can prepare a pizza quickly using a ready-to-use supermarket pizza base or Italian bread and any of our tempting toppings. But don't stop there – other kinds of breads can be used to make an instant pizza base. Try plain or wholemeal pittas, flour tortillas, matzoh or toasted English muffins. Add the topping and bake the pizza at 230°C (450°F, Gas 8) for about 10 minutes, until it is heated through.

EACH SERVING: ABOUT 570 CALORIES, 21g PROTEIN, 77g CARBOHYDRATE, 18g TOTAL FAT (5g SATURATED), 29mg CHOLESTEROL, 1005mg SODIUM

# CARAMELIZED ONION AND GRUYÈRE PIZZA

*Prep: 40 minutes    Bake: 10–12 minutes*
*Makes 4 main dish servings*

750g onions
1 tbsp olive oil
30g fresh basil leaves,
  chopped
1 large loaf, Italian bread,
  (about 450g)
150g Gruyère cheese, grated

◆ Preheat oven to 230°C (450°F, Gas 8). Half Italian loaf lengthways, then cut in each half in half again crossways.

◆ Cut each onion into 5mm thick slices. Heat olive oil in non-stick 30cm frying pan over medium heat. Stir in sliced onions until they are well coated with oil.

◆ Cook onions, stirring occasionally, 25 minutes, or until they are deep golden brown and very tender. Remove pan from heat; stir in chopped basil.

◆ Place bread pieces on large ungreased baking sheet. Spoon onion mixture over each piece of bread; sprinkle with cheese. Bake 10–12 minutes, until cheese is melted.

**Each serving: About 540 calories, 25g protein, 65g carbohydrate, 22g total fat (7g saturated), 41mg cholesterol, 735mg sodium**

## INDIVIDUAL PIZZAS

**MUSHROOM AND CHEESE** Preheat oven to 230°C (450°F, Gas 8). Grate 30g Cheddar and 30g mozzarella cheese and mix together in small bowl. Place a small pizza base on ungreased baking sheet (see above). Spread with 1 tablespoon bottled spaghetti sauce or pizza sauce; sprinkle with half of cheese mixture. Top with 15g thinly sliced mushrooms, remaining cheese mixture and 1 teaspoon chopped fresh parsley. Bake 10 minutes, or until cheese is melted and bubbly. Makes 1 serving.

Each serving: About 500 calories, 27g protein, 55g carbohydrate, 20g total fat (9g saturated), 42mg cholesterol, 990mg sodium

**BASIL, OLIVE AND TOMATO** Preheat oven to 230°C (450°F, Gas 8). Place a small pizza base on ungreased baking sheet. Arrange 1 very thinly sliced plum tomato on top; sprinkle with 60g grated mozzarella cheese. Top with 2 tablespoons chopped fresh basil, 2 tablespoons sliced stoned black olives and ⅛ teaspoon cracked black pepper. Bake 10 minutes, or until cheese is melted and bubbly. Makes 1 serving.

Each serving: About 500 calories, 24g protein, 57g carbohydrate, 21g total fat (8g saturated), 46mg cholesterol, 980mg sodium

**PEPPER AND PEPERONI** Preheat oven to 230°C (450°F, Gas 8). Place a small pizza base on ungreased baking sheet. Spread with 1 tablespoon bottled spaghetti sauce or pizza sauce; sprinkle with 30g grated mozzarella cheese. Top with 25g sliced peperoni and ¼ thinly slices small green pepper. Sprinkle with another 30g grated mozzarella. Bake 10 minutes, or until cheese is melted and bubbly. Makes 1 serving.

Each serving: About 590 calories, 28g protein, 55g carbohydrate, 30g total fat (11g saturated), 46mg cholesterol, 1360mg sodium

**SMOKED SALMON** Preheat oven to 230°C (450°F, Gas 8). Place a small pizza base on ungreased baking sheet; bake 8 minutes. Spread hot base with 2 tablespoons cream cheese. Top with 45g smoked salmon, cut into bite-sized pieces, 1 tablespoon very finely chopped red onion and 1 teaspoon canned or bottled drained and chopped capers. Garnish with fresh parsley. Makes 1 serving.

Each serving: About 455 calories, 22g protein, 52g carbohydrate, 19g total fat (6g saturated), 42mg cholesterol, 1135mg sodium

Basil, olive and tomato

Mushroom and cheese

Smoked salmon

Pepper and peperoni

# BATTER BREADS

Batter breads, which can be sweet or savoury, are the easiest of all yeast breads to prepare. The dough is simply beaten – not kneaded – and turned into a casserole or baking tin, so no shaping is required. For best results, beat the batter (which will be stickier than standard yeast-bread doughs) until it's very stiff – you should be able to stand a spoon in it.

## ONION-DILL BATTER BREAD

*Prep: 35 minutes, plus rising and cooling*   *Bake: 30–35 minutes*
*Makes 2 loaves, 8 servings each*

| | |
|---|---|
| 30g butter or margarine | 2 tsp salt |
| 1 large bunch spring onions, chopped | 60g coarse yellow cornmeal plus additional for sprinkling |
| 2 tbsp chopped fresh parsley | |
| 1 tbsp chopped fresh dill or 1 tsp dried | 600g strong plain flour |
| 1 sachet (7g) easy-blend yeast | 350ml buttermilk or soured milk (see page 392) |
| 2 tbsp caster sugar | |

**1** Melt butter in 26cm frying pan over medium heat; add chopped spring onions and cook, stirring frequently, 5 minutes, or until spring onions are tender. Remove pan from heat; stir in chopped parsley and dill. Combine yeast, caster sugar, salt, 60g cornmeal and 300g flour in large bowl. Heat buttermilk and *60ml water* in saucepan over low heat until very warm (47–52°C).

**2** Using electric mixer on low speed, gradually beat liquid into flour mixture just until blended. Increase speed to medium; beat 2 minutes.

**3** Beat in 75g flour to make a thick batter. Beat 2 minutes longer, scraping bowl frequently with rubber spatula. Using wooden spoon, stir in onion mixture and remaining 225g flour to make a stiff batter. Cover the bowl loosely with cling film; let rise in warm place (27–29.5°C) about 1 hour until doubled. Grease two 1½-litre round casseroles; sprinkle evenly with cornmeal.

**4** Using wooden spoon, stir down batter; divide in half and spoon into casseroles. Cover loosely with cling film; let rise in warm place about 45 minutes until doubled.

**5** Preheat oven to 190°C (375°F, Gas 5). Sprinkle tops of loaves lightly with cornmeal. Bake 30–35 minutes, until loaf sounds hollow when lightly tapped. Remove loaves from casseroles; cool on wire rack.

### WHAT'S IN A NAME?

Batter breads provide a quick way to enjoy yeast breads. Because they don't require kneading, the relatively soft, sticky batter usually calls for vigorous beating to develop the gluten, which gives the bread its structure and allows it to rise. Batter breads have a rustic appearance. Although the texture won't be as fine-crumbed as bread that has been kneaded, the taste will be just as delicious.

**EACH SERVING: ABOUT 155 CALORIES, 5g PROTEIN, 29g CARBOHYDRATE, 2g TOTAL FAT (2g SATURATED), 9mg CHOLESTEROL, 315mg SODIUM**

## DOUBLE-CHEESE BATTER BREAD

*Prep: 25 minutes, plus rising and cooling*
*Bake: 35 minutes*
*Makes 1 loaf, 12 servings*

1 sachet (7g) easy-blend yeast
175g mature Cheddar cheese, grated
30g Parmesan cheese, freshly grated
1 tbsp caster sugar
½ tsp salt
375g strong plain flour
2 medium eggs
½ tsp poppy seeds

◈ Combine yeast, Cheddar cheese, Parmesan cheese, sugar, salt and 225g flour in large bowl.

◈ Using electric mixer on low speed, gradually beat *175ml very hot tap water* (47–52°C) into flour mixture just until blended. Separate 1 egg and reserve white in refrigerator, covered. Beat remaining egg and egg yolk into batter.

◈ Increase speed to medium; beat 3 minutes, scraping bowl often with rubber spatula. Using wooden spoon, stir in remaining 150g flour to make a stiff batter that leaves side of bowl.

◈ Cover bowl loosely with cling film; let dough rise in warm place (27–29.5°C) 20 minutes. Grease 1½-litre round casserole. Using wooden spoon, stir down batter; spoon into casserole. Cover loosely with cling film; let rise in warm place 15 minutes.

◈ Preheat oven to 180°C (350°F, Gas 4). Using fork, beat reserved egg white in cup; brush over top of loaf. Sprinkle with poppy seeds. Bake 35 minutes, or until loaf sounds hollow when lightly tapped. Remove loaf from casserole; cool on wire rack.

**Each serving: About 175 calories, 8g protein, 20g carbohydrate, 6g total fat (4g saturated), 52mg cholesterol, 225mg sodium**

## OATMEAL BATTER BREAD

*Prep: 20 minutes, plus rising and cooling*
*Bake: 40 minutes*
*Makes 2 loaves, 12 servings each*

2 sachets (7g each) easy-blend yeast
2 tsp salt
750g strong plain flour
80g rolled oats
80g light mollasses or golden syrup
15g butter or margarine plus
    10g (optional) for glazing

◈ Combine yeast, salt and 300g flour in large bowl. Mix oats, light mollasses, 15g butter and *550ml water* together in 2-litre saucepan. Heat over low heat until very warm (47–52°C); butter need not melt.

◈ Using electric mixer on low speed, gradually beat liquid into flour mixture just until blended. Increase speed to medium; beat 2 minutes. Beat in 75g flour to make a thick batter; beat 2 minutes longer, scraping bowl frequently with rubber spatula. Using wooden spoon, stir in remaining 375g flour to make a stiff batter that leaves side of bowl.

◈ Cover bowl loosely with cling film; let dough rise in warm place (27–29.5°C) about 1 hour until doubled. Grease two 2-litre round, shallow casseroles. Using wooden spoon, stir down batter. Divide in half and spoon into casseroles. Using greased fingers, turn to grease tops and shape each into a ball. Cover loosely with cling film; let rise in warm place about 45 minutes until doubled.

◈ Preheat oven to 180°C (350°F, Gas 4). Bake 40 minutes, or until loaves sound hollow when lightly tapped. Remove loaves from casseroles. If you like, for a soft crust, rub tops with remaining 10g softened butter; cool on wire racks.

**Each serving: About 135 calories, 4g protein, 27g carbohydrate, 1g total fat (0g saturated), 2mg cholesterol, 185mg sodium**

## RAISIN BATTER BREAD

*Prep: 20 minutes, plus rising and cooling*
*Bake: 50 minutes*
*Makes 1 loaf, 20 servings*

2 sachets (7g each) easy-blend yeast
150g caster sugar
1 tsp salt
750g strong plain flour
350ml milk
90g butter or margarine, cut up
2 medium eggs
200g raisins

◈ Combine yeast, sugar, salt and 300g flour in large bowl. Heat milk and butter in 1-litre saucepan over low heat until very warm (47–52°C); butter need not melt.

◈ Using electric mixer on low speed, gradually beat liquid into flour mixture just until blended. Increase speed to medium; beat 2 minutes. Beat in eggs and 225g flour; beat 2 minutes longer, scraping bowl frequently with rubber spatula. Using wooden spoon, stir in raisins and remaining 225g flour to make a stiff batter that leaves side of bowl.

◈ Cover bowl loosely with cling film; let dough rise in warm place (27–29.5°C) 1–1½ hours until doubled.

◈ Grease 25cm tube tin. Using wooden spoon, stir down batter; spoon into tin. Cover loosely with cling film; let rise in warm place 45–60 minutes until doubled.

◈ Preheat oven to 180°C (350°F, Gas 4). Bake 50 minutes, or until loaf is golden and sounds hollow when lightly tapped. Remove from pan; cool on wire rack.

**Each serving: About 215 calories, 5g protein, 39g carbohydrate, 5g total fat (2g saturated), 34mg cholesterol, 165mg sodium**

# DANISH PASTRIES AND SWEET BUNS

A fresh, warm sweet pastry or sticky bun with your morning coffee is one of life's simple pleasures. These sweet pastries and spice-scented buns also freeze well for treats another day.

## EASY DANISH PASTRIES

◆◆◆◆◆◆◆◆◆◆◆◆◆◆◆◆◆

*Prep: 1 hour, plus standing and chilling overnight*
*Bake: 30 minutes*
*Makes 18*

4½ tsp active dried yeast
1 tsp plus 70g caster sugar
600g strong plain flour
½ tsp salt
175g butter, cut up
4 medium eggs
125ml plus 2 tbsp whipping cream
350g plus 2 tbsp cherry or apricot jam or Danish Filling (see below)
60g icing sugar

**1** Stir yeast and 1 teaspoon sugar into *125ml warm water* (47–52°C) in medium bowl; let stand 5 minutes, until foamy. Mix flour, remaining 70g caster sugar, and salt in large bowl. Using pastry blender or two knives used scissor-fashion, cut in butter until mixture resembles coarse crumbs. Whisk 3 eggs and 125ml cream into yeast mixture; stir into flour mixture until moistened. Cover and refrigerate dough overnight.

**4** Beat remaining egg with *1 tablespoon water* in cup; brush over pastries. Bake 30 minutes, or until golden, switching baking sheets on oven racks halfway through baking. Transfer pastries to wire racks set over greaseproof paper; cool. Mix icing sugar with remaining 2 tablespoons cream in small bowl to make thick glaze. Drizzle over pastries.

**2** Preheat oven to 180°C (350°F, Gas 4). Grease 2 large baking sheets. Divide dough in half. Using floured rolling pin, roll out half of dough on lightly floured surface into 30cm square. Cut into nine 10cm squares.

**3** Place 1 tablespoon filling in centre of each square. Make a 5cm cut from each corner toward centre; fold every other tip in to center. Arrange on baking sheet. Repeat with remaining dough and jam.

◆◆◆◆◆◆◆◆◆◆◆◆◆◆◆◆◆◆◆◆◆◆◆◆

### FOLDOVERS

Prepare pastries as in Steps 1 and 2 above. Place 1 tablespoon jam in centre of each 10cm square. Fold one corner in 5cm to cover jam; fold opposite corner to edge. Arrange on baking sheets and repeat with remaining dough and jam. Proceed as in Step 4.

◆◆◆◆◆◆◆◆◆◆◆◆◆◆◆◆◆◆◆◆◆◆◆◆◆

### DANISH FILLINGS

**Almond** Using electric mixer on low speed, beat 220–225g marzipan, 60g softened butter or margarine, 1 medium egg, and ½ teaspoon grated lemon rind until smooth.

**Cheese** Using electric mixer on low speed, beat 225g cream cheese, 40g icing sugar, 1½ teaspoons vanilla essence and 1 medium egg yolk until smooth.

EACH PASTRY: ABOUT 285 CALORIES, 5g PROTEIN, 41g CARBOHYDRATE, 12g TOTAL FAT (6g SATURATED), 80mg CHOLESTEROL, 165mg SODIUM

## HOT-CROSS BUNS

*Prep: 45 minutes, plus rising and cooling    Bake: 20–25 minutes*
*Makes 25*

| | |
|---|---|
| 2 sachets (7g each) easy-blend yeast | 125g butter or margarine |
| 100g caster sugar | 2 medium eggs |
| 1½ tsp ground cardamom | 75g sultanas |
| About 710g strong plain flour | 75g diced mixed fruit |
| Salt | 120g icing sugar |

◆ Combine yeast, sugar, cardamom, 225g flour and 1½ teaspoons salt in large bowl. Heat butter and *225ml water* in 1-litre saucepan over low heat until very warm (47–52°C); butter need not melt.

◆ Using electric mixer on low speed, gradually beat liquid into flour mixture just until blended. Increase speed to medium; beat 2 minutes, occasionally scraping bowl with rubber spatula. Separate 1 egg and reserve white in refrigerator, covered.

◆ Beat remaining egg, egg yolk, and 75g flour into flour mixture to make a thick batter; beat 2 minutes longer, scraping bowl often. Using wooden spoon, stir in 375g flour to make a soft dough.

◆ Turn dough onto lightly floured surface and knead about 10 minutes until smooth and elastic, working in about 35g more flour if needed to keep dough from sticking to work surface. Shape dough into a ball; place in greased large bowl, turning dough to grease top. Cover bowl loosely with cling film; let rise in warm place (27–29.5°C) about 1 hour until doubled.

◆ Knock back dough. Knead in raisins and mixed fruit. Cut dough into 25 equal pieces; let rest 15 minutes for easier shaping.

◆ Grease large baking sheet. Shape dough into balls. Arrange buns in square, 1cm apart, on baking sheet. Cover loosely with cling film; let rise about 40 minutes until doubled.

◆ Preheat oven to 190°C (375°F, Gas 5). Using fork, beat reserved egg white with ⅛ teaspoon salt in cup. Brush buns with egg white. Bake 20–25 minutes, until buns are golden and sound hollow when lightly tapped. Slide buns onto wire rack to cool.

◆ When buns are cool, prepare icing: mix icing sugar and *4 teaspoons water* until smooth. Spoon icing into small plastic bag; snip off one corner and pipe crosses on buns.

**Each bun: About 170 calories, 3g protein, 30g carbohydrate, 4g total fat (2g saturated), 28mg cholesterol, 190mg sodium**

## OLD-FASHIONED STICKY BUNS

*Prep: 70 minutes, plus rising and cooling    Bake: 25–30 minutes*
*Makes 20*

| | |
|---|---|
| 2 sachets (7g each) easy-blend yeast | 270g butter or margarine |
| 150g caster sugar | 3 medium eggs |
| 2 tsp salt | 225g walnuts, chopped |
| 2 tsp ground cardamom (optional) | 200g sultanas |
| About 1.1kg strong plain flour | 300g dark brown sugar |
| 400ml milk | 2 tbsp golden syrup |
| | 90g icing sugar |

◆ Combine yeast, caster sugar, salt, cardamom and 450g flour in large bowl. Heat milk and 90g butter in 2-litre saucepan over low heat until very warm (47–52°C); butter need not melt.

◆ Using electric mixer on low speed, gradually beat liquid into flour mixture just until blended, scraping bowl often. Beat in eggs. Increase speed to medium; beat 3 minutes. Using wooden spoon, stir in 600g flour, to make a soft dough.

◆ Turn out dough onto lightly floured surface; knead about 10 minutes, until smooth and elastic, working in about 75g more flour. Shape into ball. Cover loosely with cling film; let rest 15 minutes. Meanwhile, prepare filling: melt 90g butter in 1-litre saucepan over low heat; set aside. Mix walnuts, sultanas and 200g brown sugar in medium bowl. Grease 38 by 28cm roasting tin.

◆ Cut dough in half. Using floured rolling pin, roll half of dough, on lightly floured surface, into 45 by 30cm rectangle. Brush dough with half of melted butter; sprinkle with half filling. Starting from a long side, roll dough Swiss-roll fashion; pinch seam to seal. Using serrated knife, slice roll crossways into 10 pieces. Repeat with remaining dough, butter and filling.

◆ Arrange buns, cut-side down, in roasting tin. Cover loosely with cling film; let rise in warm place (27–29.5°C) about 30 minutes until doubled. Preheat oven to 180°C (350°F, Gas 4). Bake 25–30 minutes, until buns are golden and sound hollow when lightly tapped.

◆ Prepare glaze: heat golden syrup, remaining 100g brown sugar, and remaining 90g butter in 1-litre saucepan over medium heat until butter is melted and sugar is completely dissolved; spoon over hot buns. Cool buns in tin on wire rack. When buns are cool, mix icing sugar and *1 tablespoon water* in small bowl until smooth; drizzle icing over buns with spoon.

**Each bun: About 495 calories, 9g protein, 74g carbohydrate, 19g total fat (5g saturated), 62mg cholesterol, 365mg sodium**

# Plaits and twists

These special-occasion breads are enhanced with chocolate, sweet apples and other luscious fillings before they're baked into pretty shapes. Perfect with morning coffee or afternoon tea, they also make a delicious and thoughtful gift.

## Date-nut twist

◆ ◆ ◆ ◆ ◆ ◆ ◆ ◆ ◆ ◆ ◆ ◆ ◆ ◆

*Prep: 1 hour, plus rising and cooling*
*Bake: 40 minutes*
*Makes 1 twist, 16 servings*

**2 sachets (7g each) easy-blend yeast**
**70g caster sugar**
**1 tsp salt**
**About 675g strong plain flour**
**225ml milk**
**90g butter or margarine**
**3 medium eggs**
**125g walnuts, chopped**
**150g stoned dates, chopped**
**70g brown sugar**
**2 tsp ground cinnamon**
**175g apricot jam, melted**

**1** Mix first 3 ingredients and 150g flour in large bowl. Heat milk and 60g butter in 1-litre saucepan over low heat until very warm (47–52°C); butter need not melt. Using electric mixer on low speed, beat liquid into flour mixture just until blended. Increase speed to medium; beat 2 minutes, occasionally scraping bowl. Separate 1 egg; reserve yolk in refrigerator, covered. Beat remaining 2 eggs, egg white and 150g flour into flour mixture to make a thick batter.

**2** Beat 2 minutes. Using wooden spoon, stir in 300g flour to make a soft dough. Turn out dough onto floured surface; knead about 10 minutes, until smooth and elastic, working in about 75g more flour. Shape into ball; place in greased large bowl, turning to grease top. Cover loosely with cling film; let rise in warm place (27–29.5°C) 30 minutes, or until doubled. Grease 25 by 6cm springform tin.

**3** Preheat oven to 180°C (350°F, Gas 4). Melt remaining 30g butter in 2-litre saucepan over low heat. Remove from heat; stir in walnuts and next 3 ingredients.

**4** Knock back dough. Turn out onto lightly floured surface; cover; let rest 10 minutes. Using floured rolling pin, roll into 45 by 25cm rectangle; brush with all but 2 tablespoons jam.

**5** Sprinkle walnut mixture evenly over dough; press into dough lightly with rolling pin. Starting from a long side, tightly roll up dough Swiss-roll fashion; cut roll lengthways in half.

**6** Keeping cut sides up, twist both halves of dough roll together; place in springform pan, shaping twist into a ring. Tuck ends under to seal. Bake twist 25 minutes.

**7** Using fork, beat reserved egg yolk and *1 teaspoon water* in cup. When twist has baked 25 minutes, brush with egg-yolk mixture. Bake 15 minutes longer. Cool in tin on wire rack 5 minutes. Carefully remove side of tin; brush hot bread with remaining 2 tablespoons jam. Cool on rack slightly to serve warm. Or, cool completely on rack to serve later; re-heat if desired.

EACH SERVING: ABOUT 320 CALORIES, 7g PROTEIN, 51g CARBOHYDRATE, 11g TOTAL FAT (3g SATURATED), 54mg CHOLESTEROL, 205mg SODIUM

## APPLE-FILLED PLAIT

*Prep: 50 minutes, plus rising and cooling    Bake: 30 minutes*
*Makes 1 plait, 12 servings*

| | |
|---|---|
| 75g butter or margarine | 1 sachet (7g) easy-blend yeast |
| 2 apples, such as Cox's orange pippin, peeled, cored, and diced | ¼ tsp salt |
| | About 420g strong plain flour |
| | 75ml plus 4 tsp milk |
| 40g raisins | 1 medium egg |
| ¼ tsp ground cinnamon | 75g icing sugar |
| 100g caster sugar | |

◆ Melt 30g butter in 26cm frying pan over medium-high heat; add next 3 ingredients and 50g caster sugar. Cook 10 minutes, or until apples are tender; set aside. Combine yeast, salt, 75g flour and 50g caster sugar in large bowl. Heat 75ml milk, remaining 45g butter and *2 tablespoons water* in 1-litre saucepan over low heat until very warm (47–52°C); butter need not melt.

◆ Using electric mixer on low speed, gradually beat liquid into flour mixture just until blended. Increase speed to medium; beat 2 minutes, scraping bowl. Beat in egg and 75g flour to make a thick batter; beat 2 minutes, scraping bowl often. Stir in 225g flour to make a soft dough. Knead dough on floured surface, with floured hands, about 10 minutes until smooth and elastic, working in about 35g more flour. Shape into ball. Cover; let rest 10 minutes.

◆ Using floured rolling pin, roll out dough into 35 by 25cm rectangle on greased large baking sheet (place damp towel under sheet to prevent slipping). Place apples in 7–8cm wide strip lengthways down centre. Shape plait (see below). Cover; let rise in warm place (27–29.5°C) 40 minutes or until doubled. Preheat oven to 180°C (350°F, Gas 4). Bake plait 30 minutes, or until golden. Cool on wire rack. Mix icing sugar and remaining 4 teaspoons milk in cup. Drizzle over plait to glaze.

**Each serving: About 230 calories, 4g protein, 41g carbohydrate, 6g total fat (2g saturated), 32mg cholesterol, 110mg sodium**

◆◆◆◆◆◆◆◆◆◆◆◆◆◆◆◆◆◆◆◆◆◆◆◆◆

### SHAPING A PLAIT

Cut dough on both sides of filling into 2–3cm wide strips just up to filling. Place strips at an angle across filling, alternating sides; end of each strip should be covered by next strip. Pinch last strip to base of plait to seal.

◆◆◆◆◆◆◆◆◆◆◆◆◆◆◆◆◆◆◆◆◆◆◆◆◆

## CHOCOLATE-ALMOND PLAIT

*Prep: 55 minutes, plus rising and cooling    Bake: 50 minutes*
*Makes 1 plait, 16 servings*

| | |
|---|---|
| 1 sachet (7g) easy-blend yeast | 3 medium eggs |
| ½ tsp salt | 225g cream cheese, softened |
| About 800g strong plain flour | 200–225g marzipan |
| 100g plus 2 tbsp caster sugar | 125g plain or milk chocolate, chopped |
| 175ml milk | |
| 105g butter or margarine | |

◆ Combine yeast, salt, 150g flour and 100g sugar in large bowl. Heat milk, 75g butter and *60ml water* in 1-litre saucepan over low heat until very warm (47–52°C); butter need not melt. Using electric mixer on low speed, gradually beat liquid into flour mixture just until blended. Increase speed to medium; beat 2 minutes, scraping bowl often. Beat in 2 eggs and 300g flour; beat 2 minutes longer. Stir in 225g flour to make a soft dough.

◆ Turn out dough onto floured surface. Knead about 10 minutes, with floured hands, until smooth and elastic, working in about 75g more flour. Shape into ball; place in greased large bowl, turning to grease top. Cover; let rise in warm place (27–29.5°C) 1 hour until doubled.

◆ Prepare filling: separate remaining egg; reserve white in refrigerator, covered. Beat cream cheese, marzipan and egg yolk in large bowl, with mixer on low speed, until smooth. Stir in 90g chocolate. Refrigerate.

◆ Prepare streusel topping: mix 75g plain flour, remaining 2 tablespoons sugar and remaining 30g butter in bowl, with fingertips, until mixture resembles coarse crumbs. Refrigerate. Knock back dough. Turn onto lightly floured surface. Cover; let rest 15 minutes.

◆ Using floured rolling pin, roll out dough on a greased large baking sheet into 40 by 30cm rectangle (place damp towel under sheet to prevent slipping). Spread filling in 10cm wide strip lengthways down centre. Shape plait (see left). Cover; let rise in warm place (27–29.5°C) 30 minutes.

◆ Preheat oven to 170°C (325°F, Gas 3). Beat reserved egg white and *1 tablespoon water* lightly; use to brush over plait. Sprinkle streusel topping down centre of plait. Bake plait 50 minutes, or until browned, covering with foil after 30 minutes to prevent over-browning. Cool completely on wire rack. Melt remaining 30g chocolate in small saucepan over low heat. Drizzle over cooled plait.

**Each serving: About 380 calories, 8g protein, 49g carbohydrate, 17g total fat (7g saturated), 71mg cholesterol, 190mg sodium**

# SWEET BREADS

These sweet breads, accented with varying flavours and textures – including pecans, orange rind, cream cheese and preserves – make a tempting snack. Each of these recipes can be made ahead – wrap the cooled sweet bread well and freeze for up to one month (if you like, cut in half or into serving portions before freezing). Thaw sweet bread, still wrapped, at room temperature and re-heat, if desired, before serving.

## APRICOT-PECAN SWIRL

*Prep: 50 minutes, plus rising and cooling*    *Bake: 30 minutes*
*Makes 12 servings*

| | |
|---|---|
| 90g butter or margarine | 1 tsp salt |
| 175g pecans, finely chopped | About 675g strong plain flour |
| 70g brown sugar | 225ml milk |
| 1 tsp ground cinnamon | 2 medium eggs |
| 2 sachets (7g each) easy-blend yeast | 175g apricot jam, melted |
| 70g caster sugar | 1 medium egg yolk |

**1** Grease 25 by 6cm springform pan. Prepare filling: melt 30g butter in 2-litre saucepan over low heat. Remove saucepan from heat. Stir in chopped pecans, brown sugar and ground cinnamon until well blended; set aside. Combine yeast, caster sugar, salt and 150g flour in large bowl. Heat milk and remaining 60g butter in 1-litre saucepan over low heat until very warm (47–52°C); butter need not melt.

**2** Using electric mixer on low speed, gradually beat liquid into flour mixture just until blended. Increase speed to medium; beat 2 minutes. Add whole eggs; beat until blended. Using wooden spoon, stir in 450g flour to make a soft dough. Turn out dough onto lightly floured surface; knead about 10 minutes until smooth and elastic, working in about 75g more flour. Cover; let rest 10 minutes.

**3** Using floured rolling pin, roll dough into 45 by 25cm rectangle; brush evenly with some of melted jam. Sprinkle filling evenly over dough; press lightly into dough with rolling pin.

**4** Cut dough lengthways into 5cm wide strips. Loosely roll up 1 strip and place in centre of pan, cut-side down. One at a time, loosely wrap remaining strips around centre strip to make a spiral, matching ends of strips as you work. Cover loosely with cling film; let rise in warm place (27–29.5°C) about 30 minutes until doubled.

**5** Preheat oven to 180°C (350°F, Gas 4). Using fork, beat egg yolk lightly in cup. Brush cake evenly with egg yolk. Bake 30 minutes or until golden. Cool cake in tin on wire rack 5 minutes; brush with remaining melted jam. Carefully remove side of tin. Serve warm. Or, cool on wire rack to serve later; re-heat, if you like.

EACH SERVING: ABOUT 410 CALORIES, 8g PROTEIN, 58g CARBOHYDRATE, 17g TOTAL FAT (4g SATURATED), 72mg CHOLESTEROL, 270mg SODIUM

## ORANGE-CARDAMOM SWEET BREAD

*Prep: 35 minutes, plus rising and cooling   Bake: 50 minutes*
*Makes 1 loaf, 20 servings*

| | |
|---|---|
| 1 large orange | 235g honey |
| 2 sachets (7g each) easy-blend yeast | 60g butter or margarine |
| 1 tsp salt | 3 medium eggs |
| About 1.1kg strong plain flour | 1½ tsp ground cardamom |
| 300ml buttermilk or soured milk (see page 392) | 1 tbsp milk |
| | 60g flaked almonds |

◆ Grease 25 by 6cm springform tin. Grate 2 teaspoons rind and squeeze 60ml juice from orange. Combine yeast, salt and flour in large bowl. Heat buttermilk, honey, butter and orange juice in 2-litre saucepan over medium heat until very warm (47–52°C); butter need not melt.

◆ Using electric mixer on low speed, gradually beat liquid into flour mixture just until blended. Increase speed to medium; beat 2 minutes, occasionally scraping bowl with rubber spatula.

◆ Using fork, beat eggs lightly in cup; reserve 1 tablespoon beaten egg in refrigerator, covered. Add remaining beaten eggs with cardamom, orange rind and 225g flour to flour mixture; beat 2 minutes, scraping bowl often. Using wooden spoon, stir in 525g flour to make a soft dough.

◆ Turn dough out onto lightly floured surface and knead about 10 minutes until smooth and elastic, working in about 75g more flour while kneading. Shape dough into ball; place in centre of springform tin, turning to grease top. Cover loosely with cling film; let rise in warm place (27–29.5°C) about 1 hour, until doubled.

◆ Preheat oven to 180°C (350°F, Gas 4). Using fork, mix milk and reserved beaten egg in cup. Brush top of loaf with some of egg mixture. Sprinkle with flaked almonds; brush almonds lightly with more egg mixture. Bake 50 minutes, or until bread sounds hollow when lightly tapped, covering with foil after about 20 minutes to prevent over-browning. Remove side of tin; cool on wire rack 30 minutes to serve warm. Or, cool completely to serve later.

**Each serving: About 250 calories, 7g protein, 45g carbohydrate, 5g total fat (1g saturated), 39mg cholesterol, 160mg sodium**

## CREAM CHEESE SWIRL LOAVES

*Prep: 50 minutes, plus rising and cooling   Bake: 30–35 minutes*
*Makes 2 loaves, 12 servings each*

| | |
|---|---|
| 2 sachets (7g each) easy-blend yeast | 60ml milk |
| 70g caster sugar | 1 medium egg |
| ¾ tsp salt | 450g cream cheese, softened |
| About 525g strong plain flour | 65g icing sugar |
| 60g butter or margarine | 1 tbsp grated orange rind |
| | 2 medium egg yolks |

◆ Combine yeast, caster sugar, salt and 150g plain flour in large bowl. Heat butter, milk, and *125ml water* in 1-litre saucepan over low heat until very warm (47–52°C); butter need not melt.

◆ Using electric mixer on low speed, gradually beat liquid into flour mixture just until blended. Increase speed to medium; beat 2 minutes, occasionally scraping bowl with rubber spatula. Beat in whole egg and 135g flour to make a thick batter; beat 2 minutes. Using wooden spoon, stir in 165g flour to make a soft dough.

◆ Turn dough onto lightly floured surface and knead about 8 minutes until smooth and elastic, working in about 75g more flour while kneading. Shape dough into ball; place in greased large bowl, turning dough to grease top. Cover loosely with cling film; let rise in warm place (27–29.5°C) about 1 hour until doubled.

◆ Prepare filling: using mixer on low speed, beat cream cheese, icing sugar, grated orange rind and egg yolks in small bowl until smooth. Refrigerate until ready to use. Grease large baking sheet.

◆ Knock back dough. Turn dough onto lightly floured surface. Cut dough in half; cover and let rest 15 minutes. With floured rolling pin, roll half of dough into 33 by 20cm rectangle; spread half of filling to within 2–3cm of edge.

◆ Starting from a long side, roll dough Swiss-roll fashion; pinch seam to seal. Press ends to seal; tuck ends under. Repeat with remaining dough and filling. Place loaves, 7–8cm apart, on baking sheet; with sharp knife or single-edge razor, cut several slashes in tops. Cover loosely with cling film; let rise in warm place (27–29.5°C) about 45 minutes until doubled.

◆ Preheat oven to 180°C (350°F, Gas 4). Bake 30–35 minutes, until loaves are golden and sound hollow when lightly tapped. Remove loaves from baking sheet; cool slightly on wire racks to serve warm. Or, cool completely and refrigerate loaves to serve later; re-heat, if you like.

**Each serving: About 195 calories, 4g protein, 19g carbohydrate, 11g total fat (6g saturated), 53mg cholesterol, 170mg sodium**

# SANDWICHES 13

Sandwiches make the perfect no-fuss light meal, whether for a snack, lunch or an informal supper. Here is a guide to choosing bread, making tasty fillings, ingredients to use if you are watching your weight and how to make sandwiches for a packed lunch or picnic.

## YOU CAN TAKE IT WITH YOU

Preparing a sandwich for a school lunch, work or picnic is practical and inexpensive – it also allows you to control your diet. Pack with care or you could end up with soggy results, or even risk something dangerous to eat.

**Save time with an assembly line** If you're making several sandwiches at once, use a production-line technique. Place bread slices in rows; apply spreads; top with fillings.

**Wrap it up** To keep sandwiches fresh and moist, wrap them in cling film, greaseproof paper, plastic bags or aluminium foil immediately after preparation.

**Watch out for watery ingredients** Lettuce, sliced tomatoes or cucumbers can make bread soggy. For best results, omit these ingredients, or wrap separately and add just before serving.

**Choose the right bread** Certain sturdy, dense-textured loaves are suited to hold fillings without becoming waterlogged. They actually taste better after they absorb dressings. Best bets include focaccia, Italian ciabatta, bread rolls, sturdy baguettes and semolina bread.

**Keep sandwiches safe** To prevent the growth of harmful bacteria such as salmonella, never allow fillings containing poultry, meat, fish or eggs to sit at room temperature for longer than 2 hours.

## MAKE A SLIMMER SANDWICH

**Be selective with spreads** Avoid oil-laden spreads in favour of reduced-fat varieties. You can boost the flavour with chopped herbs or a touch of chilli sauce, or stick with low-fat relishes like mustard or chutney. Create your own spread with puréed sun-dried tomatoes or roasted garlic.

**Be skimpy with cheese** If you must add it, stick with reduced-fat varieties. A spread with a 'creamy' texture can be made from plain nonfat yogurt mixed with mustard.

**Pick a lean protein** Steer clear of fatty meats such as corned beef or sausage; opt instead for skinless chicken or turkey breast, prawn or tuna in brine.

**Pile on fat-free, high-flavour foods** Good choices include roasted peppers, chopped water-packed artichoke hearts, bottled roasted peppers or capers. Skip bland lettuces like Iceberg in favour of rocket or watercress.

## IRRESISTIBLE COMBINATIONS

• Houmous, sliced tomatoes and cucumber, and chilli sauce in warm wholemeal pitta bread.

• Sliced vine-ripened red and yellow tomatoes, mayonnaise, sea salt and freshly ground pepper on crustless white bread.

• Olive paste, roasted peppers, sliced hard-boiled egg, rocket and anchovies on a baguette.

• A grilled sandwich made with mushrooms and spinach sautéed in olive oil with Fontina cheese on ciabatta.

• Smoked turkey, cream cheese with spring onions and cranberry relish or chutney on toasted raisin-walnut bread.

• Creamy avocado with sliced red onion, tomato, cucumber, alfalfa sprouts and mayonnaise on multi-grain bread.

• Roasted aubergine, rocket and goat's cheese on focaccia.

• Sliced pork, caramelized onions and hot mustard on multi-grain bread or a sturdy bread roll.

## A WELL-BREAD SANDWICH

There is a huge range of breads available, providing delicious options for sandwich lovers. Most breads can be paired with virtually any ingredient from robust meats, such as salami and roast beef, to delicate fillings like egg salad or smoked salmon. Grilled sausage or other oily additions call for sturdy loaves. For extra flavour, try breads filled with olives, nuts or herbs. To improve day-old bread, toast the slices and spread with a relish or mustard.

White

Rye

Semolina

Ciabatta

Wholemeal

Sourdough

Focaccia

French roll

Pitta

# HOT SANDWICHES

When there's no time to cook, a simple sandwich is the obvious solution. These American-style variations on a traditional English theme are packed with fillings, combining tastes from the Mediterranean to California. Crowned with melted cheese or dripping with spicy barbecue sauce, hot sandwiches can provide inspiration for a fast supper or a weekend brunch. For a taste of New York, try our Deluxe Reubens sandwich – it is also delicious served cold.

## SALTIMBOCCA CHICKEN SANDWICHES

*Prep:* 15 minutes   *Grill:* 3–5 minutes
*Makes* 4 main dish servings

| | |
|---|---|
| 1 tbsp plain flour | 4 slices Italian bread, each |
| Coarsely ground black pepper | 2cm thick |
| 4 skinless, boneless chicken | 4 thin slices Parma ham or |
| breasts | cooked ham |
| 1 tbsp vegetable oil | 1 tomato, thinly sliced |
| 60g mayonnaise | 60g mozzarella or Provolone |
| 2 tbsp chopped fresh basil | cheese, grated |

1 Mix flour and ¼ teaspoon pepper on greaseproof paper; use to coat chicken. Heat oil over medium-high heat in 30cm frying pan; add chicken and cook about 10 minutes, turning once, until tender and golden brown and juices run clear when chicken is pierced with tip of knife.

2 Meanwhile, preheat grill. Mix mayonnaise, basil and ⅛ teaspoon pepper in small bowl. Spread mayonnaise mixture over bread slices; place on baking sheet.

3 Place baking sheet under grill at closest position to heat. Grill bread 1–2 minutes, until mayonnaise mixture is lightly browned and bubbly. Remove baking sheet; keep grill on. Place 1 slice Parma ham on each slice of bread; top with chicken, then sliced tomato. Sprinkle evenly with grated mozzarella. Grill sandwiches 2–3 minutes, until cheese is melted.

### ADDING FLAVOUR

Mayonnaise is a favourite addition for all kinds of sandwiches, and can be endlessly varied – here we've used basil for a fresh Italian flavour. But there's a whole range of other tastes for you to experiment with:

• Try whole-grain mustard for texture, or flavoured mustard with herbs or honey – good with meat or cheese.

• Tasty bean spreads or dips such as hummus are delicious with crisp greens.

• Olive spreads such as French tapenade have plenty of flavour and are especially good with tuna, fresh mozzarella or roasted peppers.

• A little pesto is the perfect partner for a tomato and mozzarella sandwich on a crusty Italian roll – or try it with bacon, roasted turkey or egg mayonnaise.

EACH SERVING: ABOUT 455 CALORIES, 42g PROTEIN, 19g CARBOHYDRATE, 23g TOTAL FAT (6g SATURATED), 124mg CHOLESTEROL, 585mg SODIUM

## CALIFORNIA SANDWICHES

*Prep: 10 minutes    Cook: 8 minutes*
*Makes 2 main dish servings*

4 slices white or sourdough
  bread, each 2cm thick
125g Cheddar cheese,
  thinly sliced
125g roasted turkey,
  thinly sliced

1 medium tomato, thinly
  sliced
½ medium avocado, thinly
  sliced
1 tbsp Dijon mustard
15g butter or margarine

◆ On 2 bread slices, layer slices of cheese, turkey, tomato and avocado. Spread remaining 2 slices of bread with mustard; place on top of filling, mustard-side down, to make 2 sandwiches. Press slightly to make sandwich halves stick together.

◆ Melt butter in 26cm frying pan over medium heat. Add sandwiches; cover and cook, carefully turning sandwiches once with metal spatula, until golden brown on both sides.

◆ To serve, cut each sandwich in half, using serrated knife.

**Each serving: About 640 calories, 39g protein, 44g carbohydrate, 34g total fat (15g saturated), 114mg cholesterol, 1015mg sodium**

## BARBECUED BEEF SANDWICHES

*Prep: 10 minutes    Cook: 30 minutes*
*Makes 4 main dish servings*

450g top round steak
2 medium red peppers
1 large onion
30ml olive or vegetable oil
1 tbsp chilli powder

225ml bottled tomato sauce
2 tbsp Worcestershire sauce
2 tbsp cider vinegar
1 tbsp brown sugar
4 hamburger buns, split

◆ Holding knife almost parallel to chopping board, cut steak crossways into paper-thin slices; transfer steak slices to bowl. Wipe chopping board clean; core and seed red peppers and then cut into 1cm wide strips. Cut onion into 5mm thick slices.

◆ Heat 1 tablespoon oil in 30cm frying pan over high heat; add steak and cook, stirring frequently, about 2–3 minutes, until steak just loses its pink colour throughout. Transfer steak to bowl.

◆ Heat remaining 1 tablespoon oil in drippings in frying pan over high heat; add peppers and onion and cook, stirring frequently, until tender-crisp and lightly browned.

◆ Stir chilli powder into vegetables in frying pan; cook, stirring, 1 minute. Add tomato sauce, Worcestershire sauce, cider vinegar, brown sugar and *175ml water*; heat mixture to boiling over high heat.

◆ Reduce heat to low; cover and simmer vegetable mixture 15 minutes, until vegetables are very tender. Return steak to pan; heat through. Serve steak slices and vegetable mixture in hamburger buns.

**Each serving: About 455 calories, 36g protein, 39g carbohydrate, 18g total fat (5g saturated), 50mg cholesterol, 730mg sodium**

## REUBENS DELUXE

*Prep: 10 minutes    Cook: 8 minutes*
*Makes 4 main dish servings*

225g bottled sauerkraut
4 tbsp bottled Thousand
  Island salad dressing
4 slices rye bread
225g roasted turkey, sliced
225g corned beef, sliced

60g Jarlsberg cheese, thinly
  sliced
30g butter or margarine
Pickles and potato crisps
  (optional)

◆ Place sauerkraut in strainer; rinse with cold running water. Drain, pressing down on sauerkraut to remove as much liquid as possible.

◆ Spread 1 tablespoon salad dressing on 1 slice rye bread. Top with half of turkey, half of corned beef, half of sauerkraut, half of Jarlsberg cheese and 1 more tablespoon salad dressing. Top with another slice rye bread. Repeat to make second sandwich.

◆ Melt 15g butter in 30cm non-stick frying pan over medium heat. Add sandwiches; cover and cook until golden brown on both sides and cheese melts, carefully turning sandwiches once and adding 15g extra butter to pan.

◆ To serve, cut each sandwich in half using serrated knife; place on 4 plates, with pickles and potato crisps passed separately, if you like.

**Each serving: About 390 calories, 36g protein, 23g carbohydrate, 17g total fat (4g saturated), 132mg cholesterol, 1375mg sodium**

### WHAT'S IN A NAME?

Corned beef, Emmenthal cheese, sauerkraut and rye bread are the ingredients of the original Reuben sandwich, said to have been invented in 1914 by Arthur Reuben, the owner of Reuben's delicatessen in New York City. The Reuben gained fame when a restaurant cook from Omaha entered his version in the National Sandwich Idea contest in 1956 and won. Reubens can be served cold, or fried in a pan like ours, which adds slices of roasted turkey for a sandwich so substantial that each one serves two.

# OPEN SANDWICHES

These sandwiches may have originated on a Swedish smorgasbord table, but the possibilities for creative toppings are endless. These main dish specialities include sliced steak with mushrooms, tender aubergine and mozzarella and a classic combination of smoked salmon and dill.

## AUBERGINE AND MOZZARELLA OPEN SANDWICHES

✦✦✦✦✦✦✦✦✦✦✦✦✦✦

*Prep: 15 minutes*
*Grill: 10–12 minutes*
*Makes 4 main dish servings*

1 medium aubergine (about 600g), cut crossways into 5mm thick slices
60ml olive or vegetable oil
225g Italian or semolina bread
250g fresh mozzarella cheese balls, drained, or 225g mozzarella cheese
1 tsp dried oregano
¼ tsp dried chilli flakes
¼ tsp salt
8 oil-packed sun-dried tomatoes, drained
1 small bunch basil

1 Preheat grill. Place aubergine slices on rack in grill pan; use half oil to brush both sides. Grill 10–12 minutes until tender and browned, turning aubergine slices once.

2 Diagonally slice both ends from loaf of bread; reserve ends for another day. Cut remaining bread diagonally into 8 slices. Thinly slice mozzarella cheese. Using fork, mix oregano, dried chilli flakes, salt and remaining oil in small bowl. Brush herb mixture over bread slices. Top bread with grilled aubergines, mozzarella slices and sun-dried tomatoes. Tuck basil leaves in between mozzarella slices.

### QUICK SANDWICH TOPPINGS

A selection of open sandwiches makes great party fare. Here are some easy ideas to try:

• Shrimp on dill mayonnaise

• Grilled cheese (Fontina, mature Cheddar) on tomato or pickle slices

• Crispy cooked bacon rashers on guacamole

• Sardines with finely chopped red onion and parsley on mayonnaise mixed with whole-grain mustard

• Parma ham and thinly sliced fresh figs on mascarpone cheese (shown above)

• Pear slices and Stilton cheese on a layer of watercress (shown above)

EACH SERVING: ABOUT 560 CALORIES, 20g PROTEIN, 53g CARBOHYDRATE, 31g TOTAL FAT (10g SATURATED), 44mg CHOLESTEROL, 825mg SODIUM

## SMOKED SALMON SANDWICHES WITH DILL-CAPER CREAM CHEESE

*Prep:* 20 minutes    *Makes* 4 main dish servings

90g cream cheese, softened
1 tbsp finely chopped shallot
1 tbsp canned or bottled
  drained and chopped capers
1 tbsp chopped fresh dill
1 tsp fresh lemon juice
4 slices pumpernickel bread

175g thinly sliced
  smoked salmon
Ground black pepper
4 tsp bottled salmon caviar
  (optional)
Dill sprigs for garnish

Prepare dill-caper cream cheese: mix cream cheese and next 4 ingredients in small bowl until blended. Spread dill-caper cream cheese evenly over bread. Arrange smoked salmon on top. Sprinkle with pepper. To serve, place 1 teaspoon salmon caviar on each sandwich, if you like, and garnish with dill sprigs.

**Each serving: About 205 calories, 12g protein, 16g carbohydrate, 10g total fat (5g saturated), 33mg cholesterol, 690mg sodium**

## SPINACH AND GOAT'S CHEESE OPEN SANDWICHES

*Prep:* 20 minutes    *Grill:* 4–5 minutes
*Makes* 4 main dish servings

1 tbsp olive oil
1 garlic clove, very finely
  chopped
350g plum tomatoes, diced
½ tsp salt
¼ tsp ground black pepper

300g spinach, rinsed and
  well drained
4 large slices white bread,
  each 10 by 8 by 1cm
60g goat's cheese, crumbled

◆ Preheat grill. Heat olive oil in flameproof casserole over medium-high heat. Add chopped garlic and cook, stirring frequently, about 15 seconds, until fragrant. Stir in diced tomatoes, salt and pepper and cook about 2 minutes until tomatoes are juicy and slightly softened. Add spinach and cook, stirring, just until spinach is wilted.

◆ Place bread on baking sheet; place under grill at closest position to heat. Grill about 1 minute per side, or until lightly toasted. Spoon spinach mixture evenly over toasted bread. Sprinkle goat's cheese on top. Grill 4–5 minutes, just until cheese begins to turn golden.

**Each serving: About 195 calories, 9g protein, 22g carbohydrate, 9g total fat (4g saturated), 11mg cholesterol, 560mg sodium**

## STEAK AND MUSHROOM OPEN SANDWICHES

*Prep:* 15 minutes    *Cook:* 25–30 minutes
*Makes* 4 main dish servings

30g butter or margarine,
  softened
1 tbsp plus 1 tsp chopped
  fresh tarragon
Ground black pepper
225g French bread cut
  horizontally in half

600g top round steak
3 tsp vegetable oil
Salt
1 medium onion, thinly sliced
350g mushrooms, sliced
Pinch dried thyme
75ml dry red wine

◆ Mix butter, 1 tablespoon tarragon and ⅛ teaspoon pepper in small bowl until blended. Spread butter mixture over cut sides of French bread. Cut each half into 4 pieces; place 2 pieces each on 4 plates.

◆ Pat steak dry with kitchen towels. Heat 2 teaspoons oil in 26cm frying pan over medium-high heat. Add steak, sprinkle with ¼ teaspoon salt and ⅛ teaspoon pepper and cook 12 minutes turning once, for medium-rare, or until desired doneness. Transfer steak to chopping board; keep warm.

◆ Reduce heat to medium. Add remaining 1 teaspoon oil to drippings in pan; add sliced onion and cook, stirring often, 5 minutes, or until tender and browned.

◆ Stir in mushrooms, thyme, ½ teaspoon salt, and ⅛ teaspoon pepper. Increase heat to medium-high and cook 8 minutes or until mushrooms are tender and liquid has evaporated. Stir in wine and bring to boil; boil 2 minutes.

◆ Holding knife almost parallel to chopping board, slice steak thinly across grain; arrange steak on bread. Spoon mushroom mixture on top and sprinkle with remaining 1 teaspoon tarragon.

**Each serving: About 540 calories, 45g protein, 38g carbohydrate, 22g total fat (7g saturated), 78mg cholesterol, 890mg sodium**

# HERO SANDWICHES

While an American-style hero sandwich goes by many names, the basic concept's always the same: take a crusty loaf, roll or baguette, split it in half, and stuff it with assorted fillings – the delicious result is guaranteed to satisfy even the largest appetite. Hero fillings can be hot or cold: our assortment includes crispy fried oysters with herbed mayonnaise; sweet sausages sautéed with peppers and onions; and an extravagant Italian meat and cheese combination drizzled with a red wine vinaigrette. Cold heroes are ideal to pack for picnics.

**1** Heat 5cm oil in saucepan to 190°C (375°F) on deep-frying thermometer. Mix mayonnaise and next 3 ingredients and ¼ teaspoon Tabasco sauce in small bowl.

**2** Combine cracker crumbs and ground red pepper on sheet of greaseproof paper. Coat 6 oysters with cracker crumb mixture.

## OYSTER PO' BOY

*Prep: 20 minutes    Cook: 30 seconds per batch*

*Makes 4 main dish servings*

**Vegetable oil for deep-frying**
**60g mayonnaise**
**1 tbsp finely chopped shallot**
**1 tbsp chopped fresh parsley**
**1 tbsp canned or bottled drained and chopped capers**
**¼ tsp Tabasco sauce, plus additional for serving**
**75g cream crackers, finely crushed**

**¼ tsp ground red pepper**
**24 oysters, shucked and drained (see page 89)**
**4 French bread rolls (each about 15cm long), split horizontally and lightly toasted**
**60g Iceberg lettuce, very thinly sliced**

**3** Using a slotted spoon, add oysters to hot oil. Fry for about 30 seconds until golden; drain on kitchen towels. Coat and cook remaining oysters, 6 at a time.

**4** Spread mayonnaise mixture on bottom halves of toasted rolls. Top with lettuce and oysters; replace tops of rolls. Serve with Tabasco sauce.

### CLAM ROLL

The clam roll is to New England what the oyster po' boy is to Louisiana. Follow the recipe above, but use 4 frankfurter rolls instead of French bread rolls and 24 shucked clams, instead of oysters. Serve rolls with Tartar Sauce (see page 119) instead of spreading with mayonnaise mixture given above.

Each serving: About 435 calories, 13g protein, 48g carbohydrate, 21g total fat (3g saturated), 23mg cholesterol, 370mg sodium

EACH SERVING: ABOUT 675 CALORIES, 34g PROTEIN, 57g CARBOHYDRATE, 33g TOTAL FAT (6g SATURATED), 8mg CHOLESTEROL, 710mg SODIUM

## DOUBLE TOMATO-BRIE HEROES

*Prep:* 20 minutes    **Makes** *8 main dish servings*

190g oil-packed sun-dried
  tomatoes, drained and
  finely chopped
2 tbsp extra virgin olive oil
2 tbsp white wine vinegar
2 long loaves Italian bread
  (about 225g each)

450g Brie cheese, sliced, with
  rind left on
60g fresh basil leaves
2 medium tomatoes, sliced

◈ Using wire whisk or fork, mix sun-dried tomatoes, olive oil and vinegar in small bowl.

◈ Cut each loaf horizontally in half. Spread sun-dried tomato mixture evenly on cut sides of bread. Arrange Brie on bottom halves of bread; top with basil and tomato slices.

◈ Replace tops of loaves. If not serving right away, wrap each hero sandwich in cling film and refrigerate. To serve, cut each hero sandwich crossways into 4 pieces.

**Each serving:** About 430 calories, 18g protein, 36g carbohydrate, 25g total fat (11g saturated), 56mg cholesterol, 750mg sodium

## SAUSAGE, PEPPER AND ONION HEROES

*Prep:* 10 minutes    *Cook:* 30 minutes
**Makes** *4 main dish servings*

450g mild Italian sausages,
  pricked all over with fork
2 medium onions, halved
  lengthways and cut into 1cm
  thick slices

2 green peppers, cored, seeded
  and cut into 1cm wide strips
4 crusty rolls (each about
  15cm long), split
  horizontally

◈ Bring sausages and *60ml water* to boil in 26cm frying pan over high heat. Reduce heat to low, cover and cook 5 minutes. Uncover pan; increase heat to medium and cook, turning occasionally, until sausages are browned and cooked through. Drain on kitchen towels.

◈ Discard all but 1 tablespoon drippings from pan. Add onions and peppers to drippings in pan and cook, stirring frequently, 15 minutes, or until tender.

◈ Slice sausages diagonally into 1cm pieces; add to pepper mixture in pan with *75ml water*, stirring until brown bits on base of pan are loosened. To serve, spoon sausage and vegetable mixture into rolls.

**Each serving:** About 585 calories, 21g protein, 41g carbohydrate, 37g total fat (11g saturated), 89mg cholesterol, 1360mg sodium

## ANTIPASTO HEROES

*Prep:* 15 minutes    **Makes** *6 main dish servings*

60ml extra virgin olive oil
2 tbsp red wine vinegar
1 tsp sugar
¾ tsp dried oregano
¼ tsp dried chilli flakes
2 loaves semolina bread (each
  40cm long)
½ small head escarole,
  coarsely chopped

½ small head radicchio,
  coarsely chopped
175g mozzarella or Provolone
  cheese, sliced
225g salami, sliced
225g cooked ham, sliced
2 medium tomatoes, sliced
100g bottled roasted red
  peppers, drained

◈ Prepare dressing: using wire whisk or fork, mix olive oil, vinegar, sugar, oregano and dried chilli flakes in small bowl until blended.

◈ Cut each loaf of bread horizontally in half. Spoon dressing onto cut sides of bread. Arrange escarole and radicchio on bottom halves of bread. Top with Provolone, salami, ham, tomatoes and roasted red peppers. Replace tops of loaves. If not serving right away, wrap each hero in cling film and refrigerate. To serve, cut each hero crossways into 3 pieces.

**Each serving:** About 600 calories, 30g protein, 45g carbohydrate, 33g total fat (11g saturated), 63mg cholesterol, 1870mg sodium

### WHAT'S IN A NAME?

A large French or Italian loaf, split and stuffed with slices of meat and cheese, peppers, pickles, lettuce and just about anything else you like, is known to most Americans as a hero sandwich, but it goes by different names in different parts of the country: a submarine in New York, a hoagie in Philadelphia and a po' boy in New Orleans. It may also be called a wedge or grinder. In Miami, a version called a Cuban sandwich is filled with pork and pickles. Other popular hero fillings include meatballs and tomato sauce, aubergine with Parmesan, and breaded, fried veal cutlets with mozzarella cheese and tomato sauce.

# TEA SANDWICHES

These pretty little morsels of crustless bread filled with a savoury or sweet filling are intended to be enjoyed in just one or two bites. Ideal for cold buffets or afternoon tea parties, you can prepare them early in the day and refrigerate them until ready to use. Try our prawn-filled hearts, cucumber and watercress sandwiches or simple pinwheels.

## PRAWN TEA SANDWICHES

❖ ❖ ❖ ❖ ❖ ❖ ❖ ❖ ❖ ❖ ❖ ❖

*Prep: 30 minutes*
*Cook: 2 minutes*
*Makes 24*

225g raw prawns peeled and
   de-veined (see page 90)
1 small celery stalk, coarsely
   chopped
60g mayonnaise
¼ tsp salt
3 drops Tabasco sauce
12 very thin slices white bread

**1** Bring *450ml water* to the boil over high heat. Add prawns; return to the boil, stirring occasionally. Boil 1 minute, or until prawns turn opaque throughout.

**2** Drain prawns. Using food processor with knife blade attached, finely chop prawns and celery. Add mayonnaise, salt and Tabasco sauce; process until blended, scraping sides with rubber spatula.

**3** Using a 5 by 3.5cm heart shaped biscuit cutter, cut 4 hearts from each bread slice. Spread prawn filling on half of hearts, using about 2 teaspoons per sandwich. Top with remaining hearts.

**4** If not serving right away, line a shallow baking tray or two with damp kitchen towels. Place tea sandwiches in tray; cover with damp kitchen towels to prevent bread drying out. Cover tray tightly with cling film and refrigerate until ready to serve.

**PINWHEEL SANDWICHES**

**1** Trim crusts from 450g unsliced wholemeal or white bread; cut lengthways into 5mm thick slices. Using rolling pin, slightly flatten each slice, then spread with 2 tablespoons of favourite smooth filling (we used soft spreadable cheese with garlic and herbs). From a short side, roll up each slice Swiss-roll fashion.

**2** Cut each roll crossways to make pinwheels.

EACH SANDWICH: ABOUT 50 CALORIES, 2g PROTEIN, 5g CARBOHYDRATE, 2g TOTAL FAT (0g SATURATED), 16mg CHOLESTEROL, 105mg SODIUM

## CUCUMBER AND WATERCRESS TEA SANDWICHES

*Prep: 30 minutes, plus chilling*
*Makes 16*

125g seedless cucumber,
    unpeeled
¼ tsp salt
½ bunch watercress
1 tbsp mayonnaise
8 very thin slices
    wholemeal bread
30g butter or margarine,
    softened

◆ Cut 16 paper-thin slices from cucumber for garnish; wrap with cling film and refrigerate. Peel remaining cucumber; cut into paper-thin slices. Toss peeled cucumber slices with salt in small bowl; let stand 30 minutes, stirring occasionally.

◆ Meanwhile, remove stalks from watercress. Reserve 16 small leaves for garnish; wrap with cling film and refrigerate. Finely chop remaining watercress leaves. Mix chopped watercress with mayonnaise in another small bowl.

◆ Trim crusts from bread; lightly spread 1 side of each slice with butter. Press salted cucumber slices with hand to drain well; pat dry.

◆ Spread watercress mixture on 4 bread slices; top with cucumber slices. Place remaining bread slices on top. Cut each sandwich diagonally into quarters.

◆ If not serving right away, line a shallow baking tray with damp kitchen towels. Place tea sandwiches in tray; cover with damp kitchen towels to prevent bread drying out. Cover tray tightly with cling film and refrigerate until ready to serve.

◆ To serve, garnish each sandwich with a cucumber slice and watercress leaf.

**Each sandwich: About 45 calories, 1g protein, 5g carbohydrate, 3g total fat (0g saturated), 5mg cholesterol, 115mg sodium**

## DATE-NUT TEA SANDWICHES

*Prep: 20 minutes    Makes 12*

90g cream cheese, softened
40g stoned dates, finely
    chopped
30g toasted walnuts, finely
    chopped
¼ tsp grated orange rind
6 very thin slices wholemeal
    bread, crusts trimmed

Mix cream cheese, dates, walnuts and orange rind in small bowl until evenly combined. Spread mixture evenly on 3 slices bread. Top with remaining bread. Cut each sandwich into 4 squares or triangles. If not serving right away, cover with damp kitchen towels then cling film and refrigerate until ready to serve.

**Each sandwich: About 70 calories, 2g protein, 7g carbohydrate, 4g total fat (2g saturated), 8mg cholesterol, 75mg sodium**

## DILLED EGG TEA SANDWICHES

*Prep: 20 minutes    Makes 18*

3 medium hard-boiled eggs
60g mayonnaise
2 tbsp chopped fresh dill
¼ tsp grated lemon rind
¼ tsp ground black pepper
12 very thin slices white or
    wholemeal bread, crusts
    trimmed

Using fork, mash eggs in medium bowl; stir in mayonnaise, dill, lemon rind and black pepper. Spread egg mixture evenly on 6 slices bread. Top with remaining bread. Cut each sandwich crossways into 3 rectangles. If not serving right away, cover with damp kitchen towels then cling film and refrigerate until ready to serve until ready to serve.

**Each sandwich: About 70 calories, 2g protein, 7g carbohydrate, 4g total fat (1g saturated), 37mg cholesterol, 105mg sodium**

## CHEDDAR AND CHUTNEY TEA SANDWICHES

*Prep: 15 minutes    Makes 16*

45g butter or margarine,
    softened
3 tbsp mango chutney
8 very thin slices white or
    wholemeal bread
125g Cheddar cheese, grated

Mix butter and chutney until combined in small bowl. Trim crusts from bread. Spread chutney mixture evenly on all bread slices. Sprinkle cheese evenly on 4 bread slices; top with remaining bread. Cut each sandwich into 4 squares or triangles. If not serving right away, cover with damp kitchen towels then cling film; refrigerate until ready to serve.

**Each sandwich: About 80 calories, 3g protein, 7g carbohydrate, 5g total fat (2g saturated), 13mg cholesterol, 120mg sodium**

# CLUB SANDWICHES

A club sandwich traditionally begins as three slices of bread or toast, which allows you to layer it with the maximum amount of fillings. Our selection ranges from Italian antipasto, to a garden of vegetables, to a spicy South-western American version of the classic club. If these hearty sandwiches seem unwieldy, pierce them with cocktail sticks to help hold them together.

## ITALIAN LOAF SANDWICH

*Prep: 25 minutes, plus chilling    Cook: 20 minutes*
*Makes 6 main dish servings*

60ml olive or vegetable oil
2 medium onions, cut into
  1cm thick slices
One loaf wholemeal bread
  (about 30cm long, 13cm
  wide and 14cm high)
3 tbsp red wine vinegar
1 bunch rocket
175g salami, thinly sliced

225g fresh mozzarella cheese,
  thinly sliced
2 red peppers, roasted and
  peeled (see page 310), or
  200g roasted red peppers in
  a jar, drained
2 medium tomatoes, sliced
150g bottled Italian hot-
  pepper slices, drained

**1** Heat 15ml oil in frying pan over medium heat. Add onions; cook, stirring occasionally, 20 minutes or until tender and golden. Set aside. Cut loaf horizontally into 3 slices.

**2** Using wire whisk or fork, mix vinegar and remaining 45ml oil in large bowl. Brush some of oil mixture over cut sides of bread. Add rocket to remaining oil mixture; toss to coat.

**3** To assemble: arrange half of rocket on bottom of loaf; top with half of salami, all of cheese and all of roasted peppers.

**4** Place middle slice of bread over peppers and arrange tomato slices on top; top with sautéed onions and hot-pepper slices, salami and rocket. Replace top of loaf. For easier slicing, wrap tightly in cling film and refrigerate 1 hour to allow juices from ingredients to moisten and flavour bread. To serve, remove clingfilm and cut sandwich into thick slices. Serve with knife and fork.

---

### SAVOURING SALAMI

A staple on antipasto platters and in robust deli-style sandwiches, salamis make some of the most tempting meats you'll find. Salami is typically made from pork or beef that has been seasoned, cured and air-dried. Some of the best known are Genoa (seasoned with black peppercorns and red wine), cotto (seasoned with white peppercorns) and varieties flavoured with garlic, herbs, chilli or fennel. Salamis are high in fat, but just a few slices add an incredible amount of taste. Once salami is cut, store it in air tight cling film in the refrigerator for up to 3 weeks.

Salami with hot pepper     French herb salami     Roman-style flat salami

---

EACH SERVING: ABOUT 505 CALORIES, 21g PROTEIN, 38g CARBOHYDRATE, 29g TOTAL FAT (10g SATURATED), 52mg CHOLESTEROL, 1390mg SODIUM

# HEALTH CLUB SANDWICH

*Prep:* 25 minutes    *Cook:* 2 minutes
*Makes* 4 main dish servings

1 tsp honey
⅛ tsp ground black pepper
2 tbsp olive oil
2 tsp plus 1 tbsp fresh lemon
   juice
3 medium carrots, grated
125g alfalfa sprouts
1 garlic clove, finely chopped
½ tsp ground cumin

Pinch ground red pepper
400g chick-peas, rinsed and
   drained
12 slices multi-grain bread,
   lightly toasted if you like
1 large tomato, thinly sliced
1 bunch watercress, tough
   stalks removed

◆ Mix honey, pepper, 1 tablespoon olive oil and
2 teaspoons lemon juice in medium bowl. Add carrots and
alfalfa sprouts; toss until evenly combined.

◆ Heat remaining 1 tablespoon olive oil with garlic, cumin
and ground red pepper in 2-litre saucepan over medium
heat; cook 30 seconds, or until very fragrant.

◆ Stir in chick-peas and remove pan from heat. Add
remaining 1 tablespoon lemon juice and *1 tablespoon water*;
using potato masher, mash until well blended.

◆ Spread chick-pea mixture evenly on 8 slices bread. Top
4 slices with tomato and watercress. Top the other 4 slices
with carrot mixture. Place chick-pea and tomato layers,
filling side-up on chick-pea and carrot layers. Top with
remaining bread to make a layered sandwich. To serve,
cut each in half.

**Each serving: About 405 calories, 15g protein, 64g carbohydrate,
12g total fat (2g saturated), 0mg cholesterol, 695mg sodium**

---

## SPROUTS

Low in calories and high in nutrients, sprouts add a bit of crunch
to sandwiches, salads and stir-fries. Most common are the fine,
thread-like alfalfa sprouts, which taste slightly nutty, and mung
bean sprouts (usually called 'bean sprouts'), which are larger,
crunchier and milder in flavour. Alfalfa sprouts are best eaten raw;
mung bean sprouts may be used raw or cooked briefly. Mustard,
with leafy tops and a peppery taste, should be eaten raw. Also
available are lentil sprouts, with a large seed and small sprout. All
sprouts are very perishable, so use within a few days of purchase.

Mung bean          Mustard          Lentil          Alfalfa
   sprouts                            sprouts          sprouts

# ROAST BEEF WALDORF CLUB

*Prep:* 20 minutes, plus standing    *Makes* 4 main dish servings

4 very thin slices red onion
2 celery stalks
½ medium Golden Delicious
   apple
½ tsp fresh lemon juice
60g reduced-fat mayonnaise
2 tbsp soured cream
1 tbsp horseradish sauce

12 slices pumpernickel bread,
   lightly toasted if you like
225g rare roast beef,
   thinly sliced
1 bunch watercress, tough
   stalks removed

◆ Combine red onion with *ice water* to cover in small bowl;
let stand 15 minutes. Drain. Meanwhile, finely chop celery.
Peel, core, and finely chop apple.

◆ Mix celery, apple, lemon juice, 2 tablespoons mayonnaise
and 1 tablespoon soured cream in another small bowl. Mix
horseradish sauce, remaining 2 tablespoons mayonnaise and
remaining 1 tablespoon soured cream in cup.

◆ Spread horseradish mixture evenly on 4 slices bread. Top
with roast beef, red onion and watercress.

◆ Spread celery mixture evenly on 4 slices bread and place
on top of roast beef layer. Top with remaining bread. To
serve, cut each sandwich in half.

**Each serving: About 445 calories, 27g protein, 52g carbohydrate,
14g total fat (4g saturated), 59mg cholesterol, 765mg sodium**

# SOUTH-WEST TURKEY CLUB

*Prep:* 20 minutes    *Makes* 4 main dish servings

60g reduced-fat mayonnaise
1 tbsp chilli sauce
12 slices sourdough bread,
   lightly toasted if you like
225g roasted turkey, thinly
   sliced

60g coriander sprigs
1 large tomato, thinly sliced
8 rashers bacon, trimmed if
   necessary, cooked and
   drained

◆ Mix mayonnaise and chilli sauce in small bowl. Spread
mayonnaise mixture evenly on 8 slices bread; top 4 slices
evenly with turkey, then coriander. Top the other 4 slices
with tomato, then bacon.

◆ Place tomato-bacon layers on turkey and coriander
layers. Top with remaining 4 slices bread. To serve, cut each
sandwich in half.

**Each serving: About 410 calories, 28g protein,
43g carbohydrate, 13g total fat (3g saturated),
63mg cholesterol, 760mg sodium**

# 14 DESSERTS

Anyone who has tasted a warm, fluffy soufflé, perfect creamy custard, or a tender fruit shortcake knows that there's an art to dessert making. The following time-honoured tricks of the trade will help you master the right methods. After all, every occasion is that much sweeter when a spectacular dessert is involved.

## COOKING WITH FRUIT

**Choosing the best fruit** Choose ripe (but not mushy) fruit that's in season. When selecting fruit, the heavier it feels in your hand, the juicier and better tasting it will be. Smell it: if there's no aroma, there will be little flavour. Feel it: fruit should yield slightly to gentle pressure. To ripen fruit, store it at room temperature in a dark place, or speed the process by placing it in a paper bag containing a whole lime.

**Reasons to rinse** Pesticides, waxy coatings or even bacteria can linger on the skin of fruit, so rinse it well before using. (Don't forget to scrub citrus fruit if you're going to use the rind.) Never soak fruit in water, however; this leaches out flavour and encourages rot. Instead, wash it quickly with gently running water, and dry immediately. Unless they are very dirty, avoid washing soft berries such as raspberries and blackberries, since they tend to become waterlogged.

**A spoonful of sugar** The sweetness of individual fruits can vary greatly, depending on ripeness, variety and growing conditions, so you may need to adjust the amount of sugar called for in a recipe. Simply taste the fruit, or the fruit mixture, before cooking and adjust the sugar as necessary.

**Prevent discoloration** When exposed to air, tannins and enzymes in fruits such as apples, peaches, pears and bananas cause them to turn brown. To prevent this, rub the fruit with a cut lemon, or briefly place it in a bowl of water with approximately 2 tablespoons of lemon juice added.

**Cook it gently** When you want to retain the shape and texture of a fruit, cook it gently just until it's tender. For poaching, keep the water at a low simmer. Sauté fruit only until it softens and begins to release its juices.

## CREAMY CUSTARD EVERY TIME

**Don't over-beat the eggs** Over-beating can make the custard foamy and cause bubbles to appear on the surface as it bakes. Beat the eggs just till yolks and whites are blended.

**Easy does it** Custards, both baked and stove-top, require gentle heat so they don't separate. For silky stove-top custards, use low heat and stir constantly to prevent boiling (and

subsequent curdling). Cook baked custards in a water bath – a larger pan of hot water. This method insulates them from the oven's direct heat so they cook evenly, without separating.

**Is it ready?** Over-baked custards may separate and turn watery. Remember that the custard is done even if the center is still shaky; it will firm as it cools. To check, insert a knife 1cm into the custard about 2–3cm from the centre; it should come out clean. A stove-top custard is ready when it's thick enough to coat a spoon well. Run your finger across the spoon; it should leave a track (see page 474).

**Be careful with cooling** Always remove the baked custard promptly from its water bath (otherwise, it will continue to cook), and then cool. Cool stove-top custards with a piece of plastic wrap pressed directly on top so a skin doesn't form.

## SOUFFLÉ SUCCESS

• It's easier to separate eggs when they're cold, so separate them straight from the refrigerator, but let the whites stand 30 minutes before beating for maximum volume.

• Perfectly beaten egg whites are a must for a light, fluffy texture; beat the whites until they're stiff but not dry.

• The best way to blend: mix in one third of the beaten egg whites to lighten mixture. Add remaining whites, half at a time, gently folding into the mixture with a rubber spatula.

• Soufflés rely on a blast of quick, even heat to rise properly, so it's essential that the oven is heated to the correct temperature before baking. Only keep the oven door open for an instant when you put in the soufflé, and don't open it during baking.

• Be sure to set the soufflé dish on a low shelf in the oven so the mixture has plenty of room to rise.

• How to tell when the soufflé is done? It should be puffed and golden with a slightly soft, barely set texture.

• For the most dramatic presentation, call everyone to the table *before* you take the soufflé out of the oven; cool air will start to shrink it in 3–5 minutes.

| **Preparing soufflé dishes** | **Folding in egg whites** |
| --- | --- |
|  |  |
| Use butter, margarine or non-stick cooking spray to grease soufflé dishes, then sprinkle with just enough sugar to coat dishes lightly. | Using a rubber spatula, gently fold one third of beaten egg whites into mixture. Then fold in the remaining egg whites, half at a time. |

## MAKING CHOUX PASTRY

This light, airy pastry is used for cream puffs and éclairs.

**Adding at boiling point**  Bring the water with the butter to a full boil and immediately add the flour. Don't let the water simmer away before adding or you'll have a dry dough.

**Egg essentials**  For best results, use room-temperature eggs (they'll blend better and rise higher). Add the eggs to the mixture one at a time, beating well after each addition to incorporate them thoroughly.

**The heat is on**  Shape and bake choux pastry immediately, while it is still warm, for maximum expansion and lightness.

**Go for the gold**  Pale, under-baked puffs will be raw inside and may collapse after they're removed from the oven. Aim for a rich, golden colour.

**Get a head-start for entertaining**  Unfilled puffs freeze successfully in plastic bags; simply recrisp them in the oven.

High-rising choux puffs produce – and retain – a lot of steam as they bake. To help them dry into a golden-crisp shell, use a paring knife to cut a small slit into the side of each puff as soon as they come out of the oven.

## PUFF PASTRY BASICS

• When buying frozen puff pastry, check the ingredients on the packet. The best brands contain only flour, butter, salt and water.

• Frozen puff pastry thaws very quickly, making it handy for last-minute treats. Allow 10–20 minutes' thawing time.

• When cutting puff pastry, be sure your knife or pastry wheel is very sharp – clean cuts will ensure maximum puffing. Always cut straight down, never at an angle, or the dough will puff unevenly as it bakes.

• If you don't want puff pastry to rise too much, prick it with a fork in several places before baking.

• Save puff-pastry trimmings; they can be re-rolled and used to make quick desserts (see page 466).

• Puff pastry demands a quick blast of heat at the beginning of baking; this melts the butter while it converts the water in the pastry to steam, making it rise. To ensure that your oven is hot enough, preheat it at least 20 minutes ahead.

## FILO FACTS

• Fragile and tissue-thin, filo dries out quickly and becomes unusable, so keep it covered with cling film until you are ready to use it. Any filo you don't use can be refrigerated, wrapped well, for up to 2 weeks.

• Frozen filo will keep for 3 to 6 months; thaw overnight in the refrigerator. Never re-freeze thawed filo dough, or it will become dry, brittle and crumbly.

• Fresh filo pastry, available at some speciality food stores and Greek and Middle Eastern shops, can be refrigerated, well wrapped, for 5 days, or frozen for up to 3 months.

• Before baking, brush filo layers with a thin coating of melted butter or margarine for extra flavour and a crisp, golden crust – and to help guard against drying.

• Let filo bake until deep golden; this gives it a toasted flavour and a wonderfully crisp crust.

• Filo pie crusts and cases can be baked a day ahead. Store them in airtight containers, and recrisp (if necessary) in the oven before filling and serving.

## GETTING TO KNOW GELATINE

• What exactly is gelatine? It's an odourless, tasteless and colourless thickening agent derived from beef and veal bones; some gelatine is a by-product of pig skin.

• For best results, measure carefully. Too much gelatine makes a mixture rubbery; with too little, it will not set firmly.

• To soften gelatine, sprinkle it over a small quantity of cold liquid; leave it without stirring for 5 minutes, or until it softens and swells to a spongy consistency that will melt smoothly when heated. The mixture to which melted gelatine is added must be warm enough to prevent the gelatine from immediately setting and forming lumps.

• Melt gelatine completely during heating, but never let the mixture boil, or its setting ability will diminish. Stirring is essential to prevent the mixture from lumping or separating.

• When adding fruit to gelatine, keep pieces small – gelatine will pull away from larger pieces. Raw pineapple, kiwifruit and papaya contain enzymes that break down gelatine.

• To quick-chill gelatine, set the bowl in a larger bowl of ice water, stirring frequently with a rubber spatula, just until the mixture begins to mound but is not lumpy. (Don't try to speed this process in the freezer; the mixture may crystallize.)

• Once set, moulded gelatine desserts have to be loosened from the mould; lower the base of the mould into a bowl of warm water and leave for 10 seconds (no longer, or the gelatine may melt). Place the serving plate on top of the mould, quickly invert it, and shake to release the dessert.

• How much gelatine? 1 sachet = 11g powdered gelatine; 1 sachet will set up to 450ml.

To check that all the gelatine crystals have fully dissolved, lift a little of the gelatine in a spoon – there should be no visible crystals.

# MAKING THE MOST OF MERINGUE

A simple mixture of beaten egg whites and sugar, meringue is essential to any dessert repertoire. There are two basic types of meringue: soft and hard. The consistency depends on the proportion of sugar to egg whites. Soft meringue has less sugar and is most often used as a swirled topping for pie. Hard meringue has more sugar; it's piped into shapes such as discs or shells (to cradle fruit or cream fillings) and baked to a crisp, brittle finish.

Properly beaten egg whites form stiff (but not dry) peaks. When the beaters are lifted from the bowl, the peaks hold their shape.

If under- or over- beaten, egg whites will be too soft and syrupy and will not hold their shape during the baking process.

For better blending and a light, fluffy texture, it's important to add the sugar to the softly beaten whites gradually – two tablespoons at a time – and to make sure it is completely incorporated. Continue beating on high speed until the mixture forms stiff, glossy peaks. To ensure that the sugar has completely dissolved, follow the foolproof test at right.

Rub a little meringue mixture between your thumb and finger to make sure all the sugar has dissolved; it should feel smooth, not gritty.

**Tricks of the trade**
- Don't make meringues on a humid or rainy day; they will absorb too much moisture from the air and end up soggy or 'weeping' (exuding little beads of moisture).
- If adding ingredients such as ground nuts, be sure to fold them in gently to avoid deflating the egg whites.
- To give meringue extra crispness and a pretty sparkle, sprinkle with caster sugar before baking.
- Is it done yet? A soft topping is ready when the peaks are brown; hard, crisp meringue will sound hollow when tapped.
- Let hard meringues dry completely in the oven for crisp results. They'll have a gummy texture if removed too soon.
- Meringue pies are best served within a few hours of baking; hard meringues can be stored in an airtight container for up to a week.

# ALL ABOUT ICE CREAM

SHOP BOUGHT
- A sticky container most likely means the product has thawed, leaked and been refrozen; choose another carton.
- For easier serving, soften ice cream in the refrigerator about 30 minutes. For speedier results, microwave rock-hard ice cream at medium-low for about 30 seconds.
- The container should be well sealed to prevent the ice cream from absorbing odours from other foods, or forming ice crystals on its surface. It's a good idea to place a sheet of plastic wrap directly against the surface of the ice cream to seal it from air. Reseal the container tightly after opening.
- Low-fat ice creams and frozen yogurt melt faster than full-fat varieties. So chill serving bowls, or add the scoops at the very last minute – or you may end up with a milky puddle over warm pies or hot, bubbling crumbles.

HOME-MADE
- For the creamiest texture (and a maximum yield), make and chill the ice cream mixture the day before you plan to freeze it (the chilled mixture will also freeze faster).
- Fill ice cream machines only two-thirds full – the mixture expands as it freezes and needs room to incorporate air.
- A freshly frozen mixture thaws quickly, so handle it as little as possible before getting it into the freezer.
- If using an old-fashioned churn, add more ice and salt as needed (the faster the freezing process, the smoother the texture of the ice cream).

ICE CREAM CLINIC (HOW TO AVOID...)
**Lumpy mixture** The mixture may have been too warm when the freezing process began. This increases churning time, which creates a less smooth texture, as well as the likelihood of flecks of butter forming. A better approach? Make sure the mixture is completely cooled (either slowly in the refrigerator or more quickly in an ice-water bath) before churning.
**Grainy texture** Pitfalls that prevent smooth results: sloppy measuring (never add extra water or alcohol to the mixture); churning the mixture too slowly (to help avoid this, add ice and salt when necessary to an old-fashioned churn to keep the mixture cold); or simply storing the finished ice cream too long.
**Bland taste** The most common culprit is a lack of sweetener. (If you're making sorbet, it's also possible that you didn't add enough lemon juice, which brightens the flavour.) To avoid this, taste the mixture prior to freezing and sweeten as necessary. You can also enhance the taste by allowing ice cream to 'ripen' in the freezer for at least 4 hours before serving; this helps it fully develop its flavour and texture.
**Ice crystals** These occur in ice cream that has been stored for too long (a practice that also creates a thick, heavy texture). To prevent ice crystals, add 1 enveope gelatine for each 1.4 litres liquid in the ice cream base. Let it soften in 60ml of the liquid, then heat until the gelatine melts and stir it into the rest of the liquid.

# FRUIT SALADS

When fruit is in its peak season, there's no better way to show it off than in a colourful fruit salad. Choose fully ripe fruit, then treat it simply: a little sugar brings out its flavour; a touch of an acidic ingredient (such as wine or citrus juice) brightens it. The result is a refreshingly light way to round off any meal from a simple lunch to a special dinner party.

## AMBROSIA

❖❖❖❖❖❖❖❖❖❖❖❖❖

*Prep: 40 minutes*
*Bake: 15 minutes*
*Makes 10 servings*

**1 fresh coconut**
**1 ripe pineapple**
**6 navel oranges**

**1** Preheat oven to 180°C (350°F, Gas 4). Prepare coconut: using hammer and screwdriver or large nail, puncture 2 eyes of coconut. Drain coconut liquid; discard. Bake coconut 15 minutes.

**2** Remove coconut from oven and wrap in tea towel. Using hammer, hit coconut to break it into large pieces. Using paring knife, pry coconut meat from shell.

**3** Using paring knife or vegetable peeler, peel outer skin from coconut meat. Coarsely grate about 150g fresh coconut and reserve remainder for use another day.

**4** Prepare pineapple: cut off crown and base from pineapple. Stand pineapple upright on chopping board; using large chef's knife, slice off rind and remove eyes. Cut pineapple lengthways into quarters. Cut out core. Cut each quarter lengthways in half; slice into chunks. Place in large bowl.

**5** Prepare oranges: cut off ends from oranges using paring knife; stand them on chopping board and slice off rind, removing all white pith.

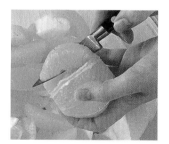

**6** Holding oranges over pineapple in bowl, cut sections and add to bowl. Squeeze juice from membranes into bowl; discard membranes. Add coconut; toss gently to combine.

EACH SERVING: ABOUT 105 CALORIES, 1g PROTEIN, 19g CARBOHYDRATE, 4g TOTAL FAT (3g SATURATED), 0mg CHOLESTEROL, 25mg SODIUM

## FRUIT AND WINE CUP

*Prep: 10–15 minutes*    *Makes 4 servings*

75ml white wine (for
   strawberries) or red wine
   (for peaches)
30g caster sugar

350g strawberries, hulled and
   each cut in half, or 350g
   peaches, peeled and sliced

Combine white or red wine and sugar in bowl, stirring until
sugar dissolves. Place strawberries or peaches in 4 goblets.
Pour wine mixture over fruit.

**Each serving: About 60 calories, 0g protein, 12g carbohydrate,
0g total fat, 0mg cholesterol, 0mg sodium**

## FRUIT WITH MARSALA CREAM AND TORTILLAS

*Prep: 25 minutes*    *Cook: 6–8 minutes*
*Makes 4 servings*

70g caster sugar
½ tsp ground cinnamon
2 flour tortillas
   (17–18cm each)
Vegetable oil
350g strawberries

2 medium kiwifruit
2 medium peaches
125g whipping cream
15g icing sugar
1 tbsp Marsala

◆ Mix caster sugar and cinnamon together in small shallow
bowl. Cut each tortilla into 6 triangles. Heat 5mm oil in
26cm frying pan over medium heat; add tortillas, a few at a
time, and cook, turning once, until golden. Drain on
kitchen towels. Immediately toss in sugar mixture; set aside.
If not using right away, store in tightly covered container.

◆ Hull strawberries and cut each in half. Peel kiwifruit and
cut into bite-sized chunks. Peel and slice peaches. Place
fruit in 4 dessert bowls.

◆ Prepare Marsala cream: using an electric mixer on
medium speed, beat cream and icing sugar until soft peaks
form; gradually beat in
Marsala. Spoon
Marsala cream
alongside fruit; serve
with tortilla triangles.

**Each serving: About
325 calories,
3g protein,
47g carbohydrate,
15g total fat
(7g saturated),
41mg cholesterol,
100mg sodium**

## BLUEBERRY-MANGO SALAD

*Prep: 15 minutes*    *Makes 6 servings*

1 tbsp caster sugar
1 tbsp dark rum
1 tbsp fresh lime juice

2 large mangoes, peeled and
   diced
400g blueberries

Combine sugar, rum and lime juice in a bowl. Add mangos
and blueberries; toss to coat.

**Each serving: About 95 calories, 1g protein, 24g carbohydrate,
0g total fat, 0mg cholesterol, 5mg sodium**

## SUMMER FRUIT BASKET

*Prep: 80 minutes*    *Makes 16 servings*

1 oblong watermelon, about
   9kg, chilled
2 large navel oranges
100g caster sugar
1 medium pineapple
350g strawberries
4 large kiwifruit
2 medium nectarines

225g red seedless grapes
Green florist wire, herb
   sprigs, clear thread or nylon
   fishing line and tiny non-
   toxic flowers such as
   gypsophila and sweetheart
   roses for handle (optional)

◆ Prepare watermelon basket: using sharp knife, cut
lengthways slice about 5cm from top of watermelon. Scoop
out pulp from both sections; cut into bited-size chunks.
Place 1.5kg watermelon chunks in large bowl (save
remainder for another day). Cut a thin slice of rind from
base of watermelon shell, if needed, so it stands level. Cut
scalloped edge around rim of watermelon shell.

◆ Using vegetable peeler, remove rind from 1 orange. Process
peel with sugar until rind is finely chopped. Cut white pith
from orange; cut rind and pith from remaining orange. Cut
sections from oranges. Cut off crown and base from pineapple.
Cut off peel; remove eyes. Cut pineapple lengthways into
quarters; cut out core. Cut pineapple into bite-sized chunks.
Hull strawberries; cut each in half if large. Peel kiwifruit; cut
into bite-sized chunks. Cut nectarines into wedges.

◆ Place fruit in bowl with watermelon. Add grapes and
orange sugar and toss to mix. Fill watermelon shell with fruit;
cover with cling film and refrigerate until ready to serve.

◆ Meanwhile, if you like, make a handle for basket: cut
florist wire into three 45cm lengths. Wrap herb sprigs
completely around wire; secure with clear thread. Tuck in
flowers. Wrap with damp kitchen towels and cling film;
refrigerate. To serve, loosely twist wires together and insert
ends into watermelon basket.

**Each serving: About 115 calories, 2g protein, 29g carbohydrate,
1g total fat (0g saturated), 0mg cholesterol, 5mg sodium**

# POACHED FRUIT AND COMPÔTES

Poaching is an easy and classic way to transform firm fresh or dried fruits into a deliciously succulent dessert. The fruit first gently simmers in a sugar syrup. The flavoured poaching liquid is then reduced to create an even richer syrup that will accompany the fruit. In these recipes we've infused the syrup with spices, herbs and citrus rind to complement different fruits. Try serving any leftover fruit for breakfast.

## HONEY-POACHED PEARS AND ORANGES

*Prep: 30 minutes, plus chilling   Cook: 35–45 minutes*
*Makes 8 servings*

| | |
|---|---|
| 165g honey | 1.9kg firm, ripe pears |
| 50g sugar | 4 small navel oranges |
| 2 tbsp fresh lemon juice | 1 small lemon, sliced |
| 6 whole cloves | Mint leaves for decoration |

**1** Stir together honey, sugar, lemon juice, cloves and *900ml water* in 5-litre flameproof casserole. Peel pears. Using melon baller, remove cores from base of pears; do not remove stalks. Immediately place pears in honey mixture, turning to coat. Bring to the boil over high heat.

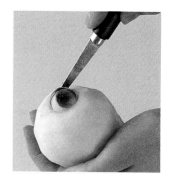

**2** Reduce heat to low; cover and simmer 10–20 minutes, until pears are tender when pierced with knife. Using slotted spoon, transfer pears to large bowl. Meanwhile, cut rind and white pith from oranges with paring knife; discard.

**3** Add oranges to poaching liquid; return to the boil over high heat. Reduce heat to medium-low; simmer, uncovered, 5 minutes, turning occasionally.

**4** Using slotted spoon, add oranges to bowl with pears. Return poaching liquid to the boil over medium-high heat; cook 10 minutes, uncovered, to reduce slightly. Pour hot syrup over fruit. Cool slightly. Cover and refrigerate, turning fruit occasionally, at least 3 hours until well chilled. To serve, stir in lemon slices. Decorate with mint sprigs.

### HONEY

One of the first sweeteners known to man, honey is made by bees from flower nectar. It is available in three forms: comb honey, complete with the wax honeycomb, which may also be eaten; cream or spun honey, which is finely crystallized; and runny honey, which is free of crystals. The flavour of honey varies according to the flower it comes from; in general, the darker the colour, the stronger the flavour. Kept covered in a cool, dark place, honey will last indefinitely. If it crystallizes, it can be liquefied by standing the opened jar in a bowl of hot water. When measuring honey for cooking, oil the measuring jug or spoon so the honey slips out easily.

EACH SERVING: ABOUT 260 CALORIES, 2g PROTEIN, 67g CARBOHYDRATE, 1g TOTAL FAT (0g SATURATED), 0mg CHOLESTEROL, 0mg SODIUM

## AUTUMN FRUIT COMPÔTE

*Prep: 20 minutes, plus chilling*
*Cook: 35–40 minutes*
*Makes 8 servings*

1 medium orange
1 medium lemon
4 Golden Delicious apples, peeled, cored and each cut into 16 wedges
225g mixed dried fruit (with stoned prunes)
125g dried figs
40g dried tart cherries or cranberries
100g sugar
1 cinnamon stick (7–8cm)

◆ Using vegetable peeler, remove rind from orange and lemon in 2–3cm wide strips. Squeeze 2 tablespoons juice from lemon.

◆ Bring orange and lemon rinds, lemon juice, apples, mixed dried fruit, figs, dried cherries, sugar, cinnamon stick and *675ml water* to the boil in 4-litre saucepan over high heat, stirring to dissolve sugar. Reduce heat to low; cover and simmer 15–20 minutes, until apples are tender. Cool slightly.

◆ Pour fruit mixture into bowl; cover and refrigerate at least 4 hours to blend flavours. Serve chilled or at room temperature.

**Each serving: About 225 calories,**
**1g protein, 55g carbohydrate, 0g total fat,**
**0mg cholesterol, 40mg sodium**

## HERB-POACHED PEACHES

*Prep: 20 minutes, plus chilling*
*Cook: 35–40 minutes*
*Makes 8 servings*

4 large lemons
100g sugar
1 bay leaf
3 thyme sprigs
1.3kg firm, ripe peaches
2 tbsp peach jam
1 small lemon, thinly sliced, for decoration

◆ Grate rind from 1 large lemon. Squeeze 125ml juice from large lemons.

◆ Stir lemon rind, lemon juice, sugar, bay leaf, 2 thyme sprigs and *1 litre water* together in 5-litre flameproof casserole.

◆ Peel peaches. As each peach is peeled, immediately place in lemon juice mixture, turning to coat completely to help prevent browning.

◆ Bring peach mixture to the boil over high heat, stirring to dissolve sugar. Reduce heat to low; cover and simmer 5–10 minutes, until peaches are tender. Using slotted spoon, transfer peaches to large bowl.

◆ Return poaching liquid to the boil over high heat; cook, uncovered, about 15 minutes, until liquid is reduced to about 350ml. Stir in peach jam until dissolved. Pour hot syrup over peaches in bowl. Cool slightly.

◆ Cover and refrigerate, turning peaches occasionally, at least 4 hours until well chilled.

◆ Discard bay leaf and serve peaches with syrup; decorate with lemon slices and remaining thyme sprig.

**Each serving: About 140 calories,**
**1g protein, 38g carbohydrate, 0g total fat,**
**0mg cholesterol, 0mg sodium**

## LEMON-ANISE POACHED PEARS

*Prep: 20 minutes, plus chilling*
*Cook: 40–50 minutes*
*Makes 8 servings*

2 medium lemons
2kg firm, ripe pears
200g sugar
2 tbsp whole star anise or 2 cinnamon sticks (7–8cm each)
1 small navel orange, thinly sliced, for decoration

◆ Squeeze juice from 1 lemon into 8-litre flameproof casserole. Thinly slice remaining lemon. Peel pears. Using melon baller, remove cores from base of pears; do not remove stalks.

◆ Add pears, lemon slices, sugar, star anise and *1.3 litres water* to casserole. Bring to the boil over high heat, stirring to dissolve sugar. Reduce heat to low. Cover; simmer 10–20 minutes, until pears are tender. Using slotted spoon, transfer pears to large bowl.

◆ Return poaching liquid to the boil over high heat; cook, uncovered, 15 minutes, or until reduced to about 675ml. Pour hot syrup over pears. Cool slightly. Cover; refrigerate, turning occasionally, at least 4 hours, until pears are well chilled. Serve pears with syrup; decorate with orange slices.

**Each serving: About 250 calories,**
**1g protein, 65g carbohydrate, 1g total fat**
**(0g saturated), 0mg cholesterol,**
**0mg sodium**

### STAR ANISE

A star-shaped seed pod from a type of magnolia shrub, star anise has a mild liquorice flavour and is a common ingredient in Chinese cooking. It is generally used whole for its attractive appearance. It is available in the spice section of some supermarkets or in Oriental food shops.

# FRUIT SHORTCAKES

Shortcakes may look fancy, but they're simply scones or cakes dressed up with sweet, juicy fruit and thick whipped cream. We have a cake-based summer classic – a strawberry shortcake; a peach and blueberry version; and a giant shortcake using mixed berries. Be sure to serve shortcakes right after they're assembled.

1 Mix first two ingredients in 3-litre saucepan until smooth. Stir in blueberries and 140g sugar; bring to the boil over medium-high heat. Reduce heat to medium; cook 1 minute. Stir in peaches; set aside.

2 Preheat oven to 220°C (425°F, Gas 7). Combine flour, baking powder, salt and 70g sugar. Using pastry blender or two knives used scissor fashion, cut in 135g butter until mixture resembles coarse crumbs.

3 Stir in milk just until mixture forms a soft dough that leaves side of bowl. Knead dough on lightly floured surface 6–8 times, just until smooth. Using lightly floured hands, pat dough 2cm thick.

## BLUEBERRY-PEACH SHORTCAKES

❖ ❖ ❖ ❖ ❖ ❖ ❖ ❖ ❖ ❖ ❖ ❖ ❖

*Prep: 30 minutes*
*Bake: 16–22 minutes*
*Makes 8 servings*

**2 tbsp fresh lemon juice**
**1 tbsp cornflour**
**600g blueberries**
**200g plus 3 tbsp caster sugar**
**900g medium peaches, peeled (see right) and each cut into 8 wedges**
**450g plain flour**
**4½ tsp baking powder**
**¾ tsp salt**
**150g cold butter or margarine**
**225ml plus 2 tbsp milk**
**225ml whipping cream**

4 Using floured 8cm round biscuit cutter, cut out shortcakes. Place shortcakes 2–3cm apart on ungreased large baking sheet.

5 Press trimmings together; cut to make 8 shortcakes in all. Melt remaining 15g butter; brush over shortcakes. Sprinkle with 1 tablespoon caster sugar. Bake 16–22 minutes, until golden. Using an electric mixer on medium speed, beat cream with remaining 2 tablespoons caster sugar to soft peaks. Split warm shortcakes in half. Spoon some fruit into each; top with cream and then more fruit.

**PEELING PEACHES**

Plunge peaches into pan of boiling water for 30 seconds. Using slotted spoon, transfer to large bowl filled with ice water to cover; cool. Slip off skin with your fingers or small paring knife. If desired, rub peeled peaches with lemon juice to prevent discoloration.

EACH SERVING: ABOUT 610 CALORIES, 8g PROTEIN, 89g CARBOHYDRATE, 27g TOTAL FAT (13g SATURATED), 85mg CHOLESTEROL, 670mg SODIUM

## BERRIES AND CREAM SHORTCAKE

*Prep: 25 minutes, plus cooling*    *Bake: 25–30 minutes*
*Makes 10 servings*

125g butter or margarine, softened
200g plus 1 tbsp caster sugar
180g plain flour
125ml milk
1½ tsp baking powder
1 tsp vanilla essence
¼ tsp salt

2 medium eggs
400g blueberries
175g strawberries, hulled and each cut in half
160g raspberries
145g blackberries
60g strawberry jam, melted
225g whipping cream

◆ Preheat oven to 180°C (350°F, Gas 4). Grease and flour two 20cm round sandwich tins.

◆ Using an electric mixer on low speed, beat butter and 200g sugar just until blended. Increase speed to high; beat about 5 minutes until light and creamy. Reduce speed to low; add flour, milk, baking powder, vanilla essence, salt and eggs; beat until well mixed, frequently scraping bowl with rubber spatula. Increase speed to high; beat 2 minutes longer, occasionally scraping bowl.

◆ Spoon mixture into tins. Bake 25–30 minutes, until cocktail stick inserted in centres of cakes comes out clean. Cool cake layers in tins on wire racks 10 minutes. Remove from tins; cool completely on racks. Meanwhile, in large bowl, gently toss all berries with strawberry jam.

◆ Using mixer on medium speed, beat cream with remaining 1 tablespoon sugar until stiff peaks form.

◆ Place 1 cake layer on plate. Spread with half of whipped cream; top with half of fruit mixture. Place second cake layer on fruit mixture; top with remaining cream and fruit.

**Each serving: About 385 calories, 4g protein, 50g carbohydrate, 20g total fat (10g saturated), 103mg cholesterol, 265mg sodium**

## CLASSIC STRAWBERRY SHORTCAKE

*Prep: 30 minutes, plus cooling*    *Bake: 30–35 minutes*
*Makes 12 servings*

225ml milk
60g butter or margarine
4 medium eggs
370g caster sugar
1½ tsp vanilla essence
265g plain flour

1 tbsp baking powder
½ tsp salt
1kg strawberries
450ml whipping cream
30g icing sugar
Mint sprigs for decoration

◆ Preheat oven to 180°C (350°F, Gas 4) and grease 33 by 20cm metal baking tin. Heat milk and butter in 1-litre saucepan over medium heat until butter melts; set aside.

◆ Using an electric mixer on high speed, beat eggs, 300g caster sugar, and 1 teaspoon vanilla essence in large bowl 2–3 minutes, until very thick and lemon-coloured. Reduce speed to low. Add flour, baking powder and salt; beat 1 minute, frequently scraping bowl with rubber spatula. Add hot milk mixture; beat 1 minute longer, or until smooth.

◆ Pour mixture into tin. Bake 30–35 minutes until cake is golden and top springs back when lightly pressed. Cool cake completely in tin on wire rack.

◆ Hull and thinly slice strawberries. Mix sliced strawberries with remaining 70g caster sugar.

◆ Cut cake lengthways into 3 strips, then cut each strip crossways into 4 pieces. Using mixer on medium speed, beat cream, icing sugar and remaining ½ teaspoon vanilla in small bowl until soft peaks form.

◆ To serve, place each piece of cake on a dessert plate; top with some sliced strawberries with their syrup, then with some whipped cream. Decorate with mint sprigs.

**Each serving: About 420 calories, 6g protein, 53g carbohydrate, 21g total fat (12g saturated), 139mg cholesterol, 300mg sodium**

### WHAT'S IN A NAME?

Strawberry shortcake is a classic American dessert, and is thought to have originated in New England in the 1850s. The most traditional version is made with fluffy, warm baking-powder scones, split and buttered, then filled with fruit. The permutations are endless, however. The scone may be individual or large, sweeter or richer, buttered or not.... It might not be a scone at all, but sponge cake, pie crust or even sweet, rich bread. Peaches and other berries also make a luscious filling, with ice cream or whipped cream to top it off.

# CRUMBLES AND COBBLERS

These ever popular desserts are quick to make and don't require any special ingredients; just choose the best and ripest fruit you can find. It takes only minutes to prepare the fruit filling and to mix up the scone or crumb topping – then just pop it in the oven and the dessert is done. For a modern twist to a traditional theme, try our Nectarine and Cherry Oat Cobbler, which substitutes a tasty oat mixture for the usual scone topping.

## RHUBARB-STRAWBERRY COBBLER WITH SPICE SCONES

❖❖❖❖❖❖❖❖❖❖❖❖

*Prep:* 20 minutes, plus cooling
*Bake:* 20 minutes
*Makes* 8 servings

600g rhubarb, cut into 2–3cm chunks

150g plus 1 tsp caster sugar

1 tbsp cornflour

350g strawberries, hulled and each cut into quarters

225g plain flour

1½ tsp baking powder

½ tsp bicarbonate of soda

¼ tsp salt

¼ tsp ground cinnamon

⅛ tsp ground nutmeg

60g butter or margarine

175ml plus 1 tbsp whipping cream

**1** Bring rhubarb and 100g sugar to the boil in 3-litre saucepan over high heat, stirring constantly. Reduce heat to medium-low; cook about 8 minutes, until rhubarb is tender.

**2** Mix cornflour and *60ml water* in cup. Stir cornflour mixture and strawberries into cooked rhubarb; cook 2 minutes longer, or until slightly thickened. Keep warm.

**3** Preheat oven to 200°C (400°F, Gas 6). Prepare scones: mix flour, next 5 ingredients, and 50g sugar together in large bowl. Using pastry blender or two knives used scissor fashion, cut in butter until mixture resembles coarse crumbs. Add 175ml cream; stir just until mixture forms a soft dough that leaves side of bowl. Turn onto lightly floured surface.

**4** Knead dough 6–8 times, just until smooth. Using floured rolling pin, roll out dough 1cm thick. Cut out scones with 8cm star-shaped biscuit cutter.

**5** Re-roll trimmings; cut to make 8 scones in all. Pour hot rhubarb mixture into shallow 2-litre ovenproof serving dish. Place scones on top of rhubarb mixture in dish.

**6** Brush scones with remaining 1 tablespoon cream; sprinkle with remaining 1 teaspoon sugar. Place sheet of foil under dish; crimp edges to form rim to catch any drips during baking. Bake 20 minutes, or until scones are golden brown and rhubarb mixture is bubbly. Cool cobbler slightly on wire rack, about 15 minutes, to serve warm.

EACH SERVING: ABOUT 315 CALORIES, 4g PROTEIN, 43g CARBOHYDRATE, 15g TOTAL FAT (8g SATURATED), 49mg CHOLESTEROL, 315mg SODIUM

## COUNTRY APPLE CRUMBLE

*Prep: 30 minutes, plus cooling    Bake: 30–35 minutes*

*Makes 8 servings*

| | |
|---|---|
| 1 large orange | ½ tsp salt |
| 1.1kg Golden Delicious apples, peeled, cored and cut into 2–3cm slices | ¼ tsp ground nutmeg |
| | 120g light brown sugar |
| | 2 tbsp plus 50g plain flour |
| 75g dried cherries or raisins | 40g rolled oats |
| 1 tsp ground cinnamon | 45g butter or margarine |

◈ Preheat oven to 220°C (425°F, Gas 7). Grate ½ teaspoon rind and squeeze 75ml juice from orange. Toss orange rind and juice, apples, next 4 ingredients, 70g brown sugar and 2 tablespoons flour in shallow 2-litre ovenproof serving dish.

◈ Prepare topping: combine oats and remaining 50g flour and 50g brown sugar in small bowl. Using pastry blender or two knives used scissor fashion, cut in butter until mixture resembles coarse crumbs. Sprinkle over apple mixture.

◈ Bake 30–35 minutes until apples are tender and topping is lightly browned, covering with foil if necessary to prevent over-browning. Cool slightly on wire rack to serve warm. Or, cool completely to serve later; re-heat if desired.

**Each serving: About 260 calories, 2g protein, 53g carbohydrate, 5g total fat (2g saturated), 12mg cholesterol, 190mg sodium**

## NECTARINE AND CHERRY OAT COBBLER

*Prep: 30 minutes, plus cooling    Bake: 1–1¼ hours*

*Makes 12 servings*

| | |
|---|---|
| 100g sugar | 140g light brown sugar |
| 3 tbsp cornflour | 1 medium egg |
| 1.3kg ripe nectarines, each cut into 6 wedges | 2 tsp vanilla essence |
| | 120g rolled oats |
| 750g dark sweet cherries, stoned | 115g plain flour |
| | ¼ tsp salt |
| 2 tbsp fresh lemon juice | ¼ tsp bicarbonate of soda |
| 120g butter or margarine | |

◈ Preheat oven to 190°C (375°F, Gas 5). Using wire whisk or fork, combine sugar and cornflour in large bowl. Add nectarines, cherries and lemon juice and toss until fruit is evenly coated. Spoon mixture into 33 by 20cm ovenproof serving dish; dot with 30g butter.

◈ Cover with foil; bake 40–50 minutes until fruit mixture is gently bubbling. Meanwhile, prepare oat topping: using an electric mixer on medium-high speed, beat brown sugar and remaining 90g butter, softened, until smooth. Add egg and vanilla essence; beat ingredients together until light and creamy.

◈ Stir in oats and remaining ingredients with wooden spoon until mixed. Cover and refrigerate until ready to use.

◈ Drop topping in large tablespoon mounds over baked fruit. Bake, uncovered, 20–25 minutes longer, until topping is browned. Cool slightly on wire rack to serve warm. Or, cool completely to serve later; re-heat if desired.

**Each serving: About 325 calories, 5g protein, 58g carbohydrate, 10g total fat (4g saturated), 40mg cholesterol, 170mg sodium**

## PLUM COBBLER

*Prep: 20 minutes, plus cooling    Bake: 45–55 minutes*

*Makes 10 servings*

| | |
|---|---|
| 1.1kg ripe plums, each cut into 4 wedges | ½ tsp bicarbonate of soda |
| | ½ tsp salt |
| 2 tbsp plus 240g plain flour | 60g white vegetable fat |
| 100g sugar | 175ml buttermilk or soured milk |
| 1½ tsp baking powder | |

◈ Preheat oven to 200°C (400°F, Gas 6). Toss plums with 2 tablespoons flour and sugar in large bowl; spoon into shallow 2-litre ovenproof serving dish. Cover loosely with foil. Bake 25–30 minutes, until plums are tender.

◈ Make scone topping: mix remaining 240g flour and next 3 ingredients in large bowl. Using pastry blender or two knives used scissor fashion, cut in vegetable fat until mixture resembles coarse crumbs. Add buttermilk and stir just until moistened. Turn out dough onto lightly floured surface and knead 6–8 times until smooth. Roll out to 1cm thick and cut out 12 rounds with 6cm biscuit cutter; place over plums.

◈ Bake, uncovered, 20–25 minutes longer, until topping is browned. Cool slightly on wire rack to serve warm. Or, cool completely to serve later; re-heat if desired.

**Each serving: About 250 calories, 4g protein, 45g carbohydrate, 7g total fat (2g saturated), 1mg cholesterol, 260mg sodium**

### MORE CRUMBLES

Crumbles are a traditional favourite and can be easily adapted to suit different tastes. Try one of the following:

• To spice up Country Apple Crumble (see left), replace the dried cherries with 2 pieces (50g) stem ginger in syrup, drained and chopped. You could also change the fruit base to rhubarb.

• To add crunch to any crumble topping, add a handful of dessicated coconut or chopped nuts (walnuts, hazelnuts or pecans would work well).

# BAKED FRUIT DESSERTS

Baking heightens the flavour of many fruits and gives them a pleasing mellow texture. Here we've wrapped apples in pastry to create tempting dumplings; given pears an Italian nuance with sweet Marsala and lemon; and enhanced ripe plums with a crumbly almond topping. These desserts are best served warm with single cream or ice cream, if you like.

## OLD-FASHIONED APPLE DUMPLINGS

❖❖❖❖❖❖❖❖❖❖❖❖❖❖❖❖❖❖❖❖❖❖❖❖❖❖❖

*Prep:* 40 minutes   *Bake:* 35–40 minutes
*Makes* 6 servings

375g plain flour
1 tsp salt
8 tbsp light brown sugar
225g white vegetable fat, diced
75g mixed dried fruit, chopped

30g butter or margarine
1½ tsp ground cinnamon
6 small Golden Delicious apples (about 175g each)
1 medium egg, beaten
6 whole cloves

**1** Combine flour, salt and 2 tablespoons brown sugar in large bowl. Using pastry blender or two knives used scissor fashion, cut in shortening until mixture resembles coarse crumbs. Stir in *5–6 tablespoons cold water* until pastry holds together; set aside. Mix dried fruit, butter, 4 tablespoons brown sugar and 1 teaspoon cinnamon together in small bowl. Preheat oven to 200°C (400°F, Gas 6).

**2** Peel apples. Using melon baller, remove cores but do not go all the way through to base. Press dried-fruit mixture into cavities. Grease Swiss-roll tin large enough to take apples in single layer.

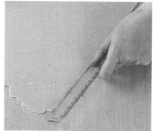

**3** Reserve 40g pastry. Roll out remaining pastry on lightly floured surface with floured rolling pin, using a ruler to help push and shape pastry into 54 by 36cm rectangle. Cut pastry into six 18cm squares.

**4** Combine remaining 2 tablespoons brown sugar and ½ teaspoon cinnamon on greaseproof paper. Roll an apple in sugar mixture. Centre apple on a pastry square; brush edges of pastry with some beaten egg.

**5** Bring pastry up over top of apple. Press to shape; seal edges. Place dumpling in baking tray Repeat with remaining apples, sugar mixture, and pastry squares, and more beaten egg, to make 6 dumplings in all.

**6** Roll reserved pastry out 5mm thick. Cut out as many leaves as possible (see page 489); re-roll scraps and cut out more leaves. Score leaves with back of knife to make veins. Brush dumplings with egg. Attach leaves; brush with egg. Press in cloves to make stems. Bake dumplings 35–40 minutes, until pastry is golden and apples are tender when pierced with knife.

EACH SERVING: ABOUT 730 CALORIES, 7g PROTEIN, 90g CARBOHYDRATE, 40g TOTAL FAT (11g SATURATED), 47mg CHOLESTEROL, 435mg SODIUM

## ROASTED ALMOND-CRUST PLUMS

*Prep: 15 minutes*   *Bake: 25–35 minutes*
*Makes 6 servings*

70g ripe plums, each cut in half
60g sliced almonds
70g brown sugar

40g plain flour
45g butter or margarine, softened
Vanilla ice cream (optional)

Preheat oven to 220°C (425°F, Gas 7). Arrange plums, cut-side up, in one layer in shallow ovenproof dish. Mix almonds and next 3 ingredients in bowl with fingertips, until mixture comes together. Sprinkle over plums. Bake 25–35 minutes, until plums are tender. Serve hot, with ice cream, if you like.

Each serving: About 205 calories, 3g protein, 31g carbohydrate, 9g total fat (2g saturated), 16mg cholesterol, 70mg sodium

## CLAFOUTI

*Prep: 20 minutes*   *Bake: 40–45 minutes*
*Makes 12 servings*

450g dark sweet cherries, stoned
100g plain flour
70g caster sugar
4 medium eggs

2 tbsp amaretto (almond-flavoured liqueur)
450ml single cream
Icing sugar for decoration

◆ Preheat oven to 180°C (350°F, Gas 4). Grease 25 by 4cm round ceramic ovenproof serving dish. Place cherries in dish. Blend flour, caster sugar, eggs, amaretto and 225ml cream together in blender on low speed for 30 seconds. With motor running, gradually add remaining 225ml cream; blend 30 seconds longer.

◆ Pour egg mixture over cherries in dish. Bake 40–45 minutes until custard is set and knife inserted 2–3cm from edge comes out clean (centre will still shake). Serve hot, sprinkled with icing sugar.

Each serving: About 160 calories, 4g protein, 20g carbohydrate, 7g total fat (3g saturated), 86mg cholesterol, 40mg sodium

### CHERRY STONER

This pliers-like tool made from aluminium or stainless steel makes short work of stoning cherries and gives a cleaner result than using a paring knife. It can also be used for stoning olives.

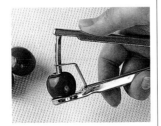

## CARIBBEAN BAKED BANANAS

*Prep: 10 minutes*   *Bake: 15 minutes*
*Makes 4 servings*

2 tbsp dark rum
½ tsp grated lime rind
4 ripe large bananas, cut into 1cm slices
2 tbsp brown sugar

30g butter or margarine, melted
50g flaked coconut
Vanilla ice cream (optional)

◆ Preheat oven to 220°C (425°F, Gas 7). Combine rum and lime rind in 23cm pie plate or shallow ovenproof serving dish. Add bananas, tossing to coat.

◆ Mix brown sugar and melted butter together in small bowl until smooth. Stir in coconut. Spoon coconut mixture evenly over bananas. Bake 15 minutes, or until coconut is golden. Serve hot, with ice cream, if you like.

Each serving: About 280 calories, 2g protein, 46g carbohydrate, 10g total fat (6g saturated), 16mg cholesterol, 100mg sodium

## BAKED PEARS WITH MARSALA

*Prep: 25 minutes, plus cooling*   *Bake: 40–50 minutes*
*Makes 8 servings*

1 medium lemon
8 firm Conference pears
2 tsp plus 70g sugar

125ml Marsala
30g butter or margarine, melted

◆ Preheat oven to 230°C (450°F, Gas 8). Using vegetable peeler or small knife, remove rind from lemon in 6 by 1cm strips; squeeze juice from lemon.

◆ Using melon baller or small knife, remove cores from base of unpeeled pears but do not remove stalks. Using pastry brush, brush insides of pears with lemon juice, then sprinkle insides with a total of 2 teaspoons sugar.

◆ Mix lemon rind strips, Marsala and *75ml water* in shallow 1½- to 2-litre ovenproof serving dish. Place remaining 70g sugar on sheet of greaseproof paper.

◆ Using pastry brush, brush pears with melted butter, then roll them in sugar to coat. Place pears, cored-ends down, in serving dish. Sprinkle any sugar remaining on greaseproof paper around pears in serving dish.

◆ Bake pears, basting occasionally with syrup in dish, 40–50 minutes, until fork-tender. Cool slightly to serve warm. Or, cool pears completely; cover and refrigerate up to 1 day and re-heat to serve warm.

Each serving: About 170 calories, 1g protein, 34g carbohydrate, 3g total fat (2g saturated), 16mg cholesterol, 30mg sodium

# RICE PUDDINGS

These creamy, mild-flavoured puddings are made of the simplest ingredients – basically rice, milk and sugar. Short-grain rice such as Italian Arborio gives an especially creamy texture, but regular long-grain rice also makes a delicious pudding. Avoid using easy-cook rice, however, because it will never become as soft. Each of these puddings is as comforting served warm as it is cold.

**1** Cut vanilla pod lengthways in half. Scrape out and reserve seeds from inside of both halves. Place pod halves and seeds in 4-litre saucepan. (If using vanilla essence, stir in with rum in Step 3.)

**2** Add milk and sugar to pan; bring to the boil over medium-high heat, stirring occasionally. Stir in rice; return to the boil. Reduce heat to low.

**3** Cover; simmer 1¼ hours, stirring occasionally, until very creamy and slightly thickened. Discard vanilla pod halves. Spoon into large bowl; stir in cherries, rum and salt.

## VANILLA RICE PUDDING WITH DRIED CHERRIES

❖❖❖❖❖❖❖❖❖❖❖❖❖

*Prep:* 15 minutes, plus chilling
*Cook:* 1½ hours
*Makes* 12 servings

½ **vanilla pod or 1 tbsp vanilla essence**
**1.3 litres milk**
**150g sugar**
**150g Arborio rice (Italian short-grain rice) or long-grain rice**
**75g dried cherries or raisins**
**2 tbsp dark rum**
**¼ tsp salt**
**125ml whipping cream**

### VANILLA PODS

The dried pod of an orchid native to Central America, vanilla adds its familiar but intriguing aroma to a vast range of sweet dishes. The bean is usually split before use and the seeds scraped out; both bean and seeds are added to the dish. Pure vanilla essence provides flavour in a more convenient form. Vanillin (unless labelled natural), imitation vanilla and 'vanilla flavour' are based on synthetic vanillin, which is strong in flavour and may have a harsh aftertaste. You can make vanilla sugar by placing a split pod in a jar with 200–400g caster sugar; leave 24 hours before using. Top up the sugar each time you use some; the bean will last up to 1 year.

**4** Cool slightly; cover and refrigerate at least 6 hours. Up to 2 hours before serving, whip cream until stiff peaks form. Fold whipped cream, half at a time, into rice pudding.

EACH SERVING: ABOUT 230 CALORIES, 5g PROTEIN, 33g CARBOHYDRATE, 8g TOTAL FAT (5g SATURATED), 30mg CHOLESTEROL, 110mg SODIUM

## LEFTOVER-RICE PUDDING

*Prep: 5 minutes    Cook: 25 minutes*
*Makes 4 servings*

| | |
|---|---|
| 450ml milk | 2 tbsp sugar |
| 200g cooked rice | 40g raisins or dried cherries |
| 1 cinnamon stick (8cm) or | (optional) |
| ⅛ tsp ground cinnamon | |

◆ Bring milk, rice, cinnamon stick and sugar to the boil in 3-litre saucepan over high heat. Reduce heat to medium-low; boil gently 20 minutes, stirring occasionally. Stir in raisins, if using, during last 5 minutes of cooking.

◆ Remove from heat. Discard cinnamon stick. Serve warm, or cover and refrigerate to serve cold later.

**Each serving: About 150 calories, 5g protein, 23g carbohydrate, 4g total fat (3g saturated), 17mg cholesterol, 60mg sodium**

## COCONUT RICE PUDDING

*Prep: 5 minutes, plus standing    Cook: 35 minutes*
*Makes 6 servings*

| | |
|---|---|
| 40g long-grain rice | 70g sugar |
| ½ tsp salt | Toasted flaked coconut |
| 425ml canned coconut milk | (optional) |

Bring rice, salt and *450ml water* to the boil in 3-litre saucepan over medium-high heat. Reduce heat to low; cover and simmer 15 minutes. Stir in coconut milk and sugar. Cook, uncovered, 10 minutes longer, stirring occasionally. Remove from heat. Let stand 20 minutes. Serve warm, or cover and refrigerate to serve cold later. Just before serving, sprinkle with toasted coconut, if you like.

**Each serving: About 280 calories, 3g protein, 32g carbohydrate, 17g total fat (15g saturated), 0mg cholesterol, 190mg sodium**

### COCONUT MILK

Canned coconut milk (not to be confused with the milky liquid from fresh coconut) is the strained blend of coconut meat and water processed to a paste. A basic ingredient in most Oriental cuisines, it adds a rich and exotic flavour to soups, sauces, meat and seafood curries, and desserts. Coconut cream is sold as a bar and must be reconstituted with boiling water before use. Cream of coconut, a richer mixture with sugar and stabilizers, is used in drinks and desserts. Once opened, canned coconut milk can be refrigerated in an airtight container for 1 week or frozen for 6 months.

## CREAMY CARDAMOM RICE PUDDING

*Prep: 5 minutes    Cook: 1¼ hours*
*Makes 6 servings*

| | |
|---|---|
| 900ml milk | ½ tsp salt |
| 70g long-grain rice | 2 medium egg yolks |
| 70g sugar | 75ml whipping cream |
| 5 cardamom pods | |

◆ Bring milk, rice, sugar, cardamom and salt to the boil in 5-litre flameproof casserole over medium-high heat, stirring occasionally. Reduce heat to low; cover and simmer 1 hour, stirring occasionally.

◆ Whisk egg yolks with cream in medium bowl. Gradually whisk in 200g hot rice pudding. Return mixture to casserole and cook over low heat, stirring constantly, 3 minutes, or until it just begins to bubble. Pour into serving bowl. Serve warm, or cover and refrigerate to serve cold later.

**Each serving: About 245 calories, 7g protein, 28g carbohydrate, 12g total fat (7g saturated), 111mg cholesterol, 265mg sodium**

## BAKED CUSTARD RICE PUDDING

*Prep: 20 minutes, plus cooling    Bake: 1¼ hours*
*Makes 8 servings*

| | |
|---|---|
| 100g long-grain rice | 3 medium eggs |
| 4 strips orange rind, | 100g sugar |
| 8 by 2cm each | 675ml milk |
| ½ tsp salt | 1 tsp vanilla essence |

◆ Preheat oven to 180°C (350°F, Gas 4). Bring rice, orange peel, salt and *450ml water* to the boil in 2-litre saucepan over medium-high heat. Reduce heat to low; cover and simmer 15 minutes. Remove and discard orange rind.

◆ Whisk eggs and sugar in large bowl until well blended. Whisk in milk and vanilla essence. Stir in hot rice. Pour mixture into shallow 1½-litre ovenproof serving dish, stirring to distribute rice. Place dish in larger roasting tin; carefully pour *boiling water* into roasting tin to come halfway up sides of serving dish.

◆ Bake 1¼ hours, or until knife inserted halfway between centre and edge of pudding comes out clean. Remove serving dish from roasting tin. Cool on wire rack 30 minutes. Serve pudding warm, or cover and refrigerate to serve cold later.

**Each serving: About 180 calories, 6g protein, 27g carbohydrate, 5g total fat (3g saturated), 92mg cholesterol, 205mg sodium**

# BAKED PUDDINGS

Baked puddings owe much of their charm to their simplicity. We've included a toffee pudding with a sticky brown-sugar topping; a delicate orange pudding that forms its own sauce; and a rich, rich chocolate pudding. For maximum pleasure, serve warm.

## STICKY TOFFEE PUDDING

❖❖❖❖❖❖❖❖❖❖❖❖

*Prep: 20 minutes, plus standing and cooling*
*Bake: 30 minutes*
*Makes 12 servings*

150g stoned dates, chopped
1 tsp bicarbonate of soda
150g butter or margarine, softened
200g caster sugar
1 medium egg
1 tsp vanilla essence
300g plain flour
1 tsp baking powder
225g brown sugar
60ml whipping cream
Whipped cream (optional)

**1** Preheat oven to 180°C (350°F, Gas 4). Grease a 33 by 20cm flameproof serving dish. Combine dates, bicarbonate of soda and *350ml boiling water* in bowl; let stand 15 minutes.

**2** Using electric mixer on medium speed, beat 90g butter in large bowl until creamy. Beat in caster sugar. Add egg and vanilla essense; beat until blended.

**3** On low speed, add flour and baking powder. Add date mixture and beat until evenly combined (mixture will be thin). Pour mixture into dish. Bake 30 minutes, or until golden and cocktail stick inserted in centre comes out clean. Meanwhile, bring brown sugar, cream and remaining 60g butter to the boil in 2-litre saucepan over medium heat; boil 1 minute. Set aside. Preheat grill.

### WHAT'S IN A NAME?

The word 'pudding' often describes a creamy, soft dessert made on the hob with milk, sugar and eggs and thickened with a starch, such as flour, rice or cornflour. It also applies to a wide range of sweet dishes, including bread pudding and steamed or baked cake-like desserts such as Christmas pudding or the Sticky Toffee Pudding on this page. Desserts in general may be referred to as 'pudding', although two of the best-known puddings are savoury: steak and kidney pudding and Yorkshire Pudding (recipe on page 184), the traditional accompaniment to roast beef. The word can also refer to an old-fashioned sausage such as black pudding.

**4** Spread brown sugar mixture evenly over hot pudding. Grill at closest position to hcat about 30 seconds, or until bubbly. Cool in dish on wire rack 15 minutes. Serve warm, with whipped cream, if you like.

---

EACH SERVING: ABOUT 355 CALORIES, 3g PROTEIN, 61g CARBOHYDRATE, 12g TOTAL FAT (7g SATURATED), 52mg CHOLESTEROL, 270mg SODIUM

# CHOCOLATE FUDGE PUDDING

*Prep: 25 minutes  Bake: 40 minutes*
*Makes 8 servings*

225ml milk
4 medium eggs, separated
100g plus 2 tbsp caster sugar
50g plain flour
90g plain chocolate, melted

1 tsp vanilla essence
¼ tsp salt
Icing sugar for decoration
Vanilla ice cream or whipped
  cream (optional)

◈ Preheat oven to 180°C (350°F, Gas 4). Grease 20cm square glass ovenproof dish.

◈ Bring milk to the boil in 3-litre saucepan over medium-high heat. Meanwhile, whisk egg yolks with 100g caster sugar in medium bowl, until smooth. Whisk in flour until combined. Gradually whisk hot milk into yolk mixture.

◈ Return mixture to pan; return to the boil over medium-high heat, whisking constantly. Reduce heat to low; cook 1 minute, whisking. Remove from heat and whisk in melted chocolate, vanilla essense and salt.

◈ Using an electric mixer on high speed, beat egg whites in small bowl until soft peaks form; beat in remaining 2 tablespoons caster sugar. Whisk one-third of whites into chocolate mixture until smooth; fold in remaining whites (mixture will be stiff). Spoon evenly into prepared ovenproof dish.

◈ Place dish in larger roasting tin; carefully pour *boiling water* into roasting tin to come halfway up sides of dish. Bake 40 minutes, or until firm. Sift icing sugar on top. Serve warm, with ice cream, if you like.

**Each serving: About 190 calories, 6g protein, 25g carbohydrate, 9g total fat (4g saturated), 111mg cholesterol, 115mg sodium**

◆ ◆ ◆ ◆ ◆ ◆ ◆ ◆ ◆ ◆ ◆ ◆ ◆ ◆ ◆ ◆ ◆ ◆ ◆ ◆ ◆ ◆ ◆ ◆

## MELTING CHOCOLATE

You can melt chocolate in a heavy saucepan or double boiler on the hob. The pan must be dry, as moisture will give the chocolate a grainy consistency. Melt over low heat, stirring constantly to prevent scorching. To melt in a microwave, place 30–125g chocolate in a microwave-safe bowl; cook on Medium (50% power) for 1½–2 minutes.

Chocolate melted in the microwave retains its shape, so it won't look melted until it's stirred (above).

◆ ◆ ◆ ◆ ◆ ◆ ◆ ◆ ◆ ◆ ◆ ◆ ◆ ◆ ◆ ◆ ◆ ◆ ◆ ◆ ◆ ◆ ◆ ◆

# INDIAN PUDDING

*Prep: 30 minutes, plus cooling  Bake: 2 hours*
*Makes 8 servings*

90g coarse yellow cornmeal
900ml milk
165g light molasses or golden
  syrup
60g butter or margarine,
  diced

50g caster sugar
1 tsp ground ginger
1 tsp ground cinnamon
½ tsp salt
¼ tsp ground nutmeg
Vanilla ice cream

◈ Preheat oven to 180°C (350°F, Gas 4). Grease shallow 1½-litre glass or ceramic ovenproof serving dish. Stir together cornmeal and 225ml milk in small bowl. Bring remaining 675ml milk to the boil in 4-litre saucepan over high heat. Stir in cornmeal mixture; return to the boil. Reduce heat to low and cook, stirring often, 20 minutes. Remove from heat. Stir in molasses and next 6 ingredients.

◈ Pour mixture into prepared dish. Cover with foil. Place dish in larger roasting tin; carefully pour *boiling water* into roasting tin to come halfway up sides of dish. Bake 1 hour. Remove foil; bake 1 hour longer. Remove from roasting tin; cool on wire rack 30 minutes. Serve warm with ice cream.

**Each serving (without ice cream): 245 calories, 5g protein, 34g carbohydrate, 10g total fat (5g saturated), 18mg cholesterol, 265mg sodium**

# ORANGE PUDDING CAKE

*Prep: 20 minutes  Bake: 40 minutes*
*Makes 6 servings*

150g sugar
40g plain flour
⅛ tsp salt
225ml milk
3 medium eggs, separated

60g butter or margarine,
  melted
60ml fresh lemon juice
60ml fresh orange juice
2 tsp grated orange rind

◈ Preheat oven to 180°C (350°F, Gas 4). Grease 20cm square glass ovenproof serving dish. Whisk sugar, flour and salt together in large bowl until combined. Whisk in milk, egg yolks and next 4 ingredients until smooth. Using electric mixer on high speed, beat egg whites to soft peaks in small bowl. Fold one-quarter of orange mixture into whites; fold whites back into orange mixture until evenly combined.

◈ Pour mixture into prepared dish. Place dish in larger roasting tin; carefully pour *boiling water* into roasting tin to come halfway up sides of dish. Bake 40 minutes, or until top is golden and set (dessert will separate into pudding and cake layers). Serve warm.

**Each serving: About 250 calories, 5g protein, 33g carbohydrate, 11g total fat (5g saturated), 133mg cholesterol, 185mg sodium**

# BAKED CUSTARDS

Crème brûlée, crème caramel and flan owe their silky smooth richness to the thick creamy custard base. Delicious results are relatively easy to achieve but take care not to over-bake, or the mixture may become watery and start to separate. The custards are done even if the centres are still slightly soft (they'll firm up as they cool). The custards work well with a wide range of flavours: here we've used butterscotch, vanilla, chocolate and pumpkin.

## BUTTERSCOTCH CRÈME BRÛLÉE

❖❖❖❖❖❖❖❖❖❖❖❖❖❖❖❖❖❖❖❖❖❖❖❖

*Prep: 20 minutes, plus cooling and chilling   Bake: 1 hour*
*Makes 12 servings*

675ml single cream
60g butter
150g plus 2 tbsp light brown
   sugar

9 medium egg yolks
1½ tsp vanilla essence
Strawberries for decoration

**1** Preheat oven to 170°C (325°F, Gas 3). Heat cream in 2-litre saucepan over medium heat until tiny bubbles form at pan edges.

**2** Meanwhile, bring butter and 150g brown sugar to the boil in 3-litre saucepan over medium heat; boil 2 minutes, stirring constantly. Gradually whisk in warm cream until mixture is completely smooth. Remove from heat. Using wire whisk or fork, beat egg yolks and vanilla essence in medium bowl until blended.

**3** Slowly beat cream mixture into egg-yolk mixture until well mixed. Pour into twelve 125ml ramekins or small ovenproof serving dishes. Place ramekins in roasting tin.

**4** Carefully pour *boiling water* into roasting tin to come halfway up sides of ramekins. Bake 1 hour, or just until set (mixture will be slightly soft in centre). Remove ramekins from roasting tin; cool on wire rack. Refrigerate at least 3 hours until well chilled.

**5** Up to 4 hours before serving, preheat grill. Place remaining 2 tablespoons brown sugar in small sieve. Using spoon, press brown sugar through sieve over top of chilled custards.

**6** Place ramekins in grill pan for easier handling. At closest position to heat, grill crème brûlée 3–4 minutes, just until sugar melts. Refrigerate until ready to serve. The melted brown sugar will form a shiny, crisp crust over the custard. Serve within 4 hours, or the crust will lose its crispness. To serve, arrange ramekins on platter and decorate platter with strawberries.

EACH SERVING: ABOUT 220 CALORIES, 4g PROTEIN, 19g CARBOHYDRATE, 15g TOTAL FAT (7g SATURATED), 193mg CHOLESTEROL, 80mg SODIUM

Delicate-textured foods such as custards and cheesecakes are commonly baked in a tin of hot water, otherwise known as a water bath or bain-marie. The water diffuses the heat of the oven so the custard does not overcook and separate. To prepare a water bath, simply set the cooking dish or dishes in a larger pan and fill partway with boiling water. The pan should be large enough to accommodate the dish with a few inches to spare on all sides; a large baking or roasting tin is ideal.

## LOW-FAT CRÈME CARAMEL

*Prep: 15 minutes, plus cooling and chilling    Bake: 30 minutes*
*Makes 8 servings*

| | |
|---|---|
| 300g caster sugar | 900ml semi-skimmed milk |
| 3 medium eggs | 1 tsp vanilla essence |
| 3 medium egg whites | |

◆ Preheat oven to 180°C (350°F, Gas 4). Grease eight 225ml ramekins or small ovenproof dishes. Heat 200g sugar and *2 tablespoons water* in 2-litre saucepan over medium heat until sugar melts and is a light caramel colour. Immediately pour into ramekins.

◆ Using wire whisk or fork, beat eggs, egg whites and remaining 100g sugar together in large bowl until well blended. Beat in milk and vanilla essence; pour into ramekins. Skim foam from tops. Place ramekins in large roasting tin. Carefully pour *boiling water* into roasting tin to come halfway up sides of ramekins. Bake 30 minutes, or until centres are just set. Remove ramekins from roasting tin; cool on wire rack. Refrigerate 3 hours, or until well chilled.

◆ To serve, using small palette knife, carefully loosen custard from ramekins; invert each custard on to a dessert plate, allowing syrup to drip from ramekin onto custard.

Each serving: About 235 calories, 8g protein, 44g carbohydrate, 3g total fat (1g saturated), 85mg cholesterol, 110mg sodium

## CHOCOLATE POTS DE CRÈME

*Prep: 15 minutes, plus cooling and chilling    Bake: 30–35 minutes*
*Makes 6 servings*

| | |
|---|---|
| 90g plain chocolate | 2 medium egg yolks |
| 600ml milk | 50g caster sugar |
| 2 medium eggs | 1 tsp vanilla essence |

◆ Preheat oven to 180°C (350°F, Gas 4). Melt chocolate and 60ml milk in 3-litre saucepan over low heat, stirring frequently. Remove from heat. Bring remaining 540ml milk

to the boil in 2-litre saucepan over medium-high heat; stir into chocolate mixture. Whisk eggs, egg yolks, sugar and vanilla essence in large bowl until well blended. Gradually whisk in chocolate mixture. Pour evenly into six 175ml ramekins or ovenproof serving dishes. Place ramekins in roasting tin.

◆ Carefully pour *boiling water* into roasting tin to come halfway up sides of ramekins. Cover roasting tin with foil, crimping edges loosely. Bake custards 30–35 minutes, until knife inserted halfway between edge and centre of custard comes out clean.

◆ Remove foil; remove ramekins from roasting tin. Cool on wire rack. Refrigerate 3 hours, or until well chilled. Serve custards in ramekins.

Each serving: About 210 calories, 7g protein, 22g carbohydrate, 11g total fat (6g saturated), 156mg cholesterol, 75mg sodium

## PUMPKIN FLAN

*Prep: 15 minutes, plus cooling and chilling    Bake: 50 minutes*
*Makes 12 servings*

| | |
|---|---|
| 220g caster sugar | 350ml evaporated milk |
| 8 medium eggs | ¾ tsp ground cinnamon |
| 450ml milk | ¼ tsp ground ginger |
| 225g canned solid-pack pumpkin | ¼ tsp ground nutmeg |

◆ Preheat oven to 170°C (325°F, Gas 3). Melt 70g caster sugar in 26cm frying pan over medium heat, stirring constantly, until a light caramel colour. Immediately pour caramel syrup into 23 by 12cm loaf tin, tilting tin to cover base completely.

◆ Using wire whisk or fork, beat eggs and remaining 150g caster sugar in large bowl until well blended. Beat in milk, pumpkin, evaporated milk, cinnamon, ginger and nutmeg until well mixed; pour mixture into loaf tin.

◆ Place loaf tin in larger baking tin. Carefully pour *boiling water* into baking tin to come halfway up sides of loaf tin. Bake about 50 minutes, until knife inserted in centre of flan comes out clean.

◆ Remove loaf tin from baking tin. Cool on wire rack. Refrigerate flan 3 hours, or until well chilled.

◆ To serve, using small palette knife, carefully loosen flan from loaf tin and invert onto a chilled large platter, allowing caramel syrup to drip from tin onto flan.

Each serving: About 190 calories, 8g protein, 25g carbohydrate, 7g total fat (3g saturated), 156mg cholesterol, 95mg sodium

# SOUFFLÉS

Dessert soufflés are dazzling whether they're baked as puffy individual servings or as one large soufflé. Despite their mystique, they are amazingly simple – follow our straightforward recipes for guaranteed light and airy results. Be sure to serve soufflés immediately from the oven, before they deflate.

## APRICOT SOUFFLÉS

❖❖❖❖❖❖❖❖❖❖❖❖

*Prep: 20 minutes, plus cooling*
*Bake: 12–15 minutes*
*Makes 6 servings*

**175g ready-to-eat dried apricots**
**175ml orange juice**
**About 2 tbsp plus 50g caster sugar**
**6 medium egg whites**
**½ tsp cream of tartar**
**1 tsp vanilla essence**

**1** Bring apricots and orange juice to the boil in small saucepan over high heat. Reduce heat to low; cover and simmer 10 minutes, or until apricots are softened. Blend apricots, with any liquid in pan, in blender or food processor with knife blade attached, until puréed. Place in large bowl; set aside to cool to room temperature. Preheat oven to 190°C (375°F, Gas 5). Grease six 175ml soufflé dishes or ovenproof dishes; sprinkle with about 2 tablespoons sugar.

**2** Using an electric mixer on high speed, beat egg whites and cream of tartar in large bowl until soft peaks form. Beat in vanilla essence. Beating at high speed, gradually sprinkle in remaining 50g sugar until mixture holds stiff peaks.

**3** Using rubber spatula or large metal spoon, gently fold one-third of beaten egg whites into apricot mixture to lighten mixture. Fold in remaining whites, half at a time. Spoon mixture into soufflé dishes.

### FRESH PEAR SOUFFLÉ

Prepare Apricot Soufflé as recipe instructs, but instead of the apricot-orange juice mixture in Step 1, make pear purée: peel and coarsely chop 5 fully ripe pears (650g). Toss with 1 tablespoon fresh lemon juice in 2-litre saucepan. Cook over high heat, covered, 15 minutes, or until pears are very tender. Uncover and cook 10–15 minutes longer, stirring occasionally, until mixture is almost dry. Transfer to blender or food processor with knife blade attached and blend until puréed. Place in large bowl; cool to room temperature. Proceed as recipe instructs.

Each serving: About 165 calories, 4g protein, 39g carbohydrate, 1g total fat (0g saturated), 0mg cholesterol, 55mg sodium

**4** Using small palette knife held at a 45° angle to soufflé, make a domed peak on each soufflé. Place ramekins on baking tray for easier handling. (If not serving right away, soufflés can be refrigerated for up to 3 hours before baking.) Bake soufflés 12–15 minutes until puffed and golden. Serve immediately.

EACH SERVING: ABOUT 150 CALORIES, 5g PROTEIN, 34g CARBOHYDRATE, 0g TOTAL FAT, 0mg CHOLESTEROL, 60mg SODIUM

## CHOCOLATE SOUFFLÉS

*Prep: 20 minutes, plus cooling    Bake: 30 minutes*
*Makes 6 servings*

50g plain flour
1 tbsp instant espresso-coffee powder
250g plus 2 tbsp caster sugar
225ml milk
45g butter, softened
175g plain chocolate, coarsely chopped
6 medium eggs, separated
2 tsp vanilla essence
¼ tsp salt
Icing sugar for decoration

◆ Combine flour, espresso powder and 250g caster sugar in 3-litre saucepan; gradually stir in milk until blended. Cook over medium heat, stirring constantly, until mixture thickens and boils; boil 1 minute. Remove from heat.

◆ Stir in butter and chocolate until melted and smooth. Beat in egg yolks all at once until well mixed. Stir in vanilla essence. Cool to lukewarm. Preheat oven to 180°C (350°F, Gas 4). Grease six 225ml soufflé dishes or ovenproof dishes; sprinkle lightly with remaining 2 tablespoons caster sugar.

◆ Using an electric mixer on high speed, beat egg whites and salt in large bowl to stiff peaks. Using rubber spatula or large metal spoon, gently fold one-third of beaten egg whites into chocolate mixture; gently fold back into remaining whites. Pour into soufflé dishes. Bake 30 minutes (centres will be fudgy). When soufflés are done, sprinkle with icing sugar; serve immediately.

**Each serving: About 485 calories, 11g protein, 60g carbohydrate, 27g total fat (10g saturated), 235mg cholesterol, 240mg sodium**

## RASPBERRY SOUFFLÉS

*Prep: 25 minutes, plus cooling    Bake: 20 minutes*
*Makes 4 servings*

45g butter
3 tbsp plain flour
⅛ tsp salt
175ml milk
7 tbsp caster sugar
3 medium egg yolks
2 tbsp orange-flavoured liqueur
4 medium egg whites
480g raspberries
80g redcurrant jelly
1 tsp cornflour
Icing sugar for decoration

◆ Melt butter in 2-litre saucepan over low heat. Stir in flour and salt until blended. Gradually stir in milk and cook, stirring constantly, until mixture thickens slightly and boils; boil 1 minute. Remove from heat.

◆ Using wire whisk, whisk in 3 tablespoons sugar. Rapidly whisk in egg yolks. Cool to lukewarm. Stir in orange liqueur. Preheat oven to 190°C (375°F, Gas 5). Grease four 300ml soufflé dishes or ovenproof dishes; sprinkle lightly with

2 tablespoons caster sugar. Using electric mixer on high speed, beat egg whites in large bowl to stiff peaks. Using rubber spatula or metal spoon, fold one-third of beaten egg whites into egg-yolk mixture; gently fold back into remaining whites. Fold in 115g raspberries. Spoon into soufflé dishes; place on baking tray for easier handling. Bake 20 minutes, or until knife inserted in soufflés comes out clean.

◆ Meanwhile, prepare raspberry sauce: reserve 80g raspberries for garnish. Press remaining raspberries through sieve to remove seeds. Heat raspberry purée, redcurrant jelly, cornflour and remaining 2 tablespoons caster sugar in 1-litre saucepan over medium heat until mixture thickens and boils; boil 1 minute. Keep sauce warm. When soufflés are done, sprinkle with icing sugar; serve immediately with sauce and reserved berries.

**Each serving: About 370 calories, 9g protein, 50g carbohydrate, 14g total fat (6g saturated), 190mg cholesterol, 250mg sodium**

## HAZELNUT SOUFFLÉ

*Prep: 25 minutes, plus cooling    Bake: 45 minutes*
*Makes 6 servings*

75g hazelnuts, toasted and skinned (see page 522)
100g plus 3 tbsp caster sugar
350ml milk
60g butter
40g plain flour
4 medium egg yolks
2 tbsp hazelnut-flavoured liqueur
¼ tsp salt
6 medium egg whites
Icing sugar for decoration

◆ Process hazelnuts with 50g sugar in food processor with knife blade attached, until very finely ground.

◆ Bring milk to the boil in 1-litre saucepan over medium-high heat. Meanwhile, melt butter in 3-litre saucepan over low heat; add flour and cook, stirring frequently, 2 minutes. Whisk in milk; bring to the boil. Cook, whisking constantly, 1 minute. Remove from heat. Whisk in egg yolks, 1 at a time. Stir in ground hazelnut mixture, hazelnut liqueur and salt. Cool to lukewarm. Preheat oven to 190°C (375°F, Gas 5). Grease 2½-litre soufflé dish; sprinkle lightly with 3 tablespoons caster sugar.

◆ Using electric mixer on high speed, beat egg whites in large bowl until soft peaks form. Gradually sprinkle in remaining 50g caster sugar, beating until mixture holds stiff peaks when beaters are lifted. Fold one-quarter of whites into hazelnut mixture until blended; gently fold back into remaining whites. Pour into soufflé dish. Bake 45 minutes, or until just set. When soufflé is done, sprinkle with icing sugar; serve immediately.

**Each serving: 330 calories, 9g protein, 28g carbohydrate, 20g total fat (7g saturated), 171mg cholesterol, 265mg sodium**

# CHOUX PASTRIES

This speciality pastry is cooked twice: choux paste, full of eggs, is mixed on the stove-top and then baked in the oven where it puffs up dramatically. The crisp – but light and airy – pastry is then filled with flavoured custards, creams or mousses.

## CHOCOLATE CREAM PUFF RING

❖ ❖ ❖ ❖ ❖ ❖ ❖ ❖ ❖ ❖ ❖ ❖ ❖

*Prep: 40 minutes, plus standing and cooling*
*Bake: 40 minutes*
*Makes 12 servings*

**Choux Paste (see page 464)**
**350g plain chocolate**
**60ml plus 1½ tsp milk**
**45g butter or margarine**
**2 medium eggs**
**450ml whipping cream**
**1½ tsp golden syrup**
**350g strawberries**

**1** Preheat oven to 200°C (400°F, Gas 6). Lightly grease and flour baking sheet. Using 17–18cm plate as guide, trace circle in flour on baking sheet. Prepare Choux Paste.

**3** Meanwhile, prepare chocolate mousse filling: heat 250g plain chocolate (reserve remaining 100g for glaze), 60ml milk and 30g butter in 3-litre saucepan over low heat, stirring occasionally, until smooth. Add eggs, one at a time, stirring constantly with wire whisk.

**2** Drop choux paste by heaped tablespoons into 12 mounds, inside circle, to form a ring. Using moistened finger, smooth tops. Bake 40 minutes, or until golden. Turn off oven; let ring stand in oven 15 minutes. Remove ring from oven; cool on baking sheet on wire rack.

**4** Continue whisking chocolate mixture about 5 minutes longer, until slightly thickened. Transfer to bowl, cover surface with cling film and refrigerate 30 minutes until cool.

**5** Using electric mixer on medium speed, beat cream until stiff peaks form. Using rubber spatula, fold whipped cream into cooled chocolate mixture, half at a time, until blended.

**6** Using long serrated knife, cut cooled ring horizontally in half. Spoon chocolate filling into base of ring. Replace top. Refrigerate until ready to serve. Prepare glaze: heat reserved 100g plain chocolate, remaining 15g butter, remaining 1½ teaspoons milk and golden syrup over low heat, stirring occasionally, until smooth. Spoon over choux ring. Fill centre of ring with strawberries.

EACH SERVING: ABOUT 445 CALORIES, 7g PROTEIN, 31g CARBOHYDRATE, 34g TOTAL FAT (15g SATURATED), 184mg CHOLESTEROL, 235mg SODIUM

## CREAM PUFFS WITH HOT FUDGE SAUCE

*Prep: 30 minutes, plus standing and cooling* **Bake:** *40–45 minutes*
*Makes 8 servings*

**Choux Paste (see below right)**
**Hot Fudge Sauce (see**
  **page 482)**
**1 litre vanilla ice cream**

◈ Preheat oven to 200°C (400°F, Gas 6). Grease and flour large baking sheet. Prepare Choux Paste. Drop paste in 8 large, slightly rounded mounds (each about 4 tablespoons), 8cm apart, onto baking sheet. Using moistened finger, gently smooth tops to round slightly.

◈ Bake 40–45 minutes until golden. Remove cream puffs from oven. Using tip of knife, poke a hole into side of each puff to let out steam. Turn off oven. Return puffs to oven and let stand 10 minutes. Transfer puffs to wire rack to cool.

◈ Using serrated knife, cut each cooled puff horizontally in half; remove and discard any moist portion inside puffs.

◈ Prepare Hot Fudge Sauce. To serve, place 125g scoop vanilla ice cream in bottom half of each cream puff; replace tops. Spoon Hot Fudge Sauce over cream puffs.

**Each serving: About 610 calories, 9g protein, 55g carbohydrate, 43g total fat (21g saturated), 209mg cholesterol, 330mg sodium**

## ÉCLAIRS

*Prep: 1 hour plus chilling, cooling, and standing* **Bake:** *40 minutes*
*Makes about 24*

**675ml milk**
**6 medium egg yolks**
**200g caster sugar**
**30g cornflour**
**4 tsp vanilla essence**
**Choux Paste (see right)**
**90g plain chocolate**
**3 tbsp whipping cream**

◈ Prepare pastry cream: bring milk to the boil in 4-litre saucepan over high heat. Meanwhile, whisk egg yolks with caster sugar in large bowl until smooth; whisk in cornflour until combined. Gradually whisk hot milk into yolk mixture in bowl.

◈ Return mixture to pan; cook over high heat, whisking constantly, until mixture thickens and boils. Reduce heat to low and cook, whisking, 2 minutes.

◈ Remove pan from heat and stir in vanilla essence. Pour pastry cream into shallow dish. Press cling film onto surface of pastry cream to keep skin from forming as it cools. Refrigerate pastry cream at least 2 hours or overnight. Preheat oven to 200°C (400°F, Gas 6). Grease and flour large baking sheet.

◈ Prepare Choux Paste. Spoon paste into large pastry bag fitted with 1cm round nozzle. Pipe paste into strips about 8cm long and 2cm wide, 2–3cm apart, onto baking sheet to make 24 éclairs. Using moistened finger, smooth any tails at ends of eclairs. Bake 40 minutes, or until golden. Transfer éclairs to wire rack to cool.

◈ Using serrated knife, cut each cooled éclair horizontally in half, leaving one side intact, or with small knife, make a hole in each end. Whisk pastry cream until smooth; spoon into large pastry bag fitted with 5mm round nozzle. Pipe into éclairs (reserve extra pastry cream for use another day).

◈ Melt chocolate with cream in 1-litre saucepan over very low heat, stirring often; remove from heat. Dip top of each éclair in chocolate mixture, smoothing with small palette knife if necessary. Let stand until chocolate sets.

**Each éclair: 160 calories, 4g protein, 18g carbohydrate, 9g total fat (4g saturated), 106mg cholesterol, 95mg sodium**

## CHOUX PASTE

❖ ❖ ❖ ❖ ❖ ❖ ❖ ❖ ❖ ❖ ❖ ❖

**125g butter**
**¼ tsp salt**
**150g plain flour**
**4 medium eggs**

1 Heat butter, salt and *225ml water* in 3-litre saucepan over medium heat until butter melts and mixture boils. Remove from heat. Using wooden spoon, vigorously stir in flour all at once until mixture forms ball and leaves side of pan.

2 Cool slightly. Add eggs to flour mixture, one at a time, beating well after each addition, until mixture is smooth and satiny. Shape and bake warm mixture as instructed in recipe.

# PUFF PASTRIES

Dozens of paper-thin layers of pastry and butter make puff pastry light and flaky. As both fresh and frozen are available at the supermarket, these elegant recipes can be made quickly. The rich, delicate pastry is lovely with a fragrant apple filling for a French-style treat or baked into little fruit-filled bundles for a less formal dessert.

## APPLE-ALMOND PASTRY

◆◆◆◆◆◆◆◆◆◆◆◆◆

*Prep:* 30 minutes, plus cooling
*Bake:* 25–30 minutes
*Makes* 10 servings

**1 medium egg**
**About 125g marzipan**
**2 tsp vanilla essence**
**450g Golden Delicious apples, peeled, cored and thinly sliced**
**2 tsp plain flour**
**500g fresh or frozen (thawed) puff pastry**
**2 tsp caster sugar**

**1** Using fork, beat egg in medium bowl. Transfer 1 tablespoon egg to cup; mix in *1 tablespoon water*; set aside. Add marzipan and vanilla essence to egg in bowl; using fork, break up marzipan and blend mixture. Toss apple slices with flour in large bowl. Place half of pastry on lightly floured surface. Using floured rolling pin, roll pastry to about 32cm square.

**2** Invert 28cm round bowl onto pastry, lightly pressing to make circle. Using sharp knife, trim pastry, leaving 2cm border around circle; discard trimmings. Transfer pastry circle to large baking sheet.

**3** Spread marzipan mixture to cover 28cm circle. Arrange apple slices on top. Roll out the remaining pastry on lightly floured surface; mark and trim as in Steps 1 and 2.

**4** Preheat oven to 190°C (375°F, Gas 5). Brush some egg mixture on pastry border around apples using pastry brush. Place second pastry circle on top of apples; press all around edge to seal.

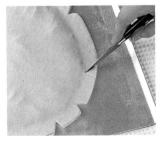

**5** Using tip of sharp knife, cut 1cm triangles from edge of pastry, about 5cm apart; discard triangles.

**6** Lightly score top crust with curved lines, starting at centre and working towards edge (do not cut all the way through). Brush pastry with remaining egg mixture; sprinkle with sugar. (Dessert can be prepared to this point and refrigerated up to 4 hours before baking.) Bake 25–30 minutes, until pastry is golden brown. Cool on wire rack at least 30 minutes before serving.

EACH SERVING: ABOUT 335 CALORIES, 6g PROTEIN, 41g CARBOHYDRATE, 17g TOTAL FAT (3g SATURATED), 21mg CHOLESTEROL, 170mg SODIUM

# FRUIT BUNDLES

*Prep: 35 minutes, plus cooling    Bake: 20–25 minutes*
*Makes 8 servings*

| | |
|---|---|
| 125g stoned prunes, coarsely chopped | 1 medium Golden Delicious apple, peeled, cored and cut into 1cm pieces |
| 125g ready-to-eat dried apricots, coarsely chopped | 50g plus 1 tbsp caster sugar |
| 175ml apple juice | 500g frozen puff pastry, thawed |
| 1 tbsp plain flour | |
| ½ tsp ground cinnamon | |

◆ Bring prunes, apricots and apple juice to the boil in 1-litre saucepan over high heat. Reduce heat to low; simmer 8–10 minutes, until fruit is soft and liquid is absorbed. Cool completely; transfer to large bowl. Stir in flour, cinnamon, apple pieces and 50g sugar.

◆ Preheat oven to 220°C (425°F, Gas 7). Place half of pastry on lightly floured surface; refrigerate remainder. Using floured rolling pin, roll pastry to 30cm square.

◆ Trim edges of pastry with sharp pastry wheel or knife; cut square into four 15cm squares. Spoon one-eighth of fruit mixture onto centre of each square.

◆ Brush edges of 1 pastry square with some *water*. Bring corners of pastry square over fruit; gently squeeze and twist pastry together to seal in filling and form a bundle. Fan out corners of pastry. Repeat to make 3 more bundles.

◆ Repeat with remaining pastry, remaining fruit mixture, and more *water* to make 4 more bundles. Place bundles, 5cm apart, on 2 ungreased large baking sheets. (If desired, refrigerate bundles on baking sheet to bake later in day.)

◆ Brush tops of fruit bundles with *water*, then sprinkle with remaining 1 tablespoon sugar. Bake 20–25 minutes until bundles are puffed and golden. Serve warm or transfer bundles to wire rack to cool.

Each serving: About 415 calories, 5g protein, 65g carbohydrate, 17g total fat (4g saturated), 0mg cholesterol, 205mg sodium

## QUICK PUFF PASTRY DESSERTS

Frozen puff pastry is great to have on hand for impressive no-fuss desserts. When working with puff pastry, remember that clean edges are important for maximum puffing. Use a biscuit cutter with very sharp edges or a very sharp knife or pastry wheel and cut straight down. If necessary, trim edges of the pastry after you've rolled it out. The following method is easy and adapts to many ideas:

Roll out the thawed pastry on lightly floured surface. Using metal biscuit cutter, cut out hearts, stars or other shapes. Or, using sharp knife or pastry wheel, trim edges of pastry and then cut out small squares, rectangles or triangles. Place on an ungreased baking sheet and prick several times with a fork.

If desired, sprinkle pastry with a little sugar or a few crushed sugar cubes. Or, brush pastry (tops only) with 1 medium egg white beaten with 1 tablespoon water (if egg mixture drips on cut edges, pastry won't puff fully), then sprinkle with finely chopped pistachios or other nuts. Bake 10–15 minutes at 190°C (375°F, Gas 5), until pastry is puffed and golden. Cool on wire rack.

Using serrated knife, carefully split each cooled pastry horizontally in half or thirds. Fill with sweetened whipped cream (flavoured with a little liqueur or vanilla essence, if you like), ice cream, berries or other fruit or Marsala Cream Cheese (see below). Try serving with any of the sauces on page 482.

**Marsala cream cheese**  Using an electric mixer on low speed, beat 225g softened cream cheese with 60g sifted icing sugar in large bowl until smooth. Gradually beat in 60ml Marsala until blended; set aside. Using mixer on medium speed, beat 225ml whipping cream in small bowl until stiff peaks form. Fold whipped cream into cream-cheese mixture. Makes about 350g.

Each 100g: About 550 calories, 7g protein, 21g carbohydrate, 48g total fat (27g saturated), 165mg cholesterol, 205mg sodium

Puff pastry hearts filled with whipped cream cheese, served with hot fudge sauce

Nut-topped puff pastry rectangles filled with kiwifruit, banana slices and whipped cream

# FILO PASTRIES

Filo pastry, fresh or frozen, makes spectacular desserts like our delicate filo cups with a berry and ricotta filling. You'll need large sheets of filo for these recipes; look for long (at least 30cm), thin packs. Filo pastry dries out quickly, so keep it covered until you are ready to use it. Wrap any unused filo and refrigerate it up to 2 weeks; do not re-freeze thawed filo or it will become dry and brittle.

## FILO CUPS WITH HONEY, RICOTTA AND MIXED BERRIES

*Prep: 45 minutes, plus draining and cooling*
*Bake: 12 minutes    Makes 6 servings*

| | |
|---|---|
| 900g ricotta cheese | 80g honey |
| 6 sheets (about 40 by 30cm) filo pastry (about 125g), thawed if frozen | 1 tsp grated orange rind |
| | 145g blueberries |
| | 125g raspberries |
| 30g butter or margarine, melted | 145g blackberries |
| | Icing sugar for decoration |

**1** Blend ricotta cheese in food processor with knife blade attached, about 1 minute, or until smooth. Place double-thick layer of white kitchen towels in medium sieve set over small bowl. Spoon ricotta cheese onto kitchen towels; cover with cling film, place in refrigerator and let drain at least 2 hours or overnight (whey will drop into bowl and ricotta will thicken).

**2** Meanwhile, preheat oven to 190°C (375°F, Gas 5). Stack filo sheets one on top of the other on work surface. Using knife, cut stack lengthways, then crossways in half (you will have twenty-four 20 by 15cm pieces).

**3** Keep filo stack covered with cling film to prevent it from drying out while assembling filo cups. Lightly brush six 300ml small ovenproof dishes or ramekins with melted butter. Place 2 pieces of filo, one on top of the other, on work surface; brush top piece with some melted butter. Arrange filo in ovenproof dish.

**4** Repeat with 2 more pieces of filo, placing them crossways over filo in ovenproof dish. Fold filo overhang to make pretty edge. Repeat with remaining filo and melted butter to make 6 filo cups in all.

**5** Place ovenproof dishes in baking tray for easier handling. Bake filo cups about 12 minutes until filo is crisp and golden.

**6** Cool filo cups in ovenproof dishes on wire racks about 15 minutes; carefully remove from dishes. (Filo cups can be made 1 day ahead and kept in air-tight container.) Just before serving, remove ricotta from refrigerator. Discard whey in bowl. Transfer drained ricotta to same bowl.

**7** Add honey and orange rind to ricotta and mix well. Toss blueberries, raspberries and blackberries together in bowl. Spoon ricotta mixture into filo cups; top with berries. Sprinkle with icing sugar. Serve immediately.

EACH SERVING: ABOUT 435 CALORIES, 19g PROTEIN, 36g CARBOHYDRATE, 25g TOTAL FAT (14g SATURATED), 97mg CHOLESTEROL, 260mg SODIUM

## SPICED PEAR STRUDEL

*Prep: 30 minutes, plus cooling    Bake: 40 minutes*
*Makes 16 servings*

| | |
|---|---|
| 800g large pears, peeled and thinly sliced | 90g dried breadcrumbs |
| 75g stoned dates, diced | 12 sheets filo pastry (each about 40 by 30cm), thawed if frozen (about 225g) |
| 70g caster sugar | |
| ½ tsp ground cinnamon | 125g butter or margarine, melted |
| ¼ tsp ground ginger | |
| ⅛ tsp salt | Icing sugar for decoration |

◈ Grease large baking sheet. Toss pears with next 5 ingredients and 30g breadcrumbs in large bowl.

◈ Cut out two 60cm lengths of greaseproof paper; overlap 2 long sides by about 5cm. Arrange 1 sheet of filo on greaseproof paper; brush with some melted butter, then sprinkle with scant tablespoon breadcrumbs. (Keep remaining filo covered with cling film to prevent it drying out.) Continue layering filo, brushing each sheet with some butter and sprinkling every other sheet with crumbs.

◈ Preheat oven to 190°C (375°F, Gas 5). Starting along 1 long side of filo, spoon pears onto pastry to about 1cm from edges to cover half of rectangle. From pear-side, roll up filo, Swiss roll fashion.

◈ Place roll on baking sheet seam-side down; tuck ends under. Brush with remaining butter. Cut 16 diagonal slashes in top. Bake 40 minutes, covering with foil during last 20 minutes if necessary to prevent over-browning.

◈ Cool on baking sheet on wire rack 30 minutes. Sprinkle cooled strudel lightly with icing sugar. Serve warm or cold.

**Each serving: About 175 calories, 2g protein, 27g carbohydrate, 7g total fat (2g saturated), 17mg cholesterol, 195mg sodium**

## HONEY-LEMON BAKLAVA

*Prep: 30 minutes, plus cooling    Bake: 1¼ hours*
*Makes 24 servings*

| | |
|---|---|
| 450g walnuts | 150g butter or margarine, melted |
| 1 tsp ground cinnamon | |
| ¼ tsp ground cloves | 325g honey |
| 200g caster sugar | 1 cinnamon stick (7–8cm) |
| 450g filo pastry (each sheet 40 by 30cm), thawed if frozen | 4 tsp fresh lemon juice |

◈ Grease 33 by 20cm glass ovenproof dish. Place first 3 ingredients and 100g sugar in food processor with knife blade attached. Pulse until walnuts are finely chopped; set aside. Preheat oven to 150°C (300°F, Gas 2).

◈ Cut filo sheets into 33 by 20cm rectangles; discard trimmings. Place 1 sheet filo in dish; brush with some melted butter. (Keep remaining filo covered with cling film to prevent it drying out.) Repeat with 5 more sheets; sprinkle with about 125g walnut mixture.

◈ Place 1 sheet of filo in dish over walnuts; brush with some butter. Repeat with 5 more sheets of filo; sprinkle with about 125g walnut mixture. Repeat layering 2 more times, ending with walnuts. Place 1 sheet of filo on top of last walnut layer; brush with some butter. Repeat until all filo sheets are used, brushing with remaining butter.

◈ Using sharp knife, cut almost but not all the way through layers to make 24 servings: cut lengthways into 3 strips; cut each strip crossways into 4 rectangles and cut each rectangle diagonally into 2 triangles. Bake 1¼ hours, or until golden.

◈ Prepare syrup: about 15 minutes before baklava is done, bring honey, cinnamon stick, *1 cup water* and remaining 100g sugar to the boil in small saucepan over medium heat; boil 5 minutes, stirring often. Reduce heat to low. Add lemon juice; simmer 5 minutes longer. Discard cinnamon stick; spoon hot syrup over hot baklava.

◈ Cool baklava in dish on wire rack at least 1 hour. Let stand at room temperature until ready to serve. To serve, finish cutting through layers.

**Each serving: About 305 calories, 4g protein, 34g carbohydrate, 18g total fat (3g saturated), 13mg cholesterol, 150mg sodium**

### FILO MILLEFEUILLES

Stack 6 sheets (40 by 30cm each), fresh or frozen (thawed) filo (about 125g), lightly brushing every second sheet with melted butter. Using pizza wheel or knife, cut stack lengthways in half; cut each half crossways into 6. Bake on baking sheet at 190°C (375°F, Gas 5) 10 minutes. Cool on baking sheet on wire rack.

Spread 4 rectangles with half of Marsala Cream Cheese (see page 466) or sweetened whipped cream; top with some berries mixed with jam. Layer with 4 more rectangles, remaining cream cheese and more berry mixture. Sprinkle remaining rectangles with icing sugar; place on top to make 4 millefeuilles.

# CRÊPES AND BLINTZES

These thin pancakes make a lovely dessert when wrapped around sweet fillings. You can freeze crêpes for up to 4 months, stacked with a sheet of greaseproof paper between each one. Thaw for about an hour before using. Blintzes, little pancake parcels filled with cheese or fruit, are made from crêpes that are browned on one side only.

## APPLE-CALVADOS CRÊPES

❖❖❖❖❖❖❖❖❖❖❖❖

*Prep: 50 minutes, plus chilling batter*
*Bake: 5 minutes*
*Makes 6 servings*

**Basic Crêpes (see page 82)**
**75g butter or margarine**
**750g Golden Delicious apples, peeled, cored and diced**
**115g caster sugar**
**60g Calvados or other apple brandy**

**1** Prepare Basic Crêpes. Preheat oven to 200°C (400°F, Gas 6). Melt 60g butter in 30cm frying pan over medium-high heat. Stir in apples and 100g sugar; cover and cook 10 minutes, or until tender.

**2** Uncover and cook about 10 minutes longer until apples begin to caramelize. Stir in Calvados. Remove pan from heat.

**3** Spread equal amount apple filling down centre of each crêpe. Roll up; arrange in shallow ovenproof dish. Dot crêpes with remaining 15g butter; sprinkle with remaining 15g sugar. Bake 5 minutes.

## PEAR- AND PLUM-FILLED CRÊPES

**Pear filling** Melt 60g butter or margarine in 30cm frying pan over medium-high heat. Add 750g peeled and diced ripe Conference pears (about 8); cook, uncovered, 10–15 minutes, stirring occasionally, until tender. Stir in 50g brown sugar, ¼ teaspoon ground cinnamon, and 2 strips (7–8cm each) lemon rind; cook 1 minute longer. Discard lemon rind. Fill and bake crêpes as instructed in Step 3. Makes 6 servings.

Each serving with crêpes: About 390 calories, 7g protein, 56g carbohydrate, 17g total fat (8g saturated), 146mg cholesterol, 370mg sodium

**Plum filling** Melt 45g butter or margarine in 30cm frying pan over medium-high heat. Add 1.1kg quartered ripe plums (about 10), 150g caster sugar and a pinch ground cloves. Cook, stirring occasionally, 15–20 minutes, until plums are tender. Fill and bake crêpes as instructed in Step 3. Makes 6 servings.

Each serving with crêpes: About 395 calories, 8g protein, 60g carbohydrate, 15g total fat (7g saturated), 141mg cholesterol, 345mg sodium

**EACH SERVING: ABOUT 465 CALORIES, 7g PROTEIN, 65g CARBOHYDRATE, 19g TOTAL FAT (8g SATURATED), 152mg CHOLESTEROL, 390mg SODIUM**

## CRÊPES SUZETTE

Prepare Basic Crêpes (see page 82). Melt 60g butter or margarine with 75ml orange juice, 2 tablespoons caster sugar and ¼ teaspoon grated orange rind in 30cm frying pan over low heat. Fold each crêpe into quarters; arrange in sauce, turning to coat. Simmer 10 minutes. Pour 60ml orange-flavored liqueur evenly over crêpes (do not stir).

Heat 1–2 minutes. Using long wooden match, carefully ignite. When flames subside, transfer crêpes to plates. Makes 6 servings.

Each serving: 275 calories, 7g protein, 22g carbohydrate, 16g total fat (8g saturated), 146mg cholesterol, 365mg sodium

## CHEESE BLINTZES

*Prep:* 40 minutes, plus chilling    *Cook:* 20 minutes
*Makes* 6 servings

Basic Crêpes (see page 82)
450g cream cheese, softened
225g cottage cheese
3 tbsp icing sugar
¾ tsp vanilla essence

1 medium egg
Blueberry Sauce (see page 482)
30g butter or margarine
Soured cream (optional)

◆ Prepare mixture as instructed in Steps 1 and 2 of Basic Crêpes. While mixture is chilling, prepare filling: using an electric mixer on medium speed, beat cream cheese, cottage cheese, icing sugar, vanilla essence and egg in bowl until smooth. Cover and refrigerate until ready to use.

◆ Cook crêpes as instructed in Steps 3 and 4 of Basic Crêpes, but cook crêpe on bottom side only. Stack cooked crêpes, browned-side up, between greaseproof paper. Prepare sauce. Place equal amount of filling in centre of browned side of each crêpe. Fold left and right sides over filling and overlap ends to make a packet.

◆ Melt 30g butter in 26cm frying pan over medium heat. Add 6 blintzes, seam-side down; cook until golden on both sides. Transfer to plates. Repeat with remaining butter and blintzes. Serve hot with Blueberry Sauce, and soured cream, if you like.

Each serving: About 595 calories, 18g protein, 38g carbohydrate, 42g total fat (24g saturated), 261mg cholesterol, 715mg sodium

## CRÊPES WITH STRAWBERRIES AND CREAM

*Prep:* 30 minutes, plus chilling    *Cook:* 20 minutes
*Makes* 6 servings

Basic Crêpes (see page 82)
60g caster sugar
350g strawberries, hulled and thinly sliced
1–2 tbsp orange-flavoured liqueur

225ml whipping cream
1 tbsp margarine or butter, melted
Icing sugar for decoration

◆ Prepare Basic Crêpes, adding 15g caster sugar to mixture in blender in Step 1. While mixture is chilling, mix strawberries, liqueur, and 30g caster sugar together in medium bowl. Let stand 20 minutes to allow sugar to dissolve and berries to marinate.

◆ Using an electric mixer on medium speed, beat cream with remaining 15g caster sugar until soft peaks form. Spoon cream into serving bowl.

◆ Strain syrup from strawberries into small bowl. Stir in melted butter and use to brush on crêpes. Fold each crêpe into quarters. Dust crêpes lightly with icing sugar. Place strawberries in small serving bowl. Serve crêpes with strawberries and whipped cream.

Each serving: About 365 calories, 8g protein, 27g carbohydrate, 25g total fat (14g saturated), 184mg cholesterol, 315mg sodium

## BROWN SUGAR CRÊPES

*Prep:* 25 minutes, plus chilling    *Cook:* 3 to 6 minutes
*Makes* 6 servings

Basic Crêpes (see page 82)
12 rounded tsp brown sugar

30g butter or margarine

◆ Prepare Basic Crêpes. Press 1 rounded teaspoon brown sugar through sieve evenly over 1 crepe. Fold crêpe into quarters. Repeat with remaining brown sugar and crêpes.

◆ Melt 10g butter in 26cm frying pan over medium-high heat, swirling to coat base of pan. Add 4 crêpes and cook 30–60 seconds per side until heated through. Transfer to 2 dessert plates. Repeat with remaining butter and crêpes in 2 more batches.

Each serving: About 225 calories, 7g protein, 22g carbohydrate, 12g total fat (6g saturated), 136mg cholesterol, 325mg sodium

# Bread Puddings

Bread pudding is filling and easy to make; it is simply bread baked in a custard of eggs, milk and sugar. Thrifty cooks make it as a way of using up day-old or stale bread – dry bread soaks up the egg mixture and all the flavours better than fresh bread. Our Bread-and-Butter Pudding is a traditional family favourite, but we have created a number of variations using different types of bread and additional ingredients. Raisins and sultanas are often added but a variety of fruit can be used; our two examples use apples and dried cherries. For a touch of luxury, our Black-and-White Bread Pudding transforms this old-fashioned dessert into a feast for chocolate lovers.

## BLACK-AND-WHITE BREAD PUDDING

*Prep: 30–40 minutes, plus standing and cooling*
*Bake: 1¼ hours*   *Makes 16 servings*

| | |
|---|---|
| **450g sliced firm white bread** | **9 medium eggs** |
| **900ml milk** | **90g plain chocolate, grated** |
| **100g caster sugar** | **90g white chocolate, grated** |
| **1 tbsp vanilla essence** | **White Chocolate Custard** |
| **½ tsp salt** | **Sauce (optional, see below)** |

### WHITE CHOCOLATE CUSTARD SAUCE

Place 90g finely chopped white chocolate in large bowl; set aside. Using wire whisk, beat 4 medium egg yolks and 50g caster sugar in small bowl until combined. Bring 225ml milk and 75ml whipping cream to the boil in heavy 2-litre saucepan over high heat. Beat small amount of hot milk mixture into egg mixture. Slowly pour egg mixture back into milk mixture in saucepan, stirring rapidly to prevent lumps from forming. Reduce heat to low and cook, stirring constantly, about 5 minutes, until mixture thickens slightly and coats back of spoon well. (Mixture should be about 67°C, but be careful not to let it boil, or it will curdle.) Pour mixture over white chocolate in bowl, stirring to combine (white chocolate will not melt completely). Transfer custard sauce to serving jug and serve warm, or refrigerate to serve cold. Makes about 600ml.

Each 100ml: About 280 calories, 5g protein, 20g carbohydrate, 20g total fat (12g saturated), 191mg cholesterol, 50mg sodium

**1** Preheat oven to 170°C (325°F, Gas 3). Place bread slices on large baking sheet; lightly toast in oven 20–30 minutes, turning once. Grease 33 by 20 glass or ceramic ovenproof dish.

**2** Arrange bread in dish, overlapping slightly. Using wire whisk or fork, mix milk, sugar, vanilla essence, salt and eggs in very large bowl until blended. Whisk in grated chocolates.

**3** Pour milk mixture over bread; let stand 30 minutes, occasionally spooning liquid over bread. Bake, covered, 1 hour. Uncover; bake 15 minutes longer, or until golden. Cool on wire rack 30 minutes. Prepare sauce, if using. Serve pudding warm, or refrigerate to serve cold later.

EACH SERVING: ABOUT 240 CALORIES, 9g PROTEIN, 28g CARBOHYDRATE, 10g TOTAL FAT (5g SATURATED), 128mg CHOLESTEROL, 285mg SODIUM

# BREAD-AND-BUTTER PUDDING

*Prep: 15 minutes, plus standing and cooling    Bake: 55–60 minutes*
*Makes 8 servings*

| | |
|---|---|
| 60g butter or margarine, softened | 70g sugar |
| 12 slices firm white bread | 1½ tsp vanilla essence |
| ¾ tsp ground cinnamon | ¼ tsp salt |
| 675ml milk | 4 medium eggs |

◆ Preheat oven to 170°C (325°F, Gas 3). Grease 20cm square glass ovenproof serving dish. Spread butter on bread slices. Arrange 4 slices of bread in dish in one layer, overlapping slightly; sprinkle with ¼ teaspoon cinnamon. Repeat, making 2 more layers.

◆ Using wire whisk or fork, mix remaining ingredients in medium bowl until well blended. Pour mixture over bread slices; let stand 10 minutes. Bake 55–60 minutes, until knife inserted in centre of pudding comes out clean. Cool on wire rack 30 minutes. Serve warm, or refrigerate to serve cold later.

Each serving: About 270 calories, 9g protein, 30g carbohydrate, 13g total fat (5g saturated), 135mg cholesterol, 385mg sodium

# LIGHT CHERRY BREAD PUDDING

*Prep: 20 minutes, plus standing and cooling    Bake: 1½ hours*
*Makes 12 servings*

| | |
|---|---|
| 125g dried cherries | 2 tsp ground cinnamon |
| 350g Italian bread | 4 medium egg whites |
| 1.3 litres semi-skimmed milk | 3 medium eggs |
| 150g light brown sugar | Icing sugar for decoration |
| 1 tbsp vanilla essence | |

◆ Bring dried cherries and *175ml water* to the boil in 2-litre saucepan over high heat. Reduce heat to low; cover and simmer 10 minutes, or until cherries are tender.

◆ Meanwhile, grease shallow 3-litre ovenproof serving dish. Cut bread into 2–3cm-thick slices. Using wire whisk or fork, mix milk and next 5 ingredients in large bowl until blended. Drain cherries, adding any liquid to egg mixture; set cherries aside. Add bread slices to egg mixture; let stand 10 minutes, carefully turning slices occasionally for even soaking.

◆ Preheat oven to 180°C (350°F, Gas 4). Arrange enough bread slices in dish in one layer, pushing slices together, to cover base; sprinkle all but 40g cherries over bread. Arrange remaining bread, overlapping slices to fit, on top. Pour any egg mixture remaining in bowl over bread.

◆ Bake bread pudding 1½ hours, or until knife inserted in centre comes out clean, covering loosely with foil during last 10–15 minutes of baking if top browns too quickly.

◆ Sprinkle pudding with remaining cherries. Dust with icing sugar. Cool on wire rack 30 minutes. Serve warm, or refrigerate to serve cold later.

Each serving: About 240 calories, 10g protein, 42g carbohydrate, 4g total fat (1g saturated), 58mg cholesterol, 270mg sodium

# APPLE BREAD PUDDING

*Prep: 40 minutes, plus standing and cooling*
*Bake: 1¼–1½ hours    Makes 12 servings*

| | |
|---|---|
| 225g unsliced rich egg bread, such as challah, cut into 2–3cm cubes | 1 tsp ground cinnamon |
| | 240g plus 1 tbsp caster sugar |
| 45g butter or margarine | 2 tbsp cornflour |
| 1.3kg Golden Delicious apples, peeled, cored, and sliced | 125ml plus 1 litre milk |
| | 5 medium eggs |
| | 1½ tsp vanilla essence |

◆ Preheat oven to 180°C (350°F, Gas 4). Spread bread cubes in baking tray; bake 15–20 minutes until lightly toasted. Meanwhile, melt butter in 30cm frying pan over medium-high heat. Stir in apples and ½ teaspoon cinnamon; cover and cook 10 minutes. Uncover; stir in 100g sugar. Cook, stirring often, 5–10 minutes, until apples are lightly caramelized. Mix cornflour and 125ml milk in cup until smooth; stir into apples. Reduce heat to low and cook, stirring constantly, 1 minute.

◆ Place half of bread in 33 by 20cm glass baking dish. Spoon apple mixture over bread; top with remaining bread. Using wire whisk or fork, mix eggs, vanilla essence, 140g sugar and remaining 1 litre milk in large bowl until well blended; pour over bread. Let stand 10 minutes, pressing bread into liquid. Combine remaining 1 tablespoon sugar with remaining ½ teaspoon cinnamon in cup; sprinkle over bread.

◆ Place dish in larger roasting tin. Carefully pour *boiling water* into roasting tin to come halfway up sides of dish. Bake 1¼–1½ hours until knife inserted in centre comes out clean. Cool on wire rack 30 minutes. Serve warm.

Each serving: 325 calories, 8g protein, 53g carbohydrate, 10g total fat (5g saturated), 120mg cholesterol, 205mg sodium

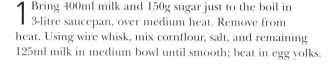

# STOVE-TOP CUSTARDS

These easy stirred custards can be served as simple puddings or used to form the basis for festive desserts like our Raspberry-Pear Trifle, laced with almond liqueur. There are also delicate brown-sugar custards, left alone to cook gently on the stove top, plus a foolproof method for classic custard sauce. The secret of making perfect custard is slow cooking over gentle heat: do not boil or the custard will curdle.

## RASPBERRY-PEAR TRIFLE

*Prep:* 1 hour, plus chilling   *Cook:* 10 minutes
*Makes* 16 servings

500ml milk
150g plus 3 tbsp caster sugar
30g cornflour
⅛ tsp salt
6 medium egg yolks
60ml almond-flavoured liqueur (amaretto)
1.3kg canned pear halves in syrup

300g fresh or frozen (thawed) raspberries
225ml whipping cream
300–350g trifle sponges, cut into 2–3cm cubes
8 pairs amaretti biscuits, coarsely crushed
Fresh raspberries for decoration

**1** Bring 400ml milk and 150g sugar just to the boil in 3-litre saucepan, over medium heat. Remove from heat. Using wire whisk, mix cornflour, salt, and remaining 125ml milk in medium bowl until smooth; beat in egg yolks.

**2** Stir small amount of hot milk mixture into yolk mixture; gradually stir yolk mixture back into milk mixture in saucepan. Cook over medium heat, stirring constantly, until mixture thickens and boils.

**3** Remove custard from heat; stir in liqueur. Pour custard into clean bowl. Press cling film onto surface of hot custard to keep skin from forming as custard cools. Refrigerate at least 3 hours until chilled.

**4** Drain pear halves, reserving 75ml syrup. Using an electric mixer on low speed, blend raspberries and reserved syrup from pears in large bowl. Using mixer at medium speed, beat cream in small bowl, gradually adding remaining 3 tablespoons sugar, until stiff peaks form. Reserve 225ml whipped cream for decoration.

**5** Gently fold remaining whipped cream into chilled custard. Place half of sponge cubes in 4-litre glass trifle or serving bowl and top with half of raspberry mixture.

**6** Arrange half of pear halves over raspberry mixture. Reserve two tablespoons amaretti biscuit crumbs for decoration; sprinkle half of remaining biscuit crumbs over pear layer in bowl.

**7** Spread half of custard over crumb layer. Repeat layering. Decorate trifle with reserved whipped cream, fresh raspberries and reserved biscuit crumbs. Cover and refrigerate at least 2 hours or up to 24 hours to blend flavours.

EACH SERVING: ABOUT 370 CALORIES, 6g PROTEIN, 53g CARBOHYDRATE, 12g TOTAL FAT (5g SATURATED), 105mg CHOLESTEROL, 105mg SODIUM

## CHOCOLATE PUDDING

*Prep: 10 minutes, plus chilling    Cook: 20 minutes*
*Makes 8 servings*

150g sugar
40g cornflour
½ tsp salt
845ml milk
5 medium egg yolks

2 tsp vanilla essence
90g plain chocolate, melted
30g butter or margarine
Whipped cream (optional)

◆ Mix sugar, cornflour and salt together in 3-litre saucepan until blended; gradually stir in milk. Cook over medium heat until mixture thickens and boils, stirring constantly; boil 1 minute, stirring. Using wire whisk or fork, beat egg yolks lightly in small bowl. Beat small amount of hot milk mixture into yolk mixture.

◆ Gradually pour yolk mixture back into milk mixture in pan, stirring rapidly to prevent lumps forming. Cook over low heat, stirring constantly, about 2 minutes, until very thick (mixture should be about 67°C).

◆ Remove from heat; stir in vanilla essence, melted chocolate and butter. Pour pudding into shallow bowl; press cling film onto surface to prevent skin forming as pudding cools. Refrigerate at least 4 hours until chilled and set. Serve with whipped cream, if you like.

**Each serving: About 280 calories, 6g protein, 32g carbohydrate, 15g total fat (6g saturated), 157mg cholesterol, 225mg sodium**

### THE PERFECT CUSTARD SAUCE

This classic sauce, also known as 'crème anglaise', goes beautifully with pies, tarts, plain cakes or fruit: bring 300ml milk to the boil in 2-litre saucepan. Meanwhile, whisk 4 medium egg yolks with 50g caster sugar in medium bowl until smooth. Gradually whisk hot milk into egg-yolk mixture. Return mixture to saucepan; cook over medium heat, stirring constantly (do not boil), just until mixture thickens slightly and coats back of wooden spoon well. (A finger run across the custard-coated spoon should leave a track.)

Remove from heat; strain mixture into clean bowl. Stir in 1 teaspoon vanilla essence, 1 tablespoon liqueur or brandy or ½ teaspoon grated lemon rind. Refrigerate if not serving right away. Makes 350ml.

Each 100ml: About 160 calories, 5g protein, 17g carbohydrate, 8g total fat (3g saturated), 223mg cholesterol, 45mg sodium

## BROWN-SUGAR CUSTARDS

*Prep: 10 minutes, plus chilling    Cook: 1 hour*
*Makes 6 servings*

4 medium eggs
100g dark brown sugar
2 tsp vanilla essence

Pinch salt
675ml milk

◆ Using wire whisk, mix eggs with sugar, vanilla essence and salt in large bowl until sugar is dissolved. Whisk in milk.

◆ Fold a tea towel in half to line base of 30cm frying pan; set six 175ml ramekins or small ovenproof dishes in frying pan. Carefully pour milk mixture into ramekins; pour *cold water* into pan to come halfway up sides of ramekins.

◆ Bring water to the boil over medium heat (it will take about 45 minutes). Cover pan and remove from heat; let stand 15 minutes. Remove custard cups from pan and refrigerate at least 2 hours, until chilled, or overnight.

**Each serving: About 200 calories, 8g protein, 24g carbohydrate, 7g total fat (4g saturated), 159mg cholesterol, 145mg sodium**

## LEMON PUDDING

*Prep: 10 minutes, plus chilling    Cook: 15 minutes*
*Makes 6 servings*

140g caster sugar
30g cornflour
1 tsp grated lemon rind
Pinch salt

600ml milk
2 medium egg yolks
75ml fresh lemon juice
Assorted berries (optional)

◆ Using wire whisk, stir sugar, cornstarch, lemon peel and salt in 2-litre saucepan until blended. Stir in a little milk until smooth; stir in remaining milk.

◆ Cook over medium-high heat, whisking constantly, until mixture thickens and boils. Boil 1 minute, whisking. Remove from heat.

◆ Whisk egg yolks and lemon juice together in small bowl. Gradually whisk half of hot milk mixture into yolks. Pour yolk mixture back into milk mixture in saucepan, stirring rapidly to prevent lumps forming. Cook over low heat, stirring constantly, about 2 minutes until very thick (mixture should be about 67°C).

◆ Spoon pudding into shallow bowl. Press cling film onto surface of pudding to prevent skin forming as pudding cools. Refrigerate at least 2 hours until chilled and set. Serve with assorted berries, if you like.

**Each serving: About 190 calories, 4g protein, 33g carbohydrate, 5g total fat (3g saturated), 85mg cholesterol, 90mg sodium**

# GELATINE-BASED DESSERTS

Gelatine works magic, turning simple cream or fruit mixtures into smooth mousses or showpiece moulded desserts. We've included a delicately flavoured cooked-cream dessert from Italy, two very different mousses and an elegant Raspberry Charlotte. The golden rules: always dissolve the gelatine completely during heating, and never allow a gelatine mixture to boil.

## PANNA COTTA WITH RASPBERRY SAUCE

❖❖❖❖❖❖❖❖❖❖❖❖

*Prep:* 20 minutes, *plus chilling*
*Cook:* 15 minutes
*Makes:* 8 servings

1 sachet (11g) powdered
 gelatine
225ml milk
½ vanilla pod or 1½ tsp vanilla
 essence
400ml whipping cream
50g sugar
1 strip (8 by 3cm) lemon rind
1 cinnamon stick (7–8cm)
300g fresh or frozen (thawed)
 raspberries
2 tbsp redcurrant jelly
1 tsp cornflour
Raspberries and mint sprigs
 for decoration

**1** Sprinkle gelatine over milk in glass measuring jug; let stand 5 minutes. Meanwhile, using knife, cut vanilla pod lengthways in half. Scrape out and reserve seeds.

**2** Bring vanilla pod halves and seeds, cream and next 3 ingredients to the boil in 1-litre saucepan over high heat, stirring occasionally. (If using vanilla essence, stir in after removing lemon rind.) Reduce heat to low; simmer, stirring occasionally, 5 minutes.

**3** Stir milk mixture into saucepan; heat 2–3 minutes, stirring constantly, until gelatine is completely dissolved (do not boil). Remove lemon rind, cinnamon stick and vanilla pod. Pour mixture into medium bowl set in larger bowl of *ice water*.

**4** Stir mixture often, 10–12 minutes, just until beginning to mound when dropped from spatula. Immediately remove from ice bath.

**5** Pour into eight 125ml ramekins or ovenproof dishes; place on baking tray for easier handling. Refrigerate at least 4 hours, or overnight.

**6** Prepare sauce: press raspberries through sieve into 2-litre saucepan. Stir in jelly and cornflour. Bring to the boil over medium heat, stirring; boil 1 minute. Transfer to bowl; cover and refrigerate.

**7** To unmould, run warm knife around edge of each ramekin, then tap side of ramekin sharply to break seal; invert onto a dessert plate. Spoon some sauce around each panna cotta and decorate.

EACH SERVING: ABOUT 260 CALORIES, 3g PROTEIN, 18g CARBOHYDRATE, 21g TOTAL FAT (13g SATURATED), 75mg CHOLESTEROL, 35mg SODIUM

## CAPPUCCINO MOUSSE

*Prep: 30 minutes, plus chilling    Cook: 2–3 minutes*
*Makes 8 servings*

| | |
|---|---|
| 1 sachet (11g) plus 1 tsp powdered gelatine | 100g plus 1 tsp sugar |
| 200ml milk | 2 tbsp coffee-flavoured liqueur |
| 225ml freshly brewed espresso coffee, or 2 tbsp instant espresso-coffee powder dissolved in 225ml boiling water | 300ml whipping cream |
| | Pinch ground cinnamon |
| | Chocolate-covered coffee beans for decoration |

◆ Sprinkle gelatine over 75ml milk in 1-litre saucepan; let stand 5 minutes. Stir in espresso coffee. Heat over low heat, stirring constantly, 2–3 minutes, until gelatine is completely dissolved (do not boil). Remove from heat and stir in 100g sugar until dissolved. Stir in liqueur and remaining 125ml milk. Transfer mixture to large bowl.

◆ Set bowl in larger bowl of *ice water*. Stir often, just until mixture mounds slightly when dropped from spoon. Immediately remove from ice bath. Meanwhile, using electric mixer on medium speed, beat 225ml cream to soft peaks in medium bowl. Fold one-third of cream into espresso mixture until incorporated. Fold in remaining whipped cream. Spoon into 8 coffee cups or 175ml ramekins. Cover and refrigerate at least 4 hours until well chilled, or overnight.

◆ To serve, using mixer, beat remaining 75ml cream with cinnamon and remaining 1 teaspoon sugar in medium bowl to stiff peaks; spoon a dollop onto each mousse and decorate with coffee beans.

Each serving: 220 calories, 3g protein, 17g carbohydrate, 16g total fat (10g saturated), 58mg cholesterol, 30mg sodium

## MANGO MOUSSE

*Prep: 20 minutes, plus chilling    Cook: 3 minutes*
*Makes 8 servings*

| | |
|---|---|
| 1 sachet (11g) powdered gelatine | 425ml canned coconut milk |
| 2 large ripe mangoes | 125ml fresh lime juice |

◆ Peel mangoes and cut into bite-sized chunks. Sprinkle gelatine over *60ml cold water* in 1-litre saucepan; let stand 5 minutes. Meanwhile, blend mango chunks, coconut milk and lime juice in blender on medium speed until smooth.

◆ Heat gelatine mixture over low heat, stirring constantly, 2–3 minutes, until gelatine is completely dissolved (do not boil). Add to mango mixture in blender and blend until combined. Pour mixture into eight 125ml ramekins or ovenproof dishes. Cover and refrigerate mousse 4 hours until well chilled, or overnight.

Each serving: 225 calories, 3g protein, 16g carbohydrate, 19g total fat (16g saturated), 0mg cholesterol, 5mg sodium

## RASPBERRY CHARLOTTE

*Prep: 25 minutes, plus chilling    Cook: 4 minutes*
*Makes 8 servings*

| | |
|---|---|
| 1 tbsp plus 50g caster sugar | 3 tbsp fresh lemon juice |
| 2 tbsp orange-flavoured liqueur | 600g fresh or frozen (thawed) raspberries |
| 160g sponge fingers | 225ml whipping cream |
| 1 sachet (11g) powdered gelatine | Fresh raspberries for decoration |

◆ Line 23 by 12cm loaf tin with cling film. Bring 1 tablespoon sugar and *2 tablespoons water* to the boil in 1-litre saucepan, stirring to dissolve sugar. Remove from heat; stir in orange flavoured liqueur.

◆ Lightly brush flat sides of sponge fingers with liqueur mixture. Line long sides and base of loaf tin with sponge fingers, flat sides in (they will not completely cover base).

◆ In clean 1-litre saucepan, sprinkle gelatine over *60ml cold water*; let stand 5 minutes. Heat over low heat, stirring constantly, 2–3 minutes, until gelatine is completely dissolved (do not boil). Remove from heat; stir in lemon juice.

◆ Blend raspberries in blender on medium speed until smooth. Press raspberries through sieve into large bowl; stir in gelatine mixture and remaining 50g sugar. Set bowl in larger bowl of *ice water*. Stir often, just until mixture mounds slightly when dropped from spoon; immediately remove from ice bath.

◆ Using an electric mixer on medium speed, beat cream to soft peaks in small bowl. Fold one-third of cream into raspberry mixture until completely incorporated; gently fold in remaining cream. Spoon into sponge finger-lined tin. Cover and refrigerate charlotte 4 hours until well chilled, or overnight.

◆ To serve, trim sponge fingers level with raspberry filling; discard trimmings. Unmould charlotte onto serving plate and remove cling film. Decorate with fresh raspberries.

Each serving: About 265 calories, 4g protein, 36g carbohydrate, 12g total fat (7g saturated), 41mg cholesterol, 190mg sodium

# MERINGUES

A mixture of stiffly beaten egg whites and sugar, meringue can be baked into many shapes. To ensure that the sugar dissolves completely – resulting in a smooth meringue – add the sugar gradually and continue beating the mixture until it stands straight in peaks when the beaters are lifted. Avoid making meringue on a humid day, because it will absorb moisture from the air and turn soggy. If not using the meringue right away, it can be stored for up to a week in an air-tight container at room temperature.

## HAZELNUT DACQUOISE

*Prep: 1½ hours, plus cooling and chilling*
*Bake: 45 minutes, plus drying in oven*    ***Makes** 12 servings*

125g hazelnuts, toasted and skinned (see page 522)
2 tbsp cornflour
180g plus 4 tbsp icing sugar
6 medium egg whites
½ tsp cream of tartar
675ml whipping cream

1 tsp vanilla essence
90g plain chocolate, melted and slightly warm
1 tbsp instant espresso-coffee powder
Chocolate Curls for decoration (see page 551)

1 Preheat oven to 150°C (300°F, Gas 2). Line 2 large baking sheets with foil. Using a cocktail stick, with 20cm round cake tin as a guide, outline 2 circles on foil on each sheet. Blend hazelnuts, cornflour and 90g icing sugar in food processor with knife blade attached, until nuts are ground.

2 Using an electric mixer on high speed, beat egg whites and cream of tartar in large bowl to soft peaks. Sprinkle 90g icing sugar, 2 tablespoons at a time, into egg whites, beating well after each addition, until sugar dissolves and whites stand in stiff, glossy peaks.

3 Fold hazelnut mixture into egg whites using rubber spatula. Spread one quarter of meringue mixture inside each circle on baking sheets, with palette knife. Bake meringues 45 minutes. Turn oven off; leave meringues in oven 1 hour to dry.

4 Transfer meringues with foil to wire racks; cool completely. Carefully loosen and remove meringues from foil using palette knife.

5 Prepare chocolate cream: using electric mixer on medium speed, beat 350ml whipping cream, 1 tablespoon icing sugar, and ½ teaspoon vanilla essence in small bowl just to soft peaks. With rubber spatula, fold half of whipped cream into slightly warm melted chocolate just until combined. Fold in remaining whipped cream. Reserve 75ml chocolate cream.

6 Prepare coffee cream: dissolve espresso powder in 30ml whipping cream in cup. Beat remaining 295ml whipping cream and remaining 3 tablespoons icing sugar in small bowl until soft peaks form. Add espresso mixture; beat until stiff peaks form.

7 Place 1 meringue layer on cake stand or plate; spread with half of chocolate cream. Top with another meringue layer and half of coffee cream. Repeat layering, ending with coffee cream. Spoon reserved 75ml chocolate cream on top. Refrigerate dacquoise at least 5 hours, or overnight, for easier cutting. Prepare Chocolate Curls. Just before serving, arrange curls on top of dacquoise.

**EACH SERVING: ABOUT 365 CALORIES, 5g PROTEIN, 24g CARBOHYDRATE, 30g TOTAL FAT (16g SATURATED), 82mg CHOLESTEROL, 50mg SODIUM**

## STRAWBERRY-LEMON MERINGUE NESTS

*Prep: 35 minutes, plus chilling and cooling*
*Bake: 2½ hours, plus drying in oven*
*Makes 6 servings*

| | |
|---|---|
| 3 large lemons | ¼ tsp cream of tartar |
| 1 tbsp cornflour | 125ml whipping cream |
| 90g butter | 350g strawberries, hulled and |
| 250g caster sugar | each cut into quarters |
| 4 medium eggs, separated | 1 tbsp strawberry jam |

◈ Prepare lemon curd: grate 1 tablespoon rind and squeeze 125ml juice from lemons. Using wire whisk, mix cornstarch, lemon peel and lemon juice in 2-litre saucepan until smooth. Add butter and 150g sugar; bring to the boil over medium heat. Boil 1 minute, stirring constantly.

◈ Beat egg yolks lightly in small bowl. Beat small amount of hot lemon mixture into yolks; pour egg mixture back into lemon mixture in pan, beating rapidly. Reduce heat to low; cook, stirring constantly, 5 minutes, or until thick (do not boil). Pour into medium bowl; cover surface with cling film. Refrigerate 3 hours, until chilled, or up to 3 days.

◈ Meanwhile, prepare meringue nests: preheat oven to 110°C (225°F, Gas ¼). Line large baking sheet with foil. Using electric mixer on high speed, beat egg whites and cream of tartar in small bowl until soft peaks form. Sprinkle in remaining 100g sugar, 2 tablespoons at a time, beating well after each addition, until sugar dissolves and whites stand in stiff, glossy peaks.

### PIPING MERINGUE STARS

For a special dessert, pipe any meringue mixture into stars: preheat oven to 110°C (225°F, Gas ¼). Line large baking sheet with foil. With a cocktail stick, using 8cm star-shape biscuit cutter as a guide, trace star outlines on foil. Spoon two-thirds of meringue into piping bag fitted with coupler and large star nozzle. Pipe meringue around outline of traced stars on foil; fill centres with meringue. Change nozzle on piping bag to medium star tip; spoon remaining meringue into piping bag.

Pipe slightly smaller star on top of each existing star. Using spoon, form small indentation in centre of each. Bake 2½ hours. Transfer meringues with foil to wire rack; cool completely. Top with lemon curd or whipped cream and fruit.

◈ Spoon meringue into 6 mounds on baking sheet. Using back of spoon, form a well in centre of each mound to create a nest. Bake 2½ hours. Turn oven off; leave nests in oven 1 hour to dry completely.

◈ Transfer nests with foil to wire rack; cool completely. Carefully loosen nests and remove from foil using palette knife. Store in airtight container at room temperature until ready to use (up to 1 week).

◈ Just before serving, using electric mixer on medium speed, beat cream to stiff peaks in small bowl. Gently fold into lemon curd. Toss strawberries with jam in medium bowl. Spoon lemon-curd mixture into nests; top with strawberry mixture.

**Each serving: About 415 calories, 5g protein, 52g carbohydrate, 22g total fat (13g saturated), 200mg cholesterol, 165mg sodium**

## BERRIES AND CREAM MERINGUES

*Prep: 25 minutes, plus cooling    Bake: 45 minutes, plus drying in oven*
*Makes 8 servings*

| | |
|---|---|
| 4 medium egg whites | 2 tbsp Marsala (optional) |
| ¼ tsp cream of tartar | 400g blueberries |
| 150g plus 1 tbsp caster sugar | 160g raspberries |
| 350ml whipping cream | 145g blackberries |
| ¼ tsp vanilla essence | Icing sugar |

◈ Preheat oven to 110°C (225°F, Gas ¼). Line 2 large baking sheets with foil. Using electric mixer on high speed, beat egg whites and cream of tartar, in small bowl, until soft peaks form. Sprinkle in 150g caster sugar, 2 tablespoons at a time, beating well after each addition until sugar completely dissolves and whites stand in stiff, glossy peaks.

◈ Using small palette knife, spread meringue on foil-lined baking sheets into eight 13cm rounds, about 1cm apart. Bake 45 minutes. Turn oven off; leave meringues in oven 1 hour longer to dry completely.

◈ Transfer meringues with foil to wire racks; cool completely. Carefully loosen and remove meringues from foil using small palette knife. Store in airtight container at room temperature until ready to use (up to 1 week).

◈ Just before serving, using electric mixer on medium speed, beat whipping cream, vanilla essence and remaining 1 tablespoon caster sugar in small bowl until soft peaks form. Beat in Marsala, if using. Spread whipped cream on meringues. Top each meringue with a mixture of berries; sprinkle berries with icing sugar.

**Each serving: About 280 calories, 3g protein, 32g carbohydrate, 17g total fat (10g saturated), 61mg cholesterol, 45mg sodium**

# ICE CREAM DESSERTS

Create impressive but easy desserts with shop-bought ice cream and sorbets. Use to fill a cake roll or top a biscuit-crumb crust, put it in the freezer – and relax.

## CINNAMON ICE CREAM ROLL

❖❖❖❖❖❖❖❖❖❖❖

*Prep: 40 minutes, plus cooling, freezing and standing*
*Bake: 12–15 minutes*
*Makes 16 servings*

80g plain flour
1 tsp baking powder
½ tsp salt
40g cocoa powder plus extra for dusting
½ tsp plus 2 tbsp ground cinnamon
4 medium eggs, separated
150g plus 2 tbsp caster sugar
¾ tsp vanilla essence
1 litre vanilla ice cream
225g whipping cream
Quick Chocolate Curls (see page 551) for decoration

**1** Preheat oven to 190°C (375°F, Gas 5). Grease 39 by 27cm Swiss roll tin; line with parchment paper. Sift flour, baking powder, salt, cocoa and ½ teaspoon cinnamon through medium-mesh sieve into small bowl. Using electric mixer on high speed, beat egg whites in another small bowl until soft peaks form. Gradually sprinkle in 50g caster sugar, beating until sugar completely dissolves and whites stand in stiff peaks.

**2** Using same beaters and with mixer on high speed, beat egg yolks, vanilla essence and 100g sugar in large bowl until very thick and lemon coloured.

**3** Using rubber spatula or wire whisk, fold in flour mixture and egg whites (this will take patience). Spread evenly in tin. Bake 12–15 minutes, until top springs back when lightly touched.

**4** Sprinkle clean tea towel with cocoa. When cake is done, immediately invert onto towel. Remove parchment paper. If you like, cut off crisp edges. From a narrow end, roll up cake with towel, Swiss roll fashion. Cool cake completely, seam-side down, on wire rack, about 1 hour.

**5** Place ice cream in large bowl; let stand at room temperature to soften slightly. Stir in remaining 2 tablespoons cinnamon. Unroll cooled cake; spread with ice cream. From same end, roll up cake without towel. Place cake, seam-side down, on freezer-proof long platter. Freeze at least 4 hours, until firm. Using mixer on medium speed, beat cream and remaining 2 tablespoons sugar in small bowl until stiff peaks form.

**6** Spoon whipped cream over top of cake. (If not serving right away, freeze cake, uncovered, until whipped cream hardens. Wrap; return to freezer. To serve, let cake stand at room temperature 15 minutes for easier slicing.) Decorate with Quick Chocolate Curls.

EACH SERVING: ABOUT 200 CALORIES, 4g PROTEIN, 25g CARBOHYDRATE, 11g TOTAL FAT (6g SATURATED), 88mg CHOLESTEROL, 145mg SODIUM

## SORBET-AND-CREAM CAKE

*Prep: 30 minutes, plus cooling, freezing and standing    Bake: 10 minutes*
*Makes 20 servings*

30 vanilla wafers
60g butter or margarine
½ tsp grated lime rind
1 litre vanilla ice cream
500ml raspberry or
   strawberry sorbet

500ml mango sorbet
500ml lemon sorbet
1 ripe mango, peeled and
   thinly sliced, for decoration
Fresh raspberries or
   strawberries for decoration

◆ Preheat oven to 190°C (375°F, Gas 5). Blend vanilla wafers in food processor with knife blade attached or in blender on medium speed, until fine crumbs form.

◆ Melt butter in small saucepan over low heat; stir in lime rind. In 22 by 8cm springform tin, with fork, stir wafer crumbs and butter mixture until crumbs are moistened. Using your hand, press mixture firmly onto base of tin; bake 10 minutes. Cool completely in tin on wire rack.

◆ While crumb base is cooling, place 500ml vanilla ice cream and all 3 fruit sorbets in refrigerator 30 minutes to soften slightly.

◆ Spoon alternating scoops of softened vanilla ice cream and sorbets over crust in 2 layers; press mixture down to eliminate air pockets. Place tin in freezer about 30 minutes to harden mixture slightly.

◆ Meanwhile, place remaining vanilla ice cream in refrigerator to soften slightly.

◆ Using palette knife, evenly spread remaining vanilla ice cream over frozen layer. Cover and freeze at least 4 hours, until firm.

◆ To unmould, place warm dampened tea towels around side of tin for about 20 seconds to soften ice cream slightly. Remove side of tin and place cake on platter. (If you like, remove tin base also.) Cover cake and keep frozen if not serving right away.

◆ Let stand at room temperature about 15 minutes for easier slicing. Before serving, garnish top of cake with mango slices and raspberries.

**Each serving: About 160 calories, 1g protein, 23g carbohydrate, 8g total fat (2g saturated), 21mg cholesterol, 85mg sodium**

## VANILLA-PECAN ICE CREAM TORTE

*Prep: 20 minutes, plus cooling, freezing and standing    Bake: 8 minutes*
*Makes 16 servings*

150g pecan halves, toasted
   and cooled
150g gingernut biscuits
2 tbsp sugar
45g butter or margarine,
   melted

1.5 litres vanilla ice cream
2 tbsp plus 1 tsp ground
   mixed spice

◆ Preheat oven to 190°C (375°F, Gas 5). Reserve 16 pecan halves for decoration. Process remaining pecan halves with gingernut biscuits and sugar in food processor with knife blade attached until mixture is finely ground.

◆ Using fork, stir biscuit mixture and melted butter together in 23 by 8cm springform tin until crumbs are moistened. Using your hand, press mixture firmly onto base of tin; bake 8 minutes. Cool completely in tin on wire rack.

◆ While crumb base is cooling, let ice cream stand at room temperature 20 minutes to soften slightly. Mix ice cream and ground mixed spice in large bowl until blended; spread over base. Place reserved pecan halves around top edge of torte, cover and freeze at least overnight, or up to 1 week.

◆ To serve, let frozen torte stand at room temperature about 15 minutes for easier slicing. Remove side of tin.

**Each serving: About 210 calories, 3g protein, 22g carbohydrate, 13g total fat (4g saturated), 28mg cholesterol, 125mg sodium**

### ICE CREAM SPECIALS

For almost-instant desserts, layer ice cream, fruit and sauce; top with crumbled biscuits or nuts

• Strawberry and vanilla ice cream layered with sliced strawberries, topped with crumbled macaroon biscuits

• Peach ice cream with fresh raspberries, Blueberry Sauce (see page 482), and toasted flaked almonds

• Cinnamon ice cream (mix in 1 tablespoon ground cinnamon per 500ml softened vanilla ice cream) with warmed maple syrup and pecans

# HOME-MADE ICE CREAM

There's nothing difficult about making delicious ice cream yourself, whether it's with an old-fashioned hand crank ice cream maker or with an electric model. Our classic, custard-based Vanilla Ice Cream is irresistible; so are the easy variations on page 482. Alternatively, make our super-simple No-Cook Vanilla Ice Cream – just stir. To add crunch, try stirring in 225g coarsely chopped nut brittle immediately *after* churning the ice cream.

## VANILLA ICE CREAM

❖❖❖❖❖❖❖❖❖❖❖❖❖❖❖❖❖❖❖❖❖❖❖❖❖❖❖❖

*Prep: 5 minutes, plus chilling and freezing   Cook: 15–20 minutes*
*Makes about 1.2 litres*

| | |
|---|---|
| **1 vanilla pod or 1 tbsp vanilla essence** | **⅛ tsp salt** |
| **150g sugar** | **225ml whipping cream** |
| **675ml single cream** | **Butterscotch Sauce (optional, see page 482)** |
| **4 medium egg yolks** | |

**1** Chop vanilla pod into 5mm pieces. Process vanilla pod and sugar in blender until mixture is very finely ground; set aside. (If using vanilla essence, stir in with whipping cream in Step 4.) Prepare custard: bring single cream to the boil in 3-litre saucepan. Meanwhile, whisk egg yolks, salt and sugar mixture in medium bowl until smooth.

**2** Gradually whisk hot single cream into egg-yolk mixture.

**3** Return mixture to pan and cook over medium heat, stirring constantly, just until mixture coats back of wooden spoon (do not boil, or mixture will curdle). Remove from heat.

**4** Strain custard mixture through sieve into clean large bowl. Stir whipping cream into custard; refrigerate at least 2 hours, until chilled, or overnight.

**5** Churn and freeze in ice-cream maker using manufacturer's instructions. Prepare Butterscotch Sauce, if you like. Serve ice cream with warm sauce.

### NO-COOK VANILLA ICE CREAM

Stir 45ml single cream, 450ml whipping cream, 150g caster sugar, 1 tablespoon vanilla essence and ⅛ teaspoon salt in large bowl until sugar is completely dissolved. Pour mixture into ice-cream maker; churn and freeze following manufacturer's instructions. Makes about 1.4 litres.

Each 100ml: 215 calories, 2g protein, 14g carbohydrate, 17g total fat (10g saturated), 62mg cholesterol, 50mg sodium

EACH 100ml: ABOUT 215 CALORIES, 3g PROTEIN, 16g CARBOHYDRATE, 16g TOTAL FAT (9g SATURATED), 121mg CHOLESTEROL, 60mg SODIUM

## PEACH OR STRAWBERRY ICE CREAM

*Prep: 20 minutes, plus chilling and freezing*    *Cook: 15–20 minutes*
*Makes about 1.4 litres*

**Vanilla Ice Cream or No-Cook**
**Vanilla Ice Cream (see**
**page 481)**
**8 medium peaches, peeled**
**and sliced, or 700g**
**strawberries, hulled**

**100g caster sugar**
**2 tbsp fresh lemon juice**

Prepare Vanilla Ice Cream as instructed in Steps 1 to 4 or prepare No-Cook Vanilla Ice Cream, but omit vanilla essence and use only 100g sugar. Mash peaches or strawberries with sugar and lemon juice in medium bowl; cover and refrigerate 30 minutes. Before churning, stir fruit mixture into ice cream mixture; churn and freeze in ice cream maker following manufacturer's instructions.

**Each 100ml: About 235 calories, 3g protein, 27g carbohydrate,**
**14g total fat (8g saturated), 103mg cholesterol, 50mg sodium**

## CHOCOLATE ICE CREAM

*Prep: 10 minutes, plus chilling and freezing*    *Cook: 15–20 minutes*
*Makes about 1.4 litres*

**Vanilla Ice Cream or No-Cook**
**Vanilla Ice Cream (see**
**page 481)**

**150g plain chocolate**
**1 teaspoon vanilla essence**

◆ Prepare Vanilla Ice Cream as instructed in Steps 1 to 4 or prepare No-Cook Vanilla Ice Cream, but omit vanilla essence and reserve 60ml whipping cream.

◆ Melt chocolate with reserved 60ml whipping cream in top of double boiler or in heatproof bowl set over pan of simmering water; remove from heat. Stir in vanilla essence.

◆ Stir 225ml ice cream mixture into melted chocolate; stir chocolate mixture back into ice cream mixture. Churn and freeze in ice-cream maker following manufacturer's instructions.

**Each 100ml: About 240 calories,**
**3g protein, 18g carbohydrate,**
**18g total fat (10g saturated),**
**103mg cholesterol, 45mg sodium**

## ICE CREAM SAUCES

These no-fuss sauces are great over ice cream and can be used for our Ice Cream Specials (see page 480). Serve a selection with different ice cream flavours and let guests assemble their own dessert. These sauces are equally delicious with sponge cake, bread pudding, dessert crêpes or cream puffs.

Hot fudge sauce

Blueberry sauce

### Hot fudge sauce
Heat 225ml whipping cream, 150g caster sugar, 125g chopped plain chocolate and 2 tablespoons golden syrup in heavy 2-litre saucepan over medium heat until mixture boils, stirring occasionally. Boil 4–5 minutes longer, until slightly thickened, stirring constantly. Remove from heat; stir in 30g butter or margarine and 2 teaspoons vanilla essence. Serve warm. Or, cool completely, then refrigerate, covered (don't cover sauce until it's cold, or the water from condensation will make it grainy); re-heat before serving. Makes about 400ml.

**Each 100ml: About 575 calories, 4g protein, 56g carbohydrate,**
**42g total fat (22g saturated), 98mg cholesterol, 95mg sodium**

### Blueberry sauce
Stir 70g sugar, 2 teaspoons cornflour, and 60ml cold water together in 2-litre saucepan until smooth. Heat to boiling over medium heat, stirring. Add 300g fresh or frozen (thawed) blueberries and return to the boil, stirring. Reduce heat to low and cook 1 minute longer. Remove from heat and stir in 1 teaspoon fresh lemon juice. Serve warm. Makes about 400ml.

**Each 100ml: About 114 calories, 0g protein, 28g carbohydrate,**
**0g total fat, 0mg cholesterol, 10mg sodium**

### Butterscotch sauce
Bring 200g brown sugar, 125ml whipping cream, 110g light corn syrup or golden syrup, 30g butter or margarine, 1 teaspoon distilled white vinegar and ⅛ teaspoon salt to the boil in 3-litre saucepan over high heat, stirring occasionally. Reduce heat to low and cook 2 minutes. Remove from heat and stir in 1 teaspoon vanilla essence. Serve warm. Makes 300ml.

**Each 100ml: About 631 calories, 2g protein, 107g carbohydrate,**
**23g total fat (14g saturated), 59mg cholesterol, 265mg sodium**

# GRANITAS AND SORBETS

Fruity, refreshing and fat-free, granitas and sorbets are made from similar mixtures of puréed fruit and sugar syrup, but granitas have a coarser texture (*granita* is derived from the verb 'to granulate' in Italian). You don't even need an ice cream maker: just whirl up the sorbets in a food processor or, for the granitas, freeze in a metal pan (metal makes the mixture freeze faster). Any of the flavours here will make a deliciously light dessert, ideal for summer or as an ending to a rich meal. Serve a crisp biscuit on the side and your guests will feel truly spoilt.

**1** Prepare sugar syrup: dissolve sugar in *300ml water* in 1-litre saucepan over medium heat, stirring occasionally. Bring to the boil. Cook, stirring, 1 minute. Transfer to small bowl to cool. Purée peach wedges in blender on medium speed or in food processor with knife blade attached until smooth; pour into medium-mesh sieve set over medium bowl.

**2** Press peach purée through sieve with back of wooden spoon; you should have 675ml. Into purée, stir lemon juice and syrup. Pour into 22cm square baking tin. Cover with foil or cling film. Freeze 2 hours; stir with fork.

**3** Freeze at least 3 hours longer, until fully frozen, or overnight. To serve, let stand 20 minutes at room temperature; using fork or spoon, scrape surface to create pebbly texture. Serve with biscotti, if you like.

## PEACH GRANITA

*Prep: 20 minutes plus freezing and standing*
*Makes about 2 litres*

**200g caster sugar**
**800g peaches or nectarines, unpeeled, cut into wedges**

**2 tbsp fresh lemon juice**
**Almond-Anise Biscotti (optional, see page 518)**

### MORE FRUIT GRANITAS

**Raspberry or blackberry granita** Prepare granita as above but substitute 1kg raspberries or blackberries and 2 tablespoons fresh lime juice for peaches and lemon juice. Makes about 2 litres.

Each 100ml: About 44 calories, 0g protein, 11g carbohydrate, 0g total fat, 0mg cholesterol, 0mg sodium

Raspberry granita

**Watermelon granita** Prepare granita as above but substitute 2.5kg piece watermelon, seeded and cut into chunks, and 2 tablespoons fresh lime juice for peaches and lemon juice; when making the sugar syrup, use only 175ml water instead of 300ml. Makes about 2 litres.

Each 100ml: About 63 calories, 1g protein, 15g carbohydrate, 0g total fat, 0mg cholesterol, 0mg sodium

Watermelon granita

**EACH 100ml: ABOUT 55 CALORIES, 0g PROTEIN, 14g CARBOHYDRATE, 0g TOTAL FAT, 0mg CHOLESTEROL, 0mg SODIUM**

## LEMON-ROSEMARY SORBET

*Prep: 25 minutes, plus standing and freezing*
*Makes about 1 litre*

250g caster sugar
80g golden syrup
2 tbsp coarsely chopped fresh
   rosemary
300ml fresh lemon juice
   (squeezed from about
   7 large lemons)

2 tsp grated lemon peel
Rosemary sprigs and lemon
   slices for decoration

◆ Dissolve sugar and golden syrup in *900ml water* in 2-litre saucepan over medium heat. Bring to the boil and cook, stirring, 1 minute. Remove pan from heat; stir in chopped rosemary. Cover pan and let syrup stand 22 minutes.

◆ Pour mixture through sieve set over medium bowl; stir in lemon juice and rind. Pour lemon mixture into 22cm square metal baking tin; cover with foil or cling film. Freeze, stirring occasionally, about 3 hours until partially frozen.

◆ Blend lemon mixture in food processor with knife blade attached, until smooth but still frozen. Return mixture to baking tin; cover and freeze at least 3 hours, or until firm.

◆ Let sorbet stand at room temperature 10–15 minutes to soften slightly for easier scooping. Decorate and serve.

Each 100ml: About 130 calories, 0g protein, 34g carbohydrate, 0g total fat, 0mg cholesterol, 6mg sodium

## BLUEBERRY SORBET

*Prep: 10 minutes, plus freezing and standing*
*Makes about 800ml*

100g sugar
2 tablespoons fresh lemon
   juice

600g frozen unsweetened
   blueberries

◆ Prepare sugar syrup: bring sugar, lemon juice and *1 tablespoon water* to the boil in 1-litre saucepan. Cook, stirring, 1 minute, until sugar dissolves; remove from heat.

◆ Process frozen blueberries in food processor with knife blade attached, until fruit resembles finely shaved ice, stopping processor occasionally to scrape down side. (If fruit is not finely shaved, sorbet will not be smooth.)

◆ With processor running, slowly pour hot sugar syrup in a thin stream through feed tube and process until mixture is smooth but still frozen. Spoon into freezer-proof container and freeze until firm.

◆ To serve, let sorbet stand at room temperature 10–15 minutes to soften slightly for easier scooping.

Each 100ml: About 85 calories, 0g protein, 21g carbohydrate, 0g total fat, 0mg cholesterol, 0mg sodium

## MORE FRUIT SORBETS

**Peach sorbet** Prepare as for Blueberry Sorbet (below left) but use 50g caster sugar, 1 tablespoon fresh lemon juice and 1 tablespoon water for sugar syrup, adding ½ teaspoon almond essence to cooked syrup; instead of blueberries, use 600g frozen unsweetened peach slices. Makes about 700ml.

Each 100ml: About 64 calories, 0g protein, 17g carbohydrate, 0g total fat, 0mg cholesterol, 0mg sodium

**Cantaloupe sorbet** Prepare as for Blueberry Sorbet (below left) but use 100g caster sugar, 2 tablespoons fresh lemon juice and 1 tablespoon water for sugar syrup; instead of blueberries, use 1 small ripe cantaloupe (about 900g), seeded, cut into small chunks, spread on shallow baking tray and frozen overnight. Makes about 1 litre.

Each 100ml: About 66 calories, 1g protein, 18g carbohydrate, 0g total fat, 0mg cholesterol, 18mg sodium

**Strawberry sorbet** Prepare as for Blueberry Sorbet (below left) but use 70g caster sugar, 1 tablespoon fresh lemon juice and 1 tablespoon water for sugar syrup; instead of blueberries, use 600g frozen unsweetened strawberries. Makes about 550ml.

Each 100ml: About 83 calories,
0g protein,
22g carbohydrate,
0g total fat,
0mg cholesterol,
0mg sodium

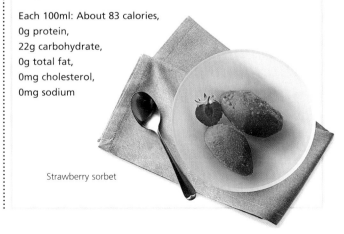

Strawberry sorbet

# PIES & TARTS

Simple or elegant, fruit-filled or fudgy, pies and tarts are welcome after practically any meal. A light, flaky crust is a pie's crowning glory and surprisingly easy to make, as long as you use the right ingredients and follow our foolproof mixing and rolling techniques.

## PERFECT PASTRY

• Start with cold ingredients (e.g. chilled butter or margarine, ice cold water). The kitchen should be cool too.
• Generally, handle the dough as little as possible, or you'll over-develop the gluten in the flour and make a tough pastry.
• For best results, use a mix of fat – butter or margarine for flavour and colour and white vegetable fat for flakiness.
• When cutting fat into the flour, work quickly so the fat remains firm and cold.
• Sprinkle in iced water just until the dough is moistened. Toss quickly and lightly with a fork; do not stir. (Use the least amount of water to avoid a tough crust.)
• Chilling dough for at least 30 minutes will make it easier to roll and also help prevent shrinkage. Wrap tightly so the edges don't dry out and crack when rolled.
• To prevent sticking, roll dough on a lightly floured surface; sprinkle surface with additional flour as necessary. Roll dough from the centre forwards and then back; rotate the dough a quarter-turn and repeat rolling and rotating to make an even circle.
• If pastry tears, just moisten the edges and press together. Or, brush a small piece of pastry with water; use as a patch.
• When fitting pastry into a pie plate, gently ease it onto the bottom with your fingertips or a small ball of dough, taking care to press out air pockets. Never stretch or pull the pastry to fit, or it may shrink during baking.

## WHICH PIE PLATE?

Crisp, flaky pastry crusts aren't dependent only on a good dough – the dish also makes a difference. For a crisp, well-browned crust, choose a glass pie plate, or a metal one with a dull finish (shiny tins are fine for crumb crusts). Use a regular pie plate (23cm across) or a deep-dish one (24cm across) as instructed so the filling won't overflow. For tarts, use a fluted pan with a removable base, which makes for easy removal of the tart.

## BLIND BAKING

Crusts with moist fillings are often partially or completely baked before they're filled for crisp results. This is called 'blind baking'. Line the pastry with foil and weight it with pie weights, dry beans or uncooked rice to prevent puffing or slipping during baking. Cool completely before filling.

For tarts and pies, remove the foil and weights after the pastry is set, then return to the oven to brown.

For tartlets, weight the crust with another tart pan before baking. Or, prevent puffing by piercing crust with a fork.

## BETTER BAKING

• For non-soggy double-crust pies, cut slits in the top crust before baking so steam can escape during cooking.
• For easy handling – and to catch drips – bake the pie on a sheet of foil with crimped edges, or use a baking sheet.
• Bake in the lower third of the oven so the bottom crust becomes crisp and the top doesn't overbrown (if pie still browns too quickly, just cover it loosely with foil).
• To check a custard pie for doneness, insert a knife 2–3cm from the centre; it should come out clean. A starch-thickened fruit pie is ready when it bubbles in the centre.
• Let pies cool before cutting so the filling can set.

## NO-FUSS CRUMB CRUSTS

Biscuit crumb crusts take no time to make – all you need is a blender or food processor. Or, crush biscuits in a sealed plastic bag with a rolling pin. Chocolate or vanilla biscuits, gingernuts or digestives are a good base. For added richness, replace some of the biscuits with ground nuts such as almonds, pecans or macadamias, or with amaretti biscuits. For spicy flavour, add a bit of ground ginger, cinnamon or nutmeg.

Regular pie plate

Deep-dish pie plate

# Pie crusts

Tender, flaky pastry is a work of art – and easy to produce. For best results, chill the ingredients before mixing and handle the pastry as little as possible (over working develops the gluten in the flour, making the pastry tough). To create a glaze, brush the top crust (not the edge) with milk, cream or slightly beaten egg white and sprinkle with sugar. Each pie crust takes about 10 minutes to prepare, plus chilling time.

## PASTRY FOR 2-CRUST PIE

340g plain flour
½ tsp salt
60g white vegetable fat, diced

125g cold butter or margarine, diced

Mix flour and salt in large bowl. Using pastry blender or two knives used scissor-fashion, cut in vegetable fat and butter until mixture resembles coarse crumbs.

Sprinkle in *4–6 tablespoons ice water*, a tablespoon at a time. Mix lightly with fork after each addition until pastry is just moist enough to hold together.

Shape pastry into 2 balls, one slightly larger. Wrap and refrigerate 30 minutes, or overnight (if chilled overnight, let stand at room temperature 30 minutes before rolling). Using floured rolling pin, roll out larger ball on lightly floured surface 5cm larger all around than inverted 23cm pie dish.

Roll pastry round gently onto rolling pin; gently ease into pie dish. Trim edge, leaving 2–3cm overhang. Reserve trimmings for decoration if you like. Fill pie.

Roll small ball of pastry into 25cm round. Cut several slashes; centre over filling. Trim edge, leaving 2–3cm overhang; fold over-hang under. Make decorative edge (see page 488).

## PASTRY FOR 1-CRUST PIE

165g plain flour
¼ tsp salt
30g white vegetable fat, diced

60g cold butter or margarine, diced

Prepare pastry as instructed for 2-Crust Pie, but in Step 2 sprinkle in *3–5 tablespoons ice water*, and in Step 3 make only 1 ball of pastry.

## PASTRY FOR 28CM TART

225g plain flour
½ tsp salt
30g white vegetable fat, diced

125g cold butter or margarine, diced

Prepare pastry as instructed for 2-Crust Pie, but in Step 2 sprinkle in *3–4 tablespoons ice water*, and in Step 3 make only 1 ball of pastry. After chilling, roll pastry to 35cm round. Ease pastry into 28 by 3cm round tart tin with removable base. Fold overhang in and press against side of tin to form rim 3mm above tin edge.

## PASTRY FOR 23CM TART

150g plain flour
¼ tsp salt
15g white vegetable fat, diced

90g cold butter or margarine, diced

Prepare pastry as instructed for 2-Crust Pie, but in Step 2 sprinkle in only *2–3 tablespoons ice water*, and in Step 3 make only 1 ball of pastry and, after chilling, roll pastry to a 28cm round. Use to line 23 by 3cm round tart tin with removable bottom as directed for 28cm tart.

### FOOD PROCESSOR METHOD

Using food processor with knife blade attached, combine flour, salt, vegetable fat and margarine. Process 1–2 seconds, until mixture forms fine crumbs. Add smaller amount of *ice water* all at once; process 1–2 seconds until pastry leaves sides of bowl. Remove pastry from bowl; with hands, shape into ball.

# DECORATIVE PIE EDGES

From classic to creative, these borders are the perfect way to add a professional finish to home-made pies. The first four pie edges shown here are pretty on any pie, whether one- or two-crust. The appliqué leaf edge is best for one-crust pies (but you will need enough pastry for a two-crust). For neat results, chill the pastry so that it is firm (not hard) when you work with it.

**Forked edge** Trim pastry edge as in Step 1 (below left) even with rim of pie plate. Using floured 4-tine fork, press pastry to rim of plate; repeat around edge.

**Fluted edge** Push one index finger against outside edge of rim; using index finger and thumb of other hand, gently pinch to form ruffle. Repeat around edge, leaving 5mm space between each ruffle.

## PREPARING PIE EDGES

1 Trim pastry edge (or top crust for 2-crust pie) with kitchen scissors to leave 2–3cm overhang. (For forked or leaf edge, trim edge even with rim of pie plate; omit Step 2 below).

2 Fold overhang under; pinch to make stand-up edge. Shape decorative edge as desired (right).

**Sharp (or pinched) fluted edge** Push one index finger against inside edge of rim; using index finger and thumb of other hand, pinch firmly to make flute. Repeat around edge, leaving 5mm space between each flute.

**Rope edge** Press thumb into pastry edge at an angle, then pinch pastry between thumb and knuckle of index finger. Place thumb in groove left by index finger; pinch as before; repeat around edge.

**Leaf edge** Prepare Pastry for 2-Crust Pie (see page 487). Use larger ball of pastry to line pie plate; trim even with rim. Roll smaller ball 2mm thick. Using knife, cut out leaves (see page 489). Lightly brush pastry edge with water. Press shapes onto edge.

# DOUBLE-CRUST PIES

A double-crust pie, which lends itself to decorative edges and adornments of cut-outs made from pastry trimmings, is a beautiful – and delicious – way to encase a fruit filling. Remember to cut a few slits in the top to allow the steam to escape during baking. Always cool the pie for a short time as the recipe instructs (even when serving it warm) so the filling can firm up for easier cutting.

## DEEP-DISH APPLE PIE

❖ ❖ ❖ ❖ ❖ ❖ ❖ ❖ ❖ ❖ ❖ ❖ ❖ ❖ ❖ ❖ ❖ ❖ ❖ ❖ ❖ ❖ ❖

*Prep: 40 minutes, plus chilling and cooling    Bake: 50–55 minutes*
*Makes 10 servings*

**Pastry for 2-Crust Pie (see page 487)**
**750g Golden Delicious apples, peeled, cored, and cut into 2mm thick slices**
**100g caster sugar**

**3 tbsp plain flour**
**2 tbsp coarsely chopped crystallized ginger**
**30g butter or margarine, diced**

**1** Prepare Pastry for 2-Crust Pie through chilling. Preheat oven to 220°C (425°F, Gas 7). Toss apple slices with next 3 ingredients.

**2** Use larger ball of pastry to line 24cm deep-dish pie plate. Spoon apple filling into pastry and dot with butter.

**3** Roll out pastry for top crust into 28cm round. Place on filling as instructed; make decorative edge (see page 488). Re-roll trimmings. Make shapes (see below); brush with water. Place on pie. Place sheet of foil underneath pie plate; crimp foil edges to form a rim to catch drips during baking.

**4** Bake 50–55 minutes until apples are tender when pierced with a knife. Cover pie loosely with foil after 30 minutes to prevent over-browning. Cool pie on wire rack 1 hour to serve warm. Or, cool completely to serve later.

❖ ❖ ❖ ❖ ❖ ❖ ❖ ❖ ❖ ❖ ❖ ❖ ❖ ❖ ❖ ❖ ❖ ❖ ❖ ❖ ❖ ❖ ❖

### DECORATIVE PASTRY SHAPES

**Apple** Roll out pastry trimmings. Use a small knife dipped in flour to cut a free-form apple shape.

**Leaves** Re-flour knife; cut out leaves from remaining pastry. Use back of the knife to mark veins in the leaves.

❖ ❖ ❖ ❖ ❖ ❖ ❖ ❖ ❖ ❖ ❖ ❖ ❖ ❖ ❖ ❖ ❖ ❖ ❖ ❖ ❖ ❖ ❖

EACH SERVING: ABOUT 370 CALORIES, 3g PROTEIN, 53g CARBOHYDRATE, 17g TOTAL FAT (4g SATURATED), 7mg CHOLESTEROL, 240mg SODIUM

## STRAWBERRY-RHUBARB PIE

*Prep:* 30 minutes, plus chilling and cooling    *Bake:* About 1¼ hours
*Makes* 10 servings

**Pastry for 2-Crust Pie (see page 487)**
**30g cornflour**
**200g plus 1 tbsp caster sugar**
**350g strawberries, hulled, each cut in half if large**

**600g rhubarb, cut into 1cm pieces**
**30g butter or margarine, diced**

◆ Prepare Pastry for 2-Crust Pie through chilling. Preheat oven to 220°C (425°F, Gas 7). Mix cornflour and 200g sugar in bowl. Add strawberries and rhubarb; toss to combine. Use larger ball of pastry to line 23cm pie plate. Spoon fruit mixture into pastry; dot with butter. Roll out top crust and place on filling as instructed; make decorative edge (see page 488). Sprinkle with remaining 1 tablespoon sugar.

◆ Place sheet of foil underneath pie plate; crimp edges to form a rim to catch drips. Bake pie 15 minutes. Turn oven control to 190°C (375°F, Gas 5); bake 80–90 minutes longer, until filling is bubbly in centre. Cool pie on wire rack 1 hour to serve warm. Or, cool completely to serve later.

**Each serving: About 355 calories, 4g protein, 49g carbohydrate, 17g total fat (4g saturated), 7mg cholesterol, 240mg sodium**

## PEAR-CRANBERRY PIE

*Prep:* 45 minutes, plus chilling and cooling    *Bake:* 80–90 minutes
*Makes* 10 servings

**Pastry for 2-Crust Pie (see page 487)**
**3 tbsp cornflour**
**⅛ tsp ground cinnamon**
**150g plus 1 tbsp caster sugar**
**150g cranberries, thawed if frozen, chopped**

**750g fully ripe pears, peeled, cored and sliced**
**30g butter or margarine, diced**

◆ Prepare Pastry for 2-Crust Pie through chilling. Preheat oven to 220°C (425°F, Gas 7). Mix cornflour, cinnamon and 150g sugar in large bowl. Add fruit; toss to combine.

◆ Use larger ball of pastry to line 23cm pie plate. Spoon pear mixture into pastry. Dot with butter. Roll out top crust and place on filling as instructed; make decorative edge (see page 488). Sprinkle pastry with remaining 1 tablespoon sugar.

◆ Place sheet of foil underneath pie plate; crimp foil edges to form a rim to catch drips during baking. Bake pie 20 minutes. Re-set oven control to 190°C (375°F, Gas 5); bake 60–70 minutes longer, until filling is bubbly in centre. Cool pie on wire rack 1 hour to serve warm. Or, cool completely to serve later.

**Each serving: About 400 calories, 3g protein, 61g carbohydrate, 17g total fat (4g saturated), 7mg cholesterol, 240mg sodium**

## HOME-STYLE PEACH AND CHERRY PIE

*Prep:* 50 minutes, plus chilling and cooling    *Bake:* 1½ hours
*Makes* 10 servings

**Pastry for 2-Crust Pie (see page 487)**
**150g light brown sugar**
**40g cornflour**
**½ tsp salt**
**1kg ripe peaches, peeled, stoned and thinly sliced**

**450g tart cherries, stoned, or 300g frozen tart cherries, thawed**
**1 tbsp milk**
**1 tbsp caster sugar**

◆ Prepare Pastry for 2-Crust Pie through chilling. Preheat oven to 190°C (375°F, Gas 5). Mix brown sugar, cornflour and salt in large bowl. Add peaches and cherries; toss to combine.

◆ Use larger ball of pastry to line 24cm deep-dish pie plate. Spoon fruit mixture into pastry. Roll remaining pastry into a 28cm round; use to make lattice top (see page 500). Brush pastry with milk and sprinkle with caster sugar.

◆ Place sheet of foil underneath pie plate; crimp foil edges to form a rim to catch drips during baking. Bake pie 1½ hours, or until filling is bubbly in centre.

◆ Cover pie loosely with foil during last 40 minutes to prevent over-browning. Cool pie on wire rack 1 hour to serve warm. Or, cool completely to serve later.

**Each serving: About 375 calories, 4g protein, 59g carbohydrate, 15g total fat (3g saturated), 0mg cholesterol, 330mg sodium**

# SINGLE-CRUST PIES

A single crust can hold luscious fruits, rich chocolate-nut creations or smooth custards. Be sure to mend any cracks that appear in the pastry during rolling: moisten the torn edges, lay a patch of pastry over the tear and carefully press into position.

## SWEET SUMMER PIE

◆◆◆◆◆◆◆◆◆◆◆◆◆◆◆

*Prep: 55 minutes, plus chilling and cooling*
*Bake: 1 hour*
*Makes 10 servings*

**Pastry for 1-Crust Pie (see page 487)**
**1 large orange**
**1 large lemon**
**4 medium eggs, separated**
**⅛ tsp salt**
**190g caster sugar**
**50g plain flour**
**1.1kg nectarines, peeled, stoned and sliced**
**160g raspberries**

1 Prepare Pastry for 1-Crust Pie through chilling. Grate 2 teaspoons rind and squeeze 75ml juice from orange. Grate 1½ teaspoons rind from lemon, then squeeze enough juice to add to orange juice to make 125ml juice in total. Using an electric mixer on high speed, beat egg yolks, salt and 70g sugar in small bowl about 3 minutes, until thick and lemon-coloured. Gradually beat in juice mixture and all of grated rind.

2 Cook yolk mixture in 1-litre saucepan over low heat, stirring constantly, 8–10 minutes until thick (do not boil or mixture will curdle). Spoon into medium bowl; cool completely. Preheat oven to 220°C (425°F, Gas 7). Mix flour and 70g sugar in large bowl. Add nectarine slices; toss to combine. Gently stir in raspberries. Use pastry to line 23cm pie plate; make decorative edge (see page 488).

3 Spoon fruit mixture into pastry. Cover loosely with lightly greased foil; bake 45 minutes, or until bubbly in centre and pastry is lightly browned. Remove from oven; re-set to 180°C (350°F, Gas 4).

### GRATING RIND

When grating rind from oranges, lemons or limes, avoid waste, messy scraping and jammed grater holes by pressing a piece of cling film over the fine side of the grater first. When you're finished, the rind will come off the wrap without any trouble – and the grater will be easier to clean.

4 Using electric mixer on high speed, beat egg whites to soft peaks in another small bowl. Sprinkle in remaining 50g caster sugar, beating to stiff peaks. Fold whites into cooled yolk mixture, one-third at a time.

5 Spread topping over filling right to edges. Return pie to oven; bake 15 minutes, or until topping is set and lightly browned. Cool pie completely on wire rack. Cover and refrigerate any leftover pie.

EACH SERVING: ABOUT 295 CALORIES, 6g PROTEIN, 49g CARBOHYDRATE, 10g TOTAL FAT (2g SATURATED), 85mg CHOLESTEROL, 160mg SODIUM

## PEACH TARTE TATIN

*Prep: 1 hour, plus chilling
and cooling
Bake: 25 minutes
Makes 12 servings*

**Pastry for 1-Crust Pie (see
   page 487)**
**200g sugar**
**90g butter or margarine**

**1 tbsp fresh lemon juice**
**1.6kg firm, slightly ripe
   peaches, peeled, stoned and
   each cut in half**

◆ Prepare Pastry for 1-Crust Pie through chilling.

◆ Bring sugar, butter and lemon juice to the boil in large
frying pan with ovenproof handle over medium-high heat.
Place peaches in pan, stoned side down. Cook 10 minutes.
Carefully turn peaches; cook 8–12 minutes longer, until
syrup is caramelized and thickened.

◆ Meanwhile, preheat oven to 220°C (425°F, Gas 7). Just
before peaches are done, using floured rolling pin, roll
out pastry on lightly floured surface into 35cm round. Place
pastry on top of peaches in pan; tuck edge under to form
a rim. Using knife, cut six 5mm slits in pastry so steam can
escape during baking. Bake 25 minutes, or until pastry
is golden.

◆ When tarte tatin is done, place large platter over top of
frying pan; carefully invert onto platter. Cool 1 hour to
serve warm. Or, cool completely to serve later.

**Each serving: 270 calories, 2g protein, 42g carbohydrate,
12g total fat (4g saturated), 0mg cholesterol, 155mg sodium**

## CHOCOLATE-PECAN PIE

*Prep: 45 minutes, plus chilling and cooling   Bake: 65 minutes
Makes 12 servings*

**Pastry for 1-Crust Pie (see
   page 487)**
**60g margarine or butter**
**60g plain chocolate**
**150g dark brown sugar**

**250g golden syrup**
**1 tsp vanilla essence**
**3 medium eggs**
**200g pecan halves**

◆ Prepare Pastry for 1-Crust Pie through chilling.

◆ Preheat oven to 220°C (425°F, Gas 7). Use pastry to line
23cm pie plate. Make decorative edge (see page 488). Line
pastry with foil and fill with pie weights, dry beans or
uncooked rice. Bake pastry 10 minutes. Remove foil with
weights; bake 10 minutes longer, or until lightly golden.

◆ Cool pastry on wire rack at least 10 minutes. Re-set oven
control to 180°C (350°F, Gas 4). Meanwhile melt butter and
chocolate in heavy 1-litre saucepan, over low heat, stirring
frequently. Cool slightly.

◆ Mix chocolate mixture, brown sugar and next
3 ingredients in large bowl, using wire whisk, until blended.
Coarsely chop 125g pecan halves; leave remainder as halves.
Stir all pecans into chocolate mixture; pour into cooled
pastry case.

◆ Bake 45 minutes, or until edges are set (centre should
shake slightly). Cool completely on wire rack. Cover and
refrigerate any leftovers.

**Each serving: About 390 calories, 5g protein, 42g carbohydrate,
24g total fat (4g saturated), 53mg cholesterol, 170mg sodium**

## SWEET POTATO PIE

*Prep: 70 minutes, plus chilling  and cooling   Bake: 40 minutes
Makes 10 servings*

**Pastry for 1-Crust Pie (see
   page 487)**
**900g sweet potatoes,
   unpeeled, or 900–950g
   canned sweet potatoes,
   drained**
**450g single cream**
**200g dark brown sugar**

**60g margarine or butter,
   melted**
**1 tsp ground cinnamon**
**¾ tsp ground ginger**
**½ tsp ground nutmeg**
**½ tsp salt**
**3 medium eggs**

◆ Prepare Pastry for 1-Crust Pie through chilling.

◆ If using fresh sweet potatoes, bring sweet potatoes and
enough *water* to cover to the boil in 3-litre saucepan over
high heat. Reduce heat to low, cover and simmer 30 minutes,
or until fork-tender; drain. Cool potatoes until easy to
handle; peel and cut into chunks.

◆ Preheat oven to 200°C (400°F, Gas 6). Using electric
mixer on low speed, beat sweet potatoes in large bowl until
smooth. Add cream and remaining ingredients; beat until
well blended.

◆ Use pastry to line 24cm deep-dish pie plate. Make
decorative edge (see page 488). Spoon sweet potato
mixture into pastry.

◆ Bake 40 minutes, or until knife inserted 2–3cm from
edge comes out clean. Cool 1 hour to serve warm. Or, cool
slightly, then refrigerate to serve later. Cover and refrigerate
any leftovers.

**Each serving: About 400 calories, 6g protein, 52g carbohydrate,
19g total fat (6g saturated), 82mg cholesterol, 320mg sodium**

# CRUMB-CRUST PIES

These crusts are simple to make. Simply blend biscuits in a food processor with knife blade attached until crumbs form; mix them together with melted fat and sugar, press into a pie plate and bake to set. For firm, easy-to-cut slices, chill the pies once filled for at least 3 hours before serving.

## STRAWBERRY-RHUBARB MOUSSE PIE

*Prep: 20 minutes, plus chilling and cooling*   *Bake: 15 minutes*
*Makes 10 servings*

450g rhubarb, cut into
  2–3cm chunks
200g sugar
2 packets gelatine
350g strawberries, hulled
1 tbsp fresh lemon juice
90g butter or margarine,
  melted

400g shortbread biscuit
  crumbs
225ml whipping cream
Mint sprigs and strawberry
  halves for decoration

**1** Bring rhubarb, sugar and *60ml water* in 2-litre saucepan to the boil over high heat, stirring constantly. Reduce heat to medium-low; cook 10 minutes, or until tender. Blend rhubarb mixture using food processor with knife blade attached, until smooth; return to pan. Sprinkle gelatine over *125ml cold water* in small bowl; let stand 2 minutes to soften.

**2** Mash strawberries in bowl with potato masher or fork. Stir into rhubarb with gelatine and lemon juice; cook 3 minutes over low heat, until gelatine dissolves completely.

**3** Pour rhubarb mixture into bowl; refrigerate, stirring occasionally, about 2½ hours until mixture mounds slightly when dropped from a spoon. (Or, for quicker setting, place bowl with rhubarb mixture in a larger bowl of *ice water* and stir every 10 minutes for about 1 hour.)

**4** Meanwhile, preheat oven to 180°C (350°F, Gas 4). Mix butter with crumbs in 24cm deep-dish pie plate; press onto base and up side. Bake 15 minutes; cool on wire rack.

**5** Using electric mixer on medium speed, beat cream to soft peaks. Fold whipped cream into rhubarb mixture using large metal spoon until blended. Spoon into crumb crust. Refrigerate at least 3 hours, or overnight. Decorate.

### WHIPPING CREAM

Whipping cream will double in volume when whipped, so use a bowl that is large enough. Soft peaks (right), when the cream forms gentle folds, are best for folding into other mixtures to add volume, as in this Strawberry-Rhubarb Mousse Pie.
Stiff peaks (right), when the cream keeps its shape, can be used to top cream pies, ice cakes or between layers of pastry.

Soft peaks

Stiff peaks

EACH SERVING: ABOUT 445 CALORIES, 5g PROTEIN, 51g CARBOHYDRATE, 25g TOTAL FAT (12g SATURATED), 43mg CHOLESTEROL, 270mg SODIUM

## DOUBLE BLUEBERRY PIE

*Prep:* 30 minutes, plus cooling and chilling    *Bake:* 8 minutes
*Makes* 10 servings

225g gingernut biscuits
2 tbsp plus 100g caster sugar
75g butter or margarine,
  melted

2 tbsp cornflour
1.2kg blueberries
Whipped cream (optional)

◆ Preheat oven to 190°C (375°F, Gas 5). Using food processor with knife blade attached or in blender on high speed, process gingernut biscuits and 2 tablespoons sugar until fine crumbs form.

◆ Using fork, mix biscuit crumbs with melted butter in 23cm pie plate. Using your hands, press mixture onto base and up side of pie plate, making a small rim. Bake crust 8 minutes. Cool on wire rack.

◆ Meanwhile, mix cornflour with *2 tablespoons cold water* in 2-litre saucepan until blended. Stir in half of blueberries and remaining 100g sugar; boil over medium-high heat, pressing blueberries against side of pan with back of spoon. Boil 1 minute, stirring constantly. Remove pan from heat; stir in remaining blueberries.

◆ Pour blueberry mixture into crumb crust. Cover with cling film and refrigerate at least 5 hours, or overnight. Serve with whipped cream, if you like.

**Each serving: About 260 calories, 2g protein, 43g carbohydrate, 10g total fat (4g saturated), 16mg cholesterol, 185mg sodium**

## CHOCOLATE PIE WITH CREAM

*Prep:* 25 minutes, plus cooling and chilling    *Bake:* 8 minutes
*Makes* 10 servings

225g digestive biscuits
75g butter or margarine,
  melted
2 tbsp sugar

Chocolate Pudding (see
  page 474)
225g whipping cream

◆ Preheat oven to 180°C (350°F, Gas 4). Using food processor with knife blade attached, blend biscuits until fine crumbs form.

◆ Using fork, mix biscuit crumbs, melted butter and sugar in 23cm pie plate. Press mixture onto base and up side of pie plate. Bake 8 minutes; cool on wire rack.

◆ Prepare Chocolate Pudding; pour warm pudding into crumb crust. Place cling film directly on surface to prevent skin forming. Refrigerate at least 4 hours, or overnight. To serve, using electric mixer on medium speed, beat cream in medium bowl until stiff peaks form. Spoon onto pie.

**Each serving: About 480 calories, 7g protein, 45g carbohydrate, 32g total fat (15g saturated), 168mg cholesterol, 415mg sodium**

## BANANA CREAM PIE

*Prep:* 30 minutes, plus cooling and chilling    *Bake:* 15 minutes
*Makes* 10 servings

120g butter or margarine
400g shortbread biscuit
  crumbs
150g sugar
80g cornflour
¼ tsp salt

845ml milk
5 medium egg yolks
1¾ tsp vanilla essence
3 medium-size ripe bananas
175ml whipping cream

◆ Preheat oven to 180°C (350°F, Gas 4).

◆ Melt 90g butter in small saucepan over low heat. Mix biscuit crumbs with melted butter in 23cm pie plate. Press mixture onto base and up side of pie plate. Bake 15 minutes, or until golden; cool on wire rack.

◆ Prepare filling: mix sugar, cornflour and salt in 3-litre saucepan; stir in milk until smooth. Cook over medium heat, stirring constantly, until mixture thickens and boils; boil 1 minute. Beat egg yolks lightly in small bowl; beat in small amount of hot milk mixture. Slowly pour yolk mixture back into milk, stirring rapidly. Cook over low heat, stirring constantly, 2 minutes, or until very thick.

◆ Remove from heat; stir in 1½ teaspoons vanilla essence and remaining 30g butter. Slice 2 bananas. Pour half of filling into crumb crust. Arrange sliced bananas on top; spoon remaining filling over. Place cling film directly on surface of filling; refrigerate at least 4 hours, or overnight.

◆ To serve, using an electric mixer on medium speed, beat cream and remaining vanilla essence in small bowl to stiff peaks; spread over filling. Slice remaining banana; arrange around edge of pie. Cover and refrigerate any leftover pie.

**Each serving: About 535 calories, 8g protein, 58g carbohydrate, 31g total fat (13g saturated), 179mg cholesterol, 395mg sodium**

# FREE-FORM TARTS

These rustic-looking tarts suggest French country bistros and homely farmhouse suppers. The pastry is simply rolled into a round and then folded up over the fruit mixture. To prevent leaking, pinch closed any cracks that form in the pastry during folding.

## FARMHOUSE CHERRY TART

❖ ❖ ❖ ❖ ❖ ❖ ❖ ❖ ❖ ❖ ❖ ❖ ❖

*Prep: 45 minutes, plus chilling and cooling*
*Bake: 45–50 minutes*
*Makes 6 servings*

**225g plain flour**
**40g plus 1 tbsp coarse yellow cornmeal**
**140g plus 1 tsp caster sugar**
**Salt**
**125g cold butter or margarine, diced**
**2 tbsp plus 1 tsp cornflour**
**750g dark sweet cherries, stoned**
**1 medium egg white**

### WHAT'S IN A NAME?

*Galette* is the French term for any round, flat, free-form tart that is baked on a baking sheet. The pastry can be either a yeast dough or a simple unleavened pastry, as in the recipes here. A galette may be sweet or savoury; possible toppings include jam, nuts, meat or cheese, as well as fruit.

**1** Mix flour, 40g cornmeal, 70g sugar and ½ teaspoon salt in medium bowl. Using pastry blender or two knives used scissor-fashion, cut in butter until mixture resembles coarse crumbs.

**2** Sprinkle in *4–5 tablespoons ice water*, 1 tablespoon at a time, mixing lightly by hand until pastry comes together (pastry will feel very dry at first). Shape into a ball.

**3** Sprinkle large baking sheet with remaining 1 tablespoon cornmeal. Using floured rolling pin, roll out pastry on baking sheet into a 33cm round, placing dampened towel under baking sheet to prevent it slipping. Using long palette knife, gently loosen pastry from baking sheet. Mix 70g sugar with cornflour in large bowl.

**4** Sprinkle half sugar mixture over centre of pastry, leaving 5–6cm border all around. Add cherries to remaining sugar mixture in bowl; toss well.

**5** Spoon cherry mixture over sugar on pastry round. Fold pastry up around cherries, leaving a 10cm opening in centre. Pinch to seal any cracks.

**6** Mix egg white and ⅛ teaspoon salt in cup. Brush over pastry; sprinkle with remaining 1 teaspoon sugar. Refrigerate at least 30 minutes. Preheat oven to 220°C (425°F, Gas 7).

**7** Place 2 sheets of foil under baking sheet; crimp edges to form a rim to catch drips during baking. Bake 45–50 minutes until crust is golden and filling is gently bubbling, covering loosely with foil during last 10 minutes to prevent over-browning. As soon as tart is baked, loosen from baking sheet with long metal spatula. Cool 15 minutes on baking sheet, then slide onto wire rack to cool completely.

EACH SERVING: ABOUT 460 CALORIES, 6g PROTEIN, 74g CARBOHYDRATE, 17g TOTAL FAT (7g SATURATED), 45mg CHOLESTEROL, 410mg SODIUM

## PEAR AND NUT TART

*Prep: 35 minutes, plus chilling and cooling    Bake: 25–30 minutes*
*Makes 4 servings*

Pastry for 1-Crust Pie (see page 487)
600g ripe pears, peeled, cored and cut into 5mm thick slices
2 tbsp plain flour
2 tbsp currants or chopped raisins

4 tsp fresh lemon juice
½ tsp ground cinnamon
70g plus 1 tbsp caster sugar
1 tbsp milk
2 tbsp chopped pecans

◈ Prepare Pastry for 1-Crust Pie through chilling. Preheat oven to 200°C (400°F, Gas 6). Toss pear slices with flour, currants, lemon juice, cinnamon and 70g sugar in large bowl. Set aside.

◈ Using floured rolling pin, roll out chilled pastry onto lightly floured surface into 30cm round. Transfer to lightly greased baking sheet.

◈ Mound pear mixture in centre of pastry, leaving a border of 5cm. Fold pastry up around pears, pleating where necessary and leaving an opening in centre. Brush tart with 1 tablespoon milk; sprinkle with 1 tablespoon sugar.

◈ Place 2 sheets foil under baking sheet; crimp foil edges to form a rim to catch any drips during baking.

◈ Bake 10 minutes. Sprinkle pecans over filling in centre of tart; bake 15–20 minutes longer, or until pastry is browned. Cool tart on baking sheet on wire rack 10 minutes to serve warm. Or, slide tart onto rack after 10 minutes and cool completely to serve later.

Each serving: About 515 calories, 5g protein, 80g carbohydrate, 21g total fat (4g saturated), 1mg cholesterol, 270mg sodium

## PEACH-BLUEBERRY TART

*Prep: 30 minutes, plus chilling and cooling    Bake: 40 minutes*
*Makes 8 servings*

Pastry for 1-Crust Pie (see page 487)
2 tbsp cornflour
70g plus 2 tbsp caster sugar
145g blueberries
6 large peaches (about 900g) peeled, stoned and each cut into 6 wedges

2 tsp fresh lemon juice
15g butter or margarine, diced

◈ Prepare Pastry for 1-Crust Pie through chilling. Preheat oven to 220°C (425°F, Gas 7). Mix cornflour and 70g sugar in large bowl. Toss in blueberries, peaches and lemon juice.

◈ Using floured rolling pin, roll out pastry on lightly floured surface to 35cm round. Trim edges; reserve scraps. Transfer pastry to large baking sheet. Spoon fruit mixture with juices in centre of pastry, leaving a 5cm border. Dot fruit mixture with butter. Fold pastry up around fruit. Brush any cracks with *water*; patch with reserved scraps.

◈ Sprinkle pastry and exposed fruit with remaining 2 tablespoons sugar. Place 2 sheets foil under baking sheet; crimp foil edges to form rim to catch any drips during baking. Bake 40 minutes, or until bubbly in centre. Cool on baking sheet on wire rack 30 minutes to serve warm.

Each serving: About 270 calories, 3g protein, 42g carbohydrate, 11g total fat (2g saturated), 4mg cholesterol, 150mg sodium

## APPLE GALETTE

*Prep: 40 minutes, plus chilling and cooling    Bake: 45 minutes*
*Makes 8 servings*

Pastry for 1-Crust Pie (see page 487)
900g Golden Delicious apples
50g caster sugar

30g butter or margarine, diced
2 tbsp apricot jam, melted

◈ Prepare Pastry for 1-Crust Pie through chilling. Preheat oven to 220°C (425°F, Gas 7). Using floured rolling pin, roll out pastry on lightly floured surface to 38cm round. Transfer to large baking sheet.

◈ Peel apples; cut each in half. Using melon-baller, remove cores. Cut crossways into 5mm thick slices. Fan apple slices in concentric circles on pastry round, leaving a 4cm border. Sprinkle apples evenly with sugar and dot with butter. Fold pastry up around apples.

◈ Place 2 sheets foil under baking sheet; crimp foil edges to form a rim to catch any drips during baking. Bake galette 45 minutes or until apples are tender. Place baking sheet on wire rack. Brush apples with jam. Cool slightly to serve warm.

Each serving: About 270 calories, 2g protein, 40g carbohydrate, 12g total fat (4g saturated), 8mg cholesterol, 165mg sodium

# TARTS

Bursting with colourful fruit, creamy custards, nuts or smooth chocolate mixtures, tarts make a superb dessert. Unlike a pie crust, a tart case must be sturdy enough to stand on its own when removed from the tin.

## PLUM FRANGIPANE TART

◆◆◆◆◆◆◆◆◆◆◆◆◆◆

*Prep:* 30 minutes, plus chilling and cooling
*Bake:* 70–85 minutes
*Makes* 12 servings

**Pastry for 28cm Tart (see page 487)**
**200–225g marzipan**
**100g caster sugar**
**60g butter or margarine, softened**
**¼ tsp salt**
**2 medium eggs**
**2 tsp vanilla essence**
**40g plain flour**
**600g large ripe plums, (about 5), stoned and each cut into 6 wedges**

1 Prepare Pastry for 28cm Tart and use to line tart tin as instructed. Preheat oven to 220°C (425°F, Gas 7).

2 Line pastry case with foil and fill with pie weights, dry beans or uncooked rice. Bake 15 minutes; remove foil with weights and bake 5–10 minutes longer, until golden. (If pastry puffs up during baking, gently press it down with back of spoon.) Remove pastry case from oven; turn oven control to 190°C (375°F, Gas 5).

3 Meanwhile, prepare filling: using electric mixer on low speed, beat marzipan, caster sugar, butter and salt together in large bowl until crumbly. Increase speed to medium-high and beat 3 minutes, frequently scraping bowl with rubber spatula. (There may be some tiny lumps.) Add eggs and vanilla essence; beat until smooth. Using wooden spoon, stir in flour until blended.

## CRANBERRY-ALMOND TART

Prepare Plum Frangipane Tart as instructed, but omit plums and bake marzipan filling only 20 minutes until golden. Cool in tin on wire rack. Bring 100g cranberries, 50g sugar, 80ml water and ½ teaspoon grated orange rind in large saucepan to the boil over high heat. Reduce heat to medium-low; simmer 5 minutes, until mixture thickens slightly and cranberries pop. Stir in additional 200g cranberries. Set mixture aside until cool. When pastry is cool, carefully remove side of pan; spoon cranberry topping over marzipan filling. Makes 12 servings.

Each serving: About 370 calories, 5g protein, 46g carbohydrate, 19g total fat (3g saturated), 36mg cholesterol, 280mg sodium

4 Pour filling into warm pastry case. Arrange plum wedges in concentric circles over filling. Bake tart 50–60 minutes until golden. Cool tart completely in tin on wire rack. When tart is cool, carefully remove side from tin. Cover and refrigerate any leftovers.

EACH SERVING: ABOUT 335 CALORIES, 5g PROTEIN, 36g CARBOHYDRATE, 19g TOTAL FAT (4g SATURATED), 47mg CHOLESTEROL, 280mg SODIUM

# RASPBERRY TART

*Prep: 20 minutes, plus chilling and cooling  Bake: 50–60 minutes*
*Makes 8 servings*

**Pastry for 23cm Tart (see**
  **page 487)**
**140g caster sugar**
**40g plain flour**

**¼ tsp ground cinnamon**
**640g raspberries**
**225ml whipping cream**
  **(optional)**

◈ Prepare Pastry for 23cm Tart, but fit pastry onto base and 2–3cm up side of 28 by 8cm springform tin. Preheat oven to 200°C (400°F, Gas 6).

◈ Combine sugar, flour and cinnamon in small bowl; sprinkle half of sugar mixture over pastry. Top with 500g raspberries; refrigerate remaining raspberries for topping. Sprinkle remaining sugar mixture evenly over raspberries in pastry. Bake tart on lowest oven rack 50–60 minutes, until raspberry mixture is bubbly.

◈ Cool tart completely in tin on wire rack. When tart is cool, carefully remove side of tin; top tart with reserved raspberries. To serve, pour 2 tablespoons cream on each plate, if you like; arrange a wedge of tart on cream.

**Each serving: About 250 calories, 3g protein, 38g carbohydrate, 11g total fat (2g saturated), 0mg cholesterol, 165mg sodium**

# MIXED BERRY TART

*Prep: 25 minutes, plus chilling and cooling  Bake: 22–27 minutes*
*Makes 8 servings*

**Pastry for 23cm Tart (see**
  **page 487)**
**225ml milk**
**2 medium egg yolks**
**70g caster sugar**
**2 tbsp cornflour**

**2 tsp orange-flavour liqueur**
**1 tsp vanilla essence**
**450g assorted berries, such as**
  **raspberries, blackberries**
  **and blueberries**
**Icing sugar for decoration**

◈ Prepare Pastry for 23cm Tart; use to line tart tin as instructed. Preheat oven to 220°C (425°F, Gas 7). Line pastry with foil; fill with pie weights, dry beans or uncooked rice. Bake 15 minutes. Remove foil with weights; bake 7–12 minutes longer until golden. (If pastry puffs up during baking, gently press it down with back of spoon.) Cool completely on rack.

◈ Meanwhile, prepare pastry cream: bring milk to the boil in 2-litre saucepan over medium-high heat. Whisk egg yolks with caster sugar in medium bowl until smooth; whisk in cornflour. Gradually whisk hot milk into yolk mixture. Return to pan. Cook, whisking constantly, until mixture thickens and boils. Reduce heat to low and cook, whisking constantly, 2 minutes. Remove from heat; stir in liqueur and vanilla essense.

◈ Pour pastry cream into clean bowl; press cling film directly onto surface to prevent skin forming. Refrigerate at least 2 hours, until cold.

◈ When pastry case is cool, carefully remove side of tin. Whisk pastry cream until smooth; spread in pastry case. Spoon berries on top. Sift icing sugar over berries. Cover and refrigerate any leftovers.

**Each serving: About 250 calories, 4g protein, 30g carbohydrate, 13g total fat (3g saturated), 57mg cholesterol, 185mg sodium**

# FIG AND CUSTARD TART

*Prep: 25 minutes, plus chilling and cooling  Bake: 34–42 minutes*
*Makes 8 servings*

**Pastry for 23cm Tart (see**
  **page 487)**
**350ml soured cream**
**70g caster sugar**
**2 tbsp plain flour**
**1 tsp vanilla essence**

**⅛ tsp salt**
**1 medium egg**
**6 large or 12 small figs or**
  **450g assorted berries**
**80g apricot jam**

◈ Prepare Pastry for 23cm Tart and use to line tart tin as instructed. Preheat oven to 220°C (425°F, Gas 7). Line pastry case with foil; fill with pie weights, dry beans or uncooked rice. Bake 15 minutes. Remove foil with weights; bake 7–12 minutes longer, until golden. (If pastry puffs up during baking, gently press down with back of spoon.) Cool slightly on wire rack. Re-set oven to 200°C (400°F, Gas 6).

◈ Using whisk or fork, beat soured cream, sugar, flour, vanilla essence, salt and egg in medium bowl, until smooth and well blended; pour into baked pastry case. Bake 12–15 minutes, just until set. Cool tart completely in tin on wire rack. Cover and refrigerate 2 hours or until cold.

◈ Carefully remove side of tin. Cut each fig into quarters, or halves if small. Arrange figs on tart. Melt apricot jam in small saucepan over low heat. Brush jam over figs. Cover and refrigerate any leftovers.

**Each serving: About 335 calories, 4g protein, 36g carbohydrate, 20g total fat (8g saturated), 46mg cholesterol, 230mg sodium**

# LEMON TART

*Prep: 20 minutes, plus chilling and cooling    Bake: 52–57 minutes*
*Makes 8 servings*

Pastry for 23cm Tart (see
  page 487)
4 large lemons
4 medium eggs

200g caster sugar
75ml whipping cream
Icing sugar for decoration

◈ Prepare Pastry for 23cm Tart and use to line tart tin as instructed. Preheat oven to 220°C (425°F, Gas 7). Line pastry with foil and fill with pie weights, dry beans or uncooked rice.

◈ Bake pastry 15 minutes. Remove foil with weights and bake 7–12 minutes longer until golden. (If pastry puffs up during baking, gently press it down with back of spoon.) Cool pastry case completely on wire rack. Re-set oven control to 180°C (350°F, Gas 4).

◈ Grate 1½ teaspoons rind and squeeze 150ml juice from lemons. Whisk together eggs, caster sugar, lemon rind and lemon juice in medium bowl until well combined. Whisk in whipped cream. Carefully pour lemon mixture into cooled pastry case.

◈ Bake on baking sheet 30 minutes, or until barely set. Cool completely on wire rack.

◈ Carefully remove side of tin; just before serving, sprinkle with icing sugar. Cover and refrigerate any leftovers.

**Each serving: About 320 calories, 5g protein, 39g carbohydrate, 16g total fat (5g saturated), 120mg cholesterol, 200mg sodium**

## CHOCOLATE TRUFFLE TART

*Prep: 20 minutes, plus chilling and cooling    Bake: 42–47 minutes*
*Makes 12 servings*

Pastry for 23cm Tart (see
  page 487)
125g butter or margarine
175g plain chocolate
50g caster sugar

1 tsp vanilla essence
125ml whipping cream
3 medium eggs
White-chocolate hearts (see
  page 552) for decoration

◈ Prepare Pastry for 23cm Tart and use to line tart tin as instructed, but trim edge even with rim of tin. Preheat oven to 220°C (425°F, Gas 7). Line pastry with foil and fill with pie weights, dry beans or uncooked rice.

◈ Bake 15 minutes. Remove foil with weights and bake 7–12 minutes longer, until golden. (If pastry puffs up during baking, gently press it down with back of spoon.) Cool pastry case in tin on wire rack 15 minutes. Re-set oven control to 180°C (350°F, Gas 4).

◈ While pastry is cooling, prepare filling: melt butter and chocolate in heavy 1-litre saucepan over low heat, stirring frequently. Stir in sugar and vanilla essence; remove from heat. Using fork or whisk, lightly beat cream and eggs in small bowl. Blend some warm chocolate mixture into egg mixture; stir egg mixture back into chocolate mixture until blended.

◈ Pour warm mixture into pastry case. Bake 20 minutes, or until just set (centre will shake). While tart is baking, prepare white-chocolate hearts. Cool tart in tin on wire rack; refrigerate to serve cold. Carefully remove side of tin; decorate with hearts. Cover and refrigerate any leftovers.

**Each serving: About 300 calories, 4g protein, 21g carbohydrate, 24g total fat (10g saturated), 89mg cholesterol, 220mg sodium**

## HOLIDAY NUT TART

*Prep: 20 minutes, plus chilling and cooling    Bake: 48–55 minutes*
*Makes 12 servings*

Pastry for 28cm Tart (see
  page 487)
100g light brown sugar
145g golden syrup
45g butter or margarine,
  melted

2 tsp vanilla essence
2 medium eggs
300–325g salted mixed nuts
Whipped cream (optional)

◈ Prepare Pastry for 28cm Tart and use to line tart tin as instructed. Preheat oven to 190°C (375°F, Gas 5). Line pastry with foil and fill with pie weights, dry beans or uncooked rice.

◈ Bake 15 minutes; remove foil with weights and bake 8–10 minutes longer, until golden. (If pastry puffs up during baking, gently press it down with back of spoon.)

◈ Meanwhile, whisk brown sugar, golden syrup, butter, vanilla essence and eggs together in medium bowl until smooth. Stir in nuts. Pour mixture into pastry case. Bake 25–30 minutes until set and deep golden brown. Cool tart in tin on wire rack. Carefully remove side of tin. Serve tart with whipped cream, if you like. Cover and refrigerate any leftovers.

**Each serving: About 405 calories, 7g protein, 35g carbohydrate, 26g total fat (6g saturated), 45mg cholesterol, 340mg sodium**

# LATTICE-TOPPED PECAN TART

*Prep:* 30 minutes, plus
chilling and cooling
*Bake:* 50–55 minutes
*Makes* 16 servings

Pastry for 2-Crust Pie (see
  page 487)
45g butter or margarine
500g golden syrup

200g caster sugar
1½ tsp vanilla essence
4 medium eggs
300g pecans, coarsely
  chopped

◆ Prepare Pastry for 2-Crust Pie through chilling. Preheat oven to 180°C (350°F, Gas 4). Using floured rolling pin, roll out larger ball of pastry on lightly floured surface to 35cm round. Use to line 28 by 4cm tart tin with removable base. Melt butter in 3-litre saucepan over low heat; remove from heat. Stir in golden syrup, sugar and vanilla essence. Separate 1 egg; set yolk aside. Using whisk or fork, beat remaining 3 eggs and egg white into butter mixture just until blended. Stir in chopped pecans; pour pecan mixture into pastry case.

◆ Mix remaining egg yolk with *2 teaspoons water* in small bowl. Roll remaining pastry into a 28cm round. Make lattice top (see right); brush with yolk mixture. Bake 50–55 minutes until knife inserted in filling 2–3cm from edge comes out clean. Cool tart in tin on wire rack. To serve, carefully remove side of pan. Cover and refrigerate any leftovers.

**Each serving: About 430 calories, 5g protein, 51g carbohydrate, 24g total fat (4g saturated), 59mg cholesterol, 195mg sodium**

## LATTICE-TOPPED FRUIT TART

*Prep:* 45 minutes, plus chilling and cooling    *Bake:* 55–60 minutes
*Makes* 12 servings

Pastry for 2-Crust Pie (see
  page 487)
600g Golden Delicious
  apples, peeled, cored and
  cut into 1cm cubes
15g butter or margarine
3 tbsp plus 140g caster sugar
Salt

200g cranberries, thawed if
  frozen
75g sultanas
1 tsp vanilla essence
2 tbsp plain flour
1 medium egg, lightly beaten

◆ Prepare Pastry for 2-Crust Pie through chilling. Using floured rolling pin, roll larger ball of pastry on lightly floured surface to 35cm round. Use to line 28 by 4cm tart tin with removable base. Cover with cling film and refrigerate.

◆ Mix apples, butter, 3 tablespoons caster sugar and ¼ teaspoon salt in 26cm frying pan; cover and cook over medium heat about 10 minutes until apples are very tender, mashing occasionally with fork. Uncover; increase heat to medium-high and cook, stirring frequently, until all liquid evaporates and apples form a thick purée. Remove pan from heat; cool completely.

◆ Preheat oven to 190°C (375°F, Gas 5). Mix cranberries, sultanas, vanilla essence, flour, remaining 140g caster sugar and ¼ teaspoon salt in medium bowl. Spread apple purée evenly over base of pastry case. Top with cranberry mixture. Roll remaining pastry into a 28cm round. Make lattice top (see below); brush lightly with beaten egg.

◆ Bake 55–60 minutes, until filling begins to bubble and pastry is golden. Cover with foil if necessary during last 30 minutes of baking to prevent over-browning. Cool in tin on wire rack. To serve, carefully remove side of tin.

**Each serving: About 315 calories, 3g protein, 47g carbohydrate, 14g total fat (3g saturated), 21mg cholesterol, 285mg sodium**

◆ ◆ ◆ ◆ ◆ ◆ ◆ ◆ ◆ ◆ ◆ ◆ ◆ ◆ ◆ ◆ ◆ ◆ ◆ ◆ ◆ ◆ ◆

### LATTICE TOP

1  Using pastry wheel or knife, cut pastry round into twenty 1cm wide strips. Place 10 strips, about 1cm apart, over tart or pie filling; do not seal ends.

2  Fold every other strip back three-quarters of its length. Place centre cross strip at right angle to first ones (place on a diagonal, if you like, for diamond lattice), and replace folded part of strips.

3  Now fold back alternate strips; position second cross strip in place, parallel to first and about 1cm away. Replace folded part of strips.

4  Repeat to weave cross strips into lattice. Trim strips almost even with tin or dish; press to inside edge of pastry case to seal.

◆ ◆ ◆ ◆ ◆ ◆ ◆ ◆ ◆ ◆ ◆ ◆ ◆ ◆ ◆ ◆ ◆ ◆ ◆ ◆ ◆ ◆ ◆

# TARTLETS

These dainty individual desserts provide a festive end to any meal. The delicate cases should be cooled in their tins. Do not fill them more than four hours in advance, or the pastry will become soggy. However, you can make the pastry cases ahead and freeze them (just bake from frozen before filling).

## LEMON-RASPBERRY TARTLETS

❖❖❖❖❖❖❖❖❖❖❖❖❖❖❖❖

*Prep:* 40 minutes, plus chilling and cooling
*Bake:* 15 minutes
*Makes* 6 tartlets (12 servings)

**4 medium lemons**
**150g caster sugar**
**175g butter**
**1 tbsp cornflour**
**6 medium egg yolks**
**Pastry for 2-Crust Pie (see page 487)**
**480g raspberries**

### CORNFLOUR

Extracted from corn kernels, cornflour thickens juicy pies, puddings and sauces; it also may be mixed with flour in biscuits, cakes and pastry for extra-tender results. Dishes thickened with cornflour are clear and glossy, while those thickened with flour are opaque.

**1** Prepare filling: grate 1 tablespoon rind and squeeze 125ml juice from lemons. Heat rind, juice, sugar, butter and cornflour in 2-litre saucepan over medium heat, stirring, until sugar dissolves and butter melts. Beat egg yolks lightly in small bowl. Beat small amount of lemon mixture into yolks; slowly pour egg mixture back into lemon mixture. Cook over low heat, stirring constantly, about 5 minutes until thick enough to coat back of spoon.

**2** Pour filling into a bowl; press cling film directly onto surface to prevent skin forming. Refrigerate 3 hours or until well chilled. Meanwhile, prepare Pastry for 2-Crust Pie through chilling, but divide pastry into 6 portions before refrigerating.

**3** Press pastry onto base and up sides of six 10cm fluted tartlet tins with removable bases.

**4** Place tins in Swiss roll pan for easy handling. Prick pastry all over with fork. Refrigerate pastry cases 20 minutes. Preheat oven to 200°C (400°F, Gas 6). Bake for 15 minutes or until golden.

**5** Transfer tartlet tins to wire rack to cool. When pastry cases are cool, carefully remove from tins. Spoon lemon filling into pastry cases and top with raspberries. Cover and refrigerate any leftovers.

EACH ½ TARTLET: ABOUT 350 CALORIES, 3g PROTEIN, 34g CARBOHYDRATE, 24g TOTAL FAT (10g SATURATED), 31mg CHOLESTEROL, 295mg SODIUM

## CHOCOLATE TARTLETS

*Prep: 50 minutes, plus chilling, cooling and standing*
*Bake: 9–12 minutes*
*Makes 36*

Pastry for 1-Crust Pie (see
  page 487)
3 tbsp apricot jam
60g plain chocolate
3 tbsp plus 60ml whipping
  cream
15g butter or margarine,
  diced

1 tsp vanilla essence
1 tsp icing sugar
Assorted berries, very thinly
  sliced kumquats or shaved
  chocolate for decoration

◈ Prepare Pastry for 1-Crust Pie through chilling. Preheat oven to 220°C (425°F, Gas 7). Using floured rolling pin, roll pastry, less than 1mm thick, on lightly floured surface. Using 6cm round cutter, cut out 36 pastry rounds (if necessary, re-roll scraps). Fill 36 mini muffin-tin cups or 4cm tartlet tins.

◈ Bake pastry 9–12 minutes, until golden. Cool in tins on wire rack. Remove tartlet cases from tins; spoon ¼ teaspoon jam into each. Melt chocolate with 3 tablespoons cream in top of double boiler over simmering water. Remove from heat; stir in butter until smooth. Stir in vanilla essence. Spoon mixture evenly into tartlets, covering jam. Let stand until tartlets are set.

◈ Using electric mixer on medium speed, beat remaining 60ml cream with icing sugar to stiff peaks. Spoon small dollop of cream onto each tartlet; decorate.

**Each tartlet: About 60 calories, 1g protein, 5g carbohydrate, 4g total fat (1g saturated), 5mg cholesterol, 35mg sodium**

## HAZELNUT TARTLETS

*Prep: 1 hour, plus chilling and cooling   Bake: 15 minutes*
*Makes 36*

Pastry for 1-Crust Pie (see
  page 487)
125g hazelnuts, toasted and
  skinned (see page 522)
120g icing sugar plus extra for
  decoration

1 medium egg
45g butter or margarine,
  softened
1 tsp vanilla essence

◈ Prepare Pastry for 1-Crust Pie through chilling. Preheat oven to 200°C (400°F, Gas 6). Using food processor with knife blade attached, process nuts with 120g icing sugar until finely ground. Add remaining ingredients; process until smooth.

◈ Using floured rolling pin, roll pastry, less than 1mm thick, on lightly floured surface. Using 6cm round cutter, cut out 36 pastry rounds (if necessary, re-roll scraps). Fit pastry into 36 mini muffin-tin cups or 4cm tartlet tins.

◈ Spoon hazelnut filling into pastry cases. Bake 15 minutes or until golden. Remove tartlets from tins and cool on wire rack. To serve, sift icing sugar on top. Cover and refrigerate any leftovers.

**Each tartlet: About 70 calories, 1g protein, 6g carbohydrate, 5g total fat (1g saturated), 3mg cholesterol, 40mg sodium**

## CREAM CHEESE AND FRUIT TARTLETS

*Prep: 45 minutes, plus chilling and cooling   Bake: 15 minutes*
*Makes 24*

Pastry for 23cm Tart (see
  page 487)
225g soft cream cheese
3 tbsp caster sugar
1 tbsp milk
¾ tsp vanilla essence

Kiwi fruit, strawberries,
  tinned mandarin orange
  sections and small seedless
  red and green grape halves
Mint leaves for decoration

◈ Prepare Pastry for 23cm Tart through chilling. Preheat oven to 220°C (425°F, Gas 7).

◈ Divide pastry in half. Roll one half into 30cm rope; cut rope into twelve 2–3cm pieces. Repeat with other half of pastry. Press each piece of pastry evenly into base and up sides of 24 mini muffin-tin cups. Prick each tartlet case several times with cocktail stick. Bake 15 minutes, or until golden. Cool pastry cases 5 minutes in tins on wire racks. Remove case from tins; cool completely on wire racks.

◈ Prepare filling: using fork, beat cream cheese, sugar, milk and vanilla essence in small bowl until blended. Spoon filling into pastry cases. Top each tartlet with some fruit. Refrigerate until ready to serve; decorate.

**Each tartlet: About 100 calories, 1g protein, 9g carbohydrate, 7g total fat (3g saturated), 11mg cholesterol, 85mg sodium**

# BISCUITS & CAKES

16

# BISCUITS KNOW-HOW

A batch of fragrant, warm-from-the-oven biscuits is a simple pleasure few can resist. They come in six basic types: drop, shaped or moulded, pressed, rolled, refrigerated and bar (which includes brownies). Drop and bar biscuits are made with a soft dough. All the others are made with a stiffer dough for ease of shaping. Although biscuit making is not complicated, you'll achieve better results if you're ready with the best ingredients, equipment and know-how. The following tips promise to help deliver delicious results.

## MAKING AND SHAPING

- Avoid adding more flour than is necessary to biscuit mixture, or over-mixing once the flour is added, or you'll have hard, tough biscuits.
- For even baking, shape biscuits to the same thickness.
- For shaped or rolled biscuits, chilled dough is easier to handle. Doughs made with butter chill to a firmer consistency and hold their shape better than doughs made with margarine or shortening.
- Roll out a small amount of biscuit dough at a time; keep remainder covered with cling film to keep it moist.

Refrigerated biscuits can be shaped, chilled and cut at your convenience. To bake, cut desired number of biscuits in even slices from log, and arrange slightly apart on baking sheets.

## ABOUT BAKING SHEETS

- Baking sheets with only 1 or 2 turned-up edges allow for the best air circulation. If using a Swiss roll tin, invert it and place dough on the reverse side.
- Baking sheets should be at least 5cm smaller in length and width than your oven, so air circulates.
- Grease baking sheets only when a recipe calls for it. Some biscuits have a high fat content, so greasing isn't always necessary. When greasing is required, use a light hand and crumpled greaseproof paper for even spreading.

- Heavy-gauge metal baking sheets with a dull finish result in the most evenly browned cookies. Aluminium is ideal. Dark-coloured sheets can over-brown the bases of biscuits.

## BETTER BAKING

- If baking with margarine, make sure it contains 80 percent fat. Spreads (which may be labelled diet, whipped, liquid, or soft) have a high water content, which will result in biscuits that are less tender and buttery.
- To make bar biscuits easier to serve, line the tin with foil before adding the mixture; when baked, the biscuits can simply be lifted out of the tin, then cut.
- For best results, bake one sheet of biscuits at a time on the centre rack of the oven. If baking two at a time, switch sheets halfway through baking so the biscuits bake evenly.
- When baking biscuits in batches, cool the baking sheet to room temperature before placing more biscuits on it. A hot baking sheet will melt the dough. If the recipe calls for greasing the sheet, regrease for each batch.
- To avoid over-cooking, check biscuits at the minimum baking time suggested in the recipe, and then watch them closely during their last few minutes in the oven.
- Straight from the oven, most drop biscuits are too soft to handle. Let them cool slightly before transferring to a rack.
- To test bar biscuits for doneness, insert a cocktail stick into the centre of tin; it should come out clean (unless the recipe specifies otherwise). Other biscuits are done when they're just firm at the edges.
- Bar biscuits should be cooled in the tin before cutting, or they'll crumble.

## STORING BISCUITS AND PACKAGING AS GIFTS

- To store biscuit dough, place in an airtight container or plastic bag (wrap logs for refrigerated biscuits first in cling film); chill up to 1 week or freeze up to 6 months (if necessary, let stand at room temperature until easy to slice).
- To store cooled baked biscuits, arrange a single layer in an airtight container; cover with greaseproof paper. Repeat layers; seal container. Store at room temperature up to 3 days.
- Freeze unbaked drop biscuits directly on baking sheets. Once biscuits are frozen, transfer to heavy-duty plastic bags.
- To freeze baked biscuits, place in plastic bags, pressing out air. Or, place in airtight containers; for cushioning, layer with crumpled greaseproof paper. Freeze up to 3 months.
- Home-made biscuits make lovely, personalised gifts. Line a gift box (you can buy these or make one yourself) with coloured tissue paper and paper doilies. To keep biscuits fresh, wrap indiviualy in cling film. Arrange the biscuits in layers with more tissue paper between the layers.

# DROP BISCUITS

These range from elegant, fragile Vanilla Wafers (see right) to biscuit-tin favourites like oatmeal biscuits. Drop biscuits are formed by dropping spoonfuls of soft unchilled dough onto a baking sheet. For even baking, distribute the dough in equal portions.

## VANILLA WAFERS

◆◆◆◆◆◆◆◆◆◆◆◆◆

*Prep:* 1 hour, plus cooling
*Bake:* 5–7 minutes per batch
*Makes* about 30

**3 medium egg whites**
**90g icing sugar**
**75g plain flour**
**90g butter, melted**
**¾ tsp vanilla essence**
**¼ tsp salt**

### ALMOND TUILES

Prepare mixture as instructed in Steps 1 to 3 above, but substitute ¼ teaspoon almond essence for vanilla essence and, before baking, sprinkle each biscuit generously with a single layer of flaked almonds; you will need about 75g almonds. Bake as instructed in Step 4, but remove warm biscuits from baking sheet and drape over rolling pin to curve. When firm, transfer to wire racks. Makes about 30.

Each biscuit: About 50 calories, 1g protein, 4g carbohydrate, 3g total fat (2g saturated), 6mg cholesterol, 45mg sodium

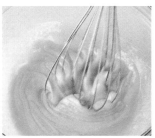

**1** Preheat oven to 180°C (350°F, Gas 4). Grease large baking sheet. Using wire whisk, beat egg whites, icing sugar and flour in large bowl until blended and smooth. Beat in remaining ingredients.

**2** Drop 1 heaped teaspoon mixture onto baking sheet. Repeat to make 4 biscuits in all, about 7–8cm apart.

**3** Using small palette knife, spread each biscuit into a 7cm round. (Do not place more than 4 on baking sheet because, after baking, cookies must be shaped quickly before hardening.)

**5** Repeat shaping with remaining biscuits on baking sheet. If biscuits become too hard to shape, return baking sheet to oven to soften biscuits slightly. Repeat Steps 2 to 4 with remaining mixture. (Mixture will become slightly thicker upon standing.) Store biscuits in tightly covered container.

**4** Bake biscuits 5–7 minutes until edges are golden. Using spatula, quickly transfer 1 biscuit to wire rack. Gently shape warm biscuit to flute edges; leave biscuits on wire rack to cool. (If you like, omit shaping biscuits and cool flat on wire rack.)

EACH BISCUIT: ABOUT 40 CALORIES, 1g PROTEIN, 4g CARBOHYDRATE, 2g TOTAL FAT (1g SATURATED), 12mg CHOLESTEROL, 45mg SODIUM

**CHOPPING NUTS**

Nuts can be tricky to keep in place while chopping. The best way is to hold down the tip of chef's knife with one hand while raising and lowering the handle with the other. Work the blade fan-wise back and forth across the nuts on a chopping board.

# JUMBO PECAN-DATE OATMEAL BISCUITS

*Prep: 30 minutes, plus cooling*
*Bake: 20–25 minutes per batch*
*Makes about 24*

225g butter or margarine, softened
150g caster sugar
150g light brown sugar
225g plain flour
1 tsp bicarbonate of soda
1 tsp vanilla essence
½ tsp salt
½ tsp ground cinnamon
2 medium eggs
240g rolled oats
300g stoned dates, chopped
125g pecans, chopped

◆ Preheat oven to 180°C (350°F, Gas 4). Using electric mixer on medium speed, beat butter and both sugars in large bowl about 5 minutes until light and creamy. Reduce speed to low; add flour and next 5 ingredients. Beat just until blended, occasionally scraping bowl with rubber spatula. Using wooden spoon, stir in oats, dates and pecans.

◆ Drop dough 4 tablespoons at a time, about 7–8cm apart, on ungreased large baking sheet. Bake biscuits 20–25 minutes until golden. Using spatula, transfer to wire racks to cool. Repeat with remaining dough. Store biscuits in tightly covered container.

**Each biscuit: About 250 calories, 4g protein, 35g carbohydrate, 12g total fat (4g saturated), 38mg cholesterol, 195mg sodium**

# PEANUT-BRITTLE BISCUITS

*Prep: 25 minutes, plus cooling*
*Bake: 15–20 minutes per batch*
*Makes about 18*

260g smooth peanut butter
125g butter or margarine, softened
100g light brown sugar
50g caster sugar
1 tsp bicarbonate of soda
½ tsp vanilla essence
¼ tsp salt
1 medium egg
150g plain flour
225g peanut brittle, coarsely chopped

◆ Preheat oven to 180°C (350°F, Gas 4). Using electric mixer on medium speed, beat first 8 ingredients in large bowl until blended, occasionally scraping bowl with rubber spatula. Reduce speed to low. Add flour; beat just until blended.

◆ Drop dough by heaped tablespoons, about 5cm apart, on ungreased large baking sheet. Top dough with chopped peanut-brittle pieces, gently pressing brittle halfway into dough.

◆ Bake 15–20 minutes until lightly browned. Cool 2 minutes on baking sheet; using spatula, transfer to wire racks to cool completely. Repeat with remaining dough and peanut brittle. Store in tightly covered container.

**Each biscuit: About 245 calories, 6g protein, 26g carbohydrate, 14g total fat (4g saturated), 27mg cholesterol, 235mg sodium**

# DOUBLE-CHOCOLATE CHUNK BISCUITS

*Prep: 30 minutes, plus cooling*
*Bake: 25–30 minutes per batch*
*Makes about 18*

350g plain chocolate, chopped
225g butter or margarine, softened
140g light brown sugar
70g caster sugar
1 tsp bicarbonate of soda
2 tsp vanilla essence
½ tsp salt
1 medium egg
300g plain flour
225g walnuts, coarsely chopped

◆ Melt 175g chocolate in heavy small saucepan over low heat, stirring frequently, until melted and smooth. Remove pan from heat; allow to cool to room temperature.

◆ Preheat oven to 180°C (350°F, Gas 4). Using electric mixer on low speed, beat butter, both sugars, bicarbonate of soda, vanilla essence and salt in large bowl until crumbly. Add melted chocolate and egg; beat until well blended, occasionally scraping bowl with rubber spatula. Using wooden spoon, stir in flour, walnuts and remaining 175g chocolate pieces until well mixed.

◆ Drop dough 4 tablespoons at a time, about 7–8cm apart, on ungreased large baking sheet. Bake biscuits 25–30 minutes, until edges are set but centres are still soft. Using spatula, transfer biscuits to wire racks to cool completely. Repeat with remaining dough. Store biscuits in tightly covered container.

**Each biscuit: About 360 calories, 5g protein, 37g carbohydrate, 24g total fat (5g saturated), 39mg cholesterol, 255mg sodium**

# CHOCOLATE-ESPRESSO WALNUT CLUSTERS

*Prep: 30 minutes, plus cooling    Bake: 15 minutes per batch*
*Makes about 36*

| | |
|---|---|
| 90g plain chocolate, melted | 2 tsp vanilla essence |
| 150g plain flour | 1 tsp salt |
| 200g sugar | ½ tsp baking powder |
| 125g butter or margarine, softened | 2 medium eggs |
| 1 tbsp instant espresso-coffee powder | 450g walnuts, coarsely broken |

◈ Preheat oven to 180°C (350°F, Gas 4). Combine all ingredients except walnuts in large bowl. Using electric mixer on low speed, beat ingredients until well mixed, occasionally scraping bowl with rubber spatula. Using wooden spoon, stir in walnuts.

◈ Drop dough by rounded tablespoons, about 2–3cm apart, onto ungreased large baking sheet. Bake 15 minutes, until set. Using spatula, transfer biscuits to wire racks to cool. Repeat with remaining dough. Store biscuits in tightly covered container.

**Each biscuit: About 160 calories, 3g protein, 11g carbohydrate, 12g total fat (3g saturated), 19mg cholesterol, 100mg sodium**

# FRUITCAKE BISCUITS

*Prep: 50 minutes, plus cooling    Bake: 12 minutes per batch*
*Makes about 66*

| | |
|---|---|
| 225g plain flour | 2 medium eggs |
| 200g dark brown sugar | 225g red glacé cherries, coarsely chopped |
| 90g butter or margarine, softened | 125g green glacé cherries, coarsely chopped |
| ½ tsp salt | 125g walnuts, coarsely chopped |
| ½ tsp bicarbonate of soda | |
| ½ tsp baking powder | |
| ½ tsp almond essence | |

◈ Preheat oven to 200°C (400°F, Gas 6). Using electric mixer on low speed, beat flour and next 7 ingredients together in large bowl until well blended, occasionally scraping bowl with rubber spatula.

◈ Reserve 125g chopped red and green glacé cherries. Using spoon, stir walnuts and remaining glacé cherries into biscuit dough. Drop dough by heaped teaspoons, about 2–3cm apart, onto ungreased large baking sheet. Decorate tops of biscuits with some of reserved cherries.

◈ Bake biscuits 12 minutes, or until golden. Using spatula, carefully transfer biscuits to wire racks to cool. Repeat with remaining dough and glacé cherries. Store biscuits in tightly covered container.

**Each biscuit: About 60 calories, 1g protein, 10g carbohydrate, 2g total fat (0g saturated), 9mg cholesterol, 45mg sodium**

# APPLE-OATMEAL BISCUITS

*Prep: 25 minutes, plus cooling    Bake: 20 minutes per batch*
*Makes about 48*

| | |
|---|---|
| 300g caster sugar | 2 medium eggs |
| 125g butter or margarine, softened | 2 medium Granny Smith's apples, peeled, cored and diced |
| 225g plain flour | 240g rolled oats |
| 1 tsp bicarbonate of soda | 150g raisins |
| 1 tsp ground cinnamon | 90g walnuts, chopped |
| 1 tsp vanilla essence | |
| ½ tsp salt | |

◈ Preheat oven to 180°C (350°F, Gas 4). Using electric mixer on medium speed, beat sugar and butter together in large bowl about 5 minutes, until light and creamy.

◈ Add flour, bicarbonate of soda, cinnamon, vanilla essence, salt and eggs; beat just until blended, occasionally scraping bowl with rubber spatula. Using wooden spoon, stir in diced apples, rolled oats, raisins and chopped walnuts until well mixed.

◈ Drop dough by heaped tablespoons, about 7–8cm apart, onto ungreased large baking sheet. Bake biscuits 20 minutes, until golden. Using spatula, transfer to wire racks to cool. Repeat with remaining dough. Store biscuits in tightly covered container.

**Each biscuit: About 120 calories, 2g protein, 16g carbohydrate, 5g total fat (1g saturated), 15mg cholesterol, 95mg sodium**

Apple-oatmeal biscuits          Fruitcake biscuits          Chocolate-espresso walnut clusters

## LACY PECAN CRISPS

*Prep: 40 minutes, plus cooling   Bake: 6–8 minutes per batch*
*Makes about 60*

175g pecan halves
90g butter, softened
100g light brown sugar

110g golden syrup
115g plain flour
½ tsp vanilla essence

◆ Preheat oven to 190°C (375°F, Gas 5). Grease large baking sheet. Set aside 60 pecan halves for decoration; finely chop remainder.

◆ Bring butter, brown sugar and golden syrup to the boil in 2-litre saucepan over medium heat (do not use margarine, because it would separate from sugar during cooking); remove from heat. Using wooden spoon, stir in chopped pecans, flour and vanilla essence.

◆ Drop 1 level teaspoon mixture onto baking sheet; top with a pecan half. Repeat to make 8 biscuits, placing them about 7–8cm apart. Bake biscuits 6–8 minutes, until lightly browned.

◆ Remove baking sheet from oven; let cool about 30 seconds to set slightly. Using spatula, quickly loosen biscuits and transfer to wire rack to cool completely. Repeat with remaining dough and pecan halves. Store biscuits in tightly covered container.

**Each biscuit: About 45 calories, 0g protein, 5g carbohydrate, 3g total fat (1g saturated), 6mg cholesterol, 15mg sodium**

## COCONUT-ALMOND MACAROONS

*Prep: 15 minutes, plus cooling   Bake: 20–25 minutes per batch*
*Makes about 18*

200g desiccated coconut
125g flaked almonds
100g sugar

¼ tsp salt
4 medium egg whites
1 tsp almond essence

◆ Preheat oven to 170°C (325°F, Gas 3). Grease large baking sheet. Using wooden spoon, mix coconut, almonds, sugar and salt in large bowl until combined. Stir in egg whites and almond essence until well blended.

◆ Drop mixture by heaped tablespoons, about 5cm apart, on baking sheet. Bake 20–25 minutes, until golden. Using spatula, transfer biscuits to wire racks to cool completely. Repeat with remaining dough. Store biscuits in tightly covered container.

**Each biscuit: About 110 calories, 3g protein, 11g carbohydrate, 7g total fat (3g saturated), 0mg cholesterol, 45mg sodium**

## SESAME CRISPS

*Prep: 20 minutes, plus cooling   Bake: 8 minutes per batch*
*Makes about 36*

90g butter, softened
140g sugar
1 tsp vanilla essence
¼ tsp salt
¼ tsp baking powder
1 medium egg
75g plus 2 tbsp plain flour

4 tsp white sesame seeds, toasted (see page 318)
4 tsp black sesame seeds (available in Oriental food shops; or use all white sesame seeds)

◆ Preheat oven to 180°C (350°F, Gas 4). Grease large baking sheet. Using electric mixer on medium speed, beat first 5 ingredients together in large bowl until blended. Add egg; beat until well combined. Using wooden spoon, stir in flour until well combined.

◆ Spoon half of dough into a small bowl; stir in toasted white sesame seeds. Stir black sesame seeds into dough remaining in large bowl. Drop doughs by rounded teaspoons, about 7–8cm apart, onto baking sheet. Bake biscuits about 8 minutes, until set and edges are golden.

◆ Remove baking sheet from oven; let biscuits cool on sheet about 30 seconds to set slightly. Using spatula, transfer to wire racks to cool completely. Repeat with remaining biscuit doughs. Store biscuits in tightly covered container.

**Each biscuit: About 45 calories, 1g protein, 5g carbohydrate, 2g total fat (1g saturated), 16mg cholesterol, 40mg sodium**

Sesame crisps

Lacy pecan crisps

Coconut-almond macaroons

# SHAPED AND PRESSED BISCUITS

For success, the dough for shaped biscuits should be firm enough to be moulded by hand. If it's too soft to handle, refrigerate it for 1 hour and try again. The dough for pressed biscuits needs to be soft enough to be forced through a piping bag or biscuit press, but still firm enough to hold its shape when baked.

## WALNUT CRESCENTS

*Prep: 45 minutes, plus chilling and cooling*
*Bake: 20 minutes per batch*
*Makes about 72*

125g walnuts
100g caster sugar
125g butter, softened
300g plain flour
125ml soured cream
2 tsp vanilla essence
¼ tsp salt
60g icing sugar

### VARIATIONS

Instead of shaping these rich, short biscuits into crescents, in Step 4 simply roll the dough into 2–3cm balls; bake and roll in icing sugar as instructed. If you like, substitute pecans or almonds for the walnuts. Or, try toasted, skinned hazelnuts (see page 522) and omit pan-toasting in Step 1.

**1** Lightly toast walnuts in 26cm frying pan over medium heat, shaking pan frequently. Set pan aside until walnuts are cool.

**2** Blend cooled walnuts and 50g caster sugar in food processor with knife blade attached, until walnuts are very finely chopped. Using electric mixer on low speed, beat butter and remaining 50g caster sugar in large bowl until blended, occasionally scraping bowl with rubber spatula.

**3** Increase speed to high; beat about 5 minutes until light and fluffy. Reduce speed to low; gradually beat in flour, soured cream, vanilla, salt and walnut mixture until blended. Divide dough in half; wrap each half in cling film and refrigerate 1 hour, or until dough is firm enough to handle. (Or, place dough in freezer 30 minutes.) Meanwhile, preheat oven to 190°C (325°F, Gas 5).

**4** Using lightly floured hands and working with half of dough at a time, shape by rounded teaspoons into 2–3 by 1cm crescents. Place crescents, about 4cm apart, on ungreased large baking sheet. Bake biscuits 20 minutes, or until lightly browned around edges. Cool biscuits on sheet on wire rack 2 minutes. Place icing sugar in small bowl.

**5** While still warm, but not piping hot, gently roll biscuits, one at a time, in icing sugar to coat. Cool completely on wire racks. Repeat with remaining dough and icing sugar. Store biscuits in tightly covered container.

EACH BISCUIT: ABOUT 55 CALORIES, 1g PROTEIN, 5g CARBOHYDRATE, 4g TOTAL FAT (2g SATURATED), 12mg CHOLESTEROL, 35mg SODIUM

## ALMOND LOGS

*Prep:* 25 minutes, plus cooling   *Bake:* 20–25 minutes per batch
*Makes* 24

400–450g marzipan, cut into     2 medium egg whites
  2–3cm chunks                       225g flaked almonds
40g icing sugar

◆ Preheat oven to 170°C (325°F, Gas 3). Grease and flour large baking sheet. Using electric mixer on low speed, beat marzipan in small bowl until crumbly. Add icing sugar and egg whites; beat until well blended (dough will be sticky and wet). Place flaked almonds on sheet of parchment paper. Using lightly floured hands, roll 1 level tablespoon dough into a 7–8cm-long log. Place dough log on almonds; gently press and stick almonds into dough to cover.

◆ Repeat with more dough and almonds to make 12 logs, placing logs on baking sheet, about 2–3cm apart, as they are formed. Bake 20–25 minutes, until golden and set. Transfer to wire racks to cool. Repeat with remaining dough and almonds. Store biscuits in tightly covered container.

**Each biscuit: About 140 calories, 4g protein, 13g carbohydrate, 8g total fat (1g saturated), 0mg cholesterol, 10mg sodium**

## GINGER BISCUITS

*Prep:* 40 minutes, plus cooling   *Bake:* 7–10 minutes per batch
*Makes* about 48

200g brown sugar                     ¾ tsp bicarbonate of soda
150g white vegetable fat,       ½ tsp salt
  softened                             ¼ tsp ground cloves
165g golden syrup                    1 medium egg
60ml milk                                  525g plain flour
2 tsp baking powder                50g caster sugar
1½ tsp ground ginger             40g crystallized ginger, cut
1 tsp ground cinnamon              into 5mm pieces (optional)

◆ Preheat oven to 180°C (350°F, Gas 4). Using electric mixer on low speed, mix first 11 ingredients and 300g flour together in large bowl until blended. Using wooden spoon, stir in remaining 225g flour. Place sugar in small bowl. Roll biscuit dough into 4cm balls; roll each ball in sugar to coat. Place 12 balls, 5cm apart, on ungreased large baking sheet.

◆ Gently press 1 piece of crystallized ginger, if using, into centre of each ball on baking sheet, flattening it slightly. Bake 7–10 minutes, or until bases are lightly browned. Transfer biscuits to wire racks to cool. Repeat with remaining dough and crystallized ginger. Store biscuits in tightly covered container.

**Each biscuit: About 85 calories, 1g protein, 14g carbohydrate, 3g total fat (1g saturated), 4mg cholesterol, 65mg sodium**

## CHOCOLATE, RASPBERRY AND ALMOND SPRITZ

*Prep:* 50 minutes, plus cooling and chilling
*Bake:* 12–14 minutes per batch
*Makes* about 30

60g blanched whole almonds      1 medium egg
150g sugar                                   60ml plus 2 tbsp whipping
340g plain flour                             cream
225g butter, softened                 175g plain chocolate, finely
1½ tsp almond essence                 chopped
¼ tsp salt                                   3 tbsp seedless raspberry jam

◆ Preheat oven to 180°C (350°F, Gas 4). Blend blanched whole almonds with sugar in food processor with knife blade attached, pulsing processor on and off, until almonds are finely ground. (Or, grind almonds with sugar in batches in blender.)

◆ Using electric mixer on low speed, beat almond mixture, flour and next 4 ingredients together in large bowl just until blended, scraping bowl occasionally with rubber spatula. Spoon dough into large piping bag with large star nozzle (about 2cm in diameter).

◆ Pipe teardrop shapes (about 5 by 4cm) or press through biscuit press, 2–3cm apart, onto ungreased large baking sheet. Bake biscuits 12–14 minutes, until lightly browned around edges. Cool slightly on baking sheet. Using spatula, transfer biscuits to wire rack to cool completely. Repeat with remaining dough.

◆ Prepare filling: bring cream to the boil in 1-litre saucepan over low heat. Place chocolate in small bowl with jam. Pour hot cream over chocolate mixture; let stand 1 minute. Stir until smooth. Refrigerate 15–18 minutes, until firm enough to spread. (If mixture becomes too firm, let stand at room temperature until slightly softened.)

◆ Using small palette knife, spread about 1 rounded teaspoon filling onto flat side of half of cooled biscuits. Top with remaining biscuits, flat-side down. Store filled biscuits in refrigerator.

**Each biscuit: About 160 calories, 2g protein, 17g carbohydrate, 10g total fat (7g saturated), 44mg cholesterol, 85mg sodium**

# ROLLED BISCUITS

These biscuits are rolled out and cut into a myriad of shapes with decorative cutters, a pastry wheel, or a sharp knife. They require a firm dough that is often refrigerated (this relaxes the gluten and yields a more tender biscuit). Biscuits made with butter (instead of margarine or a spread) hold their shape best. Cut out the biscuits as close to one another as possible to reduce excessive re-rolling of the scraps.

## TWO-TONE BISCUITS

*Prep: 1 hour, plus cooling*  *Bake: 12–15 minutes per batch*
*Makes 36*

| | |
|---|---|
| 175g butter or margarine, softened | ½ tsp salt |
| 140g plus 3 tsp sugar | 1 medium egg |
| 1 tsp baking powder | 300g plain flour |
| 1½ tsp vanilla essence | 30g cocoa powder |

**1** Grease and flour 2 baking sheets. Using electric mixer on low speed, beat butter and 140g sugar until blended. Increase speed to high; beat until light and creamy. Reduce speed to low. Add baking powder, vanilla essence, salt, egg, 225g flour and *2 tablespoons water*; beat until blended.

**2** Place half of dough in medium bowl; using wooden spoon, stir in remaining 75g flour. Stir cocoa into dough remaining in large bowl. Using floured rolling pin, roll vanilla dough on lightly floured surface until 2mm thick.

**3** Preheat oven to 180°C (350°F, Gas 4). Cut vanilla dough into as many biscuits as possible using a floured 7–8cm round scallop-shaped biscuit cutter. Reserve trimmings. Place on baking sheet, about 3mm apart. Repeat with chocolate dough, placing biscuits on second baking sheet.

**4** Cut out small round in centre of each vanilla and chocolate biscuit using 4cm round scallop-shaped biscuit cutter.

**5** Fit a small vanilla biscuit cut-out into centre of each chocolate biscuit and a small chocolate biscuit cut-out into centre of each vanilla biscuit to make two-tone biscuits.

**6** Sprinkle biscuits lightly with 2 teaspoons sugar. Place baking sheets on 2 oven racks; bake 12–15 minutes, until golden, rotating baking sheets between upper and lower racks halfway through baking time. Using spatula, transfer biscuits to wire racks to cool. Gather trimmings, re-roll, and cut out more biscuits. Sprinkle biscuits with remaining 1 teaspoon sugar and bake as above. Store biscuits in tightly covered container.

EACH BISCUIT: ABOUT 75 CALORIES, 1g PROTEIN, 9g CARBOHYDRATE, 4g TOTAL FAT (2g SATURATED), 16mg CHOLESTEROL, 90mg SODIUM

## CLASSIC SUGAR BISCUIT ASSORTMENT

*Prep: 45 minutes, plus chilling, cooling and decorating*
*Bake: 12–15 minutes per batch*    *Makes about 48*

| | |
|---|---|
| 150g caster sugar | 2 tsp vanilla essence |
| 150g butter, softened | 1 medium egg |
| 1 tsp baking powder | 300g plain flour |
| ½ tsp salt | Ornamental Icing (optional, |
| 2 tbsp milk | see below) |

◆ Using electric mixer on low speed, beat first 4 ingredients together in large bowl until blended. Increase speed to high; beat until mixture is light and creamy. Reduce speed to low. Add milk, vanilla essence and egg; beat until blended. (Mixture may appear curdled.)

◆ Using wooden spoon, stir in flour until blended. Shape dough into 2 balls; flatten each slightly. Wrap each in cling film and refrigerate 1 hour, or until firm enough to roll. (Or, place dough in freezer 30 minutes.)

◆ Preheat oven to 180°C (350°F, Gas 4). Using floured rolling pin, roll 1 piece of dough on lightly floured surface until 2mm thick, keeping remaining dough refrigerated.

◆ Cut dough into as many biscuits as possible using floured assorted 7–10cm biscuit cutters; refrigerate dough trimmings. Place biscuits, about 2–3cm apart, on ungreased large baking sheet.

◆ Bake biscuits 12–15 minutes, until golden around edges. Using spatula, transfer biscuits to wire racks to cool. Repeat with remaining dough. Re-roll trimmings; cut out more biscuits and bake as above.

◆ When biscuits are cool, prepare Ornamental Icing, if you like, and use to decorate. Set biscuits aside at least 1 hour to allow icing to dry completely. Store biscuits in tightly covered container.

**Each biscuit: About 55 calories, 1g protein, 7g carbohydrate, 3g total fat (2g saturated), 11mg cholesterol, 60mg sodium**

## DECORATING BISCUITS

These iced Christmas biscuits (made from Classic Sugar Biscuit dough on this page and Gingerbread Cut-outs, page 513) are pretty enough to be used as tree decorations. If you like, with skewer or cocktail stick, make 1 or 2 holes in top of each biscuit before baking. Thread ribbon, string or clear nylon fishing line through finished biscuits for hanging from the tree.

**ORNAMENTAL ICING**  Using electric mixer on medium speed, beat 450g icing sugar, 3 tablespoons meringue powder (see page 30) and 75ml warm water together in large bowl about 5 minutes, until icing is stiff and knife drawn through it leaves a clean cut.
 If you like, separate portions of icing and tint with assorted food colourings as desired; keep covered with cling film to prevent drying out. Using small palette knife, artists' paint brushes, or piping bags with small writing nozzles, decorate biscuits with icing. (Thin icing with a little warm water if necessary to obtain the right consistency.) Makes about 450g.

Each 100g: About 425 calories, 0g protein, 96g carbohydrate, 0g total fat, 0mg cholesterol, 50mg sodium

## HAZELNUT SPICE CUT-OUTS

*Prep: 45 minutes, plus chilling and cooling*
*Bake: 10–12 minutes per batch*   **Makes** *about 24*

| | |
|---|---|
| 60g hazelnuts, toasted and skinned (see page 522), or walnuts | ½ tsp ground cinnamon |
| 100g light brown sugar | ½ tsp vanilla essence |
| 190g plain flour | ¼ tsp ground allspice |
| 90g butter or margarine, softened | ¼ tsp salt |
| | 1 medium egg |

◈ Blend nuts with sugar in food processor with knife blade attached or in blender at high speed, until finely ground.

◈ Using electric mixer on low speed, beat nut mixture with remaining ingredients in large bowl just until mixed, occasionally scraping bowl with rubber spatula. Divide dough in half; pat each half into a 2–3cm-thick disc. Wrap each half in cling film and refrigerate 1 hour, or until firm enough to roll. (Or, place dough in freezer 30 minutes.)

◈ Preheat oven to 180°C (350°F, Gas 4). Grease large baking sheet. Using floured rolling pin, roll half of dough on well-floured surface until 2mm thick. Cut dough into as many biscuits as possible using floured assorted 7–10cm biscuit cutters; reserve trimmings.

◈ Place biscuits, about 2–3cm apart, on baking sheet. Bake biscuits 10–12 minutes, until edges are golden. Transfer biscuits to wire racks to cool. Repeat with remaining dough. Re-roll trimmings and cut out more biscuits. Store biscuits in tightly covered container.

**Each biscuit: About 80 calories, 1g protein, 10g carbohydrate, 5g total fat (2g saturated), 17mg cholesterol, 60mg sodium**

## TOASTED WALNUT CRISPS

*Prep: 30 minutes, plus cooling*   **Bake:** *20 minutes*
**Makes** *about 16*

| | |
|---|---|
| 225g walnuts | 175g butter or margarine, diced |
| 200g plain flour | |
| 120g icing sugar | 1 tbsp vanilla essence |
| 2 tbsp cornflour | 1 tbsp milk |
| ¼ tsp salt | 1 tbsp caster sugar |

◈ Reserve 40g walnuts for topping. In 30cm frying pan, toast remaining walnuts over medium heat, shaking pan frequently, until golden brown; cool and chop walnuts.

◈ Preheat oven to 170°C (325°F, Gas 3). Stir chopped toasted walnuts, flour, icing sugar, cornflour and salt together in large bowl until well mixed. Knead butter and vanilla essence into flour mixture until well blended and

mixture holds together. Gently knead dough 5–6 times on lightly floured surface, with floured hands until smooth, sprinkling with extra flour if needed.

◈ Using floured rolling pin, roll out dough 5mm thick. Cut dough into as many rounds as possible with floured 7–8cm fluted round biscuit cutter; reserve trimmings. Place biscuits on ungreased large baking sheet, about 2–3cm apart.

◈ Re-roll trimmings and cut out more biscuits. Brush biscuits with milk; sprinkle with caster sugar. Press 1 walnut into each. Bake 20 minutes, or until golden. Transfer to wire racks to cool. Store in tightly covered container.

**Each biscuit: About 240 calories, 3g protein, 18g carbohydrate, 18g total fat (5g saturated), 24mg cholesterol, 135mg sodium**

## GINGERBREAD CUT-OUTS

*Prep: 45 minutes, plus cooling and decorating*
*Bake: 12 minutes per batch*   **Makes** *about 36*

| | |
|---|---|
| 100g sugar | 125g butter or margarine, cut into chunks |
| 165g golden syrup | |
| 1½ tsp ground ginger | 1 medium egg, beaten |
| 1 tsp ground allspice | 525g plain flour |
| 1 tsp ground cinnamon | Ornamental Icing (optional, see page 512) |
| 1 tsp ground cloves | |
| 2 tsp bicarbonate of soda | |

◈ Preheat oven to 170°C (325°F, Gas 3). Bring first 6 ingredients to the boil in 3-litre saucepan over medium heat, stirring occasionally. Remove saucepan from heat; stir in bicarbonate of soda (mixture will foam up in the pan). Stir in butter until melted. Using fork, stir in egg, then flour.

◈ Knead dough on floured surface until thoroughly mixed. Divide in half. Wrap half in cling film; set aside. Using floured rolling pin, roll out remaining half of dough slightly less than 5mm thick. With floured assorted 7–10cm biscuit cutters, cut dough into as many biscuits as possible; reserve trimmings. Place biscuits, about 2–3cm apart, on ungreased large baking sheet.

◈ Bake biscuits 12 minutes, or until edges begin to brown. Transfer to wire racks to cool. Repeat with remaining dough. Re-roll trimmings and cut out more biscuits.

◈ When biscuits are cool, prepare Ornamental Icing, if you like, and use to decorate. Set biscuits aside at least 1 hour to allow icing to dry. Store in tightly covered container.

**Each biscuit: About 90 calories, 1g protein, 14g carbohydrate, 3g total fat (2g saturated), 13mg cholesterol, 100mg sodium**

## LINZER WREATHS

*Prep: 45 minutes, plus chilling and cooling*
*Bake: 10–12 minutes per batch  Makes about 20*

125g blanched whole almonds
140g caster sugar
1 tsp vanilla essence
340g plain flour
½ tsp bicarbonate of soda

225g butter or margarine,
  softened
30g icing sugar
215g seedless raspberry jam

◆ Blend almonds, 70g caster sugar and vanilla essence in food processor with knife blade attached or in blender at medium speed, until almonds are finely ground.

◆ Combine almond mixture, flour, bicarbonate of soda and remaining 70g caster sugar in large bowl. Using pastry blender or two knives used scissor-fashion, cut in butter until mixture resembles coarse crumbs. Knead until dough forms a ball. Divide ball into 2 pieces; wrap each in cling film. Refrigerate 1 hour, or until firm enough to roll. (Or, place dough in freezer 30 minutes.)

◆ Preheat oven to 180°C (350°F, Gas 4). Using floured rolling pin, roll out 1 piece of dough on lightly floured surface until 2mm thick; keep remaining dough refrigerated. Cut dough into as many rounds as possible with floured 7–8cm round biscuit cutter; reserve trimmings. Using floured 4cm round biscuit cutter, cut out centre of half of biscuits. Using spatula, place biscuits, about 2–3cm apart, on ungreased large baking sheet.

◆ Bake biscuits 10–12 minutes, until lightly browned. Using spatula, transfer biscuits to wire racks to cool completely. Repeat with remaining dough. Gather trimmings and cut-out centres, re-roll, and cut out more biscuits.

◆ Sprinkle icing sugar over biscuits with cut-out centres. Heat jam in small saucepan over low heat until melted. Brush whole biscuits with jam and top with cut-out biscuits. Store, between sheets of greaseproof paper, in tightly covered container.

**Each biscuit: About 220 calories, 3g protein, 27g carbohydrate, 12g total fat (5g saturated), 24mg cholesterol, 140mg sodium**

## APRICOT-RASPBERRY RUGELACH

*Prep: 1 hour, plus chilling and cooling  Bake: 30–35 minutes*
*Makes 48*

225g butter or margarine,
  softened
225g cream cheese, softened
1 tsp vanilla essence
¼ tsp salt
300g plain flour
150g caster sugar

125g walnuts, chopped
75g ready-to-eat dried
  apricots, chopped
50g light brown sugar
1½ tsp ground cinnamon
165g seedless raspberry jam
1 tbsp milk

◆ Using electric mixer on low speed, beat butter with cream cheese together in large bowl until blended and smooth. Beat in vanilla essence, salt, 150g flour and 50g caster sugar until blended. Using wooden spoon, stir in remaining 150g flour.

◆ Divide dough into 4 equal pieces. Wrap each piece in cling film; refrigerate at least 2 hours, until firm enough to roll, or overnight.

◆ Prepare filling: stir walnuts, apricots, brown sugar, 115g caster sugar, and ½ teaspoon cinnamon together in medium bowl until well mixed. Line 2 large baking sheets with foil; grease foil.

◆ Preheat oven to 170°C (325°F, Gas 3). Using floured rolling pin, roll out 1 piece of dough on lightly floured surface into a 23cm round; keep remaining dough refrigerated. Spread dough with 2 tablespoons jam. Sprinkle with about one quarter of filling; gently press filling onto dough.

◆ Using pastry wheel or sharp knife, cut dough into 12 equal wedges. Starting at curved edge, roll up each wedge, jelly-roll fashion. Place biscuits on baking sheet, point-side down, about 1cm apart. Repeat with remaining dough, jam and filling.

◆ Combine remaining 35g caster sugar with remaining 1 teaspoon cinnamon in cup. Brush rugelach with milk; sprinkle with cinnamon-sugar.

◆ Bake on 2 oven racks 30–35 minutes, until golden, rotating baking sheets between upper and lower racks halfway through baking time. Immediately transfer to wire racks to cool. Store in tightly covered container.

**Each biscuit: About 115 calories, 1g protein, 12g carbohydrate, 7g total fat (3g saturated), 15mg cholesterol, 70mg sodium**

Linzer wreaths

Apricot-raspberry
rugelach

# REFRIGERATED BISCUITS

The beauty of these biscuits is that you can enjoy warm-from-the-oven treats anytime. Simply prepare the dough and store it, wrapped and uncut, in the freezer for up to 2 months (or in the refrigerator for 1 week). Finish and bake the biscuits when you want them, storing them in a tightly covered container.

## COCONUT BUTTONS

❖ ❖ ❖ ❖ ❖ ❖ ❖ ❖ ❖ ❖ ❖ ❖

*Prep: 45 minutes, plus chilling and cooling*
*Bake: 20–25 minutes per batch*
*Makes about 78*

**225g butter, softened**
**100g caster sugar**
**2 tbsp milk**
**1 tsp coconut essence**
**¾ tsp baking powder**
**½ tsp salt**
**400g plain flour**
**150g flaked coconut, chopped**
**125g plain chocolate**
**1 tbsp white vegetable fat**

**BISCUIT TIP**

Although margarine and butter are equally suitable for most purposes, some biscuit recipes, such as the one above, call for butter only. This is because the dough would spread too much during baking if made with margarine. Always use butter if the recipe specifically calls for it.

1 Using electric mixer on medium-high speed, beat butter, sugar, milk, coconut essence, baking powder and salt together in large bowl until light and creamy. Using wooden spoon, stir in flour and chopped coconut (dough will be crumbly). Squeeze dough together with your hands; divide into 4 equal pieces. Shape each piece into a 25 by 2–3cm log. Wrap each log in cling film and slide onto small baking sheet for easier handling. Refrigerate dough overnight, or freeze at least 2 hours until firm enough to slice.

2 Preheat oven to 170°C (325°F, Gas 3). Cut 1 log into 1cm-thick slices (keep remaining logs refrigerated). Place slices, 2–3cm apart, on ungreased large baking sheet. Using cocktail stick, make 4 holes in each biscuit to resemble the holes of a button.

3 Bake biscuits 20–25 minutes until lightly golden. Transfer to wire racks to cool. Repeat with remaining dough. When biscuits are cool, melt chocolate with vegetable fat in small heavy saucepan over low heat, stirring frequently.

4 Dip base of each cooled biscuit into melted chocolate so that chocolate comes slightly up side of biscuit.

5 Using small palette knife, scrape excess chocolate from base of each biscuit, leaving a thin layer. Place biscuits, chocolate-side down, on parchment paper; set aside to allow chocolate to set completely. Store finished biscuits in tightly covered container.

EACH BISCUIT: ABOUT 55 CALORIES, 1g PROTEIN, 6g CARBOHYDRATE, 3g TOTAL FAT (2g SATURATED), 6mg CHOLESTEROL, 45mg SODIUM

## POPPY SEED PINWHEELS

*Prep: 40 minutes, plus chilling and cooling*
*Bake: 8–10 minutes per batch*  *Makes about 84*

| | |
|---|---|
| 375g plus 3 tbsp plain flour | 1 tsp salt |
| 325g caster sugar | 1 tsp vanilla essence |
| 3 medium eggs | 175ml milk |
| 175g margarine or butter, softened | 3 tbsp poppy seeds |
| | 100g ground almonds |
| 1 tsp baking powder | 75g sultanas, finely chopped |

◈ Using electric mixer on low speed, beat 375g flour, 200g sugar, 2 eggs and the next 4 ingredients in large bowl until well blended, occasionally scraping bowl. Divide dough in half; wrap each half in cling film and refrigerate 1 hour, or freeze 30 minutes, until firm enough to handle. Meanwhile, make filling: heat milk with remaining 125g sugar; stir until sugar dissolves. Add remaining 3 tablespoons flour, poppy seeds, almonds and sultanas. Cook until thickened. Beat in remaining egg and cool.

◈ Using floured rolling pin, roll out half of dough on a sheet of floured greaseproof paper into a 30 by 20cm rectangle; spread with half of filling. From a long side, roll dough Swiss roll fashion. Repeat with remaining dough and filling. Wrap in cling film; refrigerate overnight or freeze at least 1 hour, until firm enough to slice.

◈ Preheat oven to 180°C (350°F, Gas 4). Grease 2 baking sheets. Cut 1 log into 5mm-thick slices (keep remainder refrigerated). Place slices 2cm apart, on baking sheets. Bake 8–10 minutes, rotating halfway through cooking time, until edges are golden. Cool slightly on baking sheets. Transfer to wire rack to cool completely. Repeat with remaining dough.

**Each biscuit: About 60 calories, 1g protein, 9g carbohydrate, 3g total fat (0g saturated), 8mg cholesterol, 55mg sodium**

## SPICY ALMOND SLICES

*Prep: 25 minutes, plus chilling and cooling*
*Bake: 10–12 minutes per batch*  *Makes about 78*

| | |
|---|---|
| 525g plain flour | 1 tsp bicarbonate of soda |
| 225g margarine or butter, softened | 1 tsp vanilla essence |
| | ½ tsp ground cloves |
| 200g caster sugar | ½ tsp ground nutmeg |
| 150g dark brown sugar | 2 medium eggs |
| 1 tbsp ground cinnamon | 225g sliced blanched almonds |

◈ Using electric mixer on low speed, beat 300g flour and next 9 ingredients in bowl until well mixed. Stir in almonds and remaining 225g flour; mix well with hands. (Dough will be stiff.) Divide dough in half. Shape each half into 25 by 8 by 3cm brick; wrap in cling film. Refrigerate overnight or freeze at least 2 hours, until firm enough to slice.

◈ Preheat oven to 190°C (375°F, Gas 5). Cut 1 brick into 5mm-thick slices (keep remainder refrigerated). Place slices, 2–3cm apart, on 2 ungreased baking sheets. Bake 10–12 minutes, until browned around edges. Transfer biscuits to wire racks to cool. Repeat with remaining dough.

**Each biscuit: About 75 calories, 1g protein, 9g carbohydrate, 4g total fat (1g saturated), 5mg cholesterol, 45mg sodium**

## PECAN SQUARES

*Prep: 30 minutes, plus chilling and cooling*
*Bake: 12–15 minutes per batch*  *Makes about 60*

| | |
|---|---|
| 150g dark brown sugar | 375g plain flour |
| 125g margarine or butter, softened | ½ tsp bicarbonate of soda |
| | ½ tsp salt |
| 1 medium egg | 150g pecans, toasted and chopped |
| 2 tbsp milk | |
| 2 tsp vanilla essence | |

◈ Using electric mixer on medium-high speed, beat brown sugar and margarine together in large bowl until light and fluffy. Add egg, milk and vanilla essence; beat until smooth. Stir in flour, bicarbonate of soda and salt. When flour is almost blended, stir in pecans. (Dough will be very stiff.)

◈ Divide dough in half. Shape each half of dough on lightly floured surface into 20 by 4 by 4cm bar, using spatula to help flatten sides. Wrap each bar in cling film and slide onto small baking sheet for easier handling. Refrigerate dough overnight or freeze at least 2 hours, until very firm.

◈ Preheat oven to 180°C (350°F, Gas 4). Grease large baking sheet. Cut 1 bar into slightly less than 5mm-thick slices (keep remainder refrigerated). Place slices, about 4cm apart, on 2 baking sheets. Bake 12–15 minutes, until browned around edges. Transfer biscuits to wire racks to cool. Repeat with remaining dough.

**Each biscuit: About 60 calories, 1g protein, 7g carbohydrate, 3g total fat (0g saturated), 4mg cholesterol, 50mg sodium**

### ICED PECAN SQUARES

Prepare Pecan Squares as above. Mix 240g icing sugar and 2 tablespoons plus 2 teaspoons milk in medium bowl to make a thick icing, adding more milk if necessary. Spread some icing on top of each cooled biscuit with small palette knife; top each with a toasted pecan half (you will need about 175g toasted pecan halves). Set aside to allow icing to dry.

Each biscuit: About 90 calories, 1g protein, 11g carbohydrate, 5g total fat (1g saturated), 4mg cholesterol, 50mg sodium

# BISCOTTI

Biscotti are irresistible Italian biscuits made using a unique baking process. The dough is baked twice, first in a loaf shape, then again after the loaf has been cut into slices. The result is a dry, crunchy biscuit perfect for dipping into coffee or sweet wine. Flavours range from traditional almond and anise to modern variations made with chocolate, ginger or dried fruit.

## CRANBERRY-HAZELNUT BISCOTTI

*Prep:* 1 hour, plus cooling   *Bake:* 45–55 minutes
*Makes* about 54

560g plain flour
400g caster sugar
1 tsp baking powder
½ tsp salt
5 medium eggs
2 tsp vanilla essence

165g hazelnuts, toasted and skinned (see page 522), chopped
50g dried cranberries or currants

**1** Preheat oven to 180°C (350°F, Gas 4). Grease and lightly flour 2 large baking sheets. Combine first 4 ingredients in large bowl. Separate 1 egg; reserve white for glaze. Using wire whisk or fork, beat 4 whole eggs, 1 egg yolk, vanilla essence and *1 tablespoon water* together in small bowl. Pour egg mixture into flour mixture; stir until blended.

**2** Using your hands, knead dough until it comes together (dough will be very stiff). Knead in chopped hazelnuts and dried cranberries. Divide dough into 4 equal pieces.

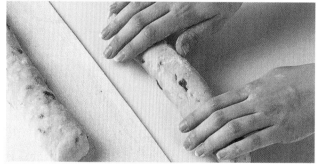

**3** Shape each piece of dough into a 28 by 5cm log on lightly floured surface with floured hands. Place 2 logs, about 10cm apart, on each baking sheet.

**4** Using fork, lightly beat reserved egg white in cup. Using pastry brush, brush logs with egg white. Bake logs on 2 oven racks 35–40 minutes, until cocktail stick inserted in centre comes out clean, rotating baking sheets between upper and lower racks halfway through baking time (logs will spread during baking and become loaf shaped). Cool loaves 10 minutes on baking sheets on wire racks.

**5** Transfer loaves to chopping board. Cut each loaf crosswise into ½-inch-thick diagonal slices using a serrated knife.

**6** Place slices, cut-side down, on same baking sheets in single layer. Bake slices on 2 oven racks 10–15 minutes, until golden, turning slices once and rotating baking sheets between upper and lower racks halfway through baking time. Transfer biscotti to wire racks to cool completely. (Biscotti will harden as they cool.) Store in tightly covered container.

EACH BISCUIT: ABOUT 85 CALORIES, 2g PROTEIN, 15g CARBOHYDRATE, 2g TOTAL FAT (0g SATURATED), 20mg CHOLESTEROL, 35mg SODIUM

## CHOCOLATE BISCOTTI

*Prep: 45 minutes, plus cooling and chilling*
*Bake: 45–50 minutes*    *Makes about 48*

200g caster sugar
225g margarine or butter, softened
375g plain flour
120g cocoa powder
1 tbsp baking powder
1 tsp instant-coffee granules
1 tsp vanilla essence
½ tsp salt
4 medium eggs
225g plain chocolate
30g flaked almonds, toasted

◈ Preheat oven to 180°C (350°F, Gas 4). Using electric mixer on medium speed, beat sugar and margarine together in large bowl until light and creamy. On low speed, beat in 150g flour and next 6 ingredients until blended. Using wooden spoon, stir in remaining 225g flour until blended. Divide dough in half. Using floured hands, shape dough into two 30 by 7cm loaves, 7–8cm apart, on ungreased large baking sheet. Bake 25–30 minutes, until firm. Cool on baking sheet on wire rack 20 minutes.

◈ Transfer loaves to chopping board. Cut each loaf crossways into 1cm-thick diagonal slices with serrated knife. Place slices, cut-side down, on 2 ungreased large baking sheets in single layer. Bake on 2 oven racks 20 minutes, turning slices once and rotating baking sheets between upper and lower racks halfway through cooking time. Transfer to wire racks to cool completely.

◈ Melt chocolate in heavy small saucepan over low heat until smooth, stirring frequently. Using pastry brush, brush top of each biscotti with some melted chocolate; sprinkle some almonds on chocolate. Refrigerate biscotti 30 minutes, or until chocolate is set. Store in tightly covered container.

**Each biscuit: About 110 calories, 2g protein, 13g carbohydrate, 6g total fat (2g saturated), 18mg cholesterol, 105mg sodium**

## ALMOND-ANISE BISCOTTI

*Prep: 25 minutes, plus cooling*
*Bake: 55 minutes*    *Makes about 84*

125g whole almonds
1 tbsp anise seeds, crushed
1 tbsp anise-flavoured aperitif or liqueur
300g plain flour
200g caster sugar
1 tsp baking powder
⅛ tsp salt
3 medium eggs

◈ Preheat oven to 170°C (325°F, Gas 3). Place almonds on Swiss roll tin. Bake 10 minutes until lightly toasted. Cool; chop very coarsely. Meanwhile, combine anise seeds and aperitif in medium bowl; let stand 10 minutes.

◈ Grease large baking sheet. Combine flour, sugar, baking powder, salt and almonds in large bowl. Whisk eggs into anise mixture. Using wooden spoon, stir egg mixture into flour mixture. Divide dough in half.

◈ Using floured hands (dough will be sticky), shape dough into two 38cm logs, 7–8cm apart, on baking sheet.

◈ Bake logs 40 minutes, or until golden and cocktail stick inserted in centre of log comes out clean. Cool on baking sheet on wire rack 10 minutes.

◈ Transfer logs to chopping board. Cut each crossways into 5mm-thick diagonal slices with serrated knife.

◈ Place slices, cut-side down, on 2 ungreased baking sheets in single layer. Bake on 2 oven racks 15 minutes, turning slices once and rotating baking sheets between upper and lower racks halfway through baking time. Transfer to wire racks to cool completely. Store in tightly covered container.

**Each biscuit: About 30 calories, 1g protein, 5g carbohydrate, 1g total fat (0g saturated), 8mg cholesterol, 15mg sodium**

## GINGER BISCOTTI

*Prep: 25 minutes, plus cooling*
*Bake: 48–50 minutes*
*Makes about 42*

450g plain flour
1 tbsp ground ginger
2 tsp baking powder
¼ tsp salt
125g margarine or butter, softened
100g caster sugar
100g brown sugar
3 medium eggs
90g crystallized ginger, very finely chopped

◈ Preheat oven to 180°C (350°F, Gas 4). Grease large baking sheet. Combine first 4 ingredients together in medium bowl.

◈ Using electric mixer on medium speed, beat margarine with both caster and brown sugar in large bowl until light and creamy. Beat in eggs, 1 at a time. On low speed, beat in flour mixture until blended. Using wooden spoon, stir in crystallized ginger. Divide dough in half.

◈ Using floured hands, shape dough into two 30cm logs, 7–8cm apart, on baking sheet.

◈ Bake 30 minutes, or until cocktail stick inserted in centre of log comes out clean. Cool on baking sheet on wire rack 10 minutes. Transfer logs to chopping board. Cut each crossways into 1cm-thick diagonal slices with serrated knife.

◈ Place slices, cut-side down, on 2 ungreased baking sheets in single layer. Bake on 2 oven racks 18–20 minutes, until golden, turning slices once and rotating baking sheets between upper and lower racks halfway through baking time. Transfer biscotti to wire racks to cool. Store in tightly covered container.

**Each biscuit: About 80 calories, 1g protein, 13g carbohydrate, 3g total fat (1g saturated), 15mg cholesterol, 70mg sodium**

# BROWNIES

The classic American brownie (so-named because of it's traditional chocolate flavour) has now become a favourite in England too. The attraction probably lies in their consistency – they can be dense and chewy or light and cake-like, studded with nuts or iced. If not using brownies within 3 days, cover tightly and freeze for future treats.

## ALMOND CHEESECAKE BROWNIES

◆ ◆ ◆ ◆ ◆ ◆ ◆ ◆ ◆ ◆ ◆ ◆

*Prep: 30 minutes, plus cooling*
*Bake: 40–45 minutes*
*Makes 24*

175g margarine or butter
250g plain chocolate, broken into chunks
400g caster sugar
6 medium eggs
2½ tsp vanilla essence
225g plain flour
¾ tsp baking powder
½ tsp salt
350g cream cheese, slightly softened
¾ tsp almond essence

**1** Preheat oven to 180°C (350°F, Gas 4). Line 33 by 20cm metal baking tin with foil; lightly grease foil. Melt margarine and chocolate in heavy 3-litre saucepan over low heat, stirring frequently. Remove from heat. Beat in 300g sugar, then beat in 4 eggs and 2 teaspoons vanilla essence until well blended. Stir in flour, baking powder and salt just until blended; set aside.

**2** Using electric mixer on medium speed, beat cream cheese until smooth. Gradually beat in remaining 100g sugar. Beat in almond essence, remaining 2 eggs and remaining ½ teaspoon vanilla essence just until blended.

**3** Spread 350g chocolate mixture evenly in base of baking tin.

**4** Spoon cream cheese mixture in 6 large dollops on top of chocolate mixture (cheese mixture will cover much of chocolate mixture). Spoon remaining chocolate mixture in 6 large dollops over and between cheese mixture.

**5** With tip of knife, cut and twist through mixtures to create marble design. Bake 40–45 minutes, until cocktail stick inserted 5cm from centre comes out almost clean with a few moist crumbs attached. Cool brownies in tin on wire rack. When cool, cut brownies lengthways into 4 strips, then cut each strip crossways into 6 pieces.

EACH BROWNIE: ABOUT 260 CALORIES, 4g PROTEIN, 27g CARBOHYDRATE, 16g TOTAL FAT (7g SATURATED), 69mg CHOLESTEROL, 185mg SODIUM

## CHOCOLATE AND PEANUT BUTTER BROWNIES

*Prep: 20 minutes, plus cooling    Bake: 25–30 minutes*

### Makes 24

| | |
|---|---|
| 120g plain chocolate, broken into chunks | 350g light brown sugar |
| 375g plain flour | 260g smooth peanut butter |
| 1½ tsp baking powder | 3 medium eggs |
| ½ tsp salt | 2 tsp vanilla essence |
| 125g margarine or butter, slightly softened | 175g plain chocolate drops |

◆ Preheat oven to 180°C (350°F, Gas 4). Melt chocolate in heavy 1-litre saucepan over low heat, stirring frequently. Remove from heat. Mix flour, baking powder and salt together in medium bowl.

◆ Using electric mixer on medium speed, beat margarine, brown sugar and peanut butter in large bowl about 2 minutes until smooth. Reduce speed to low. Beat in eggs and vanilla essence until blended. Beat in flour mixture just until combined (dough will be stiff).

◆ Place one-third of dough in another large bowl. Stir in melted plain chocolate until blended; stir in 130g plain chocolate drops.

◆ Pat half of remaining peanut butter dough into ungreased 33 by 20cm metal baking tin. Drop remaining peanut butter dough and chocolate dough in random pattern on top; pat down with hand. Sprinkle with remaining chocolate drops.

### PRALINE-ICED BROWNIES

Prepare Classic Brownies (right). While brownies are cooling, prepare topping: heat 75g margarine or butter and 75g light brown sugar in 2-litre saucepan over medium-low heat about 4 minutes, until mixture melts and bubbles. Remove from heat. Using wire whisk, beat in 3 tablespoons brandy (or 1 tablespoon vanilla essence plus 2 tablespoons water), then beat in 240g icing sugar until smooth. Using palette knife, spread topping over room-temperature brownies in tin. Sprinkle top of brownies with 60g toasted and coarsely chopped pecans. Cut brownies lengthways into 8 strips; cut each strip crossways into 8 pieces. Makes 64.

Each brownie: About 115 calories, 1g protein, 15g carbohydrate, 6g total fat (2g saturated), 20mg cholesterol, 65mg sodium

◆ Bake brownies 25–30 minutes until cocktail stick inserted in centre comes out clean. Cool in tin on wire rack. When cool, cut lengthways into 4 strips; cut each strip crossways into 6 pieces.

Each brownie: About 265 calories, 5g protein, 34g carbohydrate, 14g total fat (3g saturated), 27mg cholesterol, 185mg sodium

## COCOA BROWNIES

*Prep: 10 minutes, plus cooling    Bake: 25 minutes*

### Makes 16

| | |
|---|---|
| 125g margarine or butter | 60g cocoa powder |
| 200g caster sugar | ¼ tsp baking powder |
| 2 medium eggs | ¼ tsp salt |
| 1 tsp vanilla essence | 125g walnuts, coarsely chopped |
| 75g plain flour | |

Preheat oven to 180°C (350°F, Gas 4). Grease 22cm square metal baking tin. Melt margarine in 3-litre saucepan over medium heat. Remove from heat; stir in sugar. Stir in eggs, 1 at a time, and vanilla essence until well blended. Combine flour and next 3 ingredients in bowl; stir flour mixture into pan until blended. Stir in nuts, if using. Spread mixture evenly in tin. Bake 25 minutes, or until cocktail stick inserted 5cm from centre comes out almost clean. Cool in tin on wire rack. When cool, cut brownies into 4 strips; cut each strip crossways into 4 squares.

Each brownie: About 130 calories, 2g protein, 17g carbohydrate, 7g total fat (1g saturated), 27mg cholesterol, 115mg sodium

## CLASSIC BROWNIES

*Prep: 20 minutes, plus cooling    Bake: 35 minutes*

### Makes 24

| | |
|---|---|
| 225g margarine or butter | 6 medium eggs |
| 250g plain chocolate, broken into chunks | 2 tsp vanilla essence |
| 450g sugar | ½ tsp salt |
| | 190g plain flour |

Preheat oven to 180°C (350°F, Gas 4). Line 33 by 20cm metal baking tin with foil; grease foil. Melt margarine and chocolate in heavy 3-litre saucepan over low heat, stirring frequently. Remove from heat. Using whisk, beat in sugar, then eggs, until well blended. Stir in vanilla essence, salt, then flour just until blended. Spread mixture evenly in tin. Bake 35 minutes, or until cocktail stick inserted 5cm from centre comes out almost clean with a few moist crumbs attached. Cool in tin on wire rack. When cool, cut lengthways into 4 strips; cut each strip crossways into 6 pieces.

Each brownie: About 230 calories, 3g protein, 28g carbohydrate, 13g total fat (4g saturated), 53mg cholesterol, 150mg sodium

# BAR BISCUITS

For delicious teatime or lunchbox treats, bar biscuits are the easiest of all to make. Just spread the dough in a tin and bake, then cut the biscuits to size – as big or as dainty as you like. Our selection includes tart-sweet Citrus Bars, traditional Shortbread enriched with hazelnuts and moist Date and Nut Squares.

**1** Preheat oven to 200°C (400°F, Gas 6). Blend flour, vegetable fat, margarine, 50g caster sugar and ¼ teaspoon salt together in food processor with knife blade attached, pulsing processor on and off until crumbs form. Add *2–3 tablespoons cold water* through feed tube with motor running, 1 tablespoon at a time, pulsing processor on and off until dough comes together.

**2** Press dough onto base and 5mm up sides of ungreased 33 by 20cm metal baking tin. Using fork, prick dough all over. Bake 20–25 minutes, until golden; remove from oven. Turn oven control to 190°C (375°F, Gas 5).

**3** Squeeze 75ml juice from limes. Grate 2 teaspoons rind and squeeze 60ml juice from lemons. Whisk soured cream with eggs, remaining 200g caster sugar, and ⅛ teaspoon salt in medium bowl. Mix in lime and lemon juice and lemon rind.

## CITRUS BARS

❖❖❖❖❖❖❖❖❖❖❖❖❖

*Prep: 35–40 minutes, plus cooling and chilling*
*Bake: 30 minutes*
*Makes 32*

**260g plain flour**
**60g white vegetable fat**
**60g margarine or butter, diced**
**250g caster sugar**
**Salt**
**3 limes**
**2 lemons**
**125ml soured cream**
**5 medium eggs**
**Icing sugar for decoration**

### ORANGE BARS

For an easy variation, make Citrus Bars as above, but in Step 1, add 1 teaspoon grated orange rind to dough. In Step 3, substitute 1 teaspoon grated orange rind for lemon rind, and substitute 75ml orange juice for lime juice.

**4** Pour citrus mixture over warm crust in baking tin; bake 15 minutes, or just until set (do not overbake, or surface of citrus filling may crack). Cool completely in tin on wire rack; refrigerate until well chilled.

**5** When cool, sprinkle with icing sugar. Cut lengthways into 4 strips; cut each strip crossways into 8 pieces. To store, cover tin and refrigerate.

EACH BAR: ABOUT 100 CALORIES, 2g PROTEIN, 13g CARBOHYDRATE, 5g TOTAL FAT (1g SATURATED), 35mg CHOLESTEROL, 55mg SODIUM

Toasting hazelnuts enhances their flavour and makes it easy to remove the bitter, papery skins. Preheat oven to 180°C (350°F, Gas 4). Spread hazelnuts in a Swiss roll or baking tin; bake 10 minutes, or until lightly toasted and skins begin to crack. Wrap hot hazelnuts in clean tea towel. Roll hazelnuts around with your hands, inside towel, to remove most of skins. Cool before using.

## HAZELNUT SHORTBREAD

*Prep: 45 minutes, plus cooling    Bake: 50–60 minutes*
*Makes 36*

125g hazelnuts, toasted and skinned (see above)
340g plain flour
225g butter, softened
100g caster sugar
½ tsp vanilla essence
¼ tsp salt

◆ Preheat oven to 150°C (300°F, Gas 2). Finely chop toasted and skinned hazelnuts with 40g flour in food processor with knife blade attached.

◆ Using electric mixer on low speed, beat butter and sugar in large bowl until light and creamy. Beat in vanilla essence, salt, hazelnut mixture and remaining 300g flour just until blended. Pat dough evenly into ungreased 33 by 20cm metal baking tin. Using fork, prick dough all over.

◆ Bake shortbread 50–60 minutes until lightly browned. While still warm, cut shortbread lengthways into 3 strips; cut each strip crossways into 12 pieces. Cool in tin on wire rack 10 minutes; remove pieces from tin. Cool shortbread completely on wire rack. Store in tightly covered container.

**Each bar: About 100 calories, 1g protein, 9g carbohydrate, 7g total fat (3g saturated), 14mg cholesterol, 65mg sodium**

Vanilla and nut slices (below left), Hazelnut shortbread (below right), and Date and pecan squares (bottom)

## DATE AND PECAN SQUARES

*Prep: 15 minutes, plus cooling    Bake: 30–35 minutes*
*Makes 16*

200g light brown sugar
125g margarine or butter
200g plain flour
1 tsp bicarbonate of soda
125g pecans, chopped
150g stoned dates, chopped
2 medium eggs

◆ Preheat oven to 180°C (350°F, Gas 4). Grease 22cm square metal baking tin. Heat brown sugar and margarine in 3-litre saucepan over medium-low heat, stirring occasionally, until melted and smooth. Remove saucepan from heat.

◆ Using wooden spoon, beat in remaining ingredients until well blended. Spread batter evenly in tin. Bake 30–35 minutes, until cocktail stick inserted in centre comes out clean. Cool in tin on wire rack. When cool, cut into 4 strips, then cut each strip crossways into 4 squares. Store in tightly covered container.

**Each bar: About 220 calories, 3g protein, 30g carbohydrate, 11g total fat (2g saturated), 27mg cholesterol, 160mg sodium**

## VANILLA AND NUT SLICES

*Prep: 15 minutes, plus cooling    Bake: 35 minutes*
*Makes 12*

120g walnuts, macadamia nuts, or pecans, coarsely chopped
190g plain flour
100g caster sugar
100g light brown sugar
90g margarine or butter, softened
1¼ tsp baking powder
½ tsp salt
1½ tsp vanilla essence
2 medium eggs

◆ Preheat oven to 180°C (350°F, Gas 4). Grease 22cm square metal baking tin. Reserve 60g chopped nuts.

◆ Using electric mixer on low speed, beat flour, remaining ingredients and remaining 60g nuts in large bowl until well blended, occasionally scraping bowl with rubber spatula.

◆ Spread mixture evenly in tin; sprinkle reserved nuts on top. Bake 35 minutes, or until cocktail stick inserted in centre comes out clean. Cool in tin on wire rack.

◆ When cool, cut into 3 strips; cut each strip crossways into 4 pieces. Store slices in tightly covered container.

**Each bar: About 240 calories, 4g protein, 29g carbohydrate, 13g total fat (2g saturated), 36mg cholesterol, 220mg sodium**

# SWEETS

Home-made sweets are an old-fashioned tradition. As well as being great treats for the family and a special touch for entertaining, you can also wrap or box these sweets to make a gift with a personal touch.

## TOFFEE-ALMOND CRUNCH

❖❖❖❖❖❖❖❖❖❖❖❖❖

*Prep: 1 hour, plus cooling and standing*
*Cook: 30 minutes*
*Makes about 800g*

375g caster sugar
110g golden syrup
125g butter or margarine
225g blanched flaked almonds, lightly toasted and finely chopped
120g plain chocolate
1 teaspoon white vegetable fat

**1** Lightly grease 39 by 27cm Swiss roll tin. Bring sugar, golden syrup and *60ml water* to the boil in heavy 2-litre saucepan over medium heat, stirring occasionally until sugar dissolves. Stir in butter. Set sugar thermometer in place and continue cooking, stirring frequently, about 20 minutes, or until temperature reaches 150°C, or hard-crack stage (see below right). (Temperature will rise quickly over 147°C, so watch carefully.) Remove saucepan from heat.

**4** Transfer almond crunch in one piece from tin to chopping board. Spread melted chocolate over top; sprinkle with reserved almonds, pressing them gently into chocolate. Set crunch aside about 1 hour to allow glaze to set.

**2** Reserve 40g almonds for sprinkling on chocolate glaze. Stir remaining 185g almonds into hot syrup. Immediately pour mixture into Swiss roll tin; working quickly, spread evenly with palette knife. (Tin will become very hot.)

**5** Using knife, cut into hardened crunch to break it into pieces. Store in layers, separated by greaseproof paper, in tightly covered container up to 1 month. (Note: this almond crunch is also delicious without the chocolate layer.)

**3** Cool mixture in tin on wire rack. Meanwhile, prepare glaze: coarsely chop chocolate. Melt chocolate and vegetable fat in heavy 1-litre saucepan over low heat, stirring frequently. Remove from heat; allow to cool slightly.

### TESTING SWEETS

If you don't have a sugar thermometer, use the cold-water test: remove the syrup from the heat; drop a half spoonful into a cup or bowl of very cold water. Let stand 30 seconds.

**Thread** (102° to 104°C) Syrup forms a fine thread in the air as it falls from spoon

**Soft ball** (104° to 107°C) Syrup forms soft ball that flattens on removal from water

**Firm ball** (109° to 111°C) Syrup forms firm ball that does not flatten on removal from water

**Hard ball** (112° to 120°C) Syrup separates into hard, but not brittle, threads

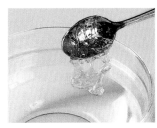

**Hard crack** (137° to 142°C) Syrup separates into hard, brittle threads (above)

PER 100g: ABOUT 645 CALORIES, 7g PROTEIN, 66g CARBOHYDRATE, 45g TOTAL FAT (13g SATURATED), 34mg CHOLESTEROL, 280mg SODIUM

# CHOCOLATE-WALNUT FUDGE

*Prep: 25 minutes, plus chilling*
*Makes 36 pieces, about 1kg*

450g plain chocolate, coarsely chopped
400ml canned sweetened condensed milk

125g walnuts, coarsely chopped
1 tsp vanilla essence
⅛ tsp salt

◈ Line 20cm square metal baking tin with cling film; smooth out as many wrinkles as possible. Heat chocolate and condensed milk in heavy 2-litre saucepan over medium-low heat, stirring constantly, until chocolate melts.

◈ Remove from heat; stir in remaining ingredients. Spoon chocolate mixture into tin; spread evenly. Refrigerate 3 hours, or until firm.

◈ Remove fudge from tin. Cut fudge into 6 strips; cut each strip crossways into 6 pieces. Store in tightly covered container at room temperature up to 2 weeks.

**Each piece: About 120 calories, 3g protein, 10g carbohydrate, 10g total fat (5g saturated), 4mg cholesterol, 20mg sodium**

# GOLD RUSH NUT BRITTLE

*Prep: 10 minutes, plus cooling    Cook: 35 minutes*
*Makes about 750g*

300g caster sugar
330g golden syrup
½ tsp salt
30g butter or margarine
2 tsp vanilla essence

1 tsp bicarbonate of soda
175g unsalted peanuts
125g blanched almonds, sliced
125g pecans

◈ Grease large baking sheet. Bring sugar, golden syrup, salt and *125ml water* to the boil in heavy 3-litre saucepan over medium heat, stirring occasionally until sugar dissolves.

◈ Set sugar thermometer in place and continue cooking, stirring frequently, about 30 minutes, until temperature reaches 137°C, or hard-crack stage (see page 523).

◈ Remove pan from heat; stir in butter, vanilla essence, bicarbonate of soda, unsalted peanuts, blanched almonds and pecans. Immediately pour onto prepared baking sheet. Using 2 forks, quickly lift and stretch nut mixture into about 35 by 30cm rectangle.

◈ Cool brittle completely on baking sheet on wire rack. Break brittle into small pieces with your hands. Store in tightly covered container up to 1 month.

**Per 100g: About 625 calories, 10g protein, 83g carbohydrate, 32g total fat (4g saturated), 9mg cholesterol, 385mg sodium**

# CHOCOLATE AND HAZELNUT TRUFFLES

*Prep: 25 minutes, plus chilling*
*Makes 32*

225g plain chocolate, broken into chunks
125ml whipping cream
45g unsalted butter, softened and diced
2 tbsp coffee-, almond-, or orange-flavoured liqueur (optional)

40g hazelnuts, toasted, skinned (see page 522) and finely chopped
3 tbsp cocoa powder

◈ Line 21 by 11cm metal loaf tin with cling film. Process chocolate in food processor with knife blade attached until finely ground.

◈ Bring cream to the boil in 1-litre saucepan over medium-high heat. Add cream to chocolate in food processor and blend until smooth. Add butter, and liqueur, if using, and blend until incorporated.

◈ Spoon chocolate mixture into loaf tin; spread evenly. Refrigerate 3 hours, or until firm enough to handle.

◈ Spread hazelnuts and cocoa on separate sheets of parchment paper. Remove chocolate mixture from tin by lifting edges of cling film and inverting onto chopping board; discard cling film. Cut chocolate mixture into 32 squares. Quickly roll each square into a ball.

◈ Roll half of truffles in chopped hazelnuts. Roll remaining truffles in cocoa. Refrigerate truffles up to 1 week. (Or, freeze in air-tight container up to 1 month; remove from freezer 5 minutes before serving.)

**Each truffle: About 65 calories, 1g protein, 3g carbohydrate, 7g total fat (4g saturated), 8mg cholesterol, 0mg sodium**

Few desserts match the festive feeling evoked by a home-made cake. Satisfying to prepare and a pleasure to serve, a home-made cake is a supremely rewarding way to put your creative energies to work. Always follow the recipe accurately for reliable – and delicious – results.

## ESSENTIAL INGREDIENTS FOR CAKES

**Fat** Margarine is a convenient and inexpensive choice but butter will give cakes a richer flavour and colour.
**Sugar** Caster sugar is favoured for its fine granules.
**Eggs** Remove eggs from refrigerator 30 minutes before using. This will help to avoid curdling cake mixtures.
**Flour** Plain flour can be used for all your baking needs. For cakes, add raising agents as instructed.

## LINING A CAKE PAN

Greasing and flouring cake tins prevents sticking, but some mixtures require a lining of greaseproof paper as well.

Place tin on greaseproof paper. Use a pencil to trace around base; cut out circle.

Fit paper in greased tin; grease paper. Lightly dust with flour; tap to remove excess.

## BAKING BASICS

• Before you begin preparing a recipe, set out all the ingredients, measuring when necessary.
• Room temperature eggs yield the best volume, but for safety, don't leave them out more than 30 minutes. Or, warm chilled eggs in a bowl of warm water 5 minutes before using.
• Use softened (not melted) butter; it's easier to blend.
• Although creamed cakes can be mixed by hand, electric mixers provide the most even blending. Scrape the bowl often while beating so ingredients are mixed well.
• To avoid air bubbles, gently tap tins on the work surface after filling with mixture.
• Bake cakes in the centre of the oven. If making more than two layers, switch the position of tins halfway through baking.
• To prevent a cake from sinking, leave the oven door shut during the first 15 minutes of baking.

## CREAMED VERSUS WHISKED CAKES

Cakes come in two basic groups: creamed and whisked cakes. Creamed cakes rely on fat for moisture and richness; they're loved for their flavour and velvety crumb. Chocolate, layer and pound cakes are the most common varieties. The 'creaming' stage is crucial; butter and sugar should be beaten together until they take on a pale colour and fluffy consistency. To ensure that all of the dry ingredients are evenly dispersed, combine them well before adding to the creamed mixture.

Whisked cakes – light, airy chiffon and angel food cakes – depend on beaten eggs or egg whites for volume and a delicate texture. Chiffon and sponge cakes contain both egg yolks and whites, and may include vegetable oil, margarine or butter; angel food cakes use only whites and contain no added fat. Adding cream of tartar to the egg whites before whisking gives them better stability; whisk until stiff peaks form when beaters are lifted. When combining ingredients, blend the mixture gently so it won't deflate. Never grease the tin for an angel or chiffon cake; the mixture needs to cling to the sides to rise. Before baking, cut through the mixture in the tin with a rubber spatula to remove any air bubbles.

## TIN SIZES AND SHAPES

Tin size and shape in relation to the amount of cake mixture influences how the cake bakes. Ideally, the tin should be the same height as the cake will be at it's highest point during baking. Unbaked, cake mixtures should fill the tin by no less than halfway.

### TIN VOLUME EQUIVALENTS

| TIN CALLED FOR | SUBSTITUTION |
| --- | --- |
| 15cm square cake tin | 18cm round tin |
| 18cm square cake tin | 20cm round tin |
| 20cm square cake tin | 23cm round tin |
| 23cm square cake tin | 25cm round tin |
| 25cm square cake tin | 28cm round tin |
| Two 18cm sandwich tins | 18 paper cake cases |

## TESTING TIPS

Professional bakers gauge doneness by how a cake looks, smells and feels, in addition to the suggested cooking time. Begin testing for doneness about 10 minutes before the end of the recommended baking time. A fully baked cake should have a toasty aroma and (except for chocolate cakes) a deeply golden surface; any cracks on the surface should look dry. Most cakes will start to pull away from the sides of the pan; a cocktail stick inserted into the centre of the cake should come out clean and dry, unless the recipe specifies otherwise. Alternatively, use the test illustrated below.

The secret's in the spring: most cakes can be tested for doneness by pressing the top lightly with a finger. When the cake is fully baked, the top should spring back.

## UNMOULDING AND COOLING

• Before unmoulding, creamed cakes should be cooled in their tins on a rack for approximately 10 minutes. Don't skimp on this resting period; it allows the cake to stabilize and further shrink from the side of the tin – and steam to build around the cake – making it easier to unmould.
• After the creamed cake has rested in its tin, unmould it without delay so air can circulate around it freely, allowing it to cool more quickly and not become soggy.
• To unmould a creamed cake, carefully run a small knife around the cake to loosen it from the side of the tin. Top cake with a wire cooling rack. Holding both the tin and the rack (if necessary, protect hands with a tea towel or oven mitts), invert cake onto rack. Carefully remove tin and top cake with second rack; flip cake, right-side up, onto second rack.
• Whisked cakes call for a slightly different approach. Angel food and chiffon cakes are too delicate to be removed from the tin until they're completely cooled. In addition, they must be cooled upside-down in the tin, which should be

Before unmoulding the cake, carefully run a small knife around the edge to loosen it from the side of the tin.

To unmould cake, place cooling rack over tin; carefully invert cake. Remove tin, then flip cake onto another rack.

inverted onto the neck of a bottle or a funnel. This position prevents the cake from sinking in the tin, while the bottle or funnel allows air to circulate evenly round the cake, and prevents the cake from touching the worktop if it has risen above the rim of the pan. Sponge cakes are sturdier and can simply be cooled in the tin on a wire rack.
• To unmould a whisked cake, carefully loosen it from the side of the tin with a palette knife, pressing it firmly against the side of the tin (to avoid tearing the cake), and turn out onto a plate.

## STORING CAKES

• All cakes should be cooled completely before they're iced or stored.
• Because of their fat content, creamed cakes stay fresher for 2–3 days. Whisked cakes are best eaten within a day or two; they contain little fat and will dry out quickly.
• Keep cakes left in the tin tightly covered. Layer cakes and iced sponge cakes are best kept under an inverted large bowl.
• Always refrigerate cakes with fillings and icings made with whipped cream, cream cheese, soured cream, yogurt or eggs.
• Freeze iced cakes, unwrapped, until firm, then wrap in cling film and aluminium foil and freeze up to 2 months.
• Freeze unfrosted creamed cakes on a baking sheet just until firm. Wrap layers in cling film, then foil, and freeze up to 4 months.
• Freeze whisked cakes in a freezer bag for up to 3 months.

## WHAT WENT WRONG?

**Curdled mixture** Each egg was not thoroughly incorporated into the mixture before the next was added; eggs were too cold when they were added. This usually corrects itself when the dry ingredients are added.
**Cake overflowed in tin** Tin too small; too much leavening.
**Tough, flat and heavy texture** Too much liquid; too much fat; too much flour; mixture under- or over-beaten.
**Sunken middle** Mixture was over-beaten, creating excess aeration that cake was unable to contain; too much sugar, liquid or baking powder was added to mixture; oven door was opened before the cake had set – or closed with too much force.
**Peaked or cracked centre** Mixture was over-beaten after flour was added (this over-activates the gluten in flour, creating a tough cake); the oven was too hot, causing the cake to rise too quickly.
**Cake did not rise properly** Too much liquid; too much fat; too large a tin; oven too cool.
**Dry crumb** Too much baking powder; too long a baking time.
**Crumbly texture** Under-beaten; too much fat.
**Pale colour** Too little sugar; too short a baking time.
**Tunnels in dough** Too much egg; too little sugar; poor mixing; oven too hot.

# LAYER CAKES

Surprisingly easy to make and yet impressive, nothing beats a layer cake for special occasions. The tender crumb and home-made taste simply can't compare with commercial mixes or shop-bought cakes. For something special try our intriguing Chequerboard Cake or sumptuous White Chocolate Cake, decorated with white chocolate curls.

## CHEQUERBOARD CAKE

*Prep:* 40 minutes, plus cooling    *Bake:* 25–30 minutes
*Make* 16 servings

225g butter or margarine,
  softened
400g caster sugar
415g plain flour
300ml milk
1 tbsp baking powder
1 tbsp vanilla essence
½ tsp salt
8 medium egg whites
225g plain chocolate,
  melted and cooled

Chocolate Buttercream
  (see page 550)

Special equipment:
2 large piping bags, each with
  1cm opening or 1cm writing
  nozzle (or use plastic bags
  with corners cut to make
  1cm opening)

**1** Preheat oven to 180°C (350°F, Gas 4). Grease three 20cm round sandwich tins. Line bases with greaseproof paper; grease paper. Dust tins with flour. Using electric mixer on low speed, beat butter and 300g sugar in large bowl until blended. On high speed, beat about 5 minutes until light and creamy. On low speed, add flour and next 4 ingredients and beat just until combined. Increase speed to medium; beat 2 minutes, occasionally scraping bowl.

**2** Using mixer on high speed, beat egg whites to soft peaks in another large bowl; gradually sprinkle in remaining 100g sugar, beating until stiff peaks form when beaters are lifted. Fold whites, one-third at a time, into cake mixture.

**3** Spoon half of cake mixture into another bowl; fold in melted chocolate and spoon into piping bag or plastic bag with corner cut. Spoon plain cake mixture into a second piping bag or plastic bag.

**4** Pipe 4cm-wide band of chocolate mixture around inside edge of two tins. Pipe 4cm-wide band of plain mixture next to each chocolate band; pipe enough chocolate mixture to fill in centre.

**5** In third tin, repeat piping, alternating mixtures, but starting with plain around edge. Stagger tins on 2 oven racks, placing 2 on upper rack and 1 on lower rack; rotate tins after 15 minutes of baking time.

**6** Bake 25–30 minutes, until toothpick inserted in centres comes out clean. Cool in tins on wire racks 10 minutes. Run small knife around edges of tins to loosen cakes; invert onto racks. Remove greaseproof paper; cool completely. Prepare buttercream. Place one of the two identical layers on cake plate; spread with 125g buttercream. Top with the reverse-design layer. Spread with 125g buttercream; top with remaining layer. Ice side and top of cake with remaining buttercream. Store any leftover cake in refrigerator.

EACH SERVING: ABOUT 550 CALORIES, 6g PROTEIN, 72g CARBOHYDRATE, 29g TOTAL FAT (11g SATURATED), 33mg CHOLESTEROL, 430mg SODIUM

## WHITE CHOCOLATE CAKE

*Prep:* 1¼ hours, plus cooling   *Bake:* 25 minutes

*Makes 16 servings*

| | |
|---|---|
| 250g white chocolate | ¾ tsp salt |
| 350ml milk | 3 medium eggs |
| 250g sugar | Quick Chocolate Curls made |
| 175g butter or margarine, | with white chocolate |
| softened | (optional, see page 551) |
| 385 plain flour | Lemon Buttercream (see |
| 1½ tsp baking powder | page 550) |
| 1½ tsp vanilla essence | 220g seedless raspberry jam |

◆ Melt white chocolate with milk in 2-litre saucepan over low heat, stirring frequently, until mixture is smooth. Remove pan from heat; cool slightly.

◆ Preheat oven to 180°C (350°F, Gas 4). Grease and flour three 20cm round sandwich tins.

◆ Using electric mixer on low speed, beat sugar and butter together in large bowl until blended. Increase speed to high; beat about 5 minutes, until light and creamy. Reduce speed to low; beat in flour, baking powder, vanilla essence, salt, eggs and cooled white chocolate mixture until blended, frequently scraping bowl with rubber spatula. Increase speed to medium; beat 2 minutes.

◆ Divide mixture evenly among tins. Stagger tins on 2 oven racks, placing 2 on upper rack and 1 on lower rack. Bake about 25 minutes, rotating tins after 15 minutes. Cakes are done when cocktail stick inserted in centre of each cake comes out clean. Cool cakes in tins on wire racks 10 minutes. Run small knife around edges of pans to loosen cakes; invert onto racks and cool completely.

◆ Meanwhile, prepare Quick Chocolate Curls, if you like, and refrigerate; prepare Lemon Buttercream.

◆ Using serrated knife, cut each cake horizontally in half to make 6 thin layers. Place 1 cake layer cut-side up on large cake plate. Spread with 75g lemon buttercream. Top with second layer; spread with 110g raspberry jam. Repeat layering to make 3 layers of buttercream and 2 layers of jam in all, ending with sixth layer.

◆ Spread remaining buttercream over side and top of cake. Using cocktail stick, carefully press chocolate curls, if using, into buttercream, completely covering cake. Store any leftover cake in refrigerator.

**Each serving: About 550 calories, 6g protein, 70g carbohydrate, 28g total fat (11g saturated), 72mg cholesterol, 425mg sodium**

## RICH CHOCOLATE CAKE

*Prep:* 50 minutes, plus cooling   *Bake:* 30 minutes

*Makes 16 servings*

| | |
|---|---|
| 200g plain flour | 400g caster sugar |
| 120g cocoa powder | 225g butter or margarine, |
| 2 tsp baking powder | softened |
| 1 tsp bicarbonate of soda | 4 medium eggs |
| ½ tsp salt | Fluffy White Icing (see page |
| 300ml milk | 550) or other icing |
| 2 tsp vanilla essence | |

◆ Preheat oven to 180°C (350°F, Gas 4). Grease three 20cm round sandwich tins. Line bases of tins with greaseproof paper; grease paper. Dust tins with flour. Combine flour, cocoa, baking powder, bicarbonate of soda and salt in medium bowl; set aside. Mix milk and vanilla esssence together in measuring jug.

◆ Using electric mixer on low speed, beat sugar and butter in large bowl until blended. Increase speed to high; beat about 2 minutes, until creamy. Reduce speed to medium-low; add eggs, 1 at a time, beating well after each addition. Alternately add flour mixture and milk mixture, beginning and ending with flour mixture; beat until mixture is smooth, occasionally scraping bowl with rubber spatula.

◆ Divide mixture evenly among cake tins. Stagger tins on 2 oven racks, placing 2 on upper rack and 1 on lower rack. Bake about 30 minutes, rotating tins after 15 minutes. Cakes are done when cocktail stick inserted in centres of cakes comes out almost clean. Cool in tins on wire racks 10 minutes. Run small knife around edges of tins to loosen cakes; invert cakes onto racks. Carefully remove greaseproof paper; cool cakes completely.

◆ Prepare icing. Place 1 cake layer on cake plate; spread with one sixth of icing. Top with second layer and another sixth of icing. Place remaining cake layer on top. Cover side and top of cake with remaining icing.

**Each serving: About 345 calories, 5g protein, 54g carbohydrate, 14g total fat (5g saturated), 86mg cholesterol, 375mg sodium**

## AMBROSIA LAYER CAKE

*Prep: 1½ hours, plus chilling and cooling*

*Bake: 35–40 minutes*

*Makes 20 servings*

| | |
|---|---|
| 4 large oranges | ¼ tsp salt |
| 1 tbsp fresh lemon juice | 2 tsp vanilla essence |
| 3 tbsp cornflour | 3 medium eggs |
| 500g caster sugar | 225ml buttermilk or soured |
| 280g butter or margarine, | milk (see page 392) |
| softened | Fluffy White Icing (see |
| 6 medium egg yolks | page 550) |
| 300g plain flour | 125g flaked coconut |
| 1½ tsp baking powder | Orange rind strips for |
| 1 tsp bicarbonate of soda | decoration |

❧ Grate 1 tablespoon rind and squeeze 300ml juice from oranges. Combine orange rind and juice, lemon juice, cornflour, and 200g sugar in heavy 3-litre saucepan. Add 120g butter; bring to the boil over medium heat, stirring. Boil 1 minute. Beat egg yolks lightly in small bowl. Into yolks, beat small amount of orange mixture; beat yolk mixture into orange mixture in saucepan. Cook over low heat, stirring constantly, 3 minutes, or until very thick. Pour filling into medium bowl; cover surface with cling film to prevent skin from forming. Refrigerate 2 hours, or until well chilled.

❧ Meanwhile, preheat oven to 180°C (350°F, Gas 4). Grease and flour 33 by 20cm baking tin. Combine flour, baking powder, bicarbonate of soda and salt in medium bowl.

❧ Using electric mixer on low speed, beat remaining 300g sugar and remaining 160g butter just until blended. Increase speed to high; beat 5 minutes, until light and creamy, scraping bowl often with rubber spatula. Reduce speed to low; add vanilla essence and whole eggs, 1 at a time, until blended. Alternately add flour mixture and buttermilk, beginning and ending with flour mixture; beat until mixture is well blended, occasionally scraping bowl.

❧ Spread mixture in tin. Bake 35–40 minutes, until cocktail stick inserted in centre of cake comes out clean. Cool in tin on wire rack 10 minutes. Run small round-bladed knife around edges of tin to loosen cake; invert onto rack to cool completely.

❧ Prepare Fluffy White Icing. Using serrated knife, cut cake horizontally in half. To remove top layer, carefully slide baking sheet in between cut layers and lift off top layer. Slide bottom layer onto serving platter; using palette knife, spread with chilled filling. Carefully transfer top layer onto bottom layer by gently sliding cake onto filling. Cover sides and top of cake with icing. Sprinkle with coconut; decorate with orange rind strips. Refrigerate until ready to serve.

**Each serving: About 360 calories, 4g protein, 52g carbohydrate, 16g total fat (6g saturated), 126mg cholesterol, 300mg sodium**

## YELLOW CAKE

*Prep: 45 minutes, plus cooling    Bake: 23–28 minutes*

*Makes 16 servings*

| | |
|---|---|
| 355g plain flour | 225g butter or margarine, |
| 1 tbsp baking powder | softened |
| ½ tsp salt | 4 medium eggs |
| 225ml milk | Orange Buttercream (see |
| 2 tsp vanilla essence | page 550) or other icing |
| 400g caster sugar | |

❧ Preheat oven to 180°C (350°F, Gas 4). Grease three 20cm round cake tins. Line bases of tins with greaseproof paper; grease paper. Dust tins with flour. Combine flour, baking powder and salt in medium bowl; set aside. Mix milk and vanilla essence together in measuring jug.

❧ Using electric mixer on low speed, beat sugar and butter in large bowl until blended. Increase speed to high; beat 2 minutes, or until creamy. Reduce speed to medium-low; add eggs, 1 at a time, beating well after each addition. Alternately add flour mixture and milk mixture, beginning and ending with flour mixture; beating until smooth, occasionally scraping bowl with rubber spatula.

❧ Divide mixture evenly among tins. Stagger tins on 2 oven racks, placing 2 on upper rack and 1 on lower rack. Bake 23–28 minutes, rotating tins after 15 minutes. Cakes are done when cocktail stick inserted in centres comes out almost clean with a few moist crumbs attached.

❧ Cool in tins on wire racks 10 minutes. Run round-bladed knife around edges of tins to loosen cakes; invert onto racks. Remove greaseproof paper; cool completely.

❧ Prepare buttercream. Place 1 cake layer on cake plate; spread with one-sixth of buttercream. Top with second cake layer and one-sixth of buttercream. Place remaining cake layer on top. Cover side and top of cake with remaining buttercream. Store any leftover cake in refrigerator.

**Each serving: About 475 calories, 5g protein, 58g carbohydrate, 25g total fat (15g saturated), 120mg cholesterol, 425mg sodium**

## CHOCOLATE-BUTTERMILK CAKE

*Prep: 30 minutes, plus cooling    Bake: 30 minutes*
*Makes 16 servings*

| | |
|---|---|
| 95g cocoa powder | 2 tsp bicarbonate of soda |
| 340g plain flour | 1½ tsp vanilla essence |
| 350g caster sugar | 1¼ tsp salt |
| 350ml buttermilk or soured | 3 medium eggs |
| milk (see page 392) | Chocolate Buttercream (see |
| 225ml vegetable oil | page 550) |

◆ Preheat oven to 180°C (350°F, Gas 4). Grease two 23cm round cake tins. Line bases of tins with greaseproof paper; grease paper. Dust tins with cocoa. Place cocoa and next 8 ingredients in large bowl. Using electric mixer on low speed, beat until mixed. Increase speed to medium and beat 3 minutes, occasionally scraping bowl with rubber spatula.

◆ Divide mixture evenly between tins and bake 30 minutes, or until cocktail stick inserted in centre of cakes comes out clean. Cool cakes in tins on wire racks 10 minutes. Run round-bladed knife around edges of tins to loosen cakes. Invert onto racks; cool completely. Prepare buttercream.

◆ Place 1 cake layer rounded-side down on cake plate; spread with one third of buttercream. Top with second layer, rounded-side up. Cover side and top of cake with remaining buttercream. Store any leftover cake in refrigerator.

**Each serving: About 475 calories, 5g protein, 56g carbohydrate, 28g total fat (7g saturated), 41mg cholesterol, 465mg sodium**

## SPICE LAYER CAKE

*Prep: 45 minutes, plus cooling    Bake: 28–30 minutes*
*Makes 16 servings*

| | |
|---|---|
| 265g plain flour | 125g butter or margarine, |
| 1 tsp baking powder | softened |
| ¾ tsp ground cinnamon | 2 medium eggs |
| ½ tsp bicarbonate of soda | 1 tsp vanilla essence |
| ½ tsp salt | 175ml buttermilk or soured |
| ½ tsp ground ginger | milk (see page 392) |
| ½ tsp ground nutmeg | Vanilla Buttercream (see |
| Pinch ground cloves | page 550) or other icing |
| 200g caster sugar | |

◆ Preheat oven to 180°C (350°F, Gas 4). Grease three 20cm round cake tins. Line bases of tins with greaseproof paper; grease paper. Dust tins with flour. Mix flour and next 7 ingredients together in bowl; set aside.

◆ Using electric mixer on medium speed, beat sugar and butter 5 minutes, or until light and creamy. Add eggs, 1 at a time, beating well after each addition. Beat in vanilla essence. On low speed, alternately add flour mixture and buttermilk,

beginning and ending with flour, beating just until mixture is smooth. Divide mixture among tins. Stagger tins on 2 oven racks, placing 2 on upper rack and 1 on lower rack.

◆ Bake 28–30 minutes, rotating tins after 15 minutes. Cakes are done when cocktail stick inserted in centre comes out clean. Cool in tins on wire racks 10 minutes. Run knife around edges of tins; invert cakes onto racks. Remove paper; cool completely. Prepare buttercream. Place 1 cake layer on cake plate; spread with one-sixth of buttercream. Top with second layer, one-sixth of buttercream and remaining layer. Cover side and top of cake with remaining buttercream. Store any leftover cake in refrigerator.

**Each serving: About 340 calories, 4g protein, 40g carbohydrate, 19g total fat (5g saturated), 47mg cholesterol, 365mg sodium**

## BANANA LAYER CAKE

*Prep: 40 minutes, plus cooling    Bake: 30 minutes*
*Makes 16 servings*

| | |
|---|---|
| 2–3 fully ripe bananas (225g), | ¼ tsp salt |
| mashed | ⅛ tsp ground nutmeg |
| 60ml buttermilk or soured | 250g caster sugar |
| milk (see page 392) | 125g butter or margarine, |
| 1 tsp vanilla essence | softened |
| 335g plain flour | 2 medium eggs |
| 1 tsp baking powder | Cream Cheese Icing (see |
| ½ tsp bicarbonate of soda | page 550) |

◆ Preheat oven to 180°C (350°F, Gas 4). Grease three 20cm round cake tins. Line bases of tins with greaseproof paper; grease paper. Dust tins with flour. Mix bananas, buttermilk and vanilla essence together in bowl; set aside. Combine flour and next 4 ingredients in another bowl; set aside.

◆ Using electric mixer on medium speed, beat sugar and butter in large bowl 5 minutes, or until light and creamy. Add eggs, 1 at time, beating well after each addition. On low speed, alternately add flour mixture and banana mixture, beginning and ending with flour mixture; beat just until smooth. Divide mixture among tins. Stagger tins on 2 oven racks, placing 2 on upper rack and 1 on lower rack.

◆ Bake 30 minutes, rotating tins after 15 minutes. Cakes are done when cocktail stick inserted in centre comes out clean. Cool in tins on wire racks 10 minutes. Run knife around edges of tins; invert cakes onto racks. Remove paper; cool completely. Prepare icing. Place 1 cake layer on cake plate; spread with one-sixth of icing. Top with second layer, one-sixth of icing and remaining layer. Cover side and top of cake with remaining icing. Store any leftover cake in refrigerator.

**Each serving: About 335 calories, 3g protein, 49g carbohydrate, 14g total fat (6g saturated), 56mg cholesterol, 265mg sodium**

# RICH CHOCOLATE CAKES AND TORTES

These eye-catching desserts will look as if they have come from an expensive bakery, but our straight-forward recipes make them easy to prepare. Chocolate lovers will be in heaven – each one promises a deep flavour, as well as a distinctive taste all of its own. The mocha torte offers tiers of espresso cream and crunchy toasted almonds; Chocolate Truffle Cake boasts a dense, decadent texture and the prune and nut torte is moist and fruity. Remember that chocolate can easily scorch when heated, so melt it carefully, over low heat, stirring often.

## TRIPLE LAYER MOCHA-ALMOND TORTE

*Prep: 45 minutes, plus cooling   Bake: 45–50 minutes*
*Makes 16 servings*

| | |
|---|---|
| 175g plain chocolate | 1 tsp baking powder |
| 1 tbsp plus 2 tsp instant espresso coffee powder | ½ tsp salt |
| 350g blanched whole almonds | 6 medium eggs, separated |
| 220g caster sugar | ½ tsp almond essence |
| 30g plain flour (yes, 30g) | 600ml whipping cream |

1 Preheat oven to 180°C (350°F, Gas 4). Grease 23 by 6cm springform tin. Line base with greaseproof paper; grease paper. Dust with flour. Melt chocolate with 1 tablespoon espresso powder and *60ml water* in small saucepan over low heat, stirring, until smooth. Remove from heat.

2 Grind 225g almonds with 50g caster sugar in food processor with knife blade attached. (Nuts should be finely ground but not paste-like.) Transfer nut mixture to medium bowl; stir in flour, baking powder and salt; set aside.

3 Using electric mixer on high speed, beat egg whites to soft peaks in large bowl; sprinkle in 100g caster sugar, 2 tablespoons at a time, until whites stand in stiff peaks when beaters are lifted. On medium speed, beat yolks, chocolate mixture and almond essence in small bowl 3 minutes, frequently scraping bowl. Fold nut mixture and chocolate mixture into egg whites just until blended.

4 Spread mixture evenly in pan. Bake 45–50 minutes, until cocktail stick inserted in centre of cake comes out clean. Cool in tin on wire rack 10 minutes. Remove side and base of pan. Remove paper; cool completely on rack.

5 Meanwhile, coarsely chop remaining 125g almonds. Toast almonds in small frying pan over medium heat until golden. Cool. Using serrated knife, cut cake horizontally into 3 layers. Dissolve 2 teaspoons espresso powder in *1 tablespoon hot water* in cup.

6 Using electric mixer on medium speed, beat cream, remaining 70g sugar and espresso mixture to stiff peaks. Place 1 cake layer on cake plate; spread with 225g cream. Top with second layer; spread with additional 225g cream.

7 Top with third layer. Spread top and side of cake with remaining cream. Reserve 1 tablespoon almonds; press toasted almonds into side of cake. Decorate with reserved almonds. Refrigerate until ready to serve.

EACH SERVING: ABOUT 380 CALORIES, 9g PROTEIN, 27g CARBOHYDRATE, 29g TOTAL FAT (12g SATURATED), 131 mg CHOLESTEROL, 135mg SODIUM

## CHOCOLATE TRUFFLE CAKE

*Prep:* 1 hour, plus chilling overnight and standing    *Bake:* 35 minutes
*Makes* 24 servings

225g butter (do not use
   margarine)
460g plain chocolate
9 medium eggs, separated

100g caster sugar
¼ tsp cream of tartar
Icing sugar for decoration

◆ Preheat oven to 150°C (300°F, Gas 2). Remove base from 23 by 8cm springform tin and cover base with foil, wrapping foil around to the underside (this will make it easier to remove cake from tin). Replace base. Grease and flour foil base and side of tin.

◆ Melt butter and chocolate in heavy 2-litre saucepan over low heat, stirring frequently. Pour chocolate mixture into large bowl; set aside.

◆ Using electric mixer on high speed, beat egg yolks and caster sugar in small bowl about 5 minutes, until very thick and lemon-coloured. Using rubber spatula, stir egg yolk mixture into chocolate mixture until blended.

◆ In another large bowl, with clean beaters, with mixer on high speed, beat egg whites and cream of tartar to soft peaks. Using rubber spatula or wire whisk, gently fold beaten egg whites into chocolate mixture, one-third at a time. Spread mixture evenly in tin.

◆ Bake 35 minutes. (Do not over-bake; cake will firm on chilling.) Cool cake completely in pan on wire rack. Refrigerate overnight in tin.

◆ To remove cake from tin, run a hot round-bladed knife around edge of tin; remove side of tin. Invert cake onto cake plate; unwrap foil on base and lift off base of tin. Carefully peel foil from cake. Let cake stand 1 hour at room temperature before serving.

◆ Just before serving, sprinkle icing sugar through fine sieve over star stencil or doily for a pretty design (see page 552), or dust top of cake with icing sugar. Store any leftover cake in refrigerator.

**Each serving:** About 200 calories, 4g protein, 15g carbohydrate, 16g total fat (9g saturated), 100mg cholesterol, 100mg sodium

## CHOCOLATE, PRUNE AND NUT TORTE

*Prep:* 1 hour, plus chilling overnight    *Bake:* 35 minutes
*Makes* 12 servings

250g plain chocolate
6 medium egg whites
100g caster sugar
½ tsp vanilla essence
325g stoned prunes, diced

175g pecans, coarsely
   chopped
1 tbsp icing sugar

◆ Grease 25 by 6cm springform tin; line base of tin with parchment paper.

◆ Finely grate chocolate. (Or, process chocolate in food processor with knife blade attached until ground.)

◆ Preheat oven to 220°C (425°F, Gas 7). Using electric mixer on high speed, beat egg whites in large bowl until soft peaks form. Beating at high speed, sprinkle in caster sugar, 2 tablespoons at a time, beating well after each addition, until whites stand in stiff peaks when beaters are lifted. Beat in vanilla essence.

◆ Using rubber spatula, gently fold prunes and pecans into beaten egg whites; gently but thoroughly fold in grated chocolate. Pour mixture into tin, smoothing top. Bake 35 minutes, or until top of torte is deep brown and edge pulls away from side of tin.

◆ Cool torte in tin on wire rack 15 minutes; remove side of tin. Invert torte onto wire rack and remove base of tin; peel off parchment paper. Cool torte completely on rack. Cover and refrigerate torte overnight.

◆ Just before serving, cut six 30 by 1cm strips of parchment paper. Place strips 2–3cm apart on top of torte. Sprinkle top of torte with icing sugar, then carefully remove parchment-paper strips. Store any leftover torte in refrigerator.

**Each serving:** About 305 calories, 6g protein, 34g carbohydrate, 21g total fat (7g saturated), 0mg cholesterol, 30mg sodium

# SWISS ROLLS

Alluring spirals of alternating cake and filling make Swiss rolls among the prettiest desserts around. Best made in advance, they're perfect for entertaining.

## WHITE-CHOCOLATE YULE LOG

❖❖❖❖❖❖❖❖❖❖❖❖❖

*Prep:* 70 minutes, plus cooling and chilling
*Bake:* 10–15 minutes
*Makes* 20 servings

10 medium eggs, separated
200g caster sugar
3 tsp vanilla essence
150g plain flour
30g icing sugar plus extra for sprinkling
White Chocolate Buttercream (see page 550)
450ml whipping cream
30g cocoa powder
½ tsp ground cinnamon
Chocolate Leaves (see page 551) and cranberries for decoration

**1** Preheat oven to 180°C (350°F, Gas 4). Grease two 39 by 27cm Swiss roll tins. Line tins with greaseproof paper; grease paper. Using electric mixer on high speed, beat egg whites in large bowl until soft peaks form. Gradually sprinkle in 100g caster sugar, 2 tablespoons at a time, beating until whites stand in stiff peaks when beaters are lifted.

**2** Using mixer on high speed, beat egg yolks, remaining 100g caster sugar, and 2 teaspoons vanilla essence until very thick and lemon-coloured; on low speed, beat in flour just until combined. Using rubber spatula, fold yolk mixture into beaten whites.

**3** Spread mixture evenly in tins. Bake on 2 oven racks 10–15 minutes, until cakes spring back when lightly touched, rotating tins between upper and lower racks halfway through baking time.

**4** Sprinkle tea towel with icing sugar. When cakes are done, immediately run palette knife around edges of tins to loosen cakes; invert onto towel, slightly overlapping a long side of each cake.

**5** Carefully peel off paper. Starting from a long side, roll cakes with towel Swiss-roll fashion. Cool completely, seam-side down, on wire rack. Meanwhile, prepare White Chocolate Buttercream; set aside.

**6** Using electric mixer on medium speed, beat cream, cocoa, cinnamon, 30g icing sugar and remaining 1 teaspoon vanilla essence to stiff peaks. Unroll cake; spread with cocoa cream, leaving 1cm border.

**7** From same long side, roll cake without towel. Cut a 5cm-thick diagonal slice from each end of roll; trim each to 6cm in diameter. Place cake, seam-side down, on long platter.

**8** Using palette knife, spread some buttercream over roll. Place end pieces on top of roll to resemble cut branches. Spread remaining buttercream over roll and branches. With four-tined fork, score buttercream to resemble bark of tree. Refrigerate cake at least 2 hours before serving. Decorate with Chocolate Leaves and cranberries. Store any leftover cake in refrigerator.

EACH SERVING: ABOUT 360 CALORIES, 5g PROTEIN, 33g CARBOHYDRATE, 23g TOTAL FAT (14g SATURATED), 166mg CHOLESTEROL, 145mg SODIUM

## FALLEN CHOCOLATE SOUFFLÉ ROLL

*Prep: 30 minutes, plus cooling and chilling   Bake: 15 minutes*
*Makes 16 servings*

| | |
|---|---|
| 180g plain chocolate | ¾ tsp ground cinnamon |
| 1 tsp instant espresso coffee powder, dissolved in 3 tbsp hot water | ¼ tsp salt |
| | ⅛ tsp ground cloves |
| | 350g whipping cream |
| 6 medium eggs, separated | 60ml coffee-flavoured liqueur |
| 150g caster sugar | 40g icing sugar plus extra for sprinkling |
| 1 tsp vanilla essence | |

◆ Preheat oven to 180°C (350°F, Gas 4). Grease 39 by 27cm Swiss roll tin. Line with greaseproof paper; grease paper. Dust tin with flour.

◆ Melt chocolate and espresso mixture in top of double boiler set over simmering water, stirring often; set aside.

◆ Using electric mixer on high speed, beat egg whites in large bowl until soft peaks form. Beating on high speed, gradually sprinkle in 50g caster sugar, 1 tablespoon at a time, beating well after each addition until whites stand in stiff peaks when beaters are lifted.

◆ Using electric mixer on high speed, beat egg yolks with remaining 100g caster sugar in small bowl until very thick and lemon-coloured. Reduce speed to low; beat in vanilla essence, cinnamon, salt and cloves.

◆ Using rubber spatula, fold chocolate mixture into yolk mixture. Gently fold one-third of whites into chocolate mixture; fold chocolate mixture into remaining whites.

◆ Spread mixture evenly in tin. Bake 15 minutes, or until firm to the touch. Cover cake with clean, dampened tea towel; cool in tin on wire rack 30 minutes.

◆ Using mixer on medium speed, beat cream in large bowl until soft peaks form. Beat in coffee liqueur and 25g icing sugar, then beat until stiff peaks form.

◆ Remove tea towel from cake; sift 15g icing sugar over cake. Run round-bladed knife around edges of tin. Cover cake with sheet of foil and a large baking sheet; invert cake onto baking sheet. Carefully peel off greaseproof paper.

◆ Spread cream evenly over cake, leaving 1cm border. Starting from a long side and using foil to help lift cake, roll cake Swiss-roll fashion (cake may crack). Place, seam-side down, on long platter. Refrigerate at least 1 hour, until ready to serve. Just before serving, sprinkle icing sugar on top.

**Each serving: About 215 calories, 4g protein, 21g carbohydrate, 14g total fat (8g saturated), 110mg cholesterol, 65mg sodium**

## BLUEBERRY-GINGERBREAD ROLL

*Prep: 30 minutes, plus cooling   Bake: 15 minutes*
*Makes 8 servings*

| | |
|---|---|
| 150g plain flour | 80g golden syrup |
| 100g caster sugar | 1 medium egg |
| 2 tsp ground ginger | 25g icing sugar plus extra for sprinkling |
| 1 tsp bicarbonate of soda | |
| ½ tsp baking powder | 225ml whipping cream |
| ½ tsp ground cinnamon | 1 tsp vanilla essence |
| ¼ tsp salt | 300g blueberries |
| ¼ tsp ground nutmeg | |
| 90g butter or margarine, melted | |

◆ Preheat oven to 180°C (350°F, Gas 4). Grease 39 by 27cm Swiss roll tin. Line with greaseproof paper; grease paper. Dust tin with flour.

◆ Combine flour and next 7 ingredients in large bowl; set aside. Whisk together butter, golden syrup, egg and *75ml hot water* in medium bowl. Whisk golden syrup mixture into flour mixture just until smooth; spread evenly in tin. Bake 15 minutes, or until top springs back when lightly touched.

◆ Meanwhile, sprinkle icing sugar onto tea towel. Run round-bladed knife around edges of tin; invert hot cake onto tea towel. Peel off greaseproof paper. Trim 5mm from edges of cake. Starting from a long side, roll cake Swiss-roll fashion. Cool completely on wire rack.

◆ Using electric mixer on medium speed, beat cream with vanilla essence and 25g icing sugar in medium bowl until stiff peaks form. Using rubber spatula, fold in blueberries. Unroll cooled cake (cake may crack); spread whipped cream evenly on top, leaving 1cm border. Starting from same long side, roll up cake and transfer, seam-side down, to long platter. Refrigerate until ready to serve.

**Each serving: About 350 calories, 3g protein, 40g carbohydrate, 20g total fat (11g saturated), 91mg cholesterol, 375mg sodium**

# ANGEL FOOD AND SPONGE CAKES

These American-style cakes share a light, springy texture. With virtually no fat, angel food cake is the most light and airy – traditionally plain, the mixture can be enriched with chocolate and other flavourings. Its delicate crumb is the result of perfectly beaten egg whites. Sponge and chiffon cakes get a bit more richness from egg yolks; chiffon, made with oil in place of vegetable fat, is the richest of the three. All are delicious on their own, lightly glazed, or simply dusted with icing sugar and served with fresh fruit.

## CHOCOLATE ANGEL FOOD CAKE

*Prep: 30 minutes, plus cooling*   *Bake: 30–35 minutes*
*Makes 16 servings*

| | |
|---|---|
| 180g plain flour | ¾ tsp salt |
| 60g cocoa powder | 1½ tsp vanilla essence |
| 12–14 (400ml) medium egg whites | 400g caster sugar |
| 1½ tsp cream of tartar | 125g plain chocolate |
| | 10g white vegetable fat |

**1** Preheat oven to 190°C (375°F, Gas 5). Sift flour and cocoa through medium-mesh sieve into bowl. Set aside. Using electric mixer on high speed, beat egg whites, cream of tartar and salt in large bowl until soft peaks form; beat in vanilla essence. Beating on high speed, gradually sprinkle in sugar, 2 tablespoons at a time, beating well after each addition, until whites stand in stiff peaks when beaters are lifted.

**2** Using rubber spatula or wire whisk, fold flour mixture into beaten whites just until flour mixture disappears. Do not over-mix. Pour mixture into ungreased 25cm angel food cake tin.

**3** Bake 30–35 minutes until cake springs back when lightly touched. Invert cake in tin on metal funnel or bottle; cool cake completely in tin.

**4** Carefully run palette knife around side of tin to loosen cake. Remove cake from tin and place on cake plate.

**5** Prepare chocolate glaze: melt plain chocolate with white vegetable fat in small saucepan over very low heat, stirring frequently, until smooth. Spread over top of cake, letting some run down side.

### ANGEL FOOD CAKE TIPS

• Use the special angel food cake tin, available from specialist kitchen shops.

• Egg whites for beating are best at room temperature. The bowl in which you beat them should be perfectly dry and free from grease or any traces of yolk.

• Over- or under-beating will cause loss of volume.

• Never grease the tin; the cake mixture must cling to the tin side as it bakes and cools. To cool, invert the tin over a funnel or bottle to let air circulate on all sides and prevent the cake from sinking.

EACH SERVING: ABOUT 190 CALORIES, 4g PROTEIN, 39g CARBOHYDRATE, 3g TOTAL FAT (2g SATURATED), 0mg CHOLESTEROL, 145mg SODIUM

## Sugar 'n' spice angel food cake

*Prep: 20 minutes, plus cooling   Bake: 30–35 minutes*
*Makes 16 servings*

120g plain flour
120g icing sugar
1 tsp ground cinnamon
1 tsp ground ginger
¼ tsp ground allspice
Salt

12–14 medium egg whites
   (400ml)
1 tsp cream of tartar
1 tsp vanilla essence
150g caster sugar
50g dark brown sugar

◆ Preheat oven to 190°C (375°F, Gas 5). Sift flour, sugar, cinnamon, ginger, allspice and ¼ teaspoon salt through medium-mesh sieve into medium bowl. Set aside.

◆ Using electric mixer on high speed, beat egg whites, cream of tartar and ½ teaspoon salt in large bowl until soft peaks form; beat in vanilla essence. Beating on high speed, sprinkle in caster sugar and brown sugar, 2 tablespoons at a time, beating well after each addition, until whites stand in stiff peaks when beaters are lifted.

◆ Using rubber spatula or wire whisk, fold in flour mixture just until flour mixture disappears. Do not over-mix. Pour mixture into ungreased 25cm angel food cake tin.

◆ Bake 30–35 minutes, until cake springs back when lightly touched. Invert cake in tin on funnel or bottle; cool completely in tin. Carefully run palette knife around side of tin to loosen cake. Remove from tin; place on cake plate.

**Each serving: About 115 calories, 3g protein, 25g carbohydrate, 0g total fat, 0mg cholesterol, 145mg sodium**

## Vanilla chiffon cake

*Prep: 20 minutes, plus cooling   Bake: 1¼ hours*
*Makes 16 servings*

265g plain flour
1 tbsp baking powder
1 tsp salt
300g caster sugar
125ml vegetable oil

5 medium egg yolks
1 tbsp vanilla essence
7 medium egg whites
½ tsp cream of tartar
Icing sugar for decoration

◆ Preheat oven to 170°C (325°F, Gas 3). Combine flour, baking powder, salt and 200g caster sugar in large bowl. Make a well in centre and add oil, egg yolks, vanilla essence and *60ml cold water*; whisk into flour mixture until smooth.

◆ Using electric mixer on high speed, beat egg whites and cream of tartar in another large bowl until soft peaks form. Beating on high speed, gradually sprinkle in remaining 100g caster sugar, 2 tablespoons at a time, beating well after each addition, until whites stand in stiff peaks when beaters

are lifted. Using rubber spatula, gently fold one-third of whites into yolk mixture; fold in remaining whites. Pour mixture into ungreased 25cm angel food cake tin.

◆ Bake 1¼ hours, or until top springs back when lightly touched. Invert cake in tin on funnel or bottle; cool completely in tin. Carefully run palette knife around side of tin to loosen cake; remove from tin and place on cake plate. Just before serving, sift icing sugar over top.

**Each serving: About 220 calories, 4g protein, 32g carbohydrate, 9g total fat (2g saturated), 67mg cholesterol, 250mg sodium**

## Golden sponge cake

*Prep: 20 minutes, plus cooling   Bake: 15–20 minutes*
*Makes 8 servings*

115g plain flour
2 tbsp cornflour
3 medium eggs
100g caster sugar

15g butter or margarine,
   melted
Whipped cream and fresh
   fruit (optional)

◆ Preheat oven to 190°C (375°F, Gas 5). Grease and flour 22cm square metal baking tin. Combine flour and cornflour in small bowl; set aside. Using electric mixer on high speed, beat eggs and sugar about 10 minutes, until thick and lemon-coloured, occasionally scraping bowl with rubber spatula. Using spatula, fold in flour mixture until well blended; fold in melted butter. Pour mixture into tin.

◆ Bake 15–20 minutes, until cake is golden and springs back when lightly touched.

◆ Cool cake in tin on wire rack 10 minutes. Run round-bladed knife around edges of tin to loosen cake; invert onto rack to cool completely. Serve cake with whipped cream and fruit, if you like.

**Each serving: About 135 calories, 3g protein, 23g carbohydrate, 3g total fat (1g saturated), 84mg cholesterol, 40mg sodium**

# FANCY DECORATED CAKES

These spectacular cakes are for grand celebrations. They rely on special icing techniques that require a steady hand and a little patience. But your guests will agree – the stunning results are well worth the effort.

## DOTTED SWISS ALMOND CAKE

❖❖❖❖❖❖❖❖❖❖❖❖❖❖❖❖❖❖❖❖❖❖❖❖❖❖❖❖❖❖

*Prep:* 1 hour, plus cooling   *Bake:* 35 minutes
*Makes* 24 servings

375g plain flour
2½ tsp baking powder
½ tsp salt
125g butter or margarine, softened
225g marzipan, diced
300g caster sugar
5 medium egg whites
1 tbsp vanilla essence
300ml milk

Amaretto Buttercream (see page 550)
6 tbsp seedless raspberry jam

Special equipment:
1 piping bag with coupler
1 writing nozzle (2mm opening)
1 writing nozzle (6mm opening)

**1** Preheat oven to 180°C (350°F, Gas 4). Grease two 20cm square metal baking tins. Line bases with greaseproof paper; grease paper. Dust tins with flour. Combine flour, baking powder and salt in medium bowl; set aside. Using electric mixer on low speed, beat butter, marzipan and sugar in large bowl 2–3 minutes, until blended, scraping bowl often.

**2** Increase speed to medium; beat about 2 minutes, until well mixed, scraping bowl often (mixture may look crumbly). Gradually beat in egg whites and vanilla essence just until blended. Reduce speed to low; alternately add flour mixture and milk to marzipan mixture, beginning and ending with flour mixture. Beat just until mixed.

**3** Pour mixture into tins. Bake 35 minutes, or until cocktail stick inserted in centres of cakes comes out clean. Cool cakes in tins on wire racks 10 minutes. Run knife around sides of tins to loosen cakes; invert onto racks. Remove paper; cool completely. Prepare buttercream. Spoon 225g buttercream into piping bag fitted with 2mm writing nozzle; set aside.

**4** Using serrated knife, cut each cake layer horizontally in half. (Use ruler and cocktail sticks to mark halfway points.)

**5** Place bottom half of 1 layer, cut side up, on cake board; spread evenly with 2 tablespoons jam. Spread about 5 tablespoons buttercream on top of jam.

**6** Repeat layering 2 times, then top with remaining cake layer. Spread remaining buttercream on top and sides of cake.

**7** Using piping bag, pipe clusters of small dots of buttercream on top of cake.

**8** Using 6mm writing nozzle, pipe rows of dots around base and top borders and down corners of cake. Store any leftover cake in refrigerator.

EACH SERVING: ABOUT 370 CALORIES, 4g PROTEIN, 40g CARBOHYDRATE, 22g TOTAL FAT (12g SATURATED), 54mg CHOLESTEROL, 180mg SODIUM

# Strawberry Basket Cake

*Prep: 1¼ hours, plus standing and cooling*
*Bake: 23–28 minutes*    *Makes 20 servings*

| | |
|---|---|
| Layers from Yellow Cake (see page 529) | 600g strawberries |
| 900ml whipping cream | **Special Equipment:** |
| 1 tbsp vanilla essence | 2 piping bags |
| 1 sachet powdered gelatine | 1 medium star nozzle (1cm opening) |
| 80g icing sugar | 1 medium basket-weave tip (2cm opening) |
| 165g strawberry jam | |

◆ Prepare Yellow Cake. While cake layers are cooling, prepare icing: combine cream and vanilla essence in large bowl. Evenly sprinkle gelatine over *3 tablespoons cold water* in small saucepan; let stand 2 minutes to soften. Cook over medium-low heat, stirring frequently, about 3 minutes, until gelatine completely dissolves. (Do not boil.)

◆ Remove pan from heat. Using electric mixer on medium-high speed, immediately begin beating cream mixture. Beat about 2 minutes, until thickened and soft peaks just begin to form. Beat in icing sugar, then beat in dissolved gelatine in a thin, steady stream. Beat cream mixture until stiff peaks form but mixture is still soft and smooth; do not over-beat.

◆ Place 1 cake layer on cake plate; spread with half of jam, then spread with 225g icing. Top with second cake layer, remaining jam, and 225g icing. Place remaining cake layer on top. Cover side and top of cake with a thin layer (about 2mm thick) of icing.

◆ Spoon about 300g icing into piping bag fitted with 1cm medium star nozzle; set aside. Spoon about 450g of remaining icing into piping bag fitted with 2cm medium basket-weave nozzle. Pipe basket-weave pattern around side of cake (see below). Add remaining icing to piping bag as necessary to complete basket weave.

◆ Using icing in bag with star nozzle, pipe decorative border around top edge of cake. Refrigerate cake until ready to serve. Just before serving, pile strawberries on top of cake. Remove berries before slicing cake; serve on the side.

**Each serving: About 455 calories, 5g protein, 46g carbohydrate, 28g total fat (13g saturated), 110mg cholesterol, 270mg sodium**

### BASKET-WEAVE ICING

Creating the basket-weave effect for our celebration Strawberry Basket Cake is easier than it looks, and the results are stunning. If you're not sure of your piping skills, have a practice run on a sheet of greaseproof paper first, before you tackle the finished cake.

1 Using basket-weave nozzle, serrated side of tip facing out, pipe vertical strip of icing up side of cake.

2 Next, pipe 3 horizontal bars, evenly spaced, across vertical strip, extending 2cm to left and right sides of vertical strip.

3 Pipe another vertical strip of icing to right of first one, just slightly overlapping ends of horizontal bars.

4 Starting at right edge of first vertical strip, pipe horizontal bars across second vertical strip in spaces between bars in first row, extending 2cm to right of second vertical strip. Repeat around cake to create a woven effect.

# CHILDRENS' CAKES

These whimsical creations are guaranteed to delight at childrens' parties. The basic cakes are made from our layer cake recipes, and are then shaped and adorned with icings and assorted sweets. Children will love helping to decorate the cakes – simply set out bowls of goodies and let their imaginations do the rest.

## MONSTER SNAKE CAKE

❖ ❖ ❖ ❖ ❖ ❖ ❖ ❖ ❖ ❖ ❖ ❖

*Prep: 80 minutes, plus cooling*
*Bake: 30 minutes*
*Makes 24 servings*

**2 layers from Yellow Cake (see page 529)**
**450g icing sugar**
**225g butter, softened**
**5 tbsp single cream**
**2 tsp vanilla essence**
**Green food-colour paste (see page 30)**
**Sweetie decorations: assorted sweets including fruit jellies, multicoloured candy-coated chocolates, black, red and white liquorice sweets and 1 small blue sweet**

**1** Prepare and cool Yellow Cake layers as instructed in steps 1 to 3 of Yellow Cake (page 529). Store remaining cake layer in airtight container for use within 3 days or wrap and freeze for use within 3 months.

**2** While cakes are cooling, prepare icing: using electric mixer on low speed, beat icing sugar, butter, single cream and vanilla essence in large bowl just until blended. Increase speed to medium and beat, frequently scraping bowl with rubber spatula, until icing is smooth and an easy spreading consistency. Stir in enough green food-colour paste to tint icing bright green; set aside.

**3** Cut 6cm round in centre of each cake layer. Without removing round, cut each layer in half to make 4 C-shaped pieces and 4 small semi-circles.

**4** Place C-shaped pieces of cake end to end, alternating directions to create a curvy snake shape, on chopping board or large piece of heavy card covered with foil. The finished cake measures approximately 70 by 23cm.

**5** Place cut side of 1 cake semi-circle against cut side of one end of snake to form tail. Repeat on other end for head. Place remaining 2 semicircles at head end of snake to form an open mouth. Ice side and top of cake.

**6** Decorate cake: cut all but 1 jelly sweet in half. Place jelly-sweet halves along top edge of cake for scales. Place whole jelly candy on head for eye, with blue sweet in centre for pupil. Use multicoloured candy-coated chocolates to decorate body. Use black and red licorice sweets for eyelashes and white liquorice sweets for teeth. Use brown candy-coated chocolate for nose. Store any leftover cake in refrigerator.

EACH SERVING: ABOUT 280 CALORIES, 2g PROTEIN, 38g CARBOHYDRATE, 14g TOTAL FAT (8g SATURATED), 63mg CHOLESTEROL, 215mg SODIUM

## CIRCUS TRAIN

*Prep:* 2 hours, plus cooling    *Bake:* 35–45 minutes
*Makes* 15 servings

Mixture for Banana Layer
 Cake (see page 530)
Cream Cheese Icing (see
 page 550)
Cocktail sticks
4 drinking straws

Sweetie decorations:
 hundreds and thousands,
 assorted liquorice sweets,
 jelly bears and liquorice
 laces and twists

◆ Preheat oven to 180°C (350°F, Gas 4). Grease and flour five 15 by 9cm mini-loaf tins (350ml capacity each) or 23 by 12cm loaf tin. Prepare mixture for Banana Layer Cake. Spread mixture evenly in mini-loaf tins. Bake 35 minutes, or until cocktail stick inserted in centres of cakes comes out clean. Cool in tins on wire rack 10 minutes. Run palette knife around sides of tins to loosen cakes; invert cakes onto rack and cool completely. (Or, if using 23 by 12cm loaf tin, bake 45 minutes; cool as above. Cut cooled cake crossways into five 4cm-wide pieces.) Meanwhile, prepare Cream Cheese Icing and cut straws in half.

◆ To assemble: using serrated knife, cut rounded tops off 3 cakes; set aside. (Do not cut tops too thin.) For engine, cut a 1cm-thick horizontal slice from 1 of the same 3 cakes. Trim slice, rounding 2 corners of a short side; attach to one end of cake with cocktail sticks for back of engine. Cut 1 rounded top crossways in half. Attach half to bottom front of engine with cocktail sticks. Cut 5cm semi-circle from second half for front of train; attach to top front of engine with cocktail sticks. Reserve remaining rounded tops for canopies.

◆ With small palette knife, ice engine and cars and tops and sides of canopies. Sprinkle canopies with hundreds and thousands. Decorate engine and cars: use round liquorice sweets for wheels; black liquorice pieces for coal car; red liquorice pieces for freight; assorted liquorice sweets on engine; and jelly bears for jelly bear carriages. Outline train borders with liquorice laces. Attach canopies to jelly bear carriages with pieces of drinking straws. Assemble train on long board or tray, using liquorice twists to attach cars. Store any leftover cake in refrigerator.

**Each serving: About 355 calories, 3g protein, 53g carbohydrate, 15g total fat (5g saturated), 41mg cholesterol, 280mg sodium**

## BALL-GAME CUPCAKES

*Prep:* 1½ hours, plus cooling    *Bake:* 25 minutes per batch
*Makes* 36

Mixture for Rich Chocolate
 Cake (see page 528)
Vanilla Buttercream (see
 page 550)
Black, red, orange and yellow
 food-colour paste (see
 page 30)

Special Equipment:
3 small piping bags
3 writing nozzles (1mm
 opening each)

◆ Preheat oven to 180°C (350°F, Gas 4). Line three standard 12-hole muffin tins with fluted paper liners. (If you do not have enough muffin tins bake cupcakes in batches.) Prepare cake mixture; pour into cups. (Bake only as many cupcakes as 1 rack in centre of oven can hold.) Bake 25 minutes, or until cocktail stick inserted in centres comes out almost clean. Cool in tins on wire racks 10 minutes. Remove from tins; cool completely on racks. Repeat with remaining mixture.

◆ Prepare buttercream. Remove 300g buttercream; divide it among 3 cups. Using food-colour paste, tint one-third black and one-third red; leave one-third white. Cover with cling film; set aside. Divide remaining buttercream among 3 more cups. Using food-colour paste, tint one-third orange and one-third yellow; leave one-third white. Ice 12 cupcakes with orange buttercream, 12 cupcakes with yellow buttercream, and 12 cupcakes with white buttercream.

◆ Spoon reserved black, red, and white buttercreams into piping bags, each fitted with a 1mm writing tip. Pipe black buttercream onto each orange cupcake for basketballs. Pipe red buttercream onto each white cupcake for baseballs. Pipe white buttercream onto each yellow cupcake for tennis balls. Store any leftover cupcakes in refrigerator.

**Each cupcake: About 210 calories, 3g protein, 25g carbohydrate, 12g total fat (3g saturated), 26mg cholesterol, 225mg sodium**

# DRIED FRUIT AND NUT CAKES

A traditional favourite at Christmas, fruit cakes can be enjoyed any time of the year as a teatime treat or an accompaniment to morning coffee. Spiced and studded with dried and glacé fruits and nuts, these dense, moist cakes have a rich, concentrated flavour that improves with time. Using brandy will further enrich the cake and ensure a moist result.

## CHRISTMAS FRUITCAKE

*Prep: 30 minutes, plus cooling and chilling    Bake: 1½ hours*
*Makes 36 servings*

| | |
|---|---|
| 160g stoned prunes, each cut in half | 225g butter or margarine |
| 300g dried figs, chopped | 300g plain flour |
| 175g ready-to-eat dried apricots, chopped | 2 tsp baking powder |
| | 1 tsp salt |
| 150g stoned dates | 1 tsp vanilla essence |
| 225g pecans | 5 medium eggs |
| 225g green glacé cherries | 60ml brandy (optional) |
| 225g red glacé cherries | 80g apricot jam, melted |
| 125g glacé pineapple wedges | Dried fruit, green and red glacé cherries and pecans for decoration |
| 125g glacé lemon rind | |
| 200g caster sugar | Wide ribbon for decoration |

1 Preheat oven to 170°C (325°F, Gas 3). Grease 25cm angel food cake tin. Line base with foil; grease foil. Combine first 9 ingredients in bowl. Using electric mixer slowly beat sugar and butter in another bowl until blended. Increase speed; beat until light and creamy. Add flour, baking powder, salt, vanilla essence and eggs. On low speed, beat until just blended, frequently scraping bowl.

2 Stir flour mixture into fruit mixture until fruit is evenly distributed. Spoon mixture into tin. Bake 1½ hours, or until cocktail stick inserted near centre of cake comes out clean.

3 Remove fruitcake from oven. Using skewer, poke holes in warm cake and drizzle with brandy, if using. Cool cake completely in tin on wire rack.

4 Run round-bladed knife around edge of tin to loosen cake; remove from tin and carefully peel off foil. Wrap fruitcake tightly in cling film or foil; refrigerate overnight so cake will be firm and easy to slice. Store in refrigerator up to 4 weeks.

5 To serve, brush fruitcake with half of melted jam; decorate with dried fruit, glacé cherries, and pecans. Brush fruit and pecans with remaining jam. If you like, wrap ribbon around cake to decorate; secure with double-sided tape. To serve, cut cake in very thin slices.

### MINIATURE FRUIT-CAKE LOAVES

Prepare fruitcake as above, but spoon mixture into six 13 by 8cm mini-loaf tins and bake 50–60 minutes. Poke holes in warm cakes and drizzle with 60ml brandy, if using; brush cakes with melted jam and garnish with fruit and pecans as instructed.

EACH SERVING: ABOUT 255 CALORIES, 3g PROTEIN, 42g CARBOHYDRATE, 10g TOTAL FAT (3g SATURATED), 43mg CHOLESTEROL, 155mg SODIUM

## COATING NUTS AND FRUIT WITH FLOUR

Tossing chopped nuts and dried or fresh fruit with a small amount of flour helps keep them separate – and suspended – in a cake mixture. Otherwise, these ingredients tend to clump together and may sink to the base of the tin while the cake is baking.

## APRICOT-PECAN FRUITCAKE

*Prep: 20 minutes, plus cooling    Bake: 70–80 minutes*
*Makes 24 servings*

| | |
|---|---|
| 425g ready-to-eat dried apricots, cut into 1cm-pieces | 5 medium eggs |
| 225g coarsely chopped pecans plus 90g pecan halves | 125ml brandy |
| | 1 tbsp vanilla essence |
| 1 tbsp plus 300g plain flour | 2 tsp baking powder |
| 250g caster sugar | 1 tsp salt |
| 225g butter or margarine, softened | 110g apricot jam, melted and strained |

◆ Preheat oven to 170°C (325°F, Gas 3). Grease 25cm angel food cake tin.

◆ Toss dried apricot pieces and chopped pecans with 1 tablespoon flour in medium bowl until coated; set aside.

◆ Using electric mixer on low speed, beat sugar and butter in large bowl until blended. Increase speed to high; beat about 2 minutes, until light and creamy, frequently scraping bowl with rubber spatula.

◆ Reduce speed to low. Add eggs, brandy, vanilla essence, baking powder, salt and remaining 300g flour; beat mixture until well blended, occasionally scraping bowl. Stir in dried apricot mixture.

◆ Spoon cake mixture into tin, spreading evenly with back of spoon. Arrange 90g pecan halves on top of levelled cake mixture to make 2 concentric circles. Bake cake 70–80 minutes, until cocktail stick inserted near centre of cake comes out clean.

◆ Cool cake in tin on wire rack 10 minutes. Run round-bladed knife around edge of tin to loosen cake; remove cake from tin and cool completely on rack.

◆ To serve, brush top of cake with melted apricot jam. Or, wrap and refrigerate cake up to 1 week; brush with jam before serving.

**Each serving:** About 295 calories, 4g protein, 32g carbohydrate, 17g total fat (4g saturated), 64mg cholesterol, 235mg sodium

## SPICE AND NUT CAKE

*Prep: 20 minutes, plus cooling    Bake: 50–60 minutes*
*Makes 12 servings*

| | |
|---|---|
| Cocoa powder for dusting | 1 tbsp ground ginger |
| 125g butter or margarine, softened | 2 tsp bicarbonate of soda |
| | 1½ tsp ground cinnamon |
| 100g dark brown sugar | 1 tsp salt |
| 1 tsp vanilla essence | ¾ tsp ground allspice |
| 2 medium eggs | 175g walnuts, coarsely chopped |
| 450g plain flour | |
| 225ml buttermilk, soured milk (see page 392), or low-fat plain yogurt | 160g stoned prunes, coarsely chopped |
| | Icing sugar for decoration |
| 250g golden syrup | |

◆ Preheat oven to 180°C (350°F, Gas 4). Grease 25cm bundt or kugelhopf tin; dust with cocoa. Using electric mixer on low speed, beat butter and next 3 ingredients in large bowl until blended. Increase speed to high; beat about 5 minutes, until light and fluffy.

◆ Reduce speed to low; add flour and next 7 ingredients. Beat until well blended, frequently scraping bowl with rubber spatula. Stir in walnuts and prunes.

◆ Spoon mixture into tin, spreading evenly with back of spoon. Bake cake 50–60 minutes, until cocktail stick inserted near centre of cake comes out clean.

◆ Cool cake in tin on wire rack 10 minutes. Remove cake from tin and cool completely on rack. Just before serving, sift icing sugar through sieve over cake.

**Each serving:** About 480 calories, 7g protein, 57g carbohydrate, 26g total fat (6g saturated), 58mg cholesterol, 605mg sodium

# APPLE, CARROT AND SPICE CAKES

Chopped or grated fruits and vegetables lend a subtle sweetness, moisture and luscious texture to these varied cakes. All these cakes keep well although our apple upside-down cake is at its best eaten fresh and still warm.

## CARROT CAKE

❖❖❖❖❖❖❖❖❖❖❖❖❖

*Prep:* 40 minutes, plus cooling
*Bake:* 55–60 minutes
*Makes* 20 servings

450g plain flour
2 tsp bicarbonate of soda
2 tsp ground cinnamon
1 tsp baking powder
1 tsp salt
½ tsp ground nutmeg
4 medium eggs
200g caster sugar
150g light brown sugar
225ml vegetable oil
1 tbsp vanilla essence
330g carrots, grated
125g walnuts, chopped
115g raisins
225g canned crushed
   pineapple in unsweetened
   juice
Cream Cheese Icing (see
   page 550)

**1** Preheat oven to 180°C (350°F, Gas 4). Grease 33 by 20cm metal baking tin. Line base with greaseproof paper; grease paper. Dust tin with flour. Combine flour, bicarbonate of soda, cinnamon, baking powder, salt and nutmeg in medium bowl.

**2** Using electric mixer on medium-high speed, beat eggs until blended. Gradually add caster sugar, then brown sugar; beat 2 minutes, frequently scraping bowl with rubber spatula. Beat in oil and vanilla essence. Reduce speed to low; add flour mixture and beat about Í minute, until smooth, frequently scraping bowl.

**3** Fold in carrots, walnuts, raisins and pineapple with its juice.

**4** Pour mixture into tin. Bake 55–60 minutes, until cocktail stick inserted in centre of cake comes out clean, with a few moist crumbs attached. Cool cake in tin on wire rack 10 minutes. Invert cake onto rack and remove paper. Cool carrot cake completely on wire rack.

**5** Prepare icing. Transfer cake to large platter or tray. Spread icing over sides and top of cake using palette knife. Store any leftover cake in refrigerator.

### COURGETTE CAKE

Prepare Carrot Cake as above, but substitute 375g grated courgettes for carrots and add ⅛ teaspoon ground cloves to flour mixture. Omit pineapple. Decorate with chopped walnuts.

Each serving: About
415 calories, 5g protein,
51g carbohydrate,
22g total fat
(5g saturated),
52mg cholesterol,
340g sodium

EACH SERVING: ABOUT 425 CALORIES, 5g PROTEIN, 54g CARBOHYDRATE, 22g TOTAL FAT (5g SATURATED), 52mg CHOLESTEROL, 345mg SODIUM

## APPLE-WALNUT BUNDT CAKE

*Prep: 25 minutes, plus cooling    Bake: 1¼ hours*

*Makes 16 servings*

| | |
|---|---|
| 450g plain flour | 3 medium eggs |
| 250g caster sugar | 600g Golden Delicious or |
| 225ml vegetable oil | Granny Smith's apples, |
| 125ml apple juice | peeled, cored and coarsely |
| 1 tsp bicarbonate of soda | chopped |
| 1 tsp ground cinnamon | 125g walnuts, coarsely |
| 2 tsp vanilla essence | chopped |
| ¾ tsp salt | 150g sultanas |
| ¼ tsp ground nutmeg | Icing sugar for decoration |

◈ Preheat oven to 180°C (350°F, Gas 4). Grease and flour 25cm bundt or kugelhopf tin. Using electric mixer on low speed, beat flour and next 9 ingredients until well mixed, frequently scraping bowl with rubber spatula. Increase speed to medium; beat 2 minutes, occasionally scraping bowl. Stir in apples, walnuts and raisins.

◈ Spoon mixture evenly into tin. Bake 1¼ hours, or until cake pulls away from side of tin and cocktail stick inserted near centre of cake comes out clean. Cool cake in tin on wire rack 10 minutes. Remove from tin and cool completely on rack. Just before serving, sprinkle with icing sugar.

**Each serving:** About 405 calories, 5g protein, 55g carbohydrate, 20g total fat (3g saturated), 40mg cholesterol, 195mg sodium

## APPLE SAUCE AND APPLE UPSIDE-DOWN CAKE

*Prep: 25 minutes, plus cooling    Bake: 35–40 minutes*

*Makes 8 servings*

| | |
|---|---|
| 175g butter or margarine, | 1 tsp ground cinnamon |
| softened | ½ tsp salt |
| 600g Granny Smith's apples, | ¼ tsp ground nutmeg |
| peeled, cored and each cut | Pinch of ground cloves |
| into 8 wedges | 140g caster sugar |
| 100g brown sugar | 2 medium eggs |
| 300g plain flour | 245g apple sauce |
| 1½ tsp bicarbonate of soda | |

◈ Preheat oven to 180°C (350°F, Gas 4). Melt 60g butter in 26cm frying pan with ovenproof handle (or wrap handle in double thickness of foil), over medium-high heat. Add apples and brown sugar and cook, stirring occasionally, 8 minutes, or until apples are tender. Remove from heat.

◈ Combine flour, bicarbonate of soda, cinnamon, salt, nutmeg and cloves in medium bowl; set aside. Using electric mixer on medium speed, beat remaining 115g butter with caster sugar until light and creamy. Beat in eggs, 1 at a time. On low speed; alternately add flour mixture and apple

sauce, beginning and ending with flour mixture, beating just until smooth. Spoon mixture evenly over apples in frying pan. Bake 35–40 minutes, until cake springs back when lightly touched and cocktail stick inserted in centre comes out clean.

◈ When cake is done, invert platter over cake. Quickly invert frying pan to unmould cake; replace any apples left in frying pan. Cool 30 minutes to serve warm.

**Each serving:** About 455 calories, 5g protein, 70g carbohydrate, 19g total fat (8g saturated), 100mg cholesterol, 590mg sodium

## GINGERBREAD

*Prep: 15 minutes, plus cooling    Bake: 55 minutes*

*Makes 9 servings*

| | |
|---|---|
| 100g sugar | 1 tsp ground cinnamon |
| 125g butter or margarine, | ½ tsp baking powder |
| softened | ½ tsp bicarbonate of soda |
| 300g plain flour | ½ tsp salt |
| 330g golden syrup | ¼ tsp ground cloves |
| 1 tbsp ground ginger | 1 medium egg |

◈ Preheat oven to 170°C (325°F, Gas 3). Grease 22cm square metal baking tin. Line base with greaseproof paper; grease paper. Dust tin with flour.

◈ Using electric mixer on low speed, beat sugar and butter until blended. On high speed, beat 1 minute or until creamy. On low speed, beat in flour, remaining ingredients and *175ml hot water* until blended. On high speed, beat 1 minute, occasionally scraping bowl. Pour mixture into tin.

◈ Bake 55 minutes, or until cocktail stick inserted in centre of gingerbread comes out clean. Cool gingerbread in tin on wire rack 10 minutes. Invert onto rack. Remove greaseproof paper and serve warm, or cool completely to serve later.

**Each serving:** About 325 calories, 4g protein, 55g carbohydrate, 11g total fat (5g saturated), 74mg cholesterol, 345mg sodium

# POUND CAKES

Dense and velvety, with a fine crumb, traditional pound cakes are leavened simply by beating air into the batter. The original pound cakes were made with a pound each of butter, sugar, flour and eggs. Modern versions, with the addition of baking powder and liquid, are a bit lighter in texture. Try the rich whisky-laced brown sugar pound cake, the Italian-style crunchy cornmeal or the refreshing vanilla. Pound cakes keep well and, in fact, are at their best the day after baking.

**1** Preheat oven to 170°C (325°F, Gas 3). Grease and flour 25cm bundt or kugelhopf tin. Combine flour, salt, baking powder and bicarbonate of soda in medium bowl; set aside.

**2** Mix milk, vanilla essence and 60ml whisky together in measuring jug. Using electric mixer on medium speed, beat brown sugar and 100g caster sugar until free of lumps. Add butter and beat 5 minutes, or until light and creamy. Add eggs, 1 at a time, beating well after each addition. Reduce speed to low; alternately add flour mixture and milk mixture, beginning and ending with flour mixture.

**3** Pour mixture into tin. Bake 80–85 minutes, until cake springs back when lightly touched and cocktail stick inserted near centre comes out clean. Cool cake in tin on wire rack 10 minutes. Remove cake from tin.

**4** Mix orange juice, remaining 2 tablespoons whisky and remaining 70g caster sugar together in small bowl; brush mixture all over warm cake. Cool cake completely on rack. To serve, slice very thin.

## LIGHT AND DARK BROWN SUGAR

Traditionally, brown sugar was simply a less-refined form of white sugar, containing molasses left over from the refining process. Today, it is more usually made by combining white sugar with molasses, though some varieties, notably muscavado, are still unrefined (raw). Brown sugar is available in light or dark varieties; the colour is determined by the molasses content. Light brown sugar is excellent for cakes, biscuits, meringues and fudge while the richness of dark brown sugar is especially suited to strongly flavoured cakes such as fruit, coffee and chocolate.

## WHISKY AND BROWN SUGAR POUND CAKE

❖❖❖❖❖❖❖❖❖❖❖❖

*Prep: 25 minutes, plus cooling*
*Bake: 80–85 minutes*
*Makes 24 servings*

450g plain flour
¾ tsp salt
½ tsp baking powder
½ tsp bicarbonate of soda
175ml milk
2 tsp vanilla essence
60ml plus 2 tbsp Scotch whisky or bourbon
300g dark brown sugar
170g caster sugar
225g butter or margarine, softened
5 medium eggs
2 tbsp orange juice

EACH SERVING: ABOUT 230 CALORIES, 3g PROTEIN, 32g CARBOHYDRATE, 9g TOTAL FAT (4g SATURATED), 65mg CHOLESTEROL, 215mg SODIUM

## VANILLA POUND CAKE

*Prep: 20 minutes, plus cooling    Bake: 60–70 minutes*
*Makes 16 servings*

| | |
|---|---|
| 450g caster sugar | ¾ tsp salt |
| 350g butter or margarine, | 6 medium eggs |
|   softened | 355g plain flour |
| 1 tbsp vanilla essence | Icing sugar for decoration |

◆ Preheat oven to 170°C (325°F, Gas 3). Grease and flour 25cm bundt or kugelhopf tin. Using electric mixer on low speed, beat caster sugar and butter in large bowl just until blended. Increase speed to high; beat about 5 minutes, until light and creamy.

◆ Add vanilla essence, salt and eggs. Reduce speed to low; beat until well blended, frequently scraping bowl with rubber spatula. Increase speed to high; beat 3 minutes, occasionally scraping bowl. Using wire whisk, fold in flour just until mixture is smooth.

◆ Spoon mixture into tin. Bake 60–70 minutes, until cocktail stick inserted near centre of cake comes out clean. Cool in tin on wire rack 10 minutes. Remove from tin; cool completely on rack. Sprinkle with icing sugar.

**Each serving: About 365 calories, 4g protein, 45g carbohydrate, 19g total fat (8g saturated), 127mg cholesterol, 320mg sodium**

## CORNMEAL POUND CAKE

*Prep: 20 minutes, plus cooling    Bake: 65 minutes*
*Makes 10 servings*

| | |
|---|---|
| 150g plain flour | 225g butter or margarine, |
| 60g coarse yellow cornmeal |   softened |
| ½ tsp baking powder | 4 medium eggs |
| ¼ tsp salt | 1 tsp grated orange rind |
| 200g caster sugar | 1 tsp vanilla essence |

◆ Preheat oven to 325°F. Grease and flour 23 by 12cm loaf tin or 25cm bundt or kugelhopf tin. Combine flour and next 3 ingredients in medium bowl. Using electric mixer on medium speed, beat sugar with butter 5 minutes, or until light and creamy. Add eggs, 1 at a time, beating well after each addition. Beat in orange rind and vanilla essence. Reduce speed to low; beat in flour mixture until combined.

◆ Pour mixture into tin. Bake 65 minutes, or until cake pulls away from sides of tin and cocktail stick inserted in centre comes out clean. Cool cake in tin on wire rack 10 minutes. Remove cake from tin and cool completely on rack. To serve, slice very thin.

**Each serving: About 340 calories, 4g protein, 35g carbohydrate, 20g total fat (8g saturated), 133mg cholesterol, 315mg sodium**

---

### POPPY SEEDS

The tiny, bluish-grey seeds of a poppy plant lend a nutty taste and crunchy bite to a variety of cakes, breads, pastries, creamy dressings, salads and noodle dishes. Because of their high oil content, poppy seeds can turn rancid quickly, so store them in an air-tight container in the freezer.

## LEMON-POPPY SEED POUND CAKE

*Prep: 25 minutes, plus cooling    Bake: 1½ hours*
*Makes 16 servings*

| | |
|---|---|
| 300g plain flour | 175g  butter or margarine, |
| 2 tbsp poppy seeds |   softened |
| ½ tsp baking powder | 350g sugar |
| ¼ tsp bicarbonate of soda | 4 medium eggs |
| ¼ tsp salt | 1 tsp vanilla essence |
| 3 large lemons | 125ml soured cream |

◆ Preheat oven to 170°C (325°F, Gas 3). Grease and flour 23 by 12cm loaf tin or 25cm bundt or kugelhopf tin. Mix flour and next 4 ingredients in bowl. Grate 1 tablespoon rind and squeeze 3 tablespoons juice from lemons.

◆ Using electric mixer on medium speed, beat butter with 300g sugar about 5 minutes, until light and creamy. Add eggs, 1 at a time, beating well after each addition. Beat in lemon rind and vanilla essence. Reduce speed to low; alternately add flour mixture and soured cream, beginning and ending with flour mixture.

◆ Spoon mixture into tin. Bake 1½ hours, or until cocktail stick inserted in centre of cake comes out clean. Cool cake in tin on wire rack 10 minutes. Remove from tin. Mix lemon juice and remaining 50g sugar together in small bowl. Brush mixture over top and sides of warm cake. Cool completely on rack. To serve, slice very thin.

**Each serving: About 255 calories, 4g protein, 34g carbohydrate, 12g total fat (5g saturated), 79mg cholesterol, 190mg sodium**

# CHEESECAKES

Few desserts are as popular as a rich, smooth cheesecake so we've included a recipe to suit every occasion. Pumpkin Swirl Cheesecake is the obvious choice for hallowe'en, but unusual enough to be special any time of year. Classic American Cheesecake uses a pastry base with a shortbread texture that combines perfectly with a classic cheese topping. Tart-sweet Lime Cheesecake is cool and creamy. To add an extra dimension to any flavour cheesecake try the crunchy pecan and brown sugar topping.

## PUMPKIN SWIRL CHEESECAKE

*Prep: 30 minutes, plus standing, cooling, and chilling*
*Bake: 70 minutes*
*Makes 16 servings*

| | |
|---|---|
| 200g digestive biscuits or cinnamon-flavoured biscuits | 4 medium eggs |
| 60g butter or margarine, melted | 450g canned solid-pack pumpkin |
| 750g cream cheese, softened | 2 tbsp cornflour |
| 200g caster sugar | 1 tsp ground cinnamon |
| 75ml brandy | ½ tsp ground allspice |
| 2 tsp vanilla essence | ½ tsp salt |
| | 225ml soured cream |

1 Preheat oven to 170°C (325°F, Gas 3). Process biscuits in food processor with knife blade attached or in blender until fine crumbs form. Using fork, stir biscuit crumbs and melted butter into 23 by 8cm springform tin, until evenly moistened. Using hand, press mixture onto base of tin. Bake biscuit base 10 minutes. Cool base completely in tin on wire rack.

2 Meanwhile, using electric mixer on medium speed, beat cream cheese in large bowl until smooth; gradually beat in sugar. Reduce speed to low; beat in brandy, vanilla essence and eggs just until blended, scraping bowl often with rubber spatula. Mix pumpkin, cornflour, cinnamon, allspice and salt together in medium bowl. Stir half of cream cheese mixture into pumpkin mixture until blended. Stir soured cream into remaining cream cheese mixture.

3 Reserve 125g pumpkin mixture. Pour remaining pumpkin mixture onto biscuit base. Carefully pour cream cheese mixture on top of pumpkin layer.

4 Spoon dollops of reserved pumpkin mixture onto cream cheese layer. Using knife, cut and twist through cream cheese layer for swirl effect.

5 Bake cheesecake 1 hour, or until edges are set (centre will shake). Turn off oven; let cheesecake remain in oven 1 hour. Remove cheesecake from oven. Run round-bladed knife around edge of tin to loosen cheesecake (this helps prevent cracking during cooling). Cool completely in tin on wire rack. Cover and refrigerate cheesecake at least 6 hours, or until well chilled. To serve, remove side of tin.

EACH SERVING: ABOUT 350 CALORIES, 6g PROTEIN, 26g CARBOHYDRATE, 23g TOTAL FAT (14g SATURATED), 110mg CHOLESTEROL, 320mg SODIUM

## CLASSIC AMERICAN CHEESECAKE

*Prep: 30 minutes, plus chilling, standing and cooling*
*Bake: 50 minutes*    *Makes 20 servings*

| | |
|---|---|
| 175g butter or margarine, softened | 5 medium eggs |
| 190g plus 2 tbsp plain flour | 2 tsp grated lemon rind |
| 250g caster sugar | 900g cream cheese, softened |
| | 3 tbsp milk |

◈ Using electric mixer on medium speed, beat butter, 190g flour, 50g caster sugar, 1 egg yolk and 1 teaspoon lemon rind in small bowl until well mixed. Shape pastry into ball; wrap with cling film. Refrigerate 1 hour.

◈ Preheat oven to 200°C (400°F, Gas 6). Press one-third of pastry onto base of 25 by 6cm springform tin. Bake 8 minutes, or until golden; cool on wire rack. Turn oven control to 240°C (475°F, Gas 9).

◈ Using electric mixer on medium speed, beat cream cheese in large bowl just until smooth; gradually beat in remaining 200g caster sugar. Reduce speed to low; beat in remaining 1 egg white and 4 eggs, milk, remaining 2 tablespoons flour and remaining 1 teaspoon lemon rind. Beat 5 minutes. Press remaining pastry around side of tin to within 3cm of top; pour filling into pastry.

◈ Bake 12 minutes. Turn oven control to 150°C (300°F, Gas 2); bake 30 minutes longer, until edges are set (centre will shake). Turn off oven; let cheesecake remain in oven 30 minutes. Remove cheesecake from oven and cool in tin on wire rack. Refrigerate at least 6 hours, or until well chilled. To serve, carefully remove side of tin.

**Each serving: About 320 calories, 6g protein, 20g carbohydrate, 24g total fat (14g saturated), 123mg cholesterol, 230mg sodium**

## LIME CHEESECAKE

*Prep: 25 minutes, plus cooling and chilling*
*Bake: 50 minutes*    *Makes 16 servings*

| | |
|---|---|
| 100g digestive biscuits | 450g cream cheese, softened |
| 60g walnuts, very finely chopped | 4 medium eggs |
| 75g butter or margarine, melted | 450ml soured cream |
| ¾ tsp ground cinnamon | 250g caster sugar |
| 3 medium limes | 1 tsp vanilla essence |
| | ½ tsp salt |
| | Lime slices for decoration |

◈ Preheat oven to 180°C (350°F, Gas 4). Process biscuits in food processor with knife blade attached or in blender, until fine crumbs form.

◈ Using fork, mix biscuit crumbs, chopped walnuts, melted butter and cinnamon in 23 by 6cm springform tin, until well blended. Press mixture onto base and 4cm up side of tin; set aside.

◈ Grate 1 tablespoon rind and squeeze 75ml juice from limes into small bowl; set aside. Using electric mixer on medium speed, beat cream cheese and eggs in large bowl until smooth. Reduce speed to low; beat in soured cream, sugar, vanilla essence, salt, lime juice and grated lime rind until well blended. Pour cream cheese mixture into biscuit crust in tin.

◈ Bake cheesecake 50 minutes. (Centre may shake slightly.) Cool in tin on wire rack. Refrigerate cheesecake at least 6 hours, or until well chilled. To serve, carefully remove side of tin; decorate cheesecake with lime slices.

**Each serving: About 315 calories, 5g protein, 22g carbohydrate, 24g total fat (12g saturated), 107mg cholesterol, 250mg sodium**

## NUT-AND-CRUMB-TOPPED CHEESECAKE

Prepare topping: using your fingertips, mix 125g chopped pecans, 100g plain flour, 100g brown sugar, 90g butter or margarine, 2 tablespoons caster sugar and ½ teaspoon vanilla essence until mixture is crumbly. Prepare Classic American Cheesecake as above, but before baking, sprinkle with topping. Bake as instructed (if top browns too quickly, cover loosely with foil). Let stand in oven, cool, and refrigerate as instructed. To serve, carefully remove side of tin. Using electric mixer on medium speed, beat 125ml whipping cream, 1 tablespoon brown sugar and ½ teaspoon vanilla essence until stiff peaks form. Spoon whipped cream into piping bag fitted with 1cm star nozzle; pipe pretty design around top edge of cheesecake. Decorate with pecan halves, if you like.

**Each serving: About 445 calories, 7g protein, 32g carbohydrate, 33g total fat (18g saturated), 140mg cholesterol, 275mg sodium**

# ICING AND DECORATING

Using a piping bag and assorted nozzles, it's easy to pipe icing or whipped cream into a vast range of attractive shapes and designs. You may want to practise piping on a sheet of parchment paper before you decorate your cake.

## WRITING TIP

**Piping dots** Hold bag fitted with small writing nozzle at a 90° angle, with nozzle just above cake. Gently squeeze bag, keeping nozzle in icing, until the dot forms. Stop pressure and lift nozzle.

**Smoothing dots** If the nozzle leaves a small 'tail' at the top of the dot, gently smooth it with finger dipped in icing sugar or cornflour.

**Squiggles and lettering** Use thinned icing for a smooth flow. With nozzle at a 45° angle, touch surface to secure icing then lift slightly to form squiggles. To finish, stop pressure and lift nozzle.

### FILLING A PIPING BAG

Place coupler base in piping bag. Attach desired nozzle with ring.

Stand bag in measuring jug or heavy glass. Fold bag over to make cuff; fill halfway with icing.

Shake down icing; twist bag shut. Use writing hand to guide nozzle and other hand to hold bag shut.

## STAR TIP

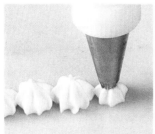

**Stars** Using star nozzle at 90° angle and just above cake, squeeze to form star, then lift slightly, keeping nozzle in icing. Stop pressure and lift nozzle.

**Rosettes** Position star tip as for stars, but as you squeeze, move tip up in a circular motion. Stop pressure and lift tip.

**Ropes** Holding bag at a 45° angle, pipe a C. Tuck tip under bottom portion of C; repeat, overlapping curves to form a rope.

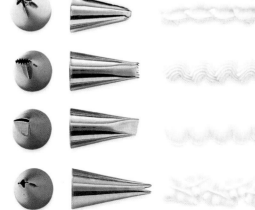

### A SELECTION OF OTHER NOZZLES

**5-POINT STAR** Use this smaller star to pipe small rosettes and fancy borders.

**BASKET** This nozzle forms the ridged lines that create the woven design for our basket cake.

**PETAL** With a wider opening at one end, petal nozzles are used to make petals, ribbons and bows.

**LEAF** The open 'V' of this nozzle gives leaves, veins and pointed tips.

# EASY ICINGS

**FLUFFY WHITE ICING**  Using electric mixer on high speed, beat 2 medium egg whites, 200g caster sugar, 60ml water, 2 teaspoons fresh lemon juice, 1 teaspoon golden syrup and ¼ teaspoon cream of tartar in top of double boiler over simmering water for 7–10 minutes, until soft peaks form. Remove double-boiler top from base; beat 7–10 minutes longer, until stiff peaks form. Makes about 500g.

Per 100g: About 145 calories, 0g protein, 38g carbohydrate, 0g total fat, 0mg cholesterol, 50mg sodium

**CREAM CHEESE ICING**  Using electric mixer on low speed, beat 360g icing sugar, 175g softened cream cheese, 90g softened butter or margarine and 1½ teaspoons vanilla essence just until blended. Increase mixer speed to medium. Beat 1 minute, or until mixture is smooth and fluffy, frequently scraping bowl with rubber spatula. Makes about 600g.

Per 100g: About 400 calories, 0g protein, 53g carbohydrate, 20g total fat (10g saturated), 65mg cholesterol, 235mg sodium

**CHOCOLATE BUTTERCREAM**  Using electric mixer on low speed, beat 240g icing sugar, 175g softened butter or margarine and 1 teaspoon vanilla essence in large bowl until almost combined. Add 185g melted and cooled plain chocolate. Increase mixer speed to high; beat about 1 minute, or until light and fluffy. Makes about 600g.

Per 100g: About 470 calories, 0g protein, 47g carbohydrate, 33g total fat (18g saturated), 63mg cholesterol, 270mg sodium

**WHITE CHOCOLATE BUTTERCREAM**  Using electric mixer on low speed, beat 225g softened butter (do not use margarine), 3 tablespoons milk, 240g icing sugar and 175g melted and cooled white chocolate in large bowl just until mixed. Increase speed to high; beat 2 minutes, or until light and fluffy, scraping bowl often with rubber spatula. Makes about 600g.

Per 100g: 570 calories, 0g protein, 53g carbohydrate, 40g total fat (27g saturated), 87mg cholesterol, 335mg sodium

**VANILLA BUTTERCREAM**  Mix 200g sugar and 75g plain flour in 2-litre saucepan until evenly combined. Using wooden spoon, gradually stir in 300ml milk until smooth. Cook over medium-high heat, stirring often, until mixture thickens and boils. Reduce heat to low; cook 2 minutes, stirring constantly. Remove from heat; cool completely. Using electric mixer on medium speed, beat 225g softened butter or margarine, in large bowl until creamy. Gradually beat in milk mixture. Beat in 1 tablespoon vanilla essence. Makes about 725g.

Per 100g: About 395 calories, 0g protein, 36g carbohydrate, 29g total fat (12g saturated), 74mg cholesterol, 325mg sodium

**LEMON BUTTERCREAM**  Prepare Vanilla Buttercream as above, but replace vanilla essence with 1 tablespoon grated lemon rind.

**ORANGE BUTTERCREAM**  Prepare Vanilla Buttercream as above, but replace vanilla essence with 1 teaspoon grated orange rind.

## AMARETTO BUTTERCREAM

*Prep: 20 minutes   Cook: 10 minutes*
*Makes about 900g*

**200g caster sugar**
**4 medium egg whites**
**450g unsalted butter, softened**
  **(do not use margarine)**

**60ml amaretto liqueur or**
  **½ teaspoon almond essence**
**Pinch salt**

◈ Bring 150g caster sugar and *75ml water* to the boil in 1-litre saucepan over high heat without stirring. Cover and cook 2 minutes longer. Uncover; set sugar thermometer in place and continue cooking, without stirring, until temperature reaches 111° to 112°C, or hard-ball stage (see page 523). Remove from heat.

◈ Just before syrup is ready (temperature will be about 97°C), using electric mixer on high speed, beat egg whites in large bowl until foamy. Gradually beat in remaining 50g caster sugar and continue beating until soft peaks form.

◈ Using mixer on low speed, slowly pour hot syrup in thin stream into beaten egg whites. Increase speed to high; beat 15 minutes longer, or until mixture forms stiff peaks and is cool to the touch.

◈ When mixture is cool, reduce speed to medium. Gradually add softened butter, about 15g at a time, beating after each addition. (If buttercream appears to curdle, increase speed to high and beat until mixture comes together, then reduce speed to medium and continue adding softened butter.) When buttercream is smooth, reduce speed to low; beat in amaretto and salt until incorporated.

Per 100g: About 460 calories, 0g protein, 28g carbohydrate, 43g total fat (28g saturated), 114mg cholesterol, 70mg sodium

# CAKE DECORATOINS

These elegant finishing touches transform home-made cakes into distinctive desserts. Arrange them to form a border or design, or simply scatter them on top. The chocolate decorations can be made ahead and stored in an air-tight container, between layers of greaseproof paper, in the refrigerator. Stencilling with icing sugar should be done just before serving, or the cake's moisture may dissolve the sugar.

## CHOCOLATE CURLS

1 Melt 175g plain chocolate pieces and 30g white vegetable fat (see page 552).

2 Scrape mixture onto baking sheet with no sides; spread to cover evenly. Refrigerate 10 minutes, or until firm but not brittle.

3 Place baking sheet on damp cloth (to keep it steady). Holding back of spatula at 45° angle, scrape chocolate into curls (if it softens or sticks to spatula, chill several minutes). Transfer to another baking sheet; refrigerate until ready to use).

## QUICK CHOCOLATE CURLS

Hold a 30g piece of plain or white chocolate between palms of hands to warm, 5 minutes. Slowly and firmly draw vegetable peeler along smooth base of square for wide curls, or along sides for short curls. Refrigerate on baking sheet until ready to use. Using cocktail stick, place curls on cake.

## LEAVES FOR DECORATIONS

The leaves of the following plants, available from florists, are safe to use and sturdy enough for making chocolate leaves: gardenia, grape, lemon, orange, magnolia, nasturtium and rose. Be sure to wash these non-toxic leaves in warm, soapy water; rinse and dry leaves thoroughly before using them.
   Do not use the following toxic leaves or let come in contact with chocolate or any other food: amaryllis, azalea, caladium, daffodil, delphinium, dieffenbachia, ivy, holly, hydrangea, jonquil, larkspur, laurel, lily-of-the-valley, mistletoe, narcissus, oleander, poinsettia and rhododendron.

## CHOCOLATE LEAVES

1 Melt 90g plain chocolate drops and 2 teaspoons white vegetable fat (see page 552). Meanwhile, rinse and dry 6 medium non-toxic leaves (see above).

2 Using clean paintbrush, pastry brush or small palette knife, spread layer of melted chocolate on underside of each leaf.

3 Refrigerate chocolate-coated leaves 30 minutes, or until firm. With cool hands, carefully peel each leaf from chocolate.

## GRATED CHOCOLATE

For an easy decoration to garnish the top or sides of cake, run a block of plain chocolate over the large holes of a grater.

## MELTING CHOCOLATE

Melt plain chocolate (with white vegetable fat, if called for) in top of double boiler over simmering water, stirring occasionally. Or, melt in heavy-based 1-litre saucepan over very low heat, stirring constantly. White chocolate should always be melted in top of a double boiler over barely simmering water; stir constantly until smooth.

## MAKING A PARCHMENT CONE

1 Cut 30 by 30cm square of parchment paper; cut in half into 2 triangles. Lay one triangle on flat surface, wide side at top. Fold left-hand point down to bottom point.

2 Take right-hand point; wrap completely round folded left-hand point, forming cone. Both points should meet at bottom point of original triangle.

3 Grasp all thicknesses of paper where original three points meet and fold point in to secure cone. Fill cone not more than two-thirds full and fold top over to seal. Snip off tip to desired size opening.

## FEATHERING

1 Ice cake. Before icing sets, melt 60g plain chocolate (see above). Spoon into parchment cone, small piping bag with small writing nozzle, or plastic bag (cut one corner off); pipe spiral on top of cake, working outwards from centre.

2 Immediately run tip of paring knife through spiral, working from centre to edge of cake. Repeat, working from centre, to mark cake in 8 segments. Divide each segment again, this time from edge to centre for feathered effect.

## CHOCOLATE SHAPES

1 Using pencil, draw outline of 12 hearts or other shapes, each 3cm across, on piece of parchment paper. Place paper, pencil-side down, on baking sheet; tape to baking sheet. Melt 40g plain or white chocolate.

2 Spoon warm chocolate into parchment cone, small piping bag with small writing nozzle, or plastic bag (cut one corner off); pipe in continuous line (not too thin, or shape will be fragile) over each tracing to form 12 shapes in all.

3 Refrigerate at least 15 minutes, or until set. Carefully peel off shapes and transfer to cake. (Create your own designs by making other shapes, such as leaves, scrolls or flowers.)

### QUICK PIPING BAG

If you don't have a piping bag, just use a plastic bag with a corner cut off. Using rubber spatula, scrape melted chocolate into bag. Seal bag, then snip off one corner with scissors to make a small opening.

## STENCILLING

1 Cut light-weight cardboard or manila file folder at least 1 inch larger all around than cake. Using scalpel or single-edge razor blade, cut out stars, triangles or other shapes of different sizes.

2 Place stencil over un-iced cake. Sift cocoa powder, icing sugar or cinnamon sugar over top. After decoration has been evenly dispersed in cut-out holes, carefully lift off stencil to reveal design.

# INDEX

## D

and nut cake 542
  -roasted pork 232
  -rubbed beef fillet 214
  wine and fruit mould 335
Spicy almond slices 516
Spicy beef
  bundles 202
  kebabs 215
  ribs with char-grilled
    pineapple 216
Spicy cheese sticks 50
Spicy corn relish 118
Spicy curried carrot soup 69
Spicy Indian creamed spinach
  278
Spicy peanut chicken 162
Spicy stir-fried prawns 103
Spinach 315
  Cheddar and bacon
    omelette 78
  chick-pea and raisin
    sauce 354
  with chick-peas and raisins,
    Italian 278
  and chick-pea salad,
    smoked turkey 340
  coleslaw, cabbage and 326
  and feta topping (for jacket
    potatoes) 299
  and goat's-cheese open
    sandwiches 434
  with mushrooms and bacon
    279
  pasta 361
  pie, Greek greens and 387
  and rice balls, baked 278
  and ricotta dumplings 277
  soup 56
  spicy Indian creamed 278
  stir-frying 280
  and tangerine salad 319
  wheat-grain salad with 332
Split pea(s) 372
  soup with smoked ham 66
Spoonbread 382
Spring greens, stir-frying 280
Spring onion and dried
  tomato couscous 380
Spring risotto 377
Spring rolls, mini 47
Spring turkey and vegetable
  piccata 156
Sprouting broccoli 269
  and anchovies, linguine
    with 353
  stir-frying 280

Squash 271
  and apple soup, winter 59
  salmon teriyaki with 130
  sauté, three- 304
  vegetable fritters 303
See also Acorn squash;
  Aubergine(s); Butternut squash;
  Courgette(s); Spaghetti squash;
  Summer squash; Winter squash
Squid 89
  calamari with spicy tomato
    sauce 99
  cleaning 89
  grilled 100
  ink 99
  Italian seafood salad 344
  salad, Thai 100
  sauce, linguine with 100
  seafood Fra Diavolo 358
Star anise 448
STARTERS AND FINGER
  FOODS 31–54
  aubergine-stuffed cherry
    tomatoes 37
  blue-cheese toasts 44
  broccoli bruschetta 43
  cheese
    bites, fast 42
    blue cheese toasts 44
    bundles, Greek 48
    chillies con queso,
      fiesta 42
    goat's herb-and-spice-
      coated 42
    goat's, marinated 41
    Parmesan dip 34
    quesadillas, tomato and
      goat's 46
    ricotta bruschetta 44
    sticks, spicy 50
    Stilton and apple
      millefeuilles 50
    toasts, Mediterranean 44
  chicken liver
    pâté 36
    and sage crostini 44
  chicken, sesame 53
  chillies con queso, fiesta 42
  corn and pepper
    quesadillas 45
  country pâté 240
  crab meat morsels 50
  crudités basket 33
  dates, Gorgonzola-
    stuffed 42
  devils on horseback 32

dip(s)
  aubergine, roasted 34
  guacamole 34
  honey-mustard 34
  Moroccan spice bean 34
  Parmesan 34
  pumpkin and roasted
    garlic 34
  quick 32
  roasted pepper and
    walnut 310
  white bean and tuna 32
empanaditas Mexican-
  style 51
know-how 32
meatballs, herbed 54
mezze platter,
  Mediterranean 32
mozzarella skewers,
  smoky 42
mushroom(s)
  caponata-stuffed 38
  triangles 48
  turnovers 52
nachos 46
olive sticks 49
Parma ham
  and goat's cheese
    roll-ups 42
  and cheese boats 38
pâté(s)
  chicken liver 36
  country 240
  smoked trout 35
  and spreads, smoked
    fish 35
pizza pronto 32
pork satay 54
potato
  crescents, spicy 52
  top hats 38
potted shrimp 40
prawn(s)
  and olives, cocktail 40
  skewers, Mexican-style 39
  with tarragon dipping
    sauce 40
quail's eggs, stuffed 32
quesadilla(s)
  corn and pepper 45
  quick 32
  salad 338
  tomato and goat's
    cheese 46
ricotta bruschetta 44
roasted aubergine dip 34

roasted pepper
  and mozzarella
    sandwiches with basil
      purée 42
  and walnut dip 310
salmon
  boats, smoked 38
  terrine, smoked 36
salsa, super 32
scallops with sage and
  bacon 54
serving 32
smoky mozzarella
  skewers 42
spring rolls, mini 47
Stilton and apple
  millefeuilles 50
Tabasco-lime spread 36
tomato(es)
  aubergine-stuffed
    cherry 37
  and goat's cheese
    quesadillas 46
  tortilla pinwheels 46
  trout pâté, smoked 35
Steak(s)
  coating with crumbs 210
  and mushroom open
    sandwiches 434
  and onion rings, barbecue-
    style 211
  and pepper fajitas 212
  with red wine sauce 200
  with yellow-pepper
    chutney 210
See also Beef, steak(s); Lamb,
  steak; Salmon, steaks; Swordfish,
  steaks
Steakhouse burgers with
  horseradish soured cream
  206
Steamed plaice 122
Steamer 13
  bamboo 122
Stew
  aubergine 308
  beef
    and barley, orange 193
    chilli con carne 196
    Chinese-spiced 194
    green chilli and
      tomatillo 196
    hearty 194
    and mixed
      mushroom 191
    oxtail 193

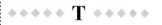

# T

## ACKNOWLEDGEMENTS

*Food preparation* Eric Treuillé,
Kathy Man, Maddalena Bastianelli
*Additional art direction*
Cherry Ramsayer
*Photographers' assistant*
Margaret-Ann Hugo
*IT Manager* John Clifford
*Typesetting* Sue Hill
*Additional editorial assistance*
Jennifer Rylaarsdam
*Additional nutrition advice*
Antonina Smith
*Proofreading* Pamela Ellis
*Index* Madeline Weston

## NUTRITIONAL VALUES

All recipes in this book carry information on levels of calories, protein, carbohydrate, fat, cholesterol and sodium per serving. These figures are provided to allow readers to make comparisons between the recipes and should be taken only as a guide. Most of the recipes in the book first appeared in *Good Housekeeping* magazine in the U.S., and there have necessarily been some small adjustments to make in converting measurements to metric, which we have made every effort to ensure are reflected in the nutritional values. In addition, differences in individual ingredients can occur either because of natural variation, as between one cut of meat and another, or because of differences in manufacturer's specifications for prepared and packaged foods. While we have tried to provide the most accurate nutritional information that we can, the values given for any recipe should therefore only be read as averages.